HANDBOOK OF LATIN AMERICAN STUDIES: No. 77

A Selective and Annotated Guide to Recent Publications in Anthropology, Geography, Government and Politics, International Relations, Political Economy, and Sociology

VOLUME 78 WILL BE DEVOTED TO THE HUMANITIES:
ART, HISTORY, LITERATURE, MUSIC, AND PHILOSOPHY

EDITORIAL NOTE: Comments concerning the *Handbook of Latin American Studies* should be sent directly to the Humanities or Social Sciences Editor, *Handbook of Latin American Studies*, Hispanic Reading Room, Library of Congress, Washington, D.C. 20540-4851 or emailed to hlas@loc.gov.

ADVISORY BOARD

Roberto González Echevarría, *Yale University*
Eric Hershberg, *American University*
Scott Hutson, *University of Kentucky*
Peter T. Johnson, *Princeton University*
Franklin Knight, *Johns Hopkins University*
Susan Ramírez, *Texas Christian University*
Ben Vinson, III, *Howard University*

ADMINISTRATIVE OFFICERS
OF THE LIBRARY OF CONGRESS

Carla Hayden, *The Librarian of Congress*
Robin L. Dale, *Deputy Librarian, Library Collections & Services Group*
Hannah Sommers, *Associate Librarian, Researcher & Collections Services*
Eugene Flanagan, *Director, General & International Collections Directorate*
Suzanne Schadl, *Chief, Latin American, Caribbean, & European Division*
Alyson Williams, *Head, Communities of Practice and Publication, LACE*

REPRESENTATIVES, UNIVERSITY OF TEXAS PRESS

Robert Devens, *Director*
Kerry Webb, *Senior Acquisitions Editor*

HANDBOOK EDITORIAL STAFF

Wendy Acosta, *Editorial Assistant*

HANDBOOK OF LATIN AMERICAN STUDIES: NO. 77

SOCIAL SCIENCES

*Prepared by a Number of Scholars
for the Hispanic Reading Room of the Library of Congress*

TRACY NORTH, *Social Sciences Editor*
KATHERINE D. McCANN, *Humanities Editor*

2025

UNIVERSITY OF TEXAS PRESS ⭐ *Austin*

International Standard Book Number: 978-1-4773-3047-0
International Standard Serial Number: 0072-9833
Library of Congress Catalog Card Number: 36032633
Copyright ©2025 by the University of Texas Press.
All rights reserved.

Requests for permission to reproduce material from this work should be sent to permissions@utpress.utexas.edu.

First Edition, 2025

The paper used in the publication meets the minimum requirements of American National Standard for Information Sciences—Permanence of Paper for Printed Library Materials, ANSI Z39.48-1984. ∞

CONTRIBUTING EDITORS

SOCIAL SCIENCES

Caroline Beer, *The University of Vermont*, GOVERNMENT AND POLITICS
Melissa H. Birch, *University of Kansas*, POLITICAL ECONOMY
Silvia Borzutzky, *Carnegie Mellon University*, POLITICAL ECONOMY
Federico Bossert, *Universidad de Buenos Aires, Argentina*, ANTHROPOLOGY
Christian Brannstrom, *Texas A&M University*, GEOGRAPHY
Jacqueline Anne Braveboy-Wagner, *The City University of New York (CUNY)*, INTERNATIONAL RELATIONS
Charles D. Brockett, *Sewanee: The University of the South*, GOVERNMENT AND POLITICS
William L. Canak, *Middle Tennessee State University*, SOCIOLOGY
Erynn Masi de Casanova, *University of Cincinnati*, SOCIOLOGY
Ernesto Castañeda-Tinoco, *American University*, SOCIOLOGY
Miguel Centellas, *University of Mississippi*, GOVERNMENT AND POLITICS
Amílcar E. Challú, *Bowling Green State University*, POLITICAL ECONOMY
David M. Cochran, Jr., *University of Southern Mississippi*, GEOGRAPHY
Jennifer N. Collins, *University of Wisconsin-Stevens Point*, GOVERNMENT AND POLITICS
Roberto Domínguez, *Suffolk University (Boston)*, INTERNATIONAL RELATIONS
Duncan Earle, *Marymount California University*, ANTHROPOLOGY
Luis Galanes Valldejuli, *University of Puerto Rico at Cayey*, SOCIOLOGY
James B. Gerber, *San Diego State University*, POLITICAL ECONOMY
Mario A. González-Corzo, *Lehman College, The City University of New York (CUNY)*, POLITICAL ECONOMY
Clifford E. Griffin, *North Carolina State University*, GOVERNMENT AND POLITICS
Daniel Hellinger, *Webster University*, POLITICAL ECONOMY
John Henderson, *Cornell University*, ANTHROPOLOGY
Guy David Hepp, *California State University, San Bernardino*, ANTHROPOLOGY
Peter H. Herlihy, *University of Kansas*, GEOGRAPHY
Silvia María Hirsch, *Universidad Nacional de San Martín, Argentina*, ANTHROPOLOGY
Jonathan Hiskey, *Vanderbilt University*, POLITICAL ECONOMY
Keith Jamtgaard, *University of Missouri*, SOCIOLOGY
Arthur A. Joyce, *University of Colorado Boulder*, ANTHROPOLOGY
Gregory W. Knapp, *The University of Texas at Austin*, GEOGRAPHY
Matthew C. LaFevor, *University of Alabama*, GEOGRAPHY
José A. Laguarta Ramírez, *The City University of New York (CUNY)*, GOVERNMENT AND POLITICS
Matthew Layton, *Ohio University*, GOVERNMENT AND POLITICS

Thomas P. Leppard, *Florida State University*, ANTHROPOLOGY
Félix E. Martín, *Florida International University*, INTERNATIONAL RELATIONS
Daniel Masís-Iverson, *Inter-American Defense College*, POLITICAL ECONOMY
Kent Mathewson, *Louisiana State University*, GEOGRAPHY
Cecilia Menjívar, *University of California, Los Angeles*, SOCIOLOGY
Mary K. Meyer McAleese, *Eckerd College*, INTERNATIONAL RELATIONS
Erika Moreno, *Creighton University*, GOVERNMENT AND POLITICS
Juan Carlos Navarro, *Instituto de Estudios Superiores de Administración (IESA), Venezuela*, GOVERNMENT AND POLITICS
Suzanne Oakdale, *University of New Mexico*, ANTHROPOLOGY
Julio Ortiz-Luquis, *Borough of Manhattan Community College and Brooklyn College, CUNY*, INTERNATIONAL RELATIONS
Enrique S. Pumar, *Santa Clara University*, SOCIOLOGY
David J. Robinson, *Syracuse University*, GEOGRAPHY
Isabel Scarborough, *Parkland College*, ANTHROPOLOGY
Joseph Leonard Scarpaci, *Center for the Study of Cuban Culture & Economy*, GEOGRAPHY
Jörn Seemann, *Ball State University*, GEOGRAPHY
Peter M. Siavelis, *Wake Forest University*, GOVERNMENT AND POLITICS
Russell E. Smith, *Washburn University*, POLITICAL ECONOMY
Jason L. Toohey, *University of Wyoming*, ANTHROPOLOGY
Brian Turner, *Randolph-Macon College*, GOVERNMENT AND POLITICS
Marygold Walsh-Dilley, *University of New Mexico*, SOCIOLOGY

HUMANITIES

Diana Alvarez Amell, *Seton Hall University*, LITERATURE
Félix Ángel, *Independent Scholar, Washington DC*, ART
José R. Ballesteros, *St. Mary's College of Maryland*, LITERATURE
Bradley Benton, *North Dakota State University*, HISTORY
Célia Bianconi, *Boston University*, LITERATURE
Amber Brian, *The University of Iowa*, LITERATURE
John Britton, *Francis Marion University*, HISTORY
Rogério Budasz, *University of California, Riverside*, MUSIC
José Cardona-López, *Texas A&M International University*, LITERATURE
Bridget María Chesterton, *Buffalo State, The State University of New York*, HISTORY
Matt D. Childs, *University of South Carolina*, HISTORY
Matthew Crawford, *Kent State University*, HISTORY
Tiffany D. Creegan Miller, *Colby College*, LITERATURE
G. Antonio Espinoza, *Virginia Commonwealth University*, HISTORY
Erin S. Finzer, *University of Arkansas at Little Rock*, LITERATURE
Raphael E. Folsom, *The University of Oklahoma*, HISTORY
Elizabeth Gackstetter Nichols, *Drury University*, LITERATURE

Myrna García-Calderón, *Syracuse University*, LITERATURE
Luis A. González, *Indiana University, Bloomington*, HISTORY
Isadora Grevan de Carvalho, *Rutgers University*, LITERATURE
Mark Grover, *Brigham Young University*, HISTORY
María-Constanza Guzmán, *Glendon College, York University*, TRANSLATIONS
Michael Huner, *Grand Valley State University*, HISTORY
Frances Jaeger, *Northern Illinois University*, LITERATURE
John Koegel, *California State University, Fullerton*, MUSIC
Erick D. Langer, *Georgetown University*, HISTORY
Alfred E. Lemmon, *Historic New Orleans Collection*, MUSIC
Peter S. Linder, *New Mexico Highlands University*, HISTORY
Daniel Livesay, *Claremont McKenna College*, HISTORY
Ryan Long, *University of Maryland*, LITERATURE
M. Angélica Guimarães Lopes, *Professor Emerita, University of South Carolina*, LITERATURE
Laura R. Loustau, *Chapman University*, LITERATURE
Mary Ann Mahony, *Central Connecticut State University*, HISTORY
Elizabeth S. Manley, *Xavier University of Louisiana*, HISTORY
Claire Emilie Martin, *California State University, Long Beach*, LITERATURE
Elaine M. Miller, *Christopher Newport University*, LITERATURE
Sarah M. Misemer, *Texas A&M University*, LITERATURE
Mollie Lewis Nouwen, *Pacific Northwest College of Art*, HISTORY
Susana Nuccetelli, *St. Cloud State University*, PHILOSOPHY
Michael O'Brien, *College of Charleston*, MUSIC
Élide Valarini Oliver, *University of California, Santa Barbara*, TRANSLATIONS
Rita M. Palacios, *Conestoga College*, LITERATURE
Suzanne B. Pasztor, *Humboldt State University*, HISTORY
Anne Pérotin-Dumon, *Historian, Alexandria*, VA HISTORY
Charles A. Perrone, *Professor Emeritus, University of Florida*, LITERATURE
Jeannine Pitas, *Saint Vincent College*, LITERATURE
Juan José Ponce Vázquez, *The University of Alabama*, HISTORY
Joshua Price, *Toronto Metropolitan University*, TRANSLATIONS
Susan E. Ramírez, *Texas Christian University*, HISTORY
Jane M. Rausch, *Professor Emerita, University of Massachusetts-Amherst*, HISTORY
Jonathan Ritter, *University of California, Riverside*, MUSIC
Francisco Solares-Larrave, *Northern Illinois University*, LITERATURE
Peter Szok, *Texas Christian University*, HISTORY
Barbara Tenenbaum, *Historian, Washington*, DC HISTORY
Giovanna Urdangarain, *Pacific Lutheran University*, LITERATURE
Peter Villella, *United States Air Force Academy*, HISTORY
Stephen Webre, *Louisiana Tech University*, HISTORY
Thomas Whigham, *Professor Emeritus, University of Georgia*, HISTORY
Steven F. White, *St. Lawrence University*, TRANSLATIONS
Chrystian Zegarra, *Colgate University*, LITERATURE

Foreign Corresponding Editors

Franz Obermeier, *Universitätsbibliothek Kiel*, GERMAN PUBLICATIONS
Mao Xianglin, *Chinese Academy of Social Sciences*, CHINESE PUBLICATIONS

Special Contributing Editors

Lucia A. Wolf, *Library of Congress*, ITALIAN LANGUAGE

CONTENTS

PAGE

EDITOR'S NOTE   XIII

ANTHROPOLOGY

ARCHEOLOGY

    Mesoamerica   *John Henderson and Guy David Hepp*   1
        General p. 4   Fieldwork and
        Artifacts p. 11   Native Sources
        and Epigraphy p. 27

    Caribbean Area   *Thomas P. Leppard*   29
        Caribbean Islands p. 30

    South America   *Jason L. Toohey*   34
        General p. 36   Argentina p. 37
        Bolivia p. 38   Chile p. 39
        Colombia p. 39   Peru p. 40

ETHNOLOGY

    Middle America   *Duncan Earle*   43

    South America

        Lowlands   *Federico Bossert, Bartholomew Dean,*
                            Silvia María Hirsch, and Suzanne Oakdale   63
            General p. 77   Brazil p. 81
            Colombia, Venezuela, and The Guianas p. 85
            Peru and Ecuador p. 90
            Paraguay, Argentina, and Bolivia p. 99

        Highlands   *Isabel M. Scarborough*   108
            General p. 108   Argentina p. 110
            Bolivia p. 111   Chile p. 114
            Ecuador p. 116   Peru p. 118

GEOGRAPHY

GENERAL	Jörn Seemann	119
THE CARIBBEAN	Joseph Leonard Scarpaci, Jr.	135
CENTRAL AMERICA	David M. Cochran, Jr. and Peter H. Herlihy	147

General p. 150 Belize p. 153
Costa Rica p. 153 El Salvador p. 155
Guatemala p. 156 Honduras p. 157
Nicaragua p. 158 Panama p. 158

MEXICO	Matthew C. LaFevor	159
WESTERN SOUTH AMERICA	Gregory W. Knapp	169

General p. 172 Venezuela p. 172
Colombia p. 172 Ecuador p. 174
Peru p. 177 Bolivia p. 180

THE SOUTHERN CONE	David J. Robinson	182

General p. 183 Argentina p. 186
Chile p. 200 Paraguay p. 209
Uruguay p. 212

BRAZIL	Christian Brannstrom	216

GOVERNMENT AND POLITICS

MEXICO	Caroline Beer	227
CENTRAL AMERICA	Charles D. Brockett	242

General p. 244 Belize p. 245
Costa Rica p. 245 El Salvador p. 248
Guatemala p. 251 Honduras p. 255
Nicaragua p. 257 Panama p. 260

THE CARIBBEAN	Clifford E. Griffin and José A. Laguarta Ramírez	261

General p. 269 Dominican Republic p. 273
Jamaica p. 275 British Caribbean p. 276
Dutch Caribbean p. 276 Puerto Rico p. 276
Trinidad and Tobago p. 279 Cuba p. 279

COLOMBIA	Erika Moreno	282
ECUADOR	Jennifer N. Collins	286
VENEZUELA	Juan Carlos Navarro	297
BOLIVIA	Miguel Centellas	305
CHILE	Peter M. Siavelis	311

ARGENTINA AND URUGUAY Argentina p. 320 Uruguay p. 323		Brian Turner	319
BRAZIL		Matthew L. Layton	324

INTERNATIONAL RELATIONS

GENERAL		Mary K. Meyer McAleese	333
MEXICO AND CENTRAL AMERICA Mexico p. 346 Central America p. 350		Roberto Domínguez	343
THE CARIBBEAN AND THE GUIANAS	Jacqueline Anne Braveboy-Wagner and Julio A. Ortiz-Luquis		351
SOUTH AMERICA (except Brazil) General p. 364 Argentina p. 367 Bolivia p. 372 Chile p. 373 Colombia p. 375 Ecuador p. 377 Peru p. 378 Venezuela p. 379		Félix E. Martín	361

POLITICAL ECONOMY

GENERAL		Jonathan Hiskey	381
MEXICO		James B. Gerber	395
CENTRAL AMERICA AND THE CARIBBEAN (except Cuba) Central America p. 410 Caribbean p. 411		Daniel Masís-Iverson	409
CUBA		Mario A. González-Corzo	415
VENEZUELA		Daniel Hellinger	419
CHILE		Silvia Borzutzky	423
ARGENTINA, PARAGUAY, AND URUGUAY Argentina p. 431 Paraguay p. 435 Uruguay p. 436		Amílcar Challú	427
BRAZIL		Melissa H. Birch and Russell E. Smith	437

SOCIOLOGY

GENERAL		Enrique S. Pumar	443
MEXICO		Ernesto Castañeda-Tinoco	448
CENTRAL AMERICA		Cecilia Menjívar	476

THE CARIBBEAN	*Luis Galanes Valldejuli*	489
COLOMBIA AND VENEZUELA *Colombia p. 501 Venezuela p. 507*	*William L. Canak*	500
ECUADOR	*Erynn Masi De Casanova*	509
PERU	*Keith Jamtgaard*	516
BOLIVIA	*Marygold Walsh-Dilley*	530

INDEXES

ABBREVIATIONS AND ACRONYMS	537
TITLE LIST OF JOURNALS INDEXED	547
ABBREVIATION LIST OF JOURNALS INDEXED	555
SUBJECT INDEX	565
AUTHOR INDEX	599

EDITOR'S NOTE

GENERAL AND REGIONAL TRENDS

As we approach publication of the first *Handbook* volume compiled entirely since the onset of the COVID-19 pandemic in March 2020, we again see research centering the impact of the global health crisis on Latin America. Coupled with this constrained situation, researchers are confronting challenges related to the environment, political conditions and security, and migration.

Researchers will not be able to avoid incorporating the impact of climate change into future research projects. Unpredictable and extreme weather events will be a consideration in terms of preserving archival materials as well as regarding human geography and migration. It is difficult to consider the future without reflecting on the past, and some researchers are wisely looking back to help inform the future. One such example is a study of hurricanes in the Caribbean. The analysis is published in a 2018 *NACLA Report on the Americas*, "Eye of the Storm: Colonialism, Capitalism, and Climate in the Caribbean" (item **970**).

A related line of study investigates the effects of the drug trade on the environment, specifically in Central America. According to the HLAS Contributing Editors (CEs) for the Central American geography section, David M. Cochran, Jr. and Peter H. Herlihy, "Most significant this biennium are the scores of geographers researching cocaine trafficking in Central America. The pioneering work of geographer Kendra McSweeney (item **478**) ignited the interest of many others and motivated them to examine narco-imprints on the region" (p. 149). Jennifer Devine and her co-authors focus on illicit economies and natural resources in Guatemala, Honduras, and Costa Rica (items **473, 480,** and **481**). While it may come as no surprise that drug trafficking has a negative impact on the environment, this research formalizes the study of land use change resulting from the drug trade.

Local, regional, and national governments must contend with climate change in ways that reflect thoughtful consideration of the real challenges people face. HLAS CE for Southern Cone geography David J. Robinson remarks on the "first book-length analysis of post-neoliberal conservation" in Argentina, in which Marcos Mendoza examines the effect of public policies on the environment (item **648**). We will continue to see more *firsts* in publications insofar as the changing climate is concerned. The challenge will be whether public policies are created in good faith or if politicians and practitioners are coopted by economic opportunities to the detriment of the people who rely on the government to implement sensible and careful policies.

The stakes are high for those in office to address climate change, among other important issues. Free and fair elections, a tenet of democracies, help ensure that politicians follow the will of the people Thus, research on voting is a relevant and welcome addition to the literature. In this volume, many contributing editors highlight the importance of security as a critical element of voting. They also note that studies of violence and insecurity go beyond voting. Taking a broad view, one study (item **1528**) looks at chronic violence and distinguishes between inhumane security (based on power) and humane security (based on social conditions) as it relates to those affected by the violence. While the authors focus on Mexico as a case study, lessons learned could be applied throughout the region.

The study of violence is a mainstay of social science research. A subset of publications focuses on the effects of gang violence and the drug trade on the region, particularly in Central America and Mexico, presumably due to the geographic proximity to the US, which is often the endpoint of the illicit trade as the US consumes more drugs than any other country (https://worldpopulationreview.com/country-rankings/drug-use-by-country). Several studies investigate the 2012-2013 truce between the state and gangs in El Salvador. Their aim is to understand why the truce was initially successful (e.g., item **866**) and why it was only temporary (e.g., item **867**). To shed light on the proliferation of gangs, *Homies Unidos* brings together testimonies by a group of former gang members in El Salvador (item **1586**).

It is worthwhile to identify and recognize the successful violence reduction initiatives. To that end, researchers in Mexico are examining when gangs choose violence and when they choose cooperation and support of local communities. In *Votes, Drugs, and Violence*, Guillermo Trejo and Sandra Ley delve into the recent uptick in drug violence in Mexico (item **843**). HLAS CE for Mexican politics and government Caroline Beer describes this work as "pathbreaking" (p. 240) as the authors attempt to determine the causes for the incessant violence in the country. Beer notes that "this book provides the most comprehensive and methodologically sophisticated analysis of drug violence available" (p. 241).

Issues of public safety and policing are not confined to Mexico and the Northern Triangle (El Salvador, Guatemala, and Honduras). Similar research on Argentina highlights the challenges of reforming the security sector (item **1102**), especially given the findings that the state cooperates with criminal groups to maintain order rather than enforcing laws. The criminal justice system in general, and police officers in particular, are tasked with ensuring public safety. What happens when police officers themselves are found to be perpetuating abuse? In one ethnographic study of a police commissary in Buenos Aires, Agustina Ugolini "addresses the problem of police abuse and violence" by analyzing how the police learn behaviors to legitimize illegal activity (item **1103**).

Violence, police corruption, and political corruption are obstacles to achieving a functional democracy. Angélica Durán-Martínez's provocative work looks at drug violence in Mexico and Colombia with an eye toward understanding why the perpetrators of violence sometimes publicize their heinous acts and other times hide their participation (item **813**). She emphasizes the link between the state and organized crime and describes scenarios in which the actions of the state vis-à-vis violence influence the decision-making of criminals. HLAS CE for general political economy Jonathan Hiskey describes the perpetuation of violence as "the most significant human, economic, and social challenge" in the region (p. 391). The goal of one edited volume, *Organized Violence: Capitalist Warfare in Latin America*, is to challenge the notion that gangs and the drug trade are solely responsible for violence in the region. The authors call out other actors, such as business and political interests, who may be the drivers of—and directly benefit from—violence (item **1273**). The community policing movement has emerged as a response to the absence of safety felt by many people. In one Mexican region, Indigenous communities have come together to form their own security organizations to protect themselves from violence (item **823**).

In a democracy, public policies should reflect the needs of the people, who in turn hold politicians accountable. To that end, several studies address political participation at all levels of government. Sofía Cordero Ponce compares and contrasts the processes that brought about new constitutions in Bolivia and Ecuador (item **1037**). She notes that, despite similar starting points, the results diverged due to the uneven approach each country took to the writing of the foundational documents. HLAS CE for Chilean government and politics Peter Siavelis reports that "there is growing scholarly literature devoted to Chile's process of constitutional reform" (p. 315).

Democracies thrive when all members of society participate in the political process. In Latin America, there has been a relatively recent recognition of the value of incorporating Indigenous people into the political process. Andean countries aim to increase political participation by considering the philosophy of sumac kawsay (*vivir bien/buen vivir*). Several works in this volume address this approach to developing public policies that benefit all citizens. It is not entirely surprising that the concept has crossed over into geographical research, where the investigation centers on improvements to land use policies based on buen vivir (item **575**). As HLAS CE for Andean ethnology Isabel Scarborough describes in her review of Orrego Echeverría's volume on the Indigenous worldview *abya yala* (item **338**): "*buen vivir* seeks to make connections with the environment" and this unique Indigenous philosophy outlines ways of being that offer "an alternative to Western development ideologies" (p. 109). Following on the new constitution of Ecuador (2008), the country launched the Plan Nacional para el Buen Vivir (2017–2021) with the intention of incorporating Indigenous ideals into the national conversation.

Disciplines offer a framework for scholarly inquiry, and theories provide the scaffolding for research and investigation. The *Handbook* has been organized around disciplines since its inception. The volume co-editors are, after all, librarians working to organize and present information to users in a systematic and meaningful way. One of the byproducts of this approach is that works may be siloed in one section and not considered as part of another. The previous discussion around political participation, public policy, and Indigenous peoples is a prime example. Within the anthropology chapter, the ethnology section focuses on studies of Indigenous people in the region. However, there is often overlap between those studies and research in other disciplines such as geography or sociology. A series of publications on children and child-rearing illustrates this point. An article by Francesca Mezzenzana examines child-rearing in Ecuadorian Amazonia by comparing the traditions of the Runa to Anglo-Americans (item **288**). She finds vast differences in how the adults address the behavior and needs of the children—as it turns out, the Runa do not share the same concerns with parental attentiveness that are considered crucial for childhood development in Western society. A related study of Indigenous children in Argentina by Pia Leavy and Andrea Szulc highlights the autonomy of the children and their participation in household activities such as taking care of younger siblings (item **322**). These important comparative approaches to studies of caring could have appeared in the sociology chapter; subject headings and keyword searches help to mitigate the disciplinary silo effect when using *HLAS Web*.

A theme that is echoed throughout this volume is the notion that understanding non-Western philosophy has value—and once again, this view cuts across disciplines. In the field of international relations, two different CEs point to an international willingness to make space for voices from the Global South. The HLAS CE for Caribbean international relations Jacqueline Braveboy-Wagner suggests that Caribbean and other small states should pursue the publication of works on their foreign policy theories rather than relying on practitioners to recount personal experiences (p. 353–354). One successful example of this approach is the chapter by Kristina Hinds in *Latin America in a Global International Relations* (item **1194**), in which she "seeks to insert Caribbean intellectual thought into a budding IR discourse on 'Global South IR' and the broader 'Global IR' (both of which seek to bring marginalized ideas and approaches into the mainstream of IR theory)" (p. 358). In a similar vein, HLAS CE for South American international relations Félix Martín expresses disappointment that most of the publications in this volume "revert to old approaches and traditional concerns just as the IR discipline calls for greater inclusion and attention to the theoretical and empirical production originating from the Global South" (p. 361).

A topic that has persisted in the scholarly literature is migration. The previous HLAS Social Sciences volume included several works about the causes of migration, ranging from climate change to violence and, of course, the search for economic opportunity. Now, we are seeing a line of inquiry that tracks migration in a circular way—from exile and diaspora to a return to the home country (items **607**, **1277**, and **1445**). A recent article from the Pew Research Center distills statistics on migration to the US and finds that the numbers are changing. Trends indicate fewer immigrants from Latin America in recent years, and an uptick in migrants from India and China (https://www.pewresearch.org/short-reads/2024/09/27/key-findings-about-us-immigrants/). All over the world, people are departing their homelands—whether by choice or by force—to seek a better life elsewhere.

Even amidst turmoil, it is important to seek joy. For me, that joy often comes in the form of chocolate. In a delicious book, Federico Paredes Umaña and Jonathan H. Kaplan turn our attention to the Maya site of Chocolá in Guatemala, where we learn about the history and civilization of this Pacific coastal plains area that was involved in sophisticated cacao production and exchange (item **64**). In another study of chocolate, Jennifer A. Loughmiller-Cardinal reassesses Maya ceramic cylinders with hieroglyphic texts referencing cacao and maize (item **71**). This study has a connection to the Library of Congress; a subset of the sample of 70 vessels are housed in the Kislak Collection at the Library of Congress, which is also available for viewing online (https://www.loc.gov/collections/jay-i-kislak-collection/). Alas, the analysis demonstrates that the vessel walls are too thin to have been functional for beverages. She concludes that they were used for dry foodstuffs that may have been used to prepare beverages. Contributions to the volume edited by Traci Ardren, *Her Cup for Sweet Cacao: Food in Ancient Maya Society* (item **11**), discuss various aspects of food and beverages with an emphasis on "the roles of food in the creation of social identities, feasting and political uses of food, and ritual consumption of food and beverages" (p. 6). I have a suspicion that the Maya may have also turned to treats during times of peril.

Expanding beyond sweet treats, two other works consider the importance of food—in one case recognizing the connection between culinary traditions and cultural heritage (item 369) and, in the other, describing contemporary cocoa production in Latin America (item 377). A related article looks at the connection between food and land use, observing the diminishing biodiversity among the Bribri Indigenous group in Costa Rica and Panama, with a focus on commercial banana and cacao production (item 492). The authors cite research that "has shown that Indigenous peoples around the world are using less of the biodiversity available to them in their home territories as a result of external encroachment and culture change" (p. 154).

Finally, a work on the ubiquitous food in Latin America, the tortilla, was published during this review period. *Volteando la tortilla: género y maíz en la alimentación actual de México* (item 242) examines the tortilla from the perspective of gender, environment, food dependency, and nutrition. The authors express concern about the adaptation of genetically modified maize in Mexico and note the role of women in tortilla-making. This study coalesces around concerns for biodiversity and sustainable energy, food sovereignty, and women's empowerment. The interconnectedness of these topics, along with the vast implications of public policies (i.e., land use policy, economic policy, etc.), are worthy of additional study.

CLOSING DATE

With some exceptions for more recent works, the closing date for works annotated in this volume was 2022. For the Bolivian sociology section, a wider date range accounts for the absence of this section in recent volumes.

ELECTRONIC ACCESS TO THE *HANDBOOK*

At the time of publication of this volume, some *HLAS* records are searchable through one open-access web site hosted at the Library of Congress, *HLAS Web*. This mobile-friendly, ADA-compliant web site can be accessed at https://hlasopac.loc.gov/ for now. However, following on the 2024 retirement of *HLAS Online*, in mid-2025 the Library plans to retire this site as a result of a change in the technology that supports Library's own online catalog (https://catalog.loc.gov/). *HLAS Web* offers robust search features such as limits; permalinks to individual records; links to thousands of open-access journal articles; and easy options for printing, saving, emailing, and exporting lists of records. The site is also compatible with the open-access bibliographic citation management software Zotero (zotero.org). *HLAS* records that did not appear in a print volume will not be annotated, and newer records are in a preliminary editorial stage. Currently Volumes 35–77 are available. In other words, reviews of publications from the 1960s to the present are searchable via *HLAS Web*. The Library is currently exploring options to continue to provide electronic access to the bibliographic citations and introductory essays for all *HLAS* volumes. As always, the print volume is available at many research institutions and we have the complete set in the Hispanic Reading Room at the Library of Congress. In addition, electronic access is available for some earlier volumes in various digital repositories. For more information about access to *HLAS*, consult this blog post from April 2024: https://blogs.loc.gov/international-collections/2024/04/hlas-online-retired.

CHANGES FROM THE PREVIOUS SOCIAL SCIENCES VOLUME

Anthropology

Guy David Hepp canvassed the Mesoamerican (non-Maya) Archeology publications for this volume. The continuity is appreciated; his PhD advisor, Arthur A. Joyce, reviewed the publications for this same section for many years.

Government and Politics

Caroline Beer took on responsibility for the Mexico section. Longtime contributor for the Venezuela section René Salgado turned over the section to Juan Carlos Navarro, who has stepped in and excelled in the role. Matthew L. Layton reviewed the copious materials for the Brazil section.

Sociology

Our newest Caribbean contributor, Luis Galanes Valldejuli, joins us from Puerto Rico. Erynn Masi de Casanova took advantage of her location at the American Sociological Association (ASA) office in Washington, DC, to prepare the Ecuador section; she has since returned to the university setting at the University of Cincinnati, but not before leaving us in a much better place. Marygold Walsh-Dilley is well-positioned to prepare the section on Bolivia with her unique interdisciplinary background in geography, sociology, and anthropology.

HLAS Style and Subject Heading Changes

Beginning with *HLAS 75*, we now capitalize the words Black and Indigenous when referring to a racial, ethnic, or cultural identity. In a related initiative, we have embarked on a project during the summer of 2024 to update language use of *HLAS* subject headings that appear in the *HLAS Subject Term Glossary*. Following the valuable work of librarian colleagues around the world that culminated in several recommendations from the SACO African American Subject Funnel Project (part of the Library of Congress Program for Cooperative Cataloging (PCC) to provide input and guidance on terminology that accurately reflects the African American experience), *HLAS* has changed a number of terms to make them more up-to-date and inclusive.

ACKNOWLEDGMENTS

The *Handbook* has always been a complex endeavor and we have continued to make enhancements and improvements to content and access. We are a very small staff and we work closely with colleagues in the Library of Congress as well as with colleagues in the related communities of librarianship, scholarship, and publishing. Ardie Bausenbach, one of our closest advisors who helped shape and shepherd the *Handbook* over the years, retired in March 2024. With Ardie's guidance, *HLAS Web* launched with enhancements to the earlier *HLAS Online* interface. She also contributed to the data conversion project where we were able to add bibliographic citations for 15 volumes (volumes 35-49) to the *Handbook* database. Thank you, Ardie, and best wishes for your next chapter!

Tracy North, *Social Sciences Editor*

ANTHROPOLOGY

ARCHEOLOGY
Mesoamerica

JOHN HENDERSON, *Professor of Anthropology, Cornell University*
GUY DAVID HEPP, *Associate Professor of Anthropology, California State University, San Bernardino*

THE RECENT RESURGENCE of interest in long-standing issues, along with an inclination to adopt orthodox approaches in Maya studies, continues. New assessments of chronologies in the Maya world involving sophisticated statistical methods are the most obvious reflection of the trend (items **61** and **72**). More nuanced approaches to classic problems in Maya archeology include the terminal classic period transformation (item **17**), the relationship between Chichén Itzá and the Toltecs (item **42**), and warfare (items **5, 28, 31, 52,** and **103**).

A trend toward increased descriptive and empirical emphasis and a corresponding decline in abstract social theory are detectable in chronological and regional syntheses (items **26, 56,** and **95**) and in site reports (items **40, 64,** and **102**) as well as in investigations focusing on obsidian (item **85**), ceramics (items **53** and **107**), and other craft items (items **66** and **104**). Topically focused investigations—of ecology, climate, and subsistence, particularly paleobotany and foodways (items **11, 51, 71, 75, 76,** and **106**); exchange (items **90, 91,** and **93**); mortuary practice and furniture (item **77**); and body adornment and modification (item **1**)—also display a stronger empirical emphasis than has been typical in the recent past. Comparison at local, regional, and societal scales (item **83**) is a common analytical strategy. Even though an empirical orientation is more visible than in the recent past, almost all analyses are explicitly informed by theoretical perspectives.

Abstract theory, particularly social theory, tends to be more salient in considerations of ontological issues, especially the nature of supernatural beings (items **41** and **108**); identity (items **55** and **63**); ritual practice (items **7, 9, 15, 22, 30–31, 47, 50,** and **99**); and urban layouts, socioeconomic hierarchies, and political strategies (items **82** and **101**).

Long-popular topics including frontiers and peripheries (items **55** and **111**), political legitimation involving patron deities and ancestors (see *HLAS 75:44* and item **73**), and bioarcheology (item **81**) continue to be represented. The impact of European culture on Maya societies, especially the effects of Christian evangelization in the colonial period (item **112**), is an increasingly common thematic focus, as are aspects of Maya belief and cosmology that have been neglected in the past (items **22** and **30**) and the history of Mesoamerican scholarship (items **54** and **102**).

The blending of text and imagery, especially in the identification of particular deities and rituals (items **5, 15, 22, 31, 41, 110,** and **115**) and literary aspects of hieroglyphic texts (item **109**), is increasingly prominent and more nuanced in studies of Maya writing. In general, epigraphers are moving beyond proposing readings for particular signs and extracting basic information about dynastic history to elaborating nuanced perspectives on Maya social and political organization (items **18, 42,** and **57**). [JSH]

NORTHERN MESOAMERICA

RECENT TRENDS in the archeology of northern Mesoamerica include the application of new technologies and approaches to answer old problems. Pox Pottery, identified by Charles Brush in Guerrero in the 1960s, has long held a contentious position as one of the early formative period's oldest proposed ceramic traditions. In their review, Kennett and colleagues find support for a model of at least two traditions of the first pottery in Mesoamerica (item **65**). Other recent works have synthesized decades of research that had not, until recently, been fully reported. These projects focus on regions such as Pacific coastal west Mexico and sites such as the epiclassic and postclassic period city of Tula in central Mexico (items **35** and **60**). Large works summarizing years of excavation and artifact analysis, including Lesure's book on Paso de la Amada in the Chiapas portion of the Soconusco (item **78**) and Pereira and Padilla Gutiérrez's edited volume about Malpaís Prieto in Michoacán (item **48**), offer readers dense sources of data on archeological context and artifact analysis, as well as imagery and synthetic interpretations. In her book about formative period anthropomorphic artifacts, Guernsey collates decades of research from across Mesoamerica about the role of human depiction at different scales (especially in ceramic figurines and public sculpture) in the establishment of complex social and political organization (item **58**). Related to this trend of synthesis is a continued focus on translating academic research for public consumption, often resulting in works published in Spanish and intended for local communities and Latin American tourists (items **8** and **60**). Notable among these are publications about rock art and archeoastronomy (items **79** and **86**). Even among more academic-style writings, there is a trend toward the exploration of cultural patrimony itself, including proposals for curation (item **67**) and theoretical discussions of how the management of cultural patrimony relates to global heritage and national identity (items **12** and **21**). This is the archeology of northern Mesoamerica turning its analytical gaze back on itself and considering its role in public and political discourse.

Another group of recent publications discusses the spatial layout and architectural history of famous sites. At the UNESCO World Heritage sites of Teotihuacán and Monte Albán, remote sensing technology and revised mapping are helping to rewrite existing models of architecture and ancient urban planning, even in areas where little or no recent excavation has been possible (items **43** and **68**). These famous sites were not originally constructed as they appear today, and projects like that of Levine and colleagues, employing nondestructive electrical resistance, ground-penetrating radar, and gradiometry in Monte Albán's main plaza, coupled with some of the best areal imagery and three-dimensional modeling ever produced for that site, are leading to new findings about the origins of one of Mesoamerica's first urban capitals. Similar projects, aided by lidar, digital architectural renderings, and excavation programs, have helped to reconstruct the layout of downtown Tenochtitlán, today mostly obscured by modern Mexico City (item 38), and the settlement system governed by the formative period capital of Izapa in modern Chiapas (item 88). Studies supported by microstratigraphic analysis (item 96), coring (item 36), lidar (item 4), and viewshed analysis in GIS (item 97) have helped readers to better understand settlement, monumental constructions, and public participation in activities such as communal ritual and ballgames. These studies make it clear that there is still much to learn about even some of Mesoamerica's best-known archeological sites.

Related to a continued interest in landscapes and spatial relationships and representing a shift from the publication trends of recent years is the growing number of studies concerning interaction. From neodiffusionist models and sourcing studies to basic artifact comparisons and explorations of identity formation, this interest in interaction and interregional influence represents a return to some of the research questions of the mid-20th century, which have been considered taboo following critiques of diffusionism (items 2, 13, and 49). A collected series of papers on Izapa (items 14, 25, 49, and 87), which appeared in the journal *Ancient Mesoamerica*, exemplifies this trend. The studies tend to appear in edited volumes and journal issues, demonstrating the multivocal, interdisciplinary nature of these new approaches to old questions.

Another pattern in the recent archeology of northern Mesoamerica represents continuity over the past five to 10 years. Bioarcheological and mortuary archeology studies (items 14, 19–20, 24, and 35) are supporting research about diachronic regional continuities, synchronic patterns of interaction and influence, paleopathology, and health and diet evinced by the analysis of human remains. Continued interests in this regard are exemplified by Pérez Rodríguez and colleagues' bioarcheological and faunal study of Cerro Jazmín and the rise of urbanism in Oaxaca's Mixteca Alta (item 24) and cultural practices involving the body, such as Tiesler and Serrano Sánchez's edited volume about the many aspects of human cranial modification (item 20).

Finally, the "material/ontological turn," broadly influential in archeological theory especially over the past two decades, continues in Mesoamerica, with the growing incorporation of Indigenous ontologies and considerations of how cultural practices and symbolism influenced native politics. Blomster and Salazar Chávez discuss the role of the Mesoamerican ball game and the formalization of an early ball court in highland Oaxaca in the development of formative period political practices (item 6). Dupey García and Vázquez de Ágredos Pascual edited a collection of papers discussing embodiment theory and the materiality of painted skins, of both humans and nonhuman social agents, such as codices (item 113). Faugère and Beekman organized an edited volume about the role of anthropomorphic imagery in highland central and west Mexico (item 34). The late archeologist Michael Lind discussed the highland Oaxaca site of Lambityeco and its role in the standardization of Zapotec religious architecture and iconography, for example of the rain/storm god Cociyo (item 69). Other works, including that by López

Luján and colleagues and that by Sugiyama and colleagues (both in the same edited volume), focus on the significance of animals and animal offerings in the establishment of complex political organization at classic period Teotihuacán and postclassic era Tenochtitlán, respectively (items **70** and **98**). Together, these works demonstrate the broad interests of archeology in northern Mesoamerica in recent years. [GDH]

GENERAL

1 The adorned body: mapping ancient Maya dress. Edited by Nicholas Carter, Stephen D. Houston, and Franco D. Rossi. Austin: University of Texas Press, 2020. 211 p., 18 unnumbered pages of plates: bibl., ill. (some color), index.

Ten chapters plus an introduction and final commentary provide a comprehensive study of precolumbian Maya dress and bodily ornamentation, including clothing, footwear, headdresses, jewelry, and body painting. Consideration is given to the symbolic, social, and political meanings of these items as well as to the techniques and materials involved in their creation. [JSH]

2 Archaeology and identity on the Pacific Coast and southern highlands of Mesoamerica. Edited by Claudia García-Des Lauriers and Michael W. Love. Salt Lake City: The University of Utah Press, 2016. 226 p.: bibl., ill., index, maps.

Edited volume about the role of identity formation and social interaction in ancient Mesoamerica. Includes chapters discussing the construction of identities as integral to complex social structures, in general, as well as specific studies of urbanization, landscape, public architecture, language diversity and change, reorganizations of space, and ancestor imagery. Contributions emphasize social elites, monumental art and architecture, and evidence for discerning between interregional and local influences on ancient identities. Several contributions offer revisions to the traditional culture-history model of identity and ethnicity as immutable and based on lists of cultural traits. Includes a synthesizing chapter by John E. Clark. [GDH]

3 Arqueología computacional: nuevos enfoques para la documentación, análisis y difusión del patrimonio cultural. Edición de Diego Jiménez-Badillo. Ciudad de México: Secretaría de Cultura, Instituto Nacional de Antropología e Historia, 2017. 305 p.: bibl., ill. (chiefly color), maps. (Cultura digital)

Edited volume synthesizing the research of the Red de Tecnologías Digitales para la Difusión del Patrimonio Cultural (RedTDPC) and comprising 18 chapters and an introduction that discuss a wide variety of applications of computer technology in archeology. Examples include multispectral analyses of historic maps, applications of 3-D modeling and photogrammetry, spectral clustering for the analysis of stone masks, the potential of virtual museum exhibits, and the modification of commercial video games as an instructional aid for the dissemination of cultural heritage information. With an emphasis on better means of sharing, analyzing, and preserving the cultural heritage of Mexico, the volume nonetheless draws on global archaeological examples and demonstrates methodologies with transnational potential. Also notable are the many color images. [GDH]

4 Arqueología de la Costa del Golfo: dínamicas de la interacción política, económica e ideológica. Edición de Lourdes Budar, Marcie L. Venter y Sara Ladrón de Guevara. Xalapa, Mexico: Universidad Veracruzana, 2017. 370 p.: bibl., ill., maps.

Edited volume focused on Gulf Coastal Mesoamerica. Major themes include landscape and interaction studies, the relationship between architecture, ideology, and political strategies, and applications of digital and experimental archeology.

Contains a prologue by Thomas W. Killion and 19 chapters by an extensive list of contributors. While many works about the Gulf Coast focus on the formative or preclassic period, this volume takes a longer-term perspective on the prehispanic period in the region, including discussions of historical continuities between the formative and classic periods. Applications of photogrammetry or Reflectance Transformation Imaging (RTI) to the study of eroded or modified monumental art and Light Detection and Ranging (Lidar) mapping to landscapes and architectural patterns provide new data for this important region. [GDH]

5   **Bassie-Sweet, Karen.** Maya gods of war. Louisville: University Press of Colorado, 2021. 324 p.: bibl., index.

Bassie-Sweet provides a comprehensive discussion of references to warfare, deities connected with warfare, and their symbolic associations in precolumbian Maya imagery and hieroglyphic texts—particularly from Palenque, Yaxchilán, Tikal, and Copán—and in colonial-period documents. She makes extensive use of the Popol Vuh, a narrative of the history and mythology Quiché people of highland Guatemala recorded in the colonial period, to interpret precolumbian materials. [JSH]

6   **Blomster, Jeffrey P. and Víctor E. Salazar Chávez.** Origins of the Mesoamerican ballgame: earliest ballcourt from the highlands found at Etlatongo, Oaxaca, Mexico. (*Sci. Adv.*, 6:11, March 2020, p. 1–9, bibl., graphs, maps)

Article presents new evidence for highland Mesoamerica's earliest known ball court, excavated at the Oaxacan early formative period site of Etlatongo. Images provide an architectural chronology of the ball court, detailing two phases of construction. Plan maps and photographs highlight the excavations, and the authors depict a figurine from Etlatongo arguably representing a ball player. They conclude that highland Mesoamerica played a larger role in the development of ball games in the region than previously supposed. The formality of ball court architecture, they argue, suggests the formality of the game(s) played there. The authors discuss connections between social complexity and the ball game among the Olmecs as a possible analogy for its role at Etlatongo, though this highland court predates known Olmec examples. [GDH]

7   **Breath and smoke: tobacco use among the Maya.** Edited by Jennifer A. Loughmiller-Cardinal and Keith Eppich. Foreword by John E. Staller. Albuquerque: University of New Mexico Pess, 2019. 262 p.: bibl., index.

This volume brings together essays on tobacco use, an underexplored aspect of Mesoamerican ritual and narrative. Five chapters analyze tobacco in ethnographic ritual and narratives, mainly among the Maya, but also among the neighboring Pipil, and as part of shamanic altered states of consciousness elsewhere in the Americas. Four chapters deal with hieroglyphic texts and imagery on archeological flasks and chemical residues of tobacco in them. [JSH]

8   **Cyphers, Ann.** Las capitales olmecas de San Lorenzo y La Venta. Ciudad de México: Fondo de Cultura Económica el Colegio de México, Fideicomiso Historia de las Américas, 2018. 187 p.: bibl., ill. (some color), maps. (Sección de obras de historia) (Serie Ciudades / Fideicomiso Historia de las Américas)

Book synthesizing decades of research about the Olmecs of the Gulf Coast. Includes chapters on Olmec origins, environmental setting, monumental art, craniofacial characteristics, and diet. The author gives special attention to the two best-known Olmec capitals of the later early and middle formative periods: San Lorenzo and La Venta. This work offers a concise, approachable summary of a foundational Mesoamerican society about which many academic texts exist. Also of note are numerous illustrations and color photographs of excavations, Olmec artifacts, and reconstructions of features and contexts. The author concludes that, while Olmec society collapsed just as others, including the Maya, were on the rise, they left millennia-long influences in Mesoamerican cultural practice and thought. [GDH]

9 **Finegold, Andrew.** Vital voids: cavities and holes in Mesoamerican material culture. Austin: University of Texas Press, 2021. 165 p.: bibl., ill., index.

Finegold explores holes or voids in Mesoamerican, particularly Maya, artifacts: "kill holes" and other perforations in ceramic vessels; perforations in sculpture; perforations of the human body; caves, tombs, pits and their representations; and, by extension, fire, produced by drilling similar to that which created perforations. All of these, he argues, can all be interpreted as relating to the flow of life energy. The "resurrection plate," an unprovenienced Maya-style ceramic dish, structures much of the discussion; many of the artifacts analyzed are similarly without documented provenience, substantially weakening the argument as well as raising ethical considerations. [JSH]

10 **The global Spanish empire: five hundred years of place making and pluralism.** Edited by Christine D. Beaule and John G. Douglass. Tucson: The University of Arizona Press, 2020. 305 p.: bibl., ill., index, maps. (Amerind studies in anthropology)

Edited volume combining diverse perspectives on the Spanish Empire. Includes chapters focused on the Old World, southern Mexico, Central America, South America, the Pacific Islands, and the American South and Southwest. Contributing authors emphasize Native American and African responses to colonialism through analysis of material culture, maps, primary and secondary historical and ethnohistorical documents, and ethnoarcheology. The volume, while published as part of a series in anthropology, weaves together the approaches of anthropology (especially archeology) and history. One notable contribution, by King, discusses the ethnic diversity of the little-studied Nejapa region of Oaxaca, Mexico, and how different native groups navigated, survived, and even exploited the changes wrought by colonialism. [GDH]

11 **Her cup for sweet cacao: food in ancient Maya society.** Edited by Traci Ardren. Austin: University of Texas Press, 2020. 383 p.: bibl., ill., index, maps. (Linda Schele series in Maya and pre-Columbian studies)

Eleven chapters, along with an introduction and concluding remarks, provide a comprehensive overview of food and drink in Maya societies. Most chapters focus on classic period lowland city-states, but coverage also include the formative period and adjacent regions including the lower Ulúa valley. Discussion considers faunal and botanical remains, serving vessels, imagery, and hieroglyphic texts. Thematic emphasis is on the roles of food in the creation of social identities, feasting and political uses of food, and ritual consumption of food and beverages. [JSH]

12 **Interpretación del patrimonio cultural: pasos hacia una divulgación significativa en México.** Coordinación de Manuel Gándara Vázquez y María Antonieta Jiménez Izarraraz. Ciudad de México: Secretaría de Cultura, Instituto Nacional de Antropología e Historia, 2018. 443 p.: bibl., graphs, ill., photos, tables. (Colección Arqueología. Serie Enlace)

Edited volume considering the management and definition of cultural patrimony in Mexico. Book is divided into three sections focused on the background and development of cultural heritage management practices, the conveyance of archeological knowledge to students and the broader public, and practical examples and proposals. The chapters tend to emphasize how cultural heritage management in Mexico has changed in recent decades and offer specific examples from museum settings, modern communities, and archeological sites like Tlatelolco, Teuchitlán, and Paquimé. The book has an overarching goal of emphasizing the value of good public outreach and education regarding archeology in Mexico. [GDH]

13 **Interregional interaction in ancient Mesoamerica.** Edited by Joshua D. Englehardt and Michael D. Carrasco. Louisville: University Press of Colorado, 2019. 412 p.: bibl, index.

Expansive edited collection providing multidisciplinary perspectives on the significance of interaction and exchange in complex Mesoamerican social dynamics.

The volume includes an introduction by the editors, 12 chapters dedicated to theoretical background or topical case studies, and a concluding chapter by David Friedel which refines but supports the continued use of the interaction sphere concept introduced in the 1960s. Contributions of particular note include a discussion of early formative period interaction on the Pacific coast of Oaxaca, linguistic and epigraphic studies, and several detailed analyses of material evidence of interaction, including artifact and architectural styles and technological developments, such as metallurgy. Contributors call on broad evidentiary support, including archeometric sourcing, studies of iconography and style, and linguistics. [GDH]

14   Lieske, Rosemary. Comparative analysis of preclassic and protoclassic burial practices at Izapa and in southeastern Mesoamerica. (*Anc. Mesoam.*, 29:2, Fall 2018, p. 289–307, bibl., ill., map, photos, table)

Article discusses changing mortuary practices at the site of Izapa, Chiapas between the formative and protoclassic periods and places those patterns in regional context. The evidence primarily comes from New World Archaeological Foundation excavations of the 1960s. The author argues that the preclassic-classic shift saw a decrease in stone monument production and site construction, as well as expansion of some peripheral areas and the abandonment of the site's center. Along with this came a shift to urn burials. The author suggests that these changes index political transitions. Burial practices appear to have been less diverse at Izapa than at contemporary sites in the region, such as Kaminaljuyu. Izapa also appears to not have had formal tombs. [GDH]

15   Looper, Matthew George. The beast between: deer in Maya art and culture. Austin: University of Texas Press, 2019. 276 p.: bibl., ill., index. (The Linda Schele series in Maya and pre-Columbian studies)

Looper presents a detailed description of the roles of deer in Maya life and thought, drawing on precolumbian imagery and material remains revealed by archeology. Emphasis is on deer symbolism in ancient Maya art and its significance in relation to social status, fertility, the sun, death, and transitional or liminal environments, but also deer hunting and the practical uses of deer remains. [JSH]

16   López Hernández, Haydeé. En busca del alma nacional: la arqueología y la construcción del origen de la historia nacional en México (1867–1942). Ciudad de México: Secretaría de Cultura: Instituto Nacional de Antropología e Historia, 2018. 389 p.: bibl., ill., map. (Colección Arqueología. Serie Logos)

Book about the origins of Mexican archeology, concerning foundational figures such as Alfonso Caso, Manuel Gamio, Matthew Stirling, and the writer Alfonso Reyes Ochoa, who began a series of essays with the same title as the book, but never finished it. Of particular interest to the author are parallels between the study of the Olmecs of the Gulf Coast, which gathered momentum in the early and middle 20th century, and the formalization of Mexican archeology as a standard of practice and as a government endeavor. Rather than an archeological work, per se, this is a historiography of the discipline as it relates to 19th- and 20th-century self-examination by Mexican society in a quest for its own identity. [GDH]

Martos López, Luis Alberto. Espacios sagrados, espacios profanos: cuevas mayas del centro-oriente de Yucatán. See item **213**.

17   **Maya kingship: rupture and transformation from Classic to Postclassic times.** Edited by Tsubasa Okoshi, Arlen F. Chase, Philippe Nondédéo, and M. Charlotte Arnauld. Foreword by Diane Z. Chase and Arlen F. Chase. Gainesville: University Press of Florida, 2021. 449 p.: bibl., ill., index, maps. (Maya studies)

Sixteen chapters, along with an introduction and two concluding commentaries, explore Maya kingship and the changes it underwent during the terminal classic period (ca. AD 750–950). These changes were central to the processes involved in the transformation of Maya societies between the terminal classic and postclassic periods—the breakdown of cities and political hierarchies and the reorganization of settlements.

Contributors provide perspectives of the process based on archeological data, hieroglyphic texts, imagery, and analogies from colonial period documentary sources. [JSH]

18   **Mayer Center Symposium, 17th, Denver Art Museum, 2017.** Murals of the Americas. Edited by Victoria I. Lyall. Denver, Colo.: Denver Art Museum, 2019. 165 p.: bibl., ill., maps. (Readings in Latin American studies)

This volume is an eclectic collection of papers on murals, ancient and modern, as expressions of social, political, and religious ideas. Four papers deal with precolumbian Mesoamerica. Claudia Brittenham's analysis of spiky multicolored serpent imagery in murals from the Temple of the Chac Mool at Chichén Itzá in northern Yucatán provides important insights into developmental relationships between Teotihuacán and Aztec iconography. A study of the Olmec painting at Oxtotitlán Cave in Guerrero by Heather Hurst and her colleagues places some of Mesoamerica's earliest murals in the context of recent settlement pattern studies and provides important enhanced documentation and a study of the painters' practice. Franco Rossi's detailed analysis of images and texts painted on the walls of a residence at Xultun in Guatemala sheds light on the important and neglected question of how knowledge of writing, mathematics, calendars, and astronomy were shared throughout the classic period Maya lowlands. Papers on the work of Chicano and Chicana muralists, contemporary Hopi muralists who draw on ancestral traditions, and rock art in the American west expand the volume's coverage. [JSH]

19   **Meza Peñaloza, Abigail.** Afinidades biológicas y contextos culturales en los antiguos teotihuacanos. Ciudad de México: UNAM, Instituto de Investigaciones Antropológicas, 2015. 169 p.: bibl., ill.

Book focused on the bioarcheology and mortuary archeology of Teotihuacán. Chapters present evidence for the organization of kinship and family life, mortuary ritual and body treatment, manipulation of human remains, and the relationship between funerary practice and social organization. The study discussed in the book is based on the analysis of 164 sets of adult human remains excavated at the site since the 1940s. Tables summarize patterns of mortuary treatment, offerings, and skeletal health, while figures compare cranial features (especially of the frontal bone) as a metric to gauge biodistance and relatedness to support the hypothesis that the people themselves were often used as ritual sacrifices or sources of human remains for manipulation. [GDH]

20   **Modificaciones cefálicas culturales en Mesoamérica: una perspectiva continental.** Edición de Vera Tiesler y Carlos Serrano Sánchez. Ciudad de México: UNAM, Instituto de Investigaciones Antropológicas; Mérida, Mexico: Universidad Autónoma de Yucatán, 2018. 2 v. (826 p.): bibl., ill., maps.

Edited volume synthesizing the bioarcheology, ritual significance, and symbolism of artificial cranial modification in ancient Mesoamerica. Comprises eight sections providing detailed information about the inspirations of cranial modification research (including 19th and early 20th-century studies in Andean South America), technological and terminological considerations for the analysis of cranial modification, the cosmological significance of the practice for Mesoamericans, and several regionally specific sections discussing the highlands, Gulf Coast, Maya area, and northern/west Mexico. Volume also includes an introduction by the editors. Figures provide numerous skeletal examples, representations of the practice in Mesoamerican two-dimensional and three-dimensional iconography, an ethnographic photograph from the Mangbetu people of Africa, regional typology maps, and reproductions of the techniques used by ancient Mesoamericans to modify the skull. [GDH]

21   **Nacionalismo, globalización y participación social: re-visiones sobre el manejo del patrimonio cultural en México.** Edición de María Antonieta Jiménez Izarraraz, María Guadalupe Espinosa Rodríguez y Blanca Paredes Gudiño. Zamora, Mexico: El Colegio de Michoacán, 2018. 267 p.: bibl., ill., index. (Colección Investigaciones)

Edited volume bringing together chapters that consider the development of laws and practices governing cultural patrimony in Mexico. Key topics include the tensions between national identity and global cultural heritage, public perceptions of the past and Mexican law, community involvement in archeology, museum curation practices, and the project of defining what is modern Mexican cultural patrimony and how best it should be managed. Chapters also consider the deployment of imagery and sentiment related to cultural heritage for modern political and social ends, including political advertisement. [GDH]

22 **Night and darkness in ancient Mesoamerica.** Edited by Nancy Gonlin and David M. Reed. Louisville: University Press of Colorado, 2021. 331 p.: bibl., ill., index, maps, photos.

This volume brings together studies of the cosmological, ritual, economic, and social significance of darkness in precolumbian and ethnographic Mesoamerica. Chapters focus on the classic period Maya, Ulúa region, Teotihuacán, and the Aztec world. [JSH]

23 **Un patrimonio universal: las pirámides de México: cosmovisión, cultura y ciencia.** Coordinación académica del proyecto por Pedro Francisco Sánchez Nava. Textos por Colette Almanza Caudillo et al. Ciudad de México: Secretaría de Cultura; Toluca de Lerdo, Mexico: Instituto Nacional de Antropología e Historia: Secretaría de Educación del Gobierno del Estado de México, 2018. 414 p.: bibl., ill. (chiefly color), plans. (Arqueología)

Edited volume focused on stone and earthen pyramids of ancient Mexico. Chapters consider the mounded monumental architecture of different regions and styles, including well-known examples at major tourist destinations and lesser-known pyramids. Several chapters also consider the religious beliefs, symbolic significance, and archeoastronomical relationships behind the production and use of these features. Notable examples of sites and regions considered here include Teotihuacán, Monte Albán, El Tajín, and the architectural traditions of the Olmec and Maya areas. Large, full-color photographs illustrate the contributing chapters. Chapters also consider the relationships between pyramids and other monumental works, including carved stone sculptures and general architectural planning of major centers. [GDH]

24 **Pérez Rodríguez, Verónica; Corina M. Kellner;** and **Ricardo Higelín Ponce de León.** Urban to the bone: isotopic and faunal dietary data from formative-period Cerro Jazmín, Mixteca Alta, Oaxaca, México. (*J. Archaeol. Sci.*, 121, Sept. 2020, 105177, p. 1–11, bibl., map, photos, table)

Article presents faunal and biorarcheological data from Cerro Jazmín, a late and terminal formative period urban center in highland Oaxaca. Partly based on stable isotope levels from human remains, the authors argue that urbanism corresponded to an extreme reliance on maize and little consumption of animal protein. Among animals consumed, dogs with a maize-based diet, rather than wild animals, were the primary resource. These results lead the authors to conclude that residents of Cerro Jazmín enjoyed little dietary diversity, perhaps due to the defensive location of the site and the danger of straying far from its hillside agricultural terraces. They also report high infant mortality, a weaning age of 3–5 years, general morbidity, and population decline by AD 300. [GDH]

25 **Pool, Christopher A.; Michael L. Loughlin;** and **Ponciano Ortiz Ceballos.** Transisthmian ties: epi-Olmec and Izapan interaction. (*Anc. Mesoam.*, 29:2, Fall 2018, p. 413–437, bibl., ill., tables)

Article reviews evidence for the interaction of late formative period centers on the Pacific and Gulf coastal sides of the Isthmus of Tehuantepec. The authors tabulate the probable sources of stylistic elements on carved stones from locales such as Izapa, Tres Zapotes, and the Maya region. They argue that late formative carved stones of the region exhibit a diverse symbology indicating extensive interaction across the isthmus, though they do describe clear evidence of Izapa influence at the Gulf Coast site of Tres Zapotes. The authors propose adopting a "communities of practice" theoretical approach to understanding the interregional influence seen in ceramics and carved stones, rather than using the traditional model based on style as a proxy for ethnolinguistic identity. [GDH]

26   **Preceramic Mesoamerica.** Edited by Jon C. Lohse, Aleksander Borejsza and Arthur A. Joyce. Abingdon, England; New York, N.Y.: Routledge, 2021. 602 p.: bibl., ill., index.

This volume includes 18 contributions that address the nature of Paleo-Indian and Archaic occupations across Mesoamerica. The main topical emphases include the peopling of Mesoamerica and the Americas generally, adaptations to late Pleistocene landscapes, the beginnings of plant domestication, sedentism, and the Mesoamerican cultural tradition. [JSH]

27   Rosenswig, Robert M. The Izapa kingdom's capital: formative period settlement patterns, population, and dating low-relief stelae. (*Lat. Am. Antiq.*, 30:1, March 2019, p. 91–108, bibl., ill.)

Article synthesizes research on the settlement system and chronology of the southern Mexican site of Izapa. The author argues that Izapa dominated a kingdom of dozens of smaller sites. He offers a reconstruction of Izapa during different periods, concluding that it reached its apex of 229 hectares and an estimated population of nearly 6,000 residents during the Escalón phase (700–500 BC). The author uses these data to argue that Izapa had a tradition of low-relief carved stone stelae well before the date of 100 BC proposed by the archeologist Takeshi Inomata and colleagues for other southern Mesoamerican sites exhibiting this style. He proposes that this discrepancy is consistent with a network of competing kingdoms in the region. [GDH]

28   **Seeking conflict in Mesoamerica: operational, cognitive, and experiential approaches.** Edited by Shawn G. Morton and Meaghan M. Peuramaki-Brown. Louisville: University Press of Colorado, 2019. 308 p.: bibl., index.

This collection of essays explores the evidence for precolumbian warfare in archeology, imagery, hieroglyphic texts, and colonial period documents. Most of the studies focus on the Maya world and several of them use precolumbian texts and imagery to sketch an emic Maya perspective on warfare. Three chapters provide enlightening comparative perspectives from archeology and imagery at El Tajín and possible Teotihuacán conquests in western Mesoamerica, as well as from the Mixtec codices. [JSH]

Sexualidades andinas: otras formas posibles del sexo y el erotismo. See item **1725**.

29   **Simposio Internacional El hombre temprano en América, 7th, Museo Nacional de Antropología, México, 2014.** Prehistoria en América: a 130 años del hallazgo del primer hombre prehistórico en México (1884–2014). Compilación de J.C. Jiménez López et al. Saltillo, Mexico: Museo del Desierto, 2018. 285 p.: bibl., ill., maps, photos.

Edited volume based on papers from the VII Simposio internacional el hombre temprano en América, which took place at Mexico's Museo Nacional de Antropología in 2014. Covers a wide variety of topics, from linguistics and craniofacial characteristics to information about early agriculture, with an emphasis on the Paleo-Indian and Archaic settlements of Mexico. Notable contributions include a summary of the Hoyo Negro project and evidence of a late Pleistocene set of human remains from the Yucatán, megafauna hunting evinced at the Clovis site of Fin del Mundo, and several chapters focused on northern and western Mexico and Baja California. One chapter discusses a site in Brazil. Images demonstrate early lithic artifacts, rock shelters, petroglyphs, floral remains, and cranial features. [GDH]

30   **Sorcery in Mesoamerica.** Edited by Jeremy D. Coltman and John M.D. Pohl. Louisville: University Press of Colorado, 2020. 409 p.: bibl., index.

This volume presents a dozen perspectives on sorcery and related aspects of belief and ritual practice as they are reflected in ethnography, colonial period documents, and precolumbian archeology and imagery. The editors provide an extended consideration of the issues raised in their introduction, but they do not attempt to create a taxonomy of these beliefs and practices, and they do not impose a consistent vocabulary for discussing them. [JSH]

31 **Šprajc, Ivan.** Venus in Mesoamerica: rain, maize, warfare, and sacrifice. (*in* Oxford research encyclopedia of planetary science. Oxford, England: Oxford University Press, 2016, https://oxfordre.com/planetaryscience)

Šprajc provides a detailed discussion of Mesoamerican understandings of Venus and associated rituals as they are reflected in architectural alignments, precolumbian books, and ethnohistorical sources. In addition to a detailed understanding of the apparent motions of the planet, Mesoamerican people shared an array of very specific beliefs about the divinatory implications of the supernatural beings associated with it for important aspects of human life including rain-summoning, maize farming, sacrifice, and warfare. [JSH]

32 **Technology and tradition in Mesoamerica after the Spanish invasion: archaeological perspectives.** Edited by Rani T. Alexander. Albuquerque: University of New Mexico Press, 2019. 284 p.: bibl., index.

Edited volume presenting 10 case studies of technological, economic, and ecological changes that followed the Spanish invasion of Mesoamerica in the 16th century. The work includes an introduction by the editor and a commentary chapter by Anthony P. Andrews. Contributions to this historical archeology collection include discussions of the understudied Nejapa region of highland Oaxaca, Afromestizo ceramic technology in the colonial port of Veracruz, continuity and change in obsidian use, and several chapters considering the ecological and economic transformations of the colonial period. Major theoretical concerns include Indigenous perseverance and ingenuity in the face of colonialism and the globalizing effects of the slave trade, resource exploitation, and the European annexation of the Americas. Beyond Mexico, geographical foci include Belize and El Salvador. [GDH]

33 **Tula y su jurisdicción: arqueología e historia.** Compilación de Francisco Luis Jiménez Abollado. Pachuca de Soto, Mexico: Universidad Autónoma del Estado de Hidalgo, 2018. 165 p.: bibl., ill., maps.

Short, edited volume about Tula and its political significance during prehispanic, colonial, and modern times. Includes chapters concerning early postclassic period Tula and the influence of the Quetzalcóatl religious group in broader Mesoamerica, the modern archeological study of ancient Tula, colonial period governance of Tula as part of the encomienda system, the treatment of Tula in film, and modern environmental issues affecting the region. Rather than a focused archeological study of a particular time, or even a particular site, the book will be of interest to readers concerned with a history of place across approximately the past 1,000 years, with a brief mention of earlier preclassic contexts in the region. [GDH]

FIELDWORK AND ARTIFACTS

34 **Anthropomorphic imagery in the Mesoamerican highlands: gods, ancestors, and human beings.** Edited by Brigitte Faugère and Christopher Beekman. Louisville: University Press of Colorado, 2019. 403 p.: bibl., index.

Edited volume focused on imagery of humans or anthropomorphic deities in the art of highland Mesoamerica, particularly central and west Mexico. Includes an introduction by the editors and 11 chapters. Contributions focus on materials such as ceramic figurines, funerary statues, earthen sculptures, masks, and murals at Teotihuacán and in Aztec contexts. Supporting theoretical concerns include embodiment, funerary practice, ancestor veneration, and Mesoamerican cosmology. Contributions include Marcus Winter's description of the Rey Kong-Oy cave sculptures of Oaxaca, editor Christopher S. Beekman's and Melissa K. Logan's photographs and scientific illustrations of west Mexican hollow figures, and Logan's reconstructions of clothing and body-art motifs depicted on the figures. [GDH]

35 **The archaeology, ethnohistory, and environment of the Marismas Nacionales: the prehistoric Pacific littoral of Sinaloa and Nayarit, Mexico.** Edited by Michael S. Foster. Salt Lake City: The University of Utah Press, 2017. 496 p.: bibl., ill., index, maps.

Edited volume summarizing a large investigation in coastal west Mexico.

Volume includes an introduction by Stuart D. Scott, who directed the original research in the Marismas Nacionales region during the 1960s and 1970s, along with 11 body chapters and a concluding chapter by Scott and volume editor Michael S. Foster. Major volume emphases include mortuary practice and the skeletal biology of 248 human burials recovered during the research, which are the focus of three chapters and eight short appendices. Other chapters summarize the setting, occupational chronology, research methods, artifacts (especially ceramics), and faunal remains. Images include site overviews, examples of ceramic and lithic artifacts, photographs and plan maps of excavations, and comparisons of human cranial and dental modification. [GDH]

36   **Arieta Baizabal, Virginia** and **Ann Cyphers.** Densidad poblacional en la capital olmeca de San Lorenzo, Veracruz. (*Anc. Mesoam.*, 28:1, Spring 2017, p. 61–73, bibl., maps, tables)

These authors employ a coring study to refine population estimates for the major Olmec site of San Lorenzo. A focus is the identification of architecture indicated by an extensive program of 2,600 coring tests and GIS spatial maps. For example, a heat map of floor remnants serves as a proxy for the architectural density of different parts of the site. The authors conclude that the population may have reached between 8,000 and 18,000 by the San Lorenzo B phase. At such a size, the settlement likely relied on the importation of resources. The authors conclude that the resulting stress on the local surroundings, coupled with internal politics, may have led to the decline of San Lorenzo. [GDH]

37   **Arqueología de la producción.** Coordinación de Emiliano Ricardo Melgar Tísoc y Linda Rosa Manzanilla Naim. Ciudad de México: Secretaría de Cultura, Instituto Nacional de Antropología e Historia: UNAM, Instituto de Investigaciones Antropológicas, 2018. 408 p.: bibl., ill., maps. (Colección Arqueología. Serie Logos)

Edited volume focused on crafting in prehispanic and early colonial Mexico, Central America, and South America. Crafting practices and materials under consideration include pottery, lithics, greenstone, shell working, bone working, and metallurgy. One notable contribution, by Valentín Maldonado, discusses hide processing and taxidermy practiced by and for the Aztecs for tribute, costume, and ritual offerings. Volume imagery includes microscopic and radiographic technical figures, stylistic artifact comparisons, codex excerpts, and workflow reconstructions based on experimental archeology. The volume's 13 chapters provide a diverse sampling of crafting practices, with an emphasis on classic and postclassic period central Mexico and the Maya region. [GDH]

38   **Barrera Rivera, José Álvaro** and **Alicia Islas Domínguez.** Arqueología urbana en la reconstrucción arquitectónica del Recinto Sagrado de Tenochtitlan. Ciudad de México: Secretaría de Cultura, Instituto Nacional de Antropología e Historia, 2018. 376 p.: bibl., ill., photos, tables. (Colección Arqueología. Serie Logos)

Co-authored book synthesizing architectural reconstructions of the great Aztec city of Tenochtitlán. Architectural renderings and digital models help the authors reconstruct buildings according to the archeological evidence. Plan maps locate major structures, such as the Templo Mayor, in spatial context with the modern urban core of Mexico City. The authors also provide background discussions of the archeology of urbanism, describe the excavations that support their arguments, and incorporate ethnohistory by seeking evidence of nearly 80 buildings mentioned in colonial period writings of the Franciscan friar Bernardino de Sahagún. The authors conclude that they have identified a 490-hectare district of ancient Tenochtitlán, in and near the modern center of Mexico City, that was the sacred precinct of the prehispanic Mexica people. [GDH]

39   **Becker, Marshall Joseph.** Ceramic roof ornaments (*almenas*) from Cihuatan, El Salvador: contexts, descriptions, and inferences from other sites. (*Anc. Mesoam.*, 28:1, Spring 2017, p. 41–60, bibl., ill., maps, photos, table)

Article discussing remnants of roof ornaments recovered in excavations in El Salvador, comparing them with archeological and iconographic finds from elsewhere in Mesoamerica, especially Mexico. Typically associated with a Teotihuacán architectural style, these ornaments are rare outside of central Mexico and after the classic period. The author identified and reconstructed the ornaments (*almenas*) from at least nine structures and concludes that the roof ornaments varied between houses at the site of Cihuatan and were in use during the postclassic period. The author argues that the ornaments support close ties to central Mexico, perhaps via the site of Tula. Contents of note include information on the context of *almenas* at Cihuatlan, images of their reconstruction, and comparison images from central Mexico. [GDH]

40 **Becquelin, Pierre** and **Dominique Michelet.** Xcalumkín: historia de un centro maya-puuc. Tomo 1, El asentamiento. Ciudad de México: Centro de Estudios Mexicanos y Centroamericanos, 2021. 173 p.: bibl., graphs, ill. (chiefly color), maps. (Cuadernos de Arqueología mesoamericana. Serie Maya)

This volume provides a detailed documentation and analysis of the settlement pattern of the Maya city of Xcalumkín in the Puuc region of northwestern Yucatán and its hinterland. The main occupation of the city is late and terminal classic (ca. AD 600–950). The distinctive Puuc style of architecture appears at Xcalumkín in the eighth century and reaches its greatest elaboration in the ninth and tenth centuries. [JSH]

41 **Beliaev, Dmitri; Albert Davletshin;** and **Sergei Vepretskii.** New glyphic appellatives of the rain god. (*in* Tiempo detenido, tiempo suficiente: ensayos y narraciones mesoamericanistas en homenaje a Alfonso Lacadena García-Gallo. Edición de Harri Kettunen *et al.* Couvin, Belgium: European Association of Mayanists WAYEB, 2018, p. 351–371)

The authors present detailed analyses of name sequences in classic period Maya texts, identifying previously unrecognized epithets for the rain god that refer to lightning and other meteorological phenomena. These extended deity designations appear most often in name sequences of Maya rulers. [JSH]

42 **Bíró, Peter** and **Eduardo Pérez de Heredia.** La organización política y el paisaje de Chichén Itzá, Yucatán, México, en el período clásico terminal (830–930 dC). (*Lat. Am. Antiq.*, 29:2, June 2018, p. 207–221, bibl., facsims., graph, photo, tables)

Using a chronological model in which the Maya (Puuc) style buildings and "Toltec" structures with stylistic features that reflect connections with central Mexico correspond to sequential periods, Bíró and Pérez propose a detailed model of the emergence of a new political organization at Chichén Itzá in the northern lowlands of Yucatán in the ninth century. In place of the single kings of earlier Maya city-states, they envision a structure in which the dominant lord presided over an administration involving two "triads" through which power was shared with less powerful lords. They identify the names and titles of these officeholders in hieroglyphic inscriptions and use their distribution to propose architectural groups corresponding to their family compounds. [JSH]

43 **Blancas, Jorge** *et al.* Estudio de conjuntos departamentales y organización de barrios utilizando sensores remotos y geofísica en el distrito de Tlajinga, Teotihuacan. (*Anc. Mesoam.*, 30:1, Spring 2019, p. 115–128, bibl., graphs, maps)

Article presents remote sensing results for the central Mexican urban center of Teotihuacán. The authors employ topographic maps, satellite imagery, magnetic gradiometry, ground-penetrating radar, and GPS to explore the shape and layout of architectural features in the Tlajinga district at the southern end of the central core of the city. Images of note include overlays of current results with the famous 1973 site map produced by René Millon and colleagues (see *HLAS* 37:659 and 7322). Significant finds include that the Avenue of the Dead extended further south (beyond the Río San Lorenzo) than previously thought. Outlines of buried walls suggest that some of the hypothetical structures reported in the Millon map are less regular than expected, while neighborhood layout itself was more regular than predicted. [GDH]

44 **Burckhalter, David.** Sleuthing Seri figurines: *Ziix Coosyat Yacaam*. (*J. Southwest*, 60:4, Winter 2018, p. 826–913, bibl., maps, photos, tables)

Long article written in a journalistic style and providing an ethnoarcheological study of the meanings of ceramic figurines of the Seri (*Comcaac*) people of Sonora. Article includes a review of the published literature on late pre-contact and early colonial Seri figurines and photos of their rediscovery and use by modern communities. Also details the production of modern figurines using local resources and comparisons of figurine styles with marine fauna. The author provides dates from thermoluminescence analysis of the figurines and concludes that the meanings and uses of Seri figurines are diverse and have changed through perhaps 1,000 years of their production. Author favors the interpretation that the figurines were been made by women potters and represented storytellers. [GDH]

45 **Castillo Bernal, Stephen; Adrián Velázquez Castro;** and **Valentín Maldonado.** Una concha esgrafiada tolteca: apuntes tecnológicos e iconográficos. (*Anc. Mesoam.*, 30:1, Spring 2019, p. 59–73, bibl., ill., map, photos)

This article describes a carved limpet (*Ancistromesus mexicanus*) shell recovered in excavations at the site of Tula, Hidalgo. The authors discuss the restoration process of the shell object, interpret the carved designs, discuss evidence for production, and explore the possible symbolic significance of the artifact. Images of note include microscopic photographs of incisions, multiple reconstructions of the carved iconography, and comparisons with Aztec art. Toltec iconography, including themes carved on the shell, was later employed by the Aztecs to reify their connections to power in central Mexico. Based on a well-documented Mexica burial, the authors suggest that the carved shell was the accoutrement of a Toltec dignitary and was likely burned as part of a funerary offering. [GDH]

46 **Castillo Bernal, Stephen** and **Bertina Olmedo Vera.** El cosmos y sus espejos: el tezcacuitlapilli entre los toltecas y los mexicas. Ciudad de México: Ediciones del Museo Nacional de Antropología, Instituto Nacional de Antropología e Historia, 2016. 115 p.: bibl., ill.

Short book focused on the symbolism and religious significance of mirrors in the cosmology of the Toltecs and Aztecs/Mexica. Includes chapters on the use of mirrors across Mesoamerica in the postclassic period, a discussion of postclassic period concepts of the universe, metaphors for and references to mirrors in other media such as carved stone monoliths and codices, and a discussion chapter. Notable contributions include color imagery of mirrors, carved stones, and codex excerpts. For these authors, *tezcacuitlapilli*, or mirrors, represented to postclassic Nahua-speaking peoples a reference to the sun and its central place in the heavens as well as a symbol of centrality and political legitimacy of the elite. [GDH]

47 **Cecil, Leslie G.** and **Timothy W. Pugh.** Souls of the ancestors: postclassic Maya architecture, incensarios, and mana. (*Anc. Mesoam.*, 29:1, Spring 2018, p. 157–170, bibl., graph, map, photos, table)

This article analyzes the incorporation of broken pieces of older pots into new incensarios and the use of rubble from older buildings in the construction of new edifices in the late postclassic (AD 1400–1525) Kowoj center of Zacpeten in the central Petén lakes district of Guatemala. The authors argue that this practice reflects potters' and architects' attempts to incorporate mana of their ancestors into their artifacts and architectural spaces. [JSH]

48 **La ciudad perdida: raíces de los soberanos tarascos.** Coordinación de Grégory Pereira y Eliseo Francisco Padilla Gutiérrez. Ciudad de México: Centro de Estudios Mexicanos y Centroamericanos; Secretaría de Cultura, Instituto Nacional de Antropología e Historia, Museo Nacional de Antropología, 2018. 121 p.: bibl., ill. (chiefly color), color map. (Museos y galerías) (Ediciones del Museo Nacional de Antropología)

Edited book accompanying an exhibit of Purépecha or Tarascan artifacts from Michoacán on display at the Mexican Museo Nacional de Antropología. The collection represents nearly 40 years of study at the site of Malpaís Prieto. The volume includes a prologue by Antonio Saborit, director of the museum, an introduction, 11 thematic chapters, and an object catalog. The catalog provides exemplary photographs, identifications, and chronological notes for 84 entries. These artifacts include polychrome pottery, diverse metallic objects, bone tools, musical instruments, and a few stone objects, of middle and late postclassic period date. Among volumes related to museum exhibits, this work is notable for providing more contextual information than most, due to the controlled nature of the research producing the collection. [GDH]

49   Clark, John E. and Thomas A. Lee Jr. A touch of Teotihuacan at Izapa: the contents of two burials from Group F. (*Anc. Mesoam.*, 29:2, Fall 2018, p. 265–288, bibl., ill., photos)

Authors discuss Pachuca green obsidian artifacts and other evidence recovered from the site of Izapa by the New World Archaeological Foundation in the 1960s as suggestive of political independence from Teotihuacán during the middle classic period. Article contains republished and new drawings and photographs, along with detailed and illustrated artifact catalogs from elite burials. The authors conclude that the preponderance of evidence at Izapa indicates limited interaction with the highland Teotihuacán state as political peers, rather than a relationship of colonial domination. Despite a prevailing model of limited middle classic period occupations at Izapa, the authors suggest more evidence from this period is overlooked as archeologists paradoxically expect to identify it via evidence for influence from Teotihuacán. [GDH]

50   Clarke, Mary E. et al. Revisiting the past: material negotiations between the Classic Maya and an entombed sweat bath at Xultun, Guatemala. (*Camb. Archaeol. J.*, 31:1, Feb. 2021, p. 67–94, bibl., ill., map, photos, tables)

This paper documents a set of offerings, including the remains of a variety of animals, especially toads and at least one juvenile human being in a buried sweat bath at the lowland Maya city of Xultun in northern Guatemala. The offering was placed in the terminal classic period (ca. AD 800–1050), two centuries or more after use of the structure ceased and it was buried. The toad bones echo the images of toads on the exterior of the sweat bath, suggesting considerable continuity in understanding of the supernatural connections of the sweat bath. [JSH]

51   Dine, Harper et al. Famine foods and food security in the northern Maya lowlands: modern lessons for ancient reconstructions. (*Anc. Mesoam.*, 30:3, Fall 2019, p. 517–534, bibl., map, photo, tables)

The authors synthesize information in the ethnographic literature on famine foods in the northern Maya lowlands and compare the results with botanical information from a study of a house garden and of *rejolladas* (sinkholes that do not reach the water table). The analysis emphasizes famine foods as strategies of resilience in response to political control of access to preferred foods. [JSH]

52   Earley, Caitlin C. "A place so far removed": dynasty and ritual in monuments from Chinkultic, Chiapas, Mexico. (*Anc. Mesoam.*, 31:2, Fall 2020, p. 287–307, bibl., ill., maps, photos)

Earley's analysis of the political implications of late classic period (ca. AD 600–850) relief sculpture from the Maya city in the Comitán valley of Chiapas brings welcome attention to a major center whose potential role in regional politics has been neglected in scholarly literature. One group of sculptures focuses on the accessions of Chinkultic lords, represented as warriors. A second set of sculptures focuses on a distinctive ritual that appears to involve relationships between the lords of Chinkultic and their subordinates. Similarities with Usumacinta cities, especially Yaxchilan and Bonampak, are striking, but their extensive hieroglyphic texts do not mention a connection, so the nature of the relationships remains to be determined. [JSH]

53   Fierro Padilla, Rafael. El consumo de cerámica entre la élite de Yaxchilán durante el clásico tardío: consideraciones a partir de la colección de contextos funerarios y ofrendas. Ciudad de México:

Instituto Nacional de Antropología e Historia, 2019. 415 p.: bibl., ill., photos, tables. (Colección Arqueología. Serie Logos)

This volume describes and analyzes the distribution of 139 ceramic vessels, mostly complete, found in late classic period (ca. AD 600–850) sealed contexts—tombs, burials, and caches—at Yaxchilán on the Río Usumacinta in eastern Mexico. The great majority of these vessels were manufactured in the Yaxchilán region, though the sample includes vessels imported from other parts of the Maya world, especially Alta Verapaz, to the south. Unsurprisingly, in comparison with simple burials, architecturally elaborate tombs contained more vessels, a greater variety of forms, and more varied decoration. All of the imported vessels were found in tombs. [JSH]

54   Frej, William. Maya ruins revisited: in the footsteps of Teobert Maler. With essays by Stephan Merk and Alma Durán-Merk et al. Santa Fe, N.M.: Peyton Wright Gallery Press, 2020. 291 p.: bibl.

This volume features dozens of b/w photographs of precolumbian architecture in the Maya lowlands by William Frej, who retraced the routes of the late 19th-early 20th century explorer and photographer Teobert Maler. Many of Maler's photographs are included as well, some juxtaposed with similar views by Frej. Maler's work is of extreme value in documenting Maya architecture before time and increased accessibility damaged them further, and many of Frej's photographs, especially of lesser-known sites, will play similar roles, but the main attraction of the volume is the esthetic quality of Frej's elegant images. Essays by Jeremy Sabloff on Maya cities, Stephan Merk and Alma Durán-Merk on Maler's work, and Khristaan Villela on Frej's photography provide helpful context. [JSH]

55   Gonlin, Nancy and William R. Fowler. Borders, frontiers, and boundaries in the Maya world: concepts and theory (special section). (*Anc. Mesoam.*, 31:3, Fall 2020, p. 451–565, bibl., ill., maps, photos)

This special section explores issues relating to zones of transition in the Maya world. An introduction (p. 453–460) summarizes recent theoretical perspectives on transitions and considers the significance and utility of the terms frontier, border, and boundary. Seven contributions provide precolumbian and post-invasion case studies that explore cultural boundaries and peripheries as they are reflected in material remains and documentary accounts. [JSH]

56   Gonlin, Nancy; James Stemp; and Jaime J. Awe. The Preceramic and early Ceramic periods in Belize and the Central Maya Lowlands (special section). (*Anc. Mesoam.*, 32:3, Fall 2021, p. 414–557, bibl., ill., maps, photos)

This special section on early occupations in the central core of the Maya lowlands in Guatemala and Belize includes eight papers along with a brief introduction. Emphasis is on Belize and the late Archaic period, but other parts of the central lowlands are covered as well, as are earlier and later occupations. Preceramic ecology and plant use, early skeletal remains, the transition to formative period occupations, formative burials, and the emergence of a recognizable Maya cultural tradition are among the topics considered. [JSH]

57   Graña-Behrens, Daniel. New evidence for political hierarchy and power in the northern Maya lowlands (A.D. 600–1000). (*Anc. Mesoam.*, 29:1, Spring 2018, p. 171–195, bibl., ill., map, photos, tables)

This paper presents the first detailed analysis of emblem glyphs and related titles from sites in the northern Maya lowlands, where royal strategies of self-aggrandizement in sculpture and hieroglyphic texts have always seemed strikingly different form contemporaneous practice in the southern lowlands. Graña-Behrens' analysis suggests that northern practices can be understood as a regional variant of better-understood southern political organization and provides a firm basis for continuing research to clarify the details of northern systems. [JSH]

58   Guernsey, Julia. Human figuration and fragmentation in preclassic Mesoamerica: from figurines to sculpture. New York, N.Y.: Cambridge University Press, 2020. 278 p.: bibl., index.

This book considers the role of anthropomorphic imagery, particularly of figurines and monumental art, in the establishment of social complexity in Mesoamerica's formative period. Combining the author's experience with the figurines and sculptures of the Pacific coastal Soconusco region with analyses of work reported in many other regions, the book synthesizes the study of anthropomorphic imagery at different scales across roughly 2,000 years of history and diverse ecological and cultural settings. Incorporating discussions of the senses (particularly sight), the intentional breakage of figurines "retired" after use, and the relationships between anthropomorphic depiction and actual human bodies, this book collates decades of research on artifacts that are often relegated to the footnotes and appendices of archeological publications. [GDH]

59 Hepp, Guy David. La Consentida: settlement, subsistence, and social organization in an Early Formative Mesoamerican community. Louisville: University Press of Colorado, 2019. 322 p.: bibl., index.

This volume is in part a detailed report on archaeological investigations of an early formative period occupation on the coast of Oaxaca, including mapping and excavation methods, the occupation history, and evidence for increasing sedentism, diet, exchange or other kinds of interaction, and social organization. These data are contextualized in relation to current perspectives on the processes of development of settled life, subsistence based on agriculture, and social, political, and economic complexity. [JSH]

60 Hernández Reyes, Carlos. Tula: capital de los toltecas, exploraciones y descubrimientos. Morelia, Mexico: Editorial Morevalladolid, 2018. 272 p.: bibl., ill., maps.

Book written for the general public synthesizes the archeological research at the postclassic central Mexican center of Tula. Provides basic overviews of the history of Tula, the symbolism of major iconographic themes in the art of Tula (such as Quetzalcóatl imagery and the Chac Mool sculptures), and summaries of other archeological materials in the region, including preclassic figurines from the nearby town of San Lucas Teacalco. The author proposes a refined chronology for Tula and provides a retrospective on his participation in excavations at the site beginning in the late 1960s. Book also provides early photographs of the research and reconstruction at Tula, including some taken by the noted archeologist Jorge Acosta. [GDH]

61 Inomata, Takeshi; Bárbara Arroyo; and Eugenia J. Robinson. Chronology building in southern Mesoamerica: comment on Love. (*Lat. Am. Antiq.*, 30:1, March 2019, p. 224–226, bibl.)

Inomata, Arroyo, and Robinson present a rejoinder to Love's 2018 critique of their 2014 paper proposing a radical revision of the early part of the chronological sequence at the key site of Kaminaljuyú in the highlands of Guatemala (see item 72). They focus on their disagreement with Love about the Bayesian statistical technique used in their original paper and about their interpretation of comparative data from other sites, but they do not address in detail the concerns he raised about stratigraphy and the ceramic sequence at Kaminaljuyú. [JSH]

62 La invención de la memoria: fotografía y arqueología en México. Madrid: Turner; Ciudad de México: Instituto Nacional de Antropología e Historia, 2019. 325 p.: bibl., ill.

Edited book combining chapters by multiple authors with no clear primary editor. The book was a companion piece to a photographic exhibit at the Museo Nacional de Antropología and other museums in Mexico, of hundreds of photographs of archeological sites, projects, and finds dating back to the 19th century and into the middle and later 20th century. These photographs, reproduced in large, glossy, b/w, provide glimpses of major archeological sites before and during their initial scientific investigations and reconstructions. Photographs include those by Alfred Percival Maudslay at Palenque, Désiré Charnay at Chichén Itzá, Teoberto Maler in the Yucatán, Rafael García at Cempoala, Hugo Brehme in highland Oaxaca, and Guillermo Kahlo at the Museo Nacional de Antropologia in the early 20th century. [GDH]

63 **Jackson, Sarah E.** Facing objects: an investigation of non-human personhood in classic Maya contexts. (*Anc. Mesoam.*, 30:1, Spring 2019, p. 31–44, bibl., ill., tables)

Jackson explores the possibility that objects depicted with anthropomorphic faces on classic period painted pottery from the Maya lowlands were considered to be persons in the sense that that they could meet the social and/or cultural expectations of community members. Her arguments are an interesting extension of current conversations about Maya concepts of ontology and long-standing debates about whether and how objects may be said to have agency. Several of the vessels analyzed do not have documented archeological provenience. [JSH]

64 **Kaplan, Jonathan H.** and **Federico Paredes Umaña.** Water, cacao, and the early Maya of Chocolá. Foreword by Arlen F. Chase and Diane Z. Chase. Gainesville: University Press of Florida, 2018. 494 p.: bibl., ill., index, maps. (Maya studies)

Chocolá, with a hundred or more platform mounds and an elegant royal portrait in low relief, is one of the largest sites overlooking the Pacific coastal plain of Guatemala. This volume summarizes Chocolá's history, with emphasis on its participation in a process of developing complexity that transformed eastern Mesoamerica between about 300 BC and AD 200, giving rise to the institutions of lowland Maya civilization. Four chapters and five appendixes describe the results of three seasons of investigation focusing on the hypothesis that Chocolá was engaged in intensive cacao production and exchange. Evidence for this claim is limited to water control features and residues of theobromine in ceramic vessels. Commentary on the colonialist dimensions of archeological investigations in Latin America and on the importance of finding appropriate collaborative modes of engaging with local communities is scattered throughout the volume. [JSH]

65 **Kennett, Douglas J.; Barbara Voorhies;** and **Josue Gomez.** Reconsidering the age and typological character of "Pox Pottery" from Guerrero, Mexico. (*Lat. Am. Antiq.*, 32:3, Sept. 2021, p. 503–516, bibl., ill., maps, tables)

Article presents a reanalysis of a well-known, but poorly understood, early ceramic tradition first identified in Guerrero in the 1960s. Authors discuss new excavations at the same sites where Charles Brush originally identified "Pox Pottery," and find that these early wares fall within the broader Red-on-Buff tradition of southern and western Mexico, as distinct from the Locona tradition primarily identified east of the Isthmus of Tehuantepec. The authors conclude that "Pox Pottery," while not supportable as a type, per se, is consistent with other early Red-on-Buff wares such as the Tlacuache phase ceramics identified at the early formative period coastal Oaxacan site of La Consentida, and support a hypothesis for at least two independent ceramic traditions in early Mesoamerica. [GDH]

66 **Kovacevich, Brigitte** and **Michael G. Callaghan.** Fifty shades of green: interpreting Maya jade production, circulation, consumption, and value. (*Anc. Mesoam.*, 30:3, Fall 2019, p. 457–472, bibl., ill., map, tables)

Analysis of jade artifacts and the contexts of their production—mostly from recent excavations of jade-working areas at the Maya city of Cancuen—does not suggest standardization of production or commodification of exchange. There is strong evidence that jade was not monopolized by elites; common people acquired and used jade ornaments and items of bodily adornment, mostly beads, and were involved in their manufacture. [JSH]

67 **Lerma Gómez, María del Carmen.** Las momias en México: propuesta metodológica para su manejo, estudio y conservación. Ciudad de México: Secretaría de Cultura, Instituto Nacional de Antropología e Historia, 2016. 112 p.: appendix, bibl., ill. (Antropología) (Colección Scientia. Serie Artífice)

Short book about mummification of human remains in Mexico, particularly in deserts, arid highland contexts, and caves. The work includes a review of the process of mummification as well as photographs and drawings of mummies of both humans and animals. A major focus for the author is her proposal, beginning in chapter 3, of a standardized methodology for recovering, studying, and conserving mummified remains. She also discusses common sources of deterioration of mummies and proposes sets of tools and methodologies for their study, including radiology, tomography, paleodietary analysis, paleopathological study, and aDNA analysis. Appendices include suggested recording paperwork and storage boxes for mummies. [GDH]

68   Levine, Marc N. *et al.* Monte Albán's hidden past: buried buildings and sociopolitical transformation. (*Lat. Am. Antiq.*, 32:1, March 2021, p. 76–98, bibl.)

Article presenting the results of recent geophysical work at Monte Albán revealing previously unknown structures located in the site's main plaza. The non-invasive remote sensing techniques employed include electrical resistance, gradiometry, and ground-penetrating radar. The survey results identify three new structures dating from 500 BC-AD 100. These findings also indicate that the present form of the main plaza has changed significantly since the site's founding in the late formative period. The authors conclude that one of the structures was likely a large temple platform and that, collectively, the remodeling of the main plaza suggests a significant political disjunction after the earliest centuries of the city's occupation. [GDH]

69   Lind, Michael. Los sumos sacerdotes de Lambityeco: la evolución de la religión zapoteca del clásico tardío al postclásico tardío. Oaxaca, Mexico: Centro INAH Oaxaca, 2017. 135 p.: bibl., ill., maps. (Arqueología oaxaqueña; 6)

In this book, the late Michael Lind has summarized excavations of the 1960s and 1970s at the highland Oaxaca site of Lambityeco, as well as subsequent laboratory analysis. Emphasizing Structure 190, and evidence for religious traditions better known from the capital city of Monte Albán, this work accompanies others by Lind and the archeologist John Paddock. It comprises 10 chapters, a preface, and a short introduction by Marcus Winter and Nicholas Johnson. Also included are many b/w excavation and artifact photos, site reconstructions, and a concluding chapter placing the site and Structure 190 in the broader context of Zapotec religion, including its role in the standardization of tomb and palace architecture and imagery of the rain/storm god Cociyo. [GDH]

70   López Luján, Leonardo *et al.* Entering the underworld: animal offerings at the foot of the great temple of Tenochtitlan. (*in* Animals and inequality in the ancient world. Edited by Benjamin S. Arbuckle and Sue Ann McCarty. Boulder: University Press of Colorado, 2014, p. 33–61)

Book chapter discussing animal sacrifice at the Aztec capital of Tenochtitlán. Synthesizes previous faunal studies and focuses on Offering 125 from the Templo Mayor Project (2007–2012). Imagery includes reconstruction of the temple, maps and photographs of excavation, and faunal remains. Tables synthesize taxa and the minimum number of individuals (MNI) from the large offering, which was placed in a stone box at the foot of the temple. Animals of note include marine mollusks and fish, freshwater mussels, a rattlesnake, quail, golden eagles, a spider monkey, and a wolf. Osteological evidence suggests some animals were kept in captivity before sacrifice. The authors conclude that diverse species were imported at considerable expense to symbolize the entrance to the underworld. [GDH]

71   Loughmiller-Cardinal, Jennifer A. Distinguishing the uses, functions, and purposes of classic Maya "chocolate" containers: not all cups are for drinking. (*Anc. Mesoam.*, 30:1, Spring 2019, p. 13–30, bibl., ill., photos, table)

This study reassesses the widely accepted function of elaborately decorated classic period (AD 250–900) Maya ceramic cylinders as drinking vessels. Hieroglyphic texts on many such vessels refer to 'uk'iib' "drinking vessel" as well as to foodstuffs, especially cacao and maize. Residue analysis of 70 cylinders detected no residues of cacao, maize, or any other food. Analysis of the vessels themselves suggests that their walls are so thin and porous that they would not have served as effective drinking vessels, though they may well have been used to store dry foodstuffs used in the preparation of beverages. This usage, rather than the function of the vessel itself, may be the referent of the hieroglyphic texts. [JSH]

72 Love, Michael W. Kaminaljuyu chronology and ceramic analysis: an alternative view. (*Lat. Am. Antiq.*, 29:2, June 2018, p. 260–278, bibl., graphs, ill., maps, tables)

Love presents a detailed critique of an influential article published in 2014 (see *HLAS 73:82*) in which Inomata and his colleagues propose a 300-year forward shift in the chronology of early occupations at the major Maya site of Kaminaljuyú in the highlands of Guatemala. Love argues that the Bayesian re-analysis of radiocarbon assays on which Inomata *et al.* rely for their redating is flawed for a variety of reasons, including their reliance on early radiocarbon assays based on uncertain, potentially problematic procedures and the unavailability of the data needed to reassess fully the stratigraphy and ceramic sequence at Kaminaljuyú. See item 61 for a rejoinder. [JSH]

73 Maza García de Alba, Rocío. *Pisom q'aq'al*: la majestad envuelta: poder, reliquias y el "poder de las reliquias" entre los mayas prehispánicos. (*Estud. Cult. Maya*, 53, 2019, p. 173–204, bibl.)

Maza García analyzes relics, especially bundled relics, relating to lineages, to founding ancestors or patron deities of communities, and to war captives and other sacrifices. Bundling relates to funerary practices and therefore to ancestors, particularly in the context of authority and its legitimation. The K'iche' *pisom q'aq'al*—"bundled majesty" or "bundle of fire"—provides a key example. [JSH]

74 Melgar Tísoc, Emiliano Ricardo; Reyna Beatríz Solís Ciriaco; and Hervé Víctor Monterrosa Desruelles. Piedras de fuego y agua: turquesas y jades entre los nahuas. Ciudad de México: Instituto Nacional de Antropolgía e Historia, 2018. 240 p.: bibl., graphs, ill. (chiefly color), maps, photos, tables. (Museos y galerías)

Co-authored book about jadeite and turquoise use by Nahua-speaking peoples of Tenochtitlán. Framed by an introduction and conclusion, the book is divided into two main sections focused on "fire stones" (turquoise) and "water stones" (jadeite). Each section discusses the procurement, transportation, classification, crafting, and symbolism of these materials. Written to accompany an exhibition at the Museo del Templo Mayor in Mexico City, the book includes hundreds of high-quality color images of greenstone artifacts, turquoise mosaics, codex imagery, distribution and transport maps, results of archeometric analyses, and even experimental archeology to reconstruct crafting practices. The authors conclude that the people of Tenochtitlán preferred high-quality stone with specific colors and manufacturing characteristics and established distant trade and tribute relations to acquire it. [GDH]

75 Morell-Hart, Shanti. Techniques for integrating macro-botanical and micro-botanical datasets: examples from pre-Hispanic northwestern Honduras. (*J. Field Archaeol.*, 44:4, 2019, p. 234–249, bibl., graphs, map, photos, tables)

Morell-Hart presents the results of collection and analysis of botanical data from four formative and classic period sites in northern Honduras. The results clearly demonstrate the importance of collecting multiple kinds of data (macro remains, phytoliths, starch grains) and adopting multiple analytical techniques. The paper provides a useful model for paleobotanical research in situations in which excavation methods, collection procedures, and preservation are all highly variable. [JSH]

76 Morell-Hart, Shanti *et al.* Cuisine at the crossroads. (*Lat. Am. Antiq.*, 32:4, Dec. 2021, p. 689–704, bibl., map, photos)

Analysis of macrobotanical remains, phytoliths, and starch grains recovered from sites in the Lake Yojoa basin, the lower Ulúa valley, the Río Amarillo valley, and the Copán valley in northern Honduras reveals a complex pattern of variability comparable to that of ceramics and other craft items. Plant exploitation in general and cuisine in particular echo indications in other material remains that the region was a frontier zone in which cultural features of South American origin and elements typical of Mesoamerican societies blended in multiple patterns. [JSH]

77 Novotny, Anna C. et al. Ritual emulation of ancient Maya elite mortuary traditions during the Classic period (AD 250-900) at Cahal Pech, Belize. (*Lat. Am. Antiq.*, 29:4, Dec. 2018, p. 641-659, bibl., ill., maps, tables)

This paper documents a tomb in the central platform of a triadic pyramid group at the Maya site of Cahal Pech in western Belize used for multiple rich burials in the early classic period (ca. AD 500-600). The interment of multiple individuals in one tomb along with the hieroglyphic texts and the style of jade ornaments and other grave goods suggest that the lords of Cahal Pech were emulating the manner of elite burials at the major city of Caracol. If so, this behavior was presumably a response to the political instability in the area occasioned by conflict between Tikal and Calakmul and their dependencies during this time. [JSH]

78 **Paso de la Amada: an early Mesoamerican ceremonial center.** Edited by Richard G. Lesure. Contributions by John E. Clark et al. Los Angeles: Cotsen Institute of Archaeology, University of California, 2021. 645 p.: bibl., ill., index, maps. (Monumenta archaeologica; 45)

Edited volume with contributions by multiple authors and especially by the editor and primary contributor Richard G. Lesure. Comprises 27 chapters divided into six thematic sections accompanied by an excavation context appendix. Contributions include syntheses of research at the site of Paso de la Amada in the Soconusco region (particularly Mounds 1, 12, and 32), several chapters dedicated to individual artifact and ecofact types, mortuary and osteological information, and three essays by several authors discussing the broader implications of the research. Also significant are the many high-quality color images. In chapter 27, Lesure provides interpretations of kinship and community organization at the site, including the presence of "multi-family households" surrounding the homes of group leaders. [GDH]

79 **Pérez Negrete, Miguel; Hans Martz de la Vega;** and **José Aguilera Almanza.** De ranas, astros y cuentas del tiempo: inspecciones arqueológicas a Piedras Grandes. Chilpancingo de los Bravo, Mexico: Gobierno del Estado de Guerrero, Secretaría de Cultura; Ciudad de México: Editorial Praxis, 2017. 141 p.: bibl., ill., maps.

Text primarily for the Spanish-speaking public about the archeoastronomy and archeology of Piedras Grandes, Guerrero, Mexico. The book summarizes a rock art survey, the geographical setting of the study, and the connections between modern communities of rural Guerrero and the archeology surrounding them. Extensive photographs and illustrations depict petroglyphs, artifacts discovered in and around modern towns, and members of local communities participating in the survey. Rock art images of note include the "Hombre de Maíz," numerous anthropomorphic and zoomorphic designs, and others likely representing ancient astronomical observations. References to postclassic codices and computer-generated astronomical reconstructions contextualize these findings. [GDH]

80 **Porcayo Michelini, Antonio** et al. Cambios y continuidades de la vida ancestral Cucapá: datos arqueológicos, arqueofaunísticos y etnográficos para su comprensión. Ciudad de México: Secretaría de Cultura, Instituto Nacional de Antropología e Historia, 2016. 84 p.: bibl., ill., maps. (Coleccion Historia. Serie Logos) (Cientifica)

Book about the Cucapá of Baja California and correspondences between archeological and ethnographic information for the Sierra El Mayor region just south of the US/Mexico border at Mexicali. The archeological data largely pertain to faunal remains, particularly of fish, but also of water birds and other animals. The authors conclude with a list of continuities and changes in cultural practices in the region beginning in the early Holocene. They report continuities in species of fish collected and in Cucapá language, dance, architecture, kinship, and residential patterns. Key changes include mid-late 20th-century shifts in fishing technology and the outside influences of industrialized agriculture, drought, and the modification of the Hardy and Colorado rivers, upon which Cucapá life has traditionally depended. [GDH]

81 Price, T. Douglas *et al.* Calakmul as a central place: isotopic insights on urban Maya mobility and diet during the first millennium AD. (*Lat. Am. Antiq.*, 29:3, Sept. 2018, p. 439–454, bibl., graphs, ill., maps, tables)

This paper reports on chemical analysis of bone collagen and tooth enamel from skeletal remains of 22 individuals excavated at the Maya city of Calakmul in Campeche, Mexico. Results suggest that the majority of people living in the city center, including at least two of its rulers, were of local origin. In general, many fewer immigrants are recognizable at Calakmul than at Tikal, Copán, and Kaminaljuyú, and those that have been identified come from nearby regions. [JSH]

82 Pugh, Timothy W.; Evelyn M. Chan Nieto; and Gabriela W. Zygadło. Faceless hierarchy at Nixtun-Ch'ich', Peten, Guatemala. (*Anc. Mesoam.*, 31:2, Fall 2020, p. 248–260, bibl., ill., maps, photos, table)

This paper documents and analyzes the layout of Nixtun-Chi'ch', a middle formative (ca. 800–400 BC) city on Lake Petén Itzá in the Maya lowlands of northern Guatemala. Nixtun-Ch'ich' has a pronounced orthogonal grid, unlike any other known Maya city. This is the kind of urban feature often associated with centralized rulership, but the absence of indications of concentrated political power suggests that in this case it arose in a relatively egalitarian context. [JSH]

83 Rice, Prudence M. Anthropomorphizing the cosmos: Middle Preclassic lowland Maya figurines, ritual, and time. Louisville: University Press of Colorado, 2018. 284 p.: bibl., index.

The focus of this volume is a collection of middle formative (ca. 800–400 BC) hand-modeled ceramic anthropomorphic figurines excavated from two sites in the Lake Petén Itzá basin in the southern Maya lowlands. In addition to detailed descriptive analysis and interpretation in terms of ritual uses and representation of sex and gender, Rice provides a brief review of interpretive approaches to figurines elsewhere in Mesoamerica and in other parts of the world along with a more extended discussion of theoretical approaches to them. Her discussion of potential relationships between figurines and head-variant glyphs in Maya scripts, especially for numbers and calendar signs, is particularly notable. This study is unique in placing figurines in the context of multiple interpretive perspectives. [JSH]

84 Rodríguez Mota, Francisco Manuel. El arte rupestre en México: guía para su estudio, conservación e interpretación. Ciudad de México: Primer Circulo, 2016. 167 p.: bibl., ill. (Colección El gabinete arqueológico; 3)

This introductory guide to rock art in Mexico includes definitions, categorizations, discussion of the techniques used by ancient artists, and details of dating and interpretation of rock art. Interpretations of rock art's meaning and use emphasize the practices of shamans or ritual practitioners. The volume also discusses modern vandalism of rock art and presents the results of a semiformal ethnographic questionnaire about the significance of cultural patrimony. Images emphasize pictographs, petroglyphs, and geoglyphs, particularly in west Mexico. [GDH]

85 Rogers, Alexander K. and Robert M. Yohe II. An equation to compute accuracy of obsidian hydration dating ages. (*IAOS Bulletin*, 67, Winter 2021, p. 5–14, bibl., graphs, table)

The authors present a very useful detailed review of the current state of obsidian hydration dating, the determination of the age of an obsidian artifact by measuring the amount of water absorbed since it was created. Emphasis is on sources of error and ways to express their impact quantitatively. The discussion is technically sound but still accessible to nonphysicists and includes a practical equation that archeologists can use to estimate the uncertainty of age determinations. [JSH]

86 Rosa Gutiérrez, Yuri Leopoldo de la. Los astros en las rocas de Coahuila: arqueología de los antiguos habitantes del desierto. Saltillo, Mexico: Gobierno del Estado de Coahuila de Zaragoza, Secretaría de Cultura de Coahuila, 2019. 136 p.: bibl., ill., maps. (Primera Piedra)

Book written primarily for the public about the archeoastronomy and rock art of the ancient hunter-gatherer-fishers of Coahuila, Mexico. The data is provided by Instituto Nacional de Antropología e Historia (INAH) projects in the state that took place in 2001, 2006, and 2008. The figures depict petroglyphs and pictographs on stone panels, cave walls, and rock shelters that, according to the author, demonstrate the systematic astronomical interests, observations, and general cosmology of desert populations of north-central Mexico dating back to at least the Archaic period. The author concludes that the nomadic ancient desert people of Coahuila used rock art to express their interpretations of specific stars, planets, the sun, and the moon, and incorporated this into a deep knowledge of the natural and sacred landscape. [GDH]

87 **Rosenswig, Robert M.** The early Izapa kingdom: recent excavations, new dating and middle formative ceramic analyses. (*Anc. Mesoam.*, 29:2, Fall 2018, p. 373–393, bibl., graphs, ill., maps, photos, tables)

Article details the results of new excavations, artifact analysis, and radiocarbon dating at the site of Izapa. Results indicate significant middle formative period construction followed by remodeling, expansion, and continued use of monumental architecture at the site into the succeeding late formative, which saw Izapa's era of greatest influence. Article presents lidar imagery of site topography, excavation locations and photographs, artifact photographs, and new radiocarbon dates supporting the regional ceramic chronology. Ceramic analysis suggests the use of distinct vessels in different parts of the site. Results are significant for detailing some of the first controlled excavations at a site primarily known for its monumental architecture and stone sculptures. [GDH]

88 **Rosenswig, Robert M.** and **Ricardo López-Torrijos.** Lidar reveals the entire kingdom of Izapa during the first millennium BC. (*Antiquity/Cambridge*, 92:365, Oct. 2018, p. 1292–1309, bibl., graphs, maps, photos, tables)

Article summarizes recent lidar analyses of late formative period Izapa and its surrounding territory. Images provide a regional lidar overview as well as digital elevation maps (DEMs) of key sites, including the Izapa capital and subsidiary centers. The authors argue that these results provide strong evidence for reconstructing the settlement and political hierarchy of the region during Izapa's rule. They speculate about the regional pattern of establishing new hierarchies in areas spatially distinct from predecessors and about Izapa's piedmont surroundings, which provided heavy rainfall for agricultural intensification. They conclude that the Izapa kingdom was internally coherent and independent and that first, second, and third-tier sites in the region qualify as "urban" based on their civic-ceremonial architecture. [GDH]

89 **Saborit, Antonio** *et al.* Cempoala: lugar de veinte aguas. Ciudad de México: Secretaría de Cultura; Xalapa, Mexico: Instituto Nacional de Antropología e Historia: Universidad Veracruzana, 2018. 239 p.: bibl., ill. (Arqueología)

Book with several contributing authors discusses the history, regional setting, and early research at the site of Cempoala in the state of Veracruz. Most notable are the large, b/w photographs recording the first scientific documentation of Cempoala, its process of reconstruction, and the local community that worked with researchers and lived atop the site in the late 19th century. The book also presents an early map of Cempoala from 1891 and photographs of buildings and finds from other sites, such as El Tajín and Papantla. The work gives much attention to the pioneering work of Francisco del Paso y Troncoso, who directed archeological investigations in Veracruz in 1890 and 1891, while also serving as director of the Museo Nacional de Antropología. [GDH]

90 **Sharpe, Ashley E.** The ancient shell collectors: two millennia of marine shell exchange at Ceibal, Guatemala. (*Anc. Mesoam.*, 30:3, Fall 2019, p. 493–516, bibl., ill., map, photos, tables)

Sharpe identifies shells and their archeological contexts dating between 1000 BC and AD 1200 at the Maya city of Ceibal and at Caobal, a subordinate community.

The frequency of specific shells used for bodily adornment and ritual fluctuated through time, but all or almost all of the specimens that could be identified to the level of species were imported from the Caribbean coast. [JSH]

91   **Sharpe, Ashley E.** *et al.* Earliest isotopic evidence in the Maya region for animal management and long-distance trade at the site of Ceibal, Guatemala. (*Proc. Natl. Acad. Sci. U.S.A.*, 115:14, April 2018, p. 3605–3610, bibl., graphs, map, table)

This paper reports on isotope studies of skeletal remains of animals from the Maya city of Ceibal in Guatemala. Results indicate that animal management had begun by 400–300 BC. Strontium values of the bones of two dogs indicate that they originated in the Maya highlands. The jaw of a large wild cat has carbon values consistent with a diet high in maize from infancy, most likely the result of having been raised in captivity. The archeological contexts of these remains, in the civic core of Ceibal, suggests that they had roles in politically charged ritual in the city center. Strontium values also identify a nonlocal tapir tooth, probably imported as a pendant. [JSH]

92   **Simposio de Arqueología del Estado de Hidalgo,** *2nd, Pachuca, Mexico, 2011.* Arqueología contemporánea del estado de Hidalgo. Coordinación de Sergio Sánchez Vázquez y Alfonso Torres Rodríguez. Ciudad de México: Secretaría de Cultura, Instituto Nacional de Antropología e Historia; Pachuca de Soto, Mexico: Universidad Autónoma del Estado de Hidalgo, 2019. 216 p.: bibl., ill., maps. (Científica) (Colección Arqueología. Serie Memorias)

Edited volume focused on recent archeological research in the central Mexican state of Hidalgo. The chapters discuss the region's petroglyphs, Toltec influence and settlements, ancient hydrology and water control, lapidary and ground stone industries, cranial modification, and research at specific sites, such as Huapalcalco and Tulancingo. The book's chapters developed from presentations at the II Simposio de Arqueología, supported by the INAH and the Universidad Autónoma del Estado de Hidalgo, in 2011. Notable contributions include ethnoarchaeological photographs of ground stone tool production and use, images of early colonial-era maps incorporating Indigenous codex-style art and landscape concepts, and photographs of modified human crania. In their introduction, the editors also offer a brief historiography of archeological research in the state. [GDH]

93   **Skaggs, Sheldon; Robert H. Tykot;** and **Terry G. Powis.** Isotopic analysis of newly discovered fragments of an Ulúa Valley marble vase at the ancient Maya site of Pacbitun, Belize. (*J. Archaeol. Sci.: Rep.*, 26, Aug. 2019, 101896, p. 1–10, bibl., graph, maps, photos)

This article reports the analysis of a carved marble vessel in an elite late to terminal classic (ca. AD 600–850) burial at Pacbitun in western Belize. Stable carbon and oxygen isotope analysis confirms that the marble of this vessel matches the composition of marble vessels manufactured at Travesía in the lower Ulúa valley in northern Honduras. The connection may have been direct or may have been mediated by any of several sites in central Belize where marble vessels and/or pottery styles indicate an Ulúa connection. Indications that the grave may have been desecrated at the time the marble vessel was deposited may indicate that connection with the lower Ulúa valley was politically charged. [JSH]

94   **Solís Ciriaco, Reyna Beatríz.** La producción de bienes de prestigio en concha, de Tula, Hidalgo. Ciudad de México: Secretaría de Cultura, Instituto Nacional de Antropología e Historia, 2019. 302 p.: bibl., ill., maps. (Colección Arqueología. Serie Fundamentos)

Book discussing the ancient shell-working industry at the central Mexican site of Tula. The chapters consider the shell artifacts recovered from the site, their archeological context, the routes along which they were traded, households as areas of crafting specialization, and experimental archeology to replicate tool marks as a means of reconstructing crafting techniques. The author focuses on shell artifacts recovered during a 1996 rescue excavation at the district of the site known as Boulevard. Microscopic and scanning electron microscope imagery provides evidence for comparing manufacturing techniques. The author concludes that shell crafting was a remarkably common, standardized, and domestic practice for this central Mexican community of the epiclassic and early postclassic periods. [GDH]

95 **Southeastern Mesoamerica: Indigenous interaction, resilience, and change.** Edited by Whitney A. Goodwin, Erlend Johnson, and Alejandro J. Figueroa. Louisville: University Press of Colorado, 2020. 343 p.: bibl., ill., index, maps.

Southeastern Mesoamerica is an essential reference for archeology and ethnohistory in northwestern Central America, especially Honduras. Eight chapters describe archeological investigations in various regions and three consider how colonial documents reflect the distributions of ethnic and linguistic groups and patterns of travel for trade and military ends. The collective perspective envisions southeastern Mesoamerica as a mosaic of cultural and social processes—sometimes labelled as communities of practice—operating at multiple scales and insists that it must be treated in its own terms, not as an array of societies that lack features typical of lowland Maya societies. [JSH]

96 **Stahlschmidt, Mareike Cordula; Emily McClung de Tapia; and María del Carmen Gutiérrez-Castorena.** A geoarcheological investigation of the street of the dead at the Tlajinga district, Teotihuacan, Mexico. (*Anc. Mesoam.*, 30:1, Spring 2019, p. 129–145, bibl., maps, photos, tables)

Article summarizing stratigraphic, microstratigraphic, and paleoethnobotanical studies in a southern district of Teotihuacán. The authors identify an obsidian workshop through microdebitage analysis, the anthropogenic alteration of bedrock to construct the southern end of the famous "Street of the Dead," and burning activities associated with a structure. Figures illustrate excavations, soil sampling techniques, maps, and microstratigraphy results. Tables synthesize botanical analyses and radiometric dating results. The authors conclude that the stratigraphy indicates the concerted efforts of Teotihuacanos to modify their environment. They also report that the "Black San Pablo Paleosol" underlying the site and found elsewhere in the valley suggests agricultural productivity in the region dating back to the middle Holocene, though botanical remains indicate periods of considerable drought. [GDH]

97 **Stark, Barbara L. and Wesley D. Stoner.** Watching the game: viewership of architectural Mesoamerican ball courts. (*Lat. Am. Antiq.*, 28:3, Sept. 2017, p. 409–430, bibl., graphs, ill., maps, tables)

The authors employ viewshed analysis to estimate the numbers of spectators able to watch ball games at major Mesoamerican urban centers, particularly in southern Veracruz. Ratios of estimated numbers of "prime viewers" to people who could occupy main plazas suggest that a limited few were able to observe a particular ball game in these major centers. The authors conclude that the restricted group of spectators is consistent with marked social inequality. Architecture adjacent to ball courts forming the basis for the analysis includes lateral and end mounds or platforms atop which spectators could gather. The authors conclude that, in most major urban centers considered in the study, 10 percent or fewer of the plaza's occupants could clearly witness ball games at a given time. [GDH]

98 **Sugiyama, Nawa et al.** Animals and the state: the role of animals in state-level rituals in Mesoamerica. (*in* Animals and inequality in the ancient world. Edited by Benjamin S. Arbuckle and Sue Ann McCarty. Boulder: University Press of Colorado, 2014, p. 11–31, bibl., ill., photos)

Book chapter about the use of animals in Mesoamerican rituals that supported complex political organization. Chapter focuses particularly on classic period Teotihuacán, and considers the role of animals as sacrifices, symbols, and elements of elite attire. Faunal remains from burials in the Pyramid of the Moon provide evidence for arguments in the chapter, including that animals were kept alive at Teotihuacán for some time before their sacrifice. The chapter includes a theoretical discussion of human-animal interaction, the background of Teotihuacán, and a detailed analysis of burials and dedicatory caches containing animal remains.

Fauna of special interest includes jaguars, pumas, eagles, snakes, and canids. [GDH]

99 **Thornton, Erin Kennedy** and **Arthur A. Demarest.** At water's edge: ritual Maya animal use in aquatic contexts at Cancuen, Guatemala. (*Anc. Mesoam.*, 30:3, Fall 2019, p. 473–491, bibl., graphs, ill., maps, photos, tables)

The densest concentrations of animal remains at the late classic period (ca. AD 600–900) Maya river port of Cancuen are found in reservoirs in the city's monumental architectural core. These reservoirs were part of elaborate hydraulic systems. The animal remains found in them have higher frequencies of symbolically important animals—such as jaguars and dogs—and unusual skeletal element frequencies compared with remains recovered from middens. These patterns, along with the location and complexity of the hydraulic systems, suggest that the reservoirs were venues for state ritual involving animals. [JSH]

100 **Vista Hermosa: nobles, artesanos y mercaderes en los confines del mundo huasteco: estudio arqueológico de un sitio Posclásico Tardío del municipio de Nuevo Morelos, Tamaulipas, México.** Vol. 3, Arte y la vida en la Huasteca posclásica. Coordinación de Claude Stresser-Péan. Ciudad de México: Secretaría de Cultura, Instituto Nacional de Antropología e Historia: Museo Nacional de Antropología: Fundación Stresser-Péan: Centro de Estudios Mexicanos y Centroamericanos, 2018. 477 p.: bibl., ill. (some color), color maps.

Third edited volume in a series concerning the Huastec region, and particularly the site of Vista Hermosa, during the postclassic period. This entry includes chapters 8–12 in the series and focuses particularly on the specialized crafting and symbolic significance of shell, other faunal remains, metal, obsidian, and other lithic materials. Microscopic imagery evinces practices of jewelry production. Chapters employ scientific illustration to explore shell pectoral iconography, metallurgy, and lithic manufacture. Significant contents include a detailed discussion of obsidian prismatic blade production, an illustrated typology of metallic objects such as copper bells, a photographic comparison of marine mollusk species of archeological import, and contextual information for the *in situ* recovery of shell pectorals, including as mortuary objects. For a review of vol. 1, see *HLAS 75:144*. [GDH]

101 **Walden, John P. et al.** Modeling variability in Classic Maya intermediate elite political strategies through multivariate analysis of settlement patterns. (*J. Anthropol. Archaeol.*, 55, Sept. 2019, 101074, p. 1–22, bibl., graphs, ill., maps, tables)

Hierarchical cluster analysis of 24 architectural features at 35 Maya sites of various sizes in the middle Belize River Valley produced a six-tier settlement hierarchy. The analysis focuses on the upper middle range, interpreted as centers occupied and controlled by "intermediate elites," a poorly understood aspect of Maya political organization. Architectural features typical of these sites suggest that the political strategies of intermediate elites included ancestor veneration, emulation of higher elites, functioning as neighborhood leaders, using ceremonies to integrate non-elites, and controlling "frontiers" between polities. [JSH]

102 **Webster, David L.** and **Joseph W. Ball.** Rehabilitating Becán. (*Anc. Mesoam.*, 32:3, Fall 2021, p. 371–395, bibl., graphs, ill., maps, photos)

Becán, the large Maya city in the south-central Maya lowlands of Mexico has little monumental sculpture and few hieroglyphic inscriptions and as a result it has become marginal to most accounts of Maya history, which emphasize dynastic history. Webster and Ball reassess the archeological record of Becán, particularly its unusual defensive wall and moat, demonstrating that architecture, ceramics, and other material remains can reveal a great deal about the political and cultural significance of precolumbian Maya cities. Successes in deciphering Maya inscriptions have not rendered conventional archeological data irrelevant. [JSH]

103 **Woodfill, Brent.** War in the land of true peace: the fight for Maya sacred places. Norman: University of Oklahoma Press, 2019. 295 p.: bibl., index.

This volume provides a historical perspective on the relatively flat region that constitutes a zone of transition between the Maya highlands and the southern Maya lowlands in Guatemala from precolumbian times until the present. The focus is on landscapes and their cultural meanings, emphasizing a nuanced ethnographic account of the ongoing struggles of the Q'eqchi' Maya to preserve and control places that are sacred to them in the face of ever-intensifying pressures emanating from economic and political forces and processes centered outside the region. [JSH]

104 **Zalaquett Rock, Francisca A.** and **Dulce S. Espino Ortiz.** Flautas triples de Jaina y Copán: un estudio arqueoacústico. (*Anc. Mesoam.*, 30:3, Fall 2019, p. 419–438, bibl., graphs, ill., maps, photos, tables)

This study documents flutes with an unusual 3-chambered form from Copán in northwestern Honduras and the Isla de Jaina off the west coast of Yucatán, Mexico. These instruments are very similar in acoustic properties as well as in their form, suggesting a relationship between the two Classic period Maya societies. The considerable distance separating the two regions and the absence of other obvious indications of connections between them problematizes the mechanism for the interaction. [JSH]

105 **Zimmermann, Mario et al.**
Metabolomics-based analysis of miniature flask contents identifies tobacco mixture use among the ancient Maya. (*Sci. Rep./London*, 11:1590, Jan. 2021, p. 1–11, bibl., graphs, map, photos, tables)

This paper reports on chemical analysis of residues in 14 small ceramic flasks excavated from Maya archeological sites in northern Yucatán, Mexico. Liquid chromatography and mass spectrometry revealed the use of two species of tobacco, almost certainly ingested for their mind-altering properties. Mexican marigold, present in several vessels, is used ethnographically as an additive to minimize the irritating effects of chewing tobacco. [JSH]

106 **Źrałka, Jaroslaw et al.** The discovery of a beehive and the identification of apiaries among the ancient Maya. (*Lat. Am. Antiq.*, 29:3, Sept. 2018, p. 514–531, bibl., graphs, ill., maps, tables)

This paper documents the discovery of a ceramic tube with ceramic caps at either end found in a late formative (ca. 100 BC–AD 300) cache within the public architectural core of the Maya city of Nakum in the lowlands of northeastern Guatemala. A review of depictions of beehives in Maya imagery and of descriptions of Maya beekeeping in ethnohistorical and ethnographic sources confirms that the ceramic tube was a beehive or a representation of a beehive. [JSH]

107 **Źrałka, Jaroslaw et al.** Political alliances and trade connections observed in the ceramic record of the Classic period: the perspective from the Maya site of Nakum, Guatemala. (*Anc. Mesoam.*, 31:3, Fall 2020, p. 461–475, bibl., ill., map, photos, table)

This paper documents external interactions reflected in elaborately decorated ceramic vessels found in excavations at the Maya city of Nakum in the northern lowlands of Guatemala. Most of these vessels date to the late classic period (ca. AD 600–800) and their style, decoration, hieroglyphic texts, and chemical composition indicate connections with multiple cities in the southern Maya lowlands, particularly Tikal and Naranjo. To judge by hieroglyphic texts on public monuments at these centers, these connections are best interpreted as reflections of social and political linkages rather than simple economic exchange. [JSH]

NATIVE SOURCES AND EPIGRAPHY

108 **Cruz Cortés, Noemí.** Hunab Ku, revisión de una deidad en la *Historia de Yucatán* de fray Diego López de Cogolludo. (*Estud. Cult. Maya*, 53, 2019, p. 239–260, bibl.)

This article undertakes a close analysis of references to a supernatural being called "Hunab Ku" in early colonial period documents written by Spanish churchmen and historians, particularly López de Cogolludo's *Historia de Yucatán*. Cruz concludes that Hunab Ku ("one, one-ness, unique" "god") was an attempt to convey the Christian characterization of their god as the one true god in the Yucatec language. [JSH]

Haskell, David Louis. The two Taríacuris and the early colonial and pre-hispanic past of Michoacán. See *HLAS 76:90.*

109 Jackson, Sarah E. Hieroglyphic texting: ideologies and practices of Classic Maya written evidence. (*Camb. Archaeol. J.*, 30:4, Nov. 2020, p. 611–628, bibl., photos)

Jackson argues that, given current interests in ontology and experiential approaches to the past, epigraphers should make serious efforts to understand how ancient readers perceived texts. Using texts painted on ceramic vessels, she speculates about ancient modes of relating to texts. The argument is weakened by reliance on vessels without documented archeological provenience. [JSH]

110 Jobbová, Eva; Christophe Helmke; and **Andrew Bevan.** Ritual responses to drought: an examination of ritual expressions of classic Maya written sources. (*Hum. Ecol.*, 46:5, Sept. 2018, p. 759–781, bibl., graphs, photos)

This paper presents a detailed analysis of activities depicted in Maya imagery as planting and rain-making rituals. Accompanying hieroglyphic texts name the rituals and the supernatural beings implicated in them, and the associated calendar dates associate them clearly with the seasonality of rain and the agricultural cycle. In the terminal classic period (ca. AD 800–900), when the timing of rains became less predictable and droughts became more frequent, the earlier emphasis on dynastic history and royal biographies in imagery and hieroglyphic texts on public monuments diminished and these rituals became more prominent. For geography specialists' comment, see item **484**. [JSH]

111 Johnson, Erlend M.; Pastor Gómez Zúñiga; and **Mary K. Kelly.** Ch'orti', Lenca, and Pipil: an onomastic approach to redefining the sixteenth-century southeastern Maya frontier. (*Ethnohistory/Columbus*, 66:2, 2019, p. 301–328)

The authors present a detailed analysis of place names, personal names, and language names in northwestern Honduras using living informants, ethnohistoric documents, and published dictionaries and maps. The results show a much greater than expected presence of speakers of Lenca and Pipil. This suggests that the orthodox interpretation that the region was occupied mainly by speakers of Ch'orti' Maya has been based partly on an inappropriate projection of the classic period Maya occupation of Copán across the region and forward in time, driven largely by the invention of a Maya history for Hondurans by the state and public intellectuals. [JSH]

112 Knowlton, Timothy. Theology and economy in the *Popol Wuj* and *Theologia Indorum*. (*Anc. Mesoam.*, 34:2, Summer 2023, p. 476–488, bibl.)

Knowlton provides a close analysis of the description of debt and obligations of people to deities in two 16th-century documents written in the K'iche' language: the *Popol Vuh*, which recounts the traditional origin and history of the K'iche' people, and the *Theologia Indorum*, a treatise produced by the Dominican friar Domingo de Vico to foster conversion to Christianity. The emphasis in the *Popol Vuh* on reciprocity contrasts sharply with the more transactional view in Vico, providing insight into Indigenous ontology and theology that is useful in understanding other Mesoamerican belief systems along with that of the K'iche'. See also *HLAS 76:125*. [JSH]

113 Painting the skin: pigments on bodies and codices in pre-Columbian Mesoamerica. Edited by Élodie Dupey García and M. Luisa Vázquez de Ágredos Pascual. Tucson: The University of Arizona Press, 2018. 284 p., 32 unnumbered pages of plates: bibl., index.

Edited collection concerning the decoration of skin, both of human bodies and non-human objects. The work includes a foreword by Stephen Houston and an epilogue by the volume editors. The volume emphases include materiality, embodiment theory, funerary practices, the archeology of the senses, objects as sentient social beings, and the correspondence of specific colors with aspects of social identity. Several chapters present the results of nondestructive technological analyses.

The volume includes numerous b/w images and over 30 high-quality color plates demonstrating the colors of pigments, the employment of iconography on human remains and artifacts, codex images, ethnographic and nature scenes, experimental reproductions, and microscopic details. [GDH]

114 Suárez Diez, Lourdes and **Martha Alicia López Díaz.** Conchas y caracoles en las pictografías de la obra de fray Bernardino de Sahagún. Ciudad de México: Secretaría de Cultura, Instituto Nacional de Antropología e Historia, 2017. 151 p.: bibl., ill. (chiefly color). (Científica) (Colección Etnohistoria. Serie Sumaria)

Co-authored book about shells referenced in the colonial-period pictographic manuscripts attributed to the Franciscan friar Bernardino de Sahagún. Produced in collaboration with native scribes, the works attributed to Sahagún that are the focus of this research include *Primeros memoriales* and the Florentine Codex. The book provides an analysis of high-quality color images excerpted from the works of Sahagún. The images depict people playing conch shell trumpets, shells used or referenced in architecture, shells incorporated in human and divine attire, and shells used in watery imagery, in general. Also included are photographs of Aztec shell and shell-referencing artifacts. The authors conclude that the Aztecs/Mexica had a broad interaction and tribute network, advanced biological concepts, and accomplished crafting practices for shell use. [GDH]

115 Valencia Rivera, Rogelio. K'awiil y el calendario maya de 819 días. (*Estud. Cult. Maya*, 53, 2019, p. 103–138, bibl.)

Valencia Rivera provides an extensive analysis of the enigmatic 819-day cycle that appears in a few Maya hieroglyphic texts. The focus is on the verbal phrase associated with these texts, which names the deity K'awiil or a related supernatural, along with one of the four world quarters and its associated color. The analysis suggests that these texts describe or prescribe a ritual circuit or procession involving aspects of K'awiil. [JSH]

Caribbean Area

THOMAS P. LEPPARD, *Archaeologist and Project Director, International Archaeological Research Institute, Inc.*

CARIBBEAN ARCHEOLOGY continues to be characterized by several trends, not least the burgeoning interest in leveraging the archeological sciences, and evident willingness to utilize modern bodies of theory in understanding the material record.

In *HLAS 75*, I observed that Caribbean scholarship was moving past 1492 as a conceptual watershed. That notion remains clear in the research described for *HLAS 77*. Whether dealing with demography, settlement, iconography, or the conceptual organization of research projects (items **123**, **126**, **128**, **130**, and **133**), the scholarship is moving towards a position in which elements of Indigenous continuity from the historic period are sought and emphasized, while also indicating an interest in tripartite cultural exchanges among Indigenous Amerindians, European colonizers, and enslaved Africans (item **130**)—often through theoretical lenses explicitly oriented away from the hegemonic view of colonialism as a process. Clearly, there continues to be a commitment to understanding the diversity of human experience within the processes of cultural contact and colonialism, moving away from monolithic narratives and models of identity towards more complex and contextual readings; either via high-resolution, multiproxy studies (item **117**) or thematically organized volumes (items **118, 125,** and **131**).

Lifeways in both pre- and postcontact Caribbean archaeology continue to be informed by the archeological sciences, notably zooarcheology and paleoethnobotany (items **116, 122, 132,** and **136**). Human bioarcheology is also evident (item **135**). Paleogenomic studies (see, for example, item **129**) will revolutionize how we think about the colonization of, and diversification within, the Caribbean—although in this instance we might be reassured that the genetic micropattern lends tangential support to our current understanding about the wider patterns and processes of Amerindian occupation.

Beyond this approach, diversity is a consistent theme; there is a willingness to move beyond traditional modes of categorization in exploring established topics in the precontact Caribbean (item **119**) as well as in considering issues of style (items **127** and **130**) and technology (items **121** and **134**).

CARIBBEAN ISLANDS

116 Antczak, María Magdalena; Andrzej T.Antczak; and Miguel Lentino. Avian remains from late pre-colonial Amerindian sites on islands of the Venezuelan Caribbean. (*Environ. Archaeol.*, 24:2, 2019, p. 161–181, bibl., map)

This paper addresses the human use of birds in the islands of the southern Caribbean in the period prior to European contact. Zooarcheological analysis of remains from several islands indicates a broad spectrum of bird hunting, but the authors show that such hunting may variously be connected to subsistence behavior (with regard to boobies and pelicans), while hunting of other taxa may instead be connected to exploitation of their plumage (e.g., flamingos, spoonbills). The authors also stress that evidence for Indigenous hunting of southern Caribbean island birds reinforces the need for a better understanding of the long-term impacts of precolumbian settlement on insular (and continental migratory) avifaunas.

117 **Archaeology in Dominica: everyday ecologies and economies at Morne Patate.** Edited by Mark W. Hauser and Diane Wallman. Gainesville: University of Florida Press, 2020. 200 p.: bibl., ill., index. (Florida Museum of Natural History: Ripley P. Bullen series)

This volume considers the historical period archeological record of the Morne Patate site in immense and multidimensional detail. Chapters address high resolution chronologies, ceramic analysis and sourcing, environmental archeology, and the archeology of domestic space—in fact, household archeology as an interpretive position informs large segments of the volume as a whole. This deep dive into the archeology of one plantation site opens up new vistas on how we conceptualize the wider impacts of the plantation process, and has relevance far beyond Dominica.

118 **Archaeology of domestic landscapes of the enslaved in the Caribbean.** Edited by James A. Delle and Elizabeth C. Clay. Gainesville: University of Florida Press, 2019. 296 p.: bibl., index. (Florida Museum of Natural History: Ripley P. Bullen series)

This volume shifts the focus of the archeology of enslaved peoples away from the artifactual record and portable material culture and towards the built environment and dwelling spaces. In exploring how enslaved peoples variously utilized their architecture to different ends and following different spatial grammars, the contributors underscore the diversity of the enslaved experience, breaking up a category that is often rendered passive and homogeneous in the archeological literature. The broad geographic sweep of the volume makes it relevant for scholars working across the Caribbean. For an additional comment on this work, see *HLAS 75:180.*

119 **Bérard, Benoît.** About boxes and labels: a periodization of the Amerindian occupation of the West Indies. (*J. Caribb. Archaeol.*, 19, 2019, p. 51–67, bibl., tables)

In this conceptual piece, the author addresses how periods of time and macroscale cultural variability are related within Caribbean precontact archeology. Rouse's scheme, as the author notes, still exercises considerable sway in how Caribbean archeologists understand the transition from colonization, to Archaic settlement, to Ceramic settlement. Bérard contextualizes this periodization and related schemata intellectually, and proposes—not the abandonment of the Rousian framework—but an update, uniting everything from the Cedrosan Saladoid to the Troumassoid into a "Ceramic" framework, for example; a periodization that increasingly finds support in the scholarship. Little mention is made of radiocarbon assays, that might be reasonably supposed to be able to more firmly anchor Caribbean chronologies.

120 **Curet, L. Antonio.** Theodoor De Booy in Puerto Rico: an untold story in the history of Caribbean archaeology. (*Caribb. Stud.*, 46:1, Jan./June 2018, p. 3–32, bibl., ill., photos, tables)

A component of the Caribbean's experience of colonialism involved the influx of European and American scholars. As a result, the early archeology of the Caribbean was dominated by archeologists from Europe and North America, primarily involving expeditions that in part sought artifacts for the purposes of enlarging European or North American museum collections. In this paper, the author considers one such expedition in detail: De Booy's expedition to southwestern Puerto Rico in 1916. This expedition was (uncharacteristically) never published by De Booy. Here, Curet relates the expedition's apparent findings in some detail, richly illustrating the discussion with a detailed photographic record. The author contextualizes the expedition in terms of the development of the national museum in the 20th century.

121 **Falci, Catarina Guzzo et al.** Lapidary production in the eastern Caribbean: a typo-technological and microwear study of ornaments from the site of Pearls, Grenada. (*Archaeol. Anthropol. Sci.*, 12, 2020, p. 1–53, bibl., maps)

This paper considers in some detail the organization and management of lapidary production at the precontact site of Pearls, on Grenada. A key node in the flow of materials between the Lesser Antilles and the South American littoral, Pearls is the only known lapidary production site from this part of the archipelago during the Ceramic Period. The presence of large numbers of nonlocal materials (including amethyst, turquoise, and jadeite) from the studied collection reinforces this understanding of the site as nodal, and indicates that it was a center of specialization in this particular industry. Manufacturing techniques and the *chaîne opératoire* parallel production sites from further north.

122 **Giovas, Christina M.** The beasts at large: perennial questions and new paradigms for Caribbean translocation research. Pt. II, Mammalian introductions in cultural context. (*Environ. Archaeol.*, 24:3, 2019, p. 294–305, bibl.)

In the second installment of this important paper (see part 1, *HLAS 75:187*), Giovas considers anthropogenic dispersal of species throughout the Caribbean. In particular, she addresses the roles of introduced fauna, from the tangible to the intangible. Giovas underlines the importance of non-native animals as sources of not only food, but also raw materials for craft production (and sometimes quite different cultural attitudes; in the case of dogs, for example). Critically, she finds that the issue of management and/or domestication of agouti and hutia remains an open question, despite clear intentional introduction.

123 **Giovas, Christina M. et al.** The Carriacou ecodynamics archaeology project: first results of geophysical survey and landscape archaeology at the Sabazan site, the Grenadines. (*J. Island Coastal Archaeol.*, 15:3, Aug. 2019, p. 421–435)

The authors report on important field activities on Carriacou, in the Grenadines. This project, a successor to sustained interest in the archeology of Carriacou and Sabazan since the 2000s, is notable in several dimensions—not least its explicit interest in spanning the precontact and historic periods, and in the multimethod applications (including GPR and shovel test pitting). The project also documented the continuing loss of archeology-bearing deposits on the island due to a combination of natural and anthropogenic factors.

124 Hanna, Jonathan A. Camáhogne's chronology: the radiocarbon settlement sequence on Grenada, West Indies. (*J. Anthropol. Archaeol.*, 55, Sept. 2019, 101075, p. 1–24, bibl.)

Continuing the Grenadine theme, Hanna discusses the radiocarbon sequence for the island in high resolution. He considers in detail the various assays available for the island, although he does not necessarily dismiss those that might potentially be considered methodologically or contextually problematic. The author finds ephemeral evidence for a late Archaic occupation, and a Ceramic occupation commencing around AD 300. This finding he takes to support Fitzpatrick's "Southward Route Hypothesis," and in contravention of the Stepping Stone model. He also discusses possible cultural differences on Grenada in the last phase of the Ceramic, prior to European contact. For a publication from the 2006 Society for American Archaeology conference that includes Fitzpatrick's paper on his hypothesis, see *HLAS 67:259*.

125 **Historical archaeologies of the Caribbean: contextualizing sites through colonialism, capitalism, and globalism.** Edited by Todd M. Ahlman and Gerald F. Schroedl. Tuscaloosa: The University of Alabama Press, 2020. 272 p.: bibl., ill., index, maps. (Caribbean archaeology and ethnohistory)

While it is no longer the case that the historical archeology of the Caribbean is entirely dominated by plantation archeology, this volume is nonetheless a welcome corrective towards any remaining bias in that direction. Contributions include important discussions of frontiers within the postcontact Caribbean, and which thereby necessarily address issues of culture contact, exchange, and hybridity. Chapters that address the archeology of sites associated with public health and the military provide useful perspectives on how state institutions intersect with quotidian experience. Finally, the plantation experience is not glossed, but is shown to be heterogenous and diversely constituted.

126 **Indígenas e indios en el Caribe: presencia, legado y estudio.** Edición y compilación de Jorge Ulloa Hung y Roberto Valcárcel Rojas. Santo Domingo: Instituto Tecnológico de Santo Domingo, Editora Búho, S.R.L., 2016. 309 p.: bibl., ill. (Los indígenas más allá de Colón; 1)

This edited volume forms part of an evident wider trend, challenging extant and now outmoded narratives regarding the intersection of pre- and postcontact worlds. In particular, contributors move beyond the moment of contact as a cultural and historical watershed, and instead emphasize evidence for continuities and cultural interactions that persist in the aftermath of the Columbian moment. Especially welcome is a consistent theoritical engagement with notions of colonialism and indigeneity. While the focus is on the Hispanophone Caribbean, this volume clearly represents part of a wider process of reconceptualizing the relationship between pre- and postcontact archeologies in the Caribbean.

127 Knight, Vernon J. Caribbean figure pendants: style and subject matter: anthropomorphic figure pendants of the late Ceramic Age in the Greater Antilles. Leiden, Netherlands: Sidestone Press, 2020. 269 p.: bibl., ill. (some color), maps. (Taboui; 7)

This book represents a comprehensive and synoptic approach to a class of portable material that, if not overlooked, is surely deserving of updated treatment. The author considers a large body of anthropomorphic pendants from the Indigenous Caribbean, and shows just how diverse the corpus is, at least in stylistic terms. Reflecting on the apparent ubiquity of the objects and their enormous diversity, Knight suggests that they be connected instead to membership in or involvement with supralocal institutions, relating to—perhaps—warfare, healing, or esoteric knowledge.

128 **Kulstad González, Pauline.** Hispaniola—hell or home?: decolonizing grand narratives about intercultural interactions at Concepción de la Vega (1494–1564). Leiden, The Netherlands: Sidestone Press, 2020. 255 p.: bibl., color ill., color map.

This volume reconsiders the archeology of the important Hispaniolan site of Concepción de la Vega from a decolonial perspective. In doing so, it emphasizes non-elite, African, and Indigenous perspectives, challenging narratives associated with the colonizing powers and institutions. The result is a richer and more complex archeology of this important site, and by extension, of Spanish colonialism in the Caribbean more broadly.

129 **Nägele, Kathrin.** Genomic insights into the early peopling of the Caribbean. (*Science/Washington*, 369:6502, 2020, p. 456–460, bibl., maps)

This important paper (now followed by other major contributions to Caribbean paleogenomics) sheds light on the macroscale process of human immigration into the insular Caribbean in the period prior to European contact. The authors analyzed 93 ancient genomes from across the Caribbean, from individuals dating from the Archaic to the late Ceramic. They detect a complex, multidispersal-event demographic history for Archaic populations in the "western" Caribbean (i.e., the westerly Greater Antilles), and then a clear South American signal in populations after around 2800 BP. This, the authors parsimoniously associated with the Ceramic horizon. They also note little apparent admixture between extant Archaic and South American-derived populations, but admit that this could be a function of the spatial and temporal distribution of samples.

130 **Ostapkowicz, Joanna et al.**
Integrating the Old World into the New: an "idol from the West Indies." (*Antiquity/Cambridge*, 91:359, Oct. 2017, p. 1314–1329, bibl., graphs, ill., photos, table)

In this paper, the authors present an analysis of a unique cemi, now housed in the Museo nazionale preistorico etnografico Luigi Pigorini in Rome. Considering the unusual mixture of styles, iconography, and materials from apparently both sides of the Atlantic, the provenance and context of the manufacture of the figure have remained contentious. The authors undertake extensive analysis of the materials and form of the figure. They show that the core is best understood (in terms of materials and method of making) in a European tradition, while the iconography and beadwork is most readily explicable within an Indigenous Caribbean context. Radiocarbon dates suggest probable manufacture in the first half of the 16th century. The rhinoceros horn remains, as the authors emphasize, enigmatic—but this paper sheds substantive light on a unique object that poses major interpretive challenges.

131 **Pieces of eight: more archaeology of piracy.** Edited by Charles R. Ewen and Russell K. Skowronek. Gainesville: University Press of Florida, 2016. 318 p.: bibl., ill., index, maps.

The historical record of the Caribbean is rich with references to piracy; this volume picks up the challenge of identifying and studying pirates and piracy via the material record. In particular, it considers the ships themselves, via underwater archeology of pirate wrecks (along with chapters on reception, identity, material culture, and conceptualization). The outcome is a rich picture of pirates, their behavior, and their material culture.

132 **Reifschneider, Meredith** and **Dana N. Bardolph.** An archaeobotanical approach to well-being: enslaved plant use at Estate Cane Garden, 19th century St. Croix. (*J. Field Archaeol.*, 45:7, 2020, p. 512–526, bibl., graphs, maps, photos, tables)

The authors present the results of paleoethnobotanical analysis from a 19th-century hospital for enslaved persons on St. Croix. This analysis reveals the presence of several taxa associated with medicinal treatment, among a wide selection of garden herbs generally. The authors also provide a comparison with assemblages from other, broadly comparable contexts. While not intrinsically surprising, these data support the identification of the site, and show active attempts to administer effective medicines to enslaved patients. The authors conclude with a call for more paleoethnobotanical analyses from historical Caribbean contexts.

133 Roura Álvarez, Lisette; Roger Arrazcaeta Delgado; and Carlos Hernández Oliva. Indios de la Habana: aproximación histórico-arqueológica. La Habana: Ciencias Sociales, 2017. 161 p.: bibl., ill.

This slim yet detailed volume constitutes an in-depth study of the Indigenous legacy of Havana. It challenges the old dichotomy between pre- and postcontact archeology, and instead emphasizes points of intersection and threads of continuity, all viewed through the lens of a rich urban archeological record. This volume, in its emphasis on bridging the Columbian divide in Cuba, clearly indicates parallels with scholarship elsewhere in the Caribbean.

134 Shearn, Isaac. Canoe societies in the Caribbean: ethnography, archaeology, and ecology of precolonial canoe manufacturing and voyaging. (*J. Anthropol. Archaeol.*, 57, March 2020, 101140, p. 1–17, bibl., maps, photos, tables)

In this paper, Shearn notes the interpretive tension between the evidence for ubiquitous inter-island contact during the precontact period of the Caribbean, but the essential paucity of archeological evidence for this technology. He approaches the problem in a novel and imaginative fashion, redefining the Amerindian Caribbean as composed of "maritime societies" and proceeds to map the distribution of species likely favorable for dugout construction. He also presents ethnographic information on canoe construction from the Kalinago of Dominica. He concludes by urging Caribbean archeologists to consider canoe making, voyaging, navigating, and concomitant cultural and ritual practices, as situated at the heart of the precontact experience.

135 Valcárcel Rojas, Roberto et al. Slavery of Indigenous people in the Caribbean: an archaeological perspective. (*Int. J. Hist. Archaeol.*, 24, 2020, p. 517–545, bibl., ill., photo)

In this paper, the authors demonstrate the impacts of the process of enslavement on Indigenous Caribbean populations. The Caribbean was the first location in the New World in which Indigenous peoples were enslaved, as the authors point out, and in this rich study they document the substantive impacts of this process. They do so by focusing on bioarcheological data from El Chorro de Maíta on Cuba, showing particularly how enslaved populations differ in terms of diet, demography, and the presence of nonlocals from precontact comparanda.

136 Wallman, Diane E. Subsistence as transformative practice: the zooarchaeology of slavery in the colonial Caribbean. (*J. Afr. Diaspora Archaeol. Herit.*, 9:2, 2020, p. 77–113, bibl.)

Wallman considers the subsistence and culinary practices of enslaved Africans, as evidenced at 15 sites across the Caribbean. Her results shed light on certain commonalities (unsurprisingly, in terms of exploitation of domesticated species), but also the exploitation of exotic or contextually unusual species, as well as marine or foreshore taxa. Wallman also connects patterns of subsistence during the 19th century with traditions of cuisine among descendent communities.

South America

JASON L. TOOHEY, *Associate Professor of Anthropology, University of Wyoming*

RECENT PUBLICATIONS focused on the archeology of South America include monograph-length treatments of particular topics; thematically focused edited volumes, which either compile archeological data collected over many years or present collections of contemporary work on one theme or time period; and articles, ranging in focus from narrow treatments of a particular archeological site to much broader, synthetic works.

Publications from outside the central Andes range widely in topic and geographic focus. While important work has been published from many countries, including Colombia, Brazil, Bolivia, and Chile, the majority of the new publications are from Argentina. As has been the case in past years, the majority of this non-central Andean research focuses on the archeology of relatively mobile hunting and gathering societies, lithic analysis, and patterns in rock art. Recent publications from the Southern Cone of Chile and Argentina indicate a continuing interest in rock art and its connections to prehistoric society in far southern regions (items **141** and **154**), as well as an ongoing focus on documenting the archeology of hunter-gatherer-fisher communities in the far south (items **146** and **156**). The latter publications highlight prehispanic construction and the use of large-scale fish traps as an intensification of economy.

The publications reviewed show an increasing interest in the study of bio-archeology in several regions outside the Andes (items **141**, **147**, and **149**). One of these works is also meant to function as a guide to best practices in the analysis of human remains in archeological contexts (item **148**).

Colombian publications focus on presenting new data on both residential and mortuary sites and contexts on the western Andean slopes (see, for example, item **158**). An important book out of Colombia takes a comparative approach to intrasite spatial organization and early urbanism in northern Colombia, with a special focus on the famous site of Ciudad Perdida (item **159**).

Publications from the central Andes continue to focus on particular time periods, ancient societies, and regions. Two recent publications focus on very early ritual architecture and monumentalism during both the formative period of the central Peruvian Andes (item **167**) and the earlier Late Archaic Period, associated with the first signs of monumental architecture (item **155**).

There is continuing interest in the archeology of the Moche societies of the northern Peruvian coast (item **173**). These studies range from very contemporary analyses of same-sex relations in figurative Moche ceramics from museum collections (item **175**) to an analysis of possible urban soundscapes at the major site of Huacas de Moche, where investigators have analyzed the sound and volume produced by large sample ceramic pipes from the site (item **172**). New data is also presented for sites of the Salinar society in the same region (item **163**).

Middle Horizon archeology both in Peru and its close southern neighbors continues to be of interest. While the Wari Empire has been strongly represented in past years, recent publications have also brought to the fore regional coverage of new discoveries related to the Tiwanaku state, centered in Highland Bolivia, but spanning broadly in the south-central Andes (item **138**). One Tiwanaku-related article stands out as a meta-archeological study of labor relations and power in archeological field projects, comparing Western conceptions of labor and leadership to those employed by Indigenous field laborers themselves (item **151**). This introspective perspective is welcome and should be of value to any archeologist working alongside local people. Elsewhere in Bolivia, the interest in rock art analysis continues with publications on Lake Titicaca's eastern shore and from Cochabamba (items **152** and **153**).

Several new works focus on long distance interaction and exchange in western South America. Coast-Highland interaction, long a major focus of Andean archeology, is addressed bioarcheologically, suggesting large-scale movement of peoples between the two zones (item **137**). Another important work focuses on the long-distance trade or exchange in tropical bird feathers from Amazonia, west into the Highlands where these exotic objects often acted as materialized authority and power. This research suggests that the advent of this trade may have been an important factor in the development and maintenance of early states and empires (item **174**).

Finally, in addition to the more regionally or thematically focused studies noted above, recent work has included both large-scale synthetic treatments and renewed efforts to publish and disseminate basic comparative data, useful to a range of investigators. A good example of the first is a richly detailed analysis of the crosscultural importance of metal artifacts in the Americas (item **139**). Basic archeological data is presented in several recent publications, including those focused on archeological site settlement data (item **165**), rock art (item **170**), and patterns of ceramic styles and their exchange during various time periods (items **164** and **169**).

GENERAL

137 Cocilovo, José A. et al. Movilidad, tráfico sur andino y diferenciación genética entre San Pedro de Atacama y la Puna de Jujuy. (*Relac. Soc. Argent. Antropol.*, 42:2, julio/dic. 2017, p. 207–229, appendix, bibl., graphs, map, tables)

The authors present new evidence for interaction and mobility between San Pedro de Atacama in Chile, and the Puna de Jujuy in Argentina based on the bioarcheological analysis of phenotypic traits on a sample of 911 individuals from various archeological sites in the two regions whose occupations overlap. The analysis, which agrees with the results of other archeological work, indicates that significant movement of people occurred between the regions for several centuries.

138 Congreso Nacional de Arqueología Chilena, *19th, Arica, Chile, 2012.* El horizonte medio: nuevos aportes para el sur de Perú, norte de Chile y Bolivia. Edición de Antti Korpisaari y Juan Chacama. Arica, Chile: IFEA: Universidad de Tarapacá, 2015. 339 p.: bibl., ill., maps.

The contributors present a wide range of new discoveries at Middle Horizon sites in the south central Andes. These sites range from large well-known centers to smaller sites. Most of the contributions focus thematically on the Tiwanaku polity, but a few also treat the contemporary Middle Horizon Wari Empire, and interaction between the two. Chapters range from those focused on intrasite spatial analysis to others dealing with mortuary patterns.

139 Falchetti, Ana María. Lo humano y lo divino: metalurgia y cosmogonía en la América antigua. Bogotá: Instituto Colombiano de Antropología e Historia-ICANH: Universidad de los Andes, Facultad de Ciencias Sociales, 2018. 318 p.: bibl., ill (chiefly color). (Arqueología y patrimonio)

This is a refreshingly broad view of metal artifacts and the process of metallurgy throughout much of the precolumbian Americas. The author analyzes a wide range of metal objects primarily from south American regions, but also from North America. The work focuses on artifact design and morphological complexity as well as how materials and color show the close relationship between some metal objects and prehispanic belief systems and cosmologies. The text is well illustrated in both b/w and color.

140 Volcanes, cenizas y ocupaciones antiguas en perspectiva geoarqueológica en América Latina. Edición de María Fernanda Ugalde. Quito: Centro de Publicaciones Pontificia Universidad Católica del Ecuador, 2017. 196 p.: bibl., ill., maps.

(Colección Estudios de antropología y arqueología; 2)
This is a well-organized volume. Its contributors present a wide range of contemporary studies of volcanism, and archeological contexts, largely from a geoarcheological perspective. Unlike most geoarcheologically focused texts, which often focus on one site or small region, the contributors in this text range broadly. Although many of the chapters focus on Ecuador, others span from Mexico in the north to Argentina in the south. These focus on precolumbian sites as well as the study of paleoenvironment from the analysis of associated volcanic deposits.

ARGENTINA

141 Carden, Natalia and Luciano Prates. Pinturas rupestres en un espacio funerario: el caso del sitio Cueva Galpón (noreste de Patagonia). (*Magallania/Punta Arenas*, 43:1, 2015, p. 117–136, bibl., graphs, ill., photos, tables)
This paper presents a formal analysis of rock art, its motifs, and the superimposition of distinct elements on panels at the mortuary site of Cueva Galpón. The authors establish that the rock art is directly associated spatially and chronologically with the two burials present at the site. The site, dated to 3000 BP, contained no domestic artifacts, and thus functioned solely as a location for burial and associated rock art production.

142 Catella, Luciana. La tecnología cerámica en la cuenca del arroyo Chasicó: una aproximación a la movilidad de las sociedades del holoceno tardío de Patagonia nororiental y de la Región Pampeana sudeste, Argentina. (*Magallania/Punta Arenas*, 45:1, 2017, p. 137–163, bibl., ill., maps, photos, tables)
The author presents a detailed and thorough characterization of the ceramic assemblage of the Chasicó area. Using vessel form, materials, and comparative decorative design analysis, the author contextualizes these ceramics within the broader region of the southeastern Pampas and northeastern Patagonia. This important work adds to our understanding of the role of ceramics within residentially mobile hunting and gathering groups of the region.

143 Cortegoso, Valeria et al. Bosques fósiles y tecnología humana: la explotación de materias primas líticas en el Bosque de Darwin, Paramillos (Argentina). (*Lat. Am. Antiq.*, 28:3, Sept. 2017, p. 317–336, bibl., graphs, maps, photos, tables)
The authors document the extensive use of petrified tree trunks located in the Darwin Forest of west-central Argentina as a valued source for lithic raw materials for precolumbian groups in the region. The paper presents the results of petrographic, geologic, and spatial datasets in order to establish the value of the material, its use in local workshops, and its movement on the local landscape.

144 Iucci, María Emilia. Producción, uso y circulación de cerámica tardía en el valle de Hualfín, (Catamarca, Argentina). Buenos Aires: Sociedad Argentina de Antropología, 2016. 320 p.: bibl., ill. (Colección Tesis doctorales)
This volume thoroughly presents the current understanding of ceramic technology, typology, and exchange in the Hualfín region of Argentina. Importantly, the text contains a wide range of color and b/w images, making it a good reference source for those working in the region. The author presents archeometric results of chemical paste analysis, as well as classic morphological analysis of vessel forms.

Lange, Victoria; Francisco Guichón; and **Josefina Flores Coni.** Lagunas de la Meseta: análisis de la distribución espacial del Registro Arqueológico en el Sur de la Meseta del Strobel (provincia de Santa Cruz, Patagonia, Argentina). See item **642**.

145 Martínez, Gustavo A. and Diana L. Mazzanti. Evidencia geoarqueológica de la transición Pleistoceno-Holoceno en reparos rocosos de Tandilia oriental (provincia de Buenos Aires). (*Relac. Soc. Argent. Antropol.*, 42:1, enero/junio 2017, p. 83–106, bibl., ill., maps, photos, tables)
The authors present evidence for significant geoarcheological shifts at the Late Pleistocene-Holocene transition, at roughly the time of the initial entry of humans into the region surrounding the Tandilia oriental region of Argentina. This transition from a

period of alternating wet and arid climates, to a long-term wetter climatic regime is noted at a series of well-excavated caves and rock shelters.

146 **Scartascini, Federico Luis.** 5000 años de pesca en la Bahía San Antonio, Río Negro, Patagonia Argentina. (*Lat. Am. Antiq.*, 28:3, Sept. 2017, p. 394–408, bibl., graphs, map, table)

This paper analyzes changes in fishing strategies by hunter-gatherer-fisher groups in Bahía San Antonio. Analysis of fish remains from a number of surface and excavated contexts shows that from the middle Holocene into the late Holocene, people increasingly take a wider range of species. Fishing during the earlier period focused more intensively on just a few species. The author shows that fishing has been a primary means for making a living in the region for the past 5,000 years.

147 **El sitio Chenque I, un cementerio prehispánico en la Pampa occidental: estilo de vida e interacciones culturales de cazadores-recolectores del Cono Sur americano.** Compilación de Mónica A. Berón. Buenos Aires: Sociedad Argentina de Antropología, 2018. 530 p.: bibl., ill. (Publicaciones de la Sociedad Argentina de Antropología)

This is an important contribution to our understanding of hunter-gatherer lifeways and mortuary patterns in the Pampas region of south-central Argentina over the past 1000 years. Chapters cover a wide range of cultural aspects from recent excavations at the site of Chenque I, from which 217 individuals were recovered. Chapters focus on mortuary patterns, technology and lithic artifacts, osteology and violence, among others. The chapters present a detailed and thorough coverage of all aspects of the work.

148 **Taller Nacional de Bioarqueología y Paleopatología, 4th, *Córdoba, Argentina, 2018*.** Metodologías para el estudio de restos esqueletales en Argentina: actualizaciones y nuevas perspectivas. Edición de Mariana Fabra et al. Córdoba, Argentina: IV Taller Nacional Bioarqueología y Paleopatología, 2019. 297 p.: bibl., ill.

The contributors to this edited volume combine discussions of best practices in contemporary bioarcheology and studies of new bioarcheological evidence from several archeological sites in Argentina. Themes range from methods and perspectives on the sexing and aging of human remains, to the investigation of rates of osteoarthritis and other degenerative joint diseases, to the investigation of dental remains.

149 **Zilio, Leandro.** Primer contexto mortuorio del holoceno medio en la costa norte de Santa Cruz (Patagonia, Argentina). (*Magallania/Punta Arenas*, 44:2, 2016, p. 219–224, bibl., ill., map, photo)

This important contribution provides details about a very early human skeleton of the late middle Holocene from the mortuary site of Punta Buque 3. Encountered in a sand dune, this young adult male is the first burial of this date in the region. Stable isotope information points to movement of the individual between the coast and the interior during this period.

BOLIVIA

150 **Ellefsen, Bernardo.** Etnias andinas de Bolivia en el periodo incaico. Cochabamba, Bolivia: Editorial Ellefsen, 2017. 199 p.: bibl., ill. (Línea histórica)

This well-written and illustrated (b/w) text presents a review of all the late prehispanic ethnic groups of what is today Bolivia. The author describes the wide range of ethnic groups that the expanding Inca empire encountered and whose territory they eventually occupied. The author also discusses non-local ethnic groups or enclaves, the mitma communities relocated from elsewhere in the Andes to this region by the Inca. The text will be of use to anyone studying the Inca Empire or late prehispanic Bolivia.

151 **Leighton, Mary.** Indigenous archaeological field technicians at Tiwanaku, Bolivia: a hybrid form of scientific labor. (*Am. Anthropol.*, 118:4, Dec. 2016, p. 742–754, bibl.)

This is a meta-archeological paper dealing with the intertwined conceptions and meanings of labor at a large-scale archeological project. The case study focuses on labor relations at a large, ongoing field project at the Tiwanaku site—one of the most well-known sites in South America. The paper investigates differences between project directors' concepts of labor and power and those of the local Indigenous peoples. The paper offers a real contribution to our understanding of archeological work in Bolivia and the rest of South America.

152   **Portugal Loayza, Jimena.** Arqueología y arte rupestre en el noreste del Lago Titicaca: una aproximación al arte rupestre y la producción de artefactos líticos, desde la arqueología del paisaje. La Paz: Plural Editores, 2017. 211 p.: bibl., ill. (some color), maps (some color).

This text presents important new data from excavated rock art-related sites along the eastern edge of Lake Titicaca in Bolivia. This is a zone that is not well known archeologically. Rock art motifs range from camelids and geometrics, to colonial period human figures on horseback. The work also includes details of test excavations and resulting artifact analyses of both ceramic and lithic materials.

153   **Querejazu Lewis, Roy.** El arte rupestre en Mizque. Cochabamba, Bolivia: Asociación de Estudios de Arte Rupestre: Gobierno Autónomo Municipal de Mizque, 2019. 188 p.: bibl., color ill.

The author characterizes the rock art of the Bolivian regions of Cochabamba and Mizque. Dating rock art is notoriously difficult and the author does a nice job of proposing a relative chronology of rock art in the region. This is a detailed analysis of both pecked and painted, immobile and mobile rock art. The text is well illustrated in color.

CHILE

154   **Muñoz S., Camila; Rosario Cordero F.;** and **Diego Artigas S.C.** El sitio Alero Picton 1: nuevo registro de arte rupestre para los canales fueguinos. (*Magallania/Punta Arenas*, 44:2, 2016, p. 225–231, bibl., ill., maps, photos)

The authors report on the discovery of two important new rock art panels at the rock shelter site of Alero Picton 1. Anthropomorphic and geometric motifs are present. The authors contextualize these findings within knowledge of other sites in the area of the Beagle Channel, attributed to hunting, gathering, and fishing peoples.

155   **Núñez, Lautaro** and **Catherine Perlès.** Tulán-52: a Late Archaic ceremonial centre at the dawn of the Neolithisation process in the Atacama Desert. (*Antiquity/Cambridge*, 92:365, Oct. 2018, p. 1231–1246, bibl., maps, photos, tables)

The authors convincingly reinterpret the Atacama site of Tulán-52 as a very early ceremonial center (3000–2200 BC) created by hunter gatherers who were just beginning to engage in simple horticulture. Reexamination of the site architecture and artifacts shows marked similarities with the later large ceremonial site of Tulán-54. Tulán-52 is characterized by semisubterranean small, niched rooms, possible feasting, intensive bead production, and imported marine shell and obsidian.

156   **Vázquez, Martin** and **Francisco Zangrando.** Estructuras de pesca en el canal Beagle. (*Magallania/Punta Arenas*, 45:1, 2017, p. 101–122, bibl., maps, photos, tables)

The authors present a detailed and useful study of the earliest known constructed fishing traps or weirs in Tierra del Fuego. This is a study of Late Holocene fishing intensification through building weirs. The piece is a good combination of ethnographic data and novel archeological data, which is not common in much of the literature. The authors present a compelling case for intensification of fishing activities in the region through the development of new technology.

COLOMBIA

157   **Aprile Gniset, Jacques.** La ciudad colombiana: la formación espacial americana prehispánica. Segunda edición. Cali, Colombia: Universidad del Valle, Programa Editorial, 2016. 226 p.: bibl., ill. (some color). (Colección de artes y humanidades. Urbanismo)

This is a very well-produced and illustrated book which will be a resource for anyone interested in the archeology of domestic buildings and urbanism in the past. Chapters focus not only on the design and organization of both archeological and modern Indigenous peoples in Colombia, but also on the wide range of spatial organizations in small to large precolumbian towns and, arguably, cities. This is a real contribution to the study of early urbanism in South America.

158 Investigaciones arqueológicas en Nariño (Colombia). Edición de Alejandro Bernal Vélez y Felipe Cárdenas Arroyo. Bogotá: Instituto Colombiano de Antropología e Historia, 2019. 284 p.: bibl., ill., maps. (Colección Arqueología preventiva)

The authors present a detailed view of new excavations at several sites in Ipiales, in the Valley of Atriz, and the Guáitara River Canyon in far southwest Colombia, near the frontier with Ecuador. This volume is detailed, presenting the excavations as well as ceramic, lithic, zooarcheological, archeobotanical, and bioarcheological results of the work. The volume is also well illustrated in b/w.

159 Salgado López, Héctor and **Carlos Armando Rodríguez.** Pautas funerarias de las sociedades prehispánicas de la región Calima, Cordillera Occidental, Colombia. Ibagué, Colombia: Programa Editorial Universidad del Tolima, 2017. 232 p.: bibl., ill. (some color). (Autores universitarios 2017) (Colección artes y humanidades)

This is a well-produced presentation and analysis of the varied mortuary practices by the prehispanic societies (the Ylama, Yotoco, and Sonso Cultures) of the Sumaria region along the west-central coast of Colombia. The text is very well illustrated with line drawings and color images, making it a good reference text for anyone interested in comparative mortuary patterns of the region. This text is made more useful because this level of detail is not common in similar volumes.

PERU

160 Apaico Flores, Aníbal. Rimaq Yupikuna: evidencias arqueológicas en el curso superior del río Urabamba, Tayacucho-Lucanas, Ayacucho. (*Investig. Soc./San Marcos*, 16:28, junio 2012, p. 223–232, bibl., ill., maps, photos)

This paper provides a detailed account and important baseline data from a large-scale archeological survey in a previously relatively understudied region of southern Ayacucho, Peru. Individual sites, including complex architectural constructions, mortuary features, corral, caves, rock shelters, and rock art are described in some detail. Survey reveals that the region has been occupied at least intermittently from the Archaic period through the Late Horizon.

161 Arqueología en Cerro Verde. Edición de Luis Valle Álvarez y Carlos Gamboa T. Arequipa, Peru: Cerro Verde, 2018. 408 p.: bibl., ill. (some color).

This is a detailed and very well illustrated volume describing all aspects of archeological survey and excavation related to the Cerro Verde mine in Arequipa, Peru. Unlike some similar volumes, this one is rich in data, maps and plans, and color images. It is thus a solid contribution and will be of use to anyone working on this region of the Andes.

162 Bikoulis, Peter et al. Ancient pathways and geoglyphs in the Sihuas Valley of southern Peru. (*Antiquity/Cambridge*, 92:365, Oct. 2018, p. 1377–1391, bibl., graphs, maps, photos, tables)

The authors report the results of digital modelling and spatial analysis seeking to better understand relationships between travel routes and small-scale geoglyphs in the Sihuas Valley. Results of the work and of associated pedestrian survey indicate a very close relationship between these two feature types. Spatial association between these and major snowcapped mountains also indicate that these geoglyphs may have been constructed and propitiated in order to petition the supernatural to ensure safe travel through the region.

163 Briceño Rosario, Jesús and **Brian R. Billman.** La ocupación Salinar en la subcuenca del río Sinsicap, parte alta del valle de Moche. (*Investig. Soc./San Marcos*, 16:28, junio 2012, p. 197–222, bibl., ill., maps, photos)

The authors present detailed and valuable basic data from a number of Salinar sites from the western slope region of Sinsicap in the upper Moche Valley. They contextualize the new data within a useful and thorough synthetic review of both archeological and ethnographic information from the region. The paper is a solid contribution to our knowledge of the Salinar culture along the north Peruvian coast.

164 **Burger, Richard L.** and **Lucy C. Salazar.** La cerámica de Coscopunta, un sitio del Periodo Intermedio Tardío en la provincia de Carhuaz, Callejón de Huaylas, Perú. (*Bull. Inst. fr. étud. andin.*, 44:1, 2015, p. 23–52, bibl., map, photos, table)

The authors present a detailed and well-illustrated record of a large collection of artifacts discovered by a landowner in 1979 near the center of an agricultural field. Importantly many of these ceramics are complete or almost complete vessels, very rare in the archeological record. The analysis of the vessels indicates local production with a wide range of variation in form, evidence for a lack of regional political or economic integration at the time. Because of the location of the find and the nearly complete state of the vessels, the authors suspect that they may have been part of an intentionally buried offering dating to the Late Intermediate Period.

165 **Dalen Luna, Pieter Dennis van.** La provincia de Huaral en la historia. Lima: Juan Gutemberg Editores e Impresores E.I.R.L., 2016. 142 p.: bibl., ill. (chiefly color).

This is a well-illustrated text which thoroughly documents the prehistoric occupations and dynamics of both the lower and upper reaches of the Chancay-Huaral River. Not only is the prehistoric period presented, but the text also includes chapters on the settlement of the regions during the subsequent colonial, and later republican periods. It is not often that a text offers such a long temporal coverage of a region.

166 **Kosiba, Steve** and **R. Alexander Hunter.** Fields of conflict: a political ecology approach to land and social transformation in the colonial Andes (Cuzco, Peru). (*J. Archaeol. Sci.*, 84, Aug. 2017, p. 40–53, bibl., graph, maps, photos, tables)

The authors present a detailed and well-developed argument for significant changes in economy, land use, and political landscape in the central Highlands due to changes in agricultural requirements brought on by the novel growing of wheat during the colonial period. This is a good example of results that can come with the use of a dynamic landscape approach to the study of changing political ecology through time, and draws from multiple forms of data including textual, archeological, and environmental sources in a GIS spatial framework.

167 **Matsumoto, Yuichi** and **Yuri I. Cavero Palomino.** Investigaciones arqueológicas en Campanayuq Rumi, Vilcashuamán-Ayacucho. (*Investig. Soc./San Marcos*, 16:28, junio 2012, p. 119–127, bibl., maps, photos)

The authors present new information on excavations at the formative period, Chavín-related mound center of Campanayuq Rumi in Ayacucho. The paper describes both architectural details of the mounds and their internal galleries, as well as associated decorated ceramics. The authors contend that this center may have formed a southern Highland interaction node between the south coast and the eastern forests.

168 **McCool, Weston C.** Coping with conflict: defensive strategies and chronic warfare in the prehispanic Nazca region. (*Lat. Am. Antiq.*, 28:3, Sept. 2017, p. 373–393, bibl., map, photos, table)

The author presents a thorough comparative study of the archeological signature of defensive architecture at a series of hillforts in the Nazca region. Datasets include GIS-based regional spatial analysis of fortified community locations, as well as statistical analysis of intrasite patterns of fortification walls and access routes. Details were also ground checked in the field. This comparative approach to fortification and defensive action will be useful to others studying societies in the midst of conflict.

169 **Pérez, Kelita** *et al.* El estilo cerámico Carmen y su presencia en el valle medio de Chincha, costa sur del Perú. (*Bull. Inst. fr. étud. andin.*, 44:2, 2015, p. 181–204, bibl., graphs, ill., maps, photos, tables)

The authors of this article characterize the vessel forms and decorative motifs of the Carmen ceramic style from a sample of sherds recovered from the sites of Cerro del Gentil and Pampa del Gentil located in the Chincha Valley. This ceramic style is associated with the Nasca and dates from approximately AD 200–400. The authors find it almost exclusively associated with domestic contexts.

170 Recientes investigaciones sobre sitios con quilcas o arte rupestre en el Perú. Edición de Pieter Dennis van Dalen Luna. Lima: Juan Gutemberg Editores Impresores E.I.R.L.: Asociación Peruana de Arte Rupestre APAR, 2019. 199 p.: bibl., ill.

This is a very well illustrated text detailing new archeological research into rock art sites in Peru. The contributions range broadly from Ancash in the northwest, to the Altiplano in the southeast. Individual sites are well contextualized and rock art ranges from painted panels to pecked designs and simple cupules.

171 Riris, Philip. Dates as data revisited: a statistical examination of the Peruvian preceramic radiocarbon record. (*J. Archaeol. Sci.*, 97, Sept. 2018, p. 67–76, bibl., graphs)

The author presents the results of a series of novel quantitative analyses of the dynamics of the Andean radiocarbon data record. This analysis of 1180 dates is the first major aggregate analysis of dates in order to study demographic change since the 1980s and its results conflict with earlier interpretations. The author, using dates as a proxy for population, argues that there was no major difference in population growth between the Peruvian coast and the Highlands from ~14,000 to ~3,000 years before present. This is an important Andean contribution to a growing literature on the use of radiocarbon dates as a "big data" proxy for studying large-scale demographic change in other areas.

172 Scullin, Dianne and **Brian Boyd.** Whistles in the wind: the noisy Moche city. (*World Archaeol.*, 46:3, Oct. 2014, p. 362–379, bibl., ill., map, photo, table)

The authors characterize the sounds and volumes produced by a sample of 419 ceramic whistles recovered from a wide variety of contexts at the well-known Moche site of Huacas de Moche. The sounds produced are both higher pitched and louder than many today would consider music. The authors suggest that aversion to particular pitch and volume are culturally relative and that the noise produced by these whistles may have held particular meaning within Moche communities.

173 Uceda, Santiago Castillo; Ricardo Morales Gamarra; and **Elías Mujica Barrera.** Huaca de la Luna: templos y dioses moches = Moche temples and gods. Investigación/research por Proyecto Huacas del Sol y de la Luna. Fotografías/photographs por Eduardo Hirose Maio. Lima: WM, World Monuments Fund Perú: BACKUS Fundación, 2016. 311 p.: color ill.

This large format book is very well illustrated in color and presents all major aspects of our current knowledge of Huaca de la Luna, perhaps the most important pyramid of the Moche culture. Huaca de la Luna is one of the most intensively studied sites in Peru and represents for many the complex architecture, artwork, and ideology of the Moche. It is moderately detailed in its presentation and one major strength for some readers will be the fact that it is presented in both Spanish and English.

174 Wilkinson, Darryl. The influence of Amazonia on state formation in the ancient Andes. (*Antiquity/Cambridge*, 92:365, Oct. 2018, p. 1362–1376, bibl., maps, photos)

This paper argues that one important cause or catalyst of late prehispanic state formation in the central Andes (principally the Wari and later Inca empires) may have been an increase in large-scale exchange of exotic tropical bird feathers from Amazonia into the Highlands. Feathered textiles became a symbol of, and perhaps a source of, political might and authority in these early states. This paper argues for the importance of this long-distance specialized exchange in state formation and maintenance.

175 Woloszyn, Janusz Z. and Katarzyna Piwowar. Sodomites, Siamese twins, and scholars: same-sex relationships in Moche art. (*Am. Anthropol.*, 117:2, June 2015, p. 285–301, bibl., ill., photos)

This important article addresses interpretations of same-sex relationships in Moche society through a critical examination of how the famous Moche erotic ceramics, particularly those depicting same-sex relations, have been studied and reported by various groups of researchers. These groups include academics, popular authors, and more socially conservative writers within Peru itself. These relatively rare ceramics are interpreted as possibly representing same-sex relations as a condoned form of sexual activity in Moche society, or possibly a reflection of power relations and ritual action within the Moche.

ETHNOLOGY
Middle America

DUNCAN EARLE, *Professor of Global Studies, Marymount California University*

Divide and Conquer, Unite and Resist: Turning the Tables

Ethnographers, informed by history and ethnohistory, appreciate the early writings of colonial period priests—despite their strong Church biases—because within and between the lines we learn about the people they served and sought to convert (item **192**). Similar feelings are evoked for many of the writings considered during this review period. Despite conscious and unconscious bias, when we sift through the texts, many jewels emerge, which we can value despite the bias (urban, cultural, political, socioeconomic, gender, religious, theoretical) embedded in the authorial voice (items **183**, **190**, **204**, and **219**). Nonetheless, we must always locate each perspective and its bias when making judgements about claims; each writer is contextualized by their own history. In academic circles, many researchers and scholars see themselves as having the most correct view on an issue, and few can fairly render points of view with which they do not agree. Negative evidence is often dismissed. Power then accrues to those with the most, the most widely circulated, the most authoritative voice (text)—and not always to the one most close to the truth. This is the bias the textual record reflects. Some authors acknowledge this notion, and some do not; this reflexivity is important in understanding some of the entries and their claims about the philosophical and ethical complexity applied to the study of those less powerful, the political Other (items **181**, **183**, and **231**).

Some prominent themes emerge in this contribution in line with this concern about bias, about interest, about power. One is the question of the relationship between Indigenous people/communities and the state/capital/everybody else (items **185** and **186**). In the past, Mesoamericanists had two dominant approaches, both tending towards facilitating (or at least documenting) the steady decline of Indigenous power, in culture, language, economy/land base, and community unity. The first saw it in the context of modernization and assimilation, the latter in terms of penetration of markets by global forces and a shifting towards a rural and migratory proletariat. Ethnic peasantry was seen as fundamentally a holdover from a feudal past, marginal and marginalized, who must inevitably exchange their native identity for progress and reason, or at least migration and acculturation. Only towards the end of the last century did any third path gain traction in the public and academic milieu, as the call from the margins was "Basta!" But, as some authors here argue, this has changed everything (item **181**).

Not unexpectedly, this voice was and remains one emerging from below, from the voices of the subjects of other people's texts, but now either making their own, or making sure their voice reflects their concerns in others' work (items **178, 195, 199, 212, 216, 219, 224, 230, 237, 240,** and **242**). Often these texts talk about autonomy, community, rights and resistance, backed by the audacious presumption that the Indigenous peasant lifestyle might not go away (and in fact might find ways to strengthen its position in the new world order.) This allows another perspective that asks of academic production whose voice is being privileged, and if the researcher's interests dovetail with those of the researched. Because if it doesn't, there is a problem for some of our authors. If First Peoples as peasants are here to stay, then what we say about them needs to be of some service—otherwise it is a kind of exploitation, an intellectual colonialism, quoting you for my sake (see item **231** for a detailed discussion of this notion of decolonization).

The question being asked by Indigenous people and by many scholars whose work appears in this section is about this consonance or dissonance of interests, the why of research. Some writings are clearly working to articulate Indigenous concerns (items **185, 200, 206, 210, 215, 218, 220, 224, 227, 235,** and **238**) while others discuss these concerns but in more academic language and focus (items **181, 188, 194, 201, 216, 228, 231,** and **232**), and still others use the knowledge provided by research to make their own claims. Many authors interrogate these texts in terms of how useful they may be to the living subjects of this production, practical, theoretical, addressing relevant policy, understanding Indigenous perspectives, interests, and concerns, or advocating for their rights. Some turn the tables, arguing that the isolated, alienated, and contaminating modern society needs to learn from the more communitarian and ecologically minded Indigenous people, as the sustainability and resilience concerns displace modernization in the Western urge (items **182, 201, 231,** and **240**).

One theme that follows from this discussion is Indigenous land tenure rights, specifically the issue of communal lands and/or collective community land management. Many communities have maintained such properties since ancient times, and with it the systems of reciprocal communal labor that correlate with land access. Several authors suggest that this approach is a key to Indigenous autonomy and a future as sustainable Indigenous communities (items **178, 185, 206, 209, 211, 215, 232, 235,** and **237**). Others seem to accept the privatization of previous community lands as a naturalized progression or an inevitable process (item **204**). Still others see renewed efforts to maintain identity through resistance to cultural loss, investment in festivals of identity reinforcement and celebration, and community aid, development, culture, and education organizations (items **180, 182, 186, 187, 193, 194, 208, 211, 222, 227, 232, 238,** and **244**). Part of the ironic social dialectic here is that just as Indigenous communities are coming apart, movements of cultural renovation and political resistance are reinforcing them in many documented instances. Those who migrate to cities or go abroad are also finding organizations of cultural revitalization and social solidarity—in alien locales (items **207, 218, 223,** and **227**). Several studies focus specifically on the role of women in cultural and political resistance (items **180, 187, 194, 195, 206, 207, 216, 221, 238, 242,** and **244**). Quite a number emphasize the environmental issues that Indigenous people, and their resistance to the destruction of their lands and ecosystem, represent (items **177, 180, 185, 201, 204, 208, 215,** and **232**).

Last, we entertain the inspirational thought addressed in these publications that in Mesoamerica, in Latin America, globally, Indigenous people and their claims to land, rights, governance, social and legal equity, and cultural practice are being heard, if inconsistently, and often only after protest and violence and protest and more violence—but they are being heard, as many of the texts indicate. These are not just the Indigenous voices and authors; many mestizos and other non-Indigenous people are now writing from this third perspective, having delved deeply into the Mesoamerican worldview, and emerged transformed (item **240**). It is a tribute to the power of Mesoamerican cultures that they now have such impact beyond the village, in the nation, and the world. Many of the publications reviewed in this section have power in their own right; they serve as documentation of those once silenced and profoundly misunderstood, and the genius of Mesoamerica is revealed.

176 **Aguirre Mendoza, Imelda.** El poder de los seres: organización social y jerarquías en una comunidad teenek de la Huasteca potosina. San Luis Potosí, Mexico: El Colegio de San Luis: Secretaría de Cultura del Gobierno del Estado de San Luis Potosí, 2018. 324 p.: bibl., ill., maps. (Colección Investigaciones)

This study of a Huastec village posits that its inhabitants believe they live in two worlds, one visible and proximate, the other located deep within a mountain canyon, but also in the sky, the sea, the graveyard, various caves, and even in dreams. This other world described in the book in numerous ways mirrors the social organization of the community, such that each reinforces and reiterates the other. The study attempts to show the hierarchy in the spirit world, and what this reveals about the uneven distribution of power in the institutions and social actors living in the township the author describes. Rich with social and religious detail, it serves as an excellent example of the agentive and creative appropriation by Mesoamericans of Catholic institutions (*cofradías*) and pantheon (saints, Jesus, virgin, devil, etc.) in order to create a system with close analog to what came before, adjusted to the current prevailing conditions of marginality. The author suggests such a ghostly system serves to maintain itself against dangerous community disruptions by way of human-nonhuman interaction, speaking and listening to a world invisible and unavailable to outsiders.

177 **Análisis de las territorialidades en México y Bolivia desde la etnografía, la historia y los imaginarios sociales.** Coordinación de José Luis Plata Vázquez y Javier Maisterrena Zubirán. San Luis Potosí, Mexico: El Colegio de San Luis, 2017. 393 p.: bibl., ill., maps. (Colección Investigaciones)

This volume brings together 15 articles discussing space and the defense of both urban and rural, agricultural and protected, peasant and Indigenous land/territory against the neoliberal and market onslaught of the last half-century. The contributions seek to problematize the naturalization of this process, to examine the many forces of resistance to this territorial encroachment and its human and environmental impacts, and to suggest what history tells us about the future. Theoretical as well as historical and ethnographic, the presentations are grouped into four sections: history of land in Indigenous and campesino communities, urban spaces, legal and jurisdictional issues tied to community governance and the state, and social movements and ethnopolitics, the organized push back. Most cases are in Mexico, but a few are in eastern Bolivia.

178   **Ángeles Contreras, Isaac.** Pedagogía de la comunalidad: herencia y práctica social del pueblo iñ bakuu. Oaxaca, Mexico: publisher not identified, 2018. 400 p.: bibl., ill., maps.

The author shares perspectives of a strong movement of teachers in the Mexican state of Oaxaca who reframe education as a community-based project, in juxtaposition to a state-based one, especially in the case of Indigenous communities such as the one presented here. In a study of a community similar to his own, the author proposes that an understanding of the institutions, practices, and shared understandings of the community provide the basis for reimagining community education along the same cultural lines. This pedagogy questions the imposed logics of individualism, avarice, acquisitiveness, consumerism, exploitation of others, and the destruction of natural resources brought on by international capital investment. The author points to the functional resistance model of a town with over 500 years of rejecting cultural conquest as a fount of understanding and inspiration for a pedagogy of the community. An example of a professional who speaks from his own biography.

179   **Antropología visual y epistemes de la imagen.** Edición de Arturo Gutiérrez del Ángel, Christoph Schabasser y Cecilia Fuentes. San Luis Potosí, Mexico: El Colegio de San Luis, 2018. 189 p.: bibl., ill. (Colección investigaciones)

Seven articles and an introduction focus on visual anthropology and raise a number of issues related to representation of "the Other" in photography and film, including early pictures of Indigenous people, pornography, the prohibition-era representation of lush Tijuana, textiles in Mexico and Colombia, and more.

180   **Aproximación a la comprensión de las comunidades indígenas y rurales desde una perspectiva multidisciplinaria.** Edición de Santa Magdalena Mercado Ibarra, María Teresa Fernández Nistal, Claudia García Hernández y Eneida Ochoa Ávila. Ciudad de México: Editorial Fontamara, 2018. 271 p.: bibl., ill., tables. (Serie Argumentos; 509)

In this work, 17 articles address diverse issues including intercultural education, the family as locus of development, addiction, rural tourism, gender equity and equality, care for the environment, human rights among seasonal migrants, the family as an economic unit, cooperative horticulture, and customs and views about death and mourning. The book's introduction emphasizes the multidisciplinary nature of the works presented.

181   **Aragón Andrade, Orlando.** De la "vieja" a la "nueva" justicia indígena: transformaciones y continuidades en las justicias indígenas de Michoacán. Ciudad de México: Universidad Autónoma Metropolitana, Unidad Iztapalapa, División de Ciencias Sociales y Humanidades, Departamento de Antropología: Ediciones del Lirio, 2016. 508 p.: bibl., ill. (Colección enfoques contemporáneos; 1)

A major contribution to the anthropology of rights and law, the author combines detailed ethnography with extensive and innovative theoretical considerations, and a deep assessment of both Indigenous concepts of law and justice and those of the state, advocating for an "inter-legality" and a multiculturalization of law in Indigenous Mexico. The author traces the last four decades of the development of the anthropology of law that, due to Indigenous struggles for rights, has influenced researchers to focus on Indigenous concepts of law and how they serve as a form of critique of the state. Proposes a new model for a comparative and critical analysis of Indigenous justice systems in relation to states.

182   **Ariel de Vidas, Anath.** Combinar para convivir: etnografía de un pueblo nahua de la Huasteca veracruzana en tiempos de modernización. Ciudad de México: Centro de Estudios Mexicanos y Centroamericanos: Centro de Investigaciones y Estudios Superiores en Antropología Social; San Luis Potosí, Mexico: El Colegio de San Luis,

2021. 499 p.: bibl., ill. (chiefly color), indexes, maps, photos, tables.

An extensive study of rituals in a Nahua town—under many acculturative pressures—that, the author argues, serve as principal mechanisms of social production/reproduction, cultural maintenance and continuity, and political authority. The focus is on how these social events promote coexistence between different groups of people, as well as getting along with nonphysical entities. Rich and nuanced ethnography, with detailed description and extensive analysis, good photography, and glossary. The rituals associated with a local hill, rain, and water are of particular note, as well as the involvement in the ritual cycle of migrants.

183   Beyond alterity: destabilizing the Indigenous other in Mexico. Edited by Paula López Caballero and Ariadna Acevedo-Rodrigo. Afterword by Paul K. Eiss. Tucson: The University of Arizona Press, 2018. 312 p.: bibl., ill., index.

Introduction, 11 chapters and an afterword by 12 scholars arising out of professional meetings that pose the question: why has identification as Indigenous become tacitly associated with alterity, with the concept of radical or essential difference? If Indigenous people are not so different from the rest of the population, are they inauthentic? Or is the problem the need to interrogate the term Indigenous itself—and how it is used in sociopolitical spaces, vis-à-vis the state? Is Indigenous an essential identity or relational to others, constantly shifting its meaning as the context shifts, and as shifts in definitions serve power? The authors provide examples of the latter conclusion, in diverse sociopolitical landscapes and times, that undermine stereotypes of what Indigenous people do and believe: cases of private property inside collective land, egalitarianism belied by power hierarchy, many native efforts to get Spanish-teaching, acculturating schools, scale Indigenous participation in regional and national political events, and supposedly land-bound Indigenous people moving all around, genetic internal diversity, and so on. These scholars address the situated and situational nature of ongoing identity dialectics when it comes to Indigenous people in Latin American states.

184   Bourdin, Gabriel. Las emociones entre los mayas: el léxico de las emociones en el maya yucateco. Coyoacán, Mexico: UNAM, Instituto de Investigaciones Antropológicas, 2014. 264 p.: bibl.

A deep dive into the way Yucatec Maya name emotions and parts of the body by a linguistic anthropologist interested in the relationship between psyche, body, and the communicative expression of emotion. Exploring the vocabulary of internal states of emotion ethnolinguistically, the author places most of the focus on documents of colonial-era vocabulary, from which he teases out emotions like the term "ool" for formal heart, which he sees as a central term relating to important and core aspects of social values.

185   Calveiro, Pilar. Resistir al neoliberalismo: comunidades y autonomías. Ciudad de México: Siglo Veintiuno Editores, 2019. 217 p.: bibl. (Sociología y política)

A critical assessment of the impact of governmentally supported neoliberalism relative to the marginalized, including Indigenous people. Focuses on two Indigenous cases, Cheran Keri in Michoacán and the CRAC-PC in Guerrero state, both in Mexico, where state violence was collectively confronted, and community organization and autonomy strengthened. The author uses these well-documented cases to advocate for the construction of alternative forms of organization to push back, and their successes in turn serve as an inspiration for alternatives to the neoliberal agenda.

186   Camacho Ibarra, Fidel. El camino de flores: mitología y conflicto interétnico en la warejma y el pajko de los mayos de Sonora. Ciudad de México: Primer Círculo, 2019. 476 p.: bibl., ill., photos, tables. (Etnología)

Large and detailed ethnography of the Mayo of Sonora. Focusing on two ceremonial moments, the workings of the cult of origin linked to the equinox and the Catholic Holy Week, and the cult of the night sun of prehispanic origin, the author maintains that their apparent passivity and inclusion of the mestizo into the rituals. Their holistic vision of the universe has helped them cope with their subordinate sociopolitical position, putting the outsider into a culturally controlled space. By incorporating the non-Indigenous as a player in the spiritual world, with a ritual role to play, the outsider has failed to undermine their traditional worldview, and in fact strengthened their resistance, even as many aspects of their daily life have evolved.

187 **Cánceres en mujeres mayas de Yucatán: pobreza, género y comunicación social.** Coordinación de Judith Ortega Canto y José Pérez Mutul. Mérida, Mexico: Universidad Autónoma de Yucatán; Ciudad de México: P y V, Plaza y Valdés Editores, 2017. 246 p.: bibl.

Consisting of eight chapters written by 13 professional authors, this book looks at cervical and breast cancer among Maya women of Yucatán, with a mix of biomedicine, social medicine, and medical anthropology. Addressing the comparatively high rates of death, the authors signal the problems of communication, medical education, disempowerment of women, and cultural barriers based in alternate understandings of illness and wellness inconsistent with biomedical, allopathic ones.

188 **Castro Neira, Yerko.** El archivo indígena: fuerzas, luchas y acomodos en el pensamiento y las visiones sobre lo indio en Oaxaca. Coyoacán, Mexico: Editora Nómada, 2019. 332 p.: bibl., ill., map.

In the face of negative and positive elements pulling apart and holding together Indigenous communities in Oaxaca state, the author uses the term Indigenous Archive to denote the corpus of writings by anthropologists, political leaders, lawyers, intellectuals, and others relevant to the place and issues, as a resource. In the introduction, he lays out his theoretical concerns (border thinking) and an outline of Oaxaca. The first chapter describes the major conflicts in the area. The second discusses the implicit orientalism and neocolonialism in much anthropological research, and shows how the situation in Oaxaca reveals this perspective.

189 **Coelho, Ruy Galvão de Andrade.** Creencias, rituales y fiestas garífunas: cuatro artículos de Ruy Coelho. Compilación y estudio introductorio por Rodrigo Ramassote. Tegucigalpa: Editorial Guaymuras, 2018. 204 p.: bibl., ill. (Colección Códices (ciencias sociales))

This compilation brings together the work of the father of Honduran Garifuna studies (Coelho). Another Brazilian (Ramassote), whose 2000 work *Days in Trujillo: A Brazilian Anthropologist in Honduras* is here translated into Spanish, examines Coelho's work including four of his major articles on the Garifuna (also included in the volume). Much of Ramassote's writing is a biographical discussion of Coelho, while the latter describes the Black Caribs in fieldwork between 1948 and 1961. The first article discusses the significance of *couvade*, the second their concept of the soul, the third their fiestas, and the last, the personality and social roles of the shaman.

190 **Lo cotidiano detrás de la lente: mujeres indígenas del Estado de México, Chiapas y Oaxaca.** Coordinación de Héctor Serrano-Barquín, Carolina Serrano Barquín, Martha Patricia Zarza Delgado y Jorge Ortega. Fotografía de Jorge Ortega. Toluca de Lerdo, Mexico: FOEM, Fondo Editorial Estado de México: Universidad Autónoma del Estado de México, 2018. 283 p.: bibl., ill. (some color), map. (Colección mayor. Patrimonio natural y cultural)

A coffee table book consisting largely of lightly labeled photographs of women, their children, and landscapes associated with their everyday life, in small communities in three states of Mexico (México, Oaxaca, and Chiapas), by photographer Jorge Ortega. These photographs are framed with a few pages about the photographer, and a few more focused on each setting, describing subjectively the place and people, and with occasional short quotes from women who are, rather disparagingly, only identified by their first names.

191 **Cruz Coutiño, Antonio.** Mitología y continuidad maya: la creación del hombre y su entorno. Tuxtla Gutiérrez, Mexico: Universidad Autónoma de Chiapas;

Puebla, Mexico: El Errante Editor, 2018. 462 p.: bibl., ill., index, maps.

A comparative examination of myths of creation by the Maya of Chiapas, Mexico, based on a corpus of 2,500 narratives and a robust review of what is known about the precontact Maya. The first half draws on classic archeology and epigraphy, and postclassic Maya ethnohistoric material, while the second half is an extensive compendium of Indigenous creation tales from Chiapas collected by ethnographers—Tzotzil, Tzeltal, Moche, Zoque, Chol, Lacandon, Mestizo, and Tojolabal. The task is to show both fundamental continuity and historically informed changes, an evolution of Maya beliefs in the context of Spanish colonialism and the unfamiliar concepts it has introduced. Departing from both notions of unchanging purity and views that claim current beliefs are largely from the colonial era, the author makes an exhaustive case for continuity-within-change by a system of cosmology wildly at odds with the West.

192   **De los dioses y sus atributos: un acercamiento a través de la cosmovisión nahua.** Coordinación de Julio César Morán Álvarez. Naucalpan de Juárez, Mexico: UNAM, Facultad de Estudios Superiores Acatlán, 2017. 560 p.: bibl., ill.

"Cosmovision"—which translates loosely to spiritual worldview or universe—has come fully into fashion as a term and subject of research in Mexico and much of Indigenous Latin America as part of a shift from class to cultural analysis. In this collection of 20 chapters, 17 authors discuss the primary pantheon of the Aztecs/Mexica and their Nahuatl-speaking neighbors, derived from 16th-century sources, and seek to correct what they see as misunderstandings and faulty interpretations, corrupted by ethnocentrism and prejudice. Applying historiographic, philological, and hermeneutic tools, they seek to tease out not just what elites revealed but the nature of everyday beliefs at the time of contact. As a whole, the volume serves as a baseline of understanding the Aztec religion, but also as a template of belief that emerges from the study of more recent (and more distant) Mesoamericans. Some authors make reference to ethnographic data to reinforce their interpretations of the meanings of the past as well as of other ethnic groups in Mexico.

193   **Enciso González, Jesús. Turismo cultural en México: un estudio de los pueblos mágicos hidalguenses.** Pachuca de Soto, Mexico: Universidad Autónoma del Estado de Hidalgo, 2019. 216 p.: bibl., ill.

An interdisciplinary study of cultural tourism in the region of Hidalgo state, a project imposed from above that had great promise and expectation, but ended up mostly helping the wealthy and outside tourism interests, and offering little local benefit, and some harm. An example of how top-down development helps those at the top and keeps the rest down.

194   **Entre el activismo y la intervención: el trabajo de organizaciones de la sociedad civil y su incidencia para la salud de las mujeres indígenas en México.** Coordinación de Clara Juárez Ramírez, Felipe José Hevia de la Jara, Ana Eugenia López Ricoy y Laura Georgina Freyermuth Joffre. Ciudad de México: Alternativas y Capacidades A.C.: Centro de Investigaciones y Estudios Superiores en Antropología Social; Ottawa, Canada: Centro Internacional de Investigaciones para el Desarrollo, 2017. 369 p.: bibl., ill., map. (Publicaciones de la Casa Chata)

An introduction, five chapters representing case studies, and a conclusion focused on issues of health, government, and other organizations attending to the health, wellness, and illness of Indigenous women. The cases include an analysis of a school for professional midwives, a coalition working for women's health, a center for environmental and health training, an organization for the rights of Nahua women, and another organization focused on Indigenous women in Oaxaca. The conclusion looks at how influence and intervention serve as more or less effective ways to improve the health conditions for Indigenous women and how these issues resonate within the discourse about Indigenous rights.

195   **Entre el despojo y la esperanza: doce ensayos sobre historia y etnografía de la Huasteca.** Coordinación de Jesús Ruvalcaba Mercado y Sergio Eduardo Carrera

Quezada. Ciudad de México: CIESAS, Centro de Investigaciones y Estudios Superiores en Antropología Social, 2019. 423 p.: bibl., ill., indexes, maps. (Publicaciones de la Casa Chata)

Twelve chapters by different authors, covering the Huasteca, one on archeology, five on history, and six ethnographic chapters. As a kind of Mesoamerican crossroads, the Indigenous cultural material is consistent with, and often goes deeply into, concepts explored in other parts of Mesoamerica. Examples include the spiritual importance of caves and mountains, the role of women in pottery (inventers?), the perennial issue of dislocation and migration, native categories of reference, kinship relations, how fish and water are conceptualized, military repression, oral mythology, sense of place, and much more. It is evident in the ethnographic entries how attentive the scholars are to local interests and concerns, and how relevant their research is to those who live there.

196 Entre minas y barrancas: el legado de Juan Luis Sariego a los estudios antropológicos. Coordinación de Séverine Durin y Victoria Novelo. Ciudad de México: Centro de Investigaciones y Estudios Superiores en Antropología Social, 2018. 219 p.: bibl., ill., photos, 1 DVD (18 min.). (Publicaciones de la Casa Chata)

An homage to mining anthropologist Juan Luis Sariego, focusing on the social history of mining in the northern regions of Mexico, an area until recently getting less anthropological attention than areas of central and southern Mexico. Fourteen former students and close colleagues discuss a variety of topics that this early investigator touched on, especially the anthropology of work, mining enclaves, critique of indigenismo (especially as regards the Tarahumara/Raramuri), and other themes that have helped give the social anthropology of northern Mexico its distinctive flavor.

Esquit Choy, Alberto. "Los indígenas también queremos ser guatemaltecos. . .": entre la exclusión y la democracia (1950–1985). See item **888**.

197 Estrada Peña, Iván Canek. Tradiciones y novedades en torno al calendario de 260 días entre los K'iche' contemporáneos: el caso del día Imox. Buenos Aires: EA, 2017. 125 p.: bibl., ill.

An historically grounded and culturally contextualized study of the Maya Cholq'ij or day count as still used by the K'iche' of Guatemala, framed within the revitalization and postcolonial cultural rights framework. The author dives into a detailed exploration of one of the 20 days, Imox (Imix in Yucatec), as an example of an evolving symbol embedded in an emerging national Indigenous effort (Movimiento Maya) to "revindicate" Maya languages, traditional dress, and religious belief and practice over and against the enculturating/deculturating pressures of the dominant half of Guatemalan society. He also demonstrates the semantic complexity of this calendric system and its ample ability to change significances in light of this Indigenous cultural movement, engaging debates about authenticity, cultural authority, and exploitation by external experts and local scholars of Guatemalan Maya knowledge.

198 Evia Cervantes, Carlos Augusto. Mitos y cavernas de Yucatán. Mérida, Mexico: Asociación de Cronistas e Historiadores de Yucatán A.C., 2018. 172 p.: bibl., ill.

A wonderfully accessible collection of 78 Yucatec stories (traditional and new myths and accounts of stories) summarized in the Spanish, Yucatecan Maya, and English languages, so the reader can easily scan between them. The tales have been introduced, contextualized, and abbreviated for space, as these texts were originally published one by one in a Yucatán newspaper. The summaries cover the essential characters, remembrances, and actions. Subjects of the tales include many involving caves, caverns, and cenotes (sinkhole wells), as well as animals and mythic figures such as the Aluxes, the childlike little people who appear in cornfields and while being tricksters, protect the cornfields of those who give offerings and prayer. The author also adds a few stories about outsiders, a "German" who gets a visit from a shadow being when he goes into a cave without permission, for example, or a priest who turns evil and sells his parishioners into slavery for schnapps.

199 Figueroa Serrano, David. La tradición oral de las comunidades mazahuas del estado de México: narrativa de la percepción del entorno natural y sobrenatural. Coordinación de David Figueroa Serrano. Toluca de Lerdo, Mexico: Secretaría de Cultura del Gobierno del Estado de México, Consejo Estatal para el Desarrollo Integral de los Pueblos Indígenas del Estado de México, 2019. 187 p.: bibl.

Mazahua perceptions of their surroundings, natural and supernatural, are revealed through the oral texts provided in this book, along with an analysis. The first part of the book discusses oral tradition and its relation to memory and myth, the types of myths presented, and how myths are connected to rituals, sacred space, and the "truths" of myths. The second part transcribes and translates 30 myths, while the final 60 pages discuss particular tales and the continuity in the Mazahua oral tradition of Mexico.

200 García Jiménez, Plutarco Emilio. Zapata en el corazón del pueblo: artículos, ponencias y testimonios sobre Zapatismo y movimiento campesino en México y América Latina. Xochitepec, Mexico: Unicam-Sur; Ciudad de México: ITACA, 2017. 377 p.: bibl., ill.

A much-needed documentation and assessment of neo-Zapatista peasant movements, some before but most after the 1994 uprising in Chiapas, Mexico. Explores and analyzes how the initial uprising gave rise to waves of progressive change in rural Indigenous communities in Mexico and beyond, with numerous local voices. The book is written as a counterpost to those from both left and right who have long dreamed of the end of the peasantry as part of the modernist project. The author, as Bartra states in the prologue, captures his own political biography in his writings from 1994 to 2014. Beginning with Chiapas, he outlines the ideals and progression of the movement that began with shouts and sticks and led to an entire region under self-government and indelible changes in Mexico's constitution. Moreover, it became a stimulus to a multitude of rural communities to revitalize the ideals of Zapata and apply them to their own rural situation. The author includes many statements, speeches, and related material that ties his voice to the historic events he narrates.

201 Gutiérrez Mannix, David Alan. Wirikuta contra la hidra capitalista: una lucha por la vida y lo sagrado. Aguascalientes, Mexico: Centro de Estudios Jurídicos y Sociales Mispat; San Luis Potosí, Mexico: Maestría en Derechos Humanos de la Universidad Autónoma de San Luis Potosí, 2019. 249 p.: bibl., ill., maps, photos. (Colección Pensamiento crítico del derecho)

This book looks at the complex struggle associated with an area in northern Mexico traditionally used by Huichol/Wixarika shamans and their initiates as a pilgrimage site, "to find our life"—but which is now threatened by the efforts to impose gold mines, funded by international capital. Using the Zapatista term "the Capitalist Hydra," the author frames the threat to this sacred and ecologically fragile space, and examines the legal and subjective landscapes, those of the inhabitants, the pilgrims, and many other social actors, utilizing this case as a microcosm of a much larger threat. The book ends with a complex exploration of rights and wrongs that concludes that local and environmental controls need reinforcing, and that the Indigenous vision that does not separate humans from nature is of particular value in reimagining the present and future, in this era of global warming impacts.

202 Guzmán Medina, María Guadalupe Violeta. La antropología social en Yucatán: panorama histórico y perspectivas de una antropología del Sur. Mérida, Mexico: UADY, Universidad Autónoma de Yucatán, 2020. 180 p.: bibl.

Less Yucatec Maya anthropology, and more an examination of the evolution of the social anthropological study of the Yucatec, this small book serves as an essay on how such study began and how it became more professional in the region as more Mexican scholars began working there and eventually the region's School of Anthropological Sciences arose. Shows how institutionalization and state and federal support for anthropological research and education have transformed the study of the subject.

203 **Hasemann, George; Gloria Lara Pinto;** and **Fernando Cruz Sandoval.** Los indios de Centroamérica. Segunda edición, ampliada y mejorada. Tegucigalpa: Universidad Pedagógica Nacional Francisco Morazán (UPNFM): Sistema Editorial Universitario (SEU), 2017. 599 p.: bibl., ill., maps (1 color).

The book is predominantly about Honduras and non-Mesoamerican Central America, with a long archeological and ethnohistoric section, and a relatively truncated review of the recent Indigenous history, again mostly focused on lower Central American groups and their relations to states. Provides a political chronology, but one that is predominantly top down. For example, it notes that Bishop Samuel Ruiz was awarded a human rights award in 1994 for defense of Indigenous people, but does not mention the Zapatista uprising that Ruiz mediated nor its impact on Indigenous rights in the Americas. The map on p. 418 captures most of the area that is explored in depth. The book serves as a solid source for Honduras' past, and the "indios" (sic) of the region, given the paucity of scholarship in this area.

204 **Hawkins, John Palmer.** Religious transformation in Maya Guatemala: cultural collapse and Christian Pentecostal revitalization. Albuquerque: University of New Mexico Press, 2021. 413 p.: bibl., ill., index, maps.

With a forward by John Watanabe, and a preface, introduction, 16 chapters, and a conclusion by Hawkins, along with 12 chapters coauthored with Hawkins and his field school students and colleagues, this book looks at changes in, and the diversity of, current K'iche' Maya religious belief and practice in two townships, with a perspective that gives greater importance, sympathy, and attention to Protestantism, but which does a good job of describing all major variants. His thesis is that Pentecostal religion, an externally imported religion which has grown over the decades among Indigenous communities in Guatemala, better fits their current social and economic reality than reform Catholicism or either the local or pan-Indigenous varieties of Maya traditionalism. As a Protestant himself with a view that Maya cultures are mostly colonial constructs (similar to some past Marxist views in Mexico), this change is seen as a welcome transformation away from community-based collective spiritual practice or pagan shamanic magicalism associated with old or revitalized Maya religion, and towards Weberian individualism.

205 **Hopkins, Nicholas A.** Chuj (Mayan) narratives: folklore, history, and ethnography from northwestern Guatemala. Louisville: University Press of Colorado, 2021. 171 p.: bibl., index.

A pleasantly empirical, nontheoretical look at the Chuj language and its oral literature by an experienced anthropological linguist. The six narratives were gathered during dissertation fieldwork in 1964–65, and they touch on topics that include legends and myths, personal narratives, and stories of diverse origins—even a rendering of Oedipus. Each chapter has a discussion of the story, plus some lexical and grammatical issues, an overview, and finally a transcription with a line for line translation. Excellent for folklorists, linguists, and those with ethnographic interest in this small Maya group in northern Guatemala and borderlands Mexico.

206 **Indigenous struggles for autonomy: the Caribbean coast of Nicaragua.** Edited by Luciano Baracco. Lanham, Md.: Lexington Books, 2019. 239 p.: bibl., ill., index, maps.

The book provides an understanding of the concepts of Indigenous autonomy and self-determination, mostly as they pertain to the social, ethnic, and political complexities of the Caribbean seacoast region of Nicaragua and adjacent lands since the original concessions by the Nicaraguan state in the 1980s. Ten authors in as many chapters follow the evolution of Indigenous autonomy—starting with the British impact, followed by the long Somoza period, the Sandinista revolution era, and finally the postrevolutionary period. This period includes the state activities associated with the Wang Jing Interoceanic canal, the ever-advancing agricultural settler frontier, the failure to have reconciliation or listen to Indigenous women's voices in the postconflict period, and the domestically disruptive post-1990 impact of narcotraffickers. It also tackles the thorny issue of language maintenance, identity, and the contradictory role of the state in both promoting it and seeking hegemonic integration.

207 Interculturalidad, arte y saberes tradicionales. Coordinación de Gabriel Medrano de Luna y Juan Manuel Franco Franco. Aguascalientes, Mexico: Universidad Autonoma de Aguascalientes: ANUIES, Centro-Occidente, 2019. 367 p.: bibl., ill.

This work brings together 16 articles and an introduction addressing interculturality, with a wide range of subjects and points of view, with about half of them touching on Mesoamerican cultures and subjects such as: Indigenous rights, the changes of flowers in Chamula, rites of death and fertility among the jnatjo of Michoacán, Wixaririka wavers in Jalisco (as feminist critique), an Otomi artist esthetics studied by students from the University of Guanajuato, and two Purépecha projects in the US tied to community service, among others. The prologue seems to define interculturality as multiculturalism, as referenced in the arena of education, as the equitable representation of diverse cultures in the classroom, although only a few articles refer to formal education. Many fascinating articles that struggle to hold together a consistent theme—a common problem with such collections.

208 Jarquín Ortega, María Teresa and **Antonio de Jesús Enríquez Sánchez.** La Virgen, los santos y el orbe agrícola en el Valle de Toluca. Zinacantepec, Mexico: El Colegio Mexiquense, A.C., 2020. 228 p.: bibl., ill., maps.

Brings together 10 studies focused on distinct facets of the maize agricultural cycle and how it ties in to the Catholic fiestas in the Toluca valley of Mexico. Documents in various parts of the valley how Mesoamerican beliefs and the Catholicism of the 16th century amalgamated into something novel to fit the agricultural cycle. The 10 chapters are organized by saint and a point in the maize cycle, Candelaria, San José, San Isidro Labrador, San Antonio, San Juan, San Pedro/Pablo, Santiago, Asunción, San Miguel, and San Francisco, each marking a step in growing corn, each with its own festivities in various towns. The study shows how much complexity has evolved in what has simplistically been called syncretism.

209 Juchari eratsikua, Cherán keri: retrospectiva histórica, territorio e identidad étnica. Coordinación de Casimiro Leco Tomás, Alicia Lemus Jiménez y Ulrike Keyser Ohrt. Michoacán, Mexico: Concejo Mayor de Gobierno Comunal de Cherán, 2018. 184 p.: bibl., graphs, ill. (chiefly color), photos, tables.

A wonderfully engaging and engaged, community-made book coauthored by members of the leadership of a Tarascan/P'urhepecha township committed to maintaining communal lands and forests, regaining local power over those lands, and celebrating Indigenous identity and practices in the face of growing threats to these collective resources by narcotraffickers, their corrupt government, as well as town elite allies—a threat that in 2011 led to open, violent conflict. Their uprising was a culmination of a decades-long struggle between those willing and those not willing to sell the communal forests and crop lands to outsiders, with resources and political forces supporting the compliant faction, and most of the residents opposed to the collective theft. Their struggle, sacrifice, and ultimate victory form the roots of the book. This situation parallels the earlier Chiapas and Oaxaca uprisings, except in this case the enemy has shifted from foreign and neoliberal privatizing profiteers to cartel-protected tree-cutters from adjacent communities paid to steal the wood, burn the forest, and plant avocados and cannabis. An excellent bottom-up perspective on how drug traffickers use government and elites to undermine communities and their collective property, and how some communities have successfully fought back, restructuring their community institutions and revitalizing their sense of community in the process. For another study on Cherán, see item **230**.

Juventudes indígenas: estudos interdisciplinares, saberes interculturais: conexões entre Brasil e México. See item 256.

210 **Lenguas minorizadas: documentación, revitalización y políticas lingüísticas.** Coordinación de Edgar Adrián Moreno Pineda y Marcos Ramírez Hernández. Chihuahua, Mexico: Secretaría de Cultura de Gobierno del Estado de Chihuahua: Programa Institucional de Atención a Lenguas y Literaturas Indígenas de la Secretaría de Cultura: Red de Archivos de Lenguas México, 2018. 344 p.: bibl., ill., maps.

This volume brings together 12 articles and two commentaries on the issue of Indigenous languages in Mexico, and how their study can be used to help revitalize their cultures and their use, as they confront language loss in the face of the dominant Spanish language. The right to the use of one's own language was reaffirmed in the Mexican constitutional order under the General Law of Linguistic Rights of Indigenous Communities (2003). At the same time, the authors point out the continued prejudice and ignorance regarding Indigenous people and their languages (often mislabeled "dialectos," as if less than real languages) and assert that it creates a kind of national negation of what the law affirms. The complaints of the costs of multilingual education are juxtaposed with the costs associated with marginalization, poor learning of Spanish, generational alienation, and numerous other social costs not typically calculated. Yet as these articles demonstrate, having the right is not the same as funding the educational infrastructure and having the mindset to reform the educational system to accommodate Indigenous languages, both of which are still lacking.

211 **Loritz, Erika** and **Irene Ragazzini.** Instituciones y prácticas económicas comunitarias: aprendiendo del sistema de reproducción de la vida de los pueblos aymara y mixteco. Los Polvorines, Argentina: Ediciones UNGS, Universidad Nacional de General Sarmiento, 2018. 220 p.: bibl., ill. (Colección Lecturas de economía social)

Comparing some Andean and Mixtec (Mexico) Indigenous communities, the authors conclude that collective land holdings and the social organization that maintains them and reproduces itself (based in socially obligatory donated reciprocal labor) are key to Indigenous power and persistence as functioning communities in the face of globalized capital and the threats of migration, land commodification, salaried labor, etc. In reviewing the processes of change surrounding these once economically autonomous societies, the authors argue that far from being isolated, the communitarian base allows for great flexibility, adaptability, and resilience not found where land is largely privatized and communities divided, whether by religion, political party, income inequality, capitalist penetration, or some combination. An example they use is the fiesta, framed here as not just symbolic reiteration of ethnic unity, but as serving the circulation and redistribution in the community economy, a system noted by some earlier scholars (e.g., James Dow). How durable a future there is for collective economic autonomy remains uncertain, in their view, as outside forces continue to erode that ancient autonomy.

212 **Luna Tavera, Francisco.** Rä Ájuä nehñu: el dios caminante; Nda kristo, ajuä nehnu: Cristo el Dios caminante; La historia otomí de la creación del mundo y de la humanidad. Pachuca de Soto Hidalgo, Mexico: Secretaría de Cultura del Estado de Hidalgo, 2019. 233 p.: bibl.

Posthumous publication of writings on the Otomi/hnunhu by Francisco Luna Tavera consisting of 41 cantos, poem-like tales written in the native language, followed by a translation into Castilian, followed in turn by an extensive glossary to explain terms, define characters, and give linguistic and anthropological background to references. An excellent example of how many Christian themes/tales have become captured and transformed by local concerns, concepts and cosmology, not so much syncretism as appropriation and "indigenization"—so that what appears like a poor or confused rendering of Christianity's stories actually has an internal logic that alters the stories to fit the culture, undermining their acculturative impact and hiding their cultural authenticity.

213 Martos López, Luis Alberto. Espacios sagrados, espacios profanos: cuevas mayas del centro-oriente de Yucatán. Ciudad de México: Instituto Nacional de Antropología e Historia, 2015. 328 p.: bibl., ill. (Colección Arqueología. Serie Logos)

A largely archeological study of Maya cave use and beliefs, with references to continuities to current and recent use. The thesis of this study, laid out in a chart on page 304, is that caves provide a counterworld juxtaposed to the profane world of daily life above ground, where many rituals associated with creation/origins, death/rebirth, rites of passage, and death/ancestors occurred (and occur), in a world viewed as imbued with the sacred. From an ethnographic perspective, demonstrates time depth for beliefs still embraced today among the traditional Maya of the region.

214 Medina Miranda, Héctor M. Los wixaritari: el espacio compartido y la comunidad. Ciudad de México: Centro de Investigaciones y Estudios Superiores en Antropología Social, 2020. 190 p.: bibl., maps.

The "barbarous Chichimecas," the many dispersed communities of Huichols, or Wixaritari, as they call themselves (sometimes), and their use of a double social space, internal and external, appear as a core idea in this book. With an assessment from colonial history to contemporary times, the author claims that this network of Indigenous communities is larger than most scholars recognize because many reside outside their Jalisco/Nayarit "homelands" as minority groups who in part define themselves in terms of opposition to the mestizos around them and who often creatively transform traditions beyond any orthodoxy—as the basis of Huichol tradition is more at a grammar of symbolism and less at fixed places, rites, or ordering of custom—and oftentimes may look like syncretism or acculturation when, if deeply examined, it is not. Excellent reading of many misreadings, past and current, of these iconic Mexicans.

215 Memoria y resistencia en Xoxocotla. Coordinación de Víctor Hugo Sánchez Reséndiz y Gabriela Videla. Mexico: Libertad bajo Palabra, 2019. 263 p.: bibl., ill.

This collection relates the processes and players, after suffering from the Morelos earthquake of 2017, who participated in an internally generated effort to not only rebuild houses and attend to those hurt, but to utilize this grave event to rebuild community and culture in the Indigenous village of Xoxocotla. It also serves to explore what processes and practices help to make a more inclusive community. From this reflection arose most of this book as a form of community memory written largely by community actors, including collective land recovery, organized protests that led to government killings, the deep and animating impact of former president Lázaro Cárdenas, and much more—a history of community resistance. Thirteen chapters by nine authors document decades of organizing against community threats, from taxes to water to airports, to show in both successes and losses the recalled trajectory of the community—as inspiration for what is yet to come.

216 México: represión, resistencia y rebeldía: L@s zapatistas, el Congreso Nacional Indígena, las madres y padres de Ayotzinapa, l@s normalistas, l@s jornaler@as, l@s maestr@s disidentes, las luchas por la autonomía y el territorio, otros movimientos sociales y la necesidad de una filosofía de la revolución. Ciudad de México: Juan Pablos Editor, 2018. 291 p.: ill.

This collectively authored book by members of the Praxis en América Latina organization speaks to the last 30 years of repression, resistance, and popular revolt in Mexico, focused on some of the most salient cases: the Zapatistas and their shift from armed revolt to an Indigenous Council of Government (1996); the response to the 43 disappeared students of Ayotzinapa (2014); the multiple teachers' protests of Oaxaca, Michoacán, and Guerrero; the fight against the new airport near Mexico City; the San Quintín (Baja California, 2015) labor strike; and protests in Ciudad Juárez against poor working conditions in the maquiladoras. The book uses these cases to call for a reform of Mexican society, from a feminist and neo-Marxist posture. An example among many of how the

Zapatista movement has altered the political landscape in Latin American theory and practice.

217 Migración de tránsito por la ruta del Pacífico mexicano: caso Sinaloa: analizando al fenómeno y sus actores. Coordinación de Brianda Elena Peraza Noriega. Culiacán de Rosales, Mexico: Universidad Autónoma de Sinaloa, 2018. 133 p.: bibl., ill., maps. (Sociología)

This collection of six essays addresses the many difficult dimensions of experiencing the route of Central American migration through western Mexico, and specifically drug cartel-plagued Sinaloa state. The authors discuss the explanatory theories of migration, the sociodemographic profile of migrants, the issue of minors and local aid efforts, the double threat of government arrest and exploitation or worse by bands of delinquents, human trafficking, and more. The book serves to personalize, theorize, and address migration policy for this important topic of what people experience before reaching the US border.

218 Monzón Flores, Martha. Los nahuas del Alto Balsas de Guerrero: migración, comercio y turismo. Guanajuato, Mexico: Universidad de Guanajuato, 2020. 414 p.: bibl., color ill., maps.

Following the theme of migration across time, the author looks at Nahuas Cuixcas of Oapan, Guerrero state, as they struggle to survive, a struggle that today still requires migration to places where tourism allows them to sell their artisanal production. The author contends the trajectory of their history has left them unable to sustain their lives based on their lands alone, and that their ability to make ends meet requires many of them to produce materials for the tourist markets. Includes extensive ethnographic material of their homeland and the places they must migrate, including Guanajuato and San Miguel de Allende.

219 Muñoz Martínez, Aurora del Socorro and José Alfredo Pineda Gómez. Movimiento y resistencia social: el caso de la Organización del Pueblo Indígena Me'phaa (OPIM) y la Organización para el Futuro del Pueblo Mixteco (OFPM). Ciudad de México: Ediciones Eón; Guerrero, Mexico: Universidad Autónoma de Guerrero, 2017. 143 p.: bibl., ill., map.

Four years after the Zapatista uprising, there was a confrontation between Indigenous communities in the state of Guerrero, Mexico, and the Mexican military, referred to as the massacre of El Charco (7/6/1998). This book looks at the background to this episode, and many later incidents of state violence and repression, rape and forced sterilization, and how, far from calming the revolt, these violent actions strengthened local organization, resistance, and identity. The book examines the Indigenous identity of the Me'phaa/Yolpe (Tlapanec) and the Na'savi/Mixtecs, the pressures of assimilation against their identity, their history, migration, and their current social context and conditions. The authors look at the major effect of the Chiapas rebellion on the Indigenous people of Guerrero, which reanimated a long tradition of revolt that in turn led to military repression. The remainder of the book describes the formation of the organizations mentioned in the title and how they responded to the military terror, including extensive documentation by human rights defenders.

220 Ochoa Nájera, José Daniel. Prácticas descoloniales: el movimiento de resistencia cultural y lingüística. Tuxtla Gutiérrez, Mexico: Consejo Estatal para las Culturas y las Artes de Chiapas: Centro Estatal de Lenguas, Arte y Literatura Indígenas, 2018. 147 p.: bibl. (Ts'ib-Jaye: textos de los pueblos originarios)

Out of the imperfect 1996 San Andrés peace accords between the Mexican government and the Zapatistas/EZLN came the birth of a new organization called the State Center for Indigenous Languages, Art and Literature (CELALI). This book, written by a Tzeltal/Bats'il k'op Maya social scientist, begins his discussion of Indigenous cultural and linguistic resistance by discussing the formation of CELALI and its efforts to translate, make educational materials, publish literature in Maya languages, and encourage the development and documentation of language, arts, and other cultural practices.

But the book does much more, advocating in its recommendations regarding education and cultural outreach to view these efforts from a perspective closer to the Indigenous peoples themselves, and exposing in this approach the negative impact of the dominant culture, lack of historical memory, lack of community, consumeristic obsession, and other negative values that Indigenous people seek to resist. He ends by questioning whether social science investigators, as individuals, are adequate or ethical, proposing community-based team research as a less ethnocentric, and more empirically valid approach to social research aimed at the Indigenous.

221 Ochoa Rivera, Teresa. Salud, alimentación y gordura en una comunidad de origen mesoamericano en México. Ciudad de México: Universidad Iberoamericana, 2017. 218 p.: bibl., graphs, ill., indexes, photos.

Studying an Indigenous community not far from the capital of Mexico, the author investigates (with many comparative references) the transformation of local diet from corn, beans, chili, and other locally produced (and healthy) foods, to industrially manufactured goods and especially a large increase in meat, sweets, and bottled sodas, representing both the loss of food autonomy and the rise of diet-related diseases and obesity. The social pressures and communal affect related to reciprocal feasting reinforce this degraded diet, and the author claims that individual appeals to healthier eating (as say in a medical consultation) are ineffectual because eating in such settings that are events of social signification fundamentally is not personal choice. Sociocultural constructions of fatness in populations previously exposed to famine have awarded it a positive esthetic, and eating is seen as a means to access an expected social practice in festivities. Thin wives suffer social opprobrium as it indicates an insufficient husband. Added to this is an etiology of illness far from the biomedical model, which involve supernatural, spiritual, and psychological concerns, and sometimes undermine the boundaries between people and spiritual entities. Failure to comprehend how food fits into culture frustrates efforts to improve health and treat illness.

222 Ojeda Dávila, Lorena. Celebración, identidad y conflicto: el concurso de Zacán y el año nuevo de los purépechas en Michoacán. Morelia, Mexico: Universidad Michoacana de San Nicolás de Hidalgo, Facultad de Historia: Secretaría de Cultura, Fondo Nacional para la Cultura y las Artes: Universidad Pablo de Olavide, El Colegio de América: Editorial Morevalladolid, 2017. 442 p.: bibl., color ill., maps, photos, tables.

The Purépecha cultural tradition, like so many in Indigenous Mexico, has robust annual festivities that incorporate ethnic expressions of collective identity, most of which have a long history that is frequently tied to the Church festival calendar, the care and feeding of saints by holders of cargos (or *cofradias*). In addition to examining traditional gatherings, this book explores two festivals that were recently initiated by township elites: the Purépecha New Year and the Artistic Concourse of the Purepucha People (Raza). Both are funded by grants and are done in collaboration with outside groups, including anthropologists. The festivals began as small celebrations but eventually grew into massive fêtes that gained the attention of tourists, television, and the world. At the same time, these new events and those who created them and benefitted from them have been criticized from groups within the community, many of whom were marginalized and who saw the development of these elites as contrary to the ideals of the community, and instead serving special interests. This pushback led the New Year group to take a more confrontational stance towards the state and federal government, while the Arts one worked closely with the government. In the decades since these two appeared, they have evolved in fascinating ways, confronting Indigenous rights issues in different ways, but both being incorporated into the larger Purépecha culture and serving as novel institutions to promote development and resist loss of land and culture.

223 Olivas Hernández, Olga Lidia. Danzar la frontera: procesos socioculturales en la tradición de danza azteca en las

Californias. Tijuana, Mexico: El Colegio de la Frontera Norte, 2018. 318 p.: bibl., ill.

Although without noting border scholars or the significant borderlands literature, this book contributes to border studies in multiple ways, first as it locates its comparison of Aztec dance groups in part on the US-Mexico border, where many mixes and mestizajes occur rather organically and synthetically. To groups in Tijuana and San Diego the author adds one in Los Angeles, Calif., which has many characteristics of the borderlands region. Far from being a direct derivation of an Indigenous dance tradition from an "Aztec" community, these danzas have a long syncretic history as a mestizo tradition, revitalizing and reworking the imagined Aztec into a basis for an alternate Mexican identity that embraces native heritage over the European, Spanish, or gringo. The author emphasizes the act of dance as an incorporation, an embodiment of identity, seated within a generalized idea of Mesoamerican cosmovision and worldview. Far from just nostalgia or folklore, these dance performances and the organizations that carry them out in this border context construct a novel counter-discourse of identity to the dominant ones. For US Chicanos, disaffected mestizos, or deculturated and displaced Indigenous alike, the dance group participation provides an architecture to push back against a surrender of identity to a secular, individuated, and prejudiced society.

224 Las palabras que en mí dormían: discursos indígenas de Bolivia, Ecuador, Chile y México. Compilación de Natividad Gutiérrez Chong. Ciudad de México: UNAM, Instituto de Investigaciones Sociales, 2019. 192 p.: bibl. (Cuadernos de investigación; 43)

The book is organized into three parts, the first regarding Indigenous thought and its critics, the second an analysis of the Indigenous voices to be presented in the third part. The third involves nine texts of Indigenous leaders, constituting the majority of the book. The objective here is less about the multitudinous Indigenous organizations and movements, and more getting at the characteristics and qualities that their leaders exhibit. The discussion of the Indigenous intellectual, formed in modern times by their struggle with the state, and their self-reflection in terms of an identity at every turn dismissed by the majority, is of note. So is the effort to identify common traits, their references to their autonomous past, their denouncing the conditions of their people's marginalization, and the certain necessity that Indigenous people manage their own affairs, and their destiny.

225 Paz Frayre, Miguel Ángel. Institucionalidad y poder: estrategias políticas y regidurías étnicas en Sonora: el caso de los Tohono O'otham. Guadalajara, Mexico: Universidad de Guadalajara, Centro Universitario del Norte; Ciudad de México: Juan Pablos Editor, 2018. 249 p.: bibl., maps.

The Mexican Papago people once functioned as collectors, hunters and gatherers with a mobile adaptation moving across the northern Sonora desert and into Arizona, where some still live today. But for the Mexican side, the impact of Jesuit missionaries and government, military officials, and INI applied anthropologists radically transformed their lives, imposing institutions based on templates from other places. This eventually led to a rejection by the communities of native authorities whose objectives and perspective reflected the state but not the people. In their politics of rejection of institutional hegemony, an evolved identity re-emerges, firmly based in their anti-politics politics.

226 Peralta de Legarreta, Alberto. Cultura gastronómica en la mesoamérica prehispánica. Ciudad de México: Universidad Anáhuac: Siglo Veintiuno Editores, 2018. 188 p.: bibl., graphs, index, tables. (Antropología)

A tasteful and detailed look at the precolumbian world of foods, the eating process, and their complex ties to Mesoamerican culture that was the baseline for current Mexican cuisine, with over half of the book serving as an inventory of foods, from the humble but piquant *chiltepin* to the mighty *maguey*. The book also documents many customs and beliefs associated with the eating process, such as eating etiquette, keeping the three-stone hearth always burning, but never stepping over it. The author points out the often-ignored process of nixtamalization, which chemically transforms this low-value food into the complex carbohydrate foundation of Mesoamerican nutrition, by way of cooking it with ash or more commonly calcium hydroxide to allow for the bioavailability of calcium, amino acids, phosphorus, fiber, and niacin. The symbolism of maize and the cornfield (milpa) is elaborated, and the author shows how the region shared a unity not just based on calendars and ball courts, but also on foods, their cultivation and preparation, and the symbolic significations associated metaphorically and metonymically with gastronomy.

227 **Pernudi Chavarría, Vilma.** Los Ngöbes del Pacífico sur. Heredia, Costa Rica: EUNA, 2017. 326 p.: bibl., ill. (some color).

A study of the Indigenous Ngobe-Bugle people of southern Pacific Costa Rica and the border with Panama (from which they began migrating in the 1930s), focused on their health, their patterns of migration to coffee-producing regions, and their identity, viewed from the perspective of cosmology and gender. Uncovering a virtually unrecognized ethnic group mostly by way of personal fieldwork, the author points to the importance of understanding their culture to addressing their pressing health and other social needs. She also raises a complex discussion of ethnicity and ethnic identity, based in her study of this heretofore virtually unstudied, unnoticed group.

228 **Pueblos indígenas y estado en México: la disputa por la justicia y los derechos.** Coordinación de Santiago Bastos y María Teresa Sierra. Ciudad de México: CIESAS, 2017. 367 p.: bibl., ill., maps. (Colección México)

An introduction and 11 chapters in three parts by authors who explore questions around Indigenous rights, justice, and political systems. These issues arise in a post-(neo)Zapatista context in Mexico, in which considerable progress has been made in legalizing alternate forms of law and political organization in Indigenous communities (*usos y costumbres*). This new legal status now confronts increasing encroachment from all sides, and does so not only by mobilization, but also in the arenas of law and legislation. In Chiapas, Guerrero, Veracruz, Oaxaca, Baja California Norte, these scholars examine cases to show how popular organization, community action, and legal push-back combine to improve the possibilities of resistance by Indigenous communities in Mexico.

229 **Religiones.** Contribuciones de Antonio Rubial García, Federico Navarrete Linares, y Carlos Garma. Ciudad de México: Secretaría de Cultura, Estados Unidos Mexicanos, 2018. 234 p.: bibl., ill. (chiefly color), map. (Historia ilustrada de México)

The three authors each take one of the prehispanic, the colonial, and the last two centuries to the present, to look at the evolution and points of continuity/similarity of Indigenous religion in Mesoamerica. They take as a starting place the all-encompassing nature of precolumbian beliefs, informing household actions and also those of the state, as well as all that lay between. Every aspect of earthly life had an analog in the world of deities, they maintain, and life was (and for many remains) experienced fundamentally as maintaining bonds of reciprocity and balance with the complex unseen world, so as to prosper in this one. It also means that politics, economics, family life, war, and so on were not separate from religion, but in a multitude of ways informed by it. A strictly secular arena of life was literally inconceivable, and as the third section reveals, this remains true today.

230 **Romero Robles, David Daniel.** Cherán K'eri: insurgencia y contrainsurgencia. Mexico: Grietas Editores, 2018. 151 p.: bibl., maps, table. (Colección Barricadas)

An Indigenous study of the Tarascan/Purepeche (Michoacán state, Mexico) town of Cherán K'eri, also studied in another work (item **209**). This book documents the community struggle against enemies external and internal, and how it managed to take political control after conflict with outside forces by way of *usos y costumbres* (uses and customs), the Indigenous right to govern by traditional means, which they used as a basis to modify their political system. Responding to the problematic of "juridical pluralism" (having different political rules within a single polity), the author concludes the book with a compelling dissertation on why such pluralism, while not always valid, applies to the case of his community. A refreshing read by an author who speaks about his own Indigenous community in great detail and with objectivity, even as he discusses legal theories of governance and the situation of rights for Indigenous communities in relation to the state in Mexico and beyond.

231 **Ruiz Ponce, Heriberto.** Resistencia epistémica: intelligentsia e identidad política en el proyecto descolonial ñuu savi. Oaxaca de Juárez, Mexico: Universidad Autónoma Benito Juárez de Oaxaca; Ciudad de México: UNAM, Programa Universitario de Estudios de la Diversidad Cultural y la Interculturalidad: Juan Pablos Editor, 2017. 269 p.: bibl., ill., photos, tables.

The author approaches and interprets contemporary Mixtec intellectuals from a perspective of decolonization, presenting their philosophy and their complex perspectives associated with a project of cultural recuperation of the Academy of the Mixtec Language. The author identifies three elements that characterize their intellectual project and concern, the discursive reverence for the past (ethnic history), a condemnation of Indigenous ethnic marginalization (racism), and the necessity for Indigenous people to take control of their own affairs and their destiny (autonomy). As such, many of the writings are aimed not only at the public but more at their own people, building a corpus of thinking in their own language—as more begin to read in Ñuu Savi. The author insists that such a project is inherently intercultural, emphasizing hospitality, solidarity, collective work for the community, and beyond this, a project of decolonization and active participation in rethinking relations with all Indigenous peoples, not just the Mixtecs, locally, nationally, and internationally.

232 **Sámano Rentería, Miguel Ángel.** La cuestión indígena en México y América Latina. Chapingo, Mexico: Universidad Autónoma Chapingo, 2017. 138 p.: bibl. (Coleccion Tlatemoa; 19)

Collection of essays by a historically informed rural sociologist, touching on relations between Indigenous communities and the state, the prospects for equitable and viable rural development in Indigenous regions, and the issue of Indigenous rights relative to general human rights. In the first two articles, he addresses ethnicity and multiculturalism in Guatemala, Mexico, and Ecuador, in the next four he discusses ethnodevelopment and sustainability, and the last two focus on Indigenous rights and their confrontation with the state, and the thorny issue of constitutional reforms that address Indigenous rights.

233 **Schumann Gálvez, Otto.** Caminos culturales mesoamericanos: obras completas de Otto Schumann Gálvez. Compilación de Rubén Borden Eng y Fernando Guerrero Martínez. San Cristóbal de las Casas, Mexico: UNAM, Centro de Investigaciones Multidisciplinarias sobre Chiapas y la Frontera Sur, 2016. 1 v.: bibl.

This homage to Guatemalan linguistic anthropologist Otto Schumann divides his work into five epochs, spanning the time from 1964 to 2013. The contributions are mainly linguistic along with some sociolinguistic work on such languages as Maya Itza, Xinca, Tuzanteco, Tojolabal, Mopan, Pocomes, K'iche', Chontal, Chuj, Q'eqchi', Chiapaneca, Mam, and several others. His writings also discuss issues such as linguistic borders, bilingual education, linguistic identity, language preservation, and translated tales, along with lively comparative assessments and interpretations.

234 **Stella, Alessandro.** L'herbe du diable ou la chair des dieux?: la prohibition des drogues et l'Inquisition. Préface d'Anne Coppel. Paris: Éditions Divergences, 2019. 194 p.: bibl.

While most drug prohibitions are relatively recent, the author notes that as an element of the Spanish Inquisition in New Spain, possession of peyote was made illegal in 1620, perhaps the first such prohibition against a psychotropic in history. The author ties this action to efforts to suppress religious-based resistance to colonial rule and the hegemony of the Church, as well as to the real beliefs of the inquisitors that the devil was at work in the use of peyote as a spiritual sacrament and a divinatory aid, by both Indigenous and mulatto/mestizo populations.

235 Trabajo colectivo en el siglo XXI: formas y contextos entre grupos étnicos de Oaxaca. Coordinación de Monzerrat Romero Luna y Camilo Sempio Durán. Ciudad de México: Secretaría de Cultura, Instituto Nacional de Antropología e Historia, 2019. 274 p.: bibl., ill. (Colección científica (Instituto Nacional de Antropología e Historia (Mexico))) (Colección Etnografía de los pueblos indígenas de México. Serie Estudios monográficos)

In this work, six articles discuss collective work, both Indigenous and ethnically mixed, in different parts of the state of Oaxaca. The authors provide diverse examples of how, in an era of increasing individualism and community decomposition, many old and some new forms of collective labor continue to operate in many parts of Oaxaca, and they show some of the social good these efforts achieve.

236 Transfiguraciones de danzas tradicionales: ensayos y entrevistas. Coordinación de Aurora Lucía Oliva Quiñones. Primera edición en Mijkskuy, movimiento, luz de razón. Terán, Mexico: Universidad Autónoma de Chiapas, 2017. 257 p.: bibl., ill., 1 map. (Mijkskuy; 1)

Eight essays and five interviews that explore and compare current and past Indigenous dance performances, in situ and as far away as the Bronx (New York), as an evolving manifestation of culture and place, based in studies emerging from the MA program in dance in the Center for Art and Cultural Studies of the Universidad Autónoma de Chiapas. Looks at Zoque, Chiapanec, Nahuatl, and conchero dances from a variety of perspectives that emphasize how dance connects to a larger cultural order.

Tzul Tzul, Gladys. Gobierno comunal indígena y estado guatemalteco: algunas claves críticas para comprender su tensa relación. See item **899**.

237 Tzul Tzul, Gladys. Sistemas de gobierno comunal indígena: mujeres y tramas de parentesco en Chuimeq'ena'. Guatemala: SOCEE, Sociedad Comunitaria de Estudios Estratégicos: Tz'i'kin, Centro de Investigación y Pluralismo Jurídico: Maya' Wuj Editorial, 2016. 220 p.: bibl., ill., maps.

In this work, a K'iche' sociologist and Indigenous activist presents a sophisticated, kin and woman-centered case for self-governing community (*gobierno comunal*) as a unit for the defense and reproduction of Indigenous society in Guatemala, rejecting the integrationist individuation forces of colonialist modernization, but also the perspective of the national Maya Movement. Her case in point is her own community and 77 adjacent ones in the region of Totonicapán, where in two tiers, extended families manage and govern their communal lands by hamlet, and come together for issues that impact all 78 of them. In this way, she maintains, they have defended themselves since colonial times from incursions of capital and government, with communal labor and extended family relations as the means by which members have political voice and agency. She questions all national projects of Indigenous cultural identity that involve integrating ("capturing") Indigenous people into the state but that do not address local governance or protection/restoration of land, insisting that territory remains fundamental to identity. A deep critique of political and community development from above.

238 Unidas tejemos la vida: testimonios de mujeres indígenas y afromexicanas radicadas en Acapulco. Entrevistas por Magdalena Valtierra García y Nadia Alvarado Salas. Chilpancingo, Mexico: Universidad Autónoma de Guerrero; Ciudad de México: Editorial Itaca, 2018. 189 p.: bibl., ill. (chiefly color), map.

Based around interviews and testimonials of members of the organization Asociación de Mujeres Indígenas y Afromexicanas Radicadas en Acapulco (Association of Indigenous and Afro-Mexican Women in Acapulco—AMIARA), this work tells of the impact of displacement and urban migration on women who seek mutual support and empowerment through organizing and sharing biographies. Sixteen testimonies make up the bulk of the book, tying the act and art of weaving to sustainable development, women's rights, gender violence, midwifery, marketing artisanal goods, tourism, and more. Part of an emerging scholarly effort to front the voices of the studied.

239 Vázquez Dzul, Gabriel. Lógicas del gusto: preferencias alimentarias y lógicas culturales en situación de migración. Zamora, Mexico: El Colegio de Michoacán, 2017. 302 p.: bibl., ill., indexes, maps. (Colección Investigaciones)

A fascinating gastronomical investigation of two displaced Indigenous communities in Quintana Roo, Mexico, one of multiethnic refugees from Guatemala, another of Yucateks migrating to the agricultural frontier. The logic of taste is applied to community foods tied to ethnicity, migration, and religious affiliation, and the tensions within and between groups based in differences in gender, age, and kinship relations, as well as on their origin, migratory trajectory, and rationale. Through the window of food, the author teases out how variation in campesino cuisine in contexts of migratory change is not just good to eat, but "good to think."

240 Velázquez Galindo, Yuribia. Porque venimos a este mundo a ayudarnos: construcción social de la persona y transmisión cultural entre los nahuas. Ciudad de México: Universidad Iberoamericana, 2018. 223 p.: bibl.

Years of sympathetic ethnography with Indigenous Nahuas in Mexico has shifted the author from seeing her work as "investigation" to apprenticeship, as her experience crushed her prior assumptions and theoretical orientation, displacing it with a view of the Nahua understandings having equal standing to the Western perspective. With this book, she seeks to demonstrate that sometimes the Nahua perspective can serve to inform hers, reversing the acculturative table. Part of a new era in anthropology working to reflect the world as seen from the view of the participants, with humility, honesty, and deep commitment to learning the culture.

241 Villegas Mariscal, Leobardo. La polisemia de los símbolos en las ofrendas rituales de los huicholes. Zacatecas, Mexico: Universidad Autónoma de Zacatecas: Taberna Libraria Editores, 2017. 154 p.: bibl., ill.

As with many groups in Mesoamerica and beyond, the author demonstrates with his symbolic analysis of Huichol offerings the reciprocal relationship between them and their deities. He sees the ritual arrows, yarn "paintings," "god eyes," tails, horns, and representations of deer and other objects presented in Huichol altars and sacred spots as a kind of parallel ritual language to the accompanying prayers that represent a kind of ritualized exchange. Offerings bring the deities close so that with petition, fasting, and good offerings, good things may continue in the profane world of hunting, farming, physical wellness, children, commerce, and so on. The book is well illustrated with b/w photographs of ritual objects and sacred locations.

242 Volteando la tortilla: género y maíz en la alimentación actual de México. Coordinación de Ivonne Vizcarra Bordi. Toluca de Lerdo, Mexico: Universidad Autónoma del Estado de México; Ciudad de México: Juan Pablos Editor, 2018. 450 p.: bibl., ill., maps.

Looking at the tortilla from the perspective of gender, environment, food dependency, and nutrition, Vizcarra decries the genetic invasion of US transgenic maize that has come to undermine native species long adapted to the microecologies of Mexico, and the national diet, in which women play a major role. She raises possibilities for alternatives that would maintain the biodiversity and social coherence of corn/tortillas, following the path of maize development as fundamentally female project, and a mainstay of not just nutrition but signification in Mesoamerican-based cultures. Sixteen cases with multiple voices provide the provocative database for her contentions, as they explore the kitchen, stove alternatives, and tortilla sustainability, based in three moves symbolic of making a handmade tortilla: food sovereignty based in native varieties, renewable/sustainable energy, and women's empowerment in the process of establishing the first two.

243 Xa' anil naj: la gran casa de los mayas. Coordinación de Aurelio Sánchez Suárez. Mérida, Mexico: Universidad Autónoma de Yucatán, 2018. 358 p.: bibl., ill., maps.

Combining the work of social scientists, biologists, architects, and construction engineers from the Universidad Autónoma de Yucatán, this collection of 14 studies approaches the Yucatec Maya house from a variety of perspectives. Central to much of the book's discussion is how culture is experientially and physically mapped onto space within and around traditional Maya houses, demonstrating that the displacement of traditional housing by foreign designs also damages the memory, lessons, and enactments of culture. Starting with preclassic archeology, the continuity of form, materials, and geomancy is amply demonstrated, as are the practices and beliefs associated with the spaces of housing, life, and death (many people used to be buried under or close by houses). Houses contain Maya "cosmovision" within the materials, construction process and techniques, space use, and terminology, and as with many Maya cultures, its parts are anthropomorphic—skin, bones, hair, etc. The contributors make the point of how the Maya habitually have constructed a habitus from their residential habitat.

244 **Xunfo Deni—Santa Rosa: trance enteogénico y ritualidad otomí.** Coordinación de Antonella Fagetti. Textos de Lourdes Baez Cubero, María Gabriela Garrett Ríos y Jorgelina Reinoso Niche. Puebla, Mexico: Benemérita Universidad Autónoma de Puebla, Instituto de Ciencias Sociales y Humanidades "Alfonso Vélez Pliego", 2019. 224 p.: bibl., ill. (chiefly color).

Four chapters by different authors addressing the consumption and offerings of a sacred plant (Santa Rosa) in the context of ritual in Otomi and adjacent communities in the southern part of the Huasteca, in Mexico. The authors document the many ways this plant and the many rituals and practices associated with it facilitate the connection with the holy, as a significant element in the Otomi worldview. She can appear as an old woman, a young girl, the Virgin, a livid blonde, in dreams and trances, and the plant plays a decisive role in the shamanic arts and ceremonies of the region. 47 pages of stunning ethnographic photographs enrich this sensitive, collaborative ethnography.

South America Lowlands

FEDERICO BOSSERT, *Researcher, CONICET, Universidad de Buenos Aires, Argentina*
BARTHOLOMEW DEAN, *Associate Professor of Anthropology, University of Kansas and Director de Antropología, Museo Regional-Universidad Nacional de San Martín, Tarapoto, Peru*
SILVIA MARÍA HIRSCH, *Professor of Anthropology, Escuela Interdisciplinaria de Altos Estudios Sociales, Universidad Nacional de San Martín, Argentina*
SUZANNE OAKDALE, *Professor of Anthropology, University of New Mexico*

WESTERN AMAZONIA

Social Change & Continuity: The Challenges of Cultural Survival in Contemporary Amazonia

Much like the remarkably diverse faunal and floral environs of Lowland South America, recent ethnological scholarship on Amazonia is complex and variegated: it reflects distinct intellectual traditions, theoretical orientations, methodological dispositions, and practical concerns. Despite the difficulty of encapsulating the diversity of the anthropological study on western Lowland South America in a single introductory essay, these remarks attempt to inform the reader of the region's broad and intellectually robust ethnological literature. The purpose is to review important contemporary anthropological concepts and writings about the region, highlighting their theoretical contributions and practical relevance. By so doing, I emphasize some existing obstacles and prospects for future ethnological research while responding to calls for more critical discussion, debate, and collaboration among scholars and the region's many stakeholders.

The ethnological reality of the area is complicated and diverse, and as a result, the challenges facing the region's inhabitants are neither isolated nor static. Radically transformative forces include colonialism, which brought violence, disease, exploitation, and displacement; capitalism, which introduced novel forms of production, exchange, consumption, and inequality; and globalization, which increased the flows of people, goods, ideas, and influences across borders and boundaries. Anthropologists have long examined how these forces have shaped and reshaped the social, political, economic, cultural, and ecological aspects of life in western Lowland South America and how Indigenous peoples have responded to and resisted them in various ways.

The historical and contemporary impacts of colonialism, capitalism, and globalization in the region have profoundly influenced the study of Lowland South America's Indigenous peoples and cultures. A compelling example of this perspective is Michael Brown's book *Upriver*, which documents the recent history and lifestyle of the Awajún, an Indigenous group living in the Peruvian Upper Amazon (item **282**). Brown's text is divided into two parts: the first provides detailed information about the Alto Mayo area of Amazonia and the Awajún during his first fieldwork period in 1976–78; the second focuses on the years 1980–2012. *Upriver* explores how the Awajún people have tried to reshape and reclaim their destiny, arguing that they have faced multiple threats to their traditional way of life, such as diseases, exploitation, and colonial violence. The book also examines local transformations in the 1990s and 2000s, such as the Awajún's adoption of land rents, greater participation in state politics and education, and the notorious 2009 deadly clash with the Peruvian army and police (*El Baguazo*). Brown shows the Awajún people's desire to redefine and actively take control of their fate despite strong historically rooted influences, particularly in a world unfriendly to their interests. The 2009 Bagua crisis made public Peru's long-standing human rights crisis between Indigenous Amazonian communities and the state over ownership of land and resources. Roberto Guevara Aranda's study methodically analyzes the horrific violence of 5 June, the tragic result of a long history of Indigenous marginalization (item **286**). Guevara Aranda's text offers a concise historical overview of the Awajún—Wampís settlers in the department of Amazonas, an analysis of their family and sociopolitical organization, and a discussion of their social conflicts between 2002–2009. The victims of the Baguazo disappearances, and the complex path to peace that involves return visits to the provinces of Bagua and Condorcanqui, are also discussed.

Lowland South American ethnology's primary concern remains in comprehending the diversity and complexity of Indigenous societies, both synchronically and diachronically. This is apparent in Carmen Laura Paz Reverol's text (item **278**), which discusses the Wayuu people's ancient communities, resistance, smuggling, and their efforts to gain political and military control. The Wayuu of northern Colombia and Venezuela are an Indo-Hispanic society marked by many cultural exchanges and a pattern of long-term survival facilitated by their strong social structure, diversification of economic endeavors, and environmental defense. The scholarship continues underscoring the diversity and creativity of Amazonian art, ritual, language, and knowledge expressions. In addition to Reverol, ethnographers such as Jon Schackt (item **280**) have documented how Amazonian peoples produce and transmit esthetic, symbolic, and cognitive forms that reflect their cosmologies, values, and experiences. Schackt's monograph discusses the imbrications of legend, myth, *maloca* (longhouse), architecture, history, and the connections between ancestry, hierarchy, and the politicization of knowledge. A valuable addition to the growing body of literature about the Indigenous peoples of the northwest Amazon, the book focuses on cultural resilience and the Yukuna's oral tradition, which includes the story of *Periyo*, the cosmos, and the conception of death, and the *Baile de los Muñecos* ("Dance of the Dolls") style of *maloca* dance.

One of the critical issues in Indigenous Amazonian ethnology over the last decade has been the investigation of the region's complex and dynamic relationships between humans and nonhumans. Ethnographers have documented how Amazonian peoples interact with animals, plants, spirits, ancestors, and other entities in ways that challenge traditional concepts of personhood, agency, and ontology. Examining the "onto-diversity" and "cosmopolitics" of South American Indigenous people, *Non-Humans in Amerindian South America* (item **251**) features nonhuman entities in ceremonial expressions, mythology, shamanism, and songs, and examine the effects of resource extraction, relocation, and modernity on Indigenous societies. Edited by Juan Javier Rivera Andía, the collection examines the importance of food sharing and exchange between humans and other species, funerary traditions, and the role of shamans.

Contemporary ethnological writing on Lowland South America is replete with pertinent philosophical reflections, continuing a growing interest in ontological issues. Elliott Oakley's incisive contribution (item **277**), for example, focuses on how the Waiwai people's perceptions of memory are produced through amalgams and associated physiological sensations. According to Elliott, remembering and forgetting are morally acceptable behaviors for the Waiwai of Guyana since they affect other people's perceptions and allow them to express positive, negative, or ambivalent sentiments. How recollections and forgetting affect Waiwai's physiologic tendencies, village coexistence, and communal connections with the state illustrates the moral power of memory and forgetting. The moral values of freedom and empathy are cherished in Indigenous Amazonia, as described in Francesca Mezzenzana's (item **288**) anthropological explanation of how moral inclinations for autonomy and social attunement are created among the Runa, an Indigenous people living in the Ecuadorian Amazon. Mezzenzana argues that two phases are required to develop this thoughtfulness: independence, self-control, and the ability to recognize and accommodate other people's desires.

In Amazonia, supralocal forces shape moral topographies. Social transformations have long been a defining characteristic of Christian conversion in Lowland South America. With this in mind, Jeffrey Luzar, Kirsten Silvius, and José Fragoso (item **276**) assess the impact of Indigenous and Christian beliefs and practices on the food taboos of the Makushi and Wapishana peoples of the Guyanese Amazon. Their innovative study shows that while Indigenous people of all religious backgrounds disregarded regional eating customs, Sabbatarian churches were more inclined to adhere to food taboos than evangelical or established churches. Despite theological resistance to shamanistic ceremonies, continuity in eating practices was observed, showing the perdurance of Makushi and Wapishana tradition in the face of cultural alterations. In a complementary fashion, Minna Opas' contribution (item **252**) explores the ambivalent relationship between Christianity and Indigenous religions in Amazonia. While intersecting various social fields, Opas investigates these two categories' apparent incompatibility and irreconcilability. This entails studying how Indigenous people's daily lives are affected by how they perceive Christianity as a category or phenomenon that fits into, overlaps with, or is distinct from Indigenous spiritualities. Similarly, Casey High's (item **287**) article on the Ecuadorian Waorani emphasizes the complexities of conversion, arguing that it is primarily a social process rather than one of commitment or faith. Religious conversion among the Waorani marks the end of a time of relative seclusion and the beginning of a new era of *civilization* involving sociocultural integration into a broader national social system.

In Lowland South America, Indigenous peoples manifest cosmogonic concerns in multiple realms, from religious conversion to shamanic relations with plant beings. Influenced by debates surrounding the theoretical stance of perspectivism, Lewis Daly and Glenn Shepard's essay (item **247**) investigates the function of sensory perception in mediating relationships between people and plants. They compare and contrast the Makushi and Matsigenka people in Guyana and Peru to examine how chemosensory perceptions permeate Indigenous conceptions of etiology and efficacy. Daly and Shepard skillfully analyze the role of the chemosensory properties of plants and associated physiological experiences among Indigenous peoples. Dieting and eating nonpsychoactive plants for sacred purification and psychic cleaning are central to Amazonian shamanism. Evgenia Fotiou explores the extent to which shamanic diets are best considered bodily technologies (item **285**). By so doing, Fotiou illustrates the critical value of anthropological and pharmacological research methods when surveying the usage of plants in Amazonian shamanism. Besides plants, animals play a foundational role in the lives of Amazonian peoples, as explicitly noted among the Wampís, who pay special attention to nonhuman primates. Also known as the Huambisa and Shuar, the Wampís live in Peruvian Amazonia and interact with many monkey species. Kacper Świerk's meticulous investigation (item **295**) identified 11 folk-generic taxa, including 14 species of locally occurring monkeys, of import to conservation ecologists and primatologists.

In contrast to Fotiou's emphasis on humans' productive relations with plants, or Świerk's demonstration of the importance of monkeys among the Wampís, Michael Cepek provides a stark counternarrative of ecocidal life in the rainforest. His monograph explores the Cofán people's struggles with oil exploration, extraction, and production in the Ecuadorian *Oriente*, or Amazon (item **284**). Cepek has written a profoundly moving account of their suffering, showing that Cofán living amidst oil exploration experience a form of slow and perplexing brutality. A thorough investigation of the intricate relationships among Indigenous peoples, global oil companies, and Ecuadorian government organizations is given by Cepek, who adeptly relies on ethnographic research, insightful first-person testimonies, and pertinent social analysis.

Ethnographers continue to examine how Amazonian peoples resist, adapt, or transform their social and political structures, economic practices, and cultural identities in response to various forms of assimilation, domination, and ethnocide. In many scholarly works regarding the Indigenous peoples of Lowland South America, political mobilization and struggles for collective rights continue to take center stage. Obstacles abound for Indigenous peoples when they mobilize for their collective rights. Juan Pablo Sarmiento Barletti and Lexy Seedhouse's essay (item **294**) questions the rise of political will to give Indigenous peoples a genuine voice in decision-making in Peru. Drawing from the experiences of the Asháninka (or Ashaninca) and the K'ana people of Espinar (Cusco), they speak to the efficacy of Peru's Truth and Reconciliation Commission (Comisión de la Verdad y Reconciliación, CVR) and Law 29785 on the Right of Prior Consultation for Indigenous Peoples, which they note have provided for a shift to a more representative democracy. Emphasized are the challenges to more democratic politics and the chances these state initiatives have afforded Indigenous peoples to engage in sociopolitical activities.

Placing particular emphasis on the connections and parallels between Indigenous organizations and political affinities in Bolivia, Chuck Sturtevant's article (item **334**) explores the history of the Mosetén Indigenous People's Organization (OPIM). For a "more nuanced understanding" of Indigenous social movements, he compared local interpretations of social change with scholarly perspectives and public debates. In a similar vein, Pablo Ortiz-T.'s 2015 essay explores Ecuador's recognition of Indigenous peoples' rights to autonomy and self-determination, the breadth of protocols established in the Political Constitution and COOTAD, and the challenges associated with establishing Indigenous Territorial Circumscriptions (CTIs) in Kichwa and Achuar territory in the central Amazon (item **290**). It reveals the conundrums that establishing CTIs present considering the tenuous relationship between the state and Indigenous nations, not to mention the broader obstacles to fashioning a plurinational, intercultural Ecuadorian state.

The Indigenous rights struggle in Colombia, which has been relatively successful compared to neighboring countries, is the principal topic of Jean Elizabeth Jackson's welcome work *Managing Multiculturalism* (item **275**). Jackson presents a perceptive account of the Indigenous rights movement's history and examines how the Colombian government has supported a modicum of regional diversity. *Managing Multiculturalism* surveys how outside perceptions play a part in the attempts of "peoples" or "nations" (*pueblos*) to restore their Indigenous identity. Jackson's astute study on inter-ethnic conflict between the Tukanoan and Nükak peoples emphasizes the significance of discursive categories that frame perspectives on racism, cultural alterity, and authenticity. Despite being forcibly driven from their homes, the Nükak are one of Amazonia's remaining Indigenous nomadic groups. As Ruth Gutiérrez Herrera's study (item **274**) recounts, they continue to have a strong desire to return to their native territories and consistently reject attempts by the West to control and acculturate them. In his essay, Patricio Trujillo Montalvo makes the provocative case that *multiculturalism* has legitimized a specific assimilationist theory based on the generation of radical alterity (item **296**). Trujillo Montalvo's work considers the violent cultural and symbolic shift among the Shuar people of Ecuador using the dual notions of multiculturalism and biopower.

In contrast, resistance to colonialism, capitalism, and elite land domination in Colombia unites the Indigenous rights movement with the non-Indigenous left. As elsewhere in Colombia, human rights violations, neoliberal expansion, and the armed forces' hijacking of local economies have meant that most Black and Indigenous communities have not exercised their rights in the department of Chocó. According to Marcela Velasco Jaramillo (item **281**), the territorialization of institutions explains the intention and the outcome of the regional changes. In short, institutions were territorialized in a setting marked by feeble public institutions, official corruption, and resource-intensive land-use practices that threatened ethnopolitical sovereignty.

From civic and political leadership to passing on ancient practices, women in Lowland South America have emerged to fill various societal roles. Pablo Felipe Gómez Montáñez and Fredy Leonardo Reyes Albarracín's contribution takes up this topic by analyzing the difficulties that Colombia's Indigenous women in leadership roles face because of their gender and sexuality (item **273**). The authors highlight these issues considering Muisca cosmogony, which holds that women represent the archetypal feminine as the source of the cosmos and humanity. Women exercise increased presence in the formal political domain and have taken part in healthcare initiatives. Daniela Peluso's perceptive essay (item **291**) explores how women, who serve as primary custodians for family well-being, got involved in a local Indigenous healthcare project in Madre de Dios, Peru. The initiative broadened the concept of health to include living well, well-being, and sustainability and calls for a broader critique of the Indigenous health agent approach to healthcare in Amazonia. This strategy is critical, especially as the region has become increasingly linked to markets and urbanization, posing many additional health issues.

Lowland South America has rapidly urbanized. This trend has been ongoing since at least the 1970s when big-scale development initiatives such as road construction, hydroelectric dam building, and oil exploration attracted many people to the region, transforming the ecosystem and traditional life patterns. The emergence of markets, transport infrastructure, and the commercialization of produce in rural Amazonia has created a new means to relieve food shortages. Still, it can also erode established authority and production networks. In the context of growing food insecurity, the study by Michael Gurven and colleagues (item **315**) determined that wealth is related to the amount of food shared with others and the number of persons with whom it is distributed. Migration and the simultaneous processes of urbanization and modernity associated with market integration continue to capture researchers' interest. A case in point is Gordon Ulmer's propitious article (item **297**) exploring how Andean Highlands migrant miners in the Peruvian Amazon cope with the transient nature of their lives and employment. Based on 75 interviews with people in rural areas, such as gold miners, loggers, agroforesters, peasants, park guardians, and boat drivers, Ulmer contends that worker deaths are a sign of the broader logic of disposability surrounding gold mining, threatening the lives of miners and the "middle ground" they so dearly want to establish. Juan Pablo Sarmiento Barletti's essay (item **293**) investigates Julián's choice to kill the jaguar-shaman and engages in multidisciplinary research on how local people interact with Latin America's burgeoning "extractive frontiers." Often dominated by studies of local collective action and social movements, Sarmiento Barletti's contribution, in contrast, reminds us of the importance of considering how individuals respond to significant extractive activity while collectively planning their lives.

Rural-to-urban migration is one of the critical drivers of urbanization in the Amazon region. Motivated by the allure of better opportunities and the prospects of improved living conditions, many people in rural areas of western Lowland South America have moved to cities, straining urban infrastructure, housing, and services. Moreover, it has resulted in in rural areas. Indigenous migrants from Lowland South America face greater challenges in urban areas due to limited access to their traditional livelihoods and cultural practices, such as language use. This is underscored by Constanza Ontaneda's article explores the potential for implementing governmental initiatives, like "prior consultation" procedures, that follow a neoliberal multiculturalist framework (item **289**). Her research on the eviction of 300 Shipibo-Konibo Indigenous residents from their homes in Lima because of plans to convert the region into a riverfront park emphasizes the difficulties Indigenous peoples face in urban environs. Despite challenges, her work illustrates how certain Shipibo seized opportunities neoliberal multiculturalism provided them with by using entrepreneurial strategies and taking advantage of the Peruvian government benefits afforded them.

Indigenous peoples can strategically adapt to urban living to negotiate and defend their unique places. Kendra McSweeney and Brad Jokisch's essay examines the connections between Indigenous Amazonians' urbanization processes and their political struggles for territorial rights (item **249**). Their contribution aims to generate a counternarrative that suggests Indigenous urbanization and territorialization coexist peacefully. Indigenous urbanism is often portrayed in policy discourses as passive, nonpolitical, and resistant to meaningful territorial continuity. While migration is tied to urbanism, it is also linked to borders that are subject to ongoing debate, made worse by competing claims to local and national identities. Claudia Carrión's book examines the Colombian-Ecuadorian-Andean border, which has shattered the territorial integrity of the area's Indigenous people (item **246**). She highlights local knowledge and proposes novel approaches to understanding autonomy among cross-border ethnic groups. Carrión asserts that borders encompass more than just physical barriers and that governments have prioritized enacting legislation instead of comprehending the region's actualities.

Anthropology has long played a prominent role in shaping national policy in western Lowland South America. For example, Roberto Pineda Camacho's book underscores the relevance of Amazonian anthropology in establishing Colombian national identity and understanding the country's many ethnic and Indigenous groups (item **279**). His expansive text is a valuable compilation of seven essays on eminent anthropologists who have worked with the country's Lowland Indigenous groups, as well as reflections on the history of anthropology in Colombia. The putative boundaries between city and jungle, civilization and barbarism, and current *yajé* consumption practices in Colombia are plumbed in Alhena Caicedo-Fernández's fascinating text (item **272**). It addresses urbanization, elitism, and government policies affected by institutional multiculturalism, and compares new rituals conducted by urban *taitas yajeceros* with those performed by traditional *yajeceros*. In neighboring Peru, a comparable cultural crisis of modernity is assessed in Thaís de Carvalho's paper (item **283**), which shows how Shipibo-Konibo children's drawings give *pishtaco* attackers and their effects meaning. Found throughout the Andean countries, a *pishtaco* is a mythical creature thought to kill people and steal their fat for various purposes. Carvalho adroitly explores the dystopian notion associated with *pishtacos* and considers the Shipibo-Konibo children's artwork as a significant visual proof based on theories regarding illusion and fantasy.

Studying the past atrocities of Amazonia reveals the current brutalities. Between 1879 and 1912, wild rubber extracted by Indigenous and migrant workers from the rainforest met the global demand for rubber. The rubber boom brought wealth, unequal development, and exploitation to the region, and cultural and environmental impacts are still felt today. We can find traces of the cruelty associated with this tumultuous time in photographs. In Amazonia, photography has long been a powerful instrument for establishing and disseminating colonial narratives. By capturing images of Indigenous peoples, landscapes, and resources, photographers shaped the perception of Amazonia as a primitive, exotic, and exploitable territory. As Carolina Sá Carvalho persuasively asserts in her study of Roger Casement's rubber boom prints, photography has long served as a potent means of control and domination, enabling colonizers to impose their gaze and categories on the colonized *other* (item **292**). Sá Carvalho explores how the British consul exploited local bodies from the Putumayo region of the Amazon to teach a particular "pedagogy of the gaze." Casement's photographs instructed the public on how to perceive the *Indigenous body*. It sheds light on a critical idea about visual evidence, particularly in times of rapacious terror. Casement's revolving roles as an oppressed person, aggressor, ethnographer, and investigator are inextricably linked to his understanding of "point of view" as a category established by imperial history.

Through photography, colonizers created a visual archive that reinforced their authority and legitimacy over Amazonia while erasing or marginalizing the agency and diversity of the Indigenous peoples. Julio César Arana's 1904 enslavement of 13,000 Indigenous peoples is remembered as one of the most brutal atrocities of the Amazon rubber boom. However, experts argue that Indigenous individuals not enticed by the whip were unaffected by rubber extraction. Robert Wasserstrom's article contends that contemporary gold miners, illicit loggers, and drug manufacturers have launched a new cycle of rapacious resource extraction in Amazonia, displacing or eradicating descendants of previous cycles (item **298**). Indeed, researching the Amazonian rubber boom can provide valuable lessons and insights into managing present issues and opportunities in Lowland South America. For instance, the boom's impact on the environment and Indigenous communities can inform current efforts to balance economic development with conservation and social justice. Additionally, studying the boom's economic and political dynamics can offer insights into contemporary debates around resource extraction and governance in the region. Overall, understanding the complexities and consequences of the Amazonian rubber boom can help us make more informed decisions about how to navigate the challenges and opportunities facing Lowland South America today. The region faces multiple threats from deforestation, degradation, climate change, and social inequality that require urgent and coordinated action from local, national, and international actors. Studying the rubber boom can help us learn from past failures and successes and inspire us to find more sustainable and equitable solutions for the challenges facing Lowland South America and its people.

Contemporary ethnological research in the region is a rich and dynamic field offering valuable insights into the diversity and complexity of human societies and cultural configurations. It also poses significant challenges and opportunities for anthropologists, who seek to understand and collaborate with Indigenous and *mestizo* peoples in a changing world. Fundamental to the ethnology of Lowland South America is how Indigenous and colonist societies have interacted and adapted to varied environmental, political, and economic situations historically and currently. This topic continues to garner interest from specialists from a variety of perspectives, including the study of religious conversion, the analysis of Indigenous resistance and agency in colonial and postcolonial settings, the examination of Indigenous movements and popular organizations in domestic and international arenas, and the investigation of Indigenous and traditional local knowledge and cultural practices concerning the conservation of biodiversity and global warming. The ethic of respectfully and collaboratively interacting with Indigenous and *mestizo* world views and epistemologies while critically reflecting on the role and positionality of the anthropologist as a researcher and interlocutor continues to shape research trends. Several developments, including the rise of Indigenous intellectuals and scholars, the recognition of Indigenous rights and autonomy, the emergence of engaged participatory research and collaborative ethnography methods, and the challenges posed by ethical quandaries and political conflicts, have all influenced this acutely progressive trend. [BD]

BRAZIL

TWO DOMINANT TRENDS among publications reviewed for *HLAS* 77 are historical works about explorers and the expeditions of Cândido Rondon, focused especially on the scientific documentation involved in these endeavors, and works focused on the more contemporary history of the Brazilian Indigenous movement. There is also a notable book that presents fascinating ideas about Amazonian esthetics and will likely shape future work in this area.

The first trend in the literature is historical volumes about explorers or scientists in the Amazonian interior during the 19th and early 20th centuries. These works include chapters on early ethnographic research, as well as research on the flora and fauna of the region. One organized by Livia Raponi (item **267**) includes a particularly interesting chapter about the 19th-century Italian explorer, geographer, and famous documenter/publisher of the Jurupari myth, Ermanno Stradelli. The chapter, written by Tukanoan scholar João Paulo Lima Barreto, focuses on the stories his father told about Stradelli's trip to the Rio Negro. Stradelli is described as a type of shape-shifting shaman who could speak with the guardians of sacred places, such as waterfalls called *wai-mahsu*. These beings then told Stradelli where to find gold and diamonds or traded some of his objects for these riches. Stradelli's use of his compass, seen as a kind of crystal rock, is also vividly described. This chapter is unusual for the way it richly presents some of the ways the Indigenous peoples perceived and remembered explorers. In the volume edited by Gilton Mendes dos Santos and Miguel Aparicio (item **261**) Stradelli's photo archive is discussed by Raponi. The wonderfully illustrated volume edited by Lorelai Kury and Magali Romero Sá (item **263**) focuses on Cândido Rondon's explorations of

Mato Grosso and Pará. Particularly interesting are the chapters describing how the Comissão Rondon constructed an ethnographic archive of the area and those discussing Rondon's positivism, and how his practices contrasted with those of missions. This volume also includes information on earlier scientific explorations. Another work by Vanderlei Sebastião de Souza (item **265**) that focuses on nationally influential physical anthropologist Edgard Roquette-Pinto, includes a fascinating chapter about his 1912 ethnographic trip into Mato Grosso carried out in conjunction with Rondon's Comissão Construtura de Linhas Telegráficas de Mato Grosso ao Amazonas. In his search for "the true Brazil," Roquette-Pinto documented the experiences of the *sertanejo* (inhabitant of the sertão) and the *seringuiero* (rubber tapper), to show that the racially mixed Brazilians were a physically robust race. He ultimately argued that the cause of the nation's problems were a lack of education and transport, as well as an inability to deal with disease, rather than racial composition. The importance of documentation for Roquette-Pinto's German-style ethnographic research shows how scientific knowledge was understood to play a role in building Brazilian national identity and how the previously ignored interior became central to this identity.

Several books have been published on the Indigenous movement in Brazil and related organizations. These tend to blend disciplinary approaches (anthropology, or at least ethnographic research, with history, education, or political science). They all include interesting interviews with Indigenous leaders or members of organizations dedicated to the Indigenous cause. One by Libertad Borges Bittencourt (item **245**) contextualizes the Brazilian Indigenous movement and Indigenous organizations within the history of Indigenous movements in Latin America, especially Mexico. The study is particularly useful for its description of the heterogeneous organizations that were created in the 1990s in Brazil at the village, ethnic, and regional levels, as well as for outlining the many non-Indigenous organizations that focus on Indigenous issues. Another by Catiúscia Custódio de Souza (item **264**) looks closely at the Indigenous movement from two regional perspectives. Yet another by Maria Dolores Campos Rebollar (item **253**) focuses on the history of Operação Amazônia Nativa (OPAN), which began as a religious organization, inspired by Liberation Theology, but later cut ties with the Church. This group focused on autodemarcation of Indigenous lands and was a player in the context of the Indigenous movement. A volume on Indigenous youth (item **256**) has several chapters written by Indigenous scholars that speak to political mobilization within Brazilian universities and William Berger's book features the life histories of three Indigenous activists in Rio (item **254**). Finally, three particularly interesting volumes examine the famous Indigenous leaders Ailton Krenak (item **257**), Álvaro Tukano (item **266**), and Biraci Yawanawá (item **270**), all of whom were involved in the União das Nações Indígenas. One of the most interesting aspects of these three books is the autobiographical accounts they include. Interestingly, spirituality is as much a focus as politics for these men. Looking at this literature as a whole, the really novel and exciting aspect is the focus on the experiences and life histories of Indigenous leaders; this has surprisingly not been as central to previous studies.

Finally, Carlos Fausto's book *Art Effects: Image, Agency, and Ritual in Amazonia* (item **248**) is an exceptional work. Drawing on his long-term fieldwork with the Tupi-speaking Parakanã of the state of Pará and the Carib-speaking Kuikuro of the Upper Xingu as well as his knowledge of Lowland peoples more generally, this book characterizes an "Amazonian esthetic." Each chapter looks at the ritual use of a different object—such as a sacred flute, a mask, and the human body in dance (in trophy form) and in effigy. He concludes, using Christian art as a foil, that the Amerindian visual regime was never interested in verisimilitude, but rather in instability and transformational flux. This is a theme developed by Els Lagrou (item **258**) as well. Images, for example, point to multiple referents, are recursively nested, and oscillate between figure and ground. *Art Effects* also picks up classic Lowland themes, for example, "the body," and rethinks them in creative ways, such as the body's different aspects (skin, flesh, and bone). It also addresses larger issues in the study of materiality and ritual, such as the relationship between people and objects, the agency of material objects, the generation of presence in ritual contexts, and the stimulation of ontological and epistemological modalities. [SO]

ARGENTINA, BOLIVIA, AND PARAGUAY

A NUMBER OF KEY TOPICS, addressed from different theoretical perspectives, continue to dominate the ethnological production of the region. One is the study of Indigenous organizations, their struggles for legal recognition and territorial recovery, and their relations with NGOs. The analysis in this field has definitively abandoned the naivete of the multicultural perspective. Many of the texts offer a critical take on the policies of "recognition" carried out by the states—even those self-described as "pluricultural"—and on the interference of indigenist NGOs in Indigenous life. And they provide a finer and more complex scrutiny of the strategies, often ambivalent, carried out by Indigenous organizations. In multiple ways, these studies give critical nuance to the formerly straightforward or optimistic notion of "resistance," to focus on the internal tensions of these movements, the differences in discourse between leaders and followers, and the ambiguities that are inherent to the processes of negotiation with the state and the resulting self-representation. In this vein, V. Hirtzel contrasts the different uses that the Yuracaré leaders and their people gave to an European linguistic documentation project, offering a stimulating case study of the dilemmas faced by the Indigenous Council and the TCOs (Tierra Comunitaria de Origen) in present-day Bolivia (item **317**). M. Glauser studies the intracommunity conflicts that decades of multicultural policies in Paraguay produced among the Angaité (item **311**). N. Fabricant and N. Postero analyze the tensions that the Bolivian government policies foster between Highland and Lowland Indigenous peoples (item **310**). M. Biocca shows the ambiguities of Qom identity after decades of agricultural socialization (in item **330**) and P. Horn studies the political age and gender tensions that arise among Guaraní of Bolivia living in urban contexts (item **318**). In these analyses, especially in writings by researchers influenced by current American anthropology (items **306**, **310**, **324**, Horst in item **328**, and J. Correia and P. Canova in item **330**), there are frequent references to the notions of "Indian forbidden" and "Indian allowed," as discussed by Charles Hale and Patricia Richards. Even when these concepts are only implied, the features defined as politically "acceptable" by the state or the surrounding society (the "limits of recognition" discussed by J. Correia) underlie many of the articles. Fabricant and Postero (item **310**) offer a clear theoretical discussion on this subject in an essay which presents indigeneity and the performative displays of the "good Indian" as a main field of political struggle in Bolivia. K. Lowrey's book pushes that criticism forward, or rather in a new direction, by taking a "disability studies" informed turn, and questioning autonomy as a main goal of the Indigenous movements, presenting arguments that may give rise to new debates. L. Grünewald's article, focused on the self-presentation of Ayoreo leaders as "poor," includes some interesting observations in this regard (item **314**). Many studies on settler colonialism are already considering the issue of "dependence" that Lowrey places at the core of Guaraní worldview; for instance, in works analyzing Indigenous agency when facing the state or landlords (items **303** and **306**).

Closely related to this topic are the problems concerning Indigenous territories—territorialization, land struggles, deforestation—which are always a primary issue in the ethnological production on the Gran Chaco, particularly the Paraguayan region. Among other works, M. Glauser addresses this issue in a study of the Angaité responses to territorial enclosure and deforestation, and a report prepared in collaboration with R. Villagra and C. Basabe Ramírez on the territorial problems of the Yshir of upper Paraguay (items **311** and **312**). Territorial dispossession is also extensively addressed from an Indigenous perspective in the book by Kalisch and Unruh (item **329**; see also Kalisch in item **330**).

Another important research topic is Indigenous labor in industrial enclaves, both agricultural and extractive, and the effects it produced in social and political organization, ethnic identity, gender roles, and language. Among works concerned with the Paraguayan Chaco are the chapter by V. Bonifacio (item **303**) on the historical memories and political strategies of the former workers of the Casado tannin factory, an article by J. Correia (item **306**) on the continuity of the boss-worker bond created in cattle ranches. Also on this topic are M. Glauser's book on the consequences of industrial colonization on what he calls the "cosmographical practices" of the Angaité, and S. Kidd's work on the daily tensions created by the market economy in Enxet communities (items **311** and **321**). And M. Biocca analyzes a less-explored enclave: the effects on Qom groups of decades of picking cotton on agricultural missions and reservations and of periodic employment on settlers' farms (item **330**).

Urbanization, which has had in general a detrimental impact on the lives of Indigenous peoples, with a dramatic reduction in living space and an increase in deleterious health situations, has also led to new forms of political participation and ethnic revitalization. A growing number of studies focus on the processes of ethnic and cultural revitalization in periurban Indigenous settlements of Argentine cities—namely to the south and north of Buenos Aires and on the outskirts of Rosario. Some authors address how crafts constitute forms of income (although not sufficient to sustain the families of craftspeople), and also become an idiom for ethnic identification (i.e., item **305**). In some cases, such as Lowland Bolivia, Indigenous urbanization involves a continuity of male leadership, blocking the emergence of new forms of leadership based on age or gender (item **318**). Other studies delve into how urban Indigenous youth engage in musical performances (such as rap), and in so doing revitalize their native language and ethnic identity (item **302**).

The situation of Indigenous communities during the COVID-19 pandemic was, not surprisingly, a broad topic of research in the past three years. Of the numerous studies on the subject, we have selected here an article by Hirsch, Müller, and Pérez, who conducted a study on the impact of the pandemic on an urbanized Indigenous Qom population and show how a lack of adequate infrastructure—in addition to their deteriorated health conditions as a result of urbanization—have had created a negative synergy with the presence of COVID (item **316**). A broad and extensive report conducted in Argentina by a wide range of scholars, contributes a panoramic view of the ways in which COVID-19 affected the lives of Indigenous peoples, both rural and urban, and makes recommendations to state institutions in order to improve the response to the public health emergency (item **299**).

Two last key topics for the region are shamanism and missionization. Regarding the first, we have selected two studies from conflicting perspectives. On one hand, an article by F. Tola which, through an analysis of native interpretations of mental "disorders" among the Qom of Argentina, deals with shamanic initiation and witchcraft accusations resorting to formulas of the "ontological turn" (item **335**). On the other, a book by K. Lowrey that plays down the relevance of the notions of predation, warcraft, or power notions that permeate the "ontological" perspective, and instead highlights the elements of conviviality and vulnerability in the shamanic healings and the omnipresent threat of witchcraft among the Guarani of Bolivia (item **324**). Problems concerning missionization are still a central field of production. There are numerous studies on Catholic and Protestant missions (items **319**, **323**, **325**, Combès in item **326**, **329**, and Ceriani in item **330**); and still others concerning subjects in which missionization plays a central role (i.e., items **314**, **319**, and **329**). An interdisciplinary collection of articles edited by N. Richard, Z. Franceschi and L. Córdoba, addressing the technological aspects of the missionary venture in Chaco, Amazonia, and the Paraná jungle (item **325**), is a particularly interesting and original work.

Along with these main topics of research, the publications reviewed for this section of *HLAS 77* include works on other growing fields of inquiry. One of them is the anthropological study of childhood by Leavy and Szulc that shows the autonomy of children in rural spaces, as well as their responsibilities for caring for their younger siblings (item **322**).

Gender continues to grow as a field of inquiry, and has diversified into new theoretical perspectives. P. Canova's study of Ayoreo women's sexual practices in exchange for money or material goods, in a tense and violent inter-ethnic context, shows how subalternized relations are also resignified by women, and how certain Indigenous groups evidence a greater exclusion from society (item **304**). In a different vein, A. Denuncio's study of motherhood, not only as a form of care within the domestic sphere, but as a political and ethnic vindication in the public sphere, addresses how women struggle for collective and cultural rights (item **307**).

Another emerging trend revisits a classical field of study that had been virtually abandoned for decades: ergology. Some studies are slowly returning to Indigenous manufactures as signs of an esthetic sensibility, merchandise inserted in commercial networks, and marks of ethnic self-representation, as in L. Cardini's study on Qom *"artesanías"* ("handicrafts" made for sale) (item **305**). Another line of these recent ergological studies analyzes manufactures as symbolic condensations, whose enormous semantic density can only be revealed through a deep knowledge of the society and its language. A paradigmatic example can be found in the writings of R. Montani (see *HLAS 75:330*); here we have reviewed, mainly because of the rarity of the area, an article by Barrientos Salinas on Tacana cotton tissues (item **301**).

A lesser, but still noticeable trend, is the discussion on the categorization of the Chaco Indigenous people as "hunter-gatherers." Research in this regard can be found, above all, in the production about Paraguay (items **303**, **304**, **306**, and **311**).

Ethnobiology, and ethnobotany in particular, is the focus of solid scholarly production in the region, ranging from systematic surveys on classic topics, such as the medicinal uses of botanical pharmacopoeia (item **325**), to works drawing deeply on the study of the group's language and worldview (item **320** on the Guaraní area of Paraguay and Suárez in item **326** on the Chaco).

Ethnoastronomy, a subdiscipline that had been virtually abandoned in the Chaco region since the classic studies of Robert Lehmann-Nitsche, has received a new impetus in the past two decades. We have reviewed the contributions of C. Gómez on the Qom temporal cycles and the Wichí cosmography (item **313**) and A. López on atmospheric phenomena as manifestations of power (item **323**). *Cosmovisiones/Cosmovisões* (Universidad Nacional de La Plata), a new Argentine journal focusing on the topic, began publication during this review period (item **313**).

Regarding the geographical distribution of the published works, the Gran Chaco continues to dominate, at least in quantitative terms, the publications reviewed in this section. A significant contribution on this region is a volume in English edited by S. Hirsch, P. Canova, and M. Biocca (item **330**), with chapters covering the three countries from an interdisciplinary perspective. The specific topics covered in the volume range from ethnohistory, shamanism, territorial disputes, and land dispossession to gender and health. The volume includes a timely introduction with an overview of the primary historical, social, political and environmental factors that have shaped this complex and inter-ethnic region. Along the same lines, another volume edited by B. Ganson (item **328**) focuses on Indigenous political struggles in Paraguay in the years after the demise of Stroessner's government. This volume also includes chapters on the impact of urbanization on Indigenous peoples' lives. Along with publications on the Chaco and, to a lesser extent, on the Guaraní forest of Paraguay (items **329** and **333**), there is a noticeable growing production on the foothills of Bolivia, whose confluence of Andean and Amazonian cultures had raised ethnological debates at the beginning of the 20th century, but had been somewhat neglected ever since. *HLAS 77* includes three contributions on Indigenous groups from that region (items **301**, **317**, and **319**).

As for theoretical currents, as in the previous volumes we notice a number of studies inspired by the "ontological turn" or perspectivism trends, which in some cases are used as a universal key of interpretation. This is mainly the case in studies on Argentina, but this perspective can also be found in works about Paraguay (items **311** and **314**) and Bolivia (item **301**). At the same time, certain studies draw on theoretical perspectives openly opposed to those trends, which until now had not been systematically applied to the Chaco region. This is the case with the study by S. Kidd on the daily life of the Angaité of Paraguay (item **321**) and the analysis by K. Lowrey on the domestic or "feminine" dimensions of shamanism and social organization of the Bolivian Guaraní (item **324**), both creatively drawing from Joanna Overing's school, and hence focusing on the microethnography of conviviality and everyday close relationships. [FB and SH]

GENERAL

245 Bittencourt, Libertad Borges. A formação de um campo político na América Latina: as organizações indígenas no Brasil. Goiânia, Brazil: Editora UFG, 2018. 247 p.: bibl.

This book focuses on the Indigenous movement within Brazil, but situates the movement within a Latin American context, with special attention to Mexico. The history of the Indigenous movement in Brazil is outlined from the first meetings of chiefs in the 1970s in Mato Grosso, to the 1988 Constitution, to the proliferation of Indigenous organizations in the 1990s. Other organizations that work with Indigenous peoples and that are linked to the state, Church, and private sector, are also discussed and listed in one chapter. The final chapter includes interviews with a variety of Indigenous leaders about their paths to leadership, the role of education, land demarcation, and watershed meetings that united people from different regions. [SO]

246 Carrión Sánchez, Claudia P. Autonomía indígena: el pueblo indígena de los Pastos en la frontera Colombia-Ecuador. Bogotá: Universidad Piloto de Colombia, 2018. 238 p. (some folded): bibl., ill.

Taking as its point of reference the Colombian-Ecuadorian-Andean border, this book is a thoughtful anthropological inquiry into the complicated cultural configuration of a modern nation-state frontier, which has shattered the territorial integrity of the Indigenous people that had long settled in the area. Carrión chronicles the fate of the marginalized, Indigenous border peoples—those whose territories have been occupied or who share borders with nation-states that disregard them. Highlighting local knowledge, the author provides a voice to community members residing along the frontier, reflects on the sociocultural conflicts that have arisen due to the artificial border that demarcates Colombia and Ecuador, and proposes novel approaches to understanding autonomy among crossborder ethnic groups. More than being a fixed position, the border is subject to an ongoing debate, made worse by the existence of any competing claims to local and national identities. Beyond the limited boundary definition, Carrión contends that it is critical to consider the entire strip or sector between two institutionally designated regions. She reminds us that borders serve as more than physical boundaries or divisions. The decisions made in these locations are influenced by local conditions and geopolitics, which impact how border settlements are handled over time and how boundaries are established but continuously change. The Colombian-Ecuadorian border has strong sociocultural ties between its residents. Still, the neglect it has experienced from both states is alarming, as evidenced by the region's high poverty and conflict rates. The book explains the border region away from the concept of integration in important administrative hubs like Quito and Bogotá, illuminating how governments have focused on passing laws rather than understanding the realities of this region. While it is true that many locations have significant legislation about integration, it frequently only applies to the points of greatest contact, neglecting the entire area surrounding these points, which is otherwise considerably larger. [BD]

247 Daly, Lewis and **Glenn Shepard.**
Magic darts and messenger molecules: toward a phytoethnography of Indigenous Amazonia. (*Anthropol. Today*, 35:2, 2019, p. 13–17, bibl., ill., photos)

As a result of current scientific findings regarding botanical cognition, anthropologists are compelled to re-examine their long-held beliefs about the vitality of plants. Through a crosscultural comparison of the Makushi and Matsigenka, this essay investigates the role of sensory experience in mediating people-plant interactions. It contrasts the Makushi people of Guyana and Matsigenka people of Peru to see how chemosensory experiences pervade Indigenous understandings of etiology (cause) and efficacy in the cosmological and microbiological realms. Due to the lack of focus on floral research, Daly and Shepard emphasize the significance of botanical beings and plant-based materials in Amazonian cosmologies. For instance, they note that the Makushi refer to plants as "people" (*pemon*) and commonly use figurative language when referring to or conversing with them. One is a person if they have a "soul" (*ekaton*), which is the living force that "brings life to things." Daly and Shepard also assess how bodily perceptions and the chemosensory attributes of plants saturate Indigenous conceptions. To recast multispecies ethnography as a phytochemical and philosophical endeavor, the authors combine emerging theories in ecosemiotics, embodiment, plant personhood, and plant intelligence with what Shepard calls "sensory ecology." Alkaloids and other micromolecules, crucial in animal-plant interactions, were first developed to transmit information across cell membranes. According to the authors, phytochemicals can be thought of as the neurotransmitters driving a cosmic nervous system, carrying information at different layers, such as intra- and intercellular, inter-organismal, biospheric, and shamanic worlds, to numerous strata and celestial creatures. This integrative approach gives fresh insight into the views of Indigenous people on "plants as teachers." [BD]

248 Fausto, Carlos. Art effects: image, agency, and ritual in Amazonia. Translated by David Rodgers. Lincoln: University of Nebraska Press, 2020. 398 p.: bibl., ill., index, maps.

This richly illustrated book focuses on artifacts that occur in rituals or within the vicinity of rituals in a variety of Amazonian societies, but mainly the Tupi-speaking Parakanã and the Carib-speaking Kuikuro. These objects include sacred flutes, masks, trophies, and effigies. The aim is to explore the relationship of persons and things, the nature of the agency of materials, the nature of personhood, the body, the genesis of presence, and the presence of patterns across the Lowlands that could be called an "Amazonian esthetic." It is based on years of fieldwork with these two groups as well as a staggering ethnographic knowledge of the Lowlands more generally. Comparisons are also made with North American and Western Christian esthetics. [SO]

249 McSweeney, Kendra and Brad D. Jokisch. Native Amazonians strategic urbanization: shaping territorial possibilities through cities. (*J. Lat. Am. Caribb. Anthropol.*, 20:1, March 2015, p. 1–21)

This article focuses on the connections between Indigenous Amazonians' urbanization processes and their political struggles for territorial rights. It accomplishes this by utilizing several wide-ranging ethnographic sources. The authors assess the interaction between Indigenous "deterritorialization" (urbanization and international migration) and "re-territorialization," or the acknowledgment, protection, and sovereign control over specific ancestral areas. The study shows how Amazonian Indigenous leaders routinely fashion migration networks linking their homelands to far-off towns in order to pursue claims for territorial recognition. McSweeney and Jokisch also show how urban life can be used to politicize Indigenous city dwellers in ways that have an ongoing impact on their territorial claims. By influencing the political consciousness of a new generation of "multi-sited" native youth, this radicalization, along with urban opportunities for education and professionalization, has arguably strengthened the Indigenous movement. The authors convincingly refute the generalization made in policy texts about Indigenous urbanization as inevitable and ultimately unstable for their territorial claims, which can be used to legitimize the takeover of Indigenous lands or commandeer their resources. They describe initiatives in Brazil to call into question existing territorial claims of Amazonian peoples using evidence of their "urbanization." Urbanization thus joins the list of archetypal practices considered to be quintessentially non-Indigenous. The article aims to generate a counternarrative that suggests Indigenous urbanization and territorialization coexist peacefully rather than being inherently in conflict. The Amazonian case offers a model because it is unique and because, in this instance, the processes tying urban residents to territorial politics appear to be much more apparent. The study contrasts ethnographic research with policy language to demonstrate that policy silences on Indigenous urbanization's territorial dynamics are more than regrettable oversights in otherwise detailed and well-intentioned policy papers. It shows how policy pronouncements unintentionally support the idea that Indigenous urbanization represents a rejection of territory and territorial enterprise by underplaying the coproduction of cityscapes and territory as Indigenous political spaces. The fluid and elaborate power dynamics affected by the cultural flows between rural and urban areas will eventually shape the territorial disputes of Amazonian peoples. The meta-analytical methodology is explicitly described to locate and evaluate academic, policy, and other sources. The three "moments" of Indigenous urbanization—the first, marked by the arrival in cities; the second, involving the consequences of city life on Indigenous urbanites; and the third, characterized by the flows between rural and urban spaces—are next arranged in counterposition to anthropological observations and policy discourses. The necessity of appointing Indigenous representatives in key positions of state authority to better advocate for collective territorial and other rights has been an important driving factor behind Indigenous relocation to urban areas. There is ample proof indicating that during the past 30 years, this urban-based movement has dramatically aided the Indigenous political resurgence. The authors turn to the epistemological distinctions between academic and policy narratives and demonstrate that it is not methodological differences that account for policy documents "overlooking" the political ties between town and homeland; instead, it is a specific modernist configuration that excludes the prospect of such interconnections. The paper skillfully highlights how policy discourses reinforce the status quo's (mis)understandings of Indigenous urbanism as submissive, apolitical, and fundamentally opposed to substantive territorial persistence. Yet urban living, according to McSweeney and Jokisch, can be one of Indigenous peoples' "strategic adaptations," or methods for negotiating and defending their various and unique places in the world, just as the use of t-shirts and DVDs. For a review of the entire journal issue, see *HLAS 73:489*. [BD]

250 **O mundo indígena na América Latina: olhares e perspectivas.** Coordenação de Beatriz Paredes. Organização de Gerson Damiani, Wagner Pinheiro Pereira e María Antonieta Gallart Nocetti. São Paulo: Edusp, 2018. 536 p.: bibl. (Cátedra José Bonifácio; 5)

This volume in honor of Mexican politician and defender of Indigenous rights, Beatriz Paredes, unites anthropologists, historians, and even an agronomist. Twelve of the 20 chapters deal with Brazilian Indigenous peoples; others deal with Mexico and Bolivia. Topics covered include colonial history and the Indigenous question during the Primeiro Reinado (1822–31) as Brazil was crafting an independent identity. Other chapters address the Anchieta missionary project and the introduction of writing and visual depictions during the 19th century. With respect to the 20th and 21st centuries, several stimulating chapters deal with representations in film, Kaxinawá myth, the oral and visual culture of the Alto Rio Negro, urban Indigenous peoples in São Paulo, and Indigenous rights in Brazil as well as internationally. An appendix by Beatriz Paredes examines the Mexican presence in Brazil. [SO]

251 **Non-humans in Amerindian South America: ethnographies of Indigenous cosmologies, rituals and songs.** Edited by Juan Javier Rivera Andía. New York, N.Y.: Berghahn, 2019. 382 p.: bibl., ill., index. (EASA series; 37)

This book, copublished by the European Association of Social Anthropology, engages critically with the contentious "onto-diversity" and "cosmopolitics" of South American Indigenous people. Relying on field research from various Indigenous societies undergoing rapid cultural transformation, adaptation, and degradation, the volume provides fresh perspectives on Indigenous formulations of humanity, selfhood, and nature typical among Native inhabitants of South America's Highlands and Lowlands. The resulting ethnographic chapters, which feature nonhuman entities that appear in ceremonial expressions, mythology, shamanism, and songs, scrutinize the circumstances and effects of unevenly positioned life forms, steadily increasing resource extraction, ongoing relocation to urban centers, and the (typically forced) introduction of contemporary manifestations of modernity into Indigenous societies. Three sections make up the collection, the first of which is a lengthy introduction by Juan Javier Rivera Andía that introduces the reader to the thinking of two proponents of the ontological turn in the ethnology of Amazonia: Eduardo Viveiros de Castro and Philippe Descola and their concepts of "perspectivism" and "new animism." The editor and contributors engage with and challenge Castro and Descola's theoretical positions while highlighting the various ways local, regional, and global Indigenous cosmologies acknowledge and interact with the Other. The volume's second section, "Cohabitation and Sharing," looks at the importance of food sharing and trade among humans and nonhumans inside the "ontological incubator," as well as death rites and the shaman's function as a conduit between the human and nonhuman worlds. In Native Amazonian cultures, kinship structures, rituals, and cosmological placemaking narratives reflect the creation and maintenance of mutual dependency among humans and nonhumans. Particularly intriguing is Bernd Brabec de Mori's use of Bruno Latour's "modes of existence" to differentiate between "ontological levels" of beings, which shows metamorphosis in storytelling within Shipibo ceremonies and songs. This section demonstrates that human and nonhuman relationships are not static but result from ongoing creative processes that guide and revitalize the community. This point is made clear in Minna Opas' chapter on the Yine people's relationship with Kaxpomyolutu, the Hand-whistler, and Alfonso Otaegui's inquiry into Ayoreo unacai songs. Part three, "Transformations and Slow Turbulences," deconstructs the poetics of Jonathan D. Hill's "musicalisation" or "the production of musical sounds and words as a way of socializing relations with affines, non-human beings, and various categories of 'others'" (p. 279). Both Jonathan Hill and Cedric Yvinec utilize musicalization as a conceptual model for understanding social transformation and reproduction, identity, embodiment, etic and emic relations, and the significance of mythological accounts in Wakuenai masculine initiation rituals and Surui expressions of religiosity. [BD]

252 Opas, Minna. Not real Christians?: on the relation between Christianity and Indigenous religions in Amazonia and beyond. (*in* Handbook of Indigenous religion(s). Edited by Greg Johnson and Siv Ellen Kraft. Leiden, The Netherlands; Boston, Mass.: Brill, 2017, p. 120–137, bibl.)

European Catholic missionaries who came to the Americas more than 500 years ago started converting the native Amazonians to Christianity. As a result, a sizable portion of the Indigenous peoples of Lowland South America practice various types of Christianity. However, their faith is frequently disregarded or not taken seriously in the scholarly literature, as indicated by Minna Opas in their chapter on Christianity and Indigenous Amazonian religiosity. One hardly ever reads, hears, or sees news about Indigenous Christians. Instead, mainstream media depicts Indigenous Amazonians as animists, spiritual rather than religious people closely connected to their ancestral lands and the environment. Opas explores the frequently ambivalent and strained relationship between Christianity and Indigenous religions in Amazonia. The author examines the ways that these two categories appear to be conflicting and irreconcilable while, at other points in time, intersecting various social fields, including missionary discursive practices, presentations of Indigenous identities, international conventions and proclamations defending Indigenous peoples' rights, Indigenous biblical discourse, as well as scholarly and media figurations. Examples for discussion are taken from online sources and the author's fieldwork (2000–2015) with the

Indigenous Arawak-speaking Yine people of the Peruvian Amazon. For practical purposes, the phrases "Indigenous religions" and "Indigenous spiritualities" are used interchangeably to refer to the traditional sociocosmological views of Indigenous peoples. These designations are the antithesis of conceptions of Indigenous Christianities or Christianity in Indigenous cultures. The chapter asserts that conflicts between stability and volatility and permanence and transformation—as well as depictions and naturalizations of these tensions—are the primary "generative problem(s)" in the interaction among Indigenous religions and Christianity in Amazonia. The essay analyzes how, why, and to what extent Christianity is perceived as a category and phenomenon that is similar to, intersects with, or is separate from Indigenous spiritualities, as well as how these perceptions affect the daily lives of Indigenous people in the Amazon. The question of how to construct Indigenous Christianities and Indigenous religions in connection to one another is raised in the chapter. [BD]

253 Rebollar, Maria Dolores Campos.
O indigenismo alternativo dos anos 1970–2000: processos formativos na Operação Amazônia Nativa (OPAN). Cuiabá, Brazil: EDUFMT, 2016. 140 p.: bibl., ill.

Based on archival research and interviews, this study looks at 40 years of the history of an NGO dedicated to the Indigenous cause. The author focuses on two periods: the origins of the organization in 1969 springing from Liberation Theology and the development of an alternative indigenismo oriented around living within Native villages and the idea of "incarnation" or "being with the other as the other" as well as a general humanism. This alternative indigenismo was in contrast to the national Indigenous policies focused on acculturation. In 1989 a second phase began in which the organization separated from the Church and became more focused on environmental issues and health, substituting for the state to provide services like many other NGOs of that era. This less revolutionary phase also promoted more professional, project-oriented work. There are many direct quotes from OPAN members throughout, providing a rich picture of the changes this key player in Indigenous Amazonia has undergone. [SO]

BRAZIL

254 Berger, William. Índios na cidade do capital: indígenas em contexto urbano na cidade do Rio de Janeiro em tempos de barbárie (2012–2017). Rio de Janeiro: Gramma, 2018. 286 p.: bibl.

This book focuses on the life histories of three Indigenous activists in Rio de Janeiro. One is a Pataxó woman, one a man who has Tupinambá and Pataxó hã-hã-hãe parents, and one woman who is reconstructing her Indigenous heritage. Along with rich interviews about their life experiences and paths to activism and leadership, interviews also cover their ideas about social rights, Indigenous rights, and racism, among other topics. The interviews discuss the way Indigenous people use the space of Rio de Janeiro and its urban context from 2012-17. [SO]

255 História ambiental e história indígena no Semiárido brasileiro. Organização de Edson Hely Silva, Carlos Alberto Batista Santos, Edivania Granja da Silva Oliveira e Eraldo Medeiros Costa Neto. Feira de Santana, Brazil: UEFS Editora, 2016. 276 p.: bibl., ill. (some color), maps.

This volume includes chapters on Indigenous peoples in the Northeast of Brazil and their historical relations with the environment, especially the arid *caatinga*. Many chapters focus on the colonial period or cover the span of time from this period to the present. Topics include environmental impacts of the railroad and industrial farming and the control of water. One chapter by Glaciene Mary da Silva Gonçalves is about the effects of agro-toxins. Other chapters cover control of space and dislocations. One focuses on the use of and relationships with animals. Two look at Indigenous peoples' memories of the environment. The Pankará, Truká, and Xukuru are among the peoples discussed. [SO]

256 Juventudes indígenas: estudos interdisciplinares, saberes interculturais: conexões entre Brasil e México.

Organização de Assis da Costa Oliveira e Lucia Helena Rangel. Rio de Janeiro: E-papers, 2017. 271 p.: bibl., ill., maps.

This volume brings together authors writing about the multiple experiences of Indigenous youth in Mexico and Brazil. The chapters that focus on Brazil include one on the political participation of urban youth, the vulnerabilities of youth in Amazonia, new technologies used by youths to mobilize, and affirmative action in universities in Bahia. Several examine the experience of being an Indigenous university student and political mobilization related to issues such as education. Many of the authors of these chapters are themselves Indigenous Brazilians who have been in positions of being university students or Indigenous youth leaders. [SO]

257 **Krenak, Ailton.** Ailton Krenak. Coordenação editorial de Sergio Cohn e Idjahure Kadiwel. Rio de Janeiro: Beco do Azougue Editorial Ltda., 2017. 155 p. (Tembetá)

Part of a series organized by Kaká Werá, this volume focuses on Ailton Krenak, Indigenous leader and philosopher. Through a collection of interviews, lectures, and testimonials from 2015–2017, this volume includes Krenak's thoughts on the history and present state of Indigenous rights in Brazil and beyond, including his role in the organization of the União das Nações Indígenas and the Aliança dos Povos da Floresta. Ailton Krenak's comments about his life experiences are woven throughout the different sections. He also discusses large philosophical topics throughout such as the fate of the planet, humanity, consumerism, the logic of beauty, art cosmology, history and myth. For comment on a volume of earlier interviews with Ailton Krenak, see *HLAS 73:353*. [SO]

258 **Lagrou, Els.** Learning to see in western Amazonia. (*Soc. Anal.*, 63:2, Summer 2019, p. 24–44, bibl., photos)

This article focuses on the shamanic songs found in ayahuasca rituals and the woven designs made by women among the Huni Kuin of western Brazil. The author argues that both teach the Huni Kuin to see hidden relational webs that are necessary for well-being. Through Huni Kuin comments about images and patterns, the author formulates an Amerindian relational esthetics, one that emphasizes change and becoming. [SO]

259 **Martins, Sckarleth; Suely Henrique de Aquino Gomes;** and **Deyvisson Pereira da Costa.** Ser semente: mulheres A'uwẽ, corpos políticos e solidariedade ecológia em Marãiwatsédé. Curitiba, Brazil: Appris Editora, 2017. 184 p.: bibl., ill. (some color). (Coleção Ciências da comunicação)

This book offers a general overview of the Brazilian Indigenous movement and how it interfaces with environmentalism. A few chapters, drawing on some of the ethnographic research with and historical work about the Xavante, focus on the Xavante's mission history, their loss of lands (in TI Marãiwatsédé), the retaking of the area, and how the latter related to socioenvironmentalism. Women's lives are a focus, including new types of organized resistance around seed collection. [SO]

260 **Pereira, Sonia Maria Couto.** Etnografia e iconografia nos registros de Hércules Florence durante a expedição Langsdorff, na província do Mato Grosso (1826–1829). Dourados, Brazil: UFGD Editora, 2016. 185 p.: bibl., ill. (some color), maps.

This book gives an account of the scientific expedition from 1825–29 of the Russian Baron Langsdorff to the area of the Upper Paraguai River near the area of the Brazilian Pantanal. The focus is the French painter who was documenting Indigenous peoples on this voyage, Hércules Florence. The groups he painted include the Arawak-speaking peoples as a group, then called the Guaná, the Gê-speaking Guató, and the Bororo. Many of these images are included in the book. This expedition is contextualized within the longer history of expeditions to this area. The work discusses Florence's biography and artistic influences, and how his images can contribute to Indigenous history. [SO]

261 **Redes Arawa: ensaios de etnologia do Médio Purus.** Organização de Gilton Mendes dos Santos e Miguel Aparicio.

Manaus, Brazil: EDUA, Editora da Universidade Federal do Amazonas, 2016. 346 p.: bibl., ill.

This volume unites a wide variety of scholars who focus on the Arawa-speaking peoples of the Middle Purus River. These include the Kulina, Kamadeni, the Eastern and Western Janamadi, Deni, Banawa, Jarawara, Suruwaha, Paumari, and Hi Merimã. These peoples have a complex system of relations marked by territorial disputes, witchcraft, and war as well as marriages, shared rituals, and trade, including of cultivated plants, knowledge, and technology. Chapters cover each of these aspects as well as some of the history of this region. There is also one chapter on archeology of the region and two chapters on the Arawa language. [SO]

262 Rolande, Josinelma Ferreira. Moços feitos, moços bonitos: a ornamentação na prática Canela de construir corpos. São Leopoldo, Brazil: Editora Oikos, 2017. 192 p.: bibl., ill. (some color), photos.

This detailed study of body ornamentation among the Canela focuses on men and women's initiation rituals and funerary rituals. These events are documented in detail with many spectacular color photos. Ideas of beauty are linked to ideas of strength by the Canela. Ideas about body painting, clothing, and feathers are discussed throughout as are human relationships with spirits. [SO]

263 Rondon: inventários do Brasil, 1900–1930. Organização de Lorelai Kury e Magali Romero Sá. Textos de Nísia Trindade Lima et al. = Rondon: inventaires du Brésil, 1900–1930. Édition par Lorelai Kury et Magali Romero Sá. Textes par Nísia Trindade Lima et al. Version française par Alain François. Rio de Janeiro: Andrea Jakobsson Estúdio, 2017. 300 p.: bibl., ill.

This volume in Portuguese and French focuses on placing into historical context the early years of Marshal Cândido Rondon's Indigenous policies and practices, particularly with respect to the longer history of colonial exploration and scientific documentation. The volume is filled with photographs, many of which are not the usually reproduced images one often sees. The images illustrate the authors' points beautifully. Of particular interest are the chapters on Rondon's use of films, style of ethnographic documentation, and the influence of positivism. One chapter by Paula Monteiro offers an interesting perspective by contrasting Rondon's posts with missions. Rondon's posts emphasized the "pacification" and militarization of Indigenous peoples in contrast to the missions that focused on the education of "already pacified" peoples. There are also noteworthy chapters on Rondon and the telegraph installation as well as the exploration of the lands of Mato Grosso and Pará states. [SO]

264 Souza, Catiúscia Custódio de. O movimento indígena e a luta por emancipação. Curitiba, Brazil: Appris Editora, 2018. 373 p.: bibl., ill. (Coleção Ciências sociais)

This book is oriented by political sociology and the ethnographic method. It provides a history of the Indigenous movement in Brazil and its organization. The author focuses on two regional groups within the national movement: Articulação dos Povos Indígenas do Sul (involving the Kaingang, Guarani, Lāklãnõ/Xokleng, Xetá, and the descendants of the Charruá) and the Comissão Guarani Yvy Rupa (involving the Guarani). Lengthy excerpts of interviews with 12 Indigenous leaders recount the history and organization of the Indigenous movement and regional organizations, as well as their own life histories. There are also sections focused on Indigenous health and education, including university education. [SO]

265 Souza, Vanderlei Sebastião de. Em busca do Brasil: Edgard Roquette-Pinto e o retrato antropológico brasileiro (1905–1935). Rio de Janeiro: FGV Editora: Editora Fiocruz, 2017. 480 p.: bibl.

Historian Souza's award-winning book studies the life of physical anthropologist and director of the Museu Nacional, Edgard Roquette-Pinto (1884–1954). The work examines Roquette-Pinto within the context of issues central to nationalism and racial relations in early 20th-century Brazil. Along with biographical material, chapters focus on Roquette-Pinto's ethnographic experiences in Mato Grosso during his 1912 trip when he formulated his ideas about the *sertanejo* or "man of the sertão" as the expression of Brazilian national identity, his classification system of "anthropological types" in Brazil, and his position within debates on racial mixture (as either the cause of Brazil's failure or its path to success). Other topics include debates about Indigenous peoples, eugenics, and the role of scientific documentation in the construction of the Brazilian nation. [SO]

266 Tukano, Álvaro. Álvaro Tukano. Coordenação editorial de Sergio Cohn e Idjahure Kadiwel. Rio de Janeiro: Beco do Azougue Editorial Ltda., 2017. 150 p. (Tembetá)

Part of a series organized by Kaká Werá, this volume focuses on Álvaro Tukano, one of the leaders who organized the União das Nações Indígenas and helped in the creation of the Federação das Organizações Indígenas do Rio Negro and the Coordinadora de las Organizáciones Indígenas de la Cuenca Amazónica. This book consists of an interview from 2017 and two sections written by Tukano on the history of the Indigenous movement, his activism, and his international travels. The third part is his account of the Tukano history of humanity. [SO]

267 A única vida possível: itinerários de Ermanno Stradelli na Amazônia. Organização de Livia Raponi. São Paulo: Editora Unesp, 2016. 256 p., 16 unnumbered pages of plates: bibl., ill., photos.

Bringing together Brazilian and Italian scholars, this collection is about the Amazonian travels of Ermanno Stradelli, the late 19th-century Italian explorer, geographer, collector, photographer, poet, and documenter of *língual geral* and the famous Jurupari myth and rituals. Many chapters discuss Stradelli's travels in the Vaupés and Orinoco Rivers. One of the more interesting chapters focuses on the author's father's story about Stradelli circulating among the Tukano people who remember him as a shaman that could talk with the supernatural guardians of sacred places. Several chapters address his interest in the Jurupary myth and his 1890 publication. Many chapters also deal with aspects of Stradelli's biography. There are several interesting photos of Ipuriná peoples included as well. [SO]

268 Vanzolini, Marina. The name of the relation: making a difference in Aweti onomastics. (*Soc. Anal.*, 63:2, Summer 2019, p. 102–121, bibl.)

This article focuses on the onomastic system of the Tupi-speaking Aweti of the Upper Xingu. The author approaches name giving as a native theory of descent that works as an explanation for positions of status such as that of the chiefship. Aweti theories about relations and names are the focus. Names are seen to produce people by evoking relations with others who have given up the name and to imbue the name receiver with certain qualities. Names for the Aweti do not so much belong to individuals as they are items given by one person to another. They mark the identity and mutual dependency between kin who share a name, as well as differentiating among them. [SO]

269 Vilaça, Aparecida M.N. Christianity + schooling on nature versus culture in Amazonia. (*Tipití*, 16:2, 2019, p. 215–234, bibl., ill., tables)

In addition to covering the mission and education history of the Wari' of Rondônia, this article offers a valuable exploration of how the categories of "nature" and "culture" or "humanity" do not have easy translations into Lowland categories. For the Wari', "human" (*wari'*) and "non-human" (*karawa*) are relative categories associated with being predator and prey, positions which an entity can occupy at different moments. Missionary teachings and school texts emphasize instead the utilitarian character of nature and its contemplative function, serving to change Wari' understandings of their place in the world. [SO]

270 Yawanawá, Biraci. Biraci Yawanawá. Coordenação editorial por Sergio Cohn e Idjahure Kadiwel. Rio de Janeiro: Beco do Azougue Editorial Ltda., 2019. 165 p. (Tembetá)

Part of a series organized by Kaká Werá, this volume focuses on Biraci Yawanawá, a political and spiritual Yawanawá leader. The volume is a collection of testimonials, interviews, previous publications, and reflections on a variety of topics such as his early involvement in the organization of the União das Nações Indígenas and the Aliança dos Povos da Floresta along with Chico Mendes. He also discusses his people's history with missions and the rubber industry, Indigenous education, spirituality, and the spread of ayahuasca in the world. Chapters include his comments from 1984–2018. [SO]

271 **Zuin, Aparecida Luzia Alzira** and **Vinicius Valentin Raduan Miguel.** A Amazônia e os povos indígenas: conflitos socioambientais e culturais. Curitiba, Brazil: Appris Editora, 2017. 222 p.: bibl., ill., maps. (Coleção Ciências sociais)

Drawing on the study of political geography, this book looks at the organization of the space of Amazonia, particularly the state of Rondônia. Topics covered include dams, agriculture, deforestation, and distribution of Indigenous lands. With respect to Rondônia, topics include the history of colonization, rubber, migration into the territory and conflicts with Indigenous peoples. [SO]

COLOMBIA, VENEZUELA, AND THE GUIANAS

272 **Caicedo-Fernández, Alhena.** La alteridad radical que cura: neochamanismos yajeceros en Colombia. Bogotá: Universidad de los Andes, Facultad de Ciencias Sociales, Departamento de Antropología, 2015. 234 p.: bibl., ill. (some color). (Colección General)

This study, which comprises a multisited ethnography conducted in various parts of Colombia, including the Putumayo-Caquetá area and Bogotá, examines the new political and social scenarios associated with identity and cultural negotiation in multicultural and multiethnic nation-states. Caicedo-Fernández's book skillfully demonstrates how the divisions between the center and the periphery, the city and the jungle, civilization and savagery, are remnants of a colonial moral topography that inter-ethnic relations and the hybridization of Indigenous and non-Indigenous worlds in the context of Colombian national multiethnic citizenship have updated. Her book introduces contemporary *yajé* consumption patterns in Colombia, including the neo-*yajé* scene, characterized by its profound eclecticism, fusing esthetic elements with the organizational and discursive fields of social movements like New Age, alternative medicine, bioconsumption, environmentalism, and Indigenous cosmologies. Caicedo-Fernández believes that Colombian *yajecero* neo-shamanism, which has opened access to the field and *yajeceros* to urban spaces, reflects a reassessment of Indianness within the national imaginary. Urban neoshamans, with their *taita* figures, express, communicate, and stimulate the complexity of the worldviews that today accompany the many roles of the *yajeceros*. The first chapter explains the dynamics of *yajé* consumption, the development of shamanic power, the skills every shaman must possess, the appropriate settings to deploy, etc. The expansion of the shamanic field as a result of the emergence of new shamanic actors in urban environments is illustrated in the second chapter through four real-world examples of new *taitas yajeceros*. To understand the contrasts and similarities between the two modalities, the book compares the new rituals performed by urban *taitas yajeceros* with the old forms of the traditional *yajeceros*. The construction of circular enclosures based on the directionality requirements of some Indigenous traditions is described in the third chapter, along with the many locations where the *yajé* is consumed. It outlines the *yajé* consumption ritual, including precautions before consumption, women's involvement, etc. The fourth chapter discusses the recent institutionalization of *yajé* drinking rituals in the "malocas." It offers some basic conclusions about the institutionalization of these activities while contrasting their diverse modalities and functions. The fifth chapter discusses urbanization, elitism, and government policies in Colombia as influenced by institutional multiculturalism. This chapter reflects on the standardization of *yajé* consumption rituals through patrimonialization or medicalization. The sixth chapter depicts the characteristics of *yajé* adherents, or new *yajeceros*, and how they construct their worlds of meaning around this practice. At the same time, an effort is made to establish some interpretive conclusions that aid in conceptualizing the outcomes and broader implications of the *yajecero* phenomenon in Colombia. [BD]

273 **Gómez Montáñez, Pablo Felipe** and **Fredy Leonardo Reyes Albarracín.** Hijas de Bachué: memoria e indigenidad desde las mujeres muiscas. Bogotá: Ediciones USTA, 2017. 192 p.: bibl., ill.

This book makes a scholarly contribution by studying the role of Indigenous women in Colombia who hold positions of authority in addition to examining the difficulties they deal with that are connected to gender and the politics of sexuality. The publication results from a project titled "Creation of indigenousness from the perspective and roles of Muisca women in Bogotá," conducted over two years through the Research Unit and the Faculty of Social Communication of the Santo Tomás University, Colombia. According to Muisca cosmogony, women represent the archetype of the feminine as the genesis of the world and humanity. The recovery of customs, routines, mythologies, and a corpus of values that ethically connect their members to their ancestors is one of the ways that diverse Muisca groups and organizations are strengthening their sense of community as part of the process of cultural re-composition. In Muisca ethnopolitical discourses, the "Mother" or "Mother Earth" world (*Jisca Guaya*) is alluded to as the figuration of the creative principle. Similar to this, Muisca myths, like the one about the first mother *Bachué*, emphasize the feminine's significance as a guiding force for the Muisca people of Colombia. In the ethnographic production on the contemporary Muiscas, researchers have given precedence to male voices, even though many women have been protagonists in the organizational processes that led to the formation of collective projects with a view to the formal recognition of their communities. Notably, the book offers an in-depth assessment of Muisca ethnopolitical processes from the viewpoint of women leaders. Muisca women have taken on a variety of societal functions, from civic and political leadership to transmitting traditional practices like healing, family care, and cuisine. In light of this, the authors remind us that Muisca indigenity also requires careful consideration of the formation and ongoing revision of gender roles and attitudes. [BD]

274 **Gutiérrez Herrera, Ruth.** Los nükak: en marcha por tierras devastadas: nomadismo y continuidad en la Amazonia colombiana. Bogotá: Instituto Colombiano de Antropología e Historia, 2016. 335 p.: bibl., ill., maps. (Terrenos etnográficos)

The Nükak are one of the few remaining Indigenous nomadic peoples of Amazonia. Based on the author's PhD dissertation, this book explains their recent history since the Colombian government contacted them in 1988. This comprehensive anthropological tome investigates how Nükak patterns of nomadism, cosmology, ceremonial behavior, and economic practices have all been altered in reaction to the turbulence of social change and the encroachment of national society. Although being forcibly removed from their lands, the Nükak still greatly desire to return to their ancestral territories, making their current situation difficult. Nevertheless, Nükak methods of cultural adaptation, as covered in various portions of the text, oppose Occidental efforts to acculturate and regulate them and illustrate the magnificence of their social independence and sense of autonomy as a unique people. [BD]

275 **Jackson, Jean Elizabeth.** Managing multiculturalism: indigeneity and the struggle for rights in Colombia. Stanford, Calif.: Stanford University Press, 2019. 308 p.: bibl., ill., index, maps.

From the perspective of an anthropologist with more than 40 years of fieldwork experience in the region, this significant book focuses on the Colombian Indigenous rights movement, which has been relatively prosperous compared to neighboring countries. Indigenous *pueblos* comprise 4 percent of Colombia's population and have acquired collective, inalienable claims to 27.3 percent of the country's land via persistent struggle. Chapter 1 provides an overview of the history of the Indigenous rights work from colonial times to the present. The subsequent chapter critically assesses how culture has been defined in anthropological theory while reflecting on the Tukanoans of the Northwest Amazon. In chapter 3, two instances of regional diversity supported by the Colombian state are analyzed, and then significant discussions regarding inter-ethnic conflict and cultural authenticity follow. The mechanics of asserting cultural rights and the politics of recognition in a multicultural state are explored in detail in the following chapter. The struggles of numerous *pueblos* to reclaim their Indigenous identity are covered in chapter 5, along with the part that outside perceptions played in these efforts. The author uses *pueblo* to denote a small local Indigenous community and a larger, formally recognized group. As Jackson demonstrates, *pueblos* are fluid; they negotiate, assert, and reinvent their Indigenous identities while interacting with and opposing various assimilationist and integrating forces like the Colombian government, religious institutions, NGOs, and the non-native Left. In their fierce resistance to colonialism, capitalism, and elite land control, the Indigenous rights movement and the non-Indigenous Left of Colombia are resolutely united. However, Colombia's non-Indigenous Left favors a unifying, cohesive proletariat and nation-state model to represent the culturally diverse peoples of the country. This stance is opposed by Indigenous activists who perceive it as integrationist. In order to manage multiculturalism and rights demands, Indigenous people and the state concurrently undergo identity alterations that, in the end, push the limits of what is considered to be "otherness," relocating concepts of Indigenousness and universal rights, and strengthen essentialist conceptions of self and cultural authenticity. In a bid to preserve their freedom and sovereignty, Indigenous *pueblos* and their organizations, like the Consejo Regional Indígena del Vaupés (CRIVA), are sometimes forced by the vocabulary and structures of the modern multicultural Colombian state to present a fixed, essentialist portrayal of their Indigenous identity. Highlighting pan-Indigenous identity might be politically astute at times, but cultural distinctiveness is required at other moments. All persons involved in the politics of recognition bear the responsibility of persuading others of their Indigenousness; in this relational process, the veracity of a *pueblo's* identity depends on others accepting their claim. Jackson's examination of inter-ethnic hostility between the Tukanoan and the nomadic Nükaks, who escaped a plague and armed fighting, highlights the significance of discursive categories that frame understandings of cultural authenticity, alterity, and racism. Although considered a failure, Tukanoan concerns were expressed over whether the 1983 state-sponsored "shaman school" was intended to enhance traditional practices and conserve culture, raising tensions between customary social structures and conceptions of pan-Indigenous identity. [BD]

276 **Luzar, Jeffrey B.; Kirsten M. Silvius; and José M.V. Fragoso.** Church affiliation and meat taboos in Indigenous communities of Guyanese Amazonia. (*Hum. Ecol.*, 40:6, Dec. 2012, p. 833–846, bibl.)

Indigenous peoples of Amazonia impact the biome by the way they manage natural resources. This helpful study evaluates the impact of Indigenous and Christian beliefs and practices on food taboos among Makushi and Wapishana peoples in the Guyana Amazon. The authors compiled empirical data during a three-year study of the socioeconomic variables influencing hunting patterns among 23 Indigenous groups. While members of Sabbatarian churches exhibit a stronger propensity to adhere to dietary taboos than Evangelicals or members of established churches, members of Evangelical and established (Anglican and Catholic) churches do not differ in terms of their compliance with dietary taboos. Contrary to predictions, the study found no discernible difference in the avoidance of meat across households affiliated with traditional and evangelical faiths. According to nutritional recommendations made by shamans, members of all faith groups disregarded Indigenous food customs. Among Makushi and Wapishana households that had converted to evangelical and Sabbatarian forms of Christianity, the authors documented continuity in food practice, despite theological resistance to shamanistic rituals connected with Indigenous taboos. [BD]

277 Oakley, R. Elliott. Being forgotten, being remembered: the affective politics of Waiwai memory in Guyanese Amazonia. (*Am. Ethnol./Washington*, 49:3, Aug. 2022, p. 345–358, bibl., photos)

The Waiwai of the Guyanese Amazon perceive memory as fashioned from amalgams and related sensations that build up in the body. Waiwai's narratives about the experiences of being forgotten and remembered operationalize historical incidents for contemporary concerns. Both remembering and forgetting are ethically germane acts because they change other people's outlooks and provide opportunities for cultivating either pleasant feelings, such as happiness, or destructive emotions, such as fury and resentment. The moral force of remembering and forgetting shapes physiological dispositions, village coresidence, and relations with the state. Whether they believe they are in other people's minds is important for state relations. According to the Waiwai, their households were fragmented in the past between Guyana and Brazil because the Guyanese state forgot about them. In contrast, in the present, the Waiwai strive to have Guyanese authorities recognize them as a form of continued political practice. Waiwai's discussions of forgetting and remembering show the importance of affective rather than symbolic forms of memory for the political dynamics of Indigenous-state relations. [BD]

278 Paz Reverol, Carmen Laura. El pueblo Wayuu: rebeliones, comercio y autonomía: una perspectiva histórica-antropológica. Quito: Ediciones Abya-Yala, 2018. 382 p.: bibl., ill., maps.

In Indigenous societies, the Wayuu of Venezuela are among the most sophisticated. Some researchers refer to it as an "Indo-Hispanic" society because of its early insertion into the world capitalist system and its many cultural exchanges with other social groupings, all of which had a substantial impact on the socioeconomic landscape of the Guajira Peninsula. Paz Reverol's historical text begins with a study of the Wayuu people's ancient communities, resistance, and "smuggling" during the Spanish monarchy in the 18th century and the early republican era. This includes a reference to the participation of the Wayuu in the independence conflict with the Spanish Empire. The subsequent chapter covers the discussion of Wayuu's social identity and the emergence of the Venezuelan nation-state. This is followed by a review of efforts at achieving political and military control of the Wayuu. Modalities of Wayuu trade, forms of autonomy, and rebellions are all assessed. The Wayuu's long-term survival and vitality have been facilitated by the culture's strong social structure, diversification of economic endeavors, adherence to reliable customs, and affiliation with mythologically associated territories. These characteristics deepen the group's connection to their homelands and vibrant history. The Wayuu's staunch defense of their environment, natural resources, and cultural survival are fundamental to their identity. [BD]

279 Pineda Camacho, Roberto. "Estrenando el oficio de etnólogas" y otros ensayos sobre la historia de la antropología en Colombia. Bogotá: Instituto Colombiano de Antropología e Historia, 2016. 249 p.: bibl., ill. (Otras miradas. Antropología)

In this important book, Pineda Camacho pays close attention to charting how institutional forces influenced anthropological practice in Colombia. His text is a compilation of seven essays on eminent anthropologists who have worked with Colombia's Lowland Indigenous groups, coupled with sustained reflections on the history of anthropology in Colombia. The text emphasizes the value of the discipline in the development of national identity and in comprehending the country's numerous ethnic and Indigenous groups. The author highlights how the institutional environment and the dynamic interactions between the contributions of foreign and local ethnologists have had an impact on how anthropology is currently practiced in Colombia. By examining the complex link between contributions from domestic and international ethnologists to the creation of a national anthropology, the book highlights significant turning points and trends in the development of Colombian anthropology. Following an introduction to the anthropologist's passion for travel, chapter 2 discusses the renowned Colombian physician and Muisca antiquities scholar Liborio Zerda. In 1883 Zerda published his major work *El Dorado* about the mythical lost Amazonian kingdom. As is evident in Pineda Camacho's rendition, Colombian anthropology has been international since at least the second half of the 19th century, a time when it came under the sway of the eminent German ethnologist Adolf Bastian and the Berlin Royal Museum of Ethnography. Bastian visited Colombia in 1876. Upon his arrival at a gathering held in the home of His Majesty the Emperor of Germany, he delivered an ethnological conference to the diplomatic community and a few office ministers. The Vaupés Basin's native esthetics are documented in the next chapter, which emphasizes the magnificent *payé*, laden with beautiful things. This is coupled with a discussion of Theodor Koch Grünberg's dubious and overtly racist evolutionist contributions to the study of Indigenous esthetics. German anthropologists and their influence on the development of Colombian anthropology are reviewed in chapter 4 in a very helpful way (1800–1970). This covers the modernization of ethnology, the decrease of German intellectual dominance within ethnology, and discussions of educational reform in Colombia. In the chapter that ensues, ethnology is examined as "a masculine universe helped by wives." In chapter 6, the discussion of "women in the field" or the trailblazing married duo, Alicia Dussán and Gerardo Reichel Dolmatoff, complements this topic. Insightful commentary on the creation of a nationalist archeology and the significance of archeology in the Araracuara region, where it thrives, are found in the concluding chapter. In contrast to the applications of "places of archeological memory," the author muses on the potential decline of Amazonian archeology in Colombia. [BD]

280 Schackt, Jon. A people of stories in the forest of myth: the Yukuna of Miritiparaná. Oslo: Novus forlag: Instituttet for sammenlignende kulturforskning, 2013. 271 p.: bibl., color ill., index, maps. (Instituttet for sammenlignende kulturforskning. Serie B; CXLVIII)

A mythological Yukuna who is more "real" than them, according to Yukuna, left behind an oral legacy that they regard as their responsibility to guard (p. 28). Knowing about something's beginnings and past gives everything its relevance and power in the present. But in the case of the Yukuna, ancestor authority is both unwavering and flexible (ibid.). Due to the lack of priesthood professionals among the Yukuna and the fact that everyone is somewhat of a shaman, seniority claims can be established through *nacimiento* (birth) or origin stories. They always start with a narrative about the patri-apical sib's ancestor and his *maloca*, "a local cooperative group settled in or around a riverside *maloca* surrounded by gardens" (p. 96), before progressing through an intricate genealogy that spans 10 or 12 generations to the present (p. 184). Schackt shows how Yukuna males establish their personas through interpretations of their lineage positions, which are contested. To bolster their claims of superiority, competitors focus on various divisions of the branching genealogical tree. Rather than gaining authority through patrilineal succession from designated ancestors, Yukuna men promote themselves through recourse to epic mythical sagas that weave historical legend into current-day events. Hosting dance parties and having a sizable *maloca* are male prerogatives (p. 21). Leadership competitions can be quickly resolved by expressing the commonly used declaration that all Yukuna are of "one *maloca*" because they all have a common *maloca* and place of origin and are all juniors to their revered ancestors. The author and his anthropologist partner Carla Matallana Laverde conducted fieldwork in Yukuna *maloca* communities that belonged to the five patrisibs in 1984–85; these communities still spoke Yukuna and recounted Yukuna history as their own today, either as a result of ancestry, affinal adoption, or borrowing. It is safe to say that the conversation is dominated by the Kamejeya patri-sib, whose members are seen as the "only real

Yukuna." The book's central themes are the imbrications of legend, myth, *maloca* architecture, history, and the connections between ancestry, hierarchy, and the politicization of knowledge. Schackt does a great job in chapter 2 of bringing the Yukuna's troubled past to life. This chapter covers the times of slave raids, the rubber boom, and missionary instruction. In the italicized text, he replicates Yukuna family history as it was related to him and appends information from missionary and historical works. The Yukuna are quoted throughout the text to illustrate particular variants of their creation myth or provide auto-anthropological clarification on topics like *maloca* dances (p. 89). This is especially true of chapter 6, where the text mostly repeats Yukuna myths, which have not been altered. Chapters 5, 6, and 7 focus on the Yukuna's oral tradition, which lies at the book's core. In chapter 5, the story of Periyo is told. Periyo is the most important ancestor of the Kamijeya sib, and all real Yukuna go to him for advice on how to run the best *maloca* community. While chapter 5 tells the tale of the Kamijeya sib's most distant ancestor, chapter 7 discusses the Yukuna cosmos and conception of death and contains an intriguing but brief description of the *Baile de los Muñecos* ("Dance of the Dolls") style of *maloca* dance, in which various species of animal spirits are invited to dance and drink in the *malocas*. The most elaborate of these dances involves impersonating more than 70 distinct species through subtly modified masks (p. 152). Chapter 8 is a reflective and critical review of Yukuna shamanism. The Yukuna contrast their shamanic tradition with that of the Makuna and other nearby groups, whose traditions are based on the ritualized consumption of the hallucinogenic brew yage; they assert that their shamanism is based on the *pensamiento* or the *thought*, of their ancestors (p. 161). The Yukuna claim their shamanic practices are based on the outlook of their forefathers (p. 161). In this regard, all Yukuna men are shamans to some extent since they have all inherited a portion of this ancestral power through the Yurupary initiation. Yukuna "appear to consider the Yurupary rituals as a kind of basic course in shamanism" (p. 172). The book is a valuable addition to the growing body of literature about the Indigenous peoples of the northwest Amazon. It explains clearly how vital the *maloca* is to Yakuna cosmologies, ideas of the self, and views of the past. [BD]

281 **Velasco Jaramillo, Marcela.** The territorialization of ethnopolitical reforms in Colombia: Chocó as a case study. (*LARR*, 49:3, Jan. 2014, p. 126–152, bibl., maps, tables)

To protect local livelihoods from resource-intensive economies, black and Indigenous ethnic movements requested communal land rights and autonomy in the Chocó department of Colombia. Most Indigenous and Black communities have not benefited from the new rights despite decentralization and state restructuring measures offering constitutional guarantees of autonomy. This has occurred because of human rights abuses, neoliberal growth, and the seizure of regional economies by armed forces, all of which have undercut attempts at self-governance. Only communities able to withstand violence and hold local or national administrations responsible could sustain autonomy in such a situation. According to the author, the territorialization of institutions, which specific political actors adjusted to address local dynamics, can explain the changes' intention and actual effect. The author claims that in the Chocó department, reforms were territorialized in an environment of weak government institutions, widespread public corruption, and resource-intensive land-use practices that undermined ethnopolitical autonomy by facilitating local intermediaries who frequently made decisions against the interests of communities. [BD]

PERU AND ECUADOR

282 **Brown, Michael F.** Upriver: the turbulent life and times of an Amazonian people. Cambridge, Mass.: Harvard University Press, 2014. 321 p.: bibl., ill., index, map.

Based on his studies from 1976 to 2012 with the Awajún, formerly known as the Aguaruna or Jíbaro, Brown has written an evocative book full of astute observations that serves as an introduction to an Indigenous Upper Amazonian society because the ethnographer comments on his experiences over a lengthy period of time. The Jivaroan-speaking Awajún reside in communities situated in northeastern Peru's Upper Amazon region; hence, the monograph's title, *Upriver*, is quite fitting. In addition to presenting readers with rich anthropological and cultural insights, Brown delivers a thorough account replete with autobiographical episodes and a wealth of knowledge about Awajún cultural endurance and social transformation. After 30 years, Brown returned to the Alto Mayo, but due to expanding colonial fronts and agribusiness, the region had undergone such drastic alteration that it was difficult for him to locate all the Awajún settlements from his earlier ethnographic research. *Upriver* is divided into two parts: the first provides extensive information about the Alto Mayo region and the Awajún during Brown's initial fieldwork in 1976–78, while the second section focuses on the years 1980–2012. The first part of the book, "Part One: 1976–1978," is a detailed and entertaining account of Brown's dissertation fieldwork in the late 1970s. In the second section, the Awajún and ideas about the emergence of state relations, hierarchical social systems, and authority are analytically related. Brown asserts that the Awajún continue to practice sorcery because they have little confidence in human interactions and because it provides comfort in the face of illness and death (p. 221). He contends that the challenges of illnesses, oppression, and colonial persecution have made the Awajún's way of life volatile; as a consequence, they no longer feel safe and secure and discern sorcery everywhere, even in intimate relationships. The book makes reference to the well-known high suicide rate among the Awajún. Brown believes that the causes of Awajún suicides, attempts, and threats to commit suicide are resentment, a lack of appropriate social support, and poor kin ties. When Brown writes honestly about his critical position in a field where children are found guilty of witchcraft and people kill to get back at them, he raises questions about ethics. In the second part, Brown highlights the local changes that occurred in the 1990s and 2000s, including the Awajún in the Alto Mayo region's use of land rents, which led to new levels of material inequality; their increased involvement in state politics and higher education; as well as the 2009 violent confrontation with the military and police (known as *el Baguazo*), which followed a two-month-long road barricade. In spite of powerful historical influences often pitted against them, this welcome book illustrates the Awajún people's yearning to redefine and take control of their fate. [BD]

283   **Carvalho, Thaís de.** White men and electric guns: analysing the Amazonian dystopia through Shipibo-Konibo children's drawings. (*Glob. Stud. Child.*, 11:1, 2021, p. 40–53, bibl., ill.)

The paper is a welcome examination of how children's drawings give *pishtaco* attackers and the effects of their onslaught meaningful substance. In Andean societies, the *pishtaco* is regarded as a man with a white complexion who covertly steals Indigenous people's organs (or fat) in return for cash. The Shipibo-Konibo peoples of the Peruvian Amazon portray *pishtacos* as high-tech assassins who use powerful laser guns to transfer voltage into their victims' hapless bodies. Through the study of images created by young Shipibo-Konibo artists, the essay explores the dystopian notion associated with *pishtacos*. It considers the Shipibo-Konibo children's artwork as significant visual proof based on theories regarding illusion and fantasy. Maps showing the neighborhood before and after a *pishtaco* attack are included, along with composite images of a *pishtaco*. While youngsters were busy portraying white men with giant needles and electrical weaponry, they debated whether modern-day organ smugglers could be mestizos. Maps of the settlement and composite sketches of the *pishtaco* comprise the two sets of drawings that form the analysis. When taken together, these parts offer perspectives before and after the attack. In light of field notes and other secondary evidence, the following conversations highlight the historical accuracy of the tales depicted in children's artwork. The article examines how *pishtaco* are evolving and the dual electricity use that children's drawings exhibit. It makes the case that kids are aware of the history of the village's changing ethnic dynamics and understand the paradox of modernity: they know that electricity can be a weapon or be used as a shield, and rather than viewing the *pishtaco* tales as colonial myths, they are placed in a post-apocalyptic present. Moreover, the children's drawings are rendered as proof of the contradictions of life in emerging Amazonia. [BD]

284 **Cepek, Michael L.** Life in oil: Cofán survival in the petroleum fields of Amazonia. Photographs by Bear Guerra. Austin: University of Texas Press, 2018. 286 p.: bibl., index, maps, photos.

Having spent decades researching the Cofán of Ecuadorian Amazonia, Cepek has penned a laudable book about these Indigenous peoples' struggles with oil exploration, extraction, and production in their ancestral homelands. In addition to the influence of the petroleum industry on Cofán customary ways of life, their fight to preserve their distinctive cultural traditions and geopolitical independence in the face of encroaching oil firms and government regulations comes center stage in the book. The author explores Cofán initiatives to mitigate oil development's adverse social and environmental effects on their territory, such as pollution, health issues, and dispossession. Through a nuanced combination of ethnographic study, personal accounts, and shrewd social analysis, Cepek paints a detailed picture of the complex interactions among Indigenous peoples, international petroleum corporations, and Ecuadorian government agencies. Written with an unwavering commitment to his subjects, the author delivers profoundly moving accounts of Cofán suffering, and shows us that *living in oil* is a form of slow, baffling brutality for some of the most defenseless yet resilient people on the earth. [BD]

285 **Fotiou, Evgenia.** Technologies of the body in contemporary ayahuasca shamanism in the Peruvian Amazon: implications for future research. (*Hum. Ecol.*, 47:1, Feb. 2019, p. 145–151, bibl., photo)

The information for this study was collected between 2003 and 2015 in and around Iquitos, Peru, primarily from *mestizo ayahuasqueros* (healers who specialize in ayahuasca rituals and are of mixed European and Indigenous origin) who engage with both locals and Western tourists. In Indigenous Western Amazonia, ayahuasca has long been a plant-based psychoactive and entheogenic brewed drink that is ceremonially consumed. Ayahuasca is typically formulated from the *Banisteriopsis caapi* vine, the *Psychotria viridis* bush or an alternative, like *Justicia pectoralis*, a *Brugmansia* species, or *Datura* species, and *mapacho* (*Nicotiana rustica*). As more and more outsiders travel to the Peruvian Amazonia to indulge in what are supposed to be its allegedly curative and transformative benefits, its international usage has recently increased exponentially. Physical purification, which is called *purga* (purge) in the area, is thought to be important for healing. It typically happens before ayahuasca ceremonies with a restricted diet and purgative plants. Consumption of ayahuasca includes a shamanic *dieta*, which comprises dieting and eating a variety of nonpsychoactive plants for purifying the body and psychic cleaning through purges and ceremonial bathing. Fotiou investigates the extent to which shamanic diets are bodily technologies. The usage of shamanic plants is portrayed by the author as a technique intimately connected to Amazonian conceptions of the self, the body, and, more broadly, to Indigenous ecocosmologies. In Amazonian shamanic complexes, a variety of plants are used as key instruments to modify the body. To wit, western Amazonia's various herbalists, such as *paleros* and *tabaqueros*, indicate a wide range of specialized shamanic knowledge. Anthropological and pharmacological approaches must be employed when researching plant use in Amazonian shamanism. [BD]

286 **Guevara Aranda, Roberto.** Bagua, de la resistencia a la utopía indígena: La "Curva del Diablo" y la lucha de los pueblos amazónicos en el siglo XXI. Lima: publisher not identified, 2013. 381 p.: color ill.

The Baguazo crisis of 2009 highlighted longstanding tensions between Indigenous communities and the government over land and resource rights in Peru. It sparked a national conversation about the need for greater respect for Indigenous rights and environmental protection. Guevara

Aranda's work reviews in some detail "El Baguazo," the violent events that occurred in Bagua province, Peru, at the "Devil's Curve" and Station 6 on 5 June 2009. In this book, Guevara Aranda analyzes and comments on the events of 5 June, which were the tragic culmination of a long process of Indigenous marginalization. The book is well illustrated with photographs, including of road blockades carried out by Awajún and Wampís Indigenous groups between January 2002 and 5 June 2009. El Baguazo, also known as the Bagua or Amazonian protests, was a conflict between the government and Indigenous communities over land and resource rights. It began as a protest against legislative decrees issued by the government that aimed to facilitate foreign investment in Peruvian Amazonia by reducing environmental and social protections. Indigenous peoples argued that the laws violated their rights to land and resources and demanded that the government repeal them. The protests turned violent when police attempted to break up a roadblock set up by protesters near Bagua in the Amazon region. The clashes between police and protesters resulted in dozens of deaths, including Indigenous protesters and police officers. The violence continued for several days, with Indigenous communities seizing control of a number of towns and blocking roads throughout the region. The first chapter provides a brief historical review of the Awajún Wampís settlement in the Peruvian department of Amazonas. This is followed by an assessment of the Awajún-Wampís family and social and political organization. The third chapter assesses the structural causes that have generated social conflicts in Amazonas and Loreto. This is followed by a study of social conflicts among the Awajún-Wampís people from 2002 to 2009. Chapter 5 provides a local perspective on the Amazonian conflict that plunged the country into mourning in June 2009. The following chapter addresses the issue of the disappearances of victims. There are reports of disappearances and unaccounted individuals after the violent clashes between police and protesters. Still, due to the chaotic nature of the events and lack of accurate records, it is difficult to determine an exact number of those missing. Human rights groups have long called for investigations into the alleged disappearances and for those responsible to be held accountable. The following chapter explores the path to reconciliation, including return visits to the provinces of Bagua and Condorcanqui. The text concludes by mentioning other zones of social conflict among Awajún inhabitants of Amazonas and Cajamarca. [BD]

287   High, Casey. "A little bit Christian": memories of conversion and community in post-Christian Amazonia. (*Am. Anthropol.*, 118:2, June 2016, p. 270–283, bibl., photos)

Conversion to Christianity is typically portrayed in Amazonia as a group action rather than a fundamental change in people's beliefs. Like other scholars, High contends the conversion process is more about social relations than commitment or faith, as exemplified by Amazonian societies that converted en masse but subsequently rejected or withdrew from Christianity. For their part, the Waorani of Ecuador relate religious conversion to individuals who underwent a fundamental rupture with the past and, in so doing, shaped the present. High explains in his essay how the Waorani see the conversion of their elders as a period of civilization involving cultural incorporation into a larger social structure following an existence marked by internal dispute and relative seclusion. Despite their 1960s conversion to Christianity, the Waorani have largely rejected Christianity. Yet they still see their religious conversion as underwriting the social change that made the ideal of communal living possible. High notes the sense of temporal breach in conversion memories, underscoring the importance of autonomy and personal experience in Waorani epistemology, and exemplifies their understanding of sociocultural transformation. In a society where Christianity has ceased to be the dominant social identity, the moral commentary of Waorani Christians is nevertheless appreciated due to the unique experiences created by recollections of communal "civilization" and the Waorani's emphasis on individual autonomy and embrace of collective values. [BD]

288 Mezzenzana, Francesca. Between will and thought: individualism and social responsiveness in Amazonian child rearing. (*Am. Anthropol.*, 122:3, Sept. 2020, p. 540–553, bibl., photos)

The study presents an anthropological explanation of how moral inclinations for autonomy and social attunement are created throughout the early years of life among the Runa, an Indigenous people that live in the Ecuadorian Amazon. Mezzenzana shows how the Indigenous concepts of *munay* (will) and *yuyay* (thought) impact how young children view themselves and their connections with others. It illustrates how a Runa child is transformed into a proper person when a particular sort of individual will (*munay*) and a specific type of social attentiveness (*yuyay*) are accorded great moral significance. The essay notes that the Runa recognize individual will (*munay*) but consciously choose not to give in to their children's requests in order to make them "thoughtful," in contrast to middle-class Anglo-Americans who believe that parental attentiveness is crucial for "healthy" child development. The paradox initially sparked the author's interest in children's social responsiveness. This behavior presented another notable aspect of local childrearing customs and, more broadly, of Runa social life: the moral requirement to respect each person's distinct identity and autonomy. Only when one's personal interests are the basis for education can learning take place, and no Runa youngster can be made to learn anything they do not want to. The type of parental blame observed in Western societies and the focus of a hefty body of sociological and anthropological research on modern parenting is much less common among the Runa since a child behaves according to their individual volition. In this regard, Runa understandings of the individual will seem somewhat "stronger" than Anglo-American concepts because, in the former case, it will inevitably entail a certain amount of responsibility (which modern Anglo-American parents would typically not wish to bestow upon very young children). Runa child rearing directs a child's individual will into constructive sociality rather than making them "bloom," as in the upper-middle-class environment. Refusing to fulfill a child's wishes is essential to fostering a child's responsiveness to others. By so doing, the Runa child gains personal self-awareness, grit, and an understanding of the hierarchy of wills and the value of being respected for embodying thought. Only when taken for the good of others is a personal action considered thoughtful; however, it might also be argued that a thoughtful action originates from a person's independent will. A Runa child must understand that *yuyay* and *munay* are inextricably intertwined in order to learn what it means to be a real "person." Despite the apparent absence of compulsion, recriminations, or strict punishment, Runa adults take great care to teach their offspring to be considerate and "decent" people. Only those who can exhibit *yuyay*, or "thinking," can have their will obeyed. Mezzenzana argues that two phases are required to develop this thoughtfulness: the first is to establish independence and self-control, and the second is to acquire the ability to recognize and accommodate other people's desires. In the subsequent section, the essay underscores how these goals can be met by employing parenting techniques that help children gradually become conscious of the hierarchy of wills. It asserts that Runa conceptions of interpersonal life result from socialization practices that emphasize a child's individual choice while promoting the growth of social attentiveness. It is important to note that the combination of individualism and social responsiveness does not exist solely in Amazonia. Anthropologists have long noted how, in many small-scale societies, the cultivation of traditions emphasizing cooperation and responsibility coincides with the stress on individual freedom and autonomy. [BD]

289 Ontaneda, Constanza. Shipibos displaced in Lima: insurgent citizens as authorized Indians in Peru. (*Lat. Am. Caribb. Ethn. Stud.*, 12:1, March 2017, p. 25–47, bibl., photos)

Over 300 Shipibo-Konibo Amazonian Indigenous community members fear eviction because of a public-private proposal to turn the region into a riverfront park after years of habitation on a dump in Cantagallo, a shantytown near Lima. Instead of resisting, Shipibos make use of the opportunities neoliberal multiculturalism gives them by adopting entrepreneurial strategies consistent with their status as "indios permitidos," or allowed Indians, and profiting from the benefits that the Peruvian government provides to such Indians. The Peruvian government encourages Indigenous exclusivity in several ways, including by rewarding the recognized Indian and restricting the achievement of full citizenship by all Indigenous peoples. The article also considers the potential of adopting state strategies intended to fit the neoliberal multiculturalist template, such as "prior consultation" procedures, which may create opportunities for Indigenous communities. [BD]

290 **Ortiz-T., Pablo.** El laberinto de la autonomía indígena en el Ecuador: las circunscripciones territoriales indígenas en la Amazonía Central, 2010–2012. (*Lat. Am. Caribb. Ethn. Stud.*, 10:1, March 2015, p. 60–86, bibl., map)

What difficulties and conflicts are encountered while creating Indigenous Territorial Circumscriptions (CTIs) regarding the right to territorial self-management and self-determination among Ecuador's Indigenous nationalities? To respond to this query, Ortiz-T.'s essay examines Ecuador's acceptance of Indigenous peoples' rights to autonomy and self-determination. It then explores the scope of the protocols established in the Political Constitution and the Organic Code of Territorial Planning and Decentralization (COOTAD). Under the framework of the definition of the Ecuadorian multinational state, it evaluates its capacity to produce a new kind of institutionality and a new territorial organization. Between 2010 and 2012, the state and the Indigenous nationalities of Amazonia reached an agreement that forms the basis for the current procedure. The article analyzes Ecuador's Indigenous rights movement, highlighting its internal developments and conflicts with other central and local state authorities and mestizo sectors. The difficulty of establishing CTIs in Kichwa territory in the provinces of Napo and Orellana and in Kichwa and Achuar territory in the area of Pastaza in the central Amazon is examined by Ortiz-T. His article is consequential for critically highlighting some of the views and conundrums that establishing CTIs present in light of the tenuous relationship between the state and Indigenous nations, not to mention the broader process of fashioning a plurinational, intercultural Ecuadorian state. [BD]

291 **Peluso, Daniela.** Gendered geographies of care: women as health workers in an Indigenous health project in the Peruvian Amazon. (*Tipití*, 18:1, 2022, p. 25–46, bibl., map, tables)

The essay explores how women, who serve as the primary custodians for family well-being, got involved as health advocates in a local Indigenous health care project in Madre de Dios, Peru's Amazonian region. It offers a cautionary tale of the processes and changes the project underwent from its outset to its ultimate incorporation of Indigenous women's health promoters into its health initiatives. The incorporation of women began in the middle of the 1980s and early 1990s, when access to Western biomedical services was even more restricted than now. A review of Madre de Dios and a discussion of the interconnections between gender and health are presented in the essay. Peluso emphasizes how women are hidden in primary healthcare and explores how and why they have been largely excluded from healthcare delivery plans. Women's role in managing current health resources is covered, as are the challenges women face as leaders concerning larger political structures, like the native federation and local government. Overall, the initiative succeeded in broadening the concept of health to incorporate concepts such as 'living well," "well-being," and sustainability as a series of caring relationships with the natural world—areas where women undeniably have key social positions. This study explores a gender-balanced perspective on processes legitimizing Indigenous healthcare practices by looking at geographic natural resource maps and plotting ideological and gender-based activities on them. In Peluso's estimation, local and international gendered healthcare politics, which frequently fail to recognize how deeply ingrained care practices are in daily social interactions, are to blame for neglecting women's responsibilities in community health. Additionally, she calls for a broader critique of the Indigenous health agent approach to healthcare in Amazonia, as noted by the exclusion of women as Indigenous health promoters. [BD]

292 Sá Carvalho, Carolina. How to see a scar: humanitarianism and colonial iconography in the Putumayo rubber boom. (*J. Lat. Am. Cult. Stud.*, 27:3, Sept. 2018, p. 371–397, bibl., photos)

This essay analyzes the photographs of Indigenous people taken by Irishman and British consul Roger Casement from the Putumayo region of the Amazon. In 1910, Casement traveled to the Putumayo watershed to look into the transgressions of the Peruvian Amazon Company, a rubber company with a British registration. Sá Carvalho says that Casement's photographs and the entries in his travel journals about how vision works shed light on a critical idea about visual evidence that is sometimes overlooked in research on early photography and the search for objective evidence. Casement asserted that it was vital to document the physical proof of torture on the bodies of the Huitoto and Bora people through writing and photographs. Still, he also stated that one's perspective on seeing their scars was subject to debate and a question of one's "point of view." Sá Carvalho contends that, for Casement, photography shows and instructs the public on perceiving the Indigenous body. She bases this claim on an analysis of Casement's concept of "point of view" and its relationship to debates from the late 19th and early 20th centuries on the function of experience in producing knowledge. The essay explores Casement's engagement with various iconographic traditions, such as the picturesque and the anthropometric. It illustrates how the British consul exploited the local body to teach the populace a particular "pedagogy of the gaze." Sá Carvalho makes the case that Casement's conception of "point of view" as a category defined by imperial history is connected to the distinctiveness of his photographic output. While the public in Britain could not see the scars left on the Putumayo bodies, the Irishman, who also bore the weight of a colonized people, could. He shared the belief of other reformists of his era that social and humanitarian sensitivity could be imparted and included photography in his educational mission. Yet, the ability to shift one's perspective made this an inherently volatile category. His alternating roles characterize Casement's writing and images of the Putumayo as an oppressed person, aggressor, ethnographer, and investigator. Casement took pictures before modern photography was established. As a result, he uses photographic aspects like attitude, decoration, and point of view (where the camera is pointed) to position himself in relation to his many subjects, whether the ideal "natives," scarred victims, armed muchachos, or Barbadians. [BD]

293 Sarmiento Barletti, Juan Pablo. Julián's choice: of jaguar-shamans and the sacrifices made for *Progreso* in Peru's extractive frontier. (*J. Lat. Am. Stud.*, 54:1, Feb. 2022, p. 103–124)

After shooting a jaguar (*Panthera onca*) that had killed two of his cows, Julián, a revered Asháninka shaman (*sheripiari*) from the town of Nueva Esperanza in the Bajo Urubamba valley (Ucayali Region), passed away less than 24 hours later. Julián had killed the jaguar-shaman to safeguard his cows, even though he knew it might retaliate by killing him. Jaguars are strong creatures, irrespective of their status as shamans, and are only encountered in dire circumstances, such as Julián's predicament after the death of his two cows. Jaguars are prominent in the cosmologies and oral histories of Indigenous peoples in the Amazon. They constantly threaten people who enter the forest to hunt or harvest wood. The Asháninka told Sarmiento Barletti that the jaguars they came across in the forest were either real jaguar-shamans who had taken on the shape of jaguars or jaguar-shamans who had died and been reincarnated as jaguars. *Sheripiari* (shamans) are treated with reverence, awe, and dread because of their strength and prowess, much like jaguars. The mysterious ways of the *sheripiari*, experts in using ayahuasca and tobacco, are only taught to men. The difficulties Julián faced in the Peruvian Amazon's degraded forests of the Bajo Urubamba valley led him to make a decision that required self-sacrifice. The essay is based on observations over 42 months of ethnographic work commencing in 2007 with Asháninka groups in the Bajo Urubamba valley. The article investigates Julián's choice to kill the jaguar-shaman and engages in multidisciplinary research on how local people interact with Latin America's burgeoning extractive frontier. Consideration of individual experiences like Julián's provides balance and a deeper understanding of the various local experiences of large-scale resource extraction. Even though most literature focuses on social movements and, to a lesser extent, the ontological aspects of such conflicts, this study helps us understand how people work toward their goals. The cornerstone of Peru's effort at rehabilitation after its internal war (1980–2000) is the extractive frontier that frames Julián's options. Resource extraction is the primary sector for economic expansion, export-led revenues, and foreign investment. Julián's actions hint at how Indigenous peoples adapt their lifestyles and means of subsistence to the uneven and shifting circumstances generated by the extractive frontier. Telling more than just the story of local activism, Julián's case illustrates the individual experiences and strategies that mediate people's wants and goals, which are just as essential to comprehend as group responses to the extractive frontier. The analysis of Julián's pursuit and its results highlights the significance of understanding how people respond to the imposition of significant extractive activity and plan their lives. Examining people's strategies can help us grasp the broader picture, which is frequently dominated by studies of local action and social movements. [BD]

294 Sarmiento Barletti, Juan Pablo and **Lexy Seedhouse.** The Truth and Reconciliation Commission and the Law of Prior Consultation: obstacles and opportunities for democratization and political participation in Peru. (*Lat. Am. Perspect.*, 46:5, Sept. 2019, p. 111–127, bibl.)

Using the complicated case of Peru as a starting point, the essay questions the rise of political will to move forward programs based on crosscultural cooperation and to give Indigenous peoples a real voice in decisions that affect their lives. Based on extensive fieldwork with Indigenous peoples of the Amazon (Ashaninka in Junin and Ucayali) and Andes (Quechua-speaking K'ana of Espinar, Cusco), the essay addresses Peru's Truth and Reconciliation Commission and the Law of Prior Consultation (Law 29785). The authors detail the challenges and prospects these programs have provided for a shift to a more representative democracy and increased political engagement by and for Indigenous peoples. In so doing, they address the efforts to remedy injustice through forging new agreements between the state and its Indigenous citizens and the unanticipated openings they have given to Indigenous peoples to participate in political life. Citing numerous cases, the authors argue that as long as the socioenvironmental injustice suffered by the Indigenous peoples of the Amazon and Andes endures, there will not be a genuine liberalization and extension of their active collaboration in national politics. The Truth and Reconciliation Commission and the Law of Prior Consultation, two important state-led initiatives to address this injustice, failed since they could not tackle the legacy of subjugation and marginalization Indigenous peoples have experienced, mainly at the state's behest. Nevertheless, Sarmiento Barletti and Seedhouse contend that their failures unintentionally strengthened Peru's Indigenous movement and increased overall political engagement. Despite their shortcomings, the Truth and Reconciliation Commission and the Law of Prior Consultation have sparked a renewed awareness of human rights, political engagement, and even examples of cultural resurgence. [BD]

295 Świerk, Kacper. Monkeys in the Wampis (Huambisa) life and cosmology in the Peruvian Amazonian rainforest. (*in* Neotropical ethnoprimatology: Indigenous peoples' perceptions of and interactions with nonhuman primates. Edited by Bernardo Urbani and Manuel Lizarralde. Cham, Switzerland: Springer, 2020, p. 311–329)

The Wampis, also known as the Huambisa and the Shuar, engage in a traditional method of sustenance that combines hunting and swidden agriculture. This chapter focuses on the interactions between monkeys and the Wampis, who live in the tropical rainforests of Peruvian Amazonia. The descriptive data presented in this chapter was collected over seven years during three separate field trips among the Wampis (2004, 2009, and 2011). The chapter emphasizes how the Wampis are closely related to their various monkey populations. This connection is mirrored in their myth and cosmology, as well as in their reliance on monkeys for food and as pets. The researchers reveal that the Wampis designated 11 folk-generic taxa, which include 14 different species of locally found monkeys. This information is relevant to conservation ecologists as well as primatologists. [BD]

296 Trujillo Montalvo, Patricio. Los Shuar y el impacto del proyecto multicultural en la amazonia ecuatoriana. (*Rev. Peru. Antropol.*, 3:4, sept. 2018, p. 42–54, bibl.)

Trujillo Montalvo discusses the Ecuadorian Shuar, traditionally known as fierce Amazonian warriors and now recognized as modern ethnic subjects. He argues that multiculturalism has validated a particular assimilationist model predicated on the production of radical alterity. This is illustrated by someone who is geographically remote, exotic, and open to subjugation, Christianization, and the forces of "civilization," including formal education and sedentism. The Ecuadorian state tasked several Christian missions with conquering Indigenous "others" as part of a multicultural civilizational and biopower agenda intended to dominate souls and bodies while surveilling Amazonian peoples. The author persuasively contends that the Catholic missions were a component of a larger scheme involving the development of biopower and multicultural project of civilization. The essay effectively deploys multiculturalism and biopower as conceptual frameworks for assessing violent cultural and symbolic transformation among the Shuar people. [BD]

297 Ulmer, Gordon. The Earth is hungry: Amerindian worlds and the perils of gold mining in the Peruvian Amazon. (*J. Lat. Am. Caribb. Anthropol.*, 25:2, June 2020, p. 324–339, bibl.)

This article explores how Andean Highlands migrant miners in the Peruvian Amazon cope with the transient nature of their lives and employment. Ulmer drew on 16 months of ethnographic fieldwork on rural labor in Madre de Dios between 2013 and 2015 to comprehend this varied arena of exchange and negotiation. He conducted 75 interviews with people in rural areas, such as gold miners, loggers, agroforesters, peasants, park guardians, and boat drivers. The essay shows how miners create a safe space where different Indigenous viewpoints may coexist and adapt to changing political realities. It underscores the struggles that Andean migrant gold miners have in the face of the disposable nature of their working lives in Peruvian Amazonia. In so doing, it sheds light on the distinctive characteristics of extractivism in the Peruvian region of Madre de Dios. It deals with a problem in the Andean and Amazonian ethnographies: these interwoven regions are frequently examined in isolation. To wit, understanding modern artisanal and small-scale mining in Madre de Dios requires an examination of political, economic, and spiritual-religious relationships that go far beyond the Andes-Amazonia divide and localized or merely regional comprehensions. With their extractive work, Andean miners in Madre de Dios create what can be considered a liminal space between rival worlds. A shared understanding between the Indigenous and non-Indigenous worlds were initially characterized by the middle-ground idea. The article expands on one account of another miner's death to demonstrate how miners must strike a balance between an agentive world, their aspirations for economic success, and the controversy surrounding resource exploitation. The essay explains how gold miners build a bridge between Indigenous and Judeo-Christian cosmologies to minimize risk during nighttime work. Ulmer contends in the article's concluding section that the notion of a middle ground is complicated because worker deaths are a sign of the broader logic of disposability surrounding gold mining. This reasoning puts other people and the environment in danger, threatening the lives of miners and the middle ground they want to establish. [BD]

Vallejo, Ivette; Cristina Cielo; and **Fernando García.** Ethnicity, gender, and oil: comparative dynamics in the Ecuadorian Amazon. See item **1695.**

298 Wasserstrom, Robert. "Yo fuí vendida": reconsidering peonage and genocide in western Amazonia. (*Adv. Anthropol.*, 7, 2017, p. 35–54)

Julio César Arana's horrific enslavement of 13,000 Indigenous peoples in Peruvian-controlled territory in the lower Putumayo River in 1904 has long been remembered as one of the most brutal atrocities of the Amazon rubber boom (1885–1930). In contrast, experts contend that Indigenous individuals not enticed by the whip were largely unaffected by rubber extraction. A contrary interpretation is supported by archival data and a reassessment of earlier ethnographies: most local laborers were forced to gather rubber because of the impact of debt peonage and forced labor, not because of widespread coercive brutality. Few Indigenous households in western Amazonia avoided the grips of this extractive industry. The common factor connecting the various rubber-tapping operations in Amazonia was debt. In the "shatter zones," as James Scott has referred to them, survivors frequently created new ethnic identities as the rubber boom faded. Backward-looking affiliation to the past was less significant as the post-rubber agrarian economy came into being than familiar places of residence, shared languages, and contemporary family connections. Allegiance remained fluid and altered according to circumstances. In this regard, modern Indigenous groups were born out of such looser ties of group affiliation. Wasserstrom concludes this far-ranging review of the impact of the rubber boom on Indigenous societies by turning his attention to contemporary Amazonia. He notes how gold miners, illicit loggers, and drug manufacturers have launched a new cycle of resource extraction in Amazonia, displacing or eradicating the descendants of previous cycles. Nonetheless, certain things remain the same. Older types of servitude remain visible in the dimly lit shadow economy of the area, such as among Indigenous youngsters serving as domestic helpers. [BD]

PARAGUAY, ARGENTINA, AND BOLIVIA

299 Abeledo, Sebastián. Informe ampliado: efectos socioeconómicos y culturales de la pandemia COVID-19 y del aislamiento social, preventivo y obligatorio en los Pueblos Indígenas en Argentina. Rosario, Argentina: Universidad Nacional de Rosario, Facultad de Humanidades y Artes, Centro de Estudios Aplicados a Problemáticas Socioculturales, 2020. 526 p.: bibl., graphs, ill., maps, photos.

Extensive report on the impact of the COVID-19 pandemic among Indigenous groups of Argentina. The report presents a collection of contributions by Argentine scholars who conducted research among Indigenous peoples. The report provides background on the living conditions, health, access to education, and infrastructure of Native people. Also shows how their situations of marginality and exclusion affect their well-being and limit their access to resources, while increasing their exposure to the virus. The report recommends that state institutions take into account the ethnic specificity and demands of the Native population in the context of the health emergency. [SH]

300 Almirón, Victoria S.; Romina M. Palma; and **Tatiana S. Barboza** Educación indígena en el Chaco (Argentina): identidad étnica, participación e interculturalidad; de la historia reciente a la actualidad. (*Runa/Buenos Aires*, 43:1, Feb. 2022, p. 153–170)

The article traces the implementation of intercultural bilingual education in the Chaco province of Argentina between 1940 and 2014. The authors take into account all of the intervening actors, and the extent of the participation of Indigenous peoples, the nature of inter-ethnic relations, as well as how public education policies considered Native peoples' demands. [SH]

Análisis de las territorialidades en México y Bolivia desde la etnografía, la historia y los imaginarios sociales. See item 177.

301 Barrientos Salinas, J. Alejandro. Hebras y nudos de marico: la vida social del tejido de algodón en el piedemonte andino-amazónico. (*Rev. Cienc. Cult.*, 45, 2020, p. 65–101)

Based on interviews carried out in two visits to the Tacana territory (department of La Paz) in 2015 and 2019, this long article examines cotton-woven products in the region, namely the bags called *marico* (*shitara* in Tacana). The first part reviews the secondary literature on the ethnohistory of the region, compiling mentions of cotton products. The second part offers a detailed first-hand and profusely illustrated description of the spinning, weaving, and dyeing techniques and the iconographic designs of the tissues, recalling a wide ethnographic literature about the Amazon foothills. The fragments of analysis, drawing from Viveiros de Castro's perspectivism, are rather hypothetical, attempting to show a link between the textiles and several beliefs and rituals. It represents a promising contribution to the scarce ethnography of the Amazonian foothills of Bolivia. [FB]

302 Beiras del Carril, Victoria and Paola Cúneo. Haciendo un freestyle con los qompas': juegos verbales y recontextualización de géneros discursivos en el rap qom. (*J. Soc. am.*, 106:1, 2020, p. 127–153)

The authors study the presence of rap music among urbanized Qom youth and how this form of musical performance incorporates bilingualism and represents specific forms of ethnic identity. The authors trace the sociolinguistic situation of the Qom, analyze the lyrics through linguistic genres, and describe how, in an urban environment marked by loss of the native language, youth are interested in recovering their language and learning about Qom cultural practices. Hence in this context, rap is seen as a form of language revitalization. [SH]

303 Bonifacio, Valentina. Da cacciatori-raccoglitori a operai: sul lavoro in fabbrica della popolazione indigena di Puerto Casado, Paraguay. (*in* Accademico impaziente: studi in onore di Glauco Sanga. A cura di Gianluca Ligi, Giovanni Pedrini e Franca Tamisari. Alessandria, Italy: Edizioni dell'Orso, 2018, p. 15–28, ill.)

Based on ethnographic interviews with former workers at the tannin factory of Puerto Casado (Paraguayan Chaco), where various ethnic groups coexisted with Paraguayan workers throughout the 20th century, this paper analyzes their different agencies. Questioning both extremes of canonical hypotheses about Indigenous work in Chaco industries (that it is either coercive or willingly adapted by the Indigenous as a complement to their hunting-gathering cycle), it postulates that Indigenous employment choices were aimed at safeguarding their individual autonomy, contrasting their practices and ideas with those of their non-Indigenous workmates. [FB]

304 Canova, Paola. Frontier intimacies: Ayoreo women and the sexual economy of the Paraguayan Chaco. Austin: University of Texas Press, 2020. 192 p.: bibl., ill., index.

Remarkable ethnography on the sexual practices of Ayoreo women (referred to as *curajodie*) of Paraguay, in which they exchange sex with non-Ayoreo men, including Mennonite settlers, for money or other material goods. The author carried out extensive research among the Ayoreo, an Indigenous group which experienced extreme violence in the process of colonization contact with surrounding society. The author addresses how these exchanges take place amidst a frontier economy. [SH]

305 Cardini, Laura Ana. El trabajo de los Qom: artesanías, cultura y construcción política en Rosario. Prólogo de Victoria Novelo Oppenheim. Rosario, Argentina: Prohistoria Ediciones, 2017. 269 p.: bibl., ill. (Colección Biblioteca de Antropología; 6)

Study of the Qom Indigenous people and their work as artisans in an urban context. The author analyzes the production and circulation of crafts, as well as the interplay of relations with government officials, organizations and state institutions involved with the production of crafts. Artisans supplement their income from the sale of crafts with other jobs. The Qom people consider the production of crafts as a marker of ethnic identity, although it does not necessarily constitute a significant form of income. [SH]

306   Correia, Joel E. Reworking recognition: Indigeneity, land rights, and the dialectics of disruption in Paraguay's Chaco. (*Geoforum/New York*, 119, Feb. 2021, p. 227–237, bibl.)

The paper analyzes actions taken in 2015 by an Enxet and Sanapaná community (due to the reoccupation of their land and the construction of the Trans-Chaco highway) as a change in their land struggle strategy aimed at challenging the limits of recognition employed by the state to perpetually delay their claims. The paper argues that the racialized "*patrón-peón*" (boss-workman) patterns of the old cattle ranches were not altered by the "multicultural turn" of the 1980s and 1990s and are still at the basis of the settler colonialism in the region, replicated in state-Indigenous relations. Correia surveys the evolution of the community leaders' claims (from better working conditions to land rights), their use of international institutions to subvert Paraguayan legal limitations, and their final break from the multicultural "*indio permitido*" ("acceptable Indian") status. The paper will be of interest to researchers focused on land struggles, settler-colonialism, political patronage, politics of recognition, and the post-multicultural debate. [FB]

307   Denuncio, Anabella Verónica. Mujeres Indígenas y espacio público: maternidad, violencias, y conciencia femenina colectiva. (*Etnogr. Contemp.*, 7:12, 2021, p. 8–31, bibl.)

The field of gender studies among Lowland groups continues to grow and diversify thematically. Denuncio's article is part of this trend, and addresses different ways of expressing motherhood among the Qom Indigenous group of Argentina. In this case, motherhood transcends the domestic sphere and engages in the public sphere, whereby women are not only caregivers, but also transmitters of cultural practices and defenders of cultural and territorial rights. In so doing, these women question notions of individual versus collective rights, as well as women's roles as caretakers. [SH]

308   Ennis, Juan Antonio. Robert Lehmann-Nitsche y Rudolf Lenz: epistolario (1897–1928). Edición y traducción de Juan Antonio Ennis y Claudio Soltmann. La Plata, Argentina: Universidad Nacional de La Plata, Facultad de Humanidades y Ciencias de la Educación; Berlin: Ibero-Amerikanisches institut; Santiago de Chile: UMCE, 2022. 306 p.: bibl., ill. (Variaciones; 3)

Transcription, translation, and commentary of correspondence between the German scientists Rudolf Lenz and Robert Lehmann-Nitsche, in Chile and Argentina. This correspondence covers more than three decades, from 1897 to 1928. Lehmann-Nitsche, physician and ethnologist (b. 1872 Radomitz-d. 1938 Berlin), worked for more than 20 years in Argentina where he was the head of the anthropology department in the Museo de La Plata. He studied Indigenous languages and ethnology (mainly the chon-language group), photographs, and objects, and wrote a study about erotic texts under the pseudonym Victor Borde. Upon retirement in 1930, he returned to Germany. Rudolf Lenz (b. 1863 Halle an der Saale-d. 1938 Santiago de Chile) worked in Chile at the Instituto Pedagógico de la Universidad de Chile as teacher and linguist and researched Araucanian languages and local folklore, Spanish in Chile, and varieties of Spanish such as the Papiamentu. In 1909, he founded the Sociedad de Folklore Chileno. [F. Obermeier]

309   **Experiencias formativas interculturales de jóvenes toba/qom, wichí y mbyá-guaraní de Argentina.** Compilación de Ana Carolina Hecht, Mariana García Palacios y Noelia Enriz. Buenos Aires: GEU, Grupo Editor Universitario, 2019. 83 p.: bibl. (Colección Las juventudes argentinas hoy)

This edited volume includes ongoing research on childhood and youth among four Indigenous groups of Argentina. The authors have been conducting work on this topic for over two decades, looking at the presence of Indigenous people in higher education, the performances of rap music among the Qom, and sexuality in interethnic contexts. [SH]

310 Fabricant, Nicole and **Nancy Postero.** Performing indigeneity in Bolivia: the struggle over the TIPNIS. (*in* Indigenous life projects and extractivism: ethnographies from South America. Edited by Cecilie Vindal Ødegaard and Juan Javier Rivera Andía. Cham, Switzerland: Palgrave MacMillan, 2019, p. 245–276, bibl.)

Insightful essay on the marches and performances organized by CIDOB (Confederación de Pueblos Indígenas del Oriente Boliviano) leaders in 2011 and 2012 to protest against the construction of a highway across the Isiboro Sécure Indigenous Territory and National Park (TIPNIS). The article states that indigeneity, as a key "ethical substance" in the country and a foundation of Evo Morales' nationalism, has become a main area of political tensions and struggles; in this case, between the state's use of images of *"indio permitido"* ("authorized Indian") to impose discipline in the communities and discredit Indigenous opposition and its discourse of "economic independence" to support new extractivist projects, and, on the other hand, the Indigenous organizations' notion of nature and quest for autonomy. The authors focus on discourses and performances of indigeneity on both sides: the state's revisiting of the contrast between Andean communities (as representatives of economic progress) and Lowlands' (as regressive), the use of environmental and gender agendas by the TIPNIS activists, and the subsequent involvement of a La Paz feminist collective (*Mujeres Creando*) in the conflict. [FB]

311 Glauser Ortiz, Marcos. Angaité's responses to deforestation: political ecology of the livelihood and land use strategies of an indigenous community from the Paraguayan Chaco. Zürich, Switzerland: LIT Verlag, 2019. 283 p., 12 pages of plates: bibl., ill., maps. (Curupira; 31)

Based on the author's PhD dissertation and long-term fieldwork, this book studies the "responses" of the Angaité living in the villages of the La Patria colony (Paraguayan Chaco) to the dramatic deforestation produced by the expansion of cattle ranches, the drastic reduction of their traditional territory, and the state's promotion of resource use practices in the surrounding ranches that are incompatible with their livelihood, focusing on the 1995–2015 period. Drawing on political ecology and political ontology and making good use of innovative cartographic software, it examines changes in the group's "cosmographical practices" (rituals, livelihood strategies, and land use patterns), the resulting internal tensions or conflicts, and the negative impact of the interventions of "Indigenist" NGOs. It puts forward the notion of "adaptive resistance" to account for these often contradictory changes and their disempowering effects. The work is a solid contribution to the literature on territorial dispossession in Chaco, and adds deep ideas to the ongoing discussion of the classic "hunter-gatherers" categorization. [FB]

312 Glauser Ortiz, Marcos; Rodrigo Villagra Carron; and **Claudio Basabe Ramírez.** El territorio Yshir a partir de las comunidades del distrito de Bahía Negra y su reclamo actual: una cartografía de su economía y ecología humanas. Asunción: Tierra viva a los pueblos indígenas del Chaco: Centro de Estudios Antropológicos de la Universidad Católica (CEADUC), 2021. 130 p.: ill., photos. (Biblioteca Paraguaya de Antropología; 114)

Report of a research project carried out between 2018 and 2021 in four Yshir villages located in upper Paraguay, aimed at documenting the territorial problems of the area. Studies the limits of the original Yshir territory, its recent deforestation, and provides extensive data and Indigenous accounts of their notions about the land, their economic activities, the native toponymy, the territorial management carried out by the Indigenous organization Unión de Comunidades Indígenas de la Nación Yshir, and the territorial claims that it promotes. Includes useful maps and statistical charts. Mostly a general overview of Yshir's territories on the upper Paraguay river with some notes on their oral history; devoid of any general analysis, it will be useful as source of data for researchers interested in Lowlands or Chaco's Indigenous territoriality or land struggles. [FB]

313 Gómez, Cecilia P. Ciclos temporales y su relación con el cielo entre los tobas del oeste formoseño. (*Cosmovisiones*, 1:1, 2020, p. 53–71, bibl., graph)

The paper studies the temporal cycles known by the Qom of Western Formosa (Argentine Chaco): their relation to celestial configurations, environmental changes (in particular the appearance and song of certain birds), ancient ritual life, their Christian-inspired reinterpretations, their uses as chronological references and their intersections with the Western calendar. It traces these notions in the Qom common knowledge on the environment and the sky and in their mythology. The brief analysis focuses on the Pleiades and the moon to sketch an interesting masculine/feminine symbolic contrast operating in those cycles. [FB]

314 Grünewald, Leif. "Apenas pobres": um conceito antropológico de pobreza do ponto de vista ayoreo (alto Paraguay). (*Maloca/Campinas*, 3, 2020, p. 1–19, bibl.)

Drawing from Marilyn Strathern's "esthetic of relations" and Viveiros de Castro's perspectivism, this piece analyzes the notion of "poverty" that underlies the self-identification of Ayoreo leaders as "poor." Based on fieldwork carried out in villages of Upper Paraguay River, it traces its genealogy to the identification of the missionaries as representatives of the demiurge Dupade, the changes promoted in relational regimes by the Salesians, their division of baptized and nonbaptized Ayoreo (the latter considered first "savages" and later "poor") and, fundamentally, the changes that took place after the departure of the missionaries and their transfer to other regions of upper Paraguay. It presents the notion of "poverty" as that of a transformation of status and relations, a means to project themselves onto the surrounding society. Theoretically grounded, it provides data and ideas on the Chaco missionization, revivalist movements and the "becoming white" debate in South American Lowlands. [FB]

315 Gurven, Michael et al. Does market integration buffer risk, erode traditional sharing practices and increase inequality?: a test among Bolivian forager-farmers. (*Hum. Ecol.*, 43:4, Aug. 2015, p. 515–530, bibl., graphs, tables)

Sharing and trading are common ways for people in rural Amazonia to reduce the risk of food shortages. Indigenous societies based on equality have found a new way to deal with risk with the rise of markets and the commercialization of their produce. However, this new lifeway can potentially destroy the established authority and domestic production networks. Gurven and associates report the results of their study on whether market involvement shields the Tsimane of the Bolivian Amazon from food insecurity and reduces their habitual pattern of shared feeding. The authors say that higher incomes and wealth among the Tsimane were not linked to food dependence on others or reciprocity. However, wealth was linked to the amount of food shared with others (deemed "providing intensity") and the number of people it was shared with (labeled "sharing breadth"). Although higher total income was linked to less reciprocity, giving intensity and sharing range between Tsimane villages were related to differences in income. While increasing market integration did not always replace traditional buffering strategies, it often raised social capital. [BD]

316 Hirsch, Silvia María; Ingrid Müller; and Laura Pérez. Desigualdades, discriminación y muerte: vivir la pandemia en los barrios Qom del Area Metropolitana Gran Resistencia, provincia de Chaco. (*Rev. Esc. Antropol.*, 28, Jan./June 2021, p. 1–28, bibl.)

Based on research conducted during the pandemic, the authors study the impact of the lockdown measures and the presence of COVID-19 in an urban Qom neighborhood in the province of Chaco. The lack of adequate infrastructure, a history of territorial dispossession and tense inter-ethnic relations, in addition to situations of structural violence, and the presence of chronic diseases, heightened the impact of the virus. [SH]

317 Hirtzel, Vincent. Entre política identitaria y narrativas autobiográficas: restituciones digitales de un proyecto de documentación lingüística en Bolivia

(Proyecto DoBeS Yurakaré 2006–2011). (*J. Soc. am.*, 107:1, 2021, p. 151–185)

Detailed account of the activities carried out between 2006 and 2011 by the DoBeS project (*Dokumentation Bedrohter Sprachen*) dedicated to documenting the Yurakaré language (Cochabamba and Beni departments, Bolivia). The article recounts how the Educational Council of the Yuracaré people used this project to seek an "identitary coming out," reinforcing a singular "national" identity to compensate for the large dispersion of this population. The study contrasts the notion of "culture" in the leaders' statements with the complex interests underlying the accounts of the footmen who actually collaborated with the project. It offers a good case study of the internal dilemmas of Bolivian Indigenous Councils after the rise of Evo Morales and his declaration of Bolivia as a "plurinational state." [FB]

318 **Horn, Philipp.** Diverse articulation of urban Indigeneity among Lowland Indigenous groups in Santa Cruz, Bolivia. (*Bull. Lat. Am. Res.*, 41:1, Sept. 2021, p. 37–52, bibl.)

Author addresses urban experiences of Lowland groups of eastern Bolivia who are settled in an urban context in Santa Cruz city. Traces the history and causes of Lowland Indigenous urbanization, and the way Indigenous rights have been denied in this context. The author takes an intracategorical intersectionality approach in order to address the dynamic character of identities in an urban context. Addresses how elderly leaders, mostly men, hold power, while downplaying the role and problems faced by young urban Indigenous women. [SH]

319 **Jabin, David.** Sédentariser les morts: conservation des os et évangélisation chez les Yuqui d'Amazonie. (*in* Valeurs et matérialité: approches anthropologiques. Édité par Frédéric Keck. Paris: Editions Rue d'Ulm Musée du quai Branly, 2019, p. 111–126)

Based on fieldwork carried out during various trips between 2004 and 2018, this article investigates the changes in the funerary practices and beliefs of the Yuqui (Bolivian Amazonia) upon their settlement in the New Tribes missions of the Chapare region between the end of the 1960s and the beginning of the 1990s. It points out a three-stage periodization of this process: the time when the bones were preserved and transported on the move; the burial in unidentified graves near the homes; and the burial in identified graves grouped in a sui generis cemetery. It shows that, below these ritual changes, the Yuqui have kept the same close relationship with the material remains of the deceased. It offers a brief overview of the little-known Yuqui ethnohistory, the peculiar social hierarchy of their groups, and the relationship between the practice of slavery and eschatological beliefs. [FB]

320 **Keller, Héctor.** La fotosíntesis de la cultura: estudios etnobiológicos en comunidades guaraníes de Misiones, Argentina. Asunción: Centro de Estudios Antropológicos de la Universidad Católica (CEADUC), 2017. 581 p.: bibl., ill. (Biblioteca paraguaya de antropología; 106)

Research on the ethnobotany of the Mbya-Guaraní, the chapters are organized by addressing the life cycles and plants used in each stage of life. Includes narratives in Guaraní language, as well as explanations of the uses of the plants for healing and rituals—and as part of the cosmology. [SH]

321 **Kidd, Stephen; Ian Skoggard; and Rodrigo Villagra Carron.** Love and its entanglements among the Enxet of Paraguay: social and kinship relations within a market economy. Lanham, Md.: Lexington Books, 2021. 298 p.: bibl., ill., index. (Anthropology of well-being: individual, community, society)

The core idea of the book is that the study of Enxet emotions through daily interactions provides the key for a deep understanding of the group's main areas of social life: economy, kinship, leadership, shamanism, etc. This close look at Enxet emotions expressed in everyday discourses provides an important insight into the contradictions and adjustments of the Indigenous dealing with deprived conditions of life in a context of latifundia, procommodities, and agrocapitalist economy promoted by the Paraguayan state. Enxet perspectives about their life in this context are analyzed through daily linguistic interactions, revealing a complex worldview from particular situations and individual points of view that are often contradictory. The book traces extensive comparisons between this and other Chaco and Amazonia groups. [FB]

322 Leavy, Pia and **Andrea Szulc.** Cuidando a los niños y niñas, cuidando el territorio: una mirada etnográfica sobre las comunidades rurales mapuche y ava-guaraní en Argentina. (*Indiana/Berlin*, 38:1, 2021, p. 79–101, bibl.)

This article compares care practices of children among the Guaraní and Mapuche of Argentina. It highlights the autonomy of children's activities and behavior in rural communities and the participation of children within the domestic sphere as caretakers of younger children. Furthermore, children participate in everyday communal activities. The article contributes to the growing field of studies of caring. [SH]

323 López, Alejandro Martín. Sobre torbellinos y otros aire: vientos y poder entre los Guaycurú del Chaco. (*in* Vida bajo el cielo estrellado: la arqueoastronomía y etnoastronomía en Latinoamérica. Edición de Stanislaw Iwaniszewski y Ricardo Moyano Vasconcellos. Warsaw, Poland: Wydawnictwa Uniwersytetu Warzawskiego, 2021, p. 275–285)

Analyzes 18th-century Jesuit accounts of Argentine Chaco Guaycurú's (currently Qom, Moqoit and Pilagá) notions about atmospheric phenomena in light of the author's own ethnographical findings on the Moqoit worldview. Drawing on the "ontological turn," it points out, behind the missionaries' "demonizing" or antishamanic readings of the Indigenous beliefs, the hints of a cosmography made of asymmetrical power relations between humans and non-humans, according to which those phenomena are considered intentional manifestations of powerful beings. [FB]

324 Lowrey, Kathleen Bolling. Shamanism and vulnerability on the North and South American Great Plains. Louisville: University Press of Colorado, 2020. 228 p.: bibl., ill., index, maps.

The book is based on research carried out by the author among the Guaraní of the Bolivian Isoso between 1997 and 2019, and between 2005 and 2009 among the western Guaraní of the Paraguayan Chaco; and, to a lesser extent, on the study of first-hand ethnohistorical sources (particularly regarding the 1892 Kuruyuki massacre, here compared in length to Wounded Knee and the Ghost Dance movement to show parallels between scientific and popular representations about Native groups of Chaco and the North American Great Plains). It applies notions from disability studies to analyze Isoseño shamanism and larger fields of Indigenous social life in Chaco, namely political organizations and their relation with the state and NGOs, aiming to highlight "feminine" aspects that, it claims, have been disregarded by mainstream scopes and official Indigenous self-representations (focused on "masculine" aspects): solidarity, family life, conviviality, caring and, above all, vulnerability and dependency. Provides nuanced ideas about revitalization movements and Indigenous struggles, such as "agency," "resistance," "self-determination," and "autonomy." It offers interesting data and ideas on these processes, shamanism, settler colonialism, development projects, and the relation between Indigenous mobilization and Western institutions. [FB]

325 La misión de la máquina: técnica, extractivismo y conversión en las tierras bajas sudamericanas. Edición de Nicolas Richard, Zelda Alice Franceschi y Lorena Córdoba. Bologna, Italy: Bononia University Press, 2021. 283 p.: bibl., ill. (DiSCi. Studi antropologici, orientali, storico-religiosi; 7)

This book gathers 13 papers by researchers from different countries and disciplines studying Indigenous peoples' encounters with Western technology in the context of missionization in Chaco, Bolivian Amazonia, and the Paraná forests of Paraguay, from the late 19th century until today. Focuses on the role played by the technologies of colonization, their residual transference towards the Indigenous societies and their resignifications: technologies of exploration, industrial exploitation, war and, above all, of "pacification" in religious missions. Villar analyzes the role played by ships in the colonization of Bolivian Amazonia; Córdoba studies the trafficking of weapons obtained in the fields of the Chaco War; Scardozzi the relationship between the Anglican missions and the sugar mills, and Bonifacio between the Anglican ones and the lumber industry in Paraguay; Franceschi, Guiteras Mombiola, and Barbosa examine the "socialization" in the schools of the Chaco, the Bolivian Amazon, and the Paraná forest; Preci then takes on the problems of the Liberation Theology missionaries in the 1960s; and Richard and Hernández address the technology transfer from the Catholic missions to the Nivaclé in the 1980s. Most of the historical chapters are based on ethnographical knowledge of the regions and inspired by current and vital ethnological questions. An important contribution to a subject rarely addressed. [FB]

326 **Montani, Rodrigo** and **Zelda A. Franceschi.** Wichí: la gente, el mundo, la palabra. (*Rev. Mus. Antropol./Córdoba*, 13:3, 2020, p. 1–14, bibl., map)

This journal issue is almost entirely devoted to ethnological papers on the Wichí of Argentine Chaco. J. Palmer analyzes the problems they face when dealing with the state, focusing on the issue of translation in trials; Z. Franceschi displays and studies Wichí women's life stories; C. Gómez reviews their cosmography and cycles; E. Suárez focuses on their botanical ethnomorphology; and A. Preci analyzes the translation of technical terms by young Wichí students. It also includes pieces by historians (I. Combès on the late 19th-century Franciscan missions of southern Bolivia; Combès and Montani on the first-known Wichí dictionary), geographers and economists (E. Zepharovich and G. Ceddia on the ideological takes on the deforestation of former Wichí territories), and linguists (V. Nercesian on the Wichí dialects). The introduction by the editors offers a general overview of the collection and the ethnological state of art, advocating for a greater collaboration between ethnography and linguistics. [FB]

327 **Morando, Agustina.** Corporalidad, emoción y discurso oral: un acercamiento a la noción de *pia* entre los Chanés del noroeste Argentino. (*Estud. Atacameños*, 67, 2021, p. 1–16, bibl.)

Focusing on how emotion is expressed in the Chané language of northwest Argentina, the study delves into how the term for "heart" embodies multiple ways of expressing emotion and corporality. It also analyzes the context of enunciation of this term. The author contributes to the growing field of sociolinguistic research in Lowland Argentina. [SH]

328 **Native peoples, politics, and society in contemporary Paraguay: multidisciplinary perspectives.** Edited by Barbara Ganson. Albuquerque: University of New Mexico Press, 2021. 175 p.: bibl., ill., index, maps, tables.

Concise interdisciplinary volume mostly on the impact of political changes on Indigenous peoples in Paraguay since the demise of the Stroessner government in 1989. Horst's chapter provides background on the participation of Indigenous peoples in national society, their lobby for constitutional changes, and their role in the demise of the Stroessner government. Reed addresses migration of Guarani to urban settings, and how this relates to land dispossession. Canova's chapter also addresses urban context, by looking at the labor experiences of the Ayoreo in a Mennonite colony. Other chapters take on a political analysis of the reform of the Paraguayan constitution, and relations between Paraguay and Mercosur. [SH]

329 **¡Que hermosa es tu voz!: relatos de los Enlhet sobre la historia de su pueblo.** Recopilación de Hannes Kalisch y Ernesto Unruh. Traducción y comentarios de Hannes Kalisch. Dibujos de Erna Ramírez. Asunción: Ya'alve-Saanga: Centro de Artes Visuales/Museo del Barro: Nengvaanemkeskama Nempayvaam Enlhet: Servilibro, 2020. 669 p.: bibl., ill., maps.

Spanish translation of *Wie schön ist deine Stimme* (2014), this volume compiles over 100 long accounts of Enlhet elders (Paraguayan Chaco) about the history of their people throughout the 20th century. These are displayed around different themes: the memories of free life in the original territory, the dramatic changes produced by the

Chaco War (1932–35, which took place on their lands) and by the arrival of Mennonites (in whose colonies many of them ended up living). The last 200 pages provide the historical context and in-depth analysis of those accounts. Complementing the editors' previous book on accounts about the Chaco War (see *HLAS 75:332*), this work represents a fundamental contribution to studies on ethnohistory, missionization, ethnic relations, and territorial dispossession of the Paraguayan Chaco. [FB]

330 **Reimagining the Gran Chaco: identities, politics, and the environment in South America.** Edited by Silvia Maria Hirsch, Paola Canova and Mercedes Biocca. Gainesville: University of Florida Press, 2021. 360 p.: bibl., index.

This timely edited volume contains 11 chapters (and an afterword by Gastón Gordillo) representing interdisciplinary scholarship, ranging from geography and history to anthropology and sociology; the contributions focus on the complex interplay of historical, social, political, and economic factors and how these impinge on Indigenous peoples and their relations with other actors, including non-Indigenous settlers, NGOs, state institutions, and political organizations. The book includes research on Argentina, Bolivia, and Paraguay, based on research conducted by the authors. The introduction by the editors constitutes a thorough panoramic view analyzing some of the most outstanding historical, political, and environmental situations which have characterized this vast ecosystem. Important contribution in English to the study of the Gran Chaco region. [SH]

331 **Rosso, Cintia N. and Gustavo F. Scarpa.** Etnobotánica médica moqoit y su comparación con grupos del Chaco argentino. (*Bol. Soc. Argent. Bot.*, 54:4, dic. 2019, p. 637–662, bibl., graphs, map, tables)

Based on systematic ethnographic research carried out in different Moqoit villages (Argentine Chaco) between 2008 and 2018, this ethnobiological piece offers a general view of medicinal plants known by the group. It presents a list of 155 species and their respective therapeutic uses (381 in total). The analysis of this data is strictly statistical: it points out the low percentage of coincidence among the Moqoit informants and between this list and botanical data offered by 18th-century Jesuit accounts; the study also indicates an intriguingly high percentage of coincidence with the ethnobotanical knowledge of the white settlers in western Chaco. The findings suggest that these statistical features could indicate a recent acquisition of many of these uses, received from migrant cotton workers. Despite the rather austere analysis, this may be the first scientific contribution to Moqoit therapeutic ethnobotany, and offers valuable data to researchers of Chaco shamanism and Lowlands ethnobotany. [FB]

332 **Ruiz, Irma.** La "conquista espiritual" no consumada: cosmología y rituales Mbyá-Guaraní. Quito: Abya Yala, 2018. 450 p.: bibl., graphs, ill., music.

The author has conducted extensive research among the Mbya-Guaraní of Argentina, focusing her studies on ritual performances, ethnomusicology, prayers, and chants. The focus on performance includes discussions of a variety of forms of communication, linguistic and nonlinguistic, such as dances, chants, and the use of material culture. In depth ethnographic account of the performance of religious rituals in everyday life. The study also includes an ethnohistorical account of the group and mythical narratives. Excellent contribution to literature on the ethnomusicology and ritual practice of the Mbya-Guaraní. [SH]

333 **Salinas, Cecilia.** Intervenciones temporales y la política de la tierra en la reserva de biosfera Yabotí. (*Etnogr. Contemp.*, 6:11, 2020, p. 134–158, bibl.)

Based on research conducted for her dissertation, Salinas focuses on the land situation of Mbya Guaraní community in Argentina who live in an area established as a biosphere reserve. The dispossession of lands has characterized the situation of the Guarani in Misiones province. The process of land grabbing affects their livelihood, and the author addresses how titling of lands is suspended for a period of time, thus delaying legal processes which endanger the subsistence of this Indigenous group. [SH]

334 Sturtevant, Chuck. Missions, unions, and Indigenous organization in the Bolivian Amazon: placing the formation of an Indigenous organization in its context. (*LARR*, 53:4, Dec. 2018, p. 770–784, bibl.)

Relying on oral narratives to recount the origin of the Mosetén Indigenous People's Organization/Organización del Pueblo Indígena Mosetén (OPIM) in Bolivia, the author emphasizes the linkages and similarities between Indigenous groups and the structures of political affiliation that precede them. A review of Indigenous political movements in Bolivia and beyond provides context to the Mosetén. The article contrasts local interpretations of social change, such as Don Braulio's, with scholarly viewpoints and public debates to achieve a "more nuanced understanding of Indigenous social movements." Mosetén people wanted to impose order on their communities and address local problems, which led to the first attempts to organize their communities. To do this, they adopted familiar modes of social organization, like the Franciscan missions and rural unions, and changed them to suit their needs. Mosetén memories of the mission time indicate their ambivalence, which manifests in more subtly expressed ways in their interactions with unions and NGOs. The political era of ethnic mobilization in the 1990s offered a chance to intensify the pursuit of Mosetén desires for cultural autonomy. Still, their internal community organizing activities and interactions with national institutions existed before that time. Initiatives to establish OPIM weren't a direct reaction to outsiders abusing Indigenous peoples, nor were they an effort by outsiders to co-opt Indigenous peoples; instead, they were an imaginative exercise that involved ongoing interactions among Mosetén aspirations, a specific historical and political context, and the creative leadership skills of the Mosetén people. [BD]

335 Tola, Florencia C. Ejercicios comparativos sobre la 'locura' en el Chaco Argentino. (*Anthropol. Dep. Cienc. Soc.*, 45, 2020, p. 63–84, bibl.)

Analyzes three cases of "mental illness" among the Qom (Argentine Chaco): the altered state of a woman who kept repeating the name of a dead relative, and thus considered to be a "witch" killer; the catatonic state of a young man caused by an encounter with a nocturnal nonhuman being; the disturbing visions of a shaman during the stage of his initiation. Drawing from the "ontological" theorists, it contrasts the Qom accounts and explanations (referring to invisible realities and etiologies) with the medical diagnoses, and analyzes them as examples of conceptions of the person and the world different from the Western and modern: a "porous" and multiple human being living together with nonhuman persons. [FB]

Highlands

ISABEL M. SCARBOROUGH, *Professor of Anthropology, Parkland College*

GENERAL

336 Beauclair, Nicolas. Éticas indígenas de los Andes y de Quebec: aportes a filosofías interculturales en las Américas. Quito: Abya Yala; Sherbrook, Canada: SoDRUS, Centre de recherche Société, Droit et Religions, 2016. 205 p.: bibl.

The current global environmental crisis together with massive movements of people and goods across territories have led to dramatic changes in Latin America's Indigenous communities. Beauclair notes that technology, industry, and capitalism are out of control in the Americas and proposes a new ethics implemented by political movements as a possible solution. The author's search for this new ethical understanding whose core lies within existing Indigenous groups is based on reading some of the first documented narratives of ethical thought in the Americas. The book compares the thinking presented in the Huarochirí manuscript and the chronicles recorded by Pachakuti Yamqui Salcamaygua in Andean Peru in the 1610s, to the narratives on the Indigenous peoples of the Quebec region reported by Jesuit missionaries Paul Lejeune and Jean de Brébeuf in 1630. The author notes that these texts represent the voices of both the colonized and colonizers, and that the line dividing colonizing from adoption is very fine. Beauclair exercises reflexivity and is aware of the power differential created by his own positionality regarding the Indigenous communities. The author concludes that the guiding ethic of Andean Indigenous communities is a philosophy of reciprocity, while the natives of the Quebec region believe in a philosophy and ethics of respect. Both these ethical beliefs are still present in the Andes and Quebecois regions. Beauclair encourages a dialogue between Western ontologies and these native schools of thought on ethics. Beauclair provides a thorough analysis of the archival texts and proposes an ethical philosophy that takes into consideration the earliest records from the original inhabitants.

337 Complejidad de la arqueología y el turismo cultural: territorios, sostenibilidad y patrimonio. Edición de Eduardo Forero Lloreda, Carlos Eduardo López Castaño y Carlos Eduardo Maldonado. Bogotá: Editorial Universidad del Rosario, 2009. 147 p.: bibl. (Colección Complejidad / Facultad de Administración)

This collection of essays on archeology and cultural heritage opens with contributions from the three coeditors. Forero surveys Mesoamerican archeology and explains how the study of archeological heritage contributed to the creation of the Latin American imaginary of the modern nation-state. He also critiques the traditional narrative of precolumbian civilizations: marked apogee followed by decay and collapse. He argues for a new approach to Latin American archeology that would abandon the positivist and processual theories imported from First World academia and focus local scholarship and new interpretations of the past. López builds on this and adds that paleontology and archeology are important for a better understanding of the deep past of this part of the world. Maldonado reflects on heritage tourism at archeological sites as the new motor of cultural policies. He asks that Latin American scholars break away from the deterministic school that was imposed on archeologists of the Global South. He calls for a participatory and diverse archeology that would inform local archeologists of the colonialist issues of past theoretical frameworks and teach them about pertinent legislation on cultural preservation. These theoretical contributions are followed by case studies from Colombia, Peru, Mexico and Argentina. Of these, the most notable is the study by María Gabriela Chaparro and Silvia Susana Soria, both Argentinian anthropologists, that describes the Inca ruins of Santa Rosa de Tastil near Jujuy. Despite being designated as a national historic landmark, the site has no help from the state and so little oversight that tourists trample the archeological features and take artifacts from the archeological park. The volume initiates an important conversation on heritage tourism and sustainability for out-of-the-way and smaller-scale archeological attractions in the Andes.

338 Orrego Echeverría, Israel Arturo. Ontología relacional del tiempo-espacio andino: diálogos con Martin Heidegger. Bogotá: Ediciones USTA, 2018. 256 p.: bibl., ill.

This volume ventures into both Western philosophy and the worldview of *abya yala* of the Andean Indigenous peoples. Orrego demonstrates how Andean thinking has a tradition of engaging and establishing conversations between its own ancestral ways of knowing and contemporary philosophies. Identifying as Indigenous is a way of being that has a history of denial and erasure. Further, indigeneity is framed within a dichotomy of the colonized and the colonizer, where the former is invisible and voiceless. Because of this, Orrego urges Andean intellectuals to break with the notion that Indigenous ways of thinking cannot be considered ontologies in their own right and stop mimicking Western ontologies. The author does not seek a way of being that is Andean; rather, he explores the senses in order to reveal where this Andean being is situated. Martin Heidegger's theories on being and authenticity, rooted in everyday life experiences, can help chart a path to a new way of being. In this book, Orrego leads the reader through an exploration of time and space in the Andes and concludes with the logic of *buen vivir* that has been presented as an alternative to Western development ideologies. While Western and Eurocentric development unravels the relational bonds of the ecosystem, he argues that *buen vivir* seeks to make connections with the environment and with the bonds created by a complementarity between the Aymara *Jiwa*, or death, and *Jaka*, or life. Thus, death, unlike Heidegger's understanding, is not the end of all temporality for the self, but a new way of experiencing movement, action, and opening. With this novel analysis and approach to the idea of *buen vivir*, the author contributes to a better understanding of this philosophy and its construction within Andean Indigenous communities.

339 **Vilar, José Rafael.** Auge y caída del socialismo del siglo XXI: una rápida visión hispanoamericana de sus recientes ciclos políticos y del fracaso de ideologizar la economía. La Paz: Plural Editores, 2017. 278 p.: bibl., ill. (some color).

In this book, political analyst Vilar offers a succinct narrative of Latin America's different versions of national socialism in the 21st century. Vilar centers this volume on the contrast between ideological narratives and political practices as, he argues, it is only by examining these differences that we can begin to understand the true impact of these movements. The book is not a history, but an exploration of the processes that led to the emergence of socialism in the region. Vilar attempts to show the political precedents of the movement and thus explain its achievements and failures. The author states that his analysis derives from an anti-populist and anti-authoritarian stance. Vilar takes the reader on a journey through the political highlights of communist Cuba in the 1960s, the right-wing military dictatorships of the 1970s in South America, and the return to democracy in these same countries in the 1980s. He then breaks down the "lost decade" of the 1990s (p. 14), the period that introduces neoliberalism to the region and triggers a structural economic crisis in every country, with a system that is proven to be unfair and inequitable. The region, he explains, was thus ripe for the Bolivarian Revolution. Vilar traces the ideological foundations for this revolution to leading Cuban socialists, European 21st century ideologues, and Brazilian intellectuals. More importantly, he produces an analysis of why the Bolivarian Revolution failed due to populism. Vilar supports his argument by detailing how this brand was built on a shaky foundation of myths, fake news, and the media's rewriting of history with a narrative centered on the victimization of the people it was meant to liberate. The book provides the political backstory of Latin America's socialist revolution in the 21st century which, despite its intellectual origins, was based on appealing to people's emotions, as well as to their sense of survival.

ARGENTINA

340 **Antropolocales: estudios de antropología en Jujuy.** Compilación de Marisel Arrueta *et al.* San Salvador de Jujuy, Argentina: Colegio de Graduados en Antropología de Jujuy: Universidad Nacional de Jujuy, 2017. 263 p.: bibl., ill. (Colección "Producción científica". Serie "Resultados")

This collection presents research essays by graduates of the anthropology program at the Universidad Nacional de Jujuy in northern Argentina. The works introduce ethnographies and literature reviews from this budding academic site, and also showcase a growing awareness of social justice in the region, wherein lies its most relevant contribution to South American ethnology.

The first section provides a comprehensive historical review of the violation of rights and demands for the autonomy of Indigenous peoples in the region and Latin America more broadly. The second section is dedicated to defining land and territory and creating a theoretical framework to justify the creation of Indigenous territories in Jujuy. The third section includes chapters that are more ethnographic and provide relevant case studies on the plight of Indigenous Jujuy peoples in the 21st century. These narratives examine Indigenous workers in local mining, Indigenous women hourly workers in the tobacco industry, and the use of recreational drugs among Indigenous youth. The last two sections demonstrate the systemic oppression and injustice faced by Indigenous peoples. The essays provide a fresh take on classic ethnography from a promising group of young scholars.

341 Pinassi, Andrés. Patrimonio cultural, turismo y recreación: el espacio vivido de los bahienses desde una perspectiva geográfica. Bahía Blanca, Argentina: EdiUNS, 2017. 404 p.: bibl., ill. (Serie Extensión. Colección Estudios sociales y humanidades)

Based on Pinassi's doctoral research, this work provides a wealth of data from in-depth interviews, surveys, and historical information on the state of cultural resource management and heritage tourism in the city of Bahía Blanca, Argentina. The definition of heritage, which implies preserving or documenting a legacy for future generations, also assumes that what is valued will vary in different communities. The author's detailed descriptions of Bahía Blanca and his collected oral histories on heritage tourism are valuable to scholars of this topic and of the Argentine social imaginary. Of special note is the discussion of cultural tourism and how its presence can provide authenticity, as well as a source of income, to a community, helping preserve or support specific aspects of community identity. Pinassi's book also analyzes cultural appropriation and the consumption of recreational tourism by Argentine society. The Bahía Blanca residents who participate in Pinassi's study cut across social lines and generations to unveil how local communities frequently have little control over their documented history. Pinassi's focus in the latter part of the book is the manipulation of space and Bahía Blanca's urban planning process. Pinassi concludes with a call for participatory projects that take into consideration the ideas and identities of the people represented in tourist attractions. The volume is an excellent contribution to the growing body of literature on heritage in South America, providing a case study that foregrounds the voices of the community.

BOLIVIA

342 Bold, Rosalyn. *Vivir bien*: a study in alterity. (*Lat. Am. Caribb. Ethn. Stud.*, 12:2, July 2017, p. 113–132, bibl.)

The author questions and breaks down idealized perspectives of indigeneity through the concept of *vivir bien* which, Bold argues, fetishizes the Indigenous rural Other in Highland Bolivia. The article explains how contemporary Bolivians identify their nation within dichotomous white/Indigenous, colonizer/colonized, and capitalist/noncapitalist tropes. The concept of *vivir bien*, which roughly translates to "living well," was adopted by urban Bolivian intellectuals in the 1990s as an alternative to neoliberal capitalism and offered a romanticized vision of the rural countryside and its Indigenous residents. The reality of Bolivia's countryside is very different. Far from being the noble savages depicted by popular media and the government, rural Indigenous youth mimic the West and migrate to urban areas to better engage with technology and consumerism. Bold argues that the notion of *vivir bien* collapses when the experiences of Indigenous rural migrants are scrutinized. Bold provides a case study of a tourism project designed by a key ideologue of *vivir bien* with funding from the Swiss Agency for Development and Cooperation (SDC). The author observed the project's planning stage and notes how the idealized alterity of indigeneity advocated by *vivir bien* reproduced familiar stereotypes of a powerless developing world. *Vivir bien* is a key part of Bolivia's new plurinational state constitution and is defined as the "non-separation of humans from their surrounding landscapes and the absence of capitalism" (p. 114). Bold challenges this definition with several examples that illustrate how animism is changing and disappearing in the highlands, where younger generations no longer pay attention to rituals linked to the landscapes as these are drastically transformed by climate change. Similarly, capitalism and the cash economy have almost completely replaced the traditional reciprocal exchanges, or *ayni*, as income flows to the countryside from the cities and from the production of coca in the tropics. Further, thanks to technology, the peripheral areas experience elements of Western culture at the same time as the center, or the cities. Because of this, the periphery is now destabilized, and the identity continuum from Indigenous to mestizo to white that defined Bolivians for centuries has become disrupted and deterritorialized. Bold concludes that *vivir bien* gazes from the city to the rural areas that it idealizes—oblivious to the changes taking place in the countryside—while at the same time presenting the more Westernized urban life as more valuable. Anthropologists understand the limitations of "static and ahistorical perspectives" (p. 129). Bold urges scholars to address *vivir bien* as one such perspective.

343 Cereceda, Verónica. De los ojos hacia el alma. La Paz: Plural Editores, 2017. 280 p.: bibl.. ill. (some color).

This beautifully crafted collection of essays showcases 50 years of ethnographic work among the Aymara and Uru-Chipayas of the Bolivian and Chilean highlands. Cereceda has made the study of these communities her life's work. She leads us on a journey among the utilitarian and specialized textiles that mark everyday experiences, as well as milestones of the agricultural cycle and its connection to myth and the divine. Only one of the essays had been previously published in Bolivia and now Cereceda's work is available for a new generation of scholars and for those with roots in the Indigenous communities to enjoy and learn from. As befits a book on textiles, the essays are punctuated with photographs and illustrations that provide the reader with visual representations of the textures and dyes that Cereceda describes in her work. The fieldwork for a couple of these articles was carried out in the 1970s, which only enhances the value of these studies as they provide a snapshot of the now dramatically changed lifestyles and customs of the Indigenous groups at the border of Bolivia with Chile. Cereceda narrates how the *talegas* or bags used to carry utensils, food, and tools create a dialogue between the hearth, the fields, and the storage sheds. The women weave a design where half of the *talega* represents the light (white) and the other half (dark) represents night. This duality and complementarity are also observed in the use of different earth tones and widths in the striping. Cereceda also delves into aspects of Andean animism and how colors can represent animals which can bring good fortune and fertility. One of her essays is centered on the *allqamari*, a bird of passage with distinct coloring whose sighting aids the most destitute as life is a matter of balance and equity. Cereceda's work among the Uru-Chipaya is strikingly depicted through her narrative and the work's illustrations. Cereceda notes the poverty and suffering among the Uru-Chipaya people, a product of centuries of isolation and exclusion, while at the same time she highlights the beauty and art found in their crafts and their relationship with the surrounding landscape. She follows this essay with a retelling of myths from the Uru-Chipaya that she heard in the field and found through archival research. She connects the semantics of these myths to the language of the textiles and weavings of these people. The visual codes noted by Cereceda tell a story of resistance and resilience, and of a production of beauty and harmony in some of the most desolate and arid corners of the planet. This book is highly recommended for anyone interested in Andean textiles and their connection to the divine and quotidian lived experiences. Cereceda's storytelling is superb, as are her theoretical musings as she reveals the meanings held in these weavings.

344 Crabtree, John. Indigenous empowerment in Evo Morales's Bolivia. (*Curr. Hist.*, 116:787, Feb. 2017, p. 55–60)

Crabtree's work begins with a summary of Bolivia's Indigenous uprisings from the 16th and 19th century, through the Indigenous political movements of the 1970s and 1980s, and ends with Evo Morales' Movimiento al Socialismo (MAS). The latter brought disparate social movements together for the defense of natural resources. Indeed, Morales' first election in 2005 was considered a milestone in the expansion of influence of Indigenous peoples globally. The UN and other similar forums helped the MAS assert a pro-Indigenous agenda worldwide, including the propagation of the notion of *vivir bien* as an alternative development parameter. However, this pro-Indigenous element of the Morales regime over time gave way to policies grounded in nationalism and state building. This was evident in the clash that this administration had with the Tipnis dispute, during which Lowland Indigenous peoples protested the plans to build a road and a national park within Indigenous territory. The conflict was exacerbated by the coca grower unions—Morales' syndicates which he continued to lead—which aimed to claim some of the protected territory. The Tipnis revealed that the government's economic agenda was increasingly driven by extractivist industries. The Bolivian example, Crabtree concludes, might have provided inspiration to other Latin American countries but, in practice, its impact on advancing pro-Indigenous policies was limited.

345 **Makaran, Gaya** and **Pabel López.**
Recolonización en Bolivia: neonacionalismo extractivista y resistencia comunitaria. Ciudad de México: UNAM, Centro de Investigaciones sobre América Latina y el Caribe: Bajo Tierra Ediciones, 2018. 351 p.: bibl., facsimiles, ill., maps, tables.

An excellent analysis of the state of indigeneity in Bolivia 15 years after the election of Evo Morales and the efforts of the Movimiento al Socialismo (MAS) to lead the majority Indigenous population of this small Andean nation into a new era of equity and decolonization. Both authors are united in the struggle against dispossession, authoritarianism, and the commercialization of life. They conclude that the MAS administration, over four terms, is implementing a recolonization process in the country due to a need to maintain ties to the multinational extractivist corporations that fund the nation-state apparatus. The defense of the nature preserve and Indigenous territory of the TIPNIS in the Bolivian Amazonian Lowlands has been spearheaded by a number of Indigenous Lowland communities who continue to protest the building of a road that would cross this territory for the benefit of mining and logging corporations. This clear anti-Indigenous and neocapitalist policy contrasts with the pro-Indigenous narrative and brand that the MAS has displayed to the democratic world. The authors build on the work of Bolivian intellectuals such as Luis Tapia, who argues that inequity and exploitation are being created anew by the MAS, hidden behind mechanisms that reorganize existing hierarchies and create new ones to gatekeep, exclude, and impose a hegemonic view in a de facto colonizing strategy. Bolivian sociologist Silvia Rivera Cusicanqui's work is the other pillar on which this book's argument is based. Rivera dubs the MAS administration as the creator of an internal colonialism which is woven into state relations and branded by a new anti-Indigenous offensive in which Lowland native communities are targeted for lands desired by foreign extractivist companies. The authors argue that the MAS' neonationalism labels itself as Indigenous, yet exploits a majority of self-identifying Indigenous who do not subscribe to the party politics. This situation, they note, is no different from that of several Bolivian administrations throughout the 19th and 20th centuries who imposed civilizing imported models for the state that were ended at the beginning of the millennium by a surge in social movements. The TIPNIS protest movement attempts to do the same with the MAS and its policies. The value of this book lies in its history of identity politics in Bolivia. Makaran and López provide a valuable and incisive analysis of the current socioeconomic and political issues that have transformed the early decolonization projects of the MAS administration into a state-based process that is the direct opposite of the shared ideals on which this party was based and elected.

CHILE

346 Castro R., Victoria. Etnoarqueologías andinas. Con la ayuda de Carlos Aldunate y José Berenguer et al. Santiago de Chile: Ediciones Universidad Alberto Hurtado, 2016. 490 p.: bibl., ill. (Colección Antropología)

This collection presents a valuable compilation of ethnographic and archeological research that provide a survey of the studies on past and present native peoples in northern Chile. The region's cultural heritage and the connections to the past are laid out in 15 chapters from the earliest precolumbian settlements to the present. The first three chapters exemplify the connections between archeology and ethnography. One chapter notes how the depictions of the *apus*, or spirits living in the surrounding mountain peaks, in archeological features are reflected in contemporary Indigenous beliefs about these same spirits. Ethnographic interviews about death and funeral practices are connected, in turn, with a vast archeological study of the *chullpas*, or mummified bodies, in Likán, and with current syncretic religious practices within the Catholic Church. Other chapters showcase archeological evidence of ancient trade with the Titikaka region, establish the unique characteristics of the Likán *chullpas* compared to other Atacama archeological sites, and describe the relation of the Inka ruler to local and regional towns from a study of purposeful architecture. There are more connections established between the past and present by two excellent chapters on rock art and the engagement of current communities with these paintings, that are further complicated with issues of preservation and the damage caused by tourism. Other chapters describe the significance of oral histories and how reciprocal relations or the concept of *ayni* can shed light on the use of architectural and archeological features and their relation to the landscape. In the Andes, quotidian agricultural practices are linked to the sacred and this vertical complementarity is translated into a new application of Murra's work on trade. Everyday interpretations of symbols and the practice of animism with icons, and their role in propitiating good crops, are analyzed in other essays in this collection, along with in-depth case studies about the complementarity of male and female in the Andean world. This collection is a much awaited and important contribution to understanding a region at the crossroads of the desert Atacama ethnic groups and the Highland groups that originated with the Aymara. The works teach about these people's social organization, and how they integrate their perception of nature with their everyday lives and the cultural landscapes that have built their shared imaginaries.

Ennis, Juan Antonio. Robert Lehmann-Nitsche y Rudolf Lenz: epistolario (1897–1928). See item **308**.

347 Gaitán-Barrera, Alejandra and Govand Khalid Azeez. Beyond recognition: autonomy, the state, and the Mapuche Coordinadora Arauco Malleco. (*Lat. Am. Caribb. Ethn. Stud.*, 13:2, July 2018, p. 113–134, bibl.)

This article argues for a new framework for Indigenous mobilization in Latin America called "revindicative autonomy." The authors provide evidence from long-term ethnographic fieldwork with the Mapuche anti-extractivism movement in Chile and in-depth interviews with Mapuche leaders who explain the struggle of the Mapuche people against multiculturalism and differentiated citizenship in leftist Chilean administrations. The latter, albeit well-meaning, continue to uphold the structure responsible for more than a century of land dispossession and assimilation imposed on the Mapuche. The authors challenge the mistaken perceptions scholars have of the activist movement led by the Coordinadora Arauco Malleco (CAM), as its difference from other Latin American Indigenous social movements lies in its "anti-statist, anti-systemic, anti-capitalist, anti-Western, anti-Christian, non-leftist, and non-anarchist" characteristics (p. 115). The movement has become stronger in the past decade and is responsible for the resurgence of violent tactics as a strategy of decolonization and declaration of war by CAM against multinational extractivist corporations, the Chilean landed elite, and the Chilean state. CAM's aim is not a secessionist state, but rather the return to a precolonial Mapuche governing structure. This notion of a true or revindicative autonomy has been discussed within the identity politics literature in Latin America. The use of Mapuche activist movements as a case study is a novel contribution to this body of intellectual production.

348 Maza, Francisca de la. Tourism in Chile's Indigenous territories: the impact of public policies and tourism value of Indigenous culture. (*Lat. Am. Caribb. Ethn. Stud.*, 13:1, March 2018, p. 94–111, bibl.)

The aim of this article is two-fold; to address what happens when culture is objectified and given a value within the tourism industry, and to show how the commercialization of culture reveals contradictions and synergies in the claiming of Indigenous rights and territories. The author was part of a research team that carried out participant observation and in-depth interviews in several Mapuche communities targeted as part of a government tourism development project. In the article, she compares the findings of her research team with those of ethnographic studies examining the impact of tourism among the Indigenous Rapa Ñui of Easter Island and Likan Antay of Atacama. She analyzes three case studies, finding that public institutions encourage the use of Indigenous culture as a tourist attraction. In all three cases, the study found that Indigenous communities who desire tourism must adapt to its demands and preconceived notions of "authentic" indigeneity, including a desire for what de la Maza terms an "extreme otherness" (p. 106). That is, tourists are attracted to essentialized and romanticized versions of authentic Indigenous life enhanced by performances, use of language, and the deployment of traditional gastronomy. Indigenous communities perform these romanticized versions for tourist consumption. At the same time, all three communities understood the importance of tourism as a path to the political recognition of Indigenous peoples and have used touristic activities, with varying degrees of success, to improve their relations with the state and claim control over territory.

349 Tomaselli, Alexandra. El derecho a la consulta de los pueblos indígenas en Chile: avances y desafíos. (*Iberoamericana/Stockholm*, 43:1/2, 2013, p. 113–142, bibl., table)

The article focuses on the application of law to the right of prior consultation and how it impacts the Indigenous peoples in Chile. The right of consultation provides Chilean Indigenous peoples with the legal right to participate in the adoption of any public policies that could affect their well-being. The author argues that the enactment of this policy has provided Indigenous communities with protections under international law after a long history of displacement and dispossession. Further, the law provides steps for the protection of cultural practices and the restitution of cultural heritage and artifacts. Tomaselli breaks down these protections in terms of language and education, electoral and political processes, and community outreach for different Indigenous groups in Chile. She details how Indigenous protections and the right to consultancy became constitutional rights in 2011 and, even though there is a long way to go for full reparation and restitution of the harm done to Indigenous communities, the right to consultancy has opened the door to present these cases in court. Indeed, several cases heard by the Chilean courts, from local courts of appeal to the Chilean Supreme Court, have ruled in favor of Indigenous rights. The author provides a series of examples that show the protection of Indigenous water sources and land from the extractive practices of forestry, mining, and other commercial entities.

350 Zomo newen: relatos de vida de mujeres mapuche en su lucha por los derechos indígenas. Coordinación de Elisa García Mingo. Santiago: LOM Ediciones, 2017. 275 p.: bibl. (Ciencias sociales y humanas. Cultura y sociedad)

There are many ethnographies that set out to collaborate with members of a community and coauthor the results of a research project. However, not many manage to share the voices of the coauthors without drowning them in theory and analysis. Elisa García sets down the words and histories of eight Mapuche women and their struggles for Indigenous rights in Chile within the domestic spheres they manage. In eight chapters, García weaves ideas and theories that complement the contributions of these women to issues of Indigenous rights. The women's narratives are written in the first person, which provides a sense of intimacy and authenticity to the words of these Mapuche activists. The narratives highlight the triple discrimination against these women for being female, Indigenous, and poor. The women's ages range from very young to elderly and their education ranges from barely literate to holding graduate degrees. They share a hunger to learn more about their roots, and a need to recreate a Mapuche lifestyle that centers around nature, language, and community. Whether in the kitchen of a humble home in a rural town, working in the fields or vegetable gardens, broadcasting their message on radio shows, or at the lecturer's podium, they challenge Mapuche gender stereotypes of women as passive and limited to the domestic sphere. In a key contribution to the literature on life histories, García's opening chapter explores how the women's stories contribute to studies on indigeneity and gender performativity. She argues that Indigenous women suffer from an "analytical invisibility" (p. 18), in that they are used as foils to revisit male-centric theories or are ignored altogether. García's work highlights this gender gap and centers her study on the political struggles and social transformation in the region.

ECUADOR

351 Colloredo-Mansfeld, Rudi et al.
Conflicts, territories, and the institutionalization of post-agrarian economies on an expanding tourist frontier in Quilotoa, Ecuador. (*World Dev.*, 101, Jan. 2018, p. 441–452, bibl., graph, maps, tables)

The article reports on an international collaborative fieldwork project carried out in the Indigenous community of Quilotoa, including interviews, land-use observations, and community mapping. The purpose of the project is to study territorial practices in conflict with state policies to identify how Indigenous peoples in the Ecuadorian Andes regularize, defend, and authorize the use of resource conservation and tourist service areas. The work revisits community heritage conservation practices through the lens of Indigenous defense of territory. The authors trace the history of land use in the area and how the Indigenous communities residing near the Quilotoa crater and lake underwent a social shift after Ecuador's agrarian reform from Indigenous land cooperatives to unionized trade associations providing tourist services, and then back to a unified community providing these services based on traditional Indigenous practices. The authors explain how rural Indigenous people have traditionally asserted their territorial identities, which is how the Quilotoa community mobilized to appropriate the tourist industry that was imposed on them by the state in the early 2010s. The gradual loss of agricultural land due to parceling and climate change, combined with a massive amount of funding earmarked by the Ecuadorian government to advance the tourist agenda, resulted in an abrupt pivot to a new form of livelihood for the region, which quickly unraveled the peasant cooperatives or *comunas* that had held the land jointly after agrarian reform. More importantly, these *comunas* then transformed into political bases that could pursue rural development projects with NGOs and the state, as well as help negotiate the many challenges that came with a reorientation toward tourism. These challenges included "the fact that none of Quilotoa's residents had tourist-service skills, no one had capital to invest... [and] the community lacked electricity and potable water" (p. 444). Quilotoans, the authors explain, turned a situation which has often ended in disaster to their advantage despite breaking off some communal ties, thanks in part to strengthening ties among local families. Focusing their fight for territory and land claims in the Quilotoa area had many benefits, including helping women join the cash economy and enabling local youth to stay in the community instead of migrating to the cities. It remains to be seen whether these positive changes will endure given the continued inequalities and poverty of the broader region. Regardless, this analysis is a meaningful contribution to Andean ethnography and heritage studies.

352 **Ferraro, Emilia.** Materialidades, cuerpos y saberes: etnografías escogidas. Quito: Abya Yala, 2018. 192 p.: bibl., ill.

Emilia Ferraro is one of Ecuador's best regarded cultural anthropologists. This book is a collection of six ethnographic studies that neatly summarize the author's work through the past quarter century. Ferraro curated the collection thinking of an Ecuadorian audience that had not necessarily had access to these essays, as all but two of the works were originally published in English in academic journals. In her prologue, Ferraro calls on her fellow anthropologists to listen to Indigenous voices and to make a concerted effort to do so without Western and Eurocentric biases. She argues that a useful approach to unveiling ancestral knowledge is through the study of quotidian tasks that connect reality to the divine. Ferraro explains her theoretical grounding as holistic, rather than positivist, and notes that a guiding thread in all her work is the notion that material culture, bodies, and different forms of knowledge can be manipulated to transform and convey meaning. Ferraro emphasizes that she practices participant observation from a decolonizing positionality, and that she attempts to practice reflexivity in all her work, being cognizant of any power relations embedded in her relations with her collaborators. An important contribution to Andean ethnography and the thread that runs through all six essays is Ferraro's critique of conventional academic debates on *vivir bien* or the Indigenous notion of "living well," and its assumptions about the connection between humans and nature. Ferraro frames *vivir bien* not as a political or spiritual idea, but instead as a lifestyle that seeks to be in harmony with nature. Ferraro's ethnographic work on the making of crafts and the role of craftspeople as makers and creators is how she approaches this concept. Her six chapters are organized not chronologically, but epistemologically, so that she builds on her research to support this argument. From kneading the dough for the Day of the Dead bread, to heating the metal for goldsmithing, to counting rosary beads and reading accounts in archives, Ferraro evidences how everyday practices in Andean Ecuador craft the path to living well.

353 **Inuca Lechón, José Benjamín.** Genealogía de *alli kawsay / sumak kawsay* (vida buena / vida hermosa) de las organizaciones kichwas del Ecuador desde mediados del siglo XX. (*Lat. Am. Caribb. Ethn. Stud.*, 12:2, July 2017, p. 155–176, bibl.)

This article provides a summary of a careful survey of current and archival uses of the Quechua terms *sumak kawsay* in Ecuador. The idea of *sumak kawsay* or "good life" has transformed into a political slogan in support of Indigenous rights in Bolivia, Ecuador, and Peru, but has as many different interpretations as it has spellings, depending on the region of the Andes in which it is used. Inuca Lechón provides a chronological history of the use of the word beginning in the late 1930s to the late 2010s in different parts of the Ecuadorian Andes. The term acquires different cultural meanings and knowledge as it is taken up as part of the discourse and narrative of not only Indigenous peoples, but also educators, NGOs, environmental activists, different churches, and the political left. The different uses of the term over the decades also reveal changes within Ecuador's racial and ethnic imaginaries, and demonstrate the importance of this concept in the struggle for Indigenous rights in the Andean Highlands. Despite claims to the contrary, there is documented evidence of the purposeful use of *sumak kawsay* in Ecuador starting in the mid-20th century in the discourse and narrative of the Quechua peoples. The continued uninterrupted use of this notion in the Quechua struggle of Indigenous rights speaks to the importance of dignity and well-being in this narrative of Indigenous identity and restitution.

354 **Velásquez, Teresa A.** Enacting refusals: mestiza women's anti-mining activism in Andean Ecuador. (*Lat. Am. Caribb. Ethn. Stud.*, 12:3, Nov. 2017, p. 250–272, bibl.)

This article centers around the refusal of the author's fieldwork collaborators to participate in a public workshop to discuss and share the results of this ethnographic study. The fieldwork collaborators are agrarian mestiza women in Andean Ecuador and members of a national all-female anti-mining movement. The author presents this refusal as an identity politics tactic by these women in their struggle to have a voice in the anti-mining movement, while distancing themselves from an Indigenous identity. The study contributes to the politics of mestizaje literature in the Andes region, as well as to subaltern and decolonization studies. The women who collaborated with Velásquez embody a folklorist romanticized vision of the rural countryside—the idealized *chola cuencana*—that feeds and sustains tropes of white supremacy, which in turn support neoliberal extractivist mining policies in the area. Much has been written—and the author cites many of these studies—on how Andean mestizo and Indigenous women deploy ideals of motherhood as a common denominator to forge cross-ethnic and cross-class alliances, as well as to justify their participation in the public sphere. These agrarian mestizo women (or *cholas*) are a silent, yet very visible and iconic part of the Cuenca region's imaginary consumed in tourist crafts and dances. When these women speak out in activist public spaces, they transgress enculturated gendered tropes and challenge political authority as well as the extractivist practices that affect their communities. Velásquez's work is valuable for drawing attention to varied forms of Indigenous political activism and, specifically, the choice these women made to deploy silence and a refusal to perform as anthropological subjects.

PERU

355 **Branca, Domenico.** Identidad aymara en el Perú: nación, vivencia y narración. Lima: Editorial Horizonte, 2017. 294 p.: bibl., ill., map. (Antropología y etnología; 17)

This classic ethnographic study seeks to answer what the Aymara nation identity means to the Indigenous groups living in the city of Puno in Peru and surrounding agricultural towns. How do these different groups interpret the concept of the nation? What does it mean to live as and be Aymara? To feel Aymara? These questions are especially relevant as the city/countryside and misti (or mestizo)/Indigenous dichotomies are no longer valid as Puno has become a rural/urban crossroad. Here the notion of an Aymara nation has been crafted and linked to a group of cooperatives formed to face climate change and its toll on the livelihood of small-scale farmers. Branca provides a solid description, based on his long stay in the area where he exercised intense participant observation and conducted in-depth interviews. He produces a picture of the complex history of the past century as the Aymara near the urban center of Puno transitioned from subsistence agriculture and pastoralism to small business management and participation in the informal economy. Because of economic challenges and the subsequent changes to Indigenous livelihoods, the story of identity formation in Puno is a political one. The Aymara of this region brought their beliefs and customs to the Puno city streets and claimed an alternative nation within a country that continued to exclude them from the Peruvian imagined community. With this book, Branca provides an excellent analysis and survey of Peru's Aymara Indigenous identity in the 21st century.

La Serna Salcedo, Juan Carlos. Sicuris, máscaras y diablos danzantes: historia de la diablada y la identidad cultural en Puno. See *HLAS 76:2091*.

Loritz, Erika and **Irene Ragazzini.** Instituciones y prácticas económicas comunitarias: aprendiendo del sistema de reproducción de la vida de los pueblos aymara y mixteco. See item **211**.

GEOGRAPHY

GENERAL

JÖRN SEEMANN, *Associate Professor of Geography, Ball State University*

AFTER THE FIRST TWO WEEKS of the epidemic, the undertakers were not able to bury all the dead in a dignified manner anymore. The coves were dug very deep to stack the bodies without coffins in three levels, leaving the ground as a sponge soaked in putrid liquids and infected blood.

This quasi-apocalyptic scene could have been reported in one of the many somber news stories and human tragedies of the COVID-19 pandemic. It strikingly evokes the drone images of Brazilian cemeteries taken in April 2020 that show dozens of rows and columns of coffins ready to be interred in hastily dug holes, while undertakers and excavating machines feverishly opened more grave sites to accommodate the steadily increasing number of corpses.

However, the first paragraph does not refer to the present-day scenario, but alludes to Gabriel García Márquez's 1985 best-selling novel *Love in the Time of Cholera*, in which the Colombian writer uses the disease as a background for a captivating story about love and passion at the turn of the 20th century. García Márquez affirms that the impacts of cholera on the Black population was devastating, though the disease affected all peoples, regardless of color or social status. Likewise, COVID-19 is a global problem, but different social and cultural populations in Latin America were disproportionately affected, leading to dramatic changes in behavior, social practices, mobility, and access to health services.

This "new" geographical reality is reflected in an increasing number of publications that address the structural impacts on the region. COVID has greatly altered people's lives during the past two years (items **360**, **379**, and **428**). Combined with neoliberal policies and uneven power relations (items **370**, **397**, and **423**), the virus has shown that the gulf between the haves and have-nots has widened. More than ever, the disparities and inequalities in regional, intraregional, and interregional contexts have been revealed in various ways: migration flows (items **401**, **402**, **406**, and **419**), natural resource exploitation and environmental justice (items **391**, **392**, **399**, and **417**), water management (item **356**), and agriculture (item **357**).

At the same time, the recent literature on the region's geography reveals a clearer definition and identification of what Latin America is for Latin Americans. Emerging concepts, such as decoloniality (item **386**), re-existence (item **370**), and mobility (items **362** and **418**), have become central for understanding the region on its own terms, together with a continuing focus on the three T's—territory, territoriality, and territorialization (item **420**)—and the impacts of globalization (item **433**). Based on the epistemologies of the South as conceived by Portuguese sociologist Boaventura de Souza Santos, Latin American considerations of space question the universality and superiority of Western theories and models, for example, the concept of gentrification (item **375**) or Anglocentric perspectives on feminism (item **432**). Latin American geographers propose new ideas and approaches adjusted to the region's reality, including South-South relations (item **396**). The studies cover a wide range of topics, among them a historical analysis of Latin American models of population control (item **365**), a Latin America-centered political ecology of waste management and trash (item **376**), the "negotiation" of everyday space (item **404**), an appraisal of social movements and the voices of activists (item **430**), and maps as tools of empowerment for marginalized communities (items **409** and **416**).

Another significant emerging trend is the consolidation of a Latin American perspective on women. Feminist geographers from the region reflect on theoretical and methodological approaches to gender studies and define a research agenda (items **385** and **407**) giving emphasis to embodied practices (items **403**, **428**, **430**, and **431**) and the frequently overlooked role of women as social actors in agriculture, mining, and tourism (items **415** and **421**).

New interfaces and intersectionalities have materialized, aiming for a deeper engagement with differences and otherness and the interrelations and interdependencies among overlapping identities shaped by race, class, gender, and other factors. For example, the study of the impacts of climate change in Latin America cannot be separated from the life of small communities, women, or groups at the margin of society, as is shown in a case study on urban floods and political clientelism (item **368**) and research on the social and political dimensions of drought, rising temperatures, and natural disasters (items **387**, **389**, **393**, and **422**).

Studies on agriculture, rural space, and peasant societies show concern with global and regional dynamics and investigate international production systems (items **364** and **377**), structures and forms of land governance (items **383**, **390**, **414**, and **419**), family and small-scale agriculture (items **358**, **383**, and **424**), water management (items **359** and **411**), and the meaning of *rural* in Latin America (item **412**). Traditional communities that are vulnerable to these changes, such as riverine and coastal populations (item **408**) and Indigenous communities (item **358**), have begun to denounce environmental injustice and the impacts of large-scale projects. This trend is also seen in studies of mining activities that examine the consequences of extractivism for marginalized groups (items **378** and **398**), though conventional environmental studies, especially environmental history (items **381** and **382**) and human-environmental relations (items **380** and **429**), have not lost significance.

Cities and urbanization processes are investigated from well-established angles, namely urban history (items **426** and **427**), development and planning (items **361**, **371**, **384**, **388**, and **405**), and transport and public services (items **394** and **425**). However, less frequently studied aspects of urban life related to culture and identities have gained more prominence, e.g., the cultural heritage of cities (item **367**) and the creative use of space (items **373** and **404**). Though appearing rather timidly, this "cultural turn" in Latin American geography has become more perceptible in publications on the geographical imagination of Latin America in the US (item **413**), space in Latin American crime fiction (item **374**), culinary heritage (item **369**), and tourism (items **363**, **366**, and **410**).

Latin America "in the time of corona" has been characterized by personal and material losses, structural changes, and involuntary adjustments with regard to the organization and transformation of space, whose consequences and effects cannot yet be foreseen. The new "normal" will undoubtedly provoke different conflicts, create alternative forms of livelihood, and spark ideas for new solutions—in short, food for thought for geographical studies in the coming years.

356 **A contracorriente: agua y conflicto en América Latina.** Edición de Gisselle Vila Benites y Cristóbal Bonelli. Quito: ABYA YALA; Wageningen, The Netherlands: Justicia Hídrica, 2017. 536 p.: bibl., ill., maps. (Serie Agua y sociedad; 25. Sección Justicia Hídrica)

The collection of 25 texts presented at the 2015 international meeting of the Water Justice Alliance in Cali, Colombia, establishes a dialogue between academics and environmental activists and engages with a wide range of themes and processes related to the conflicts about water resources in Latin America. The contributions focus on empirical regional examples and topics such as environmental justice, the impacts of mega projects, public water policies, and community management and resistance.

357 **Agrarian extractivism in Latin America.** Edited by Ben M. McKay, Alberto Alonso-Fradejas, and Arturo Ezquerro-Cañete. Milton Park, England; New York, N.Y.: Routledge, 2021. 214 p.: bibl., index. (Routledge critical development studies)

This work offers a critical assessment of the impacts of industrial-scale, profit-driven extractivist agriculture in Latin America, labeled as corporate-led, external-input plantation agriculture (CEPA). The authors of the introduction and nine chapters point out the different forms and aspects of this agricultural model. They discuss specific regions and countries (e.g., the Brazilian Cerrado and Bolivia), analyze particular crop systems (pineapple in Costa Rica and agave in Mexico), and reflect on gender exclusion and sustainability in agrarian extractivism.

358 **Agricultura familiar tradicional: experiencias rurales en México y Argentina.** Coordinación de María Guadalupe Rodriguez Galván *et al.* Buenos Aires: Instituto Nacional de Tecnología Agropecuaria; Tuxtla Gutiérrez, Mexico: Universidad Autónoma de Chiapas; Ciudad de México: P y V, Plaza y Valdés Editores, 2017. 236 p.: bibl., ill., maps.

This collaborative international research project by Mexican and Argentine scholars describes and investigates family agriculture in central and southern Mexico and Patagonia. The authors study production modes and systems, cultural traditions, the commercialization of products, and the livelihood of peasants and Indigenous communities, using examples of chicken, sheep and rabbit raising, milk production, and corn cultivation.

359 **El agua para la agricultura de las Américas.** Coordinación editorial de Víctor Villalobos Arámbula, Miguel García y Felipe Ávila. Ciudad de México: IICA: Colegio de Postgraduados: Fundación COLPOS, 2017. 132 p.: bibl. (Biblioteca Básica de Agricultura; 85. Serie Agua, innovación y productividad; 1)

Presents a state of the art of water resource management in Latin America, which holds almost 50 percent of the global waters. The authors emphasize the importance of water in the region and identify regional and international strategies for its availability and use. They give special attention to the measures and actions of the Inter-American Institute for Cooperation on Agriculture (IICA). Six examples of successful high-impact water management projects are presented.

360 Álvarez Velasco, Soledad. Mobility, control, and the pandemic across the Americas: first findings of a transnational collective project. (*J. Lat. Am. Geogr.*, 20:1, April 2021, p. 11–84, bibl.)

Álvarez Velasco discusses the impact of COVID-19 with regard to health policies and mobility. The author argues that measures such as border closings, internal policing, limited access to health services, and stricter migration and refugee laws have increased the social exclusion of migrants. The study draws from news material, official documents, and first-hand accounts by migrants in 21 countries of the Western Hemisphere that were collected by researchers participating in the trilingual collaborative digital project *(Im)mobility in the Americas/(In)movilidad en las Américas/(In)movilidad en las Américas.*

361 Aspectos estratégicos de la gestión pública para el crecimiento sostenible de las ciudades. Textos de Alejandro Navarro Arredondo et al. Caracas: CLAD, Centro Latinoamericano de Administración para el Desarrollo: CAF, Banco de Desarrollo de América Latina, 2016. 230 p.: bibl., ill. (Serie Documentos debate del CLAD; 21)

Consists of six award-winning studies of a 2015 competition organized by the Latin American Center of Administration for Development (CLAD). The authors address administrative strategies and planning for the sustainable growth of cities. The papers discuss successful local initiatives, public policies, and popular participation in several Latin American cities.

362 Automotores y transporte público: un acercamiento desde los estudios históricos. Coordinación de Ilse Angélica Álvarez Palma. Zinacantepec, Mexico: El Colegio Mexiquense, 2017. 188 p.: bibl., ill.

Insightful and original study on the history of automobiles and public transport in Latin America with a regional emphasis on Mexico and examples from Argentina and Chile. Eight thematic chapters discuss the development of the automotive industry, the introduction of taxi services, the establishment of cargo truck networks, and conflicts about public transportation in the period between the late 19th century and the first half of the 20th century.

363 The business of leisure: tourism history in Latin America and the Caribbean. Edited and with an introduction by Andrew Grant Wood. Lincoln: University of Nebraska Press, 2021. 329 p.: bibl., index.

A collection of historical-geographical studies on travel practices and the hospitality industry in Latin America. The 12 contributions in the book present different episodes, aspects, and angles of traveling and discuss a variety of cultural, economic, and political issues of tourism. The chapters address foreign investment in tourism, the promotion of national projects, the production of tourism imageries, and the more recent emergence of dark tourism—the visitation of places marked by tragedies, disasters, and crime (e.g., narco-tours in Medellín, Colombia).

364 Caficultura: panorama actual en América Latina. Edición de Guillermo Canet B. y Carlos Soto Víquez. San José: IICA; Ciudad de México: Colegio de Postgraduados: Fundación COLPOS, 2017. 134 p.: bibl., ill. (Biblioteca básica de agricultura; 90)

This work presents an analysis of coffee production in Latin American countries in the 2010s. The four thematic chapters address problems with plant diseases, environmentally friendly land use, challenges to commercialization, sustainable forms of coffee growing, and technological advances in the production process. In the conclusion, the editors point to future trends in the coffee industry, which is characterized by increasing global consumption, a growing demand for high-quality products, and an adjustment to possible climate changes.

365 Carter, Eric D. Population control, public health, and development in mid twentieth century Latin America. (*J. Hist. Geogr.*, 62, Oct. 2018, p. 96–105, bibl.)

Carter analyzes the reception of European and North American ideas of population dynamics in Latin America in the 20th century. The author argues that different from Malthusian and neo-Malthusian models embraced in the First World, Latin American countries aimed at the growth rather than the control of their populations, which is closely related to public health and nutrition issues on a national plane. The work of Brazilian geographer and physician Josué de Castro and the influence of the Catholic Church on birth control and family planning are among the examples to explain Latin American population thought.

366 Castillo Nechar, Marcelino and **Nohora Elisabeth Alfonso Bernal.** Patrimonio cultural y turismo: un estudio comparado entre México y Colombia. Toluca, Mexico: Universidad Autónoma de Estado de México, 2017. 292 p.: bibl., ill., maps.

Comparative study that explores the relations between tourism and cultural heritage in the state of México (Edomex) and in Bocayá department in Colombia. The authors identify cultural heritage related to craftwork, religion, and archeology as tourist attractions and point out the interactions and tensions among social actors, such as local communities, businesses, and visitors, and public policies implanted by the state.

367 Ciudades en diálogo entre lo local y lo transnacional/global: intersecciones entre el patrimonio, el turismo, las alteridades migrantes y el hábitat popular. Compilación de Mónica Lacarrieu. Longchamps, Argentina: Ediciones Imago Mundi, 2018. 237 p.: bibl., ill., index. (Colección Bitácora argentina)

Collection of 10 essays that analyze Latin American cities in the light of their cultural heritage and historical legacy. The authors investigate how these structures are preserved, changed, and redefined, and point out the implications for local populations. The case studies from different countries focus on urban processes such as gentrification, requalification projects, cultural tourism, and neighborhood identities.

368 Coates, Robert and **Anja Nygren.** Urban floods, clientelism, and the political ecology of the state in Latin America. (*Ann. Am. Assoc. Geogr.*, 110:5, Sept. 2020, p. 1301–1317, bibl.)

This study of urban political ecology investigates the interface between flood hazards and clientelism. How does the exchange of favors for political influence and votes produce or reinforce the vulnerability of populations and the risk of environmental disasters in cities? Two case studies on flooding and landslides from Novo Friburgo in Brazil and Villa Hermosa in Mexico are presented to point out political discourses, decision-making, and measures of mitigation and containment determined by clientelist urban governance.

369 Coloquio Internacional Patrimonios Alimentarios: Consensos y Tensiones, *UNAM,* **2015.** Patrimonios alimentarios: entre consensos y tensiones. Coordinación de Sarah Bak-Geller Corona, Raúl Matta y Charles-Edouard de Suremain. San Luis Potosí, Mexico: El Colegio de San Luis; Montpellier, France: IRD Éditions, 2019. 224 p.: bibl., ill.

The essays in this edited volume focus on food heritage in different regions of the world. The seven chapters offer a comparative look at how culinary traditions and specific recipes are increasingly recognized as official cultural heritage nationally and internationally. Examples from Latin America include a discussion of foodways in relation to Indigenous identities, ethnographic museums and the history of chocolate in Mexico, the principles and networks of Peruvian Creole cuisine, and the change in Cuban food culture caused by social and political changes.

370 Conflictos territoriales y territorialidades en disputa: re-existencias y horizontes societales frente al capital en América Latina. Coordinación de Pabel López y Milson Betancourt. Buenos Aires: CLACSO, 2021. 460 p.: bibl. (Serie Movimientos sociales y territorialidades) (Colección Grupos de trabajo)

A set of collected essays that highlights the Latin American perspective on social struggles and territory in the region in the light of neoliberal political and economic influences. The collection gathers 16 essays by renowned scholars that present theoretical reflections on and empirical examples of territorial conflicts. The essays highlight social movements and resistance of Indigenous peasant communities against capital-driven economic activities such as neo-extractivism, agribusiness, and mining.

371 Congreso Internacional sobre Sustentabilidad en los Hábitats, *1st,* *Guadalajara, Mexico,* **2016.** Sustentabilidad y territorio: herramientas para la gestion sustentable del hábitat. Coordinación de Mara Alejandra Cortés Lara, Raúl Díaz Padilla, Daniel Enrique Sardo y Carlos Petersen Farah. Guadalajara, Mexico: ITESO, Universidad Jesuita de Guadalajara, 2018. 159 p.: bibl., ill., maps. (Colección: Hábitat sustenable contemporáneo; 1)

Six essays by Latin American scholars explore the idea of sustainability of inhabited spaces based on presentations at the 2016 Habitat III Conference. The focus of the studies is "small scale" initiatives to improve urban environments: the smart city model, creative and innovative strategies, popular participation, valorization of the cultural-historical heritage, and the safety of public spaces.

372 **Convivial constellations in Latin America: from colonial to contemporary times.** Edited by Luciane Scarato, Fernando Baldraia, and Maya Manzi. New York, N.Y.: Routledge, 2020. 182 p.: bibl., ill., index. (Entangled inequalities: exploring global asymmetries)

The collection of essays focuses on the idea of conviviality, conceived as forms of living together in the light of social inequality, cultural differences, and political worldviews in Latin America. The authors of the 11 chapters present interdisciplinary approaches to the topic in different places and times and discuss a wide range of themes, including commonalities and tensions within political discourse, railways as important infrastructure for connecting people, religious syncretism and diversity, and the marginalization of peasant and Afro-descendant populations in society.

373 **Creative spaces: urban culture and marginality in Latin America.** Edited by Niall H.D. Geraghty and Adriana Laura Massidda. London: Institute of Latin American Studies, School of Advanced Study, University of London, 2019. 268 p.: bibl., ill. (some color), index, maps.

Approaches urban marginality in Latin America from an interdisciplinary cultural and artistic perspective. The editors of the collection aim to establish a dialogue between urban and cultural studies conceiving artistic expressions by marginalized populations as essentially spatial practices. In the eight thematic chapters and the afterword, the authors explore art forms such as photography, films, exhibitions, and community initiatives in several Latin American cities and invite a rethinking of the idea of urban marginality.

374 **Crime scenes: Latin American crime fiction from the 1960s to the 2010s.** Edited by Charlotte Lange and Ailsa Peate. Oxford, England; New York, N.Y.: Peter Lang, 2019. 247 p.: bibl.

In this first book-length study on Latin American crime fiction, the editors explain that this type of fiction is relatively new in the region, having emerged in the 1960s under the influence of North American novels from the 1940s. The contributors to the volume discuss particular works by both renowned and lesser-known Latin American writers and emphasize crime scenes as geographical center points. The analyses of these literary creations consider social contexts and issues such as violence, memory, discrimination, and human rights abuse.

375 **Díaz-Parra, Ibán.** Generating a critical dialogue on gentrification in Latin America. (*Prog. Hum. Geogr.*, 45:3, June 2021, p. 472–488, bibl.)

"Gentrification" is considered a rather novel research concept in Latin America. This review article covers the critical reception of the term. The author engages with the recent discussions on urban space and points out two problems in the debate: (1) the rejection of the word "gentrification" as a form of cultural and academic imperialism imported from core countries and (2) the ambiguous meaning of alternative expressions in Latin America.

376 **Ecología política de la basura: pensando los residuos desde el Sur.** Coordinación de María Fernanda Solíz T. Quito: Ediciones Abya-Yala: Instituto de Estudios Ecologistas del Tercer Mundo, 2017. 319 p.: bibl., ill.

The 13 essays in this study examine garbage and other residues through the lens of political ecology and political economy. The chapters approach trash through both theoretical reflections and empirical examples from Latin America. The authors make a plea for a Latin American strategy for waste and waste management that is based on local communities and how they defend their space and interact with the environment rather than reliance on North American and European neoliberal models of consumption and disposal.

377 **Estado actual sobre la producción, el comercio y cultivo del cacao en América.** Textos de Miguel Ángel Arvelo Sánchez et al. San José: IICA; Ciudad de México: Colegio de Postgraduados: Fundación COLPOS, 2017. 254 p.: bibl., color ill. (Biblioteca básica de agricultura; 89)

Richly illustrated book describes the present situation of the production of cocoa in Latin America. The authors discuss the commerce of cocoa in a global context and provide details about the production process, adequate cultivation methods, and land use management. Includes an exhaustive list of scientific studies and publications on cocoa and an appendix with statistical data on production, consumption, and trade.

378 **¿Fin de la bonanza?: entradas, salidas y encrucijadas del extractivismo.** Edición de Martín Ramírez y Stefan Schmalz. Buenos Aires: Editorial Biblos, 2018. 366 p.: bibl. (Sociedad)

This collection of 18 papers discusses the possibilities, limits, and risks of extractivism in Latin America. The authors debate concepts, regional trends, neoliberal policies, and the impacts of extractivism on national economies and local communities. Among the case studies are agrobusiness and mining in Argentina, salmon farms and lumber industries in Chile, and changes in the soybean production in Brazil.

379 **Finn, John C.; Cynthia Pope; and Yulia Garcia Sarduy.** COVID-19 in Latin America: Forum of perspectives. With contributions by several authors. (*J. Lat. Am. Geogr.*, 19:3, July 2020, p. 167–346)

Forum of 22 shorter essays reporting on the situation of COVID-19 in different Latin American countries at the beginning of the pandemic in 2020. The contributions address a wide range of topics from historical antecedents of pandemics in the Americas, the Cuban health model, and the role of the government in containing the virus, to strategies of religious congregations in times of social distancing, new conceptions of a sense of place, and the impacts of the virus on marginalized populations.

380 **Forest, field, and fallow: selections by William M. Denevan.** Edited by Antoinette M.G.A. WinklerPrins and Kent Mathewson. Cham, Switzerland: Springer, 2022. 451 p.: bibl., ill.

This collection of essays offers an overview of the work of the influential historical-cultural geographer William Denevan, who has studied a wide range of topics on Latin America for more than 60 years. The selection of texts is a tribute to this scholar and highlights Denevan's impactful and interdisciplinary studies on Indigenous populations in the Americas before 1492, human-environment relations, agricultural traditions, plant geography, Indigenous agroecology—especially in the Amazon, and landscapes of livestock farming. The book is divided into thematic sections, each of which offers an introduction written by an eminent geographer that contextualizes Denevan's contributions.

381 **Geografía ambiental: métodos y técnicas desde América Latina.** Edición de Humberto Reyes Hernández, Carlos Morera Beita y Óscar Reyes Pérez. Costa Rica: EUNA, 2017. 236 p.: bibl., graphs, ill., maps (some color).

This edited volume on theoretical and methodological approaches to environmental studies in Latin America was inspired by the 1955 international symposium on "Man's Role in Changing the Face of the Earth" at Princeton University and the 1987 conference on "The Earth as Transformed by Human Action" at Clark University. The authors investigate human-environment relations through the lens of landscape ecology, economic assimilation, and environmental evaluation.

382 **Geografía e historia ambiental.** Coordinación de Pedro S. Urquijo, Antonio Vieyra y Gerardo Bocco. Ciudad de México: UNAM, Centro de Investigaciones en Geografía Ambiental, 2017. 267 p.: bibl., ill., maps.

This anthology on environmental history in Latin America is comprehensive and easy to read. The authors use a historical-geographical and cultural-humanistic approach to discuss theories, historiographies, and methodologies at the intersection between geography, history, and the environment. The work gives special emphasis to the concepts of landscape, territory, and the use of historical GIS to reconstruct environments of the past.

383   **El gobierno colectivo de la tierra en América Latina.** Edición de Alejandro Diez. Lima: Pontificia Universidad Católica del Perú, Fondo Editorial, 2018. 326 p.: ill., map.

This edited volume discusses examples of community-driven land management in Latin America. The authors address subjects such as forms of governance and the right of access to land and resources among communities of peasants, small landowners, Indigenous groups, and Afro-descendants in several countries. The papers seek to contribute to a better understanding of access to and control of lands to reflect on a framework of policies for collective rights.

384   **Hábitat en deuda: veinte años de políticas urbanas en América Latina.** Edición de Michael Cohen, María Carrizosa y Margarita Gutman. Buenos Aires: Editorial Café de las Ciudades, 2016. 349 p.: bibl., ill. (Colección Hábitat)

This study presents an evaluation of the state of art of urban policies in Latin America at the dawn of Habitat III, the UN Conference on Housing and Sustainable Urban Development in Quito, Ecuador, in October 2016. Rereading the agreements from the second Habitat Conference in 1996, the authors critically engage with the achievements and persistent problems over the last 20 years in cities in six Latin American countries. The nine essays identify internal aspects (urban planning and policies) and external factors (impacts of the global economy) that had a direct impact on urban development and conclude that most of the aims defined at Habitat II (sustainability, affordable housing, gender equality, participation, and social inclusion) have not been achieved.

385   Hofmann, Susanne and **Melisa Cabrapan Duarte.** Gender and natural resource extraction in Latin America: feminist engagements with geopolitical positionality. (*Rev. Eur. Estud. Latinoam. Caribe*, 111, Jan./June 2021, p. 39–63, bibl.)

Discusses gender-related power relations in the context of natural resource extraction in Latin America from a feminist perspective. The authors argue that women's participation in these economic activities is very complex and diverse and has been widely overlooked, especially because environmentalist discourse can render women invisible in the world of labor. Particular emphasis is placed on feminist initiatives in rural communities and the situation of sex workers at male-dominated extraction sites.

386   *Íconos: Revista de Ciencias Sociales.* No. 61, May/Aug. 2018, Geografías críticas en América Latina. Edición de Sofía Zaragocin-Carvajal, Melissa Moreano-Venegas y Soledad Álvarez-Velasco. Quito: FLACSO Ecuador.

The six articles of this special journal issue discuss critical geography from a Latin American perspective, addressing questions of mobility, feminism, post- and decolonial studies, and political ecology based on the regional reality rather than Western epistemologies. The authors seek to define a Latin America-centered critical geography. Among the case studies are human-environment relations and territorial rights of Indigenous groups in Mexico and Chile, the stories of Ecuadorian women involved in cocaine trafficking, and the narratives of Central American migrants reaching the US border.

387   **International Conference on Hydrometeorological Risks and Climate Change (ICHRCC),** *2nd, Cholula de Rivadabia, Mexico, 2015.* Facing the threat: climate change: proceedings. Edited by José A. Raynal-Villaseñor. Co-edited by María E. Raynal-Gutiérrez et al. Puebla, Mexico: UDLAP, Universidad de las Américas Puebla, 2017. 270 p.: bibl., ill. (some color), color maps. (Colección Memorias)

Collection of 13 papers and keynote lectures presented at an international conference on the risks of hydrometeorological phenomena such as floods and droughts. The contributions address a wide range of topics related to global climate change and its impacts such as international policies, water resource management, air pollution, environmental health, and rainfall anomalies.

388   Jornadas Puebla: Ciudad, Capital y Cultura, 3rd, San Andrés Cholula, Mexico, 2016. Ciudad, capital y cultura. Compilación de Adrián Hernández Cordero, Anne Kristiina Kurjenoja y María Emilia Ismael Simental. San Andrés Cholula, Mexico: UDLAP, Universidad de las Américas Puebla; Ciudad de México: Itaca, 2018. 218 p.: bibl., ill.

An anthology of essays that studies urbanization in the light of the postindustrial age and neoliberalism, with a focus on Puebla, Mexico, in comparison with Brasília and Barcelona. The authors address topics such as cultural politics, self-management, gentrification, and the influences of the American dream that have become increasingly relevant in the process of shaping cities.

389   *Journal of Latin American Geography*. Vol. 19, No. 3, July 2020, Rural transformation in Latin America's changing climate. Edited by Marygold Walsh-Dilley, Jami Nelson-Nuñez, Benjamin Warner, and Chris S. Duvall. Austin: University of Texas Press.

A special journal issue that examines the impacts of environmental changes on rural communities. The editors argue that a narrow and exclusive focus on climate change provides only a limited understanding of existing problems. They believe that research should be based on an intersectional perspective that considers cultural identities and modes of discrimination and privilege as important factors in shaping rural space. The six articles address topics such as water scarcity and conservation policies in Mexico, Indigenous agroecology in Guatemala and Ecuador, and the consequences for rural communities in Bolivia of the depletion of a lake due to water withdrawal for mining, agriculture, and urban use.

390   Kröger, Markus and Anja Nygren. Shifting frontier dynamics in Latin America. (*J. Agrarian Change*, 20:3, July 2020, p. 364–386, bibl.)

Drawing on extensive fieldwork to study the dynamics of shifting territorialities, the authors discuss the concepts of resource and commodity frontiers. They present two case studies on forest clearing, land appropriation, and the occupation of protected areas for economic activities in the Brazilian Amazon and *Cerrado* and in Nicaragua. Their larger goal is to point out the impact of frontier expansion in Latin America based on regional and global economic interests.

391   Landscapes of inequity: environmental justice in the Andes-Amazon region. Edited and with an introduction by Nicholas A. Robins and Barbara J. Fraser. Lincoln: University of Nebraska Press, 2020. 347 p.: bibl., index, maps.

With a regional focus on the Andes and the Amazon region, this edited volume aims to document the struggles of marginalized groups to defend their cultural identities and traditional territories and achieve environmental justice. The nine chapters of the book discuss case studies about the environmental pollution through mining and oil prospection, the impacts of national development policies on Indigenous communities, and legal aspect of territorial rights that have produced and continue to produce landscapes of inequities.

392   Latin America in times of global environmental change. Edited by Cristian Lorenzo. Cham, Switzerland: Springer, 2020. 181 p.: bibl. (The Latin American studies book series)

This volume investigates the connections, divergences, and tensions between global environmental policies and the specific regional needs and aims in Latin America and the Caribbean for facing environmental changes. The 11 chapters written by Latin American scholars explore topics such as the peripheral role of countries from the Global South in international financing organizations for the protection of the environment, the challenges of transborder watersheds, scientific research and knowledge production on natural resources, conservation policies and agroforestry, and the relationship between tourism and climate change.

393 *Latin American Perspectives.* Vol. 43, No. 4, Special issue, July 2016, Climate change in Latin America. Edited by Andrea Santelices Spikin and Jorge Rojas Hernández. London: SAGE.

Special journal issue that focuses on the social and economic impacts of climate change in Latin America. The introduction and the six articles examine bottom-up, decolonized approaches that emphasize social movements and actors and their quest for social justice, rather than global policies. Case studies from Peru, Bolivia, and Argentina offer insights into local conflicts, potential solutions, and processes of adaptation to climate change in the light of inequality and vulnerability of communities and the decisions adopted in the 2015 Paris Climate Agreement.

394 **Libertun, Nora** and **Roberto Guerrero.** ¿Cuánto cuesta la densificación?: la relación entre la densidad y el costo de proveer servicios urbanos básicos en Brasil, Chile, Ecuador y México. (*EURE/Santiago*, 43:130, sept. 2017, p. 235–267, bibl., graphs, tables)

Researchers from the Inter-American Development Bank (IDB) provide a cost analysis of urban services in relation to population density. Using data on piped water, sewage, sanitary services, and waste collection from households in four Latin American countries (Brazil, Chile, Ecuador, and Mexico), the authors argue that the optimal demographic density to minimize expenses for urban services is close to 9,000 inhabitants per square kilometer. They suggest the promotion of specific policies to reach this ideal level considering that 85 percent of the municipalities in these four countries are less densely populated.

395 **Lois, Carla.** *Terrae incognitae*: modos de pensar y mapear geografías desconocidas. Buenos Aires: Eudeba, 2018. 283 p.: bibl., ill. (Colección Ciencia joven; 48)

A study on the history of cartography that offers a reflection on blank spaces and unknown places on historical maps. Using many examples of maps that depict Latin America or parts of the region, the author analyzes cartographic documents according to their contents, modes of representing what is unknown, and the cultural contexts of the societies and periods that produced them.

396 **Mapping South-South connections: Australia and Latin America.** Edited by Fernanda Peñaloza and Sarah Walsh. Cham, Switzerland: Palgrave Macmillan, 2019. 294 p.: bibl., ill. (Studies of the Americas)

A pioneering publication that focuses on connections and differences between Australia and Latin America with regards to culture, literature, ethnicity, and migrations. The authors affirm that there are specific Southern Hemisphere relations between the country "down under" and Latin America that are not a mere reproduction of ideas from the US and Europe. The 10 chapters compare and discuss the conceptual links, interregional encounters, crosscultural exchanges, and the geographical imagination in and of both places, including studies on the Sydney Latin American Film Festival, the decolonization of Australian and Latin American art, and the violence against Australian tourists in Mexico.

397 **Marques, Luiz C.** Capitalismo e colapso ambiental. 2a edição revista e ampliada. Campinas, Brazil: Editora Unicamp, 2016. 711 p.: bibl., ill., index.

Marques presents a detailed overview of the human impacts that have caused the environmental crisis of today and indicate an imminent environmental collapse in the near future if aggressive capitalist modes of thinking are not abandoned. In the 14 chapters, the author, a renowned Brazilian historian, discusses the decrease, decline, and degradation of important natural phenomena and systems such as forests, soils, biodiversity, and climate; points out the devastating effects of trash and fossil fuels on the environment; and carries out a critical assessment of environmental sustainability based on capitalism.

398 Martínez Espinoza, Manuel Ignacio. Jirones en el camino: pueblos indígenas y extractivismo minero en América Latina. Chiapas, Mexico: UNICACH, 2017. 190 p.: bibl., ill., maps, tables.

This work investigates Indigenous groups in Latin America, especially Mexico and Guatemala, and the impacts on them from mining and other extractivist activities. In the three chapters of the book, the author discusses Indigenous peoples from historical, political, social, economic, and juridical standpoints; analyzes the social and human rights movements of these groups; and presents a case study from Guatemala that reveals the complexity of conflicts that result from mining.

399 Megaminería en América Latina: estados, empresas transnacionales y conflictos socioambientales. Compilación de Laura Álvarez Huwiler et al. Buenos Aires: Centro Cultural de la Cooperación Floreal Gorini; Quilmes, Argentina: Universidad Nacional de Quilmes, 2018. 255 p.: bibl., ill. (Colección Pensamiento crítico)

This interdisciplinary collection of studies by Latin American authors investigates the mining boom in the region during the last two decades. The seven contributions reflect on the political, economic, and social impacts of mining at different scales, from international and national situations to local configurations. The studies also identify different stakeholders such as governments, transnational companies, and local communities, and their interests and challenges.

400 Merchán, Yelitza Osorio and Juan David Delgado. Cartografía y nación en América Latina (siglos XIX y XX): una aproximación a los casos de Argentina, México y Colombia. (*Perspect. Geogr./Bogotá*, 24:2, julio/dic. 2019, p. 49–68, bibl., maps)

Historical-geographical study examines how maps shaped nation-states in Latin America in the 19th and 20th centuries. The authors critically engage with the existing historiography that stresses the importance of maps as tools for national governments, based on the idea that measuring is knowledge and knowledge is power. Presents examples from the cartographic histories of Argentina, Colombia, and Mexico to show that maps produce a rational and imaginary idea of a country from the top to the bottom that excludes different voices and cultural diversity.

401 La migración intrarregional en América Latina: sociedad, legislación y desafíos en un mundo complejo. Edición de Loreto Correa Vera. Textos de Alejandro Salas Maturana et al. Medellín, Colombia: Ediciones Unaula: CLACSO, Consejo Latinoamericano de Ciencias Sociales, 2020. 475 p.: bibl., graphs. (Colección Grupos de trabajo. Serie Movimientos sociales y territorialidades)

This study discusses questions about international and regional migration within Latin America in the light of public policies, integration, and violence. The case studies from several countries engage with themes such as challenges for immigrants in Bolivia and Bolivians abroad, educational projects for Mexicans who returned to their country or were deported from the US, and the stigmatization of delinquent and incarcerated immigrants.

402 Migrants, refugees, and asylum seekers in Latin America. Edited by Raanan Rein, Stefan Rinke and David M.K. Sheinin. Boston, Mass.: Brill, 2020. 355 p.: bibl., index. (Jewish Latin America; 12)

Proposes a novel approach to the study of immigration in Latin America based on the immigrants' identity and self-identification on a local and national scale rather than on groups with homogeneous ethnicity and nationality. The authors engage with theoretical and methodological aspects and present a wide array of predominantly historical case studies, including Jewish migration to Argentina, Germans in Brazil, Palestinians in Chile, US immigrants in Costa Rica, and female Colombian prisoners in Ecuador.

403 Mollett, Sharlene. Resistance against the land grab: *defensoras* and embodied precarity in Latin America. (*in* Routledge handbook of critical resource geography. Edited by Matthew Himley, Elizabeth Havice and Gabriela Valdivia. London: Routledge, 2021, p. 93–102)

Mollett looks at the process of land grabbing in Latin America from a feminist geography perspective. The author argues that many studies emphasize large-scale land seizure without paying much attention to the micro level and social actors such as Indigenous and Black women who suffer both violence to their lands (dispossession and encroachment) and their bodies (sexual stereotypes and prejudice).

404 Negotiating space in Latin America. Edited by Patricia Vilches. Leiden, Netherlands; Boston, Mass.: Brill, 2020. 331 p.: bibl., indexes. (Spatial practices; 32)

A multidisciplinary collection of studies that focuses on cultural practices and social movements in Latin America and how these activities and processes shape and transform space. The authors engage with a wide variety of themes that show how space is claimed, reclaimed, contested, and negotiated in everyday life. Among the examples are femicide and women's rights in Mexico, the significance of graffiti and murals for urban renewal in Argentina, the touristic commodification of the Machu Picchu ruins, and the conception of space in Latin American travel accounts, movies, and literature.

405 New World cities: challenges of urbanization and globalization in the Americas. Edited by John Tutino and Martin V. Melosi. Chapel Hill: University of North Carolina Press, 2019. 329 p.: bibl., index.

Historians provide an engaging discussion of urbanization in Latin America and North America in the 20th century in this set of collected works. The authors argue that major cities and urban processes and politics had an essential role in shaping and transforming space in the Americas and make a plea to "urbanize" historical studies. Examples from Mexico City, Rio de Janeiro, Buenos Aires, Montreal, Los Angeles, and Houston examine aspects of urbanization such as migration, marginalization, informality, infrastructure, social movements, and ethnicity in the light of national policies and globalization.

406 *Périplos: Revista de Pesquisa sobre Migrações.* Vol. 5, No. 1, 2021, Corredores migratorios en América Latina: nuevos flujos migratorios, nuevas territorialidades, nuevas restricciones. Coordinación de Claudia Pedone, Bruno Miranda y Soledad Álvarez Velasco. Brasília: Universidade de Brasília.

Special issue of a Brazilian journal on transnational migration flows in Latin America along major corridors or routes within the region (from Brazil, Central America, and Mexico to the US) and on transatlantic migration from African countries to South America. The nine interdisciplinary papers discuss themes such as the control and monitoring of migration, the mobility of legal and illegal migrants, stories of discrimination and violence, and border crossing in times of the COVID pandemic.

407 *Perspectiva Geográfica.* Vol. 23, No. 2, julio/dic. 2018, Geografía y género: perspectivas en América Latina. Bogotá: Universidad Pedagógica y Tecnológica de Colombia.

Special issue of a Colombian journal to discuss aspects of the research agenda on women and geography in Latin America. The authors of the seven contributions report on important topics related to the situation of women in the region (mainly in Colombia and Mexico) including the female perception of space and place, safety and violence, the mobility of women in cities, and the discussion of gender-specific themes in geography and social sciences programs in college.

Pick, James B.; Avijit Sarkar; and Elizabeth Parrish. The Latin American and Caribbean digital divide: a geospatial and multivariate analysis. See item **459**.

408 Populações litorâneas e ribeirinhas na América Latina: estudos interdisciplinares. Organização de Wellington Castellucci Junior y Luiz Henrique dos Santos Blume. Salvador, Brazil: EDUNEB, 2016–2017. 2 v.: bibl., ill.

Anthology in two volumes that deals with river communities and traditional populations in coastal areas and how their ways of life and relationships with the environment are impacted by political decisions and economic initiatives. The diverse interdisciplinary case studies from Brazil,

Uruguay, and Chile pay special attention to artisanal fishing and recent environmental history.

409 Radical cartographies: participatory mapmaking from Latin America. Edited by Bjørn Sletto et al. Austin: University of Texas Press, 2020. 242 p.: bibl., ill., maps (some color).

Gathers 12 essays by Latin American scholars and activists which discuss community mapping strategies in the region. Different from traditional participatory cartography that conceives mapping as a tool to contest official maps, the authors go one step further: they focus on how marginalized groups, especially Indigenous populations and Afro-descendant communities, use maps as an instrument of resistance and an argument for territorial claims. The case studies from different countries in Latin America show how these communities apply their own conceptions of space, strengthen their cultural identity, and improve their forms of governance and resource management.

410 Repensando el turismo sustentable. Coordinación de Lilia Zizumbo Villarreal y Neptalí Monterroso Salvatierra. Ciudad de México: Ediciones Eón; Toluca, Mexico: Relidestur, Red Latinoamericana de Investigadores en Desarrollo y Turismo; Toluca, Mexico: SIEA, UAEM, 2017. 393 p.: bibl., ill., maps.

Edited volume of 13 essays that invites readers to reflect on sustainable tourism in Latin America as an economic alternative for communities beyond the capitalism-driven discourse of local development. The authors critically analyze the neoliberal model of tourism and its impact on local populations and discuss sustainable tourism in relation to real estate speculation, protected areas, rural and Indigenous communities, and cultural heritage.

411 Romano, Sarah T.; Jami Nelson-Nuñez; and G. Thomas LaVanchy. Rural water provision at the state-society interface in Latin America. (*Water Int.*, 46:6, 2021, p. 802–820, bibl., map)

The guiding question of this article is how the state can provide and support water sources in rural areas in Latin America. The authors discuss a community-based water management model that can guarantee access and sustainable use in the light of climate change. They use the examples of government water services in Costa Rica, Honduras, and Nicaragua to reveal shortcomings in state support and make suggestions for improvement, namely by strengthening national and international networks of governance and increasing the participation of local and regional water committees in the decisions made by the state.

412 Lo rural en redefinición: aproximaciones y estrategias desde la geografía. Coordinación de Hortensia Castro y Mariana Arzeno. Buenos Aires: Editorial Biblos, 2018. 349 p.: bibl., ill. (Colección Claves para la formación docente)

The aim of this edited volume by Latin American authors is to rethink the meaning and image of "rural" in the region. The authors discuss a wide range of themes related to the production and transformation of rural space in Latin American countries from territorial conflicts and migration flows to cultural-historical heritage, tourism, and agricultural activities.

413 Seemann, Jörn. Writing about "Our Good Neighbors South of the Rio Grande": moral geographies of Latin America in the early 1940s. (*Geopolitics/London*, 25:2, April/June 2020, p. 510–537, bibl., ill., photos, tables)

The article analyzes a popular American children's books series about Latin America published in the early 1940s as part of the Good Neighbor Policy. The contents of these picture books provide insights into how both images and the imagination of countries in Latin America and the Caribbean are constructed to produce a positive and frequently stereotypical impression of these places and to promote a Pan-American idea of the Western Hemisphere in the US.

414 Seminario Internacional, "Zonas Vitivinícolas, Trabajadores Inmigrantes y Transformaciones Sociales," *Mexico City, 2015.* Transformaciones productivas, inmigración y cambios sociales en zonas vitivinícolas globalizadas. Coordinación de Martha Judith Sánchez Gómez et al. Ciudad de México: UNAM, Instituto de Investigaciones

Sociales; Tijuana, Mexico: El Colegio de la Frontera Norte; Ciudad de México: Consejo Nacional de Ciencia y Tecnología (Conacyt), 2018. 440 p.: bibl., ill., maps.

This edited volume examines economic, demographic, and social changes in wine-production areas in different regions of the world. Several case studies in the book focus on places in Latin America (Mendoza, Patagonia, Uruguay, and Baja California) and how wine growing is impacted by restructuring measures and internal and external influences such as international capital, reduction of cultivation areas, sustainability, family agriculture, and local development.

415   **Silva Santisteban, Rocío.** Mujeres y conflictos ecoterritoriales: impactos, estrategias, resistencias. Lima: Centro de la Mujer Peruana Flora Tristán: DEMUS Estudio para la Defensa de los Derechos de la Mujer: Coordinadora Nacional de Derechos Humanos; Madrid: AIETI Asociación de Investigación y Especialización sobre Temas Ibeoramericanos; Barcelona: Entrepueblos, 2017. 188 p.: bibl., color ill.

Written by a Peruvian feminist activist in a lively, engaging, and highly accessible manner, the book focuses on the impacts of ecological-territorial conflicts of women in Latin America in general and Peru in particular. In six thematic chapters, the author reveals how extractivism as a biopolitical project affects women, their bodies, families, and spatial practices. In light of machismo, racism, and patriarchalism, Silva Santisteban denounces gender violence and violations of human rights and proposes concrete strategies of resistance and actions to strengthen the position of women involved in extractivist activities.

416   **Sletto, Bjørn et al.** Walking, knowing, and the limits of the map: performing participatory cartographies in Indigenous landscapes. (*Cult. Geogr./London*, 28:4, Oct. 2021, p. 611–627)

Discusses and applies innovative approaches to participatory mapping and mapmaking beyond conventional cartography. The authors argue that the concept of place and the idea of movement in the form of walking are important contributions to the decolonial study of Indigenous people in Latin America. Uses personal experiences from Brazil, Ecuador, Mexico, and Venezuela to demonstrate the potential and possibilities of this methodology for understanding Indigenous forms of knowledge and conceptions of space.

417   **Svampa, Maristella.** Neo-extractivism in Latin America: socio-environmental conflicts, the territorial turn, and new political narratives. Cambridge, England; New York, N.Y.: Cambridge University Press, 2019. 66 p.: bibl. (Cambridge elements: Elements in politics and society in Latin America)

Short and accessible introduction to the impact of the expansion of neo-extractivism, socioenvironmental conflicts, and resistance movements in Latin America. The author argues that neo-extractivism serves as a starting point for investigating the relationship between political regimes, popular participation, and human rights. She also points out the "ecoterritorial turn" in the debates over ideas such as the rights of nature, common goods, and ethics of care.

418   **Términos clave para los estudios de movilidad en América Latina.** Edición de Dhan Zunino Singh, Guillermo Giucci y Paola Jirón Martínez. Buenos Aires: Editorial Biblos, 2018. 251 p.: bibl. (Lexicón)

This work is the first comprehensive Latin American anthology of key terms related to the emerging concept of mobility in social sciences. The goal of the study is to indicate the importance of mobility as an object of study and thematic focus in research and planning. The 22 essays discuss a wide range of topics associated with movement as a social practice, such as transportation, travel, migration, as well as restrictions to mobility and gender- and age-specific forms.

419   **Territorialidades, migración y política pública en el contexto rural latinoamericano.** Coordinación de Francisco Herrera Tapia *et al.* Toluca, Mexico: Instituto de Ciencias Agropecuarias y Rurales: Centro de Investigación en Ciencias Sociales y Humanidades: Red Internacional de Procesos Participativo, Género y Desarrollo

Territorial; Ciudad de México: Ediciones y Gráficos Eón, S.A. de C.V., 2019. 296 p.: bibl., ill., maps. (Eón sociales)

This study discusses rural spaces and their territoriality in the light of public policies, migration processes, and participatory local development in different parts of Latin America. The 12 case studies deal with a wide range of topics, from the economy of solidarity and return migrations in rural Mexico to the participation of women in local development, production circuits, and food security in Mexico and Colombia.

420 **Territorialising space in Latin America: processes and perceptions.** Edited by Michael K. McCall *et al*. Cham, Switzerland: Springer, 2021. 262 p.: bibl., ill. (The Latin American Studies Book Series)

This collection of papers discusses the concept of territory and its theoretical and methodological dimensions in research in and on Latin America. Specifically, the authors analyze themes such as power relations, territorial claims, and the perception and construction of territories by the state, as well as communities and other social, political, and economic actors. They also examine mapping and mapmaking as a tool of territorialization. In the 14 chapters, case studies from different countries and themes, such as mining conflicts, Indigenous communities, land grabbing, and territorial changes in fishery, are presented to reveal a wide variety of conceptions of territory in the context of Latin American geography.

421 **Turismo y género: una mirada desde Iberoamérica.** Coordinación de Rocío del Carmen Serrano Barquín, Gregoria Rodríguez Muñoz y Yanelli Daniela Palmas Castrejón. Toluca, Mexico: Universidad Autónoma del Estado de México, 2018. 318 p.: bibl., ill., map.

Collection of 11 texts that focus on the relationship between tourism and gender in Latin America. Contributions include the discussion of theoretical and methodological approaches to the theme, the role of women in rural tourism in different countries, and the empowerment of women who work in tourism. Special emphasis is given to gender inequality and actions to improve the conditions of women in the sector.

422 **Urban climates in Latin America.** Edited by Cristián Henríquez Ruiz and Hugo Romero Aravena. Cham, Switzerland: Springer, 2019. 409 p.: bibl., graphs (chiefly color), ill. (some color), index, maps (some color).

This collection of 15 essays by Latin American scholars provides a wide range of views on urban climatology. Inspired by the three-fold classification of urban climate systems by the late Brazilian geographer Carlos Augusto Monteiro, the book is divided into three parts that indicate the close relationship between physical factors and human action: heat islands and thermal comfort; air pollution; and climate disasters, health, and recovery. The chapters are case studies from different countries and reveal not only the diversity of urban climates, but also strategies of mitigation in urban planning.

423 **Urban Latin America: inequalities and neoliberal reforms.** Edited by Thomas Angotti. Lanham, Md.: Rowman & Littlefield, 2017. 299 p.: bibl., index. (Latin American perspectives in the classroom)

This collection of 16 essays provides insights into the problems of urbanization in Latin America. The editor of the book discusses three important factors in the development of cities: violence, voluntary or involuntary segregation (gated communities and slums), and struggles for land. The chapters of the book explore urban space related to poverty, informality, and inequality and present case studies from different countries addressing informal settlements, social housing, participatory budgeting, public space, and social movements.

424 **Urquijo Torres, Pedro Sergio.** Pequeñas localidades rurales: reapropiación territorial en Argentina y México. Prólogo de Gerardo Bocco Verdinelli. Michoacán, Mexico: UNAM, Centro de Investigaciones en Geografía Ambiental, 2017. 219 p.: bibl., ill. (some color), maps (some color).

This comparative study of two rural communities in Argentina and Mexico investigates processes of depopulation and resignification of land use and tenure. The two local examples from the states of Buenos Aires and San Luis Potosí reveal common trends such as rural-urban migration and changing uses of land (from agriculture to rural tourism or irrigated agroindustry), with more recent impacts of narcotrafficking and violence in Mexico.

425 Vasconcellos, Eduardo Alcântara de. Transporte urbano y movilidad: reflexiones y propuestas para países en desarrollo. Buenos Aires: UNSAM Edita, 2015. 311 p.: bibl., ill. (Colección Ciencia y Tecnología)

This is the first Spanish translation of an influential study on transport and urban planning written by a Brazilian political scientist and urban planner. The author engages with the changes in and challenges for public and private transport in developing countries and proposes measures and solutions for the so-called urban crisis.

426 Vegliò, Simone. The urban enigma: time, autonomy, and postcolonial transformations in Latin America. Lanham, Md.: Rowman & Littlefield, 2019. 189 p.: bibl., index. (New politics of autonomy)

Comparative study of spatial dynamics in three Latin American cities, Brasília, Buenos Aires, and Ciudad de México, in the period between the late 19th century and the 1960s. The author introduces the expression "urban enigma" alluding to the contradictions between the modernization discourse for the development of cities by ruling elites and the traditional idea of Latin America as a rural space.

427 Vísperas del urbanismo en Latinoamérica, 1870–1930: imaginarios, pioneros y disciplinas. Edición de Arturo Almandoz Marte y Macarena Ibarra. Santiago: RIL Editores: Instituto de Estudios Urbanos y Territoriales UC, Facultad de Arquitectura, Diseño y Estudios, Pontificia Universidad Católica de Chile, 2018. 259 p.: bibl., index. (Colección Estudios Urbanos UC)

Presents a refreshing view and review of the historiography of urbanism in Latin American cities in its initial phase between 1870 and 1930. The six chapters of the book discuss and compare urban policies, reforms, and planning strategies in the historical and postcolonial context of cities such as Santiago de Chile, Ciudad de Guatemala, Ciudad de México, Buenos Aires, Rosario, and Rio de Janeiro.

428 Vivencias de mulheres no tempo e espaço da pandemia de COVID-19: perspectivas transnacionais. Organização de Georgiane Garabely Heil Vázquez, Joseli Maria Silva e Karina Janz Woitowicz. Curitiba, Brazil: Editora CRV, 2021. 378 p.: bibl., ill.

Collection of essays that approach the impacts of the COVID-19 pandemic from a female point of view. The 18 contributions by Latin American social scientists provide insights into the situation of women in different countries with regards to their bodies, work, and also public policies addressing themes such as pregnancy and childbirth, perception of the domestic space, social distancing, remote jobs, the challenges for nurses, access and rights to health services, and feminist social movements.

429 Voeks, Robert A. and Charlotte Greene. God's healing leaves: the colonial quest for medicinal plants in the torrid zone. (*Geogr. Rev.*, 108:4, Oct. 2018, p. 545–565, bibl., ill.)

A captivating discussion of the colonial quest for medicinal plants in the Latin American tropics driven by religious beliefs. The authors argue that Christian-inspired ideas about human-nature relations legitimized the exploration of beneficial plants downgrading the Indigenous populations to mere custodians of botanical knowledge. The example of the fever tree (cinchona) is given to draw parallels to present-day biopiracy in the region.

430 Voices of Latin America: social movements and the new activism. Edited by Tom Gatehouse. New York, N.Y.: Monthly Review Press, 2019. 285 p.: bibl., color ill., index.

This edited volume of Latin American perspectives engages with a variety of socially and politically relevant themes, based on 70 interviews with activists and leaders of social movements from 14 countries. The book consists of a collection of personal statements with editorial comments for contextualization and provides insights into topics such as machismo, LGBT rights, the struggle of Indigenous groups, the impact of mining on communities, and state violence, among many others.

431   **Zaragocin, Sofia.** Gendered geographies of elimination: decolonial feminist geographies in Latin American settler contexts. (*Antipode*, 51:1, Jan. 2019, p. 373-392, bibl.)
        Sheds light on the impacts of settler colonialism—the replacement of Indigenous population by non-native migrants—on ethnic communities in Latin America, presenting the case of the women of the Epera ethnicity in the borderlands between Ecuador and Colombia. The author provides a framework based on decolonial feminist geography to reveal how processes of cultural elimination destroy Indigenous livelihood through territorial encroachment and nontraditional agricultural practices.

432   **Zaragocin, Sofia** and **Martina Angela Caretta.** Cuerpo-territorio: a decolonial feminist geographical method for the study of embodiment. (*Ann. Am. Assoc. Geogr.*, 111:5, Sept. 2021, p. 1503-1518, bibl., photos)
        Proposes a visual methodology based on the concept of female body-territory with the intention of decentralizing Anglophone feminist geography and contextualizing decolonial debates in and about Latin America. The approach consists of a body map drawing exercise that merges the lived experience of women with collective knowledge about territories, originally used in workshops on the role of women in extractivist activities in Ecuador.

433   **Zusman, Perla.** Milton Santos: la globalización vista desde el Tercer Mundo. Buenos Aires: Ediciones UNGS, Universidad Nacional de General Sarmiento, 2018. 68 p.: bibl. (Colección Pensadores de América Latina)
        This introduction to the work of the Brazilian geographer Milton Santos (1926-2001) is part of a book series on important Latin American social scientists. The author outlines Santos' personal and academic trajectory and points out his theoretical contributions to the study of globalization, territory, development, and citizenship from a genuinely Latin American standpoint.

THE CARIBBEAN

JOSEPH LEONARD SCARPACI, JR., *Executive Director, Center for the Study of Cuban Culture & Economy*

SEVEN BROAD THEMATIC CATEGORIES, none of them particularly novel regarding published scholarly research on Caribbean geography, dominate this literature review. What is different is that tourism is not the most represented topic. Instead, the categories I construct—admittedly subjective—show the realms of social development and race as primary foci.

In the category of social development, publications call attention to the widening digital divide between the Caribbean and Latin America versus the rest of the world (item **459**), the role of parental education attainment as a predictor of children's upward mobility (item **458**), a template for integrated regional planning in Puerto Rico (item **441**), the rise of the "China threat" in the region (item **449**), post-2010 Haitian earthquake psychological trauma (item **438**), and the disparate demographic profiles in the Caribbean basin as evidenced by an aging Cuban population, which contrasts a youthful assessment of hundreds of Colombian municipalities (item **460**).

A second group embraces the broad rubric of race. These works attempt to reinsert non-European histories (item **464**) into the social and cultural records of the Caribbean. The Black Lives Matter movement has long shared parallels in the Caribbean (item **466**). Efforts to reinsert south Asian (Indian) and African diasporic healing records (item **445**) into the region's historical fabric are noteworthy. A set of comparative studies assesses key points about maritime maroons (item **442**), the rise in critical research in Atlantic Studies (item **450**), and the role of land title research in both the Barbados and slave-holding southern states in the US.

Publications that address regional and national identity, falling loosely under the rubric of "geography," register strongly in this literature review. The many labels ascribed to the Caribbean (e.g., Antilles, West Indies, Caribbean basin) (item **467**), the advantages of using physical or human-geographic descriptors in classifying places (item **436**), human-sea interactions and their literary and historical imprint on the region (item **453**), a case study on components that make up Puerto Rican national identity (item **462**), and the proposed "geotransformation" projects launched after the post-1959 Triumph of the Revolution (item **447**) are emblematic of this geographic research.

To the extent that much geographic investigation is "tied to the land" means that environmental histories receive due attention. A fascinating interdisciplinary book explores the history of Cayman "turtlemen," who expanded their exploits from their home to far corners of the Caribbean (item **440**). In doing so, they contribute greatly to clarifying international and natural-reserve boundaries. Two works offer histories of the devastating Puerto Rican earthquake of 1918. One shares lessons learned (item **451**) whilst another is an anthology about earthquakes felt in Puerto Rico since the European discovery of the island (item **439**); along the way, the reader learns of the various premodern ways that seismic activity was described and measured. Also concerning Puerto Rico is a case study of local opposition to a gas pipeline (item **454**) that mobilized from a local grassroots endeavor to an island-wide movement despite overwhelming business support for the project.

Food security and shouldering up locally produced and consumed Caribbean agriculture constitute a growing public policy and scholarly endeavor (item **455**). The nexus among water, energy, and food (item **468**), Haiti's perennial food challenges (item **434**), and the history of land reform in Puerto Rico from the 19th to the current century (item **463**) reflect this attention.

Two smaller research categories, although salient in multiple ways to the human condition in the region, close out this research review: climate change and pollution. The former documents ways of modeling drought (item **457**), risk-management approaches adopted in Jamaica (item **437**), and the need to monitor threats to biodiversity (item **461**). On pollution, two relevant works detail the rise of electronic or "e-waste" (item **456**) (electric cables, cell phones, computers, and attendant products) and the growth in plastics that pollute freshwater streams and maritime coves, keys, beaches, bays, seas, and oceans (item **435**).

434 **Agriculture et reconstruction: défis, enjeux et perspectives de l'agriculture haïtienne.** Sous la direction de Marc J. Cohen et Tonny Joseph. Port-au-Prince: Éditions de l'Université d'État d'Haïti, 2014. 339 p.: bibl., ill., maps. (Haïti-poche)

Two Oxfam America researcher-editors and three colleagues assess the state of rural food security in Haiti and the mass exodus from the countryside to Port-au-Prince and Gonaïves. Most rural Haitians rely solely on subsistence agriculture for their livelihood. National government inaction, despite the creation of several national agencies, has effectively done little over decades to enhance nonagricultural rural development. Oxfam (where 90 percent of the staff is Haitian) and other agencies have implemented the distribution of seed stock, tubers, microcredits, and food-for-work projects. Several of the chapters are reprints of Oxfam publications. Themes in this small tome are fairly standard: empower local decisionmakers; promote adequate technology; engage female workers and decisionmakers into all food security programs; and insist on transparency at state and regional levels as well as NGO engagement with all levels of government. Haiti needs to: 1) reverse several trends such as its status as the second largest long-grain US rice importer (p. 253); 2) alter the power of the rice-importer oligopoly; 3) monitor tariff increases in the first decades of the new millennium on the key products of rice, corn, sorghum wheat, and flour; 4) control inflation and exchange rates between the gourde and the US dollar; and 5) maintain focus on women in food production as the largest heads of households and the majority labor force in agriculture, among other recommendations. The devasting earthquake of January 2010 left 280,000 dead and over one million refugees. Since the book's publication, political turmoil has exacerbated the challenges for rebuilding the agricultural sector. While much of the book is an accounting of Oxfam activity in Haiti, its recommendations—while hardly novel—are both sobering and worthy of review.

435 Ambrose, Kristal K. Coordination and harmonization of a marine plastic debris monitoring program for beaches in the Wider Caribbean Region: identifying strategic pathways forward. (*Mar. Pollut. Bull.*, 171, Oct. 2021, 112167, p. 1–7, bibl., graph, maps)

Building on the UN Decade of Ocean Science and attempts to measure marine plastic debris, this paper examines peer-reviewed articles on marine debris monitoring conducted on beaches in the Wider Caribbean Region. The author concludes that there is great variation in the standardized survey protocols which can only be remedied by standardizing sampling methods and other metrics to inform policy for the Wider Caribbean Region.

436 Bojsen, Heidi. Édouard Glissant and the geography of relation. (*Karib*, 6(1):7, 2021, p. 1–8, bibl.)

This paper analyzes the readings of Édouard Glissant to assess the representations of lived relational, material, physical, and discursive geographies in the Caribbean using Danish geographic education given that nation's role as a former colonial power in the region. The author confirms a growing utilitarian and economy-focused conceptualization of geography in Denmark, where—as with studies of the Caribbean elsewhere—the teaching of physical geography tends to divorce itself from cultural and social parameters.

437 Buckland, Sarah and Donovan Campbell. Agro-climate services and drought risk management in Jamaica: a case study of farming communities in Clarendon Parish. (*Singap. J. Trop. Geogr.*, 43:1, Jan. 2022, p. 43–61, bibl., map, tables)

Caribbean farmers' use of traditional knowledge to mediate drought impacts are increasingly challenged by climate change. The authors argue that Climate Information Services (CIS) are a tool that is available to farmers even though there is little sustained research on the strategy. Some 356 farmers in one of Jamaica's breadbasket regions offer insight into the use of CIS and drought outcomes. Conclusions point to partial farmer uptake of mobile text and online climate information products; less than 5 percent of the sample had access to online CIS information. However, those small farmers who did use some elements of CIS reveal small crop losses, a smaller financial strain, and reinvestment soon after droughts.

438 Cadichon, Jeff Matherson. Narrations du sensible: récits post-traumatiques de survivants du séisme du 12 janvier 2010 en Haïti. Préface de Daniel Cerivois. Haïti: C3 Editions, 2019. 239 p.: bibl., index.

While the estimated loss of life following Haiti's devasting 2010 earthquake is 200,000, some 3 million Haitians—roughly

30 percent of the nation's population—have been impacted with both short- and long-term psychological trauma. Post-traumatic stress disorder (PTSD) is particularly acute among the 15- to 24-year-old cohort. In eight chapters, the author explores the mental health of a sample (n=723) of survivors using quantitative and qualitative analyses. The book opens with an overview of the devastation wrought by the earthquake as well as the long history of natural disasters (hurricanes and earthquakes) unleashed on Haiti. Assessing trauma draws on a tool kit that includes Post-Disaster Needs Assessment, Damage and Loss Assessment, and Rapid Initial Needs Assessment, among others. Post-earthquake amputations require both physical and psychological rehabilitation. Research by Freud, Ferenczi, and Bokanowski frames how humans react to trauma, including flashbacks, hallucinations, and other manifestations of PTSD. Chapter 2 explores psychological trauma and coping mechanisms (resilience) that often follow natural disasters. Several resilience scales are reviewed that are employed in the study population. The third chapter summarizes theoretical foundations of identity—individual and group—which offers context to chapter four, in which the population sample of survivors is broken down by gender and by adolescents and young adults six years beyond the 2010 earthquake. The fifth chapter reports that just over one third of the sample manifests severe PTSD symptoms while about half display moderate signs. Chapter 6 ratchets the scale of analysis down to eight survivors whose clinical assessments reflect the multiple layers of trauma. The seventh chapter highlights how coping with PTSD in Haiti has moved in tandem with a worsening economic situation, conditions far from ideal in coping with mental health struggles that follow a catastrophe. The role of schools is cited as paramount among adolescents. A final substantive chapter captures the contours of modeling research such as this one that employs ways of capturing dynamic achievement identity status. Cardichon concludes that comorbidities mask an accurate assessment of the myriad dimensions of PTSD in the aftermath of the January 2010 earthquake. Access to resources is highly uneven based on social and economic class, but the book does offer a way to begin the healing for the millions of earthquake survivors.

439   **Caldera Ortiz, Luis.** Historia de los terremotos en Puerto Rico. Prólogo por Luis Edgardo Díaz Hernández. Puerto Rico: Centro de Estudios e Investigaciones del Sur Oeste de Puerto Rico; Lajas, Puerto Rico: Editorial Akelarre, 2016. 132 p.: bibl., ill., maps.

The author, a historian, delves into the Puerto Rican National Archives—among other sources—to go beyond describing the well-known "strong" earthquakes of 1787, 1867, and 1918, that have rocked this Greater Antillean island. Its relative location along the edge of a tectonic plate and the Puerto Rican trench (at 28,000 feet deep, it is taller than Mt. Everest, the tallest land peak on the planet) makes it prime for frequent tremors, sea surges (maremotos), and earthquakes. The first chapter spells out the normative and historical methods used by scientists to describe seismic activity, which range from textual description, the creation and use of the seismograph, and the use of satellite images to map out epicenters along the many plates, rifts, and faults comprising the earth's crust. The subsequent chapter, "A History of Earthquakes in Puerto Rico: XVI to XVIII Century," presents an overview of the Spanish settlement of the island called Borinquén by the Taíno natives. Evidence shows that settlers documented sizeable quakes in 1528 and 1562 (epicenter in adjacent Hispaniola island), among others. A low-density and sparsely settled island meant much tectonic activity often went unreported. Both seismic tremors and hurricanes gain the attention of the Spanish crown, particularly in a one-two punch in 1615 where both types of natural disasters occurred just 10 days apart. By the 17th century, a pattern of two major earthquakes per century emerges as the norm. The following two centuries reflect more careful documentation though powerful ones were infrequent. Small towns across the island still celebrate or commemorate the dates of earthquakes. Gradually, corroborating information and improved communications among both Greater and Lesser Antillean nations led to more accurate locations of epicenters.

440   Crawford, Sharika D. The last turtlemen of the Caribbean: waterscapes of labor, conservation, and boundary making. Chapel Hill: The University of North Carolina Press, 2020. 204 p.: bibl., ill., index, maps. (Flows, migrations, and exchanges)

"Goodwill is not turtle soup, but it is an asset all the same" (p. 137). So states marine researcher Archie Carr in this complex story of sustainability, conservation, and survival of the hawksbill (called *carey* in the Spanish-speaking world) and green sea turtles (the larger of the two, ranging from 200 to 600 pounds at maturity). This book casts zoogeographic, historical, and environmental lenses on what was once a protein staple in Caribbean coastal communities and a gourmet delicacy around the circum-Atlantic region: Key West, Kingston, Philadelphia, New York, and London. Just over 100 years ago, large vessels sailed Caribbean waters to harvest tons of turtle meat. Turtlers were frequently hassled by angry customs agents and suspicious Nicaraguans and Colombians who accused the Caymanians of poaching. Turtles have offered eggs, meat, and precious shells for centuries. They proliferated in island and coastal communities of the southwestern Caribbean, especially Providencia Island, Cayman Islands, and the Miskitu communities of eastern Nicaragua. Overfishing would change that. The first two chapters trace the tradition of turtles in precolumbian and colonial economies. Exhausted turtle supplies in the Gran Caymans led to more capital intensive and longer voyages around the Caribbean basin. Canning factories at their pinnacle satisfied demand for a healthy, exotic, and affordable meat. Chapter 3 documents the growing formal and informal networks of marine information that Caymanian turtlers possessed as well as their reach into Spanish-speaking areas and their controlled waters. Claims, territorial boundaries, and disputes documented in the fourth chapter highlight how the nature of boundary-making made turtling a perilous endeavor for Caymanians. Nineteenth-century Cuba made it difficult for Caymanians to salvage wrecks and hunt turtles along the extensive archipelago off Cuba's southern coast. Depleted rookeries in the Caymans sent fishermen to Nicaragua where American investors opposed Caymanian turtlers. Imperial and nation-state policing complicated turtle fishing greatly in the early 20th century. Great Britain recruited many Caymanian seamen into the British navy as the island was still a colony. After the war, conservation and research endeavors curtailed the turtlers' livelihoods. Although the hawknose and green turtles are today on endangered species lists, the knowledge of these "last turtlemen" has done much to settle maritime boundary disputes and brace up conservation efforts to protect these resplendent reptiles.

441   Cuadrado Pitterson, Luz E. et al.
Planificación para un Puerto Rico sostenible: los fundamentos del proceso. Con la colaboración de Carlos Del Valle González, Jorge Hernández Favale y Daniel Torres Bonilla. Puerto Rico: Sociedad Puertorriqueña de Planificación, 2016. 158 p.: bibl., ill. (some color), color maps.

Five professionally licensed planners (PPL) collaborate with three other professionals in compiling this primer on the concepts that define sustainability and the challenges that the island faces. The book consists of four chapters and a rich set of annexes. Chapter 1 anchors the discussion by defining sustainability, social change, and power relationships (highlighting the contributions of French social theorist Michel Foucault and British political scientist John Gaventa). The second chapter describes basic components of the planning process that include citizen participation and their values, vision statements, decision-making, and outcome measures. Chapter 3 turns to planning implementation stages and tools, while the final chapter addresses how local communities, watershed basins, ecological regions, and the nation itself form part of a nested hierarchy that should be present in local and regional planning endeavors. The book is more of a normative outline of how a healthy and harmonious environment on the island can be achieved in participatory and democratically anchored ways versus a macro proposal of sustainability. Annexes include a glossary of key terms and suggested readings (mostly in Spanish) about the themes of democracy, social capital, development, education, governance, planning, power, sustainability, online technologies, and systems theory.

442 Dawson, Kevin. A sea of Caribbean islands: maritime Maroons in the Greater Caribbean. (*Slavery Abolit.*, 42:3, 2021, p. 428–448, facsims., ill.)

Maritime maroons used Atlantic networks of communication to select overseas locations to determine where they should escape. Reliance on African maritime techniques coupled with knowledge about Atlantic wind patterns allowed them to travel in dugout canoes and paddleboards/surfboards. At the same time, the maroons grafted African cultural, spiritual, and political knowledge onto what we now call the "Greater Caribbean." Seas connected these Africans and their descendants to a broad diaspora that shows connectivity centuries later.

443 Desarrollo y turismo sostenible en el Caribe. Textos de Silvia Mantilla V. et al. Bogotá: Universidad Nacional de Colombia, 2016. 112 p.: bibl., ill., indexes. (Colección Escuela de pensamiento)

The growing portion of the gross domestic product (GDP) derived from tourism in Caribbean basin countries has hovered between 10 and 30 percent over the past decade. This, in part, explains why "it is necessary to implement an agenda to promote [tourism] products in foreign markets and develop plans to increase the quantity and quality of what is offered" (p. 10, my translation). Three parts make up this small tome. The first situates the Mexican Riviera and historic Mayan archeological sites in Guatemala, El Salvador, Mexico, Belize, and Honduras. The multidestination "Mayan Route" encourages sustainability and community participation. Chapter 2 considers the poverty belts circling Cancún despite the latter's success at the national level. It challenges the assumptions of global capital and the exploitation of human resources. A third chapter by Johannie James shifts attention to recent developments in the San Andrés archipelago, Providencia, and Santa Catalina. He questions the benefits for the host populations. Analysts Márquez and Márquez take a step back and assess the impact of tourism on the natural environment. The Rosario and San Andrés Islands and the city of Cartagena reflect detrimental outcomes in the loss of biodiversity, real-estate speculation, and climate change. Classic or traditional tourism-development models are anachronistic in the new millennium. Part 2 synthesizes the literature pertaining to tourism strategies and models in the broader Caribbean, while part 3 focuses again on the San Andrés, Providencia, and Santa Catalina archipelago. Findings from workshops and charettes inform place-specific goals for these fragile ecosystems.

444 Fawcett, Emma. Challenges for sustainable growth through tourism in the Dominican Republic. Washington, D.C.: Global Foundation for Democracy and Development; Santo Domingo: Fundación Global Democracia y Desarrollo (FUNGLODE), 2016. 59 p.: bibl. (Research and ideas series. Sustainable development)

This primer on sustainable, inclusive growth in the Dominican Republic tourism sector outlines four challenges that the sector faces: 1) modernizing fiscal incentive frameworks, 2) generating growth in basic services and infrastructure that moves in tandem with the development of tourism, 3) linking economic development with the poorest Dominicans, and 4) staying attuned to carrying capacity and environmental concerns. Special attention is given to the Punta Cana-Bávaro tourist pole in the eastern corner of the island. The author's assessment is that the tourism sector has provided the Dominican Republic with relatively stable government, consistent foreign earnings, brand recognition, and capital and technological investment. At the time of the writing, the author signals a warning about the potential threat to the existing all-inclusive resorts operating in the Dominican Republic and the alternative in-home offerings (*pensiones*) of Cuba's budding tourist trade.

445 Fisk, Bethan. Black knowledge on the move: African diasporic healing in Caribbean and Pacific New Granada. (*Atlan. Stud. Global Curr.*, 18:2, 2021, p. 244–270, bibl.)

Many Black healers use African diasporic healing in the Caribbean and Pacific regions of New Granada (Venezuela and Colombia). Such practices draw on poisoning and ritual practice derived from criminal and ecclesiastical trials and accusations. The paper discusses how these healers create their knowledge by employing a connective and comparative approach. Mobility played a central role in the recirculation and creation of the African diaspora. Illustrative of the methodology is the retelling of a case of an African slave (called a *bozal*, a recently arrived African slave) and a *mulata* of African and European heritage who concocts a mixture of molasses and urine to treat an ailment. Her use of suspicious contaminants in the concoction led to her arrest in the Quibdó region (Colombia) and a trial ensued (led by two priests since the setting was an isolated gold mining region). Although she was acquitted, this and other case studies show how the legal proceedings (by government or the Catholic Church) document these healing practices.

446 Franzen, Sarah and **Lia T. Bascomb.**
Holding land, claiming kin: the relation between race, land, and kinship in the southern US and Barbados. (*Antipode*, 54:2, March 2022, p. 418-434)

A comparative study of race, property, and kinship draws on traditional practices of family land and heir property. Land titles are employed by racially dispossessed populations to name and practice kinship, to claim forms of belonging, and to situate their value systems within social, legal, and racial structures. This study of Black geographies can help shape US policies about agricultural support and grants. Caribbean applications include how land is used as a family resource. Central to the conclusions is the argument that dispossession means going beyond monetary losses, and considering land ownership as something other than a mere economic benefit.

447 Funes Monzote, Reinaldo. Nuestro viaje a la luna: la idea de la transformación de la naturaleza en Cuba durante la Guerra Fría. La Habana: Fondo Editorial Casa de Las Américas, 2019. 526 p.: bibl. (Ensayo histórico-social)

The allegory implied in the title, "our trip to the moon," stems from Fidel Castro's remark in 1967 about the Soviet-US Cold War space race: "[. . .] after all, the Soviets, the Americans, aren't they trying to reach the moon? Well, this project is our trip to the moon" (p. 11). The project to which the *líder máximo* referred was the quest for Cuba to take advantage of shallow seas between the main island and the Isle of Youth, the Bay of Pigs, and other sea-to-land conversion plans. As Antonio Núñez Jiménez purportedly stated, "God made the world, but the Dutch made Holland" (p. 11). Imbued into Cuban scientific research and promulgated by the cave explorer and geographer Núñez Jiménez were the concepts of "geotransformation" and "transforming nature." Three metaphoric categories structure the work. Part 1, "Preparing the Take-off: 1947-1958," explores the chimera that economic development posed conceptually for the world. It outlines developments in the island's broad field of natural resource investigation and describes the main components of large-scale swamp draining and building a highway to the Isle of Youth and its attendant efforts to reclaim shallow seas for agricultural purposes. Part 2, "The Great Acceleration Cuban Style: 1959-1970," delves somewhat uncritically into the failed 10-million-ton sugar harvest goal, swamp draining, artificial rain projects, soil reclamation, reforestation, afforestation, and national park creation. It also examines the role of geographic research within the revolution and the island's professional outreach to China and the former USSR. "A New Landscape, 1971-1991," is the title of the final part, which ends with the onset of the demise of the USSR and the beginning of Cuba's Special Period in a Time of Piece (in which Cuba lost its favored status in the Soviet trading bloc as well as key subsidies from Moscow). Topics in this part include the "Havana Ring" *(Cordón de La Habana)*—an effort to make the capital region a self-sufficient food producer that relied in good measure on weekend volunteer work—the defense of the swamps, and Las Terrazas ecotourist complex in Pinar del Río province. A metaphoric epilogue titled "Returning to Earth by a Forced Landing" takes stalk of Cuba's triumph (Las Terrazas) and failures (most of the aforementioned projects) in Cuba's geotransformations. Blame is assigned to misguided voluntarism, poor government decision-making, the long-standing US trade embargo, and Cuba's delay in implementing mass tourism (compared to other Caribbean nations). In the end, the author concludes that "transforming nature in Cuba did not become the dream of traveling to the moon, and in part it is better that way, if one takes into account the potential environmental damage of several of the more ambitious projects" (p. 480, my translation).

448 Gahman, Levi; Gabrielle Thongs; and **Adaeze Greenidge.** Disaster, debt, and "underdevelopment": the cunning of colonial-capitalism in the Caribbean. (*Development/Rome*, 64, March 2021, p. 112–118, bibl.)

Extreme weather events imposed by Hurricanes Irma and Maria in 2017 and Dorian in 2019 are examined based on structural forces that worsen the Caribbean's socioenvironmental risk. The resilience of Caribbean nations is weakened by neoliberal exploitation—the debts and practices of post-independence corruption. Social geography and political economy are key in understanding the Caribbean's vulnerability, disaster, and catastrophe, and point to the disproportionate weight of debt, underdevelopment, and imperialism in shaping the region's future.

449 Grydehøj, Adam et al. Practicing decolonial political geography: island perspectives on neocolonialism and the China threat discourse. (*Polit. Geogr.*, 85, March 2021, 102330, p. 1–11, bibl.)

The discourse about a "China threat" is increasingly used to justify how metropolitan powers operated in the former or present colonial realms of Guåhan/Guam in Oceania, Kalaallit Nunaat/Greenland in the Arctic, Okinawa in East Asia, and Jamaica in the Caribbean. This work employs a decolonial political geography to inform collaborative writing and research. Jamaica's policies have been associated with the US since the 1980s, enhanced by the USAID (US Agency for International Development) and the Caribbean Basin Trade Partnership Act. However, the new millennium witnesses many Chinese loans, credits, and grants to Jamaica, often with little restrictions. As a result, these initiatives have increased Jamaica's relationship with China as seen with the Chinese-built Kingston Logistic Hub and the 2016 Chinese financing of the 730 million US dollars North-South Highway. In the process, both public and private Jamaican entities have denounced how Chinese extractive industries have provoked deforestation, respiratory problems, groundwater pollution, and other maladies. Despite those externalities, China serves as an alternative development venue for Jamaica even though the US might directly or indirectly impose sanctions.

450 Guess, Allison. Sixteenth-century Hispaniola: a hidden geography of Solidão. (*Women's Stud. Q.*, 49, Fall/Winter 2021, p. 437–441)

This review of *Afro-Latin American Studies: An Introduction* gave high praise to the book for its timely and innovative approach to the field. Alejandro de la Fuente, one of the editors along with George Reid Andrews, is considered "an emerging scholar of racial capitalism and settler colonialism who is working at the crux of critical Black studies and early modern studies of the Atlantic world." The book fills a gap in the emerging field of Atlantic Studies, with a particular focus on the establishment of La Española (Hispaniola). The review's author also recommends the book because it is a "a robust survey of the field." For philosophy specialist's review of the 2018 publication, see *HLAS 74:2958*.

451 Jaramillo Nieves, Lorna Gisela. 11 de octubre de 1918, el terremoto en Puerto Rico: lecciones cien años después. Hato Rey, Puerto Rico: Publicaciones Puertorriqueñas, 2018. 186 p.: bibl., ill., maps.

Puerto Rico's iconic and emblematic earthquake of 1918 claimed over 100 lives and set into motion a systematic way to analyze and interpret these seismic events. The author surveys the contributions of Wegner, Richter, Copernicus, Ptolemy, Aristotle, Newton, Kepler, and Mercali to assess our contemporary understanding of mountain-building processes and plate tectonics. On 11 October 1918, records note vertical shaking with one- to two-minute intervals that were followed by horizontal shaking. In this way, the author spells out the descriptions of P-waves (primary) and S-waves (secondary) of energy moving through the ground. At that time, the Rossi Forel scale's 10 descriptors designated the intensity of the disaster. American government officials H.F. Reid and S. Taber documented much of the empirical outcomes of this powerful quake while the author fills in other elements with photographs, communications, newspaper accounts, letters, and other sources from survivors of the event. The work carefully documents the metric cubic meters of rubble across the island: Arecibo, Utuado, Gurabo, Las Piedras, Yabucoa, Maunabo, Alto Bandera, Jayuya, Mayagüez, Las Marías, Consumo, Maricao, Ponce, San Juan, and other towns. Efforts to sell bonds to aid in reconstruction were part of a strategy as was an increase in builders touting earthquake-resistant commercial and residential buildings to mitigate damage and loss of life. The book's closing chapter, "Preventing instead of lamenting," points to public policy and household proposals to reduce future losses.

452   Lewis, Patsy. Caribbean regional integration: a critical development approach. Milton Park, England; New York, N.Y.: Routledge, 2022. 284 p.: bibl., index.

This book challenges neoliberal ideology that undergirds regionalism discourse by questioning the value of neoliberal regionalism for Caribbean nations. The author employs an alternative framework for measuring the success of regional integration through a review of how the Caribbean Community (CARICOM) can confront development challenges more democratically. There are few avenues for citizens to shape the policy direction of regional integration, particularly in light of climate change and COVID-19 and its attendant variants, unstable social security and pension systems, and foreign debt.

453   Lloréns, Hilda. A passion for the sea: human-sea interactions in contemporary Caribbean art. (*Anthurium*, 17:1, 2021, p. 1–20, bibl., ill., photos)

Contemporary Caribbean artists Tony Capellán (Dominican Republic), Christopher Cozier (Trinidad), Scherezade García (Dominican-born, US-raised), El Colectivo Shampoo (Dominican Republic), Jennifer Allora (Puerto Rico), Guillermo Calzadilla (Puerto Rico), and Nadia Huggins (Trinidad and Tobago) use rich imagery of the sea to understand pressing social concerns. Their artwork visualizes local realities to illustrate broader global conditions, one of which is often referencing the sea as a pathway of escape. Caribbean history serves as a window into understanding how the "modern" and the "globalized" give artists a way to assess their critical interventions. Thus, it is essential to recognize that the Caribbean has been "modern" ever since its economies were linked to those of the North Atlantic centuries ago.

454   Massol Deyá, Arturo A. Amores que luchan: relato de la victoria contra el gasoducto en tiempos de crisis energética. 2da edición. San Juan: Ediciones Callejón, 2018. 253 p.: bibl., ill. (Colección en fuga. Ensayos)

This environmental case study is penned by a microbiologist with expertise in heavy metals. It focuses on a community center *(Casa Pueblo)* in Aguado, Puerto Rico, and its fervent opposition to a gas pipeline in the region. In 2010, the government notified residents about the use of eminent domain and the taking of private property for a so-called public good. Estimates of the project rose in short order from 150 million, to 300 million, and finally to 800 million dollars in 18 months. Nine substantive chapters document the resources used to challenge the proposal, its attendant 18 million USD advertising campaign to promote the project, and ultimately the defeat at both the Puerto Rican government level *(Estado Libre Asociado)*, which pitched the project as the Green Way *(Vía Verde)*, and the US federal government. Stakeholders in this project included professional engineers, utility companies, local residents, construction teams, and environmental groups. A 15,000-demonstrator protest at the Capitolio building in Old San Juan culminated in solidifying the opposition against the gasline as the entire book is seen through the lens of Puerto Rico's ongoing struggle as a neocolony.

455 Mohammadi, Elham et al. Food security challenges and options in the Caribbean: insights from a scoping review. (*Anthropocene Sci.*, 1, Jan. 2022, p. 91–108, bibl.)

This article examines contemporary Caribbean food policies and practices as they pertain to the second sustainable development goal (SDG2 or Zero Hunger). Methods include posing a key question to expert informants: "What constraints and enablers impact the ability of small island states to achieve the Zero Hunger goal?" Using a methodology developed by the Joanna Briggs Institute (JBI), five challenges and obstacles stem from this scoping review: 1) island geography, 2) governance deficiencies, and 3) institutional constraints, compounded by 4) collaboration barriers, and 5) externally imposed impediments (together with environmental and financial shocks). Conclusions point to three key dimensions of food security that are often overlooked: utilization, agency, and sustainability. The authors argue that more actors must be involved in rulemaking, power, conflict management, and knowledge-sharing. Such a polycentric governance system might assist islands in their search for food security.

456 Mohammadi, Elham; Simron Singh; and Komal Habib. Electronic waste in the Caribbean: an impending environmental disaster or an opportunity for a circular economy? (*Resour. Conserv. Recycl.*, 164, Jan. 2021, 105106, bibl., graph)

Electronic waste (e-waste) is no longer only a concern in the industrial North Atlantic economies. This paper estimates Electrical and Electronic Equipment (EEE) flows for five islands across 60 years (1965–2025). Estimates are that these islands will double their e-waste per capita per year, e.g., 13 kg/cap/year, which is up from a global average of 6.1 kg/cap/year in 2016. Another dimension of this looming environmental problem is that this e-waste will rise from 27,500 tons in 2010 to an estimated 59,000 tons 15 years hence. The authors conclude that small islands should retreat from the linear economy and move to a circular economy.

457 Moraes, Flávia D.; Thomas L. Mote; and Lynne Seymour. Ocean-atmosphere variability and drought in the insular Caribbean. (*Int. J. Climatol.*, 42:10, Aug. 2022, p. 1–22, bibl., graphs, maps, tables)

The insular Caribbean suffers from hurricanes, floods, earthquakes, and drought, but the latter has produced a dearth of literature on its causes and effects. By using seasonal drought in the insular Caribbean from 1950 to 2017, the paper examines similar patterns in the Eastern Pacific (EP) and Central Pacific (CP) ENSO, North Atlantic Oscillation (NAO), and Atlantic Meridional Mode (AMM). It argues that the region should be divided into the Greater Antilles and Bahamas (GA) and the Lesser Antilles (LA) to better understand the seasonality and intensity of drought over larger versus smaller islands. A high-resolution drought atlas points to a drying trend for both the GA and the LA areas. The latter is subject to more widespread drought events, recording 12 years when the midsummer dry spell (MSD; July-August) had drought >80 percent of the area, while the GA scored only two years of MSD drought that extensive. The ENSO, CP El Niño years correlated with drought in the LA from December-July, while the association between the two types of ENSO and the GA was not statistically significant.

458 Munoz, Ercio. The geography of intergenerational mobility in Latin America and the Caribbean. New York, N.Y.: CUNY Graduate Center, City University of New York, 2021. 57 p.: bibl., maps, tables. (Stone Center on Socio-Economic Inequality working paper series)

Based on data from nine censuses in 24 Caribbean and Latin American countries over the span of half a century, the study examines the probability of upward mobility among children obtaining a primary education but whose parents did not. Downward mobility meant the likelihood of not achieving a primary education among those whose parents did complete primary school. Despite the wide variances among 400 provinces and 6,000 districts, the author concludes that there is a declining trend in the so-called mobility gap between urban and rural populations as well as small differences by gender.

NACLA Report on the Americas. See item 970.

Offen, Karl H. Subsidy from nature: green sea turtles in the colonial Caribbean. See item 479.

459 **Pick, James B.; Avijit Sarkar; and Elizabeth Parrish.** The Latin American and Caribbean digital divide: a geospatial and multivariate analysis. (*Inf. Technol. Dev.*, 27:2, Aug. 2020, p. 235–262, bibl., maps)

Uneven access to digital technologies is particularly acute when the Caribbean and Latin America are compared to the rest of the world. To measure the digital divide, the authors study the spatial patterns of information and communication technology (ICT) adoption and utilization. The study maps five distinctive clusters of technology adoption and use factors. Regression findings highlight human development and infrastructural causes of this uneven geospatial divide.

460 **Retos demográficos en Colombia y Cuba.** Compilación de Andrés Castro Tobón. Bogotá: Universidad Externado de Colombia, 2019. 263 p.: bibl., some color ill., some color maps. (Cuadernos del CIDS. Serie I; 31)

Four Colombian and two Cuban social scientists author five chapters about two very different nations that hold contrasting demographic profiles, distinct positions in the demographic transition model, and attendant economic development challenges. In the former, the population forecast for more than 300 municipalities is far from sustainable. In the latter, low fertility rates and increasing out-migration of Cuban youth compound the aging of the island's population. The volume concentrates on four local development schemes to meet these challenges: decentralization, finance, planning objectivity, and community participation.

461 **Rodríguez-Rivera, Luis E.** Governance of the Caribbean marine biodiversity: complex challenges for a complex region. (*in* Biological diversity and international law: challenges for the post 2020 scenario. Edited by Mar Campins Eritja and Teresa Fajardo del Castillo. Cham, Switzerland: Springer, 2021, p. 179–203, bibl.)

This chapter assesses the current condition of biodiversity in the Caribbean Sea. Its vibrancy remains threatened, and the fabric of marine biodiversity governance is merely an "overlapping web of international and regional institutions; multilateral biodiversity, environmental and ocean management agreements; and international and regional policies, plans and initiatives implemented at the national and local levels." The author urges more flexible and locally accountable strategies to enhance the region's marine biodiversity and lead to more agile and effective governance.

462 **Rodríguez-Silva, Ileana M.** The Caribbean house of mirrors: constructing regions in area studies. (*Positions/Durham*, 29:1, Feb. 2021, p. 93–119, bibl., photo)

The author uses the house of mirrors as an analytical frame to study debates about US colonialism among Puerto Rican politicians and intellectuals in the 1910s, 1950s, and 1960s. The former reflects the 1912 War in Cuba, while the latter portrays Puerto Rico as the "Showcase of the Americas" with its Operation Bootstrap and related development programs and policies. With this approach, the paper tries to avoid reproducing a single national gaze even though there are common social, historical, and geographic factors at these distinct times. The author concludes that the house of mirrors shows how politicians and intellectuals promote their political goals.

463 **Rodríguez Vargas, Rafael A.** Hombre de la azada en Puerto Rico: opresión y libertad. Puerto Rico: publisher not identified, 2019. 441 p.: bibl.

"The Man with the Hoe" (*Hombre de la azada*) is a metaphor for the historic evolution of agrarian reform in Puerto Rico that began with the arrival of US troops on the island's shores in 1898. Derived mainly from his doctoral dissertation, the author reviews the struggles of these small farmers from sharecroppers on mostly coffee and sugar plantations to protagonists in their own livelihoods. The 1960 Mutual Aid and Self-Help Program provides a venue to examine public policy responses to housing needs. Puerto Rico's land tenure system in the 19th century was a "combination of primitive patriarchal production and a feudal regime that commenced with Spanish colonization" (p. 181). The book's eight chapters and conclusions weave a narrative that originates in Luis Muñoz Marín's commonwealth government and related policies that have tried to improve the lot of Puerto Rican farmers. Its mostly 20th-century social history is well situated within agrarian reform efforts elsewhere in Latin America and the Caribbean. Considerable attention is directed at post-WWII housing and social programs that aimed to enhance agricultural and nonagricultural employment and housing programs. Theoretical insights by John Rawls (theory of justice), anarchist Petr Alexeyevich Kropotkin (self-help and mutual aid), and Rex Tugwell, island governor and economic advisor to Franklin Delano Roosevelt (institutionalism), provide perspectives on this case study of rural social justice.

464 Samaroo, Brinsley. Changing Caribbean geographies: connections in flora, fauna and patterns of settlement from Indian inheritances. (*J. Indentureship Legacies*, 1:1, 2021, p. 16–35, bibl.)

An underreported chapter in South Asian (Indian) migration to the Caribbean is the role of agreement signers, or *grimityas*, who carried cuttings, seeds, and dried fruits in their long voyage to the New World. Their flora contribution to Caribbean plantations survived thanks to their packing within *jahaji* bundles along with the sacred Holy Qur'an and Tulsi Ranayan. Goats, poultry, and sheep formed part of the interoceanic crossing, but they were not eaten. Indian workers encouraged plantation masters to import Zebu cattle and Brahma bulls, while mongoose were released to attack venomous snakes. Not only are these contemporary features of the Caribbean landscape today, but these migrant-induced exotic species afforded meat, manure, and leather goods to island populations and offered new modes of transport in rural settlements.

465 Sheller, Mimi. Reconstructing tourism in the Caribbean: connecting pandemic recovery, climate resilience and sustainable tourism through mobility justice. (*J. Sustain. Tourism*, 29:9, 2021, p. 1436–1449, bibl.)

Extractive tourism has been deleterious for many small-island nations of the Caribbean in both the colonial and postcolonial eras. The paper first traces the history of climate change vulnerability. It then analyzes the "coloniality of climate" which entails a critique of disaster tourism during these "unnatural disasters." By reframing the ethical and political implications of tourism recovery, the author considers how prepandemic mobilities differ greatly from post-COVID-19 times. The key idea posed is that "mobility justice" is a framework to contemplate transitions to sustainable tourism, climate change, and disaster recovery. Disaster reconstruction in the Caribbean, where on average small island developing states derive 30 percent of their revenues from tourism, should focus on food sovereignty, agroecology, and regenerative economies. These strategies should be anchored in community-based organizations and people's assemblies.

466 Steinberg, Philip. Blue planet, Black lives: matter, memory, and the temporalities of political geography. (*Polit. Geogr.*, 96, June 2022, 102524, p. 1–33, bibl., map, photos)

This paper questions modernist narratives for studying the ocean's materiality, marine ecologies, and scholarship in Black and Caribbean studies. A debate in Bristol, England, in 2020 and 2021 over the handling of the unseated statue of slave trader Edward Colston uses postcolonial Caribbean theory and art to better understand how different narratives and memories of the Caribbean slaver are discussed. The roles of the Black Lives Matter movement, Frank Bowling, Matthew Fontaine Maury, and Edward Colston shape oceanic ontologies which often muddle conventional divisions between past, present, and future.

467 Williams, Ernest H. and **Lucy Bunkley-Williams.** What and where is the Caribbean?: a modern definition. (*Fla. Geogr.*, 52:1, 2021, p. 3–28, bibl.)

An overview of the many renowned origins of the meaning of "Caribbean" that include the Greater Caribbean Region, Wider Caribbean Region, West Indies, British West Indies, Antilles, Caribbean Basin, Caribbean Proper, Greater Caribbean, West Indies, and Wider Caribbean, among others. Each label presents certain weaknesses. However, the authors contend that physical geographic features are more precise than human geographic elements because the former emphasize biota, interconnectivity, and physical isolation that sidestep the myriad cultural, economic, emotional, mystical, political, and religious circumstances that are more challenging to conceptualize and operationalize.

468 Winters, Zachary S.; **Thomas L. Crisman**; and **David T. Dumke**. Sustainability of the water-energy-food nexus in Caribbean small island developing states. (*Water/Basel*, 14:3, 2022, 322, p. 1–18, bibl., maps, tables)

Small island developing states (SIDS) of the Caribbean face challenges in the water-energy-food (WEF) nexus in the near future. By 2050, some of these nations will likely fail the food and energy sectors if the assumptions behind the projections hold. The authors argue that water is the key resource for long-term sustainability. Poor governance and long-term planning for potential calamities (population growth, disasters, and climate change) will impede achieving sustainability goals for Caribbean SIDS unless they implement proactive measures.

CENTRAL AMERICA

DAVID M. COCHRAN, JR., *Professor of Geography, University of Southern Mississippi*
PETER H. HERLIHY, *Professor of Geography, University of Kansas*

THIS BIENNIAL RETROSPECTIVE of geographical research on Central America coincides with the years when the world closed itself off in response to the threat of the COVID-19 pandemic. Given the profound feelings of uncertainty and the political and economic instability that affected so many people around the world, the continued productivity of Central Americanist geographers in those years speaks to their enduring dedication to the region. This retrospective collection of publications, like others before it, showcases a variety of topics and themes in recent geographical research. More than in the past, this body of research reflects convergence around a few important themes that have captured the imaginations of geographers in recent years. Despite this convergence, however, this research continues to span the three branches of the field: physical-environmental, human-cultural, and geospatial-technological. Many of the works included in this section, especially those that focus on human-environment interactions, are interdisciplinary in nature, cutting across geography and bridging the divides among cognate disciplines. Following this interpretive essay, the annotated bibliography showcases nearly 50 exciting new works by geographers and others doing geographical research on Central America.

Physical geographers continue to produce substantive studies that highlight palynology and soil science and use proxy dating techniques to devise new interpretations of paleoenvironments in Central America. Much of this work has an interdisciplinary component and its results are clearly relevant to Central American archeology. Johnson, Horn, and Lane (item **487**) produced a 4,200-year climate chronology based on lake core sediments extracted in southwest Costa Rica. Their results provide important clues about environmental changes associated with early maize domestication and the influence of intermittent drought on prehistoric food production. Another groundbreaking study (item **482**) documents how uranium, carbon, and lead isotopes stored in a stalagmite were used to create a high-resolution climate history of the Belize River watershed that coincided with the classic and early postclassic periods of Maya civilization.

A number of physical geographers developed models to assess regional-scale landscape change and to produce tools for land-use/landcover analysis and disaster planning. Quesada-Román, Castro-Chacón, and Feoli Boraschi (item **491**) used geomorphological cartography to map natural and anthropogenic features in the urbanized Torres River watershed in Costa Rica. Similarly, Suárez and Domínguez-Cuesta (item **509**) brought together disparate data sets to produce a comprehensive landslide inventory map of Tegucigalpa, Honduras. Kjerfve, McField, Thattai, and Giró (item **476**) combined field analysis with regional-scale modeling of fluvial runoff and hurricane disturbance to measure the health of the Mesoamerican Reef in the Gulf of Honduras.

Another group of physical geographers published research that has direct relevance to natural hazards and disaster planning. Barrantes (item **486**) combined qualitative and quantitative data to create a multihazard risk model for Poás, Costa Rica. Two other research teams developed models for use in pre-event prediction and post-event assessment of earthquakes in Guatemala (items **503** and **504**). A predictive study details the impact of sea level rise in Caribbean Costa Rica (item **488**).

Several notable landcover change studies document the continuing threat of human activity on the region's most endangered ecosystems while also demonstrating new geospatial analytical capabilities. One study (item **483**) combines multiple Landsat platforms to assess the effectiveness of conservation management efforts in the Belize Barrier Reef Reserve System. Another study uses similar techniques to measure forest loss on nearby Ambergris Caye, which experienced significant urban development in recent decades. Ironically, much of this was a result of the commercial success of ecotourism (see *HLAS 75:456*). A third study integrated a modelling package in R with time-series Landsat satellite imagery to detect land clearance in tropical dry forests in Costa Rica (item **495**). Another excellent GIS study details the landscapes of urban green areas in Costa Rica (item **493**).

Cultural historical research that focuses on human-environment interactions continues to be a vibrant and diverse area of scholarship for Central Americanist geographers. Lovell (item **477**) presents an overview of postcontact epidemic disease in the Americas to draw conclusions about the global impacts of COVID-19 today. Offen (item **479**) celebrates the ecological, cultural, and commercial importance of the green sea turtle while also paying homage to the research of James Parsons, Bernard Neitschmann, and Archie Carr about this amazing species. Jobbová, Helmke, and Bevan (item **484**) use ethnographic and archeological evidence to demonstrate the historic cultural continuity of rain rituals among Maya farmers from the classic period to the present day. An image-rich ethnography of artisanal gold production in Guanacaste, Costa Rica (item **489**) combines photography with prose to tell the story of a former gold mining region whose contemporary inhabitants continue to engage in small-scale exploitation of the precious metal as part of their rural livelihoods. Rodríguez and Davidson-Hunt (item **492**) report on an Indigenous Bribri community in Costa Rica and document some of the historic influences of commercial agriculture on Bribri ethnoecology.

The legacy of colonialism and postcolonialism, inequality, and repression continues to be a focus of geographical research on Central America. Clouser (item **499**) examines how the legacy of state security, international development, and political repression has silenced Indigenous people in their efforts to bring societal change and social justice to Guatemala. A compelling historical study by Pleasant and Spalding (item **513**) uses a core-periphery lens to compare the internal dependence of Bocas del Toro province with Panama to the external dependence of Panama to the US. Another study examines lifestyle migration in Bocas del Toro, framing it as a new chapter in the ongoing history of neoliberalism in Panama (item **514**). Broad and Cavanagh (item **497**) recount an intense grassroots struggle between campesinos of the Rio Lempa watershed and a Canadian-based multinational mining company whose environmentally destructive practices and campaign of intimidation led to its expulsion from El Salvador.

Several studies examine contemporary themes in human geography. An edited volume by Borland and Adams (item **475**) examines the role of volunteer US tourism as a form of cultural interaction and progressive social change. A study by Kumar, Christakis, and Pérez-Escamilla (item **508**) examines household food insecurity and health among rural communities in western Honduras. Pope (item **485**) documents conditions in Belize during the early months of COVID-19 and another study by Caruso, Cucagna, and Ladronis (item **472**) documents a startling decrease in the flow of remittances across the region because of the pandemic. Walker (item **515**) evaluates the impacts of a private land titling campaign on patterns of forest clearance and demonstrates the continued importance of protected areas and Indigenous homelands in forest preservation in Panama. A study by Porter (item **490**) recounts the political and economic realities of informal urban residents in Costa Rica.

Most significant this biennium are the scores of geographers researching cocaine trafficking in Central America. The pioneering work of geographer Kendra McSweeney (item **478**) ignited the interest of many others and motivated them to examine narco-imprints on the region (items **469, 471, 480, 481, 501,** and **505**), most with shared authors and contents. They collectively tell how cocaine trafficking has become an illicit driver of deforestation and *narcodegradation*, especially along the region's borderlands where drug trafficking organizations engage in illegal land transactions, money laundering, and territorial control. They also show how drug trafficking has eroded governance in protected areas and Indigenous territories. Questions related to how much land cover change is actually tied to drug trafficking and how its geospatial imprint can be distinguished from other activities remain for future research to answer.

Finally, geographers continue their longstanding call for participatory governance and *in situ* conservation with sustainable development and climate change mitigation through recognition of land and resource rights (items **470** and **502**). Collective land titling for Indigenous/ladino peoples is a crucial strategy for combating deforestation, protecting cultural resources and biodiversity, and mitigating climate change. Indigenous Territorial Jurisdictions (ITJs) with collective inalienable titles now cover an astonishing 18 percent of the land area of Central America, and much of this lies in the Mesoamerican Biological Corridor (item **474**). While offering great potential, these advances must be accompanied by a greater degree of community involvement. The lands and resources of all 23 of the titled Indigenous and Black territories in eastern Nicaragua are plagued by illegal settlement and deforestation due to the absence of state enforcement (item **510**). Unfortunately, and perhaps related to concerns and restrictions during the COVID-19 pandemic, not much detailed geographical field research has focused on these relatively new territorial units. At present, we know little about this illegal settlement or the livelihoods of the settlers, let alone the geographical, political, historical, or ecological significance of this emerging phenomenon. As with other themes within Central Americanist geography, much work remains to be done.

GENERAL

Arrioja Díaz Viruell, Luis Alberto. Bajo el crepúsculo de los insectos: clima, plagas y trastornos sociales en el reino de Guatemala (1768–1805). See *HLAS 76:477*.

469   Ballvé, Teo and **Kendra McSweeney.** The "Colombianisation" of Central America: misconceptions, mischaracterisations and the military-agroindustrial complex. (*J. Lat. Am. Stud.*, 52:4, Nov. 2020, p. 805–829, maps)

The authors argue that labeling drug-related violence in Central America as "Colombianisation" of the region is misleading and perpetuates ineffective antidrug policies. The real process has more to do with the convergence of geopolitical and economic interests that have expanded the agro-industrial-military nexus in Central America. A better understanding of the drug trade is crucial for developing policies that combat drug-related violence and corruption in the region.

Bebbington, Anthony; Benjamin Fash; and **John Rogan.** Socio-environmental conflict, political settlements, and mining governance: a cross-border comparison, El Salvador and Honduras. See item **865**.

470   Bebbington, Anthony *et al.* Conflicts over extractivist policy and the forest frontier in Central America. (*Rev. Eur. Estud. Latinoam. Caribe*, 106, July/Dec. 2018, p. 103–132, bibl., maps, table)

This paper examines the relationship between extractive industries and infrastructure investments, and evaluates their impact on forest resources, community rights, and livelihoods in Central America. It identifies various drivers of this investment, describing the "contentious actions" (from forest management to outright protest) that emerge in response, exploring policy changes that might help to reduce pressure on the region's remaining forest cover.

471   Blume, Laura Ross; Laura Aileen Sauls; and **Christopher A.C.J. Knight.** Tracing territorial-illicit relations: pathways of influence and prospects for governance. (*Polit. Geogr.*, 97, Aug. 2022, 102690, p. 10–19, bibl.)

Collective land titling, especially for Indigenous peoples, is crucial for combating deforestation, protecting biodiversity, and addressing climate change. The influence of illicit activities on governance and socioecological dynamics, however, is often underestimated. This case study of the Miskitu Indigenous regions explores pathways linking land titling and illicit economies, and showcases the role of governance and institutions. Clearly Indigenous institutions are challenged by narcotrafficking, but the influence of illicit actors on political leaders and the state, as well as local stakeholders, is not tantamount to a form of "criminal governance." Fledgling governance organizations, in fact, are beginning to deal with these issues.

Brockmann, Sophie. The science of useful nature in Central America: landscapes, networks and practical enlightenment, 1784–1838. See *HLAS* 76:478.

472   Caruso, German Daniel; Maria Emilia Cucagna; and Julieta Ladronis. The distributional impacts of the reduction in remittances in Central America in COVID-19 times. (*Res. Soc. Stratif. Mobil.*, 71, Feb. 2021, 100567, p. 1–5, bibl., graphs, tables)

Data from the US labor market and economic performance indicators were used to estimate the distributional impacts of the post-COVID-19 change in remittances on Central America, a region highly dependent on this financial source. The findings indicate that remittance inflows are expected to decrease by 14 percent in the region during 2020, with varying effects among countries. El Salvador and Nicaragua are most affected, while Panama is the least affected. The study also suggests heterogeneous impacts on poverty, with a predicted 6 percent increase in poverty in El Salvador and 1 percent increase in poverty in Guatemala.

473   Devine, Jennifer A. *et al.* Narco-degradation: cocaine trafficking's environmental impacts in Central America's protected areas. (*World Dev.*, 144, Aug. 2021, 105474, bibl., ill., tables)

The researchers explore the environmental impacts of *narco-degradation* near cocaine transit nodes in protected areas of Guatemala, Honduras, and Costa Rica. Interviews, participatory mapping, and workshops with protected area managers and other actors plotted 500 narco-degradation activities between 2000 and 2018, affecting a variety of ecosystems. The intensity and types of narco-degradation vary based on transportation practices, node characteristics, and physical geography. Narco-trafficking converts natural resources into commodities, negatively affecting Indigenous communities and protected area governance. The study underscores the role of narco-capital and cocaine trafficking in global environmental change.

474   Herlihy, Peter H.; Matthew L. Fahrenbruch; and Taylor A. Tappan. Regaining ground: Indigenous populations and territories. (*in* Oxford handbook of Central American history. Edited by Robert H. Holden. New York, N.Y.: Oxford University Press, 2022, p. 57–79, bibl.)

Indigenous populations and their territories in Central America are detailed from archival and disaggregated municipal-level census data coupled with extensive fieldwork and GIS-based spatial analysis to understand demographic trends, settlement patterns, and territorial challenges of the region's Indigenous communities. Precolumbian populations and their settlement distributions, as well as their territorial and demographic collapse caused by European conquest, provide the backdrop for a resurgence of Indigenous populations and their territorial rights in the 21st century. Indigenous territorial jurisdictions (ITJs) now cover 18 percent of the land area of Central America and provide inalienable community land ownership and self-governance within the state context.

475   **International volunteer tourism: critical reflections on good works in Central America.** Edited by Katherine Borland and Abigail E. Adams. New York, N.Y.: Palgrave Macmillan, 2013. 227 p.: bibl., index.

This edited volume examines the role of volunteer US tourism as a force for social change in Central America. Introductory and concluding chapters, written primarily by the editors, create a useful historical and theoretical framework to assess the potential and limitations of volunteer tourism, which encompasses both secular and religious efforts. Eight case studies from El Salvador, Nicaragua, and Honduras illustrate the diversity of this phenomenon and demonstrate how it is an amalgam of international education, development, and progressive political action.

476   Kjerfve, Björn *et al.* Coral reef health in the Gulf of Honduras in relation to fluvial runoff, hurricanes, and fishing pressure. (*Mar. Pollut. Bull.*, 172, Nov. 2021, 112865, p. 1–7, bibl.)

This study assesses the health of the Mesoamerican Reef in the Gulf of Honduras. Using data from 24 sites along the Caribbean coasts of Belize and Guatemala, researchers evaluated reef health by measuring percent of coral coverage and fleshy macroalgae, and the populations of herbivorous and commercial fish. Published fluvial models provide estimates of water quality and hurricane impacts since 1960 that are derived from National Ocean Service data. Fluvial runoff and overfishing were found to be the most significant stressors, but hurricane-related disturbance was also important in northern Belize.

477   **Lovell, W. George.** From Columbus to Covid-19: Amerindian antecedents to the global pandemic. (*J. Lat. Am. Geogr.*, 19:3, July 2020, p. 177–185, bibl.)

This study examines the destructive outcome of epidemic disease on Indigenous peoples of the Americas. Focusing on Hispaniola, Mexico, Guatemala, and Ecuador/Peru, the author highlights the similarities and differences in how disease shaped colonial society and Indigenous peoples in these regions. The lessons of this horrific chapter in colonial and postcolonial history provide important insights into the long-term impacts of the COVID-19 pandemic today.

478   **McSweeney, Kendra.** Cocaine trafficking and the transformation of Central American frontiers. (*J. Lat. Am. Geogr.*, 19:3, July 2020, p. 159–166, bibl.)

The geographer provides a brief and definitive overview of how Central America experienced a rise in cocaine trafficking in the mid-2000s, causing notable deforestation, ecological damage, and control of land and resources by private entities. Counternarcotic efforts and militarization worsened the situation. Future research should focus on connections between drug trafficking, migration, and rural economies, emphasizing sustainable development and climate resilience through the recognition of land and resource rights.

479   **Offen, Karl H.** Subsidy from nature: green sea turtles in the colonial Caribbean. (*J. Lat. Am. Geogr.*, 19:1, Jan. 2020, p. 182–192, bibl.)

The green sea turtle *Chelonia mydas* was historically a prolific species and an abundant source of protein for the Caribbean colonial enterprise. This article pays homage to geographers James Parsons and Bernard Nietschmann and herpetologist Archie Carr for their groundbreaking research on the complex, historical linkages between green sea turtles and people in the Caribbean. The scope of the article spans the entire basin, but focuses particularly on the Central American rimlands where European, African, and Indigenous peoples relied heavily on the green sea turtle for centuries.

480   **Tellman, Beth *et al*.** Illicit drivers of land use change: narcotrafficking and forest loss in Central America. (*Glob. Environ. Change*, 63, July 2020, 102092, p. 1–17, bibl., graphs, ill., maps, tables)

Consolidated news media accounts of spatially explicit (to the departmental level) drug-related activity across Central America are used to estimate the role of drug trafficking as a driver of forest loss. The authors developed two narcotrafficking activity proxies of official drug seizures data and georeferenced news accounts. Both proxies (formulated with multiple assumptions and imprecise data) indicate that narcotrafficking is a statistically significant factor in forest loss in the region, particularly in Nicaragua, Honduras, and Guatemala. These findings highlight the need for policies that prevent the concentration of drug trafficking in ecologically and culturally sensitive areas where its presence can accelerate deforestation.

481   **Wrathall, David J. *et al*.** The impacts of cocaine-trafficking on conservation governance in Central America. (*Glob. Environ. Change*, 63, July 2020, 102098, p. 1–13, bibl., graphs, maps, photos, table)

The impact of cocaine trafficking on deforestation in Central America is examined, especially in protected areas, based on 45 interviews and 9 workshops with 70 protected areas stakeholders in drug-trafficking hotspots of the Petén, the Mosquitia, and the Osa Peninsula. Results show drug trafficking undermines conservation governance by disrupting conservation coalitions and promoting extractive activities on protected lands, thereby weakening territorial control of conservation institutions. Participatory governance offers hope to mitigate these negative impacts.

BELIZE

482   Akers, Pete D. et al. Integrating U-Th, 14C, and 210Pb methods to produce a chronologically reliable isotope record for the Belize River Valley Maya from a low-uranium stalagmite. (*Holocene/Sevenoaks*, 29:7, July 2019, p. 1234–1248, bibl., graphs, ill., map, photos, tables)

Dissolution caves and the speleothems they contain provide an important and still underutilized source of information about past environments. This study reports on the findings of a project in the Belize River watershed that used measures of multiple radioisotopes to unlock paleoclimate data stored in a recovered stalagmite. Results produced a high-resolution chronology that brings new insight about the climate history of the area during the classic and early postclassic periods.

483   Cherrington, Emil A. et al. Use of public Earth observation data for tracking progress in sustainable management of coastal forest ecosystems in Belize, Central America. (*Remote Sens. Environ.*, 245, Aug. 2020, 111798, p. 1–13, bibl., table)

This study seeks to evaluate ongoing mangrove conservation in Belize using satellite imagery from Landsat 5, 7, and 8. Based on the results of a change detection analysis of the entire Caribbean coast of Belize, researchers found little mangrove loss within the Belize Barrier Reef Reserve System protected area, but significant loss elsewhere, especially around areas associated with tourism. These findings highlight the need for an effective conservation policy both within and outside of protected areas.

484   Jobbová, Eva; Christophe Helmke; and Andrew Bevan. Ritual responses to drought: an examination of ritual expressions of classic Maya written sources. (*Hum. Ecol.*, 46:5, Sept. 2018, p. 759–781, bibl., graphs, photos)

The researchers argue that the practices of Maya farmers to mitigate drought and encourage rain, which have been described at length by ethnographers, are in fact the contemporary expressions of rituals that are represented in the written archeological record of Maya civilization during the classic and terminal classic periods. For archeology specialist's comment, see item **110**.

485   Pope, Cynthia. Coronavirus in Belize: a Central American success. (*J. Lat. Am. Geogr.*, 19:3, July 2020, p. 340–346, bibl.)

This short report merits attention because it highlights on-the-ground conditions in Belize in June 2020 during the early months of the COVID-19 pandemic. The researcher augments the social media posts of the Belize Ministry of Health with a deep knowledge of Belizean society to produce an insightful geographical explanation about how and why Belize escaped the early ravages of COVID-19 and never experienced the high rates of transmission and mortality that its neighbors did.

COSTA RICA

486   Barrantes, Gustavo. Multi-hazard model for developing countries. (*Nat. Haz.*, 92:2, June 2018, p. 1081–1095, bibl., graphs, maps)

This article presents a heuristic, multihazard risk model that was tested and deployed in Poas, Costa Rica. Drawing from a variety of quantitative and qualitative data sets, the model is capable of plotting hazard impacts at different spatial scales and portraying the interactions of multiple, simultaneous hazards. Such a model has great potential as a tool for risk assessment and disaster planning across Central America.

487   Johanson, Erik N.; Sally P. Horn; and Chad S. Lane. Pre-Columbian agriculture, fire, and Spanish contact: a 4200-year record from Laguna Los Mangos, Costa Rica. (*Holocene/Sevenoaks*, 29:11, April 2019, p. 1743–1757, bibl., graphs, maps, table)

This study presents a 4200-year chronology from lake sediments in Laguna Los Mangos, in the Gran Chiriquí culture region of southwestern Costa Rica. Results show environmental impacts of early maize agriculture, as evidenced in soil characteristics and the presence of charcoal. The chronology also contains evidence of arid periods associated with the terminal classic drought (TCD) in 1170 BP and again during the Little Ice Age when local agricultural production declined.

488 **Lizano-Araya, Melvin** and **Omar Gerardo Lizano-Rodríguez.** Creation of sea level rise scenarios for the localities of Moín and Cahuita, Limón, Costa Rica. (*Rev. Geogr. Am. Cent.*, 1:68, enero/junio 2022, p. 103–126, bibl.)

This is a predictive study of climate-change induced sea level rise in the Caribbean lowlands of Costa Rica. The model estimates future sea levels for the years 2030, 2050, 2070, and 2100, given an expected 3 mm sea-level rise per year due to global warming. The model forecasts the flooding of Moín and Cahuita by 2100.

489 **Niesenbaum, Richard A.** and **Joseph E.B. Elliott.** In exchange for gold: the legacy and sustainability of artisanal gold mining in Las Juntas de Abangares, Costa Rica. Champaign, Ill.: Common Ground Research Networks, 2019. 93 p.: bibl., color ill.

This ethnographic work, a collaboration between a biologist and a photographer, provides a vivid portrait of artisanal gold miners in Las Juntas de Abangares, a canton of Guanacaste in northwest Costa Rica. Beginning in the late 19th century, foreign investment in gold mining, mostly by US interests, transformed Las Juntas into a gold-producing region. Although the gold boom is now a thing of the past, Las Juntas residents continue small-scale exploitation of this resource as part of their diversified rural livelihoods.

490 **Porter, Jennifer.** Un proceso muy vagabundo: the use of visual research methods to explore intergenerational political behavior. (*Prof. Geogr.*, 72:1, Feb. 2020, p. 54–65, bibl., photos, tables)

Qualitative and visual ethnographic techniques are useful tools for helping geographers understand how individuals view and interact with the world around them. This article reports on a study in a Costa Rican city in which residents of informal housing were provided cameras to document the spaces and places of their everyday lives. The researcher uses the resulting images, as well as ethnographic interviews with the residents themselves, to piece together a compelling story of the political and economic realities of the informal urban sector in Costa Rica.

491 **Quesada-Román, Adolfo; José Pablo Castro-Chacón;** and **Sergio Feoli Boraschi.** Geomorphology, land use, and environmental impacts in a densely populated urban catchment of Costa Rica. (*J. South Am. Earth Sci.*, 112:1, Dec. 2021, 103560, bibl.)

The Torres River, whose catchment is situated within the Central Volcanic Cordillera of Costa Rica, has been heavily impacted by urbanization and metropolitan growth. Using the technique of geomorphological cartography, researchers integrate government topographic maps with historic and contemporary aerial and satellite imagery, and combine that with geomorphological fieldwork to map endogenic, fluvial, and anthropological landforms in the watershed. The resulting high-resolution maps combine land use and geomorphological data and are potentially valuable tools for analysis and modelling of landscape change and disaster planning.

492 **Rodríguez, Mariana** and **Iain J. Davidson-Hunt.** Resilience and the dynamic use of biodiversity in a Bribri community of Costa Rica. (*Hum. Ecol.*, 46:6, Nov. 2018, p. 923–931, bibl., map, table)

Contemporary research has shown that Indigenous peoples around the world are using less of the biodiversity available to them in their home territories as a result of external encroachment and culture change. This study, which focuses on a community in the Talamanca Bribri Indigenous Territory along the border of Costa Rica and Panama, documents how commercial banana and cacao production, as well as conservation-development initiatives, have impacted local Bribri ethnoecology.

493 **Romero-Vargas, Marilyn** *et al.* Áreas verdes urbanas, una caracterización paisajística y biológica aplicada a una microcuenca de la Gran Área Metropolitana de Costa Rica. (*Rev. Geogr. Am. Cent.*, 2:69, julio/dic. 2022, p. 23–48, bibl., maps, tables)

Geographers and biologists from the Universidad Nacional de Costa Rica characterize the landscape and biology of urban green areas (UGA) in the Bermudez River basin centering on Heredia in the northern San José metropolitan area. Geospatial data, photo interpretation, and cartography were used to analyze the landscape, while surveys, consultations, and literature review were used to study the biological characteristics of the study area. Results show that 8.95 percent of UGA are dedicated to conservation and recreation, while private UGAs dedicated to crops and pastures are four times larger. The study highlights significant differences in the landscapes and biological characteristics of UGAs and their contribution to ecosystem services for the city.

494 **Sanabria-Coto, Iván J.; Maureen A. Bonilla-Hidalgo; and Adolfo Quesada-Román.** Reconstrucción histórica y geoespacial de un sector de la ruta alternativa del ferrocarril al Atlántico (años 1871–1873), denominada: "línea de Fajardo", en un área geográfica asociada con los valles de Orosi y de Ujarrás, Cartago, Costa Rica. (*Rev. Geogr. Am. Cent.*, 2:69, julio/dic. 2022, p. 75–153, bibl., maps, tables)

The researchers combine archival research and GIS to reconstruct geospatial details of the "Fajardo line," a section of the Costa Rican Atlantic railway in Cartago province that was built from 1871–73 and then abandoned. Initiated by Tomás Guardia Gutiérrez's government, it was constructed by renowned American contractor Henry Meiggs Keith, not without issues.

495 **Smith, Vaughn et al.** Assessing the accuracy of detected breaks in Landsat time series as predictors of small scale deforestation in tropical dry forests of Mexico and Costa Rica. (*Remote Sens. Environ.*, 221, Feb. 2019, p. 707–721, bibl.)

This study utilized Landsat satellite imagery from 2013 to 2016 to measure the accuracy of the BFASTSpatial R modelling package in detecting land clearance in tropical dry forest regions of Mexico and Costa Rica. Although the researchers found that a number of models from this package had promising levels of accuracy, they emphasized the importance of local expertise in the interpretation of results.

496 **Warner, Benjamin P. et al.** Smallholder adaptation to drought in Costa Rica's crony capitalist rice economy. (*Dev. Change/Oxford*, 49:6, Nov. 2018, p. 1392–1421, bibl., graphs, maps)

Examining Costa Rica's most important rice-producing region in the Tempisque River basin, which is watered by a state-built irrigation system, the authors discuss how crony capitalism emerged during state-sponsored, neoliberal rural development whereby the *cronies* reshaped rice production and capital flows, marginalizing smallholder farmers dependent on state irrigation. These distorting policies created a scenario of winners and losers within the development project and contributed to long-term class disparities among the inhabitants of the area.

EL SALVADOR

497 **Broad, Robin and John Cavanagh.** The water defenders: how ordinary people saved a country from corporate greed. Boston, Mass.: Beacon Press, 2021. 211 p.: bibl.

This recent historical work recounts the grassroots political struggle during the early 2000s against Pacific Rim Mining Corporation, a Canadian-based multinational company responsible for widespread contamination from gold mining along the El Salvador-Honduras border and the Rio Lempa watershed. Protesters suffered brutal intimidation and repression, as well as homicide and disappearance, perpetrated by shadowy characters whose identities never came to light. The outpouring of protest from these crimes prompted the Salvadoran government to force the company to cease operations and leave El Salvador.

498 **Montoya, Ainhoa.** On care for our common home: ecological materiality and sovereignty over the Lempa transboundary watershed. (*J. Lat. Am. Stud.*, 53:2, May 2021, p. 297–322, ill., map)

Grassroots movements and NGOs in El Salvador—rooted in wartime politics, Catholic morality, and an "ethic of care towards the environment"—are pursuing legal measures, proposing development bans, and drafting a transboundary waters treaty to safeguard their water sources from polluting industrial activities like mining, given the country's largest Rio Lempa watershed covers northern borderlands with tributaries found across the border in Honduras and Guatemala.

GUATEMALA

499 Clouser, Rebecca. Security, development, and fear in Guatemala: enduring ties and lasting consequences. (*Geogr. Rev.*, 109:3, July 2019, p. 382–398, bibl.)

This article documents how security, development, and fear are closely intertwined in Guatemala. Guatemala has a long history of dictatorship, political repression, and genocide, especially towards Indigenous peoples, and this horrific legacy has coexisted with international development efforts for decades. Drawing from interviews with development practitioners, the researcher contends that development efforts, especially at the local level, work against the efforts of Indigenous communities to promote societal change and social justice.

Cook, Nathan J.; Glenn D. Wright; and Krister P. Andersson. Local politics of forest governance: why NGO support can reduce local government responsiveness. See item **886**.

500 Devine, Jennifer A. et al. Narco-cattle ranching in political forests. (*Antipode*, 52:4, July 2020, p. 1018–1038, bibl., maps)

This study reveals the impact of narco-cattle ranching on deforestation in Laguna del Tigre National Park as a core part of Guatemala's Maya Biosphere Reserve, including money-laundering practices and territorial dynamics. Importantly, the authors emphasize the relationship between drug policy and conservation, suggesting that community-based land tenure, governance, and resource management enhance residents' ability to resist drug-trafficking activities.

501 Devine, Jennifer A. et al. Tourism development as slow violence: dispossession in Guatemala's Maya Biosphere Reserve. (*in* Research agenda for geographies of slow violence: making social and environmental injustice visible. Edited by Shannon O'Lear. Cheltenham, England: Edward Elgar Publishing, 2021, p. 73–88, bibl., map)

The geographers introduce the notion of "slow violence" in tourism along with its long-term harm transforming social and ecological relations, place identities, and cultural practices looking at Guatemala's Maya Biosphere Reserve (MBR) and El Mirador Maya archeological site.

502 Einbender, Nathan and Helda Morales. Development from within: agroecology and the quest for *utziil k'asleem* in the Maya-Achí territory of Guatemala. (*J. Lat. Am. Geogr.*, 19:3, July 2020, p. 133–158, bibl.)

This research examines the efforts of Indigenous organizations in Guatemala's Maya-Achí territory to promote development that aligns with local needs and perspectives by looking at three initiatives focused on the restoration of traditional agriculture. Since the Civil War ended, these organizations have focused on endogenous development and agroecology, guided by principles of sustainable agriculture, reciprocity, and connection with the environment. Their approach, rooted in ancestral tradition of *utziil k'asleem* (well-being), aims to foster cultural recovery and improve quality of life.

503 Kalakonas, Petros et al. Exploring the impact of epistemic uncertainty on a regional probabilistic seismic risk assessment model. (*Nat. Haz.*, 104:1, Oct. 2020, p. 997–1020, bibl., graphs, maps, tables)

This article highlights a study that focused on the inherent uncertainty of probabilistic risk models for earthquakes. Simultaneously focusing on Guatemala as a whole and Guatemala City in particular, the model is based on a variety of geologic and insurance data sets to measure the exposure and potential for monetary loss within residential areas as a result of earthquakes. The researchers note the value of this model to help facilitate broader insurance coverage among homeowners in Central America to augment their resilience in the face of earthquakes and other hazards.

504 Salgado-Gálvez, Mario A. et al. Simple rules for choosing fault planes in almost real-time post-earthquake loss assessments. (*Nat. Haz.*, 104:1, Oct. 2020, p. 639–658, bibl., graphs, maps, tables)

This article focuses on a research effort to predict the likely fault planes of earthquakes, thereby providing more robust models of the geographical distribution and intensity of human risk and property loss. The researchers use two seismic events in Mexico and another in Guatemala to validate the model and demonstrate its potential for earthquake prediction and assessment.

505 **Tellman, Beth** *et al.* Narcotrafficking and land control in Guatemala and Honduras = Narcotráfico y control de la tierra en Guatemala y Honduras. (*JIED*, 3:1, 2021, p. 132–163, bibl., graphs, maps, photos, tables)

Examining secondary documents and media reports, the authors identify variations in land control related to drug trafficking activities in Guatemala and Honduras, showing how criminal organizations have significantly transformed rural livelihoods and biodiversity conservation through the usurpation of land and resources. Drug trafficking causes land control and property rights to shift from state/Indigenous/small landowners to criminals, converting public lands and Indigenous territories into large private properties. Extensive and sustained changes have consolidated narco-control over considerable land and resources in the borderlands of these two countries, but questions remain as to exactly how much.

HONDURAS

506 **Bonta, Mark.** The dilemma of Indigenous identity construction: the case of the newly-recognized Nahoa of Olancho, Honduras. (*in* Conference of Latin Americanist Geographers, *Morelia, Mexico, 2005.* Temas de geografía latinoamericana: reunión CLAG-Morelia. Coordinación de Pedro Sergio Urquijo Torres y Narciso Barrera-Bassols. Morelia, Mexico: UNAM, Centro de Investigaciones en Geografía Ambiental (CIGA), Campus Morelia, Michoacán: Conference of Latin Americanist Geographers (CLAG): Centro de Investigación y Desarrollo del Estado de Michoacán (CIDEM), 2009, p. 51–87, bibl., map, photos)

This provocative paper examines who is and who isn't Indigenous in Honduras considering the situation of the newest recognized native group in Honduras, the Nahoa (often spelled "Nahua"), examining the validity of their claims to ethnicity in light of a study by ESA Consultores (2003) that critiqued the justification for their consideration as an Indigenous federation.

507 **Galeana, Fernando.** Vernacular legibility in counter-mapping: assembling the geo-body of an Indigenous socio-territorial movement in Honduras. (*Geoforum/New York*, 128, Jan. 2022, p. 158–167, bibl.)

The author examines the impact of the first participatory mapping project in the Honduran Muskitia region in 1992 (designed by Herlihy and Leake, 1997; see *HLAS 61:1598*) that documented the subsistence lands of Indigenous and ladino communities. He concludes that the mapping project was driven by the communities' desire for legal recognition and visibility of their lands on the map. However, his analysis misrepresents the original "participatory research mapping (PRM)" methodology as "counter-mapping," when it was explicitly designed to collaborate among various stakeholders. More fundamentally, he misunderstood the PRM methodology that maps and delimits Indigenous community subsistence zones based on precise land and resource use locations, not on the project's administrative survey zones as he suggested.

508 **Kumar, Sanjeev; Nicholas A. Christakis; and Rafael Pérez-Escamilla.** Household food insecurity and health in a high-migration area in rural Honduras. (*SSM Popul. Health*, 15, Sept. 2021, 100885, p. 1–9, bibl., tables)

This large-scale study analyzes household food insecurity and physical and mental health among a sample population of 24,696 adults living in 176 communities in western Honduras. Based on a series of logistic regression models, the researchers find that females, Indigenous people, and migrants are most at risk of food insecurity. Additionally, food insecurity is found to be a significant factor in poor physical and mental health.

509 **Suárez, Ginés and María José Domínguez-Cuesta.** Improving landslide susceptibility predictive power through colluvium mapping in Tegucigalpa, Honduras. (*Nat. Haz.*, 105:1, 2021, p. 47–66, bibl., graphs, maps, tables)

This research pulls together a variety of geologic data sets to create a new landslide inventory of Tegucigalpa. Lithology, slope, distance to streams, and colluvium proved to be the most important variables explaining landslide occurrence with the colluvium data set producing the most accurate susceptibility map in the study.

Tellman, Beth *et al.* Narcotrafficking and land control in Guatemala and Honduras = Narcotráfico y control de la tierra en Guatemala y Honduras. See item **505**.

NICARAGUA

510 **Bryan, Joe.** For Nicaragua's Indigenous communities, land rights in name only. (*NACLA*, 51:1, March 2019, p. 55–64, bibl.)

The author shows that the delineation of boundaries and awarding titles to Indigenous and Black territories in eastern Nicaragua without deep community involvement and participation is not enough to slow the influx of mestizos or to protect their lands and resources. All 23 Black and Indigenous territories titled in the region now face illegal colonization and deforestation with no state enforcement of the law.

PANAMA

511 **Mendizabal, Tomás** and **Dimitrios Theodossopoulos.** The Emberá, tourism and Indigenous archaeology: "rediscovering" the past in Eastern Panama. (*Memorias/Barranquilla*, 9:18, sept./dic. 2012, p. 88–114, bibl., map, photos)

The Emberá of Eastern Panama collect colonial and precolonial ceramic fragments to learn about the past as their engagement in Indigenous tourism inspires new narratives about their history—and accidental discoveries of artifacts lead to collaborative archeology, promoting decolonization, interdisciplinary collaboration, and Indigenous representation in tourism.

512 **Mollett, Sharlene.** Racial geographies of land and domestic services in Panama. (*Ann. Am. Assoc. Geogr.*, 113:7, 2023, p. 1573–1588, bibl.)

This research, based on ethnographic methods, historical data, and policy documents, focuses on the direct connection between race and coloniality and land control, exploring the intertwined relationship between foreign land control, tourism development, and the contemporary experiences of Afro-Panamanian women household employees. The author focuses on racial and patriarchal dynamics that drive land dispossession, connecting current residential tourism to US imperial influences during the construction of the Panama Canal. Finally, she persuasively argues that foreign land acquisitions and domestic service are deeply embedded in Panama's tourism development across time and space.

513 **Pleasant, Traben** and **Ana Spalding.** Development and dependency in the periphery: from bananas to tourism in Bocas del Toro, Panama. (*World Dev. Perspect.*, 24, Dec. 2021, 100363, bibl.)

This study uses a core-periphery lens to recount the geopolitical and economic history of the Bocas del Toro province of Panama. As political-economic dependence has characterized the relationship between Panama and the US since the early 1900s, Bocas del Toro has experienced similar dependence as an internal periphery within Panama. Drawing from archival materials and ethnographic methods, the authors demonstrate how external dependence is a recurring theme in the development history of both Panama and Bocas del Toro.

514 **Spalding, Ana K.** Towards a political ecology of lifestyle migration: local perspectives on socio-ecological change in Bocas del Toro, Panama. (*Area/London*, 52:3, 2020, p. 539–546, bibl.)

Lifestyle migration, which often involves people moving from the developed world to desirable places in the developing world, has significant socioeconomic, cultural, and political-ecological implications. This study documents the impacts of lifestyle migration in the Bocas del Toro province of northwestern Panama. Drawing from interviews and focus groups with native-born residents, the researcher frames lifestyle migration as a chapter in the long history of colonialism and as a significant component in the contemporary spread of neoliberalism.

515 Walker, Kendra L. Effect of land tenure on forest cover and the paradox of private titling in Panama. (*Land Use Policy*, 109, Oct. 2021, 105632, bibl.)

Drawing from government spatial data, this study evaluates the ongoing campaign for private land titling in Panama. The researcher finds that private land titling is associated with forest transition and deforestation whereas protected areas and Indigenous *comarcas* are located in areas of forest persistence. Ironically, private land titling tends to incentivize reforestation even though it is associated with deforestation, highlighting the need to require participants involved in private land titling efforts to participate in forest conservation programs.

MEXICO

MATTHEW C. LaFEVOR, *Associate Professor of Geography, University of Alabama*

THE GEOGRAPHICAL RESEARCH on Mexico selected for *HLAS* 77 includes 41 recent works that follow 10 general subject areas. Several areas reflect longstanding interests within Geography, while others show the field is diversifying and becoming more interdisciplinary. This trend is especially evident in the edited volumes which recognize that most social issues have environmental components, and most environmental issues have social components. Geography has long recognized that cross-disciplinary synthesis is essential to addressing society's most important issues. Today, related disciplines also engage in this socioenvironmental synthesis. Welcoming this, the recent geographical research on Mexico draws on the specializations of sister disciplines to address academic and applied issues. As such, this literature is more diffuse, diverse, and integrative than in years past.

Research on urban geography in Mexico continues to explore the forms and functions of notable cities, but now integrates environmental, climatic, and environmental justice themes. The regional focus remains on the greater Mexico City metropolitan area and valley (item **520**) and the thematic focus on understanding urban forms, territories, and relationships to sustainability (item **550**). Environmental and climate factors feature prominently (items **528** and **535**), as does a recent emphasis on framing urban geography in relation to the "new rurality" in Mexico (item **547**).

Research on the geography of tourism is timely given recent initiatives to expand tourism into rural areas of southern Mexico. Among the works reviewed is an exploration of the development opportunities for nature-based tourism near Indigenous communities, framed in the context of the "new rurality" (item **538**). Lending a more critical perspective is a thorough case study of ecotourism in the Ría Celestún Biosphere and Reserve in Campeche, which emphasizes the contradictions and concerns inherent in similar development opportunities (item **545**).

As in years past, historical geographical studies abound. Historical agriculture features prominently in a case study of viticulture in Coahuila (item **552**). Other studies explore the historical geography of mining in Sinaloa (item **546**), water management in several states (item **551**), food system networks in

Aguascalientes (item **539**), mining and the dispossession of Indigenous territories in several states (item **537**), the historical geography and changing centralities of one fascinating street (Calle 11) in the city of Puebla (item **553**), and the city and municipality of Huatulco, Oaxaca (item **536**). This sample of historical geography reflects both the depth and breadth of Mexico's historical and geographical past, which studies continue to reveal.

Water studies also feature prominently. These range from a broad study of the challenges of water resources management in Mexico (item **516**) to the origins and development of one of the country's best-known colonial-era aqueducts (item **532**). A transdisciplinary study of the Rio Bravo (Grande) highlights the socioeconomic, management, and climatic drivers and impacts of water (mis)management along the northern border (item **523**). Finally, a collection of studies explores water management and the socioenvironmental conflicts that often arise in urban areas, with an eye towards sustainability and improving water management policies (item **527**).

Political ecology studies explore a diverse array of themes, though water again features prominently. Among these is research on the political ecology of water resources and land management in southwest Tlaxcala state (item **554**); a series of case studies on social mobilization around water-related activism in the greater Xalapa, Veracruz area (item **530**); and a series of case studies on the political ecology of water resource privatization, public health, and development in Mexico and Spain (item **517**). The political ecology of industrial agriculture also receives attention (item **531**), as do the socioenvironmental conflicts that arise from national and international efforts at infrastructure development, which often lead to land dispossession (item **525**).

Agricultural studies emphasize the merits of both traditional (agroecological) and conventional (industrial) approaches to cultivation across a range of environments. Other studies explore agriculture and rural development in the contexts of food and nutritional security, climate change, and the drivers and impacts of migration (item **544**). Other studies examine the potential for reforms in industrial agriculture to strengthen value chains and development in the southern state of Chiapas (item **519**) and how agroecological and indigenously developed management strategies in Veracruz and surrounding areas enhance both food production and biodiversity (item **524**). Another study charts agricultural development and business integration in northern Mexico during the 20th century, emphasizing the roles of public policy and the adaptability of the region to international markets (item **529**). Finally, a series of case studies on traditional agricultural systems explore the finer characteristics of intercropping strategies, home gardens, and terrace agriculture across a broad range of local and regional environments (item **548**).

Indigenous territorial studies also feature prominently. These include a deep ethnographic account of ejido lifeways in the Lacandon Forest in eastern Chiapas state (item **522**) and a collection of case studies on the environments and landscapes emphasizing continuity and change in Indigenous communities (Guarijío) in southern Sonora (item **549**). A final study explores the drivers and impacts of the rise and fall of the *núcleo agrario* as an active, conceptual, and legal framework for understanding Indigenous territoriality in Mexico (item **534**).

Three works address climate change and environmental planning in Mexico. The first explores links between climate change and national security in Mexico, reflecting on climate policy planning in different regions with an eye towards international efforts and policy reforms (item **540**). A second examines the impacts of climate change on urban environments, largely in Mexico City, and the local level policy changes that are needed (item **521**). Finally, a third work (item **526**) presents a series of case studies on the role of international (mostly with the US) cooperation in designing and implementing environmental public policy in Mexico. Together, these studies focus on southern Mexico and the impacts of climate change, water resources provision, food and nutritional security, and sustainable development.

Ecosystem services and restoration ecology feature prominently in three studies. The first traces the historical development of hydrologic ecosystem services provision in Mexico and Latin America (item **518**). The second presents 19 original works on restoration ecology in Mexico, primarily in Veracruz and the Yucatán (item **543**). A third explores participatory forest restoration programs in Jalisco as a means of environmental repair and of instilling a sense of stewardship (item **533**).

Finally, two studies use critical lenses to explore more abstract but revealing topics related to the social construction of spaces in Mexico. The first is an edited volume on material and symbolic spaces in both rural and urban environments (item **541**). The second focuses on the Lacandon region and the subjectivities of personal experiences to understand conservation in all its manifold dimensions, including its subtle and not-so-subtle socioenvironmental impacts (item **555**).

516 **Agua, el futuro ineludible.** Coordinación de Boris Graizbord y Jesús Arroyo Alejandre. Zapopan, Mexico: Universidad de Guadalajara; Ciudad de México: El Colegio de México; Los Angeles, Calif.: UCLA Program on Mexico; Pacific Palisades, Calif.: Profmex/World; Ciudad de México: Juan Pablos Editor, 2019. 314 p.: bibl., ill., maps. (Serie Migración y desarrollo urbano regional/Subserie de Ciclos y tendencias en el desarrollo de México; 9)

Broad exploration of water in Mexico that addresses water futures, the territorial contexts of water challenges, and the management and administration of water resources. Case studies cover both urban and rural water challenges, from direct human consumption to the development and excesses of irrigated agriculture, from the effects of climatic changes on water supply to the resulting social, economic, and political challenges.

517 **Agua y ecología política en España y México.** Coordinación de Alicia Torres-Rodríguez y Encarnación Moral Pajares. Jaén, Spain: Editorial de la Universidad de Jaén, 2018. 283 p.: bibl., ill. (Colección Sociedad y ciencias sociales. Serie Agua y medio ambiente; 2)

Studies on the political ecology of water management in Mexico and Spain. Together, the studies address water-related issues and the privatization of resources, public health, and regional development in the age of hypercapitalism and neoliberalism.

518 **Beltrán Retis, Salvador Arturo.** Diseño de sistemas y políticas públicas de pagos por servicios de los ecosistemas: experiencias del programa de pago por servicios ambientales hidrológicos en el Estado de México. Montecillo, Mexico: Editorial del Colegio de Postgraduados: Fundación Colegio de Postgraduados en Ciencias Agrícolas,

A.C: Instituto Nacional de Investigaciones Forestales, Agrícolas y Pecuarias: Universidad Autónoma Chapingo: IICA, 2017. 229 p.: bibl., color ill., color maps. (Biblioteca básica de agricultura; 82)

This study provides a description of the historical development of programs for the payment for hydrologic environmental (ecosystem) services in Latin America, with a special emphasis on programs in the state of Mexico. The book serves as a valuable reference and anchor point for current research. It primarily provides descriptive, rather than critical, analyses, and includes extensive referencing.

519 Cadenas de valor en el sistema agroalimentario de Chiapas: necesidades, retos y perspectivas. Coordinación de Rogelio Prado Ramírez, Ever Sánchez Osorio y María de Lourdes Flores López. Guadalajara, Mexico: Centro de Investigación y Asistencia en Tecnología y Diseño del Estado de Jalisco, A.C.; Ciudad de México: Juan Pablos Editor, 2018. 223 p.: bibl., ill.

A comprehensive look at current agroindustrial development in the southern state of Chiapas and its associated challenges and prospects. Chapters highlight diverse themes ranging from contextual examinations of the regional challenges and dominant cropping patterns to broader issues of international market integration, consumption, and the socioeconomic and cultural-political impacts of agrodevelopment. Together, the chapters focus on how to create and strengthen value chains in the region by making changes aligned with conventional, rather than traditional, cultivation strategies.

520 Calidad de vida en la Zona Metropolitana del Valle de México: hacia la justicia socioespacial. Coordinación de Adolfo Sánchez Almanza. Ciudad de México: UNAM, Instituto de Investigaciones Económicas: Coordinación de Humanidades: Programa Universitario de Estudios sobre la Ciudad, 2018. 356 p.: bibl., ill., maps.

This edited volume presents wide-ranging case studies on the spatial distribution of living standards in the metropolitan zone of the Valley of Mexico. Divided into three parts, the first third introduces theoretical, spatial, and legal frameworks for examining sociospatial justice. The second third examines different empirical and perceptual measures of living standards and their applications to the study area. The final third integrates related aspects of urban lifeways and their relationships to land values, elderly communities, public finance schemes, and urban natural disasters. Insightful introduction and conclusion chapters provide grounding for this diverse collection of studies on urban lifeways and related forms of sociospatial justice.

521 Cambio climático, ciudad y gestión ambiental: los ámbitos nacional e internacional. Coordinación de José Luis Lezama. Ciudad de México: El Colegio de México, Centro de Estudios Demográficos, Urbanos y Ambientales, 2018. 449 p.: bibl., ill., maps.

A diverse collection of studies on Mexico, generally, but not exclusively, focused on the greater Mexico City metropolitan area. Here, the authors broadly organize 11 chapters around the politics of climate change, urban environmental management, and public policy's role in the welfare of city residents.

522 Cano Castellanos, Ingreet Juliet. De montaña a "reserva forestal": colonización, sentido de comunidad y conservación en la Selva Lacandona. Ciudad de México: UNAM, Instituto de Investigaciones Sociales, 2018. 444 p.: bibl., ill., maps.

Ethnographic account of Indigenous lifeways on ejidos in the Lacandon Forest in eastern Chiapas state. The first half of the book focuses on understanding the sociocultural and environmental contexts through which people define their senses of community. The second half explores relationships between communities and their environments and the institutions in which they are embedded. This includes the conceptualization and formation of different conservation regimes and the transformation of the "mountain" to a "forest reserve." The book does not provide simple descriptions or answers to questions of environmental stewardship and management in the region. Instead, it revels in the complexities of human-environment interactions and the contradictions inherent in questions of identity, power, and conservation.

523 La cuenca del río Bravo y el cambio climático. Edición de Polioptro Fortunato Martínez Austria. Contribuciones de Oscar A. Aguirre Calderón *et al.* San Andrés Cholula, Mexico: United Nations Educational, Scientific and Cultural Organization, UniTwin, UNESCO Chair on Hydrometeorological Risks, Universidad de las Américas Puebla: CONACYT, 2018. 250 p.: bibl., ill., maps.

A transdiciplinary analysis of the Rio Bravo (Grande) with emphasis on socioeconomic, hydrologic, management, and climatic drivers and impacts. Though the focus in on the Mexican side of the border with the US, the impacts of land and water management on both sides of the border receive attention.

524 De la recolección a los agroecosistemas: soberanía alimentaria y conservación de la biodiversidad. Coordinación de Evodia Silva Rivera *et al.* Xalapa, Mexico: Universidad Veracruzana, 2018. 283 p.: bibl., ill. (Quehacer científico y tecnológico) (Hacia la sustentabilidad; 3)

Diverse collection of local and regional studies centered on understanding and using indigenously developed, agroecological approaches to food production and biodiversity conservation in Veracruz and surrounding areas. The chapters address issues related to food sovereignty, sustainable agriculture, maintaining and restoring agrobiodiversity, and the central question of how to continue to use natural resources while also protecting them for future use. Many of the 16 chapters represent original, primary studies from authors with expertise ranging from agronomy and agroecology to history, anthropology, and ecology.

525 Despojo, conflictos socioambientales y alternativas en México. Coordinación de Darcy Tetreault, Cindy McCulligh y Carlos Lucio. Ciudad de México: Universidad Autónoma de Zacatecas: MAPorrúa, Librero-Editor, 2019. 456 p.: bibl., ill., maps. (Medio ambiente y ecología serie)

Wide-ranging exploration of contemporary socioenvironmental conflicts in Mexico. The analyses generally frame these conflicts as the result of global and national forces imposing development and associated infrastructure and extractive industries on local communities. As several studies describe, the dispossession of land and resources often results. The book's 11 chapters are divided into three sections. The first section describes the national-level situation in Mexico and the conceptual frameworks that best explain these socioenvironmental conflicts. The second section presents case studies of these conflicts, often exploring water-related issues, industrial pollution, and megadevelopment projects. The third section explores efforts to resist dispossession through socioenvironmental conflicts using "bottom up" approaches, which have the potential to offer alternatives to dispossession.

526 La eficacia de la cooperación internacional para el medioambiente: dimensiones y alcances en México. Coordinación de Gustavo Sosa Núñez y Simone Lucatello. Ciudad de México: Instituto de Investigaciones Dr. José María Luis Mora: Consejo Nacional de Ciencia y Tecnología, 2016. 202 p.: bibl., ill. (Contemporánea, cooperación internacional y desarrollo)

This work addresses the role of international cooperation, mostly with the US, in developing environmental public policy in Mexico. Major themes include cooperation on climate policy, strengthening environmental institutions, and reforming regulatory agencies. Multiple case studies also explore water policy in southern Mexico and hydrological services provision and management, sustainable development, and food and nutritional security.

527 El estudio del agua en México: nuevas perspectivas teórico-metodológicas. Coordinación de Manuel Perló Cohen y Itzkuauhtli Zamora Saenz. Contribuciones de Nayeli Beltrán Reyna *et al.* Ciudad de México: Instituto de Investigaciones Sociales, UNAM, 2019. 396 p.: bibl., ill.

Collection of studies on water management, largely in urban environments and Mexico City, and the socioenvironmental conflicts over water access and use that often arise. Analyses focus on the socioeconomic and political dimensions of water (mis)management and how to improve decision-making processes around the sustainable development of water resource use.

528 Estudios de la forma urbana: análisis contemporáneo en México. Coordinación de Gabriela Lee Alardín. Contribuciones de Salomón González Arellano et al. Ciudad de México: Universidad Iberoamericana, 2019. 299 p.: bibl., ill. (chiefly color), maps, plans.

This volume examines different urban environments in Mexico, traces their forms and development over time, and highlights key insights for building more sustainable urban forms in the future. This edited volume comprises four parts, which address: 1) fundamentals of the study of urban form; 2) relationships between form, sustainability, and quality of life; 3) methods used in the study of urban form; and 4) case study examples by authors from a wide range of disciplines.

529 Factores del desarrollo agrícola territorial en el norte de México: historia, contemporaneidad y diversidad regional. Coordinación de Gustavo Aguilar Aguilar, Arturo Carrillo Rojas y Eva Luisa Rivas Sada. Culiacán, Mexico: Universidad Autónoma de Sinaloa: Andraval Ediciones, 2018. 234 p.: bibl., graphs, maps, photos.

Collection of studies on regional agricultural development and business integration in northern Mexico during the 20th century. Thematic emphasis is on the impacts of public policy and the adaptability of agriculture to changing national and international markets.

Gálvez, Alyshia. Eating NAFTA: trade, food policies, and the destruction of Mexico. See item **1299**.

530 Gestión para la defensa del agua y el territorio en Xalapa, Veracruz. Coordinación de Luisa Paré y Helio García Campos. Contribuciones de Luisa Paré et al. Ciudad de México: UNAM, Instituto de Investigaciones Sociales: Sendas, A.C., 2018. 212 p.: bibl., ill., maps.

Series of case studies of environmental activism and social mobilization around water and land management in the greater Xalapa metropolitan area. The book illustrates a mature environmental activism in action in the region and the success and challenges it faces. Authors are experts in their respective fields and, collectively, have extensive experience in field-based research on the human-environment relationships. Critical approaches center on the deficiencies of past governmental policies and the potential for local-level, community-based approaches to management to be more effective in the future.

531 Giraldo, Omar Felipe. Ecología política de la agricultura: agroecología y posdesarrollo. San Cristóbal de Las Casas, Mexico: ECOSUR, 2018. 211 p.: bibl.

This book includes a series of reflections on the role of industrial agriculture, and state and international organizations in appropriating not only the economic and political means of production in the Global South, but also in changing or coopting the very cultural meanings at the root of farming lifeways. The author brings these reflections into focus using the lens of political ecology and development studies. Analyses are further refined using a Marxist or post-Marxist lens, while placing special emphasis on power differentials and the extractive nature of the global complex of industrial agriculture.

532 Gómez Arriola, Luis Ignacio. El acueducto del padre Tembleque: agua, humanismo y labor comunitaria en el altiplano central mexicano. Pachuca de Soto, Mexico: Consejo Estatal para la Cultura y las Artes de Hidalgo, 2019. 217 p.: bibl., color ill.

A deep dive into the origins and development of one of Mexico's best-known aqueducts. The study combines archival research with extensive field investigation to bring to life an important piece of cultural heritage and its surrounding landscape. Water control technologies during the prehispanic, colonial, and more recent past are also examined, which adds important context to understanding links between land, water, and life on Mexico's altiplano. A scholarly work of the highest order with excellent reproductions of archival documents, indigenously developed maps, contemporary maps, photographs, and diagrams of the aqueduct and surrounding landscapes.

533   **Gutiérrez Rosete Hernández, Jorge Gastón.** Sembrar árboles, sembrar conciencias: una experiencia de restauración forestal participativa. Guadalajara, Mexico: Taller Editorial La Casa del Mago, 2015. 171 p., 16 unnumbered pages of plates: bibl., ill. (chiefly color).

This study examines participatory forest restoration programs in the state of Jalisco as a means of environmental repair, spreading awareness, and promoting stewardship ethics. The book places considerable emphasis on global and national problems of deforestation and its root causes and effects. Subsequent chapters contribute to an integrated, holistic understanding of participatory forest restoration. Included are thorough descriptions of biophysical environments and program action plans, and a focus on individual experiences in tree planting, recounted through personal reflections and poetry.

534   **Herlihy, Peter H.** *et al.* Losing ground: Indigenous territoriality and the *núcleo agrario* in Mexico. (*in* Invisible borders in a bordered world: power, mobility, and belonging. Edited by Alexander C. Diener and Joshua Hagen. Abingdon, England: Routledge Press, 2022, p. 144–175, maps, tables)

This study presents a careful analysis of the historical rise and fall of the *núcleo agrario* as an active, conceptual, and legal framework for understanding Indigenous territoriality in Mexico. The study discusses the drivers and impacts of its fall in the context of neoliberal environmental governance and the growing spatial consolidation of lands formerly held communally as ejidos. Though some hope for conserving effective Indigenous territoriality remains in remote *patrias chicas*, the study predicts that the dissolution of *núcleos* as the organizing territorial framework is likely to result in the additional loss of cultural identities and practices long tied to Indigenous lands.

Hesketh, Chris. Spaces of capital/spaces of resistance: Mexico and the global political economy. See item **1305**.

535   **Historia ambiental comparada de ciudades mexicanas.** Coordinación de Rosalva Loreto López. Puebla, Mexico: Instituto Ciencias Sociales y Humanidades "Alfonso Vélez Pliego," BUAP, 2017. 190 p.: bibl., ill. (some color), maps. (Colección Estudios Urbanos y Ambientales; 5)

This book groups urban studies into three sections that illustrate historical relationships between Mexican cities, their inhabitants, and the use of resources. The first group examines social-demographic challenges in Mexico City at the end of the 18th and beginning of the 19th centuries and their relationships to water resources and manufacturing centers. The second group explores the interdependence of cities and the agroecologcial systems that surround them. The final section explores urban markets, industrial development, and the observations of travelers through Mexican cities, especially in Mexico City, Oaxaca, and, most of all, Puebla, during the 19th century.

536   **Huatulco: espacio y tiempo.** Coordinación de Edgar Talledos Sánchez. San Luis Potosí, Mexico: El Colegio de San Luis, 2017. 232 p.: bibl., ill., maps. (Colección Investigaciones)

This work offers an historical and political geography of the municipality of Huatulco. The study traces the city's transformation from a small port city in the 16th century to its commercial growth thanks to the 17th-century cochineal trade, and from its role in coffee cultivation in the 19th century to its reorganization into a tourist destination in the 20th century. Emphasis is on the production and integration of the social and territorial spaces of Huatulco, Oaxaca, over the centuries and the roles of a diverse array of actors and institutions.

537   **López Bárcenas, Francisco.** La vida o el mineral: los cuatro ciclos del despojo minero en México. Ciudad de México: Akal, 2017. 347 p.: bibl., ill., indexes, maps. (Akal/Inter pares)

An exploration of the historical role of mining in the dispossession and deterioration of lands and resources of Indigenous communities. The book's comprehensive but unorthodox organization of themes and chapters works perfectly to outline four periods of mining dispossession in Mexico, from the colonial era to more recent (post-Article 27 constitutional reform) times. With a strong bent towards social justice and the rights of Indigenous communities, the book reflects decades of specialized work by the author in these fields. The result is a compelling perspective on mining enterprises in Mexico, which together represent one of the great drivers of socioenvironmental change and exploitation through the centuries.

538   **López Pardo, Gustavo** and **Bertha Palomino.** Turismo de naturaleza en comunidades indígenas en México. Ciudad de México: UNAM, Instituto de Investigaciones Económicas, 2019. 252 p.: bibl., graphs.

A timely exploration of nature-based tourism in Mexico as a development strategy in rural landscapes and Indigenous communities. Conceptually, the book also explores nature-based tourism in the context of the "new rurality" in Latin America. Though the potential contradictions and human-environment conflicts inherent in natural-based tourism are discussed, the primary focus is on identifying its development potential and its role in mitigating the economic crises of the agricultural sector.

539   **Martínez Delgado, Gerardo.** La experiencia urbana: Aguascalientes y su abasto en el siglo XX. Ciudad de México: Instituto de Investigaciónes Dr. José María Luis Mora; Aguascalientes, Mexico: Universidad Autónoma de Aguascalientes; Guanajuato, Mexico: Universidad de Guanajuato, 2017. 534 p.: bibl., facsimiles, ill., indexes, some color maps. (Historia urbana y regional)

This book recounts a novel aspect of the historical development of Aguascalientes during the 20th century—namely, the incremental development of food system networks and related infrastructure, which facilitated an impressive level of urban growth during the period.

Métodos cuantitativos en geografía humana. See item **649.**

540   **Miklos, Tomás.** Cambio climático y seguridad nacional: prospectiva, escenarios y estrategias. Ciudad de México: Siglo Veintiuno Editores, 2018. 198 p.: bibl., ill. (some color). (Ambiente y democracia)

Exploration of the links between climate change and national security in Mexico. Impressive for both its breadth and depth, the book explores the complexities of these issues to inform both the public and the advanced researcher. Emphatically sounding the alarm, without being alarmist in tone, the chapters systematically lay out why climates are changing, why international responses have so far been inadequate, and how Mexico can contribute to improving international efforts and public policy reforms in the future.

541   **Paisajes multiversos: reflexiones en torno a la construcción del espacio social.** Coordinación de Gabriela Contreras Pérez y Araceli Mondragón González. Ciudad de México: Universidad Autónoma Metropolitana, Unidad Xochimilco, División de Ciencias Sociales y Humanidades: Itaca, 2019. 445 p.: bibl., ill. (some color).

An edited volume exploring the social construction of spaces in Mexico through the lens of the multiversum and often at the landscape scale. Chapters delve into topics organized around both material and symbolic spaces, from rural to urban environments, tracing cultural to biophysical dimensions of "progress" and its critiques.

542   **Planeación, gobernanza y sustentabilidad: retos y desafíos desde el enfoque territorial.** Coordinación de Carlos Alberto Pérez-Ramírez y Juan Roberto Calderón-Maya. Toluca, Mexico: Universidad Autónoma del Estado de México; Ciudad de México: Juan Pablos Editor, 2018. 375 p.: bibl., ill., color maps.

This diverse collection of studies on environmental management and planning focuses on urban environments in the southern highlands. Themes range from urban planning, environmental justice, and waste management to issues of sustainability, including sustainable tourism, biodiversity conservation in Natural Protected Areas, water management, and agricultural production.

543   **La restauración ecológica productiva: el camino para recuperar el patrimonio biocultural de los pueblos mesoamericanos.** Coordinación de Silvia del Amo Rodríguez y

María del Carmen Vergara Tenorio. Xalapa, Mexico: Universidad Veracruzana, Dirección Editorial, 2019. 428 p.: bibl., ill., maps. (Quehacer científico y tecnológico)

Anthology of 19 original studies on restoration ecology in Mexico with an emphasis on forest and farm management and the valuation of biocultural resources. The regional emphasis is on Veracruz and Yucatán, though studies from other states are also included.

544 Los retos del desarrollo local en el ámbito rural. Coordinación de J. Jesús Gil Méndez y Spencer Radames Avalos Aguilar. Sahuayo, Mexico: Universidad de La Ciénega del Estado de Michoacán de Ocampo, 2016. 213 p.: bibl., ill.

Collection of investigations into rural development in local environments. Topics include food and nutritional security, climatic change, rural social and political organizations, and social reproduction. Case studies also examine rural development and the role of migration and remittances in the age of neoliberalism.

545 Retos, oportunidades y fracasos del ecoturismo: Reserva de la Biosfera Ría Celestún, México. Edición de Manuel Jesús Pinkus Rendón. Contribuciones de Mirna Rubí Aguiar Paz *et al*. Ciudad de México: UNAM, Centro Peninsular en Humanidades y en Ciencias Sociales; Mérida, Mexico: Universidad Autónoma de Yucatán, Centro de Investigaciones Regionales "Dr. Hideyo Noguchi", 2017. 241 p.: bibl., ill., maps. (Regiones; 3)

A deep dive into the history and development of the Ría Celestún Biosphere and Reserve in Campeche and the contradictions between development and conservation that emerge from ecotourism. Historians, economists, biologists, and other experts employ transdisciplinary perspectives on these dynamics. The result is a thoughtful collection of chapters on both the challenges and opportunities of promoting tourism in the reserve for the benefit of its inhabitants and for the environmental health of the region.

546 Román Alarcón, Rigoberto Arturo. La minería en Sinaloa: producción, empresas y cooperativas, siglos XIX y XX. Culiacán de Rosales, Mexico: Universidad Autónoma de Sinaloa: Guadalajara, Mexico: Pandora Impresores, 2017. 147 p., 12 pages of plates: bibl., ill. (Historia)

Historical and economic geography of mining in the state of Sinaloa during the 19th and 20th centuries. Much of the work is based on unpublished documents from the Archivo General de la Nación and from other regional and local archives. The analysis focuses on how important business activities, laws, and prominent mines developed in the state.

547 Rosique Cañas, José Antonio. Campo, ciudad y nueva ruralidad en México: hacia la urbanización total del territorio nacional. Ciudad de México: Universidad Autónoma Metropolitana, División de Ciencias Sociales y Humanidades, 2017. 229 p.: bibl., ill. (DCSH publicaciones)

A long-term history of urbanization in Mexico that traces the development of civilizations from prehispanic times through the recent era of globalization. The book emphasizes the need for an organic synthesis between urban and rural environments that protects the sovereignty and welfare of citizens in each realm. The book illustrates: (1) how these realms have been separated (conceptually and physically) for too long, and (2) why the natural complementarities of each realm require integration for a truly sustainable development to occur. The study frames these and other findings within the notion of the "total urbanization of the national territory" and how it relates to the "new rurality" in Mexico.

Salgado-Gálvez, Mario A. *et al*. Simple rules for choosing fault planes in almost real-time post-earthquake loss assessments. See item **504**.

548 Sistemas, agrícolas tradicionales: biodiversidad y cultura. Coordinación de Laura Reyes Montes, José Manuel Pérez Sánchez y Sergio Moctezuma Pérez. Zinacantepec, Mexico: El Colegio Mexiquense, A.C., 2018. 224 p.: bibl., ill., maps.

Case studies on traditional agricultural systems in Mexico with emphasis on intercropping strategies, home gardens, and terrace agriculture. Ethnographic and other field-based approaches are used to describe the persistence of ancient agricultural knowledge in the collective memories of rural communities. Analysis explores how these traditional techniques continue to come into conflict with conventional or industrial approaches to agriculture.

Smith, Vaughn et al. Assessing the accuracy of detected breaks in Landsat time series as predictors of small scale deforestation in tropical dry forests of Mexico and Costa Rica. See item **495**.

549 **Sonora: la sierra, el desierto y la costa en el contexto de los guajiríos.** Coordinación de Alba González Jácome et al. Texcoco, Mexico: Universidad Autónoma Chapingo, 2018. 308 p.: bibl., ill., maps.

Chapters explore environments and landscapes in southern Sonora while emphasizing interactions with the *guarijíos*, Indigenous communities that have long inhabited the region, but that experienced significant changes during the late 20th century. Contributions analyze historical and contemporary aspects of agricultural land use, river and water management, impacts of climatic change and mining development, and other ethnographic and geographic themes. Collectively, the chapters address a diversity of interdisciplinary topics. Researches largely use field-based and ethnographic work and employ cultural-political and agroecological lenses to contextualize findings.

550 **Transiciones territoriales, ciudad y campo: reflexiones teóricas sobre el espacio contemporáneo.** Edición de David Burbano González et al. Bogotá: Pontificia Universidad Javeriana; Tlaquepaque, Mexico: Instituto Tecnológico y de Estudios Superiores de Occidente, 2019. 235 p.: bibl., ill., maps. (Transiciones territoriales)

Edited volume exploring alternative views and epistemologies of "territories" as geographical spaces composed of social, urban, and environmental relationships. The aim of the volume is to broaden understanding of the concept of "territory" by viewing and examining territorial changes from interdisciplinary and transdisciplinary perspectives.

551 **Usos e historias del agua en México: riego, ciudad y legislación.** Edición de Sergio Francisco Rosas Salas, Mayra Gabriela Toxqui Furlong y Rogelio Jiménez Marce. Ciudad de México: Benemérita Universidad Autónoma de Puebla: Ediciones del Lirio, 2018. 221 p.: bibl., ill., index, maps, tables.

Collection of eight case studies on the historical geography of water management and how it contributed to sociopolitical change during the colonial, independent, and modern eras. These case studies span the states of Coahuila, Hidalgo, Sonora, Tlaxcala, Veracruz, Puebla, and Zacatecas. Chapters effectively use unpublished archival sources and a wealth of existing studies on historical water use in Mexico to explore river water concessions and apportionment, irrigation management, and industrial uses.

552 **Uvas, tierra y memoria: Coahuila: raíz de la vitivinicultura en América.** Coordinación de Claudia Cristina Martínez García, Juana Gabriela Román Jáquez y María Teresa del Carmen Mora Cortés. Saltillo, Mexico: Escuela de Ciencias Sociales, Universidad Autónoma de Coahuila: Colectivo Letras del Desierto: Gobierno de Coahuila, SEC, Secretaría de Cultura, 2017. 224 p.: bibl., ill. (chiefly color), maps (some color).

This book opens new vistas into the historical geography of viticulture in southern Coahuila, which served as the main point of origin for wine and aguardiente production in the Western Hemisphere beginning in the mid- to late-16th century. Based on extensive archival research and fieldwork, the authors produce a masterfully illustrated volume that includes reproductions of original maps and historical documents as well as professional-grade photography of important landmarks and modern-day cultivation sites and production operations.

553 **Valverde Díaz de León, Francisco.** Puebla, Calle 11: de borde urbano a eje de centralidad. San Andrés Cholula, Mexico: Universidad Iberoamericana Puebla, Dirección de Fomento Editorial; Puebla, Mexico: Benemérita Univesidad Autónoma de Puebla, 2017. 368 p.: bibl., ill., maps. (Lupus inquisitor)

A deep exploration of one street (Calle 11) in Puebla, Mexico, from its origins at the margins of the old city to its transformation into a central axis of urban life. This book is an essential source for anyone with interest in exploring and getting a better feel for the historic city center, from first-time tourists to long-standing residents.

554 Velasco Santos, Paola. Ríos de contradicción: contaminación, ecología política y sujetos rurales en Natívitas, Tlaxcala. Ciudad de México: UNAM, Instituto de Investigaciones Antropológicas, 2017. 295 p.: bibl., ill., maps.

Political ecology of water and land management in southwest Tlaxcala state in the municipality of Natívitas and near the confluence of two rivers: the Atoyac and the Zahuapan. The book delves into the water and land management of past eras and how its (mis)management has led to contemporary socioenvironmental, economic, and political challenges.

555 Villalobos Cavazos, Oswaldo. Del lacandón a la Selva Lacandona: la construcción de una región a través de sus representantes y narrativas. Ciudad de México: UNAM, Programa Universitario de Estudios de la Diversidad Cultural y la Interculturalidad: Instituto Nacional de Antropología e Historia: El Colegio de México: Centro de Investigaciones y Estudios Superiores en Antropología Social: Universidad Autónoma Metropolitana: Universidad Iberoamericana, 2016. 280 p.: bibl., index, maps, table. (Colección La pluralidad cultural de México; 37) (Cuadernos de la Cátedra Interinstitucional Arturo Warman)

Examines the social construction of the Lacandon region as a territory full of valuable and insightful experiences and discourses that offer windows into broader discussions of regional development, poststructuralist power relations, and conservation. The book illustrates the subjectivities of personal experience through interviews and ethnography. In turn, these subjectivities are framed within the artificial confines of "territory" as defined through different spatial-geographic lenses. The work reaches substantive depths in its exploration of the social constructivist political ecology of the Lacandon Forest (northeast Chiapas state).

WESTERN SOUTH AMERICA

GREGORY W. KNAPP, *Associate Professor Emeritus of Geography and Environment, The University of Texas at Austin*

WESTERN SOUTH AMERICA continues to be an important arena for research in geography, environmental studies, urban studies, and sustainability. Among the highlights of current writing about Venezuela, Manuel Donís Ríos presents a study of the role of travelers and explorers in integrating the southeastern part of Venezuela ("Guyana Profunda") into the nation (item **557**).

Colombia provides the site for several outstanding studies. Vargas Sarmiento's (item **566**) unique, personal examination of issues of identity and territory in Colombia in multiple time periods, regions, and scales is based in part on Sauerian cultural geography. A large-scale study of 49 municipalities in Colombia (item **565**) identifies the role of natural resources in causing or financing armed conflict, and the degree to which the conflict either harmed or benefitted the environment. The study also offers suggestions for strengthening institutions and environmental democracy. A new overview of the economic and human geography of

Colombia (item **563**) pays attention to both neoliberal and socialist perspectives. A large project (item **562**) investigates the conflicts between local people and administrations in 15 Colombian protected areas, highlighting the need to empower local park administrations and critiquing the "fortress" conservation model.

In Ecuador, the Colectivo de Geografía Crítica del Ecuador has been very active. Founded in late 2012, it coordinated with David Harvey who was invited by the Ecuadorian regime to set up CENEDET (Centro Nacional de Estrategia para el Derecho al Territorio or the National Center of Strategies for the Right to Territory) to promote goals supporting the 2008 Constitution and Buen Vivir (item **567**). CENEDET was shut down by the Ecuadorian government in 2015 (item **579**), but the Colectivo de Geografía persisted. An edited volume by the Colectivo (item **572**) includes chapters on feminist geography, Marxist geography, critical geography, geographies of hope, and case examples including mining, femicide, and abortion. Another edited volume (item **570**) reprints previously published and unpublished essays by environmentalist and activist individuals and organizations. An essay by members of the Colectivo provides examples of geographies of hope as opposed to the geographies of sacrifice supported by Correa (item **576**).

On Peru, there is a lavishly illustrated volume dealing with country's changing environments from 1700 to 1900 and beyond (item **584**). Another important book focuses on the emergence of Machu Picchu as a travel destination and a symbolic place for Peruvian nationalism and regional identity in Cusco (item **587**).

A national study on Bolivia shows that although urban populations have been growing rapidly, rural populations are also growing; a greater appreciation for changing rural strategies, including pluriactivity, is needed (item **592**). A researcher deploys grounded theory in La Paz, Bolivia, and argues that Indigenous factors and neoliberal forces are producing new, fragmented urban realities (item **596**).

There continue to be efforts to study rural and wild land resource management issues. An edited volume (item **582**) provides an overview of and multiple historical documents related to the rubber boom in Peru, in an effort to help local people deal with this tragic history. A study of deforestation inside and near protected areas in Ecuador (item **577**) shows that these areas do in fact safeguard forests. Another study of 11 communities in Ecuador (item **573**) demonstrates that payments for ecological services reduced the impact of grazing on collective lands. Participatory mapping has been deployed in Indigenous communities in the northern Peruvian Amazon to help improve the quality of governance decisions (item **591**).

In contrast, there are also examples of authorities promoting deforestation. In one case, the Peruvian government has promoted development and deforestation in Madre de Dios through its focus on short-sighted economic growth and its minimization of prior consultation (item **583**). In other cases, local Peruvian parish priests have promoted road construction (item **589**). Eleven years of progressive politics at the national level did not slow down adverse environmental consequences in the region of Santa Cruz, Bolivia (item **594**). Even conservation efforts go awry; in the Galapagos Islands, 200,000 goats were exterminated in the name of tortoise conservation, the largest large mammal eradication campaign in the world. One study examines local reactions and the politics and ethics of conservation (item **568**).

A study of palm plantations in Ecuador shows that the spread of palm oil disease and the subsequent government response strengthened capital accumulation and neoliberal agendas (item **574**). An Ecuadorian and Canadian researcher investigated their own privilege and positionality—as well as local stereotypes—while studying banana plantation workers in coastal Ecuador (item **569**).

Research on extractive activities includes a study of multiple actors and groups involved in large mining projects in Amazonian Ecuador (item **578**), identifying potential strategies for finding points of consensus. Another study focuses on the efforts of the Ecuadorian government to improve quality of life indicators and participation in three towns of southern Ecuador involved with mining; there have been improvements, but problems of coordination persist (item **575**). In Bolivia, disputes over political jurisdiction impact the management of a natural gas field (item **595**).

Natural hazards are another focus of recent publications. José Herrera (item **558**) provides a detailed monograph on the history, geomorphology, and natural hazards of the plateau of Mérida, Venezuela, with recommendations for reducing the risks of earthquakes, landslides, and flooding. A study of climate change impacts and adaptations in the vicinity (buffer zone) of Los Nevados National Park, in the Colombian Cordillera Central between Bogotá and Pereira (item **564**) finds that more clarity in government programs is needed, along with more involvement by local people. Climate change is currently perceived as less important than other factors, such as labor supply. Peruvian engineers and governments were successful in adapting to melting glaciers in the 1950s, but more recent efforts at adaptation have floundered due to local resistance (item **581**).

Commonly used frameworks for establishing water rights tend not to work well in specific situations in Peru and Bolivia and need to be calibrated for unique situations (item **556**). A group of Peruvian geographers examines agricultural adaptations in several watersheds on the coast (item **586**), finding that the boom in agricultural exports and improvements in irrigation compensated for climate change. Research continues on how to constructively confront climate change impacts. A study of three watersheds in Colombia (item **559**) demonstrates the lack of broad commitment to water quality, the influence of powerful interests, and the failure of institutions to understand local realities. A study of water issues in and near the Colca Valley of Peru (item **588**) highlights the importance of political and environmental justice approaches beyond individual adaptation.

Mercury contamination near Bogotá, Colombia, seems to be due to brick-making and other manufacturing, as well as landfills; it presents a hazard for both humans and wildlife (item **561**). A study of experiences and responses to an active volcano in Ecuador (item **571**) shows that many rural people suffered, while an urban area with a tourist economy fared much better.

In the field of urban geography, we have an examination of the history of aided self-help housing in Peru from 1954 to 1986, suggesting changes to current practice (item **585**). Urban planners call for more public and private leadership in Santa Cruz to address environmental and social issues (item **593**). Burgos Bolaños (item **560**) argues for social activism to resist globalizing forces of neoliberalism in favor of constructing a Cartagena, Colombia, that would, for the first time, serve the needs of its own people. In terms of a longer historical perspective, GIS and spatial modeling reconstruct the visual experiences of colonial people in a now-abandoned town of the Peruvian Andes (item **590**).

GENERAL

556 Seemann, Miriam. Water security, justice and the politics of water rights in Peru and Bolivia. New York, N.Y.: Palgrave Macmillan, 2016. 226 p.: bibl., ill., index, maps. (Environment, politics, and social change)

Seemann interviewed local water users in Yanque, Colca Valley, Peru, and in Cochimita, Tiraque Valley, Bolivia, to investigate the politics of water rights. The main theoretical frameworks for property rights are market-based (neoliberal) environmentalism, state-based frameworks of formalization based on the analysis of De Soto, and common property frameworks based on the work of Ostrom. Seemann argues that these three frameworks do not adequately account for power, inequality, and legal complexity of local situations. Formalization policies do not accord with local ideas of equity and security and thus bear the risk of losing legitimacy. More attention needs to be paid to the realities on the ground in specific situations.

VENEZUELA

557 Donís Ríos, Manuel Alberto. Guayana profunda: un acercamiento a la Guayana Profunda a través de algunos personajes emblemáticos, siglos XIX y XX. Caracas: Universidad Metropolitana, 2016. 312 p.: bibl., maps.

Donís Ríos specializes in territorial and cartographic history in Venezuela. In this volume, he traces the travels and activities of various explorers, adventurers, functionaries, and missionaries south of the Orinoco River during the late 19th and early 20th centuries, in what he calls *"Guayana Profunda"* or Deep Guayana. He is particularly interested in their roles in establishing Venezuelan governance and integrating local people into the Venezuelan nation; following in the intellectual tradition of geographer Pedro Cunill Grau, he argues that Venezuela should be more aware of its southern territories.

558 Herrera, José. La meseta de Mérida: sus orígenes, los terremotos y otros procesos hidro-geomorfológicos. Mérida, Venezuela: IMMECA, Imprenta de Mérida, 2016. 215 p.: ill.

Venezuelan geographer Herrera provides a detailed look at natural hazards in the plateau *(meseta)* of Mérida, focusing on earthquakes, landslides, and flooding in this unstable landscape. The first part describes the geology and geomorphology of the plateau, including its rivers. The second and third parts discuss the genesis of the plateau with a focus on tectonic faults and the history of glaciation. The fourth part discusses the earthquake history, including the earthquakes of 1812 and 1894, and points out uncertainties of future risks. The rest of the book discusses risk levels of various landscapes and buildings, describes the earthquakes of 2015, and makes recommendations to reduce risks. The book is directed at the educated general public, and Herrera makes an attempt to make the discussion lively and personal, quoting other professors and architects with interests in the theme. The text is illustrated with many photographs and diagrams.

Rodríguez Alarcón, María N. Plagas, vulnerabilidades y desastres agrícolas: la sociedad venezolana a fines del siglo XIX. See *HLAS* 76:830.

COLOMBIA

559 Buitrago Bermúdez, Oscar; Francy Viviana Bolaños Trochez; and **Zaida Patiño Gómez.** La cuenca hidrográfica como unidad de gestión del agua. Cali, Colombia: Universidad del Valle, Programa Editorial, 2017. 221 p.: bibl., color ill. (Colección Libros de investigación)

Three professional geographers analyze public water management issues in Colombia, focusing on three watersheds as territorial frameworks. The watersheds are those of the Cali, Yumbo, and Bolo-Fraile Rivers in the southern part of the Valle del Cauca Department in east central Colombia. In each watershed, the authors map geology, soils, climate, water resources and demand, and socioeconomic factors. They identify governmental and community social organizations involved with water management and interview key water managers and community leaders. This work allows them to identify conflicts and problems related to water management. Water conflict is created by competing uses for water, with some activities being deleterious to people downstream. Forests and high grasslands tend to improve the availability of reliable water downslope. There is a lack of broader commitment to water quality, with local users focusing on their own needs. Urban water systems tend to have more elaborate technology and public management, while rural people rely on communal irrigation systems, wells, and septic tanks. Water management tends to be overly determined by powerful interests who deploy their political linkages and nepotism—as well as private armed guards. Management entities tend to work from their offices with limited understanding of realities in the field.

560 **Burgos Bolaños, Santiago.** Cartagena de Indias en el sistema mundial: lectura crítica de las geografías postmodernas en una ciudad periférica. Cartagena, Colombia: Universidad de Cartagena, 2016. 462 p.: bibl.

Burgos Bolaños deploys the concepts of world systems theory (Wallerstein), postmodern urban geography (Soja), and Marxist geography (Harvey) using Cartagena, Colombia, as his case example. He argues for social activism to resist globalizing forces of neoliberalism in favor of constructing a Cartagena that would, for the first time, serve the needs of its own people.

561 **Contaminación por mercurio en Bogotá y su conurbano.** Edición de Cristian J. Díaz Álvarez y Martha C. Bustos López. Bogotá: Universidad Central, Facultad de Ingeniería y Ciencias Básicas, Departamento de Ingeniería Ambiental, 2017. 154 p.: bibl., ill. (some color).

This edited volume lays out the evidence for mercury contamination in the atmosphere, irrigation water, community aqueducts, and river sediments in urban areas near Bogotá, Colombia. These contaminated areas present hazards for food consumed from local soils. The sources of mercury here are difficult to determine, but include manufacturing (including brick factories) and landfills with mercury-added products; artisanal gold mining may be less important as a source of mercury in this urban area. Following in the tradition of Rachel Carson, the book warns of ongoing hazards for humans and wildlife if the sources of mercury are not managed and remediated.

562 **De Pourcq, Kobe et al.** Understanding and resolving conflict between local communities and conservation authorities in Colombia. (*World Dev.*, 93, May 2017, p. 125–135, bibl., graphs, map, tables)

The article reports the results of a large project investigating conflicts between local people and protected area administrations in 15 Colombian protected areas. Hundreds of interviews involved community leaders, park officers, and people living inside or along the borders of protected areas. Key problems (impairments) identified by local people include limitation on local freedom of development, restriction of access to resources, failure of park administrations to comply with previous agreements or rules, barriers to community participation in decisions, and the imposition of obligations on local communities. Local leaders point out that key drivers of conflicts were the fortress conservation model, administrative weaknesses, ongoing violence and armed conflict, conflict of interest between conservation goals and tourism or mining, and weak local community organization. The authors suggest that improvements can be achieved through making the national environmental legislative body more inclusive and by adequately empowering local park administrations.

563 **Monje Penha, Felix Eney and Hugo Ibsen Zambrano Solarte.** Geografía económica colombiana. Neiva, Colombia: CORHUILA Corporación Universitaria del Huila, 2017. 265 p.: bibl., ill.

This is a new, comprehensive overview of the economic geography of Colombia, intended for university students. It goes well beyond the basics of economic geography, including sections on human and cultural geography and geomorphology. Attention is paid to general concepts and competing ideas, including neoliberal and socialist perspectives and sustainability goals.

564 **Nates Cruz, Beatriz et al.** El tiempo que hace: estrategias e implicaciones territoriales en zonas de amortiguamiento a partir de la variabilidad y cambio climático (PNNN, Colombia). Manizales, Colombia: Editorial Universidad de Caldas, 2016. 187 p.: bibl., color ill., maps. (Libros de investigación; 61)

This study is coauthored by Colombian anthropologists, a geographer, and a rural sociologist, who benefitted from international funding to study climate change impacts and adaptations in the vicinity (buffer zone) of Los Nevados National Park in the Codillera Central between Bogotá and Pereira. This park includes volcanoes such as Nevado del Ruiz, endangered glaciers, and a variety of ecosystems; nearby communities rely on farming of potatoes and other high altitude crops, as well as cattle raising. The authors develop a regional scheme of sociospatial units of analysis and discuss agricultural practices, land tenure, transportation, tourism, and other factors influencing local life. Local meteorological stations do not clearly document changes in climate over the years from 1994 to 2009, and local people do not believe climate change has been as important as other factors (such as availability of labor) in affecting agriculture. The authors argue for more clarity in government programs and more involvement of local people so that their legitimate concerns are addressed. Numerous maps are provided.

Retos demográficos en Colombia y Cuba. See item **460**.

565 **Rodríguez Garavito, César A.; Diana Rodríguez Franco; and Helena Durán Crane.** La paz ambiental: retos y propuestas para el posacuerdo. Bogotá: Dejusticia, 2017. 128 p.: bibl., folded color ill., maps. (Documentos: ideas para construir la paz; 30)

This book analyzes the role of the environment in Colombia's armed conflict and identifies pathways toward constructing "environmental peace" after the peace accords. The authors identify 49 municipalities of special importance for this project. They discuss the role of natural resources in causing the conflict (including financing the conflict) and the degree to which the environment was harmed by or benefitted from the conflict. They then discuss challenges of land use, economic development, environmental institutions, and environmental justice in these municipalities, with suggestions for strengthening institutions and environmental democracy. The book is illustrated with several maps showing national environmental stressors such as deforestation and hydrocarbon and mining operations as they relate to the targeted municipalities.

566 **Vargas Sarmiento, Patricia.** Historias de territorialidades en Colombia: biocentrismo y antropocentrismo. Colombia: Zetta Comunicadores, 2016. 477 p.: bibl., ill. (chiefly color), maps (some color).

In this self-published volume, Vargas Sarmiento takes a deep dive into issues of identity and territory in multiple time periods, regions, and scales. The discussion is based on theories and approaches from a variety of disciplines, including Sauerian cultural geography, Marxist geography, cultural anthropology, and critical and social cartography. The result is a unique, personal vision of spatial and environmental relationships in Colombia, illustrated by maps and drawings. The book will be fascinating to cultural geographers and others who will find Vargas Sarmiento to be an engaging author with a wide-ranging vision of the past and possible futures of peoples and their landscapes.

ECUADOR

567 **Bayón Jiménez, Manuel and Manuela Silveira.** Geografiando para la resistencia: Colectivo de Geografía Crítica del Ecuador. (*J. Lat. Am. Geogr.*, 16:1, April 2017, p. 172–177, bibl., maps)

Members of the Colectivo de Geografía Crítica del Ecuador (Critical Geography Collective of Ecuador) discuss its formation by about 10 geographers in September 2012 and outline its goals of providing a critical analysis of extractivist policies in Ecuador and allying itself with popular movements of resistance. The collective has been influenced by the ideas of Milton Santos, Carlos Walter Porto Gonçalves, Carlos Walter, and David Harvey (who visited

Ecuador multiple times). This article criticizes other geography programs in Ecuador for being subservient to the military and the government.

568   Bocci, Paolo. Tangles of care: killing goats to save tortoises on the Galápagos Islands. (*Cult. Anthropol.*, 32:3, Aug. 2017, p. 424–449, bibl.)

In the name of saving endemic tortoises from extinction, the Isabela Project killed more than 200,000 goats, constituting the largest mammal eradication campaign in the world. Paolo Bocci reports on interviews with the project's assistants and local people to highlight the horrors and unanticipated consequences of this campaign. He argues that in addition to studying the politics of conservation in the Anthropocene, it is necessary to study the entanglements and contradictions of extending forms of care beyond our own species.

569   Brisbois, Ben W. and Patricia Polo Almeida. Attending to researcher positionality in geographic fieldwork on health in Latin America: lessons from La Costa Ecuatoriana. (*J. Lat. Am. Geogr.*, 16:1, April 2017, p. 194–201, bibl.)

An Ecuadorian and a Canadian researcher reflect on their fieldwork experiences studying health implications of banana plantations in coastal Ecuador. In both case studies, they encountered crude local stereotypes of coastal banana workers as well as stereotypes concerning their own positionality. They conclude that there is a need to include Latin American identities, theories, and places when planning, conducting, and interpreting fieldwork.

570   Ecología política en la mitad del mundo: luchas ecologistas y reflexiones sobre la naturaleza en el Ecuador. Compilación de Elizabeth Bravo Velásquez, Melissa Moreano y Ivonne Yánez. Quito: Universidad Politécnica Salesiana: Abya-Yala, 2017. 575 p.: bibl., 1 map.

This anthology reprints 29 essays by Ecuadorian environmentalists and activists originally published from the 1990s through 2017. Some of these articles were previously available only in manuscript form, and others are difficult to find, making this a welcome publication. In a number of cases, the authors updated their writings, condensed their work, or combined multiple articles. The articles share a critical, Marxist perspective influenced by David Harvey and others, critiquing globalized and neoliberal development and its environmental impact, and supporting alternative approaches as expressed in the Ecuadorian Constitution of 2008. For the 1990s, the volume addresses issues of oil development, mining, and Indigenous mobilization. For the 21st century, issues related to GMOs, drug fumigation on the Colombian border, shrimp fisheries mining, petroleum, dam construction, and national parks are examined; there is also extensive discussion of the pitfalls of public-private partnerships, certification programs, and the activities of the UN and other international organizations in providing smokescreens for capitalist development and suppressing popular participation. The book also addresses healthier lifestyles and feminist perspectives on sustainable development.

571   Few, Roger; Maria Teresa Armijos; and Jenni Barclay. Living with Volcan Tungurahua: the dynamics of vulnerability during prolonged volcanic activity. (*Geoforum/New York*, 80, March 2017, p. 72–81, bibl., maps)

The authors study the experiences and responses of nearby communities to eruptive activity of the Tungurahua volcano, guided in part by Ecuador's Instituto Geofísico. Social reactions vary greatly in space and time, depending on the changing characteristics of eruptions and dynamic political and economic factors conditioning resilience. In general, the nearby urban area of Baños, with its tourism-related economy, fared the best, while rural areas suffered.

572   Geografía crítica para detener el despojo de los territorios: teorías, experiencias y casos de trabajo en Ecuador. Coordinación de Manuel Bayón Jiménez y Nataly Torres. Quito: Abya Yala: Instituto de Estudios Ecologistas del Tercer Mundo: Colectivo de Geografía Crítica del Ecuador: Friedrich-Ebert-Stiftung, 2019. 220 p.: bibl., ill.

This edited volume contains articles by members of the Colectivo de Geografía

Crítica del Ecuador (Critical Geography Collective), organized in late 2012 to promote activist research addressing the deficiencies of the Correa administration in living up to the aspirations of Ecuador's 2008 Constitution. Around the same time (2013), geographer David Harvey was asked by the Ecuadorian government to set up a think tank studying territorial rights. The collective opposes most previous geographic work in Ecuador, which it views as merely promoting technical solutions to territorial problems from a supposedly apolitical perspective. Chapters focus on feminist geography, Marxist geography, critical cartography, geographies of hope (echoing Victoria Lawson), and geography of the commons. Case examples include the Yasuni preserve, the Panantza-San Carlos and Kimsacocha mining projects, the territorial struggles of the Wimbi people, countermapping femicide, and mapping the criminalization of abortion.

573   Hayes, Tanya M.; Felipe Murtinho; and Hendrik Wolff. The impact of payments for environmental services on communal lands: an analysis of the factors driving household land-use behavior in Ecuador. (*World Dev.*, 93, May 2017, p. 427–446, appendices, bibl., graph, map, tables)

The authors and their local assistants gathered data from 399 households in 11 communities to study the impacts of payments for ecological services on resource management. They determined that the payments reduced the impact of grazing on collective lands, but that communal decisions were also important.

574   Johnson, Adrienne. *Pudrición del cogollo* and the (post-)neoliberal ecological fix in Ecuador's palm oil industry. (*Geoforum/New York*, 80, March 2017, p. 13–23, bibl., map)

This paper examines a plant health emergency—the spread of the palm oil disease *pudrición del cogollo* in palm plantations in Ecuador. The government's response to the disease, through assistance measures, technical measures, the promotion of hybrid seeds, and programs of expanding the area and yield of plantations, provided benefits to varied actors, but fundamentally were oriented towards promoting capital accumulation and neoliberal agendas. The paper argues that other diseases will also present opportunities for strengthening the neo-extractivist economic agenda.

Latorre Tomás, Sara and **Katharine N. Farrell.** The disruption of ancestral peoples in Ecuador's mangrove ecosystem: class and ethnic differentiation within a changing political context. See item **1686**.

575   **Prada-Trigo, José.** Governance and territorial development in Ecuador: the Plan Nacional del Buen Vivir in Zaruma, Piñas and Portovelo. (*J. Lat. Am. Stud.*, 49:2, May 2017, p. 299–326, graph, map, tables)

The article, written by a Chilean geographer, examines changes in territorial management at the local level influenced by Ecuador's national Buen Vivir plan, which was intended to improve education, health, quality of life, the environment, and participation. Fieldwork and interviews were conducted in three towns in southern Ecuador with a strong presence of mining: Portovelo, Zaruma, and Piñas. Improvements were noted due to the national plan, including an increase in the number of decisionmakers and local capacity for action in such areas as environmental quality and deforestation, as well as improvements in quality of life indicators such as literacy, sanitation, and access to water. Challenges, however, remain due to the difficult transition from theory to reality, and translating national goals to local goals. Major problems include continuing low levels of social participation, lack of coordination at the national and local levels, and the absence of monitoring of local progress.

576   **Silveira, Manuela et al.** Geografías de sacrificio y geografías de esperanza: tensiones territoriales en el Ecuador plurinacional. (*J. Lat. Am. Geogr.*, 16:1, April 2017, p. 69–92, bibl., maps)

The authors, five members of the Colectivo de Geografía Crítica del Ecuador, analyze the impacts of, and responses to, Correa's pursuit of an extractive model of development, in the context of David Harvey's critique of neoliberalism. The extractive modernization model required spaces of sacrifice, such as oil exploitation, mining, oil palm production, banana production, and flower plantations, many of which impinged on Indigenous lands. Counterpoised to these, the authors identify spaces of hope, including Yasunidos in Yasuní National Park; the people of Quimsacocha who resisted gold mining in the Andes west of Cuenca; resistance to mining in Intag, northwest of Quito; and a massive "national march for water, life, and the dignity of the peoples" which included Indigenous people, peasants, feminists, students, and environmentalists. See also item 572.

577 **Van Der Hoek, Yntze.** The potential of protected areas to halt deforestation in Ecuador. (*Environ. Conserv./Cambridge*, 44:2, June 2017, p. 124–130, bibl., map, tables)

Using data derived from remote sensing, the author calculates the deforestation rates between 2000 and 2008 inside all the protected areas of Ecuador that were created before 2000. He also calculates deforestation rates in areas classified as forest but located outside of protected areas. Even when correcting for distance from roads, population centers, and slope, protected areas had less deforestation than unprotected areas.

578 **Vela-Almeida, Diana; Vijay Kolinjivadi; and Nicolas Kosoy.** The building of mining discourses and the politics of scale in Ecuador. (*World Dev.*, 103, March 2018, p. 188–198, bibl., tables)

This study analyzes discourses about large mining projects in Amazonian Ecuador. Snowball sampling of stakeholders includes representatives of central and local governments, National Assembly members, Indigenous organizations, civil society organizations, peasant groups, NGOs, and mining companies. Q methodology was deployed to identify four factors relating to mining discourses: responsible extractivism, local self determination, national economic development, and local economic development. Stakeholder groups employ their discourses strategically across scales to to leverage their power. The authors identify some strategies for reducing conflicts over mining, including the importance of identifying points of consensus and contestation.

579 **Wilson, Japhy.** Perplexing entanglements with a post-neoliberal state. (*J. Lat. Am. Geogr.*, 16:1, April 2017, p. 177–184, bibl., maps)

This paper discusses the circumstances surrounding the sudden shutdown of CENEDET at the end of 2015, when its findings ran afoul of authorities in Correa's government. CENEDET (Centro Nacional de Estrategia para el Derecho al Territorio or National Center of Strategies for the Right to Territory) was established by David Harvey in 2013 at the invitation of the Ecuadorian regime under Correa. Its findings involved local activism and the shutdown of a proposed university on the site of Chinese mineral development in the southern Ecuadorian Amazon. The article also discusses ideological conflicts and maneuvering between Jeffrey Sachs, Eduardo Gudynas, David Harvey, and the Ecuadorian regime regarding issues of biosocialism, friendly colonialism, and neoliberal environmentalism.

PERU

580 **Cabrera, César Humberto.** Conga. Comentarios y entrevistas. Miraflores, Peru: Centro de Investigación de Minería, Ambiente y Desarrollo, 2018. 122 p.: bibl.

The Conga copper mining project began after the approval of an Environmental Impact Statement in 2010, but construction was halted by President Humala in 2011 and eventually abandoned. This book consists of interviews and conference notes involving the authors, who strongly argue for the importance of mining and the resulting income for Peru.

581 **Carey, Mark and Holly Moulton.** Adapting to climate hazards in the Peruvian Andes. (*Curr. Hist.*, 117:796, Feb. 2018, p. 62–68)

The authors critique contemporary media for ignoring the extent to which local populations and authorities are actively addressing adaptation to climate change. For example, Peruvian engineers and governments, starting in the 1950s, developed new ways to drain and dam periglacial lakes, greatly reducing hazards of flooding downslope. These efforts were influential worldwide and helped prevent predictable hazards from melting glaciers. More recently, however, efforts to minimize risk in Huaraz, Peru, have foundered on local resistance to adaptive policies; resistance has involved both wealthy and poor residents, since wealthy residents have resisted relocation from locales seen as favorable to their status. Other recent initiatives have included lawsuits to hold international polluters responsible for local effects, and (falsely) contending that authors of glacial inventories have doctored their studies to benefit mining interests. The authors urge a shift away from an exclusive concern with abstract temperature goals, towards an appreciation for multidimensional adaptation measures in local contexts.

582   Chirif, Alberto. Después del caucho. Lima: Lluvia Editores: CAAAP, Centro Amazónico de Antropología y Aplicación Práctica; Copenhagen, Denmark: IWGIA, Grupo Internacional de Trabajo sobre Asuntos Indígenas; Lima: Instituto del Bien Común, 2017. 452 p., 3 unnumbered leaves: bibl., color maps.

This volume presents an in-depth examination of the impacts of the rubber boom on the Peruvian Amazon. Chirif provides an overview of the problem in the first article. Gasché offers an overview of Indigenous societies before and after the rubber boom. The next chapter includes a description of the voyage of Father Avencio Villarejo down the Putumayo River in 1935. The rest of the book includes transcriptions of various historical documents related to the rubber boom, and of interviews with descendents of rubber tappers and local Indigenous people. The resulting book provides a range of perspectives and evidence to help outsiders and especially local people deal with this tragic history. The book serves to combat two myths—that local Indigenous societies were static, mired in history, and opposed to change; and that the rubber tappers were bearers of civilization and progress.

583   Deforestación en tiempos de cambio climático. Edición de Alberto Chirif et al. Lima: IWGIA, Grupo Internacional de Trabajo sobre Asuntos Indígenas, 2018. 226 p.: bibl., ill. (chiefly color), color maps.

This volume is based on a workshop held in Puerto Maldonado, Madre de Dios, about the impact of road construction (including the Interoceanic Highway) on deforestation. The workshop included Indigenous community members and leaders. Many of the 12 articles were presented at the workshop; also included are invited articles by experts on Amazonian forest resources, climate change, and the impacts of resource extraction and deforestation. The editor, Alberto Chirif, is widely recognized for his lifelong scholarship and support for Indigenous rights. The essays point out the failures of the Peruvian state to reduce the adverse social and environmental impacts of illegal cultivation of coca and alluvial gold mining, among other activities. The state has instead focused on short-sighted economic growth and the minimization or abolition of Indigenous rights to consultation prior to the initiation of extractive activities.

584   Díaz Palacios, Julio et al. Historia ambiental del Perú, siglos XVIII y XIX. Lima: Ministerio del Ambiente, 2016. 464 p.: bibl., ill. (some color).

This comprehensive and lavishly illustrated volume was sponsored by Peru's Ministerio del Ambiente in commemoration of the bicentenary of Peru's independence from Spain. The team of authors includes Núnez-Carvallo, who authored part 1 on explorers, travelers, and scientists who described Peru's environment in the 18th and 19th centuries, and Torres Guevara, who authored a chapter on Peru's climate between 1750 and 1850. Díaz Palacios and Arana Cardó were responsible for other sections, based in part on interviews with historians, social scientists, and other experts. These chapters include a discussion of agricultural history with attention to technology transfer and the introduction of rodents, horses, and other exotic animals and plants. Colonial mining is addressed in a chapter on the impacts of air, water, and health. A chapter on water resources focuses on whaling and exploitation of guano. The chapter on forests discusses the impacts of various industries on firewood collection, deforestation due to pasture expansion, and commercial exploitation of quina bark for quinine. Wild fauna and domesticated and medicinal plants and urban environmental and health issues are addressed in different chapters. The volume concludes with discussions of the environmental aspects of religion, literature, and the arts. This volume is an excellent reference work, especially valuable for the wide range of illustrations, maps, photographs, and diagrams providing an overview of Peru's environmental characteristics. Although the book focuses on the period from 1700 to 1900, many of the sections go beyond this time frame to include earlier and more recent events.

585 **Gyger, Helen.** Improvised cities: architecture, urbanization & innovation in Peru. Pittsburgh, Pa.: University of Pittsburgh Press, 2019. 438 p.: bibl., index. (Culture, politics, and the built environment)

Gyger, an architectural historian, examines the trajectory of aided self-help housing *(barriadas)* in cities in Peru from 1954 to 1986. The author clarifies the multiple forms of low cost housing, including terminological and discourse issues. Aided self-help housing involves various kinds of collaborations between architects, planners, popular movements, and individual families; these relationships change over time as political regimes and dominant paradigms change. The author relies on available writings of architects, planners, anthropologists, and policymakers to document changing ideas and practices through six political regimes, both democracies and dictatorships. Particular attention is paid to architect John F. Turner, who began working with early trials of self-help housing and on-the-ground projects in Peru and subsequently focused on theoretical work in articles and books. Over time, aided self-help housing foundered over issues of funding and lack of state support and tended to give way to unaided self-help housing for the very poor. Gyger argues for revisiting the concepts and practices of aided self-help housing to reframe strategies for contemporary practice. The book is well illustrated with numerous photographs, drawings, diagrams, and plans.

586 **Ramos Bonilla, Andrea** and **Karla Vergara.** Cambios en la actividad agropecuaria en un contexto de cambio climático y estrés hídrico: el caso de las cuencas de Ica y Pampas. Lima: GRADE Grupo de Análisis para el Desarrollo: Sociedad Geográfica de Lima, 2018. 103 p.: bibl., ill.

This internationally funded study by Peruvian geographers analyzes the drainages of the Ica, Pisco, and Pampas rivers using agricultural censuses and satellite images from 1994 to 2012. Glacial area has declined during this period, but irrigation projects permit the transfer of water to lower elevations and improvements in the efficiency of irrigation technology have also helped. Improved access to markets has stimulated the production of asparagus, avocado, grapes, and pigs. The boom in agricultural exports has more than compensated for the stresses induced by climate change. At higher elevations, the increase in temperature and improvements in irrigation and fertilization have led to increases in corn production. However, longer-term processes of climate change pose severe challenges and require more research. Peruvian geographer Bernex points out in her introduction that this study provides a point of departure for more recent work in these drainage basins to constructively confront climate change impacts.

587 **Rice, Mark.** Making Machu Picchu: the politics of tourism in twentieth-century Peru. Chapel Hill: The University of North Carolina Press, 2018. 233 p.: bibl., ill., index.

This important work by an historian of tourism focuses on the emergence of Machu Picchu both as a travel destination and as a powerful symbolic place. Rice, based on analysis of data from multiple archives, argues that in this case, transnational actors played key roles in the construction of Peruvian nationalism and Cusco regional identity, performing work that would not have been possible without this type of globalization. The forces at work went beyond merely economic capitalism, neocolonialism, and neoliberalism to encompass a variety of cultural influences including the search for authenticity by modern travelers. The book provides much detail on changes in government policies, transportation and tourism infrastructure, and elite and popular discourses during widely varying political and social regimes. For historian's comment, see HLAS 76:923.

588 **Stensrud, Astrid B.** Harvesting water for the future: reciprocity and environmental justice in the politics of climate change in Peru. (*Lat. Am. Perspect.*, 43:4, July 2016, p. 56–72, bibl.)

Fieldwork on water issues in and near the Colca Valley of Peru indicates that local people at higher elevations have perceived climate change in recent decades. They have responded to uncertain water supplies by building microdams and planting trees. These were not just pursued at the local level; these projects have also been financed in part by companies making money from water based on principles of reciprocity and justice and political activism. Stensrud argues that the focus on adaptation to climate change should be replaced by a focus on political agency, and a movement away from individualized, neoliberal approaches toward environmental justice approaches.

589 **Velasco Alarcón, C. Melissa; David S. Salisbury; and Aaron A. Groth.** La religión de la infraestructura en las fronteras amazónicas: el caso del Purús. (*J. Lat. Am. Geogr.*, 16:3, Nov. 2017, p. 107–134, bibl., maps, photos, tables)

This article examines the role of Catholic Church parish media in promoting road construction in a particular location on Peru's Amazonian frontier. A quantitative analysis shows the word "road" appeared more than the word "God" or other words commonly found in religious publications. The pro-road propaganda persisted despite the social and environmental costs of road construction and Pope Francis' positions in favor of social and environmental values. The authors suggest the importance of promoting visits by communities who have experienced the costs of road development to locations such as this one.

590 **Wernke, Steven A.; Lauren E. Kohut; and Abel Traslaviña.** A GIS of affordances: movement and visibility at a planned colonial town in highland Peru. (*J. Archaeol. Sci.*, 84, Aug. 2017, p. 22–39, bibl., maps, photos)

The authors use GIS, drone-based modelling, spatial network analysis, walking models, and cumulative viewshed analysis to study visual experiences as colonial Peruvian people moved through Santa Cruz de Tuti, a well-preserved abandoned colonial town in the Colca Valley. The layout of the town would have emphasized the original Inka plaza and the colonial church, as well as elite Indigenous households. The imposition of the colonial spatial order had to accommodate the Inka predecessor and fostered a continuity of belief and practice that went against more radical objectives of colonialism.

591 **Young, Jason and Michael Gilmore.** Participatory uses of geospatial technologies to leverage multiple knowledge systems within development contexts: a case study from the Peruvian Amazon. (*World Dev.*, 93, May 2017, p. 389–401, bibl., maps, photos)

The authors worked with Maijuna Indigenous communities and their federation, located to the north of Iquitos in the Peruvian Amazon, to create a digital spatial database to influence policy decisions. An intentional effort was made to ensure that multiple perspectives were included, among them women, elders, children, healers, and farmers. This kind of participatory GIS mapping can help increase the democratic nature and quality of governance decisions. The authors also discuss the pitfalls and risks of participatory mapping, including the reinforcement of existing social and political hierarchies; the paper includes an extensive analysis of the literature on this topic.

BOLIVIA

592 **Heredia, Luis Fernando.** Desdibujando fronteras: relaciones urbanas-rurales en Bolivia. Coordinación de Luis Fernando Heredia. Equipo de investigación, Cristobal Sisco Rioja *et al.* La Paz: CIPCA Centro de Investigación y Promoción del Campesinado, 2016. 191 p.: bibl., color ill. (Cuadernos de investigación; 83)

The authors use census results and their own surveys to probe relationships between urban and rural populations and attitudes towards social inclusion in varied geographic regions of Bolivia, paying attention to ethnicity. There has been a shift in Bolivia from rural to urban, away from Indigenous identity, and a reduction in poverty. Multiple strategies (including the new rurality and pluriactivity) among rural populations have not been adequately measured in national statistics. The rural population has continued to grow despite its reduced proportion of the national population. In the east, big land holdings have consolidated, while in the west small land holdings have multiplied. Social inclusion is most valued by males and Indigenous people, and least valued by females and non-Indigenous rural people; in part, this is due to their perception of the possible negative effects of inclusion.

593 **Lineamientos estratégicos y agenda de políticas públicas para la región metropolitana cruceña.** Dirección de Fernando Prado Salmón. Con la colaboración de Isabella Prado Zanini, Carlos Schlink Ruiz y Vasilev Crispin Seoane. Santa Cruz de la Sierra, Bolivia: CEDURE, 2019. 289 p.: bibl., ill.

The coauthors draw on their experience in urban planning, economics, law, and social psychology to analyze appropriate strategies for territorial development in the metropolitan region of Santa Cruz, the largest city in Bolivia. Chapters focus on demography and characteristics of the population, the distribution of economic and sociocultural resources, and urban ecology (environmental resources and transportation infrastructure). Social organization and the distribution of power are considered, and major problems are identified. The authors call for a vision for the future and new public agendas to improve development of the metropolitan area. In particular, they call for greater governmental involvement in providing essential services, helping develop new economic activities beyond traditional agriculture, and encouraging higher density development. They also call for greater leadership in the private sector and efforts to bridge the gap between traditional and modernizing sectors of society.

594 **Prado Salmón, Fernando.** Ganadores y perdedores: actores sociales ganadoras y perdedores de la región metropolitana cruceña en los 12 años del proceso de cambio. Santa Cruz de la Sierra, Bolivia: Editorial El País, 2018. 94 p.: bibl., ill. (some color), maps.

The author, a city planner and architect with extensive experience in the region and author of numerous books about Santa Cruz, argues that 11 years of progressive politics at the national level has paradoxically seen advancements in globalized capitalism in the region of Bolivia's largest city, with adverse environmental consequences. However local elites and the middle class, as well as other groupings, have tended to lose power and legitimacy. The book has numerous maps and diagrams, and draws on data from censuses and surveys.

595 **Sandi Bernal, Ruben.** Incahuasi, un yacimiento de gas boliviano. Santa Cruz de la Sierra, Bolivia: publisher not identified, 2018. 170 p.: bibl., ill. (some color).

The author is a petroleum geologist who more recently has devoted himself to university teaching and public education. In this book, he provides an overview of the history and geology of the oil and gas fields of Bolivia, and then focuses on the specific gas field of Incahuasi-Aquio, discovered in 2004 on the border between the departments of Santa Cruz and Chuquisaca. Although the field has been determined to be entirely in the department of Santa Cruz, civic authorities and popular movements in Chuquisaca have contested this finding. The author argues that these types of dispute harm everyone and impede the kinds of development that could benefit all Bolivians.

596 **Suárez, Hugo José.** La Paz en el torbellino del progreso: transformaciones urbanas en la era del cambio en Bolivia. Ciudad de México: UNAM, Instituto de Investigaciones Sociales, 2018. 335 p.: bibl., ill., maps, photos.

In this volume, illustrated with maps and photographs, Suárez reports on his explorations of people and places in La Paz, Bolivia. He argues that theory should be grounded in reality and that it is important to be open to the most seemingly trivial data and everyday experiences. The book provides a running commentary on details of urban life in La Paz while reflecting on the literature of urbanism and modernization, including the work of David Harvey, Pierre Bourdieu, and Henri Lefebvre. This could be called "vagabond sociology" or "new anthropology," but it also has an equally strong relationship with critical urban geography. Suárez concludes that in La Paz, urban transformations are a complex mixture of Indigenous factors (related to *buen vivir*) and neoliberal forces resulting in new, fragmented urban realities.

THE SOUTHERN CONE

DAVID J. ROBINSON, *Dellplain Professor Emeritus of Latin American Geography, Syracuse University*

FOLLOWING THE PRACTICE OF *HLAS 75*, the frequency of themes and specific topics in this volume is used to identify major trends of published research over the years 2017–2020. Due to space limitations, the number of citations for some countries has required difficult selections of items listed from the evaluated pool: for Argentina and Chile, the selection represents fewer than 30 percent of the initial review corpus.

The term "territory" dominates the interest of a range of important researchers in both geography and allied disciplines during this period. The term itself has a multiplicity of meanings in varied contexts: land areas, possession, belonging, planning, power and control, heritage, etc. The list is long and complex and varies with specific contexts in both time and space. It is essentially a compound term rich in meanings. The following representative topics are found in publications on all four countries studied: governance (item **688**), conflicts (item **718**), Mapuche (item **703**), opening roads (item **725**), and planning (item **702**). Territoriality is a complex concept that is relevant in many specific research projects throughout Latin America and beyond.

Developments in, and applications of techniques of, spatial analysis are another key aspect of studies during this period (items **602**, **613**, **615**, **642**, and **668**). Patterns of political actions are also now being appraised within significant spatial contexts (items **614** and **635**).

Migration continues to be a significant area of research, whether it is shifts in population within urban areas (items **653**, **677**, and **691**) or moves between rural and urban centers (item **663**). Urban centers provide another focus of research on topics such as gentrification (item **672**), green spaces (item **628**), urban land markets (item **696**), and barrio politics (item **724**). Issues of urban waste have broached a topic that increases in proportion to population growth (item **619**).

Health issues reached the forefront with studies of the impact of COVID-19 (items **686** and **746**) and other spatial situations that demanded investigation (items **615**, **623**, and **662**). Water was also identified as a significant and poorly managed resource directly connected to clear signs of climate change (item **646**). Environmental disputes were noted in distinctive locations (items **618** and **656**); land occupancy and legitimacy of possession, especially noted in Paraguay among

Indigenous cultures, are evident in a series of excellent studies (items 730 and 732). Another set of studies confronts issues of patrimonial development, distinctive contexts, extant field evidence, and memory (items 640, 641, and 675).

Agricultural development persists as a foundational research component (items 610 and 638). Equally present are analyses of regional development and associated problems (items 644 and 655). An important newcomer to the study of mineral resources is a substance that appears to be a solution to the problems of storing energy in electric motor vehicles: lithium (items 601 and 624). Oil and gas are now being reappraised in terms of their long-life capacity: possibilities of extinction loom.

Tourism continues to be a target of analysis, especially with the ramifications of COVID-19 affecting travel possibilities and international tourists facing drastic restrictions. Cruising appears as a profitable alternative to risky land voyages (item 620); some regions have excellent electric power distribution attractive to tourists (item 630); some well-known cities have attractive segments specifically designed to entice tourists not far from home (item 634); Salta's wine route attracts increasing attention (item 665); Buenos Aires' La Boca, famous in so many contexts, witnesses an increasing interest in promoting its favorable characteristics (item 672).

In conclusion, the following publications are strongly recommended as model studies related to the geography of the Southern Cone: a superb new atlas of the Luján River basin (item 609); a classic geographical descriptive presentation of Atacama (item 692); a complete analysis and demonstration of the nature and extent of territorial order (item 657); a study of segments of the previously undocumented Buenos Aires metropolitan area (item 633); a profound analysis and examples of post-neoliberal conservation in Patagonia (item 648); an exemplary study of the worlds and crises of Bolivian migrants in Chile (item 720); a penetrating geolegal analysis of struggles over Indigenous rights and communal territories in Paraguay (item 729); political struggles over land rights in northern Patagonia—yet another story of conflicts over land and resources, superbly described in this analysis of what Carl Sauer would have titled a struggle "For Land and Life" (item 650). Finally, two studies remind us that modern techniques can expose past events and current actions as never before (items 616 and 641). Much awaits the new generation equipped with scientific methods and innovative techniques. Perhaps the moment has come that would allow larger countries of the Southern Cone to turn to help their smaller counterparts? Why not a new journal of *Geografía del Cono Sur*?

GENERAL

597 **Cebrián Abellán, Francisco** and **Carmen Delgado Viñas.** La presencia de producción científica española en la geografía de los países de América Latina y El Caribe en el cambio de milenio. (*Rev. Geogr. Norte Gd.*, 72, mayo 2019, p. 185–203, bibl., color graphs, tables)

This innovative analysis demonstrates that since 1990, there has been an increase in and diversification of the production of geographic research in Spain concerning Latin America, in terms of the number of both research articles published in geographic journals as well as doctoral theses. The works in this article are classified according to territorial and thematic criteria. Territorially, studies are grouped by large regional units or by nation states; for thematic components, larger topics have been grouped and subdivided. It is important to note that from 1990 to 2016, the Southern Cone represented the largest region studied—28 percent of all publications, the majority of which were related to human geography.

598 **Córdoba, Diana** *et al.* Fueling social inclusion?: neo-extractivism, state-society relations and biofuel policies in Latin America's Southern Cone. (*Dev. Change/Oxford*, 49:1, Jan. 2018, p. 63–88, bibl.)

An innovative analysis of the many problems of implementing "post-neoliberal" biofuel policies in Argentina, Uruguay, and Brazil, especially the many contradictions embedded in such policies. Such policies must consider the existing socioeconomic structures and the role of the many participants in economic opportunities: private corporations, international market agencies, agrarian communities, and dynamic movements.

599 **Correia, Joel E.** Territories of Latin American geography. (*J. Lat. Am. Geogr.*, 19:1, Jan. 2020, p. 132–140, bibl., map, photo)

This article represents a useful reminder of the many ways in which the concept of territory is central to the study of Latin American questions of justice, be they cultural, social, or environmental. An excellent bibliography is included.

600 **Czerny, Miroslawa** and **Andrzej Czerny.** Desarrollo territorial en América del Sur: estructuras espaciales y disparidades regionales a través del tiempo. (*Bol. Estud. Geogr.*, 114, nov. 2020/abril 2021, p. 9–32, bibl., maps)

A welcome general overview of historical and contemporary patterns of centers, paths, and spatial changes in major economic activities over the last five centuries. Such changes have modified national and regional structures, as well as the development of urban centers. South America has also experienced the effects of globalization: commercial competition and new communication systems have had a significant impact on existing patterns, and the applications of traditional spatial planning have changed. Excellent use of well-designed color maps.

601 **Dorn, Felix M.** Electro-movilidad y el triángulo del litio (Argentina, Bolivia, Chile): tendencias globales en el marco del cambio climático. (*Bol. Estud. Geogr.*, 112, julio/dic. 2019, p. 115–130, bibl., graphs, color photos, table)

The author argues that "electro-mobility polarizes." While several actors including the automotive industry, governments, and the media see electro-mobility as playing an important role in the fight against climate change and air pollution, the production of high-performance batteries is also accompanied by a growing demand for strategic resources, including lithium. Using the example of lithium mining in South America, the study describes the scarcity of raw material as an obstacle to expanding electro-mobility. Based on a field study in the region in 2018 and 2019, the author aptly describes the problems of lithium mining in the high Andean salt flats of South America.

602 **Finn, John C.** *et al.* Introducing *JLAG em Tradução*/*JLAG en Traducción*. (*J. Lat. Am. Geogr.*, 19:1, Jan. 2020, p. 246–257, bibl.)

An important statement of the editorial team's efforts to "use the JLAG to decolonize processes of knowledge production, or at least JLAG's role in these processes, in what is a historically patriarchal, white, and North-centered discipline." Their stated aim is "to intentionally recognize and confront the multi-scalar and multi-dimensional inequalities that we all, both institutionally (i.e., the journal) and individually (i.e., we as scholars), are implicit in reproducing, and to make JLAG a conduit of meaningful South-North scholarly dialogue." A necessary and welcome step in the journal's international role.

603 **Giordano, Mariana.** Expediciones, fotografía y coleccionismo entre dos siglos: itinerarios visuales de un "cultural broker" en Argentina y Paraguay. (*Rev.*

Indias, 79:275, 2019, p. 235-263, bibl., ill., map, photos)

An innovative study examining the framework of the visual, artifactual, and collectionist aspects of the photographic albums of Louis de Boccard (1866-1956), a Swiss explorer who travelled extensively from the end of the 19th century through the 1940s in the Southern Cone.

604 López-Vázquez, Carlos and **Miguel Ángel Bernabé-Poveda.** La situación de la producción científica latinoamericana en el área de la Ciencia de Información Geográfica. (*Rev. Cartogr.*, 100, enero/junio 2020, p. 173-193, bibl., graphs, tables)

The authors assess the goal for *Revista Cartográfica* to publish a minimum of 45 articles per year to be considered for participation in SciELO. They attempt to measure the feasibility of this objective by providing an estimate of the volume of scientific production of the Pan American Institute of Geography and History (PAIGH) member countries in Geographic Information Science. They perform a bibliometric analysis of the articles published in a representative set of international journals and filter those with authors from countries in the region. They exclude the US because of its high relative weight in this scientific area. The main conclusion is that the goal of capturing part of these works and thus more than duplicating the material published today in *Revista Cartográfica* seems difficult to achieve in the short term. In the future, it will be necessary to entice authors from outside the region, who typically first consider the journal's categorization, so they are somewhat hampered by their current status.

605 Martinet, Gilles *et al.* Descolonizar la producción de conocimiento sobre espacios latinoamericanos desde Europa: límites críticos y aprendizajes desde la experiencia interdisciplinaria del GRECAL. (*J. Lat. Am. Geogr.*, 17:1, April 2018, p. 257-266, bibl.)

A provocative set of opinions by members of GRECAL (Grupo de Reflexiones y Estudios Críticos sobre América Latina) on the necessity to orient geographic and other disciplinary analyses of Latin America in the Global North away from their persistent coloniality perspectives. It would have been useful to include citations of published models of such potential analyses.

606 Roniger, Luis. Changing cultural landscapes under the impact of exile, diasporas and return migration. (*Araucaria/Triana*, 20:40, 2018, p. 1-24, bibl.)

This article discusses the impact of territorial displacement from the Southern Cone during the cycle of dictatorships and democratization of the late 20th century and early 21st century. The author points out the complexities and different forms of exile, expatriation, and migration which these societies experienced, while asserting that exile could not be undone fully with democratization, as many of those who left did not come back, others left in new waves of expatriation, and even those who did return could not resume the lives they had left behind. Yet, the experience of living elsewhere broadened the social, political, and cultural perspectives. Whether returning or not, or becoming sojourners, many individuals who left during the dictatorships made substantial contributions to the societies of origin. See also item **607**.

607 Roniger, Luis *et al.* Exile, diaspora, and return: changing cultural landscapes in Argentina, Chile, Paraguay, and Uruguay. New York, N.Y.: Oxford University Press, 2017. 292 p.: bibl., index.

This innovative volume, a landmark in cultural historical geography, represents a multidisciplinary effort by a sociologist, a historian, a political scientist, and a literary scholar. The four authors examine the entire cycle of political exiles from the military regimes of South America, especially in the 1970s and 1980s: the social-political-economic circumstances that drove thousands of Argentines, Chileans, Paraguayans, and Uruguayans out of their home countries; their reception in the host countries and their efforts at social integration; the formation of exile communities and diaspora politics; the personal decision to go back and the policies of return adopted by the new democratic regimes; and the exiles' contribution to the democratization of their home countries at the end of the 20th century and beginning of the 21st, especially in Chile and Uruguay. Those considered in this forced migration are members of a selected group of an elite population: politicians, academics, lawyers, etc. The book is full of insights; each chapter deserves to become a monograph on its own, delving more deeply into some of the issues here dealt with only briefly and allowing more voices of exiles and returnees to be heard. So many critical dimensions are involved: cultural identity, experiences in exile, networks of information, significance of temporary locations, etc. The work would benefit from a flow map showing the movements of the exiles: who migrated to where, and how many returned? The authors are to be commended for their eloquent analysis of so many complex transnational cultural issues. This is a classic work. For political economy specialist's comment, see item **1277**. For sociologist's comment, see item **1445**.

ARGENTINA

608 Arboit, Mariela Edith; César Cucchietti; and Dora Silvia Maglione. Análisis comparativo preliminar de la variabilidad temporal del índice de vegetación en las áreas metropolitanas forestadas: casos de estudio: La Plata, Mendoza, Santiago de Chile y Turín. (*Bol. Estud. Geogr.*, 110, julio/dic. 2018, p. 67–86, bibl., graphs, maps, tables)

The authors offer an innovative analysis of current conditions and recent changes in urban vegetation cover through the study of temporal variability of the "normalized difference vegetation index" (NDVI) of four forested cities, comparing the images provided by satellite data for the summer periods from 1986 to 2011. They present a preliminary comparative analysis of correlations and trend estimation, which is important for understanding the relationship between urban morphology and green infrastructure. They plan to include an attempt to define criteria of urban design appropriate for forested cities, which will enable the sectors responsible for the protection of the habitat to manage, design, and implement feasible design responses toward the future, within the framework of urban and environmentally sustainable energy development.

609 Atlas de geografía humana de la cuenca del río Luján. Dirección de Gustavo D. Buzai y Sonia L. Lanzelotti. Buenos Aires: Impresiones Buenos Aires Editorial: Instituto de Investigaciones Geográficas (INIGEO), 2019. 289 p.: bibl., ill., maps. <http://www.inigeo.unlu.edu.ar/?q=node/24>

A major contribution to the knowledge of, and important use of, spatial data available for the Luján River basin. This open access electronic publication from the Universidad Nacional de Luján offers a wide range of maps representing the spatial patterns of socioeconomic variables at various scales. The appendices provide details of the GIS methodologies used to produce and map such patterns. Several recognizable scholars contributed to the atlas, which, coupled with Gustavo Buzai as one of the leads of the project, demonstrates the potential powers of a team of skilled researchers.

610 Auer, Alejandra; Laura Nahuelhual; and Nestor Maceira. Cultural ecosystem services trade-offs arising from agriculturization in Argentina: a case study in Mar Chiquita basin. (*Appl. Geogr.*, 91, Feb. 2018, p. 45–54, bibl., graphs, maps, tables)

An examination of a set of variables infrequently used in developmental analyses: trade-offs from economic processes, in this case agriculturalization, affecting such benefits as recreation and tourism. The authors analyze a selected zone to measure the impact of agricultural change in the southeast of Buenos Aires province. Results are presented on a series of well-designed color maps that allow one to clearly see the spatial pattern of the impact of landscape change.

611 Barada, Julieta. Un pueblo es un lugar: la forma urbana de un pueblo de pastores ante las lógicas del estado; Coranzulí, Puna de Jujuy, Argentina, del 1900 al hoy. (*Rev. Geogr. Norte Gd.*, 77, dic. 2020, p. 367–395, bibl., maps, photos, tables)

Andean shepherd villages, especially in Argentina, have historically faced tension between local mobility dynamics and state interests focused on their settlement. The state has concentrated on the "civilizing" process based on the rural-urban divide.

Using graphic and written documents, this article analyzes urbanization in Coranzulí (Puna de Jujuy, Argentina) from the beginning of the 20th century to the present. This study examines Argentine state actions and observes how local actors negotiate the urban form of the village based on their own interests. Some of the maps are illegible, but the author's excellent use of historic photographs enhances the study and demonstrates the changing urban form.

612 **Baxendale, Claudia A.** Análisis sociohabitacional de entornos de plazas en la Ciudad Autónoma de Buenos Aires (Argentina): exploración de su relación espacial con índices físico-ambientales. (*GeoSIG/Luján*, 12:17, 2020, p. 1–14, bibl., ill., color maps, tables)

This contribution using spatial analysis and GIS can be carried out in multidisciplinary research projects. The study, corresponding to a research project carried out by Grupo de Ecología del Paisaje y Medio Ambiente of the Universidad de Buenos Aires, focuses on 28 blocks within the Ciudad Autónoma de Buenos Aires (CABA). The work focuses on methodological issues and a spatial analysis to discover the population structure and sociohabitational characteristics of the area. The author also analyzes spatial correlations with socioresidential characteristics at the neighborhood level, and examines physical-environmental indicators constructed to evaluate green spaces.

613 **Bosisio, Andrea C.** and **Antonio Moreno Jiménez.** Análisis espacial de indicadores de vulnerabilidad y privaciones sociales basado en SIG: el caso de Santa Fe de la Vera Cruz (Argentina). (*GeoSIG/Luján*, 12:17, 2020, p. 1–19, bibl., graphs, color maps, tables)

Social factors affect how a community and its inhabitants anticipate, resist, and recover from disturbances or disasters. This work addresses the spatial distribution of vulnerable social groups in the city of Santa Fe de la Vera Cruz. The authors identify the urban populated area as the relevant study area, and select sociodemographic indicators to represent vulnerability and human deprivation to water hazards by census *radios* (small urban sections). To this end, the role of GIS technology has been fundamental. The results provide an accurate location of these critical areas, allowing the optimization of planning processes, especially those for the development of actions to protect the eventual impacts in areas where the most disadvantaged groups in Santa Fe reside.

614 **Bosque Sendra, Joaquín** and **Gustavo D. Buzai.** Geografía electoral de la Ciudad Autónoma de Buenos Aires, 2015: elecciones a Jefe de Gobierno Municipal y Presidente de la República de Argentina. (*Pers. Soc.*, 31:1, enero/junio 2017, p. 48–73, bibl., graphs, maps, tables)

This paper presents a case study of the application of exploratory spatial data analysis to better understand associations between the patterns of spatial distribution of voting, the social map of the city, and the education level of the population. Such a geographical perspective allows one to test hypotheses and advance interpretations via the spatiality of the results. All graphics are of high quality.

615 **Buzai, Gustavo D.** Análisis exploratorio de datos espaciales de los condicionantes sociales de la salud en la cuenca del río Luján, Argentina. (*Posición/Luján*, 1, 2019, p. 1–16, bibl., graphs, color maps) <http://hdl.handle.net/11336/130905>

The relationship between GIS and Spatial Decision Support Systems (SDSS) provides important possibilities for the treatment of spatial information. Focused on Exploratory Spatial Data Analysis, this study analyzes patterns of Socio-Spatial Conditioners of Health (SCH) in the Luján River basin. The conceptual definitions of the theoretical framework, the applied methodologies, the graphic representations, and the cartographic results demonstrate successive approaches towards the modeling of the underlying spatial structures as a fundamental component of territorial planning.

616 **Buzai, Gustavo D.** and **Eloy José Montes Galbán.** Megaciudad Buenos Aires: cartografía de su última expansión y conurbación mediante el procesamiento digital de imágenes satelitales nocturnas. (*Rev. Cartogr.*, 100, enero/junio 2020, p. 215–238, bibl., graphs, maps, tables)

Excellent application of a new method of identifying significant patterns of urban growth using GIS and nocturnal satellite images. It truly "sheds light" on the problem, allowing one to note the tentacular expansion of this major metropolis.

617 Cannizzo, Mariana; Claudia M. Campos; and **Gabriela Lichtenstein.** Protegiendo lo desprotegido: cambios y desafíos del sistema de áreas naturales protegidas de Mendoza. *(Bol. Estud. Geogr.,* 114, nov. 2020/abril 2021, p. 53–75, bibl., graph, map, table)

This well-documented study analyzes the history of the Protected Areas (PAs) in the province of Mendoza, as well as the socioenvironmental and management problems that currently affect it. Through bibliographic review and interviews, the authors find that the PAs of Mendoza have grown in recent decades, transforming them into a tool not only for conservation, but also for the defense of the commons. However, lingering threats and challenges require urgent attention to guarantee the conservation of biodiversity and local livelihoods.

618 Castillo, Trilce Irupé and **Claudio Rafael Mariano Baigún.** Identification of artisanal fishing territories and associated conflicts in the middle and lower Paraná River (Argentina) through participatory mapping. *(Appl. Geogr.,* 125, Dec. 2020, p. 1–13, bibl., graphs, color maps, photos, tables)

A fascinating application of participatory mapping (PM) as a method of identifying and monitoring fishing "territories" in the middle and lower Paraná River. The authors used Quantum GIS software to process the information they gathered and draft local fishing maps. They note shore activities as a specific problem given their impact on mooring facilities and other land-based needs of the fishermen. One hopes the PM method will be practiced on other larger rivers to potentially solve the many disputes facing the fishing communities.

619 Codebò, Agnese. Decolonizing the landfill: counter-maps of waste in Buenos Aires. *(J. Lat. Am. Geogr.,* 18:3, Oct. 2019, p. 30–53, bibl., ill., maps, photos)

This study examines the implications of counter-maps for decolonizing dominant perspectives on territories of waste and the people who deal with it. To study the phenomenon, the author reviews three instances of landfill counter-mapping created in Buenos Aires: Antonio Berni's 1960s series on Juanito Laguna, Iconoclasistas' contemporary *La República de los cirujas,* and the publishing house Eloísa Cartonera. Each employs artistic methods to reveal the presence and struggles of those living and working in the city's landfill. The key map of slum sites is unfortunately too small and thus illegible.

620 Cohen, Carolina; Marisol Vereda; and **Graciela Benseny.** Camarones y Puerto Deseado: estudio de atractividad de dos puertos patagónicos para el desarrollo de turismo de cruceros. *(Rev. Univ. Geogr./Bahía Blanca,* 28:2, dic. 2019, p. 57–86, bibl., graphs, maps, table)

This study analyzes the attractiveness of Camarones and Puerto Deseado for the development of cruise tourism based on the appraisals of cruise passengers and other key actors in the area of study. A qualitative-quantitative approach is adopted to surveys of cruise passengers and in-depth interviews with key informants. The results show the high potential of destinations for the development of cruise tourism according to the tourist valuation of the attractions, particularly related to natural assets.

621 Del Cid, María Concepción. La ciudad actual: un espacio con signos de fragmentación espacial; aplicación al aglomerado urbano de la ciudad de San Juan, Argentina. *(GeoSIG/Luján,* 11:13, 2019, p. 103–120, bibl., graphs, color maps, color photos)

In recent decades, urban growth has presented a series of particular patterns. In addition to the increase in consolidated urban sprawl, occupation of peripheral areas occurs discontinuously. This phenomenon manifests itself in the urban structures of cities as a process of spatial fragmentation, present in many cities, whether large or medium-sized, such as the case studied here, the urban area of the agglomerate of San Juan, Argentina. The study begins with the land cover maps of 2000 and 2010. Nice use of well-designed maps to illustrate findings.

622 **Díaz, Mariela Paula et al.** ¿Normativa urbana para quién?: el caso del nuevo barrio Parque Donado Holmberg, Ciudad de Buenos Aires, Argentina. (*Estud. Socioterritoriales*, 25, enero/junio 2019, e016, p. 1–24, bibl., ill., maps, table)

The Parque Donado Holmberg neighborhood is a new public-private real estate development in the northern zone of the city of Buenos Aires. It is located on the old pattern of the never-built Highway 3, designed during the last military dictatorship. The current project promoted by the local government plans to "rebuild" the plot in order to revitalize the neighborhood and sell public domain properties. This article analyzes the impact of modified urban regulations on the process of urban renewal in the neighborhood. The methodology is qualitative, based on nonparticipant observation in the neighborhood, in-depth interviews with key informants, and secondary sources from public and private organizations. The paper includes 11 maps, called "images": image 2 is strangely not related to the area of the newly configured barrio. A "mapeo colectivo" is mentioned but not presented.

623 **Dimas, Carlos S.** Harvesting cholera: fruit, disease and governance in the cholera epidemic of Tucumán, Argentina, 1867–68. (*J. Lat. Am. Stud.*, 49:1, Feb. 2017, p. 115–142, map)

This excellent study analyzes the impact of the 1868 cholera outbreak in Tucumán province, which led the urban-based specialists to blame the fruit-growing area as the source of the problem. Sugar cultivation was argued to be a safer agricultural base. Disease, contagion, and local politics characterized this formative period in the development of the province. An extremely well-documented study. For historian's comment, see *HLAS 76:979*.

624 **Dorn, Felix M. and Fernando Ruiz Peyré.** Lithium as a strategic resource: geopolitics, industrialization, and mining in Argentina. (*J. Lat. Am. Geogr.*, 19:4, Oct. 2020, p. 68–90, bibl., graphs, table)

Given that the world's greatest known lithium deposits are found in South America, international investors are paying major attention to the area. Future developments in mobile transportation and grid development using lithium batteries highlight the potential economic development in the "lithium triangle," hence the urgent need for more research on this strategic resource. As in past mineral booms, questions of controlling the extraction process, minimizing pollution, and maximizing the socioeconomic benefits to both local and national populations remain. The key issues involved in developing and integrating lithium products into the world economy are well-developed. The study would have benefitted from a map identifying key locations of the Argentine deposits.

625 **Easdale, Marcos Horacio.** El proceso de urbanización en un territorio pastoril trashumante del Noroeste de Patagonia, Argentina (1920–2010). (*Cuad. Geogr. Univ. Granada*, 57:2, 2018, p. 283–303, bibl., graphs, maps, tables)

Many mountainous, arid, and semi-arid regions sustain rural communities with cultural and socioproductive characteristics, which are adapted to the specific conditions of these environments, such as pastoralism tied to seasonal migration in northwest Patagonia. In these contexts, it has been proposed that the urbanization process can have implications in the sedentarization of the communities, in the ecological and agronomic fragmentation of landscapes, and in its cultural practices. These changes entail social, productive, and ecological consequences. This study analyzes whether there is evidence of urbanization in northern Neuquén, its spatial and temporal magnitude as measured by demographic and educational indicators, and its association with current regional infrastructure levels. The author discusses the results in light of proposals for territorial development and governance and their implications for transhumant pastoral activity. Excellent mapped data, linked to graphs.

626 **Edwards, Ryan C.** Convicts and conservation: inmate labor, fires and forestry in southernmost Argentina. (*J. Hist. Geogr.*, 56, April 2017, p. 1–13, bibl.)

A model study of the role of the Ushuaia prison established during the first decades of the 19th century. Prisoners worked as laborers in both the town and surrounding forests, but repeated massive fires and allegations of prisoner abuse led to the prison's closure in 1947. Symbolically, the prison became a museum in 1997 to remind residents and tourists alike of the past landscape and the former roles of the convicts, as well as the impact on the landscape of the prison as a developmental site.

627   **Engelman, Anabella** and **Pehuén Barzola Elizagaray.** Propuesta para el estudio de urbanizaciones cerradas en Latinoamérica: el caso del enclave residencial de elite "Mendoza Norte Country Club", Mendoza, Argentina. (*Bol. Estud. Geogr.*, 114, nov. 2020/abril 2021, p. 101–134, bibl., map, color photos, table)

This study analyzes a residential enclave, characterizing the process of suburbanization of the elites in the arid foothills of the Mendoza pre-cordillera. The empirical object is a gated community, Mendoza Norte Country Club, which built the first golf course in the department of Las Heras. The author emphasizes the importance of including the environmental dimension in studies of residential enclaves since its development reveals processes of dispossession in the natural commons of the piedmont. A poor-quality map and photos do not do justice to the community.

628   **Fernández Romero, Francisco.** Espacios verdes ¿para qué y para quiénes?: territorialidades en disputa en el Área Metropolitana de Buenos Aires (1944–2016). (*Estud. Socioterritoriales*, 25, enero/junio 2019, e018, p. 1–16, bibl., maps, tables)

This article identifies and describes the territorialities of green spaces in the Buenos Aires Metropolitan Area. The author focuses on recognizing the wider political, social, economic, and territorial projects which frame different ways of thinking about and taking action concerning green spaces, and on exploring the tensions surrounding these kinds of spaces. The following issues are studied for three time periods (1945–55, 1955–82, and 1982–2016): intervention by several actors to create or modify green spaces; the arguments they have invoked to justify these actions; and the types of use, users, and objectives that they have ascribed to these spaces.

629   **Fiant, Roxana E.** and **Jacqueline Salim Grau.** Metodología cualitativa en la interpretación del paisaje de la Quebrada de El Tala. (*Vientos Norte*, 6:2, dic. 2018, p. 36–47, bibl., ill., maps, photos)

The author argues that the Quebrada de El Tala, a periurban element of the city of San Fernando del Valle de Catamarca, manifests various logics of landscape relationships. The study presents a temporal analysis through inherited landscapes: prehispanic, colonial, republican, and the landscape lived during the first quinquennium of the 21st century, as well as the projected future landscape. A useful guide to how one might approach qualitative landscape interpretation. Graphics are too small to be interpreted.

630   **Furlan, Adriano.** Suministro eléctrico y desarrollo turístico en la costa atlántica de la provincia de Buenos Aires (2003–2015): articulaciones e impactos. (*Estud. Socioterritoriales*, 21, junio 2017, p. 47–70, bibl., graphs, color maps, table)

The article seeks to understand the power supply necessary for tourism in the Atlantic coastal province of Buenos Aires between 2003 and 2015. The research is part of a Latin American perspective of the study of infrastructural services, that is, in contexts of peripheral capitalism and dependent urbanization. The relationship between tourist development and electricity supply is interpreted as a local manifestation of the economic and territorial national development and whose underlying guidelines of accumulation patterns were established in 2003, but have been overbuilt in the existing spatial structure. The author analyzes the impact of tourism in three areas: seasonality of electricity demand, urban growth, and management of supply shortages. He concludes that the study of the power supply should integrate a geographic perspective to develop more effective solutions. The width of the maps should have been maximized to render them more legible.

631   **Gargantini, Daniela Mariana** and **Natalí del Valle Peresini.** Representaciones y estrategias de articulación-acción

de actores públicos y privados en relación al gobierno del suelo urbano en la ciudad de Córdoba (Argentina). (*Estud. Socioterritoriales*, 21, junio 2017, p. 155–171, bibl., table)

This study presents the progress of an investigation into urban land conflicts in the city of Córdoba. The authors review the actions of both public and private influential actors who seek to access and control land in the city. They also propose solutions to the ongoing conflicts about land use. The analysis is based principally on interview data.

632   Gómez Lende, Sebastián. Usos del territorio y psicoesfera: minería metalífera y desarrollo socioeconómico en tres provincias argentinas. (*Cuad. Geogr. Univ. Granada*, 57:1, 2018, p. 6–38, bibl., map, tables)

This study analyzes the rise of metal mining in contemporary Argentina by focusing on the "trickle-down effect" that this activity presumably would have on the economic development of the provinces of Catamarca, San Juan, and Santa Cruz. The author compares and contrasts the (pro) mining psychosphere regarding the evolution of different variables at the provincial and departmental level, such as the labor market, circumstantial and structural poverty, public finances, infrastructure, and the Human Development Index (HDI). An excellent, detailed analysis of a complexity of variables employing mostly tabular data.

633   Gómez Pintus, Ana. Las formas de expansión, 1910–1950: barrios parque y loteos de fin de semana en la construcción del espacio metropolitano de Buenos Aires. Buenos Aires: Diseño Editorial, 2018. 198 p.: bibl. (Serie Tesis de la FAU: Facultad de Arquitectura y Urbanismo/UNLP)

A valuable analysis of the historical development of distinctive landscape elements of Buenos Aires based on the author's PhD dissertation.

634   González Bracco, Mercedes and Linda Kotschack. El espacio turístico, entre el enclave y el derrame: estudio en dos barrios de Buenos Aires. (*Cuad. Geogr./Bogotá*, 26:2, julio/dic. 2017, p. 373–397, bibl., ill., maps, photos)

For this investigation, the authors carry out case studies in two neighborhoods in Buenos Aires: La Boca and Palermo, which differ in terms of history, landscape, and demographics, but are similar in touristic interest. The methodology includes ethnographic strategies, analysis of newspapers, and virtual references. Based on fieldwork, the authors observe how these neighborhoods' discourses and practices shape different tourist spaces in terms of design as well as in the use and meaning of them as determined by tourists. A well-designed research project with clear conclusions.

635   Halvorsen, Sam. The geography of political parties: territory and organisational strategies in Buenos Aires. (*Trans. Inst. Br. Geogr.*, 45:2, June 2020, p. 242–255, bibl.)

This paper addresses how and why geography informs the organizational strategies of political parties. A model for analyzing the relationship between territory and party organization draws on a case study in Buenos Aires to examine how parties strategically organize to pursue their objectives. By analyzing the Encuentro por la Democracia y la Equidad party strategy over the period 2008–2018, the paper proposes four areas—party-building, linkages, alliance-building, and electoral success—as the main strategic focal points. The study makes three key contributions: 1) it highlights the dimension and significance of space to party-building; 2) it stresses regional and local dynamics of party organizing; and 3) it demonstrates how sociospatial relations constitute parties' interactions with both the state and civil society. A truly innovative study.

636   Halvorsen, Sam; Bernardo Mançano Fernandes; and Fernanda Valeria Torres. Mobilizing territory: socioterritorial movements in comparative perspective. (*Ann. Am. Assoc. Geogr.*, 109:5, Sept. 2019, p. 1454–1470, bibl., graph)

This article develops Brazilian geographer Fernandes' notion of "socioterritorial movements" as an analytical category for social movements that seek to appropriate space in pursuit of their political project. The authors compare and contrast the concept of socioterritorial movement with those of social movement and sociospatial movement and propose four areas of analysis for socioterritorial movements. First, territory is mobilized as the central strategy for realizing a movement's aims. Second, territory informs the identity of socioterritorial movements, generating new political subjectivities. Third, territory is a site of political socialization that produces new encounters and values. Fourth, through processes of territorialization, deterritorialization, and reterritorialization, socioterritorial movements create new institutions. These axes are further elaborated through an analysis of two case studies: the Movimento dos Trabalhadores Rurais Sem Terra, a large peasant movement in Brazil, and the Organización Barrial Tupac Amaru, an urban social movement in northwest Argentina focused on the Jujeña population. An innovative, well-designed project with important conclusions.

637 Hölzl, Corinna and Roland Verwiebe. Middle-class struggles against highrise construction in Buenos Aires: urban democratization or enforcement of particular interests? (*Urban Geogr.*, 41:5, 2020, p. 713–735, bibl., graph, map, photos, tables)

This study analyzes the spatial-political outcome of protests against high-rise construction and demolitions of urban heritage in Buenos Aires. Based on a frame analysis, the authors find that the citizens' initiatives have been able to incorporate several key issues into the agenda of the public debate: the relevance of the urban heritage, the negative effects of market-oriented municipal politics, and low citizen participation.

638 Humacata, Luis. Análisis espacial de cambios de usos del suelo: aplicación con Sistemas de Información Geográfica. (*Rev. Cartogr.*, 98, enero/junio 2019, p. 239–257, bibl., graphs, color maps, tables)

The study of spatial dynamics is often used to determine the patterns of spatial distribution and land use. This study develops the conceptual and methodological aspects of spatial evolution analysis, focused on GIS as a tool for the application of cartographic resources. The methodology of detection of land use change is combined with cartographic and statistical results to assess the magnitude of changes in land use. The study area is three zones in Buenos Aires where urban growth has occurred. The results demonstrate the impact of urbanization on the natural environment, mainly affecting agricultural and forestry activities. At the same time, the process of agricultural development is noted since that advances on spaces traditionally utilized for cattle and conservation activities.

639 Humacata, Luis. Sistemas de información geográfica: aplicaciones para el análisis de clasificación espacial y cambios de usos del suelo. Buenos Aires: Impresiones Buenos Aires Editorial: Universidad Nacional de Luján, Instituto de Investigaciones Geográficas (INIGEO), 2020. 184 p.: bibl., ill, maps. <https://geoinnova.org/libro/sistemas-de-informacion-geografica-aplicaciones-para-el-analisis-de-clasificacion-espacial-y-cambios-de-usos-del-suelo/>

This important volume demonstrates the multiple benefits of using a GIS methodology in ascertaining and mapping the changing patterns of land use.

640 Jiménez Frei, Cheryl. Columbus, Juana and the politics of the plaza: battles over monuments, memory and identity in Buenos Aires. (*J. Lat. Am. Stud.*, 51:3, Aug. 2019, p. 607–638, ill., photos)

In 2013, Argentina's then-President Cristina Fernández de Kirchner sparked controversy for her decision to replace a monument of Christopher Columbus in Buenos Aires with one of 19th-century mestiza revolutionary Juana Azurduy. This article examines the history and iconography of these monuments, exploring the intersections between public space, art, politics, and memory. The author argues that these monuments—one representing Argentina's previously maligned Italian immigrant heritage, the other its forgotten Indigenous culture—demonstrate how fundamental struggles over national identity have been embedded and contested. She highlights Argentina's 1910 centennial and 2010 bicentennial as key to these efforts and examines the power and politics of place in the central plaza where various actors have fought for public commemorative representation.

641 Landa, Carlos et al. Análisis espacial de la Zanja de Alsina en la provincia de La Pampa, Argentina (1876-1879): un abordaje interdisciplinario entre la arqueología y la geografía. (*Huellas/Santa Rosa*, 21:2, dic. 2017, p. 99–120, bibl., graphs, maps, color photos)

The construction of the "Zanja de Alsina" (Alsina's trench) was a major event initiated in 1875 by the government to mark the division between the autonomous Indigenous groups of the Pampa and Patagonian cultures. The existence of the trench was the first step in a process to transform the frontier world into a rural area. This interdisciplinary study by several authors presents the results of analyses using satellite images, historical cartography, and information provided by an archeological team to locate the trench and the adjacent military forts (Machado, Alsina, and Alvear). Unfortunately, the resultant map is too small to be legible and no mention is made as to whether the project would be continued after 2017.

642 Lange, Victoria; Francisco Guichón; and Josefina Flores Coni. Lagunas de la Meseta: análisis de la distribución espacial del Registro Arqueológico en el Sur de la Meseta del Strobel (provincia de Santa Cruz, Patagonia, Argentina). (*GeoSIG/Luján*, 11:15, 2019, p. 130–145, bibl., graphs, maps, photos, tables)

This study advances existing knowledge on hunter-gatherers' mobility and landscape use in central-western Santa Cruz province (Argentina) during the last 5,000 years (Middle and Late Holocene). The authors describe the characteristics of the archeological record from the Strobel Plateau and its relationship with the environment, specifically the stability of the lagoons. Based on technological and rock art evidence, this work focuses on spatial analysis using GIS. The results suggest that the stability of lagoons is a major factor in the selection of spaces by hunter-gatherers in the past, although it was not the sole aspect in determining the location of their occupation.

643 Leguizamón, Amalia. Disappearing nature?: agribusiness, biotechnology and distance in Argentine soybean production. (*J. Peasant Stud.*, 43:1/2, March 2016, p. 313–330, bibl.)

This creative and important study attempts to assess the significance and consequences of the "distancing" of products including vegetables—in this case soybeans—from their initial place in nature to their form when consumers receive them: essentially the complex food chain process. The Argentine case of soybean production, with its shift to radical technological processes and the associated financial investment, is well described, though the "disappearance of nature" may not be of significance for those who need to purchase the end-product: the food.

644 Lema, Carolina and Paula Gabriela Núñez. Destruir para desarrollar: ciencia natural y desigualdad en el ordenamiento territorial patagónico. (*Cuad. Geogr./Bogotá*, 28:2, julio/dic. 2019, p. 255–270, bibl., maps)

This study analyzes national and scientific rhetoric that laid the foundation for the design of the Patagonian territory, while also considering the political significance of its development. The authors critique the scientific discourse that informed the development model of the region from the end of the 19th century to the beginning of the 20th century. A powerful philosophically based argument.

645 Maffini, Manuel Alfredo and Gabriela Inés Maldonado. Territorio, mercantilización de la naturaleza y turismo en la provincia de Córdoba, Argentina. (*Bol. Estud. Geogr.*, 111, enero/junio 2019, p. 61–93, bibl., maps)

The province of Córdoba, one of the most important tourist regions of the country, has increased its outreach to potential visitors by diversifying options to include ecotourism and adventure tourism. The authors argue that these new tourist practices are based on a process of commodification of nature. The study analyzes two case studies of tourism destinations to review this assessment. Well-designed maps are provided.

646 Mateos Inchauspe, Macarena and Patricia Alejandra Morrell. Problemas ambientales en el litoral del partido de Mar

Chiquita (Buenos Aires). (*Vientos Norte*, 7:1/2, dic. 2020, p. 39–52, bibl., graphs, map, photos, table)

This study examines the main environmental problems in the small coastal towns of Mar de Cobo, La Caleta, and Camet Norte, belonging to the Chiquita Mar *partido*, using data collected in seven digital diaries during the period from September 2016 to December 2018. Several environmental problems were identified in the area, including: coastal erosion, flooding, and the presence of microgarbage. To collect additional information, the authors conducted field surveys and semistructured interviews with residents. They find that the increase in population and building density, together with the absence of integrated coastal management, has permitted the environmental impacts to become ever more threatening. Excellent use of cartographic displays.

647   Maya, Mario Alejandro and María Amalia Lorda. Urbanizaciones cerradas en Mar del Plata: una aproximación desde la geografía cultural a la construcción social del territorio. (*Huellas/Santa Rosa*, 23:2, julio/dic. 2019, p. 11–29, bibl., map, photos, table)

The authors analyze the growth of gated communities in the city of Mar del Plata from a cultural approach. They note that urban developers offer various amenities to entice residents. This urban development is linked to the processes of socioterritorial fragmentation in the large metropolitan areas of the region and throughout the country. The study relies on methods of bibliographic compilation, statistical analysis, semistructured surveys, interviews, and field research. The authors also assess the link between commercial strategies and advertising for the influx of gated communities in the city. Unfortunately, the single map is not large enough to view effectively.

648   Mendoza, Marcos. The Patagonian sublime: the green economy and post-neoliberal politics. New Brunswick, N.J.: Rutgers University Press, 2018. 225 p.: bibl., index.

This is the first book-length analysis of post-neoliberal conservation, theoretically rich and with a very extensive empirical database. Not only is the Argentine embrace of "Kirchnerismo" examined in detail, but the author also analyzes the many challenges of combining development in the oil industry and ecotourism in Santa Cruz province. The author's extended fieldwork in the town of El Chaltén allows him to test his interpretation of "green productivism" with interviews conducted with diverse informants. This book should be consulted by all geographers interested in environmental-economic geography, political ecology, and comparative Latin American analysis. A classic.

649   Métodos cuantitativos en geografía humana. Compilación de Gustavo D. Buzai y Marcela Virginia Santana Juárez. Buenos Aires: Impresiones Buenos Aires Editorial: Universidad Nacional de Luján, Instituto de Investigaciones Geográficas (INIGEO), 2019. 351 p.: bibl., graphs, maps, tables. (Colección espacialidades; 2) <http://www.inigeo.unlu.edu.ar/?q=node/24>

An important collection of quantitative methodologies applied to both Argentinian as well as Mexican contexts at a variety of spatial scales. Each method is clearly defined and explained, in elegant textual descriptions, and results are illustrated in colored graphs and maps. An important example of applied geography shared between specialists in Argentina and Mexico in this new age of GIS/SIG.

650   Mombello, Laura. Por la vida y el territorio: disputas políticas y culturales en Norpatagonia. Mar del Plata, Argentina: Eudem, 2018. 409 p.: bibl. (Colección Temas de política y ciudadanía)

A short English title to this innovative study would be "For Land and Life" (a shadow of Sauer). The elegant text is replete with counterviews of persons and organizations, positions of local, regional, and the national government. The land—territory writ large—is appraised as a necessity for national identity and growth; it is variously identified as a "desert," or a frontier region of potential profitability for those who successfully domesticate it and reap the benefits of its abundant resources. But at what price?: cultural displacement and environmental damage; complex occupation processes followed by expropriational counter trends, appraisals, and challenging proposals by antagonistic cultural elements, plans and policies offering solutions to many developmental problems, repeatedly failing. Norpatagonia is fortunate to have such a skilled researcher document three generations of its history. Alas, no maps are used to show key boundaries and their evolution, places named and then renamed, or emerging urban centers linked to commercial success.

651 Montes, Nahuel. La cultura como problema territorial: la geografía humana y la superposición de espacios de producción intelectual en Argentina durante la primera mitad del siglo XX. (*Bol. Estud. Geogr.*, 114, nov. 2020/abril 2021, p. 33–52, bibl.)

Fascinating retrospective historiography of intellectual relations between geography and anthropology that laid the foundation for the study of human geography in Argentina in the first half of the 20th century. The author examines this issue by reviewing the volumes of *La Argentina, suma de geografía*, published between 1958 and 1963 by Ediciones Peuser and directed by Francisco de Aparicio and Horacio Difrieri (see *HLAS 23:2567, HLAS 24:2927*, and *HLAS 29:5125*). The goal of the study is to contribute to our understanding of the institutional and political conditions that shaped the consolidation of Argentine geography as an academic discipline in its own right.

652 Montes Galbán, Eloy José. Análisis espacial de las distancias a los principales centros urbanos de la cuenca del río Luján. (*Anu. Div. Geogr.*, 2017, p. 133–145, bibl., color maps, tables)

This innovative study analyzes the spatial distribution of urban and rural areas and their distances from the major urban centers in the Luján River basin. The author evaluates the urban areas using quantitative spatial analysis procedures. Excellent color maps, though place names are not clearly legible, even when enlarged.

653 Montes Galbán, Eloy José. Expansión y densificación urbana de Gran Buenos Aires (2012–2019). (*Geogr. Digit.*, 17:33, 2020, p. 2–16, bibl., graphs, maps, tables)

Yet another innovative project analyzing the urbanization of Greater Buenos Aires during the period 2012–2019, based on nocturnal satellite images. This methodological approach bolsters the potential of this new source of information in Argentine urban geography. The author analyzes satellite images to evaluate the density of the night lights and confirms the hypothesis that the higher the density of illumination, the greater the population density. This methodological approach made it possible to verify the potential of the night satellite images of the Earth, demonstrating the range of possible applications. Excellent maps and graphs included.

654 Montes Galbán, Eloy José. Ideas sobre tecnociencia y experimentación digital en geografía. (*Vientos Norte*, 5:2, dic. 2017, p. 7–17, bibl., ill., photo)

This paper analyzes the incorporation of technoscience in geography via GIS, how it affects knowledge production of research on geographic topics, and how it presents the opportunity for digital experimentation in geography, i.e., geodigital reality. Advances in Geographic Information Technologies (GIT) have pushed the boundaries of the field. The author highlights the promising future of digital experimentation in geography brought about by recent technological developments.

655 Monti, Alejandra I. Cambio de referentes: el Instituto de Planeamiento Regional y Urbano del Litoral (IPRUL) como vector de ingreso del planning en la Argentina. (*J. Lat. Am. Geogr.*, 17:1, April 2018, p. 34–58, bibl., maps, table)

This study examines the establishment and operations of the IPRUL (1962–65), Argentina's first regional and urban institute. The institute was the first to advocate for the notion of planning as a method of decision-making, drawing on cooperation resulting from the Alliance for Progress (1961) in Latin America. An analysis of IPRUL is useful as it serves as a lens for understanding the introduction of new topics and methods related to city and territorial planning.

656 Morea, Juan Pablo. Problemática territorial, al uso público en la Reserva de Biosfera "Parque Atlántico Mar Chiquito", Argentina. (*Cuad. Geogr. Univ. Granada*, 58:2, 2019, p. 101–120, bibl., graphs, ill., maps)

Capitalism is driving a demand for expansion, which has led to a scarcity of new productive territories and has established a territorial problem where spaces rich in natural resources and biodiversity are seen as large areas of reserve for the world. More than ever, biosphere reserves are faced with the challenge of balancing public use and conservation. With a combination of bibliographic surveys and fieldwork, this study analyzes the biosphere reserve of Mar Chiquita, characterizing the use of space and identifying the main territorial problems. The results suggest territorial problems due to poor management of public use and social conflicts arising from disputes about the use of the space and resources. Excellent, well-designed maps included.

657 Ordenar el territorio: un desafío para Mendoza. Dirección de María Elina Gudiño. Coordinación de Mirta Marre, Elena Abraham y Daniel Pizzi. Mendoza, Argentina: EDIUNC, 2017. 467 p.: bibl., ill. (some color). (Colección Territorios)

A fundamental publication related to territorial/spatial planning in Argentina. Mendoza is fortunate to have such a professional team of contributors to this innovative volume dealing with every aspect of "ordenamiento"—a term that has multiple meanings in specific contexts. Here, those meanings range spatially from the entire province to the aspects of specific urban segments, or rural developments. They also refer to the role of key political movements and social formations that have evolved over the last two centuries. Every Latin American research center will need a copy of this superbly produced book. Though many of the maps it contains are colored, one notes the complete absence of any linear scale bars: a major defect. Nonetheless, a solid contribution.

658 Palma Leotta, María et al. Aportes de la teledetección para la caracterización de amenazas para la conservación del sitio Ramsar Humedal Llancanelo, Malargüe, Argentina. (*Bol. Estud. Geogr.*, 112, julio/dic. 2019, p. 83–113, bibl., graphs, maps)

Llancanelo wetland, in the province of Mendoza, presents unique biogeographic characteristics, beauty, and genetic and ecological diversity including habitats for animal species in critical periods of their biological cycles. The site is under international protection because it is considered at risk. This study aims to analyze the threats to conservation through the application of remote sensing and satellite images with digital processing, as well as documentary and observational research. The results confirm surface reduction of the lagoon and detail land degradation, desertification, and loss of habitats of vulnerable native species. Unfortunately, problems arise in interpreting the satellite images provided due to their overabundance of data.

659 Picciani, Ana Laura. Las transformaciones productivas y tecnológicas: redefiniciones territoriales en Coronel Moldes (departamento Río Cuarto, provincia de Córdoba). (*Estud. Socioterritoriales*, 21, junio 2017, p. 13–28, bibl., color maps, table)

The "agro-export model" implemented in the southern part of Córdoba province led to the exploitation of the land. Today the approach is being redefined with a greater emphasis on the local rather than an extra-local model. This study analyzes the functioning of the territory of Coronel Moldes as it was used by companies, institutions, or the state in the 1970–2015 period. The maps would be more useful if they were extended to full-page width.

660 Piquer-Rodríguez, María et al. Drivers of agricultural land-use change in the Argentine Pampas and Chaco regions. (*Appl. Geogr.*, 91, Feb. 2018, p. 111–122, bibl., graphs, color maps, table)

A sophisticated statistical analysis of land-use change in two important ecological zones during the 2000s: the grasslands of the Pampas and the dry forests in the Chaco. The net returns model allowed the authors to calculate changes in various directions, i.e., woodlands to cropland or grazing land and grazing land to cropland. The analysis benefitted from the inclusion of such external factors as profit, or contextual spatial variations such as distance to market or soil type. All results are clearly mapped (except figure 1, which has legend issues) in color to allow one to see the variations in change factors.

661 Ponzi, Brenda Sofía. Oro o nueces: la desestructuración del sistema de riego para la implantación de la territorialidad megaminera en Andalgalá, provincia de Catamarca (Argentina). (*Estud. Socioterritoriales*, 26, julio/dic. 2019, e028, p. 1–16, bibl., graph)

In the context of a central governmental policy founded on accumulation by dispossession, during the 1990s a massive flow of capital was directed to the Argentine mining sector, with a focus on territories primarily labeled as "deserts." This important study looks at the development of a new mining model in the village of Andalgalá that dismantled the irrigation system used to secure the agricultural system. The author examines the legal and institutional arrangements that pave the way for mining in the districts of Chaquiago, Choya, Amanao, and Villa Vil—ultimately leading to repercussions felt in many other regions of the country.

662 Pou, Sonia Alexandra et al. Large-scale societal factors and noncommunicable diseases: urbanization, poverty and mortality spatial patterns in Argentina. (*Appl. Geogr.*, 86, Sept. 2017, p. 32–40, bibl., color maps, tables)

This model ecological study covers two administrative divisions of Argentina: 525 counties (510 departments and 15 communes in the city of Buenos Aires). The authors use standard statistical methods to calculate critical variables that they portray in a set of excellent maps. The patterns speak loudly of the spatial variation of mortality and poverty, reflecting the differentiation between urbanized nodes and rural margins.

663 Quirós, Julieta. Nacidos, criados, llegados: relaciones de clase y geometrías socioespaciales en la migración neorrural de la Argentina contemporánea. (*Cuad. Geogr./Bogotá*, 28:2, julio/dic. 2019, p. 271–287, bibl., maps, photos)

Throughout Latin America over the past two decades, urban middle classes have been displaced to small, rural "inland" locations in a phenomenon labeled "neoruralism." The author's ethnographic approach to the study of this internal migration from a geopolitical perspective demonstrates the underpinnings of social class and historical inequalities. She finds a stark contrast between immigrants and those born and raised in the region.

664 Quiroz Londoño, Orlando Mauricio et al. Metodología SIG para el análisis de la dinámica, monitoreo y remediación de un sistema playa-duna del sudeste bonaerense, Argentina. (*GeoFocus*, 24, 2019, p. 77–97, bibl., graphs, maps, photos, tables)

This work aims to identify sediment deposition and erosion in coastal zones and to quantify the sedimentary budget in a beach-dune system of the Atlantic coast of Buenos Aires province using GIS. Through topographic survey campaigns, the authors find that the quantity of sand fluctuated between significantly between March 2016 and March 2017 and that some coastal erosion is permanent. Excellent use of aerial photography.

665 Rainer, Gerhard. Constructing globalized spaces of tourism and leisure: political ecologies of the Salta Wine Route (NW-Argentina). (*J. Rural Stud.*, 43, Feb. 2016, p. 104–117, bibl.)

This study examines tourism and residential development in an emerging global countryside. The author analyzes the public-private efforts to nationally, and globally, position the Salta Wine region as a tourism and leisure destination. Bolstered by neoliberal policies, wineries, real estate developers, and traditional tourism destinations such as hotels have combined to portray the area as a welcome respite for high-end leisure and tourism.

666 Rausch, Gisela Ariana. Proyectos hidráulicos, ambientalismos y reescalamiento territorial: la disputa en torno a la construcción del proyecto Paraná medio en el proceso de neoliberalización de Argentina, 1995–1997. (*Rev. Geogr. Norte Gd.*, 69, mayo 2018, p. 169–190, bibl., maps)

This study analyzes the territorial-environmental conflict in Santa Fe and Entre Ríos that emerged in the context of the Paraná Medio hydroelectric project during the 1990s and its resolution in favor of the opposition coalition. The author argues that this result was due to specific global and national contexts, but also to the unusual characteristics of local environmental organizations in Argentina. Using a qualitative methodology based on interviews and documentary sources, this well-executed study examines the discursive production around the project in the context of two simultaneous processes occurring in Argentina in the 1990s: neoliberalism as political and economic ideology and environmentalism as a frame of reference.

667   **Rausch, Gisela Ariana** and **Diego Martín Ríos.** Imaginarios geográficos, grupos dominantes e ideas sobre nación: dos propuestas de transformación territorial para ámbitos fluviales argentinos. (*Rev. Geogr. Norte Gd.*, 75, mayo 2020, p. 9–33, bibl.)

Geographical imaginaries produced by dominant elites have historically operated as strategies for territorial appropriation. In river areas, those imaginaries were built on the ideas of nation, legitimizing or trying to promote territorial transformations (through the technological organization of "nature") in tune with the prevailing technocratic paradigms. Two cases located along the Paraná River highlight the significance of imaginaries in the construction of specific ideas about nation, progress, and development in Argentina. In both locations, the three ideas took shape as territorial transformation proposals. This analysis identifies the appropriation of strategies developed by dominant elites to impose an exclusive model of territorial order based on their own interests.

668   **Rocha, Heder Leandro.** Las geografías feministas y la producción científica de la geografía argentina en la última década (2008–2018): un análisis a partir de las revistas científicas. (*Huellas/Santa Rosa*, 23:2, julio/dic. 2019, p. 57–78, bibl., graphs, tables)

This innovative study examines, via social network analysis, research with a gender perspective within the published scientific production of Argentine geography. The author selected more than 1,000 research articles published in 16 geography journals in Argentina between 2008 and 2018 and available in four journal indexes: Latindex, SciELO, Redalyc, and Directory of Open Access Journals (DOAJ). With the keywords of each article, the author built a network in graph form with a focus on two main aspects: the position of topics such as "territory" and "territorial organization" and the peripheral location of research on the topics of gender and sexualities. The excellent graphics and tables allow the reader to clearly understand the changing emphases over time.

669   **Schweitzer, Mariana** *et al.* Estrategias, conflictos y tensiones en la producción del territorio: estudios de caso sobre minería, soja e hidrocarburos en Argentina. Argentina: Editorial Autores de Argentina, 2018. 140 p.: bibl., ill. (some color).

An excellent study of various types of territorial contexts, each with problems of location, boundaries, identity, and socioeconomic challenges.

670   **Schweitzer, Mariana; Santiago Pablo Petrocelli;** and **Marisa Scardino.** La producción del territorio en ciudades portuarias de la economía globalizada: tensiones e injusticias espaciales en el Área Metropolitana de Rosario, Argentina. (*Cuad. Geogr./Bogotá*, 29:1, enero/junio 2020, p. 102–117, bibl., color maps, table)

This paper analyzes the establishment of territory in two port cities with a focus on the export of agro-industrial products: San Lorenzo and Puerto General San Martín, located on the northern coast of the metropolitan area of Rosario, province of Santa Fe. The authors examine the challenges that social actors face in the appropriation and use of the territory, which often result in benefits to global corporate actors, facilitate the free circulation of capital, and generate spatial injustice.

671 Sedevich, Ana et al. Avance urbano en el cinturón verde de Guaymallén. (*GeoSIG/Luján*, 11:13, 2019, p. 138–166, bibl., color maps, color photos, tables)

The key questions in this excellent study relate to changing land use between 2005 and 2019, and especially the evolution of complexities of land occupation. The database employs cartographic, documentary, and field site investigations. Color maps (mostly without scale bars) display the complexities of land use from the viewpoints of differential sectors—urban, services, agriculture, etc.

672 Sequera, Jorge and Tomás Rodríguez. Turismo, abandono y desplazamiento: mapeando el barrio de La Boca en Buenos Aires. (*J. Lat. Am. Geogr.*, 16:1, April 2017, p. 117–137, bibl., ill., maps, photos, tables)

The La Boca neighborhood of Buenos Aires has experienced a transition from abandonment to long-term urban investment. This article presents research with the Destapiadas Collective focusing on collaborative mapping. The authors created a social cartography of the abandonment of parts of the neighborhood, along with spaces of interest to tourists and locations with the potential of higher rents. They identified sources of conflict that perpetuate the displacement of people, practices, and popular knowledge (evictions, building fires, inhabitable and abandoned buildings, street vending, homelessness, urban land speculation, and tourism). At the same time, organized resistance and plans for collective rehabilitation slow the gentrification or "touristification." Many of the maps are overloaded with iconic symbols so dense as to be illegible; others are simply too small.

673 Skarbun, Fabiana. Jerarquización del paisaje arqueológico de la Localidad Arqueológica La María, Santa Cruz, Argentina. (*GeoSIG/Luján*, 11:13, 2019, p. 11–35, bibl., color maps, tables)

The central plateau of Santa Cruz was well situated for past hunter-gathering societies. Nonetheless, the archeological evidence suggests that use of these places was highly diverse, with some characteristics of the landscape displaying attractive activities and others that generated friction and modified the landscape over time. The author uses GIS to analyze the landscape of the Localidad Arqueológica La María with different attributes defined: hills and mountains, sectors with visibility of hills and mountains, slopes, plateaus, low areas, hydrology, wellsprings, repaired places, places with visibility of repaired sectors, places with fixed resources, and culturally modified places. The author generated landscape hierarchization models that allow one to evaluate particular uses of this methodology in the future.

674 Souto, Cintia P. and Mariana Tadey. Livestock effects on genetic variation of creosote bushes in Patagonian rangelands. (*Environ. Conserv./Cambridge*, 46:1, March 2019, p. 59–66, bibl., graphs, tables)

The results of this fascinating study demonstrate the potential impacts of intensified livestock grazing patterns that could have serious consequences in an ecotone facing future climatic change.

675 Taylor, Lucy. Welsh-Indigenous relationships in nineteenth century Patagonia: "friendship" and the coloniality of power. (*J. Lat. Am. Stud.*, 49:1, Feb. 2017, p. 143–168, map)

A classic study of interactions between Welsh colonists attempting to create a new Welsh world—Y Wladfa Gymreig—in 1865 in the relatively unpopulated region of Patagonia, fatherland of the Tehuelche/Mapuche Indigenous, nomadic residents. Friendship and colonial aspirations are seen to create frequent moments of conflicting powers. Superbly documented from archival sources.

676 Trabichet, Florencia Cecilia. Caracterización de la aptitud de los suelos de la provincia de Catamarca mediante sistemas de información geográfica. (*Huellas/Santa Rosa*, 24:2, julio/dic. 2020, p. 47–63, bibl., map, photos, table)

Land suitability analysis based on GIS is effective for land planning. In this type of study, researchers employ GIS and geospatial statistical tools to assess land units and show the results in map form.

This work uses GIS to characterize the suitability of the soils in Catamarca province for pecan nuts production with six variables: rockiness, salinity, waterlogging risk, depth, texture, and drainage. The results indicate that nearly 60 percent of the total surface of the province is suitable for pecan nut production.

677 **Vaccotti, Luciana.** Migraciones e informalidad urbana: dinámicas contemporáneas de la exclusión y la inclusión en Buenos Aires. (*EURE/Santiago*, 43:129, mayo 2017, p. 49–70, bibl.)

This study analyzes the interplay between migration and urban informality in Buenos Aires (2001–2014) amid an increase in social conflict. The author presents the findings of a case study conducted at Playón de Chacarita, a Buenos Aires slum mostly inhabited by Peruvian immigrants.

678 **Valenzuela, Cristina.** Reflexiones en torno a la vulnerabilidad selectiva y el impacto ambiental en los procesos de construcción de territorios agrícolas: el caso algodonero Chaqueño. (*Bol. Estud. Geogr.*, 113, enero/julio 2020, p. 49–68, bibl., ill., color photo)

This paper uses an economic geography approach to analyze the territorial processes of the construction of productive identities and the identification of problems based on unequal exposure and the selective vulnerability of the territories to conflict, especially due to capitalism. The author examines the consolidation of cotton cultivation in the Chaco as an example that offers an illustration of the construction of cotton territoriality and the pressures exerted on it by the new dominant forms of production of business agriculture.

679 **Vazquez, Alberto** and **Marcelo Sili.** Dinámica espacial del proceso de extranjerización de la tierra en la Patagonia. (*J. Lat. Am. Geogr.*, 16:2, July 2017, p. 117–137, bibl., maps, photos)

In recent decades, foreign investors have embarked on an extensive process of land purchase in Patagonia. Land purchases have followed a spatial pattern according to how the new investors intend to use it, whether for traditional livestock activities, mining activities, or tourism. In cases where the future land use has not been clearly defined, the spatial pattern is uncertain and fragmentary. The results of the study clearly show a significant concentration of the land ownership of external investors. Very useful maps are provided.

680 **Vera, Paula.** Procesos de recualificación urbana e imaginarios de la innovación: el caso Rosario, Argentina. (*EURE/Santiago*, 43:129, mayo 2017, p. 209–234, bibl., maps, photos)

During the last decade, the city of Rosario has developed urban projects to restructure and recover degraded zones via the reclassification of spaces and activities. Such processes were defined by the notion of innovation as an engine of urban renewal.

CHILE

681 **Abufhele, Valentina.** La política de la pobreza y el gobierno de los asentamientos informales en Chile. (*EURE/Santiago*, 44:135, mayo 2019, p. 49–69, bibl., table)

This study examines in detail the concepts used to describe informal settlements between the 1940s and the 1990s. The concept of poverty was used predominantly during the military dictatorship (1973–89) and since the 1990s has been the framing used to understand informal settlements. The authors refers to this concept as "the politics of poverty" since it was instrumental in transforming informal settlements into a governable population.

Arboit, Mariela Edith; César Cucchietti; and **Dora Silvia Maglione.** Análisis comparativo preliminar de la variabilidad temporal del índice de vegetación en las áreas metropolitanas forestadas: casos de estudio: La Plata, Mendoza, Santiago de Chile y Turín. See item 608.

682 **Arboleda, Martín.** Extracción en movimiento: circulación del capital, poder estatal y urbanización logística en el norte minero de Chile. (*Invest. Geogr./Santiago*, 56, 2018, p. 3–26, bibl., maps, tables)

The author investigates extractive industries in Chile with a focus on northern port cities. The adoption of organizational steps in mining operations has spearheaded a situation where the governance of mineral flows is increasingly more important than reviews of specific sites. This territorial organization has resulted in a transpacific logistical corridor that connects multiple mineral deposits in the Chilean Andes with ports and manufacturing cities in East Asia. With an emphasis on capitalism, this study suggests that this complex socioecological system relies on the internationalization and the concentration of the political authority of the state. Only one map shows transpacific linkages of major cargo ships.

683 **Astudillo Pizarro, Francisco** and **José Sandoval Díaz.** Justicia espacial, desastres socionaturales y políticas del espacio: dinámicas sociopolíticas frente a los aluviones y proceso de recuperación en Copiapó, Chile. (*Cuad. Geogr./Bogotá*, 28:2, julio/dic. 2019, p. 303–321, bibl., color maps, photos)

This article explores the sociopolitical dynamics that resulted from the 2017 floods in the commune of Copiapó, in the Atacama region. The authors examine the relations between the local organization and others in the aftermath, especially during the rehabilitation processes. The authors analyze spatial justice related to socionatural disasters and risks. In this context, they identify and describe the sociopolitical dynamics of the local actors in urban, periurban, and rural areas of the commune of Copiapó.

684 **Barría Meneses, Jessica Araceli.** La consulta indígena en la institucionalidad ambiental de Chile: consecuencias para la minería y las comunidades indígenas Collas de la región de Atacama. (*Invest. Geogr./Santiago*, 57, 2019, p. 76–93, bibl., maps, tables)

This work looks at environmental governance related to the Indigenous consultation process in Chile. The author evaluates the repercussions of including the Indigenous and Tribal Peoples Convention (International Labor Organization-ILO 169) in the process through several case studies of interactions between the mining industry and the Colla Indigenous communities in Atacama. She analyzes governance models through quantitative analysis, exploratory interviews, and review of judicial and environmental documents. The study describes the process that led to the indictment of mining investment projects by Indigenous communities between 2008–2018. The results show that the process had unclear goals and a lack of transparency, and also neglected to consider cultural and other characteristics of the Indigenous communities. The structural limitations are evident in the major differences between stakeholders that prevent an efficient state role vis-à-vis private companies and Indigenous communities, increasing the uncertainty of private investors and the historical distrust of the Indigenous communities.

685 **Barrientos Guzmán, Teresa** and **Marfilda Sandoval Hormazabal.** El turismo accesible en Chile: articulación y pertinencia de la oferta. (*Rev. Cartogr.*, 99, julio/dic. 2019, p. 125–145, bibl., graphs, ill.)

The number of people with disabilities is increasing and the tourism sector has noticed the growth opportunities that this niche market presents. To that end, accessible tourism initiatives—including adapting physical surroundings—are now evident in both public and private organizations. A pity no locational evidence is presented; it would be helpful to know where access is currently available for people with disabilities.

686 **Bastías, Luis Eduardo** and **Pablo Pérez Leiva.** COVID-19 como fuerza motriz para el desarrollo de ciudades inteligentes: el caso de Chile. (*Invest. Geogr./Santiago*, 60, 2020, p. 35–45, bibl., graph, photo)

This study discusses the notion that the COVID-19 pandemic has served as a catalyst for the transformation of urban territories into smart cities. The theoretical framework combines systemic risk with the post-Fordist and Schumpeterian paradigm to establish—from this theoretical base—that the worldwide spread of COVID-19 during the year 2020 has accelerated urban change at a global scale. This digital transformation has created the conditions for the early evolution of urban territories into smart cities.

687 **Becerra Baeza, César** and **Jacqueline de Rurange Espinoza.** Modelo de susceptibilidad a procesos de remociones en masa en rutas cordilleranas de Chile Central: Ruta 115 CH, Paso Pehuenche, Región del Maule. (*Invest. Geogr./Santiago*, 55, 2018, p. 89–110, bibl., graphs, maps, photos, tables)

The authors develop a qualitative-quantitative model to determine the level of susceptibility of mass wasting (i.e., landslides) in central Chile. Based on terrain analysis and using geomatics to include the interaction of associated physical and natural variables, the results suggest that the area is highly susceptible to landslides, flows of detritus, and rockfalls due to other geomorphological conditions. An excellent model of applied geography.

688 **Bustos Gallardo, Beatriz** *et al.* Neoliberalismo y gobernanza territorial: propuestas y reflexiones a partir del caso de Chile. (*Rev. Geogr. Norte Gd.*, 73, 2019, p. 161–183, bibl., table)

This study analyzes governance from the perspective of Chilean spatial political economy. The authors discuss two cases of territorial governance: the Salmon Task Force (Los Lagos Region) and CREO Antofagasta (a public-private association operating in the city). They show that the governance mechanisms associated with these projects were not created to solve problems or to rethink territories in a collective manner, but rather to provide continuity to the prevailing mode of production and restore legitimacy to extractive sectors. The study argues for the need to resist a neutral understanding of governance and to recognize the need for a critical understanding that considers the context and power relations.

689 **Cárdenas-Jirón, Luz-Alicia** and **Luis Morales-Salinas.** Urbanismo bioclimático en Chile: propuesta de biozonas para la planificación urbana y ambiental. (*EURE/Santiago*, 44:136, sept. 2019, p. 135–162, bibl., maps, photo, tables)

Bioclimatic urbanism recreates an urban ecosystem vision to plan for a type of urbanization that is more protective of the environment. Since climate is a key factor in those cycles, the authors propose an approach that incorporates territorial climatic zoning to provide information for urban planners and project practitioners.

690 **Castillo, Mayarí; Iván Sandoval;** and **Carolina Frías.** Percepción y legitimación frente a las desigualdades socioecológicas en Chile contemporáneo. (*LARR*, 55:4, Dec. 2020, p. 648–661, bibl.)

An excellent detailed analysis of perceptions of inequality in Chile with a focus on the socioecological dimension. The authors present the results of a qualitative study of five cases of territories with high levels of environmental degradation. They analyze the processes through which subjects perceive and critique inequality, linking them to the connection between lives and the environment.

691 **Escolano Utrilla, Severino; Jorge Ortiz Véliz;** and **Rodrigo Moreno Mora.** Estructura espacial de la movilidad residencial en la Región Metropolitana de Santiago de Chile, 2012–2017. (*Rev. Geogr. Norte Gd.*, 77, dic. 2020, p. 313–337, bibl., graphs, maps, table)

Research on urban residential mobility generally focuses on the inflow and outflow in various spatial units. This approach does not allow for the definition of migratory areas by the origin, destination, and intensity of residential mobility. In this study, the authors use data on changes of residence between communes to examine residential mobility in the Santiago Metropolitan Region (RMS). Results demonstrate the complex and well-integrated network of residential movements, the influence of geographical proximity on changes of residence, and notable territorial differences in the effects of changes of residence on sociospatial patterns. Well-designed maps of migration flows are included.

692 **Francaviglia, Richard V.** Imagining the Atacama Desert: a five-hundred-year journey of discovery. Salt Lake City: The University of Utah Press, 2018. 435 p.: bibl., ill. (some color), index, maps (some color).

This is a modern classic of descriptive and interpretive regional geography. The author combines physical and cultural dimensions and examines them chronologically, over five centuries, to demonstrate that evolution and often remarkable change have also characterized the landscape and those living and working within it. Spanish colonial control in the mid-16th century, to independence, and integration within the Chilean state, paralleled shifts from marginal agricultural occupation to massive mining projects in the 19th and 20th centuries. Each phase is traced through textual descriptions and a plethora of maps. Anyone who has lived in or crossed the Atacama Desert will admire the author's enchantment with this singular region. It is difficult to forget the sights, smells, and sounds of this very special place.

693 Fuentes, Luis and **Mario Pezoa.** Nuevas geografías urbanas en Santiago de Chile 1992–2012: entre la explosión y la implosión de lo metropolitano. (*Rev. Geogr. Norte Gd.*, 70, sept. 2018, p. 131–151, bibl., graphs, maps, photos, tables)

This study analyzes the influence of Santiago on its regional environment and urban growth that have blurred the limits of the Metropolitan Area of Santiago. First, the limits of the city were redefined from the 34 traditional communes to 48 communes that are divided into a nucleus and a hinterland, providing a better territorial understanding of the metropolitan area. Second, the interpretation of satellite images allows for the identification of a new urban form characterized by a new geography, in which parallel growth within the city and in the periphery is evident. The application of mixed methodologies that analyze the urban area allows us to understand that urbanization is a process in which the form is only the result of many factors. Unfortunately, the small maps presented are illegible.

694 Fuenzalida Díaz, Manuel et al. Geografía, geotecnología y análisis espacial: tendencias, métodos y aplicaciones. 2 ed. Santiago, Chile: Triángulo, 2018. 260 p.: bibl., ill.

An innovative volume of essays that offers descriptions and explanations of recent geomethodologies as well as selected case studies demonstrating the benefits of their use.

695 García, Magdalena and **Monica E. Mulrennan.** Tracking the history of protected areas in Chile: territorialization strategies and shifting state rationalities. (*J. Lat. Am. Geogr.*, 19:4, Oct. 2020, p. 199–234, bibl., graphs, maps, table)

A fascinating analysis of the role of "protected areas" (PAs), frequently found in Latin America, emphasizing the broadening significance of the concept of territorialization. Given that the Chilean state currently controls one-fifth of its area as PAs, such an analysis is most valuable. It is also a pleasure to congratulate the authors for providing detailed, well-designed maps showing the location of the PAs.

696 Gasic Klett, Ivo Ricardo. Mercado del suelo urbano y reserva financiera de terrenos para producción de vivienda en el Área Metropolitana de Santiago. (*Rev. Geogr. Norte Gd.*, 76, sept. 2020, p. 71–94, bibl., graphs, color maps, tables)

Urban land in Chile is now an investment tool and a financial asset. This study offers evidence of the increase in participation of financial institutions in Santiago Metropolitan Area's land market between 2010 and 2015. Through an analysis of statistics and a systematization of agents involved in the real estate development of houses, the author finds that banks and insurers are key players in the formation of land reserves. The work discusses the effects of the financial practice of land leases on the price and availability of affordable land and concludes by describing the social exclusionary character of the urban land market. The paper uses well-designed maps.

697 González, Daniela P. et al. Risk and Resilience Monitor: development of multiscale and multilevel indicators for disaster risk management for the communes and urban areas of Chile. (*Appl. Geogr.*, 94, May 2018, p. 262–271, bibl., graphs, maps, tables)

Given that Chile suffers from a variety of natural hazards: earthquakes, volcanic activity, and tsunamis, disaster risk management policies are crucial. This study introduces multilevel indicators for measuring risk and resilience to identify and quantify spatial disparities among communes and urban areas. Indicators allow for the identification of areas that have been left relatively unprotected and require disaster risk management actions.

698 González Aliste, Fernando and **Yonatan Quintana Jara.** Análisis de impacto del incendio de 2014 en el Vergel, región de Valparaíso. (*Rev. Geogr. Chile*, 56, 2020, p. 41–61, bibl., maps, photos, tables)

In April 2014, "The Great Fire of Valparaíso" spread through seven hills of the commune of Valparaíso, affecting more than 1,000 hectares and 2,900 homes. This study analyzes the impact of the forest fire on the population and environment of El Vergel, an area close to the initial focus of the fire, which presents favorable geomorphological characteristics for the propagation of the flames, a product of the abrupt slopes, zones of urban-rural interface, and an urbanistic disorder that has been increasing, leaving the buildings more exposed. The authors perform a multitemporal study from images captured at different times by an airborne photogrammetric sensor. An excellent explanation of the methodology is presented.

699 González-Hidalgo, Marien; Sandra López-Dietz; and **Stefanie Pacheco-Pailahua.** El sentipensar extractivo colonial: geografías emocionales de la extracción en Gülumapu, el territorio mapuche en el sur de Chile. (*J. Lat. Am. Geogr.*, 18:3, Oct. 2019, p. 85–109, bibl., color map, table)

This innovative paper deals with a topic rarely addressed in studies of development and colonialism: the emotional costs of such processes. The authors introduce the concept of emotional geographies brought about by resource extraction and varieties of political emotional ecologies. They argue that environmental impacts of resource use, be they of water or forests, can precipitate extended emotional stress, whether the causes are private company or governmental activities. Yet another fact is the deeper attachment to such resources by local populations, especially Indigenous communities. This paper deserves wide circulation.

700 Höhl, Johanna. Pueblos indígenas, recursos y gobernanza: un análisis de la consulta indígena como parte de la Evaluación de Impacto Ambiental del proyecto hidroeléctrico Añihuerraqui, Región de la Araucanía, Chile. (*Invest. Geogr./Santiago*, 59, 2020, p. 28–40, bibl., graph, color map)

Governance plays a critical role in the oversight of interactions between the state, the market, and civil society. In this case, the importance of governance is seen in the inclusion of Indigenous peoples in the decision-making processes around the use of natural resources. The Indigenous consultation created as part of Chile's environmental policy in 2013 was intended to empower Indigenous communities by guaranteeing their representation in negotiations. However, the different visions of nature make the environmental impact assessment in Indigenous territories more complex. Furthermore, the system does not have a mechanism for resolution when Indigenous communities in the same territory do not agree, nor does it comply with assigning them greater control over the natural resources in their territories. A most useful analysis of key factors affecting any major hydroelectric project.

701 Ibarra, Macarena and **Beatriz Rosso.** Más allá de la catástrofe: tres propuestas urbanas para Vallenar tras el terremoto de 1922. (*Rev. Geogr. Norte Gd.*, 77, dic. 2020, p. 417–437, bibl., graphs, ill., maps, photos, tables)

Following the 1922 earthquake in the Atacama region, a debate about Vallenar's reconstruction ensued and reports containing the features that should incorporate the new city were presented. Ultimately, those proposals were not implemented, thus missing a historic opportunity to transform the city. This article reviews those proposals and attempts to determine why they were ultimately unsuccessful.

702 Imilan, Walter and **Luis Eduardo González.** Attempts at neoliberal urban planning in postearthquake Chile: master plans for reconstruction. Translated by Margot Olavarria. (*Lat. Am. Perspect.*, 44:4, July 2017, p. 10–23, bibl., photos)

Local-level plans directed urban and regional reconstruction after the 27 February 2010 earthquake and tsunami in Chile.

Based on public-private partnerships, these plans are an innovative tool for postdisaster reconstruction. The authors suggest that the plans demonstrated a commitment to the privatization of urban planning in Chile. They analyze two of the main plans based on field research and reveal that they had limited impact because of weak public-private ties, lack of comprehensiveness, and lack of legitimacy. The study concludes that the failure of implementation of reconstruction plans is a rejection of neoliberal deepening at the level of urban and regional administration.

703 **López, Mario; Andrea Valenzuela;** and **Claudio Carrasco.** Propuesta simbiótica natural-cultural en Territorio Mapuche de Arauco. (*Invest. Geogr./Santiago*, 54, 2017, p. 61–84, bibl., graphs, maps, tables)

Excellent use of maps and innovative graphics to interpret a Mapuche commune's changing intergenerational visions of territory. The authors trace the evolution in their historical spatial categories and their relationship to key natural spaces.

704 **Lukas, Michael; Maria Christina Fragkou;** and **Alexis Vásquez.** Hacia una ecología política de las nuevas periferias urbanas: suelo, agua y poder en Santiago de Chile. (*Rev. Geogr. Norte Gd.*, 76, sept. 2020, p. 95–119, bibl., maps, tables)

In recent years, the rural province of Chacabuco, north of Santiago, has been territorially transformed due to urban megaprojects intended for high-income social classes. From the perspective of suburban political ecology, this study analyzes the economic and political strategies with a focus on water and land resources through which large economic-financial groups, supported by the state, have produced an unequal landscape of archipelagos. The methods used include semistructured interviews with private, public, and community actors, and an analysis of water rights records in the province of Chacabuco. In empirical and conceptual terms, the authors demonstrate that the production of the new urban periphery and its patterns of socioterritorial and environmental fragmentation are evidence not of globalization, but of deliberate actions of commodification, concentration (of property rights), and financialization of natural resources such as land and water. Contains some excellent maps.

705 **Lunde Seefeldt, Jennapher.** Lessons from the lithium triangle: considering policy explanations for the variation in lithium industry development in the "lithium triangle" countries of Chile, Argentina, and Bolivia. (*Politics Policy*, 48:4, Aug. 2020, p. 727–765, bibl., graph, table)

A comprehensive study based on a thorough documentary foundation related to strategic interview data.

706 **Manuschevich, Daniela; Mel Gurr;** and **Carlos A. Ramirez-Pascualli.** Nostalgia for la montaña: the production of landscape at the frontier of Chilean commercial forestry. (*J. Rural Stud.*, 80, Dec. 2020, p. 211–221, bibl.)

An innovative study of the socioecological transformations in the Chilean countryside, focusing on the workings of memory and nostalgia among peasant farmers living at the fringes of major tree-farm expansion. Based on qualitative research and participatory mapping in three mountain villages, the main focus is on land use change.

707 **Miller, Jacob C.** Embodied architectural geographies of consumption and the *Mall Paseo Chiloé* controversy in southern Chile. (*Ann. Am. Assoc. Geogr.*, 109:4, July 2019, p. 1300–1316, bibl., map, color photos)

This innovative study of embodied architectural geography explores the complex relationship between human subjectivity and the materiality of landscape and affective architectural space.

708 **Molina Camacho, Francisco.** Decolonizando los riesgos naturales: poder, territorio y conocimiento ancestral en la comuna de Saavedra, Chile. (*J. Lat. Am. Geogr.*, 17:1, April 2018, p. 7–33, bibl., maps)

Using data related to the earthquake and resultant tsunami of 22 May 1960, the article assesses the differential cartographic representations of the local Indigenous Mapuche *lafkenche*, compared to that of the scientific community. Emphasis is placed on the differential meaning of such concepts as territory and the role of power in identifying features and events—as well as their representation. The paper uses as a case study the port of Saavedra, which underwent several differential impacts of the tsunami. Based on interviews with *lafkenche* and interpretations of what they determined to be sacred places, places of spirits, or safety zones, it became clear that inundated areas had more or less meaning to the local populations than to the areas mapped by trained surveyors. The question remains whether Indigenous interpretations, based on generations of experiencing tsunamis, should, or could, be integrated into mappable and more useful categories for future use. Unfortunately, the maps included in the article do not clearly portray any Indigenous countermapping results.

709 **Navarrete-Hernández, Pablo** and **Fernando Toro.** Urban systems of accumulation: half a century of Chilean neoliberal urban policies. (*Antipode*, 51:3, June 2019, p. 899–926, bibl., graphs, color maps, table)

An innovative analysis of Chile's experiences of urban policy reforms in the capital, Santiago. A genealogical thematic analysis permits the author to track changes in laws, government programs, and planning documents from between 1952 and 2014. The analysis identifies distinctive "urban systems of accumulation" by looking at the interplay of four urban policies: urban planning deregulation, social housing privatization, devolution of territorial taxes, and decreased public service provision. The multidimensional policy analysis in Santiago characterizes a fourth expression in the creative destruction process of "accumulation by dismantling"—a radical additional component. Well-designed maps and graphs.

710 **Núñez, Andrés G. et al.** Silencios geográficos en Patagonia-Aysén: territorio, nomadismo y perspectivas para repensar los márgenes de la nación en el siglo XIX. (*Magallania/Punta Arenas*, 44:2, 2016, p. 107–130, bibl., graphs, map, tables)

This important contribution provides details of the modernization process that affected much of southern Chile in the late 19th and 20th centuries, especially the Chiloe region. The perspective of the central government in Santiago was that land occupancy—farming units, rural settlement developments—was the preferred symbol of productive change, thus reducing the evident abandonment of the region by the Chono Indigenous people that had begun in the late 18th century. Well-designed map and graphs included with a very extensive bibliography.

711 **Osses, Pablo Eugenio et al.** El clima desértico costero con nublados abundantes del desierto de Atacama y su relación con los recursos naturales energía solar y agua de niebla: caso de estudio Alto Patache (20, 5°S), región de Tarapacá, Chile. (*Rev. Geogr. Norte Gd.*, 68, dic. 2017, p. 33–48, bibl., graphs, color maps, color photos, table)

Taking into account the increase of water and energy needs in arid zones, this study investigates the presence of coastal clouds as a potential water resource and solar radiation as an energy source. The authors attempt to identify the relationships between attenuation of irradiance by fog typology and the yields of associated fog water. They analyzed monthly data using GOES satellite images, data from the Standard Fog Collector (SFC), and the radiometer located at the Atacama UC Station. Results demonstrates that daily cycles of these resources complement each other and produce water during the day and energy at night. A valuable applied methodology on a very significant issue.

712 **Paulsen Bilbao, Abraham** and **Ricardo Rubio González.** Propuesta metodológica para el trabajo con fotografías de paisajes. (*Rev. Geogr. Valparaíso*, 54, 2017, p. 1–19, bibl., photos, tables)

Photography has long been a useful tool for geographic analysis, particularly for documenting reality and collecting landscape data. However, the use of photography as a resource to better undersand landscape and place, both concepts understood in the context of human geography, requires paying attention to the sociohistorical context and the technique used in image production.

This article presents a specific methodology for analyzing photography in this context.

713 **Paulsen Espinoza, Alex.** La política de vivienda de la despolitización: gobernanza neoliberal, tecnocracia y luchas urbanas; el caso del Movimiento de pobladores Ukamau, Estación Central. (*Invest. Geogr./Santiago*, 59, 2020, p. 41–58, bibl., graphs, maps, photos, tables)

This innovative study uses semistructured interviews, participatory ethnography, and data from official organizations to demonstrate that the intermediaries of the neoliberal governance structure limited, and indeed invented, the participation of the residents. The author attempts to describe the strategies used by the families of residents of the Ukamau Community Movement in their urban zone to confront these agents, and argues that it was not only by means of urban protests in public space.

714 **Rinaldi, Arturo and Kay Bergamini.** Inclusión de aprendizajes en torno a la gestión de riesgo de desastres naturales en instrumentos de planificación territorial (2005–2015). (*Rev. Geogr. Norte Gd.*, 75, mayo 2020, p. 103–130, bibl., map, color photos)

Chile has experienced many natural disasters that have resulted in human and material losses, and associated reconstruction processes have to be implemented in their aftermath. However, environmental threats do not always lead to disaster; disaster risk management can mitigate those threats. This article investigates how the natural disasters that have occurred in Chile in the last decade have influenced the incorporation of risk management within the existing urban regulations. The authors suggest that inclusion may be scarce, and when it happens, it focuses mainly on a reactive disaster risk management plan.

715 **Riquelme Brevis, Hernán and Matías Riquelme Brevis.** Representando el espacio: experiencias de movilidad cotidiana a partir de la confección de mapas en La Araucanía, Chile. (*Estud. Socioterritoriales*, 23, enero/junio 2018, p. 101–117, bibl., maps, color photo)

This article summarizes different experiences of social and visual representation of the role of the railway as daily transportation. The authors explore the use of the railway in people's daily routines and examine their destinations. The authors analyze maps that the study subjects created to identify significant places included in the maps. These places represent different mobility dynamics based on travel time, transit areas, and daily routines. The maps clearly demonstrate a variety in perceptions of places and connections.

716 **Rodríguez, Jorge et al.** ¿Perdió el Área Metropolitana del Gran Santiago su atractivo? Sí, pero no: un examen basado en datos y procedimientos novedosos para la estimación de la migración interna y sus efectos durante el periodo 1977–2013. (*EURE/Santiago*, 43:128, enero 2017, p. 5–30, appendix, bibl., graphs, table)

This detailed analysis by a group of CEPAL specialists considers the changing characteristics of the metropolitan area of Greater Santiago using a range of post-2014 censuses and a selection of socioeconomic surveys. The data reflect both significant demographic changes as well as new patterns of social and economic clusters. The study also includes a useful methodological annex but lacks cartographic representations of spatial change.

717 **Rojo Mendoza, Félix and Javier Hernández Aracena.** Colonización y nuevo territorio: la formación de la elite comercial de Temuco, 1885–1913. (*Rev. Geogr. Norte Gd.*, 73, 2019, p. 185–209, bibl., maps, tables)

The occupation of Araucania by the Chilean state followed economic principles related to annexation of new territories throughout the country. The state actively encouraged the arrival of a civilizing agent, personified in the European immigrant. This agent, together with Chilean colonists, arrived in Temuco, which became the center of the new geography of power in Araucanía. This article analyzes the commercial dynamics of the elite from 1885 to 1913. Consulting commercial records, city plans, and chronicles of the time, the authors observe differences by nationality in the type of commercial activity and occupied space, as well as strategies of economic, social, and institutional diversification that suggest the German immigrants became the local elite of the city. Well-designed maps are presented, though they could have been larger.

718 **Romero-Toledo, Hugo.** Etnicidades, etno-territorios y conflictos mineros: aportes para una geografía humana de los aymaras en Chile. (*Rev. Geogr. Norte Gd.*, 71, julio/dic. 2018, p. 211–234, bibl., graph, map)

This article analyzes Aymara ethnicity and the creation of ethno-territories in the context of mining conflicts and the impact of neoliberal policies on Indigenous people. The author looks at how the Aymara communities have evolved in northern Chile, what kind of dynamics have been established, and in what territories they have been implemented. He focuses on ethnic identity and how ethno-territories take shape as social construction and political projects. Unfortunately, the map is too small to be legible.

719 **Ruiz, Vannia; Juan Munizaga;** and **Alejandro Salazar Burrows.** Plantaciones forestales y su extensión hacia áreas urbanas en el área metropolitana de Valparaíso y su relación con el aumento de incendios forestales. (*Invest. Geogr./Santiago*, 54, 2017, p. 23–40, bibl., graphs, maps, tables)

For the past 50 years, the expansion of forest plantations has caused changes in land cover in central Chile. Considering the national context of the 2017 forest fires, the general opinion is that the occurrence of these events is related to the proximity and approach of the plantations to urban areas, especially in the Valparaíso Metropolitan Area (AMV). With this background, the authors analyze the decrease in the distance between the expansion of forest plantations and the expansion of urban land in the AMV using Landsat images predating the fires. The main results show an increase in area for forest plantations for 2015, doubling its size compared to 1989. The authors observe a greater heterogeneity in the landscape and a greater degree of forest plantations compared with other land coverings such as agriculture or shrublands.

720 **Ryburn, Megan.** Uncertain citizenship: everyday practices of Bolivian migrants in Chile. Oakland: University of California Press, 2018. 206 p.: bibl., ill., index.

This innovative volume examines the lives of Bolivian migrants in Chile with a focus on the question of citizenship. Intraregional migration is steadily increasing in Latin America, which has a significant impact on the experience of citizenship throughout the region. The author strongly argues that many migrants struggle with the notion of citizenship. Based on ethnographic research, this book adds to debates on the concept of citizenship in Latin America and throughout the world.

721 **Saavedra, Valentina** and **Paulina Gatica.** Las redes de apoyo familiar: motivación económica y doméstica para allegarse en zonas periféricas de Santiago de Chile. (*Invest. Geogr./Santiago*, 57, 2019, p. 49–62, bibl., graphs, maps, tables)

Using a mixed methods approach with quantitative and qualitative techniques such as statistical data analysis and semistructured interviews, this article tests the theory that access to housing and family support networks in two villages in the district of Puente Alto in Santiago are significant. The results suggest that the support networks influence people to stay in the peripheral communes since that is where family and neighborhood networks exist.

722 **Saelzer Canouet, Gerardo; Marcela Soto Caro;** and **Luis Álvarez.** Condiciones de desarrollo en espacios patrimoniales y remotos: caso de planificación de Río Serrano, comuna Torres del Payne, Chile. (*Rev. Geogr. Norte Gd.*, 72, mayo 2019, p. 93–112, bibl., graphs, maps, tables)

Some territories associated with natural heritage in Latin America are among the most precious destinations in the world. One example is the rural town of Villa Río Serrano, situated adjacent to the Torres del Paine National Park in Chilean Patagonia. Urban policy planning for this town is fraught with problems that are territorial, political, administrative, cultural, and economic. This article explores local and global demands in fields of natural heritage and planning, with a focus on tourism. The authors question whether the existing development plan is an efficient territorial development tool in a remote situation, and demonstrate that a special space needs specific planning tailored to that area, rather than a general approach based on urbanization. Unfortunately, many of the maps are illegible.

723 **Sandoval, Iván et al.** Capitales de liderazgo en las protestas territoriales: el caso de dos movimientos sociales en la Patagonia chilena. (*Magallania/Punta Arenas*, 48:1, 2020, p. 47–63, bibl.)

Though territorial tensions have often been reported by investigators, rarely have they provided detailed evidence of leadership qualities. This innovative article uses qualitative evidence obtained principally via interviews to assess the differential leadership components in Magallanes and Aysen provinces and their impacts on social movements in 2011 and 2012.

724 **Tapia Barría, Verónica.** Geografías de la contención: el rol de las políticas de escala barrial en el Chile neoliberal. (*Scripta Nova*, 22:592, 2018, p. 1–37, bibl., table)

Since the 1990s, researchers have sought to analyze neighborhood-scale policies according to neoliberal tenets. Chile is a case in point given that neighborhood-scale policies were implemented at the end of the military dictatorship, and the neoliberal principles have persisted during subsequent governments. This article proposes that neighborhood policies serve an ideological role since they are created with the intention of limiting conflicts that arise from the neoliberal urban policies regarding poverty and urban inequalities. Specifically, the author argues that the role of neighborhood-scale policies in neoliberal Chile is to contain conflict.

725 **Urrutia Reveco, Santiago.** "Hacer de Chile una gran nación": La Carretera Austral y Patagonia Aysén durante la dictadura cívico militar (1973–1990). (*Rev. Geogr. Norte Gd.*, 75, mayo 2020, p. 35–60, bibl., graphs)

This article examines the construction process of the Southern Highway in Chilean Patagonia during the military dictatorship (1973–90). The author analyzes the agency of the road and its territorial impact by reviewing press material, government declarations, ministerial reports, and technical studies. He proposes that the longitudinal outline of the Austral Highway implied a special process of territorial restructuring. During the study period, this highway was one of the territorial keys of the authoritarian organization of the country; it represents the biggest Chilean public work of the 20th century—a new national "orientation—opening the South": reminiscent of the US "opening the West."

PARAGUAY

726 **Blanc, Jacob.** Itaipu's forgotten history: the 1965 Brazil-Paraguay border crisis and the new geopolitics of the Southern Cone. (*J. Lat. Am. Stud.*, 50:2, May 2018, p. 383–409, bibl., map, photo)

This study describes the border conflict between the military regimes of Brazil and Paraguay that occurred between March 1965 and June 1966 that paved the way for the Itaipú project that would become the largest dam in the world. In the context of the Cold War, both governments saw the potential of a large-scale dam on the Paraná River to spur industrialization and strengthen their geopolitical standing. The Brazilian dictatorship, supported by the US, convinced Paraguay to support their position and shunned concerns voiced by the Argentine government. The conflict ultimately solidified Brazil's rising power in the region and transformed the geopolitical landscape of the Southern Cone.

727 **Boschmann, E. Eric.** Historic evolution and neoliberal urbanism in Asunción. (*J. Lat. Am. Geogr.*, 19:4, Oct. 2020, p. 140–169, bibl., maps, photos)

A standard study of the urban foundation and evolution of Asunción in some six stages, ranging from Spanish colonialism in the 16th century to the impact of late

20th-century neoliberalism on the urban fabric. The city is currently a site of intrepid tourists visiting one of Latin America's least visited (or studied) cities. The author ends his descriptive profile by offering his ideas as to a potential research agenda for the city. Excellent color photos are also provided.

728 Canese, Ricardo and **Mercedes Canese.** La lucha por la tierra en Asunción: la conveniencia de la defensa costera para los bañados. Prólogo de Ricardo Meyer. Asunción: COBAÑADOS Coordinadora General de Organizaciones Sociales y Comunitarias de los Bañados de Asunción, 2016. 182 p.: bibl., ill.

A well-told story of the effective social responses, since 2003, to the frequent floods of the Paraguay River that affected the northern limits of the city of Asunción. Once the problem was well-defined, the central focus was how to mitigate the costs for those who would have to move due to the barrier constructions involved. Belonging, even for those living in poor housing, is seen as a right worthy of protection. One rarely can read the many alternative views of options that are provided in this study. A valuable, well-documented case.

729 Correia, Joel E. Adjudication and its aftereffects in three Inter-American court cases brought against Paraguay: Indigenous land rights. (*Erasmus Law Rev.*, 1, 2018, p. 43–56, bibl.) <http://www.erasmuslawreview.nl/tijdschrift/ELR/2018/1/ELR-D-17-00018.pdf>

This innovative paper examines three Inter-American Court (IACtHR) cases on behalf of the Enxet-Sur and Sanapana claims for communal territory in Paraguay. The author argues that while the adjudication of the cases was successful, following the adjudication there are new "legal geographies" that threaten to undermine the advances made by adjudication. The author provides an overview of the opportunities and challenges to Indigenous rights in Paraguay and discusses the adjudication of the Yakye Axa, Sawhoyamaxa, and Xákmok Kásek cases. Based on extensive ethnographic research, the author considers how implementation takes place and analyzes its effects on the three claimant communities.

The paper encourages a discussion between geographers and legal scholars, suggesting that adjudication only leads to greater social justice if it is coupled with effective and meaningful implementation.

730 Correia, Joel E. Descolonizar el territorio: movimientos sociales indígenas, el giro territorial y los límites de los derechos a la tierra en la zona fronteriza entre Paraguay y Brasil. (*Etnogr. Contemp.*, 6:11, 2020, p. 160–190, bibl., map)

The "territorial turn" in Latin America has resulted in the restitution of more than 200 million hectares of land to Indigenous and Afro-descendant communities since the 1990s. While that turn has provided juridical solutions to Indigenous land claims by legally demarcating collective property rights, title does not necessarily resolve territorial disputes. Such is the case with the Kue Tuvy Aché community in the Paraguay-Brazil borderlands that successfully won collective title only to be continually confronted with (extra-)legal challenges to their land rights. Drawing from qualitative research with Kue Tuvy community members and relevant scholarship, the author analyzes the struggles that precede the turn and the conflicts that follow issuance of title. The study demonstrates how the territorial turn plays out in place, as Indigenous efforts to unsettle territory to create communal spaces for more just futures. The author argues that territorial assemblages are never finished, just as struggles for Indigenous justice do not end with territorial restitution. An excellent map is included. For an English-language version of this article, see item **732.**

731 Correia, Joel E. Soy states: resource politics, violent environments, and soybean territorialization in Paraguay. (*J. Peasant Stud.*, 46:2, Feb. 2019, p. 316–336, bibl., graph, ill., map, photo)

This paper looks at the trajectory of soy farming in Paraguay to analyze how soybean resource politics have changed environmental policy and state-society relations. The author argues that political, social, and ecological conditions affect each territorialization: agrarian reforms that altered land control, the introduction of genetically modified soy varieties, and most recently a "parliamentary coup" that was preceded by violence against campesinos. A valuable analysis.

732 **Correia, Joel E.** Unsettling territory: Indigenous mobilizations, the territorial turn, and the limits of land rights in the Paraguay-Brazil borderlands. (*J. Lat. Am. Geogr.*, 18:1, March 2019, p. 11–37, bibl., map)

The borderlands between Paraguay and Brazil continue to experience territorial conflicts. This study examines the borderland community of Kue Tuvy Aché that successfully won collective land title rights. However, following the ruling, the community continued to be confronted with challenges to those rights. The paper demonstrates how the territorial ruling played out, not only as the product of neoliberal political economic reforms, but also as Indigenous efforts to unsettle territory to create communal spaces for more just futures. The author argues that "territorial assemblages are never finished, just as struggles for Indigenous justice do not end with territorial restitution." For a Spanish-language version of this article, see item **730**.

733 **Eicher, John.** Rustic Reich: the local meanings of (trans)National Socialism among Paraguay's Mennonite colonies. (*Comp. Stud. Soc. Hist.*, 60:4, Oct. 2018, p. 998–1028, bibl.)

Fascinating details comparing distinctive Mennonite colonies' views of National Socialism and its relevance to their paths towards development. Prior experiences of such refugee migrant groups were of notable relevance. Abundant documentation is included.

734 **Mereles, Fátima et al.** La importancia del trabajo botánico de Aimé Bonpland en Sudamérica y la incógnita de las colecciones botánicas realizadas en Paraguay. (*Bonplandia*, 29:2, 2020, p. 127–139, bibl., color photos, tables)

Useful description of Bonpland's famous botanical collection in Paraguay. The authors describe challenges of identification and tracing of local specimens.

735 **Morales Raya, Eva.** Enfoques y problemáticas teórico-metodológicos de los estudios migratorios sobre Iberoamérica: el caso de la emigración catalana a Paraguay (1870–1932). (*JILAS/Bundoora*, 25:1, 2019, p. 6–21, bibl., table)

A detailed diagnosis of why, when, and how a significant group of Catalans migrated to Paraguay from 1870 onwards.

736 **Nobbs-Thiessen, Ben.** Reshaping the Chaco: migrant foodways, place-making, and the Chaco War. (*J. Lat. Am. Stud.*, 50:3, Aug. 2018, p. 579–611, map, photos)

This fascinating and superbly documented study explores the settlement of Russian Mennonites on the Paraguayan Chaco frontier in the 1930s. These colonists engaged in a range of seemingly contradictory place-making practices—from the agro-environmental and the political to the spiritual and the cultural—that served to solidify their tenuous claim to a totally unfamiliar and highly contested landscape. In the Paraguayan Chaco, these former wheat farmers experimented with a range of new crops and diets. They also initiated a campaign to evangelize the Chaco's Indigenous population with a focus on changing their diet.

737 **Pires do Rio, Gisela Aquino and Leo Name.** Patrimonialización y gestión del territorio en la triple frontera de Brasil, Argentina y Paraguay: continuidades y desafíos del parque Iguazú. (*Rev. Geogr. Norte Gd.*, 67, sept. 2017, p. 167–182, bibl., color map, tables)

The authors examine natural resources in the transboundary area between Argentina, Brazil, and Paraguay from the perspective of cultural heritage. Conceptualizing patrimonialization as an environmental instrument, they collected and processed data about the environmentally protected areas in the Triple Frontier region at the edges of these three countries. The data reveals two options of natural resource use and conservation, both related to water management. The examples of Brazilian and Argentine conservation units of Iguazú Park indicate a strategy oriented by hydrological safety. The key map included is too small for complex details to be legible.

738 Portillo, Ana. Agronegocios y la Facultad de Ciencias Agrarias de la UNA. Asunción: BASE-Investigaciones Sociales: Fundación Rosa Luxemburgo, 2018. 177 p.: bibl., ill.

This work provides a historical account of the development of the national interest in agrarian training and technologies in relation to the country's predominant economic component. Emphasis is on the role of distinctive universities and agencies and the relation of their research orientation to commercial interests. Unfortunately, graphics are of poor quality.

739 Sili, Marcelo; Claudia Ávila; and Nélida Sotelo. Modelos de acción y desarrollo territorial, un ensayo de clasificación en el Paraguay. (*Cuad. Geogr. Univ. Granada*, 58:1, 2019, p. 205–228, bibl., maps, tables)

Territorial action (TA) is a key concept for evaluating how actors, organized through public action, collective action, and private action, build and organize their territories. Analysis of such actions provides an opportunity to understand the structural conditions of the territories, as well as the representations that the actors have about the development and future of the territory. The case of Paraguay demonstrates the trajectories of the territories and allows for a review of new proposals for the construction of desired futures. Poor quality maps but well-argued text.

740 Zavattiero Tornatore, Georgina and Luis Alberto Ortiz Sandoval. Urbanización y clases sociales: la experiencia de la desigualdad en la estructuración del área metropolitana de Asunción. (*Hábitat Soc.*, 12, nov. 2019, p. 91–111, bibl., tables)

This study describes the characteristics of the link between social structure and the urban experience of inhabitants of the metropolitan area of Asunción (AMA). The methodology is mainly qualitative; the authors analyze the reflections of the city's inhabitants regarding their subjective representations about the daily experience of urban life according to their position in the country's social structure.

URUGUAY

741 Álvarez Rivadulla, María José. Política en los márgenes: asentamientos irregulares en Montevideo. Traducción de Mariana Serrano Zalamea. Bogotá: Universidad de los Andes, Facultad de Ciencias Sociales, Ediciones Uniandes, 2019. 198 p.: bibl., ill., map. (Colección General)

This is an updated version of the author's 2017 book (see item **742**) in which more details are provided of the developmental sequence of squatter settlements. From a geographical perspective, it is valuable to learn that, unlike other large cities, in Montevideo the first phase of *cantegriles* was based on very small accretions in the 1940s, and only in the 1980s did larger invasions take on more planned forms, with roads and public spaces. After 2000, the growing "asentamientos irregulares," the official name for the squatter zones, now involved active NGOs and radical Church-based participation. One should note the skillful use of newspaper cuttings to highlight critical events, as well as an attempt to show distributions cartographically. Unfortunately, the size of the map, even in this follow-up publication, is too small to make any patterning legible.

742 Álvarez Rivadulla, María José. Squatters and the politics of marginality in Uruguay. New York, N.Y.: Springer Berlin Heidelberg, 2017. 224 p.: bibl., ill. (Latin American political economy)

This book analyzes land squatting in Montevideo. The study focuses on how democratization affects the mobilization of the poor and on the role of actors such as radical Catholic priests and local leaders embedded in political networks. The methodology incorporates ethnography, historical interpretation, and time series analysis. The author skillfully reconstructs the growth and spread of the informal squatter city from the late 1940s to today, examining more than 400 specific cases of squatting. The book challenges the assumption that socioeconomic factors such as poverty cause land squatting to occur. Planning and decisions by social movements and political maneuvering are also factors to be considered. The use of diagrams in color presents ample evidence of the spatial extent of squatter settlements (*cantegriles*) over decades. Geographers will learn much from this intensive analysis of a phenomenon that has characterized most large urban centers in Latin America. Alas, the only map (p. 76) of the distribution of the *cantegriles* is too small to make them visible in any analytic mode. For an updated Spanish-language version of this book, see item **741**.

743 Borrás Ramos, Victor. Análisis exploratorio de datos espaciales de pobreza: aplicación 1996–2011 a tres ciudades de Uruguay (Montevideo, Maldonado y Salto). (*GeoSIG/Luján*, 11:15, 2019, p. 12–30, bibl., graph, color maps, tables)

The study analyzes the spatial distribution of poverty between 1996–2011 in three cities: Montevideo, Maldonado, and Salto. The author finds a reduction in poverty in all three cities during the period under review. However, the spatial analysis also shows strong spatial heterogeneity in the distribution of the phenomenon and clusters with high levels of poverty, which remain relatively stable across time, accounting for the structural nature of the spatial distribution of poverty.

744 Brida, Juan Gabriel; María Noel González; and Bibiana Lanzilotta. Análisis de los determinantes del turismo interno en Uruguay. (*Rev. Estud. Regionales*, 108, 2017, p. 43–78, bibl., map, tables)

This paper analyzes domestic tourism in Uruguay from 2010–2012. This analysis considers the bilateral flows between departments of the country, one as the source of tourism and the other as the destination. Gravity models suggest that tourist flows depend positively on the size of each department and negatively on the distance between them. The extended version includes explanatory variables to characterize the supply and demand for domestic tourism. The departments with higher income and the capital of the country (Montevideo) are the main sources of domestic tourists. The research also shows that the departments that share a border have greater tourist flows between them. In addition, departments with ocean coasts or good quality accommodation have a significant comparative advantage over the others. The article would benefit from flow maps to show tourism temporary migration paths.

745 Brida, Juan Gabriel; Virginia Carve; and Bibiana Lanzilotta. La relación entre la inversión pública en infraestructura vial y el crecimiento económico de Uruguay. (*Rev. Estud. Regionales*, 118, 2020, p. 177–211, bibl., graphs, tables)

This paper explores the relationship between public investment in road infrastructure and economic growth in Uruguay from 1988–2014. The study examines whether road infrastructure investment leads—in the long run—to economic growth, or, alternatively, economic expansion drives this investment, or a bidirectional relationship exists between the two variables. Additionally, the authors identify the direction of the causality between both variables. Finally, they analyze the response dynamics of the variables because of exogenous shocks. Based on the evidence, the authors reject the hypothesis of bidirectionality between economic growth and infrastructure investment in roads.

746 Casanova, Rosario; Miguel Gavirondo; and Eduardo Vásquez. Oportunidades y amenazas que presenta el combate al COVID-19 para la geomática en Uruguay. (*Rev. Geogr./México*, 161, 2020, p. 29–41, bibl., graph, maps)

The authors argue that the COVID-19 pandemic has allowed "geomatic" tools to be appreciated by the public and the government, both as a means of communication and as a relevant instrument to support decision-making, without demonstrating any specific tools. They also state that "this situation exposes certain weaknesses or limitations of geospatial information regarding the potentiality of its use," again without any specific details of the alleged limitations. Clearly, without the data, it is not possible to assess the utility of the techniques.

747 Ceroni, Mauricio. Megaproyectos en el espacio agrario del Uruguay: el agronegocio de la silvicultura. (*Scripta Nova*, 23:615, 2019, p. 1–23, bibl., color maps, tables) <https://revistes.ub.edu/index.php/ScriptaNova/article/view/21547/29254>

Megaprojects are a focal point of capital accumulation. With this model, transnational corporations lobby the states to support their projects. This paper critiques the 21st-century growth of agro-industrial megaprojects in the Uruguayan forestry sector that make up a large part of the agribusiness model in the framework of global capitalism. To that end, the author reviews the origin, territorial expansion, and impact in local communities of the megaprojects. He concludes that the state is subordinated to the transnational corporations.

748 **D'Angelo, Guillermo.** Análisis de riesgo de la zona costera del departamento de Canelones, Uruguay: la información geográfica como herramienta para la gestión del territorio. (*Rev. Geogr./México*, 158, 2017, p. 11–24, bibl., graph, map, photos)

To a large extent, tourism in Uruguay relies on coastal zones. The landscape is important from a cultural perspective and many of the country's residents live in vulnerable coastal areas. In the coastal zones of Canelones department, there are active cliffs, nearby housing, and infrastructure with adverse effects on the landscape. This work seeks to quantify the vulnerability of the coastal zones of Canelones. To that end, the author developed a GIS methodology to assess the damage, based on physical variables, demographics, land values, and infrastructure proximity. Using the GIS methodology, he identifies six high-risk zones. An excellent study in applied geography.

749 **Ehrnström-Fuentes, Maria** and **Markus Kröger.** Birthing extractivism: the role of the state in forestry politics and development in Uruguay. (*J. Rural Stud.*, 57, Jan. 2018, p. 197–208, bibl., tables)

This important study examines the role of states in developing contemporary extractivism based on recent investments and project plans in industrial forestry in Uruguay. The authors shed light on several unanswered questions related to the role of the state and civil society in the governance, politics, and political economy of extractivism.

750 **Gadino, Isabel** and **Germán Taveira.** Ordenamiento y gestión del territorio en zonas costeras con turismo residencial: el caso de Región Este, Uruguay. (*Rev. Geogr. Norte Gd.*, 77, dic. 2020, p. 233–251, bibl., graphs, map, photo, table)

One important element of tourism centered on Uruguay's beaches is associated with second homes. However, the impact of coastal housing has necessitated the creation of more land planning and management policies to protect the coast. In this study, the authors evaluate the implementation of these measures using quantitative, qualitative, and spatial analyses. Functional and spatial structures of residential mobility are consistent with the processes of expansion and physical, social, and functional fragmentation.

751 **Galaso, Pablo; Adrián Rodríguez Miranda;** and **Sebastián Goinheix.** Local development, social capital and social network analysis: evidence from Uruguay. (*Rev. Estud. Regionales*, 113, 2018, p. 137–163, bibl., graphs, map, tables)

This article studies local development as a socioterritorial project based on social capital. The authors propose three hypotheses describing interorganizational network properties required for the construction of a socioterritorial development project: preconditions for local development must exist, local organizations must hold central positions in territorial networks, and relations between organizations must be the result of territorial motivations. Using data from 2014 fieldwork, these requirements are analyzed for the case of Punta del Este-Maldonado-San Carlos, an urban region in southeast Uruguay. The results show that the case presents favorable conditions for the existence of a socioterritorial development project. No spatial aspects of the social networks are discussed.

752 **Groot Kormelinck, Annemarie; Jos Bijman;** and **Jacques Trienekens.** Characterizing producer organizations: the case of organic versus conventional

vegetables in Uruguay. (*J. Rural Stud.*, 69, July 2019, p. 65–75, bibl., graphs, tables)

Rural development in developing countries requires the participation of producer organizations. Scholary studies of these organizations generally focus on their impact, but do not distinguish among different types. To that end, this paper explores the organizational characteristics of different producer organizations in the vegetable sector of Uruguay.

753   **Montoya, Francisco** and **Álvaro Otero.** Is irrigating soybean profitable in Uruguay?: a modeling approach. (*Agron. J.*, 111:2, 2019, p. 749–763, bibl., graphs, tables)

Excellent report of statistical forecasting model demonstrating that irrigation could produce at least a 30 percent increase in soybean production in selected northern regions.

754   **Silveira, Ricardo Pinheiro** and **Claudinei Taborda da Silveira.** Clasificación morfológica del relieve del Uruguay basada en modelos digitales de elevación y técnicas geomorfométricas. (*GeoSIG/Luján*, 9, 2017, p. 16–33, bibl., graphs, maps, table)

Using geomorphometric techniques in GIS, this study measures the difference in elevation between central points and their relation to surrounding neighborhoods throughout Uruguay. Based on the combination of attributes and quantitative parameters, the results identified seven morphological units representing levels of dissection and slope sectors. The results highlight the potential application of modeling for preliminary surveys using automated morphological mapping, with low cost and application for various purposes.

755   **Soutullo, Alvaro et al.** Soybean expansion and the challenge of the coexistence of agribusiness with local production and conservation initiatives: pesticides in a Ramsar site in Uruguay. (*Environ. Conserv./Cambridge*, 47:2, June 2020, p. 97–103, bibl., map, tables)

In Uruguay, soybean croplands have grown to more than 1 million hectares in the past 20 years. At the same time, the government has implemented a system to preserve protected areas. This study assesses the presence of pesticides within a protected area in a basin dominated by croplands.

756   **Torrelli, Milton et al.** Mapeo de las políticas públicas vinculadas a la ESS en Uruguay (2015): una perspectiva sobre su naturaleza y orientaciones a diez años de la asunción del gobierno progresista. (*Geograficando/La Plata*, 15:1, 2019, e052, p. 1–17, bibl., tables)

This study describes public policy challenges facing the Social and Solidarity Economy (SSE) in Uruguay. These policies grew during the first 10 years of the progressive government in the country (2005–2014). However, the authors argue that a stronger commitment to more broad implementation of these policies to foster labor and social inclusion is needed. The article ends by discussing three key challenges: deepening collaboration with other actors of the SSE, improving interinstitutional linkages, and reviewing the concepts and strategies of these policies in terms of what they support.

757   **Zeballos Videla, Mabel Luz.** De Chiclayo a Montevideo: usos y prácticas de trabajadoras peruanas de/en la ciudad de Montevideo, Uruguay, 2000–2015. (*Etnogr. Contemp.*, 3:5, 2017, p. 92–119, bibl., table)

This study presents the results of an innovative event, "Andean Montevideo. Maps, Paths and Destinations," organized by Espacio de Estudios Andinos, Universidad de la República (Uruguay) in 2015. Using collective mapping, the project participants recorded narratives of 10 Peruvian women who live in Montevideo and work as household employees. Eight are from the city of Chiclayo, in northern Peru, and arrived in Montevideo with the assistance of transnational women's networks. The author details these women's lives in Montevideo, especially their working relationships, but also their access to education, culture, and recreation.

BRAZIL

CHRISTIAN BRANNSTROM, *Professor of Geography, Texas A&M University*

THE NEW AND SIGNIFICANT areas of geographical inquiry in Brazil include an agenda-setting edited book on marine geography (item **788**), which covers human and physical aspects of Brazil's ocean territories and coastline. The editors make a persuasive case for many understudied research areas with major importance for current and future resource use and policy-making. An innovative work on the water-food-energy nexus, using a children's geographies approach and a mixed methods approach, generates new insights that contrast with top-down understandings and shows considerable potential for application elsewhere in Brazil (item **782**). A third new area is found in *Lugares de memória* (item **784**), situated at the complex intersection of urban geography, violence, and memory. This book is a major contribution to geographic understandings of the military dictatorship through its compilation of 101 sites of memory in Rio de Janeiro state, inviting readers to consider the locations of contestation and state-sponsored violence during the period of military rule.

Excellent work continued in the subfield of historical geographies of the environment, with *Metamorfoses florestais* (item **787**) and *História ambiental e migrações* (item **780**) representing major accomplishments in understanding how people modified the Atlantic Forest region. Both books add important new knowledge to the now classic *With Broadax and Firebrand* by Warren Dean (1995). Another major contribution to historical geographies and understandings of the Afro-Brazilian experience is Watkins' magnificent *Palm Oil Diaspora* (item **799**), which analyzes the Dendê Coast of Bahia as a cultural landscape, showing the development of palm oil through the slave trade, the consolidation of palm oil commerce, and the impact of state-led development projects on palm oil. Marcus (item **786**) provides an excellent historical analysis of the 19th-century migration of US Southerners to Brazil. Adding to previous work on Confederados (see for example, *Americans: imigrantes do Velho Sul no Brasil;* see *HLAS 63:1781*), Marcus pays special attention to Baltimore's elites and religious leaders, while also focusing on the Confederado settlements in São Paulo state and the Campo cemetery that the Confederados established.

Hydropower, in the form of the massive Itaipu dam and reservoir, is the focus of Blanc's *Before the Flood* (item **760**), a major contribution to agrarian and energy geographies that combines previously unused archival sources with oral narratives collected from the protagonists of political movements. Known as the "project of the century" by Brazil's military leaders, the enormous reservoir supporting the Itaipu Binational hydropower site displaced people and encouraged opposition movements, which are analyzed in the book. Complementing the analysis of opposition to Itaipu are two works, *Energia, organizações e sociedade* (item **770**) and a section of *Governing the Rainforest* (item **762**), both of which offer a critique of the controversial Belo Monte hydropower plan in Pará state. A significant work on flood control in São Paulo's Tietê River analyzes the impact on low-income residents (item **779**), while another study looks at water insecurity and water supply diversification in Ceará state (item **797**).

In urban geography, policies affecting favelas receive significant attention with Prouse's study of formalization (item **791**) and Richmond's analysis of favela pacification (item **793**), while Carvalho and Carvalho Cabral (item **764**) question the utility of the favela as a category for public policy by comparing favela and non-favela census tracts in five major cities. Mobility in urban centers receives attention in Veloso's *O ônibus, a cidade e a luta* (item **798**), an analysis of popular protest for improved bus transportation in Belo Horizonte. Advances in urban historical geography include work by Davies on 20th-century Recife (items **767**, **768**, and **769**) and a paper arguing for the continued relevance of the *higienização* concept and practice (item **775**). Godfrey's outstanding *Preserving Whose City?* (item **777**) analyzes the processes of designating, reusing, and representing Rio de Janeiro's historic places.

The history of geographical thought and practice in Brazil continue to attract significant high-quality scholarship. The works of Ferretti and Davies represent major advances in our understandings of Josué de Castro, author of *Geografia da fome* (1946; see *HLAS 14:1548*). Making use of newly available archival sources, this work significantly deepens our understanding of several Northeastern geographers in terms of their context, their networks, and their influences, which in turn broadens our understandings of the discipline and of geographical thought. Davies (item **769**) shows Josué de Castro as contributing to critical work on socionatural metabolism, detailing Castro's moves from an interest in nutrition to an analysis of working-class people in Recife to publishing *Geografia da fome* (1946). Ferretti's *A Coffin for Malthusianism* (item **771**) analyzes Josué de Castro's *Geopolítica da fome* (1951), which is less well known than his 1946 book. Other significant work by Ferretti includes his analysis of Manuel Correia de Andrade, author of *Terra e homem no Nordeste* (1963), as a radical and subaltern geographer and as one of several geographers who contributed to planning processes in Northeastern Brazil (item **773**). Another notable analysis by Ferretti is his work on Mauro Mota and Josué de Castro as examples of geopoetics (item **774**).

Two significant studies offer unique analyses of geographies of human misery in the Amazon. *Escravidão por dívida* (item **783**) analyzes the workers and enabling networks involved in modern slavery conditions in Tocantins. Lopes follows workers from their recruitment in urban places to the ranches and farms where they are held in debt relationships. The first-hand accounts of workers, collected by the author, will inspire rage and disgust with the debt-slavery system and compassion for the people abused by this inhumane system. A different view of human misery appears in Simmons *et al.* (item **795**), which focuses on how the clearing of Brazil nut forest lands in eastern Pará state for cattle ranching relies upon the discipline of peasant bodies. Instead of the modernist "order and progress" ideals, we see the dystopian "discipline and punish."

758 Barbosa Jr., Ricardo and **João Roriz.**
The subversive practice of counting bodies: documenting violence and conflict in rural Brazil. (*J. Agrarian Change*, 21:4, Oct. 2014, p. 870–886, bibl., graph, maps, tables)

This analysis of the Comissão Pastoral da Terra (CPT) or Pastoral Land Commission examines its documentation of rural violence. The findings are based on qualitative interviews with CPT leaders. The authors detail how the CPT was created and its initial influences, and describe the production of reports on rural violence, known as the Conflitos no Campo Brasil series, which is based on a methodology described by the authors. The CPT's reporting is important for "creating meanings" about rural violence and conflict, or "making the invisible visible" (p. 880–881).

759 **Bittencourt, Tainá A.; Mariana Giannotti;** and **Eduardo Marques.** Cumulative (and self-reinforcing) spatial inequalities: interactions between accessibility and segregation in four Brazilian metropolises. (*Environ. Plann. B Urban Analytics City Sci.*, 48:7, 2021, p. 1989–2005, bibl.)

This analysis of São Paulo, Rio de Janeiro, Curitiba, and Fortaleza looks at spatial segregation that produces inequalities in access to formal employment and public transport. Authors rely on demographic census data from 2010 and transit itineraries. São Paulo and Curitiba have relatively high dissimilarity indices, while Fortaleza's dissimilarity index is relatively low. Presents the distributions of white upper classes and Black lower classes. Unsurprisingly, the structure of these cities is, overall, characterized by high segregation, leading to divergent levels of access to opportunity.

760 **Blanc, Jacob.** Before the flood: the Itaipu Dam and the visibility of rural Brazil. Durham, N.C.: Duke University Press, 2019. 296 p.: bibl., index.

Blanc provides an excellent historical analysis of the massive Itaipu Binational hydropower dam, completed in 1982, focusing on the struggles and activism originating from contested land flooded by the reservoir. He argues that these struggles had broader implications extending well beyond the immediate reservoir area. Blanc draws upon previously unused archival sources and oral narratives centering on two political movements that developed in opposition to the "project of the century," as Itaipu was described by the military regime. As the subtitle suggests, (in)visibility is a major theme, conceptually and empirically, that sustains the narrative.

761 **Brandão, Frederico** *et al.* The challenge of reconciling conservation and development in the tropics: lessons from Brazil's oil palm governance model. (*World Dev.*, 139, March 2021, p. 105–268, bibl.)

The study offers a critical analysis of the 2010 federal program to increase oil palm cultivation in the Amazon region through public-private partnerships while avoiding new deforestation. Governance of the program is detailed through a useful illustration and analytical framework. Surveys and spatial analysis of smallholder plots linked to firms reveal mixed outcomes for farmers. Authors conclude that approximately one percent of oil palm land was established on newly deforested land. The competitiveness of oil palm is relatively low because the program sought to incorporate, rather than displace, smallholder farmers.

762 **Bratman, Eve Z.** Governing the rainforest: sustainable development politics in the Brazilian Amazon. New York, N.Y.: Oxford University Press, 2019. 353 p.: bibl., ill., index, maps.

Bratman's analysis of sustainable development politics in the Amazon is based conceptually on Lefebvre's ideology of space. She argues that sustainable development perpetuates inequalities because social equity concerns are often ignored. The work is based on detailed and valuable case studies of BR-163 (the Cuiabá-Santarém highway), the Terra do Meio conservation unit, and the Belo Monte hydropower project. Includes a discussion of the 2005 assassination of environmental activist Sister Dorothy Stang. Also provides a useful methodological annex.

763 **Cabral, Lídia.** Embrapa and the construction of scientific heritage in Brazilian agriculture: sowing memory. (*Dev. Policy Rev.*, 39:2, 2021, p. 789–810)

This study adds to existing knowledge about Embrapa, the Agricultural Research Corporation, by focusing on environmental and social impacts of agribusiness expansion, the national seed bank, and dialogues between Embrapa's scientists and local experts. Based on interviews with Embrapa staff, this work offers a different narrative than the one present in the 2005 publication *Sol da manhã: memória da Embrapa*, an official history commemorating 40 years of Embrapa, and which the author considers to be a "branding" exercise. Includes discussion of the feeling of being *embrapiano* or *embrapiana*, the strong identification of Embrapa staff with the organization.

764 **Carvalho, Camila** and **Diogo de Carvalho Cabral.** Beyond the favelas: an analysis of intraurban poverty patterns in Brazil. (*Prof. Geogr.*, 73:2, Aug. 2021, p. 269–281, bibl.)

Based on 2010 census data, this empirical spatial analysis compares favela and non-favela residents in São Paulo, Rio de Janeiro, Salvador, Belém, and Recife. Favela and non-favela census tracts share many characteristics, including income, but they are unevenly distributed across space. Favelas are located closer to city centers than non-favelas, according to this analysis. The authors argue that as a category, the favela has many similarities to other types of low-income neighborhoods. They question the uncritical use of favela as a spatial category.

765 **Castro, Marcia C. et al.** Spatiotemporal pattern of Covid-19 spread in Brazil. (*Science/Washington*, 372:6544, 2021, p. 821–826)

This major contribution analyzes how, where, and when COVID-19 spread in Brazil during 2020. Death clusters are identified in Recife, Fortaleza, Rio de Janeiro, and Manaus. Authors are critical of the response and failure by federal and some state governments to mitigate the spread, although no single explanation was found; rather, mitigation failure was compounded by deep inequalities, leading to rapid spread of the virus.

766 **Contel, Fabio Betioli** and **Dariusz Wojcik.** Brazil's financial centers in the twenty-first century: hierarchy, specialization, and concentration. (*Prof. Geogr.*, 71:4, Oct. 2019, p. 681–691, bibl., maps, tables)

This work analyzes the changing specialization, hierarchy, and spatial concentration of Brazil's financial centers after 2000. The authors analyze employment and mergers and acquisitions data. Rio de Janeiro, which specializes in insurance, has declined in importance as a financial center, while São Paulo has a consolidated position as Brazil's financial leader, employing more than one-quarter of the financial and business services workforce. Brasília is the country's third most important financial center owing to presence of state-owned bank headquarters. Belo Horizonte, Curitiba, and Porto Alegre comprise a second tier of cities with financial, insurance, real estate, and professional services. Mergers and acquisitions within São Paulo comprise nearly 60 percent of all domestic deals.

767 **Davies, Archie.** The coloniality of infrastructure: engineering, landscape and modernity in Recife. (*Environ. Plann. D Soc. Space*, 39:4, 2021, p. 740–757, bibl.)

Davies studies the British engineers who were involved in railroads, ports, and quarries, in the making of Recife in the 1920s. In this article, he highlights scenes from the 1925 *Veneza Americana* documentary, which focused on Recife's modernized shipping infrastructure. For a comment on a related article, see item **768**.

768 **Davies, Archie.** The racial division of nature: making land in Recife. (*Trans. Inst. Br. Geogr.*, 46:2, June 2021, p. 270–283, bibl.)

This study analyzes the transformation of Recife from 1920 to 1950 through the appropriation and drying of marshes and mangroves. The work also discusses the people who resided in *mocambos* (informal housing) at the land-water interface. Davies analyzes the racial politics of the Estado Novo as they are represented in Agamenon Magalhães' writings on *mocambos*. The study also pays attention to the writers and artists who resisted anti-*mocambo* ideology and policy. For a related article by the same author, see item **767**.

769 **Davies, Archie.** Unwrapping the oxo cube: Josué de Castro and the intellectual history of metabolism. (*Ann. Am. Assoc. Geogr.*, 109:3, May 2019, p. 837–856, bibl.)

This work positions Josué de Castro as an "intellectual forebear" to political ecology (p. 838), owing to his published work on human metabolism and nutrition, understood here as contributing to critical work on socionatural metabolism. The work includes a discussion of Castro's term *homem-carangeujo* to describe how people subsisted on crabs caught in mangroves in Recife. Castro's transition from nutrition to geographical analysis begins with a study of working-class people in Recife in the 1930s, then develops into his *Geografia da fome* (1946) (see *HLAS 14:1548*). The author sees Castro's work as contributing to corporeal and anticolonial dimensions of political ecology. For a related article on Josué de Castro, see item **771**.

770 **Energia, organizações e sociedade.** Organização de Luiz Alex Silva Saraiva e Adriana Vinholi Rampazo. Recife, Brazil: Fundação Joaquim Nabuco, Editora Massangana, 2017. 281 p.: bibl.

This critical study looks at the socio-environmental impacts of large hydropower projects. The chapters analyze electricity sector reforms, the hydropower planning process, and communities affected by hydropower. Several chapters offer analyses of different aspects of the controversial Belo Monte hydropower plant in Pará state. An especially insightful chapter offers a Foucauldian analysis of hydropower discourses and governance analysis of hydropower.

771 **Ferretti, Federico.** A coffin for Malthusianism: Josué de Castro's subaltern geopolitics. (*Geopolitics/London*, 26:2, March 2021, p. 589–614, bibl.)

Based on recently opened archives and the editorial history of *Geopolítica da fome* (1951), the author argues that Castro defined geopolitics as anti-colonialist, anti-racist, and anti-Malthusian. The article includes a synthesis of Castro's biography. Also discusses Castro's correspondence with leading geographers and his teaching modules, which he delivered during 1969–73 at the Université Paris VIII in Vincennes. For a related article on Josué de Castro, see item **769**.

772 **Ferretti, Federico.** Decolonizing regional planning from the Global South: active geographies and social struggles in northeastern Brazil. (*Environ. Plann. D Soc. Space*, 39:4, 2021, p. 665–684, bibl.)

This article analyzes the 1957–64 period in which geographers (Manuel Correia de Andrade, Gilberto Osório de Andrade, Mário Lacerda de Melo, Mauro Mota, and Rachel Caldas Lins) worked with Gilberto Freyre, Josué de Castro, Milton Santos, Francisco Julião, and Celso Furtado. Interactions with the Superintendência do Desenvolvimento do Nordeste (SUDENE), led initially by Furtado, are emphasized through newly available archival holdings. The author argues that the geographers mentioned contributed to SUDENE's planning processes through "active geography" (p. 670).

773 **Ferretti, Federico.** Decolonizing the northeast: Brazilian subalterns, non-European heritages, and radical geography in Pernambuco. (*Ann. Am. Assoc. Geogr.*, 109:5, Sept. 2019, p. 1632–1650)

Ferretti's article studies the work and inspiration of geographer Manuel Correia de Andrade. He describes Andrade's social and intellectual context as a radical and subaltern geographer, emphasizing his understanding of the sertão and quilombos, and his relationships with other Brazilian geographers. The author consulted Andrade's archival records. See also *HLAS 75:754*.

774 **Ferretti, Federico.** From the drought to the mud: rediscovering geopoetics and cultural hybridity from the Global South. (*Cult. Geogr./London*, 27:4, Oct. 2020, p. 597–613)

This study examines the work of Mauro Mota and Josué de Castro as examples of geopoetics and contextualized in a useful synthesis of *literatura de cordel*, a tradition of poems and songs in the Northeast. Mota's *Paisagem das sêcas* (1958) and other work blend literary and geographical writing, while Castro's work blends anti-racism and decolonial narratives. Mota and Castro are interpreted as practitioners of geopoetics, "narrating the human dramas associated with the sertão physical conditions and the colonial histories and social geographies of their political causes" (p. 608). Unpublished archival sources support the author's interpretations.

775 **Garmany, Jeff** and **Matthew A. Richmond.** Hygienisation, gentrification, and urban displacement in Brazil. (*Antipode*, 52:1, Jan. 2020, p. 124–144, bibl.)

The authors study *higienização*, which began in Brazil with Rio de Janeiro's mayor Francisco Pereira Passos, who learned from Haussmann's reforms and destroyed *cortiços* in Rio with authoritarian, violent, and hygienist processes. The article examines contemporary forms of *higienização* by synthesizing previous work on Salvador's Pelourinho district, the Vila Autódromo favela in Rio de Janeiro, and São Paulo's "Cracolândia." The authors argue that *higienização* may help develop broader theorization of displacement processes in places where informality, state-sponsored violence, and racism are prevalent.

776 **Geografia agrária no Brasil: disputas, conflitos e alternativas territoriais.** Organização de Gustavo H. Cepolini Ferreira. Jundiaí, Brazil: Paco Editorial, 2016. 389 p.: bibl., ill., maps. (Coleção Escritos acadêmicos. Série Estudos reunidos; 13)

This edited book covers many themes important to agrarian geographies, such as the Rio São Francisco water transfers, the implications of the national policy for small farmers, identity-based issues, and foreign landownership. An especially insightful chapter analyzes rural themes in Brazilian popular music.

777 **Godfrey, Brian J.** Preserving whose city?: memory, place, and identity in Rio de Janeiro. Lanham, Md.: Rowman & Littlefield, 2021. 252 p.: bibl., index.

Analysis of designating, reusing, and representing Rio de Janeiro's historic places. Situated in the right to heritage literature. Includes concise historical geography of Rio. Case studies include the Cultural Corridor; Little Africa: the Valongo wharf, the landing site for approximately one million African slaves; the favelas and the rise of Favela Chic; and several environmental heritage sites, including the Tijuca National Park and Guanabara Bay. Argues that the cases show "expansion of the right to remember" (p. 203) across more constituencies.

Halvorsen, Sam; Bernardo Mançano Fernandes; and **Fernanda Valeria Torres.** Mobilizing territory: socioterritorial movements in comparative perspective. See item **636**.

778 **Hecht, Susanna B.** and **Raoni Rajão.** From "Green Hell" to "Amazonia Legal": land use models and the re-imagination of the rainforest as a new development frontier. (*Land Use Policy*, 96:6, July 2020, p. 1–12, bibl.)

An historical and discursive analysis of land-use models and Amazon-wide programs that were carried out before the Brazilian military implemented occupation plans for the Amazon. The authors analyze Paul Le Cointe's work on the economic potential of the Amazon, which helped encourage elites to contract scientists and attracted investors to the region. The article also synthesized the region-wide efforts to develop the Amazon during WWII. The Superintendência do Plano de Valorização Econômica da Amazônia (SPVEA), created in 1953, is also highlighted for its role in "inventing" the Amazon region using nationalist language that continues to inform public discourse.

779 **Henrique, Karen Paiva** and **Petra Tschakert.** Contested grounds: adaptation to flooding and the politics of (in)visibility in São Paulo's eastern periphery. (*Geoforum/New York*, 104, Aug. 2019, p. 181–192)

The authors analyze efforts to control flooding of São Paulo's Tietê River, which began in the late 1970s and would cause the removal of thousands of low-income families. The article highlights the complex geographies related to flood management from the perspectives of urban and feminist political ecology. The study emphasizes how flood planning neglects the needs of low-income districts, which are invisible in the process, and also describes how residents resist flood planning.

780 **História ambiental e migrações: diálogos.** Organização de Marcos Gerhardt, Eunice Sueli Nodari e Samira Peruchi Moretto. São Leopoldo, Brazil: Oikos Editora; Chapecó, Brazil: UFFS Editora, 2017. 262 p.: bibl., ill., maps.

This edited collection examines the historical geography and environmental history of southern Brazil. Notable chapters cover the agricultural frontier in Santa Catarina and Rio Grande do Sul, especially the formation of immigrant colonies in the late 19th and early 20th centuries. The chapters analyze key European writers, such as Wilhelm Vallentin, a German who wrote about Brazil's potential to receive Europeans settlers, and Paul Aldinger, a German pastor who supported immigration. Chapters also cover the tensions between European colonists and Indigenous groups.

781 **Hosannah, Luciana Dornelles.** Intermunicipal cooperation: policy transfer in São Paulo and Rio de Janeiro. (*Reg. Stud./Abingdon,* 54:7, 2020, p. 987–998)

Analyzes intermunicipal cooperation (IMC), the coordination of policies between two or more municipalities (often as a consortium) for their combined geographies in a holistic manner, in São Paulo and Rio de Janeiro metropolitan regions. Based on interviews with various stakeholders. Several cases of IMC are analyzed and categorized in types and processes of policy transfer. Contributes to geographical literature on Brazilian governance by illuminating the hierarchical and horizontal influences on municipal consortia that are responsible for policy action in solid waste, water, transport, and other policy domains.

782 **Kraftl, Peter et al.** (Re)thinking (re)connection: young people, "natures" and the water-energy-food nexus in São Paulo state, Brazil. (*Trans. Inst. Br. Geogr.,* 44:2, June 2019, p. 299–314, bibl.)

The authors analyze how young people connect to the water-energy-food (WEF) nexus. The study makes an important contribution to children's geographies in Brazil and describes empirical work in the Paraíba do Sul region in which mixed-methods approaches encourage young people to take pictures of WEF and engage in participatory cartography. The authors argue that young people have lived experiences with WEF, which should be considered in attempts to reconnect people to nature.

783 **Lopes, Alberto Pereira.** Escravidão por dívida no Tocantins-Brasil: vidas dilaceradas. Curitiba, Brazil: Appris Editora, 2018. 312 p.: bibl., ill. (Coleção Ciências sociais)

Lopes provides a qualitative analysis of workers and networks involved in modern slavery conditions in Tocantins. The work views slave labor—defined as unfree and degrading labor relations usually enforced by a debt relationship—as a determining factor in capital accumulation in frontier conditions where land concentration predominates. The slave workforce is predominantly male, but women are considered as direct and indirect victims. The study also analyzes the urban places that are key nodes in the debt-slavery network, supplying workers to ranches and farms. The brokers are viewed as key nodes in procuring indebted workers. The study is based on fieldwork, participatory collaborations, and secondary data.

784 **Lugares de memória: ditadura militar e resistências no Estado do Rio de Janeiro.** Coordenação de José María Gómez. Rio de Janeiro: Editora PUC-Rio: Clacso, 2018. 509 p.: bibl., ill. (some color), maps.

Compelling survey and description of 101 sites, ranging from newspaper publishers to high schools to the Duque de Caxias refinery, in Rio de Janeiro state that preserve the memories of violence, protest, and resistance during the military dictatorship. Sites are mapped, illustrated, and described with reference to documentary and published sources. The sites are organized according to 12 categories of violence or resistance. The first site described is the Departamento de Ordem Política e Social (DOPS).

785 **Manzi, Maya.** The making of speculative biodiesel commodities on the agroenergy frontier of the Brazilian Northeast. (*Antipode,* 52:6, Nov. 2020, p. 1794–1814, bibl.)

In this article, Manzi studies Brazil's national biodiesel program which aims to increase cultivation of the castor oil plant. The work is based on a case study of Bahia state, based on 74 semistructured interviews with family farmers producing castor beans, and includes a critical discussion of the "social inclusion" dimension of the national biodiesel policy. The article describes the political and biological risks sustained by peasants seeking to grow castor and argues that speculation over the castor bean encouraged a form of dispossession for them.

786 **Marcus, Alan P.** Confederate exodus: social and environmental forces in the migration of U.S. Southerners to Brazil.

Lincoln: University of Nebraska Press, 2021. 252 p.: bibl., index.

In this historical geographical analysis, the author studies factors encouraging the migration of US Southerners to Brazil, with special attention to Baltimore's elites, US Protestant leaders, scientific writing, and propaganda. The study focuses on the settlements in São Paulo state, where *Confederados* concentrated around Santa Bárbara do Oeste. Marcus makes significant use of new primary sources and emphasizes the role of social networks in promoting migration and facilitating settlement. Includes an analysis of the Campo cemetery. See also *HLAS 63:1781*.

787 Metamorfoses florestais: culturas, ecologias e as transformações históricas da Mata Atlântica. Organização de Diogo de Carvalho Cabral e Ana Goulart Bustamante. Curitiba, Brazil: Editora Prismas, 2016. 458 p.: bibl., ill. (some color), maps (some color).

Insightful preface by José Augusto Pádua places this valuable edited collection of historical geography and environmental history into historiographical context, especially with regard to Warren Dean's *With Broadax and Firebrand: The Destruction of the Brazilian Atlantic Forest* (1995). The chapters cover a wide range of time periods, from the Quaternary to pre-European to current conservation issues. Spatially, the chapters cover the Atlantic forest from the northeastern edges to Santa Catarina. Thematically, Indigenous land uses, forest transition, timber activities, and mining, among many other topics, are covered in this book, adding substantially to insights offered in *Broadax*.

788 Muehe, Dieter; Flavia Moraes Lins de Barros; and Lidriana Pinheiro. Geografia marinha: oceanos e costas na perspectiva de geógrafos. Rio de Janeiro: PGGM, Caroline Fontelles Ternes, 2020. 764 p.

This wide-ranging edited e-book marks the importance of geographical scholarship in Brazilian marine studies. Major sections examine dynamic processes in coastal and marine settings; monitoring and modelling; governance and management of coastal and marine environments; and case studies on a variety of topics, including planning, wind energy, tourism, and coastal erosion. The editor's introduction traces oceanographic inquiry in Brazil and its relations to geography and indicates the main lines of research, such as coastal geomorphology, tourism, vulnerability, and fishing.

789 Oliveira, Gustavo de L.T. Boosters, brokers, bureaucrats and businessmen: assembling Chinese capital with Brazilian agribusiness. (*Territ. Polit. Gov.*, 7:1, Jan. 2019, p. 22–41, bibl.)

This work provides an analysis of a Chinese-owned company that implemented an agroindustrial enterprise in Mato Grosso do Sul. Oliveira focuses on the transnational intermediaries who link Chinese funds with Brazilian agricultural experts, land, and workers. The study is informed by ethnographic application of assemblage approaches to governance and accounts of Chinese business practices. The case is contextualized within the broader realm of Chinese investments in Brazil, where little is known in terms of the practice of assembling different elements necessary to agricultural production.

790 Oliveira, Lívia de. Percepção do meio ambiente e geografia: estudos humanistas do espaço, da paisagem e do lugar. Organização de Eduardo Marandola Jr. e Tiago Vieira Cavalcante. São Paulo: GHUM, Grupo de Pesquisa Geografia Humanista Cultural: Associação de Geografia Teorética: Cultura Acadêmica Editora, 2017. 196 p.: bibl., ill.

The essays collected here pay tribute to Lívia de Oliveira, one of Brazil's leading geographers specializing in environmental and spatial perception. She was inspired by the work of Yi-fu Tuan. Some of her key texts are reproduced, allowing readers to appreciate her contributions to the field.

791 Prouse, Carolyn. Subversive formalization: efforts to (re)form land, labor, and behavior in a Carioca favela. (*Urban Geogr.*, 40:10, 2019, p. 1548–1567, bibl., map, photos, table)

This study provides an analysis of efforts to "formalize" the Complexo do Alemão favela with ethnographic methodology, including participant observation. The article contrasts state efforts at formalizing property, employment, and behavior with residents efforts to make changes, through "subversive formalization," using practices developed through a sense of community belonging.

792 **Rausch, Lisa L. et al.** Soy expansion in Brazil's Cerrado. (*Conserv. Lett.*, 12:6, Nov./Dec. 2019, p. 1–10, bibl., graph, map, tables)

Remote sensing analysis of soy expansion in the Cerrado shows that it was responsible for 22 percent of clearing from 2003 to 2014. Using boundaries of more than 580,000 properties, authors determine that half of soy farms had violated the Forest Code, which obligates on-farm conservation set-asides. The authors argue that suitable land for expansion of soy farming in the Cerrado is available on already cleared land, requiring no additional clearing of native Cerrado.

793 **Richmond, Matthew Aaron.** Hostages to both sides: favela pacification as dual security assemblage. (*Geoforum/New York*, 104, Aug. 2019, p. 71–80, bibl.)

The article uses assemblage theory and concepts to analyze pacification in Tuituti, a favela with approximately 6,000 residents in Rio de Janeiro. Argues that pacification "overlaid and fused with" security measures that drug traffickers had created, leading to "dual security assemblage" that created greater uncertainty for residents regarding security issues. The article adds to the emerging literature on the implementation of Unidades de Polícia Pacificadora (UPP) as a means to enforce state control over favelas.

794 **Silva, Ricardo Barbosa da.** Mobilidade precária na metrópole de São Paulo. São Paulo: Annablume, 2016. 362 p.: bibl., ill., maps. (Coleção Geografia e adjacências)

Silva studies urban mobility in the São Paulo metropolitan region in terms of rail and tires. The work analyzes extreme traffic congestion and attempted solutions, such as dedicated bus lanes. Also examines environmental pollution from car transport, popular protest regarding public transport, and traffic accidents.

795 **Simmons, Cynthia S. et al.** Discipline and develop: destruction of the Brazil nut forest in the lower Amazon basin. (*Ann. Am. Assoc. Geogr.*, 109:1, Jan. 2019, p. 242–265)

This article presents a comprehensive political economic analysis of clearing of Brazil nut forest lands in eastern Pará state for cattle ranching. Provides a review of a long-established literature and makes new claims regarding how land is created or made available for capitalist investment by focusing on the migration of peasants to the region, who are then preyed upon by "takers" who appropriate the results of peasant labor. This process involves "corporeal discipline" of peasant bodies. Authors are skeptical that environmental policies will protect Amazonian forests.

796 **Thaler, Gregory M.; Cecilia Viana;** and **Fabiano Toni.** From frontier governance to governance frontier: the political geography of Brazil's Amazon transition. (*World Dev.*, 85, Sept. 2016, p. 58–72, bibl., tables)

The authors deploy a "follow the policy" approach that focuses on the multiple spatial scales of policy experimentation and adoption in the Amazon region. The study offers a distinction between institutionalist and political economy scholarship as applicable to Amazonian governance studies. It argues for a "governance frontier" in which certain municipalities serve as innovative and experimental sites for policies, which are then transferred to other municipalities. Forest governance policy is followed from initial implementation in Santarém to Lucas do Rio Verde in Mato Grosso, Paragominas in Pará, and then to São Félix do Xingu. Presents a useful illustration of the complex policy pathway, showing the development of a governance frontier.

797 **Tomaz, Paula; Wendy Jepson;** and **Jader de Oliveira Santos.** Urban household water insecurity from the margins: perspectives from Northeast Brazil. (*Prof. Geogr.*, 72:4, Nov. 2020, p. 481–498, bibl., tables)

The authors deploy the Household Water Insecurity Index on a site in Ceará state, where they find that 25 percent of the population experience moderate to severe household water insecurity, even though piped water supply covers nearly 100 percent of the population. The study describes water supply diversification strategies, including informal water vending.

798 **Veloso, André.** O ônibus, a cidade e a luta. Belo Horizonte, Brazil: Impressões de Minas, 2017. 399 p., 28 unnumbered pages: bibl., ill.

This analysis of the Tarifa Zero popular movement in Belo Horizonte from 2013 to 2015 includes a synthesis of popular movements for improved urban transport from the 1970s to the 1990s. The study links the Carnaval celebration and popular culture in Belo Horizonte to the Tarifa Zero campaign.

799 **Watkins, Case.** Palm oil diaspora: Afro-Brazilian landscapes and economies on Bahia's Dendê Coast. Cambridge, England; New York, N.Y.: Cambridge University Press, 2021. 320 p.: bibl., index. (Afro-Latin America)

This historical and cultural geography of palm oil in Bahia state argues for importance of palm oil in the Afro-Brazilian economy. The study region, the Dendê Coast, is viewed as a cultural landscape and analyzed with reference to socioecological dynamics, power, and resistance. Major contributions include the analysis of the emergence of palm oil on the cultural landscape through the slave trade, the commerce of palm oil in the 19th century, and the impact of state-led development projects for palm oil in the 20th century. Analyses are based on a mixed-methods approach combining archival documents, such as probate inventories, with interviews.

Zusman, Perla. Milton Santos: la globalización vista desde el Tercer Mundo. See item **433**.

GOVERNMENT AND POLITICS

MEXICO

Caroline Beer, *John G. McCullough Professor of Political Science, The University of Vermont*

IN THE TWO DECADES since the defeat of the Partido Revolucionario Institucional (PRI) in the 2000 presidential elections and the emergence of a new era of multiparty democracy, research on Mexican politics has shifted from studying the transition to democracy to analyzing the quality of the democratic government. Overwhelmingly, scholars share a sense of disenchantment with the accomplishments of multiparty democracy.

Undoubtedly the most profound disappointment with Mexico's democracy has been the dramatic upsurge of violence since 2006 and the increasing penetration of organized crime into ever more facets of political and economic life. The inability of the state to protect citizens and enforce the rule of law has generated a national security crisis. Until recently, mainstream political science research barely addressed the problems of organized crime and drug violence, with only a few lawyers and criminologists writing about the drug trade. The challenges of studying clandestine phenomena and the related lack of reliable data leave traditional social science methodologies struggling to address the issue.

New research describes the immensity of the security crisis, from the number of dead and missing (item **810**), to the toll exacted on the free press by the killings of journalists (item **821**). Buendía Hegewisch and Esquivel Ventura (item **803**) note that as more institutional reforms to protect freedom of the press are passed, Mexico scores worse on international indices of press freedom. Others examine alternatives for addressing the security crisis. One response to the violence has been the rise of community policing or *autodefensas*, armed citizen groups that carry out their own system of justice in the face of state absence and the advance of organized crime. Horta Cruz and Aburto Espinobarro, long-time activists in community policing, provide an insider's history of the community policing movement in Guerrero (item **823**). Fuentes Díaz and Fini's more scholarly approach argues that these groups are a form of resistance against state repression and the neoliberal market (item **811**).

A new generation of scholarship has embraced innovative methodologies to answer pressing questions about organized crime and drug violence. Durán-Martínez (item **813**) and Trejo and Ley (item **843**) break important new theoretical and empirical ground to shed light on the causes of drug violence. Durán-Martínez compares cities in Colombia and Mexico to explain the frequency and visibility of violence. She identifies competitive drug markets and the cohesiveness of the state security apparatus as central causal variables. Trejo and Ley build on the findings of Durán-Martínez but point to the significance of state governments, rather than municipal governments, for understanding drug violence. State judicial police and state attorneys' general are especially important actors. Trejo and Ley highlight change in the governing party and intergovernmental conflict, and provide a more precise conceptualization of the cohesiveness of the state security apparatus. Magaloni et al. (item **827**) explain why drug trafficking organizations sometimes provide benefits to local populations and in other contexts extort them. They provide evidence that drug trafficking organizations are more likely to extort the local population when they face violent competition from other crime groups, when they are able to collude with state officials, and when their leadership is decentralized and unstable. Flores-Macías (item **816**) shows that the militarization of drug enforcement efforts undermines the capacity of the state to provide public security and extract resources. Reflecting many of these concerns, Camp and Mattiace's outstanding new edition (item **806**) of the classic introduction to Mexican politics text focuses on the challenges of building democracy and provides a new extended examination of organized crime and drug violence.

Campaign finance has been particularly important in Mexico's new democracy. Casar and Ugalde (item **809**) highlight the illegal financing and spending of political campaigns as the central weakness of Mexico's democracy. Their analysis underscores the limited capacity of electoral authorities and the ineffectiveness of existing penalties for breaking campaign finance laws. Méndez, Martínez, and Loza's survey of perceptions of electoral integrity draws attention to campaign finance in subnational elections (item **825**). Garrido de Sierra (item **818**) argues that the 1996 electoral reform ultimately brought down the one-party system, largely because of the equalizing system of campaign finance.

Several recent publications have addressed the intriguing occurrence of electoral alliances between parties with opposing ideological platforms (items **800**, **807**, **812**, and **834**). As one-party rule disintegrated, the relationship between the two major opposition parties, the Partido de la Revolución Democrática (PRD) on the left and the Partido Acción Nacional (PAN) on right, was often characterized by conflict, but on occasion the ideologically diverse opposition parties formed alliances to challenge the dominance of the centrist ruling PRI. These works try to explain why these puzzling alliances form and when they are successful. They stress the importance of the context of a declining and divided hegemonic party where opposition parties see a realistic chance of winning. While these works examine the alliance of the PRD and PAN and their attempts to oust the once-dominant PRI, the insights from this research may help shed light on the more recent ideologically diverse alliances formed in opposition to López Obrador and the Morena party.

The 2018 elections were an important focus of research in works reviewed for *HLAS 77*. In his third try for the presidency, Andrés Manuel López Obrador and his newly formed Morena party won a majority of votes for the presidency and the majority of seats in the national legislature. The landslide wins by a newly formed party produced the first majority government since the fall of one-party rule. While all observers agree that the elections and the rise of López Obrador was a consequential event, even a "critical election" (see item **814**), the scholarship mirrors much of the polarization seen in public opinion regarding López Obrador. Is López Obrador a true left alternative to traditional Mexican politics, or a continuation of the PRI's style of one-party authoritarianism? Some, such as Ackerman (item **804**), see the electoral sweep by Morena as a victory for national sovereignty and social justice, praising centralized rule as "democratic hegemony" and arguing that institutions should be subordinate to social movements and citizen participation. Others are more circumspect about the president's tendency to centralize power in his own hands and to demonize the opposition. Hernández Rodríguez (item **822**) is interested in "the craft of politics." He contrasts the traditional PRI elite with the new Morena elite and worries that the craft of politics has been lost, and as a result there is little investment in building institutions that serve the public's interest. Instead, he argues, politics has become about militancy, rather than accomplishments. Hernández Rodríguez further contends that the lack of professionalism, experience, and respect for institutions among the new elite is weakening democracy.

The adoption in 2014 of a new constitutional amendment to require gender parity in candidacies for all legislative elections has created important new opportunities for women's political participation. Franco Durán and Hernández Ramos' analysis of Aguascalientes after the 2014 constitutional reform provides an important assessment of women's political representation in the immediate aftermath of the gender parity reforms (item **832**). Two chapters in Díaz Jiménez, Góngora Cervantes, and Vilches Hinojosa's volume (item **814**) on the critical elections of 2018 examine how gender parity brought more women into formal politics in 2018, but left many gender inequalities unaddressed.

The role of Indigenous people in Mexican politics is the subject of a number of excellent studies. Magaloni *et al.* (item **828**) compare the provision of public goods in municipalities governed by traditional *usos y costumbres* to those with multiparty elections. They find that communities governed by traditional Indigenous governing structures do a better job providing water and sewage to their populations than those where mayors are chosen in multiparty elections. Price (item **836**) shows that protest is more likely in municipalities with a greater number of ethnic organizations and strong left parties, and less likely where there are strong clientelist networks. According to Ley, Mattiace, and Trejo (item **826**), Indigenous communities are better able to resist narco penetration when they have a history of Indigenous social mobilization that brings people together to form translocal networks of regional ethnic autonomy.

To conclude, I want to draw attention to a fascinating article by Francisco Cantú about the 1988 presidential elections (item **808**). Cantú uses computer image analysis to examine over 50,000 district tallies from the election and identify examples of altered tallies. He finds that one-third of the tallies had "blatant alterations," suggesting fraud. A quantitative analysis of the altered tallies shows that polling stations with no opposition representatives and states where governors had electoral experience or were close allies of the incumbent party's presidential candidate were more likely to have altered tallies. With all the discouraging news about the problems of contemporary Mexican politics, this article reminds us of how far Mexico has come since the beginning of its transition to democracy.

800 ¿Alianzas contra natura o antihegemónicas?: las alianzas PAN-PRD en los estados mexicanos. Coordinación de Diego Reynoso y Orlando Espinosa Santiago. Ciudad de México: Tirant Lo Blanch; Puebla, Mexico: BUAP, Instituto de Ciencias de Gobierno y Desarrollo Estratégico, 2017. 445 p.: bibl., graphs, tables. (Ciencia política)

This edited volume examines ideologically inconsistent electoral alliances between the leftist PRD and the rightist PAN. The research focuses on gubernatorial elections and includes 11 case studies of alliances and three cases studies where attempted alliances collapsed. These case studies include all ideologically inconsistent alliances from the 1991 gubernatorial campaign of Dr. Nava in San Luis Potosí, to the elections of 2010. The central argument is that these alliances are most likely to occur during the decline of one-party hegemony when opposition parties see the possibility of electoral victory over the hegemonic party. They also find that these alliances are more likely in gubernatorial elections that are not concurrent with federal elections, but do take place on the same day as many other gubernatorial elections. This book presents important research into state-level electoral politics during the transition to democracy and the early democratic era. It also provides important theoretical insights to explain unexpected alliance patterns.

801 Álvarez-Mingote, Cristina. How do remittances shape electoral strategies back home?: evidence from Mexico's 2006 presidential election. (*Lat. Am. Polit. Soc.*, 61:3, Aug. 2019, p. 55–79, bibl., tables)

How does international migration affect political parties' electoral strategies back home? The article argues that people receiving remittances are more likely to be targeted for clientelism and home visits during electoral campaigns because remittance recipients are more politically disengaged and therefore more likely to be receptive to campaign tactics. Using data from a panel survey of the 2006 presidential election, Álvarez-Mingote finds that people receiving remittances were more likely to be targeted by the PAN, the incumbent party at the time.

802 Bautista Arreola, Iulisca Zircey. La modernización política en México desde la perspectiva de sus actores. Ciudad de México: INE, Instituto Nacional Electoral, 2018. 204 p.: bibl., ill.

Published by the National Electoral Institute, this doctoral thesis won a competition for best research on political communication. Analyzing the transition from traditional forms of political communication (campaign rallies and meetings directed by partisan loyalists) to modern forms of media-driven campaigning (surveys, focus groups, and television advertising directed by nonpartisan consultants), the research draws on original interviews with politicians and political consultants. It focuses on professionalization, personalization, and media strategy in political campaigns. This book is a useful source of interview data for anyone interested in elections and campaigns. It also deftly maps the transition of elections from more traditional forms to more modern media-driven campaigns that took place during the first few election cycles of the 21st century.

803 Buendía Hegewisch, José and Isabella María Esquivel Ventura. Libertad de expresión y periodismo en México: situación del ejercicio y percepción de la libertad de prensa en el contexto de las alternancias políticas de 2000 a 2015. Ciudad de México: Cámara de Diputados, LXIII Legislatura, Consejo Editorial: Miguel Ángel Porrúa, 2018. 249 p.: bibl., ill., index, maps. (Serie Políticas públicas)

Examining the role of the press during the transition to democracy, the authors argue that the transition to competitive multiparty democracy has not guaranteed effective access to basic rights, especially freedom of expression and freedom of the press. They note that as more institutional reforms are passed to promote a freer press, international indicators of press freedom have declined in Mexico. The research uses interviews, a national survey, and focus groups to examine how media owners, media leaders, and reporters understand the role of the press and press freedom in Mexico since the transition in 2000.

Camaradas: nueva historia del comunismo en México. See *HLAS 76:2239.*

804 **El cambio democrático en México: retos y posibilidades de la "Cuarta Transformación".** Coordinación de John M. Ackerman. Presentación de Enrique Graue Wiechers. Prólogo por Alberto Vital. Prefacio de Pedro Salmerón y Halina Gutiérrez. Con la colaboración de Immanuel Maurice Wallerstein *et al.* Ciudad de México: Siglo Veintiuno Editores: UNAM: Instituto Nacional de Estudios Históricos de las Revoluciones de México, 2019. 853 p.: bibl. (El mundo del siglo XXI. Sociología y política)

Ackerman, a close political ally of President López Obrador, critiques liberal democracy and promotes a more "authentic" democracy. He rejects classic definitions of democracy that are built on liberal principles, but offers no alternative definition, and seems to prefer to conceive of democracy as the "voice of the people." He argues that institutions are less important than social movements and citizen participation, and praises the centralization of power as "democratic hegemony." The volume brings together papers from two international conferences in 2018. It includes a wide range of contributions from an interdisciplinary group of scholars and political officials. The book is divided into sections that address the quality of democracy in Mexico and the weaknesses that led to the election of López Obrador, the role of social movements, US-Mexico relations, and human rights.

805 **Camp, Roderic Ai.** Cabinet leadership: does it mirror democratic change in Mexico? (*Lat. Am. Polit. Soc.*, 60:2, Summer 2018, p. 83–102, bibl., tables)

Did the PRI's return to the presidency mean a return to the patterns of elite recruitment that dominated before the transition to democracy? Or are changing patterns of elite recruitment a consequence of competitive politics rather than partisan preferences? Camp provides an answer to these questions by comparing the backgrounds of cabinet members in Peña Nieto's cabinet with those from previous eras. He finds that Peña Nieto's cabinet reflected similar changes seen during the 12 years of PAN rule. Some trends even deepened from 2012–2016: more cabinet members attended private schools, and electoral careers continue to be important for cabinet members. A record 22 percent of Peña Nieto's cabinet members had served as governors. This article provides a rich set of data about cabinet members from 2012–2016 and offers a useful analysis of the impact of democratization on political recruitment.

806 **Camp, Roderic Ai and Shannan Mattiace.** Politics in Mexico: the path of a new democracy. Seventh Edition. New York, N.Y.: Oxford University Press, 2019. 395 p.: bibl., index.

The seventh edition of Roderic Camp's classic text on Mexican politics brings on a new co-author, Shannan Mattiace. This new edition focuses on the challenges of building democracy in Mexico, where criminal violence and corruption have eroded the legitimacy of democratic institutions. It includes new public opinion data and enhanced attention to social movements. Given the dramatic increase in organized crime and violence, the authors provide much greater analysis of drug trafficking organizations and the role of the military in fighting organized crime. They also make use of extensive interviews with leading politicians, all of which are available to view for free on Oxford University Press' YouTube channel "Democratizing Mexico's Politics." This book remains the go-to reference for students wanting to learn how the Mexican political system works.

807 **Cansino Ortiz, César and Faustino Pérez Morales.** Durmiendo con el enemigo: alianzas partidistas ideológicamente inconsistentes de México. Ciudad de México: Cepcom, 2017. 472 p.: bibl.

The authors of this book examine the increasingly common phenomena of electoral alliances among parties with very different ideological positions. The authors argue that "ideologically inconsistent party alliances" are most likely to succeed when their main adversary has ruled for a long time and has strongly concentrated power. This difficulty of dislodging a powerful adversary provides a justification for the alliance between incompatible ideologies. The alliance is also more likely to be successful if the candidate does not have strong ties to any of the parties in the alliance. The book includes a chapter outlining the legal status of electoral alliances in Mexico's electoral law since 1977. The final section provides case studies of ideologically inconsistent alliances in gubernatorial elections in 2010 in the states of Puebla, Oaxaca, Sinaloa, Hidalgo, and Durango.

808 **Cantú, Francisco.** The fingerprints of fraud: evidence from Mexico's 1988 presidential election. (*Am. Polit. Sci. Rev.,* 113:3, August 2019, p. 710–726, bibl.)

Francisco Cantú presents fascinating new evidence about fraud in the 1988 presidential elections. He uses computer image analysis to examine over 50,000 district tallies and identify examples of altered tallies. He finds that one-third of the tallies had "blatant alterations," suggesting aggregation fraud, in which district-level officials altered the tally sheets to bolster the votes of the incumbent party. A quantitative analysis of the altered tallies shows that polling stations with no opposition representatives and states where governors had electoral experience or were close allies of the incumbent party's presidential candidate were more likely to have altered tallies. This article is required reading for anyone interested in the mechanisms of electoral fraud generally or the specifics of Mexico's 1988 presidential elections.

809 **Casar, María Amparo** and **Luis Carlos Ugalde.** Dinero bajo la mesa: financiamiento y gasto ilegal de las campañas políticas en México. Coordinación de investigación por Ximena Mata Zenteno y Leonardo Núñez González. Ciudad de México: Penguin Random House Grupo Editorial, 2018. 341 p.: bibl., graphs, ill., maps.

These two leading scholars and anti-corruption activists (one a former director of the Federal Electoral Institute) argue that illegal financing of and spending on political campaigns are the worst problems facing democracy in Mexico. The book provides a history of campaign finance in Mexico, a detailed examination of electoral laws, and an analysis of data from electoral authorities on electoral irregularities and crimes. The final empirical chapter provides a detailed analysis of campaign spending in the 2018 elections, demonstrating the limited capacity of the electoral authorities to audit spending and the ineffectiveness of existing penalties for breaking campaign finance laws. While the authors acknowledge that illegal campaign donations by organized crime groups are a serious problem, the book focuses on the illegal diversion of public funds for political campaigns and illegal donations by businesses.

810 **La crisis de seguridad y violencia en México: causas, efectos y dimensiones del problema.** Coordinación por Carlos Antonio Flores Pérez. Ciudad de México: Centro de Investigaciones y Estudios Superiores en Antropología Social, 2018. 380 p.: bibl., ill., maps.

This edited volume argues that violence is the greatest challenge facing the Mexican state and seeks to provide a diagnostic analysis of Mexico's security crisis. The first chapter provides evidence of the magnitude of the crisis with data on crime and the justice system. Other chapters examine the role of the military and paramilitary forces in the security crisis. The second half of the book examines criminal violence in a number of states that have suffered especially high rates of organized crime.

811 **Defender al pueblo: autodefensas y policías comunitarias en México.** Coordinación de Antonio Fuentes Díaz y Daniele Fini. Puebla, Mexico: Benemérita Universidad Autónoma de Puebla, Instituto de Ciencias Sociales y Humanidades "Alfonso Vélez Pliego"; Ciudad de México: Ediciones del Lirio, 2018. 349 p.: bibl., ill., maps.

Various types of community security groups have become more active in many parts of Mexico, especially where organized crime groups are influential. These groups, often called *autodefensas,* are typically made up of armed citizens who come together to provide their own systems of justice. They carry out patrols, set up checkpoints, and detain alleged criminals. Estimates suggest that as many as 20,000 armed citizens work in networks of community security in each state. While some see these groups as vigilantes, this book argues that it is a form of popular resistance against the repression of the state and the neoliberal market. The book provides important interdisciplinary analysis of a range of different community defense organizations in Michoacán and Guerrero and examines the gray areas between legal and illegal; state, criminal, and community power; and violence and resistance.

Democracias posibles: crisis y resignificación: Sur de México y Centroamérica. See item **848**.

812   Devoto, Lisandro Martín and **Juan C. Olmeda.** "Juntos pero revueltos": estrategias electorales y coaliciones partidarias para la elección de diputados locales en los estados mexicanos (2000–2016). (*Colomb. Int.*, 90, abril/junio 2017, p. 157–187, bibl., graphs, tables)

Electoral alliances have become the norm in most Mexican elections since the transition to multiparty democracy in 2000. Most of the research to date has focused on alliances in gubernatorial elections. Many have assumed that other local elections would entail the same alliances as the state's gubernatorial election. Devoto and Olmeda find that is not necessarily the case. They use an original dataset of all electoral alliances for state legislators from 2000–2016 for a total of 180 elections. This remarkable set of data allows them to shed light on electoral alliances across districts and states over 16 years. They find that the PRI is the major party most likely to form alliances, whereas the PAN is the least likely. Though when the PAN does form alliances, it is most likely to ally with parties with opposite ideological preferences (what are sometimes called "unnatural alliances"). They find substantial cases of divergent alliances where different alliances are used in local legislative races than in the concurrent gubernatorial race. See also item **807**.

813   **Durán-Martínez, Angélica.** The politics of drug violence: criminals, cops, and politicians in Colombia and Mexico. New York, N.Y.: Oxford University Press, 2018. 308 p.: bibl., index.

Why do criminals sometimes seek to publicize violence and other times prefer to hide their violence? What explains variation in visibility of violence through time and across space? Durán-Martínez focuses on the local dynamics of drug violence and argues that violence emerges through the interaction between the state and organized crime. The cohesion of the state security apparatus and the level of competition in illegal drug markets determine the patterns of violence. The research compares the cities of Cali and Medellín in Colombia with Culiacán, Juárez, and Tijuana in Mexico. The data show that the frequency of violence increases as markets become more competitive, and the visibility of violence increases as the state security apparatus becomes fragmented. If the state is committed to either protecting or prosecuting organized crime, criminals have incentives to limit the visibility of violence. During periods of intense competition in drug markets, organized crime groups may outsource violence to local gangs, thereby losing control of discipline and often leading to spikes in violence. The subnational comparative research design, including municipalities across international borders, provides an important new strategy for analyzing organized crime and violence.

814   **Las elecciones críticas de 2018: un balance de los procesos electorales federales y locales en México.** Coordinación de Oniel Francisco Díaz Jiménez, Vanessa Góngora Cervantes y Miguel Vilches Hinojosa. Guanajuato, Mexico: Universidad de Guanajuato; Ciudad de México: Grañén Porrúa, 2019. 384 p.: bibl., ill. (Pensamiento y ciencias sociales)

As the title suggests, this book argues that the presidential elections of 2018 were critical elections with important ramifications for Mexico's future. The coordinators define critical elections as characterized by a great transformation of the electoral system, electoral behavior, and the base of support for parties. Chapters by leading social scientists examine the collapse of the party system in 2018, the return of a strong president with majority control of the legislature, gender parity in the cabinet and legislature, the extraterritorial vote and the youth vote. Two chapters provide a worthwhile comparison of elections in Guanajuato, where the PAN has dominated elections since the 1990s, and the state of Mexico, where the PRI had been able maintain control, never losing a gubernatorial election until 2023.

815   **Espinoza Valle, Víctor Alejandro.** La alternancia interrumpida: dos décadas de elecciones en Baja California. Monterrey, Mexico: Universidad Autónoma de Nuevo León: Editorial La Quincena, 2018. 246 p.: bibl., ill.

Bringing together a number of previously published papers, this edited volume examines elections in the state of Baja California from 1989 when Baja California elected the first opposition governor in the country until 2010. Electoral politics in Baja California have been characterized by the early victory of the rightist opposition to one-party rule, the development of a strong bipartisan dynamic of the PAN versus the PRI, the weakness of the left, and high rates of voter abstention. The authors examine local and state elections and provide detailed electoral data from the state.

816   **Flores-Macías, Gustavo A.** The consequences of militarizing anti-drug efforts for state capacity in Latin America: evidence from Mexico. (*Comp. Polit./New York*, 51:1, Oct. 2018, p. 1–20, bibl., graph, table)

Does militarization of antidrug trafficking efforts affect state capacity? Flores-Macías addresses this question by examining the impact of Mexico's militarization of drug enforcement starting in 2006. He argues that militarization weakens state capacity to ensure public safety and extract resources through taxation because militaries tend to escalate violence and lack the experience of traditional law enforcement in controlling crime. Moreover, when the militarized strategy fails to provide public security, public discontent and rising rates of extortion by organized crime groups are likely to decrease the government's ability to collect taxes. These expectations are tested with a subnational comparison of states where the military was deployed and states without militarization. The author also creates a synthetic model to predict what might have happened in the absence of militarization. The data show that militarization decreased state capacity in terms of public safety and resource extraction. This article provides important new theoretical and empirical insights into the consequences of law enforcement strategies that rely on the use of the military.

817   **El futuro de México al 2035: una visión prospectiva.** Coordinación de Manuel Perló Cohen y Silvia Inclán Oseguera. Contribuciones de Javier Aguilar García *et al.* Ciudad de México: Instituto de Investigaciones Sociales, UNAM, 2018. 804 p.: bibl., ill., maps.

The editors of this volume bring together a group of leading social scientists to consider possible scenarios for Mexico in the year 2035. They provide insight into the problems and potential solutions for Mexico's future. Chapters examine urban issues of transportation and housing; policy issues such as electoral reform, corruption, violence, Indigenous people, Catholic Church, higher education, labor unions; and transnational issues such as telecommunications, agriculture, environment, relations with the US, and nationalism. This collective research project provides a useful opportunity to reflect on the choices that Mexico faces today and how policy decisions might play out in the future. The essays should be of value to anyone interested in public policy in Mexico.

818   **Garrido de Sierra, Sebastián.** La reforma definitiva: un análisis de por qué y cómo la reforma electoral de 1996 desencadenó la caída del régimen priista. Ciudad de México: Centro de Investigación y Docencia Económicas, 2019. 210 p.: bibl., ill. (Investigación e ideas)

Garrido de Sierra argues that the electoral reform of 1996 is the definitive reform that brought down the PRI's hegemonic one-party system. The 1996 reform created a much more equal playing field for opposition parties, especially in terms of campaign finance. It created an autonomous electoral institute and electoral courts to adjudicate electoral conflicts. The changes, according to Garrido de Sierra, made it less risky for mid- and upper-level members of the PRI to leave the party and join opposition parties, bringing their clientelist networks with them and eroding the clientelist base of the PRI. The research includes original new datasets of PRI defections. The empirical sections show that after the reforms, members of the PRI were much more likely to defect to opposition parties, and the opposition parties who accepted the defectors benefitted electorally. The volume also includes data from interviews with leading officials responsible for the 1996 reform. This book offers a rigorous new explanation of the transition to democracy.

819   Garza Zepeda, Manuel. Insurrección, fiesta y construcción de otro mundo en las luchas de la APPO: Oaxaca 2006–2010. Oaxaca de Juárez, Mexico: Universidad Autónoma Benito Juárez de Oaxaca, Instituto de Investigaciones Sociológicas; Ciudad de México: Juan Pablos Editor, 2016. 276 p.: bibl.

In 2006 and 2007 massive protests erupted in the southern state of Oaxaca in response to the repressive and corrupt administration of the governor. In an effort to understand the meaning of what people do when they protest, Zepeda focuses on the festive, creative, artistic quality of the Oaxaca protests. He critiques the resource mobilization and new social movement approaches to theorizing collective action and instead argues for the centrality of class struggle for understanding the Oaxaca insurrection. He frames the fiestas as struggle and sees the barricades that were erected throughout the city during the uprising not as defensive positions, but rather as spaces for creating community. This book provides useful insights into the Oaxaca protests and the creative and artistic expression of political movements.

820   Género y políticas públicas: retos y oportunidades para la transversalidad en Nuevo León. Coordinación de Silvia López Estrada. Tijuana, Mexico: El Colegio de la Frontera Norte, 2017. 338 p.

This book examines the process of gender mainstreaming in the state of Nuevo León. The Instituto Nacional de Mujeres (INMUJERES) is charged with developing strategies to bring gender equality to all governing institutions. The state of Nuevo León commissioned a group of gender scholars to analyze the status of gender mainstreaming in state institutions focused on welfare, youth, transportation, transparency, public works, and security. This book presents the findings of that research project, which suggest there is still work needed to achieve gender mainstreaming throughout the state. It provides a useful example of how to evaluate gender mainstreaming projects on the ground.

821   Grecko, Témoris. Killing the story: journalists risking their lives to uncover the truth in Mexico. Translated from the Spanish by Diane Stockwell. New York, N.Y.: The New Press, 2020. 243 p.: bibl.

A journalist himself, Grecko examines the entrenched practices of censorship and the shockingly high numbers of journalists killed or harassed during the Peña Nieto presidency (2012–2018). Drawing attention to the dangerous and essential work of journalists and highlighting the crucial role of a free press in building a stable democracy and maintaining the rule of law, each chapter tells the story of an individual journalist who was killed or censored by the government. Grecko provides an engaging and personal perspective on the extraordinarily high cost of Mexico's violence and corruption for journalists. The stories also expose the corruption of some journalists who are compromised by those in power and do the bidding of corrupt leaders.

822   Hernández Rodríguez, Rogelio. El oficio político: la élite gobernante en México (1946–2020). Ciudad de México: El Colegio de México; Centro de Estudios Internacionales, 2021. 295 p.: bibl., tables.

The title of the book, *El oficio político*, is perhaps best translated as "the craft of politics," but also refers to politics as a professional career or trade. Hernández Rodríguez argues that politicians need both a vocation for politics and the skills to accomplish their goals. This comprehensive analysis of Mexico's political elites compares the profession of politics during the one-party rule of the PRI, during the transition to multiparty democracy (1982–2000), and during the era of multiparty democracy (2000–2018). The research is based on extensive interviews with leading politicians, including Dulce María Sauri, Manuel Bartlett, and Porfirio Muñoz Ledo. Hernández Rodríguez argues that the traditional PRI political elite created basic institutions that allowed for stability and economic development in the 20th century. The technocratic elite that governed after the economic collapse of the late 1970s and early 1980s modernized and restructured the economy. In contrast to the politicians of these earlier eras, President López Obrador's purpose is not to govern, but to fight for an idea, and as result he has been unable to build institutions that promote national well-being.

823   Horta Cruz, Juan and **Sabás Aburto Espinobarro.** CRAC-PC: el origen de la policía comunitaria: Montaña y Costa Chica de Guerrero. Ciudad de México: publisher not identified, 2016. 407 p.: bibl., ill., maps.

Written by two activists who have been a part of the community policing movement for many years, this book provides a history of the Coordinadora Regional de Autoridades Comunitarias—Policía Comunitaria (CRAC-PC), a group of mostly Indigenous communities in the Montaña and Costa Chica area of the state of Guerrero that formed self-defense organizations to protect themselves from government repression and criminal violence. Scholars have argued that these groups have been important in reducing violence from organized crime in Indigenous communities. The book traces the origins of community policing back to the organization of coffee producers in the 1980s. Based on the personal experience of the authors, the study provides a very important perspective on the history of community policing in southern Mexico.

824   Inclán, María. Mexican movers and shakers: protest mobilization and political attitudes in Mexico City. (*Lat. Am. Polit. Soc.*, 61:1, Feb. 2019, p. 78–100, bibl., tables)

Utilizing an innovative methodological approach, Inclán analyzes survey data from six protests in Mexico City from 2012–2013. The data are gathered at protests and include both protest participants and bystanders. Protest bystanders provide a useful control group for comparing protest participants. The data show how various factors motivate participation in different types of protests. They confirm that more politically engaged and resourceful people tend to participate in protests, but also demonstrate the diversity of mobilized voices in Mexico's civil society. The data also show that there are similarities between contentious politics in wealthier democracies and contentious politics in less wealthy, newer democracies such as Mexico.

825   Integridad electoral: México en perspectiva global. Edición de Irma Méndez de Hoyos, Ferrán Martínez i Coma y Nicolás Loza Otero. Ciudad de México: FLACSO México, 2019. 311 p.: bibl., ill., maps. (Debate renovado)

Using data from the Perceptions of Electoral Integrity (PEI) survey of elections experts, the contributors to this volume examine election integrity in Mexico in a comparative context. The leaders of the PEI survey, Pippa Norris and Ferrán Martínez, contribute chapters. The book analyzes data from Mexico's subnational PEI survey and includes comparative chapters with PEI data from Russia and India. The chapters on Mexico focus on campaign finance and subnational elections. This book provides important insights into electoral integrity in Mexico's subnational units. It will be of great interest to anyone studying the quality of democracy in Mexico.

826   Ley, Sandra; Shannan Mattiace; and **Guillermo Trejo.** Indigenous resistance to criminal governance: why regional ethnic autonomy institutions protect communities from narco rule in Mexico. (*LARR*, 54:1, April 2019, p. 181–199, bibl., tables)

Under what circumstances are Indigenous communities better able to resist narco penetration? Comparing Indigenous communities in Chihuahua and Guerrero, two areas with high levels of drug trafficking, this article seeks to explain why Indigenous communities in Guerrero have been much more effective in protecting themselves from drug violence. They find that when communities have a history of Indigenous social mobilization that brings people together to form translocal networks and regional ethnic institutions, they are more able to resist narco rule. This article provides important new insights into Indigenous politics and drug violence.

827 Magaloni, Beatriz et al. Living in fear: the dynamics of extortion in Mexico's drug war. (*Comp. Polit. Stud.*, 53:7, June 2020, p. 1124–1174, bibl., graphs, maps, tables)

Why do drug trafficking organizations sometimes target civilians with extortion and other times provide assistance to civilians living in areas they control? The authors use a survey with a list experiment to generate data on the prevalence of extortion and assistance from drug trafficking organizations. The evidence suggests that in areas where drug trafficking organizations maintain a monopoly, civilians are targeted less and provided more assistance than in areas where organized crime groups are violently competing to control territory. The authors also find that rates of extortion are higher when organized crime groups collaborate with the state actors and where crime groups are decentralized and unstable. This important paper will be of interest to anyone seeking to understand violence in Mexico.

828 Magaloni, Beatriz et al. Public good provision and traditional governance in Indigenous communities in Oaxaca, Mexico. (*Comp. Polit. Stud.*, 52:12, July 2018, p. 1841–1880, bibl.)

The authors examine *usos y costumbres*, the traditional practices of political governance used in some Indigenous communities. They ask if these traditional governance methods produce more effective provision of local public goods than multiparty elections. They find higher rates of political participation, residents more knowledgeable about politics, and municipal presidents more committed to their constituents in towns governed by *usos y costumbres*. These communities also do a better job providing water and sewage to their populations than those where mayors are chosen in multiparty elections.

829 Masferrer K., Elio. Lo religioso dentro de lo político: las elecciones de México 2018. Buenos Aires: Libros de la Araucaria, 2018. 149 p.: bibl., ill., index.

Using data from various public opinion polls, Masferrer Kan examines the role of religion in the 2018 presidential elections. The first section provides qualitative descriptions of many different religious groups and compares their beliefs and political actions. The second section compares voting behavior and political preferences between Catholics and non-Catholics. Case studies of Veracruz and Yucatán further explore the role of religion and elections. The appendix includes declarations of religious groups regarding the 2018 elections.

830 Medina Martínez, Fuensanta. El largo y sinuoso camino de la lucha contra el narcotráfico. San Luis Potosí, Mexico: El Colegio de San Luis; Tijuana, Mexico: El Colegio de la Frontera Norte, 2018. 172 p.: bibl. (Colección Investigaciones. Estudios políticos e internacionales)

Written by a former career foreign service officer, this book seeks to develop a new understanding of national security after the fall of the Berlin Wall, as drug trafficking became central to Mexico's foreign affairs and its relationship with the US. Medina Martínez provides an overview of the history of Mexican foreign policy and a comparison of drug trafficking in Colombia and Mexico focusing on Plan Colombia and Plan Mérida. Plan Colombia drew Colombia closer to the US and forced Colombian foreign policy into the shadows of US interests. Similarly, Plan Mérida brought the unprecedented influence of US intelligence into the Mexican government. But in contrast to Colombia, Calderón's war on drugs helped to discredit the Mexican military forces and did little to accomplish its goals.

831 Monreal Ávila, Ricardo. Poder legislativo. Ciudad de México: M.A. Porrua, 2020. 581 p.: bibl., ill.

Written by the former governor of Zacatecas and president of the governing Morena party in the Senate, this book begins with an historical overview of the legislative branch of government in Mexico. Multiple chapters provide descriptions of the organization, functions, and formal processes of the legislature. This book will serve as a useful reference for Mexico's national legislature.

832 **Mujeres y participación política: proceso electoral 2015-2016 de Aguascalientes.** Coordinación de Yolanda Franco Durán y Ricardo Alejandro Hernández Ramos. Toluca, Mexico: IEEM, Instituto Electoral del Estado de México, 2018. 246 p.: bibl., ill. (Política electoral incluyente; 6)

This edited volume examines women's representation in the state of Aguascalientes during the first electoral cycle after the 2014 constitutional amendment requiring gender parity in all legislatures. Chapters include an overview of women in power through history in Aguascalientes, an analysis of party activists, the results of the 2015-2016 elections, a discussion of female candidates in the media, and a report of gender violence in politics. The chapter by Diana Cristina Cárdenas Ornelas examines activists in each party and finds more female than male activists in every party in the state. The research provides an important assessment of women's political representation in the immediate aftermath of the gender parity reforms. It examines the ways in which gender inequality continues despite efforts for legal equality.

833 **Participación política indígena en México: experiencias de gestión comunitaria, participación institucional y consulta previa.** Coordinación de Claire Wright. San Pedro Garza García, Mexico: Universidad de Monterrey; Ciudad de México: Editorial Itaca, 2018. 283 p.: bibl.

The authors of this volume distinguish between two dimensions of the right to political participation for Indigenous people. The internal dimension relates to social and political organization and self-government within Indigenous communities. The external dimension reflects the relationship with the state outside of Indigenous communities, through institutions such as elections and political parties. Chapters examine internal dimensions of participation in communities in Oaxaca and Chiapas. Other chapters examine the external dimension in the Estado de México and also in terms of gender and international norms of consultation for Indigenous people. This book provides useful case studies of representation in the pluricultural context of Mexico.

834 **Petersen, German.** Elites and turnovers in authoritarian enclaves: evidence from Mexico. (*Lat. Am. Polit. Soc.*, 60:2, Summer 2018, p. 23-40, bibl., graphs, map, table)

In 2010, five states had gubernatorial elections in which the rightist PAN formed an alliance with left parties (Durango, Hidalgo, Oaxaca, Puebla, Sonora). In three of these five elections (Oaxaca, Puebla, Sonora), the opposition alliance won the election, marking the first partisan turnover in modern history in the state. In the other two (Durango and Hidalgo), the PRI managed to hold on to power. This article seeks to explain when an opposition alliance can turn out a hegemonic authoritarian party. The central finding is that opposition alliances are successful when the ruling party ruptures *and* when the opposition remains united.

835 **Política y elecciones en México: nuevas historias regionales, 1980-2015.** Coordinación de Marcela Bravo Ahuja. Ciudad de México: UNAM: Ediciones La Biblioteca, S.A. de C.V., 2017. 181 p.: bibl., ill.

Focusing on regional politics and elections, the authors of this edited volume trace the evolution of voting behavior over three decades in seven different Mexican states (Colima, Guerrero, Hidalgo, Nuevo León, Querétaro, San Luis Potosí, and Sonora). The authors show how defectors switching parties strengthened opposition parties. They examine models of retrospective voting that predict voting behavior based on the performance of incumbent governments. Local legislatures and general levels of violence emerge as key variables. Each chapter provides a close look at the elections of one state. The chapters provide detailed electoral data for each state in addition to a very useful overview of the state's recent political history.

836 **Price, Jessica J.** Keystone organizations versus clientelism: understanding protest frequency in Indigenous

southern Mexico. (*Comp. Polit.*/New York, 51:3, April 2019, p. 407–427, bibl., graph, table)

Price argues that protests are most likely in places where there are "keystone organizations." Keystone organizations are groups that have a disproportionate effect on the political environment by building networks to promote protest. Ethnic organizations and left parties are most likely to act as keystone organizations. She further argues that strong clientelist networks are likely to lower protest activities and instead funnel political participation into elections to serve the interests of the patron. She tests her model with an original dataset of protest activity during federal elections from 2000 to 2012 in Oaxaca, Chiapas, and Yucatán. This paper sheds important new light on Indigenous politics, protest movements, and clientelism.

837 **Puente Martínez, Khemvirg.** Cómo se decide el gasto público en México: congreso y proceso presupuestario durante la democratización (1994–2016). Ciudad de México: UNAM: Biblioteca Arte y Letras, 2017. 356 p.: bibl., ill.

Analyzing the changing role of the legislature in the budget process, Puente skillfully traces how the transition to democracy and the institutionalization of the national legislature transformed the budget process. During one-party authoritarianism, the executive controlled the budget. As multiparty democracy took root in the late 1990s and early 2000s, multiple parties vied for power in the national legislature and the legislature became increasingly professional and institutionalized. This development provided Congress with the capacity and incentive to participate fully in the budget process. Still, most of the executive's budgets since 1997 were passed with large majorities in the Chamber of Deputies. Puente argues that this result is because a "formalized clientelism" emerged as a mechanism to overcome ideological differences through the distribution of public funds. The process has shifted from opaque centralization dominated by the executive to a discretionary process, lacking accountability and controlled by the legislature. This book provides an extensive analysis of the institutionalization of the legislature from 1917–2010. It also clearly explains the budget-making process in the early democratic era (1997–2010). This study marshals an impressive array of institutional data and extensive interviews with legislative actors. Understanding how political systems determine the spending of public funds provides an essential view into the representation of political interests.

838 **Raymond, Christopher D.** and **Sergio Bárcena Juárez.** Constituency preferences and committee selection in the Mexican Cámara de Diputados. (*Lat. Am. Polit. Soc.*, 61:4, Nov. 2019, p. 95–117, bibl., tables)

This article examines the role played by parties in appointing members to legislative committees. The authors test theories of legislative behavior developed in US legislatures in a comparative context using data from the Mexican Chamber of Deputies. An important distinction between US legislatures and the Mexican legislature during the time period studied here is the prohibition on reelection and strong party discipline in Mexico. Mexican parties control the committee assignments and also exert substantial influence over the behavior of their members. The data analyzes deputies from 2006 to 2018 and finds that deputies are more likely to be assigned to committees whose mandates affect their constituents. Given the powerful role of parties in making committee assignments, the authors argue that their analysis provides evidence that parties use committee assignments to enhance their parties' electoral prospects.

Ristow, Colby. A revolution unfinished: the Chegomista rebellion and the limits of revolutionary democracy in Juchitán, Oaxaca. See *HLAS 76:392.*

839 **Rodríguez Sánchez Lara, Gerardo.** Seguridad nacional en México y sus problemas estructurales. Prólogo de John Bailey. San Andrés Cholula, Mexico: UDLAP; Ciudad de México: CASEDE, Colectivo de Análisis de la Seguridad con Democracia, 2017. 237 p.: bibl., ill., index.

Why is inter-agency coordination among national security, intelligence, and defense institutions so difficult to achieve? How can it be improved? Rodríguez Sánchez Lara argues that coordination among the police, military, intelligence, and justice agencies is inhibited by power maximization, the nature of the organizations, the decentralized democratic system, and a pathological culture. Data come from interviews with people who have worked in security agencies, professors who have taught for many years in military academies, and analysis of WikiLeaks documents from the US Embassy in Mexico City. The appendix includes full transcripts of the interviews, which may be useful for other scholars investigating these topics. The research draws attention to the importance of the legislature for making laws to regulate security agencies and the judiciary for enforcing the laws to avoid abuse of power. The author offers policy proposals for improving inter-agency coordination.

840 **Rodríguez Sumano, Abelardo.** México en el mundo: entre el peligro y la emergencia, desafíos y propuestas a la seguridad nacional. Ciudad de México: Universidad Iberoamericana: Editarte Publicaciones, 2019. 211 p.: bibl.

An authoritarian form of national security prevailed in Mexico during the 20th century, dominated by corruption and impunity. While scholars generally consider Mexico to have transitioned to democracy with the 2000 presidential transition from the PRI to the PAN, Rodríguez Sumano contends that an authoritarian form of national security continued through the presidencies of Vicente Fox, Felipe Calderón, and Enrique Peña Nieto. Democratic regimes tend to pursue a national security strategy focused on foreign policy, while authoritarian security strategies are largely domestic, focusing on the "enemy within." The book urges the López Obrador administration to reorient its national security strategy to a global perspective, including the national security risks posed to Mexico by the Trump administration and global warming.

841 **Seguridad y construcción de ciudadanía: perspectivas locales, discusiones globales.** Coordinación de Alfonso Valenzuela Aguilera. Ciudad de México: Bonilla Artigas Editores; Cuernavaca, Mexico: Universidad Autónoma del Estado de Morelos, 2019. 385 p.: bibl., ill., maps. (Pública social; 30)

This edited volume examines the relationship between citizenship and security. Fifteen chapters by an array of interdisciplinary scholars and public officials examine how the construction of citizenship and participatory engagement with the state and community influence violence and the rule of law in Mexico. Includes case studies of Acapulco and Monterrey.

842 **Sentido y tendencias de la transformación en México.** Coordinación de José Luis Cisneros, Martín Gabriel Barrón Cruz y José Antonio Parra Molina. Tlaxcala de Xicohténcatl, Mexico: Universidad Autónoma de Tlaxcala, 2019. 353 p.: bibl., ill. (Colección Temas estratégicos)

Written six months into the term of the new presidential administration of Andrés Manuel López Obrador, this book provides an early assessment of the "Fourth Transformation." The book brings together scholars from across the country to examine the meaning of Morena's rise to power. Chapters focus on social programs as well as security policy and the continued militarization of the fight against organized crime. This research provides a useful assessment of the López Obrador administration before the onset of the COVID-19 pandemic.

843 **Trejo, Guillermo** and **Sandra Ley.** Votes, drugs, and violence: the political logic of criminal wars in Mexico. New York, N.Y.: Cambridge University Press, 2020. 324 p.: bibl., index. (Cambridge studies in comparative politics)

This pathbreaking book employs the subnational comparative method to determine the causes of Mexico's dramatic increase in organized crime and violence. They point to state gubernatorial power, state judicial police, and state attorneys general as the central locus for determining drug violence. Security officers from authoritarian regimes were crucial players in the development of criminal networks. In states where the ruling party lost power, these officers were removed from their positions and state attorneys general were replaced. As a result, the state withdrew its protection of the cartels, so cartels armed themselves and went to war with each other. Patterns of intergovernmental cooperation and conflict help to explain the geographic distribution of violence. Where municipal, state, and federal authorities are all from the same party, there is less violence. When different levels of government are controlled by different parties, there is less coordinated action among security agencies and therefore more violence. The authors use an original databank of newspaper-reported intercartel murders, interviews with opposition governors, and comparative case studies of Baja California, Chihuahua, and Michoacán. This book provides the most comprehensive and methodologically sophisticated analysis of drug violence available.

844 **Las violencias: en busca de la política pública detrás de la guerra contra las drogas.** Edición de Laura H. Atuesta y Alejandro Madrazo Lajous. Con la colaboración de Brian T. Anderson et al. Ciudad de México: Centro de Investigación y Docencia Económicas, 2018. 234 p.: bibl., ill., maps. (Coyuntura y ensayo)

An examination of the drug policy during the Calderón presidency, this interdisciplinary, multimethod investigation begins by explaining that there was very little social science research on Mexico's drug policy before Calderón's drug war began in 2006. The research focuses on coercion as the central thread for understanding drug policy. Atuesta argues that Calderón did not have a formal policy, just an intention to put violence at the center of the government's response. Wide-ranging chapters focus on topics such as the disinformation of government statistics, the relationship between the drug trade and deforestation, case studies of drug addicts, and militarization and the increase in violence in areas where the military is deployed. There is also an analysis of the Ley de Narcomenudeo, which delegated responsibility for federal drug crimes to the states and decriminalized small amounts of drugs. The research makes use of the database created by the Centro de Investigación y Docencia Económicas (CIDE) Programa de Política de Drogas (PPD).

845 **¿Y ahora que?: México ante el 2018.** Coordinación de Héctor Aguilar Camín et al. Con la colaboración de Pedro Arturo Aguirre et al. Ciudad de México: Debate, 2018. 466 p.

Edited by a prominent journalist and public intellectual, this volume examines major problems that Mexico faced in the run-up to the 2018 presidential elections. Thirty-three short and accessible chapters written by leading public officials and academics analyze and provide possible solutions for challenges related to corruption and rule of law, democracy and governability, insecurity, poverty and inequality, and Mexico's position in the world. Each chapter provides a brief overview of a problem and concludes with three proposals to address it.

846 **Zárate, Alfonso. La generación de 1994 que marcó historia: Grupo San Ángel.** Ciudad de México: Planeta, 2019. 364 p.: bibl., ill.

Written by a member of the Grupo San Ángel, this book provides a first-hand account of the role of this group of scholars and political leaders in the elections of 1994. Jorge G. Castañeda and Carlos Fuentes brought the group together in the run-up to the presidential elections in an attempt to promote a democratic and peaceful electoral process. The book provides a description of each meeting and includes documents and publications from the group, including photographs and a list of the members with a summary of each of their professional trajectories. This a useful compilation of documents and memories from a political insider about a consequential year in Mexico's history.

CENTRAL AMERICA

CHARLES D. BROCKETT, *Professor Emeritus of Political Science, Sewanee: The University of the South*

THE TIME PERIOD COVERED by publications in this *HLAS* volume has been marked by serious setbacks for democracy and human rights throughout much of Central America. Consequently, the scholarship assessed here reflects the usual split between the more encouraging performance of Costa Rica and Panama on one side, and the more problematic political life of El Salvador, Guatemala, Honduras, and Nicaragua on the other (with too little scholarship on Belize to make a judgement). The present-day situation is captured well by the most recent book on Central America from Vanderbilt University's Latin American Public Opinion Project (LAPOP) (item **911**). The volume's specific focus is the 2018/2019 AmericasBarometer public opinion survey results for Nicaragua, but also includes substantial comparisons to all countries of the Americas. The surveys show that support for democracy is the lowest for the entire Americas in Guatemala and Honduras (item **850**). In contrast, Costa Rica has the second highest score for political tolerance, along with the highest average level of system support. Similarly, merging two leading indices of the quality of democracy as evaluated by experts finds Costa Rica at the top (with Chile and Uruguay) but Guatemala, Honduras, and Nicaragua at the bottom (with Haiti and Venezuela not included). Furthermore, the scores for each of the three have deteriorated since 2016.

On a more encouraging note, the scholarship on the region is impressive, with more solid examples of rigorous social science compared with publications of the past decade. Also worthy of note is the importance of two broader projects to scholarship on the region. The first is the continuing work of LAPOP, which has been crucial for understanding political opinion trends and their determinants across the Americas. In addition to the aforementioned book on Nicaragua, LAPOP has also released books on El Salvador (item **870**) and Guatemala (item **881**). In addition, AmericasBarometer data was used by at least five journal articles in this survey (items **850**, **858**, **895**, **903**, and **912**). Another promising project is the Central America Monitor, a collaborative effort between the Washington Office on Latin America (WOLA) and local human rights partners in El Salvador, Guatemala, and Honduras. The project produces accurate and objective data and information related to the rule of law for the Northern Triangle countries. Several reports covering the 2014–2017 period have already been released, three of which are included in this section (items **864**, **885**, and **891**).

The most disheartening situation has been in Nicaragua. The Inter-American Commission on Human Rights (item **913**) offers a clear description of the 2018 mass protests against the regime of Daniel Ortega, along with another work that provides ample documentation of the regime's widespread use of excessive force to repress the protests (item **921**). Among several publications that explain how the regime weathered the crisis, perhaps the best is Martí i Puig and Serra's account (item **914**), which draws on a variety of theoretical works to clarify Ortega's creation and consolidation of his personalistic authoritarian regime. Crucial was maintaining the support of patronage networks and especially the security forces (item **909**), with Ruhl (item **922**) providing a close examination of the steps by which the security forces were bound to Ortega before the crisis erupted. Ortega's character and ambition were forged long before his return to power in 2007. Few have better insight into the politician than Nicaraguan journalist Medina Sánchez, who has written a fascinating account (item **915**) of those earlier years. Equally captivating is Mosinger's (item **917**) evidence that the drive for dominance goes back to the earliest factional divides among Sandinista revolutionary leadership.

Many of these dynamics have been paralleled in Honduras, although less intensely. Mass protests followed the flawed election results of late 2017, which were met by regime violence. Another report by the Inter-American Commission on Human Rights (item **904**) details these events, placing them in the broader context of the continuing murders of journalists and human rights activists, usually with impunity (on this topic, see also item **907**). One of the most notorious of these cases is that of the well-known Indigenous activist Berta Cáceres. Her life, work, and murder are ably placed in their broader context by journalist Lakhani (item **905**), who also closely followed the trials that convicted her assassins. An additional challenge facing Honduras is widespread corruption. The impact of corruption on citizens' trust is put to the empirical test in Estrada and Bastida's (item **903**) well-executed examination at the municipal level. On a positive note, a large amount of land has been titled to Indigenous communities in Honduras since 2012. Based on elite interviews, Altamirano (item **901**) argues that this action was primarily done to serve the regime's security and patrimonial interests. Although President Juan Orlando Hernández was able to extend his tenure through questionable maneuvers in 2017, unlike Nicaragua's Ortega, he failed at regime consolidation when the opposition emerged victorious in the 2021 elections.

Corruption and the weakness of the rule of law continue to be the major issues in Guatemala, as well as the focus of much of the relevant scholarship. There were positive developments during this period, many of them detailed by two publications from the Central America Monitor Project—one on strengthening the judicial system (item **891**) and the other on combatting corruption (item **885**). The period began in 2015 when massive anticorruption protests brought down the government (item **880**). A significant highlight was the 2018 conviction of four senior military leaders for crimes against humanity during the civil war (item **884**). Such accomplishments registered with the public: the AmericasBarometer survey found that the percentage of the population with a lot of confidence in the ability of the judicial system to punish the guilty doubled from 2014 to 2017 (item **881**). However, this is only a partial picture of accountability. A former judge now in exile testifies to corrupt intervention in the judicial selection process (item **887**). Application of a new law criminalizing violence against women varies substantially according to class, ethnicity, and place lived (item **882**). And the two most recent presidential administrations have undermined some of the most important criminal justice advances of the immediate past (item **883**). On a different note, using case studies of Guatemalan peasant organizations, Granovsky-Larsen (item **890**) effectively explores the age-old challenge for social movements: how to gain concessions from the system without compromising their transformational potential.

A notable example of a successful social movement occurred in 2017 when El Salvador became the first country to legally ban all forms of metallic mining.

Drawing on interviews with participants, field observation, and social movement literature, two fine studies explain how this historic victory occurred (items **865** and **876**). A different type of state-social actor interaction, though, is the primary focus of the scholarship on El Salvador surveyed for this section. How the government should respond to the gangs that pervade society and the widespread violence associated with them has dominated the Salvadoran political agenda for years. Martínez-Reyes and Navarro-Pérez (item **872**) identify four phases in government policy towards gangs from 2003 to 2019 and find that each was ultimately unsuccessful. The period receiving the most scholarly attention is the truce between the state and gangs during 2012–2013—both how the truce came about and why it did not last (items **866**, **867**, **871**, and **874**). Córdova undertakes a unique approach, providing the first systematic statistical analysis for Latin America of the impact of gang dominance on political participation (item **869**). More broadly, one LAPOP study (item **870**) includes a chapter that examines public attitudes towards citizen security and violence prevention. A powerful volume about the violence of the earlier civil war period (item **878**) gives ample voice to the victims of state repression while making a strong case for restorative justice, including reparations.

Reflecting its greater social stability and democratic consolidation, the contributions on Costa Rica are more concerned with elections and electoral behavior, along with the functioning of government institutions. Perelló and Navia (item **858**) provide a well-executed analysis of both election results and public opinion trends for the 1958–2018 period to effectively argue that 2002 was a critical realigning election. Two studies examine the 2018 elections (items **854** and **859**), with the unique role religion played receiving special attention. At that time, the outgoing administration of Luis Guillermo Solís was a minority government that faced substantial social protests. Yet it also gained notable legislative successes for reasons well examined in a set of works (items **853**, **857**, and **862**). Turning to the Supreme Court (as well as the Comptroller General and the Ombudsman), Solís Avendaño's (item **861**) extensive research assesses the impact of reforms in the selection process used for its members.

Little relevant scholarship concerns Belize and Panama, but what does exist is often of high quality. Young (item **852**) takes a theory about election outcomes developed from the US experience and tests it with the case of Belize. Meanwhile for Panama, Conniff and Bigler (item **925**) have produced an outstanding book on the country's political history focusing on the post-1989 invasion period.

GENERAL

847 **Democracia y política en la Centroamérica del siglo XXI.** Coordinación de Nayar López Castellanos. Ciudad de México: UNAM: Biblioteca, Arte y Letras, 2016. 263 p.: bibl.

The chapters in the first section of this edited volume, several by leading scholars of Central America, explore political themes within the region. Their general orientation is captured by a subheading and a subtitle from two of the chapters: "neoliberal failure" and "after peace came violence." Each chapter of the second section focuses on individual countries. Although none break new ground, most provide a good summary of the political history of recent decades.

848 **Democracias posibles: crisis y resignificación: Sur de México y Centroamérica.** Coordinación de María del Carmen

García Aguilar, Jesús Solís Cruz, y Pablo Uc. Tuxtla Gutiérrez, Mexico: Universidad de Ciencias y Artes de Chiapas; San Cristóbal de las Casas, Mexico: Centro de Estudios Superiores de México y Centroamérica, Observatorio de las Democracias: Sur de México y Centroamérica, 2016. 366 p.: bibl., ill., maps.

This edited volume addresses southern Mexico and the Northern Triangle of Central America based on work presented at a series of conferences at the Universidad de Ciencias y Artes de Chiapas. The primary purpose of the volume is to critically examine the functioning of liberal democracy in the region. To accomplish this goal, general theoretical chapters along with others look more concretely at the experience of individual countries and states. The second purpose is a "counterhegemonic" one: to raise up alternative conceptions of democracy, intended as both resistance and challenge.

849 Van den Berk, Jorrit. Becoming a good neighbor among dictators: the U.S. Foreign Service in Guatemala, El Salvador, and Honduras. Cham, Switzerland: Palgrave Macmillan, 2018. 336 p.: bibl., graphs, ill., index, map.

The author, a Dutch North American studies scholar, has pored over a prodigious amount of US State Department documents to provide an in-depth and well-written examination of the implementation of US foreign policy in the Northern Triangle countries of Central America from 1930–52 with a focus on US Foreign Service personnel in the region. At the heart of the study is the tension that often developed between democratic principles and the application of the Good Neighbor Policy of non-intervention or forming relations with dictators to combat the spread of fascism or communism. This nuanced study finds variation with both place and time.

850 Velásquez Pérez, Luis Guillermo. Centroamérica: el apoyo oscilante a democracias en convulsión entre 1996 y 2018. (*Anu. Estud. Centroam.*, 46, 2020, p. 1–41, bibl., tables)

This article presents the trends in response to three questions concerning support for democracy and authoritarianism from the AmericasBarometer survey for the years 1996–2018. Support for both regime types is lower for each country at the end of the period than at the beginning. The author presents a useful discussion relating changes across the period to major political events and dynamics in each country. He also draws on a wide range of relevant scholarship.

BELIZE

851 Warnecke-Berger, Hannes. Politics and violence in Central America and the Caribbean. New York, N.Y.: Springer Science+Business Media, 2018. 281 p.: bibl.

This book's most important contribution is its chapter that provides a solid overview of contemporary Belize, especially the impact of its urban gangs. Overall, the book offers a comparative study of Belize with two other countries of the region also with very high levels of violence: El Salvador and Jamaica. Less successful is its primary objective to explain different forms of violence by developing a relational understanding of violence that combines political economy and cultural approaches. For an additional review of the book, see *HLAS 75:1020*.

852 Young, Harold A. A comparative look at success in regional party politics: US electoral prediction models in the case of Belize. (*J. Global South Stud.*, 36:2, Fall 2019, p. 341–367, tables)

This is a well-executed quantitative study testing whether a theory about election outcomes developed from the US experience applies in the very different case of Belize. The answer is yes. Despite the enormous differences between the two countries, they use the same electoral system for their national legislatures. This study shows that candidates in Belize with greater political experience are more likely to win compared to their less experienced opponents, just as in the US. An additional finding is that this advantage is greater for candidates from the opposition party.

COSTA RICA

853 Alvarado Alcázar, Alejandro and Gloriana Martínez Sánchez. De la calle a la mesa: acciones de protesta y

oportunidades políticas en el gobierno de Luis Guillermo Solís (2014-2018). (*Rev. Cienc. Soc./San José*, 166, 2019, p. 37-54, bibl., graphs)

Most of this article describes the profile of protest events in Costa Rica during the presidency of Luis Guillermo Solís (2014-18). The authors' protest events database, constructed from four domestic newspapers, contains 2,475 events for the period under review. Almost half were by workers, the majority of these through institutional mechanisms rather than non-institutional ones such as street protests. Drawing on the political opportunities literature, the article ends by developing hypotheses that might explain its major findings.

854 **Díaz González, José Andrés** and **Stephanie Cordero Cordero.** Las preferencias del electorado en la segunda ronda presidencial de 2018 en Costa Rica: un modelo de socialización política. (*Polít. Gob.*, 27:1, primer semestre 2016, p. 9-52, bibl., graphs, maps, tables)

The authors focus on the role of political socialization in explaining presidential voting preference among the general population in Costa Rica. Following a solid discussion of the relevant literature, they develop a three-level model of political socialization. Their statistical analysis of the results of a survey taken between the two rounds of presidential voting in 2018 found that primary socialization—conversations with family and other close individuals—was indeed the most important influence. Religious preference also was important, though perhaps uniquely so for this election given that one of the two finalists was the candidate of an explicitly neo-Pentecostal party.

855 **Elecciones municipales en Costa Rica 2016: contribuciones para su estudio.** Edición de María Amalia Amador Fournier. San José: FLACSO, 2017. 123 p.: bibl., ill., maps.

This edited volume, the product of a larger collaboration between FLACSO and the Konrad Adenauer Foundation, addresses the Costa Rican municipal elections of 2016. That year was the first time all local elections were held midway through the presidential term rather than conterminously with the national elections. Although the six contributions are brief, they are useful, especially those documenting the consolidation of multipartyism at the canton level, inequities in campaign financing, and imbalances in gender representation.

856 **Gallardo, Helio.** Los bárbaros ya estaban aquí: elecciones 2018. San José: Editorial Arlekín, 2018. 200 p.: bibl.

The January 2018 decision by the Inter-American Court of Human Rights legitimating same-sex marriage placed religion at the center of the then-ongoing Costa Rican national elections for the first time since 1884. Several weeks after the ruling, Fabricio Alvarado, candidate of the neo-Pentecostal Partido Restauración Nacional (PREN), placed first with a quarter of the vote. Most of this book was written during the period that followed up to the run-off, which the PREN candidate lost by a significant margin. The culture war polarization is the primary focus of this book by a leading Chilean/Costa Rican scholar. For the most part, this work consists of short essays followed by discussions based on questions, many of them quite good, directed to the author from others.

857 **Muñoz-Portillo, Juan.** Austeridad, ideología comprometida y asamblea proactiva-particularista en Costa Rica, en 2019. (*Rev. Cienc. Polít./Santiago*, 40:2, 2020, p. 259-285, bibl., graphs, tables)

In his first year in office, Costa Rican president Carlos Alvarado Quesada secured the most substantive legislative victories in over three decades even though his party had the smallest minority of seats in the Legislative Assembly for the same period. The author highlights three factors: first, the willingness of the president to move toward the center and work with the larger parties; second, an assembly willing to take the legislative initiative in recent years; third, an increasing use of particularistic legislation to facilitate coalition-building. Making good use of the relevant scholarly literature, a great value of the article is that it places the analysis of this one year in its broader context of trends across recent decades.

858 **Perelló, Lucas** and **Patricio Navia.**
Abrupt and gradual realignments: the case of Costa Rica, 1958–2018. (*J. Polit. Lat. Am.*, 13:1, April 2021, p. 86–113, bibl., graphs, tables)

There have been substantial changes in the Costa Rican party system across the last few decades, but scholars disagree as to whether they are best understood as electoral realignment or dealignment. This study effectively argues for a critical realignment occurring in 2002 followed by a gradual realignment featuring declining partisanship and party system fragmentation. The authors' quantitative analysis is based on both election results and public opinion surveys. The article includes a solid review of the relevant theoretical literature.

859 **Pignataro, Adrián** and **Ilka Treminio.**
Reto económico, valores y religión en las elecciones. (*Rev. Cienc. Polít./Santiago*, 39:2, 2019, p. 239–264, bibl., graphs, tables)

This solid article examines the Costa Rican elections of 2018, including its context, the major dynamics of the campaign, and the results and their implications. Cultural-religious issues loomed large in this election; the first round victor was an evangelical pastor. With much of the population caught between cultural conservatism and Catholic faith, in the second round the undecided voted overwhelmingly supported the opponent, the candidate of the incumbent party. Indeed, the authors' quantitative analysis found retrospective judgment of the government's performance the leading predictor of the vote in both rounds.

860 **Raventós Vorst, Ciska.** Mi corazón dice no: el movimiento de oposición al TLC en Costa Rica. Ciudad Universitaria Rodrigo Facio, Costa Rica: Editorial UCR: Instituto de Investigaciones Sociales, 2018. 213 p.: bibl., ill.

Written by a sociologist, this book analyzes the campaign promoting the "no" vote in the 2007 referendum on whether Costa Rica should join the free trade association with the US and the rest of Central America. Despite mounting what the author describes as the largest, most diverse, and most sustained popular mobilization in the country in more than a half century, the campaign narrowly lost. The most valuable contribution of the study is its analysis of the "comités patrióticos" (patriotic committees) that were formed throughout the country to promote the opposition vote. The author surveyed and interviewed participants in different regions and participated in her own neighborhood. The book also offers a solid background of the controversy but draws little on the relevant social mobilization literature. For political economy specialist's comment, see item **1336**.

861 **Solís Avendaño, Manuel Antonio.**
Costa Rica: la democracia de las razones débiles (y los pasajes ocultos). Ciudad Universitaria Rodrigo Facio, Costa Rica: Editorial UCR, 2018. 501 p.: bibl. (Instituto de Investigaciones Sociales)

The author, a Costa Rican sociologist, has written a deeply researched investigation into the impact of reforms in 1999 and 2003 on the process by which the Legislative Assembly elects members to serve in important public institutions, notably the Supreme Court, as well as the Comptroller General and the Ombudsman. The reforms were intended to reduce the role of partisan and personal considerations and strengthen professional criteria, especially through the creation of an appointments committee (Comisión de Nombramientos de la Asamblea Legislativa—CNAL). The analysis of a variety of illustrative cases draws on numerous interviews and an extensive reading of relevant government documents. The author concludes that the process is still pervaded by partisan and personal considerations but in a nontransparent fashion that erodes public confidence.

862 **Viales Hurtado, Ronny José** and **David Díaz Arias.** Costa Rica y los pactos sociales multiclasistas: la Reforma al Código Procesal Laboral (2015–2017). (*Nueva Soc.*, 273, 2018, p. 83–97, ill.)

In this concise essay, two of Costa Rica's leading historians address the passage of the significant reform of the labor code that culminated in 2015, placing this case within the context of the major sociopolitical dynamics of recent decades. Labor policy since about 1980 has been in the neoliberal direction, but with strong resistance from the previously dominant social democratic opposition. With a president in 2015 from neither of the major parties identified with these two orientations and with a willingness to continue a long tradition of compromise constructed at the elite level, this expansion of labor protections was able to pass.

EL SALVADOR

863 Acosta, Benjamin and **Melissa Ziegler Rogers.** When militant organizations lose militarily but win politically. (*Coop. Confl.*, 55:3, Feb. 2020, p. 365–387, bibl., tables)

This article is the first to provide a quantitative analysis of the infrequent transformation of a violent organization into a winning political party using a large number of cases. The authors exemplify their findings with a case study of the Frente Farabundo Martí para la Liberación Nacional (FMLN) in El Salvador. The study's primary explanatory variables for future political success are organizational size and wartime lethality. With these variables, the authors' model predicted a 56 percent likelihood of the FMLN's eventual electoral success—but only 3 percent for its counterpart in Guatemala.

864 Andrade, Laura. Combatting corruption in El Salvador: evaluating state capacity to reduce corruption and improve accountability. Washington D.C.: Washington Office on Latin America; San José: Instituto Universitario de Opinión Pública, 2019. 70 p.: bibl., graphs, tables. (Central America monitor)

This Central America Monitor Project report provides a thorough description of El Salvador's legal framework governing corruption. It also analyzes official data concerning the disposition of corruption cases during the 2014–17 period. Of particular value are the elaborate timelines provided for the successful prosecutions on corruption charges against former president Elías Antonio Saca (2004–2009) and former prosecutor general Luis Martínez (2012–15).

865 Bebbington, Anthony; Benjamin Fash; and **John Rogan.** Socio-environmental conflict, political settlements, and mining governance: a cross-border comparison, El Salvador and Honduras. (*Lat. Am. Perspect.*, 46:2, March 2019, p. 84–106, bibl.)

This article seeks to explain why El Salvador was able to ban all metal mining in 2017 while in Honduras mining instead rapidly expanded. The authors provide a clear contrast in social movement mobilization and elite behavior based on participant observation and interviews in both countries. Fundamentally, though, remains the crucial distinction that mining has always been substantially more important to the economy and elite interests in Honduras than in El Salvador.

866 Borgh, Chris van der. Government responses to gang power: from truce to war on gangs in El Salvador. (*Rev. Eur. Estud. Latinoam. Caribe,* 107, Jan./June 2019, p. 1–25, bibl., tables)

This article makes a solid contribution to the study of the gang truce in El Salvador that began in 2012 by focusing on the experience of one town, Nueva Concepción in Chalatenango. Although it was late to the process, this was one of the few municipalities that participated in a government initiative to support the truce. Drawing on six field visits between 2012 and 2017, the author contrasts the results during both the truce and the return to a more repressive approach that followed (which were mixed in both cases).

867 Borgh, Chris van der and **Wim Savenije.** The politics of violence reduction: making and unmaking the Salvadorean gang truce. (*J. Lat. Am. Stud.*, 51:4, Nov. 2019, p. 905–928)

This article explains the processes by which the 2012 truce between the government of El Salvador and the country's major gangs was developed, maintained, and disintegrated. Based on interviews with leading stakeholders, among the article's most important contributions are its discussion of the role of gang leaders in developing and maintaining the truce as well as the tensions between them and other gang members that were part of its undoing. Other aspects of the unmaking of the truce are also well explained.

868 **Comisión de Derechos Humanos de El Salvador.** Los acuerdos de paz a veinticinco años y acuerdos pendientes: los efectos de la Ley de amnistía general para la consolidación de la paz, su derogación frente a los casos señalados por la Comisión de la Verdad y su impacto. San Salvador: Comisión de Derechos Humanos de El Salvador, CDHES, 2017. 92 p.: bibl., ill.

In 1993, El Salvador adopted an amnesty law for perpetrators of the immense number of human rights violations committed during the conflict, which was justified as needed to help move the country beyond its civil war. The law came on the heels of the Truth Commission's report on 33 of the most representative of those violations. After describing these legal actions and their consequences, this short report explains the 2016 Supreme Court decision that nullified the law. It then discusses progress as of its writing to hold perpetrators accountable in four cases: the murder of Archbishop Óscar Romero, the massacre at El Mozote, and two cases involving the murders of US military personnel.

869 **Córdova, Abby.** Living in gang-controlled neighborhoods: impacts on electoral and nonelectoral participation in El Salvador. (*LARR*, 54:1, April 2019, p. 201–221, bibl., graphs, tables)

This sophisticated quantitative analysis about gangs and political participation presents important findings. In what is the first systematic statistical analysis of its topic for Latin America, the author finds that gang dominance at the neighborhood level in El Salvador reduces residents' nonelectoral political participation. Furthermore, she finds that while the standard expectation that crime victims are more likely to participate politically holds in low-gang-dominance neighborhoods, this relationship disappears where gangs are dominant. The study is based on an original dataset for 71 neighborhoods spread over six municipalities during 2010 and 2011 compiled during the author's 18 months of field research.

870 **Córdova Macías, Ricardo; Mariana Rodríguez;** and **Elizabeth J. Zechmeister.** The political culture of democracy in El Salvador and in the Americas, 2016/17: a comparative study of democracy and governance. Nashville, Tenn.: Vanderbilt University Latin American Public Opinion Project (LAPOP), 2018. 222 p.: bibl., graphs, tables.

This report focuses on contemporary political attitudes in El Salvador based on the 2016/2017 round of interviews for AmericasBarometer. These results are also compared to those for the rest of the region's countries as well as to earlier rounds for El Salvador. Notably, Salvadoran support for democracy and trust of political parties has fallen, while trust in political parties and elections are found to be the strongest predictors of democratic orientations. A particularly insightful chapter provides an in-depth examination of attitudes related to citizen security and violence prevention at the local level.

871 **Cruz, José Miguel.** The politics of negotiating with gangs: the case of El Salvador. (*Bull. Lat. Am. Res.*, 38:5, Aug. 2018, p. 547–562, bibl., graphs)

In 2012, El Salvador enjoyed a remarkable drop in its very high homicide rate. This article by the preeminent scholar on contemporary violence in the region explains this decline, both descriptively and theoretically. At the core was a truce between rival gangs and with the government. The article explains the special conditions needed for this development to occur and how they came about. When the conditions changed, the homicide rate soared once again. Crucial to developing the article's insights were interviews with former gang leaders and the government's lead negotiator.

872 **Martínez-Reyes, Alberto** and **José Javier Navarro-Pérez.** De la mano dura al enfrentamiento directo: vaivenes de las políticas públicas en El Salvador. (*Rev. Sociol. Polít./Curitiba*, 27:71, 2019, p. 1–20, bibl., tables)

This article analyzes the effectiveness of the four different phases of government policy in El Salvador towards gangs from 2003 to 2019. The authors' primary evidence is the testimony of those they interviewed during six months of fieldwork in 2016–2017. Despite variations in approach, the authors conclude that each phase had the same two counterproductive effects in common: increasing violence and strengthening the gangs.

873 **Montoya, Ainhoa.** The violence of democracy: political life in postwar El Salvador. Cham, Switzerland: Palgrave Macmillan, 2018. 303 p.: bibl., index, maps. (Studies of the Americas)

This book succeeds in its first objective of providing an ethnographic account of the types of violence that ordinary Salvadorans have experienced in the postwar period. This information is based on the author's fieldwork during 2008–2009 in Santiago Nonualco, La Paz, with most of her contacts admittedly sympathetic to the left. The author is less successful with her broader objective to critique the international community's alleged rosy view of Salvadoran democratization while downplaying the persistence of violence. A contestable characterization for 2009, it is all the more questionable for a book published in 2018.

874 **Rahman, Eric and Siniša Vukovic.**
Sympathy for the devil: when and how to negotiate with criminal gangs—case of El Salvador. (*Stud. Confl. Terror.*, 42:11, 2019, p. 935–952, graph)

This article seeks to contribute to the literature on state mediation and negotiation with socially unpopular partners, such as terrorists, insurgents, and gangs, using the example of the truce announced in El Salvador in 2012 that lasted over a year. While most of the article is devoted to elaborating the logic of the authors' three-step negotiation process, it also offers a good, concise discussion of the Salvadoran truce, drawing on the authors' own interviews with some of the main actors.

875 **Solano Ramírez, Mario Antonio.** De los acuerdos de paz al estado social y democrático de derecho. San Salvador: Universidad Tecnológica de El Salvador, 2016. 2 v.: bibl. (Colección jurídica)

This very wide ranging two-volume work begins with a concise history of El Salvador up to 1932 and ends with a discussion of the differences between neoliberalism and social democracy. A variety of other topics are also addressed, such as the 1992 Peace Accords (the text is included) and commentary on the current Salvadoran constitution and a number of related judicial decisions.

876 **Spalding, Rose J.** From the streets to the chamber: social movements and the mining ban in El Salvador. (*Rev. Eur. Estud. Latinoam. Caribe*, 106, July/Dec. 2018, p. 47–74, bibl., tables)

This solid article explains how El Salvador in 2017 came to be the first country to legally ban all forms of metallic mining. The study draws on 78 interviews over a seven-year period, thorough archival research, and a broad familiarity with the relevant social movement literature. Process tracing shows a grassroots movement growing in size and breadth over the years, strategically building alliances with institutional actors from the Catholic Church to legislators, and successfully turning public opinion. In the end, even the conservative political parties supported the ban.

877 **Sprenkels, Ralph.** Ambivalent moderation: the FMLN's ideological accommodation to post-war politics in El Salvador. (*Gov. Oppos.*, 54:3, 2019, p. 536–558, bibl.)

This article uses the concept of "ambivalent moderation" to make sense of the ideological trajectory of the Frente Farabundo Martí para la Liberación Nacional (FMLN) during the postwar period. The author knows the subject well, having lived for many years in El Salvador in close contact with FMLN activists. While the general direction of change publicly has been one of moderation in response to electoral incentives, internal to the party the situation has been much more complicated.

878 **Tribunal Internacional para la Aplicación de la Justicia Restaurativa en El Salvador.** A la paz, solo por la verdad: informe del Tribunal Internacional para la Aplicación de la Justicia Restaurativa en El Salvador 2009–2016. Edición de José Ramón Juániz Maya. San Salvador: UCA, 2017. 565 p.: bibl., ill. (chiefly color), color maps.

This important volume succeeds in its objective to give voice, name, and face to the surviving victims of the widespread human rights violations during the Salvadoran civil war—largely at the hands of the state and its agents. The volume also powerfully argues for restorative justice for victims, including reparations. The Tribunal Internacional para la Aplicación de la Justicia Restaurativa en El Salvador has held annual sessions since 2009. This volume pulls together excerpts of victim testimonies from each of the first eight years, along with helpful short essays providing explanatory context.

879   Ulloa, Félix. Democracia y financiamiento de partidos políticos. San Salvador: UFG-Editores, Universidad Francisco Gavidia, 2015. 284 p.: bibl., tables.

A Salvadoran scholar undertakes a comparative analysis of the financing of political parties in democratic systems, both in Latin America and beyond. Using ample quotations from various sources, he seeks to clarify the major issues as well as survey the variety of solutions found. Most helpful are the summary tables at the book's end. Using these findings, a second purpose is to offer support for election financing reform for El Salvador.

GUATEMALA

880   Álvarez Aragón, Virgilio. La revolución que nunca fué: un ensayo de interpretación de las jornadas cívicas de 2015. Guatemala: Editorial Serviprensa, 2016. 178 p.: bibl.

Written by a sociologist and former director of FLACSO-Guatemala, this book provides a useful description of the historic events of 2015 in Guatemala. A widening corruption scandal led to the resignations and arrests of first the vice president and then the president, as well as other members of the administration. Crucial to these events were a series of broad-based popular mobilizations. Understanding the protests is a major focus of the book. Also receiving valuable attention is the concurrent presidential campaign in which the outcome was significantly affected by the scandals. Although historic, these events were not revolutionary, which is the point of the book's title. The book concludes with a helpful extended chronology.

881   Azpuru, Dinorah; Mariana Rodríguez; and Elizabeth J. Zechmeister. Political culture of democracy in Guatemala and in the Americas, 2016/17. Nashville, Tenn.: Vanderbilt University Latin American Public Opinion Project (LAPOP), 2018. 236 p.: bibl., graphs, tables.

This report examines Guatemalan public support for the institutions at the core of democracy based on the 2016/2017 round of interviews for AmericasBarometer. These political attitudes are also compared to those for the rest of the countries in the region as well as to earlier rounds for Guatemala. Notably, political tolerance dramatically increased across the prior three years. However, support for democracy was the lowest for the entire region as was identification with a political party. Extended attention is given to attitudes relevant to migration, participation in the 2015 anticorruption demonstrations, and trust in institutions in the justice sector.

882   Beck, Erin. The uneven impacts of violence against women reform in Guatemala: intersecting inequalities and the patchwork state. (*LARR*, 56:1, March 2021, p. 20–35, bibl., graphs, tables)

This article pursues two tracks to effectively explain the shortcomings and accomplishments of Guatemala's 2008 law criminalizing various forms of violence against women. Based on a substantial number of interviews and other aspects of field research, the author explores the context for the law and how it has functioned, highlighting disparities in justice received based on class, ethnicity, and place lived. The second track powerfully presents the case of a 12-year-old girl raped by a neighbor in a remote village and the difficulties she and her family have faced in their quest for justice.

883   Brannum, Kate. Guatemala 2018: facing a constitutional crossroad. (*Rev. Cienc. Polít./Santiago*, 39:2, 2018, p. 265–284, bibl.)

This article surveys the major political issues facing Guatemala during 2018 and in advance of the 2019 elections. At the heart of the year was the struggle by President Jimmy Morales to undermine the work of the International Commission against Impunity in Guatemala (CICIG). Another major theme was the protests by, and attacks on, Indigenous and other human rights defenders. Consequently, as the author points out, the major issues in Guatemala continue to be corruption and the weakness of the rule of law.

884 **Burt, Jo-Marie.** The justice we deserve: war crimes prosecutions in Guatemala. (*LARR*, 56:1, March 2021, p. 214–232, bibl., photos)

This powerful article provides an in-depth account of the 2018 Molina Theissen trial in Guatemala that resulted in the conviction of four senior military officials for crimes against humanity, aggravated sexual violence, and forced disappearance. The author was in the courtroom for the two-and-a-half-year trial as a monitor for the Open Society Justice Initiative-sponsored project. She also interviewed the surviving victim and her family members. Burt emphasizes the transformational potential of such judicial proceedings for victims as well as the potential to generate greater public understanding of general patterns of state violence.

885 **Combatting corruption in Guatemala: evaluating state capacity to reduce corruption and improve accountability.** Compiled by the Washington Office on Latin America (WOLA) and the Fundación Myrna Mack. Washington, D.C.: Washington Office on Latin America, 2020. 54 p.: graphs, tables. (Central America monitor)

In retrospect, the 2014–17 period examined in this report was the high point for attacking corruption in Guatemala. Part of the Central America Monitor Project, the report describes the laws and institutions that have been involved in reducing corruption. Detailed information is provided on the number of cases initiated under the different types of corruption crimes and their outcomes. Attention is also given to some of the landmark cases of this period involving high-ranking public officials that demonstrated the existence of illicit networks that had captured state institutions for their own gain.

886 **Cook, Nathan J.; Glenn D. Wright; and Krister P. Andersson.** Local politics of forest governance: why NGO support can reduce local government responsiveness. (*World Dev.*, 92, April 2017, p. 203–214, bibl., graphs, tables)

This article examines whether international NGO activities in the forestry sector influence government responsiveness to local citizens. The authors analyze survey data from local governance actors in 100 randomly selected municipalities in Guatemala and Bolivia administered in 2001 and 2007. Through their regression analysis of the data collected, they conclude that local government is responsive to its citizens when domestic stakeholder pressure is strong but otherwise international NGO financial contributions can hinder responsiveness.

887 **Escobar, Claudia.** How organized crime controls Guatemala's judiciary. (*in* Corruption in Latin America: how politicians and corporations steal from citizens. Edited by Robert I. Rotberg. Cham, Switzerland: Springer, 2019, p. 235–264)

The first section of this book chapter by a former judge in Guatemala is useful; the second section is compelling and important. In the first section, the author provides a concise history of the organization of the country's judicial branch, including the methods used for selecting its highest members. In the second, she offers her own testimony about combating the corruption that pervades the judicial branch. The steps that she took against corrupt clerks and attorneys brought her death threats. Still, she persevered, bringing crucial witness against influence peddling and bribery efforts by leading government officials that ended with them in jail but Escobar and her family forced into exile.

888 **Esquit Choy, Alberto.** "Los indígenas también queremos ser guatemaltecos...": entre la exclusión y la democracia (1950–1985). Chi Iximulew, Guatemala: Maya' Wuj Editorial, 2017. 398 p.: bibl., maps.

This translation of a 2007 PhD dissertation from Vanderbilt University describes Kaqchikel Maya political leadership in four municipalities in the Guatemalan department of Chimaltenango. Written by an Indigenous anthropologist from the region, the book has three sections. The first explores the development of that leadership during the 1950–74 period. The second and most substantial section examines the participation of two deputies elected from the area to the national legislature for the 1974–78 term, while the final section does the same for those elected in 1984 to the assembly, writing a new constitution. The first is largely based on interviews, the other two on the official legislative record. In between the second and third periods, of course, the vicious state terrorism that in part was the state's response to the growing Indigenous activism described in the first two sections occurred.

889 Gillooly, Shauna N. Indigenous social movements and political institutionalization: a comparative case study. (*Polit. Groups Ident.*, 8:5, 2020, p. 1006–1021, bibl.)

This article seeks to explain why the Indigenous social movement in Guatemala was able to successfully institutionalize as a political party, comparing it to the unsuccessful case of Peru. The author's explanation emphasizes the importance of a bottom-up rather than top-down movement and especially one with charismatic leadership, such as with Rigoberta Menchú Tum in Guatemala. The party she helped form, Winaq, has had minimal success at the presidential level, some at the congressional, but most notably with electing mayors at the municipal level. The author also draws substantially on framing theory from the social movement literature to explain this successful transformation.

890 Granovsky-Larsen, Simon. Dealing with peace: the Guatemalan campesino movement and the post-conflict neoliberal state. Toronto, Canada; Buffalo, N.Y.; London: University of Toronto Press, 2019. 275 p.: bibl., ill., index, maps.

At one level, this valuable study presents an in-depth comparison of two Guatemalan peasant organizations and their varying strategies to obtain land and community development resources from the state. Further elevating the book's importance is that the comparison is guided by the critical strategic question of how to gain resources from the neoliberal state without undermining broader goals of structural transformation. The author knows the subject well, having spent considerable time over the years working with Guatemalan human rights and peasant organizations, along with doing research specific to this project. See also *HLAS 75:953*.

891 Guatemala's justice system: evaluating capacity building and judicial independence. Compiled by the Washington Office on Latin America (WOLA) and the Fundación Myrna Mack. Washington, D.C.: Washington Office on Latin America, 2019. 74 p.: graphs, maps, tables. (Central America monitor)

This Central America Monitor Project report provides a good overview and assessment of the Guatemalan judiciary. The scope is broad, including not just the courts but also the offices of prosecutors, public defenders, and forensics. Although much room for improvement remains in the Guatemalan judiciary, the report does detail several important areas where the system's capacity was expanded and strengthened during 2014–17, the focus of the report's analysis. The process for selecting members of the highest judicial offices, however, remains a key area of continuing controversy. Several contentious cases during this period are examined to illuminate the issues.

892 Juárez Elías, Erick. Reforma de la justicia civil en Guatemala. Ciudad de Guatemala: F&G Editores, 2019. 291 p.: bibl.

The author effectively argues that Guatemala is in need of a comprehensive overhaul of its Civil and Commercial Procedure Code. As he points out, a recent study placed Guatemala at 110 out of 113 countries surveyed in terms of the accessibility, affordability, and effectiveness of their civil justice systems. The book provides the appropriate historical context, including the ineffectual reforms of 1934 and 1964. A law professor, the author undertook the task of revising the code himself and succeeded in getting it introduced into the national legislature in 2016. While it has yet to make it into law, his revision is reprinted in this work.

893 **Kubota, Yuichi.** Explaining state violence in the Guatemalan Civil War: rebel threat and counterinsurgency. (*Lat. Am. Polit. Soc.*, 59:3, Fall 2017, p. 48–71, bibl., graph, maps, tables)

This article reports the results of a propensity score analysis for the relationship between state and rebel violence in Guatemala during the 1982–95 period. Using the impressive dataset compiled by the International Center for Human Rights Investigations, the study concludes that state violence did increase in response to rebel violence, especially rebel attacks targeting security forces that resulted in injuries.

894 **Montobbio, Manuel.** La perplejidad del quetzal: la construcción de la paz en Guatemala. Guatemala: F&G Editores, 2019. 250 p.: bibl.

This volume brings together essays written at different points by the author, a former Spanish diplomat and later a political scientist. Having been involved with the Guatemalan peace process as a diplomat from 1994 into 1999, the most valuable contributions concern the role of international actors, particularly Spain, especially in support of the implementation of the 1996 Peace Accords. The title of the book comes from one of the essays, a talk the author gave at a 2006 Barcelona conference, for which he was a co-organizer, that reunited many of the leading participants in the peace process. Most of the occasional citations in the book are to the author's own earlier publications.

895 **Navia, Patricio; Lucas Perello;** and **Vaclav Masek.** The determinants of perception of corruption in Guatemala, 2006–2016. (*Public Integr.*, 22, 2020, p. 435–444, bibl., graphs, tables)

Using data from the Latin American Public Opinion Project (LAPOP), this article presents a quantitative analysis of popular perceptions of political corruption in Guatemala from 2006 to 2016. The socioeconomic determinants are analyzed and the authors find that people with a higher education are more likely to perceive corruption. A second objective is to assess the impact on perceptions of the immense corruption scandals of 2015. This is made difficult by a change in question wording for the dependent variable. The authors' best effort finds little impact, perhaps because perceptions of the level of corruption were already so high.

896 **Out of the shadow: revisiting the revolution from post-peace Guatemala.** Edited by Julie Gibbings and Heather Vrana. Austin: University of Texas Press, 2020. 312 p.: bibl., ill., index.

This edited volume examines various aspects of the two democratic administrations that followed Guatemala's October Revolution of 1944 and, in some chapters, how its spirit was carried on through the following decades. The counter-revolution of 1954 and its aftermath is the shadow of the title and intentionally outside of its focus. Instead, the authors seek to highlight the diversity of experiences during the Ten Years of Spring, especially those that have been understudied. The introduction by the editors provides a solid survey of the historiography for the period while each of the subseqent chapters is worthy of attention. Some are by well-established scholars on their subjects, and all are solidly grounded in thorough research. The contributors are mainly historians and anthropologists.

897 **Sanz-Levia, Laura** and **Fernando Jiménez-Sánchez.** Breaking democracy: illegal political finance and organized crime in Guatemala. (*Crime Law Soc. Change*, 75:1, Jan. 2021, p. 21–43, bibl., tables)

Given that there is no comprehensive study of the important relationship between political corruption and organized crime in Guatemala, this article provides a useful synthesis of the available literature on the subject. The authors explain the recent development of the legislative framework for political financing and conclude by suggesting both further legislation and improved implementation to eradicate corruption in politics.

898 **Saving Guatemala's fight against crime and impunity.** Brussels: International Crisis Group, 2018. 33 p.: graphs, map, table. (Latin America report; 70)

This report presents an innovative way to assess the positive impact of the International Commission against Impunity in Guatemala (CICIG) that operated from 2007 to 2019. The authors find that beginning in 2014, Guatemala's homicide rate fell below that of a control group consisting of a weighted average of nine neighboring countries. This finding suggests that the dismantling of criminal organizations in Guatemala assisted by CICIG prevented thousands of homicides.

899 **Tzul Tzul, Gladys.** Gobierno comunal indígena y estado guatemalteco: algunas claves críticas para comprender su tensa relación. Guatemala: Instituto Amaq', 2018. 97 p.: bibl., index.

This book is a compilation of the author's previously published essays and short articles, the first of which gives the book its title. The author is a K'iche' sociologist from Tononicapán. The value of this thin volume is its defense of Indigenous communal sovereignty for self-governance, along with the elaboration of the importance of communal life as the foundation for communal governance. Communal authority, the author says, is only possible as an expression of the collective will.

900 **Weston, Gavin Michael.** Guatemalan vigilantism and the global (re)production of collective violence: a tale of two lynchings. London; New York, N.Y.: Routledge, Taylor & Francis Group, 2020. 150 p.: bibl., ill., index. (Routledge studies in anthropology; 53)

This book analyzes two lynchings that occurred in Todos Santos Cuchumatán, a small, remote, largely Maya town in Guatemala, but one well known to tourists. The first was in 1997 of a young Guatemalan man who had returned from working in the US; the second was in 2000 of a Japanese tourist and his group's bus driver. The author ably elucidates the local, regional, and national factors underlying such events. As he notes, both lynchings were connected to growing concerns about cultural changes in the area. The book is based on the author's field research in 2003 and 2004.

HONDURAS

901 **Altamirano Rayo, Giorleny D.** State building, ethnic land titling, and transnational organized crime: the case of Honduras. (*LARR*, 56:1, March 2021, p. 50–66, bibl., graphs)

In a matter of a few years beginning in 2012, Honduras granted titles to land totaling over one million hectares in the sparsely populated Mosquitia. Drawing on multiple sources, including dozens of interviews, the author explores the origins of this land distribution. Members of grassroots organizations generally credited their decades of pressure. The state officials interviewed who made the decisions, including the last two presidents, focused on their security motivations. A region with little state presence, the area had become important to transnational criminal organizations for transporting their narcotics. Communal property titles were issued to councils, which serve as the intermediary link in the hierarchical structure between their communities and national leaders.

Bebbington, Anthony; Benjamin Fash; and John Rogan. Socio-environmental conflict, political settlements, and mining governance: a cross-border comparison, El Salvador and Honduras. See item **865**.

902 **Delgado Fiallos, Aníbal.** Honduras: el retorno a la democracia. Tegucigalpa: UNAH, Universidad Nacional Autónoma de Honduras, Editorial Universitaria, 2017. 117 p.: bibl. (Colección Cuadernos universitarios)

Although not presenting new information or analysis, this short book provides a good summary of the key events in the period of its focus: Honduras' return to democracy during 1980–2002, as well as the prior period beginning with the military coup of 1963. As the author points out, during this time Honduras enjoyed six relatively free elections in marked contrast with the electoral fraud of the past (the author had been a presidential precandidate in 1996). Still, the country is plagued by acute poverty and inequality. The author apportions blame to both the devastating impact of Hurricane Mitch in 1998, as well as the imposition of neoliberalism.

903 Estrada, Lorenzo and **Francisco Bastida.** Effective transparency and institutional trust in Honduran municipal governments. (*Adm. Soc.*, 52:6, 2020, p. 890–926, bibl., graphs, tables)

Using 2014 data from the Latin American Public Opinion Project's (LAPOP) AmericasBarometer survey, this well-executed study examines trust in government at the municipal level in Honduras. The authors find that both transparency and the quality of municipal services increase the public's trust, but perceptions of corruption do not. They also provide useful recommendations concerning requirements for effective transparency.

904 Inter-American Commission on Human Rights. Human rights situation in Honduras, 2019. Washington, D.C.: Organization of American States, 2019. 159 p.: graphs, tables. (Country report: Honduras) (OEA/Ser.L/V/II; 146)

This report by the Inter-American Commission on Human Rights (CIDH) addresses the human rights situation in Honduras based on various sources, including the commission's own 2018 fact-finding visit. Particular attention is given to the disproportionate use of public force against protesters following the flawed November 2017 presidential election, as well as continuing violence against journalists and human rights defenders. The high level of impunity in all of these areas is also highlighted. At the same time, the report acknowledges positive measures adopted by the government addressing concerns raised in prior IACHR reports. This report concludes with a list of 30 recommendations for further steps to be taken.

905 Lakhani, Nina. Who killed Berta Cáceres?: dams, death squads, and an Indigenous defender's battle for the planet. London; New York, N.Y.: Verso Books, 2020. 328 p.: bibl., ill., index.

A 2015 winner of the Goldman Environmental Prize, Berta Cáceres was murdered the following year for her defense of Indigenous rights in opposition to the building of a dam in Honduras. The author of this book, a journalist for major English newspapers, ably reconstructs the story based on the extensive contacts in the country she has developed over the years. The book covers Cáceres' life, particularly her role as an effective grassroots leader; provides a concise survey of contemporary Honduran politics and society; thoroughly covers the investigation of the murder and the trial of the seven people—government officials, dam employees, and assassins—who were the direct agents of her death; and marshals substantial evidence implicating the mastermind who would be found guilty after the book's publication.

906 Muñoz-Portillo, Juan. Effects of ballot type and district magnitude on local public goods bill-initiation behavior: evidence from Honduras. (*Polit. Res. Q.*, 74:2, 2021, p. 388–402, bibl., graphs, tables)

This well-executed, quantitative study examines the impact of electoral systems on legislators' representation of their constituents. A change in Honduras' electoral system in 2004 provides the crucial contrast for the author's analysis of the 1990–2009 period. The study finds that electoral rules do matter, but at least in this case the impact coexists with that of informal clientelist rules. The author effectively presents the Honduran case material in the context of the broader theoretical literature.

907 Rodríguez, Cecilia Graciela and **Luis González Tule.** Honduras 2019: persistente inestabilidad económica y social y debilidad institucional. (*Rev. Cienc. Polít./Santiago*, 40:2, 2019, p. 379–400, bibl., graphs, tables)

Políticamente 2019 was a year of instability in Honduras. The authors highlight the avalanche of protests against the government's policies as well as the indictment in the US of President Juan Orlando Hernández's brother for narcotrafficking. The year's political dynamics are ably explored in the context of the broader social and economic trends of recent years, especially poverty and inequality rates, gang violence, and migration to the US.

NICARAGUA

908 **Antología del pensamiento crítico nicaragüense contemporáneo.** Coordinación de Juan Pablo Gómez y Camilo Antillón. Textos de Carlos Fonseca Amador *et al.* Buenos Aires: Consejo Latinoamericano de Ciencias Sociales—CLACSO, 2016. 577 p.: bibl., ill. (Colección Antologías del pensamiento social latinoamericano y caribeño)

This thick volume offers selections from the writings of 20 contemporary Nicaraguan thinkers as part of a series of anthologies compiled by CLACSO. The two editors provide a solid introduction, explaining both the overall organization and the major themes of each writer. The first two sections are the broadest and most fundamental, relating to the country's frustrating history of trying to create a viable nation-state and corresponding national identity. Two other sections continue with the theme of identity, especially the final section on the place of Indigenous and Afro-descendants in what had often been understood as a mestizo nation. The remaining section addresses the role of women in society, drawing on examples of both feminist and earlier movements.

909 Buben, **Radek** and **Karel Kouba.** Nicaragua in 2019: the surprising resilience of authoritarianism in the aftermath of regime crisis. (*Rev. Cienc. Polít./Santiago,* 40:2, 2020, p. 431–455, bibl., tables)

This article provides a good summary of the Nicaraguan protests of 2018 and their repression. However, most of the attention is devoted to how, throughout the following year, the regime of Daniel Ortega worked to survive the challenge to its rule. The patronage networks of the neopatrimonial regime remained secure, as did the loyalty of the security forces. In contrast, the very broadness of the opposition made unity highly unlikely once repression smashed the mass protests.

910 **Castro Jo, Carlos.** La democracia en el pensamiento de Sandino, Camorro y Fonseca (con un epílogo sobre Daniel Ortega). Managua: Anama Ediciones, 2019. 168 p.: bibl.

This valuable book by a Nicaraguan-born sociologist trained and teaching in the US examines the place of democracy in the thought of three giants of Nicaraguan history: Augusto C. Sandino, Pedro Joaquín Chamorro Cardenal, and Carlos Fonseca. For each, the author provides a thorough analysis of their relevant writings, along with other commentaries on their thought and some attention to their broader context. With the mass uprising of 2018 occurring as the author concluded the book, he added an epilogue with the same treatment given to President Daniel Ortega.

911 **Cruz, José Miguel; Fernanda Boidi;** and **Elizabeth J. Zechmeister.** The political culture of democracy in Nicaragua and in the Americas, 2018/19: taking the pulse of democracy. Nashville, Tenn.: Vanderbilt University Latin American Public Opinion Project, 2020. 185 p.: bibl., graphs, tables.

This thorough report on a wide range of contemporary political attitudes of the Nicaraguan adult population is based on the eighth round of AmericasBarometer surveys. This foundation enables the authors to place the results of the 2019 interviews in the context of both prior Nicaraguan results going back to 2004 as well as current responses from other countries. The consolidation of Daniel Ortega's rule has had its impact. Fear of political participation—even discussion—has increased, especially on the part of those who are not regime supporters. Meanwhile, fewer than one third of respondents claim that the best way out of the Nicaraguan crisis is for the current government to remain in power. For most questions, the determinants of variations in responses are also given. Particularly important is age, with younger citizens less supportive of the regime than their older counterparts.

912 **Dammert, Lucía** and **Mary Fran T. Malone.** From community policing to political police in Nicaragua. (*Rev. Eur.*

Estud. Latinoam. Caribe, 110, July/Dec. 2020, p. 79–99, bibl., graphs, tables)

The first part of this article describes the evolution of policing practices in Nicaragua, especially the efforts to develop a less repressive/more preventative community-oriented approach. With Daniel Ortega's return to the presidency in 2007, this shift has eroded, with defense of the regime against protesters becoming more frequent, culminating in 2018. The second part examines several related aspects of public opinion. Until recently, trust in the police surpassed that in other political institutions. The authors' analysis shows a strengthening relationship between this trust in the police and support for Ortega.

913 **Inter-American Commission on Human Rights.** Gross human rights violations in the context of social protests in Nicaragua. Washington, D.C.: Organization of American States, 2018. 93 p.: table. (Country report: Nicaragua) (OEA/Ser.L/V/II; 86)

This report presents the Inter-American Commission on Human Rights' (IACHR) findings from its working visit to Nicaragua from May 17 to 21, 2018, concerning the violent events of the prior month and subsequent events through the next month. The commission received over 1,000 testimonies, which it relies on frequently to document its findings. And the results are clear: the police under Daniel Ortega, along with allied para-police forces and other armed individuals, used excessive force to kill, wound, arbitrarily detain, and otherwise intimidate large numbers of protesters. The report also provides an account of how the crisis unfolded.

914 **Martí i Puig, Salvador** and **Macià Serra.** Nicaragua: de-democratization and regime crisis. (*Lat. Am. Polit. Soc.*, 62:2, May 2020, p. 117–136, bibl., tables)

The authors present an excellent account of Nicaraguan politics since 1990, particularly the steps by which President Daniel Ortega has created his personalistic authoritarian regime. Especially notable is their effective drawing on a variety of theoretical works to structure and clarify their explanation of the regime's consolidation and its ability to weather the mass protests of 2018.

915 **Medina Sánchez, Fabián.** El preso 198: un perfil de Daniel Ortega. Nicaragua: La Prensa, 2018. 250 p.: ill., photos.

This book does not purport to be a biography of Daniel Ortega, Nicaragua's long-time president. But it does succeed in its objective of providing a journalistic profile that clarifies what went into making a leader who would choose authoritarianism over democratic consolidation. The author, a leading Nicaraguan journalist, is well positioned for this task, drawing on over 100 interviews he has conducted over the years with people close to Ortega. The title of the book indicates its major theme: the crucial impact of seven years of imprisonment when Ortega was a young man, creating a person who would remain reclusive and suspicious. The second major theme is the important role of Rosario Murillo, his intimate and political partner and eventually the country's vice president. Given the book's objective, little attention is given to the contemporary period after Ortega returned to power in 2007.

916 **Monte, Antonio** and **Juan Pablo Gómez.** Autoritarismo, violencia y élites en Nicaragua: reflexiones sobre la crisis (2018–2019). (*Anu. Estud. Centroam.*, 46, 2020, p. 1–29, bibl.)

In this wide-ranging article, two Nicaraguan scholars seek to clarify the cultural roots of Daniel Ortega's authoritarian regime and repressive practices. As they show, discourse that "others" and dehumanizes opponents has a long history. They also trace the ample history of elite pacts that have bolstered authoritarian regimes in the country.

917 **Mosinger, Eric S.** Balance of loyalties: explaining rebel factional struggles in the Nicaraguan Revolution. (*Sec. Stud.*, 28:5, Oct./Dec. 2019, p. 935–975, graphs, tables)

The author has written a fascinating article based on impressive research. It is well known that during its years of revolutionary struggle, the Frente Sandinista de

Liberación Nacional (FSLN) was riven by factional rivalries. The usual interpretation has emphasized ideological and strategic differences. The well-supported interpretation offered here argues instead that these were fundamentally power struggles between different leaders seeking dominance. In addition to providing rich descriptive detail, the larger objective is theory-building and testing, with the crucial variable the relative size of the networks loyal to contending leaders. The author created a network database based on 31 interviews, primarily with former commanders, and consulted extensive archival and secondary research. This basis allowed him to test his successful predictions of when struggles for power would emerge during 1971–76 and their outcomes.

918 **Nicaragua, el cambio azul y blanco: dejando atrás el régimen de Ortega.** Coordinación de Edmundo Jarquín y Elvira Cuadra *et al.* Managua: Fundación para la Paz y la Democracia, 2021. 462 p.: bibl.

This volume of essays by seven leading dissenting Nicaraguan intellectuals is a useful addition to the literature on the challenges facing the country under Daniel Ortega's increasingly authoritarian and repressive regime. To set the stage, the book provides a solid overview of the confrontations of 2018 and their broader context. Other essays provide useful in-depth accounts of the levels by which the personalistic regime has increased its repressive capacity and of the international response to its human rights abuses by other governments, international organizations, and international NGOs. Several of the essays also offer recommendations for moving Nicaragua out of this crisis and in a more democratic direction.

919 **A Nicaraguan exceptionalism?: debating the legacy of the Sandinista revolution.** Edited by Hilary Francis. London: Institute of Latin American Studies, School of Advanced Study, University of London, 2020. 187 p.: bibl., ill., index.

In this edited volume, social scientists and historians from Central America, Europe, and the US assess the legacy of the Nicaraguan Revolution. Those offering the most developed analyses of the fate of the accomplishments of the revolutionary government of the 1980s under the subsequent neoliberal administrations and the current regime of Daniel Ortega examine policing, food policy, agrarian reform, and feminist and LGBTQ activism. The remaining chapters are also worthwhile. Three are based on field research in rural communities and the other describes perceptions of Soviet bloc relations.

920 **Osorio, Hloreley** and **Rony Rodríguez-Ramírez.** Crítica y crisis en Nicaragua: la tensión entre democracia y capitalismo. (*Anu. Estud. Centroam.*, 46, 2020, p. 1–42, bibl.)

This article argues that Daniel Ortega created a corporatist authoritarian regime in Nicaragua wherein privileged groups, such as economic elites and Sandinista loyalists, supported authoritarian measures in exchange for access to resources. The article gives significant attention to the viewpoints of those challenging the regime in 2018 as well as to the regime's response. Substantial attention is also given to German economic historian Wolfgang Streeck's argument about the incompatibility of democracy and capitalism as it might apply to the Nicaraguan case.

921 **Rocha, José Luis.** Autoconvocados y conectados: los universitarios en la revuelta de abril en Nicaragua. Prólogo de Elena Poniatowska. San Salvador: UCA Editores, 2019. 192 p.: bibl., ill.

This book brings a well-informed historical and theoretical perspective to its analysis of the 2018 student-led movement against the regime of Daniel Ortega. Its primary material is interviews conducted with 14 participants, supplemented by a reading of the many testimonies available online. An early chapter provides a solid summary of the student movements of the 1950s-70s against the Somoza family regime, which is then used for comparisons throughout the remainder of the study. A widely published scholar of Central American affairs, the author makes effective use of the works of leading social movement theoreticians.

922 **Ruhl, J. Mark.** Repoliticizing the Nicaraguan army: civil-military relations under Daniel Ortega (2007–2017). (*J. Polit. Mil. Sociol.*, 46:1, 2019, p. 164–189, bibl.)

The significance of this article's primary subject—civilian-military relations in contemporary Nicaragua under President Daniel Ortega—is most apparent in its contrast with the situation before Ortega. The author provides concise descriptions of the military's subservience as an arm of the political leadership during the Somoza and Sandinista regimes. He then highlights the development of a professional, nonpartisan military in the period that followed. Since returning to the presidency in 2007, Ortega has step-by-step reversed this historic accomplishment, especially by expanding the military's role and through material inducements to individual leaders and their families.

923 **Stanford, Catherine M.** Nicaragua and Agamben's state of exception: misunderstood history and current crisis. (*Lat. Am. Policy*, 10:1, 2019, p. 93–119, bibl.)

The author claims that portraying Giorgio Agamben's "state of exception" as existing in Nicaragua by the end of 2018 was both inaccurate and potentially dangerous as a euphemism for coup mongering against Daniel Ortega. She also faults the human rights community for purported imbalances in its coverage of that year's violence. Most of the article, though, is devoted to a useful summary of the last 100 years of Nicaraguan political history, especially as related to a political culture with a long tradition of authoritarian caudillo leaders.

924 **Walker, Thomas W.** and **Christine J. Wade.** Nicaragua: emerging from the shadow of the eagle. Sixth edition. Boulder, Colo.: Westview Press, 2017. 244 p.: bibl., ill., index.

This highly successful book is now in its sixth edition. When first published in 1981 (see *HLAS 45:6175*), it began with the colonial period and continued into the first days of the new revolutionary government. This new edition retains prior versions' positive view of the "nationalist" Sandinista government and its "quite moderate" policies, but acknowledges the increasing authoritarianism of Daniel Ortega following his return to power in 2007. The current edition effectively explains why Ortega remained popular with the Nicaraguan majority into the mid-2010s, but its concluding pages provide little foreshadowing of the crisis of 2018 and the aftermath.

PANAMA

925 **Conniff, Michael L.** and **Gene E. Bigler.** Modern Panama: from occupation to crossroads of the Americas. Cambridge, England; New York, N.Y.: Cambridge University Press, 2019. 346 p.: bibl., ill., index, maps.

Two well-established experts have produced an outstanding book on Panamanian politics that should serve well both students and scholars. This is the third book on Panama by the first author (see *HLAS 49:6219* and *HLAS 71:1111*), while the second was a US diplomat in the country for three years in the early 2000s. After providing a brief historical overview and analysis of the Manuel Noriega period, the book is organized in separate chapters on each of the seven presidential administrations following the 1989 invasion up to the book's publication. Throughout the book, thorough attention is given to the canal, from the negotiation of the treaties through Panama's successful management and modernization of the canal, as well as its effective integration as the driver of the national economy. While acknowledging the challenges on hand, the tone of the book is positive and optimistic.

THE CARIBBEAN

CLIFFORD E. GRIFFIN, *Associate Professor of Political Science, North Carolina State University*
JOSÉ A. LAGUARTA RAMÍREZ, *Research Associate, Center for Puerto Rican Studies (Centro) at Hunter College, City University of New York (CUNY)*

HISPANIC CARIBBEAN
The three Spanish-speaking polities of the Caribbean continue to be heavily influenced by their complicated historical relationships with the US, position within the global capitalist economy, and complex internal dynamics shaped by centuries of colonialism and marked by sharp inequalities of class, race, and gender—factors widely shared within the Caribbean region as a whole. Sustained outward migration has continued for all three countries (subsiding somewhat for Puerto Rico five years after the impact of Hurricane Maria, while increasing for Cuba as it faces renewed challenges shaped by external and internal factors), while aging populations, changing climates, "natural" disasters, and relatively weak infrastructures present additional challenges to local politics and policy-making.

The most marked political distinction between the three countries is that Puerto Rico is a US "unincorporated territory" whose residents are US citizens but lack representation and voting rights at the federal level, while Cuba and the Dominican Republic are independent nation-states. A second crucial distinction is that Puerto Rico and the Dominican Republic are formally representative democracies, while Cuba is a single-party state. Both Puerto Rico and the Dominican Republic have long been fully integrated into the US orbit of the global capitalist economy, while Cuba has been slowly transitioning from a traditional state-monopoly socialist model to a more "mixed" economic model.

Since the publication of *HLAS 75*, the ongoing global COVID-19 pandemic has become a major additional challenge facing all three Hispanic Caribbean countries (along with the rest of the world). All three countries also experienced major political events while facing these new challenges. As the summaries in this section describe, COVID-19 was a major detonator of Cuba's largest protests in a generation as it tried to consolidate its post-Castro leadership, forced the postponement (and possibly influenced the outcome) of the most significant Dominican presidential election in as much time, and generated new corruption scandals in Puerto Rico that contributed to mounting discontent and the biggest electoral threat to its two governing parties in their history. [JLR]

CUBA
On 11 July 2021, Cuba experienced its largest protests against government policy since the 1994 "maleconazo" in the midst of the "Special Period." The unprecedented protests, which took place in over 60 municipalities, were met with police repression and hundreds of arrests. At least one person died, according to the authorities (competing claims of multiple deaths have not been corroborated). As acknowledged by President Miguel Díaz-Canel, protesters included not just those long disaffected with the regime and those seeking relief and redress of immediate conditions, but many self-identified "revolutionaries" as well.

Apparently sparked by an online social media campaign with unclear origin, protesters' immediate grievances included rising COVID-19 infections and deaths, price spikes caused by recent economic reforms, and the perceived slowness of additional long-promised reforms that might alleviate a long-stagnant economy. The government attributed the worsening economic situation and lack of resources for treating COVID-19 to the six-decade-long US embargo (item **976**), while protesters argued scarcities were augmented by bureaucratic mismanagement, inefficiency, and corruption. Some protesters also sought an end to the single-party regime led by the PCC (Partido Comunista de Cuba).

Despite Díaz-Canel's initial "hard line" response, the government quickly moved to concede some of the protesters' demands, including eliminating highly restrictive tariffs on goods entering the country. Small businesses, already undergoing a very slow, drawn-out process of liberalization following the PCC's Seventh Congress in 2016 (item **980**), were almost completely legalized soon thereafter. As of mid-April 2022, Cuban officials say about 300 people have been tried and sentenced out of 790 formally arrested during the protests. Critics have noted the sentences are highly disproportionate to the charges. No new large-scale demonstrations have taken place. Protests scheduled for November 2021 failed to materialize, likely as the result of a preemptive crackdown.

Despite a campaign promise to return to the detente that characterized US-Cuba relations during the Obama years (especially after diplomatic channels were re-established in 2015), US President Joe Biden has not repealed the over 240 new sanctions imposed on Cuba during the Trump administration. In contrast, the Biden administration moved quickly, following the protests, to condemn the Cuban regime and impose additional sanctions, signaling that the anticipated thaw in relations was not likely to happen. However, in March 2022, the US State Department announced it would reopen the consular section of its embassy in Havana (closed since 2017) and resume "limited" processing of Cuban visa requests. In late April, the US held migration talks with Cuba for the first time since July 2018.

COVID-19 cases in Cuba rose sharply after the cash-starved government reopened the island to international tourism in November 2020. Further complicated by the arrival of the highly contagious Delta variant, cases skyrocketed in early June 2021, just as a mass vaccination campaign with Cuba's own homegrown vaccines was slated to begin. However, once vaccination began, cases dropped sharply. As of late April 2022, 87.8 percent of the population had been fully vaccinated, and 94.1 percent had received at least one dose (including most children over the age of 2) of one of five vaccines developed independently by Cuba. Cuban vaccines have now become a centerpiece of Cuba's long-standing soft power diplomacy efforts through the export of free medical services (item **982**).

Whether or not Cuba's single-party regime can survive the new political situation evidenced on 11 July 2021 has yet to be determined. Díaz-Canel, who became PCC First Secretary when the 92-year-old Raúl Castro stepped down during its Eighth Congress (April 2021), has been the direct recipient of much public criticism before and after the protests, and is often openly compared unfavorably to Raúl and especially to his older brother Fidel (who stepped down in 2008 and died in 2016). Born after the 1959 Revolution, Díaz-Canel is the first non-Castro to lead the country since then, and he was widely regarded as a reformer when sworn in as president in 2018. [JLR]

DOMINICAN REPUBLIC

Luis Abinader of the Partido Revolucionario Moderno (PRM) was elected president in the 5 July 2020 general election. This was the first time since the democratic "consolidation" of 1996 that a party other than the Partido de la Liberación Dominicana (PLD) or the Partido Revolucionario Dominicano (PRD) won the presidency. Originally slated for May 2020, the election was postponed due to the COVID-19 pandemic. The February 2020 municipal elections had also been postponed because of problems with voting machines, adding to frustration with the incumbent government.

Plagued by corruption scandals, the neoliberal and pro-US incumbent Danilo Medina (2012–2020) failed to secure a constitutional reform allowing him to run for a third term. His former minister of public works and communications, Gonzalo Castillo, ran for the PLD, placing second. Former President Leonel Fernández (1996–2000, 2004–2012), who left the PLD after alleging fraud in the primaries, placed third as the candidate of the emergent group Fuerza del Pueblo (FP). Despite having already served three terms, Fernández is able to run again following the 2009 constitutional reform, which allowed former presidents to run again for terms that are nonconsecutive with two consecutive terms.

The end of PLD hegemony—it ruled for 20 of 24 years since 1996, and uninterruptedly since 2004—led many to view the election as the "end of an era" (item **953**). This sense is reinforced by the virtual disappearance or absorption of the PRD and the Partido Reformista Social Cristiano (together with the PLD, the three dominant forces of the 1978–96 "transition" era). Itself largely the product of a schism in the PRD, the PRM has claimed to represent the "authentic" social-democratic politics supposedly abandoned by that party, as it gravitated towards Medina's PLD. Nonetheless, most observers continue to view Dominican politics as largely personalistic and clientelistic, with few programmatic differences among the parties and candidates (item **956**).

The Abinader administration has focused on new anticorruption measures as well as prosecuting members of the Medina administration involved in corruption schemes, especially the notorious case involving the Brazilian construction giant Odebrecht, in which bribes were paid out to government officials from 12 African and Latin American nations (item **952**). In the Dominican Republic, revelations of the government's involvement in the Odebrecht case sparked the anticorruption social movement known as the "Marcha Verde" throughout 2017 and 2018, which contributed to weakening Medina's legitimacy (item **951**).

Despite his anticorruption discourse, President Abinader has drawn attention himself after being named in the notorious "Pandora Papers" leak starting in October 2021. Abinader denies any wrongdoing, claiming that he has been "completely separated" from his family's business affairs since becoming president.

In the economic sphere, growth trends highlighted in previous *HLAS* volumes have continued. Despite contracting in 2020 (largely because of the COVID-19 pandemic) following many years of sustained yearly growth at over 4 percent (item **953**), the Dominican economy rebounded significantly in 2021.

Critics note this apparent success has been accompanied by the aforementioned corruption scandals, ongoing environmental degradation, and dramatic income inequality (item **950**). Nonetheless, there are indications of some successful social programs in areas such as education and health, due in large part to mobilization by social movement networks (item **955**). [JLR]

PUERTO RICO

In early August 2019, Pedro Rosselló stepped down as governor of Puerto Rico, following two weeks of protests sparked by a string of corruption scandals and the publication of a damning private text conversation between Rosselló and members of his inner circle (item **969**). Pedro Pierluisi became the constitutional successor when Rosselló named him secretary of state on his last day in office. Less than a week later, the Puerto Rico Supreme Court ruled that the transfer of power had been unconstitutional because the Senate had not voted to confirm. Justice Secretary Wanda Vázquez was then sworn in as governor instead. However, in the August 2020 primary of the pro-US statehood Partido Nuevo Progresista (PNP), Pierluisi handily defeated Vázquez—whose brief tenure continued to be plagued by disasters and corruption scandals—and went on to defeat a divided pro-status quo Partido Popular Democrático (PPD) in the November 2020 general election.

A nonbinding plebiscite on the territory's political status—the sixth since the enactment of the 1952 "Commonwealth" Constitution and the third since 2012 (item **971**)—was held concurrently with the election and resulted in a first-ever slim majority for US statehood. Critics of such exercises point to their nonbinding character (they do not obligate the US Congress, which holds sovereignty over Puerto Rico under the status quo) and to historically low turnout rates as undermining any potential mandate. Pursuant to the local law enacting the plebiscite, an official delegation was formed with the task of lobbying the US Congress to act on the results. As of late April 2022, neither HR1522/S780 (immediately admitting Puerto Rico as the 51st state) nor competing bill HR2070/S865 (authorizing the Puerto Rico legislature to convene a "status convention" charged with organizing a consultation funded and to be ratified by Congress) have moved beyond the House and Senate Committees on Natural Resources, which oversee territorial matters.

Also significantly, the gubernatorial candidates from the non-status oriented, left-leaning Movimiento Victoria Ciudadana (MVC), the social-democratic Partido Independentista Puertorriqueño (PIP), and the religious, conservative, non-status oriented Proyecto Dignidad received 14.2 percent, 13.7 percent, and 7 percent of the vote, respectively, in the 2020 election. Together, the MVC and PIP—both of whose candidates openly supported independence—received nearly a third of the votes, potentially signaling a dramatic realignment of the five-decades old de facto bipartisan party system (item **968**). Both parties vocally supported the 2019 uprising that ousted Rosselló (item **967**).

During the first half of its tenure, the Pierluisi administration continued to face significant challenges, including the ongoing COVID-19 pandemic (item **969**), large mobilizations by teachers and other public employees against pension cuts mandated by an unelected Fiscal Oversight and Management Board (FOMB), and widespread discontent caused by recurrent infrastructure failures (items **969** and **970**). Particularly contentious are recurrent, large-scale power outages nearly a year after the private US-Canadian venture LUMA Energy took over distribution operations from the nominally public Puerto Rico Electric Power Authority (PREPA)—a total blackout on 6 April 2022 left hundreds of thousands without power for three days or more. Protests have also targeted the illegal construction of luxury private homes on protected beaches and wetlands, as well as community displacement resulting from the buying up of properties by beneficiaries of Laws 20 and 22 (which give local tax exemptions to US investors who relocate to Puerto Rico).

Puerto Rico's special bankruptcy proceeding, authorized by the US Congress in the 2016 Puerto Rico Oversight, Management, and Economic Stability Act, which installed the FOMB (items **969** and **972**), was declared completed on 15 March 2022, following a deal to ostensibly reduce 22 billion US dollars of the territory's 74 billion dollars in public debt down to 7 billion. Critics continue to object, arguing that these deals were struck without a public accounting of irregularities and possible illegalities in the contracting of the debt, and that the purported solution ensures most bondholders are repaid at the expense of future retirees and essential public services. Some economists remain skeptical that the territory will be able to meet debt obligations under the plan, whose own projections foresee a return of budget deficits in a few decades. The FOMB will continue debt restructuring proceedings for several government agencies. [JLR]

ANGLOPHONE CARIBBEAN
"De-risking," Bank Indigenization and Political Stability in the Organization of East Caribbean States

AS OPEN MARKET and democratic societies, the political future of the Anglophone Caribbean countries is inextricably tied to their economies. The average openness ratio—the sum of exports and imports of goods and services divided by GDP—in the Caribbean amounted to 95 percent of GDP over 2011–2015, which is slightly higher than the world average of 91 percent of GDP (Alleyne et al., 2017). These economies are largely service-driven, including tourism and financial services, and are highly dependent on access to Correspondent Banking Relationships (CBRs), which are the lubricants essential to the smooth functioning of the cross-border transactions that propel today's global commercial and financial engine. Without access to CBRs, countries become susceptible to economic contraction and, quite possibly, economic implosion. The loss of CBRs can impose huge costs on an economy as financial institutions struggle to find appropriate means to settle their cross-border transactions. An increase in the cost of making payments or a disruption in the ability to make or receive international payments would seriously undermine economic activity. This is the situation in which the banks in the Eastern Caribbean Currency Union (ECCU) recently found themselves.

The economies of ECCU countries are characterized by high reliance on international trade and commerce, including tourism and related services; foreign direct investment (FDI); remittances; and the presence of offshore banking and other offshore financial services. For example, in 2021, tourism and travel amounted to 915.2 million US dollars and FDI totaled 526 billion dollars; in 2019, remittances totaled 255.52 million dollars (https://wttc.org, 2022; https://unctad.org, 2021; https://ourworldindata.org, 2021). However, many of the international banks that have long operated within the ECCU have struggled to maintain profitability along two separate, but interrelated fronts.

On the one hand, the global recession of 2007–2008 triggered huge investment losses across the Caribbean, including 1.5 billion dollars in gross impaired loans reported by Scotiabank; 835 million dollars by CIBC; and 800 million dollars by RBC (Hartnell, 2015; Kiladze, 2015). On the other hand, increased regulation of banking systems to address concerns about tax evasion and combat money laundering and the financing of terrorism has had the unintended consequence of making CBRs costlier and less attractive to global banks. Moreover, unclear regulatory expectations presented correspondent banks with the undesirable prospect of incurring huge fines for noncompliance, particularly in cases where local privacy laws prohibit the sharing of information about banks' customers. Risk aversion, therefore, triggered recission, as these international banks sold their assets, especially in the small markets in the Organization of East Caribbean States (OECS), and led to the decision to maintain and expand operations in the larger Caribbean and Latin American markets. This strategy of "de-risking" resulted in the withdrawal of CBRs from these economies long connected to and dependent upon the global banking and financial system.

Early data indicate that the ECCU countries have been among the most affected jurisdictions for termination of CBRs, with more than 75 percent of banks in Dominica and more than 50 percent of banks in Antigua and Barbuda and St. Kitts and Nevis losing their CBRs during the last five years. To date, some 13 indigenous banks and one regional bank have stepped in to fill the void left by these departing international banks. The result is bank indigenization. Is there a silver lining to bank "de-risking" and bank indigenization in the OECS? To what extent has "de-risking" been a positive development for small banking and financial institutions in this region? An empirical and strategic exploration into the challenges faced and strategies undertaken by the subregion's national and indigenous banking and financial institutions to creatively reorganize and reposition themselves to continue to provide banking services to their local and international clients reveals, among other things, that these countries need to move from single-country economic entities to multi-economy ones.

This analysis turns on the notion that countries and regions should avoid situations in which their banks are either "too big to fail" or "too small to succeed," and is informed by an analysis of the banking and financial structure in the ECCU, the impacts of anti-money laundering and counterterrorism financing (AML/CFT) enforcement on these economies, and the consequent "de-risking" strategies of the international banks that have led to the indigenization of banking and finance in this subregion. Bank indigenization reflects a paradox in the ECCU. On the one hand, it is likely to deepen regional integration by forcing members to fundamentally restructure their economies at the individual and collective levels; that is, members would move from single-country economies to multicountry economies through bank amalgamation as well as bank consortia, both within individual countries and between and among subsets of ECCU member countries. On the other hand, "de-risking" has not changed the fundamental asymmetric relationship between banks in the region, where the international banks long dominated the indigenous ones. Instead, the asymmetry has shifted to one in which a regional giant, the Trinidad and Tobago-based

Republic Financial Holdings Group (RFHL), which recently purchased assets of Scotiabank in all but one of the ECCU countries, is poised to replace the departing, powerful international banks. While RFHL's asset base for the subregion is 1.6B USD compared to 7.12B USD for the indigenous banks, its overall asset base of 16.2B USD for the broader region dwarfs the combined assets of the indigenous banks in the ECCU, thereby making it a dominant financial giant in this region. Thus, while amalgamations and consortia may alleviate the challenges associated with being "too small to succeed," the growth and expansion of the RFHL Group across the region may result in a regional institution that is "too big to fail."

A prescient former governor of the ECCB, K. Dwight Venner, noted in 2009 that the small, open, vulnerable and disaster-prone economies of the ECCU, with a population of approximately 630,000, were lagging in the Latin American and Caribbean region in growth, competitiveness, macro variables (such as fiscal policy and debt), the doing business index, and other critical elements in the Global Competitiveness Index. The viability and competitiveness of the banking system, especially the indigenous banks, he argued, demanded a rationalization of the financial sector that would entail member countries fundamentally restructuring their economies at the individual and collective levels by moving from single-country economies to a multicountry economy (Mitchell, 2015; ECCB Annual Report 2008/2009). This multistage process would be initiated with an adjustment phase from January 2012 to December 2014; next would be the economic transformational phase and the creation of a fully functional economic space from January 2015 to December 2020. The initial response was an eight-point Stabilization and Growth Plan, which, among other things, called for the amalgamation of indigenous banks to drive economies of scale and scope, efficiencies in operations, and increased opportunities for a more diverse state-of-the-art banking operation.

However, implementation was slow. Six years passed with little movement until renewed discussions in 2015 concluded that the consolidation of the sector should be undertaken, over a period of time, beginning with a shared services approach. The ECCB pushed for a shared service for the risk and compliance function, which entails: ensuring the timely establishment of an effective and efficient shared risk and compliance function; technical expertise; financial capacity; data protection capabilities; monitoring procedures; good standing within the financial services industry; and facilitating money transfers through transactions such as wire transfers, check clearing, and currency exchange. Without these banking relationships, businesses would be cut off from international trade and financing, families would be unable to collect remittances from relatives working abroad, and moreover, foreign investors may be unwilling to invest if there is a risk that they will be unable to repatriate their profits (CAB, Inc., 2019). Among the expected benefits of consolidation would be economies of scale, greater efficiency in terms of back-of-office activities such as shared software for collaboration; shared investments in ATMs, online and mobile banking; and electronic due diligence that includes greater AML/CFT oversight.

Ultimately, the decisions of the international banks—CIBC, RBC, and Scotiabank—to "de-bank" from the ECCU to refocus their investment options into bigger markets in the Caribbean and Latin America jolted the indigenous banks into action. Recognizing the trend in the global financial sector towards mergers and acquisitions, indigenous banks acknowledged that consolidation would enhance financial stability, encourage growth, and provide modern services to customers at competitive prices in a dynamic environment. This case was articulated in the ECCB's June 2018 consultative paper on consolidation of national banks in the ECCU. The evidence was clear: these individual indigenous banks were too small to succeed.

Accordingly, among the first steps were the acquisition of the assets of the departing international banks, RBC, Scotiabank, and CIBC. For example, RBC's eastern Caribbean assets were sold to a consortium of indigenous banks including the Antigua Commercial Bank (ACB), Ltd., the Bank of Montserrat, Ltd., the Bank of Nevis Ltd., the National Bank of Dominica, Ltd., and the 1st National Bank of St. Lucia, Ltd. As part of this transaction, the consortium has also acquired the Royal Bank of Trinidad and Tobago (Caribbean) Ltd. in St. Vincent and the Grenadines, majority shareholding in Royal Bank of Trinidad and Tobago (Grenada) Ltd., and the Royal Bank of Trinidad and Tobago (St. Kitts and Nevis) Ltd. According to Johnathan Johannes, managing director of 1st National Bank of Saint Lucia, "we formed the consortium for the express purpose of expanding the scale of the locally owned financial entities in the Eastern Caribbean Currency Union. This transaction gives us the size and scale to play a more active role in the development of our respective countries. We see this transaction as the first step in achieving even greater synergies, efficiencies, and crossterritory marketing opportunities" (Christopher, 2021; Gonçalves, 2019; *Loop Business News*, 12 Dec. 2019).

Risk aversion witnessed Scotiabank striking a deal with the RFHL Group in 2018 to sell banking businesses in nine Caribbean countries for US 123 million dollars. Included in this deal were all of Scotiabank's operations in the ECCU, along with those in Guyana and Saint Maarten (Zochdone, 2018). The purchase price included 25 million dollars for the business in Anguilla and 98 million for the other eight countries. De-risking, therefore, has placed banking services largely in the hands of indigenous institutions, which need larger asset bases to become more competitive. Finance and regional politics held up this deal as then prime minister of Antigua and Barbuda, Gaston Brown, became concerned about the disposal of the two branches that Scotiabank operated in his country in which approximately 75 people were employed (Padin-Dujon, 2021). The impasse was resolved via a separate agreement by Scotiabank to sell those assets to the Antigua and Barbuda-based Eastern Caribbean Amalgamated Bank (ECAB), an outcome deemed consistent with that country's national priorities that included boosting the local financial sector.

De-risking has also resulted in the following consortium of indigenous banks in the ECCU—the Bank of Nevis, Ltd., Bank of Montserrat, Ltd., Antigua Commercial Bank (ACB), Ltd., National Bank of Dominica, Ltd., and 1st National Bank of St. Lucia—which purchased the assets of RBC. Meanwhile, the assets of CIBC FirstCaribbean International Bank in St. Kitts and Nevis were purchased by the St. Kitts Nevis Anguilla National Bank; and the agreement for the assets of CIBC FirstCaribbean International Bank in St. Vincent and the Grenadines to be sold to the Bank of St. Vincent and the Grenadines is expected to be completed by May 2023. However, whether these indigenous institutions can compete with a Republic Bank and its parent company, RFHL, remains an open question. [CEG]

REFERENCES

Alleyne, Trevor et al. "Loss of Correspondent Banking Relationships in the Caribbean: Trends, Impact, and Policy Options." In *Unleashing Growth and Strengthening Resilience in the Caribbean*, Washington, D.C.: International Monetary Fund, 2017, p. 265–288 (item **1345**).

Caribbean Association of Banks' Position on Republic Bank's proposed buyout of Scotiabank's Banking Operations, *Caribbean Association of Banks, Inc.*, Press Release, 11 December 2018, https://cab-inc.com/the-caribbean-association-of-banks-position-on-republic-banks-proposed-buyout-of-scotiabanks-banking-operations/

Consultative Paper on the Consolidation of National Banks in the Eastern Caribbean Currency Union. Basseterre, St. Kitts and Nevis: Eastern Caribbean Central Bank (ECCB), June 2018, https://cdn.eccb-centralbank.org/documents/2022-04-08-07-39-32-Consultative-Paper-on-Consolidation-of-National-Banks-for-ECCB-Website.pdf

Padin-Dujon, Alejandra. "Scotiabank Wants to Leave Small Caribbean Markets. It's Not That Easy," 23 August 2021, https://blogs.lse.ac.uk/internationaldevelopment/2021/08/23/scotiabank-wants-to-leave-small-caribbean-markets-its-not-that-easy/

GENERAL

926 Beckles, Hilary. How Britain underdeveloped the Caribbean: a reparation response to Europe's legacy of plunder and poverty. Kingston: The University of the West Indies Press, 2021. 256 p.: bibl., ill., index.

The author focuses his attention on the British Empire and shows how successive governments not only have systematically suppressed economic development in their former colonies, but also have refused to accept responsibility for the debt and development support they owe their former colonies in the Caribbean. [CEG]

927 Bernal, Richard L. Globalization, trade, and economic development: the CARIFORUM-EU economic partnership agreement. New York, N.Y.: Palgrave Macmillan, 2013. 269 p.: bibl., ill., index.

This in-depth study of the economic partnership between the European Union and the 15 Caribbean countries that make up CARIFORUM, which, as the first trade agreement of its kind, represents a new type of WTO-compatible trade agreement between a group of developed countries and a group of developing ones. [CEG]

928 Cabatingan, Lee. A region among states: law and non-sovereignty in the Caribbean. Chicago, Ill.: The University of Chicago, 2023. 240 p.: bibl., index, color plates, photos, tables.

By asking why the independent, English-speaking Caribbean continues to accept the judicial oversight of their former colonizer via the British institution of the Privy Council, and what possibilities the Caribbean Court of Justice might offer for untangling sovereignty and regionhood, law and modernity, and postcolonial Caribbean identity, this work explores the possibility of constituting the Caribbean as a region on a geopolitical and ideological terrain dominated by the nation-state. [CEG]

929 Caribbean integration: uncertainty in a time of global fragmentation. Edited by Patsy Lewis, Terri-Ann Gilbert-Roberts, and Jessica Byron. Contributions by April Karen Baptiste et al. Kingston: The University of the West Indies Press, 2022. 352 p.: bibl., ill.

This collection offers diverse perspectives on the political, social, economic, cultural, and environmental dimensions of regional integration. Specific topics include the role and influence of youth, language, reparatory justice, election reform, gender-based violence, migration, trade, and climate change on the deepening and longevity of CARICOM institutions. [CEG]

930 **Caribbean migrations: the legacies of colonialism.** Edited by Anke Birkenmaier. New Brunswick, N.J.: Rutgers University Press, 2021. 305 p.: bibl., graphs, ill., index. (Critical Caribbean studies)

The contributors to this volume utilize interdisciplinary lenses to provide local and regional analyses of migration from Puerto Rico, Cuba, Jamaica, the Dominican Republic, Haiti, and diasporic communities in the US, and speak to the intersection of migration policies, identities, political agency, and colonial legacies in the cultural production of resistance and dissent. [CEG]

931 *Caribbean Quarterly.* Vol. 68, No. 2, March 2022. Kingston: University of the West Indies.

As reparation activists situate their claims within a genealogy of Caribbean Black radical responses from the Haitian Revolution to the intellectual interventions of Caribbean thinkers and the lived experiences of those impacted by native genocide, chattel slavery, and indentureship, Zaira Simone explores how contemporary claims for reparations in the Caribbean challenge us to think differently about the scope and limitations of certain strands of what Cedric J. Robinson called the Black radical tradition. [CEG]

932 **Changing continuities and the scholar-activist anthropology of Constance R. Sutton.** Edited by David Evan Sutton and Deborah A. Thomas. Kingston; Miami, Fla.: Ian Randle Publishers, 2022. 381 p.: bibl., portraits.

Constance R. Sutton was a pioneer of Caribbeanist anthropology and a political and social activist who advocated for racial and gender justice internationally. Her scholarship raised broad questions about positionality in colonial studies and challenged the male-centric authorial voice in "writing culture" more generally. This publication includes 14 of her essays across the broad themes of Caribbeanist anthropology, feminism and Black women's power, and transnationalism. [CEG]

933 **Contemporary issues within Caribbean economies.** Edited by Colin Cannonier and Monica Galloway Burke. Cham, Switzerland: Palgrave Macmillan, 2022. 295 p.: bibl., ill. (some color), index, map.

The historical approach of this volume demonstrates how tourism has emerged as the main source of foreign exchange, which is complemented by remittances, the latter of which acts as a form of social insurance. This process speaks to the lack of economic diversification, exacerbating the vulnerability of Caribbean economies to economic and climatic shocks. The authors argue that given the small size of the economies, the impact and duration of shocks are extreme, and that fiscal policy designed to smooth out these shocks has led to the rapid accumulation of debt and has been a major drag on growth. [CEG]

934 **Gonzalez-Vicente, Ruben** and **Annita Montoute.** A Caribbean perspective on China-Caribbean relations: global IR, dependency and the postcolonial condition. (*Third World Q.*, 42:2, 2021, p. 219–238, bibl.)

Situating this analysis within the context of the Belt and Road Initiative, the authors transpose a set of Caribbean-based theories that gained prominence in the 1960s and 1970s to analyze and explain China's contemporary relations with the Caribbean community. They contend that the expectations placed on the emerging "South-South" link with China are easily overstated, given China's elitist business-centric approach to development, the eschewing of participatory approaches in Sino-Caribbean ventures, and the passive incorporation of the Caribbean into China's global vision. [CEG]

935 **Guns, gun violence and gun homicides: perspectives from the Caribbean, Global South and beyond.** Edited by Wendell C. Wallace. Cham, Switzerland:

Palgrave Macmillan, 2022. 360 p.: bibl., ill., index. (Palgrave studies in risk, crime and society)

This book provides in-depth coverage of guns, gun violence, and gun homicides from a variety of perspectives, including, but not limited to, gender, suicide, "peaceology" and police (in)action. The work reflects on changes in contemporary perceptions as well as desires for scholarship emanating from underresearched areas of the globe. [CEG]

936   **Harnoncou, Julia.** Theorizing human trafficking and unfree labor. (*J. Global South Stud.*, 40:1, Spring 2023, p. 173–212)

Historicizing the issue of human trafficking within the framework of unfree labor, which, for Latin America, the Caribbean, and Africa, mostly means its connection to chattel slavery, the illegalization of unfree labor, and the development of the legal term of human trafficking and the introduction of laws against it, the author examines the emergence of today's legal, social, and political reality in order to deepen an understanding of anti-human trafficking law and its application. [CEG]

937   **Haynes, Jason.** Paradoxes and anomalies in Caribbean anti-trafficking law and practice. (*J. Global South Stud.*, 40:1, Spring 2023, p. 145–172)

The author provides a critical examination of existing state practices of human trafficking in 12 Caribbean countries by focusing on the four main contentious areas of state practice with which regional stakeholders are most concerned: the description of "trafficking in persons" as "modern slavery," the illegitimacy of the US TIP Reports, investigations into trafficking in persons, and victim identification and referral. [CEG]

938   **McIntyre, Alister.** Caribbean trade, integration and development: selected papers and speeches of Alister McIntyre. Vol. 1, Trade and integration. Edited by Andrew S. Downes *et al.* Kingston: Canoe Press, 2022. 1 v.: bibl., maps.

Sir Alister unswervingly believed that the only workable pathway for the survival of the small countries of the Caribbean was through a strategy of regional integration that would combine the synergies of the individual countries and of the region into a collective whole. This volume provides additional insights into his deep interests, such as human resource development, education, training, and the capacity to deal with the challenges of change in the 21st century, all of which are deftly addressed in his many contributions to scholarship. [CEG]

939   **McKenzie, Gabrielle.** Human trafficking in the Caribbean: developing Caribbean-centered ways to fight the crime. (*J. Global South Stud.*, 40:1, Spring 2023, p. 38–82, bibl., map, table)

Hypothesizing that Western models of analyzing human trafficking are flawed because of relatively little input from stakeholders, the author seeks to fill the data gap in the Caribbean by surveying the region's human trafficking experts—namely survivors, NGOs focused on trafficking in the Caribbean, scholars, government actors, and policymakers—in order to help advance antitrafficking solutions that are better suited to the region. [CEG]

940   **Medwinter, Sancha Doxilly** and **Tannuja D. Rozario.** Caribbean womanism: decolonial theorizing of Caribbean women's oppression, survival, and resistance. (*Ethn. Racial Stud.*, 44:14, 2021, p. 2702–2722, bibl.)

In this article, the authors theorize Caribbean womanism as an integrated decolonial, Caribbeanist, and womanist framework that reimagines and highlights the specificity of Caribbean peoples' historical and contemporary experience with European colonialism and US recolonization, and how these necessarily shape Caribbean understandings and experiences of race, class, gender, patriarchy, and sexuality. [CEG]

941   ***Meridians: Feminism, Race, Transnationalism.*** Vol. 21, No. 1, 2022, Black feminism in the Caribbean and the United States: representation, rebellion, radicalism, and reckoning. Durham, N.C.: Duke University Press.

Bringing together Black feminist conversations and debates taking place across the transnational Americas, North and South, this special issue covers, among other topics, #BlackGirlMagic, Black girlhood studies, Afro-Latina race consciousness, and a conversation with Edwidge Danticat titled "Vodou, the Arts, and (Re)Presenting the Divine." [CEG]

942   **New political culture in the Caribbean.** Edited by Holger Henke and Fred Reno. Jamaica; Barbados; Trinidad and Tobago: University of the West Indies Press, 2022. 261 p.: bibl., index.

The contributors to this volume consider recent developments precipitating significant changes in the political attitudes and discourses in the region. They contend that even the persistent themes in Caribbean political life—issues such as race, ethnicity, sovereignty, civil rights, or poverty—allow for new considerations, not only because of their longevity, but also because in their contemporary form they may speak to new dynamics in society or find different forms of expression or political impact. [CEG]

943   **Smith, Faith.** Strolling in the ruins: the Caribbean's non-sovereign modern in the early twentieth century. Durham, N.C.: Duke University Press, 2023. 280 p.: bibl., ill., index.

In this book, the author engages with a period in the history of the Anglophone Caribbean often overlooked as nondescript, quiet, and embarrassingly pro-imperial within the larger narrative of Jamaican and Trinidadian nationalism. [CEG]

944   **Sounds of vacation: political economies of Caribbean tourism.** Edited by Jocelyne Guilbault and Timothy Rommen. Durham, N.C.: Duke University Press, 2019. 234 p.: bibl., index.

The volume examines the commodification of music and sound at popular vacation destinations throughout the Caribbean in order to tease out the relationships between political economy, hospitality, and the legacies of slavery and colonialism. Drawing on case studies from Barbados, the Bahamas, Guadeloupe, Saint Martin, and Saint Lucia, the contributors point to the myriad ways that live performances, programmed music, and the sonic environment heighten tourists' pleasurable vacation experience. [CEG]

945   **Tourism resilience and recovery for global sustainability and development: navigating COVID-19 and the future.** Edited by Lloyd Waller and Edmund Bartlett. Kingston: GTRCMC, Global Tourism Resilience & Crisis Management Centre; Kingston; Miami, Fla.: Ian Randle Publishers, 2022. 291 p.: bibl., graphs, index.

This collection of essays attempts to rethink, discuss, and address the issues and challenges to Caribbean tourism before and since the pandemic. Not least among the challenges is climate change. The work makes recommendations for critical remedial actions to accelerate post-COVID-19 tourism recovery and foster enhanced resilience, including the identification of new and underexploited tourism niches. [CEG]

946   **Trade and development issues in CARICOM: key considerations for navigating development.** Edited by Roger Hosein et al. Kingston: The University of the West Indies Press, 2022. 264 p.: bibl., ill., index.

This collection of CARICOM-specific research represents a spectrum of writing on interrelated themes of trade, growth, debt, and the environment as it applies to development prospects in the Caribbean. [CEG]

947   **Williams, Eric Eustace.** The blackest thing in slavery was not the Black man: the last testament of Eric Williams. Edited by Brinsley Samaroo. Mona, Jamaica: The University of the West Indies Press, 2022. 236 p.: bibl., index.

The author demonstrates how Eric Williams provides a comprehensive view of the post-abolition world by showing how the capitalist impulse enabled Europe and the US to devise other (non-slavery) ways of further exploiting non-African people in developing countries, and how these nations fought further exploitation by creating the South-to-South Non-Aligned Movement. While most other works tend to separate these issues or deal with them on a regional basis, Williams offers a comprehensive view, tying together many themes. [CEG]

948 **Worrell, Rodney.** George Padmore's Black internationalism. Kingston: The University of the West Indies Press, 2020. 267 p.: bibl., index.

The author explores Padmore's use of Marxism and Pan-Africanism as vehicles to liberate Africa and the Caribbean from the grip of European imperialism, especially in the following roles: a leader in the Soviet Union's Black internationalism project during the early 1930s; one of the leading Pan-African activists in Britain from the mid-1930s until he migrated to Ghana in 1957, where he made his mark as a member of the International African Service Bureau and the Pan-African Federation, and as organizer of the Fifth Pan-African Congress in Manchester, England, in 1945; and as a major theorist of the unification of the African continent as Kwame Nkrumah's advisor on African affairs. [CEG]

DOMINICAN REPUBLIC

949 **Antología del pensamiento crítico dominicano contemporáneo.** Coordinación de Matías Bosch y Quisqueya Lora. Textos de Pedro Mir et al. Santo Domingo: Fundación Juan Bosch: AGN, Archivo General de la Nación; Buenos Aires: CLACSO, 2016. 542 p.: bibl., ill. (Colección Antologías del pensamiento social latinoamericano y caribeño)

As the title indicates, this groundbreaking volume gathers together key texts of Dominican political and social theory and analysis from the mid-20th century to the present. Organized into four sections ("Imperial domination and colonialism"; "Labor, production, territories, and migrations"; "Authoritarianism, ideology, and racism"; and "Identity, classes, and gender"), the book includes contributors that will be familiar to students and scholars of Dominican politics, along with lesser-known figures, such as Black and feminist thinkers, compiled and made accessible outside the Dominican Republic for the first time. [JLR]

950 **Benito Sánchez, Ana Belén.** Pobres y electores: universalidad y focalización de la política social en la República Dominicana 2006–2012. (*Rev. Int. Sociol.*, 77:3, julio/sept. 2019, e134, p. 1–16, bibl., graphs, tables)

Dominican elections since 1998 have been described as a "winner-take-all" contest maintaining the clientelistic and patrimonialist styles of the earlier post-Trujillo era, with high, stable levels of party identification lacking any real programmatic content (see item **956**). In this political context, and especially since 2004, the PLD (Partido de la Liberación Dominicana) governments led by Leonel Fernández (2004–2012) and Danilo Medina (2016–2020) instituted a series of public means-tested "programas de transferencias condicionadas" (PTCs), ostensibly for the support of those not covered by the contribution-based social security system. The author tests and confirms the hypothesis—based on the experiences of similar programs in Mexico and Brazil—that PTCs are prone to instrumentalization through clientelist strategies by analyzing spending patterns against the electoral calendar. After showing the positive correlation between election years and spending increases, the author argues that bifurcation between PTCs and contribution-based programs confirms a neoliberal tendency towards the "individual capitalization of efforts" and the "institutionalization of inequality." [JLR]

951 **Betances, Emelio.** The rise and fall of Marcha Verde in the Dominican Republic. (*Lat. Am. Perspect.*, 47:5, Aug. 2020, p. 20–34, bibl.)

The "Marcha Verde" movement emerged in 2017 to protest corruption in the Dominican Republic, sparked by revelations of the Medina administration's involvement in a bribery scheme benefiting the Brazilian construction company Odebrecht (see item **952**). Marcha Verde conducted 25 regional protests and large national marches in July 2017 and August 2018, but ultimately could not induce the Medina government to charge those implicated. As a movement for the "democratization of democracy," many observers consider it a watershed moment in Dominican political history. The author recounts the history of the Marcha Verde, arguing that ultimately it was unable to build a "social base" that would have allowed it to present an independent political challenge to the dominant parties. [JLR]

952 **Gerón, Cándido.** 172 años de corrupción en la República Dominicana: 1844–2016: cáncer globalizado. Tomo II. Santo Domingo: Serigraf S.A., 2018. 590 p.: bibl., ill., index.

Despite its sweeping title, this perplexingly organized volume in what appears to be a self-published trilogy is primarily an attempt to fastidiously document the Odebrecht scandal in the Dominican Republic. The sprawling, muckraking narrative is structured by headline-like section subtitles, interspersed with historical and philosophical considerations on "corruption" as well as discussions of Odebrecht-related and other corruption scandals from various countries. With patience, the volume may be a useful reference on the scale and impact of Odebrecht on Dominican politics, including the crucial emergence of the "Marcha Verde" movement (see item **951**), which is mentioned throughout the book. [JLR]

953 **Malamud, Carlos** and **Rogelio Núñez Castellano.** Elecciones presidenciales dominicanas: fin de época (¿y hegemonía?) en la República Dominicana. (*Rev. Elcano*, 90:1, julio 2020, p. 1–11, tables)

Published shortly before the 5 July 2020 elections, this article analyzes the historical significance of the event within the context of broader regional trends throughout Latin America. The authors begin by highlighting the broad impact of COVID-19 on the electoral process. In addition to providing a comprehensive historical background and breakdown of the Dominican party system, the authors' major line of argumentation is that the anticipated Partido Revolucionario Moderno (PRM) first-round victory would spell the end not just for Partido de la Liberación Dominicana (PLD) hegemony, but effectively of an "era" marked by major reconfigurations of the party system. According to the authors, this development was a result of the erosion of the three "pillars" of the previous era: 1) strong leaderships at the center of a dense patron-client network; 2) a cohesive dominant party facing a divided opposition, which reproduced clientelistic decision-making at the party level; and 3) a favorable international economic scenario. The authors find that this scenario fits within a larger Latin American pattern of "punishing" the incumbent irrespective of ideology, evidenced in nine of 14 regional presidential elections from 2017 to 2019. [JLR]

954 **Oliveros, Virginia** and **Christian Schuster.** Merit, tenure, and bureaucratic behavior: evidence from a conjoint experiment in the Dominican Republic. (*Comp. Polit. Stud.*, 51:6, May 2018, p. 759–792, bibl., graphs, tables)

From Max Weber's classic theorization of bureaucratic structures and behavior (the right structures create an esprit de corps around political neutrality, integrity, and commitment to public service), the authors derive two independent variables (merit examinations and job stability) and three dependent variables (corruption, work motivation, and political services). They test several hypotheses through a conjoint survey of 558 career public servants in the Dominican Republic (selected for its high levels of state politicization, as a "least likely" case to suggest generalizability of findings). They find a strong correlation between merit examinations and all three dependent variables (employees recruited through examinations are less likely to be corrupt or participate in electoral mobilization and more likely to work hard, thus enhancing the quality of both public services and democracy), but a strong correlation between job stability and only one of the dependent variables (employees with tenure are less likely to participate in electoral mobilization, thus enhancing only the quality of democracy). For political economy specialist's comment, see item **1272**. [JLR]

955 **Schrank, Andrew.** Cross-class coalitions and collective goods: the *farmacias del pueblo* in the Dominican Republic. (*Comp. Polit./New York*, 51:2, Jan. 2019, p. 259–274, graph, tables)

The "people's pharmacies" were created as part of the Dominican government's Essential Medicines Program in the late 20th century and expanded dramatically after the PLD's return to power in 2004. Today they are part of what appears to be a growing trend in some developing countries (and some developed countries), providing generic drugs at low or no cost. Such programs have become the focus of much policy debate, with critics arguing that they have been used as a source of political patronage and clientelism and/or that unless they are strictly means-tested, they "regressively" benefit middle-class clients who theoretically could afford higher prices. Using the Dominican Republic as a "least likely" case (because of its high levels of political patronage), the author tests these claims, concluding that they are not supported by the Dominican case. The author argues the variables that shaped the outcomes of this case (active civil society, "cross-class" constituencies) suggest a series of policy implications. [JLR]

956   El votante dominicano: ciudadanos y elecciones en la República Dominicana. Edición de Mariano Torcal, Leticia M. Ruiz y Gerardo Maldonado. Santo Domingo: Editorial Funglode, Fundación Global Democracia y Desarrollo, 2017. 253 p.: bibl., ill. (Política)

This book analyzes the results of the Observatorio de Opinión Pública y de Comportamiento Político Electoral Dominicano, a major survey conducted before and after the 2010 elections in the Dominican Republic, partially funded by the Spanish Agency for International Cooperation and Development and by several Dominican government agencies. Following a discussion of the historical and institutional context of the 2010 elections, the book is organized thematically according to major variables in the research design: political mobilization, sociodemographic factors, "psychological anchoring" (party identification and left-right ideology), short-term elements (performance and leadership), political intermediation (mass media, conversation, and parties), and knowledge of political issues. The conclusion offers a "profile" of Dominican voters, considers several recurring paradoxes in light of the survey findings, and suggests avenues for further research. This book provides a useful primer of contemporary Dominican electoral politics. [JLR]

JAMAICA

957   Batts, David. The law and constitution for every Jamaican. Kingston; Miami, Fla.: The Caribbean Law Publishing Company, 2022. 164 p.: bibl.

In this publication, the author provides simple information on the Jamaican legal system—its genesis, how it operates—and how the judicial system functions, and covers institutions of governance, including, among others, the Jamaica Constabulary Force, the operations of the National Land Agency, the Transport Authority and the Island Traffic Authority, the Rent Board, and the Firearm Licensing Authority. [CEG]

958   Gray, Obika. The coloniality of power and the limits of dissent in Jamaica. (*Small Axe*, 21:3, No. 54, Nov. 2017, p. 98–110)

The author argues that a second decolonization in Jamaica took place in the 1960s as a myriad of dissident organizations, personalities, and social forces challenged the country's dependency and rejected the unapologetic "coloniality of power." However, a number of serious weaknesses within this movement, including both a preoccupation with taking power and naiveté about the modern power arrayed against them, prevented dissidents from winning the majority of Jamaicans to their cause. [CEG]

959   Miller, Errol. Elections and governance, Jamaica on the global frontier: the independence years 1962 to 2016. Prelude by The Most Honourable P.J. Patterson. Foreward by The Honourable Bruce Golding. Kingston: Ian Randle Publishers, 2022. 531 p.: bibl., index.

Sketching Jamaican elections and governance through two phases—the colonial years, 1663 to 1962, and the independence years, 1962 to 2016, the author demonstrates that while Jamaica practices elections and governance within the Western model, it does so from the perspective of peoples subordinated in that world who are, nevertheless, resolutely defiant of domination because of their firm embrace of freedom. [CEG]

960 **Thame, Maziki.** Racial hierarchy and the elevation of brownness in Creole nationalism. (*Small Axe*, 21:3, No. 54, Nov. 2017, p. 111–123)

The author asserts that Creole nationalism in Jamaica is also Brown nationalism, and is rooted in notions of indigeneity and the elevation of hybridity as the basis of the state's claims to legitimacy. This phenomenon legitimized a racial hierarchy that centered Brownness, and provided a way to think about self and nation in independence through the national motto—one out of many—which served to obscure the racial order and maintain the subordinate place of Blackness in postcolonial Jamaica. [CEG]

961 **Thomas, Marc Anthony.** Participatory democracy: the case of parish development committees in Jamaica. Kingston: The University of the West Indies Press, 2021. 182 p.: bibl., index.

In this book, the author expands the existing knowledge on participatory democracy through an exploration of the institution of Parish Development Committees, which were established as a means for Jamaicans to inform government policy, and the extent to which they provided supportive institutional, infrastructural, and superstructural conditions for a robust implementation of democracy. [CEG]

962 **Walters, Shinique.** International aid under the microscope: European Union project cycle management in Jamaica. Kingston: The University of the West Indies Press, 2021. 144 p.: bibl., ill., index.

The author critically analyzes the discourse surrounding the EU's project management guidelines and their role in the development, conceptualization, management, and implementation of social development projects administered in Jamaica. Walters explores the role of the EU and its impact on aid dependency, as well as the role of environmental and social factors in achieving project success. [CEG]

BRITISH CARIBBEAN

963 **Watson, Hilbourne A.** Errol Walton Barrow and the postwar transformation of Barbados: the late colonial period. Kingston: University of West Indies Press, 2019. 315 p.: bibl., index.

The author provides an incisive and rigorous analysis of the conundrum facing a peripheral capitalist Caribbean society in explaining why Barbados, unable to break decisively with its colonial past and hamstrung by the deceit of the promise of sovereignty, is forced to make compromises with imperialism and its domestic representatives of capital. [CEG]

DUTCH CARIBBEAN

964 **Pereira, Edwina E.** and **Albert E. Steenge.** Vulnerability and resilience in the Caribbean island states: the role of connectivity. (*Net. Spatial Econ.*, 22:3, Sept. 2022, p. 515–540, bibl., graphs, tables)

In this work, the authors measure the economic vulnerability and resilience of 17 Caribbean island states—both dependent and independent—and demonstrate that the three Dutch island states—Aruba, Curaçao, and Saint Martin—which have an interest in maintaining their ties to their former colonizer, are performing comparatively well, albeit with individual differences. [CEG]

PUERTO RICO

965 **Atiles-Osoria, José M.** The COVID-19 pandemic in Puerto Rico: exceptionality, corruption and state-corporate crimes. (*State Crime*, 10:1, 2021, p. 104–125, bibl.)

This article traces the string of executive orders through which Puerto Rico's government attempted to manage the COVID-19 pandemic between April and October 2020 (all based on a recent legal framework ostensibly designed to manage the financial "crisis" and security emergencies). These steps were accompanied by multiple scandals that emerged around the procurement of testing kits, personal protective equipment, and ventilators, of which only a small number of purchased material was ever delivered, despite the fact that as a tax haven for pharmaceutical companies, Puerto Rico hosts some of the world's biggest manufacturers of medical supplies and equipment. The author has elsewhere argued that in Puerto Rico's context, the philosophical-juridical category of "state of exception" is neither a novelty, nor exceptional, but built into the politico-legal status of "unincorporated territory" itself (see *HLAS 75:1023*). For the author, these dynamics largely account for the mishandling of procurement during the pandemic and other corruption scandals in Puerto Rico. [JLR]

966   **Central Journal.** Vol. 33, No. 1, 2021, Navigating insecurity: crisis, power, and protest in Puerto Rican communities. New York, N.Y.: Centro de Estudios Puertorriqueños.

In its call for papers, the 2018 conference of the Puerto Rican Studies Association asked how insecurity resulting from "[c]olonial rule, mismanagement and corruption, migration, natural disasters, low wages, unemployment and fiscal austerity" had affected people in both the Puerto Rican archipelago and its diaspora. The articles featured in this special issue represent work presented at that conference, reflecting a varied mix of methodologies, sources, and themes. Of particular interest to students and scholars of politics is Pedro Cabán's diachronic comparison of the period extending from September 1928 (when Hurricane San Felipe devastated the territory) to 1940 with that stretching from the onset of the "fiscal crisis" in 2006 to 2020. Both periods were marked by not just economic difficulties and "natural" disasters, but also a stagnant and corrupt political system rocked by popular upheaval. In the case of the former, the political conflicts of the 1930s led to political realignment, which set the stage for Puerto Rico's post-WWII transformations. In the case of the latter, writing immediately prior to the 2020 election, the author suggested that "the collapse of politics as usual seems imminent." While that election did not produce anything as dramatic as the then-newborn Partido Popular Democrático (PPD) taking control of the Puerto Rican Senate in 1938, the outcome was significant enough to portend changes in the near future (see also item **967**). [JLR]

967   **Laguarta Ramírez, José A.** In Puerto Rico, the 2019 uprising produces an electoral opening to the left. (*New Polit./Brooklyn*, 38:2, 2021, p. 74–90)

Puerto Rico's 2020 elections, held in the midst of the COVID-19 pandemic, were the first to follow the 2019 uprising that unseated then-governor Pedro Rosselló (2017–2019). The author argues that in this context, the most significant result of the election was neither Pedro Pierluisi and the victory of the Partido Nuevo Progresista (PNP) over a divided lackluster candidate from the Partido Popular Democrático (PPD), nor the statehood option's victory in a nonbinding status referendum with very low voter participation, but the unprecedented level of support for smaller parties and unaffiliated candidates. Specifically, the combined PIP (Partido Independentista Puertorriqueño) and MVC (Movimiento Victoria Ciudadana) vote signals a major shift in the de facto bipartisan system (see item **968**), a resurgence of the political left, and the entry of social movement activists into the legislature. The author suggests that social movements and further electoral growth of the left may yet produce major reconfigurations. [JLR]

968   **Lalo, Eduardo.** Lo roto, lo mentido, lo abandonado: textos del bipartidismo terminal. Puerto Rico: Mariana Editores, 2021. 348 p.

The author is one of Puerto Rico's best-known contemporary fiction writers, as well as an insightful social, cultural, and political critic and commentator of Puerto Rican affairs. This volume gathers nonfiction essays written between 2011 and 2017, the year that Hurricane Maria struck. As the title suggests, the essays point to a generalized feeling of violence, deceit, and abandonment among the population, which the author connects to Puerto Rico's colonial territorial status. The reference to "bipartisanship" in the title further identifies the long-standing pattern of PPD/PNP alternation as responsible for both perpetuating the deteriorating situation and impeding the emergence of alternatives. While the suggestion that "bipartidismo" in itself is the structural cause of Puerto Rico's woes may be naive, Lalo's writings are representative of the views of a growing sector of the Puerto Rican population. [JLR]

969 Latin American Perspectives. Vol. 47, No. 3, Issue 232, May 2020, *Calles de la resistencia*: pathways to empowerment in Puerto Rico. Edited by Jean Hostetler-Díaz. Thousand Oaks, Calif.: Sage Publications.

Published immediately after the 2019 Puerto Rico uprising, this special issue gathers contributions from a variety of disciplines that cast light on the context in which the uprising took place. Several of the contributions (four full-length articles and three "commentaries") stand out as especially relevant for students and scholars of politics. Foreshadowing his later historical analysis in the *Centro Journal* (item **966**), Pedro Cabán offers commentary on the uprising as evidence of a "crisis of colonial authority." In another brief commentary, social movement scholar Liliana Cotto-Morales contextualizes the uprising in terms of recent Puerto Rican and global social movements. Javier Colón Morera summarizes the uprising, offering politico-juridical insights from the perspective of human rights discourse. All four of the full-length articles develop political-economic analyses. In a piece that can be read as background for his analysis of the Puerto Rican government's management of the COVID-19 pandemic (item **965**), José Atiles-Osoria analyzes the juridico-legal framework for economic policy in Puerto Rico during the 20th century through the lens of the "colonial state of exception" and "state-corporate crimes." Two additional articles, one by Ricardo Fuentes Ramírez and the other by Argeo Quiñones-Pérez and Ian Seda-Irizarry, highlight the often-neglected role of Puerto Rico's ruling classes in shaping its political economic outcomes. Finally, Sandy Smith-Nonini's article adds a crucial infrastructural component by examining the "debt-energy nexus" behind PREPA's fuel dependency and decades of neglect. [JLR]

970 *NACLA Report on the Americas.*
Vol. 50, No. 2, 2018, Eye of the storm: colonialism, capitalism, and climate in the Caribbean. Abingdon, England: Routledge, Taylor & Francis.

Published shortly after the impact of Hurricanes Irma and Maria, the articles in this special issue focus on the inter-related causes of extended humanitarian and politico-economic crises in the Caribbean from an interdisciplinary perspective. The articles on Puerto Rico include a historical analysis of the relationship between 20th-century development discourse and structural vulnerabilities by Zaire Dinzey-Flores; a reflection on the long-term crises that contextualize the hurricanes' impact by Hilda Lloréns—from the perspective of her own family's experiences of dispossession and migration; an essay focusing on the impact of the disasters on the inhabited Puerto Rican island of Vieques by Marie Cruz Soto; and an interview of environmental activist Elizabeth Yeampierre by Ricardo Gabriel. [JLR]

971 Quiñones Calderón, Antonio. El cuento de nunca acabar: la interminable danza macabra del estatus político. Ensayos críticos por Julio A. Muriente Pérez, Orlando Parga Figueroa y Juan R. Fernández. San Juan: Publicaciones Gaviota, 2016. 352 p.: bibl.

The author is a former journalist and press secretary for two Partido Nuevo Progresista (PNP) governors who has written a number of books on corruption scandals, the PNP (see *HLAS 49:6319*), and his experiences in government. Neither the central focus of this book (the "status question") nor the author's take are particularly innovative. The book is primarily useful for quick historical reference, containing a thorough series of timelines on related topics that fill the first 75 pages. This section is followed by the author's roughly chronological retelling of the juridico-legal evolution of "the status issue" and his final reflections. The book concludes with critical essays by Julio Muriente, Orlando Parga, and Juan R. Fernández, each a well-known advocate of one of the three traditional status options. [JLR]

Tiempos binarios: la Guerra Fría desde Puerto Rico y el Caribe. See *HLAS 74:947*.

972 Zambrana, Rocío. Colonial debts: the case of Puerto Rico. Durham, N.C.: Duke University Press, 2021. 264 p.: bibl., ill., index. (Radical Américas)

Although primarily a work of philosophy whose major relevance to the study of politics is theoretical rather than empirical, this book is crucial reading for anyone seeking to understand the territory's present situation. In dialogue with both Puerto Rican and also numerous Latin American and Afro-diasporic and other authors, Zambrana asks what it would mean to examine Puerto Rico's "debt crisis" and recent "natural disasters" from the standpoint of the multiple overlapping vulnerabilities and violences afflicting most of its population, albeit to different degrees. The discussion is grounded in analysis not just of colonial and neoliberal legislation, but also including instances of public discourse and cultural production that illustrate the ways in which the violences of the colonial debt regime "land on" certain gendered and racialized bodies with greater force than others. By engaging with "decolonial" feminist activists as well as scholars, the book further gives voice to the complex interpretive frames informing the activities of an important sector of contemporary Puerto Rican social movements. [JLR]

TRINIDAD AND TOBAGO

973 **Hughes, David McDermott.** Energy without conscience: oil, climate change, and complicity. Durham, N.C.: Duke University Press, 2017. 191 p.: bibl., ill., index, map.

The author centers this analysis on Trinidad and Tobago—the world's oldest petro-state—drawing parallels between Trinidad's 18th- and 19th-century slave labor energy economy and its contemporary oil industry to demonstrate that it is only by rejecting arguments that oil is economically, politically, and technologically necessary, and by acknowledging our complicity in an immoral system, that humans can stem the damage being done to the planet. [CEG]

CUBA

974 **Bertot Triana, Harold.** La Constitución cubana de 2019 en perspectiva histórica e ideológica: aproximaciones a su sistema político electoral. (*Rev. Derecho Público*, 90, primer semestre 2019, p. 11–40, bibl.)

The author compares the political system outlined by the Cuban Constitution of 2019 with that of its 1976 predecessor, taking into account "ideological" influences (the Soviet Constitution of 1936 on the latter; the current Chinese, Vietnamese, and various Latin American constitutions on the former), as well as the historical contexts in which each was drafted. Although the major "continuities" (preservation of Cuba's "socialist" economy and the single-party system) and "ruptures" (creation of an office of President separate from the Council of State, elimination of provincial and strengthening of municipal assemblies, right of *habeas corpus*) are well known, the article provides a detailed account of specific changes which should be of interest to legal and political comparativists. [JLR]

975 **The Cuba reader: history, culture, politics.** Edited by Aviva Chomsky et al. Second edition, revised and updated. Durham, N.C.: Duke University Press, 2019. 727 p.: bibl., ill., index, maps. (The Latin America readers) (The world readers)

Much has happened since the publication of the first edition of this now-classic compendium in 2003 (see *HLAS 62:3197*), not the least of which is the retirement and then death of Fidel Castro, followed by the retirement of Raúl Castro. This updated edition includes a new section titled "Cuba after Fidel: Continuities and Transitions" with 21 entries on topics such as economic reforms, emigration, tourism, race and racism, gender and sexuality, US-Cuban relations, culture and everyday life, and the death of Fidel Castro. Pre-existing sections have also been revised, with some readings added, removed, replaced, or re-edited. [JLR]

976 **López Segrera, Francisco.** Cuba: the July 11, 2021 protests. (*Lat. Am. Perspect.*, 48:6, Sept. 2021, p. 37–43, bibl.)

Written from a progovernment perspective, this brief article provides a basic overview of the 11 July 2021 protests and the Cuban regime's assessment of its causes and implications. Although the author reproduces many of the regime's talking points, he does concede that "important endogenous factors" contributed to the protests, including "increased social inequality and deterioration, especially in the slums, a food and medicine crisis, an ineffectively controlled pandemic, and poor governmental communications." The author recognizes that protesters included "revolutionaries confused and frustrated by governmental mistakes." Perhaps most notably, he indicates that the majority of protesters were young people from impoverished areas most affected by "social problems and inequality" that have emerged "over the past three decades," adding that "racial equality, one of the basic principles of the Revolution, is a key factor here." This observation suggests at least some acknowledgement that raciospatial inequality in the distribution of the above-mentioned "endogenous factors" contributed to the erosion of regime legitimacy manifested in the protests. [JLR]

977 **Mao, Xianglin** and **Yang Jianmin.**
Guba Shehuizhuyi Yanjiu (Xiudingban) = Studies on Cuban socialism. Revised edition. Beijing: Shehui kexue wenxian chubanshe [Social Sciences Academic Press, China], 2019. 534 p.: bibl., index, tables. (The senior scholars' library, Chinese Academy of Social Sciences)

Since the first edition of this book was published in 2005 (see *HLAS 69:1187*), significant changes have occurred in Cuba. This revised edition preserves the essential content of the first edition, and considers the developments in Cuba over the past 10 years. The revised edition adds three new chapters on social security, the updating of the country's economic and social models, and the policy of cultural building. Furthermore, it emphasizes that Cuba's economic performance has not been sufficient and the modernization of socialist theory is the key challenge faced by all levels of Cuban cadres. The first author is an adviser to the Center for Cuban Studies (CCS), Institute of Latin American Studies (ILAS) of the Chinese Academy of Social Sciences (CASS); and the second author is executive director of CCS. [Mao Xianglin]

978 **Muñiz Zúñiga, Viviana.** Repercusión de la muerte de Fidel Castro en Santiago de Cuba: aparición y evolución del *event* en las agendas política y mediática. (*Estud. Mensaje Periodís.*, 24:1, 2018, p. 797–816, bibl., graphs, table)

While the correlations between the "political agenda" and "media agenda" in a single-party state where all media is tightly supervised (if no longer entirely controlled) by the state might seem obvious, this article may be of interest to students and scholars of political events, especially insofar as the role of media in defining and constructing eventuality is concerned. In this case, the "event" is the death of Fidel Castro, the historical leader of the Cuban Revolution, which again might seem like an obviously "newsworthy" event—as it was treated, not just within Cuba, but internationally. The author applies a series of theoretical frameworks from the field of media studies to gauge the timing and synchronization with government messaging by local media in Santiago de Cuba, where Castro's ashes were placed after nine days of "national mourning" and a cross-island caravan. Her findings suggest more improvisation by on-the-ground journalists and less parity with official demands than might be expected. [JLR]

979 **The revolution from within: Cuba, 1959–1980.** Edited by Michael J. Bustamante and Jennifer L. Lambe. Durham, N.C.: Duke University Press, 2019. 332 p.: bibl., index.

Situated across the ideological spectrum, contributors to this volume seek to approach a historiography of post-1959 or "revolutionary" Cuba on its own terms—that is, primarily in terms of its own "internal" processes rather than the geopolitical imperatives of great-power conflicts. There is a shared interest in both taking advantage of the regime's recent relative and partial "opening" of archival sources and transcending the binary of hagiographic regime narratives and condemnatory counternarratives that have predominated. Although historiographic first and foremost, themes and approaches are diverse. Of special interest to students and scholars of politics, it is worth highlighting Lillian Guerra's essay on the "staging" of revolutionary competence for foreign journalists during the guerrilla campaign in the Sierra Maestra, Christabelle Peters' imagined (but plausible) conversation between Ernesto "Ché" Guevara and Tanzanian leader Julius Nyerere, and Ada Ferrer's reflection on the political and historiographic imbrications of the Cuban and Haitian Revolutions. [JLR]

980 Rodríguez, José Luis. La política económica en Cuba: valorando lo alcanzado y los retos a enfrentar (2011–2018). *(Int. J. Cuban Stud.*, 11:1, Summer 2019, p. 84–101, bibl., table)

The author is a former minister of economic planning (1993–2009), professor of economics, and advisor to several important research centers and ministries in Cuba. This article provides a sober assessment, from the perspective of one of the Cuban regime's foremost economic experts, of the economic policies implemented between the Sixth PCC Congress of 2011 and the date of its writing, soon after the Seventh PCC Congress of 2016. This was a period of transition from a state-led command economy to one more akin to the Chinese and Vietnamese model of "market socialism" that included, in the author's view, both significant successes and shortcomings. Regarding the latter, while identifying unforeseen "external" challenges including "natural" disasters such as hurricanes Matthew, Mitchell, and Irma, and the reversal of Obama-era US-Cuba rapprochement by the Trump administration, the author also extensively discusses "errors" in policy implementation. The article is valuable to students and scholars of politics, both as a sample of the recent economic thinking of the Cuban leadership and as a nuanced evaluation of the intricacies of a planned transition to "market socialism." [JLR]

981 Rodríguez Arechavaleta, Carlos Manuel. La democracia republicana en Cuba, 1940–1952: actores, reglas y estrategias electorales. Ciudad de México: Fondo de Cultura Económica, 2017. 388 p.: bibl. (Sección de obras de política y derecho)

This is likely the most complete and detailed analysis of the 12 years of multi-party democracy stretching from Cuba's Constitution of 1940 (itself in some ways a negotiated product of the 1933 Revolution) to Fulgencio Batista's 1952 coup. The author applies the insights of a variety of approaches in comparative politics, such as neoinstitutional and saliency theories, to examine the three-way relationship among political actors, rules (institutions), and strategies, concluding that it was the particular configuration of these three factors during the 1952 electoral campaign that led Batista—initially a proponent of the Constitution and the first President elected under its auspices (1940–44)—to opt for a military "exit" and break with the rules. Conclusions notwithstanding, the book provides rich historical detail and analytical depth not often found in discussions of this period of Cuban history. [JLR]

982 Whitehead, Laurence and Bert Hoffmann. After the protests and the pandemic: reassessing the international profile of post-Castro Cuba. Barcelona: CIDOB Edicions, 2021. 13 p.: bibl. (Monografías CIDOB; 27)

In this working paper for the Europa-Cuba policy forum, the authors argue that while some of Cuba's purported "exceptionality" may have been lost as a result of the 11 July 2021 protests, it continues to be a sui generis case that rejects facile analogies with cases in the "transitiology" literature. Specifically rejecting US President Biden's labeling of Cuba as a "failed state" (and noting that unlike Puerto Rico, Cuba is and will continue to be a sovereign state regardless of political outcomes), the authors weigh the potential local and regional consequences of regime "continuity" and rapid change, recommending that the "international community" support "some intermediate path over the coming decade." [JLR]

COLOMBIA

ERIKA MORENO, *Associate Professor of Political Science and International Relations, Creighton University*

IN RECENT YEARS, Colombia has experienced a remarkable albeit halting pacification process following over a half century of internal conflict. The scholarly literature is divided into two camps: one focuses on the remnants of internal conflict, while the other targets democratic institutions and their output.

Scholars are continuing to explore the impact of the conflict on the political realm (items **986**, **987**, **989**, and **994**). Historical analyses of the roots of the conflict are a common topic of study. Yet, few do as exhaustive a study as Gutiérrez Sanín's work in detailing the social and political clashes that helped set the stage for today's political challenges (item **989**). Some of the studies of the political ramifications of the conflict reveal nuanced interactions among armed groups, citizens, and governance structures (items **990** and **994**) and armed groups and drug traffickers (item **995**). A notable contribution by Moreno León provides a nuanced understanding of how armed actors responded to protests by noncombatants (item **994**). Meanwhile, other recent publications include studies of the peace process and its inclusion of citizen voices, especially those of marginalized groups, whether women (item **986**) or regionally marginalized—such as those from the Caribbean region (item **987**).

Among the studies of Colombia's democratic institutions, Mejía-Guinand, Botero, and Solano (item **993**) make a novel contribution to our understanding of the challenges of agency loss in presidential cabinets. At the congressional level, the literature addresses either historical developments (item **991**) or the impact of new rules for inclusion of women, as is the case with Pachón Buitrago and Aroca's multilevel analysis (item **996**). The courts are also represented in the literature, though to a lesser extent (item **988**).

Meanwhile, the literature on subnational governance structures has grown in recent years. Studies of formal democratic institutions (items **996** and **997**) mingle with studies examining the interaction of armed actors and local governance structures, including civil society organizations (CSOs) and Indigenous self-governance institutions (items **990** and **992**).

Finally, several new works turn their attention to the outputs of democratic governance, including a range of public policy outcomes (items **983** and **984**) and the potentially negative (and demobilizing) effects of citizen perceptions of corruption (item **985**).

983 **Análisis de políticas públicas en Colombia: enfoques y estudios de caso.** Compilación de Javier Armando Pineda Duque. Bogotá: Universidad de los Andes, 2018. 184 p.: bibl., ill. (some color.). (Instituciones, paz y desarrollo)

This edited volume examines several key policy areas through the use of case studies. The study makes use of competing policy streams, the role of advocacy coalitions, and policy diffusion, while emphasizing an institutional perspective. Authors examine policies related to disability, housing, and cultural change, among others. The volume provides a useful framework for understanding the case studies and contributes to our knowledge of the policy process and its key players.

984 **Anti-drug policies in Colombia: successes, failures, and wrong turns.** Edited by Alejandro Gaviria and Daniel Mejia. Translated by Jimmy Weiskopf. Nashville, Tenn.: Vanderbilt University Press, 2016. 313 p.: ill., index, maps. (Vanderbilt University Center for Latin American studies; 1)

This edited volume addresses drug policies implemented in Colombia from 1982 to the present. The contributors take on a range of topics, including the drug policy arena broadly, supply and demand, as well as domestic and international exigencies. Contributions to the volume range in scope, but address this policy concern with nuance and detail. This volume is a valuable primer on drug policies enacted from the 1980s onward, highlighting key successes and failures.

985 **Carreras, Miguel** and **Sofia Vera.** Do corrupt politicians mobilize or demobilize voters?: a vignette experiment in Colombia. (*Lat. Am. Polit. Soc.*, 60:3, Aug. 2018, p. 77–95, bibl., tables)

The authors empirically examine whether corruption inhibits voter participation. The research is designed using a vignette experiment embedded in a nationally representative survey conducted in Colombia in 2016. This particular type of study relies on presenting respondents with a vignette of a hypothetical politician, while manipulating some of the details, to determine how respondents assessed the administration in question. The authors found that the perception of corruption negatively impacted self-reported intentions to turn out to vote, even when the politician in question was painted as a good provider of district services. Thus, they find strong support for their proposition that corruption would negatively impact participation. This novel research design and question are worthy contributions to the broader literature on corruption as well as the literature on Colombian politics.

986 **Chaparro González, Nina** and **Margarita Martínez Osorio.** Negociando desde los márgenes: la participación política de las mujeres en los procesos de paz en Colombia, 1982–2016. Bogotá: Dejusticia, 2016. 122 p.: bibl., ill. (Documentos Dejusticia; 29)

This contribution presents a thorough analysis of the elections in Colombia from 2007–2011, ranging from state (departmental) to local levels. The use of geographic spatial analysis provides the study with a rigorous and visually appealing method of examining and illustrating change over time. This study is a good source of data and provides insight into trends across the country's departmental elections.

987 **Conflicto armado y transición hacia el posconflicto: una aproximación desde el Caribe.** Edición de Sergio Latorre Restrepo *et al.* Barranquilla, Colombia: Universidad del Norte Editorial; Bogotá: Grupo Editorial Ibañez, 2018. 258 p.: bibl., ill.

This study places the Colombian peace process into a broader context by examining the roles of an array of actors in the Caribbean region of Colombia. The book explores several key events and actors to uncover the lessons learned from past efforts in the hopes of finding fruitful and successful outcomes in the future. It also provides a few models and suggested topics to consider as Colombia moves towards a postconflict period.

988 **Cruz Rodríguez, Michael.** Altas cortes y clase política en Colombia: tres estudios de caso en perspectiva sociojurídica. Bogotá: Universidad Nacional de Colombia, 2017. 236 p.: bibl., index. (Colección Gerardo Molina; 66)

This book-length manuscript provides an understanding of the Colombian judicial branch as it has evolved since 1991. Chapters in the book address a series of important elements, including institutional independence, the role of new judicial tools (*la tutela*), and the impacts of partisan politics and paramilitary forces on the courts. The analysis is limited to the period following the passage of the new constitution until 2013; nevertheless, it provides a significant contribution to our understanding of this important branch of government.

Durán-Martínez, Angélica. The politics of drug violence: criminals, cops, and politicians in Colombia and Mexico. See item 813.

989 **Gutiérrez Sanín, Francisco.** La destrucción de una república. Bogotá: Taurus: Universidad Externado de Colombia, 2017. 650 p.: bibl., color ill. (Pensamiento)

This study follows the nation's path towards modernization and the role of its democratic institutions during the period prior to the internecine internal conflict (La Violencia). The study focuses on the role of the Liberal and Conservative parties, their organizations, and the institutionalization of grievances that ultimately led to internal conflict and the destruction of the pillars of a democratic republic.

Juventud y espacios de participación en Chile y América Latina. See item 1069.

990 **Larratt-Smith, Charles.** Navigating formal and informal processes: civic organizations, armed nonstate actors, and nested governance in Colombia. (*Lat. Am. Polit. Soc.*, 62:2, May 2020, p. 75–98, bibl.)

Larratt-Smith examines the interactions of civil society organizations (CSOs) and armed nonstate actors. The study focuses on two armed nonstate actors of varying ideological orientations and examines their ability to navigate a range of processes tied to local governance. By taking on these functions, ideologically distinct armed nonstate actors engage in a form of nested governance, often with similar techniques, including the use of co-optation, cultivation, and regulation of the civic sphere.

991 **Leal Buitrago, Francisco.** Estudios sobre el Congreso de la República de Colombia: la contribución de Francisco Leal Buitrago. Edición de Laura Wills-Otero y Angelika Rettberg. Bogotá: Universidad de Los Andes, Facultad de Ciencias Sociales, Departamento de Ciencia Política: Universidad Nacional de Colombia, Vicerrectoría de Investigación, 2016. 345 p.: bibl., ill. (Obra de Francisco Leal Buitrago; I)

This volume makes up part of a four-part series that highlights the contributions of Francisco Leal Buitrago's analysis of the Colombian political system. This volume focuses on the powers and behavior of the Colombian Congress from 1930–70. The volume makes a substantial contribution to our understanding of the issues, concepts, and actions of a variety of actors inside this deliberative organ.

992 **Mayka, Lindsay.** Society-driven participatory institutions: lessons from Colombia's planning councils. (*Lat. Am. Polit. Soc.*, 61:2, May 2019, p. 93–114, bibl.)

This article explores the creation of society-driven participatory institutions in Colombia. The emergence of these civil society organizations is due in part to the neglect of the Colombian state, following decades of internal conflict. The institutions filled a void left by the state and created permanent, formal, institutional spaces to debate, create, and implement public policy. Here, Mayka focuses on Colombia's planning councils which were a product of rules introduced in the 1991 Constitution and 1994 Planning Statute that required all levels of government to incorporate CSOs (civil society organizations) in mandatory planning councils. Mayka follows the trajectory of council development over the course of the 1991–2010 period, noting challenges including weak design and state hostility. The study provides useful insight into the creation of these institutions as well as the challenges they face.

993 **Mejía-Guinand, Luis Bernardo; Felipe Botero;** and **Angélica Solano.** Agency loss and the strategic redesign of the presidential office in Colombia. (*Lat. Am. Polit. Soc.*, 60:3, Aug. 2018, p. 96–118, bibl., graph, table)

This study conducts an in-depth analysis of the role of partisan identification in the organizational transformations of the presidential office from 1967–2015. The authors depart from the concern that balancing cabinet portfolios may result in agency loss, at least for presidents seeking the support of trusted advisers to pursue policy priorities. Specifically, executives redesign the office to monitor coalition partners and avoid ministry drift. The authors conduct a time-series regression analysis to identify key factors behind bureaucratic supervision of ministers or enlargement of the executive. This important contribution to our understanding of a branch of government describes a case that has rarely seen this sort of analytical rigor.

994 **Moreno León, Carlos Enrique.** Chronicle of a survival foretold: how protest behavior against armed actors influenced violence in the Colombian Civil War, 1988–2005. (*Lat. Am. Polit. Soc.*, 59:4, Winter 2017, p. 3–25, bibl., graphs, table)

This article explores the use of civilian protests to alter the strategic use of violence by other parties between 1988–2005 in Colombia. The author tests propositions about the factors that are most likely to draw a violent response from armed actors by focusing on their willingness and capacity to punish mobilized citizens. Using a zero-inflated quantitative model, the study finds that the use of violence is greater when armed actors are a dominant force in the area. All protests are seen as a sign of disloyalty. However, when protests are directed towards an armed groups' enemy, they tend to reward such actions and refrain from violence. Both the frame of strategic violence across differing actors and the quantitative analysis provide a useful means of understanding a period of conflict.

995 **Norman, Susan Virginia.** *Narcotization* as security dilemma: the FARC and the drug trade in Colombia. (*Stud. Confl. Terror.*, 41:8, 2018, p. 638–659, maps)

This article traces the troubled relationship between the FARC guerrillas and the cocaine trade in Colombia. Following the 2016 peace agreement, the FARC found itself forced to address its complicity with the drug trade. The author divides the FARC's links to the drug trade in two phases: the regulation era (1982–91) and the vertical integration era (1991–present). The author presents the FARC's involvement in the drug trade through the prism of the security dilemma. In other words, the FARC's involvement was driven by concerns over alliances struck by narcotraffickers and paramilitaries. This approach challenges other analyses that have explained the FARC's involvement with narcotraffickers as driven by greed. Furthermore, this formulation introduces a well-worn concept into a novel setting, thereby expanding our understanding of the motivations of these alliances and their implications for peace in the future.

996 **Pachón Buitrago, Mónica** and **María Paula Aroca.** Effects of institutional reforms on women's representation in Colombia, 1960–2014. (*Lat. Am. Polit. Soc.*, 59:2, Summer 2017, p. 103–121, bibl., graphs, tables)

This study is motivated by the desire to determine the effectiveness of legal reforms aimed at improving the representation of women in democratically elected positions at multiple levels of government. The authors conducted a district-level quantitative analysis of the effectiveness of three key reforms on the descriptive representation of women in national and subnational levels from 1962 to 2014. The authors focus on the effects of the 1991 constitutional reform, the 2003 electoral reforms, and the adoption of a quota law in 2011. The analysis finds that each of the institutional reforms contributed to a steady increase in the number of women competing and winning, especially at the national level. However, these findings vary depending on the office and level of government. This time serial study is a significant contribution to the broader debate on the effectiveness of institutional reforms in enhancing both the candidacies and the election of women to public office.

997 **Velasco, Marcela.** Multiculturalism, legal pluralism and local government in Colombia: Indigenous autonomy and institutional embeddedness in Karmata Rúa, Antioquia. (*J. Lat. Am. Stud.*, 50:3, Aug. 2018, p. 517–547)

The constitutional reforms of 1991 ushered in a set of rules that simultaneously allowed for political decentralization and multicultural pluralism. Velasco examines how these new instruments were employed by Indigenous communities, with special focus on the Embera Chami of Karmata Rúa (in Antioquia). Here, we see examples of a group that was empowered by the new norms and made efforts to engage in Indigenous self-governance in spite of a long history of state dominance across most of Indigenous Colombia. Velasco details the creation of new institutions inside the Embera community as well as the ways in which they addressed a range of policy issues, including environmental concerns and social and educational programs. This is an important contribution to our understanding of the formation of local institutions in existing communities following the 1991 Constitution.

ECUADOR

JENNIFER N. COLLINS, *Professor of Political Science, University of Wisconsin, Stevens Point*

THE YEAR 2029 will mark 50 years since Ecuador's transition to democracy. This nearly half century has been marked by significant social change and political volatility, including massive social protests, interrupted presidencies, political shifts between left and right, and the drafting of three constitutions. Despite or perhaps because of this recurring political churn, Ecuador has also been the incubator of innovative political ideas and dynamic social movements. From 2007–2017 under Rafael Correa, Ecuador was part of the new left. After Correa left office, the political pendulum swung back to the right under three succeeding presidents—Lenin Moreno, Guillermo Lasso, and Daniel Noboa. In recent years, this small Andean nation has struggled with the impact of the COVID-19 pandemic and increasingly with drug trafficking and the attendant rise in violence and security concerns.

The scholarship on Ecuadorian politics reviewed in this section straddles the latter half of the decade-long Citizens' Revolution headed by Correa and its unravelling under his successor, Lenin Moreno. Several of the books and articles take a longer view, attempting to assess patterns since the democratic transition and even earlier. The topics can be grouped into four overlapping categories: political development, political institutions, state and society relations, and social and political thought.

A good place to start for developing an understanding of Ecuador' political situation is the excellent anthology edited by Granda Vega and published to commemorate 40 years of Ecuadorian democracy (item **999**). This collection brings together essential articles by prominent scholars who have studied the evolution and functioning of Ecuador's political institutions, electoral and party systems, and key democratic actors. Another crucial text is Ospina Peralta's article that takes a longer time horizon as it considers the puzzle of how Ecuador avoided major political violence during the 20th century (item **1015**). The article engages in a structural analysis of the state and the key forces and class actors that shaped it, arguing that a specific constellation of power among elites and the military led to the consolidation of what the author calls a "transformative state," which explains the comparatively low levels of political violence in Ecuador during the 20th century. Ospina Peralta's analysis promises to be a key text for understanding

Ecuador's political development. A two-volume memoir by one of Ecuador's preeminent television personalities offers a granular account of the country's major political and social developments from the 1960s through the end of the Correa administration (item **1005**). Shifting from past to present and future, Ramírez Gallegos offers an assessment of the changes wrought by the Citizens' Revolution and provides a vision and roadmap for deepening Ecuador's transition towards a more equitable future (item **1017**).

Several excellent studies of Ecuadorian political institutions complement and advance the work covered in Granda Vega's anthology. Ecuador's process of decentralization and the corresponding rise in the importance of local government are ably addressed by three books (items **1002**, **1008**, and **1009**). Another work is the first to systematically study the phenomenon of "regressive political careers," those cases where, instead of running for re-election, national legislative deputies seek elected office at the local or provincial level (item **1001**). Government economic planning has not received significant attention in relation to Ecuador, so it is notable that a worthwhile book addresses the topic by providing a historical comparison of state planning in Ecuador during the 1970s when statism was dominant with the 1980s when the import substitution industrialization model was largely on the way out (item **1012**). This book not only provides a useful history and analysis of both periods, but also contributes to our theoretical understanding of the role state planning can play in a democracy. State planning came back in vogue during the Correa administration and one book examines the process undertaken during that time to develop national plans (item **1014**). The study aims to evaluate the Correa administration's implementation of participatory practices through the lens of the planning process. A number of books offer important insights into the Ecuadorian military and security services. One focuses on military involvement in politics and the challenge of asserting civilian control over the military (item **1010**). The author, a retired Ecuadorian military officer, provides an insightful comparative analysis of this struggle in Ecuador and Uruguay, drawing important conclusions about the conditions that are conducive to effective civilian control. In addition, three books are dedicated specifically to Ecuador's intelligence services. One offers a history of political intelligence agencies from the 1960s to the 1990s, arguing that Ecuador had what amounted to a secret police that was largely democratically unaccountable and responsible for numerous human rights violations (item **1019**). The other two books focus on analyzing the major reform of the country's security agencies undertaken by Correa in the wake of two major security breaches: the 2008 Colombian military's bombing raid on Ecuadorian territory (item **1011**) and the 2009 police revolt (item **1020**).

Several works grapple with different aspects of state-society relations during and immediately after the Citizen's Revolution. Correa's relationship with the private media was notoriously conflictive, but a law passed during his tenure is a model for media democratization according to Anderson (item **998**). Another point of polarization and conflict during Correa's presidency was the issue of extractivism, which became a focal point of social movement opposition. The divergent positions on drilling and mining between the government and social movements and how these differences shaped state-society relations and the politics of the Citizens' Revolution is expertly addressed by Riofrancos (item **1018**). Gaussens offers a more strident leftist critique of the Citizens' Revolution and other new left projects (item **1007**). While Riofrancos views Correa and the social movements as divergent wings of the left, Gaussens argues that the Citizens' Revolution and other new left governments are antithetical to social movement aspirations because they facilitate deeper capitalist penetration. The end of Correa's presidency and ultimately that of the Citizens' Revolution is effectively described and analyzed in a short article by Conaghan (item **1003**). The return of neoliberal policies under Moreno saw a revitalization of protest and social movement activism, with 2019 being a pivotal year. Two excellent books cover the Indigenous and popular protests that rocked the country for nearly two weeks during 2019 in response to austerity measures imposed by Moreno's government (items **1004** and **1013**).

The final group of works surveyed for this volume deals with political thought produced by Ecuadorian scholars and innovative political ideas emerging from Ecuador's political process. Herrera Mosquera has compiled an anthology of contemporary Ecuadorian critical thought (item **1000**). As with Granda Vega's anthology (item **999**), this book compiles key essays by prominent scholars, but whereas the first anthology is focused on democratic political institutions and actors, this compilation draws together significant work in the realm of political ideas and analysis. As this book attests, Ecuador, despite its small size, has been fertile ground for the production of new social and political thought and analysis. Two cutting-edge political philosophies that were expounded and experimented with during the Citizens' Revolution are explored in separate works. The Quichua term *sumak kawsay*, translated as "good living," is a core concept in Ecuador's 2009 Constitution. Gallegos-Anda explores its meaning and implementation—or lack thereof—in the context of the Citizens' Revolution (item **1006**). Another innovative idea that Correa attempted to put into practice was "universal citizenship," which is explored by Pugh (item **1016**). While Herrera Mosquera's anthology brings together critical scholarship, the book by Gallegos-Anda and the article by Pugh explore the process of putting new political ideas into practice. In both cases, the radical nature of the ideas exceeded the reality of their implementation, thus contributing to frustration over unfulfilled expectations left by the Citizens' Revolution.

Together the works covered in this section offer a nuanced and deeper understanding of Ecuadorian political development, the trials and tribulations of the last 40 years of democracy, critical assessments of the Citizens' Revolution, and the richness of political thought and analysis emerging out of this Andean nation's sometimes volatile, but also fertile political struggles.

998 **Anderson, Tim.** Media democratization in Ecuador. (*Lat. Am. Perspect.*, 45:3, May 2018, p. 16–29, bibl., table)

This article analyzes Ecuador's 2013 Communications Law, locating it within a regionwide regulatory trend aimed at democratizing national media landscapes. The author praises the law as "perhaps the most articulate version" highlighting the legislation's three central objectives: reducing monopoly control, creating mechanisms for citizen redress against media conglomerates, and incentivizing social participation and diversification of media outlets such as community media. The author contrasts this embrace of state regulation with the hands-off approach taken elsewhere that optimistically assumes the rise of new media technologies will automatically result in a democratic media landscape. Anderson disputes this notion and holds up Ecuador's media law as an example of how government can use liberal and social democratic mechanisms and principles to regulate the media such that it supports and deepens democracy. Anderson's praise of the media law stands in contrast to many critical voices that accused Correa of attacking the private media and silencing critical voices. Anderson does not address Correa's dealings with the media outside of this law nor does he describe the deliberative process in drafting it. Addressing these issues would have strengthened the article. Nevertheless, the author's assessment of the law and its merits is convincing and contributes to important debates about media regulation in a democratic polity, an issue of utmost importance in Latin America today.

999 **Antología de la democracia ecuatoriana: 1979–2020.** Edición de María Paula Granda Vega. Quito: Instituto de la Democracia: Consejo Nacional Electoral, 2020. 454 p.: ill.

This excellent compendium brings together essential academic articles on various aspects of Ecuador's democracy by 12 prominent scholars of Ecuadorian society and politics. A photo essay highlighting key historical moments of 41 years of democracy is an added feature. The main focus of the book is political institutions with chapters that analyze Ecuador's electoral and party systems, its constitution, and the extensive political reforms undertaken over the past four decades. Complementing the institutional analysis are chapters on populism, the Indigenous movement, and women's political participation. The final chapter presents a synthesis of the institutional, political, social, and economic processes discussed in the preceding chapters, and concludes that Ecuadorian democracy has been in a perpetual state of crisis that has forestalled the achievement of democracy's promise for the popular classes. The country's recurrent popular revolts, while unable thus far to revert the pattern of crisis, nonetheless offer a measure of hope that a different type of democracy is possible. This book is an excellent reference and guide for understanding Ecuador's complicated, volatile, but also vibrant dance with democracy over the last 40 years.

1000 **Antología del pensamiento crítico ecuatoriano contemporáneo.** Coordinación de Gioconda Herrera Mosquera. Textos de Agustín Cueva *et al.* Buenos Aires: CLACSO, 2018. 593 p.: bibl. (Colección Antologías del pensamiento social latinoamericano y caribeño)

This anthology of contemporary Ecuadorian critical thought brings together essential essays by 20 influential intellectuals in Ecuadorian social and political studies. Divided into five sections, the collection includes work on political economy, populism and popular identity, ethnicity and race, feminism, and a final section on the development of modern social thought and the role of the university in Ecuador's public sphere. The anthology spans work produced from the 1970s to the present, mostly in the realm of sociology and political anthropology. In her introduction, Herrera Mosquera offers an overview of the trajectory of modern critical thought in Ecuador. The choice of the 1970s as a starting point was deliberate as this decade saw the emergence of a "militant sociology" committed to social transformation and the laying of the foundations for more systematic work in the social sciences. What unites the selected texts is a concern with domination and social inequality. While it would have been helpful to provide a brief introduction at the start of each essay, background information on the authors and context for the essays is provided in the introduction. This text will be useful for those who want to become acquainted with key texts about, and understand the trajectory of, modern Ecuadorian social and political thought.

1001 **Arévalo Jaramillo, María Inés.** Ambición o estrategia: estudio de carreras políticas regresivas en Ecuador (1979–2008). Quito: CNE Consejo Nacional Electoral: Instituto de la Democracia, 2017. 159 p.: bibl., ill. (Serie Ciencia y democracia; 4)

This study, awarded best MA thesis by a government think tank, focuses on the phenomenon of "regressive" political careers: politicians elected to national legislatures who subsequently pursue election to subnational offices such as mayors or provincial prefects. Existing research has focused on federalist systems; this book represents one of the first efforts to examine this phenomenon in a unitary system. The research identifies and paints a picture of the population pursuing this path and investigates the causes for the behavior. The primary motivations identified are a desire for increased political and economic independence and greater social prestige. Most of those pursuing this path were inexperienced and utilized a brief stint in the legislature to leverage a run for office at the subnational level. Some downsides of this trend include a diminishment in the professionalism of the national legislature resulting from the election of inexperienced deputies, while subnational politics are imbued with personalism and low levels of party loyalty by these same politicians. This well-executed empirical case study contributes to our knowledge of political careers and will be of interest to those studying comparative political institutions.

1002 Armijos Velasco, Bolívar. Nuestra lucha contra la inequidad. Quito: NINA Comunicaciones, 2016. 178 p.: bibl., color ill.

Authored by the president of the National Council of Rural Parish Governments of Ecuador (CONAGOPARE), this book provides an overview of the evolution of constitutional and legal frameworks for rural governance in Ecuador, ultimately making the case for reforms. Historically rural areas had virtually no decision-making power and were subject to the rule of municipalities and the central government. A shift to decentralization in the 1990s saw reforms that among other things created a new level of government: rural parishes. Their powers were strengthened during the Correa years with the passage of the 2008 Constitution and then COOTAD, legislation codifying the country's decentralized system of local, provincial, regional, and national governments. From his perspective as a rural parish leader and president of the association representing these local governments, Armijos Velasco offers insight about the successes and limitations of the current framework and the continuing needs of rural communities. He makes a passionate plea for enhanced resources and powers for the rural parishes and to incorporate them more fully into decision-making at other levels so they can be empowered to play an even more effective role.

Assessing the left turn in Ecuador. See item **1677.**

Becker, Marc. The CIA in Ecuador. See item **1678.**

1003 Conaghan, Catherine M. Ecuador's unexpected transition. (*Curr. Hist.,* 117:796, Feb. 2018, p. 49–55)

This brief article provides a useful overview of how Correa's hold on Ecuadorian politics ended after his hand-picked successor, Lenin Moreno, won the presidency and then proceeded to distance himself, ultimately breaking with Correa. The article includes a succinct summation of Correa's time in office as well as the conditions that existed at the end of his presidency that led him to step aside in favor of a placeholder candidate who he expected would maintain the party in power until a future Correa presidency. As Conaghan details, this plan was foiled by Moreno who deftly maneuvered to "make the presidency his own and marginalize his predecessor," accusing the administration of which he had been a part of corruption and incompetence. For Conaghan, this is a cautionary tale for other radical new left Andean leaders Maduro (Venezuela) and Morales (Bolivia) that even carefully planned successions can easily go awry. Both leaders appear to have drawn this lesson, although Morales failed in his bid to remain in power. Conaghan also views these transitional moments as opportunities for democratization.

1004 Ecuador: la insurrección de octubre. Edición a cargo de Camila Parodi y Nicolás Sticotti. Textos de Adoración Guamán *et al.* Fotografía de Darwin Pizarro *et al.* Buenos Aires: CLACSO, 2020. 292 p.: bibl., color ill.

Containing a wealth of primary source materials from articles and commentary published in alternative news media to photographs and tweets, this unique book paints a vivid portrait of the October 2019 uprising against the Moreno government's adoption of neoliberal austerity measures, specifically the removal of gasoline subsidies, that shook Ecuador. The 12-day protest that resulted in blocked roads and a nationwide stoppage of much regular activity, 11 deaths, and 1,340 injured was by some accounts the largest Indigenous and popular uprising against IMF-imposed neoliberal policies in Ecuador's history. Complementing the primary source materials are six essays, commissioned for this volume and written with some distance from the actual events, that reflect on various aspects of the uprising, its outcome, and implications. Two features of the protests—the rejection of neoliberal policies and the leadership role played by the Indigenous movement—mark their similarity to the social movement mobilizations of the 1990s and early 2000s. However, the essays highlight important differences with that earlier era including the participation of urban youth and popular sectors, especially in Quito, the changing nature of the Indigenous population, the level of state violence, and the role of social media, among others. While the 2019 protests forced some concessions from the government, they did not change the government, stop the neoliberal agenda, or position the left effectively to contest power in the next election. This book is an excellent resource for making sense of the 2019 protests and their significance for Ecuadorian politics. See also item **1013**.

1005 Espinosa de los Monteros, Alfonso.
Memorias. Tomo I, 1961–1988, Entre el populismo y la dictadura. Tomo II, 1988–2016, Vaivenes de la democracia. Bogotá: Debate, 2016–2017. 2 v.: ill.

This two-volume memoir by Ecuador's longest serving television news anchor and presenter is less a personal life story than a chronicle of the country's major political and social developments and events over the span of much of the author's professional career. Espinosa de los Monteros served as television anchor, news director, and host of various popular television programs uninterrupted from 1967 until his retirement in 2023. A constant presence on Ecuadorians' television screens for more than half a century, he was a familiar and respected figure. His career provided him with an up-close view of the country's major events and access to its most important protagonists. His memoirs have an almost encyclopedic feel as they offer a detailed chronology of major events, largely political, with a bit of the author's viewpoints and assessments included as well. *Memorias* do not provide much analysis, but they are interesting and useful as a detailed recounting of major events in Ecuador's political history from the early sixties through the end of the Correa administration.

1006 Gallegos-Anda, Carlos E. Ecuador's "good living": crises, discourse and law. Leiden, The Netherlands; Boston, Mass.: Brill, 2021. 308 p.: bibl., ill., index. (Critical global studies; 13) (Studies in critical social sciences; 175)

This book engages in a critical exploration of the origins, meaning, and enforceability of "buen vivir," a concept centrally positioned in Ecuador's 2008 Constitution. Rather than focusing on the somewhat mystical and ontological origins of the term, the author instead traces its emergence to the concrete "political, legal, and social transformations" occurring in Ecuador from 1979–2008, identifying this period bookended by the transition to democracy and the drafting of the 2008 Constitution as a critical juncture. He then traces the process by which good living was included in the 2008 Constitution, arguing that the concept came to serve as an "empty signifier," following Laclau and Mouffe's use of the term. The final chapter lays out core arguments and conclusions about what the concept has come to signify. Gallegos-Anda argues that the term's revolutionary potential has been neutered and exhausted so that at the present time it is more a tool to demobilize than to empower and transform society. Retheorization is needed to revitalize and reposition good living if it is to serve as a framework for a viable political project or to have any formal legal utility. This book

1007 Gaussens, Pierre. La izquierda latinoamericana contra los pueblos: el caso ecuatoriano (2007–2013). Ciudad de México: UNAM, Centro de Investigaciones sobre América Latina y el Caribe, 2018. 390 p.: bibl.

Sociologist Gaussens develops a neo-Marxist critique of Latin America's left turn through a case study of Ecuador's Citizens' Revolution. The contention is sweeping: rather than advancing the antisystemic agenda birthed in the popular rebellions against neoliberalism, new left governments respond to reconfigurations of power and deepen capitalist penetration. While social movements helped create the conditions for the rise of the new left, new left policies represent a regression in terms of movement aspirations. The neo-Keynesian statist policies enacted by Correa and others like him respond to the interests of a new sector of the dominant class. Rather than undermining capitalism, they lay the basis for an intensification of global capitalist accumulation while perpetuating Latin America's traditional role as supplier of raw materials. In the second half of the theory-heavy book, the analysis focuses on the case demonstrating how the popular agenda was neutered and undermined by Correa administration policies. This book contributes to leftist critiques of the Citizens' Revolution by providing a broad Marxist theoretical framework and charting a future course for leftist and popular movements based on a recognition of the illusion that state power is the path to radical social change.

1008 Gobiernos intermedios: entre lo local y lo nacional. Coordinación de Francisco Enríquez Bermeo. Quito: CONGOPE; Abya-Yala Ediciones; Incidencia Pública del Ecuador, 2017. 178 p.: bibl. (Serie Territorios en Debate; 5)

The fifth in a series on decentralization in Ecuador, this slim volume focuses on what the authors call "the intermediate governments," which include provinces and regions. The 2008 Constitution envisioned the creation of a new regional level of decentralized government designed to facilitate regional economic development. However, the regions were never created and remain an unfinished constitutional mandate. Bringing together academics and provincial government officials, this book provides an overview of the history and theory behind the idea and the progress or lack thereof in consolidating this new level of government. One problem identified is the potential for overlapping competencies between the proposed regional level and the existing provincial governments. Nevertheless, the contributors agree that an intermediate level between local governments (municipalities and rural parishes) and the national government is essential. They contend that despite the provisions in the 2008 Constitution, decentralization stalled during the Citizens' Revolution, impeded by hyperpresidentialism, the concentration of power in the central government, and the persistence of the extractivist economic model. This book will be useful for scholars of decentralization and regional development as well as those who want to understand developments in this area during Correa's presidency.

1009 Gobiernos locales y descentralización en Ecuador. Edición de Wilson Araque Jaramillo y Eulalia Flor Recalde. Quito: Corporación Editora Nacional: Universidad Andina Simón Bolívar, Sede Ecuador, 2016. 246 p.: bibl. (Serie Gestión; 5)

This book serves as a primer on Ecuador's Autonomous and Decentralized Governments or GADs. The structure of the GADs was conceived in the 2008 Constitution and codified in 2010 with the passage of the major legislative bill known as the Organic Code of Territorial, Autonomous, and Decentralized Organization (COOTAD). Chapters by Ecuadorian scholars cover a range of topics from the general to the specific and technical, including overviews of the country's decentralization model and its conception in the 2008 Constitution, information sharing and coordination among the various levels of government, competencies with regards to roads and transportation infrastructure, equity in the central government's appropriations to local governments, and an evaluation of the structure's limitations in terms of ensuring integrated public policy. This book provides a useful overview of Ecuador's model of decentralized governance and will be useful to scholars looking for a straightforward description of the model and how it works. It is also designed to serve public servants in Ecuador as they work with and through this new system and consider improvements to it.

1010 Haro Ayerve, Patricio. Fuerzas armadas, pretorianismo y calidad de la democracia: Ecuador y Uruguay. Quito: FLACSO Ecuador; Sangolquí, Ecuador: ESPE, Universidad de las Fuerzas Armadas, 2017. 307 p.: bibl., ill. (Atrio)

While the military was an important topic of study during the period of military rule in Latin America, scholarly attention waned after the return to democracy. This excellent study actualizes our understanding of the military's role during the region's democratic period. The author, a retired Ecuadorian coronel, interviewed former presidents and members of military high commands for this book, which served as his doctoral dissertation. Adopting a unique case methodology, he compares military involvement in politics in Ecuador (high) and Uruguay (low). The author accepts that civilian control is crucial to democratic consolidation and seeks to understand why Uruguay has achieved this outcome where Ecuador has not. Significant contributions include describing and cataloging forms of military intervention, which is defined as any activity outside of the constitutional or legal mandate, thus including more than just military coups. The study identifies the following factors as determinant of the difference between the two cases: attitudes within the military about its proper role, public views of the military, effective legislative oversight of the military, and whether military academies teach about democracy and the proper role of the armed forces within one.

1011 Levoyer, Saudia. Los huracanes que arrasaron el sistema de inteligencia. Quito: Universidad Andina Simón Bolívar, Ecuador: Corporación Editora Nacional, 2017. 76 p.: bibl. (Serie Magíster; 222)

This short book, originally an MA thesis by an Ecuadorian journalist, examines Correa's decision to reform the intelligence services. The government framed this initiative as a response to revelations of US influence that came to light after the Colombian military's bombing of a FARC encampment within Ecuadorian territory in 2008, an incident that Correa denounced as a violation of Ecuador's sovereignty. Correa convened a commission to study the agencies and recommend reforms. The result was a major restructuring that included the disbandment of one of the central units charged with counternarcotics. Levoyer suggests that these reforms were not prompted solely by a desire to enhance the nation's sovereignty. Instead, the evidence she presents based on investigative reporting, government documents, and a few interviews points to a more subterfuge motivation related to ties between members of Correa's government, the FARC, and drug trafficking. However, the author provides no smoking gun and studiously avoids making a declarative accusation. Where she appears to be on firmer ground is in her assessment of the impact of these reforms. She contends that together with the decision to close the US base in Manta, the reforms created a vacuum that drug traffickers exploited to increase their presence in the country. This part of her analysis is significant because it provides a piece of the puzzle for explaining the fearsome incursion of cartels and the attendant violence that Ecuador is experiencing today, tracing it back in part to these reforms.

1012 Moncayo Moncayo, Patricio. La planificación estatal en el interjuego entre desarrollo y democracia. Quito: FLACSO Ecuador, 2017. 356 p.: bibl., index. (Atrio)

This study compares state planning agencies and processes in Ecuador during two periods: the nationalist military government of Rodríguez Lara in the 1970s and the first two administrations after the transition to democracy, that of Roldós and Hurtado in the 1980s. The author, who served in state planning agencies during both periods, interviewed key figures including former presidents, government ministers, and functionaries, and conducted research in the planning agency archives. He contends that despite acknowledged failures, planning succeeded in creating the foundation for the country's development during the statist period. He refutes the idea that planning is only relevant to statist models and contends that effective planning involves a practice of linking the economic and the political. Ultimately this study offers a new understanding of state planning that rejects a purely technocratic approach in favor of one that bridges the economic and the political, and in so doing, improves governance and strengthens democracy. This book makes a significant contribution to debates about economic development, statism versus neoliberalism, and state capacity, as well as to our understanding of Ecuador's modern economic development.

1013 Octubre y el derecho a la resistencia: revuelta popular y neoliberalismo autoritario en Ecuador. Coordinación de Franklin Ramírez Gallegos. Buenos Aires: CLACSO, 2020. 421 p.: bibl., ill. (some color).

This collection of 17 essays and two photo essays analyzes the massive protests that shut down the capital and large swaths of the country in October 2019. The book is divided into four sections examining protest trajectory and dynamics, the government's neoliberal agenda that provoked the crisis, the role of various social sectors, the process of dialogue that brought the protests to an end, and the long-term implications of these events for the state, democracy, and social movements. Written and published close in time to the events, the essays do not offer a unitary conclusion on the significance or implications of this event. Topics that are especially noteworthy include the role of feminist discourse and women; the emergence of support networks to provide protesters with lodging, food, and medical care; the dynamics of new and old social cleavages; analyses of the state and its interaction with the protesters; and the potential of the protests to bring about a rapprochement within the fractured Ecuadorian left. This book provides insightful analysis for those seeking a deeper understanding of this pivotal uprising and its implications for Ecuadorian politics.

1014 Orrantia, Daniela. La planificación participativa en la elaboración del Plan Nacional del Buen Vivir 2013–2017. Quito: Universidad Andina Simón Bolívar, 2018. 91 p.: bibl., ill. (Serie Magíster; 234)

This book, originally the author's MA thesis, assesses the veracity behind the Citizens' Revolution's commitment to participatory democracy through a case study of the drafting of the Plan Nacional del Buen Vivir (National Good Living Plan) for 2013–2017. The author begins by reviewing the theory of participatory democracy, then lays out the legal and institutional structure in Ecuador for implementing participatory practices, and, finally, based on government documents and direct observation, analyzes and evaluates the process in light of the theoretical model. The author finds that the apparatus purportedly designed to involve the public in decision-making was controlled and directed by the central government. The dialogues, assemblies, and councils were neither autonomous nor sufficiently diverse; the agendas were largely determined by the government; and the decisions arrived at were not binding. The whole process constituted little more than a patina of participatory democracy. Based on this case study, the author concludes that the ideological artifice of participatory democracy espoused by the Citizens' Revolution was in fact a tool to co-opt and integrate the citizenry into a project orchestrated and controlled by the central government. This careful case study provides further evidence of the distance between the Citizens' Revolution's democratic promises and reality.

1015 Ospina Peralta, Pablo. La aleación inestable: origen y consolidación de un estado transformista; Ecuador, 1920–1960. (*Ecuad. Debate*, 99, dic. 2016, p. 141–169, bibl.)

This article presents a groundbreaking theory of the Ecuadorian state that offers a solution to the puzzle of the absence of large-scale political violence for most of the 20th century in Ecuador.

While economic and social changes were accompanied by the eruption of civil wars, military dictatorships, guerrilla insurgencies, and revolutions throughout much of Latin America, Ecuador remained a placid country avoiding extreme levels of violence. Ecuador also went through a transition to capitalism but without the attendant political violence. Utilizing a Gramscian concept, Ospina argues that the development of a "transformist state" explains this anomaly, a situation in which moderates succeed in maintaining hegemony during a period of social transformation. Key structural factors account for the emergence of this state: weak and fractured regional oligarchies, a military that enjoyed autonomy from the oligarchies, and weak pushback from subaltern sectors. A particularly fascinating part of this analysis is the role played by President Velasco Ibarra, Ecuador's pre-eminent mid-20th century political figure. Difficult to categorize, Velasco Ibarra was a charismatic populist figure who nevertheless was associated with and sustained the conservative political order. Ospina offers a rich analysis of Velasco Ibarra, arguing that his popularity stemmed from his construction of a transformist state capable of transferring the declining authority of the hacienda onto the state in a way that contained social unrest and disruption. This article is required reading for understanding Ecuador's unique political development.

1016 Pugh, Jeffrey D. Universal citizenship through the discourse and policy of Rafael Correa. (*Lat. Am. Polit. Soc.*, 59:3, Fall 2017, p. 98–121, bibl., graphs)

This article examines the concept of universal citizenship and how it was utilized both rhetorically and in policy-making by the Correa administration. Associated with open borders, this concept is debated theoretically but has seen little practical implementation. The Citizens' Revolution was one of the most visible examples so far of a government that embraced and advocated for this approach. Pugh studied Correa's speeches, his policies towards migrants, and the politics surrounding this plank of the Citizens' Revolution. He found that while Correa's rhetoric entailed a radical embrace of the idea of universal citizenship, political considerations and citizen backlash ultimately led him to backtrack on implementation in ways that negatively impacted immigrant rights and political inclusion. While Correa retreated from his advocacy of migrant-friendly policies, his rhetoric and some of the policy changes implemented early in his administration provided migrants and their allies with tools, resources, and networks to push for protection of migrant rights in Ecuador. The analysis of this case highlights the inevitable political challenges and complications entailed in implementing open border policies and as such advances our understanding of the intersection between theories of universal citizenship and politics.

1017 Ramírez Gallegos, René. La gran transición: en busca de nuevos sentidos comunes. Quito: Ediciones CIESPAL, 2017. 223 p.: bibl., ill. (Libertad y conocimiento; 1)

Ramírez Gallegos held cabinet-level positions throughout the Citizens' Revolution as minister of planning and development and then of higher education. Written before the end of the Correa presidency, this book outlines a broad vision of a systemic shift that echoes Karl Polanyi's "great transformation" and identifies the Citizens' Revolution as a catalyst for a transition to a more just and sustainable economic system. The book both assesses the progress made over the previous decade and outlines the remaining work, thus implicitly arguing for a continuance of the political project. The author advocates a shift away from unfettered capitalism, inequality, and ecological destruction by breaking up great wealth concentration and the development of a new model of "Indigenous socioecological accumulation." This approach will entail a shift from industrial to knowledge-based capitalism. A key challenge is the rising expectation of a new lower middle class whose material conditions improved during the previous decade but who nevertheless feel frustrated and dissatisfied. From one of the project's most important ideologues, this book offers a compelling case for understanding the first decade of the Citizens'

Revolution as an incomplete but important step in a longer process of social and economic transformation.

1018 **Riofrancos, Thea N.** Resource radicals: from petro-nationalism to post-extractivism in Ecuador. Durham, N.C.: Duke University Press, 2020. 252 p.: bibl., index. (Radical Américas)

This important and accessible book studies political struggles over resource extraction, which became the lynchpin of conflict pitting the country's social movements against the Correa administration. The author frames it as a struggle between two lefts. "Radical resource nationalism" refers to the approach taken by Correa, which embraces using the country's mineral wealth to promote national development and social uplift. "Anti-extractivism" represents a competing left agenda and is advanced by social movements that opposed and fought the government's intensification of drilling and mining, calling instead for a radical transition away from reliance on resource extraction. Based on extensive field research—including interviews with social movement leaders and government officials as well as participant observation of protests and meetings and archival research, Riofrancos provides a richly textured and compelling analysis of these divergent visions and how they shaped political struggle in Ecuador during the Citizens' Revolution. Her analysis of politics in a petro-state is significant as a challenge to the state-centric nature of the resource curse theory in advancing an understanding of dilemmas faced by the left in an age of environmental crisis and in drawing attention to left radical ecological calls that emerged even in a resource-dependent economy. Riofrancos concludes with a cogent assessment of the current challenges and dilemmas faced by the Latin American left and argues for a political project that can bridge the need for social investment with demands for ecological care.

1019 **Rivera Vélez, Fredy; Rusia Katalina Barreiro Santana;** and **Gilda Alicia Guerrero Salgado.** ¿Dónde está el pesquisa?: una historia de la inteligencia política en Ecuador. Quito: Pontificia Universidad Católica del Ecuador, 2018. 210 p., 6 unnumbered pages: bibl. (Biblioteca de ciencias sociales)

One of few academic inquiries into Ecuador's political intelligence operations, this book uncovers the history of what the authors refer to as "secret police" (*pesquisa*). Covering the decades from the 1960s to the 1990s, the researchers describe how the mission and functioning of the intelligence services evolved from a Cold War emphasis on fighting leftist internal subversion to fighting drugs and countering Indigenous and labor movement activists during the democratic period. The authors contend that practices of secrecy and zero democratic accountability, first established during the Cold War under mostly military governments, persisted under democratic governments, leading to human rights abuses and corruption. The corrupt use of these shadowy services erupted into public view in the mid-1990s with scandals associated with President Durán Ballén and his vice president, Dahik. The authors argue that while intelligence agencies are important to a nation's security, they must be regulated and accountable to the constitution, laws, and democratic institutions, which has historically not been the case in Ecuador. This study is significant considering the major reforms undertaken by the Correa administration. Somewhat surprisingly, the authors do not comment on these more recent developments.

1020 **Vallejo, Sebastián.** Angostura, el 30-S y la (re)militarización de la seguridad interna en Ecuador. Quito: Universidad Andina Simón Bolívar Ecuador: Corporación Editora Nacional, 2018. 72 p.: bibl., ill. (Serie Magíster; 229)

This short book prepared originally as a MA thesis examines the reforms of Ecuador's security services in the wake of two important events during the Citizens' Revolution: the 2008 bombing of the FARC camp in Angostura by the Colombian military and the police revolt in 2009. The author argues that the first round of reforms served to demilitarize the security services, thus reducing the role of the military in internal affairs. However, the second round undertaken after the police insurrection that Correa interpreted as an attempted coup moved the needle in the opposite direction. The national police, now viewed as a threat to the government, had their functions curtailed. This left gaps in internal security functions that were then entrusted to the military, thus resulting in a remilitarization of the national security apparatus. Vallejo frames these developments within the broader regional context characterized by historically powerful militaries, the rise of the national security doctrine, and the persistence of these legacies within democratic structures and institutions. The author recognizes positive aspects of police reform but is concerned about the expanded role of the military in internal security and its impact on democracy.

VENEZUELA

JUAN CARLOS NAVARRO, *International Faculty, Instituto de Estudios Superiores de Administración (IESA), Venezuela*

MOST OF THE publications reviewed for the Venezuelan government and politics section of *HLAS* 77 were written between 2015 and 2020, a period full of political possibilities for a democratic renewal in Venezuela. As economic and social indicators plunged, the parliamentary election in December 2015 resulted in a two-thirds majority in favor of the united opposition to the Chavista regime in the National Assembly. After such a victory proved to be of little consequence, given Maduro's successful neutering of the Assembly's powers through a series of Supreme Tribunal decisions, the action moved to the Venezuelan streets in April 2017. Massive protests nationwide were met with hardline tactics from security forces, which resulted in over 100 fatalities. Military control of the country successfully shut down the protest movement. Subsequently, in early 2019, in response to the lack of legitimacy of the 2018 presidential elections that put Nicolás Maduro in office, the National Assembly designated Juan Guaidó as interim president. Most liberal democracies around the world joined in declaring the 2018 election illegitimate and recognized Guaidó's interim presidency. Planning for a transitional government started. Studies written at the time reflect, consequently, a sense of both hope and urgency to plan for the eventual transition to a democratic regime. These dual tendencies are accompanied by a scholarly interest in weighing the positive and negative outcomes of the preceding two decades of Bolivarian revolution.

Some of the contributions examine the very beginning of the Chávez regime. Notable examples are the two long volumes by Aguiar Aranguren that cover from the early days of the first Chávez presidency to the parliamentary election in 2015 and its consequences (item **1021**). The volumes recreate the major events of this period and offer a glimpse of how a politician and first-rate intellectual in the opposition to the Bolivarian revolution understood such events in real time, without the benefit of hindsight. The author is eloquent and analytical in describing his view of the emerging challenges to democracy. He is also unwavering in his hope for a resolution to the political conflict and a restoration of democratic institutions.

For an empirical perspective on political opinions and attitudes during the period, Trak and a team at the Universidad Católica Andrés Bello present a thorough mining of survey data collected between late 2016 and 2017 by the Barómetro de las Américas (item **1032**). Highlights of the findings reveal strong political polarization in the context of severely weakened support for the administration of Nicolás Maduro: 87 percent of the population declare that they are opposed to stripping the National Assembly of its powers. The economy is the dominant concern: scarcity, inflation, and unemployment are the most pressing problems; 67.8 of the population consider it very difficult to find the food staples needed for their families and 78 percent declare that their personal economic situation has deteriorated over the past year. Worsening economic hardship also seems to have an impact on the growing share of the population that expresses a desire to emigrate.

In a particularly noteworthy finding, Venezuelans are shown as staunch supporters of democracy and voting, yet most no longer see their country as a democracy. These facts have important implications. Venezuelan democracy before Chávez has lately been dismissed as the direct result of oil wealth. According to this perspective, a thin layer of quasidemocratic institutions covering a vast array of rent-seeking and corrupt practices defined a narrow elite that cared little for the majority and lacked a vision for the country. The volume by Schurster *et al.* is largely written in this vein (item **1029**). This view contrasts sharply with the mainstream US political science literature before Chávez, which stressed the ability of the political leadership of the main political parties to steer the country towards a real democratic regime and described the spread of a democratic culture among Venezuelans, leaving behind the legacy of one and a half centuries of dictatorships and violence. One can debate which of these two radically different assessments of Venezuelan democracy between 1958 and 1998 is closer to the truth, but only rarely does one see an empirical treatment of Venezuelans' recent political attitudes, such as Trak's book (item **1032**). The work is a necessary starting point for determining which interpretation more clearly represents the recent history of Venezuelan political culture.

The focus of the volume compiled by Alarcón and Ramírez (item **1026**) on plans and policy prescriptions for a more democratic and less conflict-ridden nation is also a product of the work's precise placement in the timeline of the political events. A broad spectrum of leading academics and activists contributed to this work. The book, published at the peak of Guaidó's interim presidency, sought to contribute to the hard work of transitioning from authoritarian rule to democracy. One requisite of implementing policy, however, is to have the capability to do it. As if inspired by Samuel Huntington's maxim that countries differ not only in the type of government they have, but also in the degree of government (meaning, their capability to carry out public policy), the volume edited by Spiritto (item **1027**) focuses on how decisions were made in the Chávez and Maduro administrations and the consequences of those decisions. The revolutionary aims of the regime are a key part of the discussion. As several of the contributions make clear, these were not administrations trying to find solutions to society's problems. They were seeking a resolution to all fundamental problems once and for all, hence the revolutionary bent. Most authors converge around the main conclusion:

Chávez did not abolish Venezuelan public institutions overnight. A "flattening" of political participation, in the expression of Urbaneja in his essay in the volume, excluded most parties, civic associations, and interest groups from the policymaking process. This was accomplished for the benefit of a new triad of dominant players: the armed forces, the Cuban government, and the core of Chávez loyalists, as shown very clearly in Briceño Montesinos' study in the book. Thus, Chávez's goal of concentrating power and displacing independent checks and balances translated into a weakening of professional management and technical policymaking capabilities in public sector agencies. Rebuilding both will have to be the first order of business in any eventual democratic transition.

Having been dealt an unprecedented defeat in the 2015 parliamentary election, the left also found the opportunity to reflect on the legacy of the Bolivarian revolution. Three seminars held in 2016 brought together several intellectuals of solid leftist credentials. Their contributions are compiled in Carosio et al. (item **1025**). The essays in this book present a noteworthy counterpoint to the previously mentioned works. Antonio Gramsci and Ernesto Laclau are explicitly recognized by several of the authors as sources for the framing of analyses, all of which are grounded in issues of cultural and political identity and hegemony, as applied to Venezuelan politics: the Punto Fijo regime fell because of an acute loss of legitimacy. Eventually a charismatic populist leader arose and was able to speak directly to the grievances of the poor and marginalized in the slums of Venezuelan cities, peasants, and Indigenous peoples—and thus articulate their demands outside mainstream political parties and traditional institutions. Then this leader reached power and proceeded to govern in direct connection to a popular coalition.

For the contributors, there is no doubt that Chávez was inspired by Marxism—as well as by his reading of Simón Bolívar—and that socialism was the core of his vision for Venezuela. Criticism of the Bolivarian revolution emerges in a few essays in the volume, which agree that the socialist model was the right one, but suggest that it was poorly implemented. Socialism did not fail. The revolution in Venezuela failed socialism. In this context, Nicolás Maduro receives most of the blame for anything that may have gone wrong: bureaucratic excesses, unbridled corruption in his entourage, damage to the environment, and, at least in Puerta's perspective, the most critical of all contributions, the undue influence of the military.

Notoriously absent from this analysis is the dismal social and economic performance of the country over this period, and the fact that all forms of democratic participation, free speech, and pluralism—typical of the pre-Chávez era—have been severely curtailed: the reader will not find economic analysis in these pages, or figures related to migration, health care, crime, or education in Venezuela. Again and again, the essays emphasize how the Venezuelan people found in Chávez a leader that they could identify with—and they may very well have done so. That they may have lost their country in the process remains unaddressed.

For a view contrasting in both political orientation and method, the outstanding volume by Torres and Casanova sees socialist policies at the root of the Venezuelan crisis (item **1024**). The book encompasses the full Venezuelan arc from despair to hope and planning for the future. Contrary to a good share of the literature, these authors argue that the economic, social, and political debacle in

Venezuela under the Bolivarian revolution was not fatally dictated by the failures of the preceding democratic era, no matter its shortcomings. They were rather a contingent, if unfortunate, outcome of the urges of Venezuelan citizens for political change in the late 1990s. A different, better future was, and still is, a possibility, according to the authors. After a comprehensive and fully corroborated discussion of the Venezuelan crisis that identifies the socialist authoritarian model implemented by Chávez and Maduro as the root cause of the country's miseries, the book dedicates itself to imagining how things could improve in the future. This discussion takes place both at the macro level, in which the future of Venezuela is a free market democracy, and, joining Alarcón and Ramírez above, in the details of sector policies and decisions that might be able to move the country in a better direction.

By early 2022, the push for a democratic transition in Venezuela seemed to have subsided. Maduro's authoritarian rule appeared to be consolidated, and the democratic opposition seemed weak and divided. A regime transition was no longer perceived as imminent in the way it had been when most of the books in this section were written. No matter that he was presiding over one of the steepest economic declines on record, Maduro seemed to have little to fear in terms of domestic political challenges in the short term.

Nonetheless, regime legitimacy is still in short supply for Maduro. The election that brought him to power is considered invalid by over 50 countries around the world. Maduro himself is under investigation for crimes against humanity in the International Criminal Court at The Hague. Sponsored by the international community, tentative dialogue with the opposition has resulted in no meaningful roadmap for future elections. And performance-based legitimacy is not an option: Venezuela's descent into poverty and dysfunctionality continues unabated while one fifth of the population has left the country. Venezuela is now on the short list of fragile or failed states, as compiled by international organizations such as the Organization for Economic Cooperation and Development, the World Bank, and the Fund for Peace.

There are early signs that the literature might be turning towards adjudicating responsibility for the dire conditions in which the country finds itself. This is not necessarily an entirely new subject, and some of the contributions highlighted here reflect this shift. The discussion is newly framed with the focus on determining whether the Maduro administration's policies are at the root of the country's economic debacle, or whether the external environment is to blame for placing obstacles in the way of a more acceptable economic performance.

A glimpse of this type of discussion can be seen in two contrasting working papers on the effect of economic sanctions on the Venezuelan economy. Weisbrot and Sachs (item **1033**) contend, based on economic analysis, that the economic sanctions imposed in 2017, and later reinforced in 2019 by the Trump administration, led to radically reduced oil revenue and international financial transactions, all of which had severe economic impacts on the welfare of Venezuelans. They admit preexisting conditions were dire, yet the sanctions made them much worse, and also made it impossible for the Venezuelan government to put together a sensible economic policy in response to the ongoing crisis. Bahar *et al.* (item **1023**) respond directly to this argument in their paper, which convincingly shows that sanctions only accentuated deep-seated negative trends.

Most of the extreme damage to society and the economy was already in place when the sanctions were imposed.

This discussion deals with only one aspect of the regime's legitimacy. Depending upon who has the better argument, the Maduro administration could claim—or not—that the sanctions, and not the adminisration's policies, are the problem. Yet this is a particularly important aspect of political legitimacy for a socialist regime in Latin America, as evidenced in the endless debate about the influence of sanctions—the over half a century blockade—on economic performance in Cuba. There is a strong possibility that soon we will see more studies published on this topic and on other aspects of political legitimacy in the forthcoming work on Venezuelan politics and government. Even more importantly, expect a renewed emphasis on transition to democracy and related issues in the literature on Venezuelan politics and public policy, since, in an unexpected but sharp turn of events, 2023 brought the opportunity for one of the most serious challenges to Maduro's hold on power, in the form of the emergence of María Corina Machado as the leader of the unified opposition and the widespread rejection of Venezuelans to the regime on the occasion of the referendum on the border dispute with Guyana.

1021 Aguiar Aranguren, Asdrúbal. El problema de Venezuela, 1998–2016. Caracas: Editorial Jurídica Venezolana, 2016. 2 v.: bibl., indexes. (Colección estudios políticos; 10)

These two volumes contain a series of essays, some of them originally read as speeches in parliament or academic settings, all of them contextualizing or assessing the key political events of the Chávez and Maduro governments, from the election of Hugo Chávez in 1998 to the date of publication. The distinctive value of this compilation is the author's front-line participation in many of the events. He was a prominent minister in the Caldera administration that immediately preceded the first Chávez presidency and then went on to keep a privileged view of most of the turbulent political circumstances that the country went through—constitutional reform, recurrent elections, massive street protests, general strikes, and more. The early alarming signals of the first Chávez administration, the dire condition of the press, the reaction of many Venezuelans against the onset of authoritarianism, the growing Cuban influence in internal Venezuelan affairs, and the questionable role played by the international community, are all themes that find a convincing treatment in these pages.

1022 Aveledo, Ramón Guillermo. El Senado: experiencia comparada y utilidad para la democracia en Venezuela. Prólogo por Andrés Zaldívar Larraín. Caracas: abediciones: Instituto de Estudios Parlamentarios Fermín Toro, 2019. 222 p.: bibl. (Colección La República de todos)

One key novelty introduced by the new constitution written at the onset of the first Chávez administration was the abolition of the Senate, replacing the bicameral system in favor of a one-chamber legislature, the Asamblea Nacional. Twenty years later, the author, a parliamentary leader, scholar, and prominent opposition figure, examines pros and cons of the current arrangement and concludes that Venezuela would be better served by a bicameral system. The country needs a Senate. This conclusion stems from an informative and balanced review of parliamentary institutions around the world, as well as from a discussion of the risks that unicameral systems pose to the checks and balances in a republic going back to Montesquieu, Constant, and The Federalist Papers. The book vehemently sends the message that rethinking the architecture of the legislative branch cannot be overlooked in the event of an eventual democratic renewal in Venezuela.

1023 Bahar, Dany et al. Impact of the 2017 sanctions on Venezuela: revisiting the evidence. Washington, D.C.: Brookings Institution, 2019. 11 p.: bibl., graphs.

Written in response to the paper *Economic Sanctions as Collective Punishment* (see item **1033**), this essay argues that most of the economic deterioration in Venezuela had already happened by the time the US sanctions were imposed (2017). Sanctions only accentuated strong pre-existing trends. Bahar et al. contend that the conclusions of the paper in question are invalid mainly because data show overwhelmingly negative trends in economic and social indicators prior to the sanctions. Imports of food and medicine decreased about 70 percent between 2013 and 2016. Financial markets were already closed to Venezuela before the sanctions, and oil production had sharply declined for over a decade during the pre-sanction Chávez-Maduro administrations.

1024 Casanova, Roberto and Gerver Torres. Un sueño para Venezuela. 2a ed. Caracas: Asociación Civil Liderazgo y Visión, 2020. 312 p.: bibl., col. ill.

This book by prominent Venezuelan economists has both analytical and pedagogical purposes. It represents an attempt to reflect on what happened to a country that by many measures was on its way to a prosperous future, yet today its economic and social indicators place it at the bottom among Latin American countries. The authors write in clear prose and include an abundance of information presented in a visually compelling way. Chapter 2 provides the best synthesis of the multifaceted Venezuelan crisis available in the scholarly literature, reviewing evidence for economic, social, and political performance. Chapter 3 turns its attention to the causes of the crisis, some rooted in unresolved issues in the country's history, but most due to the socialist regime that has systematically curtailed political and economic freedoms for the past two decades. Chapters 1 and 4 look to the future and present a vision of how far Venezuela could go, should institutions be rebuilt in the context of a modern free market democracy.

1025 Chavismo: Genealogía de una Pasión Política, *Caracas*, 2016. Chavismo: genealogía de una pasión política. Coordinación de Alba Carosio, Indhira Libertad Rodríguez y Leonardo Bracamonte. Contribuciones de Iraida Vargas Arenas et al. Caracas: CELARG, Fundación Centro de Estudios Latinoamericanos Rómulo Gallegos; Bolívar, Venezuela: CIM; Buenos Aires: CLACSO, 2017. 188 p.: bibl., ill.

This book offers a reference for the reader interested in how Venezuelan intellectuals on the left understand Chávez's and Maduro's actions. Although some nuances of opinion can be found among the many contributors to this work, most are emphatically persuaded that the socialist Bolivarian Revolution was a positive process for Venezuela. Authors repeatedly highlight the intimate connection between the leader Chávez and many Venezuelans, particularly the poor, who had felt marginalized during the previous democratic era. No reference is made to the economic and social costs of the period, however, and no empirical analysis or figures are provided. A few essays do introduce a dose of criticism to some of the outcomes of the period, particularly what some see as an excessive militarization of government and society and the failure to build a durable political party with the capacity to carry on the revolution once its charismatic leader exited the scene.

1026 La consolidación de una transición democrática: el desafío venezolano. Vol. 3. Coordinación de Benigno Alarcón Deza y Sócrates Ramírez. Caracas: Abediciones, UCAB Universidad Católica, CEPYG UCAB Centro de Estudios Políticos y de Gobierno, 2018. 561 p.: bibl., ill. (Colección Visión Venezuela)

Having laid the foundations for an understanding of the Venezuelan crisis in previous volumes of the series, this third volume, with contributions by leading Venezuelan academics, shows convincingly that there is no shortage of coherent ideas for an eventual reconstruction of the country along democratic and economically modern lines. Broad areas covered in this work include the restitution of state capacity, the recovery of rule of law, and the strengthening of democracy. Specific chapters cover economic policy, international relations, electoral institutions, citizen safety, social policy, and more. The ultimate purpose of the book is to make available a blueprint for democratic governance and reconstruction in the event of a regime transition in Venezuela. At the very least, it stands as a snapshot of how democratic forces understood the best alternative to the existing authoritarian regime by the second decade of the 21st century. For a review of Vol. 1, see *HLAS 73:1191*. For a review of Vol. 2, see *HLAS 75:1079*.

1027 Decisiones de gobierno en Venezuela: apuntes para su comprensión histórica y de políticas públicas. Coordinación de Fernando Spiritto. Caracas: AB ediciones: Universidad Católica Andrés Bello, 2018. 375 p.: bibl., ill. (Colección La república de todos)

This series of studies addresses the characteristics of decision-making in the Venezuelan state under Hugo Chávez and Nicolás Maduro. Luis Salamanca, in the most comprehensive contribution in the volume, draws a telling contrast between the Sistema Populista de Conciliación—the obsession with consensual decision-making attributed to the Venezuelan democratic polity after 1958 in the political science literature—and the Sistema Populista de Confrontación that emerged under Chávez—a substitution of consensus building by conflict as the main driver of the political system. This shift translated to an unprecedented centralization of power in the hands of the president and the loss of most of civil society's influence on policy-making. Fernando Spiritto and José Ignacio Hernández G., in their respective studies, describe the result: weakening of policy-making capabilities in public sector agencies and policy volatility. The book also contains useful sector-specific studies on oil sector policy, foreign policy, health care policy, and the media.

1028 Díaz Rangel, Eleazar. Periodismo, medios y comunicación. Caracas: Monte Ávila Editores Latinoamericana, 2018. 197 p.: bibl. (Documentos)

A reader will be left with two different takeaways from this book by a widely respected Venezuelan journalist, college professor, and editor of a major newspaper. One is a series of historical vignettes about the history of journalism in Venezuela filled with anecdotes about the key historical characters and institutions that built the profession during the early to mid-20th century. The other is a view of the role of the press in Venezuelan politics over the past 50 years. The author asserts that freedom of the press flourished during the Chávez regime, in sharp contrast with the recurring threats that it faced in the pre-Chávez years. This is a difficult position to defend against the reality of the diminished state of independent media outlets in Venezuela after two decades of Chávez and Maduro, but this book contains probably the best case that can possibly be made.

1029 A era Chávez e a Venezuela no tempo presente. Organização de Karl Schurster e Rafael Pinheiro Araujo. Rio de Janeiro: Editora Autografia; Recife, Brazil: Edupe, 2015. 322 p.: bibl.

In this book, a group of Brazilian scholars analyzes the main aspects of the Bolivarian Revolution taking place in Venezuela. For the most part, they tend to regard the Chávez regime positively, emphasizing how it emerged from the failures of the Punto Fijo political order. Ideology at times gets in the way of sound analysis and, more than once, basic facts regarding the Venezuelan polity are misrepresented, detracting from the quality of some of the chapters. One particularly egregious example is the assertion that democracy was an alien notion to the majority of Venezuelans before Chávez. Eduardo Scheidt offers the most balanced perspective in his chapter that compares assessments of Chávez and his legacy from diverse views across the ideological spectrum.

1030 Guerra fría, política, petróleo y lucha armada: Venezuela en un mundo bipolar = Cold War, politics, oil, and armed struggle: Venezuela in a bipolar world. Edición de Alejandro Cardozo Uzcátegui, Luis Ricardo Dávila y Edgardo Mondolfi

Gudat. Bogotá: Universidad del Rosario, 2019. 446 p.: bibl.

This compilation of studies by noted Venezuelan historians focuses on how the Cold War context affected the evolution of Venezuelan politics during the early decades of the country's democratic era, starting in 1958. The essays provide original and well-documented arguments that conclude that the Cold War was, indeed, fought in Venezuela, and often violently. The main theme is the left's armed and ideological challenge to the administration of President Rómulo Betancourt, a challenge directly supported by Cuba. The emergence of a consolidated Western-style democracy in Venezuela was seen by many, including the US, as a part of the anticommunist struggle worldwide. The volume, as a plus, contains a more theoretical chapter by Jessica Guillén that contrasts the work of Eduardo Galeano and Carlos Rangel, two influential Latin American intellectuals of opposite political persuasions.

1031 Samet, Robert. Deadline: populism and the press in Venezuela. Chicago, Ill.: The University of Chicago Press, 2019. 244 p.: bibl. (Chicago studies in practices of meaning)

This remarkably well researched book examines the role of the press in the context of the Chávez regime. The topic as such is not new, but the strong empirical foundation and the thoughtful approach set Samet's contribution above most of the similar literature. Years of ethnographic fieldwork went into the making of this book. The focus is the crime reporter's day-to-day work in Caracas. The rationale for this focus is the realization that crime news played an outsized role in the intense give and take between President Chávez and the opposition, becoming a key component of the dynamics of populism in Venezuela. Populism is in fact the central notion organizing the narrative in the book, understood as "...government based on appeals to the people" in contrast with representative democracy. The book is at its best when it is vividly narrating street-level interactions among journalists and common citizens. It also articulates a set of conclusions rarely found together: that the press played an important role in Chávez's ascent to power—by contributing to the loss of legitimacy of the previous democratic governments; that the press then turned around and became a major element in the opposition to Chávez—and crime news was at the center of this; and, finally, that the press may have played a role by contributing to the political salience of public safety as the first national priority and as a reaction to the highly repressive security policies under Maduro.

1032 Trak, Juan Manuel. Crisis y democracia en Venezuela: 10 años de cultura política de los venezolanos a través del Barómetro de las Américas. Coordinación de Juan Manuel Trak. Con la contribución de Lissette González y María Gabriela Ponce. Caracas: Universidad Católica Andrés Bello, Centro de Estudios Políticos, abediciones, 2017. 169 p.: bibl., color ill. (Colección Visión Venezuela)

This book reports on findings of a nationwide survey of political attitudes in Venezuela undertaken by the Barómetro de las Américas survey as a part of the international project Opinión Pública de América Latina (LAPOP) coordinated by Vanderbilt University. Since the survey has been repeated every other year starting in 2006, the evolution of political opinions over time can be observed. The book's discussion of the surveys' findings is well informed by political theory. Included are public perceptions of political polarization (very high), credibility of public institutions (very low), valuation of democracy and voting, and, crucially, given the likely influence on recent migration flows, perceptions of the economic situation as of late 2016 and early 2017. The work clearly shows that Venezuelans are greatly concerned about economic issues such as inflation and the scarcity of food staples.

Villasenin, Lucas Manuel. El camino de la Revolución Bolivariana: sus orígenes y desafíos. See *HLAS 76:834.*

1033 Weisbrot, Mark and **Jeffrey D. Sachs.** Economic sanctions as collective punishment: the case of Venezuela. Washington, D.C.: Center for Economic and Policy Research, 2019. 25 p.: bibl., graphs.

This paper advances the thesis that the US economic sanctions imposed on the Maduro regime in 2017—and reinforced in 2019—had a severe negative impact on the welfare of the Venezuelan population and the feasibility of an economic recovery. Drastically reduced oil revenues and lack of access to international financial markets as a consequence of the sanctions led to economic conditions that disproportionally harmed the poorest people by making a pre-existing economic crisis worse, deepening the ongoing recession, and producing mass migration. In addition, the authors discuss the legality of the US sanctions and conclude that they may very well be against the law. See also item **1023**.

BOLIVIA

MIGUEL CENTELLAS, *Croft Instructional Associate Professor of Sociology & International Studies, University of Mississippi*

BOLIVIA HAS UNDERGONE significant political changes since the previous *HLAS* volume. The October 2019 elections ended chaotically, with compelling evidence of fraud and widespread protests that resulted in the end of Evo Morales' presidency. Less than a month after confidently announcing that he had won an unprecedented fourth consecutive re-election, Morales and his vice president (Álvaro García Linera) boarded a Mexican Air Force Gulfstream jet and flew into exile. The government of interim president Jeanine Áñez faced immediate challenges from pro-Morales forces, complicated by the coronavirus pandemic. Nevertheless, Bolivians went to the polls a year later, on 18 October 2020, in an election that saw the MAS candidate Luis Arce win the presidency with a comfortable margin. On the surface, the return of Morales' MAS party to power suggests a return to the pre-2019 status quo. But the reality is that Bolivia is now in a post-Morales era in which many of the economic, cultural, and political changes have become established practice, including the emergence of more institutional (less personalistic) politics.

Although contemporary history dominates most of the recent scholarship, there is continuing interest in revisiting the country's political history. This trend is illustrated by an edited collection of essays, mainly by Santa Cruz-based scholars, on the 35th anniversary of the establishment of democracy (item **1051**), as well as a brief but comprehensive survey of Bolivian political thought by Eric Cárdenas (item **1036**).

Some new works on political parties are shaped by an interest in re-evaluating the past in the context of the present. An edited volume on the history of Bolivian left parties between 1920 and 1977 focuses on how they addressed "the Indian question" (item **1049**). Another edited volume on political parties since 1982 (item **1055**) includes both the major parties and the myriad of small, local, and often fleeting electoral vehicles that have emerged in recent years. Luis Meneses Herrera (item **1044**) uses the little-studied Movimiento Sin Miedo (MSM) party as a case study of the organizational structure of Bolivian political parties. Those interested in gaining a fuller understanding of the MAS in power would benefit from reading about MSM, the center-left party that dominated La Paz politics when it allied with MAS in its 2005 election victory, before slowly drifting away into the opposition, and then disappearing.

A "critical turn" in Bolivian scholarship continues, with new and increasingly nuanced critical evaluations of the Evo Morales government. While conservative and center-right voices criticized the MAS-led government from the very start, new critical voices have emerged from within the left, progressive, and Indigenous wings. Sofía Cordero Ponce's comparative analysis distinguishes Bolivia's more top-down approach to cultural and territorial autonomy from Ecuador's more flexible approach (item **1037**). Carlos Macusaya (item **1042**) and Pablo Mamani Ramírez (item **1043**) go further, arguing that plurinational cultural policies under Morales were either based on outdated "noble savages" mythologies or promoted a kind of "exoticism" that tempered Indigenous peoples' political agency and autonomy relative to the state. Most striking is the emergence of critical voices from within the circle of public intellectuals linked to Álvaro García Linera, Morales' vice president and former sociology professor (item **1038**). At the same time, a new generation of cultural progressives criticizes the "statist" or "hegemonic corporatist" trajectory of the Morales government (items **1052** and **1054**), mirroring the argument of more senior scholars like María Teresa Zegada and George Komadina (item **1056**) that the clientelist practices of the Morales government limited Indigenous and peasant actors' incorporation to a form of "controlled participation."

Unsurprisingly, a major topic within the literature is the most recent political crisis set off by the contentious 2019 election, which was marred by accusations of attempted electoral fraud and ended with the collapse of the MAS-led government headed by Evo Morales. On the whole, recent works are marked by a polemical nature, as well as by an emphasis on presenting a wide range of evidence. In some cases, the quality of the evidence is obfuscated by the sheer quantity of the material. Israel Mérida Martínez offers two provocatively titled volumes made up mostly of curated collections of newspaper clippings (items **1045** and **1046**). Manuel Morales is similarly provocative as he tries to make the case that the Morales government had close ties with narcotrafficking (item **1047**). Carlos Echazú Cortéz's collection of essays argues that the 2019 protests were politically orchestrated and part of a coup (item **1040**). This narrative is countered by established anti-Morales critic Carlos Valverde Bravo (item **1053**), and also by the well-known Asamblea Permanente de los Derechos Humanos de Bolivia (APDHB), which presents a carefully organized dossier that includes eyewitness testimonials and official documents, laying out the case that public discontent with Evo Morales was genuine and denouncing some of the actions taken to suppress protests (item **1035**). Interestingly, Valverde's volume then turns to accuse Áñez of whitewashing the Morales government and not doing enough to prevent its return to power. One final noteworthy volume is José Peralta Beltrán's book (item **1050**) on the interaction between the political crisis and the COVID-19 pandemic, and how the latter became politicized and part of the larger political crisis.

1034 Aceves López, Liza Elena. Aprender a perder: lecciones del giro latinoamericano a la izquierda: los casos de Bolivia y Venezuela. Puebla, Mexico: Instituto de Ciencias Sociales y Humanidades "Alfonso Vélez Pliego": Facultad de Economía, BUAP; Ciudad de México: Ediciones EyC, 2016. 298 p.: bibl.

This highly reflexive volume seeks to understand Latin America's "left turn" with the benefit of hindsight and using Bolivia and Venezuela as comparative cases to critically explore the Latin American left's relationship with democracy. The author concludes that, while the Bolivian and Venezuelan left transformed themselves in their resistance to neoliberalism, becoming less revolutionary and more willing to engage in electoral politics, they were unable to accept opposition and the possibility of electoral defeat as crucial democratic values.

1035 Asamblea Permanente de los Derechos Humanos de Bolivia. Relato de un Pueblo: derechos humanos y resistencia democrática en 2019. La Paz: Plural, 2021. 328 p.: ill. (chiefly color).

A detailed history of the social protests that erupted in the wake of the October 2019 election. The volume includes a trove of official documents, first-person testimonials, and other evidence chronicling both the social protests and the Morales government's response. As a document produced by the country's oldest human rights watchdog organization, the volume challenges narratives that paint the 2019 protests as politically orchestrated, rather than as an expression of widespread public discontent.

1036 Cárdenas del Castillo, Eric Luis. Historia del pensamiento político boliviano. La Paz: Libreria Editorial "G.U.M.", 2019. 223 p.: bibl.

Without treading much new ground, this volume provides a whirlwind tour of Bolivian political thought, starting with the colonial period. Noteworthy sections include the discussion of the 1928 Congreso Universitario, which led to the establishment of university autonomy, and a brief descriptive narrative of the "social Christian" and "Christian democracy" trends.

1037 Cordero Ponce, Sofía. La plurinacionalidad desde abajo: autogobierno indígena en Bolivia y Ecuador. Quito: FLACSO Ecuador; La Paz: PNUD, 2018. 222 p.: bibl. (Atrio)

A comparative analysis of Indigenous autonomy projects in Bolivia and Ecuador, two cases with many similarities and with new constitutions (2009 and 2008, respectively) that initiated a process of "reinventing" the state. An introductory chapter that provides the conceptual and theoretical framework precedes one chapter per country. The author finds that despite similar starting points, each had different experiences. In Bolivia, while the principle of territorial autonomy was more explicitly outlined in the new constitution, the top-down approach created obstacles and led to tensions. In contrast, Ecuador's more bottom-up approach allowed for experimentation and flexibility.

1038 Democracias, comunidades y estado boliviano en perspectiva histórica y multicultural. Edición de Huascar Salazar y Luis Tapia. Contribuciones de Patricia Chávez et al. La Paz: Autodeterminación, 2018. 276 p.: bibl. (Colección El horizonte interior)

This robust collection of essays explicitly sets out to go beyond the increasingly "state" political discourse focused on the question of Morales' fourth reelection. Instead, the authors offer a critical evaluation (from within leftist circles) of the tensions and contradictions inherent in "process of change" politics, in both practice and discourse. Two key recurring themes are the challenges that "process of change" discourse poses for a feminist agenda and the hopes for a different, more bottom-up articulation of genuine Indigenous cultural politics.

1039 Dunkerley, James. Rebelión en las venas: la lucha política en Bolivia, 1952–82. La Paz: Vicepresidencia del Estado Plurinacional de Bolivia, 2019. 478 p.: bibl., ill.

A Spanish translation of Dunkerley's influential history of Bolivia originally published in English (see *HLAS 48:3090* and *49:6407*). Although not updated or revised in any significant way, this volume includes an essay on the book's legacy by Carmen Soliz.

1040 Echazú Cortéz, Carlos. Fascismo y posverdad en Bolivia: reflexiones sobre el golpe de Estado de 2019 y el régimen de facto. La Paz: Ediciones Liberación, 2021. 210 p.: bibl.

This work contains a collection of short essays originally published in alternative online news outlets. While clearly partisan in nature and at times verging on conspiracy theory, the collection provides a contemporary perspective on the events leading up to, during, and immediately following the 2019 election crisis and raises thought-provoking questions and issues.

1041 Galindo, María. Feminismo bastardo. Buenos Aires: Lavaca, 2022. 262 p.: bibl.

Galindo, one of Bolivia's most vocal feminist provocateurs and the founder of the Mujeres Creando collective, offers a collection of controversial, but thoughtful essays on anarcha-feminism. Written in Galindo's sharply irreverent style, the essays articulate a vision of a "21st-century feminism" and are equally critical of Evo Morales and his government and the neoliberal order that preceded it.

1042 Macusaya, Carlos. Batallas por la identidad: indianismo, katarismo y descolonización en la Bolivia contemporánea. Lima: publisher not identified, 2019. 260 p.

This thought-provoking discussion addresses the challenges of constructing an "Indigenous" cultural and political project that goes beyond the recuperation of an idealized past or platitudes about "authenticism" or contemporary visions based on dated "noble savage" mythologies to "save our culture from culturalism."

1043 Mamani Ramírez, Pablo. El estado neocolonial: una mirada al proceso de la lucha por el poder y sus contradicciones en Bolivia. La Paz: Rincón Ediciones, 2017. 252 p., 20 unnumbered pages: bibl. (Colección Abrelosojos; 10)

The book articulates a biting critique of the trend within the Morales government towards an "exoticism" that dilutes the political power and agency of Indigenous peoples and their social movements. A long-time participant in Indigenous political organizations, Mamani traces the social history of *katarismo* and *indianismo* in Bolivia, which he distinguishes from the more performative "pachamamista" tendencies within MAS.

1044 Meneses Herrera, Luis. Estructura organizativa de los partidos en Bolivia y el caso del MSM, 1999–2014. Cochabamba, Bolivia: Fundación Centro Especializado en Estudios Políticos C.E.L.P., 2017. 202 p.: bibl., color ill.

A narrative history of political parties in Bolivia with a focus on the Movimiento Sin Miedo (MSM), a center-left party with a strong base in the city of La Paz that was a key ally of MAS from 2005 until 2014. While the book's first two parts are not particularly innovative, they are lucidly written and provide a useful overview of the history of Bolivian political parties and party systems, as well as necessary context for the chapter covering the rise and fall of MSM.

1045 Mérida Martínez, Israel. Evolución de una caída. Cochabamba, Bolivia: Escape Libros, 2020. 206 p.: bibl., ill.

Mostly a collection of excerpts from newspapers and online news websites, the book traces the "fall" of Evo Morales from January 2016 (just before the referendum to determine whether Morales could seek a fourth consecutive re-election) through the end of November 2019. Although the book offers no analysis beyond the one-page introduction, the collection of news excerpts makes this a useful documentary account.

1046 Mérida Martínez, Israel. Manual para hundir un pais. Cochabamba, Bolivia: Escape Libros, 2021. 138 p.

With its provocative title, the goal of the book is to present evidence that Evo Morales misgoverned Bolivia over 14 years, leading to massive public discontent that exploded in the aftermath of the October 2019 election. Other than brief introductions to each of the 12 chapters, the book is merely a compilation of selected excerpts from newspaper and news media outlets from October 2019 to October 2020.

1047 **Morales Álvarez, Manuel.** Narcovínculos: narcotráfico, instituciones del estado plurinacional y personajes agnados. La Paz: Ediciones Insurgente, 2019. 138 p.: bibl., ill. (some color).

This volume by a self-styled "insurgent" investigative reporter lays out evidence of a connection between the Morales government and illicit narcotrafficking. While much of the evidence relies on openly reported connections (such as campaign photographs) of MAS figures and individuals later sentenced for narcotics crimes, the large number of such connections is intriguing.

1048 **Nuevo mapa de actores en Bolivia: crisis, polarización e incertidumbre (2019–2020).** Coordinación de Jan Souverein y José Luis Exeni R. La Paz: Friedrich Ebert Stiftung, 2020. 350 p.: bibl., ill.

This volume includes essays by some of Bolivia's most well-respected social scientists and public intellections, including Fernando Mayorga, María Teresa Zegada, and Fernando Molina. The authors set out to analyze the emerging political landscape after the fall of Evo Morales. Mayorga discusses the crisis of identity within MAS, which has gone from being a party of power to a "political instrument" (as it had been before the 2005 election of Evo Morales). Eduardo Gonzales looks at Church-state relations in a pluricultural Bolivia, as well as the more open role taken by Catholic and Evangelical churches. Eliana Quiroz and Wilmer Machaca explore the role that the internet and social media played in the 2019 crisis and its implications for future political action.

1049 **Los partidos de izquierda ante la cuestión indígena, 1920–1977.** Contribuciones de Huascar Rodríguez García *et al.* Gestión editorial y cuidado de edición por Claudia Dorado Sánchez. La Paz: Vicepresidencia del Estado, Presidencia de la Asamblea Legislativa Plurinacional Bolivia, CIS Centro de Investigaciones Sociales, 2017. 272 p.: bibl., ill. (Historia política)

Collection of histories describing how leftist political organizations addressed "the Indian question" throughout the 20th century. Organized chronologically, the collection begins with an overview of syndicalism, the left, and indigenismo in pre-1952 Cochabamba. Raúl Reyes provides a history of PIR, the first significant party to explicitly incorporate "the Indian question" into its platform. Other chapters cover the Communist Party (PCB), Workers Party (POR), and MNR, as well as lesser-known leftist groups: Ejército de Liberación Nacional (ELN), Partido Revolucionario de los Trabajadores (PRTB), Partido Comunista-Marxista Leninista (PC-MIL), and Unión de Campesinos Pobres (UCAPO).

1050 **Peralta Beltrán, José Orlando.** Rebelión y pandemia: proceso político-electoral en Bolivia 2019–2020. La Paz: Plural Editores, 2021. 128 p.: bibl.

This brief volume aims to place the political crisis that followed the October 2019 election and the social crisis brought on by the COVID-19 pandemic within the broader context of social unrest predating the election itself. In particular, Peralta focuses on the ongoing resistance and challenge to the MAS government centered on Santa Cruz, and in particular the 2006 autonomy referendum as a central element in the country's subsequent polarization.

1051 **35 años de democracia: resultados y tendencias: ensayo.** Edición de Franklin Farell Ortiz. Santa Cruz de la Sierra, Bolivia: Editorial Universitaria, Observatorio Político Nacional-UAGRM, 2018. 289 p.: bibl., ill.

This collection of essays explores various themes and topics related to Bolivia's experience since the 1982 transition to democracy. Primarily reflective and descriptive, the essays are useful as an indication of contemporary *cruceño* political discourse. The volume includes a brief essay by established pundit Carlos Hugo Molina posing questions about Bolivia's transformation into an urban society. The most noteworthy essay is by José Orlando Peralta, which provides a descriptive narrative of the evolution of the political discourse of Rubén Costas, governor of Santa Cruz (2015–2021).

1052 **Uc, Pablo.** Tinku y pachakuti: geopolíticas indígenas originarias y Estado plurinacional en Bolivia. Tuxtla Gutiérrez, Mexico: Universidad de Ciencias y Artes de Chiapas; San Cristóbal de Las Casas, Mexico: Centro de Estudios Superiores de México y Centroamérica: Observatorio de las Democracias Sur de México y Centroamérica; Buenos Aires: Consejo Latinoamericano de Ciencias Sociales, 2019. 294 p.: bibl., ill., maps.

Using a contextualized ethnographic approach, the author analyzes three periods: the historical backdrop that formed modern Bolivia (*nayrapacha*), the opening of a revolutionary transformation driven by Indigenous-based social movements starting in 2000 (*pachakuti*), and the tension within the government of Evo Morales between the forces of multiculturalism and hegemonic corporatism since 2006 (*tinku*). The book also provides detailed accounts of the organizational structures and geopolitical range of different organizations within the pro-Morales coalition, as well as the drift between the "official" geopolitical discourse of "MAS and the new governing elite" and the "Indigenous originary peasant" discourse maintained by the more autonomous social movements.

1053 Valverde Bravo, Carlos. Fraude y después. . .: octubre 2019. Santa Cruz de la Sierra, Bolivia: El País, 2022. 905 p.: bibl., ill.

Polemical but thoroughly researched account of the crisis that followed Bolivia's October 2019 election, as well as its aftermath. Valverde is a well-known investigative journalist openly critical of Evo Morales. Citing numerous government documents obtained as part of his investigation, Valverde builds a case against Evo Morales and accuses the post-Áñez government of whitewashing the former president's actions.

1054 Viaña Uzieda, Jorge. Luchas para la transición: del vivir bien hacia el horizonte estratégico del socialismo comunitario. La Paz: Instituto Internacional de Integración, Convenio Andrés Bello, 2017. 178 p.: bibl.

A critical assessment of the "statist" trajectory of the Morales government after 2010 and the transition from a discourse of *vivir bien* to an institutionalized, state-centered, developmentalist "communitarian socialism" that lacks a "strategic project" and concrete plan for "emancipatory praxis."

1055 Zegada, María Teresa et al. Disonancias en la representación política: partidos aparentes y sociedad en acción (1982–2020). La Paz: Plural Editores, 2021. 382 p.: bibl., graphs, ill. (some color), maps.

An excellent and thorough overview of the history of political parties in Bolivia and changes in the party system since 1982. The analysis includes not only "major" political parties, but also the myriad of small, local parties, electoral vehicles, and other organizations that make up Bolivia's contemporary party systems. The authors conclude that Bolivia's "virtual" parties lack the strong links to civil society, posing challenges to their ability to function as institutions for social representation in a democratic society.

1056 Zegada, María Teresa; George Komadina; and **Liz Mendoza.** El intercambio político: indígenas/campesinos en el Estado Plurinacional, 2009–2016. La Paz: CERES: Plural Editores, 2017. 222 p.: bibl.

This volume critically examines the relationship between MAS, Indigenous/peasant actors, and the Bolivian state as a relationship based on "exchange" of material and symbolic benefits. The authors argue that although the rise of MAS incorporated Indigenous/peasant actors as political subjects, it often did so through "controlled participation" and "prebendalism." Anthropologists and other scholars interested in the politics of identity (re)construction will particularly appreciate the fourth chapter, which focuses on symbolic exchange and how Indigenous cultural identity was contested, formulated, and altered based on a group's standing and relationship within the MAS government.

CHILE

PETER M. SIAVELIS, *Professor of Political Science and International Affairs, Wake Forest University*

1057 Akram, Hassan. El estallido: ¿por qué? ¿hacia donde? Santiago, Chile: elDesconcierto.cl: El Buen Aire, S.A., 2020. 288 p.: bibl., graphs, ill.

Akram provides one of the first of many accounts attempting to explain the social explosion of 2019 known as the *estallido*. Rather than focusing on any one single event or even arguments about general malaise and discontent, Akram provides a comprehensive analysis of Chile's economic and social indicators going back the period of the installation of Chile's neoliberal economic model. He finds that fundamentally, governments of the two coalition parties that held sway in Chile for much of the post-authoritarian period did little to address the deep injustices and inequality embedded in the model. Also, unlike other studies, he places Chile in comparative perspective with cogent analyses of other neoliberal economies like the US and the United Kingdom. Finally, Akram concludes with a series of recommendations of how Chile can move forward to be a more just and equitable society.

1058 Arrate, Jorge. Con viento a favor. Vol. 1, Del Frente Popular a la Unidad Popular. Santiago, Chile: LOM Ediciones, 2017. 1 v. (Memorias)

As a new generation of politicians assumes power in Chile, many of the politicians of the generation of the democratic transition and the years of the Concertación have published nostalgic interviews and memoirs (see, for example, item **1065**). One of the best-known figures of the Chilean socialist movement is Jorge Arrate, who presided over the unification of the Chilean Socialist Party with the return to democracy in 1989. He served as a minister in the first two post-authoritarian governments of Patricio Aylwin (1990–94) and Eduardo Frei Ruiz-Tagle (1994–98). This memoir, part of a multivolume series, focuses on the period between 1941 with the advent of the Frente Popular (which formed in 1937) until the formation of the Unidad Popular coalition in 1970 through the ill-fated presidential government of Salvador Allende, which fell victim to the military coup of 1973. This very personal memoir follows the leader from his youth through becoming a major protagonist in the Chilean socialist movement. However, it is also an intellectual autobiography that traces the author's reflections on philosophy, Chilean history, and the forces that led to the downfall of Chile's democracy.

1059 Bril-Mascarenhas, Tomás and Antoine Maillet. How to build and wield business power: the political economy of pension regulation in Chile, 1990–2018. (*Lat. Am. Polit. Soc.*, 61:1, Dec. 2018, p. 101–125, bibl., graph, table)

Reform of the social policies implemented during the Pinochet regime have been a major focus of scholarship on Chile given the differences in the outcomes between private and public schemes. Much of the motivation for the *estallido* was rooted in a protest against injustice in social welfare provision, including education, health care, and pensions. These scholars investigate how the privatized pension system has survived given so much international and domestic scrutiny and criticism. The authors argue that a combination of the pension industry's long-term power-building investments and short-term political actions has enabled it to defeat attempts at reform. Focusing on pension regulation between 1980 and 2010, the analysis provides key insights into how businesses have achieved their goals within the context of Chile's neoliberal economic model.

1060 Cerda, Nicolás de la. Unstable identities: the decline of partisanship in contemporary Chile. (*J. Polit. Lat. Am.*, 14:1, April 2022, p. 3–30, bibl., graphs, tables)

Before the dictatorship and during the 1990s, Chile was notorious for its high level of citizen identification with parties; indeed, it usually ranked as the highest in Latin America. However, this figure plunged from over 80 percent in the 1990s to under 20 percent by 2016. This paper seeks to uncover how we can understand this dramatic decrease. The author argues that the major reason for the decline is the dissolution of the main cleavage that formed the bases of the Chilean party system during the 1990s: a division between supporters of the Pinochet regime and advocates of democracy. The author argues that as parties of the right distanced themselves from the military regime, voters lost some attachment to political parties. In essence, the paper finds that political identities need to be continually reinforced if citizen identification with them is to remain stable.

1061 La columna vertebral fracturada: revisitando intermediarios políticos en Chile. Edición de Juan Pablo Luna y Rodrigo Mardones. Santiago de Chile: Instituto de Ciencia Política, Facultad e Historia, Geografía y Ciencia Política, Pontificia Universidad Católica de Chile: RiL editores, 2017. 440 p.: bibl., ill.

Arturo Valenzuela's classic 1977 book *Political Brokers in Chile: Local Government in a Centralized Polity* (see *HLAS* 41:7454), recently republished in Spanish as *Intermediarios políticos en Chile* (item **1084**), is perhaps the most influential work on Chilean local government before the breakdown of democracy. Valenzuela underscores the central role by local mayors in extracting resources from the central government and acting as a mediating force in national politics through the web of partisan politics. In this sense, he builds on Manuel Antonio Garretón's oft-cited observation that the Chilean party system was the "backbone""of the party system. This edited volume seeks to revisit Valenzuela's thesis in light of disarticulation of party politics in the country and the increasing distance between citizens and political parties. The editors begin with a review of Valenzuela's original argument. Chapters go on to consider the new dynamics of local politics with a focus on municipal elections, the role of independents, local campaigns, and indigenous politics. Authors also discuss the transformed role of key actors and institutions like the Congress, deputies and senators, and ministries. Finally, authors address the new dynamics of policy-making in the distribution of social welfare resources and municipal funding given this transformation. The editors conclude with a useful summary of Valenzuela's contribution vis-à-vis contemporary Chilean politics.

1062 Díaz Nieva, José. Patria y Libertad: el nacionalismo frente a la Unidad Popular. Santiago, Chile: Ediciones Centro de Estudios Bicentenario, 2015. 319 p.: bibl.

Patria y Libertad was a fascist organization founded in 1970 that collaborated with the Chilean military in conspiring to overthrow the government of Salvador Allende. This comprehensive history of the group traces its origin from its successor organization, the Movimiento Cívico. This meticulously researched volume begins by exploring precursor organizations and the process by which it coalesced into the main arm of violent civilian opposition to the Allende government. It goes on to explore its relationship to the more traditional right and other groups that opposed the government including producer organizations and trade unions. The author describes in detail the lead up to the military coup and the central role of the group in facilitating the military's ultimate insurrection and violent overthrow of the government.

1063 Donoso, Sofía et al. Is it worth the risk?: grievances and street protest participation during the COVID-19 pandemic in Chile. (*J. Polit. Lat. Am.*, 14:3, Dec. 2022, p. 338–362, bibl., tables)

This article, like item **1071**, analyzes the interaction of the major political crises Chile faced simultaneously: the COVID-19 pandemic, massive street protests, and a deep political crisis. The authors examine the reasons why people continued to protest despite restrictions on protests and the potential health risks that protesting posed. They test three models in an attempt to explain this participation: biographical availability (defined as the particular characteristics and responsibilities of people that allow them to engage in protest), perception of risk, and grievances. They find that grievances appear to be more important, especially those related to Chile's massive healthcare inequalities, but also a perception that the government prioritized the economy over the safety of citizens during the pandemic. They argue that where there is a political crisis, people may be motivated to participate in politics even at the risk of their own health.

1064 Farías Antognini, Ana. Políticas sociales en Chile: trayectoria de inequidades y desigualdades en distribución de bienes y servicios. Santiago: UAH/Ediciones, Universidad Alberto Hurtado, 2019. 257 p.: bibl., ill. (Colección Ciencia política)

Studies of Chilean social policy focused on Concertación governments abound. However, few studies put these policies in the context of the wider development of the welfare state in Chile. Before the coup, Chile was characterized by a generous welfare state that had continually expanded since the first part of the 20th century. The Pinochet dictatorship abruptly halted this evolution. Subsequent democratic governments have attempted to rebuild a more equitable regimen of social benefits. This meticulously researched study takes the reader from the early origins of the Chilean welfare state through its expansion during Chile's process of industrialization between 1930 and 1970. The author then recounts the development of what she terms a "two-headed" welfare state with generous privatized benefits for the few and inadequate social benefits for the many. She outlines attempts by post-transitional democratic governments to advance reforms in the areas of health, childcare, pensions, and education. She concludes with a useful discussion of the potential future trajectory of social welfare policy. The book is valuable for understanding the injustices in the welfare system that prompted Chile's 2019 social uprising.

1065 Fernández Abara, Joaquín; Álvaro Góngora Escobedo; and **Patricia Arancibia Clavel.** Ricardo Núñez: trayectoria de un socialista de nuestros tiempos. Santiago: CIDOC, Centro de Investigación y Documentación en Historia de Chile Contemporáneo, 2013. 365 p.: color ill.

Ricardo Núñez has been a giant among leaders of the Chilean Socialist Party for the last 50 years. He was a central participant in and observer of the profound changes that occurred in Chile before and after the 1973 coup, having been a political prisoner and spending six years in exile. He went on to serve as senator for 20 years immediately following the return of democracy in 1990, and played a key role in the democratic transition. This work by three historians is based on a series of interviews undertaken with Núñez in 2010 and 2011. Among the political eras of Núñez's career covered are the period of Popular Unity, prison and exile, the creation of the Alianza Democrática, the 1988 plebiscite, and the first Concertación governments. While fundamentally a political testimony of a central player in Chilean politics, the work doubles as a fascinating account of the history of Chile from the 1950s to today. It is another in a series of biographies and autobiographies like that of Arrate (item **1058**) growing out of the process of generational change in Chilean politics.

1066 Gaudichaud, Franck. Las fisuras del neoliberalismo maduro chileno: trabajo, "democracia protegida" y conflictos de clases. Buenos Aires: CLACSO, 2015. 104 p.: appendices, bibl., ill. (Colección Becas de investigación)

Gaudichaud provides a brief but comprehensive overview of the Chilean neoliberal economic model. He examines the genesis and development of the model from the dictatorship to the first Bachelet government. While appearing successful from the outside, the author argues that the model has generated powerful divisions in Chilean society by undermining workers' rights, privatizing public services, and aggravating inequality. The major argument of the book is that it is not possible to think of just one "neoliberal" economic model; rather, the model has evolved over time and produced different kinds of social divisions and social conflict. The book is eerily prescient because the author talks about the emergence of social, labor, student, and Indigenous movements, yet it was published well before the social explosion of 2019. In this sense, it helps us understand some of the sources of discontent in Chile that became evident as protests rocked the country.

1067 Hilsenrad Grünpeter, Marcelo. Luz, camara... elección: la democracia chilena en 25 años de debates presidenciales. Prólogo de Daniel Matamal. Santiago, Chile: Catalonia, 2019. 362 p.: bibl.

Hilsenrad has been involved with presidential debates in Chile for the last 10 years as a producer and director of televised debates. This position provides the author an inside view of the mechanics of presidential debates and a keen eye for their analysis. The book begins with some key definitional terms regarding what constitutes a presidential debate and discusses controversies surrounding their significance and influence. It outlines a brief history of the role of presidential debates in Chilean politics. The author goes on to provide an analysis of each presidential debate that took place in Chile between 1989 and 2013. The analysis is geared more towards a popular rather than academic audience, but provides lively and interesting accounts of the issues, dynamics, and perceived winners of each debate.

1068 Justo, Liborio. Así se murió en Chile: reformismo y revolución en la trágica experiencia de la Unidad Popular. Buenos Aires: Editorial Maipue: Editorial Cienflores, 2018. 476 p.: bibl. (Colección "El hombre es tierra que anda")

Argentine-born Liborio Justo is a Marxist theorist and militant who died at the age of 101 in 2003. Like the many works aimed at memorializing the 50th anniversary of the 1973 coup (item **1084**, for example), this posthumously published work provides a comprehensive history of Chile from the beginning of the 20th century, recounting the socioeconomic and historical trajectories that set the stage for Marxist Salvador Allende's popular election and the eventual dramatic and violent downfall of Chile's democratic regime. Relying on interviews, political party declarations, and leftist publications in each era, the author builds on the historical context he presents to recount the victory of Allende's Unidad Popular government, its performance in office, the crisis of the "Chilean Road to Socialism," and the forces that worked to undermine the government leading to its eventually downfall. The meticulous detail presented in this work makes it stand out from standard historical analyses of the military coup.

1069 Juventud y espacios de participación en Chile y América Latina. Edición de Rodrigo Torres, Gabriel Urzúa y Juan Carlos Sánchez. Santiago de Chile: Universidad Central, Facultad de Ciencias Sociales: RiL Editores, 2018. 172 p.: bibl., ill.

Young people played a central role in sparking Chile's massive popular mobilization in 2019 and the student movements that predated it. Eventually they took the reins of government with the 2022 swearing in of Gabriel Boric, Chile's youngest president in history at age 36. This text brings together a group of young scholars from Chile, Mexico, and Colombia to analyze the new forms of popular participation and social activism of young people. The editors provide a useful overview of the text, followed by the first set of chapters of the volume that deal with the Chilean case, focusing on social mobilization for free education, the role of university students in organizing social mobilization, and reflections on the psychology of participation in social movements. The second section takes a comparative focus with chapters on social media in Mexico, collective social narratives in Colombia, and the mobilization of Afro-Colombians in the mining sector. The final chapter argues that a process of "globalization of uncertainty" is underway, with democracies in crises and ambiguity concerning young peoples' reaction to eroding democratic practices and institutions.

1070 Martínez, Christopher and Alejandro Olivares L. Chile 2021: entre un intenso calendario electoral y la acusación constitucional en contra de Sebastián Piñera. (*Rev. Cienc. Polít./Santiago*, 42:2, 2022, p. 225–253, bibl., graphs, tables)

In November 2021, then-president Sebastián Piñera was impeached by the Chilean Chamber of Deputies on charges of corruption related to the Pandora Papers scandal. This article analyzes the final year of the Piñera government with a special focus on the impeachment process and its interaction with the intense electoral calendar of the last few years, with elections for various levels of public office and the constitutional assembly. Given electoral results, the authors conclude that there is a trend toward the weakening of the center-right in Chile. In their analysis of the impeachment, they point to the possible political and electoral motivations of the sponsors. Their findings are noteworthy in terms of what has subsequently unfolded with the dramatic defeat of the proposed constitution that came out of the first constitutional assembly and the election of the Council of Experts dominated by the far right that will give the constitutional rewrite another shot.

1071 Meléndez, Carlos; Cristóbal Rovira Kaltwasser; and Javier Sajuria. Chile 2020: pandemia y plebiscito constitucional. (*Rev. Cienc. Polít./Santiago*, 41:2, 2020, p. 263–290, bibl., graphs, tables)

There is growing scholarly literature devoted to Chile's process of constitutional reform. This piece analyzes the interaction of the twin events that were most critical to shaping politics in Chile in 2020: the COVID-19 pandemic and the plebiscite on a new constitution. For the plebiscite, the citizenry was asked two questions: do Chileans want a new constitution and should it be written by a completely elected assembly or a mix of an elected assembly and Members of Congress? Chileans voted overwhelmingly to replace the constitution with a completely directly elected assembly. The authors of this study took out a series of face-to-face surveys of the population in an attempt to uncover some of the motivations of voters. They found that people who voted for the reject option held similar views to those who support populist right-wing forces, while the approve vote had a high level of heterogeneity in ideological and sociological terms. Given these findings, they conclude that conditions may be ripe for the establishment of a populist right wing force.

1072 Navia, Patricio and Nicolás Mimica. Determinants of bicameral conflict: the formation of conference committees in Chile, 1990–2018. (*Lat. Am. Polit. Soc.*, 63:4, Nov. 2021, p. 74–95, bibl., table)

Based on an analysis of 2,183 congressional bills, this article seeks to uncover the dynamics of the formation of conference committees in the Chilean legislature. In Chile, unlike in most other countries, conference committees are automatically formed if a bill is rejected in the first chamber or if the first chamber rejects modifications that the second chamber recommends. The article tests four hypotheses to explain when this automatic formation of a conference committee is likely to kick in. The authors find no difference between bills presented by the president and the Congress, but do find that conference committees are more likely to be formed when each chamber is controlled by different party or coalition majorities, when special voting thresholds are required for passage, when bills are more important for the president, and in the case of bills that were characterized by a higher number of approved amendments.

1073 Palacios-Valladares, Indira. Chile's 2019 October protests and the student movement: eventful mobilization? (*Rev. Cienc. Polít./Santiago*, 40:2, 2020, p. 215–234, bibl., graphs, tables)

This article, like others reviewed here (items **1057** and **1064**), analyzes the causes and impacts of the social protests that racked Chile in October 2019. The major question the author poses is to what extent the protest movement affected the organization, identity, and strategies of the student movement. Contrary to most interpretations, the author finds that the uprising did not in fact generate "a historical moment of change." She finds that the ability of protest movements to generate political and organization changes depends on the movement's organizational strength and its protest strategies. The author argues that other variables also affect this capacity to elicit change, including the impact of previous mobilizations and where the protest takes place.

1074 Piscopo, Jennifer M. et al. Follow the money: gender, incumbency, and campaign funding in Chile. (*Comp. Polit. Stud.*, 55:2, Feb. 2022, p. 222–253, bibl., graphs, tables)

Chile underwent a comprehensive electoral reform in 2015 including changes to its electoral law, reforms to campaign finance rules, the adoption of a gender quota, and a gendered scheme for state financing that incentivizes the nomination of women candidates. Much research has been devoted to analyzing the success of the quota in improving the representation of women. However, little has been written concerning whether gender quotas also improve campaign funding for women. This article seeks to do so. The authors find that overall, women have fewer resources from all of the sources on which men politicians traditionally rely. The major contribution of the article, though, is that it finds that women incumbents are actually better funded than men incumbents. This fact suggests that funders are unwilling to gamble on newcomers, but that incumbency sends a strong signal regarding the viability of women candidates. The findings underscore the conclusions of other scholarly literature that suggests that quotas and gender-based financing schemes may be insufficient in equalizing campaign funding between women and men.

1075 Política subnacional en Chile: instituciones, partidos, elecciones. Edición de Mauricio Morales, Bernardo Navarrete y Camilo Vial. Santiago de Chile: Universidad Autónoma de Chile: RiL Editores, 2018. 189 p.: bibl., ill.

Despite that fact that Chile is a unitary system, subnational politics have been historically important and are even more so today given recent and ongoing reforms granting additional political power to subnational institutions. In the past, subnational institutions were key to maintaining Chile's institutionalized party system, and they remain a barometer for national politics since subnational elections take place a year before national elections. Recognizing the importance of these local elections, the editors of this volume bring together a well-known set of scholars who turn their attention to subnational politics. Chapters focus on the election of regional governors and regional party organizations, the effect of the voluntary vote on local elections, campaign financing, and the effects of local politics on regional and national elections.

1076 Rodríguez Elizondo, José. Historia de la relación civil-militar en Chile: desde Eduardo Frei Montalva hasta Michelle Bachelet Jeria. Santiago: Fondo de Cultura Económica, 2018. 270 p.: bibl., ill. (some color), index. (Sección de obras de política y derecho)

The Pinochet dictatorship shattered the notion that Chile was different than other Latin American countries in terms of civil-military relations. The extended dictatorship inserted the military more directly in politics than at any time during the 20th century. This book traces the history of the growth of a political role for the military in Chilean politics beginning with the 1964 government of Eduardo Frei Montalva. The author describes the rise of the military as a political force culminating in the overthrow of Salvador Allende and explores the dynamic of civil-military relations during the dictatorship. He underscores the acumen with which Concertación governments conducted civil-military relations, walking a careful line between assuring some modicum of justice for victims while also maintaining civil-military peace. The author argues that Concertación governments were successful in finding this middle ground. However, by the second Bachelet government, there was a retrogression in civil-military relations given the transformation of the left within and outside Chile and a growing sense of citizen malaise. The analysis is prescient considering it was published before the 2019 protests where civil-military relations reached a post-transition low point.

1077 Rojas Casimiro, Mauricio. La renovación de la izquierda chilena durante la dictadura. Santiago, Chile: Piso Diez Ediciones, 2017. 538 p.: bibl.

The Chilean party system has undergone a fundamental transformation since the electoral reforms of 2015 and the social explosion of 2019. This transition has led to significant reflection within political parties regarding their political and ideological orientation and commitments. Few studies have analyzed the transformations that occurred in parties of the left during the military regime itself. This monumental and expertly researched study is based on a compilation of documents from the era, many of which were previously unpublished or clandestinely written. The book analyzes the renovation process that took place in the parties of the left given the failure of their project during the government of Salvador Allende (1970–73). The study is divided into three distinct historical periods and focuses on four parties: the Partido Socialista de Chile (PSCh), the Partido Comunista de Chile (PCCh), the Movimiento de Acción Popular Unitario (MAPU), and the Partido Izquierda Cristiana de Chile (IC). The book concludes by analyzing how this process of renovation led to a renewed convergence of the left that underwrote the foundation of the Concertación coalition.

1078 Samaniego Mesías, Augusto. Unidad sindical desde la base: la Central Única de Trabajadores, Chile 1953–1973. Santiago, Chile: Libros FAHU: Ariadna Universitaria, 2016. 286 p.: bibl. (Colección Libros FAHU)

Organized labor was one of the primary targets of the Pinochet dictatorship and Chile's main labor umbrella organization was the Central Única de Trabajadores (CUT). This book provides a comprehensive history of the CUT from its foundation in 1953 until it was attacked and suppressed following the 1973 coup. This meticulously researched work details transformations within the organization following each of its national congresses and during the various governments of the period. The most provocative section of the book recounts the central role played by the CUT during the Salvador Allende administration (1970–73). The volume's major goal is to uncover the links between the trade union movement and citizen projects for change. Although it focuses principally on two decades, the book provides a useful epilogue detailing what happened to the organization during the dictatorship and into the first Concertación governments.

1079 El sistema político de Chile. Edición de Carlos Huneeus y Octavio Avendaño. Textos de Paula Ahumada *et al.* Santiago: LOM Ediciones, 2018. 442 p.: bibl., ill. (Ciencias políticas. Ciencias Sociales y humanas)

Though written before the onset of the 19 October 2019 crisis that continued into 2020, this excellent edited volume provides a roadmap to understand how Chile got to where it stands today, with the country's major social and political institutions held in extraordinarily low esteem. As a whole, the compilation centers the nature and state of Chile's political institutions from the return of democracy until 2017. The volume's chapters identify many of the precipitants of the manifold crises that Chile faces today. One of the book's key strengths is its comprehensive breadth, with a focus on institutions, a diverse set of social actors, and the media. The point of departure is Huneeus' previous work on the "semi-sovereign" nature of Chile's political constitution under the 1980 Constitution. Topics of the chapters include the Congress, political parties, public policy formation, elections, political culture, the media, trade unions, and various judicial and oversight institutions.

1080 Somma, Nicolas *et al.* No water in the oasis: the Chilean Spring of 2019–2020. (*Soc. Mov. Stud.*, 20:4, 2020, p. 495–502, bibl.)

Like several other works reviewed here (items **1057** and **1064**), this article seeks to uncover the causes of Chile's social uprising known as the *estallido*. Referring to the uprising as the "Chilean Spring," the authors seek to analyze the roots of the most serious social outburst in Chile since the return of democracy. They contend that the combination of grievances, political attitudes, and cultural change were the main triggers of the protest movement. They study the sources of and the interaction between peaceful and violent protest. They conclude by analyzing the failure of the political class to address many of Chile's economic and social injustices and speculate on what the protests mean for the future of Chilean politics.

1081 Soto Barrientos, Francisco and **Yanina Welp.** Los "diálogos ciudadanos": Chile ante el giro deliberativo. Santiago: LOM Ediciones, 2017. 222 p.: bibl. (Ciencias Sociales y Humanas. Política)

Rarely do social movements result in widespread change to political institutions. The social explosion which translated into the process for a new constitution in Chile is in this sense unique. This volume, which was published before the 2019 *estallido*, still helps us put into perspective how this unique process played out in Chile, with a special focus on deliberative democracy and constitution-making in Chile and cross-nationally. The authors begin with an analysis of mechanisms of growing direct participation in democracy around the world, followed by a comparative analysis of the connection between democratic transitions and deliberative dialogue in Spain, Brazil, Chile, and Poland. They analyze levels of political participation in the drafting of the 1980 Constitution, then turn to the origins of constituent assemblies in Latin America and consider some of the widely held myths surrounding them, followed by a focus on citizen participation within them. The final chapters analyze the role of citizen dialogue in the process of deliberations on constitutional reform as well as a potential map for how constitutional change might take place in Chile. Given the timing of its publication, this study offers many prescient insights.

1082 Staab, Silke and **Georgina Waylen.**
Institutional change in constrained circumstances: gender, resistance, and critical actors in the Chilean executive. (*Lat. Am. Polit. Soc.*, 62:4, Oct. 2020, p. 50–74, bibl., chart)

Like item **1064**, the focus of this article is the set of social provision institutions inherited by the dictatorship and hotly debated today. The authors are interested in the role of gender and the potential for actors to elicit positive gender change in these policy areas. In particular, they study the first term of Michelle Bachelet and focus on health, pensions, and childcare. Using a theory-guided qualitative study, they analyze the relative success of actors in using, subverting, or converting existing rules. They find that strategies to elicit change, often far from the legislative arena, can actually be effective. This finding is important because gender equity actors usually do not have the power to create new institutions, so they must devise ways to transform existing ones in a gender-positive direction.

1083 Urtubia Odekerken, Ximena. Hegemonía y cultura política en el Partido Comunista de Chile: la transformación del militante tradicional, 1924–1933. Santiago: Ariadna Ediciones, 2017. 218 p.: bibl.

The Chilean Communist Party has been a constant presence in Chile since the beginning of the 20th century, though its influence has ebbed and flowed. While studies of the Communist Party abound, few focus on its early years. Luis Emilio Recabarren (1876–1924) was a driving force in the early years of the party's development. Urtubia argues that his death prompted divisions and power struggles in the party that helped lead to profound transformations in the party from the mid-1920s to the mid-1930s. In particular, she argues that the model of what a militant was expected to be changed within the party's political culture—with an increasing focus on the "bolshevization" of the party. She argues that the power struggle that was unleashed shaped the development of the party in ways that remain today.

1084 Valenzuela, Arturo. Intermediarios políticos en Chile: gobierno local en un régimen centralizado. Santiago: Ediciones Universidad Diego Portales, 2016. 316 p.: bibl. (Colección Ciencias sociales e historia)

Valenzuela's *Political Brokers in Chile*, originally published in 1977 (see *HLAS* 41:7454), is considered the quintessential work on local government and its national implications in Chile. Like other works reviewed here (e.g., item **1068**), this work's publication in Spanish in part grows from a renewed interest in pre-authoritarian politics in light of the 50th anniversary of the 1973 military coup. Valenzuela undertook research in 14 municipalities in Chile in 1968 and 1969. Central to the book's premise is the idea that local government is much more significant to Chilean politics than it seems at first blush. Rather than simply serving as local administration, these governments actually played a key role as a link in a long chain of political representation that connected citizens to national political life through party system networks. Local officials, principally mayors, acted as brokers delivering resources, jobs, and perks to localities in exchange for ensuring citizen support for Members of Congress. In this way, this network of patrons and clients helped to ease the polarization of national-level party politics. The publication of *La columna vertebral fracturada: revisitando intermediarios políticos en Chile* (item **1061**) attests to the importance of this work.

1085 Visconti, Giancarlo. Reevaluating the role of ideology in Chile. (*Lat. Am. Polit. Soc.*, 63:2, May 2021, p. 1–25, bibl., graph)

This article seeks to provide insight into the current state of the Chilean party system following the dual shake-up of comprehensive electoral reforms and the *estallido*. Its point of departure is to take on the long-held assumption that the ideological stances of politicians are an important determinant of voter choice. The author acknowledges important changes to Chile's rules and political context including electoral reform, the adoption of voluntary voting in 2012, the decline in relevance of the authoritarian/democratic cleavage (analyzed in item **1060**), and the rise of nonprogrammatic electoral strategies. Using a survey experiment conducted in low- to middle-income neighborhoods in Santiago, he finds that candidates' ideological labels are still important to understand voter choice, a tendency that is particularly strong among likely voters. In this sense, these long-held assumptions prove to be correct in this case.

ARGENTINA AND URUGUAY

BRIAN TURNER, *Professor of Political Science, Randolph-Macon College*

Argentina's political science continues to benefit from university-based collaborations focused on specific questions, such as political participation (items **1088**, **1097**, and **1099**), media policy (item **1094**), interest group politics (item **1096**), public administration (item **1098**), and the formation of elites (item **1101**). Production of excellent scholarship on matters of public safety and the police (items **1102** and **1103**) continues to contribute to a detailed understanding of the challenges of reform in this sector. Traditional concerns about populism through the prism of Argentina's experience (item **1100**) are also represented.

Future directions for research will likely include continued retrospective analyses of the nature of governing coalitions under both the neoliberal administration of Mauricio Macri and the Peronist government of Alberto Fernández, and consideration of whether the defeat in 2023 of both recognizably conservative and Peronist projects can shake the country from the long cycle of the politics of repeated economic crises. Another potential topic for consideration is whether new configurations of populist politics represent fundamental reform of patterns of political participation and policy outputs.

ARGENTINA

1086 Anderson, Leslie E. Democratization by institutions: Argentina's transition years in comparative perspective. Ann Arbor: University of Michigan Press, 2016. 292 p.: bibl., index.

Anderson argues that the postmilitary administrations of Alfonsín and Menem led a process of "democratization by institutions" rather than democracy being built on social capital, which was not abundant in Argentina during this period. The strong executive branch allowed the presidents to drive reforms, which are described across several different policy spheres (human rights, civilian supremacy over the military, labor reform, and privatization during the Alfonsín years; privatization, labor reform, and education under Menem). Congressional cooperation potentially advanced democratic reforms, while veto players in Congress occasionally derailed reform efforts, especially in the case of education.

1087 Boos, Tobias. Populismus und Mittelklasse: die Kirchner-Regierungen zwischen 2003 und 2015 in Argentinien = Populism of the middle class?: the first German-language analysis of Kirchnerism in Argentina. Vienna: DEU: Bielefeld, 2021.

In the years from 2003–2007, Néstor Kirchner and subsequently his wife Cristina Fernández de Kirchner from 2007–2015 led Argentina's political fortunes, which coined the term kirchnerismo as their system of rule. With their Frente para la Victoria movement, they kept peronismo in power for over a decade after the national bankruptcy of 2001. The study attempts to characterize the Kirchners' two periods in power, along a populist tradition specific to Argentina. In particular, the study focuses on the government's relationship with the middle class electorate and the transformations in the institutional and educational sectors. [F. Obermeier]

Bosque Sendra, Joaquín and **Gustavo D. Buzai.** Geografía electoral de la Ciudad Autónoma de Buenos Aires, 2015: elecciones a Jefe de Gobierno Municipal y Presidente de la República de Argentina. See item **614**.

1088 La democracia local en la Argentina actual: participación ciudadana en la vida política de los municipios. Coordinación de Cecilia Schneider. Buenos Aires: Editorial Biblos, 2016. 146 p.: bibl., ill. (Investigaciones y ensayos)

This study thoroughly reviews the many legal mechanisms for citizen participation in municipal decision-making, such as initiative and referendum, popular veto, recall, and participatory budget processes. The contributions identify the specific instances in provincial capitals and certain other municipalities when citizens have been called upon to participate in decision-making up to 2012 and begin to outline the specific participants. The researchers find that NGOs and foundations, neighborhood councils, religious organizations, and other groups are more likely to participate than individual citizens, raising questions about the democratizing potential of citizen participation. See also *HLAS 69:1386*.

1089 Di Mauro, José Ángel. Gobernar en minoría: el karma de la gestión Cambiemos. Buenos Aires: Corregidor, 2019. 398 p.

This is a useful and detailed journalistic history of the Cambiemos government, focusing especially on the challenges that government faced with minority support in the Senate. The author identifies this as a weakness in the origins of Cambiemos, and the opposition to the government in the Senate as a sign of strength of Argentina's democracy.

1090 Feldman, Saúl. La conquista del sentido común: cómo planificó el macrismo el "cambio cultural." Buenos Aires: Peña Lillo, Ediciones Continente, 2019. 283 p.: bibl., ill.

Feldman argues that Cambiemos began planning a communications strategy that would create a new "cosmovisión" for Argentines living in a globalized, neoliberal world where, as President Macri put it, "no hay plan B." This plan was, according to the author, thoroughly implemented and somewhat successful, in part aided by the global crisis of democracy, the concentration of capital, and the deployment of powerful new communications media.

1091 Iglesias, Fernando A. El año que vivimos en peligro: cómo sobrevivió el gobierno de Cambiemos al Club del Helicóptero. Buenos Aires: Margen Izquierdo, 2017. 394 p.: bibl., ill.

Iglesias is a polemicist who was elected to the chamber of deputies (where he has served previously) in 2017 as a member of Macri's PRO party. His style is exaggerated, in this book raising fears of deep national crisis if the Kirchnerist "Club del Helicóptero" were to force the Macri government to leave office before the end of the four-year term. No non-Peronist government had completed its elected term since 1928. Iglesias details events in this struggle month-by-month from October 2015 to May 2017.

1092 Levita, Gabriel. Movilizar la nación: trayectorias y discursos en el Senado después de 2001. La Plata, Argentina: Edulp, Editorial de la Universidad de La Plata, 2018. 223 p.: bibl., ill. (Debates)

A methodologically ambitious project to identify the "idea of the nation" represented in a selection of speeches given in the Senate between 2001 and 2011. The author identifies four types of "idea." "Cosmopolitan" refers to a vision of the nation as an expression of universal desires for the public good. "Localist" refers to a vision of a set of values and norms as distinct to the nation or to its narrowly defined localities. While not restricted to Argentina, the other two ideas of the nation have a particular resonance for the country: "conspirativist" and "decadentist" as ideas to explain Argentina's reality versus the desired vision in the first two ideas. The author probes the sociology of these expressions in the Senate, but is not able to identify clear explanatory factors for the distribution of these ideas among senators, except perhaps that those with advanced degrees in the social sciences are more likely to express cosmopolitan ideas.

1093 Malas notas: voces e ideas del Club Político Argentino. Compilación de Victoria Itzcovitz y Luis Rappoport. Buenos Aires: Eudeba, 2016. 538 p.

The Club Político Argentino was founded in 2008 by a large number of intellectuals from various political backgrounds to discuss politics but also to engage in some level of political activity. This volume brings together 133 essays written by club members between 2008 and 2016 that were published in Argentine mass media outlets about every imaginable matter of political importance in the country. The members themselves chose which essays of their own to include, so this volume gives some insight into the perspectives of this group of writers and activists.

1094 Medios públicos: políticas, actores, estrategias. Compilación de Daniela Monje y Silvina Mercadal. Villa María, Argentina: Editorial Universitaria de Villa María, 2018. 159 p.: bibl. (Cuadernos de investigación; 34)

In the first decade of the 21st century, a number of Latin American countries revised their public media policies with the goal of creating greater diversity of access to production and consumption of audiovisual technologies of communication. In one essay, Monje provides a useful comparative analysis of seven South American countries' efforts at creating media spaces that would improve public access. The other six essays (Monje is author or coauthor for each; Mercadal is coauthor of four) address aspects of the experience in Argentina. They find that the creation of regional, university-based, and Indigenous community-based not-for-profit television projects added new and diverse voices and perspectives on content, format, and message, but the public consumption of these new audiovisual materials remained limited, raising the question of "who truly participates in the public system" (p. 95).

1095 Natanson, José. ¿Por qué?: la rápida agonía de la Argentina kirchnerista y la brutal eficacia de una nueva derecha. Buenos Aires: Siglo Veintiuno Editores, 2018. 222 p.: bibl., ill. (Singular)

Similar to Feldman (item **1090**), journalist Natanson argues that Mauricio Macri capitalized on currents in Argentine society that led to his electoral success in a country with a long tradition of social solidarity and egalitarianism. The author describes Macri's movement as indeed something new in Argentina (and notably one without long traditions to which to appeal) but still mostly within a conservative vision of republican democracy. Most worrying to Natanson though was the turn to repression of political mobilizations by social movements.

Niedzwiecki, Sara. Uneven social policies: the politics of subnational variation in Latin America. See item **1129**.

1096 Nosotros que nos quisimos tanto: rupturas y continuidades en la relación con los sindicatos en las administraciones kirchneristas. Edición de María Inés Fernández y Alejandro Rossi. Buenos Aires: Zeta Ediciones, 2018. 225 p.: bibl.

This edited volume under the direction of Fernández and Rossi emanates from a project at the Universidad de Buenos Aires. The various chapters use case studies to understand the role social policies played in consolidating political support for the Kirchner governments, how unions sought to use contacts within the government to reform measures seen as anti-union in the Menem administrations, and how resource constraints after 2008 complicated the government's promotion of social policies and led to strategies of fragmentation of union support.

1097 Participación, políticas públicas y territorio: aportes para la construcción de una perspectiva integral. Compilación de Adriana Rofman. Textos de Ismael Blanco et al. Los Polvorines, Argentina: Ediciones UNGS, Universidad Nacional de General Sarmiento, 2016. 191 p.: bibl., ill. (Colección Cuestiones metropolitanas)

The six essays in this volume are dedicated to advancing the theoretical understanding of the intersections between public political participation, state institutions (in this case mostly at the level of the municipality), state intervention in society to provide "governance" over territory and to create social cohesion, and democratization and relations of power and domination. These considerations are applied to both general patterns in Argentina and to specific cases, including from municipalities in the province of Buenos Aires, Santiago del Estero, and in one essay, Barcelona, Spain.

1098 Pasaron cosas: política y políticas públicas en el gobierno de Cambiemos. Edicion de Marcelo Nazareno, María Soledad Segura y Guillermo Vázquez. Córdoba, Argentina: Facultad de Ciencias Sociales, Universidad Nacional de Córdoba: Editorial Brujas, 2019. 410 p.: bibl.

This volume is a project of 32 members of the Facultad de Ciencias Sociales at the Universidad Nacional de Córdoba, with the goal of contributing to the understanding of the nature of the Cambiemos government and of the quality of its public policy initiatives. The authors share a general understanding of the Cambiemos government that sought to impose a hegemonic vision of a "mercantile paradigm" that eroded rights achieved previously during the democratic period, and that generated significant resistance and social conflict.

1099 Políticas de juventudes y participación política: perspectivas, agendas y ámbitos de militancia. Compilación de Diego Beretta, Fernando Laredo, Pedro Núñez y Pablo Vommaro. Rosario, Argentina: UNR Editora, Editorial de la Universidad Nacional de Rosario; Buenos Aires: CLACSO, Consejo Latinoamericano de Ciencias Sociales, 2018. 303 p.: bibl. (Colección Grupos de Trabajo)

This collection of essays is the result of an ongoing series of related research projects focusing on public policy for youth and political participation by youth. Thirteen essays are divided into two sections. The first addresses young people in movements, including student movements but also as youth sections of political parties. The second section looks at policies to promote youth participation, how youth are seen by municipal leaders and by media sources, and the specific issue of precarity and death among young people. Two essays in this section address youth policy in Uruguay. An epilogue discusses similar issues from the case of the Barcelona "Indignados" movement to the 2015 Spanish elections.

1100 El populismo en la Argentina y en el mundo. Edición y compilación por Roque B. Fernández y Emilio Ocampo. Buenos Aires: Ediciones UCEMA: Claridad, 2018. 415 p.: bibl., 1 ill.

A multidisciplinary and important group of essays that consider populism's origins, maintenance, and impact on political and economic development, using the experience of Argentina to theorize a comparative approach to understanding the phenomena. The authors do not concur on all points, but do share the concern that populism threatens both the institutional stability of government and prospects for stable economic growth. Several contributors explore the deep historical roots of populist culture in Argentina and its symbolic and psychological construction, while also identifying the structural circumstances that allow for a mass movement to follow a leader unconstrained by the institutions of liberal democracy. Several essays debate the rationality of populist voters. This volume is one of solid social science analysis that does not produce a single understanding of populism but rather debates important questions about it and its "surprising" emergence in recent decades outside of Latin America.

1101 Los puentes y las puertas: las fronteras de la política argentina a través de sus elites. Compilación de Paula Canelo y Mariana Heredia. Buenos Aires: UNSAM Edita, 2019. 236 p.: bibl., ill. (Colección: Ciencias sociales) (Serie: Investigaciones)

This well-organized volume includes essays drawing from a shared database of political elites to explore the patterns of access to power and the connections between elites and social actors in the 1933–2015 period. Seven chapters are divided into three sections to explore the conformation of elites in the construction of electoral alliances (menemismo in Buenos Aires province and the Alianza in the 1990s), provincial government (Mendoza, Santa Cruz, and Santa Fe), and the ministries of the national cabinet (defense, labor and social welfare, and the "political" ministries of interior and chief of cabinet). The volume provides a strong analysis of the variability of patterns of elite access across these different political arenas.

1102 Sain, Marcelo Fabián. Por qué preferimos no ver la inseguridad, aunque digamos lo contrario. Buenos Aires: Siglo Veintiuno Editores, 2017. 154 p.: bibl. (Singular)

Sain argues that the provincial police and the provincial government in the province of Buenos Aires operate to regulate and cooperate with criminal groups engaged in narcotrafficking as a means of managing public security, rather than acting to repress criminal activity. The author details three recent cases that show how this cooperation works. He then asks what institutional factors work to keep the public from demanding an end to this criminal cooperation, even while public concern over insecurity is high.

1103 Ugolini, Agustina. Legítimos policías: etnografía de lo ilegal entre policías de la provincia de Buenos Aires. Buenos Aires: EA, 2017. 127 p.: bibl.

A fascinating ethnographic study of a police commissary in the province of Buenos Aires, focusing on how police officers use discourse to legitimize police behaviors that are objectively illegal. These discourses are how police officers learn to become members of the community and determine the boundaries of behavior established by the community itself. This work complements other studies that address the problem of police abuse and violence with direct ethnographic data (see, for example, item **1102**).

1104 Verbitsky, Horacio. Vida de perro. Conversaciones con Diego Sztulwark. 3a edición. Buenos Aires: Siglo Veintiuno Editores: Tinta Limón Ediciones, 2018. 429 p.: bibl., index. (Singular)

The veteran journalist and political activist reviews his life and his political commentary with political scientist Sztulwark.

URUGUAY

Haro Ayerve, Patricio. Fuerzas armadas, pretorianismo y calidad de la democracia: Ecuador y Uruguay. See item **1010**.

Políticas de juventudes y participación política: perspectivas, agendas y ámbitos de militancia. See item **1099**.

BRAZIL

MATTHEW L. LAYTON, *Associate Professor of Political Science, Ohio University*

THE PUBLICATIONS annotated in this section of *HLAS* 77 advance the study of Brazil's government and politics in two broad ways. First, they highlight how scholars and other observers are beginning to grapple with the socioeconomic and political crises that unfolded in Brazil between 2014 and 2018. Second, they offer methodological and theoretical innovation and illustrate the explanatory leverage scholars can achieve when they pursue answers to broad social science research questions against the backdrop of the Brazilian case. Many of the now perennial topics of Brazilian political studies including race, criminal violence, corruption, and social policy are represented in these works, as is a renewed focus on political mobilization and political party institutionalization. Several publications featured in this section analyze variation in Brazil's local municipal politics, while others exploit unique features of Brazil's national political institutions to study questions of broad interest in the social sciences.

One area of focus in recent scholarship has been Brazil's ongoing political development. Peter R. Kingstone and Timothy J. Power (item **1114**) provide the third entry in their series of edited volumes (see also *HLAS 59:4031* and *HLAS 67:1511*) about Brazil's politics and political economy; collectively, these three volumes now provide broad coverage and analysis from many leading scholars of Brazil's New Republic from 1985 through 2017. Joining this important contribution is an impressive biographical narrative of Luiz Inácio "Lula" da Silva, arguably the pivotal figure in Brazilian politics since at least 1989, from John D. French (item **1118**). Those who are interested in further reading on the importance of this entry may want to review the special symposium devoted to the biography in *Latin American Politics and Society* (Vol. 64, No. 1, Feb. 2022).

Other journalists and scholars mentioned here focus on Brazil's recent political crisis that began with the re-election of Dilma Rousseff in 2014, even after nationwide protests in 2013 had signaled rising discontent. Subsequent events like the Lava Jato corruption investigation, the 2016 impeachment of Dilma, and Jair Bolsonaro's rise to power in the 2018 election have likewise drawn the attention of Brazilianists in Brazil and abroad. Undoubtedly, this will be an area of continued interest as additional scholars publish on these topics. It is also worth noting that this edition provides an annotation for the documentary film, *The Edge of Democracy*, directed by Petra Costa (item **1113**). This film uses original and archival footage to place the political events from 2014 to 2018 into historical and personal perspective for the filmmaker and the audience and helpfully complements many of the published works featured in this section.

Despite the recent political turmoil, Brazil also continues to be a fruitful setting for scholars to study a variety of institutional research questions, many of which have broader application outside Brazil. For those who are unfamiliar with the institutional nuances in Brazil, Jairo Marconi Nicolau's book, *Representantes de quem?* (item **1128**), provides a useful introduction to unique aspects of Brazil's legislative institutions and some of the consequences of those institutional features for state-society relations, especially for the Câmara dos Deputados. Brazil's executive agencies are also a useful setting in which to study questions of institutional governance and representation. For instance, Lindsay Mayka (item **1127**) provides an in-depth qualitative study of the institutional reform of Brazil's public health sector between 1988 and 2009. This is particularly notable because, despite the reforms highlighted by Mayka, public health failings triggered many of the grievances expressed during the nationwide protests in 2013; arguably, the COVID-19 pandemic has made these concerns more relevant. Finally, electoral institutions remain an important area of study. Daniel W. Gingerich (item **1120**) uses original archival research from sources dating back to Brazil's Second Republic to uncover the history of the adoption of the secret ballot in Brazil. The analysis of returns from the 1958 and 1962 elections suggests that the reform did little to insulate voters from vote brokers and increased invalid voting in areas with high illiteracy rates; the congressional record from the same time suggests that this was both foreseen and accepted as a potentially desirable effect of the reform. Democratic backsliding in Brazil and around the world have given these historical findings new relevance in contemporary times.

Another area of research focuses on political party organizations and party supporter mobilization in Brazil, with frequent emphasis on the distinct characteristics of the Workers' Party (PT or Partido dos Trabalhadores) in its rise and fall from power in Brazil. For example, Jorge Antonio Alves and Wendy Hunter (item **1105**) provide a case study of the rise of the PT in Bahia, noting that the party set aside its programmatic approach to politics and pragmatically and instrumentally accepted the traditional politics of the region as its *modus operandi*. This argument is echoed in Peter G. Johannessen's article (item **1121**) that more systematically shows that the PT's municipal candidates across Brazil campaigned on programmatic platforms, but then followed nonprogrammatic strategies once in office. It is worth noting that several other authors listed here also find Brazilian municipalities to be a useful context in which to study important research questions, especially when paired with quasi-experimental research designs.

Finally, innovative studies on the topics of social policy, race, criminal violence, and corruption are all represented here. Two books focus on the subnational dynamics of major social policies: Sara Niedzwiecki's *Uneven Social Policies* (item **1129**) and Brian Wampler et al.'s book, *Democracy at Work* (item **1137**). These authors rely on state- and municipal-level data that add needed depth and nuance to the growing literature on the political drivers and consequences of contemporary social policy frameworks in Latin America, although it is possible that scholars will need to revisit some of their conclusions after recent moves by the Brazilian government to implement reforms to core social programs, ostensibly in response to COVID-19. Natalia S. Bueno and Thad Dunning's article (item **1109**) on the connections among race, resources, and representation in Brazil musters an impressive array of evidence to back its claims that elite behavior, rather than systematic voter bias, is responsible for disparities in white and Afro-Brazilian political representation. Two additional articles study organized criminal violence through groundbreaking research: Beatriz Magaloni et al. (item **1126**) draw on years of multimethod research, including ethnographic research, text analysis of crime reports, a survey of 5,300 favela residents, and quasi-experimental modeling of crime indicators to study interactions between organized crime and Pacifying Police Units (UPPs) in Rio de Janeiro; Benjamin Lessing and Graham Willis (item **1125**) received access to over 500 internal documents from São Paulo's Primeiro Comando da Capital (PCC) prison gang, which allow them to describe the internal governance structures of the organization in extraordinary detail. Nara Pavão's article (item **1131**) on the electoral impunity of corrupt politicians offers a new theory and multimethod empirical approach to explain that voters in high corruption contexts fail to punish corrupt officials at the ballot box because deeply ingrained cynicism leads them to discount corruption in their voting calculus. Each of these entries extends the boundaries of the theoretical and methodological approaches that are available to researchers in Brazil and raises important new questions for future research.

1105 Alves, Jorge Antonio and Wendy Hunter. From right to left in Brazil's Northeast: transformation, or "politics as usual"? (*Comp. Polit./New York*, 49:4, July 2017, p. 437–455, bibl., maps, table)

This article presents a case study of the Brazilian Workers' Party (Partido dos Trabalhadores) in the state of Bahia from the party's breakthrough presidential election victory in 2002 until about 2016. The authors note that the party's ascendency came at the expense of the traditionalist right wing political machine that had historically dominated state politics. Yet the authors argue that achieving statewide electoral success in Bahia required the Workers' Party to adapt to the traditional political strategies of the state, rather than transform local politics to align with the party's programmatic and distinctive brand of politics built through grassroots organization.

1106 Amat, Francesc and Pablo Beramendi. Democracy under high inequality: capacity, spending, and participation. (*J. Polit.*, 82:3, July 2020, p. 859–878, bibl.)

This article relies on a natural experiment among Brazilian municipalities that were randomly selected for federal fiscal audits in 2004 where the results of the audits were released prior to the 2004 municipal elections in some cases and after the elections in others. This allows the authors to test the relationship between partisan political mobilization strategies, spending decisions at different levels of contextual inequality, and state capacity. They show how contexts of high inequality and low state capacity produce favorable conditions for targeted mobilization strategies including clientelism, thus resolving an apparent paradox where developing countries with high inequality have much higher voter turnout than wealthy countries with high inequality.

1107 Avritzer, Leonardo. O pêndulo da democracia. São Paulo: Todavia, 2019. 204 p.: bibl., ill.

This book offers a critical reflection on Brazil's recent political development and makes the central argument that since 2014, Brazil has experienced a gradual institutional shift away from a normative commitment to democracy, especially among elite political actors. According to the author, this is just the latest trend in the country's long history of pendular swings between democratic enthusiasm and the reactionary impulses of antidemocratic, antipolitics actors who lie dormant in Brazil until they see a favorable critical juncture they can exploit. The author links these trends to theories of the role of the state, the role of violence in the national political culture, and the rise of religious fundamentalism and social media.

1108 Bueno, Natalia S. Bypassing the enemy: distributive politics, credit claiming, and nonstate organizations in Brazil. (*Comp. Polit. Stud.*, 51:3, Jan. 2018, p. 304–340, bibl.)

This article draws on Brazilian federal and state transfer data between 2003 and 2015 to study how incumbents strategically distribute resources to avoid credit-hijacking behavior by political opponents at lower levels of government. The results suggest that administrators use nonstate welfare providers to circumvent political opponents. For political economy specialist's comment, see *HLAS 75:1677*.

1109 Bueno, Natalia S. and Thad Dunning. Race, resources, and representation: evidence from Brazilian politicians. (*World Polit.*, 69:2, March 2017, p. 327–365, bibl., graphs, tables)

These authors use self-declared and survey-coded candidate race data from the 2008, 2010, and 2014 Brazilian legislative, gubernatorial, and municipal elections to study racial disparities in political representation in the context of Brazil. The study concludes that resource gaps, produced by the campaign investment decisions of racial and economic elites rather than systematic voter bias, perpetuate Brazil's gap in ascriptive representation based on race.

1110 Córdova, Abby and Helen Kras. Addressing violence against women: the effect of women's police stations on police legitimacy. (*Comp. Polit. Stud.*, 53:5, April 2020, p. 775–808, bibl., graphs, tables)

These authors draw on 2014 AmericasBarometer data and municipal-level data from 106 Brazilian municipalities to study the effects of designated women's police stations on trust in the police and the likelihood of reporting gender-based violence. The results suggest that women who live in a municipality with a women's police station see the police as more legitimate and effective.

1111 Crisp, Brian F. and Betul Demirkaya. Strategic entry and strategic voting in majoritarian systems. (*J. Polit.*, 82:1, Jan. 2020, p. 57–71, bibl.)

In some election years, Brazilian voters elect two senators for their state; in others, they only vote for one. This study exploits this unique feature of Brazilian electoral institutions for the selection of senators to test the differing effects of multiple nontransferable votes (MNTV) and single-member districts decided by plurality voting systems (SMDP) on elite and voter coordination strategies related to candidate entry (the number of candidates) and voter clustering (the effective number of candidates, or the number of candidates receiving a substantial vote share). Examining senatorial elections from 1994 to 2014 in comparison with gubernatorial elections across the same years, the authors show that elites coordinate better under MNTV rules, but that voters coordinate equally well across both systems.

1112 De Micheli, David. The racialized effects of social programs in Brazil. (*Lat. Am. Polit. Soc.*, 60:1, Feb. 2018, p. 52–75, bibl., graph, tables)

This article draws on AmericasBarometer data from Brazil between 2008 and 2014 to assess the distinct racialized effects of Brazil's Bolsa Família conditional cash transfer (CCT) program on self-identified whites' and Afro-Brazilians' electoral participation and vote choice. The results suggest that CCT benefits have a mobilizing effect for Afro-Brazilians but no effect on their vote choice, while white beneficiaries are more likely to vote for the incumbent Workers' Party even while there is no effect on their turnout.

1113 Democracia em vertigem: [The edge of democracy]. Um filme de Petra Costa. Brazil: Netflix, 2019. 1 DVD (123 min.).

This important documentary weaves original and archival footage, as well as political and personal narrative, to contextualize key events in Brazil's political development with a focus on the years between 2014 and 2018. The film offers "behind-the-scenes" interactions with key actors in recent presidential politics, including Luiz Inácio "Lula" da Silva, Dilma Rousseff, and Jair Bolsonaro, as well as the "view from below" through street interviews with *petistas* and *anti-petistas* alike. Although some might critique the film for its self-admitted partisan point of view, it is well-produced and useful as an entry point for conversations about many aspects of recent Brazilian and global politics.

1114 Democratic Brazil divided. Edited by Peter R. Kingstone and Timothy J. Power. Pittsburgh, Pa.: University of Pittsburgh Press, 2017. 301 p.: bibl., index. (Pitt Latin American series)

This is the third in a series of edited volumes about Brazil's democracy and political economy from Kingstone and Power (see *HLAS 59:4031* and *HLAS 67:1511* for comments on the first two volumes). In this volume, some of the world's leading Brazilianists offer assessments of Brazilian democracy under the Workers' Party (PT—Partido dos Trabalhadores), innovative aspects of Brazilian policy and governance, mass politics, and Brazil's place in global politics and international relations through 2017. Writing on the eve of the transformative 2018 presidential election, the contributing authors find that Brazil is governed by a relatively consolidated democratic regime, though it is an imperfect democracy subject to systematic corruption, rising popular demands on the political system, and significant economic headwinds.

1115 Driscoll, Amanda et al. Prejudice, strategic discrimination, and the electoral connection: evidence from a pair of field experiments in Brazil. (*Am. J. Polit. Sci.*, 62:4, Oct. 2018, p. 781–795, bibl.)

This article reports on the results of two field experiments where the researchers contacted over 7,000 state and federal candidates during and six months after Brazil's October 2010 elections to assess candidate responsiveness to requests for information from fictitious voters with randomized characteristics based on class and race. The core conclusion is that viable candidates in highly competitive elections did not discriminate in their responses to these requests while campaigning for office, but were significantly less likely to respond to individuals in lower class and less-privileged racial groups six months after the election. Less competitive elections resulted in consistent discrimination against less privileged groups before and after the election. This highlights the importance of competitive elections.

1116 Feierherd, Germán. How mayors hurt their presidential ticket: party brands and incumbency spillovers in Brazil. (*J. Polit.*, 82:1, Jan. 2020, p. 195–210, bibl., graphs, table)

This article studies election results from municipal and presidential elections in Brazil between 1996 and 2014 to show how local copartisans affect the performance of national presidential candidates. Mayoral allies' performance has more effect on presidential copartisans, for good or bad, when candidates belong to parties with strong brands; mayors from parties with weak brands do not affect presidential candidate performance.

1117 Franco, Bernardo Mello. Mil dias de tormenta: a crise que derrubou Dilma e deixou Temer por um fio. Rio de Janeiro: Objetiva, 2018. 406 p.

This book is a compilation of the author's opinion columns published in the *Folha de São Paulo* between 1 Jan. 2015 and 26 Oct. 2017. The columns cover the key events of the political crisis surrounding Dilma Rousseff's second term in office, the 2016 impeachment proceedings, and Michel Temer's efforts to avoid his own impeachment after taking power. The text is republished without edits from the original columns; the author provides some original explanatory notes with the text and introductory statements before each chapter.

1118 French, John D. Lula and his politics of cunning: from metalworker to president of Brazil. Chapel Hill: The University of North Carolina Press, 2020. 508 p.: bibl., ill., index.

This book offers an important, insightful, and deeply researched biography of Luiz Inácio "Lula" da Silva. The work focuses on Lula's life before his first successful presidential campaign in 2002, but it will be of interest to anyone who wants to understand how a rural migrant and metalworker labor activist could rise to national and international fame and become the central figure in Brazil's most recent democratic era. The book also comments on Lula's leadership style and efforts to organize and mobilize Brazil's working class which has defined his politics for decades and, despite the legal and personal challenges of his post-presidency life, arguably has continued to make him the indispensable actor for contemporary leftist politics in Brazil.

1119 Gaspar, Malu. A organização: a Odebrecht e o esquema de corrupção que chocou o mundo. São Paulo: Companhia das Letras, 2020. 639 p.: ill., index.

This book provides a journalistic account of the Odebrecht conglomerate, and draws on three years of reporting, over 120 personal interviews, police witness interviews, and documentary evidence, including from the company itself, to recreate the history of the largest documented corruption scandal in Latin America to date. The author also covers the internal dynamics of the Odebrecht family from the time of the company's founding to its restructuring in the wake of the scandal.

1120 Gingerich, Daniel W. Ballot reform as suffrage restriction: evidence from Brazil's Second Republic. (*Am. J. Polit. Sci.*, 63:4, Oct. 2019, p. 920–935, bibl.)

This article uses Brazilian municipal-level election returns for federal deputy and senator from 1958 and 1962 to study the effect of adopting the secret ballot on voter emancipation from vote brokers and voter capacity to cast valid votes. The evidence suggests that the introduction of the secret ballot led to a higher rate of invalid voting and provides little evidence that it deterred vote brokers from guiding or coercing voters. Furthermore, the author uses statements from the congressional record to show that the higher rate of invalid voting was a foreseen and intended consequence of the adoption of the secret ballot. This has important implications for scholars who study electoral reform.

1121 Johannessen, Peter G. Linkage switches in local elections: evidence from the Workers' Party in Brazil. (*Comp. Polit. Stud.*, 53:1, Jan. 2020, p. 109–143, bibl., graphs, tables)

This article draws on internal Brazilian Workers' Party (PT or Partido dos Trabalhadores) documents, a quasi-experimental analysis of municipalities where the Workers' Party narrowly won or lost elections, and text analysis of campaign platforms to assess whether the Workers' Party governed differently than nonprogrammatic, clientelistic parties at the municipal level in Brazil between 1996 and 2012. The results suggest that Workers' Party candidates campaigned on programmatic platforms, but followed nonprogrammatic linkage strategies once in government.

1122 Klašnja, Marko and Rocío Titiunik. The incumbency curse: weak parties, term limits, and unfulfilled accountability. (*Am. Polit. Sci. Rev.*, 111:1, Feb. 2017, p. 129–148, bibl., graphs, tables)

This article studies Brazilian municipal elections between 1996 and 2012 and argues that in municipalities where mayors narrowly win elections, incumbent parties are less likely to win the next election despite supposed built-in incumbency advantages. The authors provide evidence that this is due to weak institutionalization of parties and party systems as well as electoral institutions like term limits, which create perverse incentives and feedback mechanisms that perpetuate party system weakness.

1123 Kustov, Alexander and Giuliana Pardelli. Ethnoracial homogeneity and public outcomes: the (non)effects of diversity. (*Am. Polit. Sci. Rev.*, 112:4, Nov. 2018, p. 1096–1103, bibl.)

This research note uses 2010 data from Brazilian municipalities to address important limitations in previous empirical studies of the relationship between public goods provision and ethnoracial diversity. Whereas previous research has largely shown a negative correlation between diversity and public goods provision, the authors argue that these analyses are flawed. After reassessing the empirical strategy, the authors claim that, in Brazil, homogenous Afro-descendent municipalities have worse public goods provision than more diverse communities and homogenous white communities.

1124 Layton, Matthew L.; Maureen M. Donaghy; and Lúcio R. Rennó. Does welfare provision promote democratic state legitimacy?: evidence from Brazil's Bolsa Família Program. (*Lat. Am. Polit. Soc.*, 59:4, Winter 2017, p. 99–120, bibl., tables)

This article addresses the association between social policy benefits (Bolsa Família conditional cash transfers) and attitudes toward political legitimacy in Brazil. The analysis draws on public opinion data from the AmericasBarometer between 2007 and 2014 and concludes that beneficiary status reliably bolsters specific forms of legitimacy tied to institutions and incumbent political actors; no relationship is found between beneficiary status and more diffuse attitudes related to support for democratic regime principles.

1125 Lessing, Benjamin and Graham Denyer Willis. Legitimacy in criminal governance: managing a drug empire from behind bars. (*Am. Polit. Sci. Rev.*, 113:2, May 2019, p. 584–606, bibl., graphs, maps, tables)

This article analyzes a unique set of over 500 internal documents and other computer files seized from the São Paulo-based Primeiro Comando da Capital (PCC) prison gang by state prosecutors. The documents refer to the organization's criminal activity and territorial governance in the interior of São Paulo state (excluding the metropolitan area of São Paulo city) between September 2011 and October 2012. The authors leverage these data to argue that the PCC developed internal governance mechanisms that approximate rational-bureaucratic legitimacy in territory that they control, which parallels prior research on state formation. The authors argue that this helps to explain declines in violent crime in territory controlled by the PCC.

1126 Magaloni, Beatriz; Edgar Franco-Vivanco; and Vanessa Melo. Killing in the slums: social order, criminal governance, and police violence in Rio de Janeiro. (*Am. Polit. Sci. Rev.*, 114:2, May 2020, p. 552–572, bibl., graphs, map, tables)

This article draws on extensive multimethod research conducted in Rio de Janeiro between 2012 and 2018 to construct a five-part typology of criminal governance regimes used by local organized criminal groups. It highlights the role of Pacifying Police Units (Unidades de Polícia Pacificadora or UPPs) in Rio's favelas and explains why the UPP approach was more effective in some neighborhoods than others depending on the predominant local criminal regime.

1127 Mayka, Lindsay. The origins of strong institutional design: policy reform and participatory institutions in Brazil's health sector. (*Comp. Polit./New York*, 51:2, Jan. 2019, p. 275–294, bibl.)

This article draws on in-depth observational fieldwork and qualitative interviews with policy stakeholders to study path dependency and policy reform processes related to the creation of Brazil's health councils and the emergence of strong participatory institutional design under Brazil's Unified Health System (SUS). It covers the institutionalization of these reforms from the adoption of the 1988 Constitution through about 2009.

1128 Nicolau, Jairo Marconi. Representantes de quem?: os (des)caminhos do seu voto da urna à Câmara dos Deputados. Rio de Janeiro: Zahar, 2017. 175 p.: bibl., ill.

This helpful book presents readers with a data-centered empirical introduction to many unique aspects of Brazil's electoral and party systems particularly as they relate to the composition and functions of the Câmara dos Deputados and perceptions of representation in Brazil's democratic system. The book addresses many topics and misunderstandings that are frequently present in popular discourse, including the processes of translating votes to seats, party coalition formation, issues related to voter choice in legislative elections, party switching, fragmentation of the party system, malapportionment, and proposed political reforms.

1129 Niedzwiecki, Sara. Uneven social policies: the politics of subnational variation in Latin America. New York, N.Y.: Cambridge University Press, 2018. 256 p.: bibl., index.

This book adds to a growing literature that assesses the subnational dynamics of federal political systems in Latin America by studying variation in the implementation of social policy at the state/provincial and local levels in Argentina and Brazil between 1998 and 2015. The analysis draws on extensive field research, as well as pooled time series analyses, to model the contributions of attribution of responsibility, political alignment, policy legacy/feedback, and state capacity across levels of government. The analysis suggests that clear attribution of responsibility for a policy leads opposition figures to obstruct its implementation, while weak capacity stifles effective implementation; in contrast, strong state institutions, positive policy feedback, and aligned subnational leaders foster policy adoption.

1130 Novaes, Lucas M. Disloyal brokers and weak parties. (*Am. J. Polit. Sci.*, 62:1, Jan. 2018, p. 84–98, bibl.)

In Brazil, local mayors often act as vote brokers for congressional candidates who run in state-wide elections. This article draws on this feature of the Brazilian political system to study the role of local "free-agent" political brokers in shaping the organizational and electoral performance of political parties in Brazil between 2000 and 2012. The results suggest that parties perform better when their local brokers face higher barriers to partisan defection between elections, which has important implications for party building in the developing world.

1131 Pavão, Nara. Corruption as the only option: the limits to electoral accountability. (*J. Polit.*, 80:3, July 2018, p. 996–1010, bibl., graphs, tables)

This article relies on a multimethod approach, including focus groups in Brazil (2012 to 2013), a nationally representative survey run prior to the 2010 presidential election in Brazil, and the third wave of the Comparative Study of Electoral Systems (CSES) run between 2006 and 2011, to study electoral impunity of corrupt politicians. The author argues that voters are skeptical of politicians' capacity to address corruption especially when they perceive that corruption is widespread; accordingly, voters tend to discount corruption when they make their vote choice, which allows corrupt politicians to be reelected based on other aspects of government performance.

1132 Peixoto, Tiago; Fredrik M. Sjoberg; and Jonathan Mellon. A get-out-the-vote experiment on the world's largest participatory budgeting vote in Brazil. (*Br. J. Polit. Sci.*, 50:1, 2020, p. 381–389, bibl.)

This research note reports the results of a unique get-out-the-vote (GOTV) experiment conducted in June 2014 in Rio Grande do Sul, Brazil. Most GOTV studies rely on self-reported vote choice data from respondents, but these authors were able to collect both turnout and, uniquely to their design, verified vote choice data. These are tied to an indicator of an individual-level GOTV treatment in the setting of a participatory budgeting vote with over 43,000 participants. The results suggest that the GOTV campaign increased turnout, but not the distribution of voter preferences. These findings have important implications for behavioral and vote choice research.

1133 Pereira, Carlos et al. Watchdogs in our midst: how presidents monitor coalitions in Brazil's multiparty presidential regime. (*Lat. Am. Polit. Soc.*, 59:3, Fall 2017, p. 27–47, bibl., graphs, tables)

This article studies 178 minister-junior minister pairings to analyze patterns of presidential monitoring of coalition partners in the executive cabinets of the Cardoso and Lula administrations (1995–2010) in Brazil. The authors find that these presidents were increasingly likely to appoint allied junior ministers to serve in ministries assigned to coalition partners' portfolios when the ideological distance increased between the president's party and the coalition partner's party. This helps to illustrate the internal strategic dynamics of multiparty presidentialism.

1134 Sells, Cameron J. Building parties from city hall: party membership and municipal government in Brazil. (*J. Polit.*, 82:4, Oct. 2020, p. 1576–1589, bibl.)

This article draws on municipal party affiliation data from 1997 to 2009 in Brazil to study whether mayoral incumbency helps political parties attract new members. The results suggest that only institutionalized parties with a strong local organization benefit from an incumbency effect; clientelistic and decentralized parties do not.

1135 Singer, André. O lulismo em crise: um quebra-cabeça do período Dilma (2011–2016). São Paulo: Companhia das Letras, 2018. 389 p.: bibl., ill., index.

Written by a Workers' Party insider, journalist, and scholar, this book provides the author's revised, reprinted, and original analyses of Brazil's political development during Dilma Rousseff's administration (2011–2016). The author connects this analysis to the previously elaborated theory of *lulismo* (Lulaism) to argue that Dilma attempted to accelerate Lula's political project for Brazil, only to find that the structural bases of the project had shifted in ways that made it unsustainable in its second decade.

1136 Sugiyama, Natasha Borges and Wendy Hunter. Do conditional cash transfers empower women?: insights from Brazil's Bolsa Família. (*Lat. Am. Polit. Soc.*, 62:2, May 2020, p. 53–74, bibl., table)

This article draws on an original survey, focus groups, and elite interviews conducted in Brazil's Northeast region between 2009 and 2014 to argue that Brazil's Bolsa Família conditional cash transfer (CCT) program empowers women beneficiaries in terms of economic agency, enhanced physical integrity, and psychosocial growth. This may be of interest for future scholars interested in comparing outcomes under the Bolsonaro administration after the shift from Bolsa Família to Auxílio Brasil.

1137 Wampler, Brian; Natasha Borges Sugiyama; and Michael Touchton. Democracy at work: pathways to well-being in Brazil. Cambridge, England: New York, N.Y.: Cambridge University Press, 2020. 370 p.: bibl., index.

This book draws on an original dataset covering Brazil's 5,570 municipalities between 2000 and 2013 with indicators of local political institutions, social program delivery, and local state capacity, as well as fieldwork in three Northeastern municipalities, to study the importance of local democratic governance for promoting citizen well-being. The authors argue that three democratic pathways—participatory institutions, rights-based social programs, and inclusive state capacity—are the primary and potentially compounding drivers of citizen well-being and human development in terms of basic health outcomes for women and children, school attendance, access to basic income, and female empowerment.

INTERNATIONAL RELATIONS

GENERAL

MARY K. MEYER McALEESE, *Professor of Political Science, Eckerd College*

THE WORKS REVIEWED in this section appeared between 2016 and 2021, but most were published in 2017 (13 works) and 2018 (seven works). The entire set includes 20 books and four journal articles on a range of topics common to the contemporary study of Latin America's international relations, from regional integration efforts, international trade and development issues, national and human security challenges, transnational movements and transborder studies, as well as Latin America's relations with the US, China, and India. A few works also display important if overlooked Latin American scholarship in the social sciences and international relations theory. Overall, these works include an interesting if eclectic collection of scholarship from and about the region's international relations.

Giovanni Agostinis and Kevin Parthenay (item **1138**) contribute the most recent journal publication, included here because it is one of the first to link regional health governance models and responses to the COVID-19 pandemic. This interesting article compares the now defunct UNASUR intergovernmental health model to the SICA-Committee of Central American Health Ministers' (SICA-COMISA) approach to improving access to key medicines. The SICA-COMISA approach was better in addressing the pandemic, but UNASUR Health also offered effective regional health governance while it lasted.

Political shifts across Latin America led to a decline in intergovernmental regionalism in the 2017–2018 period, reflected also in an apparent decline in works published on the topic. Nonetheless, José U. Mora Mora and María Isabel Osorio-Caballero (item **1139**) compiled an outstanding peer-reviewed volume focused on the Alianza del Pacífico (Alliance of the Pacific, or AP), with contributions by an international team of scholars examining the AP's approach to the global economy and trade, international law, and various timely issues in international relations. This is one of several excellent books from Colombia reviewed in this section. Far less focused is Antônio Walber Matias Muniz *et al.*'s (item **1145**) edited collection of papers on South-South relations, notable mainly for its prologue by Theotonio dos Santos lionizing ALBA, UNASUR, and CELAC.

Three other works on regional integration offer more personal, intellectual, and historical retrospectives on regional experiments. The first is a posthumous tribute to the life and works of Ecuadorian economist and diplomat Germánico Salgado Peñaherrera (item **1156**), a key architect in the creation of the Andean Pact. Several of his essays on regional integration spanning the 1970s and 1980s are republished here and include such topics as South-South agricultural cooperation (from 1976), South-South technical cooperation (from 1977), and the role of cultural identity in regional integration (from 1987). In a second retrospective on regional integration, Argentinian diplomat Marcelo F. Valle Fonrouge (item **1160**) contributes a handy overview of CELAC, SICA, UNASUR, Mercosur, and the AP. Diego Giller et al. (item **1144**) contribute the third retrospective, this one commemorating the work of Ruy Mauro Marini, a foundational thinker of dependency theory. Giller's opening essay situates Marini's work with other key thinkers of dependency theory. Subsequent chapters honor his work with more contemporary critical theory approaches to understanding Latin America's subordinate place in the global capitalist system.

María José Brunetto (item **1141**) examines the global trading system and the evolution of special treatment for developing and lesser-developed countries from the GATT to the WTO, showing how definitions of "development" changed along the way. Extending the themes of dependency and global inequalities, editors Eloísa Martín and Barbara Göbel (item **1142**) offer an interesting volume exploring the persistent marginalization of social science scholarship originating in Latin America (and other parts of the Global South) from international centers of knowledge production. Despite some recent progress, the global political economy of knowledge production continues to be unequal, rendering innovative work by Latin American scholars largely invisible.

Along with the Martín and Göbel and the Giller et al. volumes already mentioned, another fine example of innovative work by Latin American scholars comes from Naheul Oddone and José María Ramos' (item **1146**) collection on transborder integration experiences, subnational governments, and paradiplomacy across Latin America. This fascinating work with chapters by scholars from Latin America and Europe examines a range of policy areas (environment, sustainable development, migration) and various policy actors (civil society actors, city governments, etc.) working at local, national, and international spaces. Theoretical and case study chapters show how various local actors are involved in foreign policy-making and international relations in border regions from the Rio Grande to Patagonia. Zepeda et al. (item **1158**) explore informal and illegal cross-border interactions within Latin America. In yet another excellent collection, Alberto Castillo Castañeda and César Augusto Niño González (item **1149**) gather an array of mostly Colombian (and some European) scholars and experts to rethink security studies for the 21st century, particularly the tension between national security and human security. This volume incorporates a variety of perspectives and encompasses an interesting range of issues (e.g., terrorism, migration, gender, climate change, and more) along with regionally focused topics (e.g., UNASUR, Colombian postconflict foreign policy, violence in the Northern Triangle, etc.). Less impressive yet still of some interest is Miguel Ángel Barrios' (item **1143**) effort to undertake a critical rethinking of geopolitics and the geography of security in Latin America today. Meanwhile, Leyde E. Rodríguez Hernández (item **1155**) offers a Cuban interpretation of the development of certain international relations theories for his MA-level students, with occasional revolutionary asides critical of the US.

Transnational political influences among nonstate actors feature in three works reviewed here. Manuel Alcántara Sáez and José Manuel Rivas Otero (item

1151) offer a specialized collection that discusses the transnational influences and links between Spain's Podemos party and Latin America's "pink tide" movements of the early 2000s. Moisés Garduño García (item 1153) edits a collection committed to deepening Mexican and Palestinian relationships. José J. Marulanda (item 1147) worries about Islamic extremist groups expanding their influence in Latin America. Tangentially, Yasutaka Tominaga (item 1159) shows empirically that targeted capture of a militant group's leader is a more effective strategy to deter militant group attacks than leader assassination.

Traditional state-centric or foreign policy-oriented works round out the works under review in this section. Chilean Carsten-Andreas Schulz (item 1157) refines contemporary international relations scholarship on Latin American states' diplomatic participation at the Second Hague Conference of 1907. In his excellent article, he both builds a clearer picture of Latin America's (ultimately unsuccessful) status-seeking diplomacy at the time and demonstrates the importance of careful diplomatic history in the building and testing of IR theory. Ryan A. Musto (item 1148) also contributes a fascinating diplomatic history of India's efforts to court Latin American states in the 1960s and early 1970s in its own bid to enhance its status in the Non-Aligned Movement and the UN.

Aside from occasional swipes by Rodríguez Hernández (item 1155), Thomas Andrew O'Keefe (item 1150) and Rubrick Biegon (item 1140) contribute the only two works under review that specifically address contemporary US policies vis-à-vis Latin America and the perceived US hegemonic decline. O'Keefe deftly applies various IR theories to several key policy initiatives of the George W. Bush and Barack Obama administrations, from the failed Free Trade Area of the Americas (FTAA) to the restoration of diplomatic relations with Cuba, to test the nature and extent of a US hegemonic decline. Biegon uses a neo-Gramscian approach to consider the same administrations' trade policy goals, the interests behind them, and especially the Trans-Pacific Partnership (TPP) as a (failed) means for the US to reassert its hegemony over Latin America in a post-Washington Consensus era. Perhaps the fact that only two works under review directly address US-Latin American relations is further evidence of a certain erosion of US political hegemony in the region—or of the erosion of Latin America's importance to the US foreign policy agenda.

Finally, three works focus on Latin America's relations with China. Arturo Oropeza García (item 1152) offers a Mexican perspective on the TPP as a sign of a millennial economic and political shift of hegemony from the West (Europe and the US) to East Asia (China). He considers new opportunities for Latin America's relations with China, the role of the BRICS (especially India and Russia), and the future of NAFTA/USMCA vis-à-vis East Asia. Yanran Xu (item 1161) contributes a monograph analyzing China's strategic partnerships with Argentina, Brazil, Mexico, and Venezuela in the areas of trade, investment, and political cooperation and the relative costs and benefits of those partnerships. Closing out the set, and in yet another excellent contribution from Colombia, editors Eduardo Pastrana Buelvas and Hubert Gehring (item 1154) gather a strong group of experts who analyze the full range of Sino-Latin American economic and political relations since the 1990s. Eighteen chapters analyze both bilateral (featuring Argentina, Brazil, Chile, Colombia, Mexico, Peru, Venezuela, and others) and inter-regional strategic partnerships (i.e., China's partnerships with Mercosur, CELAC, AP, APEC, and more).

Despite some unevenness across these various works, some real gems in this selection deserve attention from both IR scholars and foreign policy practitioners interested in understanding Latin America's international relations up to the start of the Trump administration and the COVID-19 pandemic. Our next biennial volume along with the bicentennial of the 1823 address that led to the Monroe Doctrine promise to provide a lot more food for thought on the international relations of Latin America and the Caribbean.

1138 **Agostinis, Giovanni** and **Kevin Parthenay.** Exploring the determinants of regional health governance modes in the Global South: a comparative analysis of Central and South America. (*Rev. Int. Stud.*, 47:4, 2021, p. 399–421, bibl., ill., tables)

The authors provide an excellent and innovative analysis of regional health governance institutions, dynamics, and efforts that developed within UNASUR and SICA. Focusing on state capacity and regional leadership as key variables, the authors compare the objectives, institutional designs, funding sources, and practical efforts of UNASUR Health and the SICA-Committee of Central American Health Ministers (SICA-COMISA) to develop regional health governance projects and improve regional efforts to procure better access to key medicines. UNASUR Health's intergovernmental governance model was endogenously driven and benefitted from strong state capacities and regional leadership from both Brazil and Argentina, resulting in promising steps toward improved regional access to medicines—until UNASUR fell apart in 2018. SICA-COMISA's technocratic governance model was exogenously driven and funded but allowed Central American states (and the Dominican Republic) to gain technocratic expertise, bargain successfully with pharmaceutical companies, lower the prices for key medicines, and increase the effectiveness of health governance efforts in the region. Ironically, this arrangement placed Central America in a better position for contingency planning in response to the COVID-19 pandemic while the subregional fragmentation of South American regional health governance modes impeded effective pandemic responses. The authors' regional health governance framework contributes to both the comparative regionalism and the global health governance literatures.

1139 **La Alianza del Pacífico: nuevos retos e implicaciones para Latinoamérica.** Compilación de José U. Mora Mora y María Isabel Osorio-Caballero. Santiago de Cali, Colombia: Pontificia Universidad Javeriana Cali, 2017. 218 p.: bibl., tables.

This scholarly compilation explores various aspects of the Alianza del Pacífico (Pacific Alliance, or AP) and its unique approach to commercial and financial integration among its member states (Chile, Colombia, Mexico, and Peru). The editors gathered scholars of international economics, international trade, international relations, and international law from Colombia, Mexico, Venezuela, Cuba, and Spain to consider the progress and challenges to deeper integration within the AP. Several chapters also analyze the AP's linkages to commercial and financial markets in other parts of the world (e.g., Mercosur, the US, and the Asia-Pacific region). Two chapters consider migration issues, particularly in terms of the founding treaty's inclusion of the principle of the free movement of labor. While this aspect has yet to be realized on a large scale, it offers the potential for the development of human capital within the AP. Two chapters explore the costs and benefits to possible monetary integration within the AP, with the EU's experience as a model. All chapters underwent peer-review and offer useful empirical data and bibliographies. Several chapters include helpful econometric tables and figures. See also *HLAS 75:1279*.

1140 **Biegon, Rubrick.** The United States and Latin America in the Trans-Pacific Partnership: renewing hegemony in a post-Washington Consensus hemisphere? (*Lat. Am. Perspect.*, 44:4, July 2017, p. 81–98, bibl.)

Biegon offers a critical neo-Gramscian analysis of the Trans-Pacific Partnership (TPP) as a vehicle for the US to salvage free trade rules and reassert its hegemony over Latin America in a post-Washington Consensus world. Insofar as TPP has collapsed, as has its support inside the US, Biegon's analysis seems to fail in explaining why. However, writing before the election of Donald Trump in the US, this analysis offers some insights into the failure of the Free Trade Area of the Americas (FTAA), the emergence of the Pacific Alliance, and the interests behind the George W. Bush and Barack Obama administrations' trade policy goals.

1141 Brunetto, María José. Los países en desarrollo y el sistema multilateral del comercio internacional: surgimiento y transformaciones del tratamiento especial y diferenciado: investigaciones pasadas, replanteo y avances recientes. Montevideo: Universidad de la República, Comisión Sectorial de la Investigación Científica, 2016. 118 p.: bibl. (Biblioteca Plural)

In this short monograph, the author focuses on the evolution of the Special and Differential Treatment Provisions of the World Trade Organization (WTO), starting with the early post-WWII origins of the global free trade system. She is especially interested in considering how the global free trade system initially did not consider any special treatment for developing and lesser-developed countries. However, their critiques of free trade rules and of the harm such rules posed to those countries guided their negotiating pressure within the GATT system and the WTO. In the process, the definitions of "development" shifted as did the obligations of developed countries to extend preferential treatment to developing countries while drawing the latter into the global free trade system.

1142 Desigualdades interdependentes e geopolítica do conhecimento: negociações, fluxos, assimetrias. Organização de Eloísa Martín e Barbara Göbel. Textos de Ana María Cetto *et al.* Rio de Janeiro: 7Letras, 2018. 150 p.: bibl., ill.

This thought-provoking collection of essays critically assesses the historically unequal impact of knowledge production between the Global North and Global South, with a particular focus on the social sciences (especially sociology) and Latin American scholarship. The structural invisibility and marginalization of Latin American social science research has slowly reversed in recent years thanks to greater access for Global South scholars to international centers of knowledge production and legitimation (e.g., core universities, core journals, international professional conferences, etc.) as well as to other parts of the Global South. Digitization may also facilitate greater global visibility and circulation of work by Latin American scholars. However, asymmetries persist, and recent funding cuts in the region threaten the little progress that has occurred. This stimulating volume succeeds in its critique without sounding whiney. The network of Latin American and European scholars who produced this volume, desiguALdades. net (Rede Internacional de Pesquisa sobre Desigualdades Interdependentes na América Latina), can help to improve the dialogue between researchers in the Global North and the Global South and to create more equal, symmetrical, and transversal knowledge production in the social sciences.

1143 Geopolítica de la seguridad en América Latina. Coordinación de Miguel Ángel Barrios. Textos de Norberto Emmerich y Yesenia Torres Curiel. Buenos Aires: Editorial Biblos, 2017. 239 p.: bibl. (Politeia)

The authors ruminate on the territorial state and its centrality to national and citizen security while attempting to develop a "new paradigm" and a deeply critical rethinking of geopolitics and the geography of security in Latin America today. Sometimes overwritten, sometimes polemical, the authors nevertheless raise important questions about the struggle to achieve real security (and justice) at all levels of society when underdevelopment, corruption, and antidemocratic politics frame the state's propensities and capabilities.

1144 Giller, Diego et al. Desafíos, perspectivas y horizontes de la integración en América Latina y el Caribe: actualidad del pensamiento de Ruy Mauro Marini. Buenos Aires: CLACSO, 2017. 404 p.: ill. (Colección Becas de investigación)

This worthy collection features the 2015 award-winning essays honoring the theoretical work of Ruy Mauro Marini, one of the foundational thinkers of dependency theory. CLACSO and the Swiss Agency for International Development sponsored these awards to honor Marini's work. Diego Giller's opening essay provides an important biographical sketch and theoretical picture of the evolution of Marini's thinking, comparing and contrasting his interpretation of Marxist analysis with those of other key dependency theorists with whom he was contemporaneous, including Furtado, Cardoso, Dos Santos, Frank, and many others, as well as with non-Marxist structuralist approaches to dependency theory developed by CEPAL. The five subsequent essays reconsider Marini's thinking in light of more contemporary theoretical frames rooted in critical theory, including constructivism, postcolonialism, and poststructuralism. A fascinating collection for those interested in the development of dependency theory as a sui generis Latin American contribution to theorizing about the region's role in the global capitalist system.

1145 Integração regional na América Latina: o papel do estado nas políticas públicas para o desenvolvimento, os direitos humanos e sociais e uma estratégia Sul-Sul. Organização de Antônio Walber Matias Muniz et al. Jundiaí, Brazil: Paco Editorial, 2016. 410 p.: bibl.

Beyond the broad theme of regional integration, this work is an unfocused collection of papers presented at a symposium held as part of the IV Congreso de la Internacional del Conocimiento at the Universidad de Santiago de Chile. Notably, Theotonio dos Santos contributes a prologue praising such regional efforts as ALBA, UNASUR, and CELAC as first steps in realizing Martí's idea of the Pátria Grande (sic) and applauding the counterhegemonic work of the BRICS in challenging the neoliberal order. But there is no centering introductory chapter to explain the purpose of the symposium or focus the volume's many chapters, and the order of the chapters is incoherent. Chapters cover such wide-ranging topics as: Brazilian and Paraguayan higher education policies; the emergence of the BRICS; the geopolitics of water resources and their challenge to regional integration (with maps and tables and a critique of US interests in those resources); and various other political and economic challenges to regional integration in South America. Additional chapter topics include: human rights law and policy in Mercosur; the internationalization (regional juridical level) and localization (national juridical level) of human rights law in the region and their interaction; the failed efforts of a Quilombola community to win land rights and recognition near the Brazil-Paraguay border; a now defunct financing mechanism in Mercosur; social rights and the social agenda of Mercosur; dictatorship and democracy; and child labor. Simply put, a very eclectic and uneven collection.

1146 Integración y paradiplomacia transfronteriza: experiencias comparadas del Río Bravo hasta la Patagonia. Coordinación de Nahuel Oddone y José María Ramos. Tijuana, Mexico: El Colegio de la Frontera Norte, 2018. 2 v.: bibl., ill.

The editors bring together an impressive and comprehensive set of scholars from Latin America and Europe who explore the international relations of subnational governments, paradiplomacy, and the formal and informal integration processes that occur in international border spaces in Latin America. After two theoretical chapters that open up critical questions about the ways the international relations literature might explore frontier spaces more deeply, the chapters present case studies that span such spaces from the US-Mexican border through Central American and Andean countries, moving into the heart of South America and down to Mercosur and Tierra del Fuego. This geographically comprehensive and comparative study is provocative and well executed. It invites IR scholars to reconsider the practical and theoretical connections at work at the local, national, and international levels/spaces and across different issue areas (environment, sustainable development, democracy, migration, nongovernmental and civil society actors, decision-making) and the ways in which subnational governments (cities and towns) participate in foreign policy-making, international integration, and international relations.

1147 Marulanda, José J. Yihad en Latinoamérica. Prólogo de José Gregorio Hernández Galindo. Bogotá: Ediciones DIPON; Buenos Aires: Ediciones Gato Azul, 2017. 206 p.: bibl., ill., map.

Could Hezbollah or the Islamic State expand their reach to Latin America? Are they? What threats could that pose? This short "dossier" speculates on the possibilities across all parts of Latin America and the Caribbean.

1148 Musto, Ryan A. Non-alignment and beyond: India's interest in Latin America, 1961–1972. (*Dipl. Statecraft*, 29:4, 2018, p. 613–637)

PhD candidate Musto presents an interesting diplomatic history after delving into forgotten records from India's Ministry of External Affairs. He uncovers a fascinating history of India's flirtation with closer diplomatic relations with Latin America in the 1960s and into the early 1970s. Though little came of several attempts at engagement with the region during that period, India's interest in playing a leadership role in the Non-Aligned Movement and at the UN drew its diplomats to consider the possibilities. This is a well-researched, beautifully written, and engaging story of a little-known aspect of Indian relations with Latin America.

1149 Nociones sobre seguridad y paz en las relaciones internacionales contemporáneas. Edición de Alberto Castillo Castañeda y César Augusto Niño González. Bogotá: Ediciones USTA, 2017. 549 p.: bibl., ill., maps.

The editors bring together 25 experts in security studies for a serious rethinking of the concept of security in a changing international and historical context. Most contributors are based in Colombia, particularly the Universidad de Santo Tomás, which published this collection, with others based in Spain or France, and several contributors have policy experience along with impressive academic credentials. The book is especially interested in grappling with the problem of national (or state) security versus human security and the changing security threats in today's world. It does so effectively from various theoretical and analytical perspectives, and includes topical chapters addressing such issues as international security, terrorism, migration, humanitarian intervention, gender, environment/climate change, postconflict democratization, and even conscientious objection in a peace and security framework. Additionally, regionally focused topics include chapters on UNASUR, child excombatants, Colombia's postconflict foreign policy, institutional weakness and violence in the Northern Triangle (and what to do about it), Russia's foreign policy under Putin, the US-Russian balance of power, and the challenge of the far right to the EU's integration and security environment. All in all, a worthy and interesting exploration of a number of salient security questions from a (largely) Colombian perspective.

1150 O'Keefe, Thomas Andrew. Bush II, Obama, and the decline of U.S. hegemony in the Western Hemisphere. New York, N.Y.; London: Routledge Taylor & Francis Group, 2018. 199 p.: bibl., index.

O'Keefe has penned a very smart, carefully documented, and even-handed analysis of the ongoing debate about the decline of US hegemony in the Western Hemisphere. He employs several theoretical frameworks used in IR theory as so many lenses for understanding "hegemony"—including classical realism, neorealism, hegemonic stability theory, classical liberalism, liberal institutionalism, regime theory, and neo-Gramscian theory. He then carefully takes the reader through a very well informed yet concise history of inter-American institutions, ideas, and practices and assesses what each theory says about that history in an effort to understand the nature and extent of "US hegemony" to the present era. O'Keefe devotes several chapters to the Bush II and Obama administrations and analyzes several policy initiatives as measures of the US hegemonic decline. Those policy initiatives are: the failed Free Trade Area of the Americas (FTAA), the Energy and Climate Partnership of the Americas, Plan Colombia, the Merida Initiative, Pathways to Prosperity in the Americas, the Central American Regional Security Initiative, the Caribbean Basin Security Initiative, 100,000 Strong in the Americas, and the restoration of normal diplomatic relations with Cuba. In addition, he assesses the role of China in the region, and elsewhere notes in passing the challenge of migration pressures from the region. O'Keefe teaches at Stanford University and from 2011 to 2016, he chaired the Western Hemisphere Area Studies Program at the US State Department's Foreign Service Institute. This would be an excellent textbook for upper-level and graduate students of inter-American relations and should also be of interest to non-academic practitioners engaged in US-Latin American relations.

1151 Los orígenes latinoamericanos de Podemos. Bajo la dirección de Manuel Alcántara Sáez y José Manuel Rivas Otero. Madrid: Tecnos, 2019. 188 p.

Ten Spanish academics explore the intellectual, political, and professional links between Spain's Podemos party and Latin America's "leftist turn" and the social movements that buoyed the "pink tide" to power in the early 2000s. As the editors note in the introductory chapter, while there have been historical precedents, Latin America's pink tide politics represent an important instance of the region's intellectual and political influence in Spanish politics. Both movements arose in moments of political crisis, are ideologically heterodox, challenge neoliberal globalization, assert social well-being and social justice policies, and remain committed to democratic processes. Three of the chapters specifically discuss the "mutual apprenticeship" of Podemos and pink tide politics in Venezuela, Ecuador, and Bolivia.

1152 Oropeza García, Arturo. Del Atlántico al Pacifico: hacia un nuevo orden global. Ciudad de México: UNAM, 2017. 404 p.: bibl. (Colección universitaria de estudios asiáticos; 4)

The author presents a Mexican perspective on the widely held idea of an historic shift occurring from an international system centered in the West for nearly a millennium, with Europe and then the US as the hegemonic centers, to one centered in Asia, with East Asia and China as the political and economic centers vying for hegemonic dominance in the 21st century. This historic shift offers Latin American countries an opportunity to move beyond being mere witnesses to history; rather, middle powers in Latin America can be key actors in this transition. They certainly have a lot at stake. Part 1 considers the main elements of this shift, which include the Trans-Pacific Partnership and the key role of the BRICS countries, especially India and Russia. Part 2 explores China's economic model and its legal/juridical system. Part 3 considers the place of NAFTA (now USMCA) and its relationship to East Asia. See also *HLAS 75:1307*.

1153 Pensar Palestina desde el Sur Global. Compilación de Moisés Garduño García. Ciudad de México: UNAM, Facultad de Ciencias Políticas y Sociales: Ediciones La Biblioteca, S.A. de C.V., 2017. 314 p.: bibl., ill.

A group of activists and researchers present a deep, interdisciplinary, and postcolonial critique of the West's policies toward Palestine and the broader Middle East while exploring Mexican-Palestinian political, academic, and literary relationships. Chapters on the "Islamic State and Palestine" and "feminist activism in Palestine" may be of interest to different researchers as well.

1154 La proyección de China en América Latina y el Caribe. Edición de Eduardo Pastrana Buelvas y Hubert Gehring. Bogotá: Pontificia Universidad Javeriana: Konrad Adenauer Stiftung, 2017. 540 p.: bibl., ill.

This excellent, comprehensive collection of chapters analyzes China's important presence, policies, and relations with Latin American and Caribbean states. Eighteen chapters written by a diverse international collection of expert scholars provide theoretical, analytical, and policy-oriented insights into Sino-Latin American economic and political-diplomatic relations since the 1990s. China's strategic partnerships with the region as a whole, its relations with key regional organizations such as Mercosur, CELAC, Alliance of the Pacific, APEC, etc., and its bilateral relations with key countries (Argentina, Brazil, Chile, Colombia, Mexico, Peru, Venezuela, and more) are covered. This is an important contribution to the discussion of China's influence in Latin America and the Caribbean.

1155 Rodríguez Hernández, Leyde E. Un siglo de teoria de las relaciones internacionales: selección de temas y lecturas diversas. La Habana: Editorial Universitaria Félix Varela, 2017. 203 p.: bibl.

This Cuban scholar-diplomat presents a brief overview of the theories of international relations and the historical development of the discipline. Aimed at MA-level students, the author introduces the subject by discussing the field's roots in early modern writings on international law and diplomacy; notably, he does not mention colonialism nor the word "sovereignty" in the introductory historical section on the early modern period. ("Sovereignty" finally appears in the next chapter.) The author goes on to outline the fundamental ontological questions of the field, the "five" debates that mark its development, and the essentials of such approaches as realism, liberalism/idealism, Grotianism, constructivism, Marxism, dependency theory, world systems theory, poststructuralism, and even a short mention of feminism along with a few other approaches. Postcolonialism and green theory are largely missing. Also missing is practically any mention of China or its recent rise, though the US, Europe, and the former Soviet Union do appear while discussing the development of the discipline during the 20th century and into the 21st. Occasional dashes of revolutionary critique round out this Cuban adaptation of an IR theory textbook.

1156 Salgado Peñaherrera, Germánico. Integración y cooperación regional en América Latina: desafíos, opciones y alternativas. Coordinación de la colección y estudio introductorio por Francisco Pareja Cucalón. Estudio introductorio por Eduardo Santos Alvite. Quito: Universidad Andina Simón Bolívar Ecuador: Corporación Editora Nacional, 2017. 334 p.: bibl. (Obras de Germánico Salgado; 2)

This is the second volume of a series highlighting the work of Germánico Saglado Peñaherrera (1925–99), a distinguished Ecuadorian economist, public servant, diplomat, and academic who advocated for Latin American regional integration and cooperation to advance meaningful and equitable development. This volume republishes several of Salgado's works featuring the sociocultural and political aspects and challenges of Latin American and Caribbean integration efforts. His remarkable career of public service ranged from the Ecuadorian Central Bank to CEPAL to the founding of the Grupo Andino (1969), to the OAS and UN, on to academia, and much more. The works reproduced in this volume include "Integración: nuevos desafíos y alternativas" (in its entirety, 1987), a work that explores the interplay of integration with cultural identity, the environment, and technological advancement, a common theme of all of the writings in this volume. Also included are a conference talk on "Worldwide vs. Regional Integration (1974)"; "La cooperación horizontal" (or South-South technical cooperation, 1977); a seminar presentation on the Ecuador-Peru dialogue on integation, culture, and environment (1998); and "Integración y cooperación entre países en desarrollo en el ámbito agrícola" (originally published in *Cuadernos de la CEPAL*, No. 12, 1976). The volume offers an appendix that includes excerpts from key documents marking the development of the idea of Latin American integration, from Bolivar's 1815 Letter from Jamaica to the founding principles of the Grupo Andino. Scholars interested in the role of political and cultural identity in the process of integration will find this collection particularly worthwhile.

1157 Schulz, Carsten-Andreas. Accidental activists: Latin American status-seeking at The Hague. (*Int. Stud. Q./Oxford*, 61:3, Sept. 2017, p. 612–622, bibl.)

Using diplomatic records and archival materials while applying contemporary international relations (IR) theoretical lenses, Schulz re-examines the role of Latin American states at the Second Hague Conference of 1907. He argues that certain Constructivist and English School works, which have become the "common interpretation," tend to overstate the "norm entrepreneurship" of Latin American states at the time of the conference because such works draw on a skewed historical record. Rather than being principled and innovative forgers of international law and multilateralism in 1907, as some pundits of the time suggested, Schulz demonstrates that the foreign policy elites in such states as Argentina, Brazil, Chile, and Mexico were more interested in seeking status in the era's hierarchical global order by "joining the club" of "civilized states." He also shows how their power rivalries with each other made them less "united" in The Hague than is commonly thought, even though something of a Latin American diplomatic epistemic community was emerging by then. He contrasts the absence of all Latin American states but Mexico at the First Hague Conference of 1899 with the broader participation of 18 Latin American states at the Second Hague Conference of 1907. He links the diplomatic politics of the emerging Pan-American system to the Hague conferences, but suggests that questions of sovereign equality and universal participation were as much due to US (and Mexican) pressure on the European hosts as to pressure from Latin American diplomats. Despite their status-seeking aims, the diplomatic posturing and confrontational style of Brazil and Argentina in 1907 were counterproductive, creating some consternation among European diplomats. Latin American delegates at The Hague thus failed to make lasting status gains, relegating the region to the margins of the international society of states for some time to come. Schulz implicitly makes a strong case for the value of good diplomatic history and regional specialization in advancing strong IR theory.

1158 El sistema fronterizo global en América Latina: un estado del arte. Edición de Beatriz Zepeda, Fernando Carrión y Francisco Enríquez. Quito: FLACSO Sede Ecuador; Ciudad de Guatemala: FLACSO Sede Guatemala; Ottawa, Canada: IDRC-CDRI, 2017. 505 p.: bibl., ill., maps. (Colección Fronteras; 1)

The fundamental theme of this compilation is the relationship between borders and illegal economies in Latin America. The authors examine several case studies where the rule of law is being threatened by illicit economies and concomitant criminal activities. Mexico, Brazil, Guatemala, Peru, and Argentina are the central focus of the analysis in several chapters. Overall, the contributors to this volume explain how legal borders and state and non-state actors shape the circuits, routes, and nodes of illegality that make up the informal cross-border interaction within Latin America. With this objective in mind, two convergent methodological approaches were developed: the idea of the themes as transversal lines and the comprehension of the national border realities as subsystems. [R. Domínguez]

1159 Tominaga, Yasutaka. Killing two birds with one stone?: examining the diffusion effect of militant leadership decapitation. (*Int. Stud. Q./Oxford*, 62:1, March 2018, p. 54–68, bibl., graphs, tables)

Tominaga combines deterrence theory and criminology to develop empirical models that test the effectiveness of leadership targeting the deterrance of militant groups and the indirect deterrence effects of such targeting on other militant groups' operations. His data set includes 186 militant groups' operations between 1970 and 2008. His findings indicate that targeted capture of a group's leader is a better strategy than killing the leader in deterring further domestic attacks by the group; it also results in indirectly deterring allied groups' attacks. Other than a passing reference in his introduction to the 1981 capture of M-19's Carlos Toledo Plata in Colombia and a later passing reference to the findings of another study on the capture of Sendero Luminoso's Abimael Guzmán in Peru, no specific Latin American cases are analyzed in this study.

1160 Valle Fonrouge, Marcelo F. Articulación de mecanismos de integración de América Latina y el Caribe. Buenos Aires: Consejo Argentino para las Relaciones Internacionales, 2018. 101 p.: bibl.

This Argentine diplomat presents a short handbook outlining recent regional integration efforts in Latin America and the Caribbean. Specifically, he describes the Comunidad de Estados de América Latina y Caribeños (Community of Latin American and Caribbean States, CELAC)—in the creation of which he played a role, the Sistema de la Integración Centroamericana (Central American Integration System, SICA), the Unión de Naciones de América del Sur (Union of South American Nations, UNASUR), Mercosur, and the Alianza del Pacífico (Pacific Alliance, AP). The author includes some inter-regional topics (e.g., CELAC-EU dialogue and migration issues) and makes some comparisons along the way, including the challenges of migration for SICA and Mercosur as well as responses to political crises in member states for SICA (e.g., Honduras in 2008) and Mercosur (e.g., Paraguay in 2012 and Venezuela in 2017). A short, useful overview of key moments, institutions, and issues of these integration experiments.

Wise, Carol. Dragonomics: how Latin America is maximizing (or missing out on) China's international development strategy. See item **1284**.

1161 Xu, Yanran. China's strategic partnerships in Latin America: case studies of China's oil diplomacy in Argentina, Brazil, Mexico, and Venezuela, 1991–2015. Lanham, Md.: Lexington Books, 2017. 157 p.: bibl., ill., index.

Based on the author's dissertation, this monograph compares China's strategic partnerships with four key Latin American countries as of 2015, with some attention to other parts of the region along the way. Xu provides a Chinese perspective on China's foreign policy toward Latin America, framing it as relatively benign and mostly mutually beneficial. She highlights the importance of China's strategic partnerships in fostering trade, financial investment, and diplomatic cooperation with the region and offers an evaluation of the relative costs (e.g., commodity export dependency for some Latin American partners) and benefits (e.g., investments) of those bilateral partnerships. Brazil is China's most important strategic partner, Mexico the most complex, Venezuela perhaps the most troubling. A brief epilogue notes leadership changes in Brazil and Argentina prior to publication that alter China's interests and opportunities. Useful (if somewhat dated) tables and graphs.

MEXICO AND CENTRAL AMERICA

ROBERTO DOMÍNGUEZ, *Professor of International Relations and Government, Suffolk University, Boston, Mass.*

SCHOLARS OF INTERNATIONAL RELATIONS (IR) and of other disciplines interested in understanding the crucial processes in Mexico and Central America are represented in the 21 publications included in this section of *HLAS* 77. The engaging and innovative literature about Mexico and Central America published in recent years is emblematic of the vivid political, economic, and social debates about the region's past, present, and future. The works in this section fall into five main areas: three groups are related to books about Mexico, including US-Mexican relations, foreign policy, and Asia; the fourth group includes books about borders in the region; and the fifth and final group is about Central America.

The first set of books is about Mexico and the US. Costero Garbarino (item **1165**) investigates various aspects of the US Metalclad Corporation's hazardous waste disposal case in Guadalcázar, San Luis Potosí, in the context of the North American Free Trade Agreement (NAFTA). The author's empirical research backs up her hypothesis about the disconnect between global and local processes in foreign direct investment and environmental regulations. Along similar lines of analysis, Lucatello (item **1166**) coordinated a volume that assesses NAFTA's environmental dimensions and investigates potential changes that could be included in the new agreement between the US, Mexico, and Canada (UMSCA). While each chapter presents a different point of view, the overall conclusion is that the environment has been marginalized, some current regulations are outdated, and the social impact has been overlooked. While progress has been made, much more work remains to meet the region's environmental challenges.

Mexican immigration to the US has been central to Mexican scholarship. Fernández de Castro (item **1167**) compiled a book based on contributions of Mexican consuls in the US and Mexican consular policy experts. Each chapter describes different consular strategies for participating in local, state, and federal discussions about protecting Mexican communities in the US. The participation of Mexicans in their circumscriptions was critical in reversing the anti-immigrant sentiments that dominated the US Congress and the White House during the Trump administration. The book coordinated by Leco Tomás and Navarro Chávez (item **1171**) provides another analysis of Mexican migration. In addition to reviewing the impact of remittances, one of the chapters in the book suggests establishing two autonomous institutions in Mexico to develop a cohesive migration policy and to support and hold accountable the National Institute of Migration in Mexico: a migration tribunal within the judicial power and an attorney office for the defense of migrants.

The second group of books examines Mexican foreign policy from various perspectives. Herrera León (item **1170**) prepared an anthology about Mexican involvement in the League of Nations. The book examines the Mexican position with regard to international aggressions against Manchuria, Leticia y El Chaco, Ethiopia, Spain, Austria, Czechoslovakia, and Finland. The author contends that between 1935 and 1939, during the turbulent League of Nations international order, President Cárdenas established a nationalist oil policy, meticulously implementing it through legal procedures to avoid international ramifications. Another anthology (item **1173**) collects the most critical articles on Mexican energy policy published in *Foro Internacional*. This timely anthology includes several articles that helped shape and continue to shape conversations about energy policy in Mexico, as well as providing reliable arguments for assessing the potential consequences of the López Obrador administration's decision to increase reliance on oil and build a new refinery. Two books examine current Mexican foreign policy events. López Montero (item **1174**) coordinates a volume on President Enrique Pena Nieto's foreign policy and whether it maintains the premises of the previous two center-right administrations or marks a new turn in Mexico's engagement with globalization. One finding shared by several chapters is that both the concept and practice of Mexican international responsibility continue to prioritize macroeconomic priorities over social benefits. In the second book,

Rodríguez Sumano (item **1175**) examines the effects of 9/11, Plan Colombia, and the 2030 Development Agenda on Mexico's national security. He concludes that the weak foundations underpinning Mexico's rule of law jeopardize national security and, potentially, the legitimacy of Mexican administrations' actions and outcomes.

As the rise of China becomes more prevalent in academic publications, three books examine the relationship between Mexico and Asia. Ambassador Carlos Almada (item **1163**) provides an intellectual and practical perspective on the 130-year history of Mexico-Japan relations. While Mexico and Japan have faced challenges and tensions throughout their bilateral history, the book contends that, since 1888, both countries have been willing and able to adapt constructively to changing internal and regional circumstances. Calvillo Unna (item **1168**) led a project that conducted archival research on one of the famous trade routes that connected Asia with Mexico more than 450 years ago: the Manila-Acapulco Galleon Trade. According to the project, religion, cultural fusion, and migration were all aspects of the connections forged between the two nations by the galleons. Another Asian and Mexican contribution (item **1164**) investigates how China has displaced Mexico as the leading trade partner of the US and considers analytical concepts, such as diverging economic strategies and competitiveness. The book also details the role of the Asia-Pacific Economic Cooperation (APEC) mechanism in establishing Asia as the leading economic magnet for Latin American economies.

The fourth thematic group discusses the borders of Mexico and Central America. Toussaint Ribot and Garzón (item **1180**) provide a sequential explanation that identifies key events and briefly explains why and how diplomats and other actors interacted in the triangular relationship between Mexico, Guatemala, and Belize from 1821 to 2017. The edited book by Zepeda, Carrión, and Enríquez presents a more general approach to borders (item **1158**). The authors examine the relationship between borders and illegal economies in Mexico, Brazil, and Guatemala, and elucidate how legal borders and nonstate actors shape the circuits, routes, and nodes of illegality that comprise Latin America's informal cross-border interaction. The third border-related book (item **1162**) is an original work based on an extensive review of historical documents that explores new lines of inquiry into Mexico's relations with Cuba, the Dominican Republic, Jamaica, and Haiti. The most recent border book is the result of an interdisciplinary project convened by El Colegio de la Frontera Norte (COLEF) and El Colegio de la Frontera Sur (ECOSUR) (item **1172**). The extensive project provides a historical overview of the significant economic, social, and environmental challenges confronting Mexico's northern and southern borders. From a conceptual standpoint, the book considers transborder areas as units, which, in an analytical breakthrough, allows for an understanding of individual interactions across borders.

The fifth and final group of books in the section focuses on Central America and includes six titles. Two books are centered on Costa Rica. In presenting the journeys of Vicente Saenz, Eunice Odio, and other important Costa Rican actors, Medina and Moreno Rodríguez (item **1169**) led a group of scholars in a discussion of original research about Costa Rican exiles. Ulibarri (item **1181**), on the other hand, explains how Costa Rican foreign policy has left a mark on international relations, which is embedded in key international conventions, such as the Paris

Agreement and the Arms Trade Treaty, as well as policies addressing democratic erosion, peace negotiations, and human rights.

Two books help us understand Nicaragua better. Benítez López (item **1176**) contributes to a better understanding of the geostrategic disputes surrounding the Fonseca Gulf in Central America. The author provides detailed information about Nicaragua, Honduras, and El Salvador regarding their vulnerabilities in managing extraregional pressures and effectively dealing with disputes around the Fonseca Gulf among themselves, from the Clayton-Bulwer Treaty to the International Court of Justice's intervention in delimiting borders. The second book (item **1178**) is based on interviews with some of the Sandinista Revolution's leading figures. Given the changes in the Nicaraguan government over the previous 10 years, this book serves as a reminder of the critical factors that contributed to the success of the 1979 revolution and the need to restore democracy to the Central American country.

Tapiero (item **1179**) covers the topic of Panama and globalization. He investigates the competing economic forces of China and the US in Latin America, particularly Panama, as globalization exacerbates economic competition. According to the book, the Silk Road in Latin America has potential benefits for the region, but will undoubtedly erode the economic position of the US. The works on Mexico and Central America also include a book (item **1177**) that studies Honduran migration and focuses on two cities on the Chiapas-Guatemala border, describing the dynamic between expelling and receiving countries, the reconfiguration of families when they arrive in Soconuco, the organization of civil mobilizations and Honduran migrants, and the transborder networks they create in Mexico.

The scholarship represented by the books included in this section of *HLAS* 77 is methodologically diverse and thematically rich. Many publications extensively use historical analysis, descriptive statistics, and qualitative tools. Some books use novel theoretical approaches from political science and embrace numerous vital concepts such as path dependency, interactive translation loops, postconflict theories, and dependency. All in all, the works are outstanding contributions to understanding better Mexico and Central America.

MEXICO

1162 Actores y temas de las relaciones de México y sus fronteras. Coordinación de Laura Muñoz Mata. Ciudad de México: Instituto de Investigaciones Dr. José María Luis Mora, 2018. 494 p.: bibl., ill., index, maps. (Historia internacional)

This book contributes to the historical understanding of Mexico's Caribbean borders. Each chapter's timeline ranges from 1820 to the late 1980s. The work focuses on events in Mexican history that, due to the overwhelming role of the US, often require more study. The co-authors' research has resulted in an original work based on an extensive review of historical documents. The contributors to this volume propose numerous new historical lines of inquiry into Mexico's relations with Cuba, the Dominican Republic, Jamaica, and Haiti. In addition, Gilberto Bosques and Enrique Creel played critical roles in strengthening cooperative relations with the Caribbean.

1163 Almada, Carlos. México y Japón: a 130 años de relaciones diplomáticas. Ciudad de México: Secretaría de Relaciones Exteriores, Dirección General del Acervo Histórico Diplomático, 2018. 243 p.: bibl., graphs, ill.

In this volume, Ambassador Almada provides an intellectual and practical perspective on Mexico-Japan relations spanning 130 years. The book, which is organized chronologically and thematically, selects the most significant episodes in the bilateral relationship and explains how both parties have established solid and consistent exchanges in the political, economic, financial, cultural, and educational domains. While Mexico and Japan have faced challenges and tensions throughout their bilateral history, the findings of the book show that both countries have been willing and able to adapt constructively to changing internal and regional circumstances since 1888.

1164 China y México en la órbita del mercado mundial del siglo XXI. Coordinación de Cuauhtémoc Calderón Villarreal y Juan González García. Tijuana, Mexico: El Colegio de la Frontera Norte, 2019. 244 p.: bibl., graphs, tables.

This book compiles articles by economists who are experts on Mexico's relations with the major Asian economies. The articles are divided into two sections. The articles in the first section explain how China has displaced Mexico as the leading trade partner with the US, considering analytical concepts such as diverging economic strategies and competitiveness. The book's second section expands on the role of the other Asia-Pacific Economic Cooperation (APEC) mechanisms in shaping Asia as the leading economic magnet for Latin American economies.

1165 Costero Garbarino, María Cecilia.
Lo internacional y lo local: estudio de caso de Metalclad Corporation en Guadalcázar, San Luis Potosí, México. San Luis Potosí, Mexico: El Colegio de San Luis, 2017. 292 p.: bibl., ill. (Colección investigaciones)

The author investigates the hazardous waste disposal case of the US company Metalclad Corporation in Guadalcázar, San Luis Potosí, in the context of the North American Free Trade Agreement (NAFTA). The empirical research conducted by the author supports her hypothesis regarding the disconnect between global and local processes in foreign direct investment and environmental standards. The lack of coordination between the federal and state governments in San Luis Potosí resulted in social mobilization in response to the hazardous waste. Metalclad's documented case teaches several lessons about the complexities of matching institutional regulations with the social impacts of productive processes.

1166 Del TLCAN al T-MEC: la dimensión olvidada del medio ambiente en América del Norte. Coordinación de Simone Lucatello et al. Ciudad de México: Instituto Mora: Siglo Veintiuno Editores, 2019. 346 p.: bibl., graphs, ill., maps. (Economía y demografía)

The primary goal of this book is to assess the environmental dimensions of the North American Free Trade Agreement (NAFTA) and to investigate potential changes that could be included in the new agreement between the US, Mexico, and Canada (UMSCA). The chapters in the book outline various aspects of the region's environmental challenges, some of which are directly related to NAFTA and UMSCA, such as Chapter 11 disputes and the North American Commission on Environmental Cooperation, and others that are more general and comprehensive, such as mitigating climate change and increasing cooperation in maritime and coastal areas. While the chapters present individual points of view, the overall conclusion is that the environment has been marginalized, some current regulations are outdated, and the social impact has been overlooked. While progress has been made, much more work remains to meet the region's environmental challenges.

1167 La diplomacia consular mexicana en tiempos de Trump. Coordinación por Rafael Fernández de Castro. San Luis Potosí, Mexico: El Colegio de San Luis; Tijuana, Mexico: El Colegio de la Frontera Norte, 2018. 285 p.: bibl., ill.

Based on the contributions of Mexican consuls in the US and experts on Mexican foreign policy, the book offers a methodical analysis of the difficulties in consular operations, particularly considering the controversial narratives that the Trump administration embraced about immigrants. Each chapter explains the various consular strategies that could be used to participate in local, state, and federal discussions about protecting Mexican communities abroad. These strategies include lobbying, education, and outreach to communities in remote locations. To counter anti-immigrant sentiments that dominated the US Congress and the White House under the Trump administration, the activity of Mexicans in their circumscriptions was essential. The book employs an intermestic approach to describe the networks of the 12 million Mexican diaspora members in the US at local, national, and transnational areas of interaction.

1168 **En torno al galeon Manila-Acapulco.** Coordinación de Tomás Calvillo Unna. San Luis Potosí, Mexico: El Colegio de San Luis; Zamora, Mexico: El Colegio de Michoacán, 2019. 190 p.: ill. (Colección Investigaciones)

One of the famous trade lines that linked Asia with Mexico more than 450 years ago was the Manila-Acapulco galleon trade. Religion, cultural fusion, and migration were all aspects of the connections that the galleon created between the two nations, making it one of the most significant events in the development of economic modernity. This collection examines the many historical effects of the Manila-Acapulco galleon, covering all facets of that relationship, from missionary activity to textile trade. In a book based on detailed research and published by El Colegio de San Luis, the historical significance of Asia in Mexico and Latin America is explained carefully.

1169 **Exilio y presencia: Costa Rica y México en el siglo XX.** Coordinación de Mario Oliva Medina y Laura Beatriz Moreno Rodríguez. Ciudad de México: UNAM, Centro de Investigaciones sobre América Latina y el Caribe; Costa Rica: Universidad Nacional de Costa Rica, 2019. 260 p.: bibl., ill. (Colección Exilio iberoamericano; 9)

This book presents original research from two perspectives. First, the literature on Costa Rican-Mexican relations has been absorbed into volumes focusing on Mexican-Central American relations. Second, research on Costa Rican exiles in Mexico has been far less extensive. The chapters are written by scholars who have completed their doctoral dissertations as well as historians who specialize in Latin American exiles and diasporas. The first section of the book contains essays on the meaning and consequences of political exiles, as well as how they create new identities in host countries. The second delves into cases of Costa Rican exiles in Mexico, presenting the journeys of Vicente Saenz, Eunice Odio, and other important Costa Rican actors.

Martínez Meléndez, Ángel. Causas de la instauración de la Ley Mexicana de Cooperación Internacional para el Desarrollo: análisis histórico-sistémico. See item **1310**.

1170 **México y la Sociedad de Naciones: una antología documental.** Selección y estudio introductorio por Fabián Herrera León. Revisión y cuidado de la edición por Guillermo López Contreras. Ciudad de México: Archivo General de la Nación, Dirección General del Acervo Histórico Diplomático; Morelia, Mexico: Coordinación de la Investigación Científica de la Universidad Michoacana de San Nicolás de Hidalgo, 2018. 579 p.: bibl., ill.

The foundation of this anthology is the author's historical knowledge and diligent study of the archives of the Mexican Foreign Affairs Secretariat. This book presents materials that show the position of Mexican foreign policy in cases of international aggression against Manchuria, Leticia y El Chaco, Ethiopia, Spain, Austria, Czechoslovakia, and Finland. Mexico was an active participant in the League of Nations. The author of the anthology offers a suggested interpretation of President Lázaro Cárdenas' foreign policy, and the selection of the documents offers the chance to review Mexican history and inspire fresh arguments. President Cárdenas established a nationalist oil policy in the tumultuous League of Nations' era, between 1935 and 1939, meticulously implementing it through legal procedures to avoid international ramifications.

1171 **Migración, remesas y actividad económica en las relaciones bilaterales México-Estados Unidos.** Coordinación de Casimiro Leco Tomás y José César Lenin Navarro Chávez. Michoacán, Mexico: Universidad Michoacana de San Nicolás de Hidalgo, Instituto de Investigaciones Económicas y Empresariales, 2018. 154 p.: bibl., ill.

This book discusses migration between Mexico and the US and its economic impacts. The authors bring together essays that address international migration in various contexts. Remittances sent to communities in Mexico, the variable of migration within the Pacific Alliance, and the case of migrants from Michoacán in the United Arab Emirates are just a few examples. Exploring how US immigration policy under the Trump administration affected undocumented migrants, the book also considers the possibility of establishing two autonomous institutions in Mexico to develop a cohesive migration policy, and support and hold accountable the Instituto Nacional de Migración in Mexico: the migration tribunal within the judicial power and the attorney office for the defense of migrants.

1172 Norte-sur: diálogos de frontera. Coordinación de Rigoberto García Ochoa y Jorge L. León-Cortés. Tijuana, Mexico: El Colegio de la Frontera Norte, 2019. 292 p.: bibl., graphs, ill.

Two essential institutions, El Colegio de la Frontera Norte (COLEF) and El Colegio de la Frontera Sur (ECOSUR), convened an interdisciplinary group of experts to present an historical overview of the main economic, social, and environmental challenges facing the northern and southern Mexican borders. From a conceptual perspective, the cohesive element of the book across all the chapters is considering transborder areas as units, which allows for an understanding of individual interactions by actors across borders, which is one of the breakthroughs of the analysis. Further contributions are made by research on migration and tuberculosis, the function of colleges, sex trafficking, and the viewpoint of cattle ranches, in addition to the main issues of environmental deterioration.

1173 La política energética y petrolera vista desde *Foro internacional*. Edición de Isabelle Rousseau. Ciudad de México: El Colegio de México, 2017. 357 p.: bibl., ill. (Antología de estudios de política y relaciones internacionales de Foro internacional; 10)

Foro Internacional has long been regarded as one of Latin America's most significant publications. For more than 50 years, *Foro Internacional* has examined Mexican energy policy from the perspectives of history, political science, and international relations due to the country's significant oil reserves. This timely anthology includes several articles that helped shape, and continue to shape, conversations about energy policy in Mexico, emphasizing the role of the US. Among the articles is a comparison of Mexican and Venezuelan oil policies, economic calculations, a discussion of efficient production, and a study of the expanding role of natural gas. The articles compiled in this collection offer reliable arguments to assess the prospective impacts of the López Obrador administration's decision to increase oil dependency and construct a new refinery.

1174 La política exterior de México: entre la responsabilidad global y el interés nacional. Coordinación de María Elena López Montero *et al.* Naucalpan de Juárez, Mexico: Facultad de Estudios Superiores Acatlán, UNAM, 2017. 333 p.: bibl., ill.

The Partido Revolucionario Institucional (PRI) was elected to lead Mexico in 2012. This multi-authored volume assesses whether President Enrique Peña Nieto's foreign policy continues to follow the established premises of the previous two center-right administrations or represents a new turn in Mexico's engagement with globalization. The chapters cover the most critical areas related to Mexico's external action, comprehensively evaluating Mexican foreign policy performance between 2012 and 2018. One of the book's main findings is that the concept and practice of Mexican international responsibility still focuses on macroeconomic priorities, rather than social benefits.

1175 Rodríguez Sumano, Abelardo. Granos de arena: ideas y marco conceptual en la seguridad nacional en México, contexto internacional y cambio político. Ciudad de México: Universidad Iberoamericana, 2018. 358 p.: bibl.

The author contributes to the study of national security in Mexico by evaluating various international relations approaches, such as idealism, interdependence, cultural perspectives, neorealism, and classic geopolitics. Through regime theory, the author examines the effects of 9/11, Plan Colombia, and the 2030 Development Agenda on Mexico's national security. The book critically evaluates national security and indicates that the foundations on which Mexico is built, such as the rule of law, are dysfunctional and could derail the euphoria of the 2018 electoral process, quickly transforming celebrations into anger and disappointment. The text compiles a selection of recent societal learnings, reflections, and analyses of Mexico's broad concept of national security.

CENTRAL AMERICA

1176 Benítez López, Jazmín. El Golfo de Fonseca como punto geoestratégico en Centroamérica: origen histórico y evolución del conflicto territorial: del siglo XVI al XXI. Ciudad de México: UNAM: Bonilla Artigas Editores; Chetumal, Mexico: Universidad de Quintana Roo, 2018. 323 p.: bibl., maps. (Pública histórica; 4)

Benítez López contributes to a better understanding of the geostrategic disputes in Central America surrounding the Fonseca Gulf. This book begins in 1850 and covers all significant battles and actions in or around this region until the end of the 2000s. From the Clayton-Bulwer Treaty to the International Court of Justice's intervention in delimiting borders with other Central American countries, the author provides detailed information about Nicaragua, Honduras, and El Salvador's vulnerabilities in managing extraregional pressures and effectively managing disputes around the Fonseca Gulf among themselves. The research gathered data from various sources, allowing the reader to understand international law disputes, national interest calculations, and regional leadership.

Broad, Robin and **John Cavanagh.** The water defenders: how ordinary people saved a country from corporate greed. See item **497**.

1177 Fernández Casanueva, Carmen. La vida en una orilla del sur: inmigración hondureña en dos ciudades de la frontera Chiapas-Guatemala. Ciudad de México: CIESAS, 2017. 223 p.: bibl., ill., maps.

This book is about Honduran migration focusing on two cities on the Chiapas-Guatemala border. The author conducted surveys and interviews in Tapachula and Huixtla, among other cities, to inform her analysis and explain why Hondurans migrate and how they adjust to their new surroundings. The analysis reveals the complexities of migration by including literature on South-South and intraregional migration in the context of Hondurans. The book describes the dynamic between expelling and receiving countries, the reconfiguration of families when they arrive in Soconuco, the organization of civil mobilizations and Honduran migrants, as well as the transborder network they form once in Mexico.

1178 García, Txema. Lava y ceniza: la revolución sandinista y el volcán de la solidaridad vasca. Donostia, Spain: Txertoa, 2019. 243 p.: ill. (Begira; 9)

Based on interviews, this book attempts to explain the Sandinista Revolution. The analysis and the interviews reveal a complex and varied language about the priorities and specifics of the revolution and its aftermath thanks to first-hand information. The debates that prevailed during the development of institutions in post-revolutionary Nicaragua are skillfully conveyed to the reader through a balanced selection of interviews and analysis. A trained and experienced journalist, the author also instructs the reader to carefully examine the substance of the chapters by reading what the interviewees stated and the subjects and viewpoints they avoided or purposefully ignored. This book serves as a reminder of the critical factors that contributed to the success of the 1979 revolution and the need to restore democracy to the Central American country considering the changes in the Nicaraguan government over the previous 10 years.

1179 Tapiero, Eddie. La ruta de la seda y Panamá: escenario prospectivo estratégico entre América y China. Segunda edición. Panama: publisher not identified, 2019. 299 p.: bibl., color maps.

The history of Panama has been shaped by its privileged position. Tapiero examines the competing economic forces of China and the US in Latin America in general and Panama in particular, as globalization exacerbates economic competition. The book contends that the Silk Road in Latin America has potential benefits for the region, but will undoubtedly erode the previous position of the US. According to the author, Panama should use its geoeconomic and geopolitical position to build production networks that benefit Panama and other Central American countries.

1180 Toussaint Ribot, Mónica and **Marisol Garzón.** México, Guatemala y Belice: tres caras de una historia fronteriza, siglos XIX-XXI. Ciudad de México: Instituto de Investigaciones Dr. José María Luis Mora, 2019. 163 p.: bibl., ill., maps. (Colección región transfronteriza México-Guatemala)

This book tells the history of the border between Mexico, Guatemala, and Belize through a chronology of significant events from 1821 to 2017. The sequential explanation identifies key events and briefly explains why and how diplomats and other actors interacted in the triangular relationship. The book enables readers to comprehend a confluence of two centuries of strategies, events, and interests in the borders of the three countries. The book's structure is aimed at a broad audience who may be unfamiliar with Mexico's relations with its southern neighbors, allowing them to become acquainted with the major stages of southern border history.

1181 Ulibarri, Eduardo. Costa Rica global: pilares y horizontes de nuestra acción en el mundo. Prólogo de Alberto Trejos. San José: Academia de Centroamérica, 2017. 290 p.: bibl.

Ulibarri develops two suggestive narratives about Costa Rican engagement in globalization. On the one hand, from the perspective of Costa Rica, the author selects the main significant variables about how the world has built international institutions, On the other, the book explains how Costa Rica has translated its identity in foreign policy initiatives to participate in global arrangements with a remarkable contribution in favor of good global governance. The Costa Rican footprint on international relations is embedded in key international conventions such as the Paris Agreement and the Arms Trade Treaty, as well as in policies addressing democratic erosion, peace negotiations, and human rights.

Van den Berk, Jorrit. Becoming a good neighbor among dictators: the U.S. Foreign Service in Guatemala, El Salvador, and Honduras. See item **849.**

THE CARIBBEAN AND THE GUIANAS

JACQUELINE ANNE BRAVEBOY-WAGNER, *Professor Emeritus of Political Science, The Graduate School and University Center, The City University of New York*
JULIO A. ORTIZ-LUQUIS, *Research Fellow, Instituto Caribeño para el Estudio de la Política Internacional, San Juan, Puerto Rico*

HISPANIC CARIBBEAN

THE SELECTION of publications for this *HLAS* volume includes different approaches and literary and scholarly tools to engage and understand Caribbean geopolitical, historical, social, and economic realities and changes. US-Cuba relations continue to be a transcendent issue in Caribbean geopolitics, diplomacy, and international relations. One methodological trend in this selection is noteworthy:

recent academic works employ structural and critical analysis to delve into the fluid reality of US-Cuba relations during the Barack Obama and Donald Trump administrations. In addition, historical approaches explore and recount the long history of US-Cuba relations since US independence. Furthermore, some publications take the form of journalistic investigative essays and current chronicles, such as in the work of the five Cuban spies arrested in the US and later released by the Obama administration (item **1197**) and the plight of Cuban medical brigades fighting the Ebola epidemic in Africa (item **1201**).

Historical analysis is employed to investigate the past, prospects, and realities of Cuba-US relations. Ramírez Cañedo reviews the history of US foreign policy towards Cuba and its diplomatic history in terms of US obstructionism in Latin American and Caribbean politics (item **1198**). Similarly, González Santamaría offers an exposition of the "deep forces" of Cuban foreign policy values and vision through a collection of Fidel Castro's speeches exhibiting a particular analysis of US history in Cuba (item **1186**).

A main concern continues to be the future of US-Cuban relations in the 21st century. The edited books compiled by Laguardia Martínez and Rosa bring together economic and geopolitical analyses to understand the challenges, opportunities, and prospects of the diplomatic normalization started by presidents Barack Obama and Raúl Castro in 2014 (items **1188** and **1189**, respectively). The uncertainty of the future of the normalization process is expressed in the volume by Castro Mariño (item **1190**), which brings together a collection of essays exploring American foreign policy towards Cuba during the Trump administration with its particular innovations and visions. Biegon uses a critical/neo-Gramscian analysis to assess the values and strategic objectives of Cuba-US normalization from a hemispheric approach and to highlight the distinctions between the Obama and Trump administrations (item **1183**). Another essay on Cuba embarks on a legal commentary on the future of Cuba-US normalization that offers insights into a possible legal framework for this new relationship at times of domestic debates over this process in American politics.

Lastly, the Puerto Rico-US relationship is also observed from a historical approach, such as in the work of Calandra, unearthing public-private efforts to experiment with the Puerto Rican population during the heyday of American eugenics in the mid-20th century (item **1185**). The book uses this case study to explore American visions of expansionism in the Caribbean during that historical moment. Rodríguez Cancel and García-Passalacqua (item **1200**) expand on the discussion and trauma of US-Puerto Rico territorial relations in a long transcription of dialogues delving into several dimensions of the stagnant relationship. The goal continues to be to find a path toward decolonization, as has been articulated publicly by various American administrators and most of Puerto Rican social forces over the years. [JOL]

NON-HISPANIC CARIBBEAN

The paucity of International Relations (IR) studies on the English-speaking Caribbean, identified in *HLAS* 75, continues into the latest round of reviews, whereas works on Haiti by Haitians continue to evolve (through collections of speeches, as well as crisis studies), a fact also noted in the last set of reviews. To some extent, this dearth of IR work in the English-speaking subregion may be related to a historical tendency of Caribbean Community scholars to focus on issues of political economy (including regionalism) to the neglect of the dominant focus on "power" or, alternatively, "norms" of the Western mainstream IR. However, this does not explain why even publications on international political economy have become rather rare. A second explanation may be that Caribbean small states have become more marginalized in the international arena in the era of globalization, not to mention in the era of COVID-19. As a result, too, once vibrant small-state diplomacies may have become less strategic and more improvisional (see *HLAS 75:1343*). A third and broader explanation may be that Caribbean scholars are more interested in a range of international studies, drawing from philosophy, sociology, anthropology, and humanities disciplines to offer their views about the international, usually with a focus on exclusionary practices around the globe. Indeed, one work in this round of reviews—Hinds' work on Caribbean intellectual thought (item **1194**)—explicitly states that because Caribbean thinkers can be found across the disciplinary spectrum, the ideas emerging from the region have normally not been connected by them to IR or framed as contributing to IR theory. Unfortunately, a byproduct of this seeming disinterest in specifically contributing to IR theory is that IR publications on the region (in the traditional sense) are almost exclusively written by diplomats and others directly involved in the practical realm, and that these are usually not theoretical, but rather policy-oriented and descriptive, which is not to say that the memoirs of public officials and their recreation of events based on personal involvement cannot provide valuable information to scholars. However, it would be helpful to the IR field if Caribbean scholars turned their attention to less insular analyses of events, and located niches in terms of regional approaches to IR and foreign policy theory, particularly at a time when some space has opened up in the Western mainstream for the inclusion of critical perspectives from the Global South.

That said, although the number of studies reviewed in this round is small, almost all offer some key insights into Caribbean diplomacy. The already-noted tendency for former diplomats and other policy participants to take the lead in IR studies is reflected in three studies, all of which can be very helpful on the academic level as well. One of these (item **1196**) is a historical discussion of the Monroe Doctrine and an attempt to implicate it, with some conceptual stretch, in contemporary events in (inter alia) Grenada, Haiti, and Venezuela today. Another (item **1192**) is a very useful discussion of Saint Vincent and the Grenadines' service as the smallest state to ever be elected to the UN Security Council (for the 2020–2022 term). The third work (item **1195**) is an account of President René Préval's two terms in office in Haiti, in which the author effectively interweaves domestic and foreign policy actions, and makes an effort to apply IR thinking on personality and leadership, human rights, and global governance. A fourth work (item **1193**), a think-tank compilation of articles by academics, edited by the think-tank director, a scholar with practical experience, offers some clear insights into Haiti's experiences and future within the Caribbean Community (CARICOM). Finally, in this genre of practice, a World Bank report on Latin American regional integration (item **1184**) as well as a think-tank report on the potential for deeper relations between India and Latin America and the Caribbean (item **1182**) are informative.

In terms of non-policy-oriented scholarship, only three works are available in this round. One, by Hinds, discusses the broad spectrum of Caribbean intellectual thought, seeking to show its applicability to a globalizing IR (item 1194). The second includes CARICOM in a discussion of how groups operate at the UN (item 1199). The third is not drawn up as an IR text per se, but is rather a lively reading of Caribbean history from slavery to Haiti (1991), which certainly has implications for cultural and identity studies in IR (item 1191). [JBW]

1182 Badri-Maharaj, Sanjay. India's relations with the Latin America-Caribbean region: prospects and constraints. New Delhi: Institute for Defence Studies & Analyses, 2017. 59 p.: tables. (IDSA occasional paper; 45)

In this relatively brief report on India's relations with the Latin American and Caribbean (LAC) region written for the Institute for Defence Studies & Analyses, New Delhi, the author profiles the LAC countries demographically and economically, and compares India's low profile, transactional, trade-oriented approach to this region with China's more strategic and deeper involvement. While India is praised for greatly increasing trade over the years with LAC, the author laments a lack of focus on adequate diplomatic representation (more LAC countries are represented in Delhi than vice versa), and too much attention to one country, Brazil. The author also suggests that India pay more attention to political cooperation, technical assistance, and defense and security cooperation (which is not very significant at the moment). Surprisingly, despite mentioning the UN Security Council and regional organizations, the author does not elaborate on the potential for better relations in this multilateral sphere where China is also active. [JBW]

1183 Biegon, Rubrick. The normalization of U.S. policy toward Cuba?: rapprochement and regional hegemony. (*Lat. Am. Polit. Soc.*, 62:1, Feb. 2020, p. 46–72, bibl.)

The article examines US foreign policy towards Cuba at times of posthegemonic regionalism in Latin America. This is a backdrop to regional debates on Cuba's access to the inter-American system. The essay uses methodology based on a neo-Gramscian approach to assess the role of policy-making, regional, hemispheric, and global transformations to assess what the author calls "oscillations in US Cuba policy," and strategic shifts that attempt to define a "hegemonic reconstitution" of US leadership in the Americas. The author concludes that the Obama administration tried to revitalize the inter-American system by normalizing diplomatic relations with Cuba in the face of the emergence of other posthegemonic regional institutions and organizations mushrooming in Latin America and the Caribbean since the first decade of the 21st century. In this way, the US attempted to revitalize mechanisms of hegemonic consensus-building. [JOL]

1184 Bown, Chad P. et al. Better neighbors: toward a renewal of economic integration in Latin America. Washington, D.C.: World Bank Group, 2017. 178 p.: bibl., color ill., color maps. (World Bank Latin American and Caribbean studies)

The Latin American and Caribbean region is known for having established many regional integration arrangements since the 1960s. Rather surprisingly, the authors of this World Bank study (supported with extensive statistics) find that, compared to the East Asia-Pacific region, Latin America and the Caribbean have not taken good advantage of the potential for regional cooperation, and that this is one of the reasons for the region's declining economic momentum in the second decade of the 2000s. While they are aware that size and geography present some hindrances (depending on definitions of the "region"), they argue for a renewed commitment to open regionalism, in the form of a balance between regional and global integration. They see room for greater tariff and nontariff liberalization, infrastructural (transportation) improvements, efficiencies through migration/labor integration, and carefully planned regional investment agreements. [JBW]

1185 **Calandra, Benedetta.** Il corpo del Caribe: le politiche sulla riproduzione tra Puerto Rico e Stati Uniti (1898–1993). Verona, Italy: Ombre corte, 2020. 285 p.: bibl., index. (Americane)

The book investigates birth control and population control in Puerto Rico as one of the first US policies as a colonial power in the Caribbean, and the role of private and public interests in the process. Through US and Puerto Rican sources, this study investigates how, from the 1920s to the 1980s, different social actors interacted, negotiated, and were involved in intense controversies on two issues that marked the singularity of Puerto Rico's history and ignited public debate: female sterilizations and the first experiments on large hormonal dosages to market the first birth control pills. The narrative is marked by the biographical events of three women who played particularly significant roles in the history of family planning: Margaret Sanger and Katharine Dexter McCormick, American activists, and Helen Rodríguez-Trías, a Puerto Rican doctor who circulated between New York and San Juan. Still little explored in the history of inter-American relations during the 20th century, the theme of birth control is centered on the politics of reproduction in Puerto Rico and constitutes a point of observation of relations between the US and Latin America since 1898. The author portrays the politically ambiguous relationship between the US and Puerto Rico as a social laboratory on which US power exercised an early "modernizing obsession" that was later promoted in the rest of the Caribbean. [JOL]

1186 **Castro, Fidel.** Fidel Castro y los Estados Unidos: 90 discursos, intervenciones y reflexiones. Compilación de Abel Enrique González Santamaría. La Habana: Editorial Capitán San Luis, 2017. 226 p.: ill. (Colección 90 aniversario del comandante en jefe Fidel Castro Ruz)

The book is a collection of speeches given by Fidel Castro in the period 1959–2016. The compiler gathered fragments of Fidel Castro's speeches pertaining to US-Cuba relations. The chapters are organized in a chronological manner allowing the reader to trace the development of Castro's thought and attitudes towards US foreign policy and presence in Cuba. The book synthesizes Fidel Castro's thoughts on the nature of the US as a world power and as a neighbor of Cuba. [JOL]

1187 **Cooperación internacional en Haití: tensiones y lecciones: los casos de Brasil, Chile y México.** Coordinación de Gabriela Sánchez Gutiérrez y Randolph Gilbert. Ciudad de México: Instituto de Investigaciones Dr. José María Luis Mora: Consejo Nacional de Ciencia y Tecnología, 2017. 400 p.: bibl., ill., index. (Contemporánea. Cooperación internacional y desarrollo)

The book presents a collection of policy analysis essays by scholars and practitioners about the impact and effectiveness of Mexican, Brazilian, and Chilean international cooperation agencies and policies towards Haiti after the earthquake of 2010. The book includes six chapters selected and edited by an editorial group formed by Haitian and Mexican experts, practitioners, and scholars. The authors analyze the trajectory and scope of Mexican, Brazilian, and Chilean international cooperation towards Latin America and the Caribbean and its impact in the Haitian crisis of the 2010–2015 period. Special attention is given to policy and technical guidelines, geopolitical calculations, South-South and triangular cooperation strategies and scope, and the authors provide recommendations for future Haitian and Caribbean cooperation engagements. The Haitian perspective and analysis is central to this volume. The essay "La cooperación Sur-Sur desde la perspectiva de los actores de Haití (South-South Cooperation from the Perspective of Haitian Actors)" by Amlin Charles evaluates the extent and effectiveness of the Chilean, Brazilian, and Mexican cooperation, assistance, and capacity-building in Haiti and makes recommendations based on lessons and shortcomings addressed according to these countries' histories of South-South cooperation with Haiti. The essays included in this volume were informed by 93 interviews with Mexican, Brazilian, Chilean, and Haitian government officials, practitioners, specialists of NGOs, and Haitian civil society actors. [JOL]

1188 **Cuba en sus relaciones con el resto del Caribe: continuidades y rupturas tras el restablecimiento de las relaciones diplomáticas entre Cuba y los Estados Unidos.** Compilación de Jacqueline Laguardia Martínez. Textos de Julio César Guanche Zaldívar et al. Buenos Aires: CLACSO, 2017. 254 p.: bibl., ill. (Colección Grupos de Trabajo)

This edited volume analyzes the impact of diplomatic normalization between Cuba and the US on Cuba's international relations with the rest of the Caribbean region. The tome opens with an introductory essay that serves as a background on US-Cuba relations in the context of Cuba's drafting of the 1940s constitutions and the ways this historical precedent set the tone for the future of US-Cuba relations. The first section of the book titled "Cuba and the Rest of the Caribbean After December 17" delves into the impact of US-Cuba bilateral diplomatic normalization within the realms of tourism and foreign investment, as well as on other Caribbean nations' exports, such as the case of Dominican Republic, along with technological-scientific cooperation and science diplomacy with the rest of the Caribbean. The second section elucidates Cuba's long-standing cooperation with other Caribbean nations such as Trinidad & Tobago, Suriname, Developing Small Island Nations, the Dominican Republic, and China's economic relations with Caribbean nations. [JOL]

1189 **Cuba, Estados Unidos y el 17D: cambios y continuidades.** Coordinación de Olga Rosa González Martín y Ernesto Domínguez López. La Habana: Editorial UH, 2018. 236 p.: bibl.

This edited volume brings together a collection of essays analyzing the events that led to the so-called process of normalization, to re-establish bilateral diplomatic relations between Cuba and the US, announced by presidents Barack Obama and Raúl Castro on 17 December 2014. The book compiles essays researched from various methodologies and theoretical perspectives within the discipline of International Relations. The transnational approach is a perspective that permeates this edited book. The origin of sources and the objectives of the analysis evident in these essays entails the consideration of multiple diplomatic relations around, and interconnected to, the issue of Cuba-US relations and its prospect in the future. Accordingly, the essay by Raúl Rodríguez, titled "Las relaciones Canadá-Cuba en el contexto del proceso de normalización Cuba-Estados Unidos: hacia una nueva dinámica triangular (Cuba-Canada Relations in the Context of the Normalization Process between the US and Cuba: Towards a New Triangular Dynamic)," examines the historical triangular dynamic among the US, Cuba, and Canada that equips Canadian diplomacy to serve as a potential mediator and guarantor with its vast experience dealing with Cuban and American government institutions. [JOL]

1190 **Donald J. Trump y las relaciones Cuba-Estados Unidos en la encrucijada.** Coordinación de Soraya M. Castro Mariño y Margaret E. Crahan. Ciudad de México: Grupo Editor Orfila Valentini, 2018. 454 p.: bibl. (Colección Geopolítica y dominación)

This edited volume analyzes the deterioration of US-Cuba relations during Donald J. Trump's presidency. The collection of essays is the result of a series of scholarly dialogues titled "XVI Serie de Conversaciones Cuba-Estados Unidos de America," sponsored by the Center of Studies of International Politics within the Superior Institute of International Relations "Raúl Roa García" (CIPI-ISRI) in Havana. From different approaches, Trump's foreign policy towards Cuba is considered as part of a crisis in the US and the concurrent political and ideological transformation in the US with the rise of the radical nationalist right led by Donald Trump. The economic stagnation and the crisis of social groups on the losing end of capitalism in developed nations set the foreground for the analysis. The political platform and foreign policy promoted by Donald Trump called "America First" is deemed throughout the text as suffering from a long- and short-term strategic view, thus hindering the role of the US in a transforming international system. The book is divided in six sections; the first deals with the Trump administration's foreign policy platform and its continuities and ruptures from Barack Obama's foreign policy views and strategies. The second section assesses the ideologies of Trump's administration and its impact on Cuba-US relations. The third section discusses Cuba-US relations during the Trump era in the midst of change and transformation in hemispheric politics. The fifth section analyzes the commercial issues, specifically the economic embargo against Cuba during the Trump era. The final section describes common US and Cuban agendas during the Trump era, such as climate change, migration, education, and security cooperation. [JOL]

1191 Dubois, Laurent and **Richard Lee Turits.** Freedom roots: histories from the Caribbean. Chapel Hill: University of North Carolina Press, 2019. 395 p.: bibl., index, maps.

There is much to inform the reader in this history of the Caribbean from the arrival of Columbus and subsequent relations between the Spanish and the Indigenous, through the tortures of slavery, the mechanics of the plantation economy, and finally, emancipation, and then on to US occupations of Caribbean countries, and more recent revolutions and resistances, including the Grenada experiment and President Aristide's rule in Haiti. This is not an IR text per se, but rather a history that aims to inform the reader about the political, social, and economic influences that have shaped the Caribbean. The writing is lively, supported by illustrative and appropriate anecdotes. Despite the broad swath of history covered, or perhaps because of it, this is a very useful work. [JBW]

1192 Gonsalves, Isis. Small, young, and female: Saint Vincent and the Grenadines on the United Nations Security Council from the perspective of the political coordinator. (*Glob. Gov.*, 28, 2022, p. 295–302)

This is a well-written and informative account of the role played by Saint Vincent and the Grenadines during its stint on the UN Security Council (2020–2022), an account written from the perspective of the embassy's political coordinator. St. Vincent is the smallest country to ever be elected to the Security Council, and this review of its tenure describes how the country managed and maximized its role by coordinating with the A3 (African group), focusing on interests such as Haitian affairs, climate change, and Council reform, promoting itself as "aligned with no one and everyone" in its foreign policy, and imbibing the procedural rules and chairing a related Informal Group. St. Vincent may not have achieved all or even a lot of what it wanted, but its overwhelmingly female and young delegation conducted itself very well. The article is a very interesting policy piece. [JBW]

1193 Haïti, la CARICOM et la Caraïbe: questions d'économie politique, d'intégration économique et de relations internationales. Sous la direction de Watson Denis. Delmas, Haiti: C3 Éditions, 2018. 502 p.: bibl., ill. (Les Publications du Centre Challenges; 2018)

In recognition of the fact that Haitians are not as familiar with CARICOM as one might expect, this text—dedicated to a number of notable regionalists—offers an in-depth look at Haiti's long effort to join the regional body. Admission, first applied for in the 1970s, was gained in 1997, though this membership was suspended in 2004 in the wake of political turmoil, only to be reactivated after a new government was installed in 2006. The contributors to this book analyze at length CARICOM's history and regulations as an integration unit, and then consider the pros and cons of Haiti's membership, including hurdles to integration such as Haiti's distance from other members on economic measures, its differential size, its linguistic status as non-English speaking, and its history of political and social unrest. The book goes beyond CARICOM itself to outline Haiti's relations with the region, including in the context of the ACP (African, Caribbean, and Pacific grouping with the European Union), CARIFORUM (CARICOM, including Haiti, and Dominican Republic), as well as the Association of Caribbean States (all the independent Caribbean states, Colombia, Venezuela, Mexico, Panama, Central American states and associated Caribbean dependencies) and other multilateral relationships. Straying a bit from the "Haiti-CARICOM" theme are useful chapters on CARICOM relations with the Dominican Republic, Cuba, Puerto Rico, and the US as a whole. In particular, a long chapter detailing the DR's rather unenthusiastic (on both sides) dance with the regional body is informative. [JBW]

1194 Hinds, Kristina. Big ideas from small places: Caribbean thought for International Relations. (*in* Latin America in global international relations. Edited by Amitav Acharya, Melisa Deciancio, and Diana Tussie. New York, N.Y.: Routledge, Taylor & Francis Group, 2022, p. 67–88, bibl.)

The author of this rather unusual work (in the IR context) seeks to insert Caribbean intellectual thought into a budding IR discourse on "Global South IR" and the broader "Global IR" (both of which seek to bring marginalized ideas and approaches into the mainstream of IR theory). Although the Caribbean is small, it has produced many thinkers of note who, while based in many disciplines and perhaps recognizing no disciplines at all, have generated and disseminated ideas that have "traveled" internationally and regionally: Frantz Fanon, Marcus Garvey, C.L.R. James, Walter Rodney, W. Arthur Lewis, and the members of the New World Group (regional theorists taking their cue from Latin America's dependency theorists) who have influenced pan-Africanism, various anticolonial approaches, and political economy. Caribbean thinkers have generated ideas about, inter alia, the impact of slavery, the plantation economy, human rights, coloniality, and postcolonialism. The author highlights the influence and development of these ideas within the context of a (continuing) racialized, colonial construction of the world. Aware that much of this work she cites has been done within a masculinist frame, the author also devotes a section to some of the feminist thought that has emerged in the last few decades, focusing on gender analyses of the particularities of Caribbean women's lived experiences and how this work can be incorporated into a broader IR. [JBW]

1195 Louis, Jean Guy-Marie. La politique étrangère de René Préval: 1996–2001/2006–2011. Haïti: publisher not identified, 2019. 318 p.: bibl.

This is one of the few books in which the author tries to incorporate some IR theory into his detailed review of the foreign policy (and domestic policy; the two areas are recognized as inter-related) of René Préval, one of the few leaders post-Duvalier to have managed to be elected to two terms in office. The author makes a brief note of realism, liberalism, and Marxism as IR theories in his first chapter, where he also details the ministries involved in foreign policy, but opts in the rest of the work to focus on personality and leadership issues as well as the peculiar domestic and international circumstances that have made Haiti developmentally deficient. Indeed, the author's interweaving of domestic and foreign policy is appropriate, although the text is sometimes bogged down by "work schedule" type details of events, state visits, dates of meetings, and amounts of aid granted. The stress throughout, rightly so, is on the major role played by the international community in Haiti as well as the struggles of the government to meet donor expectations of good governance and respect for human rights. The tension between Haitian nationalism/national pride/the desire for agency and the need to please the international community plays out on matters such as Haiti joining the Non-Aligned Movement (which was considered by the US leadership at the time as too connected to the "Axis of Evil" anti-US countries), its establishment of relations with Cuba, its membership in ALBA, its attempt to appease China in the UN Security Council (while maintaining relations with Taiwan), and Préval's desire for the UN mission in Haiti (MINUSTAH) to turn toward development goals rather than focusing only on issues of good governance. Overall, the tone is very critical, at times didactic. Préval is faulted for perceived personality flaws and attendant maneuvers to stay in/regain office, as well as for his inability to halt the economic and social decay of Haiti and to deliver some level of security to the populace. This is a very detailed and informative work. [JBW]

1196 Modeste, Denneth M. The Monroe Doctrine in a contemporary perspective. New York, N.Y.: Routledge/Taylor & Francis Group, 2020. 232 p.: bibl., ill., index, maps. (Routledge Studies in the History of the Americas; 12)

This is a very well researched book by a Grenadian diplomat who served also on the Haitian mission of the OAS. The author's aim is to link the tenets of the Monroe Doctrine to contemporary local and regional crises. Early chapters provide a solid, well-documented review of US continental expansion, the Monroe Doctrine's origins, and subsequent interventions, which were ostensibly undertaken to keep order and democracy in the hemisphere. The author also discusses US actions during the early Cold War and moves on to "contemporary" events, focusing mainly on the Grenadian and Haitian interventions where the US opposed what it viewed as undemocratic leaders. The author attempts to address more recent issues including immigration and border security policy under the Trump administration as well as the imposition of sanctions against Venezuela, but his argument loses clarity. The author's notion that the unilateralism of the Monroe Doctrine has been replaced by multilateral (regional) norms of collective self-defense is well taken. However, it seems to negate his argument that the Monroe Doctrine is still strategically important and used as such. Furthermore, actions taken on humanitarian crises such as refugee flows are hard to fit within the anti-European or antidemocratic contexts of the original or even modified Monroe Doctrine. [JBW]

1197 Morais, Fernando. The last soldiers of the Cold War: the story of the Cuban Five. Translated by Robert Ballantyne with Alex Olegnowicz. London: Verso, 2015. 275 p.: bibl.

The author, in an engaging prose, constructs the story and decades-long ordeal of five Cuban spies arrested in the US. Through various sources such as interviews, visual content, newspapers, and periodicals, the author interconnects the lives of the Cuban spies in the US and how they built different identities to join and then gather intelligence for the Cuban government about the plans, strategies, and activism of Cuban exile groups deemed by the Cuban government to be a national threat. Through the 1980 and 1990s, violent anti-Castro groups based in Florida carried out hundreds of military attacks on Cuba, bombing hotels and shooting up Cuban beaches with machine guns. The Cuban government organized the Wasp Network, a collective of men and women sent to infiltrate these organizations. This book tells the story of those spies and their eventual unmasking and prosecution by authorities in the US. [JOL]

1198 Ramírez Cañedo, Elier. La miseria en nombre de la libertad. La Habana: Editorial de Ciencias Sociales, 2017. 133 p.: bibl.

This book recounts US foreign policy toward Latin America and the Caribbean since the 19th century. The author effectively elaborates a transnational historical reconstruction that outlines a comprehensive, yet succinct, historical narrative of US efforts to avoid conflict with European powers, while advancing its expansionist interests in Latin America and the Caribbean. The US-European tensions are framed in this work as clashing interests between the corresponding mercantilist and capitalist elites that would never support the South American independence process. The author also highlights the resistance of South American elites to the revolutionary process inspired by Simón Bolívar in the early 19th century—resulting in the dissolution of Gran Colombia in 1830, the dissolution of the Peruvian-Bolivian Confederation in 1839, the dissolution of the Central American Confederation in 1848, the dissolution of the Rio de la Plata Viceroyalty, and the division of Hispaniola into Haiti and Dominican Republic. Consequently, the author interprets the dissolution of the early Latin American and Caribbean nations as the result of concerted and sometimes disjointed efforts by American and European elites and Latin American elites to fracture and stop the independence impulse that originally triggered the Atlantic revolutions in Latin America and the Caribbean. In chapter 8, the author elaborates the American diplomatic efforts to weaken and sabotage Bolívar's Amphictyonic Congress of Panama of 1826. [JOL]

1199 Ribeiro Hoffmann, Andrea. Latin American cooperation at the United Nations: exploring the role of GRULAC, CARICOM and ALBA. (*in* Group politics in UN multilateralism. Edited by Karen E. Smith and Katie Verlin Laatikainen. Leiden, The Netherlands; Boston, Mass.: Brill | Nijhoff, 2020, p. 60–75, bibl.)

In a book on group politics at the UN where the theme (as expressed by the editors in the conclusion) is that "the only sin at the UN is being isolated," the author discusses the activities and analyzes the cohesiveness of CARICOM, the Bolivarian Alliance ALBA, as well as the umbrella Latin American and Caribbean group (GRULAC). This is a straightforward, descriptive essay, with some analysis of the adverse effect of overlapping loyalties, especially between ALBA and CARICOM. [JBW]

1200 Rodríguez Cancel, Jaime L. and Juan M. García-Passalacqua. Puerto Rico y Estados Unidos: conversaciones sobre geopolítica, geocultura y postcolonialidad (2005–2007). San Juan: Editorial Luscinia C.E., 2017. 412 p.: bibl.

Between 2005 and 2007, the authors developed a series of dialogues about US-Puerto Rico territorial relations. This dialogue was recorded in 18 episodes as a program of the Universidad del Este's television circuit. As part of these dialogues, the authors discussed decolonization, free association, cultural affirmation and defense, Puerto Rican nationality, White House reports on Puerto Rico, living within a hegemony, and American geopolitics, among other subjects. The book is a transcription of this dialogue and a unique and valuable tool to understand and learn about US-Puerto Rico relations and their possible resolution. [JOL]

1201 Ubieta Gómez, Enrique. Red zone: Cuba and the battle against Ebola in West Africa. New York, N.Y.: Pathfinder, 2019. 263 p., 16 unnumbered pages of plates: bibl., ill., index, maps.

The book is a work of historical journalism that unpacks Cuba's health cooperation in Africa during the Ebola epidemic in the 2014–15 period. Cuba, with the highest ratio of doctors per capita in the world, has a history of health cooperation spanning five decades. The author traveled with a contingent of almost 300 Cuban doctors to help in the Ebola epidemic in Liberia, Sierra Leone, and Guinea. The book chronicles the request of the African countries involved to the Cuban government, the preparation in Cuba, the landing of Cuban health officials, technicians, and doctors, and the impact of the Cuban health contingent in these African countries. The chapters connect places, people, and challenges through personal recollections of the fight against Ebola in Liberia, the lives of Cuban doctors working in Africa, the challenges Cuban doctors faced in Sierra Leone, the role of religion within the Cuban contingent of doctors, the sacrifices of Cuban doctors in Guinea, the role of Cuban women doctors, and the cases of Cuban doctors that died while combating Ebola in these countries. [JOL]

1202 White, Nigel D. Ending the US embargo of Cuba: international law in dispute. (*J. Lat. Am. Stud.*, 51:1, Feb. 2019, p. 163–186)

This commentary analyzes the Cuba-US normalization process that started in 2014 from a legal standpoint, assessing international legal considerations related to a political process of diplomatic bilateral negotiations that is intended to create a peaceful relationship between the two countries. The author concludes that diplomatic and interstate normalization requires recognizing responsibilities for violations of international law and amending these violations. The US-Cuba Bilateral Commission established in 2015 is considered a positive move toward settlement of outstanding claims by both parties. For the process to become permanent and embedded in the bilateral negotiation, the author deems it necessary for both parties to share a legal discourse, thereby opening the door for each to assume legal obligations, responsibilities, and accept verifiable and sound compensations. [JOL]

SOUTH AMERICA (except Brazil)

FÉLIX E. MARTÍN, *Associate Professor of Politics and International Relations, Florida International University*

THE SECTION on South American International Relations in *HLAS 75* reported four positive trends compared to publications examined for *HLAS 71* and *73*. First, publications reviewed for *HLAS 75* reflected a wide thematic diversity. Second, the works demonstrated a refreshing, engaging, and innovative multidisciplinarity. Third, and more importantly, the works focused on traditional and nontraditional IR topics. The studies addressed the primary global concerns, such as human trafficking, drug trafficking, social mobility, regional and international migration, refugees, environmental issues, along with practical concerns like international trade, energy, natural resources, and global transportation and logistics. Finally, the works appraised for *HLAS 75* generally attempted to frame their central questions within proper theoretical positions from both positive and reflectivist epistemological perspectives and implemented rigorous methodologies. In essays for *HLAS 71* and *73*, this Contributing Editor advocated for more attention to these trends.

Disappointingly, except for seven books, the publications reviewed here for *HLAS 77* revert to old approaches and traditional concerns just as the IR discipline calls for greater inclusion and attention to the theoretical and empirical production originating from the Global South. The publications are not mindful of the potentially deleterious intellectual hegemony and academic monopoly manifested (consciously or not) in academic journals and multiple outlets and trade and university presses of the Global North.

However, seven books do adhere to the contemporary direction in the IR discipline. They frame their research topics and questions from within a specific and delineated theoretical perspective in the discipline, then explain their methodology and the empirical sources for their analyses. Their research questions are the product of theoretical reflections about specific empirical observations. They avoid pursuing ad hoc questions and answers from a purely empirical world. Also, they generally avoid asking research questions based on personal concerns. They tend to be mindful of the IR discipline's newer, more systematic, rigorous theory-building and theory-testing concerns. In other words, they attempt to build generalizable hypotheses and accumulate replicable analyses and theoretical positions in other situations and regional settings. In sum, they attempt to move forward the theoretical enterprise in IR, while studying region-specific practical aspects characteristic of intraregional, interstate relations in South America as an essential part of the Global South.

Prieto Corredor's work (item **1211**) advances a constructivist analysis of the Andean Community of Nations or Comunidad Andina (CAN), a regional project conducted by Bolivia, Colombia, Ecuador, and Peru since 1969. The CAN has been studied from rationalist-materialist approaches, mainly neorealism and neoliberal institutionalism, which emphasize material benefits as the main reason states engage in regionalism. Given that the CAN generated relatively few material benefits for its members, rationalist-materialist approaches need help explaining the permanence of the Andean Community regional project. Prieto Corredor's work emphasizes the importance of ideas that guide social action and collective identity. This book demonstrates that it is possible to explain collective identity and regional institutions for the development of regionalism based on the constructivist ontological assumption that ideas matter. Three case studies of the Andean Community of Nations establish the constitutive and causal impact of collective identity and regional institutions on the action of and between states.

A second work (item **1206**) worth underscoring contends that the restructuring of the international state system in the 1990s resulted in two essential consequences for Latin America: (1) competition among great powers for leadership and control over systemic advantages increased pressure on South American countries; (2) a window of opportunity for these countries to consolidate their joint advantages. This book aims to answer what the author considers the fundamental questions for South American countries: What strategic insertion and for what type of development? To answer these questions, Bustos proposes an eclectic theoretical approach, combining contributions from the sociohistorical school, autonomy theory, constructivism, and systemic thinking. The first part of the work consists of a sociohistorical reading of the South American integration process from 1985–2015. The book's second part analyzes the same events, but from the vantage point of a systemic perspective.

A third impressive work is an edited volume by Brizzio, Espósito, and Ortega (item **1205**). The monograph explores the following position: The long historical process of Latin America's rise did not result in a homogeneous or unified space. Instead, it resulted in a profound fragmentation of the region into multiple nation-states. This work seeks to clarify the process of disintegration and understand the history of efforts to promote Latin American integration. The authors engage in a thorough, systematic, and concise exploration of Latin American integration efforts: ALBA, ALADI, CAN, UNASUR, and most recently, the Pacific Alliance, among others, with a particular emphasis on Mercosur. The beginning of the 21st century has presented Latin America with a new opportunity. This work can help readers consider how to promote a sound and successful integrationist project for Latin America.

The fourth work advancing the current direction of the IR discipline in the Global South is *Small Builds Big: How Ecuador and Uruguay Contributed to the Construction of UNASUR* (item **1242**). This work introduces an innovative model for studying the role of small states in regional organizations. It conceptualizes small states into region-engaging, region-constraining, and region-adapting actors, according to their particular type of engagement in regional politics. According to this model, Ecuador and Uruguay are region-engaging small states. The work argues that elements of a shared collective identity are a major factor of influence on the region-engaging character of Ecuador and Uruguay in the construction of the South American Union of Nations (UNASUR). The study employs a constructivist approach to exploring the reasons why these states have supported the creation and consolidation of UNASUR. The work is based on an analysis of documents, political speeches, and semistructured interviews, while also considering various historical events from 2000 to 2012. A significant component of the research concerns the shared factors of a South American identity. A comparison with other countries facilitates an understanding of the aspects of identity influencing the behavior of Ecuador and Uruguay in the consolidation of UNASUR.

The fifth book, coordinated by Daniel Pontón (item **1241**), is less theoretically driven. However, it is still a rigorous analysis worth highlighting for its contribution to testable hypotheses and replicable analyses from the Global South. From a theoretical-conceptual perspective, this book indicates the particularities and complexities of the Colombian peace process. The author places the evolution of the peace process within a historical context, building on various political scenarios that might offer alternative plans, and assesses how different evolutions of the conflict could affect Ecuador. In particular, the work examines the social, political, economic, and geopolitical dynamics of the Ecuador-Colombia Border Integration Zone.

The sixth book is a short work (item **1236**), the product of Zamora's MA thesis. It deserves a mention here because it shows how the current direction of the IR discipline is influencing newer graduate study works on South America. The author's contention is that although international phenomena have been treated as an almost exclusive problem of national states, multiple international transformations (i.e., economic, political, social, cultural) occurred at the end of the 20th century, leading to changes in the theoretical focus of the discipline of International Relations. Among multiple transformed aspects in the external environment, the author argues that the range of relevant actors for the discipline expanded considerably beyond the nation-state. These public actors included entities at subnational, local, or regional order, and even private actors and others from the community at large. In this sense, it is evident how civil society influences the external environment. Thus, the author argues, traditional IR theories must include actors beyond national state actors. The author looks particularly at the case of Santafé de Bogotá, Colombia (2001–2013).

Finally, the edited volume by María Andrea Nicoletti *et al.* (item **1213**) is a noteworthy compilation of 14 chapters by researchers from both sides of the Andean or Patagonian mountain range, separating Argentina and Chile. The book comprises Argentine-Chilean cross-border studies. The analytical approach followed by the researchers in this project adhered to three research dimensions: first, circuits, relationships, and representations of political and economic practices; second, territories, itineraries, and material expressions; and third, cultural and social practices within the framework of interculturality. The intention is to consolidate the imaginary of familiar territory in time and space with the mountain range as an integrating aspect, not as a national political limit.

Although classes to study international political questions began in 1898 at the University of Wisconsin and in 1910 at Columbia University, the discipline of International Relations took its first formal organizational steps in 1919 when Aberystwyth University in Wales established its first Department of International Studies and founded the first IR professorship. During those early years, the practitioners focused their attention on the study of diplomacy, international organizations, security matters, and the causes of wars, mainly among great powers in the aftermath of the Great War or World War I.

In the late 1950s, the discipline took a systematic and theoretical turn. The Rockefeller Foundation promoted a scholarly effort to systematize the theoretical study of international relations. A committee of IR scholars met in New York and scholars from several British universities, known at the time as the British Committee, met periodically to discuss questions related to international relations. These meetings led to a greater formalization of the IR discipline, leading to four great theoretical debates from the 1950s to the new millennium's first decade.

Even when IR scholars called for greater attention to the periphery, the Third World, and now the Global South, the evolution of the discipline was dominated by attention to great power politics and other aspects of external politics among states of the core Global North. Nonetheless, since the early 2000s, there has been greater emphasis and effort from Global South scholars to draw attention to IR scholarly production from different regions of the Global South. Thus, one is dismayed when one reviews the publication record from South America in this section and confirms that most of the production still lingers on traditional approaches and adopts theories and methodologies mainly developed in the Global North. It is hoped that there will be a more significant effort to produce and disseminate theoretical and empirical studies that grow out of the historical reality of the Global South. South American IR scholars must strive to achieve a greater theoretical and empirical impact on the development of the IR discipline. Such an endeavor should be the goal for publications that will be reviewed in *HLAS 79*.

GENERAL

1203 **El ALBA-TCP: origen y fruto del nuevo regionalismo latinoamericano y caribeño.** Compilación de Maribel Aponte García *et al*. Buenos Aires: CLACSO, 2015. 423 p.: bibl., ill. (Colección Grupos de trabajo)

This edited volume examines the origins, evolution, and future of Latin American and Caribbean regionalism. The 16 contributors to this volume examine Latin American and Caribbean countries to demonstrate how the regional integration process has evolved in different countries. The contributors reveal the difficulties and benefits of the integration process in each country over the years. The authors enable readers to understand the multiple manifestations of the "new regionalism and integration" in the Americas. This approach allows readers to grasp the basic principles of interstate integration. Theoretical contextualization is central to the first chapter by editor Maribel Aponte García, who begins by carefully theorizing about the new strategic regionalism. At the book's outset, she defines the notion of regional integration and explains why Latin America is failing to establish a sound and prosperous level of integration.

1204 **Bas Vilizzio, Magdalena.** América del Sur frente a los tratados bilaterales de inversión: ¿hacia un retorno del estado en la solución de controversias? Montevideo: Universidad de la República, Comisión Sectorial de Investigación Científica, 2017. 94 p.: bibl., ill. (Biblioteca Plural)

This book contributes to the debate on investor-state dispute resolution mechanisms provided for in the bilateral investment treaties in force in the South American states. The work analyzes public international law in light of the theory of international economic regimes. Further, it addresses the investor-state dispute resolution mechanisms that entail exceptions to state sovereignty, the cornerstone of public international law. The focus is on the characteristics of the 1965 Convention on the Settlement of Investment Disputes between States and Nationals of Other States (also referred to as the Washington Convention).

1205 **Brizzio, Jacquelina; Santiago Martín Espósito;** and **José Emilio Ortega.** Integración latinoamericana: experiencias. Córdoba, Argentina: Encuentro Grupo Editor: Editorial Universidad Nacional de Córdoba, 2017. 268 p.: bibl.

The monograph posits that the long historical process promoting Latin America's rise did not result in a homogeneous or unified space. Instead, it resulted in the profound fragmentation of the region into multiple nation-states. This work seeks to clarify this process of disintegration and understand efforts to promote integration in Latin America. Thus, this book aims to unpack the difficulties and complexities of the construction and development of Latin America. This work will establish a basis for understanding and explaining why regional integration is complex and challenging, eluding multiple attempts over the years. The authors examine various phases of Latin American integration: ALBA, ALADI, CAN, UNASUR, and most recently, the Pacific Alliance, with particular emphasis on Mercosur. The beginning of the 21st century has presented Latin America with a new opportunity to think about a sound and successful integrationist project. Two significant sections comprise this book. The first part examines the conceptualization and analysis of the origins of the integration process in Latin America. It also looks at notions of interstate integration, regionalism, and regionalization and explores the historical antecedents of integration in the Americas. The second part of this book examines the transitions and perspectives needed for a successful regional integration process.

1206 Bustos, Gonzalo. Inserción estratégica suramericana: alcances y límites de los intereses conjuntos en América del Sur (1985–2015). Buenos Aires: EUDEBA, 2016. 381 p.: bibl., ill. (Temas. Política)

Bustos claims that the restructuring of the international state system in the 1990s produced two essential consequences in Latin America. On the one hand, the competition among great powers for leadership and control over systemic advantages (i.e., productive, commercial, financial, and technological capacities) increased the pressures on the South American countries; on the other, it opened a window of opportunity for these countries to grow, based on their common factors and the strategic density of their integration projects. This book aims to answer what the author considers the fundamental question for South American countries: Which strategic insertion and for what type of development? To answer this question, Bustos proposes an eclectic theoretical approach. It combines contributions from the sociohistorical school, autonomy theory, constructivism, and systemic thinking. The author provides an historical narrative of events that influenced relations between Mercosur and UNASUR member states like Argentina and Brazil. Within this context, the author presents a two-level analysis of the regional and global tensions, and examines how these tensions weaken or strengthen shared interests. The first part of this work provides a sociohistorical reading of the South American integration process from 1985 to 2015 and is structured around three hypotheses. First, based on similar structural and situational historical junctures, Argentina and Brazil articulated a joint interest whose content changed based on the political, economic, strategic, and sociocultural variables that affected both countries. The second hypothesis maintains that since the beginning of the 21st century, two central factors conditioned the integrationist strategy and impacted the collective interests of these states: first, the struggle among great powers to lead and control economic connections in South America; and, second, the fundamental differences among countries in the Mercosur regarding development strategies, globalization, and regional integration. The third hypothesis posits that despite some strategic consolidation of interests among Mercosur member states, advancement was minor and partial. The book's second part analyzes the same events, but from a systemic perspective.

1207 Cooperación Sur-Sur, política exterior y modelos de desarrollo en América Latina. Edición de Maria Regina Soares de Lima, Carlos R.S. Milani y Enara Echart Muñoz. Textos de Bruno Ayllón Pino *et al*. Buenos Aires: CLACSO, 2016. 263 p.: bibl., ill. (Colección Grupos de Trabajo)

This edited volume combines the investigations of a CLACSO working group on South-South Cooperation and Development Policies and the Insertion Project of

Rio de Janeiro in FAPERJ's Decentralized South-South Cooperation Agenda. The contributions share a critical view of South-South cooperation and its intersection with foreign policy, developmental models, and the contradictory role of regional firms and companies regarding globalization. The chapters examine foreign policy, geopolitics, and developmental models; the governance of South-South cooperation; the confrontation of Latin America with the post-2015 agenda; the regional dimension of South-South cooperation as revealed in the case study of ALBA-TCP; cooperation and Ecuador's well-being; South-South cooperation and Brazil, Chile, and Venezuela's foreign policies; the participation of Brazilian civil society in the process of South-South cooperation; public policies and private interests, Brazilian multinational corporations, and cooperation in Latin America; the expansion of Brazilian construction enterprises in South America; and a final chapter dedicated to South-South cooperation, practices, actors, and narratives.

1208 Davydov, Vladimir Mikhaïlovich.
Latinoamérica y Rusia: rutas para la cooperación y el desarrollo. Buenos Aires: CLACSO, 2018. 169 p.: bibl.

The author of this book contends that the Latin American and Caribbean macro-region is unique. According to Davydov, the exceptional character of the region derives from its shared linguistic, confessional, and historical trajectories and its role in the international context. Nevertheless, at the same time, the development of this macro-region provides a wide variety of models and paths. According to the author, the fundamental Latin American paradox is reflected in the contrast of mutually exclusive qualities. In other words, Latin America and the Caribbean represent a unit with variants or, conversely, a variety of unit frameworks. Recognizing this peculiarity, this book covers many of the common denominators and tries to demonstrate the diversification of the regional development problem. The work reflects the Russian background and outlook of its author.

1209 Más allá de las fronteras: integración, vecindad y gobernanza: Colombia, Ecuador, Perú. Dirección de Carlos Enrique Guzmán Mendoza y Luis Fernando Trejos Rosero. Textos de Sebastián Bitar Giraldo *et al.* Barranquilla, Colombia: Universidad del Norte Editorial, 2017. 170 p.: bibl., ill.

This multidisciplinary and interdisciplinary work is based on the premise that given the transformations within the international system since 1992 and particularly since 2008, borders can no longer be understood as hard limits and/or static lines. In six chapters, contributors to this work examine the challenges of improving cross-border neighborhood relations and the demands and dynamics of territories in border areas, particularly those in Colombia, Peru, and Ecuador. Chapter 1 examines neighborhood relations and governance in the Andean region. Chapter 2 explores communitarian policy and its impact on regional integration and border development. Chapter 3 analyzes the areas of development and integration in the context of two border zones—the Colombo-Peruvian and the Colombo-Ecuadorian Zones. Chapter 4 assesses the insecurity and the socioeconomic development gaps in Colombia's borders. Chapter 5 focuses on improvements in neighboring communities on the Colombian border and indicates avenues for improvement. Finally, chapter 6 concludes by analyzing the prospect for successful governability or governance, and the role of nonstate actors in facilitating this process.

1210 El no al ALCA diez años después: la Cumbre de Mar del Plata y la integración latinoamericana reciente. Compilación de Julián Kan. Textos de Luiz Alberto Vianna Moniz Bandeira *et al.* Buenos Aires: Editorial de la Facultad de Filosofía y Letras, Universidad de Buenos Aires, 2016. 239 p.: ill. (Colección Saberes)

This book examines the conditions that led to the defeat of the Free Trade Area of the Americas (FTAA), an initiative supported by the US, and the consequences of the debacle 10 years later, after the 2005 Summit of the Americas in Mar del Plata. The book argues that the rise of progressive governments in Latin America in the late 1990s and early 2000s with decidedly anti-US leadership and the wave of popular discontent and public protests in the region caused the denouement of the proposed free trade initiative. In its place emerged alternative integrationist projects and a new type of regionalism. The free trade area initiative waned by 2015. Since then, US and the Latin American countries more amenable to the neoliberal dynamic have pursued bilateral free trade agreements in place of the FTAA.

1211 Prieto Corredor, Germán Camilo.
Identidad colectiva e instituciones regionales en la Comunidad Andina: un análisis constructivista. Bogotá: Pontificia Universidad Javeriana, 2016. 353 p.: bibl.

This book provides a constructivist analysis of the Andean Community of Nations or Comunidad Andina (CAN), a regional project developed by Bolivia, Colombia, Ecuador, and Peru in 1969. The CAN has been studied from rationalist-materialist approaches—mainly neorealism and neoliberal institutionalism—which emphasize material benefits as the main reason that states engage in regionalism. Given that the CAN generated relatively few material benefits for its members, rationalist-materialist approaches need help explaining the deepening and permanence of the Andean Community regional project. Therefore, this work takes a constructivist approach that emphasizes the importance of the ideas that guide social action and collective identity. To explain the approach used in this book, the first chapter reviews some constructivist approaches to regionalism that highlight the role of collective identity and regional institutions. These approaches acknowledge the constitutive role of these ideational structures, but sometimes also suggest the causal effects of ideas in making agents act in specific ways. Once the author teases out the constructivist conceptual and theoretical framework, he proceeds to explore the permanence of the Andean Community in the absence of significant material gains and benefits. Through an interpretive analysis of three case studies, he establishes the constitutive and causal effects of collective identity and regional institutions on the actions of individual member states and among them.

1212 Las relaciones entre Sudamérica y Asia-Pacífico en un mundo incierto: los casos de Argentina, Chile y Brasil.
Coordinación de María Clelia Guiñazú y Alejandro Pelfini. Buenos Aires: FLACSO Argentina: Ediciones CICCUS, 2018. 251 p.: bibl., ill.

The editors of this volume start from the following contention: At the center of the Asia Pacific, a new global axis of power has been evolving and reconfiguring the preexisting balance of power in the international system. This power rivalry is creating an increasingly uncertain and volatile global context that has influenced Latin America. Hence, many countries in the region are developing their strategies for international insertion within this new power-balancing equation. How do Latin American elites perceive the growing role of Asia-Pacific? What are—and have been— the visions that guide the strategies and political decisions towards that region? Do these perceptions converge or diverge when identifying opportunities and evaluating current and future initiatives for international cooperation and political coordination between both regions? In this book, the classic dilemmas of the international insertion of the countries of the Southern Cone gain new light, reexamined from the perspective of the Asia Pacific axis of power. In-depth interviews of technopolitical and social elites in Argentina, Brazil, Chile, and with Mercosur officials help round out the discussion. The work constitutes an essential contribution for those interested, not only in international relations, but also in the history of development models in the region and the conformation of the elites of the countries of the Southern Cone.

ARGENTINA

1213 Araucanía-Norpatagonia. Vol. 1, Discursos y representaciones de la materialidad. Edición de María Andrea Nicoletti et al. Viedma, Argentina: IIDYPCA, CONICET, URNR: Editorial UNRN, 2016. 440 p.: bibl., ill. (Aperturas. Serie Sociales)

This book is a compilation of 14 chapters by researchers from both sides of the Andean or Patagonian mountain range separating Argentina and Chile. The book comprises Argentine-Chilean cross-border studies. The analytical approach followed by the researchers in this project adhered to three research dimensions: first, circuits, relationships, and representations of political and economic practices; second, territories, itineraries, and material expressions; and third, cultural and social practices within the framework of interculturality. The work proposes that the mountain range territory acts as an integrating agent, not as a national political limit.

1214 **Araucanía-Norpatagonia.** Vol. 2, La fluidez, lo disruptivo y el sentido de la frontera. Compilación por Paula Gabriela Núñez. Buenos Aires: LUA; Viedma, Argentina: Editorial UNRN: Río Negro Universidad Nacional, 2018. 535 p.: bibl., ill. (Aperturas. Serie Sociales)

This work seeks to understand the constructions of the social senses of the space called Araucanía-Norpatagonia. Furthermore, it is essential to understand that the meanings are not univocal. In this case, the plurality of the territorial is intuited in the different perspectives, showing both the multiple meanings and the tensions behind concepts such as space, border, and representation. The researchers and social scientists who contributed to this volume assumed the center-periphery debate, understanding that the particular view developed from a territory of late integration, such as Patagonia in Argentina and Chile. The work builds a necessary and singular epistemological view. Thus, Patagonia adopts a plural character, nations diversify, and the meanings and practices of the state become complex. In addition, territorialities and subjectivities are part of the challenges addressed in this 18 chapter compilation of the binational space. See also item **1213**.

1215 **Argentina y Brasil: industrialización, contexto internacional y relaciones bilaterales (1940–2010).** Edición de Alberto J. Sosa y Cristina Dirié. Buenos Aires: AmerSur, 2018. 574 p.: bibl.

The book offers a seven-decade analysis of the key players and public policies in Argentina and Brazil that impacted industrialization and bilateral relations between the two South American giants. The work places their relations in the context of the interstate system from the beginning of WWII to the US unipolar moment and the aftermath of the 2008 financial crisis. The authors review the employment and social situation. They classify the industrial performance of both countries into three stages: the industrial, the neoliberal, and the resistance to the globalizing neoliberal regime. According to the authors, the Brazilian armed forces did not hesitate to support the industrialization policy initiated by "Varguismo" (as an extension of Getúlio Vargas' industrial and public policies and Estado Novo ideology), a popular current not too different from the one led and founded by Perón in Argentina. Nonetheless, the ideological prejudice instilled in the Argentine armed forces (due to Peronism and its justicialism ideology) deprived Argentina of critical support from the military to promote industrial and public policies similar to those of Brazil. The authors suggest the importance of considering the Brazilian school of geopolitics, of which General Golbery do Couto e Silva (a veteran of the Brazilian Expeditionary Force that fought in Italy during WWII) was a prominent representative and intellectual. Brazilian geopoliticians represented Brazil's attempts to establish the country as a relevant player in the world. The authors see greater industrial policy success in Brazil than in Argentina. There was nothing similar in Argentina, although individually, specific military officers advocated for industrialization and greater autonomy in national decisions.

1216 **Cangiano, Fernando.** Malvinas: la cultura de la derrota y sus mitos. Buenos Aires: Editorial Dunken, 2019. 173 p.

Providing an in-depth study of the trauma Argentinians experienced in the aftermath of the 1982 Falkland/Malvinas War, Cangiano examines two contrasting and powerful narratives about the war. Notwithstanding the broad national consensus about Argentine sovereignty over the South Atlantic, Cangiano claims that the postwar period revealed a profound dispute between two fundamental narratives about the outcome of the war. On the one hand were those who saw the war as a "senseless madness" and favored a quick "reconciliation" with the UK. On the other hand were those who emphasized the war's anti-imperialist objective. Thus, they rejected the policy of silence about the war's true meaning. In the opinion of the author and ex-combatant, Fernando Cangiano, these fundamental disagreements demonstrate a more profound debate in Argentina, whose origins stem from the country's independence. The first narrative evolved from a dominant power structure in Argentine society that is servile to the interests of the great powers (the US and Great Britain, in the first place) and distorted the meaning of the 1982 war. According to the author, the war's purpose was to restore the semicolonial status of the country. War veterans, critical of this perspective, coined the term "demalvinization," a concept that the author examines extensively in his work. Veterans opposed this notion because it implied purging the collective, national psyche of Argentina's sovereign right over the South Atlantic archipelago. War veterans did not support the view that the war was a disastrous event in Argentina's national history, leading to tragic consequences for Argentina's national identity. The author proceeds to dismantle the myths propping up the "demalvinizing" story. He links them with the imperatives of the neoliberal offensive of the time, which imposed, according to the author, the need to dissolve the concept of "national sovereignty" over the South Atlantic for the sake of a mythical process of "globalization," a euphemism that concealed the voracity of big international capital in the Global South. In addition to this sociological analysis, Cangiano also describes his active combat experiences between April and June 1982.

1217 **Dalbosco, Hugo Luis.** Los diplomáticos profesionales y la formación de la política exterior 1983–2007. Buenos Aires: EDUCA, Editorial de la Universidad Católica Argentina, 2017. 258 p.: bibl., ill.

This work focuses on the role of career diplomats and their influence on Argentina's foreign policy. The book covers a range of topics from the formation of the state bureaucracy—where questions related to recruitment, the stability of the professional administration, and the existence of links between the administration and the political system prevail—to the study of national elites. Due to the composition of the diplomatic corps and its intervention in the national political process, this elite group is different from other leadership groups in the national policy process. Career diplomats are a specialized portion of the state bureaucracy, whose recruitment and career development are aimed at other areas of the national administrative process. The author maintains that the diplomatic elite have legitimacy, based on the individual capacity of its members and an aptitude for interdisciplinary work, as well as on the acceptance of the group and its rules of selection and career. The book describes this bureaucratic elite and its participation in the formulation of foreign policy. In summary, it explores the attributes of members of the diplomatic corps and the conditions for developing a career in Argentina's diplomacy between 1983 and 2007. This original study allows us to understand the exceptional nature of the diplomatic profession and how a diplomatic career fits within the state bureaucracy. The Argentine institutional fabric is highly indebted to the diplomatic career and its leadership.

1218 **De militares a policías: la "guerra contra las drogas" y la militarización de Argentina.** Edición de Juan Gabriel Tokatlian, Marcelo Fabián Sain y Germán Montenegro. Buenos Aires: Capital Intelectual, 2018. 278 p.: bibl. (Claves del siglo XXI)

This book advances a critical analysis of the state's position on illegal drugs and the relationship with the armed forces in Latin America, in general, and in Argentina, in particular. The work examines the policies implemented during the so-called "war on drugs" and their impact on the role of the military in the context of Latin American democracies from the Cold War to 2018. The book is divided into three chapters, titled "The United States and the Militarization of the Drug Phenomenon in Latin America," by Juan Gabriel Tokatlian; "The Armed Forces and the 'War on Drugs' in Argentina (2011–2018)," by Marcelo Fabián Sain; and "Antecedents, Strategies, and Forms of Intervention by the DEA," by

Germán Montenegro. A brief two-page conclusion highlights the significance of the three-chapter work. Although these three chapters are independent and self-standing, they share common threads: first, the fight against illicit drugs and, second, the role of the military in carrying out the task. The first aspect is central in inter-American relations, despite the repeated failures of the strategies deployed during the anti-drug crusade in the region. The second is paramount for designing public and institutional policies in Latin America, particularly after the advent of democracy in the region in the mid-1980s and early 1990s.

1219 García, Marcelo. La agente nazi Eva Perón y el tesoro de Hitler: los archivos desclasificados del FBI de Hoover: la trama de acuerdos y traiciones entre la Alemania nazi y la Argentina de Juan Domingo Perón. Buenos Aires: Sudamericana, 2017. 334 p.: bibl., ill.

Historian Marcelo García examines the complex relationship between Juan Domingo Perón, Eva Duarte, and Nazism based on declassified FBI documents from the Hoover era. Nazi Germany's defeat rearranged international politics in the mid-1940s. The author argues that Juan Domingo Perón, encouraged by Hitler's loss of strength and influence, set out to establish Argentina as a leading nation in South America, trying to replicate Germany's expansionist goals in the region. García examines how Perón intended to finance his plans for domination. The author claims that Perón planned to use the vast, looted fortunes that German National Socialists stole and transferred to Buenos Aires. However, Perón's most significant obstacle was his wife, Eva Duarte, who utilized her powerful connections to safeguard the looted German treasures. García's work is based on hundreds of declassified documents—including those from Hoover's FBI investigations. Historian García builds a compelling thesis that connects the unexpected agreements and betrayals between Nazi Germany and Perón's Argentina. The author's impressive research has resulted in a book that explores the mysteries of Peronism from a new perspective: the conflicts of interest between Juan Domingo Perón and his wife, Eva Duarte.

1220 Gianola Otamendi, Alberto. Aires de guerra sobre las aguas de Tierra del Fuego. Buenos Aires: Instituto de Publicaciones Navales, 2018. 182 p.: bibl., ill. (some color). (Colección historia; 60)

The work examines the factors leading up to the Beagle Channel military crisis between Argentina and Chile in December 1978. The highly descriptive narrative work is based on secondary and primary sources, including academic articles, journalistic accounts, and multiple interviews of participants in the crisis. The author discusses Argentina's military plans and preparations, defensive and offensive schemes, and the mobilization and deployment of the branches of the Argentine navy stationed in Tierra del Fuego. The book also briefly describes the Chilean navy and army preparations and deployment in the disputed territory. According to the author, the actions of the Argentine navy during the Beagle crisis of 1978 set a precedent for organization and joint action to take advantage of the experience gained and lessons learned by the Argentine military. Also, he affirms that the mobilization and deployment in Tierra del Fuego prepared the Argentine navy for its subsequent participation in the Falkland/Malvinas War of April 1982. Thus, the experience gained ultimately influenced the Argentine armed forces' confrontation with British forces.

1221 González, Julio C. Desde la Patagonia hacia Hispanoamérica unida: a propósito del libro de Juan Domingo Perón *Toponimia patagónica de etimología araucana y lo acaecido con el territorio patagónico*. Buenos Aires: Editorial Docencia, 2016. 508 p.: bibl., ill. (Obras selectas; 6) (Biblioteca testimonial del Bicentenario)

The author engages in an intensive analysis of the 1950 book by Juan Domingo Perón, *Toponimia patagónica de etimología araucana*. After a critical introduction, he discusses Argentina's economic and juridical structures from the 16th century to present day. Chapter 2 opens with a toponymic and etymological analysis of concepts and names that appear in Perón's book. Chapter 3 engages in an intensive anthropological discussion of Perón's lineage. The book finally arrives at its primary purpose in chapter 6. Here the reader discovers that the author aims to examine the industrial history of Patagonia. The highly detailed narrative examines the following topics: agreements between Argentina and the People's Republic of China; Argentina's economic and military links with Russia; the long march to the BRICS's destiny; and an epilogue that offers a wealth of information and data. In addition to being a reference source, this book serves many purposes from a historical and linguistic perspective, ranging from a contemporary analysis of Argentina's economic relations to an exploration of the Patagonia region.

1222 Gregorio-Cernadas, Maximiliano.
Una épica de la paz: la política de seguridad externa de Alfonsín. Buenos Aires: Eudeba, 2016. 797 p.: bibl. (Hecho y por hacer)

President Raúl Alfonsín ushered in the transition to democratic governance in Argentina after the collapse of the military dictatorship in 1982. He was the first democratic president in Argentina's modern democracy. He served as president from 1983 to 1989. Forty years later, the figure of President Alfonsín continues to exalt, prompting routine demonstrations of widespread affection based on his ethical contribution as a respectable politician, the father of modern Argentine democracy, and world champion of human rights. However, as the author Gregorio-Cernadas notes, little or nothing is known about another of President Alfonsín's contributions on an international level: his tireless efforts for Argentina to combine the extraordinary technological advances prior to 1983 with a new and powerful commitment to peace, disarmament, and world security. This book fills that void with an exciting story enhanced with original and primary sources. A wealth of unpublished information, entertaining and painstaking prose, and a mixture of genres—presidential biography, contemporary history, investigative journalism, diplomatic memory, political science essay, and international intrigue novel—come together in *Una épica de la paz*. Gregorio-Cernadas was, as a young diplomat, witness to the events described in this book. He immerses us in the complex personality of President Alfonsín who confronted multiple and simultaneous challenges—political, technological, and ethical. With this work, the author deepens our understanding of this contemporary Argentine president and the recent history of Argentina, the region, and the world.

1223 Morgenfeld, Leandro Ariel. Bienvenido Mr. President: de Roosevelt a Trump, las visitas de presidentes estadounidenses a la Argentina. Prólogos de Cecilia Nahón y Max Paul Friedman. Buenos Aires: Octubre Editorial, 2018. 385 p.: bibl.

The book analyzes the visits to Argentina by seven US presidents from the 1930s to 2018. From President Franklin D. Roosevelt's visit in 1936 to President Donald Trump's within the framework of the G20 Summit in Buenos Aires, these presidential visits comprised different agendas and degrees of complexity. Leandro Morgenfeld aims to identify and explain the ruptures and continuities in the historically tense bilateral relationship between Argentina and the US by analyzing the presidential visits and other notable US political personalities. The author discusses different national political experiments in Argentina as reflected in the bilateral link and considers how an unstable and ambivalent Argentine domestic policy has traditionally guided the partnership with the US. Indeed, the study of this relationship suggests alternative perspectives to address specific trajectories of Argentina's national history, the projection of its actors, and how they were conditioned by the dense network constituting various actors who participated in the Argentine-American relationship. The author establishes the notion of the "Yankee Pan-American" line versus the Argentine universalist line. He examines, first, US intentions in the Southern Cone and its perennial insistence on consolidating an economic and military alliance with Argentina. These objectives intensified in the post-WWII period and after the collapse of the Soviet Union. All the presidential visits prompted public protests, allowing the author to confirm that the protests were not just a sporadic or isolated anti-imperialist reaction. These public reactions to US presidential visits suggest a permanent modality of popular intervention that facilitates analyzing modalities of collective action in Argentina.

BOLIVIA

1224 **Alcázar Chávez, Luis Fernando.** El problema marítimo. Vol. 1, Los escenarios del despojo, 1842–1904. Bolivia: Imprenta "Beonova Gráficos", 2016. 1 v.: bibl., ill. (Enciclopedia del problema marítimo; 1)

This book is the first of two volumes dedicated to examining the maritime dispute between Bolivia and Chile from 1842 until 1904. It provides extensive historical evidence of the diplomatic clashes between these two Andean states over their litoral in the Pacific Ocean. According to the author, this volume aims to detail all 29 wasted opportunities that could have been instrumental in resolving the maritime problem peacefully. The author is highly critical of Chile's apparent lack of serious commitment to resolving the maritime problem. The author favors Bolivia's position. He argues that had Chile been fully committed, the bilateral issue would have been resolved over a century ago to the satisfaction of Bolivia. Alcázar Chávez discusses what he terms Chile's "strategy of interests." These consist of Chile's noncommittal diplomatic approach: a willingness to negotiate only when danger or threats loomed ominously over its national interests; then, when normalcy returns in the bilateral relations, reverting to a position of indifference, retraction, ignorance, and ultimately threats. According to the author, Chile's approach has prevailed for more than a century, preventing a solution to the maritime problem. For comment on Vol. 2, see item **1225**.

1225 **Alcázar Chávez, Luis Fernando.** El problema marítimo. Vol. 2, Los escenarios de la "Fuerza de la Razón," 1905–2016. Bolivia: Imprenta "Beonova Gráficos", 2016. 1 v.: bibl., ill. (Enciclopedia del problema marítimo; 2)

This book is the second of a two-volume work dedicated to examining the maritime dispute between Bolivia and Chile from 1905 until 2016. Again, the author's argument linking these two volumes is that Chile has behaved irresponsibly and has been uncommitted to ending the maritime problem between these Andeans nations in a peaceful and just manner. The author poses the following question: Was Chile not ready to engage in conversations and negotiations to resolve the maritime problem? In this work, Alcázar Chávez argues that, while Chile appeared ready to negotiate a solution to the problem, it never truly was amenable to finding a just, sound, and lasting solution to the problem. Thus, the author asks rhetorically: What is the use and purpose of diplomatic conversations in the absence of the Chilean will to negotiate a just and lasting solution? Accordingly, this work examines 111 years of continuous and failed attempts to negotiate a reasonable solution to the maritime problem. It is evident that the author squarely blames Chile for the failure, irrespective of the ideological projection of the government in Santiago. For comment on Vol. 1, see item **1224**.

1226 **Sánchez, Gabriel.** Regulación de conflictos: el enfoque de UNASUR en la intervención de Pando. Buenos Aires: UAI Editorial: Teseo, 2015. 213 p.: bibl. (Colección UAI—Investigación. Tesis)

The rise of minor and internal conflicts in the last 20 years reveals that, together with the end of the Cold War, the conception of conventional warfare needs to be revised. Confrontations between states have been replaced by intrastate disputes that respond to deeply rooted and long-term animosities, linked to claims for the collective rights of identity groups. These conflicts have consequences that cross borders, creating international disputes and regional instability. With increasing numbers of disputes, conflict regulation has arisen as a complementary discipline for international relations. In response to the acts of violence in the department of Pando (Bolivia) in September 2008, UNASUR intervened to prevent an extreme radicalization of the confrontation. The author analyzes

UNASUR reports concerning those events to explain what type of conflict regulation (management, resolution, or transformation of conflicts) was used in the Pando case.

CHILE

Alcázar Chávez, Luis Fernando. El problema marítimo. See item **1224**.

1227 América Latina y Chile en el mundo global: algunas tendencias en el siglo XXI. Edición de Raúl Allard Neumann y Manfred Wilhelmy von Wolff. Valparaíso, Chile: Ediciones Universitarias de Valparaíso, Pontificia Universidad Católica de Valparaíso, 2017. 415 p.: bibl., ill.

The editors of this volume provide 15 essays analyzing the behavior of Latin America and Chile in global politics. The first six chapters cover questions ranging from the politics of international law in times of crisis, Latin America's discomfort with globalization, to the Colombian peace process. The second part focuses on international political-economic topics and the role of nontraditional international actors. Specifically, the essays examine strategic scenarios in the Asian Pacific region, Latin America, and Chile, describe relative investment differences among foreign investors and state investments, and provide a critical analysis of the situation of Latin America circa 2017. The third part centers on diplomatic dimensions, culture, communications, and technology. The four chapters comprising this part analyze topics such as the role of Chile in the global world, cyberdiplomacy, and the role of big data in international relations. The idea for this excellent volume stems from critical reflections on the progress of the international system based on the work of students and professors of the MA program in international relations at the Pontificia Universidad Católica de Valparaíso. The sources for this volume are interdisciplinary, predominantly from the discipline of international relations. The volume proposes a different perspective on international relations in the post-Cold War era and the process of open globalization. This new approach views the rapprochement of economies and the globalization of markets as fundamental characteristics of international economic relations, while considering how to politically inject increasing degrees of progressive governance into the process of globalization. Despite the absence of a world government, this volume assumes the possibility of a global community trying to reckon with an increasingly complex international order and an ever-larger number of new actors interacting with traditional ones.

1228 Bustos, Carlos. Diplomacia chilena: una perspectiva histórica. Santiago: RiL Editores, 2018. 633 p.: bibl.

Reminiscing about his visit to the Blenheim Palace, Winston Churchill's birthplace in the UK, the author reflects on a Spanish inscription on the palace's coat of arms that is affixed to the front doors. It is a motto, referring to Prime Minister Churchill, that reads, "loyal but unfortunate." Bustos claims the message may accurately describe Chile's diplomatic corps for over two centuries. In this work, the author exalts the heroics of Chile's diplomats and recognizes their exemplary and patriotic work. The author offers an in-depth historical study of Chilean diplomacy that spans from independence to the present day. The volume focuses mainly on Chile's diplomatic relations with its closest regional neighbors. The volume also emphasizes the contributions of Chilean diplomacy in areas as diverse as the codification of international law, law of the sea, aeronautics and space, disarmament, environment, decolonization, human rights, nuclear nonproliferation, and the peaceful use of nuclear energy, among other topics.

1229 Gutiérrez Tapia, Cristian. La contrasubversión como política: la doctrina de guerra revolucionaria francesa y su impacto en las FF.AA. de Chile y Argentina. Santiago: LOM Ediciones, 2018. 141 p.: bibl., ill. (Historia)

Imbued with the atmosphere of the Cold War, the Latin American armed forces began early (at the end of the 1950s) to become familiar with the new ways that military and, above all, political conflicts would manifest themselves. Thus, the experiences of France in Indochina and Algeria, or that of the US in Vietnam, were internalized as eminently political battles, where the decisive factor was no longer technological or human superiority on the battlefield. However, the civilian population and other internal political actors became the preponderant force that would ultimately lead to the defeat of well-armed and trained regular armies. This experience transformed the military mission and training from external confrontations toward internal and national threats. The book examines Argentina's and Chile's military schooling and training thoroughly.

1230 McPherson, Alan L. Ghosts of Sheridan Circle: how a Washington assassination brought Pinochet's terror state to justice. Chapel Hill: The University of North Carolina Press, 2019. 382 p.: bibl., ill., index.

This book examines the role of the Dirección de Inteligencia Nacional or DINA, Chile's secret police during the dictatorship of Augusto Pinochet, in the murder of Orlando Letelier, the former Chilean ambassador to the US under President Allende, and his colleague Ronni Moffitt, on 21 September 1976. They were assassinated with a car bomb in Sheridan Circle, in the heart of Washington, DC. It shocked the Washington establishment and the world and put the US government in a highly uncomfortable and embarrassing position. Augusto Pinochet was a close political ally of the US at the height of the Cold War. It appeared that Washington failed to warn him against assassinating Letelier and hesitated to blame him afterward, and it was a heinous political crime that could not be swept under the rug. Despite heavy foot-dragging by the US government, the murder investigation began thanks to public and international pressure, and the tenacity of Letelier's widow and her allies. After two decades, the killers were identified and a link to Pinochet's DINA was established. This book questions if justice was attainable. Interviews from three continents, never-before-used documents, and recently declassified sources conclude that Pinochet himself ordered the hit and then covered it up. Alan McPherson has produced the definitive history of one of the Cold War's most consequential assassinations. According to the author, the Letelier car bomb forever changed counterterrorism, human rights, and democracy. This page-turning, real-life political thriller combines a police investigation, diplomatic intrigue, courtroom drama, and survivors' tales of sorrow and tenacity.

1231 Olivares Dysli, Luis Benjamín. La paz en 1978: el pueblo de Chile y su ejército. Segunda edición. Santiago: Luís Benjamín Olivares Dysli, 2018. 710 p.: bibl., ill.

The historical narrative addresses aspects of the Beagle Channel dispute between Argentina and Chile in 1978. This book examines an unprecedented perspective. The author contends that previous historiography of the crisis has focused mainly on the presidential and diplomatic levels. That focus ignores the critical role played by the people of Chile; the national structure (state, municipal and private institutions); the distribution of population; participatory organizations; and interactive actions—such as the national mobilization that summoned 1,027,661 Chileans to form a new land force or a second army (the largest in the history of Chile), a vital part of the Carabineros de Chile—the Red Cross, a member of war hospitals; the Rodeo Clubs; and huasos and campesinos organized by combat. These were critical actors that previous historical studies of the 1978 crisis failed to examine. This work narrates the reaction of the Chilean people and its army and the path to regional peace. The study also discusses critical military events between January 1978 and January 1979. In sum, the work provides essential information that has previously escaped the attention of military historians, journalists, politicians, and the general public.

1232 Selección de *Realidad y Perspectivas*. Dirección de José Rodríguez Elizondo. Edición de Sergio Cortés Beltrán, Sebastián Flores Díaz y Matías Letelier Eltit. Santiago: RIL Editores, 2017. 359 p.

This book is a selection of articles published in the Chilean journal *Realidad y Perspectivas*. The journal focuses on regional questions, domestic-level issues in Latin American countries, and some global or international issues. Director José Rodríguez Elizondo and the three editors made excellent choices when selecting articles for this work. The first part focuses on articles from special issues of the journal. The topics covered include the Malvinas question and Bolivian-Chilean bilateral relations. The second part is a selection of articles by invited columnists. The articles explore Latin America and Europe, Chilean strategy, world order, and domestic issues in countries like Argentina, Bolivia, Cuba, and Peru. The third part combines multiple authors' postscripts, short notes, and rejoinders. These postscripts include topics from corruption in Central America to issues in Venezuela. The next five chapters are titled: Questions for Individuals; Notes on Strategy and Grand Strategy; Original Articles Published in the Journal; Research Notes on Various Books; and Reviews of Films.

COLOMBIA

1233 Estado y perspectivas de las relaciones colombo-brasileñas. Edición de Daniel Flemes, Eduardo Pastrana Buelvas y Mariana Carpes. Bogotá: Pontificia Universidad Javeriana Bogotá; Germany: Konrad Adenauer Center for International Relations and Security Studies; Rio de Janeiro: Escola de Comando e Estado-Maior do Exército; Hamburg, Germany: GIGA German Institute of Global and Area Studies, 2017. 368 p.: bibl., ill.

The editors of this book contend that among all the Latin American states, Brazil and Colombia have the greatest potential to influence the political, economic, and social future of South America. At the time of the writing and publication of this work, Brazil was experiencing a profound internal crisis affecting the country's socioeconomic and political spheres. According to the editors, the concurrence of Brazil's internal situation and the resolution of Colombia's internal conflict has generated a more balanced or symmetrical relationship between the two state actors. The book examines the state and future prospects of Colombian-Brazilian relations based on a research project carried out by academics from the Pontificia Universidad Javeriana, the German Institute of Global and Area Studies, and the Escola de Comando e Estado Maior do Exército. The work shows how the projection of regional power in Brazil from the 1990s onward influenced its relations with Colombia. The essays explore the cooperative and competitive factors of Colombian-Brazilian relations and attempt to project the trajectory of the bilateral relations and the potential influence on the region's future. Following an introduction, the 12 chapters are organized into five sections: security, economic relations, Colombia's internal conflict, geographical parameters, and the effect of the great powers on the bilateral relations.

1234 Fronteras: fuentes de conflicto y cooperación. Edición de Luis Fernando Trejos Rosero. Textos de Angélica Rodríguez Rodríguez et al. Barranquilla, Colombia: Universidad del Norte Editorial; Bogotá: Grupo Editorial Ibañez, 2016. 170 p.: bibl., ill.

This set of collected essays by members of the International Agenda Research Group of the Universidad del Norte explores aspects of international borders. The book also includes studies from academics affiliated with other research groups who study the question of "internal borders." Most of the essays use elements of political-cultural regional geography and critical geopolitics. Avoiding the classic, state-centric vision, the guiding thread of this work is an interpretation of borders as a space through which sociospatial differences communicate, interact, and develop. The first part of the work, Colombian Borders, comprises four works that approach, from different perspectives, trade and binational integration, security, public policies, and the history of the country. The second part, Frontiers of the World, includes two chapters on new threats, specifically drug trafficking and its impact on the security agenda and redrawing borders in the Middle East.

1235 Montoya Ruiz, Sandra. Política exterior y diplomacia cultural: hacia Colombia en posconflicto. Bogotá: Universidad

Católica de Colombia, 2017. 331 p.: bibl. (Colección Jus público; 19)

This monograph studies the role of cultural diplomacy in Colombia's foreign policy formulation and implementation. The author believes that cultural diplomacy is fundamental for Colombia today, helping to make the country better known and strengthening ties with other countries. Further, emphasizing Colombia's internal cultural strength provides greater foreign policy coherence. The author contends that cultural strength endured during the long-running armed conflict and continues to regenerate and revitalize the country. Thus, studying Colombia's successful cultural diplomacy can be beneficial for the international community. In the first chapter, the author examines the theoretical foundations of deep cultural diplomacy from a constructive vantage point; in the second, the analysis focuses on foreign policies in the 21st century; in the third, it addresses the relationship between Colombia's foreign policy and cultural diplomacy; in the fourth, it examines Colombia's international role in the aftermath of the internal armed conflict; and, in the fifth, the book closes with the author's reflections and conclusions about Colombia's future.

1236 Zamora, Edgar. La "política exterior" de Bogotá en el siglo XXI: agenda política e institucionalidad para la internacionalización (2001–2013). Quito: Universidad Andina Simón Bolívar Ecuador: Corporación Editora Nacional, 2015. 96 p.: bibl., ill. (Serie Magíster; 197)

Based on an MA thesis, this work contends that while international phenomena have been treated as the almost exclusive problem of national states, multiple international transformations (i.e., economic, political, social, cultural) at the end of the 20th century resulted in changes to the theoretical focus of the discipline of international relations. The author argues that the range of relevant actors for the discipline expanded beyond the nation-state to subnational, local or regional, and even private actors. Thus, the author argues, IR theories must include these significant actors. The book discusses noncentral governments as international actors and the possibility that they develop a kind of "local state foreign policy" that does not challenge the central government, and distances itself from simple ad hoc international participation. The work looks at the case of Santafé de Bogotá DC (2001–2013), based on two variables: political agenda and institutionalization for internationalization, and applies a discrete quantification model to the level of the international participation that the city reached as a significant international actor, parallel to the Colombian state. The results indicate the growing importance of the para-diplomatic activities of these nonstate actors in the international system. This short monograph includes two chapters, bookended by an introduction and a conclusion. The first chapter focuses on the theoretical framework and methodology, and the second offers the case study on Santafé de Bogotá. The author emphasizes that, given their paradiplomatic behavior, subnational actors should be incorporated into the study of world politics and international relations.

1237 Zárate Botía, Carlos Gilberto et al.
Perfil de una región transfronteriza en la Amazonia: la posible integración de las políticas de frontera de Brasil, Colombia y Perú. Leticia, Colombia: Universidad Nacional de Colombia, 2017. 291 p.: bibl., color ill., maps. (Colección Nación)

This book examines the complex dynamics of the border region comprising Brazil, Colombia, and Peru. It is not simply an ad hoc narrative, or a portrait and a map. Instead, the work aims to advance the research tools, theoretical framework, and methodology needed to promote regional visualization, recognition, and positioning in the international context. The authors and co-authors of this book contend that in recent years there has been a significant increase in the number of speeches, announcements, laws, and adaptations of existing laws to encourage regional integration in an uncertain global context. Notwithstanding these efforts, there has been little progress. The authors blame the lack of progress in regional integration on public and academic ignorance of the complex reality of border regions and the lack of executable proposals to support and advance regional integration, particularly at the boundaries of contiguous countries in South America, like Brazil, Colombia, and Peru. This excellent multidisciplinary work aims to address this current lack of understanding by bringing together sociologists, demographers, anthropologists, political scientists, and international relations experts. The five chapters cover towns and peoples on the borders of Brazil, Colombia, and Peru; the economic profiles of the border regions of the three countries; environmental policies and natural resources in the trilateral border region; customs policies in the border region; and the public policies addressing the integration of the tri-state border region.

ECUADOR

1238 Carrión Mena, Francisco. Ecuador: entre la inserción y el aislamiento: política exterior, 2000–2015. Quito: FLASCO Ecuador: Universidad Central del Ecuador: Esquel, 2017. 346 p.: bibl., index.

This monograph examines Ecuador's role in the international context since 1995. The author explores how the 1995 peace treaty with Peru; the transformation of Ecuador's economic, political, social, and institutional structures; and the prevalence of radically different international scenarios dating back to the late 20th century impacted the country. The author focuses on Ecuador's foreign policy objectives and strategies and their implementation in contemporary history. Ecuador's foreign relations during the past seven years were deeply influenced by internal political instability caused by four presidential changes. The author assesses whether the country has managed to insert itself into a globalized world or if it has remained isolated from the global context. Specifically, the author looks at whether the peace agreements with Peru enabled Ecuador to act more freely in the international arena. The book encourages further discussion of the impact of the international environment on Ecuador's internal political-economic conditions.

1239 Luna Osorio, Luis. Las relaciones económicas del Ecuador y Colombia. Quito: Centro Andino de Estudios Internacionales, Universidad Andina Simón Bolívar, Ecuador: Corporación Editora Nacional, 2016. 228 p.: bibl. (Serie Estudios Internacionales; 12)

Historically, Ecuador and Colombia have maintained an excellent friendship that has allowed their shared border to remain open at the Rumichaca Bridge, the border site through which most of the binational trade circulates. This book exhaustively analyzes the economic and social ties of the two countries with an overview of the primary data and indicators of each one, focusing on the main binational problems of recent years. The work addresses legal and institutional frameworks and the foreign policies of Colombia and Ecuador, highlighting their evolution, and plans for regional integration. Finally, the monograph presents the conclusions of the analysis with recommendations for better binational cooperation, and bilateral integration with the rest of the world.

1240 Lyko Marczak, Halina; Anibal Robayo Lemarie; and **María Belén Wong.** Comercio exterior entre Ecuador y los mercados de países de Europa del Este: Bulgaria, Eslovaquia, Hungría, Polonia, República Checa, Rumania (miembros de la Unión Europea, período 2007–2016). Quito: Centro de Publicaciones Pontificia Universidad Católica del Ecuador, 2018. 299 p.: bibl., color ill., color maps.

This book explores Ecuador's trade perspectives and relations with several Eastern European countries: Bulgaria, Slovakia, Hungary, Poland, Czech Republic, and Romania. This work's methodology is quantitative and qualitative. It uses primary and secondary sources, such as direct observations, interviews, analyses of economic indicators published by the Central Bank of Ecuador during the 2007–2014 period, and trade agreements, as well as articles from academic journals. The analysis includes data from the current and applicable official regulations of Ecuador's Ministerio de Relaciones Exteriores y Movilidad Humana. The results demonstrate that the Ecuadorian economy is complementary to the economies of the Eastern European countries and that foreign trade volume between Ecuador and those countries is still incipient, with the potential for expansion in the coming years. Thus, the findings reveal many options for improving and diversifying Ecuador's trade relations with Eastern Europe.

1241 Negociación de paz, escenarios para el desarrollo y la integración fronteriza Ecuador-Colombia. Coordinación de Daniel Pontón. Quito: Instituto de Altos Estudios Nacionales, Universidad de Posgrado del Estado, 2016. 186 p.: bibl., ill. (some color). (Colección Editorial Informes de investigación; 6)

From a theoretical-conceptual perspective, this book highlights the historical complexities of the peace process in Colombia and its impact on Ecuador. With special concern for the Ecuador-Colombia Border Integration Zone, the author reviews the region's social, political, economic, and geopolitical dynamics. The work includes eight chapters, bookended by an introduction (chapter 1) and a conclusion (chapter 10). Chapter 2 examines methodological processes and chapter 3 reviews the theoretical considerations. Chapter 4 considers alternative diagnoses of the peace process. Chapter 5 analyzes the historical junctures within which the peace process in Colombia evolved. Chapter 6 explores the construction of future scenarios for 2022. Chapter 7 is an analysis of the possible effects of the Colombian conflict on the planning process. Chapter 8 centers on political advice on the process. Chapter 9 analyzes the possible effects of signing the peace process on the binational plan for border integration between Colombia and Ecuador.

1242 Salgado Espinoza, Raúl. Small builds big: how Ecuador and Uruguay contributed to the construction of UNASUR. Quito: FLACSO, 2017. 218 p.: bibl., ill. (Serie Atrio)

This investigation introduces an innovative model for studying the role of small states in regional organizations. It defines small states as region-engaging, region-constraining, or region-adapting actors, depending on their particular type of engagement in regional politics. This model defines Ecuador and Uruguay as region-engaging small states and argues that elements of a shared collective identity are a major factor of influence on the region-engaging character of Ecuador and Uruguay in the construction of the Union of South American Nations (UNASUR). The study employs a constructivist approach to exploring why these states have supported the creation and consolidation of UNASUR. It takes a cross-case-oriented approach based on the analysis of documents, political speeches, and semistructured interviews, while also considering various historical events from 2000 to 2012. Each case study delves into various historical events to provide specific foci on elements of a shared collective identity, left-oriented ideology, the failure of economic integration projects, the overpowering influence of exterior agents, the need for national and regional peace, as well as the prospect of leading roles and a new type of political cooperation. A significant component of the research concerns the elements of a shared South American identity. The comparison facilitates an understanding of the aspects of identity influencing the behavior of Ecuador and Uruguay in the consolidation of UNASUR.

PERU

1243 Curay Ferrer, José Joshua. Los intereses nacionales de la República de Corea y su relación con el Perú. Lima: Fondo Editorial Cultura Peruana, 2018. 184 p.: bibl., color ill.

This theoretically sophisticated book analyzes South Korean relations with Peru from the point of view of a high-ranking Peruvian diplomat. In the first chapter, the author underscores the importance of South Korea in the international system and, specifically, for Peru. In the second chapter, the author discusses the historical development of South Korea as an independent state. The first two chapters offer more an analysis of South Korea itself than of South America's international relations. However, this focus changes drastically in the third chapter, in which the author analyzes the bilateral relations between South Korea and Peru.

1244 Rubio Correa, Jorge Félix. Las negociaciones políticas en el Tratado de Libre Comercio del Perú con los Estados Unidos. Lima: FADP Fundación Academia Diplomática del Perú, 2016. 278 p.: bibl. (Colección Negociación internacional; 1)

This book praises the Peruvian diplomatic corps for their capacity, quality, and ingenuity in successfully negotiating the free trade agreement with the US. According to the author, they accomplished this feat amid a complicated and changing political context where different visions of the world and divergent interests confronted each other. The author stresses that reaching a free trade agreement with the US was one of the first expressions of a national state policy. He also argues that this was a political accomplishment that transcended the temporality of governments and projected an image of a stable, predictable country. The author describes efforts by officials and private businesspeople over two consecutive Peruvian administrations to overcome obstacles that arose from the first signing to the approval of the FTA by the US Congress. This occurred amid the political uncertainty of the 2006 elections in Peru and the midterm elections in the US Congress, which meant a defeat for the Republicans and political control of Congress by the Democratic Party. The latter was less committed to the bilateral free trade agreement with Peru. In sum, gaining the approval of the free trade agreement with the US was an outstanding achievement of Peruvian foreign policy. This book describes this achievement.

1245 Wu Brading, Celia. Diplomacia y cañones en la Guerra del Pacífico: testimonios británicos de la ocupación de Lima, enero de 1881. Lima: BNP Biblioteca Nacional del Perú, 2016. 224 p.: bibl., ill. (Colección La calandria de fuego)

This short monograph constitutes a highly focused and intensive historical analysis of Chile's occupación de Lima in 1881. This occupation was central to Peru's ultimate defeat at the hand of Chile in the War of the Pacific, 1879–84. In four chapters, the author presents and analyzes testimonies by British naval officers and military observers of the war. It is a rich historical analysis that adds direct evidence of how the British viewed the war and assessed its progress.

Zárate Botía, Carlos Gilberto et al. Perfil de una región transfronteriza en la Amazonia: la posible integración de las políticas de frontera de Brasil, Colombia y Perú. See item **1237**.

VENEZUELA

1246 Salcedo Ávila, Gustavo Enrique.
Venezuela, campo de batalla de la Guerra Fría: los Estados Unidos y la era de Rómulo Betancourt (1958–1964). Caracas: Academia Nacional de la Historia: Fundación Bancaribe para la Ciencia y la Cultura, 2017. 294 p.: bibl. (Colección Premio Rafael María Baralt)

This work examines Venezuelan and US relations during a short but critical stretch of the Latin American Cold War. Historian Gustavo Salcedo Ávila argues that US fears regarding continental security were focused on Venezuela. The work draws on research in the John F. Kennedy Presidential Library, the archive of the Ministerio del Poder Popular para Relaciones Exteriores (Venezuelan Ministry of Foreign Affairs), and the archive of the Rómulo Betancourt Foundation, as well as press releases, declassified US Department of State and CIA documents, and six interviews with Venezuelan policymakers. The author presents Venezuela as one of Latin America's main battlefields of the Cold War. Chapter 1 provides historical background that explains why 1958 was a significant turning point. Chapter 2 addresses a moment of transition in Venezuela and Latin America. Chapter 3 deals with the significant disagreements and mistrust between Venezuela and the US, in part regarding the sensitive oil issue. In chapter 4, Salcedo describes "the slow road to trust," in which two issues were fundamental: the president's clash with the communists and Venezuela's collaboration in confronting Cuban "radicalism." The beginnings of a "special relationship" between Presidents Kennedy and Betancourt are the focus of chapter 5.

As the author points out, there was a "powerful empathy" between the Venezuelan and his American counterpart. Chapter 6 covers the the bilateral relationship of the US with Venezuela during 1963. In short, *Venezuela, campo de batalla* constitutes an approach to a crucial moment in Venezuelan and hemispheric history that, according to the author, is still valid and has a robust impact on the present.

POLITICAL ECONOMY

GENERAL

JONATHAN HISKEY, *Professor of Political Science, Vanderbilt University*

REFLECTING THE PERSISTENT and pernicious challenges confronted by governments and citizens across the Americas over the first two decades of the 21st century, the works reviewed for this volume address a range of issues and themes that continue to plague both the political and economic development processes of the region. Notable among these emerging topics for scholars of Latin America's political economy are the destabilizing role that crime and violence play in efforts to achieve sustainable economic growth; the myriad implications of the informal sector for both labor and capital; the political and economic consequences of migration; and, continuing a recent trend, the ongoing and increasing Chinese presence in the region. Alongside these relatively new lines of political economy research, we also find longstanding topics of inquiry such as Latin America's role in the global economy, the proliferation of post-neoliberal development strategies across the region, work on the drivers and impact of social and redistributive policies, and, lastly, the oft-researched question of the role of the economy in the decision calculus of voters. Taken together, these themes and strands of investigation represent the state of political economy research on the region as scholars move beyond a singular focus on the implementation and impact of the neoliberal model.

Though attention to the neoliberal era has waned in recent years, interest in development strategies and state-building has remained strong among scholars of Latin America's political economy. A fairly new element to this longstanding interest in macroeconomic development trends across the Americas is greater attention to the features of these development paradigms that were conducive to the construction of an effective state. Centeno and Ferraro's volume (item **1281**) on Latin American and Spanish development processes during the rise and fall of the state-led development strategy, alongside Pérez Caldentey and Vernengo's nod to Acemoglu and Robinson's 2012 *Why Nations Fail*, entitled *Why Latin American Nations Fail* (item **1283**), both represent an effort to re-examine the era of state-led development and assess its long-term impact on the development trajectories of countries across the region, as well as the quality and effectiveness of state institutions that emerged during that period. Works from Orihuela (item **1274**), Montero and Chapple (item **1276**), Martins (item **1269**), and Kingstone (item **1267**) provide a range of useful perspectives on these questions, looking back at the legacies of the developmental state models that prevailed across the region during the second half of the 20th century, and an assessment of the neoliberal and post-neoliberal models that have been implemented since the 1980s.

Works with a more explicit focus on the post-neoliberal era include those of Etchemendy (item **1257**), who examines the emergence of "segmented neocorporatism" in Argentina and Uruguay, alongside studies by Foxley and Stallings (item **1266**) and Medina Garzón (item **1270**) that offer regional comparisons of development innovations and responses to economic crisis across the countries of Latin America and East Asia. Finally, the article by Garfias (item **1260**) offers a fine example of growing efforts to understand the sources of state capacity through the lens of historical analysis, in this case, using archival data from Mexico's postrevolutionary period. Similarly, Schenoni's study (item **1279**) offers an insightful look at the role that winning or losing an international conflict plays in the state-building process through an analysis of historical data across Latin America between 1865 and 1913, assessing the impact of such interstate conflicts as the Paraguayan War, the War of the Pacific, and the War of Reunification on subsequent state capacity levels. Taken together, these works represent a significant step forward in our attempts to understand the legacies of past development models and state-building efforts as well as more recent development strategies being pursued by certain countries across the region.

As noted, what most distinguishes the body of works reviewed for this volume is the greater attention paid to specific policy and societal challenges that many countries in the region confront in their efforts to achieve sustained economic development. First and foremost among these challenges is the high level of crime and violence that continues to plague much of the region. Further, the emergence of new intraregional migration flows, in particular the significant exodus of Venezuelans in recent years, and the persistence of the substantial informal economies in many countries also represent issues for which policymakers across the region seek answers. The increasing attention such issues are garnering among political economy scholars underscores a trend toward research on the day-to-day, microlevel obstacles faced by Latin American economies and away from (notwithstanding the works discussed above) concerns with the politics of macroeconomic development strategies and models. This trend is also likely a product of the post-neoliberal vacuum that has left the region without a clear paradigmatic development model. Scholars have thus turned their analytical lens toward such issues as crime and migration as essential components of the region's current political economy landscape.

Among the most notable works on the political economy of crime across Latin America is Bergman's *More Money, More Crime* (item **1249**), which offers a comprehensive assessment of the institutional and economic drivers of crime across the region. Nicely complementing this work is the research by Ch et al. (item **1256**) on the local-level fiscal implications of paramilitary and rebel violence in Colombia that highlights the ways in which armed factions, whether criminal or ideological in nature, can fundamentally reshape local and regional fiscal policy processes and outcomes. Similarly, Holland and Rios (item **1264**) provide an innovative assessment of the ways in which a climate of crime and insecurity can alter the fiscal policy preferences of even the business sector in countries such as Mexico. In an edited volume, Paley and Granovsky-Larsen (item **1273**), along with their contributing authors, provide a scathing indictment of the aiding and abetting of Latin America's high levels of crime and violence that come from vested business and political interests with much to gain from the many incidents of organized violence and crime across the region. Other chapters in this collection explore how specific economic entities such as multinational corporations use repression and the criminalization of resistance as a means to gain access to coveted lands and resources. This work provides an important perspective on the sources and implications of crime and violence that moves us beyond the more common focus on narcotrafficking groups and gangs as the main purveyors of such activities in the region. In a somewhat similar vein, Sexton, Wellhausen, and Findley (item **1280**) examine the empirical consequences of the inherent fiscal policy tradeoffs that governments must make in a context of high violence and insecurity, finding—not surprisingly—that areas such as health care suffer significantly when spending on security forces increases. Lastly, González (item **1263**) provides an important contribution to this line of work by focusing on the reasons for the many ineffective police forces across the Americas in an effort to better understand why attempts at reforming these institutions so rarely result in improved performance.

Another topic that has received greater attention in recent years concerns a long-standing feature of Latin American economies—the informal sector. Several works reviewed for this volume offer novel and important insight into the workings of the informal economy across the region, the implications for those who work within it, and the forces that serve to push individuals into it. The study by Berens (item **1248**), for example, explores the ways in which poor governance, low levels of institutional trust, and a tattered social safety net push individuals into the informal economy. Turning to the consequences of membership in the informal economy, Altamirano (item **1247**) explores how economic vulnerability, a feature strongly associated with work in the informal sector, undermines individuals' attachments to political parties, highlighting the political consequences of work in the informal sector. These studies offer an encouraging sign of heightened attention to the economic and political implications of the informal sector that plays such a prominent role across many of the economies in the Americas.

In a similar vein, numerous studies reviewed in this section explore the issue of redistributive policy and its impact on poverty and inequality across the region. Several works address the question of the drivers of public support for such policies, including the piece by Borges (item **1252**) that examines, among other issues, crossnational variations in support for redistributive policies among those in lower income brackets. Menéndez González (item **1271**) offers an innovative approach to understanding the sources of support for such policies through the implementation of a survey-based experiment that highlights the role of risk in individual assessments of social policies. More broadly, Boulding and Holzner's work on poverty and political participation in Latin America provides tremendous insight into the ways in which lower-income individuals across the Americas overcome the "participation bias" and engage in substantively important ways in the politics of their respective countries (item **1253**). Turning to the question of the sources of social policy itself, Bonvecchi and Scartascini (item **1251**) provide a comprehensive analysis of the policy-making landscape across Latin America as it pertains to redistributive policy. This study is replete with analyses of the various forces at work in the development and implementation of social policy. Finally, on the consequences of such policies, authors such as Houel and Miller (item **1265**) offer important contributions to our understanding of the ways in which paths out of poverty can influence individual attitudes toward democracy and the degree to which individuals are willing to express support for democratic rule.

Economic voting, or the degree to which the decision calculus of voters is shaped by economic conditions, remains a principal area of research for political economy scholars across the region. Carlin and Hellwig (item **1255**) continue to make significant contributions to this research agenda with their part in a "Scholarly Dialogue," along with Zucco and Campello (item **1286**), that debates the role of global economic forces, rather than purely domestic conditions, in shaping the contours of economic voting in the region. Moving beyond the question of economic voting, Rueda and Ruiz (item **1278**) explore the prospect for electoral accountability when the quality of elections is in question. Such efforts to incorporate the current, quite varied, state of democracy across Latin America into analyses of economic voting and other forms of electoral accountability are surely to increase as the political systems of the region develop along distinct paths.

Finally, two other recent trends in political economy research remain relevant in this volume with work on the economic and political impact of China in Latin America and the myriad economic, political, and social consequences of increased migration flows across the region. Campello and Urdinez (item **1254**) tackle the former question through an analysis of the ways in which voters and politicians have responded to the ups and downs of Chinese trade relations with Brazil in recent years. Wise (item **1284**) also continues to make important contributions to our understanding of the implications of the growing Chinese presence in the region with her assessment of the opportunities gained and lost in the region's varied relations with China in recent years, a topic of ongoing interest for political economy scholars.

Similarly, work on the political economy of migration across the region continues to grow, particularly given the ongoing exodus of Venezuelans and the economic and political implications of one of the largest migration outflows from one country in the past 20 years. Germano's work (item **1261**) on the welfare impact of remittances is an outstanding example of the ways in which research into these questions has progressed in recent years, while Roniger et al. (item **1277**) provide a notable contribution to this line of investigation in their monograph on how the various exile communities that emerged during the authoritarian era of the 1970s have influenced the political and economic dynamics of their home countries over the past several decades.

Nearly all of the works reviewed for this section are part of an exciting, innovative wave of political economy research in Latin America that has moved beyond the period in which scholars understandably were primarily concerned with the causes and consequences of, and variations in, the neoliberal strategy of development. These works represent, in contrast, a desire among scholars to identify and investigate those questions and issues that have persisted throughout the region regardless of the economic paradigm in place. With such efforts, buttressed by novel methodological research strategies, interested observers may find increasing signs that progress is being made in identifying concrete solutions for tackling these seemingly intractable obstacles to sustained economic development in the future.

1247 **Altamirano, Melina.** Economic vulnerability and partisanship in Latin America. (*Lat. Am. Polit. Soc.*, 61:3, Aug. 2019, p. 80–103, bibl., graphs, table)

This study examines the erosion of partisan ties among members of the informal sector across Latin America. Through analysis of survey data across 17 countries, the author finds a strong negative relationship between economic vulnerability/informality, as measured by lack of health insurance, and the lack of ties to a political party. The work highlights the need to better understand the political implications of informal economies and those who work within them across the Americas. This study adds to a small but growing group of works that explicitly focuses on the attitudinal and behavioral profiles of the substantial number of informal sector workers. Given the size of this sector in many of the region's countries, the need for more such work is clearly evident.

1248 **Berens, Sarah.** Opting for exit: informalization, social policy discontent, and lack of good governance. (*Lat. Am. Polit. Soc.*, 62:2, May 2020, p. 1–28, bibl., graphs, tables)

An insightful study of the ways in which a weak and poorly governed welfare system can push individuals into the informal sector through, in part, its impact on individuals' trust in institutions. Through analysis of survey data collected across Latin America and the Caribbean, the author finds individual dissatisfaction with the social safety net, flawed governance institutions, and low levels of trust all are associated with entry into the informal sector.

1249 **Bergman, Marcelo.** More money, more crime: prosperity and rising crime in Latin America. New York, N.Y.: Oxford University Press, 2018. 392 p.: bibl., index.

An important and tremendously rich study on the political economy of crime in Latin America that is replete with a wide range of data, insightful analyses, and an in-depth look at the flawed institutional environments in which crime thrives across many countries in the region. As crime continues to plague the region, works such as this are essential in moving forward our understanding of the causes, consequences, and potential remedies to this issue.

1250 **Boas, Taylor C.; F. Daniel Hidalgo; and Guillermo Toral.** Competence versus priorities: negative electoral responses to education quality in Brazil. (*J. Polit.*, 83:4, Oct. 2021, p. 1417–1431, bibl., graphs, tables)

This study offers an innovative approach to a growing body of research that seeks to expand upon decades of work on economic voting through the assessment of how an array of government services such as public education influence voters' decision-making process. Here the authors employ a field experiment and a regression discontinuity design to evaluate the degree to which the vote choice in Brazil is swayed by the quality of local schools. They find, interestingly, that only among parents do high-quality schools bolster support for the incumbent, while among other voters, higher-quality schools are associated with lower levels of incumbent support.

1251 **Bonvecchi, Alejandro and Carlos Scartascini.** Who decides social policy?: social networks and the political economy of social policy in Latin America and the Caribbean. Washington, D.C.: World Bank Group: IDB, 2020. 158 p.: bibl., color ill. (Latin American development forum)

As part of the Inter-American Development Bank's Latin American Development Forum series, this monograph offers a fine example of the high quality of work done in the IADB in providing resources of use for a wide audience of policymakers and scholars. The volume offers a comprehensive overview and assessment of the political economy of social policy across Latin America as well as detailed case studies of certain countries including Argentina, Bolivia, Trinidad and Tobago, and Bahamas. For anyone interested in the dynamics of social policy-making, the social networks that underlying these processes, and the factors involved in determining the outcome of such policies, this resource is full of insight and provides a wealth of data on social policy in the region.

1252 Borges, Fabián A. It's not me, it's you: self-interest, social affinity, and support for redistribution in Latin America. (*Lat. Am. Polit. Soc.*, 64:3, Aug. 2022, p. 1–36, bibl., graphs, tables)

This study tackles the important and oft-studied question of who supports redistributive policies and why. What makes this article stand out is its attention to the multiple levels of influence that are at play in shaping the public's preferences for such policies across the regions. Analyzing a significant quantity of survey data across the 18 Latin American countries, the author finds that the extent and depth of cultural divisions within a country influence the degree to which the public, particularly those in low-income brackets, support redistribution. In countries that are relatively homogenous, the poor tend to support redistributive policies, but in countries that are more diverse, the author finds that this support among low-income individuals is lower. This useful study contributes to our understanding of where and why we might find the incongruity of the poor opposing policies designed to help those in the lower income segment of society. In answering these questions, the author highlights the role that cultural and ethnic divisions play in reducing support for redistributive policies.

1253 Boulding, Carew E. and Claudio Holzner. Voice and inequality: poverty and political participation in Latin American democracies. New York, N.Y.: Oxford University Press, 2021. 244 p.: bibl., index.

The authors provide an important contribution to our understanding of political participation among members of different income sectors across Latin America with a specific focus on the scope and depth of participation among the poor. Among the many notable findings is a significant challenge to conventional understandings of the "participation bias" that sees low-income individuals as less engaged in politics. Harkening back to the innovative edited volume of Seligson and Booth over 40 years ago entitled *Political Participation in Latin America, Vol. 2: Politics and the Poor* (1979; reviews of most chapters appeared in *HLAS 43*), *Voice and Inequality* makes a strong case for the vitality of the poor's engagement with politics across the region. The bulk of the work relies on analysis of survey data from the Latin American Public Opinion Project (LAPOP) and highlights the role that electoral competition and institutional performance play in shaping the participation patterns of the poor.

1254 Campello, Daniela and Francisco Urdinez. Voter and legislator responses to localized trade shocks from China in Brazil. (*Comp. Polit. Stud.*, 54:7, June 2021, p. 1131–1162, bibl., graphs, map, tables)

Trade relations between countries have long been recognized as often producing specific winners and losers *within* each trading partner, and often these sector-specific winners and losers are geographically concentrated in such a way as to dramatically affect the electoral connection between voters and their elected representatives. In this study, the authors explore the implications of this phenomenon as it has played out in trade between China and Brazil. Through analysis of survey data, measures of local trade shocks brought on by China, and opinions of legislators, the study provides an important addition to our understanding of the ways in which citizens and legislators respond to the ups and downs of trade with China. The study underscores the differential effects such patterns have on the winners and losers of trade in finding that it is those most negatively affected by trade that were most vocal in their opposition to China, while the winners were relatively quiet with respect to supporting continued trade with the country.

1255 Carlin, Ryan E. and Timothy Hellwig. The world economy, political control, and presidential success. (*J. Polit.*, 82:2, April 2020, p. 786–799, bibl.)

This brief contribution to the journal's "Scholarly Dialogue" feature offers a valuable discussion of the ways in which the world economy does and does not influence domestic politics in the form of public support for the executive. Responding to research that found economic voting in Latin America to be largely a product of the vicissitudes of the world economy rather than the policy performance of the incumbent (item **1286**), the authors make a compelling case for the role that executive policy choices can play in shaping voters' evaluations of their president. The larger debate this research is a part of highlights the continued vitality of work on understanding the drivers of vote choice among the emerging democracies of Latin America.

1256 Ch, Rafael *et al.* Endogenous taxation in ongoing internal conflict: the case of Colombia. (*Am. Polit. Sci. Rev.*, 112:4, Nov. 2018, p. 996–1015, bibl., graphs, maps, tables)

A fascinating account of the relationship between violent nonstate actors and the capacity of local governments to collect tax revenue through analysis of the armed conflict in Colombia between 1988 and 2010. The authors compile an impressive array of data on local tax revenues, land values, elections, and guerrilla/paramilitary attacks that allow for a fine-grained analysis of the ways in which armed groups capture local governments and shape the nature and direction of tax collection. In the process, this study advances our understanding of how civil war can undermine state-building, and also highlights critical issues with decentralization that have long been noted, such as elite capture and the facilitation of subnational authoritarian regimes.

Córdoba, Diana *et al.* Fueling social inclusion?: neo-extractivism, state-society relations and biofuel policies in Latin America's Southern Cone. See item **598**.

1257 Etchemendy, Sebastián. The rise of segmented neo-corporatism in South America: wage coordination in Argentina and Uruguay (2005–2015). (*Comp. Polit. Stud.*, 52:10, Sept. 2019, p. 1427–1465, bibl., graphs, tables)

Argentina and Uruguay stand out among Latin American countries in terms of their development of "neocorporatist" institutions following the turbulent decades of the 1980s and 1990s. In this rich and comprehensive study of the development of these institutions, the author provides insights into the challenges faced by countries in constructing such policy regimes. The disintegration of neocorporatist arrangements in both countries over the past several years underscores the difficulties identified by the author. The study offers an important addition to work on the increasing variation in economic policy regimes across the Latin American region following the somewhat homogenizing period of neoliberal reforms in the 1980s and 1990s.

1258 Falleti, Tulia Gabriela and **Thea N. Riofrancos.** Endogenous participation: strengthening prior consultation in extractive economies. (*World Polit.*, 70:1, Jan. 2018, p. 86–121, bibl.)

Through a focus on participatory institutions, such as local oversight committees, this study explores the questions of how, when, and why certain institutions become stronger over time while others become weaker. Latin America has been a source of great innovation with respect to the development of institutions specifically designed to create a space for citizens to participate in the business of politics—to varying degrees of success. The authors focus on participatory institutions in Bolivia and Ecuador and find that one key to the strengthening of these forms of citizen participation is the incorporation of the citizen protagonists whose mobilization efforts played a role in the creation of such institutions. Through their subsequent inclusion into the formal political system, the institutions they fought for have a greater chance of becoming stronger and more durable.

1259 Garfias, Francisco. Elite coalitions, limited government, and fiscal capacity development: evidence from Bourbon Mexico. (*J. Polit.*, 81:1, Jan. 2019, p. 94–111, bibl., graphs, tables)

This excellent historical study looks at the strengthening of state capacity—this time with a focus on the way in which an institution that can lower coordination costs for economic elites in an effort to constrain the state may lead to an enhanced ability of the state to impose and collect taxes on various economic sectors. Drawing from data during the late colonial period in Mexico, the author offers a compelling explanation of how institutions that organize elites may in fact lead those elites to be less resistant to tax impositions on the part of the ruler.

1260 Garfias, Francisco. Elite competition and state capacity development: theory and evidence from post-revolutionary Mexico. (*Am. Polit. Sci. Rev.*, 112:2, May 2018, p. 339–357, bibl.)

Another piece that relies on archival work to explore the question of state development processes. The author examines the case of postrevolutionary Mexico to evaluate an argument that sees a source for state capacity development rooted in the shock to Mexico's postrevolutionary system that came in the form of the Great Depression. When such a shock occurs it can undermine economic elites in such a way that allows rulers to expropriate land and consolidate power, thereby increasing incentives for investment in state capacity. While elements of this account seem specific to Mexico, the author does also briefly discuss the cases of Chile and Dominican Republic to highlight the ways in which this process may play out in other settings. This is an important addition to the increasing number of works devoted to identifying and understanding the mechanics of state capacity building across the region.

1261 Germano, Roy. Outsourcing welfare: how the money immigrants send home contributes to stability in developing countries. New York, N.Y.: Oxford University Press, 2018. 227 p.: bibl., ill., index.

What role does migration play in the lives of the millions of poor people living in countries with tattered safety nets that tend to be least effective during times of economic crisis when they are most needed? This important addition to the political economy of migration research explores the role that remittances play in patching together a lifeline for those for whom a safety net does not exist. The author provides a compelling account of both the direct impact of remittances in sustaining recipient households during times of crisis as well as an examination of how remittances can shape recipients' economic outlook and their receptivity to populist appeals. Lurking behind these positive first- and second-order effects of remittances, however, is the fact that in general the poorest of the poor do not tend to emigrate, leaving many more households in dire need and, potentially, creating yet another divide within Latin American countries based on remittance and nonremittance households. Nonetheless, this is certain to become an essential resource for those interested in the political consequences of migration moving forward.

1262 Giraudy, Agustina et al. The impact of neopatrimonialism on poverty in contemporary Latin America. (*Lat. Am. Polit. Soc.*, 62:1, Feb. 2020, p. 73–96, bibl., graphs, tables)

This innovative study focuses on the concept of neopatrimonialism, understood as a situation in which rulers have great discretion in the application of state power and exhibit a tendency to expropriate private property. After a discussion of the novel measurement approach deployed to capture this concept, the authors examine the consequences of neopatrimonialism on key indicators of poverty, finding that it has a clear impact on poverty in that it produces heightened levels of economic inequality in countries where such ruler characteristics prevail. Though much work remains to be done on these issues, this study represents a significant step forward in terms of the conceptualization and measurement of neopatrimonialism and its role in poverty levels across the region.

1263 González, Yanilda María. The social origins of institutional weakness and change: preferences, power, and police reform in Latin America. (*World Polit.*, 71:1, Jan. 2019, p. 44–87, bibl., graphs, tables)

An important contribution to work on crime and violence in Latin America with a focus on the electoral implications of and impediments to police reforms faced by elected officials across the region. Through analysis of the cases of Argentina, Brazil, and Colombia, the study attempts to explain the persistence of flawed police institutions throughout the region and the ways in which reforms, in a context of limited political competition, can fall apart. Flawed and dysfunctional police forces continue to pose a significant threat to individuals across the Americas and works such as this one are invaluable in advancing our understanding of the ways in which police reforms may achieve their intended impact.

1264 Holland, Bradley E. and **Viridiana Rios.** Violence and business interest in social welfare: evidence from Mexico. (*Comp. Polit. Stud.*, 55:11, Sept. 2022, p. 1844–1876, bibl., graphs, table)

This study takes a novel approach to understanding the link between violence and the fiscal policy preferences of members of an influential business organization in Mexico. Through a unique experiment embedded in the organization's internal member survey that includes respondents from all of Mexico's states, the authors test for the impact on respondents' policy preferences when primed to think about violence in society. They find that when respondents have such concerns about violence first and foremost in their mind, they tend to exhibit a greater receptivity to antipoverty spending proposals and lower support for tax cuts than those respondents who did not receive the "violence" treatment. Though these findings have important caveats, the work represents a significant step in research on the many ways in which high levels of crime and violence may influence the policy preferences of critical actors in Latin America.

1265 Houle, Christian and **Michael K. Miller.** Social mobility and democratic attitudes: evidence from Latin America and Sub-Saharan Africa. (*Comp. Polit. Stud.*, 52:11, Sept. 2019, p. 1610–1647, bibl., graphs, tables)

The importance of social mobility and reduction of inequality for the inculcation of democratic attitudes has long been noted but there remains a limited understanding of where and why such a connection may exist. In this study, the authors examine survey data across 33 countries in Latin America and Africa to assess the connection between intergenerational mobility and support for democracy. Though limited by the cross-sectional nature of the data, the authors find fairly robust support for conventional view that individuals who have been able to move beyond the economic rung of their parents are more likely to embrace democracy and the principles that serve as its foundation. Conversely, those who have experienced downward mobility exhibit less support for democratic rule. These findings highlight the connection between economic opportunity (or lack thereof) and citizens' level of support for democracy.

1266 Innovation and inclusion in Latin America: strategies to avoid the middle-income trap. Edited by Alejandro Foxley and Barbara Stallings. New York, N.Y.: Palgrave Macmillan, 2016. 235 p.: bibl., index. (Studies of the Americas)

A welcome addition to the long-running research agenda centered on comparing the development prospects of East Asian countries with those of Latin America. In this edited volume, the focus is largely on the role that technology and innovation can play in increased productivity, as well as the need for greater economic inclusion in Latin America of previously marginalized sectors in order to escape from the "middle income trap" in which many of the region's countries find themselves. Chapters address such topics as the state of technological innovation in Latin America, the lessons on innovation that can be drawn from East Asia, and a case study of productivity in Mexico.

1267 Kingstone, Peter R. The political economy of Latin America: reflections on neoliberalism and development after the commodity boom. Second edition. New York, N.Y.; London: Routledge, Taylor & Francis Group, 2018. 206 p.: bibl., index.

This second edition of a work (first published in 2011) that is emerging as a foundational introductory text to Latin America's political economy of development offers a concise treatment of the watershed moments in the region's development process over the past century, including the post-neoliberal era of the early 21st century. The underlying theme of the work is the role that key institutions play in shaping a country's development prospects, alongside the myriad global forces at play. The book stands out for its even-handed and comprehensive analysis of the factors that have most influenced economic development patterns over the years and is certain to be of value for students of Latin America's political economy.

1268 Mangonnet, Jorge and **María Victoria Murillo.** Protests of abundance: distributive conflict over agricultural rents during the commodities boom in Argentina, 2003–2013. (*Comp. Polit. Stud.*, 53:8, July 2020, p. 1223–1258, bibl., graphs, maps, tables)

Social movements and protests are common across Latin America and Argentina stands outs a country particularly prone to such forms of political engagement. This study provides tremendous insight into the dynamics that drive protest among one key sector of Argentina's society—agricultural export producers. Through analysis of a unique subnational data set of producer lockouts that serve as one of the most effective forms of protest for this sector, the authors identify the conditions under which such protests occur. They find, perhaps not surprisingly, that among soy producers, these forms of protests were most likely to occur during periods in which the government sought to increase the export tax burden faced by farmers—even if such tax increases occurred during times of high international prices for the product. The article underscores the degree to which specific economic interest groups recognize and respond to fiscal policy pressures exerted by the state.

1269 Martins, Carlos Eduardo. Dependency, neoliberalism and globalization in Latin America. Translated by Jacob Lagnado. Leiden, The Netherlands; Boston, Mass.: Brill, 2020. 343 p.: bibl., index. (Studies in critical social sciences; 150) (Critical global studies; 10)

A wide-ranging treatment of Latin America's place in the global economy through a renewed dependency theory analytical lens. The work highlights the new (and old) forms of dependency that persist under the current globalization paradigm that has characterized the past 30 years of economic development patterns. In the process, the author identifies many of the challenges countries across the region face and links them to the region's ties to the dominant economic powers in the global economy—the US and China. A useful perspective on recent economic development patterns.

1270 Medina Garzón, Camilo Andrés. Contagio financiero internacional en países emergentes de Asia y América Latina: aplicación de un DCC-MGARCH. Bogotá: Universidad Central, Facultad de Ciencias Administrativas, Económicas y Contables, 2018. 149 p.: bibl., ill. (some color). (FCAEC/Tesis)

An insightful and comprehensive assessment of the phenomenon of financial contagion which entails the spreading of economic crisis from one country to the next in quick succession. The author examines the cases of the "Great Recession" of 2008 in the US and the relatively rapid slowdown of China's economy in the period of 2015–2017. In both cases, the study looks at the extent to which select countries in East Asia and Latin America suffered from "contagion" as defined by the author. Through this exercise, a core finding is that in order to assess the impact of such global economic shocks, a more nuanced understanding of the type of contagion that is at work is necessary.

1271 Menéndez González, Irene. Insiders, outsiders, skills, and preferences for social protection: evidence from a survey experiment in Argentina. (*Comp. Polit. Stud.*, 54:14, Dec. 2021, p. 2581–2610, bibl., graphs)

Another study that examines the redistributive policy preferences of a specific group of economic actors—in this case it is "privileged workers," or "insiders," who serve as the analytical focus. Through a survey experiment in Argentina, along with a crossnational survey analysis, the author evaluates the proposition that the degree of risk faced by low- and high-skilled workers will shape their preferences with respect to social protection policies. The variations in the type and magnitude of risk will thus lead to a polarization of policy attitudes among workers in the formal sector with high and low skill sets.

1272 Oliveros, Virginia and **Christian Schuster.** Merit, tenure, and bureaucratic behavior: evidence from a conjoint experiment in the Dominican Republic. (*Comp. Polit. Stud.*, 51:6, May 2018, p. 759–792, bibl., graphs, tables)

A well-executed exploration of the institutional sources of variations in bureaucratic behavior through application of a conjoint experiment among government workers in the Dominican Republic in an online survey. The authors find support for the proposition that merit-based hiring and promotion procedures are associated with perceived greater political neutrality among bureaucrats and lower corruption. Job stability, on the other hand, only appeared to be associated with a more apolitical civil service—not one that is less corrupt. This study adds to a growing body of work on the role and workings of the bureaucracy in Latin American development processes. For Caribbean political scientist's comment, see item **954.**

1273 Organized violence: capitalist warfare in Latin America. Edited by Dawn Paley and Simon Granovsky-Larsen. Regina, Canada: University of Regina Press, 2019. 284 p.: bibl., ill., index, maps.

A collection of essays that directly confronts and challenges the dominant narrative concerning the sources, perpetrators, and beneficiaries of the high levels of violence that confront many of Latin America's societies. Rather than being solely a product of criminal organizations and the drug trade, many of the chapters in this edited volume argue that consideration of the role that business and political interests play in the perpetuation of violence in the region is essential for a more complete understanding of what is arguably that most significant human, economic, and social challenge confronting countries across the region. To varying degrees, the works here offer a compelling counternarrative that forces a reconsideration of the drivers of such violence and those who may directly benefit from it. A welcome addition to the burgeoning literature on the political economy of crime and violence in Latin America and the Caribbean.

1274 Orihuela, José Carlos. The political economy of the developmental state in Latin America. (*in* Oxford research encyclopedia of politics. Oxford, England: Oxford University Press, 2019, https://oxfordre.com/politics)

This essay offers both a retrospective and prospective assessment of the developmental state in Latin America during what might be called the post-neoliberal era of economic policy. The author provides a fairly concise overview of the golden era of statist development policies during the 1950s and 1960s, and gives an assessment of what went right and wrong during that era where the state emerged as a primary driver of development. The essay then offers a compelling discussion of the prospects for the emergence of a more central role of the state in 21st-century development patterns across Latin America.

1275 Palmer-Rubin, Brian and **Ruth Berins Collier.** Work and demand making: productionist and consumptionist politics in Latin America. (*Comp. Polit. Stud.*, 55:10, Sept. 2022, p. 1631–1662, bibl., graphs, tables)

Representative of an increasing research focus on Latin America's labor sector and the drivers of workers' attitudes and behaviors both inside and outside the workplace, this study examines the ways in which work conditions themselves shape workers' demand making within the workplace and in the political realm outside of the workplace. Working with data from four Latin American cities (Buenos Aires, Caracas, Lima, and Santiago), the authors offer support for their contention that common features of the modern workplace, such as income volatility, weak organized labor protections, and the dramatic increase in the "gig economy" all have served to weaken the political voice of many workers, helping to explain the low level of demand making seen from this sector in many countries across the region.

Políticas proactivas en lo fiscal y financiero: México y América Latina. See item **1318**.

1276 Regiones periféricas, gobernanza frágil: desarrollo económico local desde América Latina. Compilación de Sergio Montero y Karen Chapple. Bogotá: Universidad de los Andes, 2018. 231 p.: bibl., ill. (some color). (Planificación, gobernanza y desarrollo territorial)

A fascinating collection of chapters on dynamic centers of economic growth across Latin America with a focus on pockets of innovation in certain countries. Along with case studies of cities like Córdoba, Argentina, and Arauco, Chile, are essays that examine the development prospects of rural areas in the region and development policies that target peripheral areas. A useful addition to the body of work that shines a light on the vast *intranational* variations that characterize much of Latin America.

1277 Roniger, Luis et al. Exile, diaspora, and return: changing cultural landscapes in Argentina, Chile, Paraguay, and Uruguay. New York, N.Y.: Oxford University Press, 2017. 292 p.: bibl., index.

A long-needed assessment of the economic, social, and political contributions and consequences of the many exile communities that formed as a result of Latin America's era of authoritarian rule in the 1960s and 1970s. As such communities are full of individuals with myriad skills and potential contributions who were forced to flee their countries, this work offers one of the few systematic explorations of what was lost and, as importantly, what has been gained as these diasporas have developed over the years and begun to return to their home countries. This is an outstanding contribution to a body of work that should continue to grow as we witness more and more voluntary and forced returns among individuals, both exiles and others, that have left their countries over the past several decades. Greater attention to the potential role such communities play while living abroad and when they return will be an important addition to Latin America's political economy research in the future. For geography specialist's comment, see item **607**. For sociologist's comment, see item **1445**.

1278 Rueda, Miguel R. and Nelson A. Ruiz. Political agency, election quality, and corruption. (*J. Polit.*, 82:4, Oct. 2020, p. 1256–1270, bibl., graphs, tables)

An abundance of research over the years has examined the role of elections in citizens' efforts to hold their elected officials accountable but very few works have explored this question in situations where the quality of the election itself was in doubt. Asking the question "What forms of electoral accountability emerge when winners enter office under questionable circumstances?" this work offers a novel contribution to our understanding of elections and accountability. The authors find that those officials who enter office amidst allegations of vote buying tend to be more likely to be prosecuted and found guilty of violations while in office. These results add to our understanding of the accountability mechanisms at work in the many flawed democracies across the region in an era of democratic backsliding.

1279 Schenoni, Luis L. Bringing war back in: victory and state formation in Latin America. (*Am. J. Polit. Sci.*, 65:2, April 2021, p. 405–421, bibl., graphs, tables)

Though the role of international conflict, and winning or losing such conflicts, in the development of states has long been a question of interest for scholars in Europe and elsewhere, very little research on this question has been carried out in Latin America. This paucity of research makes this study on state formation in Latin America a particularly welcome addition. The author contends that the outcome of war for specific countries can have long-term consequences for the development of a state's capacity, with winners and losers experiencing distinct state development trajectories. The author finds, for example, that losing a war has a robust, statistically significant effect on per capita government revenue and railroad mileage. These types of findings are important additions to extant work on the distinct development trajectories that characterize postcolonial Latin America.

1280 Sexton, Renard; Rachel L. Wellhausen; and Michael G. Findley. How government reactions to violence worsen social welfare: evidence from Peru. (*Am. J. Polit. Sci.*, 63:2, April 2019, p. 353–367, bibl., tables)

This study takes a novel approach to the age-old "guns and butter" question of fiscal policy in a context where the "guns" side of the debate too often wins the day. Through analysis of subnational data on solider deaths and public service budgets in Peru, the authors find compelling evidence of the second-order effects that the budgetary prioritization of short-term security concerns over such areas as health care can have—in this case resulting in a significant increase in infant mortality rates. This study adds to the numerous studies examined for this *HLAS* volume on the various ways in which crime, insecurity, and government responses to these issues can shape myriad outcomes of interest in the field of political economy.

1281 State and nation making in Latin America and Spain: the rise and fall of the developmental state. Edited by Augustin E. Ferraro and Miguel A. Centeno. Cambridge, England; New York, N.Y.: Cambridge University Press, 2019. 436 p.: bibl., index.

This edited work represents the second of a trilogy on state-building and development in Latin American and Spain, covering the critical period of 1930–90—a time during which the region moved from a state-led development strategy to one driven, at least in part, by adherence to market-based principles in the economic policy realm. The editors and contributors offer a wide-ranging assessment of Latin America and Spain during this period driven by the question of how and why Spain was able to move ahead of most countries in Latin America during this time. Most chapters grapple with and explore the legacy of the developmental state that characterized the region throughout much of the time period and provide useful assessments of this period in Latin America's development process that depart from the stylized characterizations that emerged in the 1980s and 1990s. As such, this is an important addition to work on this critical period in the region's history. For a review of the first volume, see *HLAS 71:986*.

1282 Steinberg, David A. and Stephen C. Nelson. The mass political economy of capital controls. (*Comp. Polit. Stud.*, 52:11, Sept. 2019, p. 1575–1609, bibl., graphs)

The prevailing view of public opinion is decidedly skeptical in terms of the degree to which most in the general public hold meaningful opinions on the majority of the specific economic policy choices made by elected officials that affect their collective pocketbook. In this study, this view is challenged through analysis of Argentines' views of capital control policies. Despite being a relatively arcane policy issue that from afar most might assume a relatively uninformed public, the author offers robust support for the contention that Argentines in fact know quite a bit about their government's capital control policies and use this information to shape their assessments of their elected officials. These findings highlight the importance of contextual factors in assessing the degree to which a particular policy sector may or may not be relevant to the mass public.

Ugarteche, Oscar. Arquitectura financiera internacional: una genealogía (1850–2015). See item **1329**.

Vilar, José Rafael. Auge y caída del socialismo del siglo XXI: una rápida visión hispanoamericana de sus recientes ciclos políticos y del fracaso de ideologizar la economía. See item **339**.

1283 Why Latin American nations fail: development strategies in the twenty-first century. Edited by Esteban Pérez Caldentey and Matías Vernengo. Oakland: University of California Press, 2017. 224 p.: bibl., index.

From the title alone, this work clearly seeks to give credit to and extend the analysis of Acemoglu and Robinson's *Why Nations Fail* (2012) by homing in on the institutional obstacles to sustained economic development in Latin America. As such, the chapters in this edited volume offer further insight into the ways in which various economic and political institutions continue to hamper growth patterns across the Americas. Mixed in with the chapters that highlight the role of institutions in the economic development process are those that offer more of an overview of economic development trends across the region during the past several decades. This combination of approaches makes for a useful collection of studies on the ways in which politics and economics have intersected in myriad ways to produce periods of both success and failure in recent years.

1284 Wise, Carol. Dragonomics: how Latin America is maximizing (or missing out on) China's international development strategy. New Haven, Conn.: Yale University Press, 2020. 308 p.: bibl., ill., index.

Reflective of the growing body of research on the rise of China in Latin America, this work is certain to be an essential part of this agenda moving forward as the author offers a comprehensive assessment of the ways in which Latin American countries have both benefitted from and "missed out" on economic relations with China. Though confined to a focus on selected countries—Argentina, Brazil, Chile, Peru, Costa Rica, and Mexico—Wise offers an abundance of insights and recommendations for countries across the region, with an emphasis on the importance of adequate oversight institutions and efforts to diminish the rent-seeking behavior that has been common among the region's foreign economic relationships.

1285 Yashar, Deborah J. Homicidal ecologies: illicit economies and complicit states in Latin America. Cambridge, England; New York, N.Y.: Cambridge University Press, 2018. 418 p.: bibl., index, maps, tables. (Cambridge studies in comparative politics)

This work addresses a simple but tragic question that has plagued much of Latin America, and particularly Central America, for many years: "Why do so many people die due to homicide?" The core argument regarding the answer is perhaps not surprising in its emphasis on the drug trade and larger illicit economy, weak states that are largely unable (and/or unwilling) to enforce the law, and the frequent turf battles that occur between nonstate factions. Through its focus on northern Central America, a region with some of the most violent countries in the world, the study is a welcome addition to scholarship on an issue that remains, arguably, the largest obstacle to economic development and one of the most powerful drivers of migration. For Central American political scientist's comment, see *HLAS 75:935*.

1286 Zucco, Cesar and **Daniela Campello.** Endogenous policy making. (*J. Polit.*, 82:2, April 2020, p. 800–807, bibl.)

The authors respond to the critiques of their original work offered in part one (item **1255**) of this "Scholarly Dialogue" regarding the role that exogenous, global economic conditions play in shaping the presidential vote across Latin America. While the initial critique focused on the impact that domestic policy choices have on voting patterns in the region and discounted to some extent the role international factors play, this rejoinder provides compelling support for the role of global forces in domestic election outcomes. In the end, it appears that there is an influence of both domestic and international factors on the voting patterns of Latin American publics and the importance of these factors may ebb and flow based on the dynamics surrounding a particular electoral contest.

MEXICO

JAMES B. GERBER, *Professor Emeritus of Economics, San Diego State University*

MEXICO'S LACKLUSTER ECONOMIC GROWTH over the last several decades continues to be a major focus of research and scholarly publication. There are good reasons for this line of investigation since, according to IMF data, real per capita income grew at a disappointingly slow annual compound rate of 0.2 percent between 2000 and 2021. Even with the omission of the pandemic years of 2020 and 2021, low rate of growth of 0.6 percent per year would take 120 years to double income per capita. The negative consequences of this level of stagnant growth are enormous since it means poverty remains a major problem, inequality is impossible to address, and confidence in the future wanes.

In publications highlighted in previous *Handbook* volumes, researchers approached the problem of slow economic growth mainly through criticisms of the neoliberal economic reforms of the 1980s and 1990s and other macroeconomic policy choices. *HLAS 77* continues to register those critiques, but they are complemented by a larger number of inquiries into the roles of firms, markets, and the policy environment in fostering innovation, competitiveness, and increased productivity. It is a subtle shift, but it appears that scholars are currently more interested in understanding the specific factors holding back increased productivity than they are in producing another critique of NAFTA and neoliberalism.

Three works set the stage for this discussion. Huerta González (item **1306**) discusses Mexico's growth failure in the context of internal and external conditions and questions whether the successes of populists in the US and elsewhere are an indicator that the era of globalization is over. Ten chapters produced through a series of workshops held by the UNAM Facultad de Economía (item **1292**) also focus on the lack of growth and high rates of poverty. The authors consider structural reforms as one element but add several other factors such as lagging innovation, the lack of public investment, the quality of jobs, and the type of work available. UNAM's Programa Universitario de Estudios del Desarrollo (PUED) introduces two additional dimensions that have not been spotlighted (item **1287**). One is the Great Recession of 2007–2009 and the slow recovery that followed and the second is an investigation into the resilience of the economy after natural disasters. Chapters consider not only the institutional strengths and vulnerabilities in the face of major earthquakes, but also the hundreds of smaller, more regionalized disasters and emergencies and the ability of institutions to respond.

Economic growth flourishes with supporting environments at all levels of government, but ultimately it depends on the ability of firms and markets to innovate and to implement changes that enhance productivity. Many works, both single-authored and collaborative, analyze conditions in specific markets or specific regions. For example, the mold and die (tool-making) industry in Querétaro, Puebla, and the state of Mexico, is the subject of a collaborative work (item **1290**) that adopts a perspective of globalized production systems. The goal is to understand how small firms acquire technical knowledge, skilled workers, and market information. Another work offers a similar investigation into Mexico's auto industry (item **1324**), focusing on innovation and the changing technology of autos and automobile production. Meraz Ruiz's work (item **1311**) on micro-, small-, and medium-sized firms in the wine industry illustrates a similar focus on issues of productivity and competitiveness, although on a much smaller stage. Since micro-, small-, and medium-sized firms are the largest employers, their performance matters greatly to Mexico's economy even if any individual firm is a statistically insignificant part of the national economy. A collaboration between the Universidad Veracruzana and Renmin University in Beijing compares small- and medium-sized firms in China and Mexico (item **1331**). Researchers at the Colegio de la Frontera Norte (COLEF) have also joined the discussion of more microrelated factors affecting economic growth. In some cases, the obstacle to a deeper understanding has been the lack of data. A book comprised almost entirely of data tables (item **1301**) is designed to fill this gap for multinational firms operating in Mexico by publishing the results of a survey that was coordinated with several other country studies of multinationals carried out in Europe and South America.

Oil, like automobile and auto parts manufacturing, continues to be a significant part of Mexico's economy, but unlike the automotive sector, private firms play a smaller role in production. With its size and the extent of its recent regulatory changes, the 14 chapters by academics, government officials, consultants, lawyers, and industry insiders offer a deep dive into the new energy model and its relation to climate change (item **1316**). For background on Pemex, the state-owned company, a collection of essays by Miguel Wionczek published in the 1970s and 1980s describes the history of petroleum markets, their condition at the time, and his view of their future prospects (item **1312**). At the request of the president of the Colegio de México, Wionczek directed a research program on Mexico's petroleum industry and its prospects.

In addition to firm and market-level perspectives, researchers also examine the growth issue from the perspective of regions. This work continues a long and vibrant tradition of regional studies in Mexico. COLEF researchers produced a diagnostic of the states of Coahuila and Chihuahua, which is part of a series financed by CONACYT, Mexico's national science foundation (item **1325**). The diagnostic analyzes science, technology, and innovation capacity in the two states, including their socioeconomic characteristics, through case studies and interviews. More of the research in this *Handbook* volume concerns the state of Sonora than any other state. Overall economic conditions (item **1327**) and entrepreneurship in Sonora's maquilas (item **1323**) approach the topic of growth and competitiveness, while a study of poverty in the southern part of the state (item **1302**) adds a socioeconomic dimension. Finally, an analysis of Jalisco (item **1322**) questions the causes of its slow growth and relatively lagging economic performance.

Labor studies also have a strong tradition in Mexican scholarship. Several works approach the topic from different perspectives. Mexico's high rate of informality in the labor market, and the attendant negative consequences for economic growth, make work in this area useful (item **1296**). A related topic is the status of Mexico's rural labor force (item **1294**) and their transformation into rural laborers in place of small farmers. Two works examine migration. The first is a comparative work relating migration to technological innovations and the growth of the knowledge economy (item **1320**) and the second examines return migration and problems of social mobility (item **1304**).

In addition to the microeconomics of lagging economic growth, several works address the socioeconomic consequences of slow growth, especially poverty and inequality. One of the most valuable works from a policy perspective uses a social accounting framework to analyze the socioeconomic consequences of economic changes in seven mesoregions, each of which is comprised of multiple states (item **1314**). Social accounting matrices are built around input-output models of the economy but have the added advantage of incorporating payments to capital, labor, and foreigners. Additional studies elaborate the many dimensions of inequality (item **1303**), the structural roots of inequality (item **1288**), and a Marxian perspective on comparative Mexican and US salaries (item **1330**). Poverty and inequality are not equivalent, and two works tackle the issue of poverty specifically. One analyzes poverty traps from a new institutionalist perspective (item **1313**) while the second is a descriptive narrative focused on NAFTA (item **1328**).

Arguments against neoliberalism and Mexico's structural reforms of the 1980s and 1990s continue to occupy the attention of scholars. Two noteworthy discussions that focus more narrowly on particular problems both concern Mexico's loss of its traditional foodways and the horrendous consequences for public health in the country. The first describes the changes to food production and consumption within the context of NAFTA and globalization (item **1299**) while the second offers a sociopolitical analysis of different options for regulating junk food (*comida chatarra*) to combat high rates of diabetes and other health problems (item **1315**).

Finally, a series of works of economic history with political economy implications is commendable. CIDE (Centro de Investigación y Docencia Económica) in Mexico City provides open access to over 40,000 press clippings on the topic of bank nationalization and government debt spanning more than a century, from the first third of the 19th century to the last decade of the 20th (item **1326**; https://repositorio-digital.cide.edu/handle/11651/3764). Three works examine finance and banking, including one on banking in San Luis Potosí from the late colonial period through the end of the 19th century (item **1295**), banking and the growth of international liabilities before the 1982 crisis (item **1289**), and the development of the international financial architecture of the 20th century (item **1329**). Two outliers of significant interest are studies on the growth of markets for meat production and consumption from the 18th to the 20th century (item **1308**) and the link between global progressive movements in the late 19th and 20th centuries and Mexico's science and engineering apostles, as told through the biography of ingeniero Modesto Rolland (item **1293**).

1287 A 10 años de la gran recesión: desastres y desarrollo. Coordinación de Rolando Cordera Campos y Enrique Provencio Durazo. Ciudad de México: UNAM, 2019. 193 p.: bibl., ill. (chiefly color), color maps. (Colección Informe del desarrollo en México)

This is the third Development in Mexico Report from the Programa Universitario de Estudios del Desarrollo (PUED) at UNAM. Two major themes are addressed. One is a general overview of economic and social recovery from the Great Recession (2007–2009). The other is an examination of resilience, well-being, institutional strengths, vulnerabilities, and questions arising from the institutional response to disasters, both natural and human caused. Individual chapters offer a detailed quantitative look at slow growth and persistent poverty since 2009 and the socioeconomic effects of major earthquakes and the many smaller but regionally important disasters and emergencies that occurred over the last two decades. Particular attention is given to rural and vulnerable communities.

1288 Aguilera Gómez, Manuel and **Felipe Riva Palacio Guerrero.** Las raíces estructurales de la desigualdad en México: el lado oscuro de un desarrollo suspendido. Ciudad de México: UNAM, Programa Universitario de Estudios del Desarrollo: Miguel Ángel Porrúa, 2018. 225 p.: bibl. (Serie Estudios críticos del desarrollo)

The six chapters of this ambitious book attempt to uncover the structural causes of inequality in Mexico. Chapter 1 provides an historical panorama since colonial times while chapter 2 reviews the relevant theories of Ricardo, Marx, Kuznets, Kalecki, and Pinto, and hypothesizes a role for monopolies that is further explored in chapter 3. Chapter 4 emphasizes the loss of occupational and socioeconomic mobility among working class people, while chapter 5 differentiates the working class from the top 10 percent. In the last chapter, the author argues that the failure of Mexico's economy to generate sufficient economic growth caused its leaders to excavate the dead ideas of pre-Keynesians and led to the minimal state model of neoliberalism. The authors follow the final chapter with a series of reflections.

1289 Alvarez, Sebastian. Venturing abroad: the internationalisation of Mexican banks prior to the 1982 crisis. (*J. Lat. Am. Stud.*, 49:3, Aug. 2017, p. 517–548, appendix, graphs, tables)

The debt crisis that began in 1982 is usually discussed as a problem of sovereign debt. Alvarez notes how the oil crisis decade of the 1970s increased the international exposure of Mexican banks. This research examines the banking crisis aspect of the debt crisis. In Mexico, between 1975 and 1982 international claims on Mexican bank balance sheets rose from 0.7 percent of total assets and liabilities to 20 percent. The author argues that bank balance sheets were deteriorating before the 1982 crisis, as evidenced by increased leverage and a greater reliance on debt in place of equity. The article reviews the historical background and the growth of foreign funding from the mid-1970s onward. An econometric model estimates the relationship between foreign borrowing and risk levels.

1290 Aprendizaje para el mercado global: moldes y troqueles en el centro de México. Coordinación de Carmen Bueno, Rebeca de Gortari, Alejandro Mercado y María Josefa Santos. Ciudad de México: Universidad Iberoamericana: Universidad Autónoma Metropolitana, Unidad Cuajimalpa, 2017. 299 p.: bibl., ill.

The 10 chapters of this edited volume examine tool making of various kinds but especially molds and dies. The goal of the study is to understand how small firms acquire technological knowledge, skills, experience, and awareness of production trends to survive and prosper within globalized production systems. The analysis is concentrated in the three states of central Mexico (Querétaro, Puebla, and México) where the development of complex production processes accelerated over the last 20 years. The researchers conducted a statistical analysis of the production of molds and dies, carried out 24 case studies of firms, and compared the experiences of Mexican firms with firms in production centers outside Mexico.

1291 Bennett, Abigail and **Xavier Basurto.** Local institutional responses to global market pressures: the sea cucumber trade in Yucatán, Mexico. (*World Dev.*, 102, Feb. 2018, p. 57–70, bibl., graphs, maps, table)

Small scale fisheries account for 90 percent of the world's fishers and 50 percent of output. Consequently, issues of sustainability, rulemaking, and enforcement in small scale fisheries are an important consideration for the long-term health of the world's food supply. This study adopts Ostrom's institutional framework for analyzing the management of common pool resources to the study of production relations, rulemaking, and rules enforcement. Two communities are studied in depth, one with a production system based on cooperatives and the other with a client-patron system of individual producers. Increased world demand for sea cucumbers has put pressure on both communities. Formal regulations were less effective, particularly when they did not consider local relations of production. Cooperatives were more effective at enforcing rules than individual patrons.

1292 Cambio de rumbo: desafíos económicos y sociales de México hoy. Coordinación de Eduardo Vega López. Con la colaboración de Jaime Ros *et al.* Ciudad de México: UNAM, Facultad de Economía, 2018. 233 p.: bibl.

The 10 essays in this book are the result of a series of meetings held by the UNAM Facultad de Economía to discuss and debate current conditions in Mexico. The first essay makes the case for changes in Mexico's economic policies. Among the most important reasons are stagnant growth and persistently high rates of poverty. Individual chapters analyze the relationship between economic stagnation and structural reforms, trade opening, and lagging innovation. Chapters also consider public investment as an economic multiplier, the impact of inflation on income distribution, the quality of jobs and work, inequality, and out migration and return migration.

1293 Castro, J. Justin. Apostle of progress: Modesto C. Rolland, global progressivism, and the engineering of revolutionary Mexico. Lincoln: University of Nebraska Press, 2019. 310 p.: bibl., index.

Modesto Rolland was born in 1881 in La Paz, Mexico. He trained as a teacher and followed with engineering studies at the National School of Engineering in Mexico City. Castro's biography is a narrative of the life of the adult Rolland as he directed a wide range of infrastructure projects, promoted land reform, and advocated for progressive social change across Mexico. Rolland was at times a government official and at others a private citizen. Throughout most of his life, he was an important contributor to Mexico's economic development. A primary goal of the book is to explore the connections between the scientific-engineering-progressive outlook of the late Porfiriato and revolutionary eras with global progressive movements. For historian's comment, see *HLAS 76:421.*

1294 Contreras Molotla, Felipe. Población rural y trabajo en México: de productores agrícolas a trabajadores rurales. Ciudad de México: UNAM, Centro de Investigaciones Interdisciplinarias en Ciencias y Humanidades, 2017. 228 p.: bibl., ill. (Colección Alternativas)

The focus of this monograph is the transition of the rural labor force in recent decades. The main concern is the lack of improvements in its well-being, particularly during the era of neoliberal policies. The primary data sources are the censuses of population and housing for 2000 and 2010. Key variables of interest are the changes in non-agricultural employment, including occupational structure, regional variations in rural work and income, and the importance of income earned outside agriculture. The book begins with a literature review of sociodemographic conditions, rural occupations, and family survival strategies. Chapter 2 traces the history of rural labor from the 1940s to 2010. Chapters 3 and 4 analyze the occupational structure and labor conditions in rural areas and the final chapter examines household economics.

1295 Corral Bustos, Adriana. Estrategias de asociación para la inversión: el desarrollo del sistema financiero en San Luis Potosí entre 1850 y 1900. San Luis Potosí, Mexico: El Colegio de San Luis, 2017. 434 p.: bibl., ill. (some color), maps. (Colección Investigaciones)

Corral Bustos' monograph on 19th-century banking in the state of San Luis Potosí is focused on local credit dynamics before the creation of a regional bank of emission and on the characteristics of the social and financial networks that led to the development of a financial elite. The work is presented in two parts. The first explores the general situation of financial intermediation, including the role of national banks, informal lending, and the dual nature of credit-providing institutions. The important roles of national and state finances and tax policies are discussed at length. Part 2 examines the creation of the Banco de San Luis Potosí, S.A., towards the end of the 19th century. The emphasis is on social actors that made possible the development of a formal bank of emission, the strategies of association they employed, and their rise as a financial elite.

1296 Cruz Vásquez, Miguel. La reforma laboral y sus desafíos: formalidad, informalidad y migración. Ciudad de México: UPAEP: MAPorrúa, Librero-Editor, 2018. 175 p., 4 unnumbered pages: bibl. (Serie Las ciencias sociales)

Definitions of informality in the labor force are not standardized and different definitions lead to significantly different estimates of the size of the informal labor force in Mexico. The definition aside, Cruz Vásquez argues that the growth of formal employment has been inadequate. The result has been a large informal sector and massive out migration. The first chapter of this work reviews the history of labor reforms from the 19th century to the present. The second chapter describes recent rates of open unemployment and formal employment, defined as employment with social benefits. Chapter 3 offers a comparison between formality and informality, and chapter 4 analyzes out migration due to labor market imbalances. A short conclusion summarizes the analysis.

1297 Desempeño institucional y desarrollo en países tardíos. Coordinación de Mario Humberto Hernández López. Textos de Ángel Ávila Ramírez et al. Ciudad de México: Publicaciones Empresariales UNAM FCA Publishing, 2017. 235 p.: ill.

This work combines economics with administration to investigate several issues of importance to late developing economies. A key goal is to understand the institutional systems that promote or hinder the ability of firms to effectively use technology. The notion of corporate governance is discussed throughout the text and plays a key role in differentiating the performance of countries (Brazil, China, India, Mexico, South Korea) in chapters 1 and 5, in management of value chains (chapter 2), and in the overall performance of the economy (chapter 4). Chapter 6 compares public policies to support microelectronics industries in China and Mexico and the last two chapters are focused on Mexico, its development model, and its small- and medium-sized businesses.

1298 Las fronteras: espacios estratégicos para la globalización. Coordinación de Héctor Antonio Padilla Delgado et al. Ciudad Juárez, Mexico: Universidad Autónoma de Ciudad Juárez: Benemérita Universidad Autónoma de Puebla, 2017. 367 p.: bibl., ill., maps.

The first six chapters of this work explore the concept of the US-Mexico border within the framework of a global North America deemed essential for the advancement of transnational capitalism. Concepts such as securitization and militarization are examined from the perspective of border communities. The second part of the book is focused on the impact of globalization and militarization on various social groups. Specific chapters consider environmental security and access to shared water resources, the plight of deported exconvicts, migration and its impact on a small border community, and the impact of migration on Mexico's southern border. The authors of this interdisciplinary work represent a variety of social science disciplines.

1299 Gálvez, Alyshia. Eating NAFTA: trade, food policies, and the destruction of Mexico. Oakland: University of California Press, 2018. 270 p.: bibl., ill., index.

The author of this monograph used ethnographic fieldwork, discourse analysis, and other methods to examine Mexico's food system and changing foodways. The goal of the study is to understand the forces responsible for the loss of Mexico's traditional "milpa diet" of local corn products and vegetables and its replacement with an industrially based diet of processed food that contributes to diabetes and various comorbidities such as problems of excess weight. The book also seeks to understand the responses of national, state, and local governments to growing health problems caused by the transformation of traditional foodways. After an introductory chapter, Gálvez narrates the history of Mexico's food traditions, the dramatic changes represented by the free trade agreement, and the growth of diabetes and other noncommunicable diseases.

1300 **García Zamora, Rodolfo.** México, la nación desafiada: análisis y propuesta ante la migración y la falta de desarrollo en México. Ciudad de México: Universidad Autónoma de Zacatecas: MAPorrúa, Librero-Editor, 2019. 238 p.: bibl., ill., maps. (Serie Estudios críticos del desarrollo)

Written in the run-up to the 2018 election of President Andrés Manuel López Obrador, García Zamora makes the case that the absence of economic development requires Mexico to change its economic model. At times polemical and at times analytical, the work refers to the neoliberal model as an economic model of death, citing data on the thousands that have died in drug wars and the social costs of institutionalized corruption and impunity. The bulk of the book explores the challenges of mass migration, including the potential role of Mexican migrants residing in the US and the impact of return migration on both the nation and their communities of origin.

Garfias, Francisco. Elite coalitions, limited government, and fiscal capacity development: evidence from Bourbon Mexico. See item **1259**.

1301 **Gomis, Redi; Jorge Carrillo;** and **Jordy Micheli.** Las multinacionales en datos: empleo, recursos humanos e innovación en México. Tijuana, Mexico: El Colegio de la Frontera Norte, 2018. 263 p.: bibl., tables.

Although it is self-contained, this work is part of a study of multinational firms spread across approximately nine countries. The goal of both this publication on multinationals in Mexico and its associated research on other countries is to fill the gaps in primary data on multinational firms. The importance of this volume can be found in the 150 pages of tables containing the results of a survey of multinationals operating in Mexico between 2008 and 2009. A short essay contextualizing the survey's focus is followed by a detailed discussion of sample selection and other methodological issues.

1302 **González Barajas, María Teresa; Antonio Emmanuel Pérez Brito;** and **Martha Isabel Bojórquez Zapata.** La competitividad en la region sur del estado de Sonora: análisis de los efectos de los programas sociales en la reducción de la pobreza. Yucatán, Mexico: Ediciones de la Universidad Autónoma de Yucatán, 2017. 157 p.: bibl., some color graphs, chiefly color ill., color map.

The researchers for this volume administered 96 surveys designed by the Secretary for Social Development. They also collected official data on socioeconomic conditions in seven municipalities of southern Sonora. Using the definition of poverty given by CONEVAL (Consejo Nacional de Evaluación de la Política de Desarrollo Social), they determined that the municipality of Alamos had the highest poverty rate. The goal of their research was to determine the relative effectiveness or ineffectiveness of each of seven different social programs in reducing poverty. Chapters 1 and 2 discuss the definition of poverty and chapter 3 describes the methodology employed. The results are presented in chapter 4 and the final chapter offers conclusions and recommendations.

1303 **Las grietas del neoliberalismo: dimensiones de la desigualdad contemporánea en México.** Coordinación de María Cristina Bayón. Ciudad de México: UNAM, Instituto de Investigaciones Sociales, 2019. 416 p.: bibl., ill.

This volume presents an interdisciplinary analysis of the many dimensions of inequality. Bayón introduces the book with an overview of Bourdieu's work on social classes and their symbolic and cultural meanings. The 10 essays on different dimensions of inequality are by scholars drawn from sociology, social science, economics, anthropology, and demography. The first part of the book focuses on material issues of wealth, work, and income. Part 2 considers welfare policies and inequality, part 3 education, and part 4 culture and social relations. Key questions asked by researchers concern how much inequality Mexico will tolerate, the relationship of inequality to neoliberal policies, and what policies might lead to desired changes.

1304 Hagan, Jacqueline Maria and **Joshua T. Wassink.** Return migration and social mobility in Mexico. (*Curr. Hist.*, 118:805, Feb. 2019, p. 50–55)

During the last 15 years, net migration to the US from Mexico has been zero or slightly negative, with more Mexican citizens leaving the US than arriving. Consequently, the opportunities open to Mexico's return migrants have become an increasingly significant social issue. This essay describes in general terms several cases of return migration to illustrate the larger issues. Migrant characteristics such as education and skills attained before leaving Mexico, skills acquired in the US, and ability to speak English are keys to mobility when migrants return. Some US-acquired skills are not transferable, however, and individual savings and rural-versus-urban location are also important factors.

1305 Hesketh, Chris. Spaces of capital/spaces of resistance: Mexico and the global political economy. Athens: University of Georgia Press, 2017. 223 p.: bibl., index. (Geographies of justice and social transformation; 37)

Hesketh analyzes the 1994 Chiapas uprising and the 2006 teachers strike in Oaxaca within the context of a hybrid theoretical framework combining history, geography, and sociology. Chapter 1 emphasizes the importance of spatial analysis and how space is produced in capitalist societies. Chapter 2 focuses on Latin America's integration into the global economy as well as its role as a site where globalism is produced. Chapter 3 turns toward Mexico and the relations between the state, space, and class formation. Chapters 4 and 5 apply the concepts developed in the previous chapters to analyzing resistance to Mexican and global capitalist notions of space in Chiapas and Oaxaca.

Holland, Bradley E. and **Viridiana Rios.** Violence and business interest in social welfare: evidence from Mexico. See item **1264**.

1306 Huerta González, Arturo. El ocaso de la globalización. Ciudad de México: UNAM, Facultad de Economía, 2017. 253 p.: bibl., graphs, ill.

Huerta González's well-written book is a response to two main trends. One is Mexico's seeming inability to grow its economy at a rate that leads to widespread increases in prosperity. The second is the appearance of populist policies in several high-income economies, including the US and the United Kingdom. The book begins with an analysis of internal and external conditions affecting Mexico's economy and a discussion of the inability of the country to adjust to external shocks. Subsequent chapters consider the limits of monetary policy and export-oriented growth, the decline of China as a motor of growth, and the rise of populism in the forms of Brexit (UK's removal from the EU) and the election of Donald Trump in the US.

1307 Impactos de la homologación del IVA en zonas fronterizas: análisis desde la plataforma informática OCEF. Edición de Noé Arón Fuentes Flores, Héctor Alejandro Vázquez y Ricardo Alberto Vero. Tijuana, Mexico: El Colegio de La Frontera Norte, 2017. 243 p.: bibl., ill., map, tables.

OCEF (Observatorio de Coyuntura de la Frontera Norte) is the Border Economic Situation Observatory in the Economics Department of El Colegio de la Frontera Norte. Its purpose is to report regularly on social and economic conditions along Mexico's border. In 2013, Mexico raised the value added tax in northern border communities from 11 percent to 16 percent, the same as the rest of the country. (In 2019, after publication of this work, President López Obrador reduced the value added tax in border communities to 8 percent but imposed requirements that excluded many individuals.) This work analyzes the economic impacts of the 2013 tax increase on consumer prices, food baskets, retail trade, and overall economic activity, including estimates of its growth and employment effects.

1308 Integración y desintegración del espacio económico mexicano: mercado interno y abastecimiento de las carnes desde la colonia al siglo XX. Coordinación de Enriqueta Quiroz. Ciudad de México: Instituto de Investigaciones Dr. José María Luis Mora: Consejo Nacional de Ciencia y

Technología, 2017. 374 p.: bibl., ill., maps. (Historia económica)

This edited volume consists of 10 case studies of geographically and temporally diverse regional markets. Most of the chapters are set in central Mexico (Michoacán, Mexico City and environs, Zacatecas, Aguascalientes). Each chapter attempts to understand the relationship between livestock production and meat consumption by examining prices, numbers of animals, local linkages between production centers and markets, and the existence of supporting policies, if any. Five chapters are set in the colonial period of the 18th century, three in the late colonial and early republican era, and two in the 20th century. The *longue durée* adopted in this work is intended to provide insight into the several centuries of changes that occurred in market supply and consumer demand.

1309 **La lógica neoliberal y su impacto en el estado mexicano: un enfoque multidisciplinario.** Compilación de Óscar Diego Bautista y Lauriano E. Rodríguez Ortiz. Toluca, Mexico: Centro de Investigación en Ciencias Sociales y Humanidades (CICSyH) de la Universidad Autónoma del Estado de México (UAEMex); Tuxtla Gutiérrez, Mexico: Universidad Autónoma de Chiapas, 2018. 188 p.: bibl., tables.

The six chapters of this edited volume are a multidisciplinary exploration of two variables. The first is the situation of the Mexican state and its deviation or adherence to the principles of the Constitution of 1917. The second is the implementation of neoliberal policies and the role of globalization. A key question is whether neoliberal policies are consistent with the Constitution of 1917. The first essay is a philosophical discussion that subverts neoliberalism with a number of ethical considerations. Subsequent essays explore the congruences and contradictions between neoliberalism and the constitution, the political economy of the nation-state, impunity, and the political situation of Indigenous peoples in Chiapas.

1310 **Martínez Meléndez, Ángel.** Causas de la instauración de la Ley Mexicana de Cooperación Internacional para el Desarrollo: análisis histórico-sistémico. Ciudad de México: Acervo Histórico Diplomático, Secretaría de Relaciones Exteriores, México, 2018. 269 p.: bibl.

The Development Assistance Committee of the OECD designated a class of countries that give and receive foreign aid as "emerging donors." Mexico falls into that group and is a member of the OECD, unlike China, Brazil, and India, who are not members and have resisted the designation since it entails a gradual evolution into net foreign aid donors. Mexico's Law of International Cooperation for Development institutionalized its status as a donor country and created a legal framework for providing development assistance. This work explores the reasons for the Mexican law from an international relations and political-institutional perspective. The first two chapters discuss international cooperation from the perspective of international relations theory. Chapter 3 narrates Mexico's experiences and a fourth chapter presents the author's analysis of the need for the law.

1311 **Meraz Ruiz, Lino.** Estrategias de competitividad de las micro, pequeñas y medianas empresas vinícolas de la ruta del vino del valle de Guadalupe. Mexicali, Mexico: Universidad Autónoma de Baja California, 2015. 346 p.: bibl., ill., maps. (Colección Tesis)

Those who are unfamiliar with Mexico, or only casually familiar, are usually surprised to discover that it produces world-class wines. Its best-known region has approximately 82 (as of 2011) wineries located in northern Baja California, primarily in the Valle de Guadalupe. These wineries range from microenterprises to small- and medium-sized firms. Meraz Ruiz's monograph contextualizes the industry within the literature on firm competitiveness and analyzes three specific strategies to increase competitiveness: interfirm cooperation in production and marketing, the uses of information and communication technologies (ICTs), and the supply of wine-tourism activities. The results are obtained from questionnaires distributed to a nonrandom sample of 64 wineries, of which 57 responded. The core of the study is a correlational analysis of increased competitiveness with the three strategies.

1312 Miguel S. Wionczek y el Prointergemex: travesías en el petróleo mexicano. Ensayo preliminar y selección de Joseph Hodara. Ciudad de México: El Colegio de México, 2017. 455 p.: bibl. (Colección Estudios sobre energía)

An introductory chapter by Joseph Hodara presents the author of the essays that comprise the bulk of this volume. Wionczek was a Polish migrant who became a naturalized Mexican citizen in the 1950s. Working as a journalist and with Mexico's national science foundation, he became familiar with international economic trends. In 1979 he was selected by the president of Colegio de México to direct a research project on the recent history of petroleum markets, their current circumstances, and future trends. The program was called *Prospectiva internacional en relación con la política mexicana de energéticos* (Prointergemex), which roughly translates as "Mexican energy policy and its international prospects." The bulk of the book is a revised selection of his texts on petroleum markets and international trends written in the 1970s and 1980s during the expansion of petroleum production and the international oil crisis.

1313 Millán Valenzuela, Henio. Instituciones y trampas de la pobreza en México: economía política e historia. Zinancantepec, Mexico: El Colegio Mexiquense, A.C., 2018. 338 p.: bibl., ill.

The author of this monograph on poverty traps in Mexico approaches the subject from the perspective of new institutionalism and the works of North and Acemoglu and Robinson. Mexico is definitely in a poverty trap, he asserts, because it has spent great sums on poverty alleviation, mostly to no avail. A review of efforts to combat poverty lead him to conclude that institutional explanations buried partly in Mexico's history are the reason why most policies to reduce poverty have failed. After examining political and economic macro factors, he considers a quantitative multilevel hierarchical model and estimates it econometrically. A concluding chapter emphasizes political factors over economic ones.

1314 Modelos económicos de las regiones de México. Coordinación de Alejandro Dávila Flores. Ciudad de México: Universidad Autónoma de Coahuila: MA Porrúa, 2019. 322 p.: bibl., ill. (Serie Las ciencias sociales, Cuarta década)

This volume presents seven quantitative and technical studies of economic regions in Mexico. The studies use a social accounting matrix (SAM). An introductory chapter explains the concepts, methodology, and utility of a SAM for measuring the socioeconomic effects of economic changes and defines seven mesoregions in Mexico. The seven regionally focused chapters examine structural economic changes in northwest Mexico, the role of exports in the economies of the northeast and western regions, income distribution in the north central region, the economic structure of central Mexico, the impact of declining oil production in the Gulf and southeast regions, the disarticulation of southern Mexico, and the effects of an export shock on the nation's seven mesoregions.

1315 Montes de Oca Barrera, Laura Beatriz. Comida chatarra: entre la gobernanza regulatoria y la simulación. Ciudad de México: UNAM, Instituto de Investigaciones Sociales, 2019. 258 p.: bibl.

Mexico, like the US, is infamous for its consumption of excess sugar and other unhealthy foodstuffs. Junk food (*comida chatarra*), defined as food high in salt, fat, and sugar, or as food of high caloric and low nutritional value, is widely available and consumed in large quantity. This study analyzes three institutional innovations for regulating junk food. Drawing from her previous analysis and her training as a political sociologist, Montes de Oca Barrera notes that the problem of regulation requires a reconfiguration of relations between the interests of the state, the market, and society. She suggests three institutional options, each favoring one of the three interests, and a method for judging whether the regulations are effective governance or a simulation of governance.

1316 **Nuevo modelo energético y cambio climático en México.** Coordinación de Erik Manuel Priego Brito y Rafael Loyola Díaz. Con la colaboración de Georgina Trujillo Zentella *et al.* Ciudad de México: H. Cámara de Diputados, LXIII Legislatura: Miguel Ángel Porrúa, librero-editor, 2018. 437 p.: bibl., ill., maps. (Serie Las ciencias sociales. Tercera década)

The 21 authors of the 14 chapters included in this edited volume are a diverse group of academics, government officials, industry insiders, consultants, and lawyers. All or nearly all have extensive background in energy markets, from production to distribution, marketing, and regulation. A short prologue explains the main goals of the energy reform of 2013. An introductory essay discusses energy reforms in the context of Mexican history and current national and international conditions. The rest of the book is divided into two parts. The first explores the new rules for the energy sector and contrasts Mexico with other Latin American hydrocarbon producers. The second and larger part explores the impacts of the reforms on hydrocarbon production, alternative energy, climate change policies, and public opinion.

1317 **Pérez Pineda, Jorge A.** Consideraciones sobre el papel del sector privado en la cooperación internacional para el desarrollo, una mirada desde México. Ciudad de México: Instituto de Investigaciones Dr. José María Luis Mora: Consejo Nacional de Ciencia y Tecnología, 2018. 149 p.: bibl. (Contemporánea, cooperación internacional y desarrollo)

In this relatively short work, the author undertakes a broad investigation of the international cooperation of Mexico's private sector in promoting economic development and poverty reduction. After a review of recent international efforts, the author considers the reactions of the private sector through social entrepreneurship, corporate social responsibility, and notions of good corporate citizenship. Chapter 2 examines the specific case of Mexico, including the evolution of concepts related to socially responsible entrepreneurship, philanthropy, public-private partnerships, and several forms of inclusive investing, such as business for the bottom of the pyramid. A final chapter debates the efficacy of the private sector in supporting economic development and poverty reduction.

1318 **Políticas proactivas en lo fiscal y financiero: México y América Latina.** Coordinación de María Irma Manrique Campos. Ciudad de México: UNAM, Instituto de Investigaciones Económicas, 2018. 244 p.: bibl., ill.

This collection of essays by academic specialists tackles two major problems in middle-income countries: finance and fiscal policy. The book is divided into three parts. Part one has chapters devoted to problems of international sovereign debt, including the debt crisis of the 1980s, the role of exchange rates, and historical episodes of debt crises in Latin America. Part two considers new fiscal and monetary policies, the fiscal cost of monetary restrictions, and inefficiencies in tax administration. The final section analyzes the availability of financial services in Mexican states, instability and chaos in Mexican capital markets, and the financial integration of Latin America. The analysis is quantitative and theoretically sophisticated.

1319 **Ramírez Hernández, Roberto.** La expansión metropolitana de la Ciudad de México y la dinámica de su estructura policéntrica: un análisis de las fuerzas de dispersión y concentración económicas como factores de crecimiento urbano entre 1993 y 2008. Ciudad de México: UNAM, Instituto de Investigaciones Económicas, 2016. 182 p.: bibl., ill., maps.

Ramírez Hernández's work uses regional science and location theory to describe the growth of Mexico City. The first chapter reviews the literature on location theory and defines several concepts, such as spatial economic concentration, spatial economic dispersion, and polycentric versus monocentric urban spaces. A model of urban expansion is proposed based on the interactions of land rents with concentrating and dispersing forces and the economics of agglomeration. Chapter 2 describes the evolution of Mexico City and chapter 3 analyzes its polycentrism both qualitatively and quantitatively with several statistical tests. Chapter 4 sets out the complete mathematical model and performs a series of econometric tests to measure the forces of concentration and dispersion.

1320 **La reciente crisis financiera y el debate sobre migración y desarrollo: propuestas para América Latina y México.** Coordinación de Ana María Aragonés. Ciudad de México: UNAM, Instituto de Investigaciones Económicas, 2016. 267 p.: bibl., ill.

This work explores the relationships between structural economic changes, including increased rates of innovation and the rapid growth of the knowledge economy, economic development, and patterns of migration. The perspective is interdisciplinary and pluralistic in the use of theory. Several authors note that migration patterns in the 21st century are no longer dominated by movements from less developed to more developed economies, and that climate change and other factors often force movement. Five of the 8 chapters are focused on Mexico; two others are general and one examines remittances in the Andean Community.

1321 **Reconfiguraciones socioterritoriales: entre el despojo capitalista y las resistencias comunitarias.** Coordinación de Gisela Espinosa Damián y Alejandra Meza Velarde. Puebla, Mexico: Benemérita Universidad Autónoma de Puebla; Ciudad de México: Universidad Autónoma Metropolitana, Unidad Xochimilco, 2019. 301 p.: bibl., ill. (Mundos rurales)

The 12 chapters of this mosaic of case studies are drawn from the experiences of communities across different regions of Mexico. While the chapters are heavily heterogeneous in their disciplinary approaches, regional focuses, and the resistance movements described, each emphasizes the concept of territory. The goal is to use a territorial framework to identify the key themes in the political debates over the impacts of megaprojects, the exploitation of natural resources, the dislocation of Indigenous and other communities, and the forms of resistance to dominant economic forces. A primary motivation for this work was the perception that the exploitation of communities and the environment by the owners of capital crossed a threshold from worrisome to extremely alarming.

1322 **Rezagos de la economía de Jalisco en la apertura económica (1980–2015).** Coordinación de Rubén Chavarín Rodríguez, Carlos Fong Reynoso y Carlos Riojas López. Zapopan, Mexico: Arlequín, 2017. 197 p.: bibl., ill. (Estudios globales, de población y región; III)

The five essays presented in this book explore the causes of the lagging economic performance of the state of Jalisco during the last three decades. An introductory essay outlines different theories of economic growth and provides quantitative information about Jalisco's relative underperformance. Five main factors are highlighted as important for understanding the case of Jalisco: geography, a predatory state government, the role of entrepreneurs and competition, retail trade and innovation, and the role of economic groups in the economic opening of the state. Individual chapters examine each of these factors.

1323 **Robles Robles, María del Rosario Fátima.** Las maquiladoras de exportación y sus actores: una visión de los empresarios. Hermosillo, Mexico: El Colegio de Sonora, 2016. 286 p.: bibl., ill.

Entrepreneurship in Sonora's maquiladora industry is the focus of this work. The author begins with a literature review of the concept of entrepreneurship, the role of entrepreneurs, and their relationship to economic development, from Weber and Schumpeter to Bourdieu and other more recent scholars. She then turns to a focus on Sonora, with chapters on the state's entrepreneurs and an economic profile. Two chapters examine conditions in Sonora's main urban centers and the actions of entrepreneurs in those locales. A concluding chapter draws together the previous chapters to present a longer-run view of industrialization and the future of the maquiladora.

1324 **Rumbo al auto del futuro: innovación, sistemas de calidad y trabajo en la industria automotriz de México.** Coordinación de Sergio A. Sandoval

Godoy y Alex Covarrubias Valdenebro. Ciudad de México: AM Editores, Clave Editorial; Hermosillo, Mexico: CIAD: El Colegio de Sonora, 2017. 301 p.: bibl., ill. (some color), color maps. (Ciencias sociales)

Mexico is the largest producer of vehicles in Latin America and seventh largest in the world. It is also the fourth largest global exporter of vehicles. Consequently, the transformation of the automobile and the processes used in its manufacture are of great importance to the nation's economy. The first of the book's three parts examines the technological changes confronting the industry, including supply chain issues, alternative energy sources, big data, and the social impacts of smart cars. Part two focuses on quality control, the organization of production, and systems for environmental sustainability. Part three examines the industry from the perspective of its workforce. An English language introduction summarizes the book.

1325 **Santos, Saúl de los** *et al.* Ecosistemas de innovación en la frontera norte: Chihuahua y Coahuila. Tijuana, Mexico: El Colegio de la Frontera Norte: COMECSO, 2017. 440 p.: bibl., ill., maps.

This work is part of a series of diagnostics financed by Mexico's national science foundation (CONACYT) examining science, technology, and the innovation capacities of states and regions within Mexico. This analysis of Chihuahua and Coahuila utilizes detailed cases studies of firms and industries along with semistructured interviews with businesspeople, academics, and government officials. The broad goal of the research is to measure the "ecosystems of innovation." The book presents five chapters on each state, covering (1) socioeconomic characteristics, (2) regulatory frameworks, (3) indexes of science, technology, and innovation, (4) key institutions and actors, and (5) conclusions and recommendations. The purpose is to understand how states establish priorities and assign resources, and how those actions complement national policies.

1326 **Selección de los Archivos Económicos de la Secretaría de Hacienda y Crédito Público, Biblioteca Miguel Lerdo de Tejada.** Ciudad de México: Centro de Investigación y Docencia Económicas (CIDE), 2021. <https://repositorio-digital.cide.edu/handle/11651/3764>

These digitized files consist of a large collection of press articles in the archives of the Mexican Finance Ministry. There are more than 40,000 folders of press clippings spanning a period from the first third of the 19th century to the last decade of the 20th century. The digitized material covers two main topics: government debt and the nationalization of banks in Mexico. This material is contained in the digital repository of CIDE (Centro de Investigación y Docencia Económicas), an institution of higher education in Mexico City, and is publicly available. All the materials are in Spanish.

1327 **Sonora: problemas de ayer y hoy, desafíos y soluciones.** Coordinación de Gabriela Grijalva Monteverde. Sonora, Mexico: El Colegio de Sonora, 2017. 267 p.: bibl., ill.

The eight chapters of this work offer an introduction to economic conditions in the state of Sonora. An introductory essay notes the relatively disappointing results from the broad transformation of the economy in the last four decades. Individual chapters examine why employment remains too scarce and precarious, how externalities such as the effects of manufacturing on water resources are undervalued, the challenges presented by the return migration of children from the US, and the need for more inclusive policies for Indigenous people and communities. Additional essays trace the history of economic development policies in Sonora, describe the challenge of the state's political cycles, and propose an agenda for state public policy.

1328 **Staudt, Kathleen A.** How NAFTA has changed Mexico. (*Curr. Hist.*, 117:796, Feb. 2018, p. 43–48)

NAFTA remains one of the most controversial North American policies of our time. This article associates most of Mexico's current challenges to the effects of NAFTA. In some cases, the association is explicit, in others implicit. The discussion focuses on the enormous gap between incomes in the US and Mexico, the widening inequality inside Mexico, the dire circumstances of small-scale farming, and the growth of new industries such as aerospace and automotive value chains where wages for Mexican workers continue to lag behind their US counterparts even as productivity differences shrink or disappear altogether. The story of NAFTA presented in this article is one where the trade agreement is the mechanism used to keep Mexico dependent on the US.

1329 Ugarteche, Oscar. Arquitectura financiera internacional: una genealogía (1850–2015). Ciudad de México: Akal: UNAM, Instituto de Investigaciones Económicas, 2018. 382 p.: bibl., ill. (Inter pares. Serie Ayer, hoy, mañana)

This book, a revision of the author's 2007 PhD dissertation, provides an extensive description of the distinct events that created and changed the international economy's financial architecture from the 19th century to the present. The book begins with a definition of key concepts before proceeding to the beginnings of modern international finance in the late 19th and early 20th centuries. The author describes the main historical events and international challenges that led to the creation of new institutions and the modification of existing ones, including the Bretton Woods systems, the IMF, the Washington Consensus, and approaches to resolving international debt problems. A final chapter addresses the current problems of risk and industries and corporations that are deemed "too big to fail."

1330 Valle Baeza, Alejandro and **Blanca Gloria Martínez González.** Los salarios de la crisis. Segunda edición. Ciudad de México: UNAM, Facultad de Economía, 2017. 191 p.: bibl., graphs, ill., tables.

This is the second edition of a short monograph on Mexican salaries in the neoliberal era. The authors use Marxist theory to analyze industrial salaries in Mexico (chapter 3), to compare them to salaries in the US (chapter 4), and to explore their relationship in real terms to productivity (chapter 5). A final chapter measures the increasing rate of surplus value and explains higher salaries in the US as due to a lower rate of extraction of surplus value by the owners of capital. The appendices provide a large amount of quantitative data on wages, real and nominal, and the text is illustrated with many time series graphs.

1331 Zottele Allende, Aníbal; Li Yan; and **Mario Alberto Santiago.** Las Pymes mexicanas y chinas: ante el crecimiento acelerado de las relaciones económicas entre ambas naciones. Xalapa, Mexico: Universidad Veracruzana, Dirección General de Relaciones Internacionales: MEXCHAM China: Centro de Estudios China-Veracruz, 2017. 191 p.: bibl., ill., maps.

This work is a collaboration between authors at Renmin University (Beijing) and the Universidad Veracruzana. It brings together official Chinese and Mexican data to describe micro-, small-, and medium enterprises in both countries. The researchers begin with a review of China-Mexico relations followed by a discussion of the concepts of micro-, small-, and medium-sized enterprises. Given that international standards for classifying enterprises by size do not exist, they examine the different definitions used in China and Mexico. The book then discusses the regional and sectoral distributions of micro-, small, and medium enterprises in both countries. The last two chapters compare Mexican and Chinese systems of financing and the various systems of support offered.

CENTRAL AMERICA AND THE CARIBBEAN (except Cuba)

DANIEL MASÍS-IVERSON, *Professor, Department of Studies, Inter-American Defense College*

THE CURRENT SET OF WORKS on the political economy of Central America and the Caribbean (except Cuba) for *HLAS* 77 includes studies of Costa Rica, El Salvador, and Guatemala in Central America, and the Dominican Republic, Haiti, Jamaica, Saint Vincent and the Grenadines, Puerto Rico, and the Caribbean as a whole. The underlying theme of the publications is achieving economic and social development, with attention given to domestic economic, social, and political conditions, and also to the wider global context within which the countries' economies and societies find themselves inserted.

Contributions by Piedras Feria (item **1335**) and the ICEFI (item **1337**) recommend domestic policy reforms for Guatemala. Piedras Feria suggests that public policy recognize cultural production as an economic sector equally important to others, while the ICEFI study proposes the establishment of a modest universal basic income for Guatemalans, which would necessarily require additional reforms in other areas, including, among others, fiscal policy.

González Orellana (item **1333**) and Arias Peñate (item **1332**) focus on the close relationship between international forces and domestic outcomes in El Salvador. González Orellana examines the effects of what he considers an excessive reliance on remittances by this Central American country. Arias Peñate provides an in-depth analysis of what he argues are the deleterious effects of the adoption of the US dollar by El Salvador as its official currency. Both authors propose the de-dollarization of the Salvadorian economy.

Raventós Vorst (item **1336**) and Gudmundson (item **1334**) provide contributions to the political history surrounding Costa Rica's economic and social development. Gudmundson builds on previous historical work as he documents the evolution of the cooperative movement in coffee production and distribution, including exports, in the 20th and 21st centuries, and provides a novel interpretation of the interplay of the movement and the ideological development of the country's most important political party for over 60 years. Raventós Vorst examines the history, the fraught politics, and the shift toward neoliberal economic policy surrounding the national referendum leading to the approval of Costa Rica's participation in the Dominican Republic-Central America Free Trade Agreement with the US.

The entries on the Caribbean span a wide spectrum of views. Editors Alleyne et al. offer detailed contributions covering many discrete topics viewed from a market-oriented perspective (item **1345**). Thompson centers on Jamaica but also includes the Caribbean generally (item **1343**). Both he and Montás, who focuses on the Dominican Republic (item **1341**), also present a traditional economic approach, and offer varied practical recommendations. Werner, who examines economic conditions in the Dominican Republic and Haiti (item **1347**), and Gonsalves, who analyzes the evolution of the labor movement in Saint Vincent and the Grenadines (item **1340**), on the other hand, hew closely to a Marxist perspective and offer a highly critical view of the current development path, squarely inserted in its global context, in those three countries.

Finally, the entries on Puerto Rico all have as their backdrop this US territory's special status and its people's complex relationship with the mainland. The volume edited by Fuentes Ramírez offers analyses that contribute to the understanding of the formidable challenges Puerto Rico faces in its quest to achieve economic and social development, including the 1996 repeal of Section 936 of the US Internal Revenue Code (item **1339**). Córdova Iturregui provides an in-depth study of the process leading to the repeal of Section 936 and the effects of the latter on industrial employment on the island (item **1338**). Trigo sharply critiques the establishment of a federal Financial Oversight and Management Board for Puerto Rico in 2016 (item **1344**). For their part, Mora, Dávila, and Rodríguez share the results of their detailed research on the demographic shifts between the island and the US mainland, with an emphasis on the impact on the Puerto Rican economy (item **1342**).

CENTRAL AMERICA

1332 Arias Peñate, Salvador. Regreso del colón a El Salvador y el derrumbe del imperialismo del dólar. La Libertad, El Salvador: Asociación para el Desarrollo Económico y Social de El Salvador, 2017. 551 p.: bibl., ill.

The author provides an in-depth critical analysis of the results of El Salvador's decision to replace its domestic currency, the *colón*, with the US dollar in the year 2000. He argues that the adoption of the dollar has negatively affected economic growth and development, as well as equality and social welfare. He further argues that El Salvador should shake itself of US "financial imperialism" and return to a national currency. His context includes a review of the rise of the dollar as a global currency and the relationship of Latin America with the dollar, with particular attention to Ecuador and Argentina. This book is well-worth reading for anyone interested in studying the dilemmas facing developing countries regarding their foreign currency policies.

Caruso, German Daniel; Maria Emilia Cucagna; and Julieta Ladronis. The distributional impacts of the reduction in remittances in Central America in COVID-19 times. See item **472**.

1333 González Orellana, Mauricio. El Salvador: enfermedad holandesa, educación, y crecimiento. San Salvador: UFG Editores, Instituto de Ciencia, Tecnología e Innovación, 2016. 152 p.: bibl.

The author argues that El Salvador suffers from "Dutch Disease," a term that refers to the appreciation of a country's currency, usually due to the excessive reliance on a valuable natural resource such as oil. In El Salvador's case, the dependency is on emigrant remittances. The constant inflow of remittances from abroad has led to a physical and human decapitalization of the country. In particular, the returns to education, a theoretically important capital (and hence development) enhancer, have decreased over time. To overcome these and other deleterious effects of remittances, an important policy measure that should be adopted is the de-dollarization of the Salvadoran economy.

1334 Gudmundson, Lowell. Costa Rica después del café: la era cooperativa en la historia y la memoria. San José: EUNED, Editorial Universidad Estatal a Distancia, 2018. 190 p.: bibl., ill., maps.

The author seeks to provide a detailed account of the "historiographically elusive" small and medium-sized Costa Rican coffee growers, some in the country's Central Valley and some outside of it, with particular attention to their relationship with the cooperative movement that began in the 1950s alongside a novel interpretation of the ideological evolution of the country's National Liberation Party, which governed the country during most of the years between 1948 and 2014. This book is a natural sequel to the author's previous volume, *Costa Rica before Coffee: Occupational Distribution, Wealth Inequality and Elite Society in the Village Economy of the 1840s* (see *HLAS 50:1408*). This book is also available in English as *Costa Rica after Coffee: The Co-op Era in History and Memory* (2021).

Pérez Sáinz, Juan Pablo. La redefinición de las relaciones de poder con los sectores subalternos en Centroamérica hacia fines del siglo XX. See *HLAS 76:526.*

1335 **Piedras Feria, Ernesto.** Guatemala: un análisis de la contribución económica de la cultura. Guatemala: Editorial Cultura, 2017. 150 p.: bibl., color ill. (Ensayo) (Colección economía y cultura; 2)

In this slim, beautifully illustrated volume, the author documents the economic importance of cultural production in Guatemala. He treats the sector as conceptually equal to agriculture, industry, and services, as classified by the country's national accounts system. The competitive and dynamic cultural industries sector provides employment, encourages foreign exchange, and drives investment, which taken together warrant public support for its development.

1336 **Raventós Vorst, Ciska.** Mi corazón dice no: el movimiento de oposición al TLC en Costa Rica. Ciudad Universitaria Rodrigo Facio, Costa Rica: Editorial UCR: Instituto de Investigaciones Sociales, 2018. 213 p.: bibl., ill.

In August 2004, Costa Rica, El Salvador, Guatemala, Honduras, Nicaragua, the Dominican Republic, and the US signed the Dominican Republic-Central America FTA (CAFTA-DR). It entered into force in 2006 for El Salvador, Guatemala, Honduras, Nicaragua, and the US, in 2007 for the Dominican Republic, and for Costa Rica in 2009. The process to reach the agreement, however, was not uniformly smooth. In this study, the author takes the reader through the fraught politics of its congressional approval in Costa Rica. The process culminated in a referendum on the agreement, for this country a treaty, following (mostly peaceful) mass mobilizations of tens and even of hundreds of thousands of citizens against the treaty in a broad coalition of farmers, public sector trade unions, Indigenous organizations, environmental activists, and student organizations, among others. The referendum resulted in a narrow victory in favor of the treaty. As Raventós reports, 51.6 percent voted for it, 48.4 against it, with an abstention rate of 40 percent. The backdrop of her careful account and analysis are the also fraught political times and the movement of the country towards neoliberal economic policies from the 1980s and particularly the 1990s onward. For political scientist's comment, see item **860**.

1337 **Renta básica universal: más libertad, más igualdad, más empleo, más bienestar: una propuesta para Guatemala (2019-2030).** Guatemala: ICEFI, Instituto Centroamericano de Estudios Fiscales, 2017. 168 p.: bibl., ill. (chiefly color).

This book begins with an analysis of the nature and effects of socioeconomic inequality on a global scale, including the dangers it poses to democracy. It then studies inequality in Guatemala and its relation to, *inter alia,* the labor market, nutrition, children's access to education, discrimination and violence against Indigenous communities, and the patriarcal framework women live in. A universal basic income (UBI) of 175 Quetzales per month from 2019 to 2030 (approximately 23.00 USD/month) would go a long way toward reducing inequality and its nefarious effects on democracy and development. To make this proposal viable, additional steps are needed, such as better management of public debt, tax reform to eliminate odious fiscal privileges and tax evasion, and a more progressive taxation system; higher wages and universal and improved access to public goods are also important. The authors maintain that these measures would substantially increase economic growth and employment, reduce inequality, and increase welfare and freedom.

Rodríguez Solano, Pablo Augusto. La cuestión fiscal y la formación del estado de Costa Rica, 1821–1859. See *HLAS 76:530.*

CARIBBEAN

Agriculture et reconstruction: défis, enjeux et perspectives de l'agriculture haïtienne. See item **434**.

1338 **Córdova Iturregui, Félix.** La eliminación de la Sección 936: la historia que se intenta suprimir. Río Piedras, Puerto Rico: Publicaciones Gaviota, 2020. 273 p.: bibl., ill.

Section 936 of the US Internal Revenue Code, enacted in 1976, provided a tax exemption for US corporations operating in Puerto Rico and other US possessions, with a view to promoting employment in those locations. President Bill Clinton signed legislation in 1996 to begin phasing out Section 936 over a period of 10 years. Córdova details the political process leading to this outcome, with a special focus on Puerto Rican politics. He argues that, although the decision was in the hands of the US Congress and the president, Puerto Rican political players were decisive in the initiative to eliminate the section from the US tax code. Governor Pedro Roselló and his New Progressive Party were on the side of achieving statehood for the island and Section 936 stood in the way. Among others, the effects of the elimination of Section 936, accompanied by neoliberal economic policies, included a steady decline in industrial employment in Puerto Rico over the next 10 years and a higher level of worker exploitation in those industries that remained on the island. The author contends, moreover, that the responsibility for this unfortunate outcome, and for not having an alternative plan in place, is shared by the US and Puerto Rican governments.

1339 Desarrollo económico de Puerto Rico: ensayos para una nueva economía. Edición de Ricardo R. Fuentes Ramírez. Textos de Edwin Irizarry Mora et al. San Juan: Ediciones Callejón, 2017. 351 p.: bibl., ill. (Colección En fuga. Ensayo)

This book of essays is intended for multiple uses: in university class settings, for policymakers, and for the public at large. Written from different perspectives, as the foreword explains, the authors are in agreement that Puerto Rican public policy over the last few decades has been ineffective. Following the introductory essay, the chapters are organized into three categories: the current economic situation, the requirements for human development, and Puerto Rico's status as a US territory and its effect on the island's economic development planning. The chapters in the first two sections include essays that take the broader view and others that are more focused, e.g., on income distribution, women's participation in the island's economy, agricultural development, and water as a resource. The essays in the third section examine, *inter alia*, the effects of the Jones Act (regulating maritime commerce in the US) on Puerto Rican trade competitiveness and the possible economic effects of an eventual Puerto Rican independence. This is a valuable collection for scholars as well as the lay reader interested in understanding the daunting development challenges facing the island and the possible ways to overcome them.

Gahman, Levi; Gabrielle Thongs; and Adaeze Greenidge. Disaster, debt, and "underdevelopment": the cunning of colonial-capitalism in the Caribbean. See item **448**.

1340 Gonsalves, Ralph E. The political economy of the labour movement in Saint Vincent and the Grenadines. Kingstown, St. Vincent and the Grenadines: Strategy Forum, Inc., 2019. 352 p.: bibl., indexes. (Caribbean ideas; 5)

The author, at the time of writing into his third term as prime minister of Saint Vincent and the Grenadines, provides a history of the labor movement in his country from 1935 to 2018. He writes from a historical-materialist perspective, establishing close connections between evolving economic and social conditions on the one hand, and political developments on the other. Historical scholarship intertwines with personal political experience, weaving a complex tapestry of Saint Vincent and the Grenadines politics over nearly a century and constituting a valuable contribution to the literature.

1341 Montás, Juan Temístocles. Crisis, políticas y reformas: lecciones aprendidas en República Dominicana. Santo Domingo: Juan Temístocles Montás: Alfa y Omega, 2017. 396 p.: bibl., ill.

This book is the product of considerable research and deep thinking on Dominican economic, social, and institutional development. The author begins by reviewing the global context in which the Dominican Republic finds itself inserted. Among other notable changes on a world scale, the share of global gross domestic product (GDP) of the "Emerging 7" or "E7" countries, the largest emerging economies of Brazil, China, India, Indonesia, Mexico,

Russia, and Turkey, has surpassed that of the "Group of Seven" or "G7" countries, comprised of Canada, France, Germany, Italy, Japan, the UK, and the US. The author is squarely in the camp of those who believe globalization has been largely beneficial and he wishes the Dominican Republic to position itself to take advantage of it fully. Throughout the volume, Montás provides his views on what he considers to be the six main public policy priorities for his country, i.e., macroeconomic policies to minimize growth volatility; development policies that foster growth with equity; policies regarding the Dominican Republic's insertion in the global economy; policies to ensure social cohesion; environmental and intergenerational equity policies, and consensus-based policies for institutional development. This book constitutes a thought-provoking and fascinating primer for any reader interested in the socioeconomic development of the Dominican Republic, and also provides a basis for the comparative analysis of the development process in other Latin American and Caribbean countries.

1342 **Mora, Marie T.; Alberto Dávila;** and **Hávidan Rodríguez.** Population, migration, and socioeconomic outcomes among island and mainland Puerto Ricans: La Crisis Boricua. Foreword by Francisco L. Rivera-Batiz. Lanham, Md.: Lexington Books, 2018. 217 p.: bibl., ill., index.

In this admirably researched book, Mora, Dávila, and Rodríguez document and explain the demographic shifts of Puerto Ricans between this US territory and the mainland, closely linking them with the variations in the island's economic fortunes and misfortunes since its acquisition by the US following the Spanish-American War (1898). Their focus, however, is on the period before and the period following the steep escalation of the "Boricua Crisis" in 2006 and ensuing years, where the "perfect storm" of a fiscal crisis met a long-term period of economic stagnation. Among the intervening variables, the reader will find the secular unequal income distribution, the expiration of corporate tax breaks (see item **1338** in this section) and its effect on industry, the collapse of the housing market, the rise in energy prices, weak labor markets, and others. All are brought to bear in this statistically rich analysis of the migration patterns between the island and the mainland and the outcomes for Puerto Ricans on one side or the other of the Caribbean Sea. The book is scholarly, yet accessible to the lay reader as well.

Rodríguez, José Luis. La política económica en Cuba: valorando lo alcanzado y los retos a enfrentar (2011–2018). See item **980**.

1343 **Thompson, Canute S.** Education and development: policy imperatives for Jamaica and the Caribbean. Foreword by P.J. Patterson. Kingston: The University of the West Indies Press, 2020. 147 p.: bibl., index.

In this multifaceted book, the author examines several related challenges to development in Jamaica particularly, but with wider applicability to the Caribbean as a whole. Among these challenges, within the wider framework of globalization, are productivity, governance, management of the public sector, and crime, the latter seen using the lens of public health. The provision of quality education at all levels is a key to success in economic and social development. Thompson calls for citizen action, particularly among university academics, to address the issues he carefully examines. His book is a clarion call and a very valuable source for all those interested in Caribbean development.

1344 **Trigo, María de los Angeles.** Los Estados Unidos y la promesa para Puerto Rico: un análisis de la Ley para la Supervisión, Administración y Estabilidad Económica de Puerto Rico. San Juan: América Libros, 2017. 263 p.: bibl.

The author carries out a detailed, critical analysis of chapter 20 of Title 48 of the US Code on "Puerto Rico Oversight, Management and Economic Stability," amended in 2016. She is particularly critical of the establishment of a US federally mandated Financial Oversight and Management Board, whose powers she sees as excessive and that, in her view, does not properly or adequately serve the inhabitants of the island. She further criticizes, *inter alia*, provisions regarding the minimum wage, the privatization of state-owned assets, and the process for the approval of fiscal plans and budgets. The author also provides a narrative regarding the politics of the bill's passage into law. This book is a valuable contribution to the literature on the current relationship between the US and its territory.

1345 Unleashing growth and strengthening resilience in the Caribbean. Edited by Trevor Alleyne, Inci Ötker, Uma Ramakrishnan, and Krishna Srinivasan. Washington, D.C.: International Monetary Fund, 2017. 364 p.: bibl., color ill., index.

This book is comprised of 15 chapters written by 31 contributors affiliated with the International Monetary Fund (IMF), the Inter-American Development Bank (IDB), or the World Bank. Although each chapter is independent and self-sufficient, there is an over-arching perspective. Central to it is the notion that the countries' business climates and hence growth prospects are stymied by three basic structural weaknesses: the high cost of energy, the emigration of skilled workers, and violent crime, to which is added natural disasters of increased frequency and destructiveness. Among the topics addressed in the chapters are: tourism, tax incentives, economic citizenship programs (these programs, not exclusively of the Caribbean, offer citizenship or residency in exchange for investment), sovereign debt and other financial and banking issues, emigration and remittances, energy, and the cost of violence. Throughout the volume, the reader will find the results of careful research and documentation, along with policy recommendations, making it a very valuable contribution to the literature on Caribbean development.

1346 The W. Arthur Lewis reader. Edited by Hamid A. Ghany. Kingston: Ian Randle Publishers, 2019. 138 p.: bibl., index.

This volume gathers contributions of scholars from the University of the West Indies celebrating the life, ideas, and scientific accomplishments of the 1979 Nobel Memorial Prize winning economist from St. Lucia, W. Arthur Lewis. Within a discussion of the elements of Lewis' thought, the authors touch upon his contributions to international development economics, his thinking on the effects of colonization, and his political philosophy. This delightful book is a wonderful introduction to one of the most important development economists of the 20th century.

1347 Werner, Marion. Global displacements: the making of uneven development in the Caribbean. Southern Gate, England: Wiley-Blackwell, 2016. 215 p.: bibl., index. (Antipode book series)

The author combines social and geographic theory with ethnographic research, providing an important contribution to the study of contemporary globalization. The context for the ethnographic studies, focused on the Dominican Republic and Haiti, starts with the shift toward export-oriented industrialization (towards Northern markets) in Latin America and the Caribbean, and the abandonment of import substitution industrialization (ISI). This new approach occurs within a general neoliberal policy framework that includes free trade agreements that accommodate the interests of multinational corporations. Overall, this process is related to the restructuring of the global factory, accompanied by a discourse treating global production as a stage of development in general, against which Werner develops and opposes the Marxist concept of uneven development, combined with a feminist approach that reveals gendered differences in the production processes of the garment industry in both Haiti and the Dominican Republic. This deep, nuanced book is well-worth careful reading.

Zambrana, Rocío. Colonial debts: the case of Puerto Rico. See item **972**.

CUBA

MARIO A. GONZÁLEZ-CORZO, *Associate Professor, Department of Economics and Business, Lehman College, The City University of New York*

CUBA IS FACING the worst economic crisis since the 1990s, when Gross Domestic Product (GDP) fell by an estimated 32 percent (in real terms), severely reducing the living standards of the Cuban population. Gross Domestic Product (GDP) fell 0.2 percent in 2019 and 10.9 percent in 2020 (after the COVID-19 crisis); between 2013 and 2020, Cuba's GDP *decreased* at an annual average rate of 1.3 percent. The fiscal deficit reached close to 30 percent in 2021; between 2019 and 2022, Cuba experienced an unprecedented rise in inflation. Official statistics indicate that the inflation rate rose from 18.5 percent in 2019 to 40 percent in 2022; however, estimates from independent experts suggest that in 2021, the inflation rate ranged between 140 and 470 percent, reaching close to 500 percent in 2022 (item **1356**).

Since 2020, the Cuban peso (CUP) has been on a downward spiral reminiscent of its rapid devaluation during the worst years of the "Special Period" (1989–93). Despite the introduction of a program of monetary unification in January 2021, the informal exchange rate between the Cuban peso (CUP) and the US dollar (USD) remains well above the 120 CUP/USD exchange rate established by the Cuban government in August 2022. The depreciation of the CUP/USD exchange rate in the informal sector has been primarily driven by increased demand for dollars by Cubans wishing to migrate to the US. In 2022, an estimated 280,000 Cuban migrants entered the US (mainly via the US-Mexico border), compared to an estimated 40,000 in 2021.

Production indicators across multiple sectors of the Cuban economy reflect the severity of the current economic crisis. Industrial production has fallen by more than 62 percent since reaching a post-1989 peak in 2013 (item **1357**); non-sugar agriculture continues to suffer from notable declines in the area harvested, physical output levels, and agricultural yields, and domestic (agricultural) output remains unable to satisfy consumer demand (contributing to the aforementioned historically high inflation) (item **1354**). Cuba imports more than 80 percent of the food and agricultural products consumed by its population. Sugar production also continued on its (seemingly endless) downward spiral (item **1358**). During the 2020–2021 sugar harvest, Cuba produced a total of 480,000 tons of sugar, or 52 percent of the planned level of output, representing the lowest output level in 120 years (or since 1901 when sugar output reached 695,189 tons).

In recent years, particularly in 2021 and 2022, the Cuban economy has also been impacted by massive nationwide power outages (*"apagones"*). The country's electrical power infrastructure collapsed in 2022 due to decades of deferred maintenance, insufficient capitalization, and the damage caused by Hurricane Ian, which hit the island on 26 September 2022. Later that month, the nation's state-run electrical monopoly Unión Eléctrica de Cuba (UNE) announced new blackouts due to a generation capacity deficit of 23.5 percent during peak demand hours. For the rest of 2022 and into 2023, UNE predicted a generation capacity deficit of more than 50 percent, resulting in extended nationwide blackouts (in some cases lasting 12 consecutive hours or more). Cuba's energy crisis triggered large numbers of popular protests and social unrest throughout the island in 2022 and was a contributing factor to the massive exodus of close to 300,000 Cubans that year. While some measures to confront the energy crisis have been introduced, and the minister of Energy and Mines was replaced in late 2022, in February 2023, the UNE announced that Cuba (once again) would be facing major, extended, nationwide blackouts due to continued power generation deficits (into the foreseeable future). The magnitude and persistence of Cuba's energy crisis casts a dark cloud over the country's short-term and mid-range economic prospects for economic growth. The Cuban government has recognized this dire situation by revising their GDP estimates for 2023 downward and appealing to the Cuban people to "make more sacrifices," "work harder," and prepare for more economic hardships, scarcity, and difficulties.

Unlike "the economic crisis of the 1990s," which marked the beginning of the "Special Period," Cuba's current economic crisis is not the result of the collapse of its principal trading partners (i.e., the Soviet Union and the Council for Mutual Economic Assistance—CMEA); instead, the island's current economic crisis is the result of a combination of internal and external factors (item **1357**). On the domestic (or internal) front, the most significant causes of Cuba's economic crisis include the inefficiency and distortions associated with its socialist system of centralized economic planning and the process of monetary unification and economic restructuring (*"tarea de reordenamiento"*) launched by the Cuban government in January 2021. On the external front, the Cuban economy has been impacted by the worsening economic and social conditions in Venezuela (Cuba's principal trading partner) and the continued effects of the COVID-19 pandemic, particularly on the tourism sector.

Cuba's highly inefficient and restrictive socialist system of centralized economic planning, under which the state retains ownership of the majority of the means of production, remains the principal obstacle to the island's economic growth and development. Despite the introduction of some limited economic reforms since 2007, excessive levels of state control and intervention in output markets, input markets, the labor market, international trade, the financial sector, etc., combined with state-imposed restrictions on private property rights and the use of market-based mechanisms to coordinate economic activities, continue to plague the Cuban economy and limit its ability to achieve the levels of economic growth and development needed to improve the living standards of the majority of the Cuban population.

The much officially touted monetary unification and economic restructuring plan (*"tarea de reordenamiento"*) introduced in January 2021 has contributed to historically high inflation, massive reductions in the real purchasing power of pensions and wages, notable reductions in the value of the Cuban peso (CUP), and severe shortages of basic necessities and consumer goods (item **1362**). In 2020, the inflation rate was approximately 18.5 percent; the inflation rate reached close to 500 percent in 2021 and 175 percent in 2022 (although Cuban government officials claim that for 2022 the inflation rate was just 40 percent). In 2022, the Cuban peso (CUC) lost an estimated 71 percent of its value vis-à-vis the US dollar (USD).

In early 2023, the Cuban government once again announced a series of policy measures in response to the economic crisis. These proclamations primarily focus on "moral incentives" and appeal to workers to "work harder" and "make more sacrifices," rather than on the implementation of profound institutional and structural changes to confront Cuba's worst economic crisis since the 1990s.

1348 Anuario Estadístico de Cuba. 2021. La Habana: Oficina Nacional de Estadísticas.

The most recent volume of Cuba's national statistical yearbook contains a wide range of socioeconomic statistics, mostly covering the 2017–2021 period. National account series remain questionable given recent (2001) changes in the methodology used to estimate gross domestic product (GDP) (at constant prices), and the increased role of the service sector in the Cuban economy. Coverage of external sector statistics has been expanded to include merchandise exports and imports according to their corresponding Standard International Trade Classifications (SITC), as well as balance of payments and external debt statistics. The current (2021) version is available online through the official website of the national statistics office (http://www.onei.gob.cu/).

1349 Co-operativism and local development in Cuba: an agenda for democratic social change. Edited by Sonja Novkovic and Henry Veltmeyer. Leiden, The Netherlands: Brill, 2018. 263 p.: bibl., index. (Studies in critical social sciences; 121)

Examines the principal characteristics of production cooperatives in Cuba and their linkages with local development. Also explores the potential contributions of cooperatives to the country's economic growth and development.

1350 Cuba, empresas y economía: memorias del primer viaje de estudios de la Universidad de Puerto Rico, Facultad de Administración de Empresas. Coordinación de Maribel Aponte García, Isabel Allende Karam y Luis Suárez Salazar. Textos de Jessica Acosta *et al.* Buenos Aires: CLACSO, 2016. 363 p.: bibl., ill.

A compendium covering various aspects of Cuba's economy and society in 2015–2016. The topics discussed include: restructuring the economic model, foreign investment, international relations, agricultural transformations, state-owned enterprises (SOEs), among others.

1351 Cuba rural: transformaciones agrarias dinámicas sociales e innovación local. Coordinación de Arisbel Leyva Remón, Dayma Echevarría León, y Rubén Villegas Chádez. Con la colaboración de un colectivo de autores. La Habana: Ciencias Sociales, 2018. 417 p.: bibl., ill., maps.

Examines the evolution of Cuba's agricultural sector since 2007. Topics discussed include: agricultural transformations, structural and demographic dynamics of Cuba's rural regions, and local agricultural development experiences.

1352 Deere, Carmen Diana. The special relationship and the challenge of export diversification: Cuban exports of fruits and vegetables to the United States, 1900 to 1962. (*Cuba. Stud.*, 47, 2019, p. 247–276, graph, tables)

Explores trends in Cuban exports of fruits and vegetables during the 1900–62 period, focusing on Cuba's special (trade) relationship with the US during this period. Shows that between 1900 (shortly before the birth of the Cuban Republic on 20 May 1902) and 1962 (a short period after the 1959 Revolution), US trade preferences with regard to Cuba played different roles at different times, providing incentives and contributing to the export of nontraditional fruits and vegetables to the US.

1353 Feinberg, Richard E. Open for business: building the new Cuban economy. Washington, D.C.: Brookings Institution Press, 2016. 264 p.: bibl., index.

Analyzes Cuba's (limited) reform policies to permit the (small-scale) expansion of selected entrepreneurial activities in the incipient nonstate sector, attract foreign investment, and promote joint ventures (with Cuban SOEs) during the short-lived "thawing" (*deshielo*) of US-Cuba relations initiated in December 2014.

1354 González-Corzo, Mario A. Agrarian policy changes and the evolution of land tenure in Cuba. (*Econ. Pap.*, 39:3, 2020, p. 239–258, bibl., tables)

Analyzes the agrarian reforms introduced in Cuba since 2007 and their impact on the evolution of land tenure (and management) in the nonsugar agricultural sector. Discusses the principal lessons from Cuba's experiences with agricultural reforms for other developing and emerging economies.

1355 **González-Corzo, Mario A.** Entrepreneurship in post-Soviet Cuba: self-employed workers and non-agricultural cooperatives. (*Int. J. Entrep. Small Bus.*, 21:2, 2020, p. 197–226, bibl., tables)

Examines the evolution of entrepreneurship and self-employment in Cuba since 2010 and the emergence of nonagricultural cooperatives as an alternative mode of nonstate production. Argues that the expansion of entrepreneurial activities is one of the pillars of Cuba's strategy to adopt a less paternalistic economic model in which the nonstate sector is expected to play a larger role. While the expansion of self-employment has unleashed an unprecedented level of entrepreneurial activities in one of the last bastions of communism in the Western Hemisphere, Cuba's emerging (and relatively small) "entrepreneurial class" faces a wide range of institutional and economic barriers that limits its economic contributions and potential for growth. The elimination of these barriers and radical changes in state policies towards the emerging nonstate sector are essential requirements for the development and expansion of small and medium enterprises (SMEs) and for improving the living standards of the Cuban people.

1356 **Mesa-Lago, Carmelo.** Assessing the conundrums of the Cuban economy under the revolution (1959–2019). (*St. Petersburg Univ. J. Econ. Stud.*, 36:3, 2020, p. 455–482, bibl., graphs, tables)

Examines the principal challenges confronted by the Cuban economy during the 1959–2019 period, with a particular emphasis on its historical external sector economic dependency on the Soviet Union (1960–90) and Venezuela (2000-present), and analyzes the adverse economic effects of the deterioration and termination of such relationships. Discusses the principal causes of Cuba's recent economic crisis and its impact on key economic indicators such as GDP, capital formation, the financial sector, and selected sectors of the Cuban economy including agriculture, industry, services, and tourism. Concludes that to confront the current crisis, Cuba needs to implement deeper economic reforms.

1357 **Mesa-Lago, Carmelo** and **Jan Svejnar.** The Cuban economic crisis: its causes and possible policies for a transition. Miami: Florida International University, Steven J. Green School of International and Public Affairs, Vaclav Havel Program for Human Rights and Diplomacy, 2020. 66 p.: bibl., graphs, photos, tables.

Examines the principal causes of Cuba's current economic crisis and its impact on selected macroeconomic indicators, such as: GDP, merchandise trade balance, foreign direct investment (FDI), foreign debt, remittances, and international tourism. Analyzes Cuba's policy responses to the crisis and recommends a series of economic reform measures and strategies for economic growth and development.

1358 **Mesa-Lago, Carmelo** and **Mario A. González-Corzo.** Agrarian reform and usufruct farming in socialist Cuba. (*J. Econ. Policy Reform*, 24:2, 2021, p. 1–15, bibl., tables)

Analyzes the evolution, progress, and hurdles of usufruct farming in Cuba since its inception in 2008, as well as its impact on agricultural output, exports, and imports. Proposes a series of market-based economic reform measures to improve agricultural production and yields in Cuba.

1359 **Pérez, Louis A.** Rice in the time of sugar: the political economy of food in Cuba. Chapel Hill: The University of North Carolina Press, 2019. 249 p.: bibl., ill., index, maps.

Discusses the importance of rice production, consumption, and trade as an intrinsic part of Cuban culture and national identity and analyzes the role of rice in the island's socioeconomic development during the Republican era (1902–58). Explores trends in Cuban rice production during this period in the complex, but very important, context of US-Cuban trade relations and dependency.

1360 **Sanguinetty, Jorge A.** Obra selecta. Prólogo por Elías Amor Bravo. Valencia, Spain: Aduana Vieja, 2019. 320 p.: bibl. (Colección Obra selecta; 2)

A compendium of selected articles (from the early 1990s to the present) covering a wide range of areas related to Cuba's economy and society. Some topics include culture, economics, international relations, national identity, politics, and social issues.

1361 Torres Pérez, Ricardo. La transformación productiva en Cuba y las propuestas contenidas en el Plan Nacional de Desarrollo hasta 2030. (*Econ. Desarro./Habana*, 164:2, 2020, p. 1–16, bibl., ill., tables)

Discusses the principal elements of Cuba's National Development Plan for 2030 and analyzes Cuba's economic transformations since the early 1990s. Discusses Cuba's transition towards a service-based economy and the changing nature of employment in the context of Cuba's changing patterns of global integration. Examines the (potential) effects of these trends on the country's prospects for economic growth and development.

1362 Vidal Alejandro, Pavel. Cuban macroeconomic trends and the pending monetary reform. (*Cuba. Stud.*, 47, 2019, p. 277–294, bibl., graphs, table)

Uses a multivariate version of the Dynamic Factor Model (DFM) to analyze Cuba's principal macroeconomic trends and policies between 1985 and 2013. Demonstrates that while fiscal policy during this period was procyclical, monetary policy, by contrast, was countercyclical and (accurately) predicted that monetary reform (which was pending at the time of the writing of the article) could contribute to adverse economic effects such as higher aggregate price levels (or inflation) and drastic output contractions across multiple sectors of the Cuban economy. Concludes that greater levels of international openness are needed to counterbalance (or offset) the effects of these negative economic shocks.

VENEZUELA

DANIEL HELLINGER, *Professor Emeritus of International Relations, Webster University*

IN BOOM OR BUST, the political economy literature on Venezuela confronts rentierism. With the country still enmeshed in the deepest social and economic crisis since the devastating War of Independence, most of the works on Venezuelan political economy reviewed here are debating not only the legacy of the late Hugo Chávez but also the broader question of whether the country is entering a "post-rentier" era. For Carvajal (item **1365**) and Noguera Santaella (item **1371**), the crisis is almost wholly due to the errors in Chávez's domestic economic policies. These two authors see Chávez's populist rentierism as the root cause of the present crisis, and, in their view, President Nicolás Maduro (2013 to the present) has done nothing but deepen and extend these policies through the crisis. On this latter point, every political economist represented here would agree—even Curcio Curcio (see *HLAS 75:1606*), a Marxist economist who is more sympathetic, though not uncritically, to Chávez.

The contributors to Peña's collection (item **1373**) and the coauthored work by Abadí and García Soto (item **1363**) take a longer-range view. Peña's approach is aptly titled "su tradición rentista" ("its rentist tradition"), as collectively the volume explores the rentierism entrenched in Venezuelan political culture from the colonial era onward. However, several contributions (notably that of Catalina Banko on the middle decades of the last century) usefully narrate the way that rentierism deepened in those years, as both conservative and social democratic governments attempted to "sow the oil" in development.

In some ways, Abadí and García Soto reinforce this thesis; however, the authors are singularly focused on price controls in the book, published by a libertarian NGO. To be consistent, the authors might have also noted the heavy dependence of Venezuelan businessmen and women on subsidies from the state. Gómez Naranjo's book (item **1367**) is very different methodologically, and though it has little sympathy for populist rentierism, it also lacks libertarian analysis. For Gómez Naranjo, sympathetic accounts of Chávez's economic policies often romanticize the peasant communities that he has advised throughout a long career. At the same time, he would chide the libertarians for failing to understand that allowing market forces to run their course can be very destructive of rural social solidarity. Curcio Curcio represents the other end of the spectrum, attributing more responsibility for the crisis to the sanctions and hostility of transnational corporations and banks and the Venezuelan bourgeoisie (see *HLAS 75:1606*). Both books provide concrete analyses of the impact of price control and economic policies.

Bull and Rosales' article (item **1364**) on Venezuela's crisis sees a synergistic relationship among rentierism, failed policies, and sanctions. Straka's collection (item **1370**) focuses more on the impact of the oil industry on Venezuelan society. The contributions diverge theoretically, but the historically rooted ones shed considerable light on the legacy of rentierism without the usual assumption that it brings only bad results. Rosales' study (item **1372**) could easily be a chapter in this work in the way he analyzes Chávez's oil policies as "hybrid nationalism," eschewing the usual view that the late populist leader "re-nationalized oil." Read in tandem with Yin-Hang To and Acuña (item **1374**), one might wonder whether Chinese investors and the Venezuelan state oil company would find the bargain obsolete. The authors explore the thorny question of whether Chávez-era oil agreements with China are consonant with the theory of economic dependency. They find that Chinese companies exemplify policies and behavior similar to their Western counterparts, but tensions arise because the Chinese state is eager not to replicate Western economic aid programs.

Two works by Bernard Mommer (items **1368** and **1369**) provide a very different take on both rentierism and oil nationalism in Venezuela. Mommer worked toward both goals in the Venezuelan oil ministry during the Chávez years and has for 45 years written influential, if not controversial, works on oil history and policy. Mommer's eulogy to his friend and sometime collaborator, Asdrúbal Baptista, serves as an excellent, short introduction to their mutual views on the economic origin and impact of international oil rents. As for Mommer's book, likely to be his last extended work on oil, Arturo Sosa, the distinguished Venezuelan historian who also serves as superior general of the Jesuit Order, writes in the prologue, "Among the virtues of this book is to offer a detailed and complex analysis of Venezuela as an oil country without stopping there. He proposes [that] the Venezuelan case is an illuminating example of the relationships among capitalism, globalization, and natural resources... without which it is not possible to visualize a better future for humanity."

1363 Abadí, Anabella and **Carlos García Soto.** El control de precios en Venezuela (1939–2015): de la Segunda Guerra Mundial a la "guerra económica". Presentación por Vladimir Chelminski. Prólogo por Richard Obuchi. Caracas: CEDICE Libertad, 2016. 208 p.: bibl., ill.

The authors demonstrate the futility of government-imposed price controls from 1939, when Venezuela first imposed price restraints in response to dislocations caused by the outbreak of war in Europe. Most recently, new controls were decreed by the government of Nicolás Maduro in response to what he charged was an "economic war" waged against his government by the opposition and by the US. The analysis, to the extent that it goes beyond description of laws, decrees, and administration of controls in each of seven different periods, is deeply rooted in the libertarian ideology of CEDICE, the publisher. In sum, the authors argue that price controls have done nothing but drive inflation by disincentivizing production.

1364 Bull, Benedicte and **Antulio Rosales.** Into the shadows: sanctions, rentierism, and economic informalization in Venezuela. (*Rev. Eur. Estud. Latinoam. Caribe*, 109, Jan./June 2020, p. 107–133, bibl.)

The authors argue that international sanctions on Venezuela's rentier economy and the government's response have together resulted in an increase in barter and de facto dollarization; the expansion of extractive activities and use of cryptocurrency; and the spread of labor informality, illegal actors, and military involvement in key sectors of the economy. These effects are attributed to the way that rent-seekers both inside and outside official circles have to adapt to new strategies and opportunities to appropriate rents.

1365 Carvajal, Leonardo. Noventa miradas sobre el chavismo: en lo económico, social, gerencial, político, jurídico e ideológico. Caracas: AB abediciones, 2018. 440 p.: bibl. (Colección Visión Venezuela)

This thick volume contains 90 polemical, thin essays, mostly two to five pages each, including a section of works (21 pages) focused on economic policies in the Chavista era. Carvajal, a professor of education, largely reduces the social, economic, and humanitarian disaster of Venezuela today to a single cause: Hugo Chávez. The author's historical interpretations adhere to the orthodox version of history from the perspective of the Punto Fijo era. Some arguments may stand up well, but in this book there is no room for more recent and ideologically varied revisions of oil history.

1366 Fronjosa Lasalle, Ernesto. Auge y caída de un petroestado: la historia de la industria petrolera en Venezuela. Caracas: Universidad Metropolitana, 2018. 558 p.: bibl., index.

In some ways this book covers well-trodden ground in narrating the history of oil policy and the oil industry from the earliest period of concessions, through nationalization, the reopening to foreign capital in the 1990s, and the struggles over control of the state oil company (PDVSA) between the Chávez government and company executives. The latter culminated in the crisis of the industry and, more broadly, of the entire society in the Bolivarian era. The author worked in executive positions in the industry before and after nationalization, so there is little sympathy for oil nationalism. At the same time, his insider perspective permits him to add important details on state-company relations that may be of interest to economic historians.

1367 Gómez Naranjo, Manuel. Mitos y desafíos del desarrollo. Estado Miranda, Venezuela: Acción Campesina, Acción Popular, 2019. 162 p.: bibl.

The author pens 44 short essays offering lessons taken from 25 years as a rural field advisor for the Venezuelan NGO CESAP (Social Centro al Servicio de la Acción Popular), drawing on development thinkers ranging from the Peruvian Hernando de Soto to the Bengali Amartya Sen. Much of the book, engagingly peppered with illustrative stories, reflects the author's search for reconciliation between incentivizing production by ensuring property rights for small holders and defending communities threatened by market forces.

1368 Mommer, Bernard. Asdrúbal Baptista: más allá del optimismo y del pesimismo. (*Agroalimentaria*, 26:51, julio/dic. 2020, p. 389–392)

A memorial essay on the work of Asdrúbal Baptista, the Venezuelan economist who, like Mommer, explored the source and implications of "international oil rents" using frameworks taken from the classical writings of Ricardo, Smith, and Marx. Baptista and Mommer, sometimes working together (see *HLAS 51:2109*), sometimes apart, created a statistical method for separating international ground rents from actual gross national product in national accounts data. Baptista was the first Venezuelan economist to challenge the "sow the oil" thesis and move beyond the simple Dutch disease thesis. This essay serves as a highly useful introduction, not only to the work of Baptista, but to Mommer's as well. For examles of Baptista's earlier works, see *HLAS 43:3376* and *HLAS 71:1747*.

1369 Mommer, Bernard. Recursos naturales y globalización: petróleo y Venezuela como ejemplos. Prólogo por Arturo Sosa. Caracas: AB abediciones: Universidad Católica Andrés Bello, 2022. 310 p.: ill. (Colección Letraviva)

Mommer offers both a revisionist interpretation of Venezuela's oil history and a challenge to the view that the country's reliance on oil rents was an abject failure. During the concessionary era (1935–74), the country rapidly and successfully modernized as it asserted its sovereign ownership of natural resources to maximize the capture a normal rate of profit. This experience made it a pioneer in forging OPEC. Nationalization in 1974 weakened Venezuela's sovereign control over natural resources by ceding key oil policies, including relations with foreign oil companies, to the state oil company. Around this same time, the OPEC oil boom brought a torrent of petrodollars into the country, far exceeding the ability of the country to absorb the capital. Failure to adjust adequately—under both the oil regime and the post-1998 Chávez government—brought about social and economic collapse.

1370 La nación petrolera: Venezuela, 1914–2014. Compilación de Tomás Straka. Caracas: Universidad Metropolitana, 2016. 332 p.: bibl.

This book compiles seven studies to mark the centenary of Venezuela's oil industry. Two previously published essays by Bernard Mommer and Asdrúbal Baptista recount the history of relations between the Venezuelan state and foreign oil companies through the lens of classical political economy and theories of ground rent. Straka's contribution examines oil's transformative impact on the state of Zulia and Lake Maracaibo. Catalina Banko looks at how oil fostered a proclivity toward state "intervention" in the domestic economy. Three shorter essays examine the postnationalization era and oil policy, but in contrast to other contributions largely trod ground covered in critiques of the Chávez era.

1371 Noguera Santaella, José. Venezuela en el nudo gordiano: lecciones para la reconstrucción de la democracia y la prosperidad económica. Venezuela: Dahbar, 2018. 426 p.: bibl. (Ensayo)

Noguera Santaella, a mathematician by training, professor of economics, and lifelong member of the social democratic Acción Democrática Party (AD) in his native Venezuela, adds another critique of populism to the growing critical examinations of the Chávez era. He provides a historical context that closely adheres to AD orthodoxy, which forms the basis for his contention that rational economic policy and liberal democracy reinforce one another. His policy prescriptions are drawn largely from neoclassical economics, as befits his stint as an advisor to neoliberal Chilean president Sebastián Piñera.

1372 Rosales, Antulio. Pursuing foreign investment for nationalist goals: Venezuela's hybrid resource nationalism. (*Bus. Polit.*, 20:3, Sept. 2018, p. 438–464, bibl.)

Rosales analyzes Chávez's oil reforms and his negotiations with foreign oil companies as a modified version of obsolescing bargaining theory, the notion that changed global market conditions and extractive technologies lead to pressures to revise contracts in extractive industries. In this case, the rising demand and pricing for oil created incentives for the Venezuelan landlord state to insist on renegotiating contracts with foreign investors, but at the same time it remained open to new associations with other companies, especially state oil companies and Chinese investment. Rosales argues that the obsolescing bargaining model needs to take into account that actors on both sides, and especially on the host country side, are not monolithic actors. Synthesizing constructivist and ideational theories with bargaining theory helps us explain why Chávez did not simply renationalize the oil industry, but preferred instead to renegotiate relationships with foreign capital, in essence, "hybrid resource nationalism."

1373 **Venezuela y su tradición rentista: visiones, enfoques y evidencias.** Compilación de Carlos Peña. Contribuciones de Catalina Banko et al. Primera edición en español. Caracas: IIES, 2017. 234 p.: bibl., ill.

Nine contributors provide articles, all highly critical of the Chávez era, but unlike many other negative assessments, the analyses attempt to put the Bolivarian regime and the disastrous social, economic, and political implosion of the last 10 years in a broader historical, cultural, and international context. The intellectual frameworks employed generally draw upon modernization theory and the idea of the Dutch disease—that is, natural resource wealth as a curse that has reinforced tendencies toward rent-seeking and a patrimonial political culture that at least two of the authors trace back to colonialism.

1374 **Yin-Hang To, Emma Miriam** and **Rodrigo Acuña.** China and Venezuela: South-South cooperation or rearticulated dependency? (*Lat. Am. Perspect.*, 46:2, March 2019, p. 126–140, bibl.)

Using the case of Venezuela, the authors argue that the state-to-state relationship between China and Latin America departs from the typical dependent relationship between North and South in the financial and aid cooperation agreements. However, Chinese companies involved in implementing commercial and aid programs often replicate the relationship between Northern transnational corporations, despite innovative financial arrangements and programs intended to transfer technology. The authors also acknowledge that domestic economic policies, including decapitalization of the Venezuelan state oil company, also played an important role in reinforcing dependency.

CHILE

SILVIA BORZUTZKY, *Teaching Professor of Political Science and International Relations, Heinz College of Information Systems and Public Policy, Carnegie Mellon University*

ANÍBAL PINTO'S book *Chile: un caso de desarrollo fustrado* (item **1382**) was first published in 1959 and now is in its fourth edition. This book has been a critical source of information and inspiration for many generations of social scientists and serves as the pillar for this essay.

While it is impossible to summarize Pinto's many contributions to the historical analysis of the Chilean economy, two ideas that he discusses, *desarrollo hacia afuera* (export-oriented development) and inequality, have remained constant features of the Chilean economy. This essay focuses on inequality, which has been a permanent characteristic of the Chilean economy and the source of social mobilization and political crisis.

The policies of the Pinochet dictatorship dramatically intensified the historically unequal distribution of land, wealth, income, and resources in Chile. The neoliberal policies designed and implemented by the Chicago Boys had a strong impact on the economy and wages. By 1975, the implementation of the market policies contracted GDP by 12.9 percent. This recession was followed by the 1982 crisis that produced a 14.5 percent reduction in GDP. By 1983, unemployment was 23.9 percent and real wages were 14 percent below their 1970 level (Banco Central de Chile, p. 24; and García H. and Wells). Simultaneously, a handful of economic groups or conglomerates enriched themselves from the privatization of state-owned enterprises and the reallocation of credit and other resources. By 1989, when President Aylwin took office, social policies had been decimated and 45 percent of the population was below the poverty level, 27 percent of Chileans were extremely poor (indigents), and wages were 20 percent below their 1981 level. It is important to note that in 1970 the poverty rate was 17 percent (Perry and Borzutzky). As the comprehensive and rigorous analysis of *Complicidad económica con la dictadura chilena: un país desigual a la fuerza* (item **1377**) clearly shows, the unequal policies implemented by the dictatorship were fully supported by international financial organizations, by the Chilean economic elites, and by their supporters in the media. The repression, the elimination of political parties and unions, and the misuse of natural resources by extractive corporations all contributed to the economic, political, and social oppression of Chileans.

Because of the arrangements made during the transition period, the postdictatorship political and economic systems were built on a continuation of the neoliberal model and a political system that has become known as elitist democracy or *democracia de acuerdos*. Thus, while the socioeconomic policies of the Concertación—the new governing coalition—led to massive poverty reductions, the same policies did not produce a substantial reduction in inequality. By 1996, the highest 20 percent of the population captured 56.7 percent of the income, while the lowest 20 percent received only 4.1 percent of the income. At the beginning of the 21st century, Chile's Gini coefficient of 0.58 was the third highest in Latin America and 12th highest in the world. However, by 2017, the Gini coefficient had declined to 0.46 (*Gini Index-Chile* (World Bank)). As the extensive data in *Desiguales* (item **1378**) clearly shows, there are very large disparities, not only between the different income quintiles, but also between women and men and between urban and rural areas, with urban income at the time being 87 percent higher than rural income.

The Concertación coalition brought political stability, democratically held elections, and a partial reckoning with the past to Chile, but underpinning the political and economic system was a new form of political engagement known as *democracia de acuerdos* (Siavelis) or elitist democracy. In this system, political leaders sought to build consensus, including with members of Congress who had supported Pinochet's regime. *Democracia de acuerdos* was rooted in the very nature of the Chilean transition to democracy, steered by the 1980 Constitution, which constrained the ability of elected governments to move away from market economy policies. Thus, political and socioeconomic reforms were partial at best as they resulted from multiple agreements, both within the governing coalition and with the right-wing opposition that held a veto power over the system. While this type of elitist democracy gave the country political stability, its legitimacy declined as more and more Chileans felt excluded from the system. The massive October 2018 social movement demonstrated the depth of Chilean discontent. The "social explosion" disrupted the *acuerdo* by mobilizing approximately one million people in the streets of Santiago. They demanded a decent education, pensions, and gender and ethnic equality, as well as a new constitution that would provide the framework needed to carry out substantial socioeconomic reforms. As the protesting students argued, it was not about the 30-peso increase in the metro fare, but the 30 years of economic inequality.

Change appeared to be on the horizon as Chileans elected delegates to a constitutional convention in 2021 and elected Gabriel Boric—who was supported by a leftist coalition—to the presidency in 2022. However, in September 2022, Chileans resoundingly rejected the constitutional draft proposed by the convention. This rejection comes in the context of the socioeconomic impact of the COVID-19 pandemic and worldwide inflation. How Chileans will react to these political and economic issues is uncertain because none of the substantial reforms that could have reduced inequality have been implemented and now the future of constitutional reform is unclear. To paraphrase Aníbal Pinto, Chileans are frustrated with the state of the economy and of the country—and the next steps are uncertain.

FOOTNOTES

García H., Alvaro and John Wells, "Chile: A Laboratory for Failed Experiments in Capitalist Political Economy." *Cambridge Journal of Economics*, 7:3/4, Sept./Dec. 1983, p. 287–304.

Indicadores económicos y sociales 1960–1982. Santiago: Banco Central de Chile, Dirección de Política Financiera, 1983 (*HLAS 47:3546*).

Perry, Sarah and Silvia Borzutzky, "'The Revolution Will Be Feminist—Or It Won't Be a Revolution': Feminist Response to Inequality in Chile." *Social Inclusion*, 10:1, 2022, p. 46–57, https://www.cogitatiopress.com/socialinclusion/article/view/4784/ (open access)

Siavelis, Peter, "Crisis of Representation in Chile?: The Institutional Connection." *Journal of Politics in Latin America*, 8:3, 2016, p. 61–93, https://doi.org/10.1177/1866802x1600800303 (open access)

World Bank Open Data Poverty and Inequality Platform. *Gini Index-Chile*, https://data.worldbank.org/indicator/SI.POV.GINI?locations=CL (open access)

1375 Álvarez, Roberto and **Rodrigo Fuentes.** Minimum wage and productivity: evidence from Chilean manufacturing plants. (*Econ. Dev. Cult. Change*, 67:1, Oct. 2018, p. 193–224, bibl., graphs, tables)

The authors argue that a 22 percent increase in the minimum wage between 1998–2000 in Chile had a negative effect on firms' total factor productivity (TPF). Their estimates show that the wage increase reduced TPF by 5.8 percent in industries that do not use low-skilled workers intensely and 9.7 percent in ones that do. However, the authors also conclude more work needs to be done to explain changes in firms' productivity.

1376 Cavarozzi, Marcelo. Los sótanos de la democracia chilena, 1938–1964: las esferas de "protección" de los empresarios industriales—la CORFO, represión a los obreros y la inflación. Santiago, Chile: LOM Ediciones: USACH, Facultad de Humanidades, 2017. 147 p.: bibl., ill. (Historia) (Colección Enzo Faletto)

Cavarozzi's analysis successfully addresses a number of points about Chilean industrialization: how it developed, the role of CORFO (Corporación de Fomento), how CORFO financed private sector entrepreneurial activities, industrial evolution under the second Ibáñez administration, and the undermining of CORFO in the context of an aborted capitalist revolution under President Jorge Alessandri. A second set of questions raises critically important issues dealing with the nature of what Cavarozzi calls the political party governments and their deterioration in the 1950s under the Ibáñista earthquake. Cavarozzi successfully argues that while the Ibáñez and Alessandri administrations were profoundly different, they both succeeded in reducing the power of the working class and enhancing entrepreneurial political and economic power.

1377 **Complicidad económica con la dictadura chilena: un país desigual a la fuerza.** Edición de Juan Pablo Bohoslavsky et al. Santiago, Chile: LOM Ediciones, 2019. 475 p.: bibl., ill. (Historia)

This edited volume presents 26 chapters that cover the many ways in which the Chilean economic elite was an accomplice of the multiple crimes committed by the Pinochet dictatorship. While it is impossible to summarize the content in a few words, the authors successfully achieved their intended goal of demonstrating the multiple connections between the brutal repression of the dictatorship and the economic repression experienced by millions of Chileans during those years. Additionally, they show how these actions were at the center of the profound socioeconomic inequalities that the country experienced during the dictatorship and that have continued since the transition to democracy. The authors also provide an analysis of the support that the US provided to the dictatorship and the economic elite. The book concludes with a series of case studies that highlight the intimate connections between the economic elite and the military dictatorship.

1378 **Desiguales: orígenes, cambios y desafíos de la brecha social en Chile.** Edición de Andrea Palet y Pilar de Aguirre. Santiago: PNUD: Uqbar Editores, 2017. 411 p.: bibl., color ill.

That Chile is an unequal country is amply and widely demonstrated by the very thorough historical and quantitative analysis in this excellent study. The book defines the nature of Chilean inequality, offers a historical perspective on the inequality, describes what it is like to live in an unequal society, and explores its impact on people. These initial sections are followed by specific analyses of inequality at work, income redistribution and social security, education, and political inequality. At the end of each chapter, the authors raise critical issues and propose policies to reduce inequality.

1379 **Martner, Gonzalo.** Economía: una introducción heterodoxa. Santiago, Chile: LOM Ediciones, 2018. 361 p.: bibl.

Economist and professor Gonzalo Martner has written a textbook on economic theories, a historical analysis of the evolution of contemporary economies from the agricultural revolution to the 2008 Great Recession, as well as a critique of market economic theory. In his critique of market economics, Martner presents a detailed analysis of its failures in several areas, including natural resources, innovation, pensions, and health. He clearly shows that what the experts call externalities or market inefficiencies produce grave consequences for society and for the environment. The last chapter of this comprehensive book provides an analysis of inequality, poverty measurements, and the capacity of public policies to alter poverty and distribution.

1380 **Matus Acuña, Alejandra.** Mitos y verdades de las AFP. Santiago, Chile: Aguilar, 2017. 207 p.: bibl.

The journalist Alejandra Matus provides a comprehensive and critical analysis of the birth and evolution of the Pension Fund Administrators (AFPs), which are in charge of administering Chilean pensions. Interesting aspects of the analysis include the development of the system during the Pinochet dictatorship, the critical role played by labor minister José Piñera, and the attempts to partially reform the system in 2008 and beyond.

1381 **Navia, Patricio** and **Rodrigo Osorio.** "Make the economy scream"?: economic, ideological and social determinants of support for Salvador Allende in Chile, 1970-3. (*J. Lat. Am. Stud.*, 49:4, Nov. 2017, p. 771-797, graphs, tables)

Using polling and municipal-level data, the authors show that support for President Allende, both at the time of his election and in 1973, was determined by ideology and not by the country's economic performance or economic concerns. In brief, according to the authors, support for Allende remained strong among the poor and working class and the left despite deteriorating economic conditions.

1382 Pinto Santa Cruz, Aníbal. Chile: un caso de desarrollo fustrado. Prólogos de Ricardo Lagos E. y Dante Contreras G. Cuarta edición. Santiago: Editorial Universitaria, 2018. 302 p.: bibl. (Imagen de Chile)

The fourth edition of this emblematic book which first appeared in 1959 (see *HLAS 25:1692*) is undoubtedly a well-deserved homage to its author who pioneered the academic analysis of Chile's political economy. Pinto provides one of the most comprehensive analyses ever written of Chile's economic history—from colonial time to the 1950s—which justifies the decision to issue a new edition. In addition to the historical overview, Pinto delves into the adoption of the import substitution industrialization (ISI) model which was central to Chile's mid-century economy. In a country where the political system and political demands were expanding rapidly, the consequences of ISI were budget deficits and inflation fueled by the "empate político" or political tie that characterized Chilean politics. As President Ricardo Lagos notes in the prologue, "can we say that this book reveals the seeds of what Chile experienced in the years to come?" The answer is yes.

1383 Vega Tapia, Héctor. Capitalismo del siglo XXI: una mirada desde los bienes públicos. Santiago, Chile: Editorial Forja, 2017. 277 p.: bibl.

The chapters of this ambitious book address new economic principles, predictions for the 21st century, partial rents and the social reproduction of work, ethics and the value of work, the labor market and the aging of the population, the economy of debt and the impact of the Great Recession, the iron logic of the model—which is debt, the vulnerabilities of emerging economies based on the export of commodities, and transitions toward a citizenship economy of public goods. In the words of the author, the book searches for a new social economy based on solidarity.

ARGENTINA, PARAGUAY, AND URUGUAY

AMÍLCAR CHALLÚ, *Associate Professor of History, Bowling Green State University*

THE LITERATURE on the political economy of the Southern Cone countries continues to be dynamic and vibrant, reflecting not just the continued production of knowledge but also the centrality of the economic experience in public discourse. For *HLAS 77*, I selected 34 works, mostly from and about Argentina. They range from sectorial analysis to in-depth local or firm studies, to histories of institutions, to macroeconomic analysis. Particularly in the case of Argentina, the selection reflects a broad arc of production: from strongly partisan books to descriptive books often celebrating local or regional identities or institutional milestones, to scholarly works with more rigorous methodologies, but perhaps less influence in shaping public opinion. These selections balance the trends in academic fields with economic discourses in the public sphere. While selected early in 2023, the topics reflected here became dominant themes in the Argentine presidential election of 2023, which resulted in the election of an economist in the Austrian tradition who ran on an economic platform proposing the elimination of the national currency and central bank. In this essay, I present an overview of common topics: inflation, long-term economic development, economic crises and economic policy cycles from 2001 to the present, regional economies, and the energy sector.

Inflation and monetary policies have taken center stage in studies of the Argentine economy. With annual inflation rates averaging 50 percent in the past few years, this is not a surprising development. An interest in monetary and banking institutions—perhaps drawing inspiration from present-day concerns—is reflected in the works by Gómez on the first convertibility system (item **1394**), by Rougier and Sember on the Central Bank (item **1395**), and by Plotinsky on cooperative banks (item **1402**). These historical studies present nuanced interpretations of the relationship of money, the national state, the banking system, and general society that have relevance in today's world. Beker and Escudé's homage to Dr. Julio Olivera (item **1406**) shows how Argentine economists developed unique insights on inflation and macroeconomic theory by drawing on the national experience. From different intellectual traditions and ideological lenses, studies have paid considerable attention to the return of inflation during the Kirchners' years (2003–15) and the Macri administration (2015–19), ranging from interpretations that privilege money emission (item **1397**), the relationship with the external sector (item **1391**), and redistributive struggles (item **1401**).

A cluster of studies focuses on economic development in the long term. For Argentina, Della Paolera and Cortés Conde take a long-term view in their compilation of studies inspired by New Economic History, an approach that rigorously applies economic theory and quantitative methodology to an analysis of the past (item **1400**). While New Economic History often points to factor endowments and technological innovation and institutions, it is significant that, at least in the essays dealing with the most recent periods, the building of political coalitions plays a stronger explanatory role. Other works, while limited to more recent history, also place emphasis on the preeminence of politics in setting the course of institutions and their impact on the economy as a whole (items **1386**, **1391**, and **1401**). By contrast, recent publications from Uruguayan and Paraguayan authors place more emphasis on the continuities in economic policies of their countries. The essays in the collective history of Uruguay's planning and budgeting office (item **1412**), while recognizing the connections with the political world, tend to emphasize the process of learning and institution building, indicating a stronger long-term continuity; Román and Willebald (item **1415**) highlight long-term dynamics within a complex economy, again downplaying the role of specific policy moments. A study of Paraguay's economic policies under democratic governments from 1989 to the present (item **1411**) also highlights continuities, such as lower rates of inflation, greater rates of investment in infrastructure, and economic growth, although it is certainly a balanced picture that shows the shortfalls in terms of low public investments and strong dependence on the export of natural resources.

The analysis of crises, recessions, and depressions is a major trope in the literature about the Southern Cone and occupies an important part of the attention of any book focused on economic policies in the long run (e.g., item **1411**). In the case of Argentina, the crisis of 2001 still attracts considerable attention and studies often point to neoliberalism as an ideological bias that conditioned policymaking (items **1398** and **1410**). The previous works still rely on neoliberalism as an ideological framework, but provide a more nuanced reading, relying on theories of elites and coalition building. Gerchunoff and Llach (item **1391**), by contrast, eschew neoliberalism entirely to favor a macroeconomic perspective of external conditions and domestic political constraints.

The 2001 crisis casts a long shadow in the narratives about Argentine economic policies in the postconvertibility era (2002 to the present). Rapoport (item **1403**) identifies the Kirchner administrations as a turning point marked by a swift adaptation to new international realities and a viable model to restore industrial growth and a more equal distribution of income. There has been less interest in the so-called popular or social economy of the postconvertibility era; there is, however, interest in cooperative financial institutions and their transformations during these years (item **1402**). Vigil's edited volume about agricultural machinery (item **1396**) intersects macro and sector-specific policies, concluding that despite pro-industrialist policies, industrial development was elusive in the neodevelopmentalist model of the Kirchners' years. By contrast, in the conversation between Gerchunoff and Hora (item **1392**), the Kirchner policies (particularly after the initial years of government) are presented as invested in a traditional nationalist-populist framework that had served its goals in the 20th century but, in their view, it is no longer adapted to the present-day configuration of Argentina and the world. Similarly, Schorr's edited volume (item **1409**) emphasizes the long-term continuities in the concentration of economic power despite the "return of the state" in those years. The literature on Uruguay during these years presents an interesting contrast with Argentina. The essays edited by Hernández Veleros, Velázquez Orihuela, and Willebald (item **1413**) on the 2008 global recession problematize different national and subnational experiences, while Notaro's study of inequality (item **1414**) similarly eschews a reading based on domestic politics.

Works about the more recent conservative administration of Mauricio Macri (2015–19) are still scarce, but they fall under a similar range of opinions. The majority of the works reviewed here present the Macri years as a repeat of neoliberal policies described as a high dependence on the external sector and financing (item **1386**), fiscal adjustment (item **1384**), and concentration of power and authoritarianism (items **1403** and **1405**). These studies highlight the continuities between market-friendly and deregulation policies from the military dictatorship to the right-leaning administrations of the democratic era. By contrast, Gerchunoff in his interview with Hora (item **1392**) and Tigani (item **1407**) are more interested in the novelty of the Macri coalition and policies. In this reviewer's opinion, the usefulness of the neoliberal category is in a phase of diminishing returns, quite often flattening diverse contexts and policy decisions.

Moving away from more immediate matters of economic performance and decision making, another cluster of production focuses on regional (or even local) economic trajectories. The edited book *Time and Space* (item **1417**) is a milestone in the economic history of Latin America since it reconstructs subnational GDP estimates roughly from 1900 to 2015. Interestingly, the regional trajectories of Argentina and Uruguay (and Brazil and Chile as well) are remarkably different and contrast with trends at the global level. While insertion in international markets is a major factor singled out by the contributors, it is also significant that the creation of the regional common market Mercosur was not a force of convergence at least at the subnational level. Regional economic divergence has deep roots in Argentine history. The collection of essays edited by Santilli (item **1399**) features similar emphasis on local economies through the construction of real wage series using a common methodology. Focused on the 19th century, the contributions problematize the simple characterization of Argentina as a frontier economy becoming part of broader trade flows. Moving forward to the 20th century, Girbal-Blacha (item **1393**) convincingly shows that the innovative economists who envisioned the transition to import substitution industrialization (ISI) were not able to conceptualize a plan that addressed the pronounced regional inequalities in Argentina. Other works focus on specific sectors and activities such as agriculture (items **1390** and **1408**), energy (items **1387** and **1416**), and industry (items **1385**, **1389**, **1396**, and **1404**). These texts are often couched as a nostalgic commemoration of the locality's industrial past suggesting the important role of economic memory in shaping regional identities.

Often having a strong localized approach, a small group of works presents interesting contrasts among different countries and different types of energy. Stuhldreher and Morales (item **1416**) describe the transition to clean energy in Uruguay's northern region, highlighting the positive externalities that it created for sustainable economic development in the 21st century. Essays in Borda and Masi (item **1411**) similarly evaluate Paraguay's increasing investments in hydraulic infrastructure. By contrast, the analysis of Argentine energy policies by Guzowski, Ibañez Martín, and Rojas (item **1388**), while broader in focus, highlights the shortfalls of the same transition in Argentina, focusing on the regulatory framework and the investment climate as obstacles to the transition, while noting the broader geopolitical context of energy policies. Hopes for future economic growth in Argentina are pegged to the development of extractive activities. These include mining (and particularly lithium) and the development of shale oil and gas fields. This approach is analyzed from a regional perspective in Burton's history of energy in Neuquén (item **1387**), the province that has the Vaca Muerta oil field, one of the largest deposits in the world.

A final note is that the selection of works tends to feature publications from Argentina, mostly from the capital city, Buenos Aires. This is not necessarily an overrepresentation, since Buenos Aires is the predominant publishing market in the region. As the main platform to reach the country as a whole, books from the capital city focus more on national issues and national policies, and they tend to be more influenced by a national political agenda. They emphasize the neoliberal-developmentalist policy pendulum. By contrast, the voices from other geographies make a difference in the tone of the discourse. Books published in the Argentine provinces bring a stronger focus on specific sectors, such as energy or manufacturing, and regional economies. Sometimes this approach comes at the expense of having a more descriptive bent. Works from Uruguay and Paraguay, just a few in this selection, are more analytical, lean less towards partisanship (while retaining a critical approach), and often highlight continuities and institutional learning.

ARGENTINA

1384 Ajustados: de la revolución de la alegría al crecimiento invisible. Contribuciones de Diego Rubinzal y Carlos Heller. Buenos Aires: Colihue, 2018. 284 p.: bibl., ill. (Encrucijadas)

A study of the policies of the Macri administration from a leftist perspective. The authors pay strong attention to the public discourse of the Cambiemos (Macri) and how it was used to justify policies that reduced the role of the state and increased indebtedness in the tradition of previous neoliberal experiences in the country.

1385 Altos Hornos Zapla: historias en torno al primer centro siderúrgico integral de Argentina. Edición de Liliana Bergesio y Laura Golovanevsky. Rosario, Argentina: Prohistoria Ediciones, 2016. 210 p.: bibl., ill. (some color). (Colección Universidad; 50)

A collection of essays about the impact of the privatization of the most important steel mill in Argentina, located in a remote area in the northwestern province of Jujuy. The essays weave discussions of economic policies, workers' oral histories, analysis of everyday life, and representations of the company in public discourse, with an emphasis on the significance of this industrial behemoth at the local level.

1386 Brenta, Noemí. Historia de la deuda externa argentina: de Martínez de Hoz a Macri. Buenos Aires: CI, Capital Intelectual, 2019. 239 p.: bibl., ill.

The book espouses the view that Argentina's foreign debt is a shackle that constrains the country's growth and the egalitarian distribution of income. The "debt problem" started in the military dictatorship of the 1970s and democratic administrations did not seek a solution until the 2001 crisis. The postconvertibility policies were able to lower the pressure of debt payments through difficult negotiations, but the Macri administration (2015–2019) threatened to repeat the experience.

1387 Burton, Gerardo. Crónica del subsuelo: el petróleo en Neuquén (1918–2013). Neuquén, Argentina: Ediciones con Doblezeta, 2017. 281 p.: bibl., ill.

A chronicle of the oil industry in Neuquén, the province that concentrates half of the production and two-thirds of the known reserves. Of particular interest is the fast adoption of shale oil and shale gas in Argentina. The book emphasizes the importance of energy independence and the generation of income, while neglecting to acknowledge the environmental impact of the industry.

1388 Los desafíos de la política energética argentina: panorama y propuestas. Compilación de Carina Guzowski, María Ibañez Martín y Mara Leticia Rojas. Buenos Aires: Editorial Dunken, 2016. 175 p.: bibl., ill.

A compilation of research essays about the energy sector in Argentina, including discussions of sustainability, technological innovation, and global geopolitical conditions. Of particular relevance is the slow transition to renewable sources of energy and the increased dependence and vulnerability to external conditions despite the immense reserves of fossil fuels.

1389 Eliano, Ezequiel. Escenarios para innovar: trayectoria tecnológica de la cementera Loma Negra entre 1990 y 2010. Buenos Aires: Lenguage Claro Editora: Área de Estudios sobre la Industria Argentina y Latinoamericana, Instituto Interdisciplinario de Economía Política de Buenos Aires, Facultad de Ciencias Económicas, Universidad de Buenos Aires, 2017. 152 p.: bibl., ill.

This study presents a history of technological and organizational innovation through a case study of one of the major producers of cement in Argentina. Of particular interest is the discussion of research and development policies in the firm and the national state.

Etchemendy, Sebastián. The rise of segmented neo-corporatism in South America: wage coordination in Argentina and Uruguay (2005–2015). See item **1257**.

1390 Fernández, Diego. El desierto verde: un estudio sobre la naturaleza y causas del proceso de concentración económica en la agricultura pampeana. Buenos Aires:

Ediciones Imago Mundi, 2018. 354 p.: bibl., ill., index. (Colección Bitácora argentina)

This book documents the concentration of ownership and operation of the Argentine Pampas, highlighting the continuities despite the significant contrast in terms of macroeconomic and social policies. Particularly noteworthy are the author's discussions of technical innovations, the less progressive taxation of the 2000s compared to the 1990s, and the profit margins by scale of producers. Although the book does not address the conflicts between agrarian organizations and the state in the 2010s, it is still a valuable contribution to the understanding of the transformation of cereal agriculture in Argentina.

1391 Gerchunoff, Pablo and **Lucas Llach.** El ciclo de la ilusión y el desencanto: políticas económicas argentinas de 1880 a nuestros días. Edición corregida y aumentada. Buenos Aires: Crítica, 2018. 613 p.: bibl., ill. (Memoria crítica)

A new edition of a book first published in 1998 (see *HLAS 61:3302*). The authors equate the crisis of the convertibility regime with another Great Depression, evaluating external conditions and the nature of domestic alliances that conditioned economic policy. The early economic successes of the postconvertibility regime are first attributed to favorable external conditions with prudent management of monetary policy, but eventually led into unhinged external and fiscal unbalances.

1392 Gerchunoff, Pablo and **Roy Hora.** La moneda en el aire: conversaciones sobre la Argentina y su historia de futuros imprevisibles. Buenos Aires: Siglo Veintiuno Editores, 2021. 339 p.: ill. (Singular)

A lively, conversational reflection about Argentine politics and economic policy based on edited interviews between Pablo Gerchunoff and economic historian Roy Hora. Gerchunoff is a prominent public intellectual and former high-ranking officer in economic planning under the radical governments of Alfonsín and De la Rúa. Organized around Gerchunoff's trajectory and his views of economic history, the book provides a balanced perspective that is rather unusual in contemporary economic discourse. The chapters on recent economic policy offer a highly critical analysis of what Gerchunoff calls the "backward-looking policies" of the Kirchner administrations, while also addressing the move towards open-trade and deregulatory policies during the Macri administration.

1393 Girbal-Blacha, Noemí María. ¿"La Argentina que no fue"?: las economías regionales norteñas en la *Revista de Economía Argentina*. Rosario, Argentina: Prohistoria Ediciones, 2018. 78 p.: bibl.

An intellectual history of the influential group of Argentine economists and intellectuals led by Alejandro Bunge in the mid-20th century. Concerned about economic independence, modernization, and equality, the group had a complex relationship with political movements of the 1930s and 1940s. The author focuses on their visions for the relatively underdeveloped regions of northern Argentina, concluding that they lacked a consistent and innovative proposal, mimicking the lack of attention to these regions in the realm of public policies as well.

1394 Gómez, Mónica. Avatares de un sistema monetario: la primera Caja de Conversión argentina y su transformación final en Banco Central (1890–1935). Buenos Aires: Teseo; Córdoba, Argentina: Facultad de Ciencias Económicas, Universidad Nacional de Córdoba, 2018. 204 p.: bibl., ill.

This book provides a history of Argentina's first Caja de Conversión in the early 20th century and its transformation into the Banco Central in the 1930s. Well documented and clearly argued, the book shows that for a short period (1900–1914), the office functioned as expected, but in other periods, the need for a lender of last resort and some discretion in monetary policy made the office and the nation's bank operate in tandem like a central bank. The process of creation of the central bank was gradual and based on existing institutions.

1395 Historia necesaria del Banco Central de la República Argentina: entre la búsqueda de la estabilidad y la promoción del desarrollo. Coordinación de Marcelo

Rougier y Florencia Sember. Buenos Aires: Ediciones CICCUS, 2018. 470 p.: bibl., ill.

A collection of essays by prominent scholars of the history of banking. Organized chronologically, the work starts with the interwar context that led to creation of the bank, continues into its initial formation in the 1930s with the leadership of Raúl Prebisch, the transformation of its mission during the import substitution industrialization (ISI) era, the neoliberal moment leading to convertibility, and the postconvertibility aftermath that saw a return to the paradigms of the ISI era. Rather than narrowing down its focus to the Central Bank and the specific handling of its mandate, the book highlights that throughout its different phases, the bank had strong impacts on the economy and society.

Mangonnet, Jorge and **María Victoria Murillo.** Protests of abundance: distributive conflict over agricultural rents during the commodities boom in Argentina, 2003–2013. See item **1268**.

1396 **La maquinaria agrícola argentina: desafíos de la producción nacional en el nuevo desarrollismo.** Edición de José Ignacio Vigil et al. Santa Fe, Argentina: Ediciones UNL, Secretaría de Planeamiento Institucional y Académico, Universidad Nacional del Litoral, 2018. 151 p.: bibl., ill. (Colección Ciencia y tecnología)

Focuses on the post-2001 policies that encouraged the development of a domestic industry of agricultural machinery in Argentina. Mostly based on national economic surveys and statistics, the book carefully documents the policies and assesses their effectiveness in terms of production and social impact.

Menéndez González, Irene. Insiders, outsiders, skills, and preferences for social protection: evidence from a survey experiment in Argentina. See item **1271**.

1397 **Milei, Javier Gerardo** and **Diego Giacomini.** Maquinita, infleta y devaluta: ensayos de economía monetaria: para el caso argentino. Prólogo de José Luis Espert. Buenos Aires: Grupo Unión, 2016. 271 p.: bibl., ill.

A highly partisan account of economic policy in Argentina written by an emerging leader of the brand of libertarianism inspired by Ayn Rand and the Austrian School. In colloquial and vitriolic language, the authors harshly criticize the Kirchner administrations for their populism and expansionary monetary policies. A well-known economic journalist and media character, Milei was eventually elected president in 2023 running on a platform of fiscal austerity and elimination of the national currency that were the main themes of this book.

1398 **El modo de acumulación en la Argentina contemporánea.** Compilación de Alberto Bonnet y Adrián Piva. Buenos Aires: Ediciones Imago Mundi, 2019. 251 p.: bibl., ill. (Colección Bitácora argentina)

This work provides an analysis of the concentration of economic power since the 1970s from a structuralist perspective. It portrays the last quarter of the 20th century as a period of deaccumulation of capital, followed by a new balance of political forces that was sufficient to block neoliberal policies, but insufficient to redesign the productive structure of the economy.

1399 **Niveles de vida en un país en ciernes: dimensiones de la desigualdad en la Argentina en el largo plazo, 1700–1900.** Compilación de Daniel Santilli. Rosario, Argentina: IIE, Instituto de Investigaciones Económicas, Escuela de Economía, FCEyE, UNR; Buenos Aires: Instituto de Historia Argentina y Americana Dr. Emilio Ravignani; Mendoza, Argentina: CONICET, INCIHUSA; Buenos Aires: Prometeo Libros, 2020. 276 p.: bibl., ill. (Colección Historia argentina)

Building on a growing network of Argentine (and other South American) scholars interested in the history of real wages, this volume collects contributions that present new measurements and methodological advances in the study of living standards and inequality. The opening section is a fine introduction to the measurement methods and their application in Argentine history. The book advances beyond the more documented case of Buenos Aires to include studies of different regions as well as urban and rural areas. A welcome addition to long-term studies of the Argentine economy that seldom rely on these comprehensive metrics.

1400 Nueva Historia Económica de la Argentina: temas, problemas, autores; el último medio siglo: ensayos de historiografía económica desde 1810 a 2016. Dirigido por Roberto Cortés Conde y Gerardo Della Paolera. Textos de Roberto Cortés Conde et al. Buenos Aires: Edhasa, 2018. 342 p.: bibl., ill.

New Economic History requires the rigorous application of economic theory and econometric methods to historical economies. This book presents a state-of-the-art study by leading economic historians from Argentina. Rather than presenting a uniform narrative, the chapters focus on the treatment of three broad areas in different historical periods: economic growth, money and debt, and labor and business. Also noteworthy are the chapters about archival sources and the intellectual lineages of New Economic History.

1401 Pensar la economía argentina: por una macroeconomía compatible con el desarrollo. Edición de Matías Kulfas y Guido Zack. Ciudad de México: Siglo Veintiuno Editores, 2018. 206 p.: bibl., ill.

This compilation of essays examines the challenges of the Argentine economy. The discussion of inflation in 21st-century Argentina is a strength of this work, arguing that neither strict monetarist nor antimonetarist explanations are sufficient to account for inflation and should not be sole targets of policy. Another topic is the aim of a more industrial composition of an export-driven, but not foreign-dependent economy. Finally, the work discusses the balance between growth and inequality. This economic analysis based on econometric techniques served as a roadmap for the policies initially pursued by the Fernández administration.

1402 Plotinsky, Daniel. El dinero de los argentinos en manos argentinas: historia del cooperativismo de crédito. Buenos Aires: Ediciones Idelcoop, 2018. 300 p.: bibl.

Plotinsky traces the history of credit cooperatives since the 1950s in Argentina. He narrates the explosive growth of cooperativism under a favorable regulatory framework. Deposits quickly accrued to almost 10 percent of the entire banking system, but the expansion was followed by a conflictive relationship with the Central Bank and military governments. Even under the return of democracy, cooperative banks became more concentrated and less responsive to their popular origins. Only one cooperative bank survives today. The book argues that the vibrancy of credit cooperativism is intimately related to the democratic governance of the institutions and the broader political economic context.

1403 Rapoport, Mario. Parece cuento que la Argentina aún exista: la crisis del neoliberalismo en el espejo del mundo y de la historia. Buenos Aires: Octubre Editorial, 2020. 494 p.: bibl.

A collection of op-ed pieces about the Argentine political economy written by a prominent economist in the tradition of Latin American structuralism. In Rapoport's argument, the conservative government of Mauricio Macri damaged the restoration of the industrialist and egalitarian policies of the Kirchner years, misreading the larger global economic context and catering to well-entrenched interests that rally behind neoliberal banners.

1404 Robertini, Camillo. Quando la Fiat parlava argentino: una fabbrica italiana e i suoi operai nella Buenos Aires dei militari (1964–1980). Firenze, Italy: Le Monnier, 2019. 266 p.: bibl., ill. (Quaderni di storia)

An account of the establishment of the Italian firm FIAT as one of the main automakers in Argentina. The book tracks the origins of the company in the 1960s through the early 1980s when the Italian management left the company after a series of mergers and acquisitions with other business groups. Of particular interest are the interviews with workers and the treatment of the relationship between the labor force and Italian management.

Steinberg, David A. and **Stephen C. Nelson.** The mass political economy of capital controls. See item **1282.**

1405 **Susani, Bruno.** La economía oligárquica de Macri: endeudar, empobrecer y fugar. Buenos Aires: Ediciones CICCUS, 2019. 191 p.: bibl.

A highly critical account of the economic policies of the Macri administration. The critique focuses on policies that increased the concentration of economic and political power and opened the economy to international trade and capital movements. The author sticks primarily to the analysis of economic discourse and leans on rather conspiratorial thinking.

1406 **Teoría y política económica: ensayos en honor al profesor Dr. Julio H.G. Olivera.** Compilación de Víctor A. Beker y Guillermo J. Escudé. Buenos Aires: EUDEBA, 2019. 237 p.: bibl., ill. (Homenaje)

This book is an homage of the disciples of Argentine economist Julio Olivera to the topics studied by their mentor. In this sense it serves as a testimony of the state of macroeconomics in Argentina, with a particular emphasis on the contributions of Olivera to understanding inflationary processes from a structuralist perspective.

1407 **Tigani, Eugenio Pablo.** 2001: FMI, tecnocracia y crisis. Buenos Aires: Editorial Dunken, 2018. 275 p.: bibl., ill.

An analysis of the 2001 crisis based on conceptualizations about technocratic elites. The author considers that technocrats were largely responsible for the 2001 crisis in that they lacked democratic legitimacy, but they were at the same time the outcome of a shrinking coalition to sustain the government. A strength of the book is the careful examination of cabinet compositions.

Time and space: Latin American regional development in historical perspective. See item **1417**.

1408 **Vidoni, Flavio.** Don Juan B.V. Mitri: el pionero del cooperativismo en Sunchales (1881–1954): pequeña historia de un gran hombre. Buenos Aires: Intercoop, Editora Cooperativa Limitada, 2017. 162 p.: bibl., ill.

This biography of Mitri, a leader of the cooperativist movement in the dairy belt of the Pampas region, tracks the organization of producers in the 1930s, eventually increasing its scale to become "SanCor," the most important dairy company in Argentina. The appendixes complement the main narrative with brief histories of northern Italian migration in Argentina, cooperativism, and the region. There is much of interest about cooperativism and the formation of an entrepreneurial elite in the aftermath of the Great Depression.

1409 **El viejo y el nuevo poder económico en la Argentina: del siglo XIX a nuestros días.** Edición de Martín Schorr. Buenos Aires: Siglo Veintiuno Editores, 2021. 240 p.: bibl., ill. (Sociología y política)

An edited volume about big business in Argentina. Written by a network of business history scholars, the book is organized by time period and topic. Recurrent themes are the centrality of big business in the crafting of economic and social policy, the question of whether there is a national bourgeoisie pushing economic development, the importance of foreign capital, and the relationship between state and business. Of particular importance is the assessment that the state was a dynamic force in the private sector during the import substitution industrialization era—a position which it never recovered, even after the "return of the state" in the 21st century.

1410 **Zícari, Julián.** Camino al colapso: cómo llegamos los argentinos al 2001. Buenos Aires: Peña Lillo, Ediciones Continente, 2018. 477 p.: bibl., ill.

A detailed historical account of the 2001 economic crisis in Argentina. Carefully analyzes the political developments and social struggles. It argues that the convertibility regime was not viable and was inevitably headed for a collapse.

PARAGUAY

1411 **Políticas públicas en Paraguay: avances y desafíos 1989–2020.** Edición de Dionisio Borda y Fernando Masi. Prólogo por Milda Rivarola. Asunción: Centro de Análisis y Difusión de la Economía Paraguaya, 2021. 336 p.: graphs, ill.

A review of economic policies and performance of Paraguay in the democratic period from 1989 to 2020. During this period, Paraguay transitions from being considered a low-income country in the World Bank metrics to a medium-high income country. The commodity boom cycle of the early 21st century is at the center of this transformation. The articles also highlight the reduction in poverty levels and increase in public investment, although they are still not comparable to countries of similar income. The book deals with the impact of the COVID pandemic, highlighting the precariousness of the public health sector. Overall, the book highlights progress, but also the need to diversify the economy, limit the environmental degradation of the dynamic agro-export sector, and meet the challenge of clientelism and corruption, while pursuing the long-term prospects for growth.

URUGUAY

1412 50 años de historia de la OPP. Coordinación de Luis Bértola. Contribuciones de Jorge E. Álvarez Scanniello et al. Montevideo: Editorial Fin de Siglo, 2018. 253 p.: bibl.

This work is a history of Uruguay's Oficina de Planeamiento y Presupuesto (Office of Planning and Budget) since its creation in 1967. Written by leading Uruguayan economists and historians, the study is organized around shifting paradigms of economic planning: developmentalism, neoliberalism (in its dictatorial and democratic phase), and 21st-century pragmatism that seeks to balance social policies and growth. The authors approach the legal framework of the office, assess its effectiveness in planning and execution, and articulate different visions of the state and engagement of stakeholders. An important work that helps readers understand the institutional underpinning of changing economic policies.

Etchemendy, Sebastián. The rise of segmented neo-corporatism in South America: wage coordination in Argentina and Uruguay (2005–2015). See item **1257**.

1413 México y Uruguay ante la Gran Recesión. Coordinación de Zeús Salvador Hernández Veleros, Daniel Velázquez Orihuela y Henry Willebald. Pachuca de Soto, Mexico: Universidad Autónoma del Estado de Hidalgo, 2019. 199 p.: bibl., ill., maps.

This edited collection is the fruit of a collaboration between the departments of economics at the Universidad de la República in Montevideo, Uruguay and the Universidad Autónoma del Estado de Hidalgo in Mexico. The essays focus on the economic trajectories and government policies of the two during the Great Recession (2008–2009). The two countries are paradigmatic examples of opposite trajectories: while Uruguay came away unscathed, Mexico was hit hard by the recession. The essays focus on public policies at the national and local level using tools of econometric analysis.

1414 Notaro, Jorge. La distribución social del ingreso: el caso de Uruguay, 2008–2014. (*Cuad. CLAEH*, 37:107, 2018, p. 11–37, bibl., graphs)

The article introduces the concept of "social distribution of income" to estimate income gaps across social groups defined by their insertion in the economy. The study relies on tax records and other sources to refine the measurement of capital income across different social categories, such as foreign and domestic capital owners, laborers and employees, mixed income worker-entrepreneurs, retirees, and the state. Concludes that the distribution of income was stable throughout the period.

1415 Román, Carolina and **Henry Willebald.** Structural change in a small natural resource intensive economy: switching between diversification and reprimarization, Uruguay, 1870–2017. (*Econ. Hist. Dev. Reg.*, 36:1, 2021, p. 57–81, bibl., graphs, tables)

The essay creates a novel synthetic indicator of the complexity of the Uruguayan economy in the long run. It concludes that during periods of crisis, the economy reverted to a simpler structure based on the export of natural resources.

1416 Stuhldreher, Amalia Margarita and **Virginia Morales Olmos.** Energías renovables y desarrollo territorial sustentable: el caso de la región Noreste del Uruguay. (*Cuad. CLAEH*, 36:105, 2017, p. 141–167, bibl.)

The article discusses the transition towards renewable energy in Uruguay, a country that in 2016 had the highest percentage of energy produced by wind turbines in the world and has the highest level of clean energy investment in the continent. The authors focus on the northeastern region and how clean energy served as a driving factor of sustainable development.

1417 Time and space: Latin American regional development in historical perspective. Edited by Daniel A. Tirado, Marc Badia-Miró and Henry Willebald. Cham, Switzerland: Palgrave Macmillan, 2020. 407 p.: bibl., ill., index, maps. (Palgrave studies in economic history)

This edited volume is the first compilation of regional GDP in Latin America covering the late 19th century to the present. Inspired by economic geography and history questions, this volume examines paths of regional convergence and divergence within several Latin American countries. Of particular relevance are the trajectories of Argentina and Uruguay. Despite their regional integration, the two countries show quite different paths: persistent regional inequalities between the north and the capital city and southern regions in Argentina, and a long-term decline of regional inequalities in Uruguay (briefly reversed during the last third of the 20th century). The authors tend to emphasize location of natural resources and integration within the international economy as major factors explaining regional economic trends.

BRAZIL

MELISSA H. BIRCH, *Associate Professor of International Business, University of Kansas*
RUSSELL E. SMITH, *Professor Emeritus of Economics, Washburn University*

THE BRAZILIAN ECONOMIC POLICY literature reviewed for *HLAS* 77 continues to examine the theoretical underpinning of Brazilian economic policy and performance. The homage to Edmar Bacha provides a comprehensive review of Brazilian economic policy from the beginning of the Brazilian Miracle years (1969–73) to the middle of the 2010s (item **1419**). *The Brazilian Economy Today* (item **1418**) is a welcome addition to the literature on the Brazilian economy in that it gives voice to Brazilian authors in English.

The broader discussion in the books reviewed here centers around the rise of developmentalism in Brazil, contrasting it with more traditional, free-market theories. Volumes from Pereira (item **1426**) and Resende (item **1427**) typify this ongoing analysis. Through the lens of new developmentalism, Pereira provides a big picture of Brazilian economic development since World War II. Resende provides a more personal account, contrasting Eugenio Gudin and Roberto Simonsen in a discussion of the role of monetary and fiscal policy in Brazilian development. Taylor (item **1432**) provides a fresh look at Brazil's experience with proactive development policy. His use of an institutional complementarities framework provides a sobering assessment of what can go wrong, and his concept of the developmental hierarchical market economy is illuminating.

Mirroring the structuralist/monetarist debates of the 1960s and 1970s, there is a continuing dialogue among scholars seeking to understand the ways in which economic theory evolved in the mid-20th century and how these ideas were understood and adopted by various actors. *Estado, empresários e política* (item **1423**) examines the debate from the perspective of two business leaders with radically different perspectives on how to achieve economic growth and development for Brazil. *A grande imprensa "liberal" carioca* (item **1425**) challenges the idea that large newspapers uncritically supported liberal (free market) policies, reflecting the position of powerful economic elites. Instead, it notes that Brazilian journalism itself was developing, its readership was evolving, and its coverage of the economic debate was necessarily more nuanced.

Taken together, the books on Brazilian macroeconomics reviewed here constitute an important next step in understanding the complexity of Brazilian economic policy and development. This more forward-looking glance is bolstered by two volumes that seek to understand the impact of two important Brazilian economic policy decisions. A very granular assessment of the impact of the Bolsa Família program on individuals and families contributes to our understanding of cash transfer policies, a hallmark of the first Lula administration (item **1424**). The impact of Brazil's decision in 2016 under the Temer government to freeze federal spending in real terms for 20 years is analyzed in a collection edited by Rossi, Dweck, and Oliveira (item **1420**). The researchers take issue with the wisdom of this approach to government spending and highlight its impact on income inequality.

The publications reviewed for this volume also include some valuable contributions to our understanding of microeconomic considerations such as antitrust (item **1428**) and the impact of mega-events on the informal sector (item **1422**). There seem to be fewer volumes in the 2018–2021 period that examine regional economies and labor markets. A notable exception is the study of the evolution of the footwear industry in Franca (item **1429**). Evidence of the continued interest in Brazilian economic history is evident in several volumes (items **1421, 1423,** and **1429**).

The impact of the global pandemic can be seen in the smaller number of volumes collected by the Library of Congress during this period. The impact on the Brazilian economy of the pandemic itself will no doubt be the focus of future research. While a smaller number of volumes is reviewed here, the quality remains strong and the emergence of new authors and new perspectives is encouraging.

Boas, Taylor C.; F. Daniel Hidalgo; and **Guillermo Toral.** Competence versus priorities: negative electoral responses to education quality in Brazil. See item **1250**.

1418 The Brazilian economy today: towards a new socio-economic model? Edited by Anthony W. Pereira and Lauro Mattei. Houndmills, England: New York, N.Y.: Palgrave Macmillan, 2016. 204 p.: bibl., ill.

The availability in English of this edited collection of essays on the Brazilian economy written by (mostly) Brazilian economists is noteworthy. The essays focus on economic performance in the first 15 years of the 21st century. While by no means comprehensive, it provides short, readable chapters on a variety of economic and social policy topics from the perspective of Brazilian academics and professionals.

Campello, Daniela and **Francisco Urdinez.** Voter and legislator responses to localized trade shocks from China in Brazil. See item **1254**.

1419 **De Belíndia ao real: ensaios em homenagem a Edmar Bacha.** Organização de José Carlos Carvalho *et al.* Textos de Affonso Celso Pastore *et al.* Rio de Janeiro: Civilização Brasileira, 2018. 516 p.: bibl., ill.

This multi-authored volume includes papers on economic theory and fiscal and monetary policy, growth, economic development and balance of payments, and economics and contiguous disciplines. The 21 papers were written in honor of Edmar Lisboa Bacha, the prominent Brazilian academic economist whose career included many years in public service, and were presented at a conference held in February 2017. The periods covered in the papers in this volume begin in the 1970s and continue until shortly before publication.

1420 **Economia para poucos: impactos sociais da austeridade e alternativas para o Brasil.** Organização de Pedro Linhares Rossi, Esther Dweck e Ana Luíza Matos de Oliveira. São Paulo: Autonomia Literária, 2018. 370 p.: bibl., ill.

The articles in this volume analyze the impact of macroeconomic austerity following Emenda Constitucional 95 of 2016, a constitutional amendment that limited the real value of the federal budget to its 2016 level for 20 years. While nominal spending levels could rise in line with official inflation, the needs of a growing population and the real value of needed federal expenditure would be ignored. This forces difficult choices among competing needs, especially in the social sectors. In periods of economic downturn when countercyclical measures would be desirable, the government's hands will be tied. Austerity is experienced, not as a consequence of macroeconomic policy choices, but as the result of a single policy choice, Emenda Constitucional 95. The first papers present general discussions of austerity, while the later papers consider specific areas of government responsibility.

1421 **Huertas, Daniel M.** Território e circulação: transporte rodoviário de carga no Brasil. São Paulo: Editora Unifesp, 2018. 558 p.: bibl., ill., maps, tables.

This doctoral dissertation presents a detailed study of the development of the long-haul trucking industry as an instrument of national integration. The author likens the change to a transition from an *"arquipelago econômico,"* meaning dispersed islands connected by roads, around 1930, to a Brazilian *"rodoviário,"* meaning a "Brazil of highways," by the end of the 20th century. The image is of an integrated network of roads supporting the military's (1964–85) national integration project, followed by continued subsequent development and division of labor unconstrained by distance. The book includes a large number of maps and tables. The author notes that Brazil's highway system predates the country's system of rail transportation, in contrast to the US where the trains came generations earlier. The discussion of carriers includes both large long-haul carriers and smaller local and autonomous carriers.

1422 **Hummel, Calla.** Do poor citizens benefit from mega-events?: São Paulo's street vendors and the 2014 FIFA World Cup. (*Lat. Am. Polit. Soc.*, 60:4, Nov. 2018, p. 26–48, bibl., graphs)

This original study based on surveys, interviews, and participant observation examines the impact of the World Cup on the income of street vendors in São Paulo. It concludes that these poor citizens are more likely to benefit from such mega-events when "officials who depend on their votes or bribes make event laws inclusive and minimize disruption" (p. 27). The authors conclude that forbearance (selective enforcement of relevant laws) is more likely to occur when a "broker" can bundle the needs of poor citizens and represent them to political actors.

1423 **Margalho, Maurício.** Estado, empresários e política: a hegemonia em construção (1930–1945). Rio de Janeiro: Autografia, 2018. 368 p.: bibl.

This book examines the political participation of business leaders between 1930 and 1945 during the administration of Getúlio Vargas. It is a sociopolitical history of the Brazilian economy using a Gramscian framework of analysis. In particular, the book focuses on Euvaldo Lodi (the first president of the CNI, Conselho Nacional da Industria) and Valentim Bouças (general manager of IBM in Brazil, among other roles).

While the former favored a restricted role for foreign capital, the latter maintained a close relationship with US businesses and politicians. The inherent conflict between these interests is examined along with the impact of WWII on the Brazilian economy and the interests of Brazilian business elites.

1424 Marins, Mani Tebet A. de. Bolsa família: questões de gênero e moralidades. Rio de Janeiro: Editora UFRJ, 2017. 311 p.: bibl., ill.

This book presents the results of an interview-based study of the impact of the Programa Bolsa Família, an income transfer program, on school attendance and meeting health requirements. This research considers the impacts of the program, not only on its stated goals, but also on variables normally within the scope of sociology. Following an experimental stage, the program started in 2003 during President Lula da Silva's first term and by March 2013, it had 13 million participants. The volume itself is based on research done for a doctoral dissertation and was conducted in a community in the periphery of Rio de Janeiro.

1425 Martins, Luis Carlos dos Passos. A grande imprensa "liberal" carioca e a política econômica do segundo governo Vargas (1951–1954): conflito entre projetos de desenvolvimento. Porto Alegre, Brazil: ediPUCRS, 2016. 381 p.: bibl. (Série História; 71)

This scholarly analysis of the position taken by the Rio de Janeiro press toward the economic reforms introduced during the second Vargas administration challenges current interpretations. The author argues that rather than simply reflecting the interests of certain economic groups, newspapers in Rio during this period were fighting to establish themselves with their readers. While *Jornal do Brasil* was most closely associated with the free-market principles espoused by Gudin that favored natural resource exports rather than rapid industrialization, Brazilian journalism in the 1950s faced a growing interest among readers in the ideas of economic development and national sovereignty. The author's careful assessment of newspaper coverage of the Vargas government's economic policy reveals a more nuanced picture of journalism in the period and suggests it was more reflective of the policy debates taking place globally.

1426 Pereira, Luiz Carlos Bresser. The political construction of Brazil: society, economy, and state since independence. Boulder, Colo.: Lynne Rienner Publishers, 2017. 419 p.: bibl., index.

This structuralist analysis of Brazilian economic policy-making from the colonial period to the Rousseff administration is both rigorous and readable. A series of Brief Theory text boxes found throughout the volume provide concise explanations of relevant economic theories in the Brazilian context or explanations of specific economic events in Brazil. The volume also stands as a comprehensive application of new developmentalism theory to Brazil.

1427 Resende, André Lara. Juros, moeda e ortodoxia: teorias monetárias e controvérsias políticas. São Paulo: Portfolio Penguin, 2017. 186 p.: bibl.

This book begins with brief biographies of two icons of economic debate in Brazil: Eugenio Gudin for liberalism and Roberto Simonsen for the developmentalists. Later chapters discuss the decline of monetarism and the Quantity Theory of Money and the rise of neo-Keynesian theory through the end of the 20th century, each with their own views of the role of money in economic policy-making. A new orthodoxy regarding inflation and interest rate targets is discussed. The book concludes with a discussion of macroeconomics for less developed countries and the impact of global financial crises, with a focus on the crisis of 2007–2008.

1428 A revolução do antitruste no Brasil: a era dos cartéis. Organização de César Costa Alves de Mattos e Alexandre Cordeiro Macedo. São Paulo: Editora Singular, 2018. 475 p.: bibl., ill.

This edited volume provides a rigorous microeconomic analysis of market concentration and antitrust regulation in Brazil. It is the third volume in a series on the development of antitrust policy in Brazil that emerges with Law 8.884/94 at the end of the 20th century. The various chapters, written primarily by economists, provide both a theoretical analysis of optimal enforcement as well as case studies of monopoly power and regulation in specific sectors from medicine to building maintenance.

1429 Rezende, Vinícius de. Vidas fabris: trabalho e conflito social no complexo coureiro-calçadista de Franca-SP (1950–1980). São Paulo: Alameda, 2017. 532 p.: bibl.

This book presents a study of the workers in the leather and shoemaking industry in the municipality of Franca in the northeastern corner of the state of São Paulo from 1950 to 1980. A traditional leatherworking region located in cattle country, Franca prospered under import substitution industrialization and also as an export platform for men's shoes. The book focuses on the lives of all workers in and out of the workplace, especially in the context of the corporatist "old unionism," since the period under study predates the "new unionism." A chapter on social peace and class conflict at the time is based on the labor rights cases brought in the labor courts. Other chapters consider how technological change does not necessarily lead to lower skill levels nor the end of traditional self-management. Instead, new technology can be adopted while retaining elements of self-management, *"gesto operário,"* in production.

1430 Rougier, Eric; François Combarnous; and Yves-André Fauré. The "local economy" effect of social transfers: an empirical assessment of the impact of the *Bolsa Família* program on local productive structure and economic growth. (*World Dev.*, 103, March 2018, p. 201–215, bibl., graphs, tables)

This paper analyzes the impact of the Bolsa Família conditional cash transfer program beyond its original goals of poverty reduction and the improvement of educational performance, recognizing that the program was successful in distributing income. The authors note that the program operates on both demand and supply sides, increasing both buying power and labor supply. They also find that the program has differential impacts on productive structures in the most and least industrialized municipalities, with the tendency to promote light industrialization in the poorest jurisdictions, while in higher income municipalities the impact of the program was more clearly on the consumption side.

1431 Silva, Bernardino Coelho da and Claudio Tognolli. A caixa preta do BNDES: como o dinheiro público abasteceu Cuba, Venezuela, Angola e a JBS USA. São Paulo: Matrix, 2019. 246 p.: ill.

Less ambitious than the title would suggest, this volume is written through a legal lens and brings together public documents and media reports regarding several major corruption scandals in Brazil. The book focuses primarily on the scandals involving JBS, the Brazilian meat processing giant.

1432 Taylor, Matthew MacLeod. Decadent developmentalism: the political economy of democratic Brazil. Cambridge, England; New York, N.Y.: Cambridge University Press, 2020. 365 p.: bibl., index.

This examination of Brazilian development uses the concept of institutional complementarities to explain the failure of Brazilian policy to deliver sustained growth, superior education, and ample infrastructure. Instead, the author argues, Brazil has fallen into a low-growth equilibrium characterized by low productivity and persistent income inequality. He identifies five domains through which these complementarities work to hold Brazil back: the developmental state, coalitional presidentialism, weak control, autonomous bureaucracy, and what he terms the developmental hierarchical market economy (DHME). His discussion of the developmental state pays special attention to the way the private sector in Brazil has rooted itself within public institutions. JBS, the global meatpacking company (see item **1431**), and the better-known construction firms associated with the Lava Jato scandal are examined.

SOCIOLOGY

GENERAL

ENRIQUE S. PUMAR, *Fay Boyle Endowed Professor and Chair of Sociology, Santa Clara University*

THE PUBLICATIONS included in volume 77 of the *Handbook* reflect the state of Latin American sociology before the COVID-19 pandemic took effect in March 2020. This observation at least partly explains the diverse topics and methodologies featured herein. The reader might notice, for instance, that none of the entries refer to public health concerns despite the distressing social effects of COVID-19 in the region. After considering the uneven impact of the pandemic across and within countries, the Economic Commission for Latin America and the Caribbean (ECLAC) concluded that the prolonged health crisis abated the effectiveness of public health systems and the impact of social protection policies. The World Bank, among other financial institutions, avows that the region experienced the sharpest economic contraction among developing regions. Despite being topics of great interest and contention among sociologists, we'll have to wait and see if they will be featured in, or perhaps even dominate, future research.

One common theme that ties the readings together is an exploration of the social aspects of citizenship. The representative sample of books reviewed can be grouped into three distinct clusters. The first examines how inequality persistently affects some social groups, primarily Afro-Latinos, women, and Indigenous communities. Sagot Rodríguez presents a fine exposition of this topic when she argues that the admission of intersectional effects on inequality is in itself a topic of great contentiousness since identities are highly politicized by power relations (item **1436**). The case studies in Sagot's book also establish how feminist insights cast further understandings on the dispersion of social inequality. Another provocative exposition of this genre is the volume by Horbath Corredor and Gracia about the fate of Indigenous communities in major urban centers throughout the region (item **1439**). This insightful study shows how after migrating to the city in search of better economic opportunities, Indigenous populations find themselves marginalized and facing discrimination. Their deprivation and relative social isolation also motivate civic engagement in the forms of advocacy and social activism beyond resistance. The recent volume of social mobilization in Ecuador and Chile, among other nations, supports the finding (item **1444**). Finally, another illustration of the nexus between discrimination and empowerment is the collection of essays captured by Campoalegre Septien (item **1434**). This book shows how Afrocentric resistance movements frame questions related to race and racial relations in the contexts of national historical experiences to make them more meaningful. Besides demanding that racial stigmatization be considered a violation of fundamental human rights, these essays examine how, throughout history, racial suppression became a mechanism for sustaining the legacy of colonialism and domination.

A second theme is displacement. While most migration patterns still follow a South/North divide, Neira Orjuela's comparative study of irregular urban mobility reminds us that a South/South trajectory is on the rise (item **1442**). In part, this is the outcome of inhospitable deterrent border policies and the rise of nativism, but cost considerations and historical ties also played a part in decisions to move nearby. One lesson we could draw from this analysis is that in the Southern Hemisphere immigrant families face a similar marginalized context of reception, and community NGOs in the "third sector" often must intervene to mitigate the hardships immigrants face even in neighboring societies.

The fate and contributions of returning exile expatriates present another exciting analytical edge of the complex question of displacement. This is the research topic Roniger and his collaborators thoroughly investigate (item **1445**). This book discerns the many contributions returning exiles offer to sending societies. The Southern Cone's comparative focus is understandable. Starting in 1964 these fragile democracies broke down and were replaced by bureaucratic-authoritarian regimes that consolidated power by terrorizing and exiling the mobilized opposition. As Roniger and his collaborators point out, while residing abroad, dissident groups learned fresh cultural norms and political mechanisms that would contribute to consolidating pluralism throughout the region. Not all was lost for exile intellectuals who after years of living abroad came back to revitalize the cultural spheres in their native countries.

Finally, the third category of papers ventures into epistemological questions. Two books from this group are worth highlighting. López Nájera explains in a brief but insightful study how paradigm shifts are often the result of political defeats (item **1440**). López Nájera asserts that one of the unintended consequences of the transition from authoritarianism to more pluralistic politics after the 1980s was the rise of southern epistemologies which explore the intriguing effects of neocolonialist policies affecting the hemisphere. Mejía Navarrete, obviously inspired by the pioneering work of Edward Said, proposes a fitting follow-up to this argument when he argues that Eurocentric notions of modernity sustained hegemonic empires (item **1441**). Mejía Navarrete also argues that after independence the push to become modern along Western lines was responsible for fostering a distorted national reality among Latin American societies. One can think of how the modernization perspective inflicted serious material and cultural distortions in the postwar era only to be rebutted by more critical development perspectives after the unsettling decades of the 1960s.

After reviewing this provocative literature, one concluding thought is the extent to which Latin American sociologists represent in many respects what Aldo Morris has called "the scholar denied." That is, sometimes discerning scholars are pushed to the margins by other more resourceful colleagues who promote theories and scopes of research that conform to mainstream perspectives. The social science community will be remiss if it does not pay closer attention to the literature published by our Southern neighbors. The intellectual merits of these rich and insightful publications should not be denied.

1433 Afro-Asian connections in Latin America and the Caribbean. Edited by Luisa Marcela Ossa and Debbie Lee-DiStefano. Lanham, Md.: Lexington Books, 2019. 240 p.: bibl., ill., index. (Black diasporic worlds: origins and evolutions from New World slaving)

To analyze cultural representations and identity formations, this collection explores how the intersectionality among gender, race, and ethnic nationality manifests itself in different genres throughout the Americas. One of the major contributions of this conceptual approach is the incorporation of the transnational dimension of intersectional social relations. The authors also examine how the interactions between African and Asian groups contribute to unique cultural productions. Finally, interracial relations are problematized presenting us with a more vivid understanding of ethnic relations in the region.

1434 Afrodescendencias: voces en resistencia: en homenaje al centenario de Nelson Mandela. Edición de Rosa Campoalegre Septien. Textos de Rosa Campoalegre Septien *et al.* Buenos Aires: CLACSO, 2018. 334 p.: bibl., ill. (Colección Antologías del pensamiento social latinoamericano y caribeño. Serie Pensamientos silenciados)

The authors in this collection investigate the various links between colonialism and racism throughout the Americas. Their approach consists in exploring marginalized voices and modalities of emancipation taking a historical posture into account. The contributions of African American voices and praxis in such topics as the struggle against social inequality, identity suppression, fundamental human rights, and antiracist movements are noted. Taken together, this rich compilation transforms these suppressed views into voices leading to anticolonial and self-determination struggles. Finally, the volume captures essays from scholars with a wide variety of institutional affiliations contributing to the inclusive representation of African American studies.

1435 América Latina en movimiento: migraciones, límites a la movilidad y sus desbordamientos. Coordinación de Blanca Cordero, Sandro Mezzadra y Amarela Varela. Madrid: TDS, Traficantes de Sueños; Ciudad de México: UACM, Universidad Autónoma de la Ciudad de México; Buenos Aires: Tinta Limón Ediciones, 2019. 335 p.: bibl., color ill.

The 10 essays in this book analyze how migration from Latin America to the US is characterized by tensions and struggles within and among migrant movements and other social actors. Often this contentiousness does not manifest itself in traditionally violent ways; rather, the contestation is often intersubjective—diasporic identities and geographies of power are two manifestations. The essays conclude that displacement modalities are conditioned on the one hand by the limits of institutional capacities among NGOs and states, and on the other by the impacts of the stigma associated with marginality.

Antropología de la violencia. See item **1448**.

Charles Tilly: sobre violencia colectiva, política contenciosa y cambio social: antología selecta. See item **1457**.

Desigualdades interdependentes e geopolítica do conhecimento: negociações, fluxos, assimetrias. See item **1142**.

Elsey, Brenda and **Joshua Nadel.** Futbolera: a history of women and sports in Latin America. See *HLAS 76:248*.

1436 Feminismos, pensamiento crítico y propuestas alternativas en América Latina. Coordinación de Montserrat Sagot Rodríguez. Textos de Alba Carosio *et al.* Costa Rica: CIEM, Centro de Investigación en Estudios de la Mujer; Buenos Aires: CLACSO, 2017. 225 p.: bibl., ill. (Colección Grupos de trabajo)

The 12 chapters in this collection explore how feminist perspectives provide dissenting and critical views of the social milieu in Latin America. All the chapters problematize the conditions of women's subordination and exclusion to discern the sophisticated elements of power relations not just in the realm of gender, but also when gender intersects with race, ethnicity, and nationality. The essays emphasize that feminism is not a homogeneous perspective and that there are many versions of feminism, which may even be in contention with one another. The diverse number of case studies captured in this volume reaffirms that feminist thinking is one of the vital critical perspectives being debated throughout Latin America.

1437 Galli, Carlos María. La alegría del evangelio en América Latina: de la Conferencia de Medellín a la canonización de Pablo VI (1968–2018). Buenos Aires: Agape Libros, 2018. 169 p.: bibl. (Colección Escritos teológico-pastorales; 28)

In this essay, Galli contends that after the 1968 Medellín Conference, the Catholic Church in Latin America developed an evangelical strategy rooted in principles of Catholic social teachings to attract and energize marginalized groups and rejuvenate the Church. The book opens with a historical account focusing on the continuities of values embedded in Catholic discourse from 1968 to 2018, emphasizing how the spirit of renewal has been a constant tenet. This argument is followed by a more detailed analysis of the Puebla Conference and the formulation of the doctrine of preferential option for the poor. The book closes with a thoughtful reflection on how Laudato si' and other recent papal encyclicals reassert the need for renewal amid many contemporary existential problems.

1438 Género, sexualidades y mercados sexuales en sitios extractivos de América Latina. Coordinación de Susanne Hofmann y Melisa Cabrapan Duarte. Ciudad de México: UNAM, Centro de Investigaciones y Estudios de Género, 2019. 334 p.: ill.

The essays in this edited volume examine gender relations in the context of extractive local economies in Mexico, Argentina, Ecuador, Peru, Bolivia, and Brazil. Whereas other volumes exploring this subject tend to portray individuals working in extractive economics as trapped in a cycle of poverty, this book explores social ties and the relations between individuals and ecological factors to give meaning to human agency. Following an ethnographic approach, the essays discern how extractive economies reproduce new forms of gender domination, power, and authority relations.

1439 Indígenas en las ciudades de las Américas: condiciones de vida, procesos de discriminación e identificación y lucha por la ciudadanía étnica. Coordinación de Jorge Enrique Horbath Corredor y María Amalia Gracia. Buenos Aires: Miño y Dávila Editores, 2019. 443 p.: bibl., ill., maps.

The essays in this volume explore different social, cultural, economic, and political aspects of the internal migration experiences of Indigenous populations in cities throughout Latin America. While the original motivating factor to migrate might have been to improve their livelihoods, the encounters with urban life also marginalized and raised the collective consciousness of Indigenous populations after they faced recurrent discrimination, segregation, and stigmatization. One of the themes that cuts across these essays is how Indigenous actors also developed agency through activism and resistance in unwelcoming environments. The collection consists of 18 case studies organized along seven topical sections contrasting similarities and differences in regional experiences.

1440 López Nájera, Verónica Renata. Derrota política, crisis teórica y transición epistémica: los estudios pos/de/descoloniales en América Latina. Coyoacán, Mexico: UNAM, 2018. 151 p.: bibl.

Following Karl Mannheim's classic approach to knowledge production, López Nájera asserts that to understand the rise of recent critical postures in Latin America, one needs to associate paradigmatic shifts with specific regional political trends. The rise of authoritarian politics gave rise to dependency and neodependency debates. More recent political transformations have given way to what de Sousa refers to as "southern epistemologies" or the concerns for postcoloniality and emancipation. Recent critical perspectives in Latin America manifest themselves not just in the field of theoretical interpretations, but at specific moments in everyday discourse and symbolism. Finally, the essay proposes that new paradigms are pluralistic and often entertain debates and tensions calling for further reflections.

1441 Mejía Navarrete, Julio Víctor.
América Latina, modernidad y conocimiento: el desarrollo de otro discurso epistémico. Lima: Universidad Nacional Mayor de San Marcos, Fondo Editorial, Facultad de Ciencias Sociales, 2016. 177 p.: bibl. (Colección Ensayos)

This brief but provocative essay examines the evolution of social science epistemology as it relates to Latin American social thought. Mejía Navarrete argues that the development of knowledge in the region was originally tied to the question of modernity, a movement that was Eurocentric and could not incorporate the complexities of Latin American societies. Modernity sustained colonial rule and was promoted by many public intellectuals in the 19th century. The postwar years incrementally gave way to alternative paradigms that not only questioned Eurocentrism, but also introduced alternative views grounded in Latin American critical thinking, such as the ideas promoted by Mariátegui. One component of this argument that might disappoint the reader is that the reasons and conditions contributing to paradigm shifts are not attentively examined.

Munoz, Ercio. The geography of intergenerational mobility in Latin America and the Caribbean. See item **458**.

1442 Neira Orjuela, Fernando. Migración irregular andina en tres países y capitales sudamericanas: sus efectos sobre las políticas, programas y actores institucionales. Ciudad de México: Bonilla Artigas Editores: UNAM, Centro de Investigaciones sobre América Latina y el Caribe, 2019. 224 p.: bibl. (Diásporas)

This book reminds us that the question of irregular migration is not just a South/North population movement, but also a South/South. To illustrate this point, Neira Orjuela investigates irregular migration in Chile, Argentina, and Brazil. The first of five chapters sets the tone for the rest of the book with an impressive review of the literature. This chapter is followed by a demographic analysis and an impact assessment of programs designed to assist irregular migrant populations. The book closes with an analysis of the economic, social, and cultural tensions associated with migration to urban areas. The author concludes that many of the problems confronted by migrants are racialized, and assistance dispersement by NGOs and religious organizations is primarily responsible for the survival of these marginalized groups.

1443 Ortiz Ocaña, Alexander; María Isabel Arias López; and **Zaira Esther Pedrozo Conedo.** Decolonialidad de la educación: emergencia/urgencia de una pedagogía decolonial. Santa Marta, Colombia: Editorial Unimagdalena, 2018. 153 p.: bibl. (Colección Ciencias sociales. Serie Educación y pedagogía)

This study embarks on the exploration of one of the major topics of our time, the nature and implication of epistemology contentions. The book depicts relations of knowledge in terms of power. To accomplish this task, the authors examine how a particular pedagogical conception was imposed by colonial powers to sustain their rule in the Americas. They also argue that our quest must be to decolonize science to help us understand the complex realities we confront. To decolonize education, the authors argue, is to incorporate the experiences and knowledge of marginalized groups such as Indigenous populations. The book spells out these complex concepts in layman's terms.

1444 Pleyers, Geoffrey. Movimientos sociales en el siglo XXI: perspectivas y herramientas analíticas. Prefacio de Boaventura de Sousa Santos. Posfacio de Breno Bringel. Buenos Aires: CLACSO, 2018. 229 p.: bibl. (Colección Democracias en movimiento)

The new wave of social movement organizations that proliferated after 2011 marks a significant departure from the traditional patterns and composition of social mobilization. Whereas social movements in the 1990s were primarily protesting the disrupting effects of neoliberalism through advocacy networks of Indigenous groups and committed intellectuals, Pleyers argues, after 2011, social movements consist of cross-class alliances demanding further democratic participation and support for a dignified way of life. The risks associated with the rise of progressive politics have resulted in the proliferation of countermovements by the far right and frequent contentiousness. These cleavages have repercussions for public life as well as for the field of social movement studies, which now must attempt to understand not just radical mobilization, but also the rise of renegades.

¿Qué hacemos con la(s) masculinidad(es)?: reflexiones antipatriarcales para pasar del privilegio al cuidado. See item **1689**.

1445 Roniger, Luis *et al.* Exile, diaspora, and return: changing cultural landscapes in Argentina, Chile, Paraguay, and Uruguay. New York, N.Y.: Oxford University Press, 2017. 292 p.: bibl., index.

Focusing on four nations from Latin America's Southern Cone, this book examines the contributions of displaced public intellectuals in the cultural and political fields. During the wave of authoritarianism that dominated the region after 1964 many academics and intellectuals were forced into exile, but continued to write despite different political and social realities. The return to democracy presented the exiles with an opportunity to contribute to the public life of their countries of origin in significant ways. To explore these contributions, the book follows a comparative historical approach to post-dictatorial politics, emphasizing the importance of transnational advocacy networks. Readers should note that the book makes a noteworthy contribution to the study of migration and the emerging focus on the roles and influence of immigrant intellectuals. For geography specialist's comment, see item **607**. For political economy specialist's comment, see item **1277**.

1446 Trabajadores y sindicatos en Latinoamérica: conceptos, problemas y escalas de análisis. Compilación de Silvia Simonassi y Daniel Dicósimo. Buenos Aires: Ediciones Imago Mundi, 2018. 301 p.: bibl. (Colección Bitácora argentina)

This comprehensive comparative sociohistorical examination of labor unions in South America analyzes the complex world of organized labor from different perspectives, encompassing labor activism, the linkages between professions and types of labor representations, the manifested contentiousness, and the current transformations experienced by labor organizations. One important takeaway from the book is the challenges unions face with the proliferation of the informal sector and transnational post-Fordism. In the Argentine case, for instance, the return of many political exiles has contributed to the proliferation of new forms of activism and this, the authors assert, might be the future for other industrial sectors in the region.

Vilar, José Rafael. Auge y caída del socialismo del siglo XXI: una rápida visión hispanoamericana de sus recientes ciclos políticos y del fracaso de ideologizar la economía. See item **339**.

MEXICO

ERNESTO CASTAÑEDA-TINOCO, *Associate Professor of Sociology and Director, Center for Latin American and Latino Studies (CLALS), Immigration Lab, American University*

THE PUBLICATIONS included in this section in many ways represent the state of sociological inquiry in Mexico today. The authors employ a variety of methodologies to investigate questions pertaining to a range of topics. Of notable prevalence among the topics are feminist scholarship; corruption, violence, and organized crime in Mexico; labor issues; gender and sexuality studies; social movements; and migration. As these works emanate from sociologists, there is a greater emphasis on qualitative methods. Numerous scholars employ methods like ethnography and interviews to develop a deeper understanding of various cultural groups and phenomena. Nonetheless, some of the publications offer mainly demographic data and tables on specific indicators.

Among those studies with feminist themes, scholars explore the exclusion of disabled women from feminist scholarship and activism (item **1460**), gendered experiences of Mexico City (item **1519**), persistent inequalities faced by Mexican women (item **1467**), women's rights to make decisions surrounding maternity and pregnancy (items **1489** and **1516**), and feminist social action (item **1515**).

The issue of state sanctioned/organized corruption and violence in Mexico is clearly of great concern among sociologists today, with many placing focus on both recent and historical human rights violations at the hands of the Mexican government (items **1458**, **1466**, and **1498**), including violent acts and disappearances (items **1476** and **1484**).

Several scholars explore changing labor trends, often through studies of specific groups of workers/occupations such as "planted houseworkers" (item **1470**), workers in call centers (item **1487**), and women entrepreneurs (item **1503**).

Related to the demonstrated focus on feminist issues, many scholars are keen to investigate issues of gender and sexuality (items **1490**, **1495**, and **1525**), especially through exploration of identity construction (items **1464**, **1485**, and **1507**).

Given the discussion of historical and current social issues, it is fitting that scholars have also examined the related social movements within Mexico. Included in this section are studies that explore both national and regional social movements (item **1529**), public policy as a mode of resistance (item **1514**), grassroots movements and their complex relationships with communities (item **1530**), and filmmaking as a tool for social activism (item **1534**). We also have a translated collection of the work of renowned sociologist Charles Tilly (item **1457**).

A wealth of migration scholarship has come out in recent years, much of which offers new perspectives to the traditional modes of examining Mexican migration. Scholars analyze migration among adolescents (items **1479** and **1522**), as well as women and the family (items **1486** and **1518**). They privilege previously underrepresented perspectives from the Global South (item **1540**), migration and work (item **1500**), and underrepresented topics such as internal migration within Mexico (items **1501** and **1545**).

Finally, this section offers perspectives from numerous scholars who examine various subcultures within and around Mexico, including the cult of La Santa Muerte (items **1527** and **1549**), gangs in the El Paso-Juárez region of the US and Mexico (item **1537**), and understudied religious groups like Latino Muslims (item **1496**).

1447 Acuña Villavicencio, John Kenny and Ever Sánchez Osorio. La escuela y la necropolítica del trabajo en el estado de Guerrero. (*in* Cotidianidad, educación y violencia en el estado de Guerrero: otras prácticas y haceres en un mundo turbulento. Coordinación de John Kenny Acuña Villavicencio y Ever Sánchez Osorio. Acapulco, Mexico: Hipócrates Universidad; Iztapalapa, Mexico: Ediciones del Lirio, 2020, p. 21–39, bibl.)

Explores the effect of organized crime on everyday life and necropolitics of work and school in Guerrero state.

1448 **Antropología de la violencia.** Coordinación de Yerko Castro Neira. Puebla, Mexico: Benemérita Universidad Autónoma de Puebla: Dirección General de Publicaciones, 2019. 301 p.: bibl., ill., maps. (Colección homo ludens)

This study provides an overview of conflict and violence in various parts of Latin America. The book presents an ethnological analysis of trends of violence in Mexico, Chile, Ecuador, Colombia, France, Spain, Argentina, Brazil, and Costa Rica. The book is organized in three sections: Ethnographies in the Context of Multiple Violences (Etnografías en contextos de múltiples violencias); Ethnographies of Displaced Communities and Migratory Circulation (Etnografías en comunidades en desplazamiento y circulación migratoria); and Ethnography and Ethnographer Awareness (La toma de conciencia de la etnógrafa y el etnógrafo). Within these sections, violence in Latin America is considered structurally and as it affects the lives of citizens. The contributions focus on the acts of violence that perpetuate throughout the region, as well as on the stereotypes and stigmas that characterize Latin America as a "violent" continent. The authors critique how the concept of violence is constructed in Latin America and how stigmatization reproduces brutality. Overall, this work uses ethnography to both understand and critique how violence is described in Latin America.

1449 **Ávila García, Virginia.** Las mujeres creyentes y el Opus Dei: identidades en el trabajo mediante la fe. Ciudad de México: UNAM, Facultad de Filosofía y Letras: Dirección General de Asuntos del Personal Académico: Ediciones Eón, 2018. 185 p.: bibl.

An investigative piece on the history of women in Opus Dei, specifically in Mexico, which was the religious entryway to the Americas. Specifically, the author explores the female condition in the realm of Catholicism and the Westernized look into the changes from the 20th and 21st centuries.

1450 **Ávila Ortiz, María Natividad.** Presiones socioculturales y la percepción de la imagen en estudiantes universitarios. (*in* Estudios críticos sobre políticas y problemáticas sociales. Coordinación de Elisa Cerros Rodríguez y Verónica Martínez Flores. Mexico: Universidad Autónoma de Nuevo León, 2018, p. 167–188, bibl.)

This study analyzes family, peer, and media pressures and their association with body weight and body image perception amongst college students studying nutrition ranging in ages between 18 and 25.

1451 **Benavides Rincón, Guillermina.** La coordinación interinstitucional en el Programa de Desarrollo Humana Oportunidades: un estudio de caso. (*in* Estudios críticos sobre políticas y problemáticas sociales. Coordinación de Elisa Cerros Rodríguez y Verónica Martínez Flores. Mexico: Universidad Autónoma de Nuevo León, 2018, p. 21–60, bibl.)

This case study analyzes how the inter-institutional coordination of a human development program (Prospera) can be accomplished. The results show that at the federal level it is coordinated by three macromechanisms: hierarchy, networks, and markets.

1452 **Berlanga Gayón, Mariana.** Una mirada al feminicidio. Ciudad de México: Universidad Autónoma de la Ciudad de México: Itaca, 2018. 250 p.: bibl., ill., photos.

Feminicidio, or femicide, describes the phenomena in which women and girls around the globe are victims of murder because of their gender and/or sexuality. Femicide is an unfortunately frequent occurrence in Latin America, and particularly in Mexico. This study examines how the construction of gender and its relationship to power is manifested through femicides. The book is divided into three chapters: A "Glimpse" at Femicide (Una "mirada" del feminicidio); Image Narratives: Framing of Life and Death (Narrativas de la imagen: encuadres de la vida y la muerte); and The Color of Femicide: Shades of Vulnerability (El color del feminicidio: tonalidades de la vulnerabilidad). Within these chapters, the author provides the reader with an in-depth analysis of the nature of femicide in Latin America and the social and political factors—such as patriarchy, race, social class, and migration status—that have contributed to the reality of gender-based violence.

1453 Bienestar subjetivo en México. Coordinación de René Millán y Roberto Castellanos. Colaboración de René Millán *et al.* Ciudad de México: UNAM, Instituto de Investigaciones Sociales, 2018. 437 p.: bibl., ill., maps.

Researchers in Mexico have done extensive work on the subject of well-being—which refers to an individual's personal evaluation of their happiness and quality of life. They have found that most Mexicans find employment, income, and education to be among the top indicators when assessing their well-being. Health, social life, and safety are the next most important indicators on the evaluation. Additionally, age and gender play a role in their assessments as, for example, young women have a more positive outlook than older men. They argue their work can be used to help create public and social programs to improve well-being.

1454 Bórquez Bustos, Rodolfo. Violencia y miedo en Acapulco. (*in* Cotidianidad, educación y violencia en el estado de Guerrero: otras prácticas y haceres en un mundo turbulento. Coordinación de John Kenny Acuña Villavicencio y Ever Sánchez Osorio. Acapulco, Mexico: Hipócrates Universidad; Iztapalapa, Mexico: Ediciones del Lirio, 2020, p. 39–60, bibl.)

This study examines the prevalent violence and insecurity in Mexico through empirical findings in Acapulco and historical efforts to gain workers' rights and the violent response of the state.

1455 Calvario Parra, José Eduardo. Bríncale, no seas miedoso: masculinidad y peligro en jornaleros agrícolas de Sonora. Hermosillo, Mexico: El Colegio de Sonora: Centro de Investigación en Alimentación y Desarrollo: Universidad de Sonora, 2017. 295 p.: bibl., ill.

A normative structure has enforced a set of damaging sanctions or ideologies that promote an understanding of how the roles of masculinity or femininity are placed in the workspace of agriculture. Laborers are assigned dangerous tasks and face health risks. An investigation in Hermosillo, Sonora, seeks to understand the relationship between masculinity and the preceding acts of danger within the labor market and the consequences of social and gender violence.

1456 Cantoral Cantoral, Guadalupe. Mujeres y varones en búsqueda de cambio: el malestar como vía. San Cristóbal de Las Casas, Mexico: Universidad de Ciencias y Artes de Chiapas, Centro de Estudios Superiores de México y Centroamérica, 2018. 273 p.: bibl., ill. (Colección Thesis; 7)

Using discomfort as a tool, Cantoral examines the social construct of what it means to be masculine and feminine in San Cristóbal de las Casas, Chiapas, and challenges encountered in both identities. Through learned gender norms, the author assesses how women and men spend their free time, their frustrations with the division of labor at home, power in relationships, domestic violence, mental health, and more. Additionally, the author notes the discrepancies of family dynamics based on surveys of the town in relation to family dynamics that mothers and fathers encounter.

1457 Charles Tilly: sobre violencia colectiva, política contenciosa y cambio social: antología selecta. Edición de Ernesto Castañeda y Cathy Lisa Schneider. Ciudad de México: UNAM, Instituto de Investigaciones sobre la Universidad y la Educación, 2022. 587 p.: bibl.

Charles Tilly was one of the towers of contemporary social sciences, the author of over 50 books and 700 articles and chapters; his influence is large in sociology, political science, and history. This book brings together original pieces by Tilly that put his overall oeuvre in context. It also includes an introduction to put the work and contributions further into context. Of interest to the general reader and to those doing research on social movements and contentious politics, inequality, cultural sociology, historical change, and democratization. For the review of a 1986 chapter by Tilly on urban history, see *HLAS 58:823*.

1458 Contreras Orozco, Javier H. Es el mensaje: la estrategia de comunicación del narcotráfico. Ciudad de México:

MA Porrúa librero-editor, 2017. 283 p.: bibl., ill.

The author explores the linkage between violence, drug trafficking, and the media in Mexico. Some of the themes are strategies narcotraffickers utilize for scare tactics through acts of violence, disinformation in the media and news outlets, and through religion. The author concludes by offering ways to reduce violence and delinquency.

1459 Cruz Herrera, Victor Manuel. Rudimentos para la formación de agencia democrática y paz positiva en el estado de Guerrero: educación para la democracia. (*in* Cotidianidad, educación y violencia en el estado de Guerrero: otras prácticas y haceres en un mundo turbulento. Coordinación de John Kenny Acuña Villavicencio y Ever Sánchez Osorio. Acapulco, Mexico: Hipócrates Universidad, 2020, p. 115–130, bibl.)

This investigative article explains and analyzes the conditions that favor or restrain education about democracy in Guerrero, taking into consideration formal and nonformal educational institutions.

1460 Cruz Pérez, María del Pilar. De cuerpos invisibles y placeres negados: discursos y prácticas en torno a la sexualidad y la reproducción de las mujeres con discapacidad en México. Ciudad de México: Universidad Autónoma Metropolitana, Unidad Xochimilco, División de Ciencias Sociales y Humanidades: Universidad Iberoamericana, Ciudad de México, 2017. 253 p.: bibl. (Colección Teoría y análisis; 71)

Cruz Pérez addresses the lack of public policy advocating for the rights and access for disabled women in Mexico, particularly related to reproduction, sexuality, and sexual health. Through a bibliographic review and intensive fieldwork, she uncovers the marginalization of this population. She unpacks the exclusion of disabled women in gender and feminist studies and argues that certain groups and topics are often omitted from these fields. Cruz seeks to shift the narrative regarding disabled women from personal tragedies to instead highlight the resilient, fighting attitudes that they live with every day. The book's first section navigates through caring for and understanding people with disabilities, as she frames disability as dynamic and socially constructed. She works through how historically, scholars have justified their social exclusion. In the second section, she discusses feminism and disability, and how the body is viewed as well as recognizing reproductive and sexual rights. She raises the importance of eliminating obstacles to making access to these rights a certainty for all women. Cruz also acknowledges the advances that have been made in the realm of gaining rights for disabled women. The third section of this book discusses the policies and programs regarding disabilities in Mexico, as Cruz offers an overview of the ways (such as treaties and international conventions) that Mexico has worked towards rights for women and disabled persons. Additionally, she describes the programs and actions of the Mexican government, as well as the current status of reproductive and sexual rights of disabled women. In the fourth section, the author discusses the different practices and narratives regarding motherhood and sexuality of disabled women. Cruz brings awareness to and shares the importance of rights for disabled women, as well as the need to stop marginalizing them within gender studies.

1461 Cruz Vasquez, Miguel and **Renato Salas Alfaro.** Algunos casos de emprendimiento de migrantes retornados. (*in* Emprendimiento y migración de retorno: raíces y horizontes. Coordinación de Miguel Cruz Vásquez y Alfredo Cuecuecha Mendoza. Ciudad de México: Universidad Popular Autónoma del Estado de Puebla: El Colegio de Tlaxcala: MAPorrúa, 2018, p. 133–151)

An analysis of return migrants turned entrepreneurs in their home of origin in Mexico and other parts of the world. The author detects various motivations for migrating based on budgeting, investing, place of origin, community, and logistical purposes.

1462 Cuecuecha, Alfredo. ¿Es la migración de retorno la causa de la reducción de mexicanos viviendo en Estados Unidos? (*in* Emprendimiento y migración de retorno: raíces y horizontes. Coordinación de Miguel Cruz Vásquez y Alfredo Cuecuecha

Mendoza. Ciudad de México: Universidad Popular Autónoma del Estado de Puebla: El Colegio de Tlaxcala: MAPorrúa, 2018, p. 35–47)

The author examines various variables related to the reduction of Mexican migration to the US in 2008. Cuecuecha Mendoza makes a strong argument that one important reason was the growing number of formal jobs in Mexico that decreased the need to migrate.

1463 Cuéllar Vázquez, Angélica. Reflexiones desde la sociología jurídica en torno a las leyes y políticas públicas hacia las mujeres en México. (*in* Reflexiones interdisciplinarias sobre la ciudadanía de género: mujeres en la Ciudad de México. Coordinación de Lorena Margarita Umaña Reyes. Ciudad de México: Grupo Editor Orfila Valentini, SA de CV: UNAM, 2018, p. 129–131)

This qualitative analysis examines a variety of laws aiming to end gender violence and promote equity among men and women. The author addresses women's freedom in Mexico and how society adjusts according to preset social norms. For a review of the entire volume, see item **1519**.

1464 Cuerpos, subjetividades y (re)configuraciones de género. Coordinación de María Eugenia Flores Treviño y Rosa María Gutiérrez García. Ciudad Juárez, Mexico: Universidad Autónoma de Ciudad Juárez, 2018. 313 p.: bibl., ill. (Colección Discurso(s) en Frontera(s); 3)

Product of the III Coloquio de Discursos en Fronteras at the Universidad Autónoma de Ciudad Juárez, this volume gathers multidisciplinary studies that explore the semiotics, discourses, languages, and cultures of power and violence, as well as their impacts on the body and sexual identity. The book is divided into four sections: Bodies and Subjectivities, Femme Bodies in Intervened Spaces, The Feminine Body and its Literary Metaphorizations, and The Performativity of Gender Violence. The contributions offer readers the opportunity to reflect on the female experience, ever-evolving patriarchies, social marginalization, and various gender configurations from different perspectives. Furthermore, the book holds a particular interest in bodies and the meanings they generate depending on the space in which they find themselves.

1465 La cultura y sus efectos sobre la psicología del mexicano. Coordinación de Rolando Díaz-Loving y Alejandra del Carmen Domínguez Espinosa. Ciudad de México: Universidad Iberoamericana, 2019. 228 p.: bibl.

The authors, both social psychologists, compile a diverse collection of works that address pressing questions regarding the influence of culture on psychology, specifically within Mexico. The empirical research considers issues of socialization as a process as well as social constructions and their historical trajectories and new interpretations. Specifically, the chapters explore Mexican culture in comparison with the dominant cultures in other countries; common practices of parents and the role of the family; critical reflections on the concept of social desirability in Mexico; assertiveness in Mexican culture; Mexican resilience to economic and social crises; "universal" Mexican values—compared among those living near the northern border; the nuanced cognitive and behavioral patterns of love in Mexican culture; and the construction of gender through a historical-social-cultural lens.

1466 Derechos humanos y violencia en México. Coordinación de Laura Loeza Reyes y Analiese Richard. Ciudad de México: UNAM, Centro de Investigaciones Interdisciplinarias en Ciencias y Humanidades, 2018. 209 p.: bibl.. ill. (Colección Alternativas)

This edited volume examines the systemic issues in the justice system and the institutional design that results in a lack of rights for victims. The authors explain that rates of impunity and corruption have been increasing for over a decade, allowing for a humanitarian crisis. To examine these issues, they compare similar experiences and situations in other Latin American countries, as well as giving voice through testimony to those who have worked to defend and fight for victims. The works included in the edited volume cover several related topics. For example, Jairo Antonio

López Pacheco compares legal opportunities in Mexico and Colombia and discusses collective action, accountability in security policy, and human rights. Through this, he discusses structures of legal opportunity and the defense of human rights, as well as politics of national security and militarization in Colombia and Mexico and the limits to personal freedom in that context. Another piece focuses on the Valley of Mexico and analyzes environmental citizenship and the human right to water there. The author examines the different discourses and actors regarding water as a resource, as well as the structural violence that arises from the geopolitics of water. The volume also offers three works that are testimonies from participants in civil and victimization organizations. They discuss the movement for missing persons in Mexico and recount their struggle for a law, as well as the challenges that victims and their organizations experience through the severe human rights violations in Mexico. The authors give a voice to and tell the story of people who are experiencing these issues in real life, and give the reader an even better picture of the significant concerns addressed in the volume.

1467 Desigualdades: mujer y sociedad. Coordinación de Concepción Company Company, Linda Rosa Manzanilla Naim y María Elena Medina-Mora. Con la colaboración de Sabina Berman *et al*. Ciudad de México: El Colegio Nacional, 2020. 266 p.: bibl.

This volume explores gender inequality in Mexico. In the section on women and work, the authors examine the gender gap in employment along with the participation of women in the professional workforce and the discrimination they face. In the section on women and health, they discuss women's living conditions, violence against women, and the prevalence of HIV among women. Finally, in the section on women, education, and culture, the authors explore the role of women in scientific and cultural institutions and misogyny in academia.

1468 Domínguez, Anna R. Unisur: una experiencia de educación comunitaria. (*in* Cotidianidad, educación y violencia en el estado de Guerrero: otras prácticas y haceres en un mundo turbulento. Coordinación de John Kenny Acuña Villavicencio y Ever Sánchez Osorio. Acapulco, Mexico: Hipócrates Universidad, 2020, p. 131–154, bibl.)

A brief analysis of the economic, political, and human rights conditions of Guerrero for facilitators of the Universidad de los Pueblos del Sur (Unisur).

1469 Duarte Cruz, Jóse Maria. Modelo multicomponente para la prevención/intervención de la violencia escolar y familiar. (*in* Estudios críticos sobre políticas y problemáticas sociales. Coordinación de Elisa Cerros Rodríguez y Verónica Martínez Flores. Mexico: Universidad Autónoma de Nuevo León, 2018, p. 91–124, bibl.)

A proposal for violence prevention and the promotion of a peaceful coexistence between school and family through the development and strengthening of prosocial competencies. The proposal is designed to encourage a culture of peace among teachers, principals, students, and parents of seven elementary schools in the municipality of San Cristóbal de las Casas, Chiapas.

1470 Durin, Séverine. Yo trabajo en casa: trabajo del hogar de planta, género y etnicidad en Monterrey. Ciudad de México: Centro de Investigaciones y Estudios Superiores en Antropología Social, 2017. 414 p.: bibl., ill. (Publicaciones de la Casa Chata)

This book features qualitative research done in Monterrey, Mexico, that dives into the complexities of domestic work, mainly done by Indigenous (often migrant) women, and the associated class, gender, ethnicity, and labor rights injustices. The author discusses how domestic and household work are not only highly feminized jobs (and the implications of that), but also ethnicized jobs, since Indigenous and migrant workers perform much of this labor. She also discusses the biopolitics of domestic work, as well as workers' treatement by their employers. Durin writes about being young in the city, and the experiences of that beyond the workplace. Within this domestic work, she addresses the attachment and (at times symbiotic) dependence that can arise during a life at service. Specifically, Durin questions whether these workers are part of the family, and the attachment that can arise between the nannies and the children. Furthermore, the book documents the social challenges and potential exploitation faced by young domestic workers in the homes of the privileged upper class.

1471 Economía social y solidaria, migración y género: hacia la búsqueda de alternativas de "desarrollo": una reflexión interdisciplinaria desde México. Coordinación de Leïla Oulhaj y Ximena Gallegos. Ciudad de México: Universidad Iberoamericana, 2017. 230 p.: bibl.

This book is composed of four chapters that explore the social economic policies that impact migration and gender as well as alternate development avenues. The final part is a case study of the Purépecha women of Nahuatzen, Michoacán de Ocampo, and an analysis of the use of remittances in their efforts to promote social change and development.

1472 Emprendimiento y migración de retorno: raíces y horizontes. Coordinación de Miguel Cruz Vásquez y Alfredo Cuecuecha Mendoza. Ciudad de México: Universidad Popular Autónoma del Estado de Puebla: El Colegio de Tlaxcala: MAPorrúa, 2018. 163 p.: bibl., ill. (Desarrollo y migración)

A text by various authors addressing the problems of return migration in Mexico and the rise of Anglo-Saxon entrepreneurial pursuits since the 1930s in response to the hardships migrants faced upon their return. Several individual contributions are reviewed separately in this *HLAS* volume.

1473 Espacios del consumo y el comercio en la ciudad contemporánea. Coordinación de José Gasca Zamora. Ciudad de México: UNAM, Instituto de Investigaciones Económicas, 2017. 322 p.: bibl., ill., maps.

This work brings together 14 chapters by a wide array of authors. The chapters deal with how consumerism and commerce have become key elements in the origin and growth of contemporary Mexican cities. The chapters use and discuss distinctive theoretical arguments and concepts to explain each of the book's themes. Empirical evidence is also used, much of it coming from the results of the "Programa de Apoyo para Proyectos de Investigación e Inovación Tecnológica." The book looks at several contemporary urban themes such as: how the restructuring of the cities influences the dynamics between the center and periphery; processes of gentrification promoted by the growth of certain sectors, like real estate and commerce; differences between agents of corporations and traditional retailers; impact of globalization; new social practices, and the conflicts that arise from these new changes. The book seeks to explain how certain spaces, such as markets and plazas, represent the elements of edification and functionality of the urban landscape. Accompanying these themes are several attempts to understand the expressions of consumption and commerce within cities. This expression is addressed through different theoretical frameworks and analysis, including: the social space where urban cities have transformed and produced; the influence of political and public management in regards to regulations and legislation; and the participation of actors with distinctive natures that operate under different rationalities. The expression of consumption and commerce is impacted by the trends of globalization and gentrification. Globalization has brought in major streams of capital, commerce, finance, and real estate for cities. Arrival and use of new fields have created a competition between different segments and their strategies of expansion, which has impacted retail businesses and transformed places of consumption. Furthermore, this new mobilization of capital and finance has led to the production of residential developments, large corporate buildings, offices, and other centers for commerce. Gentrification has partnered with this trend by converging commercial firms, real estate, and urban political business to reactivate and provide new functions for the cities. This process has amplified goods and services and contributed to a higher standard of living; however, some authors have looked at the growth of displacement faced by established forms of commerce and how polarizing and fragmenting urban areas are. The book notes that these processes are not the only ones involved in the changes of cities. The financing of urban areas and the mobilization of real estate capital cannot be explained without the involvement of governments, new institutions, and the participation of other elements such as private agents and urban management. Thus, with these dynamics, there has been major internal reorganization of cities, which has impacted the relations between the center and periphery, as seen with the rise of suburbs and "peri-urbanization." With more specification, readers who are interested in: post-gentrified city centers, the consumption and gentrification in CDMX, commercial centers of CDMX, historical perspectives, new commercial enclaves in CDMX, the restructuring of urban landscape such as Toluca, and the spaces of social movements within contemporary cities will find this book valuable.

1474 Flores Mejía, Jesús Guillermo and **Belén Velázquez Gatica.** Los estudiantes universitarios y su política de negociación interna. (*in* Cotidianidad, educación y violencia en el estado de Guerrero: otras prácticas y haceres en un mundo turbulento. Coordinación de John Kenny Acuña Villavicencio y Ever Sánchez Osorio. Acapulco, Mexico: Hipócrates Universidad, 2020, p. 165–172, bibl.)

Examines the new competency models in Public Education Institutions (IEP) in Mexico and the outcomes of alllowing student participation in their education.

1475 Gabayet González, Natalia. El tigre escondido: memoria ritual de los pueblos negros de la Costa Chica. Ciudad de México: UNAM, Dirección General de Publicaciones y Fomento Editorial: Editorial Turner, 2020. 278 p., 32 unnumbered pages of plates: bibl., ill. (chiefly color).

This work focuses on the denied identity of Afro-Mexican populations, a group that faces immense challenges and discrimination in Mexico. A relatively understudied and poorly documented racial and ethnic group, the Afro-Mexican population is analyzed in its entirety in this work—including its cultural and social impact in the country. La Costa Chica of Guerrero and Oaxaca is a cultural landscape in Mexico in which a vast Black population lives. The region has a rich, diverse cultural history that has remained intact after the arrival of enslaved Black Africans in the 16th and 17th centuries. The book's objective is to provide an in-depth ethnographical account of the region and its residents, describing its history of agriculture, religion, dance, rituals, and spiritual beliefs and practices. Although observing from an outside perspective, the author does an excellent job explaining the history of Afro-Mexicans living in La Costa Chica and provides a panoramic view of a group that is underrepresented in the scholarly literature.

1476 Gamiño Muñoz, Rodolfo. La patria de los ausentes: un acercamiento al estudio de la desaparición forzada en México. Ciudad de México: Universidad Iberoamericana, 2020. 393 p.: bibl.

The author examines the forced disappearance of people during Mexico's Dirty War of the 1970s and 1980s, and the war against drug trafficking and organized crime in the early 2000s. He presents historical explanation of tactics of violent drug traffickers, corrupt government members turned drug traffickers, and testimonies of survivors. The book ends with stories of missing people and, in some cases, groups in various states across Mexico. Most of the disappeared were human rights activists whose survivors pleaded for local investigations, but were often denied the opportunity.

1477 Gilas, Karolina Monika. Los derechos políticos de las mujeres en la Ciudad de México: ¿MujerEs CdMx? (*in* Reflexiones interdisciplinarias sobre la ciudadanía de género: mujeres en la Ciudad de México. Coordinación de Lorena Margarita Umaña Reyes. Ciudad de México: Grupo Editor Orfila Valentini, SA de CV: UNAM, 2018, p. 67–87)

A theoretical analysis of the idea of the "universal citizen" in Mexico City as it is found to carry a masculine connotation that is not gender inclusive. The author finds that Mexico is closing the gender gap through political reform and, in turn, the number of women in the General Council has increased. For a review of the entire volume, see item **1519**.

1478 González, Beatriz Pico. El emprendimiento como solución a la migración de retorno. (*in* Emprendimiento y migración de retorno: raíces y horizontes. Coordinación de Miguel Cruz Vásquez y Alfredo Cuecuecha Mendoza. Ciudad de México: Universidad Popular Autónoma del Estado de Puebla: El Colegio de Tlaxcala: MAPorrúa, 2018, p. 123–132)

Research conducted on return migrants' labor skills, human capital, and savings acquired during their stay in the US and how practices and aspects of US business culture cannot always be applied in Mexico.

1479 González Anaya, Ana Gabriela. La construcción del sueño americano en la vida de los adolescentes acatiquenses. Guadalajara, Jalisco, Mexico: Universidad de Guadalajara, 2017. 254 p.: bibl., maps.

In this study, González Anaya uses mixed-methods research to provide an in-depth analysis of adolescents' ideas about migration. Focused in the city of Acatic, Jalisco, González Anaya administered surveys and conducted interviews and focus groups to develop a well-rounded understanding of not only what youth in this region believe, but how they construct their beliefs surrounding immigration, life in the US, and the American Dream.

1480 González Corona, Rosa María. Vulnerabilidad social y vida familiar: cómo las familias experimentan, sienten y enfrentan la pobreza en la frontera. Mexicali, Mexico: Universidad Autónoma de Baja California, 2017. 329 p.: bibl., index. (Selección anual de libro universitario)

With data collected through semi-structured interviews with poor families living near the US-Mexico border, González Corona seeks to develop deeper understanding of their objective and subjective experiences. She reviews a series of related theories from various disciplines to contextualize her work. This is supplemented with an exploration of previous studies of poverty and inequality in Tijuana, as well as an analysis of relevant statistics and demographic information. From there, she presents an analysis of her own findings by characterizing the families who participated in the study. In the final four chapters, González Corona offers a detailed analysis of the condition of poverty and social vulnerability, focusing specifically on the different ways families experience, feel about, and confront their circumstances.

1481 González Ulloa Aguirre, Pablo Armando and **Laura Nayeli Pedraza Álvarez.** Ciudadanía y limitaciones para las mujeres de la Ciudad de México. (*in* Reflexiones interdisciplinarias sobre la ciudadanía de género: mujeres en la Ciudad de México. Coordinación de Lorena Margarita Umaña Reyes. Ciudad de México: Grupo Editor Orfila Valentini, SA de CV: UNAM, 2018, p. 13–30)

A critical review of limitations women face in public spaces compared to their male counterparts through conclusions based on evidence from mass surveys in Mexico City. One conclusion the authors note is that while both men and women use public spaces differently and are both prone to insecurities and violence, women face them at a higher rate than men. For a review of the entire volume, see item **1519**.

1482 Guillén, Marquina Terán. La violencia escolar: disciplina, control y poder en la interacción en el aula. (*in* Cotidianidad, educación y violencia en el estado de Guerrero: otras prácticas y haceres en un mundo turbulento. Coordinación de John Kenny Acuña Villavicencio y Ever Sánchez Osorio. Acapulco, Mexico: Hipócrates Universidad, 2020, p. 87–96, bibl.)

The author analyzes school violence, the negative and positive viewpoints of discipline, and how it affects students' learning capabilities.

1483 Gutiérrez Zúñiga, Cristina and **Renée de la Torre.** Cambio religioso en Guadalajara: perfiles y comportamientos en tres décadas (1996–2016). Zapopan, Mexico: El Colegio de Jalisco; Guadalajara, Mexico: Universidad de Guadalajara, 2020. 350 p.: bibl., graphs, ill. (Investigación)

Religious change has been known to emerge in societies because of a tendency toward subjectivity and deinstitucionalización. This leads religious practitioners to follow an individualist "spiritual journey."

The purpose of this research study conducted in Guadalajara, Mexico is to understand how the Catholic religion has changed over the years (between 1996 and 2016). The study provides a historical context on the contraction of the Catholic religion; tendencies of religious change in Guadalajara; and the role of age, gender, socioeconomic status, and education in religious change within the Tapatíos.

1484 Hernández, Anabel. A massacre in Mexico: the true story behind the missing forty-three students. Translated with an introduction by John Washington. London; New York, N.Y.: Verso, 2018. 404 p.: index, maps.

Mexican journalist Anabel Hernández details the events of a crime that occurred in Iguala, Guerrero, Mexico, in September 2014. After being intercepted by the police while traveling to a protest, a group of students were killed or injured, and 43 of them went missing. Hernández's comprehensive investigation into the crime reveals important details about the history and current reality of state violence and impunity in Mexico.

1485 Hernández Cabrera, Porfirio Miguel. Identidad gay en construcción: el activismo del Grupo Unigay en la Ciudad de México. Ciudad de México: Universidad Autónoma de la Ciudad de México, 2020. 624 p.: bibl.

An ethnographic analysis of a group of 18-year-olds and older who identify as LGBTQ, better known as "Unigay" in Mexico City. The study focuses on a range of topics, including the process of coming out, HIV campaigns, the history of LGBTQ, and social, academic, and political movements. Hernández Cabrera takes a closer look at the LGBTQ contributions and diversity in Mexican society and abroad.

Hesketh, Chris. Spaces of capital/spaces of resistance: Mexico and the global political economy. See item **1305**.

1486 Hogares y familias transnacionales: un encuentro desde la perspectiva humana. Coordinación de J. Guadalupe Rodríguez Gutiérrez, Miguel Moctezuma Longoria y Óscar Calderón Morillón. Ciudad de México: Universidad de Sonora: Benemérita Universidad Autónoma de Puebla: Jua Pablos Editor, 2017. 396 p.: bibl.

This volume presents a thematic compilation of texts and research about transnational migration, a field of study that considers the complex experience of mobility and transportation through migration. The authors present research on Mexico and cities on the American side of the US-Mexico border, such as El Paso, Texas; Brownsville, Texas; Douglas, Texas; Laredo, Texas; Nogales, Arizona; Calexico, California; and San Diego, California. The authors address several topics related to transnationalism and transnational migration, including but not limited to social relationships, family in the process of migration, family dynamics, employment, education, maternity, migration status in the US, and the effects of migration on sexual and reproductive health. This collection of texts uses a multidisciplinary approach to understanding transnational migration and the human experience.

1487 Hualde Alfaro, Alfredo. Más trabajo que empleo: trayectorias laborales y precariedad en los call centers de México. Tijuana, Mexico: El Colegio de la Frontera Norte, 2017. 252 p., 4 unnumbered pages: bibl.

An investigation of call centers, including their history and increasing numbers due to globalization, their target demographic of young professionals, and employees' work experience in Tijuana, Guadalajara, and Mexico City. The lack of job security and benefits at the call centers negatively impacts Mexico's job market.

1488 Jiménez, Javier Donoso and Ricardo del Carmen Gallardo. Morfología de la muerte en Acapulco. (*in* Cotidianidad, educación y violencia en el estado de Guerrero: otras prácticas y haceres en un mundo turbulento. Coordinación de John Kenny Acuña Villavicencio y Ever Sánchez Osorio. Acapulco, Mexico: Hipócrates Universidad, 2020, p. 61–86, bibl.)

The authors discuss homicides in Acapulco and the criminalization of victims as a way of avoiding responsibility for public safety and access to justice and truth.

1489 Lamas, Marta. La interrupción legal del embarazo: el caso de la Ciudad de México. Ciudad de México: Fondo de Cultura Económica: UNAM, Centro de Investigaciones y Estudios de Género, 2017. 190 p.: bibl., ill. (Sección de obras de política y derecho)

A decade after legislation was passed in Mexico City allowing legal abortion under certain circumstances, Lamas explores the history of abortion policy in Mexico City. She begins with a thorough historical review to contextualize the issue, followed by a discussion of the decriminalization of abortion in various Mexican states and the implications of such laws, the political and ideological tensions the issue creates, activist efforts, and challenges yet to come.

1490 Larios Deniz, Jonás. Mujeres lesbianas: educación, inclusión y no inclusión. Colima, Mexico: Colima, Gobierno del Estado: Puertabierta Editores, 2017. 182 p.: bibl., ill.

This work is a compilation of interviews with lesbian and bisexual women, exploring their struggles of expression and belonging and discussing the social constraints they experience in Mexico. Additionally, Larios Deniz makes connections to the lack of institutional support for providing education in sexuality and sexual health—education that would be instrumental in creating a more inclusive community.

1491 López, Octavio Tixtha. Trascendiendo el conflicto en un contexto de violencia: educación para la ciudadanía. (*in* Cotidianidad, educación y violencia en el estado de Guerrero: otras prácticas y haceres en un mundo turbulento. Coordinación de John Kenny Acuña Villavicencio y Ever Sánchez Osorio. Acapulco, Mexico: Hipócrates Universidad, 2020, p. 97–114, bibl.)

A research piece focused on high school students in the city of Ecatepec to help raise awareness of their rights as citizens and right to live in a peaceful state away from violence.

1492 Luna Alfaro, Ángel Christian. Políticas para vidas en situación de prostitución: aportes desde la antropología. Lagos de Moreno, Mexico: CULagos Ediciones, 2020. 127 p.: bibl., maps. (Diálogos académicos)

An investigation from 2011 to 2020 of sex workers in Tlaxcala, Puebla, and Veracruz. The author explores the historical sexual exploitation of women and addresses patriarchal norms that reinforce harmful practices against women sex workers. Further, Luna Alfaro investigates the lack of government intervention against drug traffickers and machismo, often leading to sexual exploitation and femicides. Then he explores the stigmatization of sex work due to lack of health education, the rise of feminism, and the struggle for sex worker rights.

1493 Maciel, David. La otra cara de México: ensayos acerca del pueblo chicano. Ciudad de México: UNAM, 2018. 494 p.: bibl.

This anthology describes the Chicano population—defined as Mexicans living in the US—and their experiences connecting with their community, culture, roots, and even land, while living in the US. The book is divided into five parts: 1) Panoramic Visions (Visiones Panorámicas), 2) Immigration and Borders (Inmigración y Frontera), 3) Culture and Society (Cultura y Sociedad), 4) Cinematographic Images (Imágenes Cinematográficas), and 5) Current Situation (Coyuntura Actual). The book invites readers to learn more about the Chicano population through art, politics, education, and media. The Chicano community faces a complex situation with respect to maintaining its Mexican, Chicano, and, for those born in the US, American identity. Maciel addresses these complexities by compiling several historical and current accounts that offer a panoramic view—as the title of the first part suggests—of a large community in the US that has had a major impact on the nation's dominant culture.

1494 Martínez Flores, Verónica and Elisa Cerros Rodríguez. Entre el texto y el contexto: el papel del promotor en la política social. (*in* Estudios críticos sobre políticas y problemáticas sociales. Coordinación de Elisa Cerros Rodríguez y Verónica Martínez Flores. Mexico: Universidad Autónoma de Nuevo León, 2018, p. 61–90, bibl.)

This study examines the implementation of Programa Comedores Comunitarios (Community Kitchen Program) and the roles of the community promoters of a social policy idea in Juárez, Chihuahua. They are seen as agents of change, as they adjust institutional procedures and rules to achieve bureaucratic requirements.

1495 **Masculinidades, familias y comunidades afectivas.** Coordinación de Rocío Enríquez Rosas y Oliva López Sánchez. Guadalajara, Mexico: ITESO, Universidad Jesuita de Guadalajara; Tlalnepantla de Baz, Estado de México, México: Universidad Nacional Autónoma de México, Facultad de Estudios Superiores Iztacala, 2018. 243 p.: bibl. (Colección Emociones e interdisciplina; 03)

This edited volume is divided into two parts: the first part is titled Masculinities and Emotions, and the second is called Families and Affective Communities. The work is written largely through the lens of emotions and how emotional expressions and experiences shape interactions and social structures. In each part, five papers written by different authors cover topics under the larger umbrella of the section. In the first half, most of the research presented is qualitative and explores how men handle emotions in several facets of life. The authors explore male conceptions of love and heartbreak through music, how employment impacts men's emotional life, emotional processes in heterosexual couples working towards equity, and more. In the second half, they analyze emotions during oncological treatment and emotions of people giving and receiving care for older people, relationships and interactions in blended families, and more. In sum, works regarding masculinity, families, and affective communities examine how emotion plays a role in these facets.

1496 **Medina, Arely.** Islam-latino: identidades étnico-religiosas: un estudio de caso sobre los mexicanos musulmanes en Estados Unidos. Zapopan, Mexico: El Colegio de Jalisco; Tijuana, Mexico: El Colegio de la Frontera Norte, 2019. 400 p.: bibl., ill. (Investigación)

This ethnological and empirical research investigation explores the ethnic and cultural identity of Muslim Latinos. The work is organized into seven parts: 1) Islam in Motion (Islam en movimiento); 2) Racial and Cultural Heterogeneity and the United States (Heterogeneidad racial y cultural y Estados Unidos); 3) Islam in the United States (Islam en Estados Unidos); 4) Mapping the Cyberenvironment of Latin Islam (Cartografía del ciberentorno del Islam latino); 5) The Proposals of Latin Islam (Las propuestas del Islam latino); 6) The Latino Muslim Association of America (La Asociación Latino Musulmana del América); and 7) Identity Processes in Muslim Mexicans (Procesos de identidad en Mexicanos musulmanes). Before defining what it means to be a Latino and a practicing member of Islam, Medina describes contemporary and transnational Islamic religion. In various parts of the world, Islam is a widely contested and misunderstood religion, similar to the Latino/Hispanic ethnic identities. Through research, Medina illustrates the relationship between the two and how this intersection of identities can lead to discrimination and oppression on multiple levels. The work contextualizes the discourse about both communities in the US and how they interact.

1497 **Mendoza García, Leticia.** Política religiosa en Michoacán: las diversidades evangélicas 1910–1932. Morelia, Mexico: Instituto de Investigaciones Históricas, Universidad Michoacana de San Nicolás de Hidalgo, 2017. 371 p.: bibl.

A historical overview (1910–32) of Protestant political and social movements in Michoacán and the way they navigated state regulations as a minority religion to the dominant Catholic Church.

1498 **Mexico's human rights crisis.** Edited by Alejandro Anaya-Muñoz and Barbara Frey. Philadelphia: University of Pennsylvania Press, 2019. 326 p.: bibl., index. (Pennsylvania studies in human rights)

This volume argues that within the past decade, Mexico has faced a human rights crisis, as both state and nonstate actors have systemically violated the rights of citizens with near-total impunity. These violations have been categorized as extrajudicial killings, disappearances, and torture. In addition to exploring instances of this violence, the book discusses the historical formation of the present crisis and the institutional forces that allow it to perpetuate. Although there exist substantial data to provide evidence for the egregious frequency of these human rights offenses, it is difficult to accurately determine the proportion that may be attributed to government actors, organized crime groups, or private citizens. Even without the concrete evidence of government personnel carrying out these forms of violence, the perpetuation of these crimes and the failure of the government to investigate and adjudicate them constitutes a human rights violation in its own right. The authors make various recommendations for addressing these systemic issues. In general, the volume calls for minimizing state violence and impunity, though more specific actions are offered as well, including developing processes to collect more accurate human rights data and offering economic and social support for victims of these violations.

1499 Migración miradas y reflexiones desde la universidad. Coordinación de María Elena Rivera Heredia y Rodrigo Pardo Fernández. Ciudad de México: Miguel Ángel Porrúa; Michoacán, Mexico: Universidad Michoacana de San Nicolás de Hidalgo, Centro Nicolaita de Estudios Migratorios, 2018. 347 p.: bibl., ill., maps. (Colección centenario universidad y sociedad; 6)

Product of the Universidad Michoacana de San Nicolás de Hidalgo's Center for Migration Studies (CENIEM), this edited book seeks to exhibit the university's work in the migration studies field, particularly its contributions to understanding the migratory phenomenon in Michoacán and Mexico in general. This book is divided into four main sections. The first section analyzes the role of universities in understanding migration trends and migrants' experiences. The second section consists of contributions that study the implications of migration of individuals of all ages. While this section may seem straightforward, the topics range considerably. Obregón-Velasco's study, "Recursos psicológicos y fortalezas de jóvenes hijas e hijos de padres migrantes en Michoacán," examines the psychological impact of migration on children whose parents migrate every so often and identifies the resources the children rely on to carry on with their everyday routines. This entry is in stark contrast to Rivera Loaiza and Domínguez Mota's chapter, "Diseño centrado en el usuario," on user-friendly app designs for Mexican migrants in the US, which sheds light on the communicative challenges that arise once migrants begin to assimilate to a new country. The third section of the book collects studies on the educational processes and interculturality present in highly transited communities. The fourth section centers on migrant organizations and their impact on transnational communities. The book provides a multidisciplinary perspective into a very broad subject and offers a comprehensive view of the state of migration within Mexico and from Mexico to the US.

1500 Migración: nuevos actores, procesos y retos. Coordinación de Magdalena Barros Nock y Agustín Escobar Latapí. Ciudad de México: Centro de Investigaciones y Estudios Superiores en Antropología Social, 2017. 1 v.: bibl., ill., index, maps. (Colección México)

Since the beginning of 2010, Mexico has experienced a drastic change in the mobility of immigrants. As migration has increased internationally, immigrants have established themselves in Mexico. But Mexico has not properly designed a political and social plan to sustain these movements. This gap has led to an abrupt change in how migrants circulate and creates social, economic, and political change within the border and between the two countries. This volume seeks to show various investigations to understand how different regions are affected by migration. The investigations exhibit the social, political, and cultural reality of Mexican migration within Mexico itself and to the US. In this first volume of a two-volume edited series, the authors explore the international face of migration as it relates to the Mexican state. The volume is divided into two parts. The first part focuses on the challenges that arise with international migration. The studies discuss a range of issues that extend from the institutional perspective of dual citizenship, to the political activism of DACA recipients, to the social meanings of money and its role in the bidirectional flows of remittances. The second part focuses on immigrants' participation in US and Mexican labor markets and their social impact on migrants. The studies in this section discuss topics such as work visas, human rights coalitions, international business turnover, domestic work and labor laws, and criminalization. Given the variety of authors, the methodologies and perspectives employed in each study differ considerably. However, the unifying element among all these studies is the authors' commitment to reveal the social, political, and cultural realities of immigration in the Mexican context, which includes Mexicans migrating to the US and foreign individuals migrating to Mexico. Immigration and emigration are seen as phenomena that were imposed on a state and a population that do not necessarily have the resources and institutions to address the massive amounts of exits and entries that take place in the country. As such, they are seen as products of a variety of external factors rather than internal. Among those referenced in these studies are anthropologist James Clifford, philosopher Michel Foucault, sociologist Saskia Sassen, sociologist Viviana Zelizer, and anthropologist J. Clyde Mitchell.

1501 Migraciones y movilidades en el centro de México. Coordinación de Norma Baca Tavira *et al*. Ciudad de México: Juan Pablos Editor, 2018. 206 p.: bibl., ill., maps.

This edited book sheds light on internal migration and mobilization trends observed in the center of Mexico. The editors note the widespread misconception that Mexicans typically migrate internationally when in fact most Mexicans migrate within their home country and move from city to city for a variety of reasons. To understand the reasons behind this internal migration, this book brings together a range of perspectives and methodological approaches that make clear what migration and mobilization look like in the center of Mexico, why these phenomena take place, and what the implications of migration are for urban planning decisions and general policy-making. The authors indicate the phenomena of mobility, not just with respect to migration to another residence, but also to work, school, and anywhere else that requires reliable transportation. Ten sections of the book analyze the theoretical-methodological standpoints that offer insight into the migration discourse in Mexico as well as solutions for facilitating mobility within the region. Topics range from unequal access to healthcare to workers' and students' commuting patterns to living conditions for elderly populations, intermetropolitan migration, rural migration, access to health and medical services in the state of Mexico, the well-being of Mexican migrants, transportation trends for employment and education, economic participation, and aging of the Mexican population. In sum, the authors contextualize the life of migrants to, from, and within Mexico and discuss how their mobility is defined by their relationship to the state, the economy, and social and political spheres.

1502 Mojica Madrigal, Óscar Ariel and **Gustavo López Castro.** "Duele ser hombre": migración de retorno y emociones en los procesos de reinserción. (*in* Emprendimiento y migración de retorno: raíces y horizontes. Coordinación de Miguel Cruz Vásquez y Alfredo Cuecuecha Mendoza. Ciudad de México: Universidad Popular Autónoma del Estado de Puebla: El Colegio de Tlaxcala: MAPorrúa, 2018, p. 53–68)

An investigative piece on the social and psychological effects that return migrants face upon arrival in Mexico. The authors look at the separated families, reintegration with community, and the struggles to find employment that matches skills acquired in the US.

1503 Montoya Zavala, Erika. Mujeres empresarias y autoempleadas: nuevas identidades femeninas y empresariales en construcción. Culiacán, Mexico: Facultad de Estudios Internacionales y Políticas Públicas, Universidad Autónoma de

Sinaloa; Ciudad de México: Edición de Juan Pablos Editor, 2017. 246 p.: bibl., ill.

This book addresses the persistent gender gap in wages, employment, education, etc., in Mexico by investigating women's participation in economic activities. Montoya Zavala describes the prevailing theoretical perspectives regarding women workers and entrepreneurs, analyzes existing studies to compare the circumstances across different countries, and uses statistics to explain the economic context and the participation of self-employed women nationwide and within the state of Sinaloa. She then compares findings on these topics across different contexts, including in Culiacán, Phoenix, and Tuscon.

1504 Mujeres en la policía: miradas feministas sobre su experiencia y su entorno laboral. Coordinación por Olivia Tena Guerrero y Jahel López Guerrero. Textos de Abigain Dely García López et al. Ciudad de México: UNAM, Centro de Investigaciones Interdisciplinarias en Ciencias y Humanidades, 2017. 413 p.: bibl., ill. (Colección Diversidad feminista; 19)

This book unites different investigations with different authors using a feminist insight focused mostly in Mexico. This book addresses the challenges of being a policewoman in a field that has been mostly dominated by men and that has been described as a "manly job." This perception has an impact on the well-being of women and men in the police workspace, leading to a valid concern for the safety of the whole country. The investigation covers how women experience oppression within the workplace, the challenges they must overcome, and how they attempt to achieve gender equality. Topics include sexual harassment of policewomen, strategies for the achievement of gender equality in police work, and reflections on what has been done.

1505 Niñez detenida, los derechos de los niños, niñas y adolescentes migrantes en la frontera México-Guatemala: diagnóstico y propuesta para pasar del control migratorio a la protección integral de la niñez. Coordinación de Pablo Ceriani Cernadas. Ciudad de México: Distribuciones Fontamara, 2013. 300 p.: bibl., ill. (Colección Argumentos; 140)

The human rights of migrants at the border between Mexico and Guatemala has received increased attention in recent years. Reports from NGOs and from national and international organizations that supervise the situation of human rights have shown evidence of the existence and persistence of practices and politics that have not fully adjusted to the international standards of human rights (p. 13), including some reports from Mexico that have given counts of numerous deaths of migrants at the border. At times, the reports have specifically discussed the question of children. There is a growing necessity for initiatives aimed at addressing the rights and needs of children and adolescents who migrate or intend to do so. The existing information indicates that children and adolescents who migrate unaccompanied or separated from their parents, when they have entered Mexico without a residence permit, suffer in ways that are inconsistent with international human rights standards, especially those arising from the UN Convention on the Rights of the Child. This study identified 10 issues in immigration policy and children's rights in Mexico specifically. Recommendations are provided to various sectors of the federal government, to the state of Chiapas, to the countries of origin (El Salvador, Guatemala, and Honduras), to the US, and to civil society organizations.

1506 Nostti, Raúl Bringas. Los primeros migrantes de retorno que trajeron a México el espíritu emprendedor anglosajón en la década de 1930. (*in* Emprendimiento y migración de retorno: raíces y horizontes. Coordinación de Miguel Cruz Vásquez y Alfredo Cuecuecha Mendoza. Ciudad de México: Universidad Popular Autónoma del Estado de Puebla: El Colegio de Tlaxcala: MAPorrúa, 2018, p. 13–30)

An in-depth look at the start of Mexican migration to the US during the 19th century and the Great Depression. The author explores the methods of Anglo-Saxon entrepreneurship that Mexican migrants learned in the US and the challenges encountered when they attempted to implement those methods upon their return to Mexico.

1507 Olvera Muñoz, Omar Alejandro and José Arturo Granados Cosme. La experiencia de varones homosexuales y bisexuales en torno al rechazo social, la violencia y su impacto en la salud mental. Ciudad de México: Universidad Autónoma Metropolitana, 2017. 142 p.: bibl.

In this book, the authors discuss the impact of violence on the mental health of homosexual and bisexual men in Mexico. They explain that to maintain power dynamics and reinforce discrimination, violence is often the chosen tool. They examine the differences between the experiences and mental health of bisexual and gay men. This work is the outcome of an investigation that examined a group of gay and bisexual men in Mexico City. The authors first explain their social medicine methodology for characterizing both the violence and the mental health damage inflicted on this group of men. They then utilize a bibliographic review to analyze the health damage among the population of the study. Next, they analyze the process through which gay and bisexual people are forced into a heteronormative social system, thereby leading to violence, social rejection, and exclusion. Then they work through the construction of gay and bisexual identities as well as negative experiences, such as violence and damage to mental health. They conclude that these experiences and circumstances illustrate the dire need to fight inequality in mental health experiences.

1508 Onofre Rodríguez, Dora Julia and Reyna Torres-Obregón. Asertividad sexual en mujeres del Noreste de México. (*in* Estudios críticos sobre políticas y problemáticas sociales. Coordinación de Elisa Cerros Rodríguez y Verónica Martínez Flores. Mexico: Universidad Autónoma de Nuevo León, 2018, p. 149–166, bibl.)

A study of sexual assertiveness among women in northeastern Mexico and its relationship to sexual functioning and response. Sexual assertiveness is also relevant as a protective mechanism against risky sexual behaviors and the sexual victimization and coercion of women from northeastern Mexico.

1509 Palacios, Hugo and Ángela Ávila. Las diferentes comunidades que confluyen en las experiencias cotidianas de las personas: humanización inclusiva. (*in* Cotidianidad, educación y violencia en el estado de Guerrero: otras prácticas y haceres en un mundo turbulento. Coordinación de John Kenny Acuña Villavicencio y Ever Sánchez Osorio. Acapulco, Mexico: Hipócrates Universidad, 2020, p. 155–164, bibl.)

A study of diverse cultural beliefs and the development of socializing children and teenagers.

1510 Pardo Montaño, Ana Melisa. Migración y transnacionalismo: extrañando la tierrita.... Ciudad de México: FLACSO México, 2017. 170 p.: bibl., ill., maps.

This study focuses on mobility within US-Mexican migration. The author uses a geographic and demographic approach to study transnational migration, which describes how people move across nation-state borders. The work is organized into four chapters: 1) Space and Migration: Theoretical Approaches and Perspectives (Espacio y migración: enfoques y perspectivas teóricas); 2) Time to Migrate: Background to the Migratory Flow (Tiempo de migrar: antecedentes del flujo migratorio); 3) Material Practices: Political and Economic Aspects of the Axochiapa-Ciudades Gemelas Migratory Flow (Las prácticas materiales: aspectos políticos y económicos del flujo migratorio); and 4) Here and There, Present and Past: The Imaginary and the Symbolic of the Axochiapan-Ciudades Gemelas Migratory Flow ("Aquí y allá, presente y pasado": lo imaginario y lo simbólico del flujo migratorio Axochiapan-Ciudades Gemelas). Using the Axochiapan-Ciudades Gemelas as an example of transnationalism, the book concludes that the principal catalyst for immigration in this region was the global economic crisis of 2007–2008. Migrants also moved through Chicago, Ill., Los Angeles, Calif., and the state of Minnesota because of the devastating impact of the crisis on the Mexican economy and its population.

1511 **Pensar Ayotzinapa.** Coordinación de Rosaura Martínez Ruiz, Mariana Hernández Urías y Homero Vázquez Carmona. Ciudad de México: UNAM: Almadía, 2018. 220 p.: bibl.

This book is part of a larger research project titled Philosophies After Freud (Filosofías después de Freud), which focuses on how Freudian psychoanalysis is a principal part of the body of philosophical thought in the 20th century. During this research in 2014, 43 students from the Escuela Normal Rural Raúl Isidro Burgos in Ayotzinapa disappeared. The researchers decided to analyze the judicial system's faulty response to the disappearances as evidence of a flawed sociopolitical reality. The authors use a critical lens to address the injustices and violations of the government when investigating such a crime. The research project thus turned its attention to the Mexican criminal justice system and its participation in marginalization, inequality, organized crime, corruption, manipulation, and state violence. Dedicated to the families of the 43 missing students, this investigative project provides insight into the political institutions in Mexico and how they contributed to an insufficient and inadequate response to the disappearances.

1512 **Pobreza y vulnerabilidad: debates y estudios contemporáneos en México.** Coordinación de Mercedes González de la Rocha y Gonzalo Andrés Saraví. Ciudad de México: CIESAS, 2018. 303 p.: bibl., ill. (Colección México)

This book examines the relationship between poverty and vulnerability and how the two concepts are deeply interconnected. The authors explain that the more vulnerable a subject or group is, the more likely it is to fall into poverty or worsen its poverty level; the poorer, the more tenuous the layer of protection that can prevent the risk of catastrophe. They often use the framing of risk and disaster while discussing vulnerability, but differentiate between them. The authors first examine the history and tendencies of poverty in Latin America generally and Mexico specifically. They discuss the notion of the working poor, i.e., people whose jobs (and the income that comes with them) cannot satisfy their basic needs. They explain that this situation is a result of systematic issues—not laziness—including both economic marginalization and cultural social structures. The authors then describe the accumulation of disadvantages and vulnerability. Additionally, they outline and assess four properties of vulnerability: differentiate, differential, global, and progressive. They consider the extension and intensity of vulnerability, vulnerability and political participation, and the retraction of social security in Mexico. The authors discuss inequality and the concept of "weak citizenship" in Mexico, as well as how poverty and public policy interact. They describe the labor structure in Mexico, focusing on labor income and polarization. The authors also make note of microfinance and poverty. Further, they discuss youth vulnerability: the risks that poor youth face and how they are excluded from experiencing the transition to adulthood. In sum, this book provides an in-depth look at the reciprocal relationship between poverty and vulnerability and how they exist in Mexico both individually and together.

1513 **Política migratoria y derechos de los migrantes en México.** Edición de Velia Cecilia Bobes León. Ciudad de México: FLACSO México, 2018. 212 p.: bibl., ill., maps.

This volume analyzes the existing academic discourse regarding the intersection between migration policy and migrant rights. Bobes describes several laws recently enacted in Mexico that are designed to support the human rights of migrants. However, this new regulatory framework—which in theory protects migrants from discrimination, supports their health and education, and increases social inclusion—has not been successful in its goals. The book is divided into six chapters by different authors who utilize research to illustrate the shortcomings of policy-making for Mexican migrants. Each chapter addresses the need for the political and social integration of migrant populations to sustain Mexican democracy. The book's sections are: 1) Human Rights and Migration Approach (Enfoque de derechos humanos y migración); 2) Protection and

Inclusion of the Foreigner in Mexico: the Institutionalization of Migrant Human Rights (2007–2016) (Protección e inclusión del extranjero en México: la institucionalización de los derechos humanos del migrante (2007–2016)); 3) Transit Migrants: (De)protection, Exclusion and Non-Access to Rights (Migrantes de tránsito: (des)protección, exclusión y (no) acceso a derechos); 4) Political Migration and Protection of the Foreign Population: the Risk of Natural Phenomena in the South of Mexico (Política migratoria y protección a población extranjera: el caso del riesgo por fenómenos naturales en el sur de México); 5) From Discourse to Action on the Right to Free Transit for the Foreign Population Resident in Mexico (Del discurso a la acción en el derecho al libre tránsito para la población extranjera residente en México); and 6) Migration and Access to Rights: an Analytical Perspective from the Reality of Cuban Migrants in Mexico (Migración y acceso a derechos: una perspectiva analítica desde la realidad de los migrantes cubanos en México).

1514 Políticas y estrategias de resistencia. Coordinación de Manuel Garza Zepeda y Eduardo Bautista Martínez. Con la colaboración de Eduardo Bautista Martínez *et al.* Oaxaca de Juárez, Mexico: Universidad Autónoma Benito Juárez de Oaxaca; Ciudad de México: Editorial ITACA, 2018. 223 p.: bibl., maps.

This edited volume discusses how individuals resist marginalization through public policy. The work is divided into three sections, each covering a different form of resistance and mobilization among social actors in response to public policy. In the first section, "Public Policy and Mobilization," the authors examine agricultural public policies. They analyze initiatives of coffee producers in Oaxaca and their social and economic politics and strategies in the context of neoliberal globalization. They present the effects of negative programs aimed at the rural sector in Mexico and the resistance that has arisen. The second section, "Against Exclusion," includes a report on the Afro-Mexican Council regarding the interconnected relationship of political identities and opportunities. They use the perspectives of subjects on the council to serve as evidence of this theory. The other entry in this section discusses the National Creole Council and the identity mobilization initiatives among Afro-Belizean Creoles. The last section, "Building Alternatives in Struggle," contains two chapters that discuss different communities in Oaxaca: one covers the Indigenous youth and their community participation and the other describes the strife in their efforts toward social self-determination. The final piece in this section discusses struggles in everyday life, and more specifically how resistance leads to hope, as well as hope as a form of resistance. In sum, this edited volume pulls together numerous examples to discuss resistance, the relationship between politics and identity.

1515 Prácticas comunicativas y prefiguraciones políticas en tiempos inciertos. Coordinación de Amaranta Cornejo Hernández. San Cristóbal de Las Casas, Mexico: Universidad de Ciencias y Artes de Chiapas, Centro de Estudios Superiores de México y Centroamérica, 2018. 243 p.: bibl.

Cornejo and a group of activists focusing on social change and feminism created a collective book that presents 10 different experiences in Mexico and Honduras. They share a sociopolitical aspect that focuses on understanding how social change and feminism have been communicated in different political and social realms. This book offers fresh insight on lived experiences, with the purpose of providing different communication practices in order to be able to have a better understanding of complex realities. These varied lived experiences have implications for the fields of feminism and social change, and touch on topics such as the political proposals of cyberfeminism in Mexico and the discourses of gender violence for Indigenous women.

1516 Quintal López, Rocío. Maternidad, el derecho a elegir: significados y experiencias de mujeres mexicanas que eligieron "no ser madres." Mérida, Mexico: Ediciones de la Universidad Autónoma de Yucatán, 2018. 280 p.: bibl.

Quintal López explores the interrelated concepts of womanhood and motherhood in Mexico. As more women make the decision not to become mothers, this study offers valuable insights into the experiences of those who make such a choice. The book includes a detailed review of the social construction of maternity in Mexico, discussion of the legal rights related to maternity and the difficulties women might face in exercising these rights, the motivating factors and life experiences of Mexican women who chose not to be mothers, and an exploration of how new conceptions of femininity may be constructed through these changing trends in maternity.

1517 Racismo y desigualdad: una visión multidisciplinar. Coordinación de Ana María Cárabe, Eduardo Luis Espinosa y Olivia Leyva. Ciudad de México: Universidad Autónoma de Guerrero: Miguel Ángel Porrúa, 2018. 225 p.: bibl., graphs, ill. (Serie Las ciencias sociales. Cuarta década)

This study examines the social construction of race in the context of Latino/Hispanic identity. "Race" has had many implications for communities of color in the US that affect peoples' lives politically, economically, culturally, socially, and educationally. With the created concept of race, the Hispanic community faces barriers to the benefits granted with white citizenship in the US. The first part of the book, "En la interculturalidad de México," contextualizes racial identity in Mexico and efforts to combat racial discrimination, especially among Indigenous and Black Mexicans. The second part, "In Other Latitudes," expands the discussion to include the experiences of Latinos in the Spanish-American colonial society with an emphasis on slavery and its detrimental effects. The book also considers gender identities, religion, socioeconomic class, ethnicity, and sociopolitical institutions. The book provides an overview of the racial status of Latinos/Hispanics in the US and how their experiences reimagine the construction of postcolonial freedom.

1518 Ramírez López, Dulce Karol.
Mujeres migrantes en la frontera sur de México: aproximaciones desde la interseccionalidad. Chiapas, Mexico: Universidad de Ciencias y Artes de Chiapas; San Cristóbal de Las Casas, Mexico: Centro de Estudios Superiores de México y Centroamérica, 2017. 208 p.: bibl., ill.

This feminist examination of the experiences of migrant women in Mexico is based on qualitative data collected by Ramírez López. The discussions she had are analyzed here with respect to the particular social and political contexts in which she spoke with these women. Following a feminist Latin American theoretical tradition, Ramírez López provides a basis for her analysis with five central ideas, which serve as lenses through which she analyzes the qualitative data. These central themes include: the intersectionality of gender and other social categories; issues of sexuality, reproduction, and women's rights; the necessary contribution of voices of marginalized groups, including the women interviewed here; and the importance of an analytical framework that not only investigates women's experiences of oppression, but actively seeks to reduce that oppression.

1519 Reflexiones interdisciplinarias sobre la ciudadanía de género: mujeres en la Ciudad de México. Coordinación de Lorena Margarita Umaña Reyes. Ciudad de México: Grupo Editor Orfila Valentini, SA de CV: UNAM, 2018. 159 p.: bibl., ill. (Serie Política y sociedad)

A compilation of seven multidisciplinary reflections associated with citizenship in Mexico City through the social construct of gender beyond men and women. Each contribution is reviewed separately in this section (see items **1463**, **1477**, **1481**, **1533**, **1535**, **1538**, and **1541**).

1520 Religiosidades transplantadas: recomposiciones religiosas en nuevos escenarios transnacionales. Coordinación por Renée de la Torre y Patricia Arias. Tijuana, Mexico: El Colegio de la Frontera Norte; Ciudad de México: Juan Pablos Editor, 2017. 315 p.: bibl., ill.

Following the 2017 gathering of La Red de Investigadores del Fenómeno Religioso en México (RIFREM), themed Religion and Migration in Greater Mexico, this book compiles several of the most notable works presented at the conference. The collection seeks to emphasize the various religious modalities occurring transnationally, between the US and Mexico, with particular focus on the distinct characteristics across evangelical and Pentecostal congregations, Native American groups, Latino Muslims, and Catholics. The authors explore such questions as how religion can be an important factor in creating a sense of community and ethnic identity transnationally. They specifically consider the impact of different migratory dynamics on religious practices and related social ties. In the book's first section, various authors discuss how religious practices may be considered migratory cultural practices and they should be considered in the context of changing border policies. The second section addresses themes related to the reconfiguration of ethnic identity, mediated through religious identity/practice, in transnational contexts. The final section explores the role of migration in changing religious identities.

1521 Reyes Morales, Rafael G. and **Alicia Sylvia Gijón-Cruz.** Modelo interdisciplinario de migración, economías familiares y fuentes de ingreso que impactan el bienestar familiar. (*in* Emprendimiento y migración de retorno: raíces y horizontes. Coordinación de Miguel Cruz Vásquez y Alfredo Cuecuecha Mendoza. Ciudad de México: Universidad Popular Autónoma del Estado de Puebla: El Colegio de Tlaxcala: MAPorrúa, 2018, p. 97–120)

A multisector analysis of three rural economies in the Valles Centrales del Estado de Oaxaca, Mexico. The study examines sources of income and social human capital that influence the overall well-being of families.

1522 Rivera García, Óscar Bernardo. Las redes sociales en el proceso migratorio de adolescentes en México. Hermosillo, Mexico: El Colegio de Sonora, 2019. 274 p.: bibl., ill.

How do vulnerable adolescents navigate the migratory process by themselves? This book examines the role that social networks play in helping Mexican adolescents determine whether migrating is an option for them and, if so, how adolescents draw on their social networks to receive the support they need to get through the migratory process. The book describes the migratory context in which Mexican adolescents find themselves, as well as the theoretical and methodological approaches utilized to understand the three phases of the migratory process (mobilization, migration, and involuntary return). It then presents two case studies that assess and compare adolescents' interactions with different types of social networks, thereby demonstrating the impact these networks can have on adolescents' decision making and general experiences with the migratory process. The book concludes by offering recommendations on how to approach adolescents' migratory processes and mitigate the perils they may face throughout.

1523 Robledo Silvestre, Carolina. Drama social y política de duelo: las desapariciones de la guerra contra las drogas en Tijuana. Ciudad de México: El Colegio de México, Centro de Estudios Sociológicos, 2017. 223 p.: bibl., 1 map, photos, tables.

The war against drugs in Mexico has had consequences, creating a "social drama." As social and political violence arises, thousands of individuals have disappeared. This has left families with the constant pain of having lost loved ones. Robledo Silvestre experienced this situation with her son. While fighting for justice, she found herself fighting for families experiencing the same pain. She wrote this book to create an ethnographic investigation of how families react to social drama due to the war against drugs, and the inquiries they must make and strategies they must follow in order to be heard within the corrupt government and societies.

1524 Rodríguez Hernández, Rogelio and **Raúl Teobaldo de Jesús Quintero Novoa.** El divorcio en México: procesos y oportunidades para la intervención. (*in* Estudios críticos sobre políticas y problemáticas sociales. Coordinación de Elisa Cerros Rodríguez y Verónica Martínez Flores. Mexico: Universidad Autónoma de Nuevo León, 2018, p. 125–148, bibl.)

An investigative piece on the increasing number of divorces in Mexico and the consequences for women, men, and children and a proposal for care for families going through marriage dissolution.

Los "rostros invisibles" de la desigualdad social: un estudio sobre arte, política, educación y consumo cultural en América Latina: los casos de Lima y la Ciudad de México. See item **1723**.

1525 Russo Garrido, Anahi. Tortilleras negotiating intimacy: love, friendship, and sex in queer Mexico City. New Brunswick, N.J.: Rutgers University Press, 2020. 191 p.: bibl., index.

An ethnography of three generations of women within queer spaces in Mexico City, this book provides new insights into the changing landscape of intimacy in these communities. Russo Garrido explores lesbian polyamory and the alternative imaginaries it offers, while investigating a shift in queer spaces to include polyamory and nonmonogamy more openly. She discusses lesbian friendships and their potential for challenging norms regarding gender, sexuality, class, race, and ethnicity, as well as the boundaries within various types of relationships. In mapping out the prevalence of various erogenous zones in women's sexual encounters, Russo Garrido aims to redefine the practice of sex in queer spaces. Finally, through a geographic lens, she examines the social networks of queer women in Mexico City, offering a more comprehensive understanding of queer physical space.

1526 Salas Alfaro, Renato. Inversión en pequeños negocios entre los migrantes retornados del estado de Mexico. (*in* Emprendimiento y migración de retorno: raíces y horizontes. Coordinación de Miguel Cruz Vásquez y Alfredo Cuecuecha Mendoza. Ciudad de México: Universidad Popular Autónoma del Estado de Puebla: El Colegio de Tlaxcala: MAPorrúa, 2018, p. 71–91)

This article examines the investments of remittances by returning migrants in Mexico. The author examines various investments, honing in on small business investments, and deciphers whether migrants are keen on staying or migrating again based on their investment decisions.

1527 La Santa Muerte in Mexico: history, devotion, & society. Edited by Wil G. Pansters. Albuquerque: University of New Mexico Press, 2019. 230 p.: bibl., ill., index.

This collection of essays explores a relatively recent addition to the canon of Mexican religious iconography: La Santa Muerte. In addition to discussing the cultural significance of La Santa Muerte and the cult of her worshippers, the anthology offers greater context to the historical and current social landscape relevant to the figure's rise in popularity. The essays challenge traditional notions of what types of people are included in the Santa Muerte cult and describe the various expressions of their allegiance.

1528 Seguridad humana y violencia crónica en México: nuevas lecturas y propuestas desde abajo. Edición de Gema Kloppe-Santamaría y Alexandra Abello Colak. Ciudad de México: Instituto Tecnológico Autónomo de México: Miguel Ángel Porrúa, Librero-Editor, 2019. 299 p.: bibl. (Políticas públicas serie)

This book serves as a "methodological response" to issues of violence faced in Latin America, particularly in Mexico. The book draws on participatory action research to address the issue from the perspectives of those who are most affected by it, ultimately reframing the view of chronic violence. The authors argue that the labels "war" and "post-war" serve as potential vehicles for erasure, and should be reexamined to find terms that more adequately describe how the people living in areas experiencing violence are chronically affected by it. They describe the elasticity of Mexican criminal organizations, making them immune to conventional tactics of combatting crime, as was demonstrated by the Calderón government's unsuccessful utilization of the army to combat the cartels in the early 2000s. Criminal organizations are seen as manifestations of the chronic violence in Mexico as they are a response to the socioeconomic conditions that make them necessary and, in turn, become more violent to combat threats to their existence. The authors draw a contrast between inhumane security, which is based on power and ultimately ineffective when dealing with chronic violence, and humane security, which considers not just security from violence, but also food and other forms of security. Humane security is a solution which does not view people as creators of violence (and thus does not create the need to eliminate them), but instead posits that violent social conditions create reactions by people.

1529 Seminario Institucional La Crisis, el Poder y los Movimientos Sociales. Los movimientos sociales en la vida politica mexicana. Coordinación de Aguilar García. Ciudad de México: UNAM, Instituto de Investigaciones Sociales, 2019. 365 p.: bibl.

This book assesses the current landscape of social movements in today's globalized world by analyzing particular movements that have arisen during the end of the 20th and beginning of the 21st centuries. The social movements discussed are situated within the context of the development of the welfare state and neoliberalism as distinct stages in the development of capitalism. The book is divided into two sections, the first addresses social movements at the national level, and the second addresses those at the regional level. The first section explores contemporary social movements in Mexico and the state's failure to meet people's demands; the primary Mexican social movements of the 21st century and the historic nature of this period; the often complex relationship between democracy and social movements; labor reform movements and their relation to neoliberalism; neo-Zapatismo movements in Mexico; anti-authoritarian protests in Veracruz; and the resistance of neoliberalism via community radio in rural Oaxaca and Guerrero. In the second section, topics discussed include the fragmentation of power across North America as a result of globalization and democratization; the social movements of Indigenous Ecuadorians; and an overview of the most important books on social movements published between 2010 and 2016.

1530 Serna Pérez, María Guadalupe. Entre caridad y solidaridad: las organizaciones mexicanas del Tercer Sector. Ciudad de México: Instituto de Investigaciones Dr. José María Luis Mora: Consejo Nacional de Ciencia y Tecnología, 2017. 204 p.: bibl. (Contemporánea. Sociología)

What prevents Mexicans from reaching a basic agreement on a subject and working together to create an organized movement? This is the guiding question of Serna's book, an in-depth look into why Mexicans seem chronically incapable of finding common ground on even the most trivial issues and coming together to act on them. The author focuses specifically on grassroots movements, which often face backlash from their own communities. The book provides an exploration of the contexts in which disagreements have historically taken place and the economic and social implications that arise as a result of these disputes. Furthermore, the book focuses on organizations stemming from the "Third Sector," or the sector composed of grassroots movements that require a certain degree of solidarity and reciprocity in order to advance their work. As such, the book furthers the scholarly understanding of the "Third Sector," while also offering a comprehensive answer to a challenging question: Why is Mexico one of the countries with the fewest social organizations? The book aims to understand what role social solidarity plays. This study provides a historical context for understanding the organizational landscape and how associative processes have developed from the 17th to 21st centuries.

1531 Soboroff, Jacob. Separated: inside an American tragedy. First Custom House Paperback Edition. New York, N.Y.: Custom House, 2021. 419 p.

The Trump administration deliberately and systematically separated thousands of migrant children from their parents and, according to humanitarian groups and child welfare experts, there was an unparalleled abuse of the human rights of children (p. xvii). Over the course of a year, the Trump administration carried out widespread family separations at the border. Soboroff and other journalists were invited to

Casa Padre in Brownsville, Tex., where the Rio Grande and the Gulf of Mexico meet. Casa Padre was a former Walmart—which Soboroff and other journalists were told was a "shelter." This "shelter" held nearly 1,500 migrant boys, 10 to 17 years old. Hundreds of these boys had been separated from their parents due to Trump's zero-tolerance immigration policy. The Trump administration lacked a plan to reunite these families. The story of Juan and his son, José, appears in this book, describing their almost five-month-long separation. Since the summer of 2017, the Trump administration took at least 5,556 children from their parents; but to this day, it is unclear how many families were separated. In February 2020, the US Government Accountability Office (GAO) noted that it was also unclear the extent to which Border Patrol has accurate records of separated families in its data system. Some of the families were quickly reunited and other children were permanently orphaned. US Customs and Border Protection separated 2,814 children during the zero-tolerance policy, and later admitted it had separated 1,556 more before the policy officially started.

1532 **Sociología y género: estudios en torno a performances, violencias y temporalidades.** Edición de Karine Tinat y Arturo Alvarado. Ciudad de México: El Colegio de México, 2017. 299 p.: bibl., ill.

This book provides a general survey of research on gender in Latin America. The volume features sections on the topics of performances of gender, intimate partner violence, and the different uses of time by gender. In the first section, authors examine trans masculinity and how this gendered performance both subverts and legitimizes traditional ideals of masculinity and the relationship between sexuality and body image. In exploring issues of intimate partner violence, authors in the second section unpack important sociological concepts like habitus, agency, and victimhood. They also investigate the relationship between alcohol consumption and domestic violence as well as between progress toward equality and homicide. The final section explores how gender and socioeconomic background play a role in youth's discontinuation of schooling and the differentials of time spent on productive and nonproductive activities between girls and boys.

1533 **Sosa Hernández, Guadalupe Georgina.** Estereotipos de género: la construcción de la imagen de la mujer en la propaganda del gobierno de la Ciudad de México (2012–2017). (*in* Reflexiones interdisciplinarias sobre la ciudadanía de género: mujeres en la Ciudad de México. Coordinación de Lorena Margarita Umaña Reyes. Ciudad de México: Grupo Editor Orfila Valentini, SA de CV: UNAM, 2018, p. 87–108)

An analysis of gender, gender stereotypes, and propaganda depictions created by Mexico City's local initiatives. The analysis examines multiple campaigns that cover topics such as encouraging breastfeeding and social inclusion for human development. The author's conclusion suggests that local government campaigns should be re-evaluated as they have produced images and slogans that reinforce gender, racist, and classist stereotypes that affect both men and women. For a review of the entire volume, see item **1519**.

1534 **Stone, Livia K.** Atenco lives!: filmmaking and popular struggle in Mexico. Nashville, Tenn.: Vanderbilt University Press, 2018. 202 p.: bibl., index. (Performing Latin American and Caribbean identities)

Stone provides an in-depth exploration of The Community Front in Defense of Land of Atenco, or the Frente, a well-known activist group in Mexico, focusing particularly on the role of filmmaking in the group's social movements. After describing the origins of the Frente and their commonly used tactics, Stone turns attention to the experiences of several filmmakers involved in the movement to demonstrate that the role of cameras as tools of either surveillance or liberation is dependent on the cultural context. She contrasts the concept of *protagonismo*, often policed in these social movements, with that of *compañerismo*, as well as using a widely known documentary about the Frente to juxtapose approaches to film activism centered on resistance against those that center on autonomy. Stone argues that the work of the Frente demonstrates how films may be used to build "transformative noncapital material economies," and puts this mode of activism in the context of today's landscape in the anticapitalist struggle.

1535 Tacher Contreras, Daniel. Incorporación de la perspectiva de género en los instrumentos de derechos humanos. (*in* Reflexiones interdisciplinarias sobre la ciudadanía de género: mujeres en la Ciudad de México. Coordinación de Lorena Margarita Umaña Reyes. Ciudad de México: Grupo Editor Orfila Valentini, SA de CV: UNAM, 2018, p. 31–50)

An explanation of the history of the legality and ethics of human rights and the lack of inclusion of gender, specifically women. For a review of the entire volume, see item **1519**.

1536 Tamez Valedez, Blanca Mirthala. Dependencia en el adulto mayor: estudio comparativo entre contextos urbanos y rurales en Nuevo León. (*in* Estudios críticos sobre políticas y problemáticas sociales. Coordinación de Elisa Cerros Rodríguez y Verónica Martínez Flores. Mexico: Universidad Autónoma de Nuevo León, 2018, p. 189–220, bibl.)

A comparative analysis of women and men in urban and rural Nuevo León and the needs of the elderly.

1537 Tapia, Mike. Gangs of the El Paso-Juárez borderland: a history. Albuquerque: University of New Mexico Press, 2019. 188 p.: bibl., index.

Tapia investigates the historical context of the criminal subcultures that exist in the El Paso-Juárez borderland region, including southern New Mexico, western Texas, and northern Chihuahua, Mexico. By using newspaper archives, police records, oral histories, and various other data sources, Tapia first builds a chronology of neighborhoods and gang cultures in El Paso from the 1920s to the 1960s. He performs a similar analysis for the city of Las Cruces, N.M., though this chronology extends to the present day, and Anthony, N.M., a city which serves in many ways to connect networks between El Paso, Juárez, and Las Cruces. Tapia traces the history of criminal activity in El Paso and Juárez to the Prohibition era and explores the relationship between the two cities, including details on the oft-discussed spillover effects, as well as the lack thereof. This history is contrasted with an examination of present-day El Paso and its current gang subcultures.

1538 Téllez Contreras, León Felipe and Mayra Angélica Ascencio Martínez. #YoTeRespeto: género, espacio público y Acoso Callejero en Tlalpan, 2014. (*in* Reflexiones interdisciplinarias sobre la ciudadanía de género: mujeres en la Ciudad de México. Coordinación de Lorena Margarita Umaña Reyes. Ciudad de México: Grupo Editor Orfila Valentini, SA de CV: UNAM, 2018, p. 109–130)

An exploration of street harassment and gender-based violence in public spaces in order to find interventions and improve a local government campaign, Campaña Contra el Acoso Callejero (Campaign Against Street Harassment), in Tlalpan between 2012 and 2015. For a review of the entire volume, see item **1519**.

1539 Tirado Villegas, Gloria. El 68 en Puebla y su universidad. Puebla, Mexico: Benemérita Universidad Autónoma de Puebla, Dirección General de Publicaciones: Instituto de Ciencias Sociales y Humanidades "Alfonso Vélez Pliego", 2019. 229 p.: bibl., facsimiles, ill., portraits.

An overarching view on the Mexican Movement of 1968, known as the Movimiento Estudiantil. Its foundation in Puebla was during an expected industrial development peak with opportunities for employment, financial investments, and the social movements that were ignited by university students against President Gustavo Díaz Ordaz. Through ethnographic research, the author distinguishes the diverse social student-led organizations that demanded national support for democracy, civil liberties, and human rights while encountering fatal consequences from the government.

1540 ¡Tú, migrante!: la construcción de las representaciones de la migración en el contexto de América del Norte y Centroamérica. Coordinación de Aaraón Díaz

Mendiburo y Andrea Meza Torres. Ciudad de México: UNAM, CISAN—Centro de Investigaciones sobre América del Norte, 2017. 254 p.: bibl., ill.

There has been a thematic shift in migration studies to the imaginaries, representations, and perceptions of migrants and migration, in general. This edited book provides a brief look into the literature Mexican scholars have produced regarding the perceptual and discursive elements affecting migrants' experiences and representations in the Global North. The book's goal is to provide a Global South perspective that contrasts mainstream perspectives on the impacts and realities of migration, most of which have been conceived by Global North scholars. The book consists of articles that shed light on the imaginaries, representations, and perceptions of North and Central American migrants found in the US, Canada, and Mexico as examined by Mexican scholars. The comprehensive articles explore representations of North and Central American migrants in the press, museums, and films, as well as migrants' perceptions of their cultures and communities.

1541 Umaña Reyes, Lorena Margarita. Ciudadanía de género desigual: análisis de programas sociales de apoyo a la mujer en la Ciudad de México desde la teoría de las representaciones sociales. (*in* Reflexiones interdisciplinarias sobre la ciudadanía de género: mujeres en la Ciudad de México. Coordinación de Lorena Margarita Umaña Reyes. Ciudad de México: Grupo Editor Orfila Valentini, SA de CV: UNAM, 2018, p. 131–156)

A cumulative review of three local government departments run by different political parties with separate social issues affecting women. The research aims to compare the different approaches to foster and implement new social programming benefiting women of Mexico City between 2010 and 2016. For a review of the entire volume, see item **1519**.

1542 Universidad Nacional Autónoma de México. Seminario Permanente Cultura y Representaciones Sociales. Las culturas hoy. Compilación de Gilberto Giménez y Natividad Gutiérrez Chong. Ciudad de México: UNAM, Instituto de Investigaciones Sociales, 2019. 227 p.: bibl.

This book compiles the works presented at the 2016 meeting of El Seminario Permanente Cultura y Representaciones Sociales, during which scholars discussed various themes relating to the theory and analysis of culture. The papers presented here explore topics such as the relationship between culture and ethnic identity, the various definitions of culture and the implications of having so many, and the inception of new cultural artifacts as a result of emerging phenomena. The collection is a useful tool for understanding theories and expressions of culture in Latin America.

1543 Vasquez, Jessica M. Mexican Americans across generations: immigrant families, racial realities. New York, N.Y.: New York University Press, 2011. 301 p.: bibl., ill., index.

Paul Zagaga, a 62-year-old, second-generation Mexican American lawyer, described his representation of racial identities of Mexican immigrants and how their descendants change with each generation with the following metaphor comparing "Coca-Cola, 7-Up, and Evian water." For example, to him, the Mexican immigrant generation is the "Coca-Cola" generation due to them being rich in their tradition and hanging on to it in their new context. The children of these immigrants are the "7-Up" generation since they lose some of the "color" of their culture and are more assimilated to the US compared to their parents. The third generation are the "Evian water" since they have lost both their color and their cultural vibrancy. Vasquez's research "finds that Mexican immigrants, their children, and their grandchildren become increasingly embedded in US institutions and ways of life with each successive generation" (p. 4). Vasquez interviewed members of middle-class families to learn how "these economically successful and structurally integrated Mexican Americans are racialized" (p. 6). Vasquez conducted 67 interviews with 29 families in California. She finds "that integration in language, education, income, occupation, and civic participation occur over generations and yet Mexican-origin people may live out their ethnic heritage by choosing either to loosen or to tighten their grip on Mexican culture" (p. 237). The findings indicate that race-based policies like affirmative action are essential measures to prevent historical and contemporary exclusionary mechanisms.

1544 **Vega, Rosalynn A.** No alternative: childbirth, citizenship, and Indigenous culture in Mexico. Austin: University of Texas Press, 2018. 238 p.: bibl., ill., index. (Louann Atkins Temple women & culture series; 44)

Through ethnographic observation, Vega explores two forms of childbirth and midwifery in Mexico, humanized and traditional. Humanized births are those which are attended by professionally trained midwives, often in private clinics, while traditional births occur in medical settings with experience-based, often Indigenous midwives. Although the practices of professional midwives are learned from Indigenous tradition, their knowledge and skill are viewed as the superior alternative to what is offered by traditional midwives. Vega problematizes the rhetoric surrounding modern midwifery, in which these practices are said to be empowering expressions of free choice, despite being only available to select classes of women. The book discusses the commodification of Indigenous culture, the humanized birth movement as a new facet of the pressure women face to "correctly produce future citizens," and intersectional racialization processes and how these contribute to systemic violence in medicine.

1545 **Velasco Ortiz, M. Laura** and **Carlos Hernández Campos.** Migración, trabajo y asentamiento en enclaves globales: indígenas en Baja California Sur. Tijuana, Mexico: El Colegio de la Frontera Norte; Ciudad de México: CDI, Comisión Nacional para el Desarrollo de los Pueblos Indígenas, 2018. 339 p., 22 pages of plates: bibl., ill. (some color), maps.

In the Mexican state of Baja California Sur, migration within Indigenous communities has arisen thanks to the lack of jobs, the crisis in the agriculture industry, and violence due to drug trafficking. These factors have contributed to an increase in migration to cities where elites reside, such as Los Cabos. This investigation seeks to understand the migration movements from 1990 to the present, with the purpose of seeing how these communities live and how the processes of segmentation, segregation, and ethnicization play a role. This study sets out to understand how to create sustainable societies where social inequality is reduced.

1546 **Velázquez García, Mario Alberto.** No hay constitución ni leyes que valgan: los recursos del estado mexicano frente a los movimientos sociales. Puebla, Mexico: Benemérita Universidad Autónoma de Puebla, Instituto de Ciencias Sociales y Humanidades "Alfonso Vélez Pliego", 2017. 270 p.: bibl.

This study examines the relationship between social movements and the Mexican state, and in particular the broad range of mechanisms that the state possesses and has used to manage social movements. The study begins by exploring the utility of Foucault's concept of "biopower" to understand how the Mexican state responded to social movements. Beginning with the period following the end of the Mexican Revolution, there was an uneasy coexistence between the emerging new state and the various groups that participated in the revolution, any of which could easily become rivals. The book examines the state's approach to managing this situation. Other cases examined include: the case of the "Pacto Ribereño", the Mexican activities of state intelligence organizations beginning with the Dirección Federal de Seguridad (DFS), and the actions of the state in response to the armed guerrilla groups that emerged during the late 1960s and 1970s. [K. Jamtgaard]

1547 **La vida en el centro: feminismo, reproducción y tramas comunitarias.** Edición y notas por Mariana Menéndez y Carolina Conze. Ciudad de México: Bajo Tierra A.C., 2021. 259 p.: bibl.

This book poses a question in response to a call for feminists to place life at the center by disputing patriarchal, colonial, capitalist modes of reproduction: what does it mean to put life at the center? The essays included here address the debates surrounding the feminist struggle and the production of the commons.

1548 Violencia y crisis social en el último rincón de la frontera: Piedras Negras y Acuña. Coordinación de Socorro Arzaluz Solano. Tijuana, Mexico: El Colegio de la Frontera Norte, 2017. 247 p.: bibl.

This work has a clearly defined objective: "to describe and analyze the different situations that attract violent conditions in two cities on the Mexico-US border: Piedras Negras and Acuña" (p. 9). The book is divided in three sections: 1) contextualizing the issue; 2) analyzing family dynamics, the role of education, and social media to explain violence across the two cities; and 3) evaluating how social capital and the culture of legality are potential factors of this violence. Piedras Negras and Acuña are ideal locations for international migration, one of the reasons that it is crucial to study how violence manifests in these regions. Types of violence present in Piedras Negras and Acuña include, but are not limited to, organized crime and narcotrafficking, robbery and assault, intrafamilial violence, assassinations, automobile accidents, sexual violation and abuse, physical fighting, and violence in educational institutions. Most victims of these violent crimes in Mexico are women and children. The contributions consider the economic, social, political, and transnational components that contribute to violence in Piedras Negras and Acuña.

1549 Yllescas Illescas, Jorge Adrián. Ver, oír y callar: creer en la Santa Muerte durante el encierro. Ciudad de México: UNAM, 2018. 238 p.: bibl., some color ill. (Colección Posgrado; 78)

Since its emergence, the cult of Santa Muerte has captivated scholars both in Mexico and the US who have sought to understand its origins and dynamics. Yet despite the considerable scholarship on the topic, little has been said about its practice outside the cult hub in Tepito, Mexico. This book aims to fill the scholarly void by revealing how the cult of Santa Muerte manifests itself among individuals who are or have been imprisoned. The book provides a comprehensive overview of the Mexican prison system, particularly focusing on the obstacles the bureaucracy creates for those looking to interact with it. The book then presents the author's study of the cult of Santa Muerte as observed from a Mexican male prison. The book provides key insights into the way cult members practice and understand their faith while navigating a particularly repressive environment. Through this book, the author contributes a rare perspective of an elusive religious community that has gained a significant following in the past few years.

1550 Zamora Carmona, Gabriela. Las niñas también migramos. (*in* Estudios críticos sobre políticas y problemáticas sociales. Coordinación de Elisa Cerros Rodríguez y Verónica Martínez Flores. Mexico: Universidad Autónoma de Nuevo León, 2018, p. 221–240, bibl.)

A closer look into the growing number of young girls migrating from Central America and Mexico in hopes of reaching the US and their high degree of vulnerability relative to other migrants.

1551 Zendejas Romero, Sergio. Etnografía histórica de una elite burguesa. Zamora, Mexico: El Colegio de Michoacán; Ciudad de México: Fideicomiso "Felipe Teixidor y Monserrat Alfau de Teixidor", 2018. 410 p.: bibl., ill., indexes, maps. (Migajas y protagonismo; I) (Colección Investigaciones)

This study provides an ethnographic description of "empresarios" from the Ecuandureo municipality, located in the northeast part of Michoacán. These "empresarios" were an elite agricultural class that dominated the political, economic, and social landscape of Ecuandureo. However, at the start of the 20th century, Mexico began to experience significant changes. Mass urbanization, industrialization, and the postrevolutionary presidential regime would modify the structure of rural and agricultural communities. Zendejas Romero notes that despite the disfavorable conditions created by new corporations, bureaucracies, and other institutions, the "empresarios" and their families continued to fight to maintain the socioeconomic and political status that has existed for generations. The book presents an ethnographic analysis of the empresarios and ejidatarios. Zendejas Romero looks at the living conditions of each group, the challenges and opportunities they faced, and what aspects of the processes most influenced their heightened protagonism and subsequent marginalization. The book is designed in a chronological order that starts with the formation of the elite in Ecuandureo in the early 1900s and follows to their demise by the late 1990s. The overall aim of the chapters is to link theoretical-methodological ideas to research and historical ethnography to analyze the interconnections between different historical processes and how they impacted the municipality. The book is divided into four main parts. The first part focuses on the origins of the main social groups in Ecuandureo from 1906–42. It also addresses the organizational and hierarchical social structure and the main social institutions that support it: haciendas. In the second part, Zendejas Romero analyzes the changes and continuities of "los ricos" and their allies. The section looks at how their businesses and identity were impacted by agrarian distributions, which subsequently led to economic difficulty as they were exposed to substantial outside competition. The third part studies the ensuing conflicts, changes, and continuities in the period from 1958–98, such as the business crisis and major migratory waves. The final part reflects on the strategy and research conducted by the author and how it leads into a forthcoming second volume.

CENTRAL AMERICA

CECILIA MENJÍVAR, *Professor of Sociology and Dorothy L. Meier Social Equities Chair, University of California, Los Angeles*

THE SOCIOLOGICAL SCHOLARSHIP on Central America reflects a reality where concerns about violence, the future of youth, employment, social movements, religion, migration, and trafficking are ever-present. This review highlights these topics and a few others to depict a dynamic scholarly landscape that continues to deepen our understanding of pressing issues in the region.

Migration is a central feature of Central American societies and shapes lived experiences across spheres of life; as such, it emerges prominently as a theme in the works reviewed here. Most authors take a structural approach to examining and explaining migrations within and from the region. Some examine emigrations from Central America from a historical, macrostructural perspective and delve into the roots of violence to provide context to contemporary migration flows (item **1563**), sometimes examining these factors through a personal lens in memoir format (item **1582**). Others center on population movements, especially forced internal displacements, to connect them to the violence that ravaged the region during the years of political conflicts in the 1980s (item **1566**). Others argue that neoliberal capitalism lies at the root of migratory flows in the region, whereby neoliberal capitalism intersects with violence, humanitarian crises, and women's inequality experiences (item **1593**). Following a similar approach, but with a focus on what Central Americans face when they arrive in the US, some focus on the construction of fear and crises to create hostile border policies for these immigrants (item **1577**). Similarly, other authors examine how borders in the region are defined, reconfigured socially, and contested by the activities of migrants and communities in migration corridors (item **1603**). An interesting approach emerges when migratory flows are reconceptualized through the lens of social movements to understand unauthorized migration from the region as a political act of disobedience (item **1595**). The challenging and complex experiences of migrant youth are captured when they arrive unaccompanied (item **1597**) and when they are deported, with a special focus on how Indigenous youth fare in enforcement systems (item **1576**). Migrant women also face special challenges as they travel, experiences that come to the fore when examined through a feminist lens (item **1587**). And migration is also examined through the lens of Hollywood, to reveal how Central American migrants are depicted in film during periods of heightened migration from the region (item **1561**).

As has been the case for some time, various dimensions of violence have generated quite a bit of research attention. Some authors take a theoretical standpoint to interrogate the meaning of violence and the sociological lens we use to study this topic (item **1575**), while others shed light on a long-standing theme of the enduring significance of the genocidal violence of the 1980s (item **1572**). Others examine how violence manifests in institutions, especially in the carceral system, where it intersects with gender (item **1574**). Also examined are institutional responses to gang violence, understood as an outcome of the civil wars in the region (item **1594**), while others take an in-depth look at the internal organization and stratification of gangs (item **1586**). Manifestations of violence can be found in other forms and spaces, such as bullying in schools (item **1600**) and the general violence permeating school settings which disrupts learning despite student resilience (item **1591**).

Gender-based violence is a recurring theme, with some authors looking at its legal and political history (item **1588**), the close ties between political power and sexual violence (item **1559**), and the theoretical and empirical links between gender-based violence and migration (item **1571**). Along these lines, some authors look specifically at this connection in the context of sex trafficking in the region (item **1580**) and, through a feminist lens, examine how drug trafficking, carceral conditions, and women's lives intersect (item **1590**).

The topic of social movements continues to garner scholarly attention in the region. Some authors use a historical lens to look at working-class social movements and union organizing (item **1552**); others highlight how working-class movements and unions impact social reform (item **1592**); and still others examine peasant movements within historical memory projects (item **1581**). Others look at resistance and tensions between worker movements and illicit power structures, such as cartels (item **1584**), while others examine how youth participate and organize in social movements to advocate for issues important to them (item **1596**), and others study women's political art that exposes difficult social conditions (item **1568**).

Another constant in research from and about Central America is race and ethnicity, and the works reviewed here approach this topic broadly. Some use a theoretical lens to examine constructions of race and identity as it intersects with gender and social class in Indigenous communities (item **1602**), situating this discussion within debates about multiculturalism in a postconflict context (item **1598**), and focusing on Indigenous writers to call for a rethinking of frameworks, methodologies, and ethics to approach these debates (item **1556**). Others show a broader range of experiences and examine contemporary notions of race as it is linked to national identity in the Central American region (item **1565**).

Religion continues to attract scholarly attention as well. Some authors look at the lives of martyrs and prominent religious leaders to highlight their social justice service and pastoral leadership (item **1562**) and to show the social context and inequalities that influenced their work (item **1558**), as well as their influence on social movements through liberation theology work (item **1578**). Two works take a historical approach to draw comparisons between Christian groups in the region and religiously influenced, non-Christian groups in other parts of the world (item **1599**), and to examine the development of particular groups, such as Masonic lodges, which are not formally a religious group, but share key characteristics with predominant religious groups in the region (item **1557**).

An interesting set of works focuses on theoretical thought and the study of culture in the region. Two volumes compile writings by contemporary critical thinkers in the region with essays on globalization, democracy, inequality, and insecurity with the aim of countering popular narratives on these issues; one from El Salvador (item **1555**) and the other from Honduras (item **1554**). Also taking a critical approach, two other volumes examine cultural narratives and archetypal figures in popular culture (item **1560**), as well as cultural identities through the concepts of coloniality and power inequalities (item **1589**).

The lives of young and older Central Americans occupy an important space in this scholarship. Some authors take a historical view of the experiences of youth as students across the 20th century (item **1579**), while others take a contemporary look at issues that affect youth, such as their labor exclusion and marginalization in the context of urban violence (item **1601**). And others focus on institutional policies central to youth's lives, such as school accreditation for public educational institutions (item **1553**). However, youth are not the only age group examined in the works reviewed here; there is also attention on aging through a human rights perspective and citizenship (item **1567**).

A set of works examines important demographic topics, such as work, family, health, and aging. Topics studied include work and employment under neoliberal policies in rural and urban areas, among adults and youth; minimum wage inequalities; and social rights across the region (item **1570**). Others focus on families through transgender parenting, which challenges gender relations within the family under neoliberalism (item **1573**), and others examine the medicalization of childbirth and the role of midwifery in birthing practices (item **1564**). Works also take a historical view to look at the health effects of disease-eradication campaigns, such as malaria (item **1585**).

Finally, some works examine broadly societies and economies of the region aiming to propose policy solutions to improve living conditions. A group of publicly engaged scholars considers development processes and tools for transformations into democratic institutions (item **1569**), while another group observes that government solutions will only be effective if traditional approaches are abandoned in favor of engaging deeply with communities (item **1583**).

1552 Acevedo Granados, Napoleón. La clase obrera hondureña: su papel histórico. Tegucigalpa: Editorial Guaymuras, 2017. 269 p.: bibl., ill., photos.

This book delves into the long history of the working class in Honduras from the late 19th century through the early 21st century. In 12 sections, divided by themes and time periods, the author explores topics ranging from banana plantation workers and factory workers to miners, the effects of neoliberalism, and key political moments like coups. The book begins with an analysis of precursors to unions in Honduras and ends with recommendations for how to continue developing workers' rights and collective bargaining.

1553 Aguilar Arce, Marianela. Diseño de una política pública regional de acreditación de la educación superior en Centroamérica (1993–2003). Costa Rica: Editorial UCR, 2018. 283 p.: bibl., ill.

This book analyzes public policy on higher education accreditation in Central America. Case-study analyses are organized to evaluate policies of quality assurance in global contexts and reveal the political and technocratic influences that shape them. The analysis informs the audience of the historical efforts the Central American Higher Education Council (CSUCA) made to spearhead regional collaboration on improving the quality of postsecondary education. This movement sought to modernize university management to support efficiency and promote equity in public higher education in this region.

1554 Antología del pensamiento crítico hondureño contemporáneo. Coordinación de Ramón Romero. Contribuciones de Ventura Ramos *et al.* Buenos Aires: CLACSO, 2019. 485 p.: bibl., ill. (Colección Antologías del pensamiento social latinoamericano y caribeño)

The themes in this collection include national and international political dynamics, economic and social development, and national identity. The volume is part of a series coordinated by the Latin American Council on Social Sciences to democratize access to prominent sociological perspectives of each country in the region. The editors gathered academic research from the last five decades that radically reinterprets Honduran historical and contemporary realities. While methodologies vary, all authors provide historical and economic analyses that counter mainstream narratives on the issues discussed.

1555 Antología del pensamiento crítico salvadoreño contemporáneo. Coordinación de Loida Mariela Castro y Roberto Oswaldo López Salazar. Buenos Aires: CLACSO, 2018. 561 p.: bibl., ill. (Colección Antologías del pensamiento social latinoamericano y caribeño)

This anthology on contemporary Salvadoran critical thought includes themes ranging from identity, globalization, democracy, social liberation, poverty, and inequality to migration, urban development, insecurity, and violence. This volume is part of an effort coordinated by the Latin American Council on Social Sciences to democratize access to the prominent sociological perspectives of each country. In the case of El Salvador, the editors gathered academic research from the last five decades that provides insight into the changing political and social dynamics that influence Salvadoran identity.

1556 Arias, Arturo. Recuperando las huellas perdidas: el surgimiento de narrativas indígenas contemporáneas en Abya Yala. Guatemala: Editorial Cultura, 2016. 268 p.: bibl. (Colección ensayo. Serie Luis Cardoza y Aragón; 56)

Arias examines contemporary Indigenous literatures in Abya Yala (the Kuna name for Latin America), which has seen significant growth in recent years. With a focus on Luis de Lión, Gaspar Pedro González, and Víctor Montejo, Arias sheds light on the power of Indigenous authors and literary production. This book, the first in a three-part series, is a call to rethink conceptual frameworks, methodologies, and ethics in work on Indigenous texts.

1557 Arias Castro, Tomás Federico. Historia de las logias masónicas de Costa Rica: (siglos XIX, XX y XXI). San José: Editorial Costa Rica, 2017. 185 p.: bibl., ill., portraits. (Colección Nueva biblioteca patria; 12)

This book details the history of Masonic lodges in Costa Rica from their inception to their current organizational structure in the region. Based on archival research that informs about Masonic beliefs and their role in the formation of the nation-state, the author also discusses how Costa Rican Masonic authorities extended their influence to Colombia, Cuba, and Guatemala. The text includes a collection of profiles for each of the 22 Masonic lodges that exist throughout Costa Rica.

1558 Artiga González, Álvaro. Una sociedad según el corazón de Dios: la polis cristiana en el pensamiento de Monseñor Óscar A. Romero. San Salvador: UCA Editores, 2017. 262 p.: bibl., ill. (Coleccion La iglesia en America Latina; 23)

This book introduces the sociopolitical factors that ultimately influenced Archbishop Óscar Romero's pastoral leadership. The author focuses on the social context in which Romero lived before and during his time as San Salvador's archbishop. This historical context focuses on the vast gaps in social inequality that motivated Romero's advocacy for the poor. The subtitle refers to Romero's utopian vision for El Salvador, which is referenced consistently through Romero's homilies and speeches that the author quotes and analyzes. A brief reflection on the role of Christians in society and associated social leadership is also included.

1559 Bateson, Ian. "Justice is afraid of the priest's robe": rape and power in Nicaragua. (*World Policy J.*, 34:3, Fall 2017, p. 36–40, photo)

Through the case study of a 15-year-old girl in Nicaragua and a comparison to the president's daughter, the author explores the themes of power and sexual violence in Nicaragua, which range from priests to the president. This article highlights the complete ban on abortion in Nicaragua, which has led to high rates of teen and young women pregnancy. Some organizations assist (e.g., the Axayacatl Association of Women) with counseling and a safe space for pregnant women. The article highlights the close ties between power, masculinity, and sexual violence.

Beck, Erin. The uneven impacts of violence against women reform in Guatemala: intersecting inequalities and the patchwork state. See item **882**.

1560 Bolaños Davis, Alejandro. El Nicara[güe]güense: la incultura de nuestra cultura y transformación de la incultura en cultura: un análisis antropológico, psicológico, sociopolítico, con una propuesta para la alternativa de un diálogo nacional. Con un epílogo, Atlas cultural de Nicaragua, de Julio Valle-Castillo. Managua: PAVSA, 2018. 231 p.: bibl., ill., map.

Based on anthropological research, the author seeks to transform negative characteristics associated with the archetype of the *güegüense*, into the positive figure of the *Güegüense-sabio*. The author argues that this archetype arose as a defense mechanism against colonialism and that it is possible to transform it into a positive image. The author discusses culture, symbols, and archetypes, and presents a methodology to transform the current archetype through technology. There is a description of Nicaraguan culture, including religion, food, dance, and theater.

1561 Carballo, Willian. Centroamérica, una película de Hollywood: representación de los países del área y sus migrantes en series y filmes estadounidenses de 1990 a 2015. Santa Tecla, El Salvador: Escuela de Comunicación Mónica Herrera, 2016. 101 p.: bibl., color ill.

This study focuses on the representation of Central America in Hollywood from 1990–2015, a period with a high influx of Central American immigrants to the US. The study asks how Central Americans who migrated to the US and compatriots who stayed in their home countries are represented. Based on discursive analysis of 114 works, the volume dedicates a chapter each to Guatemala, El Salvador, Honduras, Nicaragua, Costa Rica, and Panama.

1562 Cardenal, Rodolfo. Vida, pasión y muerte del jesuita Rutilio Grande. San Salvador: UCA Editores, 2017. 564 p.:

bibl. (Colección La Iglesia en América Latina; 22)

A comprehensive biography of Salvadoran priest Rutilio Grande that combines two biographies that the author previously wrote and adds an examination of Grande's spiritual legacy. Cardenal relies on Grande's letters and homilies, archival religious documents, and local journalism to provide an in-depth view of the formative experiences that transformed Grande's religious identity during missionary service, pastoral leadership, and political organizing. Moving away from focusing on his assassination, Cardenal honors Grande's religious guidance, social justice fervor, and unconditional love—Grande's guiding principles.

1563 **Chomsky, Aviva.** Central America's forgotten history: revolution, violence, and the roots of migration. Boston, Mass: Beacon Press, 2021. 306 p.: bibl., index.

This book seeks to inform readers about the intertwined histories of the US and Central America. It discusses how the past is remembered and what narratives have dominated modern understandings of Central American political and migration crises. In efforts to demystify racist and xenophobic assumptions about Central American immigration, Chomsky examines the region's colonial and postcolonial history and foreign relations during the Cold War, and provides a comprehensive description of the social, economic, and political consequences of US foreign policies in Guatemala, El Salvador, Honduras, and Nicaragua.

1564 **Cosminsky, Sheila.** Midwives and mothers: the medicalization of childbirth on a Guatemalan plantation. Austin: University of Texas Press, 2016. 303 p.: bibl., ill., index. (Louann Atkins Temple women & culture series; 43)

Attacks on midwives and their reproductive health services by the medicalization of childbirth are at the center of this book. This longitudinal study of a *finca* and the author's ethnographic research provide insight into how different models of birthing impact culture and society. Cominsky explores birth, illness, death, and survival on Guatemalan coffee and sugar plantations with a focus on how traditional birthing practices clash with technological developments and changes in the plantation system. Midwives are willing to consider changes while also advocating for local midwifery knowledge to be respected.

Cruz, José Miguel. The politics of negotiating with gangs: the case of El Salvador. See item **871**.

1565 **DeLugan, Robin Maria.** *"Turcos"* and *"chinos"* in El Salvador: orientalizing ethno-racialization and the transforming dynamics of national belonging. (*Lat. Am. Caribb. Ethn. Stud.*, 11:2, July 2016, p. 142–162, bibl., photo)

This article explores the historical and contemporary notions of race and ethnicity in El Salvador and their role in the construction of national identity. The author analyzes how Palestinian-Salvadorans and Chinese-Salvadorans are racialized and Othered—such as their exclusion from the mestizaje ideology and the common vernacular identifiers, "turco" and "chino," used for them. She points to a potential new era in which the state attempts to be more inclusive and represent a more diverse nation, but there is still much work to be done to continue advancing social equality.

1566 **Desplazamiento forzado interno en Guatemala: diagnóstico 2010–2016.** Coordinación de Sindy Hernández Bonilla. Guatemala: Instituto de Investigación y Proyección sobre Dinámicas Globales y Territoriales (IDGT), 2018. 178 p.: bibl., map.

More than 30 years after the end of Guatemala's conflict, and more than 20 years since the Peace Accords, rates of violence in the country are still four times higher than the global average. Within this context, this report seeks to understand the reasons for forced displacement within Guatemala. The reasons vary and are related to structural violence, processes that were cut short with the almost nullified Peace Accords, and neoliberal policies that resulted in corruption. The study notes that the Guatemalan government neglects forced displacement. The report explains the roots of forced displacement and calls attention to the need for protection for those affected.

1567 Díaz-Tendero Bollain, Aída. Envejecimiento en Centroamérica y el Caribe. Ciudad de México: UNAM, Centro de Investigaciones sobre América Latina y el Caribe, 2018. 247 p.: bibl., ill. (Colección Política, economía y sociedad en América Latina y el Caribe; 32)

This is the first book to comparatively analyze aging in Central America and the Caribbean through a sociodemographic, socioeconomic, and human rights perspective. The author discusses the theoretical frameworks and statistical analyses used to study aging populations and uses—but also criticizes—traditional demographic and socioeconomic methods to research this population in the Latin American region. She addresses the intersection of aging with human rights developments and how this influences the relationship between the citizen and the state.

1568 Dobinger-Álvarez Quioto, Josefina. Recordar para volver al corazón: el cuerpo, territorio de sentido y resistencia. Tegucigalpa: Editorial Guaymuras: MUA, Mujeres en las Artes Leticia de Oyuela: COSUDE, Agencia Suiza para el Desarrollo y la Cooperación, 2017. 272 p.: bibl., ill. (chiefly color).

This book combines poems, brief chapters, art pieces, and photography related to reflections of the body, through the positionality of the author who identifies as a Black Garifuna woman. The book critiques the way that culture is handled in Honduras, and explores how culture has flourished in certain spaces, like MUA (Mujeres en las Artes), an institution that the author helped fund. The author highlights the role of women in art in Honduras, and the connections among social conditions, politics, culture, and the artist's personal life.

1569 El Salvador en construcción. Coordinación de Carolina Ávalos Burgos. San Salvador: Istmo Editores, 2017. 354 p.: bibl., ill., maps. (Colección Perfiles)

Scholars contributing to this collection have a personal and intellectual investment in discussing how El Salvador can develop into a democracy and progress economically and socially. The eight chapters discuss various processes of development in postwar El Salvador through a global and interdisciplinary analysis. The topics range from economic transformation to culture and philosophy. The aim is not to provide definitive answers, but to give Salvadoran citizens guidelines with which to reflect on change, which can eventually lead to action.

1570 Empleo y desigualdad en Centroamérica. Textos de Rocío Elizabeth Maldonado Tomás et al. Prólogo de Dídimo Castillo Fernández. Buenos Aires: CLACSO, 2018. 163 p.: bibl., ill. (Colección Estudios sobre desigualdades) (Colección Becas de investigación)

Employment and inequality in Guatemala, El Salvador, and Honduras are examined in depth in this collection. It contains theoretical debates on labor and social inequalities in relation to specific economic models institutionalized in Central America. Case studies by country include: employment accessibility for Guatemalan rural youth, minimum wage inequality in El Salvador, labor and social rights following the Guatemalan Peace Accords, and the degradation of salaried employment for Honduran youth. This compilation ultimately underlines how neoliberal policies contribute to making labor conditions more precarious.

1571 Entre dos fuegos: naturalización e invisibilidad de la violencia de género contra migrantes en territorio mexicano. Coordinación de Hiroko Asakura y Marta W. Torres Falcón. Ciudad de México: CIESAS: Universidad Autónoma Metropolitana, Azcapotzalco, 2019. 365 p.: bibl., ill. (some color). (Publicaciones de la Casa Chata)

This book, divided into eight chapters, delves into gender violence within the migration process. The topics range from strategies of survival, sexual violence, and processes of criminalization of migrant women. The authors deploy a range of methodologies and theoretical frameworks. Ultimately, the authors aim to contribute to novel academic debates and new forms of analysis.

1572 Flores, Carlos Y. El caso por genocidio de Ríos Montt y la elaboración cultural del terror entre los Q'eqchi' de

Guatemala. (*Investig. Soc./San Marcos*, 20:36, enero/junio 2016, p. 261–274, bibl.)

The author explores the construction and disputes over historical memory related to war crimes and genocide experienced by Maya-Q'eqchi' communities in Alta, Verapaz, Guatemala. The focus is on how the traumas of social violence have distorted this community's spiritual beliefs in the absence of cultural mechanisms to confront their harrowing past. General Efraín Ríos Montt's systematic campaign of military violence and his religious discourse and criminalization of counterinsurgency complicated the ability of Q'eqchi' communities to remain unified. Ultimately, they undergo a process of social and cultural reconstruction to counter narratives promoted by Guatemala's military dictatorships.

1573 **Flórez-Estrada, María.** La notable maternidad de Luis Gerardo Mairena. Costa Rica: Editorial UCR, 2017. 193 p.: bibl. (Colección Identidad cultural)

This book focuses on transgender adoptive parenting within the heteronormative, neoliberal Costa Rican culture by exploring the case of Luis Gerardo Mairena and her adoptive son. The author relies on an ethnographic survey and utilizes a queer framework to examine Costa Rican research on the family, modern maternity, national identity, and transgenderism. Flórez-Estrada seeks to understand how a socially conservative country's legal system ruled in favor of providing custody rights to a transgender citizen over a child's biological mother. This case study shows how transgender parenting defies gender relations dictated by neoliberalism.

1574 **Fontes, Anthony W.** and **Kevin L. O'Neill.** La visita: prisons and survival in Guatemala. (*J. Lat. Am. Stud.*, 51:1, Feb. 2019, p. 85–107, table)

Survival in Guatemalan prisons is analyzed through 15 years of ethnographic research that explores the interdependencies between male prisoners, female visitors, and the carceral system. The authors give attention to male prisoners' visitation privileges to reveal how women's labor triages the role and responsibility of the state. The authors explore the emotional complexities of prison survival through the lived experience of one relationship. By focusing on affection, readers learn how interpersonal relationships can organize prison spaces, sustain drug economies, and subjugate women to state policies that reproduce gendered prejudices.

1575 **García Aguilar, María del Carmen.** Violencia y globalización: reflexiones marginales desde el sur de México y Centroamérica. Ciudad de México: Universidad de Ciencias y Artes de Chiapas, Centro de Estudios Superiores de México y Centroamérica: Juan Pablos Editor, 2019. 249 p.: bibl.

This book asks the question, what is violence? And what is our perspective when considering violence? These questions animate a phenomenological study of thought and history. The book covers violence and philosophy and brings together reflections by Walter Benjamin, Jacques Derrida, and Hannah Arendt. It compares violence in the 20th and 21st centuries through a sociological lens and then focuses on violence south of the Mexican border. It includes an examination of violence against migrants traveling through Mexico to the US.

1576 **Heidbrink, Lauren.** Migranthood: youth in a new era of deportation. Stanford, California: Stanford University Press, 2020. 213 p.: bibl., ill., maps.

Through ethnographic research, Heidbrink examines the experiences of Indigenous migrant youth in various places, such as their homelands in Guatemala, zones of transit, and detention centers in Guatemala, Mexico, and the US. Despite their hardships, Heidbrink argues that migrant youth are able to draw on social, cultural, and political resources to navigate precarity and marginality. By focusing on the youth, she underscores the youth's role as contributors to household economies, local social practices, and global processes. The author observes that migrant management, called "development," only entraps young migrants.

1577 **Heyman, Josiah; Jeremy Slack;** and **Emily Guerra.** Bordering a "crisis": Central American asylum seekers and the reproduction of dominant border enforcement practices. (*J. Southwest*, 60:4, Winter 2018, p. 754–786, bibl.)

Given drastic declines in border apprehensions, why has border immigration enforcement increased (not declined)? The authors explore various themes, including contention around Central American migration, the political construction of the border "crisis," and the symbolic and material saliency of the US-Mexico border in immigration debates. They examine actors on all sides, pro- and anti-immigration, and Central American actors as well, and argue that understanding processes of contestation and crisis is essential to understanding how the Trump administration was able to mobilize mass support for its anti-immigration platform.

1578 Ibarra Chávez, Héctor Angel. En busca del Reino de Dios en la tierra: la teología de la liberación durante la revolución salvadoreña. San Salvador: Secretaria de Cultura de la Presidencia, Dirección de Publicaciones e Impresos (dpi), 2016. 212 p.: bibl., ill., maps. (Colección unámonos para crecer; 3)

This book narrates the historical background of Liberation Theology in El Salvador. In collaboration with the government, the objective is to reveal the role of progressive Christians and Catholics in the Salvadoran civil war. A close analysis of different Christian beliefs, such as the concept of the Kingdom of God, is used to evaluate how these beliefs motivated religious community members to become involved in this conflict. It is based on a series of interviews with members of religious and political communities that supported revolutionary forces.

1579 La inolvidable edad: jóvenes en la Costa Rica del siglo XX. Edición de Iván Molina Jiménez y David Díaz Arias. Heredia, Costa Rica: EUNA, 2018. 238 p.: bibl., ill., index.

Based on a collaborative project, this volume explores the role of youth in Costa Rican history. This study takes a historical approach to exploring the lives of Costa Rican youth as students, including during historical events, such as efforts to gain admittance to public colleges and street protests against Alcoa (Aluminum Company of America). The six chapters are organized chronologically through the 20th century.

1580 Izcara Palacios, Simón Pedro and Karla Lorena Andrade Rubio. Migrantes centroamericanas transportadas por redes de tráfico sexual. Ciudad de México: Editorial Fontamara, 2018. 129 p.: bibl. (Argumentos; 467)

Based on qualitative data, this book examines how sex trafficking networks operate in the North American region and analyzes the strategies used to recruit Central American women who migrate to Mexico and the US. The work provides an introduction to the ongoing debate on women's rights in the context of legal and illegal sex work and the commercialization of sex trafficking in a globalizing world. The authors discuss the difficulties in accessing this population of migrant women and argue that sex trafficking is becoming feminized. Women experience precarious labor conditions, but also challenge traditional assumptions about trafficker behavior.

Juárez Rodríguez, Ángel Adalberto. La fe cristiana como fuerza de liberación histórica en El Salvador. See *HLAS 76:518*.

1581 Lara Martínez, Carlos Benjamín. Memoria histórica del movimiento campesino de Chalatenango. San Salvador: UCA Editores, 2018. 536 p.: bibl., ill. (Colección Estructuras y procesos; 50)

Through ethnographic fieldwork, the author explores the historical memory of communities in Chalatenango, specifically Guarjila and Los Ranchos. The book combines memory, discourse analysis, and history, with the aim of understanding how residents understood and continue to understand the Salvadoran armed conflict. Through analysis of collective memory and "academic" memory, a better understanding of the conflict can be gained. This book is useful as a pedagogical tool for a holistic anthropology that aims to understand the humanity of the communities being investigated.

1582 Lovato, Roberto. Unforgetting: a memoir of family, migration, gangs, and revolution in the Americas. New York, NY: Harper, an imprint of HarperCollinsPublishers, 2020. 325 p.: bibl.

Through reporting on gang life, state violence, and US-bound Salvadoran migration, Lovato weaves the personal and political as the child of Salvadoran immigrants. He explores the history of his father, who grew up in El Salvador during a period of intense political conflict, and the effects it had on him as a child. Lovato covers multiple perspectives: as a child of immigrants growing up around gangs in San Francisco, as a guerilla fighter in El Salvador fighting against the US-backed fascist military government, and as a journalist when he returns to the US.

1583 Martínez, Edin. Barrios: una mirada desde la ciudad profunda. Prólogo de Enrique Ortiz Flores. El Salvador: KFW, 2016. 322 p.: bibl., ill. (some color).

This book takes an urban-sociological approach to documenting the history of poor neighborhoods in El Salvador. The author directed the Salvadoran Foundation for Development and Basic Housing (FUNDASAL), where he obtained the data for this study. Martínez compares the experiences of participating families in various programs and the social and technical proposals designed to overcome poverty. To improve the lives of the poor, the author contends that government policies will only be effective if they steer away from traditional approaches to resolving housing inequality and begin engaging deeply with communities.

1584 Molenaar, Fransje. Power shortcircuited: social movement organisation under cartel rule in rural Guatemala. (*J. Lat. Am. Stud.*, 49:4, Nov. 2017, p. 829–854)

This article examines the effects that diffuse licit and illicit power structures have on Guatemalan citizens, specifically the tension between a cartel and the FRENA (People's Rights and Natural Resources Defense Front), the Guatemalan electricity movement. The article presents Guatemala as a fragmented sovereign state, where the state's authority does not have legitimate political power, and is instead ineffectual, or collaborates with organized crime networks, undermining the state's legitimacy. For political science specialist's comment, see *HLAS 75:958*.

1585 Mora-García, Claudio A. Can benefits from malaria eradication be increased?: evidence from Costa Rica. (*Econ. Dev. Cult. Change*, 66:3, April 2018, p. 585–628, appendix, bibl., graphs, tables)

This study explores the causal effects that early-life exposure to malaria during periods of eradication propagation had on adults' years of education and wages. Based on government archives and historical records, the author contextualizes the impact that malaria had throughout Costa Rica and evaluates the results of malaria eradication campaigns in the late 1940s and early 1970s. School conditions and the child labor market affected malaria prevalence. Ultimately, policies designed to eliminate children's employment can contribute to eradicating malaria.

1586 Moreno Hernández, Hugo César and Mónica Elivier Sánchez González. Homies Unidos: estrategias de reestratificación desde la sociedad civil. Ciudad de México: Universidad Iberoamericana, 2018. 295 p.: bibl.

This book explores the conditions that stratified Salvadoran street gangs in the 1990s and 2000s. This ethnography focuses on Homies Unidos El Salvador, an organization composed of gang members no longer active, and their testimonies introduce radical approaches to analyzing the gang phenomenon. Theoretical frameworks discussing systems theory, self-intervention, and social stratification are used to assess the gangs' social impact. Advocacy efforts push society to recognize gang members' right to participate in society.

1587 Mujeres, migración centroamericana y violencia: un diagnóstico para el caso de Puebla. Coordinación de Almudena Cortés y Josefina Manjarrez. Puebla, Mexico: Benemérita Universidad Autónoma de Puebla, Facultad de Filosofía y Letras, 2017. 94 p.: bibl., ill. (some color), color maps.

This collaborative project employs a feminist lens to examine Central American women migrants' experiences as they travel through the state of Puebla in Mexico, a key point in this migration corridor. This study argues that even though the state of Mexico and the Puebla government have implemented policies aimed at eradicating violence against women, lack of effective application, resources, interest, and corruption have meant that women migrants continue to suffer violence as they travel through Mexico.

1588 Neumann, Pamela J. Transnational governance, local politics, and gender violence law in Nicaragua. (*Lat. Am. Polit. Soc.*, 60:2, Summer 2018, p. 61–82, bibl., tables)

Neumann provides a legal and political history of gender-based violence laws in Nicaragua with a focus on Law 779. Initially celebrated as progressive legislation, the law was subject to swift legislative backlash. This analysis questions state legitimacy and the limitations of transnational governance when addressing violence against women. Based on ethnographic data from June 2012 and December 2014, newspaper articles, and government records, Neumann details the configurations of power in the country that derailed Nicaraguan women's right to lives free of violence.

1589 Orellana Peña, Jorge Humberto. Cultura silenciosa: creencias, costumbres y tradiciones como expresiones de identidad cultural en la región occidental de Honduras. Tegucigalpa: Editorial Universitaria, 2017. 178 p.: bibl. (Colección Raíces)

This book explores cultural expressions, beliefs, customs, and traditions that remain a part of the collective imaginary in communities in the western part of Honduras. Orellana utilizes the concepts of coloniality of power, knowing, and being to delve into community change over time. The book is divided into four chapters starting with context about the region and ending with an overiew of studies—interviews, short stories, testimonies, and anecdotes—on beliefs, customs, and traditions.

1590 Palma Campos, Claudia. Me puse a jugar de narco: mujeres, tráfico de drogas y cárcel en Costa Rica. Ciudad Universitaria Rodrigo Facio, Costa Rica: Editorial UCR, 2018. 311 p.: bibl., color ill., maps.

This book focuses on how the drug trade has impacted Costa Rican women and their representation in the country's prison system. The author provides historical and sociocultural context to understand narcotrafficking and maps the sociology of drug-related crimes. The author uses intersectional analytic methods drawn from feminist theories to place the lived experiences of incarcerated Costa Rican women in sociological, political, and economic contexts. The focus is not simply on women jailed for this crime, but rather on their experiences with the drug-related offenses that resulted in their incarceration.

1591 Picardo Joao, Óscar and Suyapa Padilla. Educación y violencia, una mirada a las escuelas de El Salvador y Honduras: las perspectivas sobre clima escolar, resiliencia y aulas disruptivas. San Salvador: UFG, 2017. 191 p.: bibl., ill.

This study explores school climate, student resilience, and classroom disruption in disadvantaged schools that are plagued by violence in El Salvador and Honduras. The authors review social theories with the goal of developing practices that improve the quality of student life. They also provide a demographic profile of the two countries complemented with empirical data gathered from schools they observed in both sites. Student behavior and students' family background are evaluated to measure the influence personal dynamics have on their academic performance.

1592 Posas, Mario. Las luchas de los trabajadores hondureños organizados (1880–1993). Tegucigalpa: Editorial Universitaria, Universidad Nacional Autónoma de Honduras, 2017. 523 p.: bibl. (Colección Sociedad y pensamiento)

This study focuses on the role of workers and labor movements in Honduras from 1880 to 1993. It focuses on export sector workers, miners, and banana workers and their impact on the economic, social, and political history of Honduras. The book is divided into 11 chapters, each focusing on different themes and time periods, ranging from the appearance of the working class to the impact of unions on social reforms. The author argues that the working class has had a defining role in Honduran social and political life.

1593 **Procesos migratorios en la Centroamérica del siglo XXI.** Coordinación de Nayar López Castellanos. Ciudad de México: La Biblioteca: UNAM, Facultad de Ciencias Políticas y Sociales, 2018. 215 p.: bibl., ill.

This book is a multidisciplinary effort by several established researchers with two key objectives: first, to contribute to the recovery of the Central American region within Latin American studies; and second, to analyze the complex migration patterns that disrupt society, the economy, and politics in the region. The authors analyze migration in the context of neoliberal capitalism with chapters on violence, humanitarian crises, and women's experiences.

Raventós Vorst, Ciska. Mi corazón dice no: el movimiento de oposición al TLC en Costa Rica. See item **860**.

1594 **Reséndiz Rivera, Nelly Erandy.** Violento luego existo: pandillas y maras en Guatemala. Ciudad de México: UNAM, Centro de Investigaciones sobre América Latina y el Caribe, 2018. 224 p.: bibl., ill., map.

The author analyzes gang violence in Guatemala in the contexts of Barrio 18 and Mara Salvatrucha, as "necro-empowered" groups. The author starts out with a historical analysis of the Guatemalan civil war to show how it created a culture of political violence that continues today. The author also conducted an ethnography in Guatemalan prisons with officials and active and non-active gang members to present identities and lived experiences that shape violent actions. Gang networks dominate the realities where structural violence is materialized, and the absence of institutional strategies will only prolong their existence.

1595 **Rocha, José Luis.** La desobediencia de las masas: la migración no autorizada de centroamericanos a Estados Unidos como desobediencia civil. San Salvador: UCA Editores, 2017. 367 p.: bibl., ill. (Colección Estructuras y Procesos; 44)

This work, based on engaged ethnographic research, offers a different lens through which to view migration. The author does not want to dismiss or belittle the impact of ever-present immigration policies but seeks to highlight the power that migrants hold. The author then invites us to view migrants as political actors, as workers who refuse to be passive victims and who exert civil disobedience. In doing so, Rocha contributes to theories of citizenship, membership, and undocumented migration in the US.

Solís Avendaño, Manuel Antonio. Costa Rica: la democracia de las razones débiles (y los pasajes ocultos). See item **861**.

1596 **Stocker, Karen.** Millennial movements: positive social change in urban Costa Rica. Toronto, Canada; Buffalo, N.Y.; London: University of Toronto Press, 2020. 123 p.: bibl., color ill., index. (Teaching culture: ethnographies for the classroom)

Through ethnographic research, particularly participant observation and interviews, this research delves into social movements led by the youth in Costa Rica in recent years. The author notes that these social movements differ from those of the 1980s, in their positive, solution-oriented attitude and willingness to work with people from various backgrounds. Each chapter in the book addresses a different social movement, including environmental sustainability, freedom from sexual assault, food security, LGBTQ+ rights, and more. It is a resource for activists and non-activists alike.

1597 **Undocumented and unaccompanied: children of migration in the European Union and the United States.** Edited by Cecilia Menjívar and Krista Perreira. Abingdon, England; New York, N.Y.: Routledge, 2022. 155 p.: bibl., ill., index. (Research in ethnic and migration studies)

This book examines contexts that minors encounter when they migrate alone to the US and the EU. Originally published in the *Journal of Ethnic and Migration Studies*, this collection highlights the common vulnerabilities of minors and the challenges that governments face when developing policy responses. Relying on various methods and disciplinary angles, they interrogate the legal and ethical frameworks used to understand minors.

1598 Valdéz Rodas, Julio Alejandro. Entre monólogos y sorderas: las paradojas del multiculturalismo y el discurso etnicista en Guatemala. Prólogo de David Stoll. Guatemala: Litografía Mercurio, 2018. 150 p.: bibl.

The years after the Guatemalan Peace Accords in 1996 gave way to new discourses. Composed of eight chapters, this book aims to encourage conversations around multiculturalism and ethnic identity in Guatemala. The author attempts to break down binaries common in Western discourse, such as man and woman, Indigenous and Ladino, the proletariat and capitalist, which he argues are not reflective of reality. The book can be read in any order and chapters range from topics such as the Left in Guatemala, Indigenous and Maya peoples, and linguistic diversity.

1599 Valdéz Rodas, Julio Alejandro. Los Talibanes del trópico: el fundamentalismo cristiano en el conflicto armado centroamericano. Guatemala: Julio Alejandro Valdez Rodas, Litografía Mercurio, 2018. 154 p.: bibl.

The author narrates the Guatemalan civil war from a religious perspective. Valdéz Rodas acknowledges that there is no fundamental relation between Afghanistan's Taliban's movement and Guatemala's evangelical leadership other than their similar ultraconservative religious and political opposition to communism during the late 1980s and early 1990s. The author provides an historical background for these two religion-based movements and explains how the religious left took up arms and how this militant shift took place through covert action, poetry, and music.

1600 Vargas Morúa, Elizarda and María Martha Durán Rodríguez. Bullying en Costa Rica: consideraciones generales, legislación y jurisprudencia. San José: EUNED, 2017. 70 p.: bibl., ill. (Colección Ágora. Serie Cuadernos; 14)

This study provides a holistic overview of this form of school violence for families, students, and education and other professionals who deal with bullying issues. It differentiates the various forms of bullying and provides recommendations for detection, prevention, and intervention. It discusses which type of bullying is considered a crime under Costa Rican law. The authors' legal and psychological backgrounds help them define the responsibilities of the state and society in designing integrated solutions to improve students' quality of life.

1601 Vidas sitiadas: jóvenes, exclusión laboral y violencia urbana en Centroamérica. Edición de Juan Pablo Pérez Sáinz. San José: Facultad Latinoamericana de Ciencias Sociales (FLACSO), Sede Académica Costa Rica, 2018. 238 p.: bibl., ill., graphs.

This volume contains five papers that evaluate the difficulties Costa Rican and Salvadoran youth face in the labor market in poor urban communities. Based on surveys, the author details the sociodemographic characteristics of select neighborhoods to illustrate that youth's lives are besieged by gang violence. To estimate the magnitude of labor exclusion, the author examines risk assessments to better determine existing vulnerabilities. Findings challenge existing strategies that promote inclusive economic opportunities by uplifting the desires and hopes of marginalized youth seeking social mobility.

Weston, Gavin Michael. Guatemalan vigilantism and the global (re)production of collective violence: a tale of two lynchings. See item **900**.

1602 Xiap Riscajché, Rosa Liberta. Identidades y relaciones de género, clase y etnia en Almolonga, comunidad Maya K'iche' de Guatemala. Chiapas, Mexico: Universidad de Ciencias y Artes de Chiapas, Centro de Estudios Superiores de México y Centroamérica, 2018. 337 p.: bibl. (Colección Thesis; 8)

This book explores ethnic identity, gender, and class in the Maya K'iché community of Almolonga in Guatemala.

Through historical analysis, gender theory, cultural control theory, and intersectionality with a decolonial focus, Xiap Riscajché explores ethnic identity, collective construction of class, and exclusion of outsiders in Almolonga. The book reflects the work of a politically engaged Indigenous scholar who discusses issues that Indigenous identity and culture face against the threats of neoliberal capitalism, which affects everyone.

1603 **Zepeda, Beatriz; Matilde González-Izás;** and **Carmen Rosa de León-Escribano.** Guatemala: fronteras y mercados ilegales en la era de la globalización. Ciudad de Guatemala: FLACSO Guatemala; Quito: FLACSO Ecuador; Ottawa, Canada: IDRC-CRDI, 2018. 364 p.: bibl., ill., maps. (Fronteras; 6)

This book, sponsored by FLACSO, is part of a regional project on the global political economy of violence along various border regions. The focus is on how the territorial dimension of illicit markets reshapes the physiognomy of a border. It includes case studies of the Guatemala-Mexico border, northern Central America, and the Pacific Coast, which highlight historical context and give an overview of sociodemographic factors for each region. As communities adapt to new landscape dynamics for survival, so does the illicit trade of drugs, humans, and arms.

THE CARIBBEAN

LUIS GALANES VALLDEJULI, *Professor of Anthropology, University of Puerto Rico at Cayey*

AMONG THE 36 TEXTS selected for review in *HLAS* 77 for the period 2015–2020, there is one that deserves special mention: *Saamaka Dreaming* (item **1635**), in which renowned Caribbean anthropologists Richard and Sally Price revisit field notes and diaries from their joint Saamaka fieldwork from 1966–86. They retell their experiences in autobiographical format, revealing details of daily life that are often left out of formal ethnographic texts. The publication is an incredible story, marvelously told, of the experiences of two white North American anthropologists doing research in a Black maroon community deep within the South American jungle, a place typically prohibited to whites, in a country immersed in civil war. They become absorbed in an intense ritual-driven life consisting of daily, hours-long drum-beating ceremonies of possessions, divinations, consultations with oracles, etc., and adhering to strict rules for women during their menstrual periods. The text invites reflection on the hardships, obstacles, dangers, and contradictions of conducting ethnographic fieldwork. The authors conclude that, if the Saamaka they encountered in 1966 resembled a "dreamworld," the reality of that same territory today "most closely resembles a nightmare."

Race, as demonstrated by *Saamaka Dreaming*, has for many years been a staple topic in Caribbean sociological and anthropological literature, and is certainly the most significant topic within the literature reviewed here. Seven of the works reviewed for *HLAS* 77 explore topics related to race and racial identity. Interestingly, the seven publications come from two easily demarcated and identifiable Caribbean regions: Puerto Rico and the Anglophone Caribbean.

Four studies of race in Puerto Rico are concerned with the cultural practice of *blanqueamiento* or whitening. Hilda Lloréns' "Beyond *Blanqueamiento*" (item **1627**), for example, invites us to go beyond an understanding of *blanqueamiento* as a mere racist ideology or identity complex, and instead, following the work of James Scott, to view it as an "everyday form of resistance" played out in a highly contested terrain, where "whiteness" is "sometimes affirmed, other times denied," but never fully internalized. Sherina Feliciano-Santos (item **1618**) documents a similar ambivalence in her research on Indigenous identity among Puerto Ricans. While claims to Indigenous identities in Puerto Rico have been broadly conceived as related to *blanqueamiento* practices—or, more precisely, as a mechanism for disguising African heritage—the ambivalent and heterogeneous linguistic usages and meanings that Puerto Rican neo-Tainos attribute to the term "Indian" give way to a conception of Indianness that is fluid and negotiable, and defies monolithic representations. The concern with race and *blanqueamiento* is present once again in Rafael Ocasio's *Race and Nation in Puerto Rican Folklore* (item **1631**), which documents the ethnographic work conducted by anthropologists Franz Boas and John Alden Mason in Puerto Rico in the 1910s. The author questions why valuable information collected by Mason among Afro-Puerto Ricans from Loiza in the 1910s, including evidence of the survival of a "Congolese" language and vocabulary, was never published; he condemns the tendency among early American anthropologists to become complicit with the process of "whitening" the Puerto Rican population by emphasizing and publishing only their work on Jibaro heritage and identity.

While the concern with race and identity seems to be equally prominent in the context of the Anglophone Caribbean, the theorization about race in this region takes a different turn. Anglo-Caribbean writers are less interested in *blanqueamiento* practices than in exploring the problematic dimensions of constructing an Afro-Antillean identity after the shattering experience of slavery and forced removal from the motherland. In Rhonda Cobham-Sander's *I and I* (item **1612**), for example, the problematic aspect of Afro-Caribbean identity results from its dependence on a white referent (I as opposed to the Other). This is in contrast with white identity, which takes its own world as its sole reference (I and I). This situation becomes problematic insofar as it condemns Afro-Caribbean subjects to see themselves through the "autoscopic" lens of the white other, a mere derivate reflection or mirror image of the white gaze. G.A.E. Griffin (item **1620**) and Kevin Adonis Browne (item **1608**) further delve into the use of literature and photography, respectively, as mechanisms for transcending the white gaze. Employing Derek Walcott's metaphor of Afro-Caribbean identity as a broken vase whose scattered pieces cannot be put back together again, both of these authors suggest that Afro-Caribbean subjects are nonetheless capable of looking at the pieces and recognizing that an intact vase once existed, and that an identity can be constructed based on such certainty.

Afro-Caribbean syncretic religion, particularly santería, also proved to be a salient topic among the texts reviewed in this volume. Both N. Fadeke Castor (item **1611**) and Krista L. Cortes (item **1614**), for example, document the uses of santería in Trinidad and Puerto Rico, respectively, as a political act meant to vindicate an African heritage. Cortes further documents the emergence of a "light" (lite) version of santería, practiced mostly by Puerto Rican women, where the vindication of Blackness is achieved without needing to submit to the burdensome ritual life demanded by more formal santería practitioners, thus making santería compatible with their modern lifestyles. Clemente Hugo Ramírez Frías (item **1636**) documents the effects of a religious awakening or santería boom in Cuba, where religious tourists have transformed La Habana into "the Rome of santería." Collectively, these texts document the transformations of Afro-Caribbean religions within the Caribbean region and beyond.

Migration and migrants are a significant topic in the literature, with six of the reviewed texts devoted to this theme from a multiplicity of perspectives. Several of the authors show a particular interest in the phenomenon of post-national identity among diasporic Caribbean communities in the US and Europe, including Cubans living in the US mainland (item **1622**), Jamaicans and Haitians in England and France (item **1610**), and Puerto Ricans in Orlando (item **1616**). All these communities create long-distance affective ties with the countries of their forefathers, even when they left long ago, and even among second- and third-generation migrants who have never set foot on ancestral lands.

Focusing instead on migration patterns within the Caribbean region, Orlando Inoa's outstanding work *Trabajadores inmigrantes en República Dominicana* (item **1623**) documents the ethnic and racial groups that migrated to the Dominican Republic throughout its republican history, from 1844 to the present. Special attention is devoted to the migration of Black "cocolos" from the Caribbean Windward Islands from 1870 to 1933. The book reminds us that the mobility of peoples within the insular Caribbean has historically been far greater and much more fluid than is commonly assumed.

While studies based on women and gender were not numerous, two of the texts reviewed for *HLAS 77* deserve mention. Lorraine Bayard de Volo's *Women and the Cuban Insurrection* (item **1607**) challenges common misconceptions of the 1959 Cuban revolutionary movement as excessively masculinized, led by bearded macho men. Instead, the author engages in a retelling of the Cuban Revolution from the perspective of women, documenting not only the active participation of women in the revolutionary activities since 1953, but also the intentional utilization by the revolutionary forces of gendered roles as a "tactic of war" in the parallel struggle for hearts and minds. In Luis Galanes Valldejuli and Otomie Vale Nieves' "Feminism and Difference" (item **1619**), the topic of women's activism within a militarized context is again explored. Drawing on ethnographic data collected in the Puerto Rican island-municipality of Vieques, the authors argue that the departure of the US navy from the island in 2003, after more than 60 years of presence, provoked a shift in the gender of civic leaders from male to female. As the tasks required from civic leaders shifted from physical confrontation during the navy occupation period, to taking care of the sick and decontamination of the island during the post-US navy period, the leadership positions in civic organizations evidenced a radical shift from men to women, each obeying norms and expectations traditional of their respective genders.

While the topic of poverty was not salient for the Caribbean region in general, it did become a topic of heated discussion in the context of Cuba. Both Ángela I. Peña Farias' *Regímenes de bienestar y pobreza familiar en Cuba* (item **1633**) and Katrin Hansing and Bert Hoffmann's "When Racial Inequalities Return" (item **1621**) document rising levels of poverty and class differentiation in Cuba in the context of deteriorating economic conditions after the collapse of the Soviet Union in 1990s. Both authors also reveal the unequal distribution of wealth and poverty along racial lines, with Black Cubans being the most negatively impacted sector. This is a topic that has traditionally received little attention in Cuba, primarily because within the Cuban socialist model there is no sector of the population officially categorized as "lower class" or "poor," thus making the problem invisible and ignored.

1604 Aboy Domingo, Nelson. Orígenes de la Santería cubana: transculturación e identidad cultural. La Habana: Editorial de Ciencias Sociales, 2016. 325 p.: bibl., ill. (Colección Echú Bi)

The author traces the historical roots of contemporary Afro-Cuban santería to two separate major spiritual systems that originated in medieval Africa: the cult of the Orishas and the cult of Ifá; and further documents their syncretic union after their arrival on Cuban soil, giving birth to santería. The author suggests that the insularity of the small Caribbean island probably helped preserve the original medieval versions of the rites, divinations, and oracular consultations of the two spiritual systems, maintaining their immunity from changes witnessed by these spiritual systems in their African context where the two are still practiced.

1605 Allen, Reuben. Investigating the cultural conception of race in Puerto Rico: residents' thoughts on the U.S. Census, discrimination, and interventionist policies. (*Lat. Am. Caribb. Ethn. Stud.*, 12:3, Nov. 2017, p. 201–226, bibl., tables)

Based on 31 in-depth semistructured interviews conducted with island-based Puerto Ricans in 2013, and using an ingenious combination of qualitative and quantitative methodological approaches, this paper attempts to arrive at a Puerto Rican "emic understanding" of race and racial classification systems and their interpretation of the racial categories that appear in the US Census. The paper reveals that a majority of Puerto Ricans reject racial categories imported from the US, and instead express a preference for an alternative system that incorporates intermediary admixture categories.

1606 Alverio Ramos, Zulmarie. La gran ausente: la maestra Celestina Cordero Molina. Segunda edición revisada y aumentada. Hato Rey, Puerto Rico: EDP University, 2015. 126 p.: bibl.

This book pays homage to the life and work of 19th-century Afro-Puerto Rican schoolteacher Celestina Cordero (1787–1862), sister of the also renowned schoolteacher Rafael Cordero. While brother and sister were equally active and committed to providing and promoting the education of poor children, it is only the brother who has been widely remembered, immortalized by renowned 19th-century Puerto Rican painter Francisco Oller in his painting "Maestro Cordero's School" (c. 1890). Celestina, on the other hand, has been systematically excluded from history books, becoming thus one among a relatively long list of Black women whose voice has been silenced. The book both celebrates Celestina's life and critiques the society that condemned her to anonymity.

Antología del pensamiento crítico caribeño contemporáneo: West Indies, Antillas Francesas y Antillas Holandesas. See *HLAS* 76:2252.

1607 Bayard de Volo, Lorraine. Women and the Cuban insurrection: how gender shaped Castro's victory. New York, N.Y.: Cambridge University Press, 2018. 272 p.: bibl., index.

Based on archival research of Cuban sources, this book has two major objectives: first, excavating and documenting the role played by women in the Cuban Revolution during the 1953–1960 period; second, showing the way gender was employed by the revolutionary movement as a "tactic of war," always including women in high-level positions within the rebel's circle, and strategically injecting a humanizing feminine dimension to the rebel movement. These strategies of inclusion may have been low-key, but they were vital to the movement. This retelling of the Cuban Revolution from the women's perspective serves to correct traditional misconceptions of the revolution as excessively masculinized, led by armed bearded macho men.

1608 Browne, Kevin Adonis. High Mas: carnival and the poetics of Caribbean photography. Jackson: University Press of Mississippi, 2018. 245 p.: bibl., ill., index.

This is a book of photography of Trinidad's carnival or, more specifically, of the central disguised characters of Mas and Carnival, including blue devils, la *diablesse*, moko jumbies, and others. The author's extended commentaries propose a poetics of Caribbean carnival where the production of beauty is interpreted as a response to suffering and to "the violence that brought us here." Employing Derek Walcott's metaphor of the Caribbean subject as a broken vase, whose scattered pieces cannot be put back together again, the author views photographs as one among the "pieces" of this broken vase. In this sense, they are meant to capture the "beauty [that is] filtered through the chambers of our infinite suffering."

1609 Byrd, Brandon R. The Black Republic: African Americans and the fate of Haiti. Philadelphia: University of Pennsylvania Press, 2020. 297 p.: bibl., ill., index. (America in the nineteenth century.)

The book explores the ideas held by African American in general, and African American intellectuals in particular, about Haiti and the Haitian experience during the post-emancipation period, 1860s-1930s. For most African American intellectuals of the period, including Monroe Work, William Pickens, and W.E.B. DuBois, it was imperative that Haiti succeed as an independent nation, as a form of corroboration of the capacity of Black people for self-governance. Moreover, for these African-American intellectuals, the success of Haiti was only possible through a process of "racial uplifting," under which the brightest of the Haitian Blacks would need to undergo formal education and be imbued with US middle-class cultural norms, thus giving birth to a New Negro: the *fin de siècle* Renaissance Negro. African-American intellectuals of the period saw it as their moral duty—the "Black man's burden"—to aid Haiti in the process of racial uplifting, ensuring in this way the political success of the country.

Cadichon, Jeff Matherson. Narrations du sensible: récits post-traumatiques de survivants du séisme du 12 janvier 2010 en Haïti. See item **438**.

1610 Casseus, Clara Rachel Eybalin. Geopolitics of memory and transnational citizenship: thinking local development in a Global South. New York, N.Y.: Peter Lang, 2019. 245 p.: bibl., ill., index, map. (Cultural memories; 9)

This book explores the phenomenon of "transnational citizenship" among Jamaican and Haitian migrants in France and England. Different from the classical meaning of citizenship derived from the French republican model, and based exclusively on national origin, the phenomenon of transnational citizenship allows immigrants to develop long-distance affective ties with their ethnicity and country of origin, even if they left those countries a long time ago, and even among second- and third-generation migrants, some of whom have never set foot on their ancestral countries. Lastly, the author explores the possible role of these transnational citizens in fomenting development in the country of origin, by means of remittances and other forms of associative engagements and contributions.

1611 Castor, N. Fadeke. Spiritual citizenship: transnational pathways from Black power to Ifá in Trinidad. Durham, N.C.: Duke University Press, 2017. 228 p., 8 pages of plates: bibl., ill. (some color), index.

This book documents the development of the cult of Ifá and the cult of the Orishas in Trinidad, but goes beyond the local specificities of the Trinidadian case to reveal the existence of a globally connected "diasporic space" built around the practice of African and Afro-Caribbean syncretic religions, and that extends across the Caribbean to Central and South America, to their diasporic communities living in the US mainland, to the Nigerian Ilé-Ifá region, and further on to the afterworld of the ancestors. The inhabitants of this diasporic space are bound together by a shared "spiritual citizenship" and an allegiance to a "sacred praxis." Thus, in the present, becoming a practitioner of Afro-Caribbean religions is best understood as a political act, a mechanism for revindication of African heritage, and for the expression of solidarity with Black people's struggle against racism and oppression.

1612 Cobham-Sander, Rhonda. I and I: epitaphs for the self in the work of V.S. Naipaul, Kamau Brathwaite and Derek Walcott. Kingston: The University of West Indies Press, 2016. 302 p.: bibl., index.

Based on an exploration of selected works by canonical Caribbean writers V.S. Naipaul, Kamau Brathwaite, and Derek Walcott, the author documents and critically assesses their respective attempts to transcend the most problematic aspect of Caribbean identity, as originally posed by Frantz Fanon: namely, the fact that Black identity is necessarily dependent on its white referent (I and the Other), whereas white identity operates on its own, without the need of a racialized Other (I and I). The author argues that their privileged position within Western literary tradition, as well as their old age and proximity to death, enabled these three authors to fantasize about a Caribbean Black identity that takes its own world as its sole reference.

1613 Congreso de Afrodecendencia en Puerto Rico, 1st, San Juan, 2015. ¡Negro, negra!: memorias del Primer Congreso de Afrodescendencia en Puerto Rico. Compilación de Lester Nurse Allende. San Juan: Facultad de Estudios Generales, Universidad de Puerto Rico, Recinto de Río Piedras, 2018. 417 p.: bibl., ill.

The book gathers a collection of 33 essays delivered during the Primer Congreso de Afrodescendencia en Puerto Rico, which took place at the University of Puerto Rico's Río Piedras campus in November 2015. The essays cover a variety of topics, including Afro-Puerto Rican art, literature, architecture, and social movements. Two details make this edited text unique: first, the explicit declaration that the congreso was "organized by Afro-Puerto Ricans"; and second, the explicit concern with the absence of activism and involvement assumed by Afro-Puerto Ricans themselves in Black social movements.

1614 Cortes, Krista L. Brujería lite: centering Blackness-as-practice in everyday Afro-Puerto Rican spiritualities. *(Cent. J.*, 33:3, Fall 2021, p. 128–157, bibl., table)

This paper explores the increasing popularization of Afro-Caribbean syncretic religions, particularly santería and witchcraft *(brujería)*, as a mechanism for reclaiming an African identity among Puerto Rican women. Drawing inspiration from a multiplicity of female orishas of santería often portrayed as "badass brujas," including Oya, Oshun, or Yemaya, contemporary Puerto Rican Black women reclaim and reappropriate the *bruja* identity as an outward mechanism for the expression of their Blackness. Moreover, and because of the complex ritual life demanded from santería practitioners, these women often adopt simplified or "light" (lite) versions of these practices to make them compatible with their modern lifestyles.

1615 De Onis, Catalina M.; Hilda Lloréns; and **Ruth Santiago.** ¡Ustedes tienen que limpiar las cenizas e irse de Puerto Rico para siempre!: la lucha por la justicia ambiental, climática y energética como trasfondo del verano de Revolución Boricua 2019. Cabo Rojo, Puerto Rico: Editora Educación Emergente, 2020. 84 p.: bibl., ill.

The authors document the history of two major community-based ecological movements that took place in Puerto Rico in the past two decades: first, the social movement against a carbon power plant in the town of Guayama, commencing in 2002; second, the struggle for the creation of an energetically self-sufficient community, Pueblo Coquí, in the Salinas-Guayama area, commencing in 2014. In both cases, the authors argue, the movements revealed a new type of heterogeneous social activism and organization, carried out by a multiplicity of actors and coalitions that included, but were not limited to, ecologically based organizations. The authors argue that these two cases, among others, served as preamble to the also heterogenous "revolutionary" activism of the 2019 Ricky Renuncia movement that culminated with the pacific ousting of the then governor Ricardo Rosselló.

1616 Delerme, Simone Pierre. Latino Orlando: suburban transformation and racial conflict. Gainesville: University Press of Florida, 2019. 181 p.: bibl., index. (Southern dissent)

Based on ethnographic work conducted in 2010–2012, the book documents the cultural profile and racial conflicts of Puerto Rican migrants in the Greater Orlando Region, Florida. The author focuses specifically on island-Puerto Rican migrants who moved to Orlando during and after the 2008 economic crisis. Different from their pre-2008 counterparts, these post-2008 Puerto Rican migrants are well-educated professionals, exhibiting middle-class values and cultural tastes, and mostly identifying as white in the census. Their arrival upset traditional settlement patterns along class and race, insofar as the post-2008 migrants increasingly seek housing in neighborhoods historically occupied by non-Latino whites, who in turn consider their new neighbors non-white. Post-2008 Puerto Rican migrants, on the contrary, reject the Southern-based, binary Black-and-white racial ideology dominant in their host community, and replace race categories with national origin as their preferred mode of self-identification.

1617 Encuentro Conjunciones Complejas: Encuentro Transdisciplinario para el Estudio de la Violencia, 3rd, San Juan, P.R., 2015. Entre violencias. Edición y compilación de Madeline Román. Cabo Rojo, Puerto Rico: Editora Educación Emergente, 2017. 153 p.: bibl.

This book gathers the works of nine authors who participated in the "Third Encounter of Complex Conjunctions: Transdisciplinary Encounter on the Study of Violence" held in April 2015 at the Universidad de Puerto Rico. The essays address the different manifestations of violence that can be witnessed in contemporary Puerto Rican society, with a focus on modes of violence typical of the contemporary digital era. The contributors share the conviction that increased visibility of violence through the media and social networks has helped to normalize and reproduce violent behaviors.

1618 Feliciano-Santos, Sherina. A contested Caribbean indigeneity: language, social practice, and identity within Puerto Rico Taíno activism. New Brunswick, N.J.: Rutgers University Press, 2021. 227 p.: bibl., ill., index. (Critical Caribbean studies)

Based on linguistically oriented ethnographic research on neo-Indigenous movements and organizations in Puerto Rico and within the Puerto Rican diaspora, the author explores discursive practices that contest the generalized perception that native Indigenous groups in Puerto Rico became extinct very soon after colonization. Feliciano-Santos reveals a linguistic field that she indistinctively describes as cacophonous, dissonant, ambiguous, ambivalent, incongruous, and "altogether heterogeneous." The multiple linguistic uses and ambiguous meanings that neo-Tainos attribute to the term "Indian" gives way to a concept of Indianness that is fluid and negotiable, and defies monolithic representations. In line with the work of Cuban writer Antonio Benítez-Rojo, the author warns that "the process[es] involved in homogenizing historical narratives are always partial, positioned and problematic."

1619 Galanes Valldejuli, Luis and Otomie Vale Nieves. Feminism and difference: women activism in Vieques in the post-Navy period. (*Cent. J.*, 32:1, Spring 2020, p. 116–142, bibl., photo)

This article documents female activism on the small Puerto Rican island of Vieques during the post-2003 period. Two-thirds of the island were occupied by the US marine corps from 1941–2003. A years-long civilian struggle finally succeeded in its objective during that last year. As the tasks required from civic leaders shifted from physical confrontation during the navy occupation period, to taking care of the sick, and decontamination of the island during the post-navy period, the leadership positions in civic organizations evidenced a radical shift from men to women, each obeying traditional norms and expectations of their respective gender. A series of focus groups conducted with female Viequense civic leaders further revealed a generalized rejection of "feminism" as an adequate label to define their work and the adoption of discourses typical of the third-wave feminist movement.

1620 Griffin, G.A.E. In the penumbra of the Antillean hallucination. (*Small Axe*, 21:2, No. 53, July 2017, p. 1–20, ill.)

This article offers a psychologically informed commentary on a series of photographs of Black young men accused of committing criminal acts, and printed on the front pages of the sensationalistic newspaper *St. Kitts and Nevis Observer* from 2008–2016. The author explores the problematic aspects of "the psychic process of identity-building among Antillean blacks," and, drawing on the works of Jacques Lacan and Frantz Fanon, argues that the criminalizing effects of the photographs are a reflection of the "hallucinatory autoscopic" lens through which Antillean Blacks are condemned to see themselves, a mirror image of the white gaze. While Lacan and Fanon provide a useful interpretive tool for the analysis of the photographs, the author rejects their pessimistic conclusions, which practically deprive Antillean Blacks of the possibility of ever transcending the autoscopic gaze.

1621 Hansing, Katrin and **Bert Hoffmann.** When racial inequalities return: assessing the restratification of Cuban society 60 years after revolution. (*Lat. Am. Polit. Soc.*, 62:2, May 2020, p. 29–52, bibl., map, tables)

This text documents the economic problems and rising levels of poverty in Cuba during the critical periods of 1991, 2008, and 2011, and is based on data obtained through a nationwide quantitative survey with 1,049 respondents. Part of the value of this publication resides in its capacity to offer trustworthy quantitative data on poverty for a socialist country that claims to be the most egalitarian in the world, and where the category of "poor" is absent from government-produced official statistics. The research reveals not only rising levels of poverty in some sectors of the community, but also an unequal distribution of wealth and poverty along racial lines, with Black Cubans as the most negatively impacted sector.

1622 Identidad y postnacionalismo en la cultura cubana. Edición de Laura Alonso Gallo y Belén Rodríguez Mourelo. Valencia, Spain: Advana Vieja, 2019. 288 p.: bibl. (Colección de estudios culturales. Serie Reading Cuba)

This book gathers fiction and non-fiction contributions from 16 writers centered on post-nationalist consciousness and identity among Cuban-Americans, as can be evidenced through their cultural and literary productions. Such post-nationalist consciousness and identity, the authors argue, must have emerged during the very early stages of migration history, and must have been strongly present among the first wave of migrants in 1959 and before, most of whom probably left the island knowing with a high degree of certainty that there would be no return. Moreover, and insofar as their identity remains tied to a distant and imaginary Cuba, that identity is best conceived metaphorically as a fire that existed at some point in the past, but that history put out long ago.

1623 Inoa, Orlando. Trabajadores inmigrantes en República Dominicana. Santo Domingo: Letragráfica, 2018. 414 p., 84 unnumbered pages of plates: bibl., ill., maps.

This scholarly work provides a broad and detailed history of major migration movements to the Dominican Republic throughout its republican history, 1844 to present. The author devotes individual chapters to different ethnic and racial groups that migrated to the island during this period, including African, Middle Eastern, Chinese, Haitian, etc. But the emphasis of the book is on the "cocolo" migrants from the Caribbean Windward Islands, who migrated to the Dominican Republic between 1870 and 1933 to work on the sugar plantations. The author documents the mismatch between a racist and idealistic national political project aimed at whitening the population by promoting Caucasian migration, and the actual migration movements that took place, which consisted mainly of Black workers from the Windward Islands and Haiti.

1624 La invariable crisis. Edición de Alexis Rodríguez Ramos. Río Piedras, Puerto Rico: Publicaciones Gaviota, 2020. 284 p.: bibl., ill.

This book contains a collection of essays on different aspects of Puerto Rican society during the 2010–2020 period, a decade marked by multiple economic, political, and environmental crises. It includes 10 articles written by 15 authors, most of them professors of the Social Sciences Department of the Universidad de Puerto Rico, Cayey campus. As such, it includes contributions from sociologists, psychologists, economists, geographers, etc., on a diversity of topics, including social movements, civilian activism, and health crisis, among others.

1625 Kahn, Jeffrey S. Islands of sovereignty: Haitian migration and the borders of empire. Chicago, Ill.; London: The University of Chicago Press, 2019. 355 p.: bibl., ill., index, maps. (The Chicago series in law and society)

This book explores the impact of the "offshore migrant interdiction program" implanted by the US Citizenship and Immigration Services from 1981–92, with emphasis on Haitian immigrants fleeing political violence. The program, which allows US immigration authorities to intercept migrants while still en route to the US, or before reaching US eastern shores, has the effect of transporting the jurisdictional authority from federal US courts to the blurry legal arena of international waters, thus depriving Haitian migrants the benefits of the federal legal asylum program. In the case of Haiti, the author argues, the program had the effect of creating a fictional "floating Berlin wall" encircling Haiti.

1626 Kivland, Chelsey L. The magic of guns: scriptive technology and violence in Haiti. (*Am. Ethnol./Washington*, 45:3, Aug. 2018, p. 355–366, bibl., photos)

Based on ethnographic fieldwork conducted in Port-au-Prince during the period 2008–2013, this paper documents the process by which guns used in the underground criminal world are conceived as being endowed with magical powers, giving way to a black market of "magical weapons" custom manufactured by sorcerers for individual clients. In this context, guns are conceived as possessing their own agency, and capable of becoming co-complicit in the act of killing. Drawing from the logic of Azande witchcraft, according to which "two spears" are necessary in order to produce death, the author argues that, under Haitian local understanding of death, the gun becomes the second spear.

Latin American Perspectives. See item **969**.

1627 Lloréns, Hilda. Beyond *blanqueamiento*: Black affirmation in contemporary Puerto Rico. (*Lat. Am. Caribb. Ethn. Stud.*, 13:2, July 2018, p. 157–178, bibl.)

This paper explores the discursive strategies and "race talk" practices of island-based Afro-Puerto Rican subjects, centering on the topic of whitening *(blanqueamiento)*. The author challenges traditional assessments of *blanqueamiento* practices as self-deceiving ideology or pathological complex. Following James Scott, she instead argues that *blanqueamiento* is best understood as an "everyday form of resistance," that is, as an ideology that is played out in a highly contested terrain, where it is "sometimes affirmed, other times denied," but always strategically employed within a system of racial ascription that is "messy, polyvalent, inconsistent and contradictory."

López Segrera, Francisco. Cuba: the July 11, 2021 protests. See item **976**.

1628 Mahabir, Joy. Communal style: Indo-Caribbean women's jewelry. (*Small Axe*, 21:2, No. 53, July 2017, p. 112–122, ill., photos)

This essay documents the changing meanings behind pieces of jewelry traditionally worn by Indo-Caribbean women in Suriname, Guyana, and Trinidad. Beyond the esthetic value of the tradition, the author argues that the pieces are more than mere items of fashion. They are objects charged with powers, often found as offerings on the altars of Hindu deities, Lucumí orishas, or

Vodou loas. Their continued use among contemporary Indo-Caribbean women grants them new meaning as a "text of resistance" that condemns the exploitation of women within traditional Hindu gendered division of labor.

Munoz, Ercio. The geography of intergenerational mobility in Latin America and the Caribbean. See item **458**.

1629 Murillo Garnica, Jacqueline. La escritura decimonónica cubana como reflejo del complejo de "blanqueamiento." (*Caribb. Stud.*, 47:2, July/Dec. 2019, p. 3–24, bibl.)

This paper explores the social strategies of whitening *(blanquamiento)* employed in 19th-century Cuba, as they are revealed in three novels and one testimonial text belonging to what is usually referred to as the 19th-century antislavery literary tradition. The texts include Anselmo Suarez y Romero's *Francisco* (1840); Cirilo Villaverde's *Cecilia Valdés o la Loma del Angel* (1882); Martín Morúa Delgado's *Sofía* (1891); and Juan Francisco Manzano's *Autobiografía de un esclavo* (1874). The paper attempts to reveal the fundamental role played by fiction writers in 19th-century nation-building efforts in Cuba, and as promoters of racial mixing and *blanqueamiento*.

1630 Negotiating gender, policy and politics in the Caribbean: feminist strategies, masculinist resistance and transformational possibilities. Edited by Gabrielle Jamela Hosein and Jane L. Parpart. London; New York, N.Y.: Rowman & Littlefield International, 2016. 220 p.: bibl., index.

Collection of 10 essays that aim to document and assess the successes of the feminist movement in the Anglophone Caribbean, incorporating data from Jamaica, Trinidad and Tobago, Guyana, Dominica, and St. Lucia. The contributors point to the lessons learned in the process, and the transformational possibilities of feminist activism in their struggle for gender justice in and beyond the Caribbean.

1631 Ocasio, Rafael. Race and nation in Puerto Rican folklore: Franz Boas and John Alden Mason in Porto Rico. New Brunswick, N.J.: Rutgers University Press, 2020. 239 p.: bibl., index. (Critical Caribbean studies series)

This book summarizes the anthropological findings of the *1913 Scientific Survey of Porto Rico and the Virgin Islands*, conducted under the direction of renowned anthropologists Franz Boas and John Alden Mason. Of particular relevance to the author is Mason's findings from research conducted on the Black enclave of Loiza, where he documented the existence of a rich culture and folklore and the presumed survival of a "Congolese" language and vocabulary. The author interrogates why these findings from Loiza were never published, and condemns the tendency among early American anthropologists to "whiten" the Puerto Rican population by emphasizing their Jibaro heritage and identity.

1632 Patterson, Orlando. The confounding island: Jamaica and the postcolonial predicament. Cambridge, Mass.: The Belknap Press of Harvard University Press, 2019. 409 p.: bibl., ill., index.

More than 50 years after the publication of his canonical text *The Sociology of Slavery* (1967; see *HLAS 30:1730*), renowned Jamaican historical sociologist Patterson reflects on the "perplexing" and "head-scratching paradoxes" of postcolonial Jamaican society at the beginning of the 21st century. Statistically speaking, the island tends to score among either the very top or the very bottom in the world on almost everything: economic growth, violence, democratic participation, happiness surveys, etc. The confusion this creates, the author argues, is responsible for most of the political and economic failures of the country.

1633 Peña Farias, Ángela I. Regímenes de bienestar y pobreza familiar en Cuba. La Habana: Editorial Ciencias Sociales, 2017. 189 p.: bibl.

The deterioration of the Cuban economy in 1990 and afterwards has contributed to the emergence of a social sector that lives under conditions of extreme poverty. Moreover, because within the Cuban socialist and welfare model there is no sector of the population officially categorized as "poor," the problem is made invisible and left unattended. In this sense, the study, based on in-depth interviews with families in two of the poorest sectors of La Habana during 2009–2013, reveals the emergence of incipient forms of "social classes," or what the author calls differentiated "regimes of welfare." It also reveals a profile of those who are most affected by poverty: namely women, the elderly, and Blacks.

1634 Pérez-Lizasuain, César. Rebelión, no-derecho y poder estudiantil: la huelga de 2010 en la Universidad de Puerto Rico. Cabo Rojo, Puerto Rico: Editora Educación Emergente, 2018. 211 p.: bibl. (Otra universidad)

The book documents the 2010 student's strike at the University of Puerto Rico, based on interviews with 14 students and professors directly involved in the movement. The author argues that the students strike of 2010 shows similarities with a new mode of social mobilization and organization that is global, heterogeneous, and civic-based. The events of 2010, the author finally argues, laid the foundation for the subsequent 2017 strike at the same university.

1635 Price, Richard and **Sally Price.** Saamaka dreaming. Durham, N.C.: Duke University Press, 2017. 252 p.: bibl., index.

This is a fascinating book written by two canonical Caribbean anthropologists, in commemoration of the 50th anniversary of the authors' first contact with Saamaka maroon society in 1966 in Suriname. The structure of the book deviates from the formal academic essay, and more closely resembles an autobiographical text of the couple's professional life deep inside the South American jungle, revealing details about the dangers and hardships of anthropological fieldwork that are often left out of the formal ethnographic text. The authors conclude that, if the Saamaka they encountered back in 1966–86 resembles a "dreamworld," the realities of the territory today "most closely resemble nightmares."

1636 Ramírez Frías, Clemente Hugo. Turismo y religión en Cuba: viabilidad y antípodas de una relación. La Habana: Editorial de Ciencias Sociales, 2017. 242 p.: bibl., ill.

The book documents the surge in religious tourism in Cuba during the past two decades. While the surge in visitors can be evidenced for all religious congregations, including Catholics, Protestants, and Jews, it is particularly the Afro-Cuban syncretic religions, and mainly santería, that attract the highest number. In this sense, as the author argues, Cuba has become "the Rome of santería."

1637 Regional discourses on society and history: shaping the Caribbean. Edited by Jerome Teelucksingh and Shane J. Pantin. New York, N.Y.: Peter Lang Publishing, Inc., 2020. 228 p.: bibl.

This book contains a collection of 12 essays by different authors on a multiplicity of topics related to the Caribbean region, including race, ethnicity, nationalism, culture, gender, identity, politics, literature, cricket, Pentecostalism, Calypso music, language, development, and resistance to colonialism. While most of the essays focus on the Anglophone Caribbean, and particularly on Trinidad and Tobago, the book also includes two essays based on the Hispanic Caribbean, one on Cuba and one on Puerto Rico.

1638 Reyes, Raimy and **Nairoby Chalas.** Personas retornadas en condiciones de vulnerabilidad: dominicanos/as deportados/as desde los Estados Unidos (2012–2016). Santo Domingo: INMRD, Instituto Nacional de Migración de la República Dominicana, Ministerio de Interior y Policía, 2018. 109 p.: bibl., ill.

This book documents trends of both migration of Dominicans to the US mainland and deportations of Dominicans back to the Dominican Republic, for the period 1960 to 2010. Both migrations and deportations increased drastically after the fall of the Trujillo dictatorship, which ended in 1961. The majority of deportations are related to criminal offenses. The aim of the book is to offer public policy recommendations for the reception and reinsertion of deported subjects in the Dominican Republic.

1639 Turning tides: Caribbean intersections in the Americas and beyond. Edited by Heather Cateau and Milla Cozart Riggio. Kingston; Miami, Fla.: Ian Randle Publishers, 2019. 344 p.: bibl., ill., index.

This book gathers 17 essays presented in the international conference "Turning Tides: Caribbean Intersections in the Americas and Beyond," held on the University of the West Indies' St. Augustine Campus, in Trinidad, February 2016. The essays cover a wide variety of topics, including music, the visual arts, gender, sexuality, feminism, religion, migration, race and identity, and the interconnections between two or more of them. Collectively, the book initiates a transdisciplinary conversation about the most important issues of the Grand Caribbean, but with special emphasis on Trinidad and Tobago and the Anglophone Caribbean.

COLOMBIA AND VENEZUELA

WILLIAM L. CANAK, *Professor Emeritus of Sociology, Middle Tennessee State University*

COLOMBIA

COLOMBIA'S RECENT academic sociological research focuses on a range of topics, including family, demographics, social inequality, political violence, drug trafficking, employment and labor, feminists and gender, and urbanization. One major contribution has been the study of social inequality and its impact on Colombian society. Researchers examine the ways in which poverty, unemployment, and social exclusion contribute to the perpetuation of inequality, and propose policy solutions to address these issues. Additionally, there has been a focus on the intersection of race, gender, and class in shaping inequality (for example, items **1643**, **1650**, and **1660**). Another important area of research has been the study of political violence and its effects on Colombian society. Scholars examine the roots of the country's decades-long armed conflict, as well as the challenges of building peace and reconciliation in the aftermath of the conflict (items **1644** and **1663**). They also explore the ways in which drug trafficking and organized crime contribute to violence in the country (item **1648**). In terms of contributions to theory and methodology, Colombian sociologists have made significant strides in developing innovative research methods and approaches. For example, some researchers utilized participatory action research (PAR) to engage communities and stakeholders in the research process, while others have employed mixed-methods approaches to combine quantitative and qualitative data (item **1640**). Colombia's academic sociological research in recent years has contributed significantly to our understanding of social inequality intersections with a rich range of societal structures and relationships. By addressing these challenges head-on, researchers have proposed new solutions and strategies for building a more just and equitable society in Colombia.

VENEZUELA

VENEZUELAN SOCIOLOGY has been shaped by a range of contexts and influences in recent years. One of the most significant is the country's political and economic crisis, which began in the late 2000s and has continued to impact the country to this day. This crisis has led to a range of social problems, including high levels of poverty, crime, and political instability (items **1671** and **1675**). In response to these challenges, Venezuelan sociologists are increasingly focusing their attention on understanding and addressing the social and economic issues facing the country. Many have become involved in social movements and political activism, seeking to promote social justice and economic reform (item **1669**). There has been growing recognition of the importance of interdisciplinary approaches to social research, with sociologists increasingly collaborating with scholars in other fields, such as economics, anthropology, and political science. This has led to the development of new research agendas that seek to address complex social issues from a range of perspectives. Venezuelan sociology is deeply embedded in the country's political and economic context, yet recent research has reasserted links to traditional themes and methodologies once dominant in the body of research.

COLOMBIA

1640 Arjona, Ana. Rebelocracy: social order in the Colombian civil war. New York, N.Y.: Cambridge University Press, 2016. 401 p.: bibl., index. (Cambridge studies in comparative politics)

Using multiple research methods spanning qualitative (community studies, in-depth interviews) and quantitative surveys, this remarkable contribution to the literature on conflict and functioning community institutions offers an insightful and original understanding of civil society's resilience when coping with armed conflict. Research spanning many years engages with a field study of a nuanced interplay between armed insurgents and civil communities during periods of intense violence.

1641 Bogotá en la encrucijada del desorden: estructuras socioespaciales y **gobernabilidad metropolitana.** Compilación de Óscar Alfredo Alfonso Roa. Bogotá: Universidad Externado de Colombia, 2017. 564 p.: bibl., ill., maps. (Serie Economía institucional urbana; 13)

An important contribution to Colombian urban studies that analyzes the complex social and spatial structures of Bogotá, the capital city of Colombia, and how they impact its governance. Roa concludes that the city is facing a crisis of governability due to a combination of factors, including inequality, informal economies, social and spatial fragmentation, and the lack of effective public policies. Governance structures have created a fragmented urban landscape, with stark inequalities between different neighborhoods and social groups. Roa also highlights the challenges faced by the city's governance structures, including weak institutional capacity, corruption, and a lack of effective coordination between different levels of government. Overall, the study provides a comprehensive analysis of the complex sociospatial dynamics of Bogotá and their impact on its governance.

1642 Cárdenas, Roosbelinda. "Thanks to my forced displacement": blackness and the politics of Colombia's war victims. (*Lat. Am. Caribb. Ethn. Stud.*, 13:1, March 2018, p. 72–93, bibl.)

After Colombia's 1991 constitutional recognition of racial and ethnic diversity, the country saw the emergence of a political-victim identity merging with status as displaced persons among populations relocated to Bogotá and employed by them as a political narrative and a tool for political organization.

1643 Castillo Vargas, Elizabeth. No somos etcétera: veinte años de historia del movimiento LGBT en Colombia. Prólogo de Brigitte Baptiste. Bogotá: Penguin Random House Grupo Editorial, 2018. 227 p.: ill. (Noficción)

A collection of testimonials, interviews, and essays that aims to give a voice to the marginalized communities within the LGBTQ spectrum in Colombia, including transgender people, bisexuals, and non-binary individuals. The stories shared in the book highlight the struggles and discrimination faced by these individuals in a country where LGBTQ rights are still not fully recognized. Through these narratives, Castillo Vargas seeks to raise awareness about the diverse experiences of LGBTQ people and the importance of recognizing and respecting their identities. The book also explores the intersectionality of LGBTQ identity with other marginalized identities, such as race, class, and religion. The author challenges the notion that the LGBTQ community is a monolith and emphasizes the need to recognize and celebrate the diversity within the community. Overall, *No somos etcétera* is an important contribution to the ongoing conversation about LGBTQ rights and representation, particularly in Latin America, and serves as a powerful reminder of the ongoing struggles faced by marginalized communities within the LGBTQ spectrum.

1644 Chaparro Rodríguez, Juan Carlos. El ocaso de la guerra: la confrontación armada y los procesos de paz en Colombia. Bogotá: Editorial Universidad del Rosario, 2017. 218 p.: bibl. (Colección Textos de ciencias humanas)

This work covers 70 years of Colombian domestic conflict, negotiations, efforts by governments and guerrillas to gain advantage or establish peace, leading to disruptions and displacement for millions of Colombians. Explores the "dirty war" and the inflexible ideological positioning by government, military, and other actors that served partisan interests sustained by continuing conflict.

1645 Ciudadanías emergentes y transiciones en América Latina. Coordinación de José Javier Niño Martínez, Paula Andrea Valencia Londoño y Gabriel Ruiz Romero. Medellín, Colombia: Universidad de Medellín; Toluca, Mexico: Universidad Autónoma del Estado de México, 2017. 177 p.: bibl., ill. (some color).

The chapters of this edited volume chart the emergence of new forms of citizenship and political participation in Latin America, particularly in the context of the region's ongoing democratic transitions. The book's contributors examine a range of topics, including social movements, participatory budgeting, Indigenous rights, and the role of the media in shaping public opinion. Drawing on case studies from across the region—with a focus on Colombia, the book offers a comprehensive analysis of the complex relationship between citizens, the state, and civil society in Latin America today.

1646 Colombia en la Encrucijada. El Proyecto LAMP Colombia Sobre Migración, *Bogotá, 2015.* Migración internacional, patrones y determinantes: estudios comparados Colombia-America Latina-Proyecto LAMP. Compilación de María Gertrudis Roa Martínez. Cali, Colombia: Universidad del Valle, Programa Editorial, 2016. 298 p.: bibl., ill., maps. (Colección Ciencias sociales. Sociologia)

This collected work includes a series of studies on the patterns and determinants of international migration in Colombia and Latin America. The book was published as part of the Latin American Migration Project (LAMP) in 2016 by the Editorial Program of Universidad de Cali. The Andean Migration Program within LAMP was an interdisciplinary research initiative that aimed to understand the dynamics of migration in the Andean region, with a focus on Colombia, Ecuador, and Peru. The book includes 10 chapters, each authored by an expert in the field of international migration. The chapters cover a range of topics, including the causes and consequences of migration, the role of social networks and family ties in migration decision-making, and the experiences of migrants in host countries. The studies draw on both quantitative and qualitative methods, including surveys, interviews, and secondary data analysis. Provides a comprehensive overview of the complex factors that drive migration in Colombia and Latin America, and contributes to our understanding of the broader global phenomenon of international migration.

Descolonizando mundos: aportes de intelectuales negras y negros al pensamiento social colombiano. See *HLAS 76:2264*.

1647 **Desencuentros territoriales.** Tomo II, Caracterización de los conflictos en las regiones de la Altillanura, Putumayo y Montes de María. Edición de Carlos Arturo Duarte Torres. Bogotá: Instituto Colombiano de Antropología e Historia, 2015. 1 v.: bibl., color maps. (Terrenos etnográficos)

A significant addition to Colombian socioeconomic research that focuses on the extractive industry's impact on peripheral regions through investment by multinational mining and agricultural corporations. Duarte describes the territorial impact through three case studies that trace a disruption and disarticulation of traditional social relations and economic activity, links to extensive armed conflict, and the legal and illegal initiatives that sustain ongoing instability.

1648 **Exclusión, mujeres y prisión en Colombia: un caso en la región Caribe: (Investigación-acción en el Centro de Rehabilitación Femenino El Buen Pastor de Barranquilla).** Compilación por Francisco José del Pozo Serrano et al. Barranquilla, Colombia: Editorial Universidad del Norte; Bogotá: Uniediciones, 2017. 201 p.: bibl., ill.

Ten chapters explore the topic of exclusion and gender-based violence in the context of women's incarceration in Colombia. The first chapter provides an overview of the current state of the Colombian prison system and the challenges faced by incarcerated women. The subsequent chapters delve into issues such as the impact of drug trafficking on women's incarceration, the role of the state in perpetuating violence against women in prison, and the experiences of transgender women in the Colombian prison system. The book also examines the various forms of violence and exclusion that incarcerated women face, including sexual violence, institutional violence, and the stigmatization of incarcerated women by society. The authors argue that these forms of exclusion are not only perpetuated by the prison system, but are also deeply ingrained in Colombian society. These studies shed light on the complex and multifaceted issues surrounding women's incarceration in Colombia, and provide important insights into the ways in which gender-based violence and exclusion intersect in this context.

1649 **Familias fragilizadas en el contexto colombiano: el caso de Medellín.** Edición de Nadia Semenova Moratto Vásquez y Adriana Patricia Arcila Rojas. Textos de Carolina Andrea Benjumea Herrera, Cecilia Cardona Vélez y Jenny Tatiana Espitia Moya. Medellín, Colombia: Universidad de San Buenaventura de Medellín: Federación Internacional de Universidades Católicas, 2016. 168 p.: bibl. (Colección Señales)

Overall, a valuable contribution to the literature on family fragility that provides important insights into the challenges faced by families in Medellín. The book is recommended for scholars, practitioners, and policymakers working on issues related to family welfare, social inequality, and violence in Colombia and other similar contexts. Chapters explore the concept of fragile families and establish a model for empirical studies that includes consideration of constitutional and legal frameworks that impact family composition and a cultural assessment of family morphology and structure with implications for future research.

1650 **Feminismos y estudios de género en Colombia: un campo académico y político en movimiento.** Compilación de Franklin Gil Hernández y Tania Pérez-Bustos. Bogotá: Universidad Nacional de Colombia, 2018. 332 p.: bibl., ill., index. (Biblioteca abierta; 463. Colección general Estudios de género)

A series of chapter contributions frame feminist and gender studies with reference to the state and feminist movements.

Additional chapters address the range of academic research within feminist and gender studies, as well as pedagogical experiences dealing with these topics. In sum, these essays provide a valuable and needed introduction to feminist, gender, and queer studies in Colombia.

1651 **Fox-Hodess, Katy.** Worker power, trade union strategy, and international connections: dockworker unionism in Colombia and Chile. (*Lat. Am. Polit. Soc.*, 61:3, Aug. 2019, p. 29–54, bibl., ill.)

A comparative analysis of dockworker union strategies in Colombia and Chile with substantive implications for union mobilizations elsewhere; concludes that coordinated shop floor action produces significantly more workplace union power than legalistic initiatives focused on themes of human rights.

1652 **García Ubaque, Juan Carlos; César Augusto García Ubaque;** and **Camilo Alberto Torres Parra.** Habitabilidad de la vivienda: una perspectiva de salud. Bogotá: Universidad Nacional de Colombia, 2017. 99 p.: bibl., color ill. (Colección Salud pública y nutrición humana)

This publication from the Universidad Nacional de Colombia provides a comprehensive analysis of the relationship between housing and health. The book delves into various aspects of housing, such as ventilation, lighting, and water supply, and their impact on the physical and mental health of occupants. The authors argue that inadequate housing can lead to various health issues, including respiratory diseases, mental health problems, and infectious diseases. The book includes recommendations for improving housing conditions to promote better health outcomes. It highlights the need for policies and interventions that promote equitable access to adequate housing and address the root causes of inadequate housing. The authors also emphasize the importance of community participation in housing interventions and the need for interdisciplinary collaboration between health and housing professionals. Overall, the book provides a valuable resource for policymakers, researchers, and practitioners interested in improving housing conditions and promoting health equity.

1653 **Giraldo Prieto, Cristina.** Entre el azadón y el smartphone: jóvenes rurales entre políticas culturales. Bogotá: Pontificia Universidad Javeriana-Bogotá, Facultad de Ciencias Sociales, Editorial Pontificia Universidad Javeriana, 2018. 131 p.: bibl., color ill. (Intervenciones en estudios culturales)

A study of the cultural and political experiences of young rural people in Colombia. The book focuses on the intersection of technology and traditional rural practices and how young people navigate the tensions between them. Giraldo Prieto examines how government policies aimed at promoting rural development intersect with the cultural and economic realities of rural youth. Through interviews and observations, the author explores how these young people negotiate their identities in a rapidly changing society and the challenges they face in accessing education and employment opportunities. Ultimately, the book sheds light on the complex realities of rural youth and highlights the need for policies that take into account their unique experiences and perspectives.

1654 **Lizarazo, Tania.** Alongside violence: everyday survival in Chocó, Colombia. (*J. Lat. Am. Cult. Stud.*, 27:2, June 2018, p. 175–196, bibl., photos)

Study of two Chocó-based women's groups and their everyday use of narratives that provide pathways to collective emotional and cognitive survival in a context of profound violence and cultural stress. These narratives become a self-constructed resource that charts visions of a healthy, ethical grounded future.

1655 **Muñoz Sánchez, Hernando.** Hacerse hombres: la construcción de masculinidades desde las subjetividades. Medellín, Colombia: Fondo Editorial FCSH, Facultad de Ciencias Sociales y Humanas, Universidad de Antioquia, 2017. 273 p.: bibl., index. (FCSH investigación. Trabajo social)

This book explores the construction of masculinity within the hacker subculture. Specifically, the book studies the intersection of gender, technology, and power, and how they manifest within the hacker community. Muñoz Sánchez argues that the construction of masculinity within the hacker subculture is heavily influenced by societal norms and values surrounding gender, power, and technology. Through in-depth interviews with hackers, the author provides insights into the ways in which masculine identities are constructed and performed within this subculture, and how identities intersect with race, class, and sexuality. Overall, the book provides a nuanced and insightful analysis of the complex ways in which gender and technology intersect within the hacker community.

1656 **Muñoz Velasco, Luis Alfredo; Jenny Lisseth Avendaño López; and José Jardani Giraldo Uribe.** Espacio público e informalidad en el microcentro de Neiva. Neiva, Colombia: Universidad Surcolombiana, Facultad de Economía y Administración, Ediciones de la U, 2016. 103 p.: bibl., color ill.

A brief monograph describing urban socioeconomic structure and activity with the particular goal of understanding the rise and role of informal economic organization and its relationship with the formal economic institutions and markets.

1657 **Paisajes laborales postfordistas en el sur occidente colombiano.** Vol. 1, Organización y condiciones de trabajo en diferentes sectores de la economía. Edición de Carlos Alberto Mejía Sanabria y Deidi Maca Urbano. Cali, Colombia: Universidad del Valle, Programa Editorial, 2017. 1 v.: bibl., ill. (Colección Ciencias sociales)

A substantial contribution to the long standing excellent Colombian research on employment practices and the world of work. Chapters present empirical studies of labor conditions in different economic sectors, such as Afro-Colombian women, urban transportation, informal economies, cooperatives, health, coffee, warehouses, computer controlled industry, refineries, recent university graduates and more. An essential reference for those interested in employment and labor relations.

1658 **Paisajes laborales postfordistas en el sur occidente colombiano.** Vol. 2, Cambios en el mundo del trabajo y sus impactos en las trayectorias laborales, la subjetividad y la identidad. Edición de Carlos Alberto Mejía Sanabria y Deidi Maca Urbano. Cali, Colombia: Universidad del Valle, Programa Editorial, 2017. 1 v.: bibl., ill. (Colección Ciencias sociales)

A valuable contribution to the established Colombian socioeconomic research on labor market structures that spans formal and flexible informal domains. Regulated employment systems exist in a flexible relationship, facilitating adaptation during times of stability and uncertainty.

1659 **Paz en el territorio: diálogo intercultural y justicia social.** Bogotá: Universidad Nacional de Colombia: El Colectivo, 2017. 200 p.: ill. (Colección Gerardo Molina; 68)

A significant contribution to current analyses of Colombia's national advances beyond an era of urban/rural divide and post-armed conflict social movements, focusing on rural social movements and efforts to gain access to land, Afro-Colombian identity, and progress beyond national accords. An excellent review of organizations associated with these developments.

1660 **Perdomo Gamboa, Óscar.** Lecturas sobre la afrocolombianidad. Ibagué, Colombia: Caza de Libros, 2016. 149 p.: bibl., ill. (Colección Pensamiento contemporáneo; 15)

Perdomo focuses on the cultural and historical contributions of Afro-Colombians in Colombian society. The book is a collection of essays, articles, and research studies that examine the experiences of Afro-Colombians in various aspects of Colombian society, including politics, education, and literature. It also explores the complex issues of racism and discrimination that many Afro-Colombians still face today, and offers insights on how to promote greater awareness and understanding of Afro-Colombian culture and identity. Overall, the book provides a valuable addition to the growing body of research into the rich and diverse heritage of Afro-Colombians.

1661 **Poder(es) en movimiento(s): procesos y dinámicas (re)constituyentes en Colombia durante el siglo XXI.** Edición de

Carolina Jiménez Martín, Sergio Moreno Rubio y José Francisco Puello-Socarrás. Bogotá: Universidad Nacional de Colombia, 2017. 406 p.: bibl., ill. (Colección Gerardo Molina; 62)

This volume brings together a set of eight studies examining the role of popular movements in response to capitalist transformation and widespread violence in Colombia. The authors trace the emerging power of grassroots social justice movements in the early decades of the 21st century and the bridges to a potential resolution of conflict and establishment of a just and stable social order.

1662 **Radiografía de la violencia regional: indicadores de diversos tópicos de violencia en el departamento de Antioquia.** Medellín, Colombia: Instituto Nacional de Medicina Legal y Ciencias Forenses, Regional Noroccidente: Corporación Universitaria Remington, Fondo Editorial Corporación Universitaria Remington, 2017. 2 v.: bibl., ill. (some color).

The first volume offers a report on various topics associated with violence in one Colombian department. Descriptions cover homicides, suicides, interpersonal violence, family violence, sexual violence, transportation accidents, accidents, and disappearances. Volume 2 focuses on children and adolescents. This report provides a grounded and comprehensive description that may inform future research.

1663 **Ramírez Gröbli, María del Pilar.**
Paisajes sonoros del retorno: palma de aceite, despojo y culturas de paz en el postconflicto colombiano. Madrid: Iberoamericana; Frankfurt am Main: Vervuert, 2020. 424 p.: bibl. (Nexos y diferencias; 58)

Paisajes sonoros focuses on the impact of the Colombian conflict on rural communities, particularly those involved in palm oil production. It also explores the consequences of palm oil production on the environment, social relations, and cultural traditions in the post-conflict period. Ramírez Gröbli argues that palm oil production has been a significant driver of land displacement, violence, and environmental degradation in rural areas of Colombia. She explores the experiences of communities affected by these issues and their efforts to rebuild their lives and create cultures of peace. The book also examines the role of the state and multinational corporations in exacerbating these problems and the challenges faced by those seeking to hold them accountable. Overall, *Paisajes sonoros* sheds light on the complex intersections between economic development, environmental sustainability, and social justice in Colombia's postconflict landscape.

1664 **Rodríguez López, Mercedes.** Mujeres en las gerencias de Cartagena de Indias: "traspasando el techo de cristal." Cartagena de Indias, Colombia: Universidad de Cartagena, Editorial Universitaria, 2017. 267 p.: bibl., ill.

Qualitative and quantitative methods provide insight to a group of women leaders and to their management and career trajectories in large and medium-sized companies. The book examines the challenges and barriers that women face in their careers and explores strategies that could help them break the glass ceiling and achieve their professional aspirations. It highlights the importance of addressing gender inequalities in the workplace. Research findings show that women face a range of challenges, including cultural and societal expectations, lack of support from their families and employers, and limited access to networks and opportunities. The book also offers recommendations for companies and policymakers to promote gender equality and create a more inclusive and diverse workplace. In brief, a valuable contribution to the literature on gender and management.

1665 **Velásquez Atehortúa, Juan Fernando.**
Barrio women and energopower in Medellín, Colombia. (*J. Lat. Am. Stud.*, 49:2, May 2017, p. 355–382, graphs)

Focusing on Medellín, Velásquez Atehortúa explores the implementation of Colombia's "pre-payment" for access to electricity policy, echoing similar policies established elsewhere in South America to avoid fiscal crises when displaced populations failed post-usage plans. In Colombia these prepayment for electricity plans were viewed by neoliberal governments as a means of socializing populations to self-discipline their consumption practices, while stabilizing energy infrastructure finances.

VENEZUELA

1666 Abbott, Jared A.; Hillel David Soifer; and Matthias vom Hau. Transforming the nation?: the Bolivarian education reform in Venezuela. (*J. Lat. Am. Stud.*, 49:4, Nov. 2017, p. 885–916, appendix, bibl., tables)

Based on analysis of educational curricula, texts, and interviews with education officials and teachers, this study explores the tensions and conflicts that developed as the Chávez government used mass public education to promote its nationalist ideology, but faced resistance from teachers leading to their marginalization from political leadership.

1667 Briceño-León, Roberto. La modernidad mestiza: estudios de sociología venezolana. Caracas: Editorial Alfa, 2018. 308 p.: bibl., ill. (Colección Trópicos; 130) (Sociología)

Examines the concept of mestizaje, or the mixing of different racial and ethnic groups, and argues that it has taken on a new form in modern times. According to Briceño-León, this new form of mestizaje is characterized by the blending of global and local cultures, as well as the intersection of various social identities, such as gender, class, and sexuality. Through a series of case studies, the author explores how this modernized mestiza plays out in various aspects of Venezuelan society, including politics, media, and popular culture. Venezuela now grapples with new forms of identity and culture. Briceño-León argues that the country must find ways to reconcile its diverse cultural heritage with the demands of modernity, while also addressing issues such as inequality, corruption, and political instability. Overall, *Modernidad mestiza* offers a thought-provoking analysis of the social and cultural landscape of contemporary Venezuela, and provides important insights into the challenges and opportunities facing the country in the years ahead.

1668 Elfenbein, Rachel. Engendering revolution: women, unpaid labor, and maternalism in Bolivarian Venezuela. Austin: University of Texas Press, 2019. 263 p.: bibl., index.

An important ethnographic analysis of Venezuela's Chávez-led transformation of the constitution to recognize women's reproductive labor, and also to incorporate women's unpaid labor as a fundamental and exploited resource, sustaining family, community, and government. Gender inequality became woven into laws, education, political rhetoric and policy, even as formal institutional, legal, and government projects promoted a vision of women's rights and importance for revolutionary ambitions.

1669 Espejo de la crisis humanitaria venezolana: Encuesta Nacional de Condiciones de Vida 2017: ENCOVI 2017. Coordinación por Anitza Freitez Landaeta. Caracas: abediciones, 2018. 259 p.: bibl., ill. (Colección Visión Venezuela)

This report provides an in-depth analysis of the worsening humanitarian crisis in Venezuela. The report was published by three prestigious universities in Venezuela and serves as a valuable tool for understanding the country's social, economic, and political situation. The report reveals that poverty, hunger, and lack of access to basic services have reached unprecedented levels, with the poorest sectors of society being the most affected. According to the report, the percentage of Venezuelans living in poverty increased from 48 percent in 2014 to 87 percent in 2017, with extreme poverty reaching 61 percent. Additionally, the report shows that access to basic services such as electricity, water, and health care has deteriorated significantly, with many Venezuelans lacking access to even the most basic necessities. The report concludes that the crisis is a result of a combination of factors, including economic mismanagement, corruption, and political repression, and that urgent action is needed to alleviate the suffering of the Venezuelan people.

1670 El éxodo venezolano: entre el exilio y la emigración. Edición de José Koechlin y Joaquín Eguren. Lima: Konrad Adenauer Stiftung: Universidad Antonio Ruiz de Montoya, Instituto de Ética y Desarrollo: OIM, Organización Internacional para las Migraciones; Madrid: OBIMID, 2018. 367 p.: bibl., ill. (some color). (Colección OBIMID; 4)

Eleven reports on Venezuelan emigration to other Latin American nations, including Colombia, Peru, Brazil, Argentina, Chile, Uruguay, Mexico, Dominican

Republic, plus Spain. This diaspora's encounter with public policy, cultural and economic challenges, adaptation and collective community identity, and demographic composition, gets varied degrees of investigation, but in sum this work provides a distinctive review of this important and unprecedented modern migration.

1671 López Ortega, Antonio. La gran regresión: crónicas de la desmemoria venezolana (2000–2016). Prólogo por Nelson Rivera. Selección por Samuel González Seijas. Venezuela: AB abediciones: Konrad Adenauer Stiftung; Montalbán, Caracas: Universidad Católica Andrés Bello, 2017. 802 p. (Colección Visión Venezuela)

The book explores the social, economic, and political situation in Venezuela between 2000 and 2016 and offers a critical analysis of this recent history. Specifically, it analyzes the events and decisions that led to the country's decline and regression, highlighting the factors that contributed to the loss of democracy, the deterioration of the economy, and the erosion of social rights. Those factors include the rise of populism, the mismanagement of the economy, and the erosion of democratic institutions. The author argues that Venezuela's decline was not inevitable, and that it was the result of a series of decisions made by the country's leaders.

1672 Rangel Cáceres, Antonio. Luces y sombras: Iglesia, poder y Estado en Venezuela: la Conferencia Episcopal frente a Hugo Chávez. Mérida, Venezuela: ICH, Instituto de Altos Estudios del Pensamiento del Comandante Supremo Hugo Rafael Chávez Frías: Pequiven, 2016. 324 p.: bibl.

Rangel's work explores the complex relationship between the Catholic Church, political power, and the state in contemporary Venezuela. The author traces the history of the Catholic Church in Venezuela from colonial times to the present day, highlighting the role of the Church as a social and political force in Venezuelan society. Rangel argues that the Church has played a significant role in shaping Venezuela's political landscape and has often been a source of both support and resistance to the government. Rangel examines the Church's relationship with the Chávez and Maduro governments, the role of the Church in the opposition movement, and the Church's response to the ongoing economic and political crisis in Venezuela. He also analyzes the Church's role in shaping public opinion, the media, and civil society in Venezuela. Through this detailed analysis of the Church's history and its contemporary role in Venezuelan society, Rangel provides a unique perspective on the complex interplay between religion, politics, and power in this deeply divided country.

1673 Uribe Castro, Hernando; Germán Ayala Osorio; and Carmen Jimena Holguín. Ciudad desbordada: asentamientos informales en Santiago de Cali, Colombia. Santiago de Cali, Colombia: Programa Editorial, Universidad Autónoma de Occidente, 2017. 452 p.: bibl., color ill.

Offers a comprehensive analysis of informal settlements in the city of Cali. The book focuses on the spatial, social, and economic characteristics of these settlements, examining their origins, evolution, and current state. The authors draw on extensive fieldwork, including interviews with residents, community leaders, and local officials, to provide a nuanced understanding of the dynamics that shape informal settlements. The book argues that informal settlements in Cali are not just a result of poverty or inadequate housing policies, but rather the consequence of complex historical and social factors. The authors explore how informal settlements are both shaped by and shape the wider urban landscape, and the implications of this for social inequality and urban development in Cali. Overall, they provide a rich and detailed account of informal settlements in Cali, shedding light on the challenges facing marginalized communities and offering insights into the potential paths towards more inclusive and sustainable urban development.

1674 Vecchio, Carlos. Libres: el nacimiento de una nueva Venezuela. Presentación de Leopoldo López. Prólogo por Luis Almagro. Venezuela: Dahbar, 2018. 246 p.: bibl. (Ensayo / Dahbar)

A detailed account of the current crisis in Venezuela, with a focus on the rise of the opposition movement and the struggle for democracy in the country. Vecchio argues that the crisis in Venezuela is the result of the failure of the socialist policies of the government, and that the only way to solve the crisis is through the establishment of a democratic system that respects human rights and the rule of law. The book is divided into four parts, each focusing on a different aspect of the crisis. The first part provides an overview of the political and economic situation in Venezuela, while the second part focuses on the opposition movement and its efforts to bring about change. The third part examines the role of the international community in the crisis, and the final part offers a vision for the future of Venezuela. This timely and insightful book provides a comprehensive analysis of the crisis in Venezuela and offers a path forward for the country.

1675 **Venezuela: la caída sin fin ¿hasta cuándo?: Encuesta Nacional de Condiciones de Vida 2016.** Coordinación de Anitza Freitez Landaeta. Caracas: AB Ediciones, 2017. 187 p., some folded: bibl., ill. (Colección Visión Venezuela)

Freitez explores the socioeconomic and political crisis in Venezuela. She delves into the historical and cultural factors that have contributed to the current situation, including the country's dependence on oil, corruption, and authoritarianism. The book provides a critical analysis of the policies of the Chávez and Maduro governments, which have led to hyperinflation, food and medicine shortages, and mass emigration. Freitez also highlights the voices of ordinary Venezuelans who have been directly affected by the crisis, and offers a call to action for national and international solutions to address the ongoing humanitarian crisis.

ECUADOR

ERYNN MASI DE CASANOVA, *Professor and Head, Sociology Department, University of Cincinnati*

THE ANNOTATED BIBLIOGRAPHY that follows covers a period—2012 to 2021—that may seem a strange slice of time to select, but is also advantageous. Because there had not been a stable contributing editor for the Sociology: Ecuador section for several years, I was asked to go back and review works from 2012 on, in order to ensure that all noteworthy publications were considered for inclusion in this volume. I call this somewhat random period advantageous because it includes works published both during the late phase of the regime of President Rafael Correa, and the post-Correa phase, nearly up to the present. As shown in the recent volume chronicling the trajectory of Correa's government (item **1677**), the later years were characterized by reduced petroleum and other income for state programs and by increased hostility between Correa allies and other political and social movement leaders and constituencies. Because this is an extended period, nearly a decade, it is not possible to sum up all the important contributions to sociology in and on Ecuador, but I will highlight here a few interesting trends in the publications that seemed most innovative and potentially impactful.

Sociologists have been studying race and ethnicity in Ecuador for decades, and so it may not be surprising that I have included several works focused on this topic here. While earlier research on race and ethnicity emphasized structural and formal political aspects, and in particular the national-level political projects of

Indigenous people, social scientists are studying and theorizing local experiences and identity in new ways. These new takes on race and ethnicity show how ethnic identity is not only relational, but is also a social process (items **1686, 1692, 1693**, and **1695**). Latorre and Farrell (item **1686**), for example, contribute to this understanding of ethnicity in a context in which there are severe constraints on the ways that groups can place demands on the state; that is, the state is more amenable to and feels more obligated to groups of people that identify as sharing a minoritized ethnic category. These authors' discussion of debates over indigeneity in a coastal location is also important. Researchers, those highlighted here and others, are contributing to sociology on Ecuador by examining locations that are understudied in the "racial geography" of the nation (item **1693**), such as Manabí province and the city of Guayaquil.

Rather than employing a structuralist approach, the social scientists whose work is featured here examine social processes, how decisions get made, and individual and collective agency. They assume uncertainty and instability as the everyday context in which Ecuadorians live their lives, and they show how Ecuadorians cope with, anticipate, and adapt to these conditions. Andrea Aguirre Salas' book *Incivil y criminal* (item **1676**), for example, stands out for its intersectional analysis of resistance and coping strategies among the people most affected by systems of punishment in Quito, and for its lively and approachable writing style, unique in such a rigorous study. Juan Pablo Pinto (item **1688**), in an article on amateur filmmaking in Manabí, takes us into the process of producing films that elites dismiss as low culture, showing how these cultural products allow directors and audiences to see themselves. Christien Klaufus (item **1685**) likewise complicates our suppositions about architecture and class by showing how working-class residents design their homes and how architects strive to produce particular esthetics in Riobamba and Cuenca. The edited collection *Grado cero* (item **1682**) takes readers on an informative and yet entertaining ride through diverse cultural and literary studies of what might be called equatorial perspectives and concepts.

Sociological publications tend to follow a relatively predictable organization and use particular types of academic language. Most of the studies I read in the process of selecting what to include fit that description. Some of the works featured here, however, are not typical academic books—in the best way possible (items **1679, 1680**, and **1681**). They often come from authors situated outside the academy and introduce concepts that are good for social scientists to consider. For example, Juan García Salazar and Catherine Walsh's discussion of the Afro-Ecuadorian ideal of *"estar bien colectivo"* (collective well-being) provides a useful comparison with the Quichua term *sumak kawsay (buen vivir)*, which has been influential even among non-Indigenous political leaders (item **1680**). Both concepts are described in opposition to deterritorialization of minority groups and misuse or exploitation of environmental resources. García Salazar and Walsh's book, similar to that of José F. Chalá Cruz (item **1679**), is unlike any other scholarly book I have read, and the departure from Western academic style and organization is intentional. This may make the works challenging for some scholars to read, and that is also intentional. It is past time to pay attention to Indigenous and African-descended intellectuals, and we must be willing to read their words and ideas in the way that they choose to present them, rather than forcing these thinkers to adopt the style and format of outsiders/oppressors.

Thus, the trends I found most inspiring as I reviewed many sociological works on Ecuador published since 2012 were these: new perspectives on race and ethnicity in understudied settings; a focus on social process over social structure; and a willingness to explore innovative formats and writing styles. It is also my hope that future selections for this section of the *HLAS* always strive to include contributions by Black and Indigenous Ecuadorian scholars; two decades into the 21st century, there is no valid reason for not doing so.

1676 **Aguirre Salas, Andrea.** Incivil y criminal: Quito como escenario de construcción estatal de la delincuencia entre los decenios 1960 y 1980. Quito: Universidad Andina Simón Bolívar: Abya-Yala: Corporación Editora Nacional, 2019. 273 p.: bibl., ill. (Biblioteca de historia; 50)

Drawing on archival materials and oral histories, this book examines how Quito's criminal justice system operates, in the streets and in police stations, courtrooms, and jail cells. The author centers the perspectives of people (often called *rateros*) seen as driving crime, people engaged in informal work and embedded in cooperative survival networks created and sustained by women. Analyzing punishment of small-scale property crimes and gendered treatment of defendants and prisoners, Aguirre Salas sketches a "geography of punitive power in Quito" (p. 11). This artful "ethnography of the state" reveals that, except for some women's correctional facilities, Ecuadorian jails are not isolated institutions; instead they remain connected to the urban informal economy, mostly through women's efforts on behalf of incarcerated family members.

Antología del pensamiento crítico ecuatoriano contemporáneo. See item **1000**.

1677 **Assessing the left turn in Ecuador.** Edited by Francisco Sánchez and Simón Pachano. Cham, Switzerland: Palgrave Macmillan, 2020. 373 p.: bibl., ill. (some color). (Studies of the Americas)

This edited volume claims that Ecuador has been studied less than similar cases in which neoliberal governments were replaced by populist, left-leaning ones (e.g., Bolivia and Venezuela), despite the transformation in Ecuador being in some ways more radical. Chapters by political scientists, sociologists, economists, anthropologists, and others analyze the rhetoric and actions of former President Rafael Correa, as well as the consequences of the changes that took place during his administration. The authors do an excellent job of explaining why Correa rose to power, how his policies changed the political landscape, and whether those changes appear to be lasting ones. Recommended for course adoption; each chapter can stand alone, and in combination, they represent the best scholarly overview of this topic.

1678 **Becker, Marc.** The CIA in Ecuador. Durham, N.C.: Duke University Press, 2020. 317 p.: bibl., ill., index. (American encounters/global interactions)

Using declassified CIA reports from the post-WWII period, this book provides a view of Ecuadorian politics and social movements. Although we might assume that such reports were too biased to provide useful information, Becker argues that "in the absence of other sources of information, police surveillance can provide an important opportunity to reconstruct the history of popular movements" (p. 6). The movements discussed in the book include leftist, communist, and other social and political movements operating in the context of internal politics as well as US imperialist and Cold War policies. The book would pair well for researchers and students of social movements with *El pensamiento político de los movimientos sociales* (item **1687**).

1679 Chalá Cruz, José Franklin. Representaciones del cuerpo, discursos e identidad del pueblo afroecuatoriano. Quito: ABYA-YALA; Cuenca, Ecuador: Universidad Politécnica Salesiana, 2013. 195 p.: bibl., ill. (some color). (Investigaciones; 24)

The main argument of this book is that African-descended people of the Chota Valley in Ecuador have created a system of cultural signs and meanings to preserve—and sometimes hide—their knowledge and worldview. This rebel knowledge (*sabiduría cimarrona*), as opposed to *el saber ventrílocuo*, is a powerful "survival mechanism." The book explores Afro-Ecuadorian identities and collective memory by studying self-representation and cultural practices from within, rejecting Western epistemology. These include stories, wordplay, singing games, and forms of popular education. The insistence on Black people's joy and beauty, not only pain and oppression, is a primary element of the *afrochoteña* cosmovision Chalá Cruz describes. Another element is the centrality of the body as a vehicle for thinking and feeling simultaneously—*senti-pensar*.

1680 García Salazar, Juan and **Catherine Walsh.** Pensar sembrando/sembrar pensando con el Abuelo Zenón. Quito: Cátedra de Estudios Afro-Andinos, Universidad Andina Simón Bolívar, Sede Ecuador: Abya Yala, 2017. 263 p.: bibl., ill.

This book uses "ancestral-collective Afro-Ecuadorian thought and knowledge" to show that knowledge is produced not just in the academy, but in praxis. Abuelo Zenón, who embodies this knowledge, is the real name of García Salazar's grandfather, but also a symbolic character: an older, wise Black man from the "gran territorio," a geographic and cultural region encompassing parts of Ecuador and Colombia. The book explores cultural practices (popular songs, "oral literature"), Afro-Ecuadorians' political and territorial struggles, and links to anticolonial resistance in the African diaspora. Through the words of Abuelo Zenón, printed in a different font from those of each author, the metaphor of *sembrar* (to plant/cultivate both land and knowledge) emphasizes the communal use of resources and resistance to extractive capitalism.

Gaussens, Pierre. La izquierda latinoamericana contra los pueblos: el caso ecuatoriano (2007–2013). See item **1007**.

1681 Gomezjurado Zevallos, Javier. Historia de la muerte en Quito. Quito: PPL Impresores, 2017. 340 p.: bibl., ill.

This is a unique work, emerging from outside of the academic presses that we tend to see producing more typical scholarly and historical works. The book traces the social, cultural, economic, and political practices related to death from the precolonial (Inca) period through the 20th century, incorporating diverse sources and stunning images of photographs and paintings. (Some readers may be uncomfortable with actual photographs of dead bodies and unsure about the cultural sensitivities involved in showing mummified remains.) On the whole, the book is enlightening, providing background on paid funeral mourners (*lloronas*), the Day of the Dead (*Día de los Difuntos*) as it has been celebrated over time, and the trappings of funeral rites, including carriages and coffins.

1682 Grado cero: la condición equinoccial y la producción de cultura en el Ecuador y en otras longitudes ecuatorianas. Edición de Esteban Ponce Ortiz. Textos de Karina Borja *et al.* Guayaquil, Ecuador: Universidad de las Artes, 2016. 415 p. (Colección Ensayo)

This edited volume aims to examine the production of culture "in-from-toward" Ecuador, while avoiding the limitations imposed by "nationalism, localisms, [and] regionalisms" (p. 11). The authors ask, what does it mean to theorize or imagine the world from the center of the planet, which is not a center of power? Drawing on postmodern theories, each chapter presents literary, historical, or cultural analysis of one case or set of texts, for example, travel narratives of geographers obsessed with the equator, or the made-up novelist Marcelo Chiriboga. The final section considers the paradox of taking national identity from an imaginary line, delving into the representation of that line on maps. A truly innovative and interdisciplinary work.

1683 Hernández, Maricarmen. Building a home: everyday placemaking in a toxic neighborhood. (*Sociol. Perspect.*, 62:5, Oct. 2019, p. 709–727, bibl., photos)

This ethnographic article explores why residents of an informal settlement in the city of Esmeraldas remain in their neighborhood despite knowing that it is contaminated by a nearby petrochemical plant. In explaining this paradoxical decision-making, Hernández attends to the individual and collective narratives of the residents and shows that the struggle to self-construct houses and neighborhoods, as well as the presence of dense family and friend networks, motivate people to stay and fight for better living conditions. The piece makes a contribution because it features an understudied site, particularly within environmental studies, and because of the central focus on research participants' voices and experiences. This would be an excellent article to assign in courses on ethnographic methods or environmental studies.

1684 Iglesias Martínez, Juan. Stay or go?: Ecuadorian immigrants in Spain in times of crisis. (*Bull. Lat. Am. Res.*, 36:4, Oct. 2017, p. 477–492, bibl.)

This article shows the complexity of migrants' decision-making processes through a qualitative case study of Ecuadorian migrants in Spain during an economic crisis (2008–2013). The author asks: how do immigrants decide whether to remain in Spain or return to Ecuador? Iglesias Martínez found three main patterns: deciding to stay ("permanence"), "wait and see," and return migration. When deciding, migrants considered how much progress they had made toward the goals that motivated their initial journey to Spain, and how rooted they felt in the new country. Ecuadorian government programs for return migrants did not factor into the decision. The valuable contributions of the article include focusing on the largest immigrant group in Spain and centering migrants' own accounts of their decisions.

1685 Klaufus, Christien. Urban residence: housing and social transformations in globalizing Ecuador. Translated by Lee Mitzman. New York, N.Y.: Berghahn Books, 2012. 313 p.: bibl., index, maps, photos, tables. (CEDLA Latin America studies; 100)

This book fills a gap by comparing working-class neighborhoods in Cuenca and Riobamba, in an exploration of the "mechanisms driving development" in smaller cities. Klaufus attends to the perspectives of working-class residents (as builders and consumers of urban architecture) and architects (as residents and experts/practitioners) in this unique example of simultaneously studying up and studying down. The description of debates over what counts as appropriate and tasteful architecture will interest social scientists who study consumption, taste, class, and colonialism. The abundant, high-quality photos illustrate the process of home-building in these two cities, and how that process differs based on resources, esthetic preferences, and trends, some of which are tied to international migration of Ecuadorians to the Global North.

1686 Latorre Tomás, Sara and Katharine N. Farrell. The disruption of ancestral peoples in Ecuador's mangrove ecosystem: class and ethnic differentiation within a changing political context. (*Lat. Am. Caribb. Ethn. Stud.*, 9:3, Nov. 2014, p. 293–317, bibl., map)

Mangroves provide homes for coastal fauna and maintain water and soil quality in estuaries, hence the global push for their conservation. In Ecuador, mangroves officially belong to the government (as natural patrimony) and local communities care for and use them, yet for-profit shrimp farmers have encroached. This article charts the emergence of a unique social movement for local control of mangrove ecosystems. The movement splits, with some groups beginning to claim ethnic labels (Afro, Montubio) and others rejecting these labels. The study contributes to understanding ethnic identity as relational and a process, particularly in Ecuador, where there are severe constraints on how to place demands on the state. The discussion of indigeneity in a coastal site is also noteworthy.

1687 El pensamiento político de los movimientos sociales. Introducción y selección de Carolina Larco C. y León Espinosa O. Quito: Ministerio de Coordinación de la Política y Gobiernos Autónomos Descentralizados, 2012. 290 p.: bibl., ill. (Pensamiento político ecuatoriano)

This reader features primary sources related to Ecuadorian politics, with texts dating from 1931–98 from groups such as the Frente Popular, the FEI (Federación Ecuatoriana de Indios), the CTE (Confederación de Trabajadores Ecuatorianos), and prominent individuals, including Ecuadorian presidents, politicians, party officials, and social movement leaders. The overview essay by the editors, contextualizing the political thought of social movements, is on its own a noteworthy contribution to the literature on social movements in Ecuador. This would be an excellent supplementary text for courses on Andean/Ecuadorian history or Latin American social movements.

1688 Pinto, Juan Pablo. La irrupción del "otro": economías audiovisuales populares en contextos poscoloniales. (*Ecuad. Debate*, 100, abril 2017, p. 117–131, bibl.)

This article explores popular films ("popular" here meaning both produced by everyday people and well-liked) in a location not often seen on screen nor written about by scholars. Because intellectual elites and critics impose their ideas of "quality," they misunderstand these films, which are set in rural parts of Manabí province and build on vernacular traditions and local myths. Self-taught and self- and community-funded directors address issues of local importance, especially violence and gangs. The films they produce may reinforce stereotypes about Manabí and its people, but they also address actual historical and contemporary practices, for example, murder for hire. Pinto's valuable contribution is in showing how even hyperlocal cultural products are embedded in globalized networks and worthy of serious discussion.

1689 ¿Qué hacemos con la(s) masculinidad(es)?: reflexiones antipatriarcales para pasar del privilegio al cuidado. Edición de Gustavo Endara. Quito: Friedrich-Ebert-Stiftung (FES-ILDIS) Ecuador, 2018. 240 p.: bibl., ill.

The book opens with anecdotes of gendered violence and argues that men must find out how to move "from the use of force to empathy; from domination to respect; from traditional to non-conventional roles" (p. 11). The use of the plural "masculinities" allows for many ways to be a man. This is a transnational collaboration, with examples of men rethinking and remaking masculinity from diverse authors based in Ecuador, Colombia, Cuba, and the Dominican Republic. The blending of personal, scholarly, and political writing in one work demonstrates the book's feminist approach. Chapters are short, easy to read, and rich in new ideas, making this book ideal for use in a course or as an orientation to the topic for researchers.

1690 Rahier, Jean Muteba. Blackness in the Andes: ethnographic vignettes of cultural politics in the time of multiculturalism. New York, N.Y.: Palgrave Macmillan, 2014. 243 p.: bibl., index.

This collection features essays that Rahier, one of the foremost thinkers on the topic of Blackness (and anti-Blackness) in Ecuador, published over two decades, plus two new pieces. The book tackles "race in Ecuadorian popular culture; Afro-Ecuadorian cultural politics, cultural traditions, and political activism; mestizaje... race and gender relations," and more. The historical and cultural context for these essays is the "multicultural turn" in Ecuador beginning in the late 1990s (as reflected in the 1998 Constitution), a movement away from what Rahier calls "monocultural mestizaje." The book is noteworthy for the range of topics covered, from literary genres to cultural festivals to beauty pageants to sports journalism, along with essays that provide theoretical grounding for the empirical work.

1691 Rahier, Jean Muteba and Jhon Antón Sánchez. Anti-discrimination law in two legal cases in multicultural Ecuador: Afro-Ecuadorian organizations and individuals versus Bonil/*El Universo*, and Michael Arce and Liliana Mendez versus Lieutenant Fernando Encalada/Escuela Superior Militar Eloy Alfaro (ESMIL). (*Lat. Am. Caribb. Ethn. Stud.*, 14:3, Oct. 2019, p. 270–293, bibl., ill.)

This article describes two very different legal cases, both of which ended in victories for the Afro-Ecuadorian claimants, with the goal of showing how anti-discrimination laws are viewed and applied in Ecuador. Although the primary method is analysis of media portrayals of the cases, the study benefits from interviews with key figures in each case. The article is noteworthy for its discussion of the contradictions between antidiscrimination laws and what the authors call "race regulation customary law," the set of common understandings that structures public debates about race and racism in Ecuador. Readers may also appreciate the nuanced discussion of the Correa administration, which the article describes as an unreliable ally for racial justice.

1692 Rodas Ziadé, Fadia Paola. Discriminación y luchas de poder entre "baisanos": identidad étnica y estrategias de integración social de la colonia libanesa de Guayaquil. Quito: FLACSO Ecuador, 2012. 321 p.: bibl., ill. (Tesis)

The prologue to this anthropological study emphasizes "the need for ethnographies about Guayaquil" and studies reflecting the diversity of the city, and this book rises to the challenge. Rodas Ziadé explores the community of migrants and their descendants from Lebanon, Syria, and Palestine, who have been known as "libaneses" or, erroneously, "turcos." She highlights two main themes: 1) the changes in ethnic identity over time, including the role of the Sociedad Unión Libanesa, and 2) the experiences of community members, with a focus on one prominent family. The connections of wealthy migrants to processes of urban development and politics (especially through links to the Partido Social Cristiano, PSC) are important for anyone interested in understanding the city and its history.

1693 Smith, Kimbra. Practically invisible: coastal Ecuador, tourism, and the politics of authenticity. Nashville, Tenn.: Vanderbilt University Press, 2015. 254 p.: ill., maps.

In Ecuador's "racialized geography," collective ethnic identity on the coast is equated with Afro-Ecuadorianness, but this study focuses on descendants of Manteños, a coastal Indigenous group. Extending Bourdieu's concepts of field and habitus, Smith's fine-grained ethnography examines one small town's residents' decision to claim Indigenous identity and defend collectively held land. She places everyday practices in the context of development, modernization, globalization, and ideas of racial difference in Ecuadorian political and public life. This book is ideal for use in courses: Smith defines terms clearly when introducing them and engages in exemplary discussions of reflexivity and methodology. Readers come to see ethnic identification as a process, as Agua Blancans reject top-down definitions and attempt to expand who counts as Indigenous.

1694 Tuaza Castro, Luis Alberto. Liderazgo indígena tras la disolución de la hacienda. (*Ecuad. Debate*, 102, dic. 2017, p. 33–44, bibl., ill.)

Based on interviews with people living in two rural areas of Chimborazo province, this article describes forms of Indigenous leadership during the hacienda system and after its demise. Tuaza Castro focuses on the influence and duties of *jipus*, the lowest-level leaders overseeing peasant farmers for hacienda owners. This is an important, understudied social role whose activities reverberated even after land reforms. In the shift to elected councils (*cabildos*) and increasing Indigenous social and political movement, some descendants of *jipus* were elected, but others found ways to exercise power outside of formal governance structures. The major contributions are in discussions of the continued impact of colonial-era social structures and possible solutions to combat these lingering effects, which undermine Indigenous liberation and self-determination.

1695 Vallejo, Ivette; Cristina Cielo; and Fernando García. Ethnicity, gender, and oil: comparative dynamics in the Ecuadorian Amazon. (*Lat. Am. Perspect.*, 46:2, March 2019, p. 182–198, bibl., photos)

Gender relations in processes of oil production on Indigenous territory is an understudied topic, making this comparative case study of gender and ethnic strategies among two groups of Amazonian Indigenous women particularly interesting. The study uses qualitative methods and a feminist political ecology approach to examine responses to oil enterprises' encroachment on collectively held land. The authors find these enterprises encounter more resistance where women remain more tied to the land (through farming and other activities), and in both cases, show how women's gender roles can affect the collective behavior of communities. This is an excellent text to assign in courses on race, class, gender, and indigeneity, and offers a necessary gender perspective for the burgeoning scholarship on extractivism in Ecuador.

PERU

KEITH JAMTGAARD, *Senior Research Associate, Institute of Public Policy, Truman School of Public Affairs, University of Missouri*

THE PERUVIAN sociological publications reviewed for this volume cover an impressive range of topics and reflect a discipline that is actively involved in examining the problems of the larger society. One area that receives considerable attention is environmental concerns, which scholars analyze at several levels. Castro Carpio critiques the approaches that have been used to understand and address climate change, arguing that the connections between the scientific method and its ties to economic interests limit the usefulness of this tool for the state (item **1701**). Instead, he argues, policymakers need to employ different intellectual tools and a rich tradition of engaging nonstate actors to help enact climate policy. Returning to the principal tenets of an Andean philosophy offers the best path forward for society, suggests Chacón Málaga (item **1702**). Such a philosophy places a high value on a harmonious relationship between humans and the environment. This approach to navigating the climatic challenges that lie ahead has the potential to lead to a more successful society.

Rural communities of Indigenous peoples, neighboring extractive industries, and the state have developed an uneasy coexistence during the 21st century. While fees that mining companies pay are a significant boon for the regions in which they are located, corruption among public officials has also increased, limiting the economic benefits. Urquizo Valdeiglesias assembled a database of the environmental conflicts that have occurred between 1999 and 2015 in Peru (item **1726**). At a higher level, Hinostroza Rivera published a broad analysis of corruption in Peru and its associated costs (item **1708**). The author argues that international conventions to which Peru is a party offer an option for combatting corruption. At the midpoint of the Fujimori decade, the government initiated a program to encourage birth control. However, with the collapse of the Fujimori administration, a wave of rejection of corrupt practices began, including a rejection of the family planning program—alleging that 300,000 forced sterilizations had taken place. Villegas argues that a coalition of conservative interests and the Catholic Church were active in bringing about the demise of the family planning program (item **1729**).

Several analyses of the changing status of religion, both past and present, were published during this review period. In examining the diminishing role of the Catholic Church in Peruvian society, Lecaros argues that cultural change is responsible (item **1709**). Even though most Peruvians state that they are believers, the proportion that participate in church services is declining markedly. Another publication documents how struggles have taken place between Christian congregations and groups representing sexual diversity (item **1717**). Violent confrontations against the Andean LGBTQ community have occurred. Madrigal Sánchez considers the broad outlines of what a preconquest theology in the Americas might have looked like (item **1711**). Ramírez Bautista looks to the Andean community of Huamatanga in the department of Lima to explore how Christian traditions fused with preconquest beliefs to create a unique celebration that marks the beginning of the agricultural calendar (item **1719**). A member of the Jesuit mission in Peru contributed a book documenting the experience of the Jesuits during the period in which Sendero Luminoso was active in the country (item **1712**). The Jesuits operated missions in four areas in Peru during this time: San Juan de Jarpa (Junín), Juamanga and nearby provinces (Ayacucho), El Agustino (Lima), and Chimbote. The Jesuit response in the four areas under siege was to accompany the people during this time of great distress.

Scholars have written much about the 12-year period between 1980 and 1992 in which Sendero Luminoso emerged and became active in Peru as well as about the conditions that precipitated this outbreak of violence. A new contribution to this body of literature (item **1703**) suggests that events that took place two decades earlier set the stage for the subsequent political violence. In October 1963, violence related to land seizures in the province of Andahuaylas in the department of Apurimac resulted in 17 deaths and many injuries. In response to this episode, in 1964 the Belaúnde Terry administration passed an agrarian reform law to address the inequities that were then apparent. This book argues that the promised, but unrealized, reforms in this region initiated the discontent that eventually led to the 20-year period of violence beginning in 1980. Another event that rocked Peruvian society in 1983 concerned the deaths of eight journalists who were visiting the community of Uchuraccay, Ayacucho, in an attempt to better understand the issues that were producing armed conflict in the region. A judicial process took place in which three members of the community were accused of causing the deaths of the eight journalists. A contemporary analysis of this process was published in 2010 by one of the defense attorneys for the three community members. This same attorney has since published a reanalysis of the events that took place (item **1705**), and in light of additional information, concluded that it was very likely that there was involvement of the Peruvian armed forces in the original incident, as well as in the proceedings that followed, and that evidence of this connection has been suppressed.

A 2016 essay competition titled "Shrapnel of Hate" took place among contemporary youth regarding their perceptions of Sendero Luminoso. Twelve of the essays were selected and published (item **1713**) to represent the current state of reflection from today's young people regarding the period of violence that took place before they were born. The contributions contain many insights into the young people of this period that have often been overlooked by adults, such as the failure to clearly distinguish between the actions of adherents of Sendero Luminoso and the young people who were captured and forced to carry out actions on behalf of the group. An ethnography (item **1728**) studies the former guerrillas as social beings in a prison setting. The author seeks to understand the guerrilla organizations of which they were once members by better understanding the organizations that the former guerrillas (now prisoners) have constructed in their penitentiary surroundings. Another publication (item **1706**) resulted from a colloquium on gender and social class relationships, both within the Sendero Luminoso and Movimiento Revolucionario Túpac Amaru movements, and in their vision of what these would look like in the society that they envisioned. A psychological perspective was also brought to bear on this period of violence in Peru. In a demonstration of the social responsibility of psychoanalysis, Herrera Abad (item **1707**) sees a pattern in which rebellions and subversive movements throughout Peru's history have tended to result in profoundly authoritarian outcomes, thus reproducing the very dynamic that they seek to overthrow. The author argues that this is a result of the multiracial and multicultural identities that Peruvians embody.

Barriaga (item **1698**) offers a conceptual exploration of some of the ways that different cultures can interact, as well as a case study of the intercultural challenges in Peru. He argues that the greatest intercultural challenge that Peru faces today is that the Indigenous population does not share fairly in the wealth produced by the minerals in the lands that they occupy. Feedback from efforts at introducing intercultural education suggest that these efforts did not align well with the goals of the Indigenous communities. Parents wanted their children to learn language and other skills that would allow them greater access to opportunities. In another study (item **1723**), youth consumer cultures were compared for Lima and Mexico City. A series of cultural consumption indicators were reviewed, including reading patterns, museum attendance, and television and internet usage. Based on this analysis, researchers argue that the youth consumer cultures in these two settings were quite similar and worthy of comparison. Similar patterns were found in each of the countries in the relationship between income levels and access to different types of cultural resources.

A review of what is known about the cultural practices related to sexuality in Peru prior to the arrival of the Europeans in the early 16th century was written by Barra Ruatta (item **1725**). Evidence was based upon observations from archeological materials, as well as reports from early European arrivals and their Inca informants. The chroniclers described the existence of the well-established tradition of trial marriage known as *"servinacuy"* that typically preceded longer term relationships. The book also documents what has been learned about the existence of homosexuality, transvestism, prostitution, and other aspects of sexual life. Motta (item **1714**) presents a series of 17 short essays on the topics of sexual violence and violence based on gender and LGBTQ status. It is also a statement in defense of the notions of participatory democracy and human rights as they concern individuals from diverse orientations. Also included is a discussion of the frequently stated objections to these arguments as represented by some of Peru's more culturally conservative sectors and organizations. Santi Huaranca (item **1730**) presents a collection of five articles written by undergraduate students concerning the economic and labor impacts of violence against female employees in Peruvian businesses. Four of the studies gathered information from female and male employees from places of business in Lima, and one article had a national scope, using data from a survey conducted by the Instituto Nacional de Estadística e Informática (INEI). A study was conducted concerning gender relations and labor rights for female live-in domestic service workers from 16 districts within Lima (item **1727**). Both employers and employees were interviewed by the author, an attorney. One of the conclusions from the study is that, as females, both employer and employee are often subject to similar processes of devaluing in a male-dominated society. Bermúdez Valdivia (item **1700**) argues that it is through the political process that doors will be opened to Peruvian women. She reviews the degree to which women's political participation has increased in Peru, as well as in other countries in the region.

Regional studies were among the selections reviewed for this volume. Two publications by the same author discuss the social history and cultural contributions of Afro-Peruvians, particularly from the north of Peru, but also the Malambo neighborhood in Lima. The first concerns Bartola Sancho Dávila, an Afro-Peruvian woman from Zaña in the north of the country, who popularized song and dance from the Afro-Peruvian population during the early 20th century (item **1720**). This study is one of the few available on Afro-Peruvian women from this period, their family lives, as well as, in her case, her life as a performing artist. Her impact on criollo dance forms were lasting. The second publication (item **1721**) is a catalog of some of the other cultural forms that were created and used by Afro-Peruvians, including songs, stories, and poems. The content contained in these forms includes anticlerical and sexual themes, and one that specifically represents content from Afro-Peruvian women. The book contains many examples of the language used in these forms.

Another series of regional analyses was reviewed this year. One of these involved coca leaf growers and their organizations distributed along the eastern slope of the Andes (item **1704**). The study looks at how the organizations and their membership responded to the opening of political space following a long period of lockdown and silence during the conflict with the Sendero Luminoso. The growers and their organizations quickly grew in their sophistication and exercise of power to respond to new opportunities from national and international agencies. Love (item **1710**) explores the unique culture of Arequipa, Peru's second largest city located in the far south of the country. The author argues that the origins of its famously independent culture parallel in part its geographical location midway between the coastal criollo culture and the Andean Indigenous Highlands. Arequipa was focused on its mestizo identity long before this became popularized across the rest of Latin America during the 20th century. Lima and its institutions and history of attending to the needs of the mentally ill are described by Prieto Sánchez (item **1718**). The institutions in Lima that attended to those considered to be mentally ill are enumerated, illustrated, and described, beginning with early days of European settlement, through and including the establishment of insane asylums in Lima. This exploration of the lives, places, and ways in which the mentally ill lived is an effort to better appreciate the contradictions that sometimes lead to the categorization of mental illness. The book includes a selection of the stories, art, and poems of those who were interned. Another inquiry focuses on Trujillo, Peru's third largest city, also located in Peru's north. Becerra (item **1699**) examines the growth of organized crime in Trujillo. The author describes the evolution of criminal activities from individual actors to groups working as an organization. Ultimately, the network of organizations became instrumental in the overseas distribution of illegal drugs.

A recent publication about femicide sheds light on this phenomenon through four case studies of victims (item **1715**). The author describes the relationships between the victims and their accused assassins, along with the judicial proceedings and outcomes. She also provides a statistical review of many of the aspects of femicide in Peru. In another analysis of crime in Peru, Sánchez Aguilar (item **1724**) looks at the social class characteristics of both perpetrators and victims. The author also highlights the role that information can play in addressing crime. Forty years after Webb and Figueroa published their study of Peru's income distribution in the mid-1970s (see *HLAS 39:3474*), Alarco et al. (item **1696**) have examined the status of Peru's income distribution following the economic upheavals and violence of the 1980s and early 1990s, followed by the two-decade long period to the present which has been dominated by neoliberal policies. Their analysis includes a discussion of the methodological challenges associated with studying those Peruvians with the highest incomes. Other topics include: a review of earnings, the evolution of the role of international capital since the 1970s, changes in the relative share of GDP represented by wages and salaries, and income distribution with associated Gini coefficients with a comparison to earlier periods in Peru and to other Latin American countries. The authors find that income distribution is less concentrated than that reported previously, and improvements were generally larger than those reported by Chile, Mexico, and Colombia.

To ensure continued access to some classic works produced in Peru, two publications look back on works by journalists and social scientists. Concerned that the quality of Peruvian journalism could easily be lost in the internet age, Coaguila (item **1716**) assembled some of the best work from living journalists of different media, including newspapers, magazines, essays, poems, and television journalism. Tanaka (item **1697**) was part of an effort that spanned Latin America to ensure that today's students are aware of their own rich heritage of social thought produced in the region over the past 50 years. Peru is richly represented in this publication with 21 articles from a selection of sociologists, anthropologists, historians, and others, highlighting an important body of critical social thought that emerged from Peru during this period.

1696 Alarco, Germán; César Castillo; and Favio Leiva. Riqueza y desigualdad en el Perú: visión panorámica. Lima: Oxfam, 2019. 196 p.: bibl., color ill.

Forty years after Webb and Figueroa published their study of Peru's income distribution in the mid-1970s (see *HLAS 39:3474*), this study revisits the topic after the economic upheavals and terrorism of the 1980s followed by the neoliberal policies of the next 20 years beginning in the early 1990s. The book examines five areas, starting with the methodological issues related to studying those Peruvians with the highest incomes. The second section reports on the how the generation of earnings has evolved over the period under review. The third section provides a comparative international perspective, with a look at how the presence and importance of international capital has evolved over the time period. A fourth section analyzes changes in the share of the GDP represented by wages and salaries, in which a decline in its share took place over the period under review—larger than several other Latin American economies. The fifth section reviews the distribution of personal income and resulting Gini coefficients. The results indicate that income distribution was less concentrated compared to earlier periods. Likewise, spending was also more evenly distributed than was the case previously. In a comparative analysis, the Gini coefficient for Peru's income distribution showed improvements that were generally larger than those of three other Latin American countries: Chile, Mexico, and Colombia. For a review of Webb's 1977 study, see *HLAS 41:7364*.

1697 Antología del pensamiento crítico peruano contemporáneo. Coordinación de Martín Tanaka. Textos de José Matos Mar *et al*. Buenos Aires: CLACSO, 2016. 796 p.: bibl., ill. (Colección Antologías del pensamiento social latinoamericano y caribeño)

This selection of 21 articles from sociologists, anthropologists, historians, and others, represents an important body of critical social thought that emerged in Peru during the past 50 years. The collection was published with the intention of raising awareness of the rich heritage of social thought produced in Latin America. It presents a critical analysis of the status quo and conceptualizes options for moving beyond the discriminatory outcomes from the diverse and complex settings in which exploitation and exclusion are found. The texts are organized by historical period beginning with the time period preceding and eventually producing the military takeover and subsequent reforms led by General Velasco. The contributions in this section document the fragmented nature of relations among classes and ethnic groups. The second period under review includes the second stage of the military government and an eventual return to democracy along with an economic focus on the extreme poverty in the rural Andes. The earlier military policies directed toward restructuring the economy are replaced by a greater focus on rural development to combat poverty. The political left experienced a period of growth as demonstrated by the role that the Izquierda Unida (IU) played in electoral politics in the 1980s. This influence declined as a more radical left represented by Sendero Luminoso (SL) and the Movimiento Revolucionario Túpac Amaru (MRTA) initiated a violent armed struggle. The third period encompasses the economic collapse that followed years of hyperinflation, the election of Alberto Fujimori in 1990, and the eventual capture of the leadership of SL. Neoliberal policies dominated the subsequent decade.

1698 Barriga, Tomás Carlos. Interculturalidad y comunicación intercultural: el desafío del diálogo intercultural en el Perú. La Molina, Peru: Universidad Nacional Agraria La Molina, 2017. 146 p.: bibl., ill.

Settings with more than one culture present both the uncertainties of relations between different cultures as well as opportunities for collaboration and understanding. This work provides a conceptual exploration of some of the ways that cultures may interact, as well as a case study of one country confronting intercultural challenges at many levels: Peru. The author presents a framework for distinguishing different levels of the integration of cultures existing in the same geographic space, and contemplates domination and conflict among the levels. Peru has the largest population of Indigenous inhabitants in Latin America and the Caribbean, with by far the largest share living in the Andean region. Simultaneously, the Andean region is the source of Peru's most important economic resource: minerals extracted from mines for export. The largest intercultural challenge in Peru today is that the Indigenous population does not share fairly in the wealth produced by the minerals in the lands that they occupy. There have been efforts at introducing intercultural education; however, feedback suggests that these efforts did not align well with the goals of the Indigenous communities. Parents wanted their children to learn language and other skills that would offer them greater access to opportunities. The author reports on a research project that he led with the support of students at the Universidad Nacional Agraria La Molina. The goal was to explore the intercultural image of self and others among 474 subjects selected randomly across Lima. Respondents reported that while they did not perceive themselves as prejudiced against those of other cultural backgrounds, they felt that others in society were more likely to be prejudiced. The book concludes with a series of proposals regarding how to help Peru become a more inclusive society.

1699 Becerra, Charlie. El origen de la hidra: crimen organizado en el norte del Perú. Lima: Aguilar, 2017. 179 p.: bibl., ill.

Trujillo is Peru's third largest city and, similar to Lima, rural-to-urban migration has contributed to much of its growth. This book presents a personal account of the proliferation of organized crime in Trujillo from the perspective of a Trujillo native. This book consists of a series of stories of the people who were involved in criminal activities, both lawbreakers and their victims. Becerra describes the evolution of their activities from individuals acting alone to groups working as an organization. Eventually, with the role that illegal drug production has played in Peru, northern Peru became a center for overseas distribution, with Trujillo playing a leading role.

1700 Bermúdez Valdivia, Violeta. Género y poder: la igualdad política de las mujeres. Lima: Palestra Editores, 2019. 263 p.: bibl.

Over 40 years have passed since the UN approved the Convention on the Elimination of All Forms of Discrimination against Women (CEDAW) in 1979. This study looks at the degree to which women have achieved equality in their political participation. The author argues that this engagement is critically important, as it is through involvement in the political process that other doors will be opened to women. Women began seeking suffrage early in the 20th century, but it was not achieved at the national level in Peru until 1963. The author compares Peru to the experience of other Latin American countries. She then analyzes the degree to which political equality for women has progressed in Peru, and how this progress has impacted equality for women throughout society.

1701 Castro Carpio, Augusto. El desafío de un pensar diferente: pensamiento, sociedad y naturaleza. Buenos Aires: CLACSO, 2018. 373 p.: bibl.

This study attempts to explore the interplay among three areas: a critique of modern thought regarding society, ideas about the role of the state in today's world, and connections between these topics and issues regarding the environment. The argument the author pursues is that these three areas have always been extraordinarily complex. What is relatively new is a greater awareness of the limitations to the approaches that have been employed to explore these complexities to date. To illustrate this point, the author gives the example of the scientific method and its close relationship with economic interests. He argues that there is a need to explore the world's complexities with intellectual tools from elsewhere in the rich human tradition of approaches to problem-solving. Peru as a case study advances the discussion of complexities associated with a state, specifically the experiences of class and ethnicity and the role of the state. The possibilities for addressing climate change are then examined in light of the observations about available intellectual tools and alternative roles for the state.

1702 Chacón Málaga, Hugo. Nación andina. Lima: Fondo Editorial IIPCIAL, Instituto de Investigación para la Paz, Cultura e Integración de América Latina, 2017. 280 p.: bibl.

The author is a poet, novelist, and essayist who adds to a tradition established by other well-known Peruvians dating back to the country's origins. Unlike many of his predecessors, however, Chacón Málaga argues that the Indigenous prehispanic Andean culture, far from being the central problem, is in fact at the heart of the Peruvian soul and represents the ideal path forward for the society. The Andean peoples value a harmonious relationship between humans and the environment, as illustrated by the ancestors' achievements in the areas of irrigation and construction. This work outlines the principal tenets of an Andean philosophy and the author suggests that these could be the foundation of a successful society.

1703 Chati Quispe, Guido. De quién es la tierra: historia y memoria campesina sobre política por la tierra, la represión y masacre en Ongoy, 1960 a 1969. Lima: Lluvia Editores, 2019. 207 p.: bibl., ill.

(Colección Historia y memoria. Serie Movimientos campesinos; 1)

Much has been written about the deadly decades of violence between 1980 and 2000 that began initially in Ayacucho department, involving the Sendero Luminoso guerrilla movement. This study looks at the origins and legacy of another instance of violence that took place in the decade of the 1960s in the neighboring department of Apurimac in the town of Ongoy, located in the province of Andahuaylas. An incident that occurred in October 1963 resulted in the deaths of 17 members of the Ongoy community along with many who were injured. This tragedy was not an isolated case; the first months of the Belaúnde administration (1963–68) were marked with numerous instances of land seizures, resulting in an Agrarian Reform Law in 1964. The author argues that the social movements that were unleashed by the events of this period, and the failings of the promised agrarian reform, came to represent the foundation upon which, in this same region, the violence of the period between 1980 and 2000 was constructed.

1704 Durand Guevara, Anahí. La irrupción cocalera: movilización social y representación política en los productores de hoja de coca del Perú (2000–2008). Lima: Universidad Nacional Mayor de San Marcos, Fondo Editorial, Facultad de Ciencias Sociales, 2018. 238 p.: bibl.

Following the end of the Fujimori period at the conclusion of the year 2000, the political landscape in Peru began to open up to diverse actors and interests. Many areas which had been under a strict lockdown resulting from the long conflict with leftist guerrilla organizations began to see expanded political participation from groups that had long been silenced. This case study takes the perspective that coca leaf growers organizations are an example of a social movement. The author studied the activities in the valleys along the eastern slope of the Peruvian Andes, one of the areas where coca leaf growers and their organizations increased their sophistication in the exercise of increased power as they responded to new initiatives on the part of national and international agencies. The book also documents the history of growers' attempts to influence national policy in this area.

1705 Falconí Gonzales, Julio. Hipótesis y conclusiones sobre el caso Uchuraccay: el juicio oral y el procedimiento ante la CIDH. Lima: Fondo Editorial, Asociación Nacional de Periodistas del Perú, 2017. 384 p.: bibl., ill.

This is the second book by the author regarding the tragic incident resulting in the deaths of eight journalists in January 1983 in the community of Uchuraccay, in the department of Ayacucho, Peru. The first was *El caso Uchuraccay: las claves de un complot contra la libertad de expresión: Ayacucho, Perú, enero de 1983* (2010). The reporters were visiting the Andean community in an effort to better understand the conflict that was raging in the region between the Sendero Luminoso (SL) guerrilla movement and the Peruvian armed forces. A trial was held in Lima, which resulted in sentences for three members of the Uchuraccay community. The defense had argued that the member of the Uchuraccay community assumed the visiting journalists were members of the SL and killed them for that reason. The author was a member of the team of attorneys representing the accused and their families. In this book on the Uchuraccay case and subsequent trial, the author expands on the additional information that has come to light since the trial. The author also explores in depth the nature of the involvement of the Peruvian armed forces in the war against terrorism in the Ayacucho region, and the likelihood that the Peruvian armed forces were involved either directly or indirectly in the deaths of the journalists.

1706 Género y conflicto armado en el Perú. Textos de Anouk Guiné, Maritza Felices-Luna, Luisa Dietrich et al. Prólogo de José Luis Rénique. Epílogo de Milena Justo y Jimmy Flores. Lima: La Plaza Editores; Le Havre Cedex, France: Groupe de Recherche Identités et Cultures GRIC, Université Le Herve Normandie, 2018. 283 p.: bibl., ill.

This volume is the result of a colloquium concerning gender, class, and peacemaking, which was held in Huamanga,

Ayacucho, Peru in July 2014. The goal of the contributions is to review the involvement of women guerrillas in the armed conflict and to analyze how gender intersected with social class. The authors examine how Sendero Luminoso and Movimiento Revolucionario Túpac Amaru (MRTA) conceptualized gender and class relationships, both within their movements and in the wider society, as well as their ideal vision of these relationships in the society they wished to construct.

1707 Herrera Abad, Luis. Reflexiones psicoanalíticas sobre la violencia y el poder en el Perú. Miraflores, Peru: Biblioteca Peruana de Piscoanálisis, 2018. 165 p.: bibl.

This series of essays views violence in Peru from a number of psychoanalytical perspectives. It is, in a sense, an examination of the social responsibility of psychoanalysis. The author suggests that with Freudian psychoanalysis, there are always more questions than answers. A successful result for an individual could be changing out the questions asked by a patient for a new set of questions, rather than receiving answers to the original questions. In the case of Peru's history, the author sees a pattern in which rebellions and subversive movements become profoundly authoritarian—essentially reproducing the very dynamic that they seek to overthrow. Another example is that it is challenging to speak of a singular Peruvian identity; a fractured identity is a more useful concept due to the multiracial and multicultural identities in Peru. This situation suggests that violence among the fragments is the inevitable result, with domination as the most successful way to move forward.

1708 Hinostroza Rivera, Dino. Gobernabilidad democrática, corrupción y derechos humanos: los vínculos entre corrupción y derechos humanos en el Perú, 1990-2000: cómo evitar que se repita. Lima: Centro de Políticas Públicas y Derechos Humanos Perú Equidad, 2018. 113 p.: bibl., ill.

As this study points out, corruption is the confluence of a complex set of social phenomena, which is often poorly defined—in its methods and scope, as well as in its reason for existence and its impact on areas such as culture and democracy itself. The first section of this publication attempts to bring clarity to this situation by examining corruption in Peru and in particular how it interacts with human rights. The second section looks at the Fujimori decade (1990 through 2000) and investigates how the forms of corruption that emerged during this period created the basis for the practices that have persisted since then. The third section examines the costs associated with corruption in Peru, particularly in terms of "large scale" corruption, at the upper levels of government, and "small scale" corruption, examples of which are the bribes necessary to advance routine governing. The last section looks at the international conventions to which Peru is a party and the possibilities that they offer to combat the impact of corruption on human rights.

1709 Lecaros, Véronique. Fe cristiana y secularización en el Perú de hoy. Pueblo Libre, Peru: Universidad Antonio Ruiz de Montoya, 2018. 219 p.: bibl., ill., maps.

This work analyzes the process of change underway in Peru regarding Catholicism and its impacts on Peruvian society as well as on the Catholic Church itself. The argument the author elaborates is that the Church is not the victim of a process of secularization, but rather, it is subjected to the consequences of a cultural process that is taking place. The Church is no longer supported by the dominant culture in Peru. Even though surveys suggest that most Peruvians consider themselves believers, and that a third say they regularly attend church services, data collected at services report that actual numbers of attendees are typically lower. The author sees a major challenge for the Church in the need to reconcile faith with science in the minds of its followers.

Lobatón, Javier. El sueño peruano. See *HLAS 76:2092.*

1710 Love, Thomas F. The Independent Republic of Arequipa: making regional culture in the Andes. Austin: University of Texas Press, 2017. 321 p.: bibl., ill., maps. (Joe R. and Teresa Lozano Long series in Latin American and Latino art and culture)

Arequipa is Peru's second largest city, located in the far southern region of the country. It possesses a unique (within Peru) regional culture. The people are proud and independent. To that end, this work explores Arequipeñan culture, its origins, and the forces that sustain it through the present time. Its geography and culture represent a midway point between coastal Lima with its Criollo culture and the Andean Highlands with strong Indigenous origins. Notably, the author makes the case that Arequipa was focused on its mestizo identity long before it became popularized across Latin America during the 20th century.

1711 Madrigal Sánchez, Víctor. Teología en Abya Yala. San Salvador: Editorial Universidad Don Bosco, 2018. 147 p.: bibl.

This book is the result of an effort to derive a vision of a preconquest theology. The author attempts to provide some answers to questions about the beliefs of the Indigenous population prior to the imposition of Christianity in North and South America. He argues that the 20th-century conversion en masse was made possible by the Second Vatican Council which had the effect of encouraging and giving increased attention to the cultural identity of Indigenous peoples. The book discusses some of the characteristics of the theologies likely to have been practiced by Indigenous peoples throughout the Americas.

1712 Martínez, Emilio. Los jesuitas en tiempos de la violencia, 1980–1992. Lima: Antonio Ruiz de Montoya Universidad Jesuita: Compañía de Jesús en el Perú, 2018. 102 p.: bibl.

The Catholic Church found that it had become an unwitting participant in Peru's 10-year guerrilla war at the end of the 20th century. The author was a member of a Jesuit mission in Peru during this period. Sendero Luminoso (SL) represented an outlier in its relationship to the Catholic Church. Other Latin American revolutionary groups have been somewhat sympathetic to the goals of the Catholic Church; this was clearly not the case with SL. The principal issue that the book addresses is how the Jesuits responded to the violence between 1986 and 1992 in their effort to accompany the people in four areas where they had missions in Peru: San Juan de Jarpa (Junín), Juamanga and nearby provinces (Ayacucho), El Agustino (Lima), and Chimbote. The sources of information that the author consulted consisted almost entirely of members of the mission living in these four regions, along with a number of individuals from the laity in these same areas.

1713 Memorias del presente: ensayos sobre juventud, violencia y el horizonte democrático. Edición de Álvaro Maurial. Lima: Ministerio de Cultura, LUM—Lugar de la Memoria, la Tolerancia y la Inclusión Social, 2017. 245 p.: bibl.

This publication contains essays submitted to a 2016 competition titled "Esquirlas del Odio: Percepciones de los Jóvenes Hoy sobre Sendero Luminoso." The three winning essays were selected for publication, along with nine additional essays judged to be worthy of inclusion. Together, the editor considered this group of essays to be a useful sample of the current state of reflection on this period from today's youth. The book is divided into four sections, the first of which presents the three winning essays. One analyzes a class of cadets situated in the heart of the region of violence in Ayacucho and examines their curriculum of violence and terror. Another winning essay looks at the role of universities in contributing to the development of Sendero Luminoso in light of the fact that these institutions were ignored by the state during this period. The next section presents essays based on testimonials focused on an understanding of the period of violence. These first-hand accounts address the impacts of the perception that Sendero Luminoso was present in the social science departments of the Universidad Nacional Mayor de San Marcos in Lima. Another looks at the failure to distinguish between the actions of Sendero Luminoso adherents and those youth who were captured and forced by SL members to carry out actions on their behalf. The final section examines the different ways that young people in the postconflict period responded to the new environment with its challenges and potential.

1714 **Motta, Angélica.** La biología del odio: retóricas fundamentalistas y otras violencias de género. Lima: La Siniestra Ensayos, 2019. 146 p.: bibl., ill.

This series of 17 short essays covers the topics of sexual violence and violence based on gender and LGBTQ status. It is also a statement in defense of the notions of participatory democracy and human rights as concerns individuals from diverse orientations. The book includes a discussion of the frequently stated objections to these arguments as represented by some of Peru's more culturally conservative sectors and organizations.

1715 **Muñoz-Nájar Rojas, Teresina.** Morir de amor: un reportaje sobre el feminicidio en el Perú. Lima: Aguilar, 2017. 145 p.

This publication consists of four case studies of the victims of femicide and those who were accused of murdering them. The women were killed between 2010 and 2015. Simona was the oldest at 45, and the sister of the author. The other three women were under the age of 25. Those accused of the crimes were similarly young. Each chapter describes the history of the relationship between the victim and her partner, the involvement of family members in the proceedings, as well as the actions of the criminal justice system and the eventual fate of the accused. The author provides a statistical background for many aspects related to the occurrence of femicide in Peru.

1716 **Perú: crónicas y perfiles.** Selección de Jorge Coaguila. Lima: Revuelta Editores, 2018. 299 p.

Concerned about the disappearance of outlets for quality journalism in Peru, Coaguila set out to publish some of the best work of living Peruvian journalists from a broad spectrum of media, including newspaper and magazine articles, essays, poems, and even television. One of the common threads joining the selections is the perception of quality, along with the concern that an appreciation for solid and reliable publications and programs could easily be lost in the internet age.

1717 **Poder(es) en contexto: lecturas teológicas, socioculturales y de género en torno al poder.** Edición de Juan Carlos Chávez Quispe y Ángel Eduardo Román-Lopez Dollinger. La Paz: ISEAT, 2016. 227 p.: bibl.

Sponsored by the Instituto Superior Ecuménico Andino de Teología (ISEAT), this book reviews the origins of power and the ways that it is exercised. One section looks at how people experience power by reviewing publications in which Bolivia's president and vice president use symbols, often originating from the preconquest era, with the goal of achieving societal change in the country. Another analysis of power looks at gender and the use of Andean ideals as models to ensure the continued domination of males over female bodies. The Andean concept of Pachamama as a feminine virtue is contrasted with the reality of continued domination of females by males. In another example, a struggle takes place between Christian churches and groups representing sexual diversity. In this scenario, the LGBTQ community experiences acts of violence and oppression.

1718 **Prieto Sánchez, Roberto.** Guía demente: soñadores y manicomios en la historia de Lima. Chorillos, Peru: Autor-Editor Roberto Rachid Antonio Prieto Sánchez, 2017. 316 p.: bibl., ill. (some color).

The author, an architect by training, describes this book as an homage to the irrational. He argues that this distinction is important because the line between brilliance and absurdity is often not clearly drawn. One who does things that are out of the ordinary risks being categorized as "insane." To that end, beginning with individuals well known to Western civilization, this work explores the lives, places, and ways in which these people lived, in an effort to better appreciate the contradictions that sometimes lead to people being categorized as mentallly ill. The book offers a window into the ways that mental illness was perceived in Lima, beginning with the descriptions from native peoples as recorded by the first European arrivals. The institutions in Lima that attended to those considered to be mentally ill are enumerated and described from the early days of European settlement, through and including the insane asylums of Lima, and the book includes a selection of the stories, art, and poems of those who were interned.

1719 Ramírez Bautista, Bernardino. La fiesta de las cruces y la danza de los negritos: el sincretismo cristiano-indígena en Huamantanga, Canta. Lima: Centro de Estudios y Proyectos Surco Andino (CEPSA), 2018. 94 p.: bibl., color ill.

This study explores how cultural traditions that emerged in Spain following the "reconquista" of Moorish-held lands were introduced to Spanish-held areas following the Spanish conquest in America. Two such traditions became popular in many areas: the celebration of the crosses and the dance of the African descendents of enslaved people who were brought to the region by the Spanish—though some eventually escaped to Andean communities. This study focuses on how these traditions merged and were adapted to meet the needs of one isolated setting in the Andes: Huamatanga, in the province of Canta, department of Lima. The celebration of the crosses of the department became associated with the beginning of the agricultural calendar in early January, replacing prehispanic symbols previously used to mark the occasion. Thirty-eight crosses, each with its own sponsors, are distributed across the two main sectors of the community and painted and decorated with flowers and fruits from the area. In a procession on 6 January, the crosses are brought to the central plaza near the church, and following a ceremony, they are carried to the village's agricultural and pasture lands by community members portraying themselves as Africans. The purpose of this activity is to encourage the arrival of seasonal rains—beneficial for both livestock and agriculture.

1720 Rocca Torres, Luis. Bartola Sancho Dávila: bailarina de Malambo. Zaña, Peru: Museo Afroperuano de Zaña, 2018. 119 p.: bibl., ill.

This biography examines the life of Bartola Sancho Dávila, an Afro-Peruvian woman who was born in 1882 in the north of Peru and who popularized Afro-Peruvian song and dance during the early 20th century. Her biography is important not only for her lasting impact on song and dance, but also as an Afro-Peruvian woman. The information available about her life represents one of the few sources on Afro-Peruvian women from this period, their family lives and, in her case, her life as a performing artist. She gained national recognition and performed more than once at the Presidential Palace, as well as in the homes of Lima's upper class. Her early dance was primarily in the style of the "vieja zamacueca," a dance form that preceded and is a precursor of "La Marinera," an evolutionary process that she was very much involved with. La Marinera remains at the heart of dance culture of the Peruvian coast.

1721 Rocca Torres, Luis. El libro prohibido: afrodescendientes, sexo y religión. Zaña, Peru: Museo Afroperuano de Zaña, 2018. 73 p.: bibl.

Africans were forcibly brought to Peru as enslaved people soon after the conquest; slavery was abolished in 1854 by presidential decree. This book documents the cultural forms that Afro-Peruvians have created, including songs, stories, and poems. Three categories of these cultural forms are presented and discussed, including anticlerical, sexual, and women's voices. The use of these forms varied greatly by location, with a stark contrast between urban and rural areas. Over time, Afro-Peruvians learned to employ Spanish literary techniques using metered verses such as quatrains and "décimas," a popular 10-line stanza.

1722 Rodríguez Pastor, Humberto. El peón y empresario Nikumatsu Okada y la comunidad japonesa del valle de Chancay, 1900–1950. Lima: APJ Asociación Peruano Japonesa, Fondo Editorial, 2018. 108 p.: bibl., ill. (Serie Memorias de la inmigración japonesa)

The first migration of Asians to Peru in modern times originated from China in the third quarter of the 19th century. The second large migration took place in the first two decades of the 20th century from Japan. The Japanese migration was less than one-fifth the size of the Chinese migration. This study examines the Japanese agricultural settlement in the lower Chancay Valley in the region just north of Lima.

The typical labor contract for Japanese agricultural workers upon arrival was for four years. By the beginning of the 1920s, a number of Japanese immigrants began renting agricultural properties themselves and exporting cotton, often to Japan. The author describes the cultural adaptations that took place, in which the Japanese arrivals became part of the Chancay region, and there were marriages between Peruvians and immigrants. Periods of anti-Japanese sentiment followed, coinciding with the economic depression of the 1930s and the war in the Pacific in the 1940s. Beginning in December 1941, there was evidence of coordination with Washington, D.C., regarding limitations placed on Japanese Peruvians. An anti-Japanese bias was evident in the Peruvian news media. This development was followed by expulsions of an estimated 1,771 Japanese Peruvians, many sent to internment camps in the US. Some from this group opted to remain in the US following the end of the war, while others attempted to return to Peru, but were denied re-entry.

1723 Los "rostros invisibles" de la desigualdad social: un estudio sobre arte, política, educación y consumo cultural en América Latina: los casos de Lima y la Ciudad de México. Coordinación de Vivian Romeu Aldaya. Mexico: Universidad Iberoamericana, 2018. 207 p.: bibl., ill.

This unique study offers a comparative perspective of youth consumer culture from the urban centers in two Latin American countries: Mexico and Peru. Both countries are exposed to powerful market forces directed at their populations, particularily in their urban centers, and both face conditions of severe social inequality. The study provides an overview of cultural consumption among the youth of both countries and analyzes indicators related to reading patterns, attendance at museums, consumption of television and internet usage—with similar results between the two populations. The authors find similar patterns in each country regarding the relationship between income levels and access to different types of cultural resources.

1724 Sánchez Aguilar, Aníbal. Criminalidad y seguridad ciudadana en el Perú del siglo XXI: hacia un sistema integrado de estadísticas de la criminalidad y seguridad ciudadana. Lima: V & S Editores, 2018. 171 p.: bibl., color ill.

The author describes the purpose of this book as twofold: first, to examine criminal activity in terms of the social characteristics of perpetrators and victims, along with some policy recommendations aimed at enabling Peru to be more successful in achieving its full potential; and second, to highlight the availability of and role that information can play in addressing crime itself. The primary sources of concern regarding crime, as expressed by the general public in Peru, may be thought of in terms of social class. The largest category concerns corruption—"white collar" crime, followed closely by delinquency, in which crimes involve a more direct interaction between perpetrator and victim such as theft, and which may potentially be violent, involving various types of assault. The author provides an international context for certain crimes, as well as a longitudinal perspective for Peru. In addition, he recommends specific actions to positively impact crime prevention and other efforts.

1725 Sexualidades andinas: otras formas posibles del sexo y el erotismo. Compilación de Abelardo Barra Ruatta. Argentina: publisher not identified, 2018. 89 p.: bibl.

This study reviews existing knowledge about the cultural practices related to sexuality in Peru prior to the arrival of the Europeans in the early 16th century. Observations are based on archeological discoveries, including erotic depictions, as well as contacts between the European arrivals and Inca informants. The chroniclers from the period described the existence of a well-established tradition of trial marriage that preceded longer term relationships, known as *servinacuy*. The author suggests that the purpose of this practice would likely have been to provide greater assurance of the longer-term happiness of the couples. The book also documents findings about the existence of homosexuality, transvestism, prostitution, and other aspects of sexual life.

1726 Urquizo Valdeiglesias, Luis. El rol de las relaciones públicas comunitarias en una década de conflictos sociales en el Perú. Lima: USMP Universidad de San Martin de Porres, Fondo Editorial, Facultad de Ciencias de la Comunicación, Turismo y Psicología, 2017. 341 p.: bibl., color ill.

This book describes the process that Peru, like other Latin American countries, has experienced due to the growth in extractive industries between 2009–2014. The increase in this sector has been accompanied by a progressively uneasy relationship between mining corporations and nearby communities. However, another notable trend has been the dramatic increase in mining fees that have benefited the regions in which the extractive industries are located. Yet standards of living in the mining areas have not improved significantly during this time, and corruption among public officials has been widespread. Also on the increase have been social protests ending in violence with deaths and injuries occuring in the conflicts. A three-sided conflict often develops among the extractive industry, local communities—often consisting of Indigenous peoples, and the state. The principal achievement of this book is that it provides a description and analysis of the major socioenvironmental conflicts during the period 1999–2015. From this data, support is found for the notion that to the degree that greater Corporate Social Responsibility (CSR) is practiced, social conflict has been reduced.

1727 Valdez Carrasco, Bettina. Revelando el secreto: relaciones de género entre empleadoras y trabajadoras del hogar cama adentro. Lima: Siete Ensayos Ediciones, 2018. 237 p.: bibl., ill.

This study examines gender relations and labor rights for those Peruvian households with live-in domestic service workers. The purpose of the study is to understand the historical background and current status of this activity so the various institutions involved in policy-making may have access to empirically based information. The author, an attorney, interviewed 16 employers and 15 domestic workers from 16 districts within the Lima metropolitan area. In this work, she provides an extensive review of the literature as well as an analysis of her data from the perspective of gender, race, ethnicity, social class, and legal considerations, as well as interactions among these. An additional consideration is that as females, both employers and employees are often subjected to similar processes of devaluing in a male-dominated society.

1728 Valenzuela Marroquín, Manuel Luis. Cárcel dominio: una etnografía sobre los senderistas presos en el Establecimiento Penitenciario Miguel Castro, 2008–2010. Lima: Revuelta Ediciones, 2019. 185 p.: bibl., ill.

The period between 1980 and 2000 in which armed conflict between the Sendero Luminoso and MRTA on the one hand, and the armed forces on the other, has been thoroughly examined. This study uses a novel approach by taking a closer look at the former guerrillas, now prisoners. Previous studies have focused on the actions undertaken by these individuals during the period of violence. This author, in contrast, seeks to understand these individuals as social beings to better understand how they became involved in the guerrilla organizations. His method is to attempt to understand the organizations that the prisoners built within the penitentiary—and the relationship that the prisoners had with these organizations. From this research, the author produces an ethnography of the Castro Castro Prison and the sections where the Sendero Luminoso prisoners resided.

1729 Villegas, María Cecilia. La verdad de una mentira: el caso de las trescientas mil esterilizaciones forzadas. Lima: Planeta, 2017. 176 p.: bibl., ill.

This study addresses the belief that during the government of Alberto Fujimori, some 300,000 forced sterilizations took place in Peru. This book describes the process by which this narrative was widely distributed by an alliance of diverse interests. At the beginning of Fujimori's second administration, measures were promulgated in which vasectomy and tubal ligation were recognized as legal methods to achieve birth control. Women were also granted the right to choose sterilization without the consent of their spouses or partners. A program to encourage reproductive health among the low income population was also initated by the Fujimori administration in the mid-1990s. This program was widely opposed by the Catholic Church and conservative interests in Peru. When Fujimori resigned at the end of 2000 following a failed attempt to secure a third presidential term, a wave of rejection of corrupt practices raced across country, and the efforts at birth control were swept aside as well. This book traces the emergence and disappearance of the family planning program during this period.

1730 La violencia contra las mujeres en las empresas: nuevas visiones de jóvenes valores. Coordinación de Inés Fanny Santi Huaranca. Lima: Universidad de San Martín de Porres, Fondo Editorial, 2017. 216 p.: bibl., ill.

This collection of five articles based on theses written by undergraduate students concerns the economic and labor impacts of violence against female employees in various businesses in Peru. Four of the studies gathered information from female and male employees from places of business in Lima, such as shopping and manufacturing centers, and provide an account of the proportion of employees who reported being victims or victimizers of aggression against women and the frequency of such attacks. In three of the studies, the economic consequences of this violence were estimated based on lost salaries and lost productivity. One study had a national scope, using survey data concerning demographic and family health indicators collected by the Instituto Nacional de Estadística e Informática (INEI). The authors evaluate the responses to the ENDES survey and assess the categories of violence reported, along with regional differences.

BOLIVIA

MARYGOLD WALSH-DILLEY, *Associate Professor of Geography and Environmental Studies, University of New Mexico*

OVER THE PAST FIVE YEARS, Bolivian sociology has been—as one would expect—disproportionately occupied with the great transformations brought about by the rise of Evo Morales, the Movimiento a Socialimso (MAS), and their "process of change." Morales was elected president in 2005 after several years of political instability related to social movements and protests against the neoliberal reforms of the 1990s and beyond. Grounded in democratic socialist and indigenist ideologies, Morales and the MAS advocated for radical, revolutionary change—an Indigenous world reversal. Mark Goodale's ethnography of the first 10 years of the Morales administration highlights many of the challenges it faced as it transitioned from a social movement to a political administration (item **1738**). This question of the possibilities of and on-the-ground realities of the *masista* process of change was a dominant theme in recent social scientific research in Bolivia (items **1737, 1739, 1746,** and **1748**). Much of this work examines the consequences of this process of change for Bolivian national identity (item **1750**).

In line with the national identification of the process of change as "descolonizador y despatriarcalizador," much recent Bolivian sociology focused on the possibilities for inclusion and recognition of previously marginalized groups, especially Indigenous peoples, women, and LGBTQ+ individuals. Works that make visible the experiences of women in Bolivia include Itxaso Arias Arana's ethnography of women in Christian denominations (item **1734**), Natalie L. Kimball's study of women's experiences of abortion and unwanted pregnancy (item **1740**), and a catalog from a photo exhibition of the iconic *pollera* skirt and the *chola* women who wear them (item **1735**). A two-volume set (items **1744** and **1745**) highlights women's political participation in Bolivia, both historically and in the 2015 Plurinational Legislative Assembly—which achieved gender parity for the first time in Bolivia. The works confirm a pattern of study that highlights the diversity of Bolivian women, and also emphasizes women's agency and dynamism.

Continuing a theme from past years, there was also a fair amount of research on marginalized or vulnerable populations, but with an added emphasis on how these groups negotiate their political and economic surroundings to build more sustainable livelihoods and support shared identity. Julio Cesar Mita Machaca gives us a lovely ethnography of the *q'ipiri minitransportistas* of the Villa Dolores open air market of El Alto (item **1741**). These men, who transport market wares on their backs, have organized to form a union and legitimize their labor. Well-known agricultural economist Miguel Urioste presents a study on the multiple activities of rural people in the Highlands, emphasizing how they build livelihoods that engage with urban spaces and global markets without undermining their existence and identities as campesinos (item **1749**). This work departs from questions of "lo andino," to instead explore what is special and unique about Bolivian identities without reifying rural and Indigenous communities as static or weak.

Indeed, some of the most inspiring works of Bolivian sociology over the past five years are those that explicitly build spaces of counterhegemonic envisioning and knowledge formation. The Morales process of change created this space by highlighting Indigenous worldviews as a basis for an alternative political-economic system. The possibilities for learning from Indigenous, feminist, LGBTQ+, and other epistemological points of departure are explored in a volume of 10 essays edited by Harry Soria Galvarro Sánchez de Lozada (item **1733**). Renowned Bolivian sociologist Silvia Rivera Cusicanqui's slim collection of essays presents the Aymara concept of *ch'ixi* as a way forward for Bolivian society that doesn't reproduce the hegemonic binaries of colonial racial hierarchy, but which nonetheless respects the heterogeneity and complexity of Bolivian society (item **1747**). And a volume on feminist disobedience (item **1743**) presents this activism as an exercise of unbridled imagination that gives voice to—and generates strength from—the vulnerability, fear, rage, and longing of women and Indigenous peoples.

Trends in Bolivian social scientific scholarship reveal the process of change that began with the rise of Bolivia's first Indigenous president and the social revolution he facilitated. Recent work has increasingly focused on meaningful inclusion of previously excluded, oppressed, or marginalized peoples; respect for and curiosity about difference; and counterhegemonic envisionings for possible futures.

1731 **Álvarez, Sandra.** En justicia depende de tu suerte...: derechos humanos, medios de comunicación y la población LGBTI en Bolivia, Ecuador y Perú. Lima: Adelante Diversidad Sexual: Instituto de Estudios en Salud, Sexualidad y Desarrollo Humano IESSDEH, 2018. 141 p.: bibl., color ill.

This book is part of a project aimed at respecting and protecting the human rights of LGBTI persons in the Andean region. The book brings together five essays that separately address a particular issue in one of the countries of focus. The first part includes three essays discussing violence and human rights abuses experienced by the LGBTI community in Peru, Bolivia, and Ecuador. These essay cover issues such as violence within same-sex couples (Bolivia), the experience of coming out for gay men and trans women in Lima (Peru), and a participatory diagnostic study about human rights of the LGBTI community (Ecuador). The second part presents two shorter essays on the representation of LGBTI communities in the media in Bolivia and Ecuador.

1732 **Andia Fagalde, Elizabeth** and **Jimmy Leaño Espejo.** Un camino sin retorno: trata y tráfico de niñ@s, adolescentes y mujeres en la ciudad de La Paz desde el género y la identidad cultural 2012–2015. La Paz: Universidad Mayor de San Andrés, Facultad de Ciencias Sociales, Instituto de Investigaciones Antropológicas y Arqueológicas, 2018. 303 p.: bibl., color ill.

Human trafficking is the third most lucrative trade in the world after the illegal drug trade and contraband weapons. This book presents a study of human trafficking and exploitation in the city of La Paz, focusing on the causes and consequences, and examining the effect of the 2012 Law 263 combatting human trafficking and related crimes. This study first presents quantitative data from the Bolivian national police and other sources before presenting qualitative data from interviews with rescued victims and observations of locations connecting with human trafficking. The authors highlight the interconnections between migration and human trafficking, emphasizing the vulnerability of migrants to exploitation. The book ends with a proposal for a registration and tracking system for human trafficking cases.

1733 **Aproximaciones al pensamiento crítico: reflexiones epistemológicas sobre la realidad social boliviana.** Edición de Harry Soria Galvarro Sánchez de Lozada. Cochabamba, Bolivia: Fundación para la Educación en Contextos en Multilingüismo y Pluriculturalidad (FUNPROEIB Andes), 2018. 324 p.: bibl., ill.

This volume brings together 10 essays that examine, from different academic points of departure, epistemological models for comprehending reality. It seeks to identify and explore alternative forms of knowledge and social practices marginalized within occidental ways of thinking. With essays focusing on Indigenous, feminist, and LGBTQ knowledges among other ways of knowing, this volume builds new theoretical tools for understanding and learning from counter-hegemonic epistemologies.

1734 **Arias Arana, Itxaso.** La experiencia de ser mujer en las iglesias de La Paz y El Alto: un análisis crítico del ethos del patriarcado religioso. La Paz: ISEAT Instituto Superior Ecuménico Andino de Teología, 2017. 202 p.: bibl., ill.

This book focuses on violence against women in Christian ecclesiastic spaces in La Paz and El Alto, Bolivia. Beginning from the fact that Bolivia has one of the highest incidences of violence against women in Latin America, this study notes that religion can often be a context where women are silenced, discriminated against, and made invisible. Using participatory action methods, this study combines an examination of Christian theology with an exploration of the lived experiences of contemporary Christian women to investigate possibilities for confronting gendered violence within Christian denominations. The study finds that faith and religion are important sources of support in moments of difficulty, and argues that there are possibilities for emancipation and inspiration in the fight against gender-based violence, exclusion, and oppression.

1735 Cárdenas Plaza, Cleverth C.; Yenny Espinoza Mendoza; and **Ladislao Salazar Cachi.** Realidades solapadades: la transformación de las polleras en 115 años de fotografía paceña. La Paz: Museo Nacional de Etnografía y Folklore, 2015. 220 p.: ill., photos.

This volume is the catalog for an exhibit at the Museo Nacional de Etnografía y Folklore (National Museum of Ethnography and Folklore), which presented 151 photographs selected from the institutional archives. The exhibit and volume posit that the traditional skirt called the pollera, and the women who wear them, are important symbols of La Paz identity over time. The photographs help us to abandon two principal ideas about La Paz cholas: first, the idea of cultural continuity and static ethnic identity; and second, the common association of the pollera as a symbol of elite status. The photographs in this exhibit, instead, help make visible the dynamic histories of rural-urban migration, social mobility, and diversity of the La Paz cholita.

1736 Chicha y limonada: las clases medias en Bolivia. Contribuciones de Roberto Laserna *et al.* La Paz: CERES: Plural Editores, 2018. 140 p.: bibl., ill.

This slim volume brings together six essays by renowned Bolivian social scientists on the theme of the middle class in Bolivia. The conditions for an emerging middle class came with new social mobility brought about by a long process of urbanization, the expansion of the educational system, and the economic expansion of the last decade. The six pieces in this book examine this emerging social class, and its implication for the democratization of the country.

1737 Del estado nacional al estado plurinacional. Edición de María Silvina Irusta y María Susana Bonetto. Villa María, Córdoba, Argentina: Eduvim, 2016. 239 p.: bibl. (Colección Poliedros)

This volume brings together eight essays by Bolivian sociologists examining the political processes and outcomes put in motion with the landslide election of Evo Morales Ayma in 2005. These essays reflect on the combination of indigenism, nationalism, and Marxism that came with the success of Morales' party, Movimiento al Socialismo (MAS). The MAS promoted the idea of plurinationality, upending dominant social ideology. The essays in this volume examine different aspects of this process, including social movements, class alliances, and debates over the nature of Bolivian democracy.

1738 Goodale, Mark. A revolution in fragments: traversing scales of justice, ideology, and practice in Bolivia. Durham, N.C.: Duke University Press, 2019. 299 p.: bibl., ill., index.

Goodale offers an ethnography of the first 10 years of the revolutionary project of Evo Morales and his MAS party. The central claim of this book is that the process of transformation in Bolivia was deeply hybrid, ideologically ambiguous, often disconnected from well-defined theories of history, and built upon often contradictory concepts of both Indigenous world reversal and neoliberal rights-infused cosmopolitanism. Goodale presents several tensions within Bolivia's revolutionary project: between ideologies of class and those surrounding indigeneity; between the goals of radical transformation and the necessity to govern once in power; and between Indigenous cosmovisions and the MAS government's emerging framework for economic and social development.

1739 Inclusión social en Bolivia: avances y desafíos, 2006–2014: política pública, estructura económica y tierra. Coordinación de Verónica Paz Arauco *et al.* La Paz: Vicepresidencia del Estado, Presidencia de la Asamblea Legislativa Plurinacional, Bolivia, CIS Centro de Investigaciones Sociales, 2017. 228 p.: bibl., ill. (Economía y desarrollo)

Ten years after the initiation of a process of change under President Evo Morales, Bolivia entered a new period of social transformation. This book presents three essays about this process of change, from the perspectives of the economy, the body politic, and land distribution. These essays focus in particular on the possibilities for inclusion of previously excluded sectors of the population. The combination of strong economic growth and social inclusion was an important achievement during this period and both incomes and equality improved. The two threads tying the essays in this volume together are first, the question of the distributional effect of this process of change, and second, attention to both the goals and the on-the-ground reality of this process.

1740 Kimball, Natalie L. An open secret: the history of unwanted pregnancy and abortion in modern Bolivia. New Brunswick, N.J.: Rutgers University Press, 2020. 351 p.: bibl., index.

This book focuses on women's experiences with abortion and unwanted pregnancies in La Paz and El Alto, Bolivia. Using oral histories, medical records, and interviews with health care workers, government officials, and activists, the study finds that different ethnic groups use different forms of health care, ranging from allopathic to more traditional forms, and they also speak differently about health care choices as alternatively, individual choice or a more collective decision. However, nearly all women in this study who had abortions say they were obligated to end their pregnancy—by life circumstances, economic difficulties, or unsupportive families or partners. This contrasts with a more liberal notion of abortion rights, which contends that reproductive decisions are individual.

1741 Mita Machaca, Julio Cesar. Los artesanos del transporte en El Alto: de q'ipiris a minitransportistas. La Paz: Vicepresidencia del Estado, Presidencia de la Asamblea Legislativa Plurinacional, Bolivia, CIS, Centro de Investigación Sociales, 2019. 264 p.: bibl., ill. (chiefly color).

This book presents an ethnography of the daily lives and experiences of the "q'ipiris" in a large open-air market in El Alto, Bolivia—the men who carry the wares of the market on their backs. Julio Mita highlights how these carriers collectively construct their shared identity as "minitransportistas" through the formation of a union and the self-organization of their work. Mita gives us an embodied sociology of this overlooked and vulnerable group of laborers, how they work together to claim space and legitimacy within the chaos of a large urban market, and how they build shared meaning to overcome the stigmatization of their work and present the importance of the service they provide.

1742 Molina, Fernando. Modos del privilegio: alta burguesía y alta gerencia en la Bolivia contemporánea. La Paz: Vicepresidencia del Estado, Presidencia de la Asamblea Legislativa Plurinacional Bolivia, CIS Centro de Investigaciones Sociales, 2019. 146 p.: bibl. (Economía y sociedad)

This book presents the findings of a study on the "high bourgeoisie" as a social class, and the social group marked by high status and social prestige locally called "jailón." The book argues that there is a convergence between class and status in Bolivia that is often grounded in a social capital derived from an ethnic status detached from indigeneity. Using a microsociological lens and ethnographic and historical methods, this project describes and analyzes the social and economic relations of the people in Bolivia with access to great economic power. It highlights the preponderance of inherited wealth and professional positions within this group, and concludes that Bolivia is situated in a "quasi caste society" not all that different from colonial hierarchies.

1743 Morales Franco, Fabiola. La desobediencia: antología de ensayos feministas. Santa Cruz de la Sierra, Bolivia: Fundación Simón i Patiño: Dum Dum Editora, 2019. 235 p.: bibl.

This anthology brings together 11 feminists writing around the theme of "disobedience." As Liliana Colanzi writes in the introduction, women engage in acts of disobedience to both negate their own complicity within an oppressive system and also to imagine something different. Feminism, she writes, is an exercise in simultaneous disobedience and unbridled imagination. Bolivia is in a vital moment of rupture and action, in which a new feminist force and voice has emerged. Colanzi describes this moment as one of urgency and euphoria, but also of doubt. Thus, Colanzi writes, acts of feminist disobedience—and the essays in this volume about them—require not just a show of strength, but also necessarily vulnerability, fear, rage, and longing.

1744 Mujeres bolivianas: desde el Parlamento hasta la Asamblea Legislativa Plurinacional. Vol. 1, Insurgencias femeninas hacia el epicentro del poder (siglos XX-XXI). Edición de Daniela Franco Pinto. La Paz: Vicepresidencia del Estado, Presidencia de la Asamblea Legislativa Plurinacional Bolivia: CIS Centro de Investigaciones Sociales: ONU Mujeres, 2017. 1 v.: bibl., ill. (Género y política)

This volume is the first in a series on women's political participation in Bolivia. Using archival and oral histories, it traces the role of women in Bolivian politics since the events leading up to the National Revolution in 1952. Women were important leaders and had an impact on previous periods of political activities, but they became particularly influential during the period leading up to the Constituent Assembly in 2006–2009 that resulted in a new national constitution. During that time, women were central to the reenvisioning of a new national narrative where Indigenous people and women became included as full citizens and political participants. For comment on Vol. 2, see item **1745**.

1745 Mujeres bolivianas: desde el Parlamento hasta la Asamblea Legislativa Plurinacional. Vol. 2, Paridad y diversidad en la escena legislativa. Edición de Bianca de Marchi Moyano y Noelia Gómez Téllez. La Paz: Vicepresidencia del Estado, Presidencia de la Asamblea Legislativa Plurinacional Bolivia: CIS Centro de Investigaciones Sociales: ONU Mujeres, 2017. 1 v.: bibl., ill. (Género y política)

This volume presents the results of research undertaken in the Plurinational Legislative Assembly (ALP) between 2015 and 2016. In line with then-President Evo Morales' goals for "decolonization and depatriarchization," the ALP that was elected in 2014 was highly diverse in terms of racial, cultural, individual and political identities and achieved gender parity for the first time. This volume, the second in a series on women's political participation in Bolivia, examines the composition, participation, and parliamentary experiences of women legislators. For comment on Vol. 1, see item **1744**.

1746 Pensando Bolivia desde México: estado, movimientos, territorios y representaciones. Coordinación de Guadalupe Valencia García, Börries Nehe y Cecilia Salazar de la Torre. Ciudad de México: UNAM, Programa de Posgrado en Estudios Latinoamericanos; Bolivia: Posgrado en Ciencias del Desarrollo de la Universidad Mayor de San Andrés, 2016. 461 p.: bibl., ill.

This volume is the fruit of a rich collaboration between academics and students at the Universidad Nacional Autónomo de México (UNAM) in Mexico City and Universidad Mayor de San Andrés (UMSA) in La Paz. The essays work to interpret recent changes in the Andean region, putting them in dialogue with the contemporary realities in Mexico. This volume highlights the rich common ground of social movements and Indigenous organizing. The volume is organized in four parts: 1) reflections on the transformation of the Bolivian process of change after the rise of Evo Morales; 2) the question of identity in Indigenous and popular social movements; 3) an examination of the new and reconstituted territories; and 4) reflections on the cultural representations and theorization of Bolivian reality.

1747 Rivera Cusicanqui, Silvia. Un mundo ch'ixi es posible: ensayos desde un presente en crisis. Buenos Aires: Tinta Limón, 2018. 169 p.: bibl., ill. (Colección Nociones comunes)

This volume presents a collection of essays by Bolivian sociologist, feminist, and activist Silvia Rivera Cusicanqui, one of the most important Bolivian social theorists and a key decolonial thinker in Latin America. Here Rivera presents the concept of *ch'ixi*, a metaphor that she uses to imagine an understanding of the world that doesn't reproduce hegemonic binaries, but which nonetheless respects the heterogeneity and complexity of Bolivian society. Pushing back on ideas of mestizaje and multiculturalism, Rivera describes *ch'ixi* as a "spotted gray" (p.16), the combination of black and white that doesn't quite mix into gray; which is "neither white nor black [but] the two things at the same time" (p. 78). In these essays, Rivera Cusicanqui highlights the potential for non-hegemonic knowledges (like the knowledge emergent from oral traditions) to create alternative worlds in our current moment of crisis.

1748 ¿Todo cambia?: reflexiones sobre el "proceso de cambio" en Bolivia. Coordinación de Hugo José Súarez. Ciudad de México: UNAM, Instituto de Investigaciones Sociales, 2018. 445 p.: bibl.

This volume brings together essays by 15 Bolivian academics reflecting on the "process of change" provoked by the election of Evo Morales in 2005. The starting point for these essays is that Bolivia, in the 10 years since Morales became president, went through an important state, political, economic, social, cultural, and symbolic transformation. But there is little consensus about the impact that these transformations have had. In 2015, authors in this collection gathered for an international colloquium titled "What changed in the Bolivian process of change?" With a focus on culture and daily life, the contributions to this volume articulate a vision of Bolivia's process of change as complex and multidimensional.

1749 Urioste Fernández de Córdova, Miguel. Investigaciones Foro Andino Amazónico de Desarrollo Rural: pluriactividad campesina en tierras altas: con un solo trabajo no hay caso de vivir. La Paz: Foro Andino Amazónico de Desarrollo Rural, 2017. 106 p.: bibl., color ill.

This small volume presents a study of the multiple activities undertaken by rural people in the Highlands of Bolivia. There, agriculture does not provide a sufficiently stable income, and the people who live there are obligated to seek other sources of employment or pursue informal or precarious work. One key strategy is temporary employment in cities; rural households often are deeply connected to urban centers without abandoning their economic and social relationship with the rural sphere. Using focus groups, interviews, and oral life histories, this study disrupts the view of rural people as encapsulated in their own world, nearly impermeable to the expansion of market logics. It shows the rural and urban worlds of Bolivian *campesinos* as relational, with rural people interacting with urban spaces without undermining their rural identities and existence.

1750 Zurita, Alfonso. La sociedad multiétnica boliviana: riesgos de fragmentación social y amenazas a la formación de la identidad nacional. Prólogo por Carlos R. Fernández Liesa y J. Daniel Oliva Martínez. Cizur Menor, Spain: Thomson Reuters Aranzadi, 2017. 196 p.: bibl., ill. (The global law collection. Legal studies series)

This book focuses on the multiethnic nature of Bolivian society. Before the Inca and Spanish conquests, the region was marked by extreme cultural and linguistic diversity albeit with significant interaction and exchange. Under Spanish colonization, the principal social groups that now characterize Bolivia were firmly established: a minority of whites, a fluid and diverse group of mestizos or "cholos" with both Spanish and Indigenous roots, and an Indigenous majority made up mostly of Quechua and Aymara peoples. Since the 2005 election of Evo Morales and the social and political transformation of his administration, there has been a much greater emphasis on social inclusion and integration. This book examines the balance between the ideas of plurinationality and autonomy, on one hand, and the integration and inclusion of different perspectives, voices, and experiences, on the other. It asks how these dynamics shape the possibilities for a national Bolivian identity.

ABBREVIATIONS AND ACRONYMS

Except for journal abbreviations which are listed: 1) after each journal title in the *Title List of Journals Indexed* (p. 547); and 2) in the *Abbreviation List of Journals Indexed* (p. 555).

ALADI	Asociación Latinoamericana de Integración
a.	annual
ABC	Argentina, Brazil, Chile
A.C.	antes de Cristo
ACAR	Associação de Crédito e Assistência Rural, Brazil
AD	Anno Domini
A.D.	Acción Democrática, Venezuela
ADESG	Associação dos Diplomados de Escola Superior de Guerra, Brazil
AGI	Archivo General de Indias, Sevilla
AGN	Archivo General de la Nación
AID	Agency for International Development, US
a.k.a.	also known as
Ala.	Alabama
ALALC	Asociación Latinoamericana de Libre Comercio
ALEC	*Atlas lingüístico etnográfico de Colombia*
ANAPO	Alianza Nacional Popular, Colombia
ANCARSE	Associação Nordestina de Crédito e Assistência Rural de Sergipe, Brazil
ANCOM	Andean Common Market
ANDI	Asociación Nacional de Industriales, Colombia
ANPOCS	Associação Nacional de Pós-Graduação e Pesquisa em Ciências Sociais, São Paulo
ANUC	Asociación Nacional de Usuarios Campesinos, Colombia
ANUIES	Asociación Nacional de Universidades e Institutos de Enseñanza Superior, Mexico
AP	Acción Popular
APRA	Alianza Popular Revolucionaria Americana, Peru
ARENA	Aliança Renovadora Nacional, Brazil
Ariz.	Arizona
Ark.	Arkansas
ASA	Association of Social Anthropologists of the Commonwealth, London
ASSEPLAN	Assessoria de Planejamento e Acompanhamento, Recife, Brazil
Assn.	Association
Aufl.	Auflage (edition, edición)
AUFS	American Universities Field Staff Reports, Hanover, N.H.
Aug.	August, Augustan
aum.	aumentada
b.	born (nació)
B.A.R.	British Archaeological Reports
BBE	Bibliografia Brasileira de Educação
b.c.	indicates dates obtained by radiocarbon methods

BC	Before Christ
bibl(s).	bibliography(ies)
BID	Banco Interamericano de Desarrollo
BNDE	Banco Nacional de Desenvolvimento Econômico, Brazil
BNH	Banco Nacional de Habitação, Brazil
BP	before present
b/w	black and white
C14	Carbon 14
ca.	*circa* (about)
CACM	Central American Common Market
CADE	Conferencia Anual de Ejecutivos de Empresas, Peru
CAEM	Centro de Altos Estudios Militares, Peru
Calif.	California
cap.	capítulo
CARC	Centro de Arte y Comunicación, Buenos Aires
CARICOM	Caribbean Common Market
CARIFTA	Caribbean Free Trade Association
CBC	Christian base communities
CBD	central business district
CBI	Caribbean Basin Initiative
CD	Christian Democrats, Chile
CDHES	Comisión de Derechos Humanos de El Salvador
CDI	Conselho de Desenvolvimento Industrial, Brasília
CEB	comunidades eclesiásticas de base
CEBRAP	Centro Brasileiro de Análise e Planejamento, São Paulo
CECORA	Centro de Cooperativas de la Reforma Agraria, Colombia
CEDAL	Centro de Estudios Democráticos de América Latina, Costa Rica
CEDE	Centro de Estudios sobre Desarrollo Económico, Universidad de los Andes, Bogotá
CEDEPLAR	Centro de Desenvolvimento e Planejamento Regional, Belo Horizonte
CEDES	Centro de Estudios de Estado y Sociedad, Buenos Aires; Centro de Estudos de Educação e Sociedade, São Paulo
CEDI	Centro Ecumênico de Documentos e Informação, São Paulo
CEDLA	Centro de Estudios y Documentación Latinoamericanos, Amsterdam
CEESTEM	Centro de Estudios Económicos y Sociales del Tercer Mundo, México
CELADE	Centro Latinoamericano de Demografía
CELADEC	Comisión Evangélica Latinoamericana de Educación Cristiana
CELAM	Consejo Episcopal Latinoamericano
CEMLA	Centro de Estudios Monetarios Latinoamericanos, Mexico
CENDES	Centro de Estudios del Desarrollo, Venezuela
CENIDIM	Centro Nacional de Información, Documentación e Investigación Musicales, Mexico
CENIET	Centro Nacional de Información y Estadísticas del Trabajo, Mexico
CEOSL	Confederación Ecuatoriana de Organizaciones Sindicales Libres
CEPADE	Centro Paraguayo de Estudios de Desarrollo Económico y Social
CEPA-SE	Comissão Estadual de Planejamento Agrícola, Sergipe
CEPAL	Comisión Económica para América Latina y el Caribe
CEPLAES	Centro de Planificación y Estudios Sociales, Quito
CERES	Centro de Estudios de la Realidad Económica y Social, Bolivia
CES	constant elasticity of substitution
cf.	compare
CFI	Consejo Federal de Inversiones, Buenos Aires
CGE	Confederación General Económica, Argentina
CGTP	Confederación General de Trabajadores del Perú

chap(s).	chapter(s)
CHEAR	Council on Higher Education in the American Republics
Cía.	Compañía
CIA	Central Intelligence Agency, US
CIDA	Comité Interamericano de Desarrollo Agrícola
CIDE	Centro de Investigación y Desarrollo de la Educación, Chile; Centro de Investigación y Docencias Económicas, Mexico
CIDIAG	Centro de Información y Desarrollo Internacional de Autogestión, Lima
CIE	Centro de Investigaciones Económicas, Buenos Aires
CIEDLA	Centro Interdisciplinario de Estudios sobre el Desarrollo Latinoamericano, Buenos Aires
CIEDUR	Centro Interdisciplinario de Estudios sobre el Desarrollo Uruguay, Montevideo
CIEPLAN	Corporación de Investigaciones Económicas para América Latina, Santiago
CIESE	Centro de Investigaciones y Estudios Socioeconómicos, Quito
CIMI	Conselho Indigenista Missionário, Brazil
CINTERFOR	Centro Interamericano de Investigación y Documentación sobre Formación Profesional
CINVE	Centro de Investigaciones Económicas, Montevideo
CIP	Conselho Interministerial de Preços, Brazil
CIPCA	Centro de Investigación y Promoción del Campesinado, Bolivia
CIPEC	Consejo Intergubernamental de Países Exportadores de Cobre, Santiago
CLACSO	Consejo Latinoamericano de Ciencias Sociales, Secretaría Ejecutiva, Buenos Aires
CLASC	Confederación Latinoamericana Sindical Cristiana
CLE	Comunidad Latinoamericana de Escritores, Mexico
cm	centimeter
CNI	Confederação Nacional da Indústria, Brazil
CNPq	Conselho Nacional de Pesquisas, Brazil
Co.	Company
COB	Central Obrera Boliviana
COBAL	Companhia Brasileira de Alimentos
CODEHUCA	Comisión para la Defensa de los Derechos Humanos en Centroamérica
Col.	Collection, Colección, Coleção
col.	colored, coloured
Colo.	Colorado
COMCORDE	Comisión Coordinadora para el Desarrollo Económico, Uruguay
comp(s).	compiler(s), compilador(es)
CONCLAT	Congresso Nacional das Classes Trabalhadoras, Brazil
CONCYTEC	Consejo Nacional de Ciencia y Tecnología (Peru)
CONDESE	Conselho de Desenvolvimento Econômico de Sergipe, Brazil
Conn.	Connecticut
COPEI	Comité Organizador Pro-Elecciones Independientes, Venezuela
CORFO	Corporación de Fomento de la Producción, Chile
CORP	Corporación para el Fomento de Investigaciones Económicas, Colombia
Corp.	Corporation, Corporación
corr.	corrected, corregida
CP	Communist Party
CPDOC	Centro de Pesquisa e Documentação, Brazil
CRIC	Consejo Regional Indígena del Cauca, Colombia
CSUTCB	Confederación Sindical Única de Trabajadores Campesinos de Bolivia
CTM	Confederación de Trabajadores de México
CUNY	City University of New York

CUT	Central Única de Trabajadores (Mexico); Central Única dos Trabalhadores (Brazil); Central Unitaria de Trabajadores (Chile; Colombia); Confederación Unitaria de Trabajadores (Costa Rica)
CVG	Corporación Venezolana de Guayana
d.	died (murió)
DANE	Departamento Nacional de Estadística, Colombia
DC	Demócratas Cristianos, Chile
d.C.	después de Cristo
Dec./déc.	December, décembre
Del.	Delaware
dept.	department
depto.	departamento
DESCO	Centro de Estudios y Promoción del Desarrollo, Lima
Dez./dez.	Dezember, dezembro
dic.	diciembre, dicembre
disc.	discography
DNOCS	Departamento Nacional de Obras Contra as Secas, Brazil
doc.	document, documento
Dr.	Doctor
Dra.	Doctora
DRAE	*Diccionario de la Real Academia Española*
ECLAC	UN Economic Commision for Latin America and the Caribbean, New York and Santiago
ECOSOC	UN Economic and Social Council
ed./éd.(s)	edition(s), édition(s), edición(es), editor(s), redactor(es), director(es)
EDEME	Editora Emprendimentos Educacionais, Florianópolis, Brazil
Edo.	Estado
EEC	European Economic Community
EE.UU.	Estados Unidos de América
EFTA	European Free Trade Association
e.g.	*exempio gratia* (for example, por ejemplo)
ELN	Ejército de Liberación Nacional, Colombia
ENDEF	Estudo Nacional da Despesa Familiar, Brazil
ERP	Ejército Revolucionario del Pueblo, El Salvador
ESG	Escola Superior de Guerra, Brazil
estr.	estrenado
et al.	*et alia* (and others)
ETENE	Escritório Técnico de Estudos Econômicos do Nordeste, Brazil
ETEPE	Escritório Técnico de Planejamento, Brazil
EUDEBA	Editorial Universitaria de Buenos Aires
EWG	Europaische Wirtschaftsgemeinschaft. *See* EEC.
facsim(s).	facsimile(s)
FAO	Food and Agriculture Organization of the United Nations
FDR	Frente Democrático Revolucionario, El Salvador
FEB	Força Expedicionária Brasileira
Feb./feb.	February, Februar, febrero, febbraio
FEDECAFE	Federación Nacional de Cafeteros, Colombia
FEDESARROLLO	Fundación para la Educación Superior y el Desarrollo
fev./fév.	fevereiro, février
ff.	following
FGTS	Fundo de Garantia do Tempo de Serviço, Brazil
FGV	Fundação Getúlio Vargas
FIEL	Fundación de Investigaciones Económicas Latinoamericanas, Argentina
film.	filmography

fl.	flourished
Fla.	Florida
FLACSO	Facultad Latinoamericana de Ciencias Sociales
FMI	Fondo Monetario Internacional
FMLN	Frente Farabundo Martí de Liberación Nacional, El Salvador
fold.	folded
fol(s).	folio(s)
FPL	Fuerzas Populares de Liberación Farabundo Marti, El Salvador
FRG	Federal Republic of Germany
FSLN	Frente Sandinista de Liberación Nacional, Nicaragua
ft.	foot, feet
FUAR	Frente Unido de Acción Revolucionaria, Colombia
FUCVAM	Federación Unificadora de Cooperativas de Vivienda por Ayuda Mutua, Uruguay
FUNAI	Fundação Nacional do Indio, Brazil
FUNARTE	Fundação Nacional de Arte, Brazil
FURN	Fundação Universidade Regional do Nordeste
Ga.	Georgia
GAO	General Accounting Office, Wahington
GATT	General Agreement on Tariffs and Trade
GDP	gross domestic product
GDR	German Democratic Republic
GEIDA	Grupo Executivo de Irrigação para o Desenvolvimento Agrícola, Brazil
gen.	gennaio
Gen.	General
GMT	Greenwich Mean Time
GPA	grade point average
GPO	Government Printing Office, Washington
h.	hijo
ha.	hectares, hectáreas
HLAS	*Handbook of Latin American Studies*
HMAI	*Handbook of Middle American Indians*
Hnos.	hermanos
HRAF	Human Relations Area Files, Inc., New Haven, Conn.
IBBD	Instituto Brasileiro de Bibliografia e Documentação
IBGE	Instituto Brasileiro de Geografia e Estatística, Rio de Janeiro
IBRD	International Bank for Reconstruction and Development (World Bank)
ICA	Instituto Colombiano Agropecuario
ICAIC	Instituto Cubano de Arte e Industria Cinematográfica
ICCE	Instituto Colombiano de Construcción Escolar
ICE	International Cultural Exchange
ICSS	Instituto Colombiano de Seguridad Social
ICT	Instituto de Crédito Territorial, Colombia
id.	*idem* (the same as previously mentioned or given)
IDB	Inter-American Development Bank
i.e.	*id est* (that is, o sea)
IEL	Instituto Euvaldo Lodi, Brazil
IEP	Instituto de Estudios Peruanos
IERAC	Instituto Ecuatoriano de Reforma Agraria y Colonización
IFAD	International Fund for Agricultural Development
IICA	Instituto Interamericano de Ciencias Agrícolas, San José
III	Instituto Indigenista Interamericana, Mexico
IIN	Instituto Indigenista Nacional, Guatemala
ILDIS	Instituto Latinoamericano de Investigaciones Sociales

ill.	illustration(s)
Ill.	Illinois
ILO	International Labour Organization, Geneva
IMES	Instituto Mexicano de Estudios Sociales
IMF	International Monetary Fund
Impr.	Imprenta, Imprimérie
in.	inches
INAH	Instituto Nacional de Antropología e Historia, Mexico
INBA	Instituto Nacional de Bellas Artes, Mexico
Inc.	Incorporated
INCORA	Instituto Colombiano de Reforma Agraria
Ind.	Indiana
INEP	Instituto Nacional de Estudios Pedagógicos, Brazil
INI	Instituto Nacional Indigenista, Mexico
INIT	Instituto Nacional de Industria Turística, Cuba
INPES/IPEA	Instituto de Planejamento Econômico e Social, Brazil
INTAL	Instituto para la Integración de América Latina
IPA	Instituto de Pastoral Andina, Universidad de San Antonio de Abad, Seminario de Antropología, Cusco, Peru
IPEA	Instituto de Pesquisa Econômica Aplicada, Brazil
IPES/GB	Instituto de Pesquisas e Estudos Sociais, Guanabara, Brazil
IPHAN	Instituto de Patrimônio Histórico e Artístico Nacional, Brazil
ir.	irregular
IS	Internacional Socialista
ITESM	Instituto Tecnológico y de Estudios Superiores de Monterrey, Mexico
ITT	International Telephone and Telegraph
Jan./jan.	January, Januar, janeiro, janvier
JLP	Jamaican Labour Party
Jr.	Junior, Júnior
JUC	Juventude Universitária Católica, Brazil
JUCEPLAN	Junta Central de Planificación, Cuba
Kan.	Kansas
KITLV	Koninklijk Instituut voor Tall-, Land- en Volkenkunde (Royal Institute of Linguistics and Anthropology)
km	kilometers, kilómetros
Ky.	Kentucky
La.	Louisiana
LASA	Latin American Studies Association
LP	long-playing record
Ltd(a).	Limited, Limitada
m	meters, metros
m.	murió (died)
M	mille, mil, thousand
MA	Master of Arts
MACLAS	Middle Atlantic Council of Latin American Studies
MAPU	Movimiento de Acción Popular Unitario, Chile
MARI	Middle American Research Institute, Tulane University, New Orleans, La.
MAS	Movimiento al Socialismo, Bolivia; Venezuela
Mass.	Massachusetts
MCC	Mercado Común Centro-Americano
Md.	Maryland
MDB	Movimiento Democrático Brasileiro

Me.	Maine
MEC	Ministério de Educação e Cultura, Brazil
Mich.	Michigan
mimeo	mimeographed, mimeografiado
min.	minutes, minutos
Minn.	Minnesota
MIR	Movimiento de Izquierda Revolucionaria, Chile and Venezuela
Miss.	Mississippi
MIT	Massachusetts Institute of Technology
ml	milliliter
MLN	Movimiento de Liberación Nacional
mm.	millimeter
MNC	multinational corporation
MNI	minimum number of individuals
MNR	Movimiento Nacionalista Revolucionario, Bolivia
Mo.	Missouri
MOBRAL	Movimento Brasileiro de Alfabetização
MOIR	Movimiento Obrero Independiente y Revolucionario, Colombia
Mont.	Montana
MRL	Movimiento Revolucionario Liberal, Colombia
ms.	manuscript
MS	Master of Science
msl	mean sea level
MST	Movimento Sem Terra; Movimento dos Trabalhadores Rurais Sem Terra
n.	nació (born)
NBER	National Bureau of Economic Research, Cambridge, Mass.
N.C.	North Carolina
N.D.	North Dakota
NE	Northeast
Neb.	Nebraska
neubearb.	neubearbeitet (revised, corregida)
Nev.	Nevada
n.f.	neue Folge (new series)
NGO	nongovernmental organization
N.H.	New Hampshire
NIEO	New International Economic Order
NIH	National Institutes of Health, Washington
N.J.	New Jersey
NJM	New Jewel Movement, Grenada
N.M.	New Mexico
no(s).	number(s), número(s)
NOEI	Nuevo Orden Económico Internacional
NOSALF	Scandinavian Committee for Research in Latin America
Nov./nov.	November, noviembre, novembre, novembro
NSF	National Science Foundation
NW	Northwest
N.Y.	New York
OAB	Ordem dos Advogados do Brasil
OAS	Organization of American States
OCLC	Online Computer Library Center
Oct./oct.	October, octubre, octobre
ODEPLAN	Oficina de Planificación Nacional, Chile
OEA	Organización de los Estados Americanos

OECD	Organisation for Economic Cooperation and Development
OIT	Organización Internacional del Trabajo
Okla.	Oklahoma
Okt.	Oktober
ONUSAL	United Nations Observer Mission in El Salvador
op.	opus
OPANAL	Organismo para la Proscripción de las Armas Nucleares en América Latina
OPEC	Organization of Petroleum Exporting Countries
OPEP	Organización de Países Exportadores de Petróleo
OPIC	Overseas Private Investment Corporation, Washington
Or.	Oregon
OREALC	Oficina Regional de Educación para América Latina y el Caribe
ORIT	Organización Regional Interamericana del Trabajo
ORSTOM	Office de la recherche scientifique et technique outre-mer (France)
ott.	ottobre
out.	outubro
p.	page(s)
Pa.	Pennsylvania
PAN	Partido Acción Nacional, Mexico
PC	Partido Comunista
PCCLAS	Pacific Coast Council on Latin American Studies
PCN	Partido de Conciliación Nacional, El Salvador
PCP	Partido Comunista del Perú
PCR	Partido Comunista Revolucionario, Chile and Argentina
PCV	Partido Comunista de Venezuela
PD	Partido Democrático
PDC	Partido Demócrata Cristiano, Chile
PDS	Partido Democrático Social, Brazil
PDT	Partido Democrático Trabalhista, Brazil
PDVSA	Petróleos de Venezuela, S.A.
PEMEX	Petróleos Mexicanos
PETROBRAS	Petróleo Brasileiro
PIMES	Programa Integrado de Mestrado em Economia e Sociologia, Brazil
PIP	Partido Independiente de Puerto Rico
PLN	Partido Liberación Nacional, Costa Rica
PMDB	Partido do Movimento Democrático Brasileiro
PNAD	Pesquisa Nacional por Amostra Domiciliar, Brazil
PNC	People's National Congress, Guyana
PNM	People's National Movement, Trinidad and Tobago
PNP	People's National Party, Jamaica
pop.	population
port(s).	portrait(s)
PPP	purchasing power parities; People's Progressive Party of Guyana
PRD	Partido Revolucionario Dominicano
PREALC	Programa Regional del Empleo para América Latina y el Caribe, Organización Internacional del Trabajo, Santiago
PRI	Partido Revolucionario Institucional, Mexico
Prof.	Professor, Profesor(a)
PRONAPA	Programa Nacional de Pesquisas Arqueológicas, Brazil
PRONASOL	Programa Nacional de Solidaridad, Mexico
prov.	province, provincia
PS	Partido Socialista, Chile

Abbreviations and Acronyms / 545

PSD	Partido Social Democrático, Brazil
pseud.	pseudonym, pseudónimo
PT	Partido dos Trabalhadores, Brazil
pt(s).	part(s), parte(s)
PTB	Partido Trabalhista Brasileiro
pub.	published, publisher
PUC	Pontifícia Universidade Católica; Pontificia Universidad Católica
PURSC	Partido Unido de la Revolución Socialista de Cuba
q.	quarterly
rev.	revisada, revista, revised
R.I.	Rhode Island
s.a.	semiannual
SALALM	Seminar on the Acquisition of Latin American Library Materials
SATB	soprano, alto, tenor, bass
sd.	sound
s.d.	*sine datum* (no date, sin fecha)
S.D.	South Dakota
SDR	special drawing rights
SE	Southeast
SELA	Sistema Económico Latinoamericano
SEMARNAP	Secretaria de Medio Ambiente, Recursos Naturales y Pesca, Mexico
SENAC	Serviço Nacional de Aprendizagem Comercial, Rio de Janeiro
SENAI	Serviço Nacional de Aprendizagem Industrial, São Paulo
SEP	Secretaría de Educación Pública, Mexico
SEPLA	Seminario Permanente sobre Latinoamérica, Mexico
Sept./sept.	September, septiembre, septembre
SES	socioeconomic status
SESI	Serviço Social da Indústria, Brazil
set.	setembro, settembre
SI	Socialist International
SIECA	Secretaría Permanente del Tratado General de Integración Económica Centroamericana
SIL	Summer Institute of Linguistics (Instituto Lingüístico de Verano)
SINAMOS	Sistema Nacional de Apoyo a la Movilización Social, Peru
S.J.	Society of Jesus
s.l.	*sine loco* (place of publication unknown)
s.n.	*sine nomine* (publisher unknown)
SNA	Sociedad Nacional de Agricultura, Chile
SPP	Secretaría de Programación y Presupuesto, Mexico
SPVEA	Superintendência do Plano de Valorização Econômica da Amazônia, Brazil
sq.	square
SSRC	Social Sciences Research Council, New York
STENEE	Empresa Nacional de Energía Eléctrica. Sindicato de Trabajadores, Honduras
SUDAM	Superintendência de Desenvolvimento da Amazônia, Brazil
SUDENE	Superintendência de Desenvolvimento do Nordeste, Brazil
SUFRAMA	Superintendência da Zona Franca de Manaus, Brazil
SUNY	State University of New York
SW	Southwest
t.	tomo(s), tome(s)
TAT	Thematic Apperception Test
TB	tuberculosis

Tenn.	Tennessee
Tex.	Texas
TG	transformational generative
TL	Thermoluminescent
TNE	Transnational enterprise
TNP	Tratado de No Proliferación
trans.	translator
UABC	Universidad Autónoma de Baja California
UCA	Universidad Centroamericana José Simeón Cañas, San Salvador
UCLA	University of California, Los Angeles
UDN	União Democrática Nacional, Brazil
UFG	Universidade Federal de Goiás
UFPb	Universidade Federal de Paraíba
UFSC	Universidade Federal de Santa Catarina
UK	United Kingdom
UN	United Nations
UNAM	Universidad Nacional Autónoma de México
UNCTAD	United Nations Conference on Trade and Development
UNDP	United Nations Development Programme
UNEAC	Unión de Escritores y Artistas de Cuba
UNESCO	United Nations Educational, Scientific and Cultural Organization
UNI/UNIND	União das Nações Indígenas
UNICEF	United Nations International Children's Emergency Fund
univ(s).	university(ies), universidad(es), universidade(s), université(s), universität(s), universitá(s)
uniw.	uniwersytet (university)
Unltd.	Unlimited
UP	Unidad Popular, Chile
URD	Unidad Revolucionaria Democrática
URSS	Unión de Repúblicas Soviéticas Socialistas
UNISA	University of South Africa
US	United States
USAID	*See* AID.
USIA	United States Information Agency
USSR	Union of Soviet Socialist Republics
UTM	Universal Transverse Mercator
UWI	University of the West Indies
v.	volume(s), volumen (volúmenes)
Va.	Virginia
V.I.	Virgin Islands
viz.	*videlicet* (that is, namely)
vol(s).	volume(s), volumen (volúmenes)
vs.	versus
Vt.	Vermont
W. Va.	West Virginia
Wash.	Washington
Wis.	Wisconsin
WPA	Working People's Alliance, Guyana
WWI	World War I
WWII	World War II
Wyo.	Wyoming
yr(s).	year(s)

TITLE LIST OF JOURNALS INDEXED

For journal titles listed by abbreviation, see *Abbreviation List of Journals Indexed*, p. 555.

Administration & Society. Sage Publications. Beverly Hills, Calif. (Adm. Soc.)
Advances in Anthropology. Scientific Research Pub. Irvine, Calif. (Adv. Anthropol.)
Agroalimentaria. Universidad de los Andes, Facultad de Ciencias Económicas y Sociales, Centro de Investigaciones Agroalimentarias. Mérida, Venezuela. (Agroalimentaria)
Agronomy Journal. American Society of Agronomy. Madison, Wis. (Agron. J.)
American Anthropologist. American Anthropological Association. Washington, D.C. (Am. Anthropol.)
American Ethnologist. American Anthropological Association, American Ethnological Society. Washington, D.C. (Am. Ethnol./Washington)
American Journal of Political Science. Midwest Political Science Association; Wiley-Blackwell Publishing. Hoboken, N.J. (Am. J. Polit. Sci.)
American Political Science Review. American Political Science Association. Washington, D.C.; Michigan State University, College of Social Science, Department of Political Science. East Lansing, Mich. (Am. Polit. Sci. Rev.)
Ancient Mesoamerica. Cambridge University Press. New York; Cambridge, England. (Anc. Mesoam.)
Annals of the American Association of Geographers. Taylor & Francis Group. Philadelphia, Pa. (Ann. Am. Assoc. Geogr.)
Anthropocene Science. Springer Nature. Singapore. (Anthropocene Sci.)
Anthropologica del Departamento de Ciencias Sociales. Pontificia Universidad Católica del Perú, Departamento de Ciencias Sociales. Lima. (Anthropol. Dep. Cienc. Soc.)
Anthropology Today. Royal Anthropological Institute. London. (Anthropol. Today)
Anthurium: A Caribbean Studies Journal. University of Miami. Coral Gables, Fla. (Anthurium)
Antipode. Basil Blackwell. Oxford, England; Cambridge, Mass. (Antipode)
Antiquity. Antiquity Publications Ltd. Cambridge, England. (Antiquity/Cambridge)
Anuario de Estudios Centroamericanos. Universidad de Costa Rica. San José. (Anu. Estud. Centroam.)
Anuario de la División Geografía. Universidad Nacional de Luján, Departamento de Ciencias Sociales, División Geografía. Buenos Aires. (Anu. Div. Geogr.)
Anuario Estadístico de Cuba. Dirección General de Estadística. La Habana. (Anu. Estad. Cuba)
Applied Geography. Butterworths. Sevenoaks, England. (Appl. Geogr.)
Araucaria. Universidad de Sevilla, Miño y Dárila Editores. Triana, Spain. (Araucaria/Triana)
Archaeological and Anthropological Sciences. Springer. Berlin. (Archaeol. Anthropol. Sci.)
Area. Institute of British Geographers. London. (Area/London)
Atlantic Studies: Global Currents. Taylor & Francis. Abingdon, England. (Atlan. Stud. Global Curr.)

Boletín de Estudios Geográficos. Universidad Nacional de Cuyo, Facultad de Filosofía y Letras, Instituto de Geografía. Mendoza, Argentina. (Bol. Estud. Geogr.)

Boletín de la Sociedad Argentina de Botánica. Buenos Aires. (Bol. Soc. Argent. Bot.)

Bonplandia. Instituto de Botánica del Nordeste, CONICET, Universidad Nacional del Nordeste. Corrientes, Argentina. (Bonplandia)

British Journal of Political Science. Cambridge University Press. London. (Br. J. Polit. Sci.)

Bulletin de l'Institut français d'études andines. Lima. (Bull. Inst. fr. étud. andin.)

Bulletin of Latin American Research. Blackwell Publishers. Oxford, England; Malden, Mass. (Bull. Lat. Am. Res.)

Business and Politics. Cambridge University Press. Cambridge, England. (Bus. Polit.)

Cambridge Archaeological Journal. Cambridge University Press. Cambridge, England. (Camb. Archaeol. J.)

Caribbean Quarterly: CQ. University of the West Indies, Vice Chancellery, Cultural Studies Initiative. Mona, Jamaica. (Caribb. Q./Mona)

Caribbean Studies. Universidad de Puerto Rico, Instituto de Estudios del Caribe. Río Piedras, Puerto Rico. (Caribb. Stud.)

Centro Journal. Centro de Estudios Puertorriqueños. New York. (Cent. J.)

Colombia Internacional. Universidad de los Andes, Centro de Estudios Internacionales. Bogotá. (Colomb. Int.)

Comparative Political Studies. Sage Publications. Thousand Oaks, Calif. (Comp. Polit. Stud.)

Comparative Politics. City University of New York, Political Science Program. New York. (Comp. Polit./New York)

Comparative Studies in Society and History. Society for the Comparative Study of Society and History; Cambridge University Press. London. (Comp. Stud. Soc. Hist.)

Conservation Letters. Society for Conservation Biology. Washington, D.C.; Blackwell Publishers. Malden, Mass. (Conserv. Lett.)

Cooperation and Conflict. Nordic Committee for the Study of International Politics. Stockholm. (Coop. Confl.)

Cosmovisiones / Cosmovisões. Universidad Nacional de La Plata, Facultad de Ciencias Astronómicas y Geofísicas. Buenos Aires. (Cosmovisiones)

Crime, Law, and Social Change. Kluwer Academic Publishers. Dordrecht, Netherlands; Boston, Mass.; London. (Crime Law Soc. Change)

Cuadernos de Geografía. Universidad Nacional de Colombia, Facultad de Ciencias Humanas, Departamento de Geografía; Instituto Colombiano para el Fomento de Educación Superior. Bogotá. (Cuad. Geogr./Bogotá)

Cuadernos del CLAEH. Centro Latinoamericano de Economía Humana. Montevideo. (Cuad. CLAEH)

Cuadernos Geográficos de la Universidad de Granada. Universidad de Granada. Granada. (Cuad. Geogr. Univ. Granada)

Cuban Studies. University of Pittsburgh Press. Pittsburgh, Pa. (Cuba. Stud.)

Cultural Anthropology: Journal of the Society for Cultural Anthropology. American Anthropological Association, Society for Cultural Anthropology. Washington, D.C. (Cult. Anthropol.)

Cultural Geographies. Arnold. London. (Cult. Geogr./London)

Current History. Philadelphia, Pa. (Curr. Hist.)

Development and Change. Blackwell Publishers. Oxford, England; Malden, Mass. (Dev. Change/Oxford)

Development: Journal of the Society for International Development. Rome. (Development/Rome)

Development Policy Review. Sage. London. (Dev. Policy Rev.)

Diplomacy and Statecraft. Frank Cass and Co. Ltd. London. (Dipl. Statecraft)

Economía y Desarrollo. Universidad de La Habana, Facultad de Economía; Asociación Nacional de Economistas de Cuba. La Habana. (Econ. Desarro./Habana)

Economic Development and Cultural Change. University of Chicago Press. Chicago, Ill. (Econ. Dev. Cult. Change)

Economic History of Developing Regions. Routledge Taylor & Francis. Abingdon, England; Unisa Press. Pretoria, South Africa. (Econ. Hist. Dev. Reg.)

Economic Papers: A Journal of Applied Economics and Policy. Economic Society of Australia. Sydney. (Econ. Pap.)
Ecuador Debate. Centro Andino de Acción Popular. Quito. (Ecuad. Debate)
Environment and Planning: B, Urban Analytics and City Science. Sage. London. (Environ. Plann. B Urban Analytics City Sci.)
Environment and Planning: D, Society & Space. Pion Ltd. London. (Environ. Plann. D Soc. Space)
Environmental Archaeology: The Journal of Human Palaeoecology. Maney for the Association of Environmental Archaeology. Leeds, England. (Environ. Archaeol.)
Environmental Conservation. Cambridge University Press. Cambridge, England. (Environ. Conserv./Cambridge)
Erasmus Law Review. Erasmus School of Law. Rotterdam, The Netherlands. (Erasmus Law Rev.)
Estudios Atacameños. Universidad del Norte, Museo de Arqueología. San Pedro de Atacama, Chile. (Estud. Atacameños)
Estudios de Cultura Maya. UNAM, Instituto de Investigaciones Filológicas, Centro de Estudios Mayas. Ciudad de México. (Estud. Cult. Maya)
Estudios sobre el Mensaje Periodístico. Universidad Complutense, Facultad de Ciencias de Información, Departamento de Periodismo I. Madrid. (Estud. Mensaje Periodís.)
Estudios Socioterritoriales: Revista de Geografía. Universidad Nacional del Centro de la Provincia de Buenos Aires, Centro de Investigaciones Geográficas. Tandil, Argentina. (Estud. Socioterritoriales)
Ethnic and Racial Studies. Routledge & Kegan Paul. London. (Ethn. Racial Stud.)
Ethnohistory. American Society for Ethnohistory. Columbus, Ohio. (Ethnohistory/Columbus)
Etnografías Contemporáneas. Universidad Nacional de San Martín, Instituto de Altos Estudios Sociales, Centro de Estudios en Antropología. Buenos Aires. (Etnogr. Contemp.)
EURE: Revista Latinoamericana de Estudios Urbano Regionales. Pontificia Universidad Católica de Chile, Facultad de Arquitectura y Bellas Artes, Instituto de Estudios Urbanos. Santiago. (EURE/Santiago)

Florida Geographer. Florida Society of Geographers. Boca Raton, Fla. (Fla. Geogr.)
GeoFocus. Grupo de Métodos Cuantitativos Sistemas de Información Geográfica y Teledetección; Asociación de Geógrafos Españoles. Madrid. (GeoFocus)
Geoforum. Pergamon Press. New York; Oxford, England. (Geoforum/New York)
Geografía y Sistemas de Información Geográfica. Universidad Nacional de Luján, Departamento de Ciencias Sociales, Programa de Docencia e Investigación en Sistemas de Información Geográfica. Luján, Argentina. (GeoSIG/Luján)
Geográfica Digital. Universidad Nacional del Nordeste. Instituto de Geografía. Resistencia, Argentina. (Geogr. Digit.)
Geograficando. Universidad Nacional de La Plata, Facultad de Humanidades y Ciencias de la Educación, Departamento de Geografía. La Plata, Argentina. (Geograficando/La Plata)
Geographical Review. American Geographical Society. New York. (Geogr. Rev.)
Geopolitics. Frank Cass. London. (Geopolitics/London)
Global Environmental Change: Human and Policy Dimensions. Butterworth-Heinemann. Guildford, England. (Glob. Environ. Change)
Global Governance: A Review of Multilateralism and International Organizations. Lynne Rienner Publishers, Inc. Boulder, Colo. (Glob. Gov.)
Global Studies of Childhood. Sage Publications. London. (Glob. Stud. Child.)
Government and Opposition. Cambridge University Press. London. (Gov. Oppos.)

Hábitat y Sociedad. Universidad de Sevilla, Máster Propio en Gestión Social del Hábitat. Sevilla, Spain. (Hábitat Soc.)
The Holocene. Edward Arnold. Sevenoaks, England. (Holocene/Sevenoaks)
Huellas. Universidad Nacional de la Pampa, Facultad de Ciencias Humanas, Instituto de Geografía. Santa Rosa, Argentina. (Huellas/Santa Rosa)

Human Ecology. Kluwer Academic Publishers. Dordrecht, N.Y. (Hum. Ecol.)

Iberoamericana: Nordic Journal of Latin American Studies/Revista Nórdica de Estudios Latinoamericanos. Stockholm University, Institute of Latin American Studies. Stockholm. (Iberoamericana/Stockholm)
Íconos: Revista de Ciencias Sociales. FLACSO Ecuador. Quito. (Íconos/Quito)
Indiana. Gebr. Mann. Berlin. (Indiana/Berlin)
Information Technology for Development. Oxford University Press; UNESCO; UK Council for Computing Development. Oxford, England. (Inf. Technol. Dev.)
International Association for Obsidian Studies Bulletin. San José State University, Department of Anthropology. San José, Calif. (IAOS Bulletin)
International Journal of Climatology. Royal Meteorological Society; Wiley. Chichester, England. (Int. J. Climatol.)
International Journal of Cuban Studies. London Metropolitan University, International Institute for the Study of Cuba. London. (Int. J. Cuban Stud.)
International Journal of Entrepreneurship and Small Business. Inderscience Enterprises. Olney, England. (Int. J. Entrep. Small Bus.)
International Journal of Historical Archaeology. Plenum Press. New York. (Int. J. Hist. Archaeol.)
International Studies Quarterly. Blackwell Publishers. Malden, Mass.; Oxford, England. (Int. Stud. Q./Oxford)
Investigaciones Geográficas. Universidad de Chile, Departamento de Geografía. Santiago. (Invest. Geogr./Santiago)
Investigaciones Sociales: Revista del Instituto de Investigaciones Histórico Sociales. Universidad Nacional Mayor de San Marcos, Facultad de Ciencias Sociales. Lima. (Investig. Soc./San Marcos)

JILAS: Journal of Iberian and Latin American Studies. Association of Iberian and Latin American Studies of Australasia; La Trobe University, School of History. Bundoora, Australia. (JILAS/Bundoora)
Journal de la Société des américanistes. Paris. (J. Soc. am.)
Journal of African Diaspora Archaeology and Heritage. Maney Publishing. Leeds, England. (J. Afr. Diaspora Archaeol. Herit.)
Journal of Agrarian Change. Blackwell Publishers. Oxford, England; Malden, Mass. (J. Agrarian Change)
Journal of Anthropological Archaeology. Academic Press. New York. (J. Anthropol. Archaeol.)
Journal of Archaeological Science. Academic Press. London. (J. Archaeol. Sci.)
Journal of Archaeological Science: Reports. Elsevier. Amsterdam. (J. Archaeol. Sci.: Rep.)
Journal of Caribbean Archaeology. University of Florida, Florida Museum of Natural History. Gainesville, Fla. (J. Caribb. Archaeol.)
Journal of Economic Policy Reform. Routledge, Taylor & Francis Group. London. (J. Econ. Policy Reform)
Journal of Field Archaeology. Boston University. Boston, Mass. (J. Field Archaeol.)
Journal of Global South Studies. Association of Global South Studies, Inc. Americus, Ga. (J. Global South Stud.)
Journal of Historical Geography. Academic Press. London; New York. (J. Hist. Geogr.)
Journal of Illicit Economies and Development. LSE Press. London. (JIED)
Journal of Indentureship and its Legacies. Ameena Gafoor Institute for the Study of Indentureship and its Legacies. London. (J. Indentureship Legacies)
Journal of Island & Coastal Archaeology. Taylor & Francis Group. Philadelphia, Pa. (J. Island Coastal Archaeol.)
The Journal of Latin American and Caribbean Anthropology. University of California Press, Journals Division. Berkeley. (J. Lat. Am. Caribb. Anthropol.)
Journal of Latin American Cultural Studies. Carfax Publishing. Abingdon, England. (J. Lat. Am. Cult. Stud.)
Journal of Latin American Geography. Conference of Latin Americanist Geographers. Tucson, Ariz. (J. Lat. Am. Geogr.)
Journal of Latin American Studies. Cambridge University Press. Cambridge, England. (J. Lat. Am. Stud.)

Title List of Journals Indexed / 551

The Journal of Peasant Studies. Frank Cass & Co. London. (J. Peasant Stud.)

Journal of Political and Military Sociology: JPMS. Northern Illinois University, Department of Sociology. DeKalb, Ill. (J. Polit. Mil. Sociol.)

The Journal of Politics. Blackwell Publishers. Abingdon, England; Williston, Vt.; Southern Political Science Association; University of North Carolina. Chapel Hill. (J. Polit.)

Journal of Politics in Latin America. Institute of Latin American Studies; German Institute of Global and Area Studies. Hamburg, Germany. (J. Polit. Lat. Am.)

Journal of Rural Studies. Pergamon Press. New York; Oxford, England. (J. Rural Stud.)

Journal of South American Earth Sciences. Elsevier Science Ltd. New York. (J. South Am. Earth Sci.)

Journal of Sustainable Tourism. Multilingual Matters. Clevedon, England. (J. Sustain. Tourism)

Journal of the Southwest. University of Arizona, Southwest Center. Tucson. (J. Southwest)

Karib: Nordic Journal for Caribbean Studies. Novus forlag. Oslo, Norway; Stockholm University Press. Stockholm. (Karib)

Land Use Policy. Butterworths. Guildford, England. (Land Use Policy)

Latin American and Caribbean Ethnic Studies. Taylor & Francis. Colchester, England. (Lat. Am. Caribb. Ethn. Stud.)

Latin American Antiquity. Society for American Archaeology. Washington, D.C. (Lat. Am. Antiq.)

Latin American Perspectives. Sage Publications, Inc. Thousand Oaks, Calif. (Lat. Am. Perspect.)

Latin American Policy. Wiley Periodicals, Inc. Malden, Mass. (Lat. Am. Policy)

Latin American Politics and Society. University of Miami, School of International Studies. Coral Gables, Fla. (Lat. Am. Polit. Soc.)

Latin American Research Review. Latin American Studies Association; University of Texas Press. Austin. (LARR)

Magallania. Universidad de Magallanes, Instituto de la Patagonia. Punta Arenas, Chile. (Magallania/Punta Arenas)

Maloca: Revista de Estudos Indígenas. Universidade Estadual de Campinas, Instituto de Filosofia e Ciências Humanas, Centro de Pesquisa em Etnologia Indígena. Campinas, Brazil. (Maloca/Campinas)

Marine Pollution Bulletin. Pergamon Press. Oxford, England. (Mar. Pollut. Bull.)

Memorias: Revista Digital de Historia y Arqueología desde el Caribe. Universidad del Norte. Barranquilla, Colombia. (Memorias/Barranquilla)

Meridians: Feminism, Race, Transnationalism. Duke University Press. Durham, N.C. (Meridians)

Mesoamérica. Plumsock Mesoamerican Studies. South Woodstock, Vt.; Centro de Investigaciones Regionales de Mesoamérica. Antigua, Guatemala. (Mesoamérica/Antigua)

NACLA: Report on the Americas. North American Congress on Latin America (NACLA). New York. (NACLA)

Natural Hazards. Kluwer Academic Publishers. Dordrecht, The Netherlands. (Nat. Haz.)

Networks and Spatial Economics. Kluwer Academic Publishers. Norwell, Mass. (Net. Spatial Econ.)

New Politics. New Politics Associates. Brooklyn, N.Y. (New Polit./Brooklyn)

Nueva Sociedad. Fundación Friedrich Ebert. Caracas. (Nueva Soc.)

Périplos: Revista de Pesquisa sobre Migrações. Universidade de Brasília. (Périplos/Brasília)

Persona y Sociedad. Instituto Latinoamericano de Doctrina y Estudios Sociales. Santiago, Chile. (Pers. Soc.)

Perspectiva Geográfica. Universidad Pedagógica y Tecnológica de Colombia. Bogotá. (Perspect. Geogr./Bogotá)

Política y Gobierno. Centro de Investigación y Docencia Económicas, División de Estudios Políticos. Ciudad de México. (Polít. Gob.)

Political Geography. Butterworth-Heinemann. Oxford, England. (Polit. Geogr.)

Political Research Quarterly. University of Utah. Salt Lake City. (Polit. Res. Q.)

Politics & Policy. Georgia Southern University. Statesboro, Ga. (Politics Policy)

Politics, Groups, and Identities. Western Political Science Association; Routledge, Taylor & Francis Group. Abingdon, England. (Polit. Groups Ident.)

Posición. Universidad Nacional de Luján, Instituto de Investigaciones Geográficas. Luján, Argentina. (Posición/Luján)

Positions: East Asia Cultures Critique. Duke University Press. Durham, N.C. (Positions/Durham)

Proceedings of the National Academy of Sciences of the United States of America. Washington, D.C. (Proc. Natl. Acad. Sci. U.S.A.)

The Professional Geographer. Association of American Geographers. Washington, D.C.; Blackwell Publishers. Abindgon, England; Williston, Vt. (Prof. Geogr.)

Progress in Human Geography. E. Arnold. London. (Prog. Hum. Geogr.)

Public Integrity. American Society for Public Administration; M.E. Sharpe. Armonk, N.Y. (Public Integr.)

Regional Studies. Routledge, Taylor & Francis Group. Abingdon, England. (Reg. Stud./Abingdon)

Relaciones de la Sociedad Argentina de Antropología. Buenos Aires. (Relac. Soc. Argent. Antropol.)

Remote Sensing of Environment. American Elsevier Pub. Co. New York. (Remote Sens. Environ.)

Research in Social Stratification and Mobility. JAI Press. Greenwich, Conn. (Res. Soc. Stratif. Mobil.)

Resources, Conservation, and Recycling. Elsevier. Amsterdam; New York; Pergamon. Oxford; New York. (Resour. Conserv. Recycl.)

Review of International Studies. British International Studies Association; Cambridge University Press. London. (Rev. Int. Stud.)

Revista Cartográfica. Instituto Panamericano de Geografía e Historia (IPGH), Comisión de Cartografía. Ciudad de México. (Rev. Cartogr.)

Revista Ciencia y Cultura. Universidad Católica Boliviana. La Paz. (Rev. Cienc. Cult.)

Revista de Ciencia Política. Pontificia Universidad Católica de Chile, Instituto de Ciencia Política. Santiago. (Rev. Cienc. Polít./Santiago)

Revista de Ciencias Sociales. Editorial Universidad de Costa Rica. San José. (Rev. Cienc. Soc./San José)

Revista de Derecho Público. Universidad de Chile. Santiago. (Rev. Derecho Público)

Revista de Estudios Regionales. Universidad de Málaga, Facultad de Ciencias Económicas y Empresariales. Málaga, Spain. (Rev. Estud. Regionales)

Revista de Geografía Norte Grande. Pontificia Universidad Católica de Chile, Facultad de Historia, Geografía y Ciencia Política, Instituto de Geografía. Santiago. (Rev. Geogr. Norte Gd.)

Revista de Historia de América. Instituto Panamericano de Geografía e Historia (IPGH). Ciudad de México. (Rev. Hist. Am./México)

Revista de Indias. Consejo Superior de Investigaciones Científicas, Instituto de Historia, Departamento de Historia de América. Madrid. (Rev. Indias)

Revista de la Escuela de Antropología. Universidad Nacional de Rosario, Facultad de Humanidades y Artes, Escuela de Antropología. Rosario, Argentina. (Rev. Esc. Antropol.)

Revista de Sociologia e Política. Universidade Federal do Paraná, Departamento de Ciências Sociais, Area de Ciência Política. Curitiba, Brazil. (Rev. Sociol. Polít./Curitiba)

Revista del Museo de Antropología. Universidad Nacional de Córdoba, Facultad de Filosofía y Humanidades, Museo de Antropología. Córdoba, Argentina. (Rev. Mus. Antropol./Córdoba)

Revista Elcano. Real Instituto Elcano. Madrid. (Rev. Elcano)

Revista Europea de Estudios Latinoamericanos y del Caribe = European Review of Latin American and Caribbean Studies. Center for Latin American Research and Documentation = Centro de Estudios y Documentación Latinoamericanos. Amsterdam. (Rev. Eur. Estud. Latinoam. Caribe)

Revista Geográfica. Instituto Panamericano de Geografía e Historia (IPGH). Ciudad de México. (Rev. Geogr./México)

Revista Geográfica de América Central. Universidad Nacional. Heredia, Costa Rica. (Rev. Geogr. Am. Cent.)

Revista Geográfica de Chile. Instituto Geográfico Militar. Santiago. (Rev. Geogr. Chile)

Revista Geográfica de Valparaíso. Universidad Católica de Valparaíso. Valparaíso, Chile. (Rev. Geogr. Valparaíso)

Revista Internacional de Sociología. Consejo Superior de Investigaciones Científicas, Instituto de Estudios Sociales de Andalucía. Madrid. (Rev. Int. Sociol.)

Revista Peruana de Antropología. Centro de Estudios Antropológicos Luis Eduardo Valcárcel. Lima. (Rev. Peru. Antropol.)

Revista Universitaria de Geografía. Universidad Nacional del Sur, Departamento de Geografía. Bahía Blanca, Argentina. (Rev. Univ. Geogr./Bahía Blanca)

Runa. Archivo para las Ciencias del Hombre; Universidad de Buenos Aires, Facultad de Filosofía y Letras, Instituto de Antropología. Buenos Aires. (Runa/Buenos Aires)

Science. American Association for the Advancement of Science. Washington, D.C. (Science/Washington)

Science Advances. American Association for the Advancement of Science. Washington, D.C. (Sci. Adv.)

Scientific Reports. Nature Publishing Group. London. (Sci. Rep./London)

Scripta Nova: Revista Electrónica de Geografía y Ciencias Sociales. Universitat de Barcelona, Centre de Recursos per a l'Aprenentatge i la Investigació. Barcelona. (Scripta Nova)

Security Studies. Frank Cass. London. (Sec. Stud.)

Singapore Journal of Tropical Geography. University of Singapore, Department of Geography. Singapore. (Singap. J. Trop. Geogr.)

Slavery and Abolition. Taylor and Francis. Oxon, England. (Slavery Abolit.)

Small Axe: A Journal of Criticism. Ian Randle Publishers. Kingston. (Small Axe)

Social Analysis. Berghahn Books. New York. (Soc. Anal.)

Social Movement Studies. Routledge. London. (Soc. Mov. Stud.)

Social Science Medicine, Population Health. Elsevier Ltd. London. (SSM Popul. Health)

Sociological Perspectives. Pacific Sociological Association; University of California Press. Berkeley. (Sociol. Perspect.)

St. Petersburg University Journal of Economic Studies. St. Petersburg University. Russia. (St. Petersburg Univ. J. Econ. Stud.)

State Crime: Journal of the International State Crime Initiative. Pluto Journals. London. (State Crime)

Studies in Conflict and Terrorism. Taylor and Francis. London. (Stud. Confl. Terror.)

Territory, Politics, Governance. Routledge, Taylor & Francis Group. Abingdon, England. (Territ. Polit. Gov.)

Third World Quarterly. Taylor & Francis Group, Carfax Publishing. London; New York. (Third World Q.)

Tipití: Journal of the Society for the Anthropology of Lowland South America. Society for the Anthropology of Lowland South America (SALSA). New Orleans, La. (Tipití)

Transactions—Institute of British Geographers. Institute of British Geographers. Oxford, England. (Trans. Inst. Br. Geogr.)

Urban Geography. V.H. Winston. Silver Spring, Md. (Urban Geogr.)

Vientos del Norte. Universidad Nacional de Catamarca, Facultad de Humanidades, Departamento de Geografía. Catamarca, Argentina. (Vientos Norte)

Water. MDPI. Basel. (Water/Basel)

Water International. International Water Resources Association. Urbana, Ill. (Water Int.)

Women's Studies Quarterly. Feminist Press. Old Westbury, N.Y. (Women's Stud. Q.)

World Archaeology. Routledge & Kegan Paul. London. (World Archaeol.)

World Development. Elsevier Science; Pergamon Press. Oxford, England. (World Dev.)

World Development Perspectives. Elsevier. Amsterdam. (World Dev. Perspect.)

World Policy Journal. World Policy Institute. New York. (World Policy J.)

World Politics. Johns Hopkins University Press. Baltimore, Md. (World Polit.)

ABBREVIATION LIST OF JOURNALS INDEXED

For journal titles listed by full title, see *Title List of Journals Indexed*, p. 547.

Adm. Soc.   Administration & Society. Sage Publications. Beverly Hills, Calif.

Adv. Anthropol.   Advances in Anthropology. Scientific Research Pub. Irvine, Calif.

Agroalimentaria.   Agroalimentaria. Universidad de los Andes, Facultad de Ciencias Económicas y Sociales, Centro de Investigaciones Agroalimentarias. Mérida, Venezuela.

Agron. J.   Agronomy Journal. American Society of Agronomy. Madison, Wis.

Am. Anthropol.   American Anthropologist. American Anthropological Association. Washington, D.C.

Am. Ethnol./Washington.   American Ethnologist. American Anthropological Association, American Ethnological Society. Washington, D.C.

Am. J. Polit. Sci.   American Journal of Political Science. Midwest Political Science Association; Wiley-Blackwell Publishing. Hoboken, N.J.

Am. Polit. Sci. Rev.   American Political Science Review. American Political Science Association. Washington, D.C.; Michigan State University, College of Social Science, Department of Political Science. East Lansing, Mich.

Anc. Mesoam.   Ancient Mesoamerica. Cambridge University Press. New York; Cambridge, England.

Ann. Am. Assoc. Geogr.   Annals of the American Association of Geographers. Taylor & Francis Group. Philadelphia, Pa.

Anthropocene Sci.   Anthropocene Science. Springer Nature. Singapore.

Anthropol. Dep. Cienc. Soc.   Anthropologica del Departamento de Ciencias Sociales. Pontificia Universidad Católica del Perú, Departamento de Ciencias Sociales. Lima.

Anthropol. Today.   Anthropology Today. Royal Anthropological Institute. London.

Anthurium.   Anthurium: A Caribbean Studies Journal. University of Miami. Coral Gables, Fla.

Antipode.   Antipode. Basil Blackwell. Oxford, England; Cambridge, Mass.

Antiquity/Cambridge.   Antiquity. Antiquity Publications Ltd. Cambridge, England.

Anu. Div. Geogr.   Anuario de la División Geografía. Universidad Nacional de Luján, Departamento de Ciencias Sociales, División Geografía. Buenos Aires.

Anu. Estad. Cuba.   Anuario Estadístico de Cuba. Dirección General de Estadística. La Habana.

Anu. Estud. Centroam.   Anuario de Estudios Centroamericanos. Universidad de Costa Rica. San José.

Appl. Geogr. Applied Geography. Butterworths. Sevenoaks, England.

Araucaria/Triana. Araucaria. Universidad de Sevilla, Miño y Dárila Editores. Triana, Spain.

Archaeol. Anthropol. Sci. Archaeological and Anthropological Sciences. Springer. Berlin.

Area/London. Area. Institute of British Geographers. London.

Atlan. Stud. Global Curr. Atlantic Studies: Global Currents. Taylor & Francis. Abingdon, England.

Bol. Estud. Geogr. Boletín de Estudios Geográficos. Universidad Nacional de Cuyo, Facultad de Filosofia y Letras, Instituto de Geografia. Mendoza, Argentina.

Bol. Soc. Argent. Bot. Boletín de la Sociedad Argentina de Botánica. Buenos Aires.

Bonplandia. Bonplandia. Instituto de Botánica del Nordeste, CONICET, Universidad Nacional del Nordeste. Corrientes, Argentina.

Br. J. Polit. Sci. British Journal of Political Science. Cambridge University Press. London.

Bull. Inst. fr. étud. andin. Bulletin de l'Institut français d'études andines. Lima.

Bull. Lat. Am. Res. Bulletin of Latin American Research. Blackwell Publishers. Oxford, England; Malden, Mass.

Bus. Polit. Business and Politics. Cambridge University Press. Cambridge, England.

Camb. Archaeol. J. Cambridge Archaeological Journal. Cambridge University Press. Cambridge, England.

Caribb. Q./Mona. Caribbean Quarterly: CQ. University of the West Indies, Vice Chancellery, Cultural Studies Initiative. Mona, Jamaica.

Caribb. Stud. Caribbean Studies. Universidad de Puerto Rico, Instituto de Estudios del Caribe. Río Piedras, Puerto Rico.

Cent. J. Centro Journal. Centro de Estudios Puertorriqueños. New York.

Colomb. Int. Colombia Internacional. Universidad de los Andes, Centro de Estudios Internacionales. Bogotá.

Comp. Polit./New York. Comparative Politics. City University of New York, Political Science Program. New York.

Comp. Polit. Stud. Comparative Political Studies. Sage Publications. Thousand Oaks, Calif.

Comp. Stud. Soc. Hist. Comparative Studies in Society and History. Society for the Comparative Study of Society and History; Cambridge University Press. London.

Conserv. Lett. Conservation Letters. Society for Conservation Biology. Washington, D.C.; Blackwell Publishers. Malden, Mass.

Coop. Confl. Cooperation and Conflict. Nordic Committee for the Study of International Politics. Stockholm.

Cosmovisiones. Cosmovisiones / Cosmovisões. Universidad Nacional de La Plata, Facultad de Ciencias Astronómicas y Geofísicas. Buenos Aires.

Crime Law Soc. Change. Crime, Law, and Social Change. Kluwer Academic Publishers. Dordrecht, Netherlands; Boston, Mass.; London.

Cuad. CLAEH. Cuadernos del CLAEH. Centro Latinoamericano de Economía Humana. Montevideo.

Cuad. Geogr./Bogotá. Cuadernos de Geografía. Universidad Nacional de Colombia, Facultad de Ciencias Humanas, Departamento de Geografía; Instituto Colombiano para el Fomento de Educación Superior. Bogotá.

Cuad. Geogr. Univ. Granada. Cuadernos Geográficos de la Universidad de Granada. Universidad de Granada. Granada.

Cuba. Stud. Cuban Studies. University of Pittsburgh Press. Pittsburgh, Pa.

Cult. Anthropol. Cultural Anthropology: Journal of the Society for Cultural Anthropology. American Anthropological Association, Society for Cultural Anthropology. Washington, D.C.

Cult. Geogr./London. Cultural Geographies. Arnold. London.

Curr. Hist. Current History. Philadelphia, Pa.

Dev. Change/Oxford. Development and Change. Blackwell Publishers. Oxford, England; Malden, Mass.

Dev. Policy Rev. Development Policy Review. Sage. London.

Development/Rome. Development: Journal of the Society for International Development. Rome.

Dipl. Statecraft. Diplomacy and Statecraft. Frank Cass and Co. Ltd. London.

Econ. Desarro./Habana. Economía y Desarrollo. Universidad de La Habana, Facultad de Economía; Asociación Nacional de Economistas de Cuba. La Habana.

Econ. Dev. Cult. Change. Economic Development and Cultural Change. University of Chicago Press. Chicago, Ill.

Econ. Hist. Dev. Reg. Economic History of Developing Regions. Routledge Taylor & Francis. Abingdon, England; Unisa Press. Pretoria, South Africa.

Econ. Pap. Economic Papers: A Journal of Applied Economics and Policy. Economic Society of Australia. Sydney.

Ecuad. Debate. Ecuador Debate. Centro Andino de Acción Popular. Quito.

Environ. Archaeol. Environmental Archaeology: The Journal of Human Palaeoecology. Maney for the Association of Environmental Archaeology. Leeds, England.

Environ. Conserv./Cambridge. Environmental Conservation. Cambridge University Press. Cambridge, England.

Environ. Plann. B Urban Analytics City Sci. Environment and Planning: B, Urban Analytics and City Science. Sage. London.

Environ. Plann. D Soc. Space. Environment and Planning: D, Society & Space. Pion Ltd. London.

Erasmus Law Rev. Erasmus Law Review. Erasmus School of Law. Rotterdam, The Netherlands.

Estud. Atacameños. Estudios Atacameños. Universidad del Norte, Museo de Arqueología. San Pedro de Atacama, Chile.

Estud. Cult. Maya. Estudios de Cultura Maya. UNAM, Instituto de Investigaciones Filológicas, Centro de Estudios Mayas. Ciudad de México.

Estud. Mensaje Periodís. Estudios sobre el Mensaje Periodístico. Universidad Complutense, Facultad de Ciencias de Información, Departamento de Periodismo I. Madrid.

Estud. Socioterritoriales. Estudios Socioterritoriales: Revista de Geografía. Universidad Nacional del Centro de la Provincia de Buenos Aires, Centro de Investigaciones Geográficas. Tandil, Argentina.

Ethn. Racial Stud. Ethnic and Racial Studies. Routledge & Kegan Paul. London.

Ethnohistory/Columbus. Ethnohistory. American Society for Ethnohistory. Columbus, Ohio.

Etnogr. Contemp. Etnografías Contemporáneas. Universidad Nacional de San Martín, Instituto de Altos Estudios Sociales, Centro de Estudios en Antropología. Buenos Aires.

EURE/Santiago. EURE: Revista Latinoamericana de Estudios Urbano Regionales. Pontificia Universidad Católica de Chile, Facultad de Arquitectura y Bellas Artes, Instituto de Estudios Urbanos. Santiago.

Fla. Geogr. Florida Geographer. Florida Society of Geographers. Boca Raton, Fla.

GeoFocus. GeoFocus. Grupo de Métodos Cuantitativos Sistemas de Información Geográfica y Teledetección; Asociación de Geógrafos Españoles. Madrid.

Geoforum/New York. Geoforum. Pergamon Press. New York; Oxford, England.

Geogr. Digit. Geográfica Digital. Universidad Nacional del Nordeste. Instituto de Geografía. Resistencia, Argentina.

Geogr. Rev. Geographical Review. American Geographical Society. New York.

Geograficando/La Plata. Geograficando. Universidad Nacional de La Plata, Facultad de Humanidades y Ciencias de la Educación, Departamento de Geografía. La Plata, Argentina.

Geopolitics/London. Geopolitics. Frank Cass. London.

GeoSIG/Luján. Geografía y Sistemas de Información Geográfica. Universidad Nacional de Luján, Departamento de Ciencias Sociales, Programa de Docencia e Investigación en Sistemas de Información Geográfica. Luján, Argentina.

Glob. Environ. Change. Global Environmental Change: Human and Policy Dimensions. Butterworth-Heinemann. Guildford, England.

Glob. Gov. Global Governance: A Review of Multilateralism and International Organizations. Lynne Rienner Publishers, Inc. Boulder, Colo.

Glob. Stud. Child. Global Studies of Childhood. Sage Publications. London.

Gov. Oppos. Government and Opposition. Cambridge University Press. London.

Hábitat Soc. Hábitat y Sociedad. Universidad de Sevilla, Máster Propio en Gestión Social del Hábitat. Sevilla, Spain.

Holocene/Sevenoaks. The Holocene. Edward Arnold. Sevenoaks, England.

Huellas/Santa Rosa. Huellas. Universidad Nacional de la Pampa, Facultad de Ciencias Humanas, Instituto de Geografía. Santa Rosa, Argentina.

Hum. Ecol. Human Ecology. Kluwer Academic Publishers. Dordrecht, N.Y.

IAOS Bulletin. International Association for Obsidian Studies Bulletin. San José State University, Department of Anthropology. San José, Calif.

Iberoamericana/Stockholm. Iberoamericana: Nordic Journal of Latin American Studies/Revista Nórdica de Estudios Latinoamericanos. Stockholm University, Institute of Latin American Studies. Stockholm.

Íconos/Quito. Íconos: Revista de Ciencias Sociales. FLACSO Ecuador. Quito.

Indiana/Berlin. Indiana. Gebr. Mann. Berlin.

Inf. Technol. Dev. Information Technology for Development. Oxford University Press; UNESCO; UK Council for Computing Development. Oxford, England.

Int. J. Climatol. International Journal of Climatology. Royal Meteorological Society; Wiley. Chichester, England.

Int. J. Cuban Stud. International Journal of Cuban Studies. London Metropolitan University, International Institute for the Study of Cuba. London.

Int. J. Entrep. Small Bus. International Journal of Entrepreneurship and Small Business. Inderscience Enterprises. Olney, England.

Int. J. Hist. Archaeol. International Journal of Historical Archaeology. Plenum Press. New York.

Int. Stud. Q./Oxford. International Studies Quarterly. Blackwell Publishers. Malden, Mass.; Oxford, England.

Invest. Geogr./Santiago. Investigaciones Geográficas. Universidad de Chile, Departamento de Geografía. Santiago.

Investig. Soc./San Marcos. Investigaciones Sociales: Revista del Instituto de Investigaciones Histórico Sociales. Universidad Nacional Mayor de San Marcos, Facultad de Ciencias Sociales. Lima.

J. Afr. Diaspora Archaeol. Herit. Journal of African Diaspora Archaeology and Heritage. Maney Publishing. Leeds, England.

J. Agrarian Change. Journal of Agrarian Change. Blackwell Publishers. Oxford, England; Malden, Mass.

J. Anthropol. Archaeol. Journal of Anthropological Archaeology. Academic Press. New York.

J. Archaeol. Sci. Journal of Archaeological Science. Academic Press. London.

J. Archaeol. Sci.: Rep. Journal of Archaeological Science: Reports. Elsevier. Amsterdam.

J. Caribb. Archaeol. Journal of Caribbean Archaeology. University of Florida, Florida Museum of Natural History. Gainesville, Fla.

J. Econ. Policy Reform. Journal of Economic Policy Reform. Routledge, Taylor & Francis Group. London.

J. Field Archaeol. Journal of Field Archaeology. Boston University. Boston, Mass.

J. Global South Stud. Journal of Global South Studies. Association of Global South Studies, Inc. Americus, Ga.

J. Hist. Geogr. Journal of Historical Geography. Academic Press. London; New York.

J. Indentureship Legacies. Journal of Indentureship and its Legacies. Ameena Gafoor Institute for the Study of Indentureship and its Legacies. London.

J. Island Coastal Archaeol. Journal of Island & Coastal Archaeology. Taylor & Francis Group. Philadelphia, Pa.

J. Lat. Am. Caribb. Anthropol. The Journal of Latin American and Caribbean Anthropology. University of California Press, Journals Division. Berkeley.

J. Lat. Am. Cult. Stud. Journal of Latin American Cultural Studies. Carfax Publishing. Abingdon, England.

J. Lat. Am. Geogr. Journal of Latin American Geography. Conference of Latin Americanist Geographers. Tucson, Ariz.

J. Lat. Am. Stud. Journal of Latin American Studies. Cambridge University Press. Cambridge, England.

J. Peasant Stud. The Journal of Peasant Studies. Frank Cass & Co. London.

J. Polit. The Journal of Politics. Blackwell Publishers. Abingdon, England; Williston, Vt.; Southern Political Science Association; University of North Carolina. Chapel Hill.

J. Polit. Lat. Am. Journal of Politics in Latin America. Institute of Latin American Studies; German Institute of Global and Area Studies. Hamburg, Germany.

J. Polit. Mil. Sociol. Journal of Political and Military Sociology: JPMS. Northern Illinois University, Department of Sociology. DeKalb, Ill.

J. Rural Stud. Journal of Rural Studies. Pergamon Press. New York; Oxford, England.

J. Soc. am. Journal de la Société des américanistes. Paris.

J. South Am. Earth Sci. Journal of South American Earth Sciences. Elsevier Science Ltd. New York.

J. Southwest. Journal of the Southwest. University of Arizona, Southwest Center. Tucson.

J. Sustain. Tourism. Journal of Sustainable Tourism. Multilingual Matters. Clevedon, England.

JIED. Journal of Illicit Economies and Development. LSE Press. London.

JILAS/Bundoora. JILAS: Journal of Iberian and Latin American Studies. Association of Iberian and Latin American Studies of Australasia; La Trobe University, School of History. Bundoora, Australia.

Karib. Karib: Nordic Journal for Caribbean Studies. Novus forlag. Oslo, Norway; Stockholm University Press. Stockholm.

Land Use Policy. Land Use Policy. Butterworths. Guildford, England.

LARR. Latin American Research Review. Latin American Studies Association; University of Texas Press. Austin.

Lat. Am. Antiq. Latin American Antiquity. Society for American Archaeology. Washington, D.C.

Lat. Am. Caribb. Ethn. Stud. Latin American and Caribbean Ethnic Studies. Taylor & Francis. Colchester, England.

Lat. Am. Perspect. Latin American Perspectives. Sage Publications, Inc. Thousand Oaks, Calif.

Lat. Am. Policy. Latin American Policy. Wiley Periodicals, Inc. Malden, Mass.

Lat. Am. Polit. Soc. Latin American Politics and Society. University of Miami, School of International Studies. Coral Gables, Fla.

Magallania/Punta Arenas. Magallania. Universidad de Magallanes, Instituto de la Patagonia. Punta Arenas, Chile.

Maloca/Campinas. Maloca: Revista de Estudos Indígenas. Universidade Estadual de Campinas, Instituto de Filosofia e Ciências Humanas, Centro de Pesquisa em Etnologia Indígena. Campinas, Brazil.

Mar. Pollut. Bull. Marine Pollution Bulletin. Pergamon Press. Oxford, England.

Memorias/Barranquilla. Memorias: Revista Digital de Historia y Arqueología desde el Caribe. Universidad del Norte. Barranquilla, Colombia.

Meridians. Meridians: Feminism, Race, Transnationalism. Duke University Press. Durham, N.C.

Mesoamérica/Antigua. Mesoamérica. Plumsock Mesoamerican Studies. South Woodstock, Vt.; Centro de Investigaciones Regionales de Mesoamérica. Antigua, Guatemala.

NACLA. NACLA: Report on the Americas. North American Congress on Latin America (NACLA). New York.

Nat. Haz. Natural Hazards. Kluwer Academic Publishers. Dordrecht, The Netherlands.

Net. Spatial Econ. Networks and Spatial Economics. Kluwer Academic Publishers. Norwell, Mass.

New Polit./Brooklyn. New Politics. New Politics Associates. Brooklyn, N.Y.

Nueva Soc. Nueva Sociedad. Fundación Friedrich Ebert. Caracas.

Périplos/Brasília. Périplos: Revista de Pesquisa sobre Migrações. Universidade de Brasília.

Pers. Soc. Persona y Sociedad. Instituto Latinoamericano de Doctrina y Estudios Sociales. Santiago, Chile.

Perspect. Geogr./Bogotá. Perspectiva Geográfica. Universidad Pedagógica y Tecnológica de Colombia. Bogotá.

Polit. Geogr. Political Geography. Butterworth-Heinemann. Oxford, England.

Polít. Gob. Política y Gobierno. Centro de Investigación y Docencia Económicas, División de Estudios Políticos. Ciudad de México.

Polit. Groups Ident. Politics, Groups, and Identities. Western Political Science Association; Routledge, Taylor & Francis Group. Abingdon, England.

Polit. Res. Q. Political Research Quarterly. University of Utah. Salt Lake City.

Politics Policy. Politics & Policy. Georgia Southern University. Statesboro, Ga.

Posición/Luján. Posición. Universidad Nacional de Luján, Instituto de Investigaciones Geográficas. Luján, Argentina.

Positions/Durham. Positions: East Asia Cultures Critique. Duke University Press. Durham, N.C.

Proc. Natl. Acad. Sci. U.S.A. Proceedings of the National Academy of Sciences of the United States of America. Washington, D.C.

Prof. Geogr. The Professional Geographer. Association of American Geographers. Washington, D.C.; Blackwell Publishers. Abingdon, England; Williston, Vt.

Prog. Hum. Geogr. Progress in Human Geography. E. Arnold. London.

Public Integr. Public Integrity. American Society for Public Administration; M.E. Sharpe. Armonk, N.Y.

Reg. Stud./Abingdon. Regional Studies. Routledge, Taylor & Francis Group. Abingdon, England.

Relac. Soc. Argent. Antropol. Relaciones de la Sociedad Argentina de Antropología. Buenos Aires.

Remote Sens. Environ. Remote Sensing of Environment. American Elsevier Pub. Co. New York.

Res. Soc. Stratif. Mobil. Research in Social Stratification and Mobility. JAI Press. Greenwich, Conn.

Resour. Conserv. Recycl. Resources, Conservation, and Recycling. Elsevier. Amsterdam; New York; Pergamon. Oxford; New York.

Rev. Cartogr. Revista Cartográfica. Instituto Panamericano de Geografía e Historia (IPGH), Comisión de Cartografía. Ciudad de México.

Rev. Cienc. Cult. Revista Ciencia y Cultura. Universidad Católica Boliviana. La Paz.

Rev. Cienc. Polít./Santiago. Revista de Ciencia Política. Pontificia Universidad Católica de Chile, Instituto de Ciencia Política. Santiago.

Rev. Cienc. Soc./San José. Revista de Ciencias Sociales. Editorial Universidad de Costa Rica. San José.

Rev. Derecho Público. Revista de Derecho Público. Universidad de Chile. Santiago.

Rev. Elcano. Revista Elcano. Real Instituto Elcano. Madrid.

Rev. Esc. Antropol. Revista de la Escuela de Antropología. Universidad Nacional de Rosario, Facultad de Humanidades y Artes, Escuela de Antropología. Rosario, Argentina.

Rev. Estud. Regionales. Revista de Estudios Regionales. Universidad de Málaga, Facultad de Ciencias Económicas y Empresariales. Málaga, Spain.

Rev. Eur. Estud. Latinoam. Caribe. Revista Europea de Estudios Latinoamericanos y del Caribe = European Review of Latin American and Caribbean Studies. Center for Latin American Research and Documentation = Centro de Estudios y Documentación Latinoamericanos. Amsterdam.

Rev. Geogr. Am. Cent. Revista Geográfica de América Central. Universidad Nacional. Heredia, Costa Rica.

Rev. Geogr. Chile. Revista Geográfica de Chile. Instituto Geográfico Militar. Santiago.

Rev. Geogr./México. Revista Geográfica. Instituto Panamericano de Geografía e Historia (IPGH). Ciudad de México.

Rev. Geogr. Norte Gd. Revista de Geografía Norte Grande. Pontificia Universidad Católica de Chile, Facultad de Historia, Geografía y Ciencia Política, Instituto de Geografía. Santiago.

Rev. Geogr. Valparaíso. Revista Geográfica de Valparaíso. Universidad Católica de Valparaíso. Valparaíso, Chile.

Rev. Hist. Am./México. Revista de Historia de América. Instituto Panamericano de Geografía e Historia (IPGH). Ciudad de México.

Rev. Indias. Revista de Indias. Consejo Superior de Investigaciones Científicas, Instituto de Historia, Departamento de Historia de América. Madrid.

Rev. Int. Sociol. Revista Internacional de Sociología. Consejo Superior de Investigaciones Científicas, Instituto de Estudios Sociales de Andalucía. Madrid.

Rev. Int. Stud. Review of International Studies. British International Studies Association; Cambridge University Press. London.

Rev. Mus. Antropol./Córdoba. Revista del Museo de Antropología. Universidad Nacional de Córdoba, Facultad de Filosofía y Humanidades, Museo de Antropología. Córdoba, Argentina.

Rev. Peru. Antropol. Revista Peruana de Antropología. Centro de Estudios Antropológicos Luis Eduardo Valcárcel. Lima.

Rev. Sociol. Polít./Curitiba. Revista de Sociologia e Política. Universidade Federal do Paraná, Departamento de Ciências Sociais, Area de Ciência Política. Curitiba, Brazil.

Rev. Univ. Geogr./Bahía Blanca. Revista Universitaria de Geografía. Universidad Nacional del Sur, Departamento de Geografía. Bahía Blanca, Argentina.

Runa/Buenos Aires. Runa. Archivo para las Ciencias del Hombre; Universidad de Buenos Aires, Facultad de Filosofía y Letras, Instituto de Antropología. Buenos Aires.

Sci. Adv. Science Advances. American Association for the Advancement of Science. Washington, D.C.

Sci. Rep./London. Scientific Reports. Nature Publishing Group. London.

Science/Washington. Science. American Association for the Advancement of Science. Washington, D.C.

Scripta Nova. Scripta Nova: Revista Electrónica de Geografía y Ciencias Sociales. Universitat de Barcelona, Centre de Recursos per a l'Aprenentatge i la Investigació. Barcelona.

Sec. Stud. Security Studies. Frank Cass. London.

Singap. J. Trop. Geogr. Singapore Journal of Tropical Geography. University of Singapore, Department of Geography. Singapore.

Slavery Abolit. Slavery and Abolition. Taylor and Francis. Oxon, England.

Small Axe. Small Axe: A Journal of Criticism. Ian Randle Publishers. Kingston.

Soc. Anal. Social Analysis. Berghahn Books. New York.

Soc. Mov. Stud. Social Movement Studies. Routledge. London.

Sociol. Perspect. Sociological Perspectives. Pacific Sociological Association; University of California Press. Berkeley.

SSM Popul. Health. Social Science Medicine, Population Health. Elsevier Ltd. London.

St. Petersburg Univ. J. Econ. Stud. St. Petersburg University Journal of Economic Studies. St. Petersburg University. Russia.

State Crime. State Crime: Journal of the International State Crime Initiative. Pluto Journals. London.

Stud. Confl. Terror. Studies in Conflict and Terrorism. Taylor and Francis. London.

Territ. Polit. Gov. Territory, Politics, Governance. Routledge, Taylor & Francis Group. Abingdon, England.

Third World Q. Third World Quarterly. Taylor & Francis Group, Carfax Publishing. London; New York.

Tipití. Tipití: Journal of the Society for the Anthropology of Lowland South America. Society for the Anthropology of Lowland South America (SALSA). New Orleans, La.

Trans. Inst. Br. Geogr. Transactions—Institute of British Geographers. Institute of British Geographers. Oxford, England.

Urban Geogr. Urban Geography. V.H. Winston. Silver Spring, Md.

Vientos Norte. Vientos del Norte. Universidad Nacional de Catamarca, Facultad de Humanidades, Departamento de Geografía. Catamarca, Argentina.

Water/Basel. Water. MDPI. Basel.

Water Int. Water International. International Water Resources Association. Urbana, Ill.

Women's Stud. Q. Women's Studies Quarterly. Feminist Press. Old Westbury, N.Y.

World Archaeol. World Archaeology. Routledge & Kegan Paul. London.

World Dev. World Development. Elsevier Science; Pergamon Press. Oxford, England.

World Dev. Perspect. World Development Perspectives. Elsevier. Amsterdam.

World Policy J. World Policy Journal. World Policy Institute. New York.

World Polit. World Politics. Johns Hopkins University Press. Baltimore, Md.

SUBJECT INDEX

Abortion. Bolivia, 1740. Mexico, 1489. Nicaragua, 1559.
Acapulco, Mexico (city). Homicide, 1488. Maritime History, 1168. Political Violence, 1454. Women, 238.
Acatic, Mexico (city). Teenagers, 1479.
Aceros Zapla (firm), 1385.
Acueducto del Padre Tembleque (Zempoala, Hidalgo and Otumba de Gómez Farías, Mexico), 532.
Adolescents. See Teenagers; Youth.
Adoption. Costa Rica, 1573. Law and Legislation, 1573.
African-Americans. See Black People.
African Influences. Caribbean Area, 445. Peru, 1719, 1721. See Also Santería.
Afro-Americans. See Black People.
Aged. Caribbean Area, 1567. Central America, 1567. Mexico, 1536.
Agrarian Reform. See Land Reform.
Agribusiness. Argentina, 610, 643, 659. Brazil, 763. South America, 598. Uruguay, 747, 755. See Also Agroindustry.
Agricultural Development. Argentina, 610, 638. Cuba, 1349. Mexico, 529. See Also Agricultural Technology; Development Projects; Economic Development.
Agricultural Development Projects. See Development Projects.
Agricultural Ecology. Argentina, 625. Paraguay, 311. See Also Ecology.
Agricultural Geography. Argentina, 625. Brazil, 799. Ecuador, 574. See Also Agriculture; Geography.
Agricultural History. Brazil, 799. Colombia, 1663.
Agricultural Industries. See Agroindustry.
Agricultural Labor. Economic Conditions, 1749. Guatemala, 890. Mexico, 200.
Agricultural Policy. Argentina, 1268, 1390, 1396. Brazil, 731, 785, 792. Cuba, 1351, 1354. Mexico, 529, 1299. Puerto Rico, 463. See Also Land Reform; Rural Development.

Agricultural Productivity. Argentina, 660. Climate Change, 586. Cuba, 1358.
Agricultural Systems, 357, 414. Cuba, 1358. Mexico, 531.
Agricultural Technology. Argentina, 1396. See Also Agricultural Development.
Agricultural Workers. See Agricultural Labor.
Agriculture, 380, 412, 419. Costa Rica, 487. Haiti, 434. Industry and Industrialization, 519, 531, 548. Water Supply, 516. See Also Sustainable Agriculture.
Agroindustry. Brazil, 789. Paraguay, 738. See Also Agribusiness.
Aguaruna (indigenous group). Political Participation, 282. Social Life and Customs, 282. Witchcraft, 282.
Aguascalientes, Mexico (city). Urbanization, 539.
Aguascalientes, Mexico (state). Politicians, 832.
Aisén, Chile (prov.). Human Geography, 710.
Aldinger, Paul, 780.
Alfonsín, Raúl, 1222.
Alianza Bolivariana para los Pueblos de Nuestra América—Tratado de Comercio de los Pueblos, 1203.
Allende Gossens, Salvador, 1068, 1381.
Alvarado Quesada, Carlos, 857.
Amazon Basin. Boundaries, 1237. Land Use, 778. Sustainable Development, 762.
Amazonia. See Amazon Basin.
American Influences. See US Influences.
Amulets. Caribbean Area, 127.
Andean Region. Migration, 1442.
Andrade, Manuel Correia de Oliveira, 773.
Angaité (indigenous group). Deforestation, 311.
Animal Remains. Mesoamerica, 15. Mexico, 67, 80. Mortuary Customs, 98. See Also Animals.
Animals. Archeology, 15. Art, 15. Cosmology, 295. Environmental Conservation, 568. Sacrifice, 98. See Also Animal Remains; Livestock.

Anthropologists. Caribbean Area, 932. Mexico, 196. US, 1631.
Anthropology. Colombia, 279.
Anthropometry. Mexico, 19. *See Also* Anthropology.
Antioquia, Colombia (dept.). Violence, 1662.
Aqueducts. Mexico, 532.
Arab-Israeli Conflict, 1153.
Arabs, 402, 1153.
Arana, Julio César, 298.
Araucanía Region (Chile). Colonization, 717. Economic Conditions, 1214. Elites, 717.
Araucanian (indigenous group). *See* Mapuche (indigenous group).
Araucano (indigenous group). *See* Mapuche (indigenous group).
Arawak (indigenous group). Marriage, 261. Purus River Valley (Peru and Brazil), 261. *See Also* Indigenous Peoples.
Archeoastronomy. Mexico, 79, 86.
Archeological Dating. Argentina, 148–149. Belize, 482. Caribbean Area, 130. Costa Rica, 487. Grenada, 124. Human Remains, 149. Mesoamerica, 61, 72. Mexico, 27. Obsidian, 85. Peru, 171.
Archeological Sites. Bolivia, 152. Chile, 346. Labor and Laboring Classes, 151. Mexico, 35, 62. Photography, 62. Tourism, 337.
Archeological Surveys. Caribbean Area, 125. Methodology, 119. Peru, 166.
Archeologists. Education, 337. Mexico, 16.
Archeology. Mesoamerica, 95. Methodology, 3, 25. *See Also* Artifacts.
Architecture. Chile, 707. Ecuador, 1685. Mesoamerica, 39.
Arequipa, Peru (city). Cultural Identity, 1710. History, 1710.
Arequipa, Peru (dept.). Excavations, 161.
Argentina. Caja de Conversión, 1394.
Argentina. Congreso de la Nación Senado de la Nación, 1092.
Armaments. *See* Weapons.
Armed Forces. *See* Military.
Arrate, Jorge, 1058.
Articulação dos Povos Indígenas do Brasil, 264.
Artifacts. Andean Region, 138. Caribbean Area, 127, 130. Mexico, 21, 29, 78. Peru, 164. Precolumbian Civilizations, 139. Symbolism, 9. *See Also* Archeology.
Artisanry. Caribbean Area, 122.
Asamblea Popular de los Pueblos de Oaxaca, 819.
Ashaninca (indigenous group). Myths and Mythology, 293. Political Participation, 294.
Asians, 402, 1433.
Asociación de Administradoras de Fondos de Pensiones (Santiago, Chile), 1380.
Assassination. Washington, DC (city), US, 1230.
Astronomy. Mesoamerica, 31. *See Also* Cosmology.
Asunción, Paraguay (city). City Planning, 740. Coastal Areas, 728. History, 727. Housing, 740. Social Structure, 740.
Atacama, Chile (region). Environmental Policy, 684. Floods, 683. Minerals and Mining Industry, 684. Natural Disasters, 683.
Atacama Desert (Chile). Description and Travel, 692. Discovery and Exploration, 692.
Atlases. Argentina, 609. *See Also* Maps and Cartography.
Austerity Measures. Brazil, 1420.
Authoritarianism. Central America, 850. Nicaragua, 914, 916, 918, 920, 923. *See Also* Dictatorships.
Automobile Industry and Trade, 362. Argentina, 1404. Labor Supply, 1324. Mexico, 1324. *See Also* Transportation.
Aweti (indigenous group). Kinship, 268. Names, 268.
Ayacucho, Peru (city). Rock Art, 160.
Ayahuasca. Brazil, 258. Colombia, 272. Peru, 285.
Aymara (indigenous group). Economic Conditions, 211. Ethnic Groups and Ethnicity, 355. Ethnic Identity, 718. Human Geography, 718. Myths and Mythology, 343. Peru, 355. Social Conditions, 211. Textiles and Textile Industry, 343.
Ayoreo (indigenous group). *See* Moro (indigenous group).
Aysén, Chile (prov.). *See* Aisén, Chile (prov.).
Aztecs. Artifacts, 38, 46. Dance, 223. Mexico, 19. Rites and Ceremonies, 114.
Azurduy de Padilla, Juana, 640.
Bacha, Edmar Lisboa, 1419.
Bagua, Peru (prov.). Indigenous Peoples, 286.
Bahia, Brazil (state). Agricultural Policy, 785. Palms, 799. Political Parties, 1105.
Bahía Blanca, Argentina (city). Tourism, 341. Urbanization, 341.

Baja California, Mexico (region). Commerce, 1311. Economic Development, 1311. Excavations, 80. Tourism, 1311. *See Also* Baja California Sur, Mexico (state); Baja California, Mexico (state).

Baja California, Mexico (state). Elections, 815. *See Also* Baja California, Mexico (region).

Baja California Norte, Mexico (state). *See* Baja California, Mexico (state).

Baja California Sur, Mexico (state). Indigenous Peoples, 1545. Migration, 1545. Social Conditions, 1545.

Balance of Trade. Cuba, 1359. *See Also* Commerce.

Ball Games. Mesoamerica, 6, 97. *See Also* Rites and Ceremonies.

Banco Central de la República Argentina, 1394–1395.

Banco de San Luis Potosí (Mexico), 1295.

Banco Nacional de Desenvolvimento Econômico e Social (Brazil), 1431.

Banking and Financial Institutions. Argentina, 1394, 1402. Brazil, 766. Mexico, 1289, 1295, 1326. Nationalization, 1326.

Baptista, Asdrúbal, 1368.

Barrow, Errol Walton, 963.

Beaches. Argentina, 664. Caribbean Area, 435. Dominican Republic, 444. Refuse and Refuse Disposal, 435. Uruguay, 750. *See Also* Coastal Areas.

Beagle Channel (Argentina and Chile), 1220, 1231.

Becan Site (Mexico). Precolumbian Architecture, 102.

Beliefs and Customs. *See* Religious Life and Customs; Social Life and Customs.

Belize. Ministry of Health, 485.

Belize River Valley. Archeological Surveys, 482.

Belo Horizonte, Brazil (city). Transportation, 798.

Bernardino, *de Sahagún*, 114.

Betancourt, Rómulo, 1246.

Bilingual Education. Argentina, 300. *See Also* Education.

Bioarcheology. Argentina, 137. Chile, 137.

Biodiversity. Argentina, 617. Caribbean Area, 461. Costa Rica, 492. Patagonia (region), 674.

Biotechnology. Argentina, 643. *See Also* Technological Development; Technology.

Birds. Caribbean Area, 116. Hunting, 116.

Birth Control, 365. Peru, 1729. Puerto Rico, 1185.

Black Carib (indigenous group). Honduras, 1568. Religion, 189. Social Life and Customs, 189.

Black Market. Guatemala, 1603. *See Also* Crime and Criminals.

Black People, 1433–1434. Brazil, 1123. Caribbean Area, 931–932, 941, 943, 1620. Collective Memory, 1679. Colombia, 1660. Cuba, 1604, 1621. Dance, 1720. Ecuador, 1679–1680, 1690–1691. Elections, 1112. Intellectual History, 1680. Intellectuals, 1609. Land Tenure, 403, 446, 510. Mexico, 1475, 1514. Peru, 1721. Philosophy, 450. Puerto Rico, 1613–1614, 1627. Religion, 1721. Social Movements, 1613. Teachers, 1606. Trinidad and Tobago, 1611. US, 1609. Women, 238.

Boas, Franz, 1631.

Bocas del Toro, Panama (prov.). Geopolitics, 513. Migration, 514. Political Ecology, 514.

Boccard, Louis de, 603.

Bogotá, Colombia (city). Environmental Pollution, 561. Foreign Policy, 1236. Housing, 1652. Indigenous Peoples, 273. Social Conditions, 1641.

Bolsa Família (program), 1112, 1124, 1136, 1424, 1430.

Bonpland, Aimé, 734.

Books. Children, 413.

Border Disputes. *See* Boundary Disputes.

Borderlands. Guatemala/Mexico, 1603. Mexico, 1172. South America, 737. *See Also* Mexican-American Border Region.

Botany. Caribbean Area, 464. Paraguay, 734.

Boundaries. Argentina/Chile, 1220, 1231. Belize/Guatemala, 1180. Bolivia, 1224–1225. Chile, 1224–1225. Colombia, 1209, 1234, 1241. Colombia/Ecuador, 246. Crime and Criminals, 1158. Economic Conditions, 1158. Ecuador, 1209, 1241. Guatemala/Mexico, 1180. Mesoamerica, 55. Peru, 1209. Philosophy, 599. *See Also* Boundary Disputes.

Boundary Disputes. Brazil/Paraguay, 726. *See Also* Boundaries.

Brathwaite, Kamau, 1612.

Brazil. Comissão de Linhas Telegráficas Estratégicas de Mato Grosso ao Amazonas, 263.

Brazil. Congresso Nacional Câmara dos Deputados, 1128.
Bribri (indigenous group). Agriculture, 492. Land Use, 492.
British Influences. Brazil, 767.
Brush, Charles, 65.
Budget. Argentina, 1088. Mexico, 837.
Buenos Aires, Argentina (city). City Planning, 622, 628, 633, 637. Civil Society, 637. Demography, 612, 653. Elections, 614. Housing, 612. Human Geography, 635. Land Use, 634, 638. Maps and Cartography, 619, 672. Migration, 677. Political Parties, 635. Political Systems, 635. Population, 653. Public Spaces, 622, 628, 640. Social Conflict, 677. Tourism, 634, 672. Urban Renewal, 638, 672. Urbanization, 616.
Buenos Aires, Argentina (prov.). Electricity, 630. Land Use, 424. Urbanization, 630.
Bunge, Alejandro Ernesto, 1393.
Bureaucracy. Argentina, 1407. Chile, 713. Dominican Republic, 954, 1272.
Burials. *See* Cemeteries; Mortuary Customs; Tombs.
Business Administration. Cuba, 1350. Ethics, 1317. Mexico, 1297. Puerto Rico, 1338. *See Also* Government-Business Relations.
Businesspeople. Argentina, 1408. Colombia, 1664. Mexico, 1478, 1551. Political Participation, 1423.
Caboclos. *See* Mestizos and Mestizaje.
Cacao. History, 64.
Cáceres, Berta, 905.
Calakmul Site (Mexico), 81.
Cali, Colombia (city). City Planning, 1673.
Calle 11 (Puebla de Zaragoza, Mexico). Urbanization, 553.
Camacho, Bolivia (prov.). Rock Art, 152.
Cambiemos (Argentina), 1089–1091, 1098, 1384.
Campaign Funds. Chile, 1074. Costa Rica, 855. El Salvador, 879. Women, 1074.
Campeche, Mexico (state). Precolumbian Architecture, 40. Precolumbian Civilizations, 81.
Cancuén Site (Guatemala), 99.
Canella (indigenous group). Mortuary Customs, 262. Rites and Ceremonies, 262.
Canelo (indigenous group). Children, 288.
Canoes and Canoeing. Caribbean Area, 134.
Canta, Peru (prov.). Religious Life and Customs, 1719.

Capital. Argentina, 1282. Peru, 1696.
Capitalism. Argentina, 648. Bolivia, 342. Chile, 1383. Economic Development, 947. Environmental Degradation, 397. Mexico, 1305, 1321, 1529. Natural Resources, 656. Nicaragua, 920. Violence, 1273.
Cárcel de Mujeres de Quito, 1676.
Cárdenas, Lázaro, 1170.
Cardoso, Fernando Henrique, 1133.
Caribbean Community (CARICOM), 452, 929, 946, 1199.
Caribbean Court of Justice, 928.
Caribbean Forum, 927.
Caribbean Sea. Biodiversity, 461.
CARICOM. *See* Caribbean Community (CARICOM).
Carnival. Caribbean Area, 1608.
Carriacou Island (Grenada). Archeological Surveys, 123.
Cartagena, Colombia (city). Urbanization, 560.
Cartography. *See* Maps and Cartography.
Casement, Roger, 292.
Cashinawa (indigenous group). Rites and Ceremonies, 258.
Caso, Alfonso, 16.
Castañeda, Jorge G., 846.
Castro, Fidel, 978, 1186, 1607.
Castro, Josué de, 769, 771, 774.
Catamarca, Argentina (prov.). Irrigation, 661. Land Use, 629, 676. Minerals and Mining Industry, 661. Soils, 676.
Catholic Church, 1437. Costa Rica, 856. Environmental Degradation, 589. Mexico, 1168, 1449. Peru, 1709. Venezuela, 1672. *See Also* Catholicism; Christianity.
Catholicism. Mexico, 1483. Peru, 1709. Women, 1449. *See Also* Catholic Church.
Cattle Raising and Trade. Brazil, 795. Guatemala, 500. Mexico, 1308. Paraguay, 311. *See Also* Food Industry and Trade; Meat Industry.
Cauca, Colombia (dept.). Labor Market, 1658.
Cave Paintings. Mesoamerica, 18. *See Also* Indigenous Art; Rock Art.
Caves. Folklore, 198. Guatemala, 103. Peru, 160.
Ceará, Brazil (state). Water Supply, 797.
Cement Industry, 1389.
Cemeteries. Bolivia, 319. *See Also* Mortuary Customs.
Cempoala Site (Mexico). Pictorial Works, 89.

Censuses. Puerto Rico, 1605. See Also Population Forecasting; Population Growth.
Central Americans. Mexico, 217.
Central Intelligence Agency. See United States. Central Intelligence Agency.
Central-Local Government Relations. Brazil, 1108, 1129. Chile, 1075, 1084. Colombia, 1236. Ecuador, 1002. Mexico, 219. See Also Municipal Government.
Central Unica de Trabajadores (Chile), 1078.
Centro de Rehabilitación Femenino El Buen Pastor de Barranquilla (Colombia), 1648.
Centro Estatal de Lenguas, Arte y Literatura Indígenas (Chiapas, Mexico), 220.
Ceramics. Argentina, 142. Mesoamerica, 44, 65, 87. Peru, 164, 167, 169, 175.
Ceremonies. See Rites and Ceremonies.
Chacabuco, Chile (prov.). Urbanization, 704.
Chaco, Argentina (prov.). Agribusiness, 678. Bilingual Education, 300. Cotton Industry and Trade, 678. COVID-19 (disease), 316.
Chaco, Argentina (region). Ethnobotany, 331. Land Use, 660.
Chaco, Paraguay (region). Mennonites, 736.
Chaco War (1932–1935). Indigenous Peoples, 329.
Chalatenango, El Salvador (dept.). Collective Memory, 1581.
Chamorro Cardenal, Pedro Joaquín, 910.
Chané (indigenous group). Emotions, 327. Language and Languages, 327.
Chávez Frías, Hugo, 1025, 1029, 1031, 1365, 1373, 1666.
Chavín Culture. Mounds, 167.
Chenque I Site (Argentina), 147.
Cherán, Mexico (village). Indigenous Peoples, 209, 230. Political Conditions, 230.
Chiapas, Mexico (state). Agricultural Development, 519. Education, 1469. Indigenous Languages, 220. Indigenous Peoples, 190–191. Political Conditions, 1309. Precolumbian Pottery, 53.
Chicanos. See Mexican Americans.
Chichén Itzá Site (Mexico). Architecture, 42.
Chihuahua, Mexico (state). Drug Traffic, 826. Economic Conditions, 1325. Social Conditions, 1537. Technology, 1325.
Childbirth. Guatemala, 1564. Mexico, 1544.
Children. Education, 1469. Human Rights, 1505. Malaria, 1585. Mexico, 1509, 1532. Nature, 782. See Also Family and Family Relations; Youth.

Chiloé Island (Chile). Land Tenure, 710.
Chimane (indigenous group). Economic Conditions, 315.
Chimborazo, Ecuador (prov.). Indigenous Peoples, 1694. Political Leadership, 1694.
Chinese. Brazil, 789. El Salvador, 1565.
Chinese Influences, 1154. Central America, 1179. Ecuador, 579.
Chocó, Colombia (dept.). Autonomy, 281. Land Tenure, 281. Political Conditions, 281. Women, 1654.
Cholera. See Diseases.
Chono (indigenous group). Land Settlement, 710.
Chorti (indigenous group). Language and Languages, 111.
Christian Democracy. Bolivia, 1036.
Christianity. Bolivia, 1734. History, 1711. Mexico, 229. Peru, 1719. See Also Religious Life and Customs.
Christians. El Salvador, 1558.
Chuj (indigenous group). Language and Languages, 205. Oral Tradition, 205.
Chuquisaca, Bolivia (dept.). Natural Gas, 595.
Church and State. See Church-State Relations.
Church History, 1437.
Church-State Relations. Bolivia, 1048. Costa Rica, 856. El Salvador, 1578. Mexico, 1497.
CIA. See United States. Central Intelligence Agency.
Cinchona, 429.
Cinema. See Film.
Cities and Towns, 361, 367, 373, 423. Argentina, 621. Chile, 686. Colombia, 157. Colonial History, 590. Economic Conditions, 539. Forests and Forest Industry, 608. Mexico, 550, 1319, 1473. Modernization, 426. Uruguay, 743. See Also City Planning.
Citizenship, 1610. Chile, 720. Colombia, 1645. Ecuador, 1016. Guatemala, 888. Mexico, 841, 1519. Women, 1477.
City Planning, 371, 394, 425, 427. Argentina, 611, 633, 655. Bolivia, 593. Chile, 689, 702, 724. Colombia, 560. Ecuador, 1685. Mexico, 528, 542, 553. See Also Cities and Towns; Urbanization.
Civil-Military Relations. Chile, 1076. Ecuador, 1010, 1020. Nicaragua, 922. Uruguay, 1010.

Civil Rights. Colombia, 1643. Honduras, 904. Mexico, 219. *See Also* Human Rights.
Civil Society, 1253. Bolivia, 1055. Colombia, 990, 992. Mexico, 1530.
Civil War. Colombia, 994, 1640, 1644. El Salvador, 1578.
Civil War, 1861–1865 (US). Refugees, 786.
Civilization. Honduras, 1589.
Class Conflict. *See* Social Classes; Social Conflict.
Clientelism. Costa Rica, 861. Dominican Republic, 950, 955. Honduras, 906.
Climate. Argentina, 145. Urban Areas, 422.
Climate Change, 387, 389, 392–393, 397. Caribbean Area, 465, 468, 970. Central America, 471. Colombia, 564. Costa Rica, 488. Jamaica, 437. Mexico, 521, 523, 540, 1316. Patagonia (region), 674. Peru, 581, 583, 586, 588, 1701. Southern Cone, 601. Water Supply, 411.
Climatology. Caribbean Area, 457. Chile, 689. *See Also* Rain and Rainfall.
Clothing and Dress. Bolivia, 1735. Central America, 1. Mexico, 1. Pictorial Works, 1735. *See Also* Textiles and Textile Industry.
Clothing Industry. Caribbean Area, 1347.
Coahuila, Mexico (state). Economic Conditions, 1325. Rock Art, 86. Technology, 1325. Wine and Wine Making, 552.
Coal Mining. *See* Minerals and Mining Industry.
Coalitions. Chile, 1077. Costa Rica, 857. *See Also* Political Parties.
Coastal Areas, 408. Argentina, 646, 664. Belize, 483. Central America, 476. Uruguay, 748, 750. *See Also* Beaches.
Coastal Ecology. Chile, 711. Ecuador, 1686.
Coca. Peru, 1704. *See Also* Cocaine.
Cocaine. Central America, 473, 478. *See Also* Coca.
Cocoa Industry and Trade, 377.
Cocopa (indigenous group). Cultural History, 80.
Códice florentino, 114.
Codices. Mesoamerica, 113.
Cofán (indigenous group). Environmental Protection, 284.
Coffee Industry and Trade, 364. Costa Rica, 1334. Mexico, 536.
Cold War. Chile, 1229. Venezuela, 1030, 1246.

Colectivo de Geografía Crítica del Ecuador, 567.
Colima, Mexico (state). Social Conditions, 1490.
Colla (indigenous group). Environmental Protection, 684.
Collective Memory, 374. Argentina, 640. Dictatorships, 784. Ecuador, 1679. Guatemala, 896.
Colleges. *See* Higher Education.
Colombia. Congreso, 991.
Colonial Administration. Dominican Republic, 128.
Colonial History. Peru, 166.
Colonization, 10. Caribbean Area, 926. Chile, 717. Human Geography, 699. Jamaica, 958. Patagonia (region), 675.
Colston, Edward, 466.
Comisión Internacional contra la Impunidad en Guatemala, 898.
Comissão Guarani Yvy Rupa, 264.
Comissão Pastoral da Terra (Brazil), 758.
Commerce. Caribbean Area, 927, 1345. Cuba, 1353. Mexico, 1473. Mexico/Philippines, 1168. Peru, 1244. *See Also* Balance of Trade.
Commercial Policy. *See* Trade Policy.
Commodities. Argentina, 1268.
Common Markets. *See* Economic Integration.
Communication. Ecuador, 998.
Communism and Communist Parties, 948. Chile, 1083.
Community Development. El Salvador, 876. Guatemala, 899. Jamaica, 962. Mexico, 1494.
Community Policing. Mexico, 185, 811. Nicaragua, 912. *See Also* Police.
Competition. Mexico, 1311.
Comunidad Andina, 1211.
Concepción de la Vega, Dominican Republic (site). Archeological Sites, 128.
Confederación de Pueblos Indígenas de Bolivia, 310.
Confederacy. *See* Confederate States of America.
Confederate States of America. Migration, 786.
Conflict Management. Bolivia, 1226. Colombia, 1644.
Congress. *See* Legislative Bodies; Legislative Power.
Conquest. *See* Spanish Conquest.

Conquest and Exploration. *See* Discovery and Exploration.
Conservation and Restoration. Brazil, 777.
Conservation (environment), 381, 389. Argentina, 617, 626, 648. Belize, 483. Caribbean Area, 440. Central America, 473, 481. Chile, 695. Colombia, 562, 564. Ecuador, 576–577, 579, 1686. Panama, 515. Patagonia (region), 648. Peru, 584. Social Movements, 1686. Uruguay, 755. *See Also* Environmental Protection.
Constitutions. Bolivia, 1037, 1744. Chile, 349, 1070, 1079, 1081. Colombia, 1642. Cuba, 974. Ecuador, 1037. El Salvador, 875. Guatemala, 883. Paraguay, 328.
Construction Industry. Argentina, 637.
Consumption (economics). Chile, 707. Mexico, 1473.
Contact. *See* Cultural Contact.
Contemporary Art. *See* Modern Art.
Contraceptives. *See* Birth Control.
Cooperatives. Agriculture, 1334. Argentina, 1408. Cuba, 1349, 1355. Mexico, 1291.
Coordinadora Arauco Malleco (CAM), 347.
Coordinadora Regional de Autoridades Comunitarias-Policía Comunitaria, 185, 823.
Copán Site (Honduras), 104.
Copper Industry and Trade. Peru, 161, 580.
Cordero Molina, Celestina, 1606.
Córdoba, Argentina (city). Land Use, 631. Public Policy, 631.
Córdoba, Argentina (prov.). Agroindustry, 659. Land Use, 659. Nature, 645. Social Conditions, 663. Tourism, 645.
Corn. Mexico, 242. Syncretism, 208.
Corporación de Fomento de la Producción (Chile), 1376.
Corporations. *See* Business Administration.
Correa, Rafael, 1003, 1016, 1677.
Corruption. Argentina, 1102–1103. Central America, 469. Guatemala, 885. Honduras, 907. *See Also* Political Corruption.
Cosmology. Mesoamerica, 22, 34. Precolumbian Civilizations, 139. *See Also* Astronomy.
Cost and Standard of Living. Argentina, 1399.
Costa Chica, Mexico (region). Community Policing, 823. Rites and Ceremonies, 1475. Social Life and Customs, 1475.
Costa Rica. Asamblea Legislativa, 857, 861.
Costa Rica. Corte Suprema de Justicia, 861.

Costume and Adornment. Caribbean Area, 1628. Shells and Shell Middens, 90.
Cotton Industry and Trade. Bolivia, 301.
Counterinsurgency. Guatemala, 893.
Coups d'Etat. Bolivia, 1040.
Courts. Caribbean Area, 928. Guatemala, 891. Jamaica, 957.
COVID-19 (disease), 360, 379, 477. Argentina, 299, 316. Belize, 485. Bolivia, 1050. Brazil, 765. Caribbean Area, 945. Central America, 472. Chile, 686, 1063, 1071. Human Geography, 428. Migration, 406. Uruguay, 746.
Crafts. *See* Artisanry.
Credit. Argentina, 1402.
Crime and Criminals, 374, 1143, 1158, 1249. Argentina, 1102. Belize, 851. Brazil, 1125–1126. Caribbean Area, 935, 1620. Central America, 1285. Colombia, 1662. Ecuador, 1688. El Salvador, 866–867, 869. Guatemala, 884, 898, 1603. Haiti, 1626. Mexico, 811, 813, 842, 1466, 1528. Peru, 1724. Political Economy, 1249. Public Policy, 1264. Tourism, 363. US, 1638. Venezuela, 1031.
Criminals. *See* Crime and Criminals.
Crops, 357.
Cueva Galpón (site). Mortuary Customs, 141.
Cuicatec (indigenous group). Education, 178. Social Life and Customs, 178.
Cults. Mexico, 1527.
Cultural Contact. Caribbean Area, 125–126. Mesoamerica, 104.
Cultural Development. Guatemala, 1335.
Cultural Geography, 404. Caribbean Area, 436. Chile, 707. *See Also* Human Geography.
Cultural History. Caribbean Area, 930. Cuba, 975. Grenada, 124. Guatemala, 1335. Mexico, 12.
Cultural Identity, 369. Argentina, 341. Caribbean Area, 1639.
Cultural Pluralism. *See* Multiculturalism.
Cultural Property, 366. Guatemala, 103. Mexico, 3.
Cultural Relations. Colombia, 1235. Latin America/Australia, 396. Latin America/Spain, 1151. Latin America/US, 413. Mexico/Palestine, 1153. *See Also* Intellectual Cooperation.
Culture. Mexico, 1465, 1542.
Currency. *See* Money.

Cyclones. *See* Hurricanes.
Dairy Industry. Argentina, 1408.
Dams. Brazil, 760.
Dance. Mexico, 236. Peru, 1720.
De Booy, Theodore, 120.
Death. Brazil, 765. Ecuador, 1681. Mexico, 1527, 1549. Religious Life and Customs, 1527, 1549. *See Also* Mortality.
Debt. *See* External Debt; Public Debt.
Debt Bondage. Peru, 298.
Debt Crisis. Mexico, 1289.
Decentralization. Ecuador, 1002, 1009.
Decolonization, 1440. Africa, 948. Caribbean Area, 948, 1346. Teaching, 1443.
Defense Budgets. Peru, 1280.
Deforestation. Argentina, 626. Belize, 483. Brazil, 761. Central America, 470–471, 478, 480–481. Costa Rica, 495. Ecuador, 575, 577. Guatemala, 500. Mexico, 495, 543. Nicaragua, 510. Panama, 515. Paraguay, 312. Peru, 583.
Deities. Warfare, 5.
Democracy, 1034, 1253, 1278. Argentina, 1100. Bolivia, 1035. Brazil, 1107, 1114, 1137, 1432. Central America, 847–848, 850. Chile, 1079. Cuba, 981. Dominican Republic, 954, 1272. Economic Conditions, 1265. Ecuador, 999, 1010, 1012, 1014. El Salvador, 870, 873, 875, 879. Guatemala, 881. Honduras, 902. Mexico, 804, 845–846, 848. Nicaragua, 910–911, 920. Peru, 1713. Uruguay, 1010. Venezuela, 1026, 1030, 1371, 1671.
Democratization, 1285. Argentina, 1086, 1218. Bolivia, 1038, 1051. Chile, 1081. Ecuador, 998–999, 1003. El Salvador, 873, 877, 1569. Mexico, 803, 805–806, 809, 840. Venezuela, 1022.
Demography. Bolivia, 592. Colombia, 460. Cuba, 460. Peru, 171.
Demonstrations. *See* Protests.
Denevan, William M., 380.
Dependency, 1269, 1440. Caribbean Area, 926. Cuba, 1356. Jamaica, 958. Mexico, 1313. Panama, 513. Puerto Rico, 969. Theory, 1144. Venezuela, 1374.
Deportation. Dominican Republic, 1638.
Depression. *See* Mental Health.
Desaparecidos. *See* Disappeared Persons; Missing Persons.
Description and Travel. Peru, 584. Southern Cone, 603.
Detective and Mystery Stories, 374.

Development. Amazon Basin, 778. Caribbean Area, 1346. Panama, 513. Paraguay, 739. *See Also* Underdevelopment.
Development Projects. Argentina, 669. Costa Rica, 496. Guatemala, 499, 502.
Dictatorships. Chile, 725, 1230, 1377. Guatemala, 1572. *See Also* Authoritarianism.
Diet. *See* Nutrition.
Diplomacy, 1146. Colombia, 1235–1236. Saint Vincent and the Grenadines, 1192.
Diplomacy, Mexican. US, 1167.
Diplomatic History, 1155, 1157, 1198. Argentina, 1217, 1223. Central America/Mexico, 1180. Chile, 1228, 1231. Cuba, 1189. Cuba/US, 1202. Haiti, 1195. Latin America/India, 1148.
Diplomats. Argentina, 1217. Chile, 1228.
Disabled People. *See* People with Disabilities.
Disappeared Persons. Guatemala, 884. Mexico, 1476, 1511, 1523. *See Also* Missing Persons.
Disaster Relief. Mexico, 215. Puerto Rico, 970.
Discovery and Exploration. Brazil, 263, 267. *See Also* Spanish Conquest.
Discrimination. Brazil, 1115. Colombia, 1643, 1664. Ecuador, 1676, 1691. Law and Legislation, 1691. Mexico, 820, 1467, 1503, 1517. Peru, 1722. Puerto Rico, 1605. Women, 1467.
Diseases, 379, 477. Africa, 1201. Agriculture, 574. Argentina, 662. Mexico, 187. Puerto Rico, 965. Women, 187. *See Also* Epidemics.
Displaced Persons. Food, 239. Mexico, 239.
Distribution of Wealth. *See* Income Distribution.
Divorce. Mexico, 1524.
Documentaries. Mexico, 1534.
Dollarization. El Salvador, 1332.
Domestic Violence. *See* Family Violence.
Domestics. *See* Household Employees.
Dominican Republic-Central America-United States Free Trade Agreement, 860, 1336.
Dress. *See* Clothing and Dress.
Droughts. Caribbean Area, 457. Costa Rica, 487. Jamaica, 437.
Drug Control. *See* Drug Enforcement.
Drug Enforcement. Argentina, 1218. Central America, 469, 478, 481. Colombia, 830. Mexico, 830, 1458, 1523.

Subject Index / 573

Drug Traffic. Argentina, 1102, 1218. Bolivia, 1047. Brazil, 793. Central America, 469, 471, 473, 478, 480–481. Colombia, 984, 995, 1011. Corruption, 1102. Deforestation, 480. Ecuador, 1011. Environmental Degradation, 473, 505. Guatemala, 500, 505, 1603. Honduras, 505. Mass Media, 1458. Mexico, 209, 813, 816, 827, 830, 843–844, 1458. Public Policy, 984. Violence, 1528.

Drug Utilization. Mexico, 844.

Drugs and Drug Trade. *See* Drug Enforcement; Drug Traffic; Drug Utilization.

Dwellings. Ecuador, 1685.

Earthquakes. Guatemala, 503–504. Haiti, 438. Mexico, 504, 1287. Puerto Rico, 439, 451. Venezuela, 558.

Ecological Crisis. *See* Environmental Protection.

Ecology. Argentina, 660. Caribbean Area, 465. Chile, 682, 695. Costa Rica, 493. Patagonia (region), 674.

Economic Assistance. Mexico, 1302, 1310, 1317.

Economic Assistance, Brazilian. Haiti, 1187.

Economic Assistance, Chilean. Haiti, 1187.

Economic Assistance, Chinese. Venezuela, 1374.

Economic Assistance, European. Jamaica, 962.

Economic Assistance, Mexican, 1317. Haiti, 1187.

Economic Conditions, 339, 378, 1269. Argentina, 1093, 1384, 1398, 1407. Bolivia, 1739, 1748. Brazil, 1418–1419, 1426. Caribbean Area, 934, 964. Central America, 1593. Chile, 1057, 1064, 1377–1379, 1382–1383. Colombia, 1656. Crime and Criminals, 1249. Cuba, 977, 1350, 1356, 1360, 1621, 1633. Ecuador, 1238. El Salvador, 1333, 1555. Honduras, 1554. Jamaica, 1632. Mexico, 1172, 1314. Panama, 925, 1179. Puerto Rico, 969, 1338–1339. Uruguay, 1415. Venezuela, 1023–1024, 1026, 1033, 1363–1364, 1369–1370, 1669, 1671.

Economic Crises, 1270. Argentina, 1407, 1410. Cuba, 1356–1357. Dominican Republic, 1341. Mexico, 1320, 1330.

Economic Development, 1139, 1208, 1266–1267, 1274, 1276, 1281, 1283. Argentina, 632, 1386, 1391, 1393, 1401. Brazil, 1418, 1421, 1425, 1432. Caribbean Area, 926, 933, 938, 946, 1343, 1345–1347. Cuba, 1349, 1361. Dominican Republic, 444, 1341. Ecuador, 578, 1018. El Salvador, 1333, 1569. Emigrant Remittances, 1471. Jamaica, 449, 962. Mexico, 538, 545, 1287–1288, 1292, 1297, 1300, 1305–1306, 1313, 1317, 1320. Public Opinion, 1425. Puerto Rico, 1339. Southern Cone, 1206. Uruguay, 745. Venezuela, 1367.

Economic Development Projects. *See* Development Projects.

Economic Geography, 600. Argentina, 648, 678. Colombia, 563.

Economic Growth. *See* Economic Development.

Economic History, 1329. Argentina, 1391, 1393, 1400. Brazil, 1423. Chile, 1382. Costa Rica, 1334. Cuba, 1356. Mexico, 1259–1260. Saint Vincent and the Grenadines, 1340. Venezuela, 1365.

Economic Indicators. Caribbean Area, 1345. Cuba, 1348, 1356–1357.

Economic Integration, 1139, 1144–1146, 1152, 1156, 1160, 1184, 1203, 1207, 1210. Argentina, 1417. Caribbean Area, 452, 938, 1144, 1193. Southern Cone, 1206. Uruguay, 1417. *See Also* Free Trade; Regional Integration.

Economic Models, 1281. Cuba, 1350. Mexico, 1300.

Economic Planning. *See* Economic Policy.

Economic Policy, 1267, 1274, 1281, 1284. Argentina, 1257, 1391–1392, 1397, 1401, 1405, 1409. Bolivia, 1739. Brazil, 1423, 1432. Caribbean Area, 933. Chile, 1379. Cuba, 980, 1349, 1353, 1357, 1360. Dominican Republic, 1341. Ecuador, 1006, 1012, 1017. El Salvador, 1332. Honduras, 907. Mexico, 1288, 1292, 1303, 1310, 1313, 1318, 1413. Migration, 1261. Paraguay, 1411. Public Opinion, 1255, 1286. Puerto Rico, 972, 1339. South America, 598. Uruguay, 1257, 1412–1413. Venezuela, 1024, 1366, 1371, 1675. *See Also* Political Economy.

Economic Reform. Cuba, 980, 1361.

Economic Sanctions. Venezuela, 1023, 1033.

Economic Sanctions, US. Cuba, 1202.

Economic Theory. Argentina, 1400, 1406. Brazil, 1425–1427. Venezuela, 1368, 1372.

Economists. Brazil, 1427. Venezuela, 1368.

Ecotourism. Argentina, 645. Caribbean Area, 443. Mexico, 538, 545. Patagonia (region), 648. *See Also* Tourism.

Education. Mexico, 1474, 1482, 1491. Social Mobility, 458. Venezuela, 1666. *See Also* Bilingual Education.
Education and State. *See* Educational Policy.
Educational Policy. Central America, 1553. Mexico, 1469.
Educational Sociology. Mexico, 1723. Peru, 1723.
Ejército Zapatista de Liberación Nacional (Mexico), 200.
Ejidos. Mexico, 534.
El Alto, Bolivia (city). Abortion, 1740. Markets, 1741.
El Mirador Site (Guatemala). *See* Mirador Site (Guatemala).
Elderly Persons. *See* Aged.
Elections, 1278. Argentina, 1090. Belize, 852. Bolivia, 1035, 1040, 1050. Brazil, 1106, 1109, 1111, 1115–1116, 1120–1122, 1128, 1130–1131. Chile, 1067, 1070, 1074–1075. Colombia, 986. Costa Rica, 854, 856, 859. Dominican Republic, 950, 953. Honduras, 906. Jamaica, 959. Mass Media, 802. Mexico, 800, 802, 807, 809, 814, 819, 825, 834–835, 838, 846. Political Corruption, 808, 1278. Puerto Rico, 967. Social Classes, 1115. *See Also* Campaign Funds; Local Elections; Voting.
Electricity. Colombia, 1665. Guatemala, 1584.
Elites. Argentina, 667, 1101, 1217. Bolivia, 1735, 1742. Businesspeople, 1408. Chile, 1377. El Salvador, 865. Elections, 1111. Forced Migration, 606–607, 1277, 1445. Honduras, 865. Mesoamerica, 2. Mexico, 1259, 1551. Nicaragua, 916. Political Participation, 805. Precolumbian Civilizations, 46. Spanish Conquest, 128.
Embera (indigenous group). Ethnohistory, 511. Political Conditions, 997. Tourism, 511.
Emigrant Remittances, 1261. Central America, 472. El Salvador, 1333. Haiti, 1610. Jamaica, 1610. Mexico, 801, 1171, 1471, 1500, 1526.
Emigration and Immigration. *See* Internal Migration; Migration; Return Migration.
Emotions. Mexico, 1495.
Employment. Colombia, 1657. Cuba, 1355, 1361. El Salvador, 1570. Guatemala, 1570. Mexico, 1294, 1296, 1462, 1487, 1502. Peru, 1730. Urban Areas, 759.
Violence, 1730. *See Also* Public Service Employment.
Empresa Brasileira de Pesquisa Agropecuária, 763.
Endangered Species. Caribbean Area, 479.
Energy Consumption, 973. Argentina, 1388.
Energy Policy. Argentina, 1388. Ecuador, 1018. Mexico, 1173, 1312, 1316. Puerto Rico, 454. South America, 598. Uruguay, 1416.
Energy Sources. Chile, 711. Trinidad and Tobago, 973. Uruguay, 1416.
Energy Supply. Mexico, 1316.
Engineers. Brazil, 767. Mexico, 1293.
Entrepreneurs. Chile, 1376.
Entrepreneurship. Cuba, 1353, 1355. Mexico, 1317, 1461, 1472, 1506. *See Also* Small Business.
Environmental Conservation. *See* Conservation (environment).
Environmental Degradation, 368, 397. Argentina, 646. Central America, 473. Chile, 683, 690. Colombia, 1663. Dominican Republic, 444. Guatemala, 501. Mexico, 530, 537, 1166, 1172. Puerto Rico, 1615.
Environmental History, 386. Chile, 695.
Environmental Policy, 389, 392–393. Amazon Basin, 391. Andean Region, 391. Brazil, 781. Caribbean Area, 448, 456. Chile, 684, 689, 697, 700, 714. Colombia, 565. Cuba, 447. Ecuador, 570, 573, 576, 1018, 1686. El Salvador, 498, 865. Guatemala, 886. Honduras, 865. International Agreements, 526. Mexico, 521, 526, 1166. Paraguay, 731, 739. Peru, 1701, 1726. Puerto Rico, 454. Uruguay, 749–750, 755.
Environmental Pollution, 387, 397. Amazon Basin, 391. Andean Region, 391. Brazil, 794. Caribbean Area, 435. Ecuador, 1683. El Salvador, 497–498. Indigenous Resistance, 284. Mexico, 525. Peru, 581. Urban Areas, 422.
Environmental Protection. Argentina, 666. Caribbean Area, 440, 456. Central America, 470. Chile, 697. Ecuador, 570, 573, 1695. El Salvador, 497. Honduras, 905. Mexico, 545. Puerto Rico, 970. *See Also* Conservation (environment).
Environmental Sustainability. *See* Sustainable Development.
Epidemics, 477. Argentina, 623. *See Also* Diseases.

Epistemology. Bolivia, 1733.
Equality, 372, 1265–1266. Chile, 1057, 1064, 1378. Cuba, 976. Ecuador, 1002. El Salvador, 1555, 1565, 1570. Guatemala, 1570. Mexico, 1303, 1517, 1723. Peru, 1696–1697, 1723. *See Also* Income Distribution.
Erosion. *See* Soil Erosion.
Escuela Normal Rural de Ayotzinapa, 1484, 1511.
Esmeraldas, Ecuador (city). Environmental Degradation, 1683. Social Conditions, 1683.
Espinosa de los Monteros, Alfonso, 1005.
Espionage. Cubans, 1197. *See Also* Intelligence Service.
Ethics. Andean Region, 336. *See Also* Philosophy.
Ethnic Groups and Ethnicity, 402. Bolivia, 150, 342, 1750. Chile, 348, 718. Ecuador, 351, 353–354. Honduras, 506. Mesoamerica, 2. Mexico, 183, 224. Nicaragua, 908. Paraguay, 303. Peru, 1701, 1707.
Ethnic Identity, 402. Bolivia, 1056, 1735, 1742, 1746–1747. Colombia, 1642. Cuba, 1622. Ecuador, 353–354, 1693. El Salvador, 1565. Guatemala, 1598. Mexico, 183. Peru, 1710. Puerto Rico, 1616, 1618. Venezuela, 1667.
Ethnobotany. Amazon Basin, 247. Argentina, 320, 331.
Ethnoecology. Amazon Basin, 391. Andean Region, 391. Costa Rica, 492.
Ethnohistory. Honduras, 203. Mesoamerica, 95.
Eurocentrism, 1441.
European Union, 962.
Evita. *See* Perón, Eva.
Excavations, 337. Argentina, 144, 146. Caribbean Area, 118. Colombia, 158. El Salvador, 39. Mexico, 60, 78, 89. Peru, 165. Urban Areas, 38.
Executive Power. Argentina, 1086, 1101. Colombia, 993.
Exiles. Mexico, 1169. Southern Cone, 606–607, 1277, 1445. *See Also* Refugees.
Expeditions. Puerto Rico, 120. Southern Cone, 603.
Exploration. *See* Discovery and Exploration.
Exports. Agricultural Policy, 1268. Argentina, 1268. Cuba, 1352, 1359. Mexico, 1314. Uruguay, 1415. *See Also* International Trade.
Expropriation. Poverty, 1262.

External Debt, 1329. Argentina, 1386. Puerto Rico, 1344.
EZLN. *See* Ejército Zapatista de Liberación Nacional (Mexico).
Falkland Islands, 1216.
Family and Family Relations. Chile, 721. Colombia, 1649. Costa Rica, 1573. Mexico, 1465, 1495, 1523–1524.
Family Planning. *See* Birth Control.
Family Violence. Colombia, 1649, 1662. Guatemala, 882. Mexico, 1452, 1463–1464, 1467, 1532, 1548.
FARC. *See* Fuerzas Armadas Revolucionarias de Colombia.
Farms, 358. Brazil, 792. Costa Rica, 496. Cuba, 1358. Jamaica, 437. Social Conditions, 531.
Favelas. *See* Slums; Squatter Settlements.
FDI. *See* Foreign Investment.
Feather-Work. Andean Region, 174.
Feminism, 385, 428, 1436, 1547. Argentina, 668. Bolivia, 1041, 1743. Caribbean Area, 932, 941, 1630. Colombia, 1650. Ecuador, 1000. Geography, 403, 432. Mexico, 1515. Peru, 1714. Puerto Rico, 1619. Research, 668.
Fernández de Kirchner, Cristina, 1087.
FIAT Concórd (firm), 1404.
Fiction. Cuba, 1629.
Fieldwork. Ecuador, 569.
Film. Central America, 1561. Ecuador, 1688.
Finance, 1318. Mexico, 1331.
Financial Crises. *See* Economic Crises.
Financial Institutions. *See* Banking and Financial Institutions.
Financial Markets. Brazil, 766.
Fire. Chile, 698, 719. Costa Rica, 487.
Fiscal Crises. *See* Economic Crises.
Fiscal Policy. Brazil, 1420. Cuba, 1362. Mexico, 1318. Puerto Rico, 972, 1344.
Fish and Fishing, 408. Central America, 476. Chile, 156.
Fisheries. Argentina, 618. Caribbean Area, 440. Sustainable Development, 618.
Floods, 368. Costa Rica, 488. Paraguay, 728.
Florence, Hercules, 260.
Florida, US (state). Cubans, 1197.
FMLN. *See* Frente Farabundo Martí para la Liberación Nacional (El Salvador).
Folk Dance. California, US (state), 223. Mexican-American Border Region, 223. Mexico, 223, 236.

Folk Medicine. *See* Traditional Medicine.
Folklore. Chile, 308. Puerto Rico, 1631.
Fonseca, Gulf of, 1176.
Fonseca Amador, Carlos, 910.
Food, 369. Advertising, 1315. Brazil, 769, 771. Caribbean Area, 122, 136. Cultural Contact, 76. Diseases, 221. Mesoamerica, 226. Mexico, 221, 1315. Paraguay, 736. Urban Areas, 24.
Food Industry and Trade. Argentina, 643. Mexico, 1299, 1315. Uruguay, 752.
Food Insecurity. *See* Food Supply.
Food Supply. Argentina, 643. Bolivia, 315. Caribbean Area, 455, 468, 479. Cuba, 1359. Haiti, 434. Honduras, 508. Mexico, 221, 539, 1291, 1308.
Forced Migration. Central America, 1593.
Foreign Affairs. *See* Foreign Policy.
Foreign Aid. *See* Economic Assistance.
Foreign Debt. *See* External Debt.
Foreign Direct Investment. *See* Foreign Investment.
Foreign Economic Relations. *See* International Economic Relations.
Foreign Intervention, US, 1198. Central America, 849. Drug Traffic, 1011.
Foreign Investment. Cuba, 1350, 1353, 1357. Patagonia (region), 679. Venezuela, 1372. *See Also* Investments.
Foreign Investment, Chinese, 1161, 1284.
Foreign Investment, US. Puerto Rico, 1338.
Foreign Policy, 1146, 1207, 1255, 1286. Caribbean Area, 1191. China, 1161. Costa Rica, 1181. Cuba, 982, 1186, 1188, 1201, 1360. Haiti, 1193, 1195. History, 1157. Mexico, 1174. US, 1198. *See Also* International Relations.
Foreign Policy, US. Central America, 849. Cuba, 1183, 1190.
Foreign Relations. *See* International Relations.
Foreign Trade. *See* International Trade.
Foreign Workers. *See* Migrant Labor.
Forest Restoration. *See* Reforestation.
Forests and Forest Industry, 390. Argentina, 626. Belize, 483. Brazil, 787. Central America, 470. Chile, 698–699, 706, 719. Costa Rica, 495. Guatemala, 886. Mexico, 495. Panama, 515. Uruguay, 747, 749.
Fortifications. Peru, 168.
Francis, *Pope*, 1437.
Francisco de Tembleque, *Father*, 532.

Free Trade, 1141. Costa Rica, 860, 1336. Mexico, 1299. North America, 1328. *See Also* Economic Integration.
Free Trade Area of the Americas (FTAA), 1150, 1210.
Free Trade Areas, 1140, 1150.
Freedom of Information. Mexico, 803, 821.
Freemasonry. Costa Rica, 1557.
Frente del Pueblo en Defensa de La Tierra (Mexico), 1534.
Frente Farabundo Martí para la Liberación Nacional (El Salvador), 863, 877.
Frente Nacionalista Patria y Libertad (Chile), 1062.
Frente Sandinista de Liberación Nacional. *See* Sandinistas (Nicaragua).
Frontiers. Archeology, 125. Argentina, 641. Land Use, 390. Mesoamerica, 55.
FSLN. *See* Sandinistas (Nicaragua).
FTAA. *See* Free Trade Area of the Americas (FTAA).
Fuentes, Carlos, 846.
Fuerzas Armadas Revolucionarias de Colombia, 995.
Fujimori, Alberto, 1708.
Galápagos Islands, Ecuador. Environmental Conservation, 568.
Gamio, Manuel, 16.
Gangs. Belize, 851. Central America, 1601. Ecuador, 1688. El Salvador, 866–867, 869, 871–872, 874, 1586. Guatemala, 1594. Mexico, 1537. US, 1582.
Garbage. *See* Hazardous Wastes; Refuse and Refuse Disposal.
García-Passalacqua, Juan M., 1200.
Garifuna (indigenous group). *See* Black Carib (indigenous group).
Gated Communities. Argentina, 647.
GATT. *See* General Agreement on Tariffs and Trade (GATT).
Gays. Colombia, 1643. Discrimination, 1643. Mexico, 1485. *See Also* Homosexuality.
Gender Relations, 385. Andean Region, 1717, 1725. Brazil, 1110. Caribbean Area, 1639. Chile, 1082. Ecuador, 1695. Mexico, 1467. *See Also* Sex and Sexual Relations.
Gender Roles, 1436. Caribbean Area, 940, 1628. Chile, 1082. Colombia, 1650, 1655, 1664. Ecuador, 1695. Guatemala, 1602. Mexico, 832, 1464, 1503, 1518, 1532. Peru, 1714. Venezuela, 1668. *See Also* Sex Roles.

General Agreement on Tariffs and Trade (GATT), 1141.
Genocide. Guatemala, 1572, 1599.
Geoglyphs. Peru, 162.
Geographers, 380, 433. Brazil, 772–773, 790. Fieldwork, 569. Social Conflict, 567.
Geographic Information Systems. Archeology, 673. Argentina, 609, 613, 638–639, 642, 649, 654, 676. Chile, 694. Costa Rica, 494. Land Use, 673. Mexico, 649. Peru, 591. Soils, 676. Uruguay, 748, 754.
Geographical History. Argentina, 667. Brazil, 772. Peru, 590. See Also Historical Geography.
Geographical Names. Caribbean Area, 467. Honduras, 111.
Geography. Argentina, 668. Epistemology, 599. Feminism, 668. Methodology, 432, 649, 694. Research, 597, 602, 605, 668, 694. Technological Innovations, 654. Translating and Interpreting, 602.
Geology. Guatemala, 503. Honduras, 509. Precolumbian Civilizations, 140.
Geomorphology. Chile, 687. Costa Rica, 491. Uruguay, 754.
Geopolitics, 1143, 1145, 1152. Argentina, 1388. Boundaries, 1237. Colombia, 1234. Mexico, 1305. Panama, 1179. Puerto Rico, 1200. Research, 599. Southern Cone, 726.
Germans. Chile, 717.
GIS. See Geographic Information Systems.
Glaciers. Peru, 581.
Glissant, Édouard, 436.
Global Financial Crisis, 2008–2009, 1270, 1320. Brazil, 1427.
Globalization, 405, 433, 1141, 1267, 1269. Argentina, 670. Caribbean Area, 934, 1347. Chile, 1227. City Planning, 600. Costa Rica, 1181. Dominican Republic, 1341. Economic Policy, 1255, 1286. Ecuador, 1008, 1017. Mexican-American Border Region, 1298. Mexico, 1305–1306, 1309, 1487, 1529.
Goajiro (indigenous group). Social Life and Customs, 278.
Gold Mines and Mining. Costa Rica, 489. El Salvador, 497.
González, Gaspar Pedro, 1556.
Good Neighbor Policy, 413.
Government. See Bureaucracy.
Government, Resistance to. Peru, 1706.
Government-Business Relations. Mexico, 1317. See Also Business Administration.
Governors. Elections, 834.
Gran Chaco (region). Environmental Policy, 330. History, 330.
Grande, Rutilio, 1562.
Grassroots Movements. See Social Movements.
Grazing. Ecuador, 573.
Grupo San Ángel, 846.
Grupo Unigay, 1485.
Guadalajara, Mexico (city). Religious Life and Customs, 1483.
Guajiro (indigenous group). See Goajiro (indigenous group).
Guarani (indigenous group). Argentina, 320. Bolivia, 324. Children, 322.
Guayana Region, Venezuela. Description and Travel, 557.
Guayaquil, Ecuador (city). Ethnic Identity, 1692. Social Conditions, 1692.
Guaycuru (indigenous group). Cosmology, 323.
Guaymi (indigenous group), 227. Agriculture, 487.
Gudin, Eugenio, 1427.
Guerrero, Mexico (state). Community Policing, 823. Democracy, 1459. Disappeared Persons, 1511. Drug Traffic, 826. Economic Conditions, 219, 1468. Education, 1447, 1459. Excavations, 65. Human Rights, 1468. Murder, 1511. Organized Crime, 1447. Political Conditions, 219, 1468. Social Conditions, 219. Violence, 1447.
Guerrillas, 1159. El Salvador, 1582.
Habana, Cuba (city). See La Habana, Cuba (city).
Haitian Revolution (1791–1804), 1609.
Handicapped. See People with Disabilities.
Harbors. See Ports.
Havana, Cuba (city). See La Habana, Cuba (city).
Hazardous Wastes. Mexico, 1165.
Health Care. See Medical Care.
Heidegger, Martin, 338.
Herders and Herding. Argentina, 625.
Hidalgo, Mexico (state). Artifacts, 92. Development, 193. Tourism, 193.
Higher Education. Caribbean Area, 1343. Central America, 1553. Mexico, 1450. Paraguay, 738. See Also Universities.
Hinduism. Caribbean Area, 1628.
Hispanic Americans. See Hispanics.
Hispanics. Florida, US (state), 1616.

Historia de Yucatán, 108.
Historic Sites. Brazil, 777.
Historical Demography. Caribbean Area, 129. Mesoamerica, 36. Mexico, 535.
Historical Geography, 382, 395, 400, 405, 420, 426. Brazil, 780. *See Also* Geographical History.
Hizballah (Lebanon), 1147.
Homicide. Mexico, 1488.
Homies Unidos, 1586.
Homosexuality. Andean Region, 1717. Colombia, 1650. Discrimination, 1507. Ecuador, 1731. Mexico, 1490, 1507. Peru, 1714, 1731. *See Also* Gays.
Horticulture. Chile, 155.
Hospitals. Peru, 1718. Psychiatry, 1718.
Hotel Industry. Argentina, 665.
Household Employees. Mexico, 1470. Panama, 512. Peru, 1727. Social Conditions, 1727. Uruguay, 757.
Housing, 384. Argentina, 677. Banking and Financial Institutions, 696. Brazil, 764, 768. Chile, 691. Ecuador, 1685. Peru, 585. Slaves and Slavery, 118.
Housing Policy. Chile, 681, 713, 721. Colombia, 1652. El Salvador, 1583.
Huaca de la Luna Site (Peru), 173.
Hualfín Inka Site (Argentina), 144.
Huambisa (indigenous group). Animals, 295. Myths and Mythology, 295.
Huao (indigenous group). Christianity, 287. Religion, 287.
Huaorani (indigenous group). *See* Huao (indigenous group).
Huaral, Peru (prov.). History, 165.
Huari (indigenous group). Ethnic Identity, 269. Language and Languages, 269.
Huastec (indigenous group). Archeology, 100. Ethnography, 195. History, 195. Religion, 176. Social Life and Customs, 176.
Huasteca Region (Mexico). Archeology, 195.
Huichol (indigenous group). History, 214. Land Tenure, 201. Religion, 241. Rites and Ceremonies, 241. Social Life and Customs, 214.
Huixtla, Mexico (city). Migration, 1177.
Human Capital. *See* Human Resources.
Human Ecology, 382. Costa Rica, 489. Cuba, 447. Mexico, 543. Peru, 584.
Human Geography, 382, 386, 409, 458, 572. Argentina, 609, 614–615, 649, 651. Belize, 485. Bolivia, 177. Caribbean Area, 436, 458. Chile, 699, 712, 718. Colombia, 460, 563, 566. Costa Rica, 490. Cuba, 460. Diseases, 379. Ecuador, 1693. Mexico, 177, 649, 1510. Paraguay, 729. Patagonia (region), 710. Race and Race Relations, 446. Research, 597. Southern Cone, 606–607, 1277, 1445. Women, 407. *See Also* Cultural Geography.
Human Remains. Argentina, 148. Mexico, 19, 67.
Human Resources. Mexico, 1301.
Human Rights, 415, 417. Bolivia, 1035, 1732. Central America, 1567. Chile, 1651. Colombia, 1651. Ecuador, 1019, 1731. El Salvador, 868, 878. Guatemala, 883, 893, 896. Honduras, 904. Mexico, 219, 1466, 1498. Nicaragua, 913, 918. Paraguay, 729. Peru, 294, 1708, 1731. Puerto Rico, 969. Women, 1535. *See Also* Civil Rights.
Human Trafficking, 936. Caribbean Area, 937, 939. Central America, 1580. Guatemala, 1603. Mexico, 1580. Minerals and Mining Industry, 1438. US, 1580.
Hurricanes. Caribbean Area, 970. Central America, 476. *See Also* Natural Disasters.
Hydration Rind Dating. *See* Archeological Dating.
Hydroelectric Power. Argentina, 666. Brazil, 770. Chile, 700.
Hygiene. *See* Public Health.
Ideology. Peru, 1702.
Illness. *See* Diseases.
Immigrants, 396, 401. Citizenship, 720, 1016. Civil Rights, 1513. COVID-19 (disease), 360. Ecuador, 1016. Human Rights, 1513. Mexico, 1478, 1513, 1571. Religious Life and Customs, 1520. Social Conditions, 1442.
Immigration. *See* Migration.
Imperialism. Dominican Republic, 949.
Imperialism, US. Puerto Rico, 462, 969.
Imports and Exports. *See* Exports; International Trade.
Incas. Bolivia, 150. Cosmology, 338. Philosophy, 338. State-Building, 174.
Income. Guatemala, 1337. Mexico, 1294, 1314, 1521. Peru, 1696.
Income Distribution, 1252. Chile, 690, 1064, 1378. El Salvador, 1570. Guatemala, 1337, 1570. Mexico, 1288, 1328, 1723. Paraguay, 740. Peru, 1696, 1723. Uruguay, 1414. *See Also* Equality.
Indigenismo and Indianidad. Bolivia, 1042, 1049. Mexico, 183.

Indigenous Art. Mesoamerica, 34.
Indigenous Languages. Acculturation, 210. Argentina, 308. Chile, 308. Honduras, 111. Mexico, 210, 233.
Indigenous Medicine. *See* Traditional Medicine.
Indigenous/Non-Indigenous Relations, 398, 429, 431. Amazon Basin, 277. Argentina, 331, 641. Bolivia, 342, 345, 1738. Brazil, 263, 267. Caribbean Area, 126, 130, 135. Chile, 348–349. Ecuador, 353. Mexico, 230, 534, 537. Paraguay, 303, 306, 314. Peru, 355, 582.
Indigenous Peoples, 380, 386, 409. Acculturation, 348. Agrarian Reform, 351. Amazon Basin, 248, 253. Animals, 122. Argentina, 309. Artisanry, 84, 94, 352. Autonomy, 206, 211, 290. Bilingual Education, 300. Bolivia, 150, 317, 344–345, 1037, 1042–1043, 1746. Brazil, 245, 250, 254–255, 264, 266, 270, 787. Caribbean Area, 126, 130. Chaco Boreal (Paraguay and Bolivia), 321, 329. Chile, 346, 349, 700. Christianity, 252. Civil Rights, 353. Climate Change, 583. Colombia, 157, 275. Colonization, 10. Conservation (environment), 255. Cosmology, 22, 86. COVID-19 (disease), 299, 477. Craniology, 20. Cuba, 133. Cultural Destruction, 431. Cultural Identity, 257. Dance, 236. Debt Bondage, 298. Description and Travel, 162. Development Projects, 499, 502. Disaster Relief, 215. Discrimination, 1439. Diseases, 477. Drug Utilization, 234. Economic Anthropology, 211. Economic Conditions, 351. Ecuador, 352, 354, 1037. Education, 180. Emotions, 321. Employment, 303. Environmental Degradation, 255. Epidemics, 477. Ethics, 336. Ethnic Identity, 224, 275, 302. Family Violence, 1515. Farms, 358. Food, 221, 226, 239, 276, 524. Forests and Forest Industry, 522. Gender Roles, 318. Guatemala, 499, 889, 899. History, 10. Honduras, 203, 506–507. Household Employees, 1470. Human Geography, 177. Human Rights, 232, 250, 290, 398, 729. Intellectual History, 257. Internal Migration, 1439. Labor and Laboring Classes, 340. Land Reform, 228. Land Settlement, 474. Land Tenure, 177, 286, 306–307, 310, 312, 383, 403, 471, 474, 507, 510, 534, 537, 729–730, 732, 901. Law and Legislation, 181, 228, 349. Maps and Cartography, 416, 507, 591. Massacres, 286. Material Culture, 37, 248. Medical Care, 194, 291, 331. Mesoamerica, 2, 13, 20, 95. Mexico, 12, 92, 183, 538, 833. Midwives, 1544. Migration, 1545. Minerals and Mining Industry, 398. Mortuary Customs, 346. Myths and Mythology, 251. Natural Resources, 700. Nature, 269, 352. Nicaragua, 206, 510. Nongovernmental Organizations, 253. Nutrition, 226. Paraguay, 312, 328. Peru, 163. Photography, 179, 292. Pictorial Works, 179, 190, 260. Plants, 247. Political Activism, 344. Political Conditions, 245, 828. Political Participation, 215, 237, 256–257, 266, 310, 328, 833, 836, 889, 899, 1056, 1694, 1750. Political Violence, 499. Popular Music, 302. Public Health, 194. Public Policy, 1327. Religion, 229, 251–252, 1711. Religious Life and Customs, 234. Rites and Ceremonies, 248, 267. Rubber Industry and Trade, 298. Rural Development, 232. Rural-Urban Migration, 249. Shamanism, 251. Slaves and Slavery, 135. Social Conditions, 190, 224, 232, 245, 1439. Social Life and Customs, 251, 522. Social Movements, 264, 826, 1043, 1052. Social Structure, 113. Spanish Conquest, 32. State, The, 306. Syncretism, 208. Technology, 325. Tourism, 348, 351, 1693. Truth Commissions, 294. Urban Areas, 318, 1439. Urbanization, 249. Views of, 179. Women, 194, 238, 273. Youth, 256.
Indigenous Policy. Argentina, 641. Bolivia, 345. Colombia, 275, 281. Ecuador, 290. Mexico, 228, 230. Peru, 289.
Indigenous Resistance. Capitalism, 370. Ecuador, 576. Mexico, 209, 228, 230.
Industrial Development Projects. *See* Development Projects.
Industrial Policy, 1267. Chile, 1376.
Industry and Industrialization. Argentina, 1215. Brazil, 1215. Chile, 347, 1376. Mexico, 1325.
Inequality. *See* Equality; Income Distribution.
Infant Mortality. Peru, 1280.
Inflation. Argentina, 1406. Venezuela, 1363.
Informal Sector, 1247. Colombia, 1656–1657. Mexico, 1296. Social Welfare, 1248. Venezuela, 1364.
Information Technology. Argentina, 654.
Inquisition. Drug Utilization, 234.

Instituto de Planeamiento Regional y Urbano del Litoral (Argentina), 655.
Instituto Movilizador de Fondos Cooperativos, 1402.
Instruments. See Musical Instruments.
Insurance. Guatemala, 503.
Insurrections. Colombia, 987. Peru, 1706.
Intellectual Cooperation, 1142. Argentina, 655. Latin America/Spain, 597. See Also Cultural Relations.
Intellectual History, 1441. Argentina, 651, 1393. Puerto Rico, 462.
Intellectuals. Caribbean Area, 1194. Ecuador, 1000.
Intelligence Service. Ecuador, 1011, 1019. See Also Espionage.
Intercultural Communication. Peru, 1698.
Internal Migration. Argentina, 663. Chile, 716. Guatemala, 1566. Mexico, 1499, 1501. See Also Forced Migration; Rural-Urban Migration.
Internal Stability. See Political Stability.
International Agreements. Mexico, 1328.
International Centre for Settlement of Investment Disputes, 497.
International Economic Relations, 390, 1139, 1141, 1152, 1184. Argentina/Italy, 1404. Brazil/China, 1254. Caribbean Area, 1193. Caribbean Area/China, 934. Caribbean Area/EU, 927. Caribbean Area/Great Britain, 926. Chile, 1227. Chile/China, 682. Colombia/Ecuador, 1239, 1241. Cuba, 1356, 1359. Cuba/US, 1352–1353. Ecuador, 1242. Ecuador/Eastern Europe, 1240. Jamaica/European Union, 962. Latin America/Asia, 1212. Latin America/China, 1161, 1284. Latin America/US, 1210. Mexico, 1306, 1310. Mexico/China, 1164, 1331. Mexico/US, 1165. Panama/China, 1179. Peru/US, 1244. Puerto Rico, 1339. Puerto Rico/US, 972, 1338. Venezuela, 1364. Venezuela/China, 1374. Venezuela/US, 1023.
International Finance. History, 1329.
International Law, 1155. Chile, 1228. History, 1157. Venezuela, 1033.
International Migration. See Migration.
International Peace Conference, 2nd, Hague, Netherlands, 1907, 1157.
International Relations, 1146, 1149, 1199, 1232. Argentina/Germany, 1219. Argentina/US, 1223. Brazil/Colombia, 1233. Brazil/Paraguay, 726. Caribbean Area, 1194. Caribbean Area/Cuba, 1188. Caribbean Area/Haiti, 1193. Caribbean Area/India, 1182. Caribbean Area/Mexico, 1162. Caribbean Area/US, 1150, 1196. Central America, 1176. Central America/Mexico, 1180. Central America/US, 475, 849, 1563, 1595. Colombia, 1236. Colombia/Ecuador, 1011. Colombia/US, 830. Costa Rica/Mexico, 1169. Cuba/Africa, 1201. Cuba/US, 1183, 1186, 1188–1190, 1197–1198, 1202. Ecuador/Peru, 1238. Ecuador/US, 1678. Haiti/US, 1609. History, 1155. Jamaica/China, 449. Latin America/China, 1154, 1284. Latin America/India, 1148, 1182. Latin America/Iran, 1147. Latin America/Middle East, 1147, 1153. Latin America/Pacific Area, 1152. Latin America/Russia, 1208. Latin America/Spain, 1151. Latin America/US, 1140, 1150, 1196. Mexico, 1170, 1174–1175. Mexico/Japan, 1163. Mexico/Pacific Area, 1164. Mexico/US, 830, 1167. Nicaragua/US, 924. Panama/US, 513. Peru/South Korea, 1243. Puerto Rico/US, 971, 1185, 1200, 1342, 1344. Saint Vincent and the Grenadines, 1192. Theory, 1155, 1157. See Also Foreign Policy.
International Trade, 1141, 1184. Brazil, 1254. Cuba, 1348, 1352. Haiti, 1193. Mexico, 1314. See Also Exports; International Economic Relations.
International Trade Relations. See International Economic Relations; International Trade.
Internet, 459.
Investment. See Public Investments.
Investments. Mexico, 1526. Venezuela, 1364. See Also Foreign Investment.
Irrigation. Argentina, 661. Costa Rica, 496. Uruguay, 753.
Islam. Mexico, 1496.
Islas Malvinas. See Falkland Islands.
Itaipu (power plant), 726, 760.
Izapa Site (Mexico). Archeological Dating, 27. Artifacts, 49. Excavations, 87. Mortuary Customs, 14. Remote Sensing, 88. Stelae, 27.
Jade. Mesoamerica, 66. Mexico, 74.
Jails. See Prisons.
Jaina Island Site (Mexico), 104.
Jalisco, Mexico (state). Economic Conditions, 1322. Economic Development, 1322. Reforestation, 533.

Japanese. Peru, 1722.
JBS (firm), 1431.
Jesuits. El Salvador, 1562. Peru, 1712. Sources, 323.
Jewelry. *See* Costume and Adornment.
Jews, 402.
Jihad, 1147.
Jivaro (indigenous group). *See* Shuar (indigenous group).
Jobs. *See* Employment.
Jornal do Brasil, 1425.
Journalism. Peru, 1716. Venezuela, 1028, 1031. *See Also* Mass Media; Newspapers.
Journalists. Argentina, 1104. Mexico, 821. Peru, 1705, 1716.
Judges. Costa Rica, 861.
Judicial Power. Colombia, 988.
Judicial Process. Chile, 1070. El Salvador, 875. Guatemala, 887, 891–892.
Jujuy, Argentina (prov.). Herders and Herding, 611. Indigenous Peoples, 340. Land Tenure, 611. Steel Industry and Trade, 1385.
Kaminaljuyú Site (Guatemala), 61, 72.
Kekchi (indigenous group). Religion, 103. Sacred Space, 103.
Kennedy, John F., 1246.
Kidnapping. Mexico, 1476.
Kirchner, Néstor, 1087.
Krenak, Ailton, 257.
La Consentida Archaeological Project, 59.
La Habana, Cuba (city). Indigenous Peoples, 133.
La Paz, Bolivia (city). Abortion, 1740. Description and Travel, 596. Human Trafficking, 1732. Social Conditions, 596.
La Venta Site (Mexico), 8.
Labor and Laboring Classes, 936, 1446. Bolivia, 151, 1741. Brazil, 783, 795, 1429. Chile, 1066, 1376, 1651. Colombia, 1651, 1657–1658. Costa Rica, 862. Honduras, 1552, 1592. Law and Legislation, 862. Mexico, 1294. Public Opinion, 1275. *See Also* Labor Market; Labor Supply; Migrant Labor.
Labor Market. Argentina, 1257. Political Anthropology, 1247. Political Participation, 1275. Public Policy, 1271. Uruguay, 1257.
Labor Movement. Ecuador, 1687. Saint Vincent and the Grenadines, 1340. *See Also* Labor Policy.
Labor Policy. Argentina, 1096. Costa Rica, 862. Mexico, 1296. *See Also* Labor Movement.
Labor Supply. Mexico, 1324. *See Also* Labor and Laboring Classes.
Labor Unions. *See* Trade Unions.
Lacandona Forest (Mexico). Environmental Protection, 522. Rural Development, 555.
Lambityeco Site (Mexico). Excavations, 69.
Land Invasions. Uruguay, 741–742.
Land Ownership. *See* Land Tenure.
Land Reform. Brazil, 760. Colombia, 1659. Cuba, 1354, 1358. Ecuador, 351. Guatemala, 890. Honduras, 901. Mexico, 228, 547, 1534. Puerto Rico, 463. *See Also* Agricultural Policy.
Land Settlement. Mesoamerica, 88. Patagonia (region), 644.
Land Tenure, 383, 424, 1262. Argentina, 333. Barbados, 446. Bolivia, 177, 345, 1739. Brazil, 259, 776. Central America, 471, 474. Colombia, 1647, 1659. Cuba, 1354. Drug Traffic, 505. Honduras, 507, 901. Mexico, 177. Nicaragua, 510. Panama, 512, 515. Paraguay, 328, 729–730, 732. Patagonia (region), 679. Peru, 286, 1703. Protests, 723. Puerto Rico, 463.
Land Use, 370, 383, 431. Amazon Basin, 795. Argentina, 627, 629, 639, 660, 669, 671. Brazil, 761, 781, 787, 792, 796. Chile, 688, 706, 719. Colombia, 1647. Costa Rica, 486, 491, 493. Drug Traffic, 505. Geographic Information Systems, 642. Mexico, 209, 554, 1321. Paraguay, 739. Patagonia (region), 679. Peru, 166.
Landscape Architecture. Mexico, 541.
Landslides. Chile, 687. Honduras, 509.
Language and Languages. Mexico, 210.
Latin American Influences. Spain, 1151. *See Also* Hispanics.
Latin American Migration Project, 1646.
Latin American Public Opinion Project, 1032.
Law and Legislation. Chile, 1072. Ecuador, 998, 1691. El Salvador, 875–876. Guatemala, 885, 891–892. Jamaica, 957. Nicaragua, 1588. Puerto Rico, 1344. Rape, 882.
Le Cointe, Paul, 778.
League of Nations, 1170.
Lebanese. Ecuador, 1692.
Legislation. *See* Law and Legislation.
Legislative Bodies. Argentina, 1089. Chile, 1072. Costa Rica, 857. Mexico, 831, 837. Venezuela, 1022.

Legislative Power. Mexico, 837.
Legislators. Argentina, 1092.
Lehmann-Nitsche, Robert, 308.
Lenca (indigenous group), 905. Language and Languages, 111.
Lenz, Rudolf, 308.
León, Luis de, 1556.
Letelier, Orlando, 1230.
Leticia Dispute, 1932–1934, 582.
Lewis, William Arthur, 1346.
LGBT. *See* Gays; Homosexuality.
Liberation Theology, 1711. El Salvador, 1578.
Libertarianism. Argentina, 1397.
Lima, Peru (city). Black People, 1720. Musicians, 1720. Social Conditions, 1727. War of the Pacific, 1879–1884, 1245. Women, 1727.
Linguistics. Mexico, 233.
Literary Criticism. Caribbean Area, 1612.
Lithics. *See* Stone Implements.
Livestock. Caribbean Area, 464. Mexico, 1308. Patagonia (region), 674.
Living Standards. *See* Cost and Standard of Living.
Local Elections. Chile, 1075, 1084. Costa Rica, 855.
Local Government. *See* Municipal Government.
Local Transit, 362. Chile, 715.
Lockouts. *See* Strikes and Lockouts.
Loma Negra (firm), 1389.
López Cogolludo, Diego, 108.
López Obrador, Andrés Manuel, 842.
Lovato, Roberto, 1582.
Luján, Argentina (city). Social Indicators, 615.
Lula, 1118, 1133, 1135.
M-19 (Colombian guerrilla group), 1159.
Machiguenga (indigenous group). Ethnobotany, 247.
Machismo. *See* Sex Roles.
Machu Picchu Site (Peru). Tourism, 587.
Macri, Mauricio, 1090, 1095, 1384, 1403, 1405.
Macusi (indigenous group). Ethnobotany, 247.
Magalhães, Agamenon, 768.
Maids. *See* Household Employees.
Maize. *See* Corn.
Malaria. Costa Rica, 1585.
Maler, Teobert, 54.
Malnutrition. *See* Nutrition.
Malpaís Prieto Site (Mexico), 48.
Malvinas, Islas. *See* Falkland Islands.

Manabí, Ecuador (prov.). Social Conditions, 1688.
Mangrove Plants. Belize, 483. Ecuador, 1686.
Mangrove Swamp Ecology. Ecuador, 1686.
Manta (indigenous group). Ecuador, 1693.
Manufactures. Mexico, 1324.
Maps and Cartography, 395, 409. Archeological Sites, 43. Argentina, 609, 641. Brazil, 782. Cities and Towns, 616. Colombia, 566. Fish and Fishing, 618. Honduras, 507. Peru, 591. Refuse and Refuse Disposal, 619. Research, 597, 599, 602. State-Building, 400. Uruguay, 746. *See Also* Atlases.
Mapuche (indigenous group). Children, 322. Civil Rights, 350. Colonization, 699. Discrimination, 350. Ethnobotany, 331. Language and Languages, 308. Maps and Cartography, 708. Natural Disasters, 708. Natural Resources, 699, 703. Political Activism, 347, 350. Sustainable Development, 703. Women, 350.
Mar Chiquita, Argentina (town). Environmental Policy, 646. Soils, 646.
Mar del Plata, Argentina (city). Housing, 647.
Marginalization. *See* Social Marginality.
Marine Biology. Caribbean Area, 461.
Marine Resources. Brazil, 788. Caribbean Area, 136, 461, 466, 479.
Marini, Ruy Mauro, 1144.
Maritime History. Caribbean Area, 440, 442.
Maritime Law. Caribbean Area, 461.
Maritime Policy. Bolivia, 1224. Caribbean Area, 461. Chile, 1224–1225.
Markets. Chile, 1379.
Maroons. Caribbean Area, 442. Colonial History, 442. Suriname, 1635.
Marriage. Andean Region, 1725.
MAS. *See* Movimiento al Socialismo (Bolivia).
Masculinity, 1689. Colombia, 1655. Mexico, 1455, 1495, 1532.
Mason, John Alden, 1631.
Masons. *See* Freemasonry.
Mass Media. Argentina, 1094. Cuba, 978. Ecuador, 998. Immigrants, 1540. Law and Legislation, 1094. Mexico, 803. Peru, 1716. Politicians, 1067. Public Policy, 1094. Venezuela, 1028, 1031. Violence, 1617. *See Also* Journalism.
Massacres. Peru, 286, 1703.

Mataco (indigenous group). Argentina, 326. Cosmology, 326. Youth, 309.
Material Culture. Caribbean Area, 131. History, 37.
Mato Grosso, Brazil (state). Indigenous Peoples, 260.
Mato Grosso do Sul, Brazil (state). Agroindustry, 789.
Matsigenka (indigenous group). *See* Machiguenga (indigenous group).
Maya Biosphere Reserve (Guatemala). *See* Reserva de la Biosfera Maya (Guatemala).
Mayas. Animal Remains, 91, 99. Animals, 15. Archeological Dating, 61, 72. Architecture, 243. Artifacts, 73, 83, 105. Boundaries, 55. Cacao, 64. Calendrics, 115. Caves, 213. Ceramics, 105–107, 109. Cities and Towns, 82, 102. Clothing and Dress, 1. Cosmology, 191, 243. Costume and Adornment, 90. Death, 47. Deities, 5, 41, 108, 112, 115. Diseases, 187. Droughts, 110, 484. Elites, 101. Emotions, 184. Epigraphy, 109. Etymology, 184. Famines, 51. Folklore, 198. Food, 11, 76, 91. Food Supply, 51. Frontiers, 55. Geographical Names, 111. Guatemala, 888, 1572. History, 17. Housing, 243. Human Remains, 81. Hunting, 15. Hydrology, 99. Iconography, 71. Incense, 47. Insects, 106. Jade, 66. Kings and Rulers, 17, 42, 52–53, 57. Land Settlement, 56, 101. Language and Languages, 111, 184, 233. Lexicology, 184. Linguistics, 233. Literature, 1556. Material Culture, 9, 47, 102. Medical Anthropology, 187. Medicine, 7. Meteorology, 41. Monuments, 107. Mortuary Customs, 47, 50, 53, 73, 77. Musical Instruments, 104. Myths and Mythology, 5, 191, 205. Paleobotany, 75. Pentecostalism, 204. Photography, 54. Pictorial Works, 54. Political Leadership, 42, 57, 101. Political Participation, 888. Political Systems, 101, 107. Pottery, 53. Precolumbian Architecture, 40, 54. Precolumbian Land Settlement Patterns, 40. Precolumbian Pottery, 63, 71, 93. Rain and Rainfall, 41, 110, 484. Religion, 108, 112, 204, 213. Religious Life and Customs, 47. Rites and Ceremonies, 50, 73, 83, 99, 115, 213. Sculpture, 52. Semantics, 184. Social Change, 204. Social Conditions, 896. Social Life and Customs, 11, 30. Symbolism, 9. Tobacco Use, 7, 105. Violence, 1572. Warfare, 5, 28. Witchcraft, 30. Writing, 109–110, 484.
Mayo (indigenous group). Religion, 186. Rites and Ceremonies, 186.
Mayors. Brazil, 1130, 1134. Chile, 1084. Elections, 1116, 1122.
Mazahua (indigenous group). Folklore, 199. Oral Tradition, 199. Religion, 199.
Mbya (indigenous group). Ethnomusicology, 332. Land Tenure, 333. Religious Life and Customs, 332. Rites and Ceremonies, 332. Youth, 309.
McCormick, Katharine Dexter, 1185.
Meat Industry. Brazil, 1431. Mexico, 1308. *See Also* Cattle Raising and Trade.
Medellín, Colombia (city). Energy Policy, 1665.
Media. *See* Mass Media.
Medical Anthropology. Argentina, 335.
Medical Care, 1138. Argentina, 299. Bolivia, 1740. Brazil, 1127. Fieldwork, 569. Public Policy, 1127. Women, 194.
Medical Policy. Cuba, 1201.
Medicinal Plants, 429. Caribbean Area, 132. Colombia, 272. Peru, 285.
Medicine. Argentina, 623. *See Also* Medical Care; Traditional Medicine.
Memory. *See* Collective Memory.
Mendes, Francisco Roberval, 270.
Mendoza, Argentina (city). Elites, 627. Gated Communities, 627.
Mendoza, Argentina (prov.). Conservation (environment), 658. Environmental Degradation, 617, 658. Natural Resources, 617. Regional Planning, 657. Sustainable Development, 657.
Mennonites. Indigenous/Non-Indigenous Relations, 329. Paraguay, 304, 733, 736.
Mental Health. Haiti, 438. Honduras, 508. Mexico, 1507. Peru, 1718.
Mercosur, 1145, 1206.
Mérida, Venezuela (state). Earthquakes, 558. Natural Disasters, 558.
Mestizos and Mestizaje. Ecuador, 354. Peru, 1710.
Metalclad Corporation, 1165.
Metallurgy. Precolumbian Civilizations, 139.
Metropolitan Areas. *See* Cities and Towns.
Mexica. *See* Aztecs.
Mexican-American Border Region. Social History, 1537. Violence, 1548. *See Also* Borderlands.

Mexican Americans. Acculturation, 1543. Ethnic Identity, 1543. Historiography, 1493. Race and Race Relations, 1543. Social Conditions, 1543. Social Life and Customs, 1493.

Mexicans. Migration, 1540. US, 1496, 1520.

México, Mexico (city). Artifacts, 38. Citizenship, 1477, 1519. City Planning, 1319. Description and Travel, 535. Economic Conditions, 1319. Family Violence, 1538. Gender Roles, 1533. Homosexuality, 1525. Police, 1504. Protests, 824. Public Spaces, 1481, 1538. Sex and Sexual Relations, 1525. Social Policy, 1541. Women, 1477, 1481, 1519, 1533, 1538, 1541.

México, Mexico (state). Indigenous Peoples, 190. Migration, 1501. Social Conditions, 186. Transportation, 1501.

Mexico. Congreso Cámara de Diputados, 1309.

Mexico. Oportunidades, 1451.

Michoacán, Mexico (state). Festivals, 222. Indigenous Peoples, 181. Land Tenure, 222. Law and Legislation, 181. Migration, 1499. Protestantism, 1497. Religion, 1497.

Microelectronics Industry. Mexico, 1297.

Middle Classes. Argentina, 1087. Bolivia, 1736. Mexico, 1551.

Midwives. Guatemala, 1564. Mexico, 1544.

Migrant Labor. Children, 1505. Mexico, 1500. Peru, 297. *See Also* Agricultural Labor.

Migrant Labor, Bolivian. Chile, 720.

Migrant Labor, Mexican. US, 1486, 1500.

Migrants. *See* Immigrants.

Migration, 418–419, 1320. Caribbean Area, 129, 930. Central America, 1595. Children, 1505. Colombia, 1646. Ecuador, 1016, 1684. Elections, 801. Entrepreneurs, 1461. Family and Family Relations, 1177, 1486. Food, 239. Guatemala, 1505, 1566. Honduras, 907. Human Rights, 1732. Labor and Laboring Classes, 1296. Mass Media, 1540. Mexico, 1300, 1499–1500, 1505. Nicaragua, 919. Panama, 514. Political Conditions, 1577. Public Opinion, 1577. Puerto Rico, 1342. Social Conditions, 1486. Social Marginality, 1435. Social Mobility, 1304. Women, 1550. Youth, 1531. *See Also* Immigrants; Internal Migration; Return Migration.

Migration, African, 406. Dominican Republic, 1623.

Migration, Bolivian, 401. Chile, 720.

Migration, Caribbean. Dominican Republic, 1623.

Migration, Catalan. Paraguay, 735.

Migration, Central American, 1593. US, 1561, 1563. Women, 1587.

Migration, Chinese. Dominican Republic, 1623.

Migration, Cuban. Mexico, 1513.

Migration, Dominican. US, 1638.

Migration, Ecuadorian. Spain, 1684.

Migration, El Salvadoran. US, 1582.

Migration, German. Brazil, 402, 780. Paraguay, 733.

Migration, Guatemalan. Mexico, 1576. US, 1576.

Migration, Haitian. Dominican Republic, 1623. England, 1610. France, 1610.

Migration, Honduran. Mexico, 1177.

Migration, Indian. Caribbean Area, 464.

Migration, Internal. *See* Internal Migration.

Migration, Italian. Argentina, 1408.

Migration, Jamaican. England, 1610. France, 1610.

Migration, Japanese. Peru, 1722.

Migration, Jewish. Argentina, 402.

Migration, Latin American, 406. US, 1435.

Migration, Mexican, 401. US, 1171, 1462, 1479, 1506, 1510.

Migration, Palestinian. Chile, 402.

Migration, Peruvian. Argentina, 677. Uruguay, 757.

Migration, Puerto Rican. US, 1616.

Migration, Russian. Paraguay, 736.

Migration, US. Brazil, 786. Costa Rica, 402.

Migration, Venezuelan, 1670.

Migration Policy, 401. Central America, 1597. Colombia, 1646. Mexico, 217, 1167, 1171, 1513. US, 1171, 1531.

Militarism. Ecuador, 1020. Mexican-American Border Region, 1298.

Military. Crime and Criminals, 884. Ecuador, 1010. Guatemala, 884. Nicaragua, 922. Uruguay, 1010. Violence, 810, 816.

Military History. Argentina, 641, 1216, 1220. Central America, 1176. Chile, 1220, 1229, 1231. Nicaragua, 922.

Military Occupation, US. Puerto Rico, 1619.

Military Policy. Argentina, 1218. Nicaragua, 922.

Minerals and Mining Industry, 378, 399, 417. Argentina, 624, 632, 661, 669, 705. Bolivia, 705. Chile, 682, 684, 705. Colombia,

561, 1647. Ecuador, 354, 578, 1018. El Salvador, 865, 876. Honduras, 865. Law and Legislation, 876. Mexico, 196, 537, 546. Migrant Labor, 297. Peru, 161, 297, 580, 1726. Social Conditions, 1438. Southern Cone, 601. Transportation, 682.
Mining. *See* Minerals and Mining Industry.
Mirador Site (Guatemala), 501.
Miskito (indigenous group). Land Tenure, 471.
Missing Persons. Mexico, 1466. *See Also* Disappeared Persons.
Missions. South America, 325.
Mitri, Juan Bautista Vicente, 1408.
Mixtec (indigenous group). Economic Conditions, 211. Intellectuals, 231. Political Participation, 219, 231. Social Conditions, 211.
Mizque, Bolivia (prov.). Rock Art, 153.
Moche (indigenous group). *See* Mochica (indigenous group).
Moche River Valley (Peru). Archeological Surveys, 163.
Mochica (indigenous group). Homosexuality, 175. Musical Instruments, 172. Peru, 173.
Mocobi (indigenous group). Ethnobotany, 331. Shamanism, 331.
Modern Art. Caribbean Area, 453.
Modernization. Argentina, 1393. Bolivia, 596. Chile, 725.
Moffitt, Ronni Karpen, 1230.
Molina Theissen Family, 884.
Monetary Policy. Argentina, 1394–1395. Brazil, 1419, 1427. Cuba, 1362. El Salvador, 1332–1333. Mexico, 1306.
Monetary Reform. Cuba, 1362.
Money. Venezuela, 1364.
Monopolies. Brazil, 1428.
Monroe Doctrine, 1196.
Monte Albán Site (Mexico). Political Conditions, 68. Remote Sensing, 68.
Montejo, Víctor, 1556.
Montevideo, Uruguay (city). Social Conditions, 741–742. Squatter Settlements, 741–742.
Monuments. Argentina, 640.
Moquegua, Peru (dept.). Artifacts, 138.
Morales Ayma, Evo, 1045–1047, 1053–1054, 1737–1738, 1748.
Morals. *See* Ethics.
Morelos, Mexico (state). Indigenous Peoples, 215.

Moreno, Lenin, 1003.
Morne Patate Site (Dominica). Plantations, 117.
Moro (indigenous group). Paraguay, 314. Poor, 314. Sex Roles, 304.
Mortality. Argentina, 662. *See Also* Death.
Mortuary Customs. Argentina, 147. Colombia, 159. Ecuador, 1681. Mesoamerica, 14, 35, 113. Mexico, 19. *See Also* Cemeteries; Tombs.
Moseten (indigenous group). Social Change, 334. Social Structure, 334.
Mosquito (indigenous group). *See* Miskito (indigenous group).
Mota, Mauro, 774.
Motherhood. Mexico, 1516.
Motion Pictures. *See* Film.
Mounds. Peru, 167.
Movimento dos Trabalhadores Rurais Sem Terra (Brazil), 636.
Movimiento al Socialismo (Bolivia), 1052, 1056, 1737.
Movimiento Regeneración Nacional (Mexico), 842.
Movimiento Revolucionario Túpac Amaru (Peru), 1706, 1712.
Movimiento Sin Miedo, 1044.
Multiculturalism, 372. Bolivia, 1747. Colombia, 275. Ecuador, 290, 296, 1690. Educational Models, 1443. Guatemala, 1598. Mexico, 207, 1542. Peru, 1698.
Multinational Corporations. Colombia, 1647. Mexico, 1301. Uruguay, 747.
Mummies. Conservation and Restoration, 67. Mexico, 67.
Municipal Government. Argentina, 1088, 1097. Brazil, 1106. Chile, 1075, 1084. Colombia, 990. Ecuador, 1002, 1008–1009. Honduras, 903. Jamaica, 961. *See Also* Central-Local Government Relations.
Murals. Mesoamerica, 18.
Murder. Caribbean Area, 935. Central America, 1285. Honduras, 905. Mexico, 1476. Peru, 1705, 1715. Women, 1452.
Museo preistorico-etnografico Luigi Pigorini, 130.
Museums. Artifacts, 120. Mexico, 21.
Music. Caribbean Area, 944.
Musical Instruments. Mesoamerica, 104. Peru, 172.
Muslims, 1496.
Mystery Stories. *See* Detective and Mystery Stories.

Myths and Mythology. Animals, 293. Chile, 346. Mexico, 1527, 1549.
NAFTA. *See* North American Free Trade Agreement (NAFTA).
Nahuas (indigenous group). Ethnography, 240. Folklore, 192. Philosophy, 240. Religion, 192. Rites and Ceremonies, 182, 192. Social Life and Customs, 182. Tourism, 218.
Naipaul, Vidiadhar Surajprasad, 1612.
Narcotics Policy. Central America, 480. Guatemala, 500.
Nariño, Colombia (dept.). Excavations, 158.
Nasca (indigenous group). *See* Nazca (indigenous group).
Nation-Building. *See* State-Building.
National Characteristics, 369. Argentina, 1092, 1216. Bolivia, 1750. Brazil, 265. Caribbean Area, 1637, 1639. Cuba, 1622. Jamaica, 1632. Mexico, 1465. Nicaragua, 1560. Peru, 1702. Puerto Rico, 1200, 1631. *See Also* National Identity.
National Defense. *See* National Security.
National Identity, 402. Argentina, 640. Ecuador, 1682. Nicaragua, 908. Peru, 1707. *See Also* National Characteristics.
National Parks. *See* Parks and Reserves.
National Patrimony. Environmental Policy, 737. Mexico, 12, 21, 84.
National Security, 1143, 1149, 1159. Argentina, 1222. Brazil, 1233. Colombia, 1233. Ecuador, 1019–1020. Guatemala, 499. Mexico, 540, 839–840, 1175.
Nationalism. Caribbean Area, 943, 960. Chile, 1062. Ecuador, 1690. Mexico, 1170.
Nationalization. Mexico, 1326. Petroleum Industry and Trade, 1366, 1372. Venezuela, 1369, 1372.
Nationbuilding. *See* State-Building.
Nativitas, Mexico (municipality). Waterways, 554.
Natural Disasters. Argentina, 613. Caribbean Area, 448, 457, 465. Chile, 697–698, 701–702, 708, 714. Costa Rica, 486. Ecuador, 571. Guatemala, 503. Mexico, 1287. Public Policy, 451. Puerto Rico, 439, 970. *See Also* Hurricanes.
Natural Gas. Bolivia, 595. Protests, 454. Puerto Rico, 454.
Natural History. Argentina, 644. Paraguay, 734.
Natural Resources, 378, 383, 385, 392. Amazon Basin, 276. Argentina, 624, 656, 705.

Bolivia, 705. Central America, 471. Chile, 699–700, 703–705, 711. Economic Theory, 1368. Ecuador, 567, 573, 1018. Guatemala, 1584. Mexico, 543, 555. National Patrimony, 737. Peru, 584. Public Policy, 411. South America, 598. Southern Cone, 601. Uruguay, 1415. Venezuela, 1373.
Nature, 417. Argentina, 667. Cuba, 447. Peru, 584.
Nazca Culture. Peru, 168.
Nazca (indigenous group). Ceramics, 169. Social Life and Customs, 169.
Nazism. Argentina, 1219. Paraguay, 733.
Negotiation. El Salvador, 866–867, 874.
Neiva, Colombia (city). Informal Sector, 1656.
Neoliberalism, 370, 410, 1267. Argentina, 666, 1384. Caribbean Area, 448. Chile, 688, 709, 724, 1066. Economic Development, 576. Ecuador, 1004, 1013. Guatemala, 890. Honduras, 902. Mexico, 185, 534, 1300, 1303, 1309. Uruguay, 727.
Neuquén, Argentina (prov.). Land Tenure, 650. Land Use, 650. Petroleum Industry and Trade, 1387. Regional Development, 625. Urbanization, 625.
Newspapers. Brazil, 1425. Caribbean Area, 1620. Mexico, 803.
NGOs. *See* Nongovernmental Organizations.
Nicaragua. Ejército, 922.
Nixtun-Ch'ich' Site (Guatemala), 82–83.
Non-Aligned Nations, 1148.
Nongovernmental Organizations. Argentina, 1088. Guatemala, 886.
North American Free Trade Agreement (NAFTA), 1166, 1299, 1328.
Nuevo Encuentro por la Democracia y la Equidad (Argentina), 635.
Nuevo León, Mexico (state). Gender Roles, 820. Social Conditions, 1536.
Nukak (indigenous group). Acculturation, 274. Land Settlement, 274. Social Change, 274.
Núñez, Ricardo, 1065.
Nutrition. Brazil, 769, 771. Caribbean Area, 455. Mexico, 221, 1299.
Oaxaca, Mexico (city). Description and Travel, 535. Political Conditions, 828.
Oaxaca, Mexico (state). Archaeological Sites, 6. Archaeological Surveys, 59. Ethnology, 188. Indigenous Peoples, 59, 190. Indigenous Policy, 188. Protests, 819. Social

Conditions, 235. Social Life and Customs, 235.
Obsidian. Archeological Dating, 85.
Occupational Training. Paraguay, 738.
OceanaGold, 497.
Oceanography. Caribbean Area, 457, 466. Costa Rica, 488.
Odebrecht, Emílio, 1119.
Odebrecht, Marcelo Bahia, 1119.
Odebrecht (firm), 952, 1119.
Oidores. *See* Judges.
Okada, Nikumatsu, 1722.
Older People. *See* Aged.
Oliveira, Lívia de, 790.
Olmecs. Cultural History, 8. Mesoamerica, 8.
Ongoy, Peru (town). History, 1703.
Operação Amazônia Nativa, 253.
Opposition Groups. Argentina, 1091. Bolivia, 1034. Ecuador, 1007. Nicaragua, 909. Venezuela, 1034, 1674.
Opus Dei (society), 1449.
Organización Barrial Tupac Amaru, 636.
Organización del Pueblo Indígena Me'phaa, 219.
Organización del Pueblo Indígena Mosetén (OPIM), 334.
Organización para el Futuro del Pueblo Mixteco, 219.
Organized Crime. Guatemala, 887, 897. Honduras, 901, 905. Mexico, 810–811, 813, 827, 843, 1528, 1548. Peru, 1699.
Orlando, Florida (city). Hispanics, 1616.
Ortega, Daniel, 909–910, 914–916, 918, 920.
Otomi (indigenous group). Folklore, 212. Religion, 212, 244. Rites and Ceremonies, 244.
Pacific Alliance (organization), 1139.
Pacific Rim Mining Corporation, 497.
Padmore, George, 948.
Paleo-Indians. Mesoamerica, 26. Mexico, 29.
Paleobotany. Honduras, 75–76. Mesoamerica, 96. Saint Croix (United States Virgin Islands), 132.
Paleoclimatology. Belize, 482.
Paleoindians. *See* Paleo-Indians.
Palestinians. El Salvador, 1565.
Pampas, Argentina (region). Agriculture, 1390. Land Use, 660.
PAN. *See* Partido Acción Nacional (Mexico).
Pan American Institute of Geography and History, 604.
Pan-Americanism. History, 1198.

Pando, Bolivia (dept.). Conflict Management, 1226.
Paramilitary Forces. Taxation, 1256.
Parks and Reserves. Argentina, 612, 617, 656. Belize, 483. Central America, 473, 481. Chile, 695. Colombia, 562. Ecology, 564.
Parliamentary Systems. *See* Political Systems.
Parque Nacional Laguna del Tigre (Guatemala), 500.
Parque Nacional Lihué Calel (Argentina). Antiquities, 147.
Parque Nacional Natural Los Nevados (Colombia). Conservation (environment), 564.
Partido Acción Nacional (Mexico), 800–801, 805, 812, 834.
Partido Comunista de Chile, 1083.
Partido de la Revolución Democrática (México), 800, 805, 812, 834.
Partido dos Trabalhadores (Brazil), 1105, 1121, 1135.
Partido Revolucionario Institucional (Mexico), 818, 1174.
Partido Trabalhista Brasileiro, 1113.
Paso de la Amada Site (Mexico), 78.
Paso y Troncoso, Francisco del, 89.
Pasto (indigenous group). Political Conditions, 246. Social Conditions, 246.
Pastoral Systems. *See* Herders and Herding.
Patagonia, Argentina (prov.). Economic Conditions, 1214. Industry and Industrialization, 1221. Regionalism, 1213.
Patronage, Political. *See* Clientelism.
Paz, Bolivia (city). *See* La Paz, Bolivia (city).
Peace, 1149. Colombia, 986–987. Conservation (environment), 565. Ecuador/Peru, 1238. El Salvador, 868, 874. Guatemala, 894.
Peace-Building. Colombia, 1659, 1661.
Pearls Site (Grenada). Precolumbian Civilizations, 121.
Peasant Movements. Guatemala, 890. Mexico, 200.
Peasants. Bolivia, 1052, 1749. Brazil, 785. Peru, 1703. Political Participation, 1581. Puerto Rico, 463.
Peddlers. *See* Informal Sector.
Peña Nieto, Enrique, 1174.
Pensions. Chile, 1059, 1380.
Pentecostalism. Guatemala, 204.
People with Disabilities. Chile, 685. Civil Rights, 1460. Mexico, 1460.

Pérez Molina, Otto, 880.
Periodization. Caribbean Area, 119.
Perón, Eva, 1219.
Perón, Juan Domingo, 1219, 1221.
Pesticides. Uruguay, 755.
Petén, Guatemala (dept.). Archeological Surveys, 82. Excavations, 83.
Petrochemical Industry. Ecuador, 1683.
Petroglyphs. See Rock Art.
Petroleum Industry and Trade. Argentina, 669. Bolivia, 595. Ecuador, 284, 1695. Foreign Investment, 1161. Mexico, 1173, 1312. Trinidad and Tobago, 973. Venezuela, 1366, 1368–1370, 1373–1374.
Pharmacy. Dominican Republic, 955.
Philosophy. Andean Region, 1702. See Also Epistemology; Ethics.
Philosophy of Liberation. See Liberation Theology.
Photographers. Southern Cone, 603.
Photography. Caribbean Area, 1608. Chile, 712. Human Geography, 712. Mexico, 179. Southern Cone, 603.
Physical Anthropology. Brazil, 265.
Physical Geography. Caribbean Area, 436, 467. Chile, 692. Modern Art, 453. Puerto Rico, 439.
Physicians, Cuban. Africa, 1201.
Pictorial Works. Mexico, 179.
Piedras Grandes, Mexico (town). Rock Art, 79.
Piñera, Sebastián, 1070.
Pinto, Edgard Roquette, 265.
Pipil (indigenous group). Language and Languages, 111.
Pirates. Caribbean Area, 131.
Place Names. See Geographical Names.
Plan Nacional de Desarrollo (Cuba), 1361.
Plantations. Diseases, 574. Dominica, 117.
Plants. Caribbean Area, 136. Diseases, 574.
Pluralism. Colombia, 997.
Podemos (Spanish political party), 1151.
Police. Argentina, 1102–1103. Belize, 851. Brazil, 793, 1110. Corruption, 1103, 1263. Ecuador, 1020, 1676. Mexico, 1504. Nicaragua, 912–913. Women, 1504. See Also Community Policing.
Policía de la Provincia de Buenos Aires, 1103.
Political Activism. Argentina, 1104. Puerto Rico, 967.
Political Boundaries. See Boundaries.
Political Campaigns. See Elections.

Political Candidates. See Politicians.
Political Conditions, 372, 1247. Argentina, 1091, 1093, 1095, 1098, 1101. Barbados, 963. Bolivia, 1034, 1037, 1045, 1048, 1051, 1737. Brazil, 1107, 1113, 1124. Caribbean Area, 1637. Central America, 847–848, 850. Chile, 1057, 1061, 1066, 1076, 1079–1080. Colombia, 991. Costa Rica, 853, 857. Cuba, 975–977, 979, 982. Dominican Republic, 949, 952, 955–956. Ecuador, 999, 1003–1004, 1007, 1010, 1013, 1037. El Salvador, 863, 873, 1555. Guatemala, 880, 888, 895. Honduras, 902, 907, 1554. Jamaica, 958–959, 1632. Mesoamerica, 49, 88. Mexico, 806, 815, 822, 837, 848. Nicaragua, 908, 914, 918, 920, 924. Panama, 925. Peru, 1697, 1701, 1704. Public Opinion, 942. Puerto Rico, 966, 968–969, 971, 1344, 1624. Uruguay, 1010. Venezuela, 1021, 1025, 1029–1030, 1032, 1034, 1672, 1674–1675.
Political Corruption, 1278. Argentina, 1102. Bolivia, 1047, 1053. Brazil, 1114, 1117, 1119–1120, 1131, 1431–1432. Colombia, 985. Dominican Republic, 951–952, 954, 1272. El Salvador, 864. Guatemala, 880, 883, 885, 887, 895, 897. Honduras, 903, 905. Law and Legislation, 864. Mexico, 806, 808–809, 821, 825, 840, 845. Peru, 1708. Puerto Rico, 965. Venezuela, 1669, 1671. See Also Corruption.
Political Culture, 1247. Argentina, 1101. Bolivia, 1046, 1052, 1054, 1056. Brazil, 1107. Caribbean Area, 942. Economic Policy, 1252. El Salvador, 870. Guatemala, 881. Mexico, 1723. Nicaragua, 908, 911, 916, 923. Peru, 1723. Venezuela, 1373.
Political Development. Ecuador, 1015.
Political Ecology. Ecuador, 1695. Mexico, 517.
Political Economy. Argentina, 1403. Chile, 688. See Also Economic Policy.
Political Geography, 420. Brazil, 271. Caribbean Area, 466. Jamaica, 449.
Political History. Argentina, 1089. Bolivia, 1039. Caribbean Area, 1191. Central America, 847, 1563. Chile, 1061–1062, 1068, 1083, 1381. Cuba, 975, 979, 981. Ecuador, 1005, 1012, 1015, 1678, 1687. El Salvador, 875. Guatemala, 896. Nicaragua, 910, 919, 923–924. Panama, 925. Puerto Rico, 462, 966. Venezuela, 1021, 1365.

Political Ideology. Argentina, 1087. Bolivia, 1738, 1750. Chile, 1077, 1085. Ecuador, 1006. El Salvador, 877. Nicaragua, 917. Venezuela, 1666. *See Also* Political Thought.
Political Institutions, 1258. Argentina, 1086, 1088. El Salvador, 876. Guatemala, 881. Informal Sector, 1248. Mexico, 839. Warfare, 1279.
Political Leadership. Ecuador, 1001, 1694.
Political Left, 1151. Argentina, 1384. Chile, 1077, 1381. Ecuador, 1007. Puerto Rico, 967.
Political Opposition. *See* Opposition Groups.
Political Participation, 430, 1253, 1258. Argentina, 1088, 1097, 1099. Bolivia, 1038. Brazil, 1109, 1111, 1114, 1132, 1422. Chile, 1060, 1063, 1069, 1081. Colombia, 985, 1645. Costa Rica, 490, 854–855. Dominican Republic, 956. Ecuador, 1014. El Salvador, 869. Guatemala, 889, 899. Jamaica, 961. Mexico, 801, 804, 824, 828–829, 841, 846, 1515, 1534. Municipal Government, 1088. Nicaragua, 206, 911. Peru, 1700. Puerto Rico, 1634.
Political Parties, 1247. Bolivia, 1044, 1049, 1055. Brazil, 1108, 1122, 1128, 1130, 1134. Chile, 1060–1061, 1077, 1079, 1085. Colombia, 989. Costa Rica, 858. Dominican Republic, 950, 953. Ecuador, 1677. El Salvador, 863, 870, 877, 879. Elections, 812. Guatemala, 889. Mexico, 806–807, 812, 814, 838. Puerto Rico, 967–968.
Political Patronage. *See* Clientelism.
Political Persecution. Mexico, 1476, 1484, 1546.
Political Prisoners. Peru, 1728.
Political Prisoners, Cuban. US, 1197.
Political Reform. Argentina, 1086. Brazil, 1120. Chile, 1071. Colombia, 996. Costa Rica, 861. Cuba, 974, 982. Ecuador, 1677. Guatemala, 892. Mexico, 818.
Political Repression. *See* Political Persecution.
Political Sociology, 1457.
Political Stability. Bolivia, 1055. Colombia, 992. Ecuador, 1238. Guatemala, 894. Honduras, 907.
Political Systems. Belize, 852. Chile, 1060, 1085. Colombia, 991. Costa Rica, 855, 858. Cuba, 974. Dominican Republic, 953. El Salvador, 879. Honduras, 906. Puerto Rico, 966–967.

Political Thought, 1440. Bolivia, 1036, 1051. Caribbean Area, 1194. Dominican Republic, 949. Ecuador, 1000. *See Also* Political Ideology.
Political Violence, 1457. Chile, 1229. Colombia, 987, 989, 994, 1640, 1644, 1663. Conservation (environment), 565. El Salvador, 878. Guatemala, 499, 884, 893. Mexico, 1498, 1511. Nicaragua, 913, 923. Peru, 1706–1707, 1712. *See Also* Violence.
Politicians. Belize, 852. Brazil, 1113, 1118, 1131, 1133. Chile, 1058, 1074. Colombia, 996. Ecuador, 1001. Honduras, 906. Mexico, 806, 822. Women, 1074.
Pollution. *See* Environmental Pollution.
Poor. Brazil, 1424. City Planning, 779. Colombia, 1652. Cuba, 1633. Economic Policy, 1252. El Salvador, 1558, 1583. Income, 1422. Jamaica, 1632. Mexico, 1480. Political Participation, 1253. Uruguay, 741–742. Venezuela, 1668. *See Also* Poverty.
Popol Vuh, 112.
Popular Culture. Brazil, 798. Caribbean Area, 1608. Ecuador, 1682, 1690. Nicaragua, 1560.
Popular Movements. *See* Social Movements.
Population. Puerto Rico, 1342.
Population Forecasting. Colombia, 460. Cuba, 460.
Population Growth, 365. *See Also* Birth Control.
Population Studies. *See* Demography.
Populism. Argentina, 1087, 1100. Chile, 1071. Venezuela, 1371, 1671.
Ports. Argentina, 620, 670. Chile, 682.
Pottery. Argentina, 144.
Poverty, 1253. Argentina, 662. Brazil, 1430. Central America, 472. Chile, 681, 1379. Cuba, 1621. Ecuador, 1002. Guatemala, 1337. Land Tenure, 1262. Mexico, 1313, 1512. Peru, 1697. Public Policy, 1264. Uruguay, 743. Venezuela, 1669. *See Also* Poor.
PRD. *See* Partido de la Revolución Democrática (Mexico).
Precolumbian Civilizations. Agriculture, 487. Animals, 15, 116, 122. Architecture, 23. Argentina, 147. Art, 34. Artifacts, 25. Astronomy, 31. Ball Games, 6. Canoes and Canoeing, 134. Caribbean Area, 126, 129, 134. Ceramics, 25, 142, 164. Climate, 145. Clothing and Dress, 1, 34. Corn, 24. Costa Rica, 487. Costume and Adornment, 127. Cuba, 133. Feather-

Work, 116. Fire, 487. Fish and Fishing, 146. Food, 226. Grenada, 121, 124. Horticulture, 155. Human Fertility, 31. Marriage, 1725. Mesoamerica, 95. Mexico, 92. Mortuary Customs, 141, 159. Nutrition, 24. Peru, 160, 167. Political Conditions, 49. Puerto Rico, 120. Rain and Rainfall, 31. Religious Life and Customs, 23. Rites and Ceremonies, 46. Sacrifice, 31. Sex and Sexual Relations, 1725. Social Mobility, 137. Stone Implements, 143. Warfare, 28. Windwards Islands, 123.

Precolumbian Land Settlement Patterns. Argentina, 642. Mesoamerica, 26, 56.

Precolumbian Pottery. Belize, 93. Mesoamerica, 63.

Precolumbian Sculpture. Caribbean Area, 127.

Precolumbian Trade. Mesoamerica, 66.

Pregnancy. Mexico, 1460, 1544. Nicaragua, 1559.

Prehistory. *See* Archeology.

Presidential Systems. *See* Political Systems.

Presidents. Bolivia, 1040. Brazil, 1118, 1133. Chile, 1067. Colombia, 993. Costa Rica, 856. Ecuador, 1003. Elections, 829, 1116. Mexico, 814. Nicaragua, 915. US, 1223.

Press. *See* Mass Media.

Préval, René, 1195.

PRI. *See* Partido Revolucionario Institucional (Mexico).

Prices. Venezuela, 1363.

Prime Ministers. Barbados, 963.

Primeiro Comando da Capital, 1125.

Prisoners. Argentina, 626. Ecuador, 402. Gangs, 1125. Guatemala, 1574. Women, 1648, 1676.

Prisons. Argentina, 626. Colombia, 1648. Costa Rica, 1590. Guatemala, 1574. Violence, 1648.

Private Enterprises. Mexico, 1317.

Produce Trade. *See* Food Industry and Trade.

Production (economics). Mexico, 1290.

Productivity, 1266. Chile, 1375. Mexico, 1328, 1330.

Programa de Educación, Salud y Alimentación (Mexico), 1451.

Property. Paraguay, 730, 732.

Propuesta Republicana (Argentina), 1090.

Prostitution. Mexico, 1492. Minerals and Mining Industry, 1438.

Protected Areas. *See* Parks and Reserves.

Protest Movements. *See* Protests.

Protestantism. Mexico, 1497.

Protests. Agricultural Policy, 1268. Argentina, 1268. Bolivia, 1035, 1050. Brazil, 256. Chile, 713, 1063, 1073, 1080. Costa Rica, 853, 860, 1336. Cuba, 976. Dominican Republic, 951. Ecuador, 1004, 1013. Guatemala, 880. Mexico, 824, 836, 1546. Nicaragua, 909, 913–914. Puerto Rico, 454.

Psychiatry. Peru, 1718.

Psychoanalysis. Peru, 1707.

Psychology. Mexico, 1465, 1495. Peru, 1707.

PT. *See* Partido dos Trabalhadores (Brazil).

Public Administration. Chile, 702. Ecuador, 1008. El Salvador, 864. Honduras, 903. Puerto Rico, 965. Venezuela, 1027.

Public Debt, 1318. Mexico, 1326. Puerto Rico, 972, 1344. Sources, 1326.

Public Education. Voting, 1250.

Public Finance. Argentina, 1282. Brazil, 1108.

Public Health, 360, 379. Argentina, 299, 623. Brazil, 1137. Costa Rica, 1585. Cuba, 1201. Dominican Republic, 955. Honduras, 508. Mexico, 194, 221, 1299. Puerto Rico, 965. Regionalism, 1138.

Public Investments. Uruguay, 745.

Public Opinion. Argentina, 1282. Bolivia, 1046. Brazil, 1124. Chile, 1081. El Salvador, 870. Guatemala, 881, 895. Mexico, 806. Nicaragua, 911. Venezuela, 1032.

Public Policy. Amazon Basin, 796. Argentina, 1093, 1098. Brazil, 781. Chile, 1079. Colombia, 983, 992. Ecuador, 575, 1017. El Salvador, 866–867, 872, 876. Mexico, 817, 837, 845, 1327. Paraguay, 1411. Peru, 1280. Tourism, 366. Uruguay, 746, 756.

Public Safety, 1143. Mexico, 841.

Public Service Employment. Dominican Republic, 954, 1272. *See Also* Employment.

Public Spaces. Argentina, 612. Chile, 713. Mexico, 541. Women, 1481, 1538.

Public Transportation. *See* Local Transit; Transportation.

Public Utilities. *See* Public Works.

Public Welfare. *See* Social Welfare.

Public Works. Chile, 725.

Publishers and Publishing. Geography, 604.

Puebla, Mexico (state). Cultural Policy, 388. History, 1539. Migration, 1587. Social Life and Customs, 240.

Puebla de Zaragoza, Mexico (city). Description and Travel, 535.

Puno, Peru (city). Indigenous Peoples, 355.

Punta Buque 3 Site (Argentina), 149.
Purépecha (indigenous group). Artifacts, 48. Migration, 1471. Political Participation, 185. Rites and Ceremonies, 222. Social Life and Customs, 222.
Putumayo River Basin. Ethnography, 292. Rubber Industry and Trade, 292.
Puuc Region (Mexico). Precolumbian Architecture, 40.
Pyramids. Mexico, 23.
Quality of Life, 1471. Ecuador, 575, 1014. Honduras, 508. Mexico, 520, 1453. Venezuela, 1669.
Quechua (indigenous group). Ecuador, 353.
Quiché (indigenous group). Calendrics, 197. Ethnic Identity, 1602. Language and Languages, 197.
Quintana Roo, Mexico (state). Indigenous Peoples, 239. Internal Migration, 239.
Quito, Ecuador (city). Crime and Criminals, 1676. Social Life and Customs, 1681. Women, 1676.
Race and Race Relations, 1433–1434. Barbados, 446. Bolivia, 1747, 1750. Brazil, 768, 1109, 1112, 1123. Caribbean Area, 931, 940, 960, 1620, 1637. Colombia, 1642, 1660. Cuba, 1629. Dominican Republic, 1623. Ecuador, 1679, 1690–1691. El Salvador, 1565. Florida, US (state), 1616. Guatemala, 1598. Mexico, 1517. Panama, 512. Peru, 1721. Philosophy, 450. Puerto Rico, 1605, 1627, 1631. Venezuela, 1667. *See Also* Racism.
Racism, 1434. Colombia, 1660. Ecuador, 1691. Mexico, 1517. Puerto Rico, 1613. *See Also* Race and Race Relations.
Radio. Argentina, 1094.
Railroads. Chile, 715. Costa Rica, 494.
Rain and Rainfall. Central America, 476. Deities, 41. Mesoamerica, 41.
Rape. Guatemala, 882. Nicaragua, 1559.
Realidad y Perspectivas, 1232.
Rebellions. *See* Insurrections.
Recabarren, Luis Emilio, 1083.
Recessions. Mexico, 1287, 1413. Uruguay, 1413.
Recife, Brazil (city). Labor and Laboring Classes, 769. Modernization, 767–768.
Reclamation of Land. *See* Land Invasions; Land Reform; Land Tenure.
Redemocratization. *See* Democratization.
Redistribution of Wealth. *See* Equality; Income Distribution.

Reforestation. Mexico, 522, 533. Panama, 515.
Refugees. Haiti, 1625. International Law, 1625. Southern Cone, 606–607, 1277, 1445. *See Also* Exiles.
Refuse and Refuse Disposal, 376. Argentina, 619. Caribbean Area, 435. *See Also* Environmental Pollution.
Regional Development. Argentina, 670. Caribbean Area, 938. Patagonia (region), 644. Southern Cone, 1417. Uruguay, 751. *See Also* Regional Planning.
Regional Integration, 1160, 1199. Caribbean Area, 452. South America, 1237.
Regional Planning, 1156, 1276. Argentina, 655, 657, 670. Chile, 702, 704, 714, 722. Mexico, 542. Puerto Rico, 441. *See Also* Regional Development.
Regionalism, 1145–1146, 1160, 1184, 1203, 1205, 1207, 1232. Andean Region, 1211. Argentina, 1213. Caribbean Area, 929, 1183. Chile, 1213. Medical Care, 1138. Peru, 1710. South America, 1242. Southern Cone, 1206.
Religion. History, 229. Mexico, 229. Peru, 1709.
Religion and Politics. Costa Rica, 856. Mexico, 829. Venezuela, 1672.
Religious Life and Customs, 429. Andean Region, 1717. Bolivia, 1734. Cuba, 1604, 1636. Guatemala, 1599. Mexico, 1520, 1527, 1549. Peru, 162, 1719. Puerto Rico, 1614. Trinidad and Tobago, 1611. US, 1520. *See Also* Religion.
Remains. *See* Human Remains.
Remittances. *See* Emigrant Remittances.
Remote Sensing. Costa Rica, 495. Mexico, 495.
Repression. Argentina, 1095. Chile, 1377. Mexico, 823. Nicaragua, 909, 913, 918.
Research. International Relations, 1142.
Reserva de la Biosfera Maya (Guatemala), 501.
Reserva de la Biosfera Ría Celestún (Mexico), 545.
Reserves. *See* Parks and Reserves.
Restoration. *See* Conservation and Restoration.
Return Migration, 401, 419. Dominican Republic, 1638. Ecuador, 1684. Investments, 1526. Mexico, 1300, 1304, 1461, 1472, 1478, 1502, 1506, 1522, 1526. Southern Cone, 606.

Revista Cartográfica, 604.
Revista de Economía Argentina, 1393.
Revolutionaries. Argentina, 640. Peru, 1706. *See Also* Revolutions and Revolutionary Movements.
Revolutions and Revolutionary Movements. Central America, 1563. Nicaragua, 917, 919, 1178. Venezuela, 1025. *See Also* Revolutionaries.
Reyes Ochoa, Alfonso, 16.
Rice and Rice Trade. Costa Rica, 496. Cuba, 1359.
Rio de Janeiro, Brazil (city). Historical Geography, 777. Indigenous Peoples, 254. Slums, 1126. Squatter Settlements, 793.
Rio de Janeiro, Brazil (state). Dictatorships, 784.
Rio Grande do Sul, Brazil (state). Elections, 1132.
Río Negro, Argentina (prov.). Land Tenure, 650. Land Use, 650.
Rites and Ceremonies. Ecuador, 1681. Mesoamerica, 84.
Rituals. *See* Rites and Ceremonies.
River Basins. *See* Waterways.
Rivers, 408.
Roads. Brazil, 1421. Chile, 725. Peru, 589. Uruguay, 745.
Rock Art. Archeological Dating, 84, 153. Argentina, 141. Bolivia, 152–153. Chile, 154. Mesoamerica, 18. Mexico, 79, 84, 86. Peru, 170. *See Also* Cave Paintings.
Rock Paintings. *See* Cave Paintings; Rock Art.
Rockshelters. *See* Caves.
Rodríguez Cancel, Jaime L., 1200.
Rodríguez-Triás, Helen, 1185.
Rolland, Modesto C., 1293.
Romero, Óscar Arnulfo, *Saint*, 1558.
Rondon, Cândido Mariano da Silva, 263.
Rondônia, Brazil (state). Colonization, 271. Indigenous/Non-Indigenous Relations, 271.
Rosario, Argentina (city). Development Projects, 680. Land Use, 680.
Rouse, Irving, 119.
Rousseff, Dilma, 1117, 1135.
Rúa, Fernando de la, 1407.
Rubber Industry and Trade. Peru, 298, 582.
Runa (indigenous group). *See* Canelo (indigenous group).
Rural Conditions, 389, 412, 419. Argentina, 625, 652, 1390. Brazil, 758. Colombia, 1647, 1663. Ecuador, 1002. Mexico, 541, 1294, 1521. Nicaragua, 919.
Rural Development, 1276. Argentina, 641. Cuba, 1351. Haiti, 434. Mexico, 544, 1321. Peru, 1697. Uruguay, 752.
Rural Poverty. *See* Poverty.
Rural-Urban Migration, 424. Amazon Basin, 249. Bolivia, 342, 592, 1749. Mexico, 238. *See Also* Migration.
Salaries. *See* Wages.
Salta, Argentina (prov.). Tourism, 665.
San Antonio Bay, Argentina. Fish and Fishing, 146.
San Cristóbal de las Casas, Mexico (city). Social Conditions, 1456.
San Fernando, Argentina (city). Geography, 629.
San Juan, Argentina (city). Land Use, 621. Population Growth, 621.
San Lorenzo Site (Mexico), 8. Population, 36.
San Luis Potosí, Mexico (state). Economic History, 1295. Finance, 1295. Human Rights, 201. Land Use, 424. Minerals and Mining Industry, 201.
San Pedro de Atacama, Chile (city). Artifacts, 138.
Sancho Dávila, Bartola, 1720.
SanCor Cooperativas Unidas Limitada, 1408.
Sandinistas (Nicaragua), 917, 919, 924. Interviews, 1178.
Sandino, Augusto César, 910.
Sanger, Margaret, 1185.
Sanitation. *See* Public Health.
Santa Cruz, Argentina (prov.). Archeology, 673. Land Settlement, 673.
Santa Cruz, Bolivia (city). Indigenous Peoples, 318. Urbanization, 593.
Santa Cruz, Bolivia (dept.). Natural Gas, 595.
Santa Cruz de la Sierra Metropolitan Area, Bolivia. Conservation (environment), 594. Globalization, 594.
Santa Fe, Argentina (city). Natural Disasters, 613. Social Conditions, 613.
Santa María Huatulco, Mexico (city). Economic Conditions, 536.
Santa Muerte (Mexican deity), 1527, 1549.
Santería, 1636. Cuba, 1604. Puerto Rico, 1614. *See Also* African Influences.
Santiago, Chile (city). City Planning, 709. Demography, 716. Housing, 696, 721. Land Tenure, 696. Social Conditions, 691. Urbanization, 693.

Santos, Milton, 433.
São Paulo, Brazil (city). Floods, 779. Income, 1422. Transportation, 794.
São Paulo, Brazil (state). Crime and Criminals, 1125. Nature, 782.
Saramacca (Surinamese people). Social Life and Customs, 1635.
Sariego Rodríguez, Juan Luis, 196.
Satellites. Argentina, 616, 653.
Savings and Investment. Argentina, 1398.
Schools. Costa Rica, 1600. Violence, 1482, 1591.
Science. Publishers and Publishing, 604.
Scientific History. Argentina, 644.
Sculpture. Precolumbian Civilizations, 58.
Security. *See* National Security.
Seibal Site (Guatemala), 90–91.
Self-Determination. *See* Sovereignty.
Sendero Luminoso (guerrilla group), 1706, 1712, 1728.
Separation. *See* Divorce.
Seri (indigenous group). Ceramics, 44.
Sex and Sexual Relations. Andean Region, 1725. Mexico, 1460, 1490, 1508, 1518. *See Also* Gender Relations.
Sex Roles, 1689. Bolivia, 1734. Mexico, 1456, 1464, 1492, 1532. Minerals and Mining Industry, 1438. Peru, 1727. *See Also* Gender Roles.
Shamanism. Animals, 293. Argentina, 331. Bolivia, 324. Colombia, 272. Peru, 285.
Shantytowns. *See* Squatter Settlements.
Shells and Shell Middens. Archeological Dating, 90. Excavations, 45. Mesoamerica, 90, 94, 114.
Shining Path (guerrilla group). *See* Sendero Luminoso (guerrilla group).
Shipibo-Conibo (indigenous group). Children, 283. Citizenship, 289. Myths and Mythology, 283. Urban Areas, 289.
Shoe Industry. Brazil, 1429.
Shuar (indigenous group). Acculturation, 296. Animals, 295. Myths and Mythology, 295.
Silva, Luiz Inácio da. *See* Lula.
Simonsen, Roberto, 1427.
Sinaloa, Mexico (state). Artifacts, 35. Migration, 217. Minerals and Mining Industry, 546.
Sipibo (indigenous group). *See* Shipibo-Conibo (indigenous group).
Slaves and Slavery, 936. Brazil, 783. Caribbean Area, 118, 135, 445, 931, 937, 947.

Cooking, 136. Dominica, 117. Food, 136. Medical Care, 132. Religious Life and Customs, 445. Trinidad and Tobago, 973.
Slums. Argentina, 677. Brazil, 764, 791. Chile, 681. El Salvador, 1583. *See Also* Squatter Settlements.
Small Business. Mexico, 1290, 1331. *See Also* Entrepreneurship.
Social Change, 375, 1436, 1441, 1457. Bolivia, 1748. Caribbean Area, 942. Central America, 475. Chile, 1057, 1073, 1080, 1082. El Salvador, 1569, 1586. Guatemala, 896. Mexico, 1515. Nicaragua, 1560.
Social Classes. Argentina, 623, 663. Bolivia, 594, 1736, 1742. Cuba, 1633.
Social Conditions, 374, 400, 404, 1444. Andean Region, 1717. Argentina, 1093. Bolivia, 592, 1733, 1738, 1743, 1747–1748. Brazil, 1137. Caribbean Area, 1637, 1639. Chile, 1057, 1064, 1073, 1080, 1378. Colombia, 1653, 1656. Cuba, 975–976, 1360. Dominican Republic, 949. Ecuador, 1680. El Salvador, 873, 1555. Guatemala, 204, 900. Honduras, 902, 1554. Mesoamerica, 13. Mexico, 216, 554, 817, 845, 1172, 1453, 1464, 1512, 1515, 1528, 1548. Peru, 1697–1698, 1707, 1724. Puerto Rico, 1342, 1624. Venezuela, 1024, 1367, 1369, 1669, 1671–1672, 1674–1675.
Social Conflict, 370, 1457. Argentina, 1098. Colombia, 994, 1661. Conservation (environment), 415. Ecuador, 572. Mexico, 216, 525, 1321. Peru, 1726.
Social Control. Ecuador, 1676. Peru, 1729.
Social Customs. *See* Social Life and Customs.
Social Development. Mexico, 1451.
Social History. Caribbean Area, 1191. Mexico, 196. Puerto Rico, 1185. Saint Vincent and the Grenadines, 1340. Venezuela, 1365.
Social Justice, 430. Ecuador, 1676. Guatemala, 499. Mexico, 520.
Social Life and Customs. Chile, 707. Ecuador, 352, 1680, 1682. Honduras, 1589. Mexico, 1478, 1509, 1530, 1532. Peru, 172, 1702.
Social Marginality, 372. Central America, 1601. Mexico, 1480, 1512. Migration, 1435.
Social Mobility, 458, 1265. Bolivia, 1736. Caribbean Area, 458. Mexico, 1304.

Social Movements, 430, 1444, 1457. Argentina, 636, 1095. Black People, 1434. Bolivia, 1038, 1737, 1746. Brazil, 636. Chile, 723. Colombia, 1069, 1661. Costa Rica, 490, 1596. Dominican Republic, 951. Ecuador, 1678, 1686–1687. El Salvador, 865, 876, 1581. Guatemala, 883, 889–890, 1584. Honduras, 865. Mexico, 216, 219, 804, 819, 1321, 1485, 1514, 1529–1530, 1534, 1546. Peru, 1704. Puerto Rico, 969, 1615.

Social Organization. *See* Social Structure.

Social Policy, 1248, 1251. Argentina, 1096, 1271, 1409. Bolivia, 1739. Brazil, 1129, 1137. Caribbean Area, 1251. Central America, 1595. Chile, 1059, 1064, 1082. Cuba, 982, 1349. Ecuador, 1006, 1017. El Salvador, 872. Mexico, 1303, 1315, 1451, 1494, 1514. Peru, 1697, 1729. Public Opinion, 1271. Venezuela, 1027.

Social Relations. *See* Social Life and Customs.

Social Sciences, 1142.

Social Structure. Colombia, 1640. Mesoamerica, 97, 113. Venezuela, 1667.

Social Thought, 1441. Peru, 1697.

Social Values. Mexico, 1317.

Social Welfare, 1248, 1264. Argentina, 1271. Brazil, 1124, 1136, 1424, 1430. Colombia, 1649. Cuba, 1633. Peru, 1280.

Socialism and Socialist Parties, 339. Bolivia, 1054. Chile, 1065, 1077. Cuba, 977, 980. Ecuador, 1017. Latin American Influences, 1151. Paraguay, 733. Venezuela, 1365, 1674.

Sociolinguistics. Mexico, 233.

Sociology. Research, 1142.

Soconuso, Mexico (region). Artifacts, 78.

Soil Erosion. Argentina, 646, 664.

Solís Rivera, Luis Guillermo, 853.

Sonora, Mexico (state). Agricultural Labor, 1455. Economic Conditions, 1327. Economic Development, 1302. Entrepreneurship, 1323. Environmental History, 549. Indigenous Peoples, 225. Industry and Industrialization, 1323. Maquiladoras, 1323. Political Conditions, 1327. Poverty, 1302. Rural Conditions, 180. Social Conditions, 180, 549, 1455. Water Resources Development, 549.

Sorcery. *See* Witchcraft.

South Asian Influences. Caribbean Area, 464.

Sovereignty, 1155. Cuba, 982. Ecuador, 1011. Guatemala, 899.

Soybeans. Argentina, 643, 669, 1268. Brazil, 792. Paraguay, 731. Uruguay, 753, 755.

Spanish Conquest. Caribbean Area, 128. Economic Conditions, 32. Environmental Degradation, 32.

Spiritualism. Caribbean Area, 445.

Sports. Caribbean Area, 1637.

Squatter Settlements. Brazil, 791. Colombia, 1673. Peru, 585. Uruguay, 741–742. *See Also* Slums.

Standard of Living. *See* Cost and Standard of Living.

Stang, Dorothy, 762.

State, The. Economic Development, 1409. El Salvador, 874. Guatemala, 893. Land Tenure, 1262. Mexico, 1259–1260. Warfare, 1279.

State-Building, 1281. Brazil, 265, 1421. Cuba, 1629. Dominican Republic, 949. Venezuela, 557.

State Violence. *See* Political Violence.

Statehood. Puerto Rico, 971.

Statistics. Cuba, 1348.

Steel Industry and Trade. Argentina, 1385.

Stirling, Matthew, 16.

Stone Implements. Argentina, 143, 147.

Stradelli, Ermanno, 267.

Strikes and Lockouts, 1446. Honduras, 1592. Puerto Rico, 1634.

Student Movements. Argentina, 1099. Chile, 1073. Mexico, 1539. Nicaragua, 921.

Students. Mexico, 1450, 1474. Political Participation, 921. Puerto Rico, 1634. Strikes and Lockouts, 1634.

Subsistence Economy. Haiti, 434.

Suchitepéquez, Guatemala (dept.). History, 64.

Sugar Industry and Trade. Cuba, 1359. Dominican Republic, 1623.

Suicide. Colombia, 1662.

Sustainable Agriculture. Guatemala, 502. Mexico, 524. Paraguay, 311.

Sustainable Development, 361, 371, 410, 1283. Amazon Basin, 391. Andean Region, 391. Argentina, 608, 618. Brazil, 762. Caribbean Area, 443, 456, 468. Chile, 608. Colombia, 1673. Costa Rica, 489. Dominican Republic, 444. Jamaica, 1343. Mexican-American Border Region, 1298. Mexico, 528, 542. Puerto Rico, 441. Uruguay, 1416.

Sutton, Constance R., 932.
Syncretism. Chile, 346.
Syndicalism. Bolivia, 1049. Chile, 1078.
Taino (indigenous group). Ethnic Identity, 1618. Puerto Rico, 1618.
Tamaulipas, Mexico (state). Excavations, 100.
Tapachula, Mexico (city). Migration, 1177.
Tarasco (indigenous group). *See* Purépecha (indigenous group).
Tax Reform. Mexican-American Border Region, 1307. Puerto Rico, 1338.
Taxation. Colombia, 1256. Mexican-American Border Region, 1307. Mexico, 1259. Puerto Rico, 1338.
Technological Development, 459. Argentina, 654. Mexico, 1290.
Technological Innovations, 1266, 1276. Argentina, 680. Mexico, 1325.
Technology. Mexico, 1297. Missions, 325.
Technology Transfer. Venezuela, 1374.
Teenagers. Mexico, 1479, 1509, 1522. Migration, 1522.
Tegucigalpa, Honduras (city). Natural Disasters, 509.
Telecommunication, 459.
Telegraph. Brazil, 263.
Television. Argentina, 1094. Ecuador, 1005. Elections, 1067.
Temer, Michel, 1117.
Templo Mayor (Mexico City), 38. Animal Remains, 70. Sacrifice, 70.
Tenochtitlán Site (Mexico). Artifacts, 74.
Teotihuacán Site (Mexico), 19. Agricultural Productivity, 96. Animals, 98. Excavations, 96. Remote Sensing, 43.
Territorio Indígena Parque Nacional Isiboro-Sécure (Bolivia), 345.
Terrorism, 1147, 1159. Guatemala, 1599. Peru, 1712.
Textiles and Textile Industry. Bolivia, 301. Women, 238.
Theologia Indorum, 112.
Tiahuanaco Site (Bolivia). *See* Tiwanaku Site (Bolivia).
Tierra del Fuego (region). Fish and Fishing, 156.
Tijuana, Mexico (city). Poor, 1480.
Tilly, Charles, 1457.
Tiwanaku Culture. Andean Region, 138.
Tiwanaku Site (Bolivia). Labor and Laboring Classes, 151.
Tlapanec (indigenous group). Political Participation, 219.
Toba (indigenous group). Artisanry, 305. COVID-19 (disease), 316. Employment, 305. Ethnic Identity, 305. Motherhood, 307. Rites and Ceremonies, 313. Shamanism, 335. Social Life and Customs, 335. Time, 313. Youth, 309.
Tobacco Use. Mesoamerica, 7. Rites and Ceremonies, 7.
Tohono O'odham (indigenous group). Autonomy, 225. Political Conditions, 225.
Toltecs (indigenous group). Artifacts, 46. Mortuary Customs, 45.
Toluca Valley (Mexico). Religious Life and Customs, 208.
Tombs. Belize, 77.
Tools. Mexico, 1290.
Totalitarianism. *See* Authoritarianism.
Totonac (indigenous group). Pictorial Works, 89.
Totonicapán, Guatemala (dept.). Community Development, 237. Indigenous Peoples, 237.
Tourism, 363, 366, 404, 410, 412, 418. Argentina, 620, 630, 665. Brazil, 788. Caribbean Area, 443, 465, 933, 944–945. Central America, 475. Chile, 685, 722. Cuba, 1636. Dominican Republic, 444. Ecuador, 1693. Electricity, 630. Environmental Degradation, 501. Gender Roles, 421. Guatemala, 501. Mexico, 218, 536. Nature, 645. Panama, 511–512. Patagonia (region), 679. People with Disabilities, 685. Peru, 587. Sustainable Development, 443, 465. Uruguay, 744, 750. *See Also* Ecotourism.
Towns. *See* Cities and Towns.
Trade. *See* Balance of Trade; Commerce.
Trade Policy, 1140–1141, 1204–1205. Ecuador, 1240. Mexico, 1164.
Trade Unions, 1446. Argentina, 1096, 1404. Brazil, 1118, 1429. Chile, 1078, 1651. Colombia, 1651. Ecuador, 1687. Honduras, 1552, 1592.
Traditional Farming. Argentina, 358. Mexico, 358, 548.
Traditional Medicine. Caribbean Area, 445. Colombia, 272. Guatemala, 1564. Peru, 285. *See Also* Medicine.
Trans-Pacific Partnership Agreement, 1140.
Transnational Corporations. *See* Multinational Corporations.
Transportation, 362, 418. Brazil, 759, 794, 1421. Chile, 682. Maps and Cartography, 715. Mexico, 1501. Urban Areas, 425.

Trash. *See* Refuse and Refuse Disposal.
Travel. *See* Description and Travel.
Travelers. Peru, 587.
Treaties, 1204. Central America, 1176. Costa Rica, 1181.
Trees. Argentina, 143. Chile, 706. Mexico, 533.
Trials. Guatemala, 884. Peru, 1705.
Trujillo, Peru (city). Crime and Criminals, 1699. Drug Traffic, 1699.
Trump, Donald, 1190.
Truth Commissions. El Salvador, 868, 878. Peru, 294.
Tsimane (indigenous group). *See* Chimane (indigenous group).
Tuan, Yi-fu, 790.
Tucano (indigenous group), 591.
Tucumán, Argentina (prov.). Epidemics, 623.
Tukano, Álvaro, 266.
Tukano (indigenous group). *See* Tucano (indigenous group).
Tula de Allende, Mexico (city). Political Conditions, 33. Precolumbian Civilizations, 33.
Tula Site (Mexico). Chronology, 60. Iconograpy, 60. Precolumbian Civilizations, 45. Shells and Shell Middens, 94.
Tulán-52 Site (Chile), 155.
Tulán-54 Site (Chile), 155.
Turquoise. Mexico, 74.
TV. *See* Television.
Uchuraccay, Peru (city). Terrorism, 1705.
UN. *See* United Nations.
Underdevelopment. Caribbean Area, 448. *See Also* Development.
Underwater Archeology. Caribbean Area, 131.
Unemployment. Mexico, 1296.
Unidad Popular, 1068.
Unidad Revolucionaria Nacional Guatemalteca, 894.
Unión de Naciones Suramericanas, 1242.
United Nations, 1199.
United Nations. Commission on the Truth, 868.
United Nations Conference on Human Settlements, 384.
United Nations. Security Council, 1192.
United States. Central Intelligence Agency, 1678.
United States. Foreign Service, 849.
United States-Peru Free Trade Agreement, 1244.

Universidad Autónoma de Puebla, 1539.
Universidad Nacional de Asunción. Facultad de Ciencias Agrarias, 738.
Universities. Bolivia, 1036. *See Also* Higher Education.
University of Puerto Rico (system), 1634.
University Reform. Costa Rica, 1579.
Urban Areas. Agriculture, 608. Argentina, 608, 621, 631, 652, 662, 670–671. Brazil, 759, 764, 775, 791. Chile, 608, 686, 693, 696, 704. Climate Change, 521. Costa Rica, 490, 493. Economic Conditions, 423. Economic Geography, 600. Historical Geography, 427. Mesoamerica, 88. Mexico, 1473. Population, 394. Research, 375. Satellites, 616, 653. Uruguay, 743. *See Also* Urban Renewal.
Urban Conditions, 371, 422. Bolivia, 596. Mexico, 528, 541.
Urban History. Uruguay, 727.
Urban Planning. *See* City Planning.
Urban Policy, 361, 384. Argentina, 611, 622. Chile, 686, 709, 724. Globalization, 600. Mexico, 388. Population, 394.
Urban Renewal. Argentina, 622, 680. Chile, 693. *See Also* Urban Areas.
Urban Sociology, 373. Bolivia, 592. Chile, 681, 691. Ecuador, 1685.
Urbanization, 361, 405, 423, 426–427. Argentina, 627–628, 633, 653, 671. Bolivia, 593. Chile, 689, 707. Colombia, 157, 1641. Costa Rica, 491. Ecuador, 1008. Mexico, 530, 547. Paraguay, 740. Research, 375.
Uruguay. Oficina de Planeamiento y Presupuesto, 1412.
U.S. Citizenship and Immigration Services, 1625.
US Influences. Mexico, 1162.
Vallenar, Chile (city). City Planning, 701. Earthquakes, 701.
Vallentin, Wilhelm, 780.
Valparaíso, Chile (city). Fire, 698.
Velasco Ibarra, José María, 1015.
Veracruz, Mexico (state). Archeology, 4. Sustainable Agriculture, 524.
Verbitsky, Horacio, 1104.
Vieques, Puerto Rico (island). Social Movements, 1619.
Violence, 406, 1448, 1689. Belize, 851. Brazil, 758. Caribbean Area, 935. Central America, 469, 1285, 1575, 1593. Costa Rica, 1600. Economic Conditions, 1273. Ecuador, 1688. El Salvador, 870–871, 873,

1586, 1591. Gangs, 1582. Guatemala, 882, 898, 900, 1594. Honduras, 907, 1591. Mexico, 810, 816, 821, 823, 826–827, 841, 843, 1264, 1448, 1466, 1469, 1484, 1491, 1498, 1507, 1523, 1528, 1548, 1575. Military, 844. Peru, 1280, 1713, 1724, 1730. Philosophy, 1575. Police, 1263. Political Participation, 869. Puerto Rico, 1617. Social Conditions, 1548. Squatter Settlements, 793. Taxation, 1256. Women, 1559, 1715, 1730. *See Also* Political Violence.
Virginity. *See* Sex and Sexual Relations.
Vista Hermosa Site (Tamaulipas, Mexico), 100.
Volcanoes. Ecuador, 571. Precolumbian Civilizations, 140.
Volunteers. Central America, 475. Tourism, 475.
Voting, 1255, 1286. Argentina, 614. Brazil, 1128. Colombia, 985. Costa Rica, 854, 859. Dominican Republic, 950, 956. Economic Conditions, 1250. Mexico, 835. *See Also* Elections.
Wages. Argentina, 1257, 1399. Chile, 1375. Mexico, 1330. Peru, 1696. Uruguay, 1257.
Waiwai (indigenous group). Collective Memory, 277. Social Life and Customs, 277.
Walcott, Derek, 1612.
Wambisa (indigenous group). *See* Huambisa (indigenous group).
Waorani (indigenous group). *See* Huao (indigenous group).
Wapishana (indigenous group), 276.
War of the Pacific, 1879–1884. Peru, 1245.
Warfare, 1226. Economic Conditions, 1279. Guatemala, 1599. Mesoamerica, 28. State-Building, 1279.
Wari (indigenous group). *See* Huari (indigenous group).
Water Conservation. Colombia, 559. Mexico, 523.
Water Distribution, 359. Colombia, 559. Mexico, 516, 551. *See Also* Water Resources Development.
Water Policy, 356.
Water Resources Development. Congresses, 387. Mexico, 517–518, 526–527. Peru, 588. Spain, 517. *See Also* Aqueducts; Water Distribution.
Water Rights. Bolivia, 556. Mexico, 517, 551. Peru, 556.
Water Supply, 356, 359, 389. Bolivia, 556.

Brazil, 776, 797. Caribbean Area, 468. Chile, 704. Colombia, 559. Guatemala, 64. Mexico, 516, 525, 527, 530, 532, 535. Peru, 556, 586, 588. Rural Conditions, 411.
Water Use. Mexico, 551.
Waterways. El Salvador, 497–498. Modern Art, 453.
Wayu (indigenous group). *See* Goajiro (indigenous group).
Weapons. Haiti, 1626.
Weaving. *See* Textiles and Textile Industry.
Welfare. *See* Social Welfare.
Welsh. Argentina, 675.
Wenner-Gren Foundation International Symposium, 381.
Wetlands. Argentina, 658. Belize, 483.
Wheat. Peru, 166.
Wichí (indigenous group). *See* Mataco (indigenous group).
Wildlife Refuges. *See* Parks and Reserves.
Wine and Wine Making. Argentina, 665. Demography, 414. Mexico, 552, 1311. Social Change, 414. Tourism, 665.
Wionczek, Miguel S., 1312.
Witchcraft. Central America, 30. Haiti, 1626. Mexico, 30.
Women. Agriculture, 242. Bolivia, 1041, 1735, 1740, 1743–1745. Businesspeople, 1503. Caribbean Area, 932, 940–941. Central America, 1593. Ceramics, 44. Chile, 350. Colombia, 996, 1664. Conservation (environment), 415. Costa Rica, 1590. COVID-19 (disease), 428. Crime and Criminals, 1590. Cuban Revolution (1959), 1607. Cultural Identity, 307. Drug Traffic, 1590. Economic Conditions, 385, 1136. Employment, 1467, 1730. Equality, 832, 1700. Geography, 432. Guatemala, 882, 1602. Homosexuality, 1525. Honduras, 1568. Household Employees, 1470. Human Geography, 407. Immigrants, 1518. Labor and Laboring Classes, 385. Land Tenure, 403. Medical Care, 291, 428. Mexico, 832, 1449, 1452, 1464, 1467, 1492, 1503, 1515–1516. Migration, 1571. Murder, 1715. Nicaragua, 1559, 1588. People with Disabilities, 1460. Peru, 1700, 1714–1715, 1730. Police, 1110, 1504. Political Participation, 354, 832, 986, 996, 1074, 1477, 1700, 1744–1745. Prostitution, 304. Public Health, 194. Puerto Rico, 1619. Revolutionaries, 1706. Sex

and Sexual Relations, 1508. Social Conditions, 1516. Social Policy, 1541. Teachers, 1606. Textiles and Textile Industry, 258. Tourism, 421. Uruguay, 757. Venezuela, 1668. Violence, 403, 415, 882, 1452, 1571, 1587–1588, 1654, 1734.

Women's Rights, 404, 1580. Caribbean Area, 1630. Venezuela, 1668.

Working Class. *See* Labor and Laboring Classes.

World Cup (soccer), *Brazil, 2014*, 1422.

World Trade Organization, 1141.

Xavante (indigenous peoples). Brazil, 259.

Xcalumkín Site (Mexico), 40.

Yawanawá, Biraci, 270.

Yaxchilán Site (Mexico), 53.

Youth. Argentina, 1099. Central America, 1597. Chile, 1069. Colombia, 1653. Costa Rica, 1579, 1596. Guatemala, 1576. Mexico, 1723. Migration, 1550, 1597. Peru, 1713, 1723. Political Participation, 1069, 1099. Protests, 1579. Quality of Life, 1600. Rural Conditions, 1653. Urban Areas, 256, 1601. Violence, 1594, 1600.

Yucatán, Mexico (state). Anthropology, 202. Caves, 213. Ethnology, 202. Fisheries, 1291. Medical Care, 187. Small Business, 1291.

Yucatán Peninsula. Caves, 198. Housing, 243.

Yucuna (indigenous group). Myths and Mythology, 280.

Yuqui (indigenous group). Mortuary Customs, 319.

Yura (indigenous group). *See* Yuracare (indigenous group).

Yuracare (indigenous group). Language and Languages, 317.

Zacapú, Mexico (city). Artifacts, 48.

Zapatistas. *See* Ejército Zapatista de Liberación Nacional (Mexico).

Zapotec (indigenous group). Religious Life and Customs, 69.

Zooarcheology. *See* Animal Remains.

AUTHOR INDEX

A contracorriente: agua y conflicto en América Latina, 356.
A 10 años de la gran recesión: desastres y desarrollo, 1287.
Abadí, Anabella, 1363.
Abarca, Cristóbal, 716.
Abbott, Erin, 765.
Abbott, Jared A., 1666.
Abeledo, Sebastián, 299.
Abello Colak, Alexandra, 1528.
Aboy Domingo, Nelson, 1604.
Abrams, Jesse, 598.
Abufhele, Valentina, 681.
Aburto Espinobarro, Sabás, 823.
Acevedo Granados, Napoleón, 1552.
Acevedo Rodrigo, Ariadna, 183.
Aceves López, Liza Elena, 1034.
Achim, Miruna, 62.
Ackerman, John M., 804.
Acosta, Benjamin, 863.
Acosta Ochoa, Guillermo, 43.
Actores y temas de las relaciones de México y sus fronteras, 1162.
Acuña, Rodrigo, 1374.
Acuña Villavicencio, John Kenny, 1447.
Adamo, Susana B., 412.
Adams, Abigail E., 475.
Adams, Emily C., 483.
Adelante con la Diversidad Sexual (project), 1731.
The adorned body: mapping ancient Maya dress, 1.
Afro-Asian connections in Latin America and the Caribbean, 1433.
Afrodescendencia en Puerto Rico, 1613.
Afrodescendencias: voces en resistencia: en homenaje al centenario de Nelson Mandela, 1434.
Agostinis, Giovanni, 1138.
Agrarian extractivism in Latin America, 357.
Agricultura familiar tradicional: experiencias rurales en México y Argentina, 358.

Agriculture et reconstruction: défis, enjeux et perspectives de l'agriculture haïtienne, 434.
Agua, el futuro ineludible, 516.
El agua para la agricultura de las Américas, 359.
Agua y ecología política en España y México, 517.
Aguayo, Sergio, 1523.
Aguiar Aranguren, Asdrúbal, 1021.
Aguiar Paz, Mirna Rubi, 545.
Aguilar, Diego, 622.
Aguilar Aguilar, Gustavo, 529.
Aguilar Arce, Marianela, 1553.
Aguilar Camín, Héctor, 845.
Aguilar García, Javier, 817, 1529.
Aguilar-González, Bernardo, 473, 480–481.
Aguilar-Robledo, Miguel, 534.
Aguilera Almanza, José, 79.
Aguilera Gómez, Manuel, 1288.
Aguirre, Pedro, 845.
Aguirre, Pilar de, 1378.
Aguirre Mendoza, Imelda, 176.
Aguirre Molina, Alejandra, 70.
Aguirre Salas, Andrea, 1676.
Ahlman, Todd M., 125.
Ainstein, Luis, 361.
Ajustados: de la revolución de la alegría al crecimiento invisible, 1384.
Akers, Pete D., 482.
Akram, Hassan, 1057.
Alarco, Germán, 1696.
Alarcón Deza, Benigno, 1026.
El ALBA-TCP: origen y fruto del nuevo regionalismo latinoamericano y caribeño, 1203.
Alcántara Sáez, Manuel, 1151.
Alcázar Chávez, Luis Fernando, 1224–1225.
Aldrich, Stephen, 795.
Aldunate, Carlos, 346.
Alejandro Vázquez, Héctor, 1307.
Alexander, Rani T., 32.
Alfaro-Sánchez, Marvin, 493.

Alfayate, Emmanuel, 641.
Alfonso Bernal, Nohora Elisabeth, 366.
Alfonso Roa, Óscar Alfredo, 1641.
La Alianza del Pacífico: nuevos retos e implicaciones para Latinoamérica, 1139.
¿Alianzas contra natura o antihegemónicas?: las alianzas PAN-PRD en los estados mexicanos, 800.
Aliste A., Enrique, 710.
Allard, Raúl, 1227.
Allen, Reuben, 1605.
Allende Karam, Isabel, 1350.
Alleyne, Trevor Serge Coleridge, 1345.
Almada, Carlos, 1163.
Almandoz Marte, Arturo, 427.
Almanza Caudillo, Colette, 23.
Almeida, Alfredo Wagner Berno de, 409.
Almeida, Patricia Polo, 569.
Almirón, Victoria S., 300.
Alonso Fradejas, Alberto, 357.
Alonso Gallo, Laura, 1622.
Altamirano, Melina, 1247.
Altamirano Rayo, Giorleny D., 901.
Alternativas y Capacidades, A.C., 194.
Altos Hornos Zapla: historias en torno al primer centro siderúrgico integral de Argentina, 1385.
Alvarado Alcázar, Alejandro, 853.
Alvarado Mendoza, Arturo, 1532.
Alvarado Salas, Nadia, 238.
Álvarez, Luis, 722.
Álvarez, Roberto, 1375.
Álvarez, Sandra, 1731.
Alvarez, Sebastian, 1289.
Álvarez Alonso, José, 583.
Álvarez Aragón, Virgilio, 880.
Álvarez Huwiler, Laura, 399.
Álvarez-Mingote, Cristina, 801.
Álvarez Palma, Ilse Angélica, 362.
Álvarez Rivadulla, María José, 741–742.
Álvarez Scanniello, Jorge E., 1412.
Álvarez Velasco, Soledad, 360, 386, 406.
Alverio Ramos, Zulmarie, 1606.
Alves, Jorge Antonio, 1105.
Amador Fournier, María Amalia, 855.
Amat, Francesc, 1106.
Ambrose, Kristal K., 435.
América Latina en movimiento: migraciones, límites a la movilidad y sus desbordamientos, 1435.
América Latina y Chile en el mundo global: algunas tendencias en el siglo XXI, 1227.
Amescua Chávez, Cristina, 1540.
Amézquita, Gloria, 1203.
Amo Rodríguez, Silvia del, 543.
Análisis de las territorialidades en México y Bolivia desde la etnografía, la historia y los imaginarios sociales, 177.
Análisis de políticas públicas en Colombia: enfoques y estudios de caso, 983.
Anaya, Alejandro, 1498.
Ancona Aragón, Iliana, 105.
Anderson, Eric R., 483.
Anderson, Leslie E., 1086.
Anderson, Tim, 998.
Andersson, Krister P., 886.
Andia Fagalde, Elizabeth, 1732.
Andrade, Ariana, 641.
Andrade, Laura, 864.
Andrade Rubio, Karla Lorena, 1580.
Ángeles Contreras, Isaac, 178.
Angotti, Thomas, 423.
Antczak, Andrzej T., 116.
Antczak, María Magdalena, 116.
Anthropomorphic imagery in the Mesoamerican highlands: gods, ancestors, and human beings, 34.
Anti-drug policies in Colombia: successes, failures, and wrong turns, 984.
Antillón, Camilo, 908.
Antología de la democracia ecuatoriana: 1979–2020, 999.
Antología del pensamiento crítico dominicano contemporáneo, 949.
Antología del pensamiento crítico ecuatoriano contemporáneo, 1000.
Antología del pensamiento crítico hondureño contemporáneo, 1554.
Antología del pensamiento crítico nicaragüense contemporáneo, 908.
Antología del pensamiento crítico peruano contemporáneo, 1697.
Antología del pensamiento crítico salvadoreño contemporáneo, 1555.
Antropolocales: estudios de antropología en Jujuy, 340.
Antropología de la violencia, 1448.
Antropología visual y epistemes de la imagen, 179.
Antunes, Aghane, 795.
Anuario Estadístico de Cuba, 1348.
Apaico Flores, Aníbal, 160.
Aparicio, Miguel, 261.
Aponte García, Maribel, 1203, 1350.

Aponte Motta, Jorge M., 1237.
Aprendizaje para el mercado global: moldes y troqueles en el centro de México, 1290.
Aprile Gniset, Jacques, 157.
Aproximación a la comprensión de las comunidades indígenas y rurales desde una perspectiva multidisciplinaria, 180.
Aproximaciones al pensamiento crítico: reflexiones epistemológicas sobre la realidad social boliviana, 1733.
Aragón Andrade, Orlando, 181.
Aragonés, Ana María, 1320.
Arana Cardó, Martín, 584.
Arancibia Clavel, Patricia, 1065.
Arancio, Mariel, 669.
Araque Jaramillo, Wilson, 1009.
Araucanía-Norpatagonia, 1213–1214.
Araujo, Rafael Pinheiro, 1029.
Arboit, Mariela Edith, 608.
Arboleda, Martín, 682.
Archaeology and identity on the Pacific Coast and southern highlands of Mesoamerica, 2.
The archaeology, ethnohistory, and environment of the Marismas Nacionales: the prehistoric Pacific littoral of Sinaloa and Nayarit, Mexico, 35.
Archaeology in Dominica: everyday ecologies and economies at Morne Patate, 117.
Archaeology of domestic landscapes of the enslaved in the Caribbean, 118.
Arcila Rojas, Adriana Patricia, 1649.
Ardren, Traci, 11, 51.
Arévalo Jaramillo, María Inés, 1001.
Argentina y Brasil: industrialización, contexto internacional y relaciones bilaterales (1940-2010), 1215.
Arias, Arturo, 1556.
Arias, Patricia, 1520.
Arias Arana, Itxaso, 1734.
Arias Castro, Tomás Federico, 1557.
Arias López, María Isabel, 1443.
Arias Peñate, Salvador, 1332.
Ariel de Vidas, Anath, 182.
Ariel Ortega, Fernando, 362.
Arieta Baizabal, Virginia, 36.
Arima, Eugenio, 795.
Arjona, Ana, 1640.
Armijos, Maria Teresa, 571.
Armijos Velasco, Bolívar, 1002.
Arnauld, Marie-Charlotte, 17.
Aroca, María Paula, 996.

Arqueología computacional: nuevos enfoques para la documentación, análisis y difusión del patrimonio cultural, 3.
Arqueología de la Costa del Golfo: dinámicas de la interacción política, económica e ideológica, 4.
Arqueología de la producción, 37.
Arqueología en Cerro Verde, 161.
Arques, Facundo, 1088.
Arrate, Jorge, 1058.
Arrieta, Mario Alberto, 148.
Arriola V., Luis A., 1172.
Arroyo, Bárbara, 61.
Arroyo Alejandre, Jesús, 516.
Arrúa, Rosa Degen de, 734.
Arrueta, Marisel, 340.
Artero, Chloé Nicolas, 605.
Artiga González, Álvaro, 1558.
Artigas S.C., Diego, 154.
Arts, Bas, 562.
Arvelo Sánchez, Miguel Ángel, 377.
Arzaluz Solano, Socorro, 1548.
Arzeno, Mariana, 412.
Asakura Sato, Hiroko, 1571.
Asamblea Permanente de los Derechos Humanos de Bolivia, 1035.
Ascencio Martínez, Mayra Angélica, 1538.
Asociación Iberoamericana de Historia Urbana, 427.
Asociación para el Desarrollo Económico y Social de El Salvador, 1332.
Asociación Uruguaya de Ciencia Política, 1099.
Aspectos estratégicos de la gestión pública para el crecimiento sostenible de las ciudades, 361.
Assessing the left turn in Ecuador, 1677.
Astudillo Pizarro, Francisco, 683.
Asún, Rodrigo, 723.
Atiles-Osoria, José M., 965.
Atlas de geografía humana de la cuenca del río Luján, 609.
Atuesta, Laura H., 844.
Auer, Alejandra, 610.
Automotores y transporte público: un acercamiento desde los estudios históricos, 362.
Avalos Aguilar, Spencer Radames, 544.
Ávalos Burgos, Carolina, 1569.
Aveledo, Ramón Guillermo, 1022.
Avendaño López, Jenny Lisseth, 1656.
Ávila, Ángela, 1509.

Ávila, Claudia, 739.
Ávila, Felipe, 359.
Ávila García, Virginia, 1449.
Ávila Ortíz, María Natividad, 1450.
Avritzer, Leonardo, 1107.
Awe, Jaime J., 56, 77, 101, 482.
Ayala Osorio, Germán, 1673.
Azeez, Govand Khalid, 347.
Azpuru, Dinorah, 881.
Baca Tavira, Norma, 1501.
Bacha, Edmar Lisboa, 1419.
Badia-Miró, Marc, 1417.
Badillo, Alex E., 68.
Badri-Maharaj, Sanjay, 1182.
Báez Cubero, María de Lourdes, 244.
Báez-Jorge, Félix, 89.
Bahar, Dany, 1023.
Baigún, Claudio Rafael Mariano, 618.
Baldraia, Fernando, 372.
Baldwin, Kate, 828.
Balestieri, Jose Antonio Perrella, 782.
Ball, Joseph W., 102.
Ballvé, Teo, 469.
Bandeira, Moniz, 1210.
Baracco, Luciano, 206.
Barada, Julieta, 611.
Barba, Luis, 43.
Barberia, Lorena, 765.
Barbosa Jr., Ricardo, 758.
Barboza, Tatiana S., 300.
Bárcena Juárez, Sergio, 838.
Barclay, Jenni, 571.
Bardolph, Dana N., 132.
Bargsted, Matías, 1080.
Barra Ruatta, Abelardo, 1725.
Barrantes, Gustavo, 486.
Barreiro Santana, Rusia Katalina, 1019.
Barrera, Saira, 1570.
Barrera de la Torre, Gerónimo, 416.
Barrera Rivera, José Álvaro, 38.
Barría Meneses, Jessica Aracelí, 684.
Barrientos Guzmán, Teresa, 685.
Barrientos Salinas, J. Alejandro, 301.
Barriga, Tomás Carlos, 1698.
Barrios, Edy, 76.
Barrios, Miguel Ángel, 1143.
Barrón Cruz, Martín Gabriel, 842.
Barros, Flavia Moraes Lins de, 788.
Barros, Magdalena, 1500.
Bartlett, Edmund, 945.
Barzola Elizagaray, Pehuén, 627.
Bas Vilizzio, Magdalena, 1204.
Basabe Ramírez, Claudio, 312.

Bascomb, Lia T., 446.
Bascopé, Grace, 51.
Bassie-Sweet, Karen, 5.
Bastías, Luis Eduardo, 686.
Bastida, Francisco, 903.
Bastos, Santiago, 228.
Basurto, Xavier, 1291.
Bateson, Ian, 1559.
Batista, Mariana, 1133.
Batts, David, 957.
Baumann, Matthias, 660.
Bautista, Stefanie, 162.
Bautista Arreola, Iulisca Zircey, 802.
Bautista Martínez, Eduardo, 1514.
Baxendale, Claudia A., 612.
Bayard de Volo, Lorraine, 1607.
Bayón, María Cristina, 1303.
Bayón Jiménez, Manuel, 567, 572.
Beauclair, Nicolas, 336.
Beaule, Christine D., 10.
Bebbington, Anthony, 470, 865.
Becerra, Caren, 671.
Becerra, Charlie, 1699.
Becerra Baeza, César, 687.
Beck, Erin, 882.
Becker, Ignacio, 716.
Becker, Marc, 1678.
Becker, Marshall Joseph, 39.
Beckles, Hilary, 926.
Becquelin, Pierre, 40.
Beekman, Christopher, 34.
Beiras del Carril, Victoria, 302.
Beker, Víctor A., 1406.
Beliaev, Dmitri, 41.
Bell, Martha, 602.
Bello M., Álvaro, 710.
Beltrán, Boris, 50.
Beltrán Retis, Salvador Arturo, 518.
Benavides Rincón, Guillermina, 1451.
Benemérita Universidad Autonóma de Puebla. Instituto de Ciencias de Gobierno y Desarrollo Estratégico, 800.
Benessaiah, Karina, 473, 480–481.
Benítez López, Jazmín, 1176.
Benito Sánchez, Ana Belén, 950, 956.
Benjumea Herrera, Carolina Andrea, 1649.
Bennett, Abigail, 1291.
Benseny, Graciela, 620.
Beramendi, Pablo, 1106.
Bérard, Benoît, 119.
Berenguer, José, 346.
Berens, Sarah, 1248.

Beretta, Diego, 1099.
Bergamini, Kay, 714.
Berger, William, 254.
Bergesio, Liliana, 1385.
Bergman, Marcelo, 1249.
Berlanga Gayón, Mariana, 1452.
Bermúdez, Damián, 1212.
Bermúdez-Rojas, Tania, 493.
Bermúdez Valdivia, Violeta, 1700.
Bernabé-Poveda, Miguel Ángel, 604.
Bernal, Richard L., 927.
Bernal Vélez, Alejandro, 158.
Berón, Mónica A., 147.
Bértola, Luis, 1412.
Bertot Triana, Harold, 974.
Betances, Emelio, 951.
Betancourt Santiago, Milson, 370.
Bevacqua, Michael Lujan, 449.
Bevan, Andrew, 110, 484.
Beyond alterity: destabilizing the Indigenous other in Mexico, 183.
Biegon, Rubrick, 1140, 1183.
Bienestar subjetivo en México, 1453.
Bigler, Gene E., 925.
Bijman, Jos, 752.
Bikoulis, Peter, 162.
Billman, Brian R., 163.
Biocca, Mercedes, 330.
Birkenmaier, Anke, 930.
Bíró, Peter, 42.
Bishop, Ronald, 107.
Bissio, Beatriz, 1145.
Bittencourt, Libertad Borges, 245.
Bittencourt, Tainá A., 759.
Blanc, Jacob, 726, 760.
Blancas, Jorge, 43.
Blomster, Jeffrey P., 6.
Blume, Laura Ross, 471.
Blume, Luiz Henrique dos Santos, 408.
Boas, Taylor C., 1250.
Bobes, Velia Cecilia, 1513.
Bocci, Paolo, 568.
Bocco, Gerardo, 382, 424.
Bogotá en la encrucijada del desorden: estructuras socioespaciales y gobernabilidad metropolitana, 1641.
Bohoslavsky, Juan Pablo, 1377.
Boidi, Fernanda, 911.
Bojkowska, Dorota, 107.
Bojórquez Zapata, Martha Isabel, 1302.
Bojsen, Heidi, 436.
Bolaños Davis, Alejandro, 1560.
Bolaños Trochez, Francy Viviana, 559.

Bold, Rosalyn, 342.
Bonelli, Cristóbal, 356.
Bonelli, Regis, 1419.
Bonetto, María Susana, 1737.
Boni Noguez, Andrew, 420.
Bonifacio, Valentina, 303.
Bonilla-Hidalgo, Maureen A., 494.
Bonilla-Soto, Sebastián, 493.
Bonnet, Alberto, 1398.
Bonta, Mark, 506.
Bonvecchi, Alejandro, 1251.
Boos, Tobias, 1087.
Borden Eng, Rubén, 233.
Borejsza, Aleksander, 26.
Borges, Fabián A., 1252.
Borgh, Chris van der, 866–867.
Borja, Karina, 1682.
Borland, Katherine, 475.
Bórquez Bustos, Rodolfo, 1454.
Borrás Ramos, Victor, 743.
Bosch Carcuro, Matías, 949.
Boschmann, E. Eric, 727.
Bosisio, Andrea C., 613.
Bosque Sendra, Joaquín, 614.
Botero, Felipe, 993.
Boulding, Carew E., 1253.
Bourdin, Gabriel, 184.
Bourne, Compton, 938.
Bown, Chad P., 1184.
Boyd, Brian, 172.
Bracamonte, Leonardo, 1025.
Branca, Domenico, 355.
Brandão, Frederico, 761.
Brandão Jr., Amintas, 792.
Brannum, Kate, 883.
Bratman, Eve Z., 762.
Bravo Ahuja, Marcela, 835.
Bravo Velásquez, Elizabeth, 570.
The Brazilian economy today: towards a new socio-economic model?, 1418.
Breath and smoke: tobacco use among the Maya, 7.
Brenta, Noemí, 1386.
Briceño-León, Roberto, 1667.
Briceño Rosario, Jesús, 163.
Brida, Juan Gabriel, 744–745.
Bril-Mascarenhas, Tomás, 1059.
Bringas Nostti, Raúl, 1472.
Bringel, Breno M., 1444.
Brisbois, Ben W., 569.
Brizzio, Jacquelina, 1205.
Broad, Robin, 497.
Brock, Fiona, 130.

Brockmann Quiroga, Erika, 1055.
Brook, George A., 482.
Brown, Michael F., 282.
Browne, Kevin Adonis, 1608.
Brownstein, Korey J., 105.
Bruckmann, Mónica, 1145.
Brunetto, María José, 1141.
Bryan, Joe, 409, 510.
Buben, Radek, 909.
Buckland, Sarah, 437.
Budar, Lourdes, 4.
Buendía Hegewisch, José, 803.
Bueno, Carmen, 1290.
Bueno, Natalia S., 1108–1109.
Buitrago Bermúdez, Oscar, 559.
Bull, Benedicte, 1364.
Bunkley-Williams, Lucy, 467.
Burbano González, David, 550.
Burckhalter, David, 44.
Burger, Richard L., 164.
Burgos Bolaños, Santiago, 560.
Burke, Monica Galloway, 933.
Burt, Jo-Marie, 884.
Burton, Gerardo, 1387.
The business of leisure: tourism history in Latin America and the Caribbean, 363.
Bustamante, Ana Goulart, 787.
Bustamante, Michael J., 979.
Bustos, Carlos, 1228.
Bustos, Gonzalo, 1206.
Bustos, Sebastián, 1023.
Bustos Gallardo, Beatriz, 688.
Bustos López, Martha C., 561.
Butler, Megan, 501.
Butsic, Van, 660.
Buzai, Gustavo D., 609, 614–616, 649, 694.
Byrd, Brandon R., 1609.
Byron, Jessica, 929.
Cabatingan, Lee, 928.
Cabral, Diogo de Carvalho, 764, 787.
Cabral, Lídia, 763.
Cabrapan Duarte, Melisa, 1438.
Cabrera, César Humberto, 580.
Cadenas de valor en el sistema agroalimentario de Chiapas: necesidades, retos y perspectivas, 519.
Cadichon, Jeff Matherson, 438.
Caffentzis, Constantine George, 1547.
Caficultura: panorama actual en América Latina, 364.
Caicedo-Fernández, Alhena, 272.
Calandra, Benedetta, 1185.
Caldera Ortiz, Luis, 439.

Calderón-Maya, Juan Roberto, 542.
Calderón Morillón, Óscar, 1486.
Calderón Villarreal, Cuauhtémoc, 1164.
Calidad de vida en la Zona Metropolitana del Valle de México: hacia la justicia socioespacial, 520.
Caliri, Martina Noel, 658.
Callaghan, Michael G., 66.
Calvario Parra, José Eduardo, 1455.
Calveiro, Pilar, 185.
Calvillo Unna, Tomás, 1168.
Camacho Ibarra, Fidel, 186.
Cambio climático, ciudad y gestión ambiental: los ámbitos nacional e internacional, 521.
Cambio de rumbo: desafíos económicos y sociales de México hoy, 1292.
El cambio democrático en México: retos y posibilidades de la "Cuarta Transformación", 804.
Camp, Roderic Ai, 805–806.
Campbell, Donovan, 437.
Campello, Daniela, 1254, 1286.
Campoalegre Septien, Rosa, 1434.
Campos, Arminda Eugenia Marques, 782.
Campos, Claudia M., 617.
Campos Cuevas, Arturo, 362.
Cánceres en mujeres mayas de Yucatán: pobreza, género y comunicación social, 187.
Canelo, Paula, 1101.
Canese, Mercedes, 728.
Canese, Ricardo, 728.
Canet B., Guillermo, 364.
Cangiano, Fernando, 1216.
Cannizzo, Mariana, 617.
Cannonier, Colin, 933.
Cano, Gabriela, 1532.
Cano Castellanos, Ingreet Juliet, 522.
Canova, Paola, 304, 330.
Cansino Ortiz, César, 807.
Cantoral Cantoral, Guadalupe, 1456.
Cantú, Francisco, 808.
Cárabe, Ana María, 1517.
Carballo, Willian, 1561.
Carden, Megan E., 50.
Carden, Natalia, 141.
Cardenal, Rodolfo, 1562.
Cárdenas, Roosbelinda, 1642.
Cárdenas Arroyo, Felipe, 158.
Cárdenas del Castillo, Eric Luis, 1036.
Cárdenas-Jirón, Luz-Alicia, 689.
Cárdenas Plaza, Cleverth C., 1735.
Cardini, Laura Ana, 305.

Cardona Vélez, Cecilia, 1649.
Cardozo Uzcátegui, Alejandro, 1030.
Carena, María Laura, 669.
Caretta, Martina Angela, 432.
Caretti, Florencia, 641.
Carey, Mark, 581.
Caribbean integration: uncertainty in a time of global fragmentation, 929.
Caribbean migrations: the legacies of colonialism, 930.
Caribbean Quarterly, 931.
Carlin, Ryan E., 1255.
Carneiro Filho, Arnaldo, 792.
Carnoy, Martin, 1190.
Carosio, Alba, 1025, 1436.
Carpes, Mariana, 1233.
Carr, Barry, 975.
Carrasco, Claudio, 703.
Carrasco, Michael, 13.
Carrera Quezada, Sergio Eduardo, 195.
Carreras, Miguel, 985.
Carrillo Rojas, Arturo, 529.
Carrillo Viveros, Jorge, 1301, 1325.
Carrión, Fernando, 1158.
Carrión Mena, Francisco, 1238.
Carrión Sánchez, Claudia P., 246.
Carrizosa, María, 384.
Carter, Eric D., 365, 602.
Carter, Nicholas, 1.
Carty, Emily, 1262.
Caruso, German Daniel, 472.
Carvajal, Leonardo, 1365.
Carvalho, Camila, 764.
Carvalho, José Carlos, 1419.
Carvalho, Thaís de, 283.
Carve, Virginia, 745.
Casanova, Roberto, 1024.
Casanova, Rosario, 746.
Casar, María Amparo, 809.
Casseus, Clara Rachel Eybalin, 1610.
Castañeda, Ernesto, 1457.
Castañeda, Heide, 217.
Castellanos Cereceda, Roberto, 1453.
Castellucci Junior, Wellington, 408.
Castillo, César, 1696.
Castillo, Mayarí, 690.
Castillo, Trilce Irupé, 618.
Castillo Bernal, Stephen, 45–46.
Castillo Castañeda, Alberto, 1149.
Castillo Fernández, Dídimo, 1570.
Castillo Nechar, Marcelino, 366.
Castillo Vargas, Elizabeth, 1643.
Castor, N. Fadeke, 1611.

Castro, Fidel, 1186.
Castro, Hortensia, 412.
Castro, J. Justin, 1293.
Castro, Loida Mariela, 1555.
Castro, Marcia C., 765.
Castro, Silvina, 143.
Castro, Soraya, 1190.
Castro Carpio, Augusto, 1701.
Castro-Chacón, José Pablo, 491.
Castro Jo, Carlos, 910.
Castro Neira, Yerko, 188, 1448.
Castro R., Victoria, 346.
Castro Tobón, Juan Andrés, 460.
Cateau, Heather, 1639.
Catella, Luciana, 142.
Cavalcante, Tiago Vieira, 790.
Cavanagh, John, 497.
Cavarozzi, Marcelo, 1376.
Cavero Palomino, Yuri I., 167.
Cebrián Abellán, Francisco, 597.
Cecil, Leslie G., 47.
Centeno, Miguel Angel, 1281.
Central Journal, 966.
Centre d'études mexicaines et centraméricaines (Mexico City), 48, 100.
Centro de Artes Visuales (Asunción), 329.
Centro de Investigación y Asistencia en Tecnología y Diseño del Estado de Jalisco, 519.
Centro de Investigación y Promoción del Campesinado (Bolivia), 592.
Centro de Investigaciones Regionales "Dr. Hideyo Noguchi." Unidad de Ciencias Sociales, 545.
Centro de Investigaciones y Estudios Superiores en Antropología Social (Mexico), 194, 1571.
Centro Internacional de Estudios Superiores de Periodismo para América Latina, 1017.
Centro Latinoamericano de Administración para el Desarrollo, 361.
Centro Peninsular en Humanidades y Ciencias Sociales, 545.
Cepaluni, Gabriel, 1115.
Cepek, Michael L., 284.
Cerda, Nicolás de la, 1060.
Cereceda, Verónica, 343.
Ceriani Cernadas, Pablo, 1505.
Cermelo, Leonardo, 664.
Ceroni, Mauricio, 747.
Cerros Rodríguez, Elisa, 1494.
Céspedes, Gloria, 734.
Cetto, Ana María, 1142.

Ch, Rafael, 1256.
Chacama, Juan, 138.
Chacón Málaga, Hugo, 1702.
Chalá Cruz, José Franklin, 1679.
Chalas, Nairoby, 1638.
Chan Nieto, Evelyn M., 82.
Changing continuities and the scholar-activist anthropology of Constance R. Sutton, 932.
Chaparro González, Nina, 986.
Chaparro Rodríguez, Juan Carlos, 1644.
Charles, Amlin, 1187.
Charles Tilly: sobre violencia colectiva, política contenciosa y cambio social: antología selecta, 1457.
Chase, Arlen Frank, 17, 64.
Chase, Diane Z., 17, 64.
Chati Quispe, Guido, 1703.
Chavarín Rodríguez, Rubén A., 1322.
Chaves Castaño, Juana, 564.
Chávez, Patricia, 1038.
Chávez Balderas, Ximena, 70.
Chávez Quispe, Juan Carlos, 1717.
Chavismo: Genealogía de una Pasión Política, *Caracas, 2016*, 1025.
Chelminski, Vladimir, 1363.
Cheng, Hai, 482.
Cherkinksy, Alex, 482.
Cherrington, Emil A., 483.
Chiappe, Marta, 598.
Chibana, Megumi, 449.
Chicha y limonada: las clases medias en Bolivia, 1736.
Childers, Daniel L., 496.
China y México en la órbita del mercado mundial del siglo XXI, 1164.
Chirif, Alberto, 582–583.
Chomsky, Aviva, 975, 1563.
Christakis, Nicholas A., 508.
Cielo, Cristina, 1695.
50 años de historia de la OPP, 1412.
Cisneros, Héctor, 658.
Cisneros, José Luis, 842.
La ciudad perdida: raíces de los soberanos tarascos, 48.
Ciudadanías emergentes y transiciones en América Latina, 1645.
Ciudades en diálogo entre lo local y lo transnacional/global: intersecciones entre el patrimonio, el turismo, las alteridades migrantes y el hábitat popular, 367.
Clark, John E., 49.

Clarke, Mary E., 50.
Clay, Elizabeth C., 118.
Clouser, Rebecca, 499.
Club Político Argentino, 1093.
Co-operativism and local development in Cuba: an agenda for democratic social change, 1349.
Coaguila, Jorge, 1716.
Coates, Robert, 368.
Cobham-Sander, Rhonda, 1612.
Cocilovo, José A., 137.
Codebò, Agnese, 619.
Coelho, Ruy Galvão de Andrade, 189.
Cohen, Carolina, 620.
Cohen, Marc J., 434.
Cohen, Michael A., 384.
Cohn, Sergio, 257, 266, 270.
Colectivo Copal, 1659.
Colectivo de Estudios Poscoloniales/Decoloniales en/de América Latina (Universidad Nacional de Colombia), 1659.
Colectivo de Geografía Crítica del Ecuador, 572.
Colectivo Letras del Desierto, 552.
Colegio de la Frontera Norte (Tijuana, Mexico), 1146.
Coles, Benjamin, 782.
Coll, Luis Vicente, 641.
Collier, Ruth Berins, 1275.
Colloredo-Mansfeld, Rudi, 351.
Colombia en la Encrucijada. El Proyecto LAMP Colombia Sobre Migración, *Bogotá, 2015*, 1646.
Coloquio Internacional Patrimonios Alimentarios: Consensos y Tensiones, *UNAM, 2015*, 369.
Coltman, Jeremy D., 30.
La columna vertebral fracturada: revisitando intermediarios políticos en Chile, 1061.
Combarnous, François, 1430.
Combatting corruption in Guatemala: evaluating state capacity to reduce corruption and improve accountability, 885.
Comisión de Derechos Humanos de El Salvador, 868.
Company Company, Concepción, 1467.
Complejidad de la arqueología y el turismo cultural: territorios, sostenibilidad y patrimonio, 337.
Complicidad económica con la dictadura chilena: un país desigual a la fuerza, 1377.
Conaghan, Catherine M., 1003.

Conflicto armado y transición hacia el posconflicto: una aproximación desde el Caribe, 987.
Conflictos territoriales y territorialidades en disputa: re-existencias y horizontes societales frente al capital en América Latina, 370.
Congreso de Afrodecendencia en Puerto Rico, *1st, San Juan, 2015*, 1613.
Congreso Iberoamericano de Historia Urbana, *1st, Santiago, Chile, 2017*, 427.
Congreso Internacional sobre Sustentabilidad en los Hábitats, *1st, Guadalajara, Mexico, 2016*, 371.
Congreso Latinoamericano de Ciencia Política, *9th, Montevideo, 2017*, 1099.
Congreso Nacional de Arqueología Chilena, *19th, Arica, Chile, 2012*, 138.
Congreso Nacional de Ciencia Política (Argentina), *13th, Buenos Aires, 2017*, 1099.
Conniff, Michael L., 925.
Consejo Mexicano de Ciencias Sociales, 1325.
La consolidación de una transición democrática: el desafío venezolano, 1026.
Contaminación por mercurio en Bogotá y su conurbano, 561.
Contel, Fabio Betioli, 766.
Contemporary issues within Caribbean economies, 933.
Contreras Molotla, Felipe, 1294.
Contreras Orozco, Javier H., 1458.
Contreras Pérez, Gabriela, 541.
Contreras Romero, Carlos, 1174.
Convivial constellations in Latin America: from colonial to contemporary times, 372.
Conze, Carolina, 1547.
Cook, Nathan J., 886.
Cooperación internacional en Haití: tensiones y lecciones: los casos de Brasil, Chile y México, 1187.
Cooperación Sur-Sur, política exterior y modelos de desarrollo en América Latina, 1207.
Corbridge, Stuart, 1346.
Cordera, Rolando, 1287.
Cordero Cordero, Stephanie, 854.
Cordero Díaz, Blanca Laura, 1435.
Cordero F., Rosario, 154.
Cordero Ponce, Sofía, 1037.
Córdoba, Diana, 598.
Córdoba, Lorena I., 325.
Córdova, Abby, 869, 1110.
Córdova Iturregui, Félix, 1338.
Córdova Macías, Ricardo, 870.
Cornejo Hernández, Amaranta, 1515.
Corona, Sarah Bak-Geller, 369.
Corona-Vásquez, Benito, 387.
Corporación Andina de Fomento, 361.
Corporación Editora Nacional (Quito), 1009.
Corral Bustos, Adriana, 1295.
Correa, Javiera, 723.
Correa Vera, Loreto, 401.
Correia, Joel E., 306, 599, 729–732.
Cortegoso, Valeria, 143.
Cortés, Almudena, 1587.
Cortes, Krista L., 1614.
Cortés Beltrán, Sergio, 1232.
Cortés Conde, Roberto, 1400.
Cortés Lara, Mara Alejandra, 371.
Cosminsky, Sheila, 1564.
Costa, Deyvisson Pereira da, 259.
Costa, Petra, 1113.
Costa Neto, Eraldo Medeiros, 255.
Costero Garbarino, María Cecilia, 1165.
Lo cotidiano detrás de la lente: mujeres indígenas del Estado de México, Chiapas y Oaxaca, 190.
Covarrubias V., Alejandro, 1324.
Crabtree, John, 344.
Crahan, Margaret E., 1190.
Crawford, Sharika D., 440.
Creative spaces: urban culture and marginality in Latin America, 373.
Crime scenes: Latin American crime fiction from the 1960s to the 2010s, 374.
La crisis de seguridad y violencia en México: causas, efectos y dimensiones del problema, 810.
Crisman, Thomas L., 468.
Crisp, Brian F., 1111.
Crispin Seoane, Vasiliev, 593.
Cruz, José Miguel, 871, 911.
Cruz Cortés, Noemí, 108.
Cruz Coutiño, Antonio, 191.
Cruz Herrera, Victor Manuel, 1459.
Cruz León, Artemio, 549.
Cruz Pérez, María del Pilar, 1460.
Cruz Rodríguez, Michael, 988.
Cruz Santana, Salvador, 203.
Cruz Vásquez, Miguel, 1296, 1461, 1472.
Cuadra L., Elvira, 918.
Cuadrado Pitterson, Luz E., 441.

Cuba, empresas y economía: memorias del primer viaje de estudios de la Universidad de Puerto Rico, Facultad de Administración de Empresas, 1350.
Cuba en sus relaciones con el resto del Caribe: continuidades y rupturas tras el restablecimiento de las relaciones diplomáticas entre Cuba y los Estados Unidos, 1188.
Cuba, Estados Unidos y el 17D: cambios y continuidades, 1189.
The Cuba reader: history, culture, politics, 975.
Cuba rural: transformaciones agrarias dinámicas sociales e innovación local, 1351.
Cucagna, Maria Emilia, 472.
Cucchietti, César, 608.
Cuecuecha, Alfredo, 1462, 1472.
Cuéllar Vázquez, Angélica, 1463.
La cuenca del río Bravo y el cambio climático, 523.
Cuerpos, subjetividades y (re)configuraciones de género, 1464.
La cultura y sus efectos sobre la psicología del mexicano, 1465.
Cúneo, Paola, 302.
Curay Ferrer, José Joshua, 1243.
Curet, L. Antonio, 120.
Currit, Nate, 500.
Cyphers, Ann, 8, 36.
Czerny, Andrzej, 600.
Czerny, Miroslawa, 600.
Dalbosco, Hugo Luis, 1217.
Dalen Luna, Pieter Dennis van, 165, 170.
Dalto, Carlos, 664.
Daly, Lewis, 247.
D'Amato, Laura, 1400.
Damiani, Gerson, 250.
Dammert, Lucía, 912.
D'Angelo, Guillermo, 748.
Davidson-Hunt, Iain J., 492.
Davies, Archie, 767–769.
Davies, Gareth R., 121.
Dávila, Alberto E., 1342.
Dávila, Anayasi, 480–481, 505.
Dávila, Luis Ricardo, 1030.
Dávila Flores, Alejandro, 1314.
Davis, Sasha, 449.
Davletshin, Albert, 41.
Davydov, Vladimir Mikhaïlovich, 1208.
Dawson, Kevin, 442.
De Belíndia ao real: ensaios em homenagem a Edmar Bacha, 1419.
De Giacomi, Brisa, 756.
De la recolección a los agroecosistemas: soberanía alimentaria y conservación de la biodiversidad, 524.
De los dioses y sus atributos: un acercamiento a través de la cosmovisión nahua, 192.
De Micheli, David, 1112.
De militares a policías: la "guerra contra las drogas" y la militarización de Argentina, 1218.
De Onis, Catalina M., 1615.
De Pourcq, Kobe, 562.
Decisiones de gobierno en Venezuela: apuntes para su comprensión histórica y de políticas públicas, 1027.
Deere, Carmen Diana, 1352.
Defender al pueblo: autodefensas y policías comunitarias en México, 811.
Deforestación en tiempos de cambio climático, 583.
Del Cid, María Concepción, 621.
Del estado nacional al estado plurinacional, 1737.
del Rio, Camilo, 711.
Del TLCAN al T-MEC: la dimensión olvidada del medio ambiente en América del Norte, 1166.
Delerme, Simone Pierre, 1616.
Delgado, Juan David, 400.
Delgado, Roger Arrazcaeta, 133.
Delgado Fiallos, Aníbal, 902.
Delgado López, Tanya, 377.
Delgado Viñas, Carmen, 597.
Della Paolera, Gerardo, 1400.
Delle, James A., 118.
DeLugan, Robin Maria, 1565.
Demarest, Arthur Andrew, 99.
Demirkaya, Betul, 1111.
Democracia em vertigem: [The edge of democracy], 1113.
La democracia local en la Argentina actual: participación ciudadana en la vida política de los municipios, 1088.
Democracia y política en la Centroamérica del siglo XXI, 847.
Democracias, comunidades y estado boliviano en perspectiva histórica y multicultural, 1038.
Democracias posibles: crisis y resignificación: Sur de México y Centroamérica, 848.
Democratic Brazil divided, 1114.

Denevan, William M., 380.
Denis, Watson, 1193.
Denuncio, Anabella Verónica, 307.
Denyer Willis, Graham, 1125.
Derechos humanos y violencia en México, 1466.
Los desafíos de la política energética argentina: panorama y propuestas, 1388.
Desarrollo económico de Puerto Rico: ensayos para una nueva economía, 1339.
Desarrollo y turismo sostenible en el Caribe, 443.
Desempeño institucional y desarrollo en países tardíos, 1297.
Desencuentros territoriales, 1647.
Desigualdades interdependentes e geopolítica do conhecimento: negociações, fluxos, assimetrias, 1142.
Desigualdades: mujer y sociedad, 1467.
Desiguales: orígenes, cambios y desafíos de la brecha social en Chile, 1378.
Desplazamiento forzado interno en Guatemala: diagnostico 2010–2016, 1566.
Despojo, conflictos socioambientales y alternativas en México, 525.
Devine, Jennifer A., 473, 480–481, 500–501, 505.
Devoto, Lisandro Martín, 812.
Di Mauro, José Ángel, 1089.
Díaz, Maria del Pilar, 662.
Díaz, Mariela Paula, 622.
Díaz Álvarez, Cristian J., 561.
Díaz Arias, David, 862, 1579.
Diaz-Cayeros, Alberto, 827–828.
Díaz González, José Andrés, 854.
Díaz Hernández, Luis Edgardo, 439.
Díaz Jiménez, Oniel Francisco, 814.
Díaz-Loving, Rolando, 1465.
Díaz Mendiburo, Aaraón, 1540.
Díaz Nieva, José, 1062.
Díaz Padilla, Raúl, 371.
Díaz Palacios, Julio, 584.
Díaz-Parra, Ibán, 375.
Díaz Rangel, Eleazar, 1028.
Díaz-Tendero Bollain, Aída, 1567.
Dicósimo, Daniel, 1446.
Diego Bautista, Óscar, 1309.
Dietrich Ortega, Luisa María, 1706.
Diez Hurtado, Alejandro, 383.
Dimas, Carlos S., 623.
Dine, Harper, 51.
La diplomacia consular mexicana en tiempos de Trump, 1167.
Dirie, Cristina, 1215.
Dobinger-Álvarez Quioto, Josefina, 1568.
Dobson, Jerome E., 534.
Domínguez, Anna R., 1468.
Domínguez, Judith, 521.
Domínguez-Cuesta, María José, 509.
Domínguez Espinosa, Alejandra del Carmen, 1465.
Domínguez López, Ernesto, 1189.
Donaghy, Maureen M., 1124.
Donald J. Trump y las relaciones Cuba-Estados Unidos en la encrucijada, 1190.
Donís Ríos, Manuel Alberto, 557.
Donoso, Sofia, 1063.
Dorado Sánchez, Claudia, 1049.
Dorn, Felix M., 601, 624.
Douglass, John G., 10.
Doval, Jimena, 641.
Downes, Andrew S., 938.
Driscoll, Amanda, 1115.
Duarte, Melisa Cabrapan, 385.
Duarte Cruz, Jóse Maria, 1469.
Duarte Torres, Carlos Arturo, 1647.
Dubois, Laurent, 1191.
Dumke, David T., 468.
Dunkerley, James, 1039.
Dunn, Claire, 1262.
Dunning, Thad, 1109.
Dupey García, Elodie, 113.
Durán-Apuy, Alejandro, 493.
Durán Crane, Helena, 565.
Durán-Martínez, Angélica, 813.
Durán-Merk, Alma, 54.
Durán Rodríguez, María Martha, 1600.
Durand Guevara, Anahí, 1704.
Durin, Séverine, 196, 1470.
Duvall, Chris S., 389.
Dweck, Esther, 1420.
Earley, Caitlin C., 52.
Easdale, Marcos Horacio, 625.
Ebert, Claire E., 101, 482.
Echart Muñoz, Enara, 1207.
Echazú Cortéz, Carlos, 1040.
Echevarría León, Dayma, 1351.
Echeverría, Bolívar, 1000.
Ecología política de la basura: pensando los residuos desde el Sur, 376.
Ecología política en la mitad del mundo: luchas ecologistas y reflexiones sobre la naturaleza en el Ecuador, 570.
Economia para poucos: impactos sociais da austeridade e alternativas para o Brasil, 1420.

Economía social y solidaria, migración y género: hacia la búsqueda de alternativas de "desarrollo": una reflexión interdisciplinaria desde México, 1471.
Ecuador: la insurrección de octubre, 1004.
Edwards, R. Lawrence, 482.
Edwards, Ryan C., 626.
La eficacia de la cooperación internacional para el medioambiente: dimensiones y alcances en México, 526.
Eguren, Joaquín, 1670.
Ehrnström-Fuentes, Maria, 749.
Eicher, John, 733.
Einbender, Nathan, 502.
Eiss, Paul K., 183.
El Salvador en construcción, 1569.
Las elecciones críticas de 2018: un balance de los procesos electorales federales y locales en México, 814.
Elecciones municipales en Costa Rica 2016: contribuciones para su estudio, 855.
Elfenbein, Rachel, 1668.
Eliano, Ezequiel, 1389.
Ellefsen, Bernardo, 150.
Elliott, Joseph E.B., 489.
Emery, Kitty F., 91.
Emmerich, Norberto, 1143.
Empleo y desigualdad en Centroamérica, 1570.
Emprendimiento y migración de retorno: raíces y horizontes, 1472.
En torno al galeon Manila-Acapulco, 1168.
Enciso González, Jesús, 193.
Encuentro Conjunciones Complejas: Encuentro Transdisciplinario para el Estudio de la Violencia, 3rd, San Juan, P.R., 2015, 1617.
Endara, Gustavo, 1689.
Energia, organizações e sociedade, 770.
Engelman, Anabella, 627.
Englehardt, Joshua, 13.
Ennis, Juan Antonio, 308.
Enríquez Bermeo, Francisco, 1008, 1158.
Enríquez Rosas, Rocío, 1495.
Enríquez Sánchez, Antonio de Jesús, 208.
Enriz, Noelia, 309.
Entre dos fuegos: naturalización e invisibilidad de la violencia de género contra migrantes en territorio mexicano, 1571.
Entre el activismo y la intervención: el trabajo de organizaciones de la sociedad civil y su incidencia para la salud de las mujeres indígenas en México, 194.

Entre el despojo y la esperanza: doce ensayos sobre historia y etnografía de la Huasteca, 195.
Entre minas y barrancas: el legado de Juan Luis Sariego a los estudios antropológicos, 196.
Eppich, Keith, 7.
A era Chávez e a Venezuela no tempo presente, 1029.
Erdösová, Zuzana, 1309.
Escobar, Claudia, 887.
Escobar, Rodrigo, 711.
Escobar Latapí, Agustín, 1500.
Escolano Utrilla, Severino, 691.
Escoto, Ana, 521.
Escudé, Guillermo, 1406.
Espacios del consumo y el comercio en la ciudad contemporánea, 1473.
Esparza, Ilse, 1325.
Espejo de la crisis humanitaria venezolana: Encuesta Nacional de Condiciones de Vida 2017: ENCOVI 2017, 1669.
Espert, José Luis, 1397.
Espino Ortiz, Dulce S., 104.
Espinosa, Eduardo Luis, 1517.
Espinosa Damián, Gisela, 1321.
Espinosa de los Monteros, Alfonso, 1005.
Espinosa O., León, 1687.
Espinosa Rodríguez, María Guadalupe, 21.
Espinosa Santiago, Orlando, 800.
Espinoza Mendoza, Yenny, 1735.
Espinoza Valle, Víctor Alejandro, 815.
Espitia Moya, Jenny Tatiana, 1649.
Espósito, Santiago Martín, 1205.
Esquit Choy, Alberto, 888.
Esquivel Ventura, Isabella María, 803.
Estado actual sobre la producción, el comercio y cultivo del cacao en América, 377.
Estado y perspectivas de las relaciones colombo-brasileñas, 1233.
Estrada, Lorenzo, 903.
Estrada Peña, Iván Canek, 197.
El estudio del agua en México: nuevas perspectivas teórico-metodológicas, 527.
Estudios de la forma urbana: análisis contemporáneo en México, 528.
Etchemendy, Sebastián, 1257.
Evia Cervantes, Carlos Augusto, 198.
Ewen, Charles R., 131.
Exclusión, mujeres y prisión en Colombia: un caso en la región Caribe: (Investigación-acción en el Centro de Rehabilitación Femenino El Buen Pastor de Barranquilla), 1648.

Exeni R., José Luis, 1048.
Exilio y presencia: Costa Rica y México en el siglo XX, 1169.
El éxodo venezolano: entre el exilio y la emigración, 1670.
Experiencias formativas interculturales de jóvenes toba/qom, wichí y mbyá-guaraní de Argentina, 309.
Ezquerro-Cañete, Arturo, 357.
Fabra, Mariana, 148.
Fabricant, Nicole, 310.
Factores del desarrollo agrícola territorial en el norte de México: historia, contemporaneidad y diversidad regional, 529.
Fagetti, Antonella, 244.
Fahrenbruch, Matthew L., 474.
Falchetti, Ana María, 139.
Falci, Catarina Guzzo, 121.
Falconí Gonzales, Julio, 1705.
Falkin, Camila, 756.
Falleti, Tulia Gabriela, 1258.
Familias fragilizadas en el contexto colombiano: el caso de Medellín, 1649.
Farell Ortiz, Franklin, 1051.
Farías Antognini, Ana, 1064.
Farrell, Katharine N., 1686.
Fash, Benjamin, 470, 865.
Faugère, Brigitte, 34.
Fauré, Yves-André, 1430.
Fausto, Carlos, 248.
Fawcett, Emma, 444.
Feierherd, Germán, 1116.
Feinberg, Richard E., 1353.
Feldman, Saúl, 1090.
Feliciano-Santos, Sherina, 1618.
Femenia, Alfredo, 671.
Feminismos, pensamiento crítico y propuestas alternativas en América Latina, 1436.
Feminismos y estudios de género en Colombia: un campo académico y político en movimiento, 1650.
Feoli Boraschi, Sergio, 491.
Fernandes, Bernardo Mançano, 636.
Fernández, Abel, 169.
Fernández, Diego, 1390.
Fernández, Federico, 340.
Fernández, Juan Ramón, 971.
Fernández, Karina, 1377.
Fernández, María Inés, 1096.
Fernández, Octavio, 622.
Fernández, Roque B., 1100.
Fernández Abara, Joaquín, 1065.
Fernández Casanueva, Carmen, 1177.
Fernández de Castro, Rafael, 1167.
Fernández Nistal, María Teresa, 180.
Fernández Romero, Francisco, 628.
Ferraro, Augustin E., 1281.
Ferraro, Emilia, 352.
Ferreira, Gustavo H. Cepolini, 776.
Ferretti, Federico, 771–774.
FES Acatlán (institution), 1174.
Few, Roger, 571.
Fiant, Roxana E., 629.
Fierro Padilla, Rafael, 53.
Figueroa, Alejandro J., 95.
Figueroa Serrano, David, 199.
¿Fin de la bonanza?: entradas, salidas y encrucijadas del extractivismo, 378.
Findley, Michael G., 1280.
Finegold, Andrew, 9.
Fini, Daniele, 811.
Finn, John C., 379, 602.
Fisk, Bethan, 445.
FLACSO (organization). Sede Costa Rica, 1601.
Flemes, Daniel, 1233.
Flores, Carlos Y., 1572.
Flores-Anderson, Africa I., 483.
Flores Coni, Josefina, 642.
Flores Díaz, Sebastián, 1232.
Flores Flores, Álvaro, 842.
Flores López, María de Lourdes, 519.
Flores-Macías, Gustavo A., 816.
Flores Mejía, Jesús Guillermo, 1474.
Flores Pérez, Carlos Antonio, 810.
Flores Treviño, María Eugenia, 1464.
Flórez-Estrada, María, 1573.
Folan, William J., 81.
Fong Reynoso, Carlos, 1322.
Fonseca Amador, Carlos, 908.
Fontes, Anthony W., 1574.
Forero Lloreda, Eduardo, 337.
Forest, field, and fallow: selections by William M. Denevan, 380.
Foster, Michael S., 35.
Fotiou, Evgenia, 285.
Fowler, William R., 55.
Fox-Hodess, Katy, 1651.
Foxley, Alejandro, 1266.
Fragkou, Maria Christina, 704.
Fragoso, José M.V., 276.
Francaviglia, Richard V., 692.
Franceschi, Zelda Alice, 325–326.
Francis, Hilary, 919.
Franco, Bernardo Mello, 1117.
Franco Durán, Yolanda, 832.
Franco Franco, Juan Manuel, 207.
Franco Pinto, Daniela, 1744.

Franco-Vivanco, Edgar, 1126.
Franzen, Sarah, 446.
Fraser, Barbara J., 391.
Frederick and Jan Mayer Center for Ancient and Latin American Art, 18.
Freeman, J. Brian, 362.
Freitez Landaeta, Anitza, 1669, 1675.
Frej, William, 54.
French, John D., 1118.
Frey, Barbara, 1498.
Freyemuth Joffre, Laura Georgina, 194.
Frías, Carolina, 690.
Frid, Carina, 1399.
Friedman, Max Paul, 1223.
Fronjosa Lasalle, Ernesto, 1366.
Las fronteras: espacios estratégicos para la globalización, 1298.
Fronteras: fuentes de conflicto y cooperación, 1234.
Fuchs, María L., 137.
Fuentes, Cecilia, 179.
Fuentes, Luis, 693.
Fuentes, Rodrigo, 1375.
Fuentes Díaz, Antonio, 811.
Fuentes Flores, Noé Arón, 1307.
Fuentes Ramírez, Ricardo R., 1339.
Fuenzalida Díaz, Manuel, 694.
Fundación Myrna Mack, 885, 891.
Fundación Puertorriqueña de las Humanidades, 1613.
Fundación Stresser-Péan, 100.
Funes Monzote, Reinaldo, 447.
FUNPROEIB Andes, 1733.
Furlan, Adriano, 630.
Furlong, Aurora, 1298.
El futuro de México al 2035: una visión prospectiva, 817.
Gabayet González, Natalia, 1475.
Gadino, Isabel, 750.
Gahman, Levi, 448.
Gaitán-Barrera, Alejandra, 347.
Galanes Valldejuli, Luis, 1619.
Galaso, Pablo, 751.
Galeana, Fernando, 507.
Galindo, María, 1041.
Gallardo, Helio, 856.
Gallardo, Ricardo del Carmen, 1488.
Gallart Nocetti, María Antonieta, 250.
Gallegos, Franklin R., 1013.
Gallegos-Anda, Carlos E., 1006.
Gallegos Toussaint, Claudia Ximena, 1471.
Galli, Carlos María, 1437.
Gálvez, Alyshia, 1299.

Gamboa T., Carlos, 161.
Gamiño Muñoz, Rodolfo, 1476.
Gándara Vázquez, Manuel, 12.
Gang, David R., 105.
Ganson, Barbara, 328.
García, Fernando, 1695.
García, Magdalena, 695.
García, Marcelo, 1219.
Garcia, Redlich, 711.
García, Txema, 1178.
García Aguilar, María del Carmen, 848, 1575.
García Campos, Helio, 530.
Garcia de León, Armando, 694.
García-Des Lauriers, Claudia, 2.
García Hernández, Claudia, 180.
García Jiménez, Plutarco Emilio, 200.
García Mingo, Elisa, 350.
García Ochoa, Rigoberto, 1172.
García Palacios, Mariana, 309.
García-Passalacqua, Juan M., 1200.
García Salazar, Juan, 1680.
Garcia Sarduy, Yulia, 379.
García Soto, Carlos, 1363.
García Ubaque, César Augusto, 1652.
García Ubaque, Juan Carlos, 1652.
García Winder, Miguel, 359.
García Zamora, Rodolfo, 1300.
Garduño García, Moisés, 1153.
Garfias, Francisco, 1259–1260.
Gargantini, Daniela Mariana, 631.
Garma Navarro, Carlos, 229.
Garmany, Jeff, 775.
Garrett Ríos, María Gabriela, 244.
Garrido de Sierra, Sebastián, 818.
Garrocho, Carlos, 521.
Gärtner, Philipp, 660.
Garza Zepeda, Manuel, 819, 1514.
Garzón, Marisol, 1180.
Gasca Zamora, José, 1473.
Gasic Klett, Ivo Ricardo, 696.
Gaspar, Malu, 1119.
Gasparri, Nestor I., 660.
Gatehouse, Tom, 430.
Gatica, Paulina, 721.
Gaudichaud, Franck, 1066.
Gaussens, Pierre, 1007.
Gavier Pizarro, Gregorio, 660.
Gaviria, Alejandro, 984.
Gavirondo, Miguel, 746.
Gehring, Hubert, 1154.
Género, sexualidades y mercados sexuales en sitios extractivos de América Latina, 1438.

Género y conflicto armado en el Perú, 1706.
Género y políticas públicas: retos y oportunidades para la transversalidad en Nuevo León, 820.
Geografia agrária no Brasil: disputas, conflitos e alternativas territoriais, 776.
Geografía ambiental: métodos y técnicas desde América Latina, 381.
Geografía crítica para detener el despojo de los territorios: teorías, experiencias y casos de trabajo en Ecuador, 572.
Geografía e historia ambiental, 382.
Geopolítica de la seguridad en América Latina, 1143.
Geraghty, Niall H.D., 373.
Gerber, Mónica, 1063.
Gerchunoff, Pablo, 1391–1392.
Gerhardt, Marcos, 780.
Germano, Roy, 1261.
Gerón, Cándido, 952.
Gestión para la defensa del agua y el territorio en Xalapa, Veracruz, 530.
Ghaffari, Zahra, 473.
Ghany, Hamid A., 1346.
Giacomini, Diego, 1397.
Giannotti, Mariana, 759.
Gianola Otamendi, Alberto, 1220.
Gibbings, Julie, 896.
Gibbs, Holly K., 792.
Gign, Annelou Van, 121.
Gijón-Cruz, Alicia Sylvia, 1521.
Gil Hernández, Franklin, 1650.
Gil Méndez, J. Jesús, 544.
Gilas, Karolina Monika, 1477.
Gilbert, Randolph, 1187.
Gilbert-Roberts, Terri-Ann P., 929.
Gildo de la Cruz, María Gabriela, 835.
Giller, Diego, 1144.
Gillooly, Shauna N., 889.
Gilmore, Michael, 591.
Giménez, Gilberto, 1542.
Gingerich, Daniel W., 1120.
Giordano, Mariana, 603.
Giovas, Christina M., 122–123.
Giraldo, Omar Felipe, 531.
Giraldo Prieto, Cristina, 1653.
Giraldo Uribe, José Jardani, 1656.
Giraudy, Agustina, 1262.
Girbal-Blacha, Noemí María, 1393.
Giró, Ana, 476.
Giucci, Guillermo, 418.
Glauser Ortiz, Marcos, 311–312.
The global Spanish empire: five hundred years of place making and pluralism, 10.
Göbel, Barbara, 1142.
El gobierno colectivo de la tierra en América Latina, 383.
Gobiernos intermedios: entre lo local y lo nacional, 1008.
Gobiernos locales y descentralización en Ecuador, 1009.
Godfrey, Brian J., 777.
Godfrid, Julieta, 399.
Gogol, Eugene, 216.
Goinheix, Sebastián, 751.
Golovanevsky, Laura, 1385.
Gomes, Suely Henrique de Aquino, 259.
Gómez, Cecilia P., 313.
Gómez, José María, 784.
Gomez, Josue, 65.
Gómez, Juan Pablo, 908, 916.
Gómez, Mónica, 1394.
Gómez Arriola, Luis Ignacio, 532.
Gómez Lende, Sebastián, 632.
Gómez Montáñez, Pablo Felipe, 273.
Gómez Montes, Liliana, 536.
Gómez Naranjo, Manuel, 1367.
Gómez Pintus, Ana, 633.
Gómez Téllez, Noelia, 1745.
Gómez Zúñiga, Pastor, 111.
Gomezjurado Zevallos, Javier, 1681.
Gomis, Redi, 1301.
Góngora Cervantes, Vanessa, 814.
Góngora Escobedo, Álvaro, 1065.
Gonlin, Nancy, 22, 55–56.
Gonsalves, Isis, 1192.
Gonsalves, Ralph E., 1340.
Gonzales, Anthony P., 946.
González, Beatriz Pico, 1478.
González, Daniela P., 697.
González, Fabián, 664.
González, Julio C., 1221.
González, Lissette, 1032.
González, Luis Eduardo, 702.
González, María Noel, 744.
González, Yanilda María, 1263.
González Aliste, Fernando, 698.
González Anaya, Ana Gabriela, 1479.
González Arellano, Salomón, 528.
González Barajas, María Teresa, 1302.
González Bracco, Mercedes, 634.
González Corona, Rosa María, 1480.
González-Corzo, Mario A., 1354–1355, 1358.
González de la Rocha, Mercedes, 1512.
González García, Juan, 1164.

González Granillo, José Luis, 521.
González-Hidalgo, Marien, 699.
González-Izás, Matilde, 1603.
González Jácome, Alba, 549.
González León, Diego, 377.
Gonzalez-Macqueen, Felipe, 162.
González Martin, Miranda, 309.
González Martín, Olga Rosa, 1189.
González Orellana, Mauricio, 1333.
González Romo, Adrián, 1171.
González Santamaría, Abel Enrique, 1186.
González-Seijas, Samuel, 1671.
González Torres, Claudia Cecilia, 361.
González Tule, Luis, 907.
González Ulloa Aguirre, Pablo Armando, 1481.
Gonzalez-Vicente, Ruben, 934.
Goodale, Mark, 1738.
Goodwin, Whitney A., 95.
Gookool, Rebecca, 946.
Gorla, Nora B.M., 658.
Gortari, Rebeca de, 1290.
Goss, Catriona, 1201.
Grabendorff, Wolf, 1209.
Gracia Sain, Amalia, 1439.
Grado cero: la condición equinoccial y la producción de cultura en el Ecuador y en otras longitudes ecuatorianas, 1682.
Graizbord, Boris, 516, 521.
Graña-Behrens, Daniel, 57.
Granados Cosme, José Arturo, 1507.
Granda Vega, María Paula, 999.
Granovsky-Larsen, Simon, 890, 1273.
Graue Wiechers, Enrique, 804.
Gray, Obika, 958.
Grecko, Témoris, 821.
Green, Charlotte, 429.
Greenidge, Adaeze, 448.
Gregorio-Cernadas, Maximiliano, 1222.
Las grietas del neoliberalismo: dimensiones de la desigualdad contemporánea en México, 1303.
Griffin, G.A.E., 1620.
Griffin, Robert E., 483.
Grijalva Monteverde, Gabriela, 1327.
Groot Kormelinck, Annemarie, 752.
Groth, Aaron A., 589.
Groupe de recherche identités et cultures, 1706.
Grünewald, Leif, 314.
Grupo de Análisis para el Desarrollo (Lima, Peru), 586.
Grydehøj, Adam, 449.

GTRCMC (research institute), 945.
Guadiana, Pablo, 362.
Guanche, Julio César, 1188.
Guatemala's justice system: evaluating capacity building and judicial independence, 891.
Gudiño, María Elina, 657.
Gudmundson, Lowell, 1334.
Guernsey, Julia, 58.
Guerra, Bear, 284.
Guerra, Emily, 1577.
Guerra fría, política, petróleo y lucha armada: Venezuela en un mundo bipolar = Cold War, politics, oil, and armed struggle: Venezuela in a bipolar world, 1030.
Guerrero, Roberto, 394.
Guerrero Martínez, Fernando, 233.
Guerrero Salgado, Gilda Alicia, 1019.
Guess, Allison, 450.
Guevara Aranda, Roberto, 286.
Guevara H., Francisco, 358.
Guía Ramírez, Andrea, 80.
Guichón, Francisco, 642.
Guilbault, Jocelyne, 944.
Guillén, Marquina Terán, 1482.
Guimarães, Feliciano de Sá, 1115.
Guiñazú, María Clelia, 1212.
Guiné, Anouk, 1706.
Guns, gun violence and gun homicides: perspectives from the Caribbean, Global South and beyond, 935.
Gurr, Mel, 706.
Gurven, Michael, 315.
Gurzenda, Susie, 765.
Gutiérrez, Natividad, 224, 1542.
Gutiérrez Báez, Celso, 51.
Gutiérrez-Castorena, María del Carmen, 96.
Gutiérrez del Ángel, Arturo, 179.
Gutiérrez García, Rosa María, 1464.
Gutiérrez Herrera, Ruth, 274.
Gutiérrez Mannix, David Alan, 201.
Gutiérrez Rosete Hernández, Jorge Gastón, 533.
Gutiérrez Sanín, Francisco, 989.
Gutiérrez Tapia, Cristian, 1229.
Gutiérrez Zúñiga, Cristina, 1483.
Gutman, Margarita, 384.
Guzmán Medina, María Guadalupe Violeta, 202.
Guzmán Mendoza, Carlos Enrique, 1209.
Guzmán Vargas, Daniela, 1055.
Guzowski, Carina, 1388.
Gyger, Helen, 585.

Habib, Komal, 456.
Hábitat en deuda: veinte años de políticas urbanas en América Latina, 384.
Hadfield-Hill, Sophie, 782.
Hagan, Jacqueline Maria, 1304.
Haïti, la CARICOM et la Caraïbe: questions d'économie politique, d'intégration économique et de relations internationales, 1193.
Hale, Charles R., 409.
Halvorsen, Sam, 635–636.
Hammerstedt, Scott W., 68.
Hanna, Jonathan A., 124.
Hannigan, Elizabeth M., 50.
Hansing, Katrin, 1621.
Harnoncou, Julia, 936.
Haro Ayerve, Patricio, 1010.
Hartlyn, Jonathan, 1262.
Hasemann, George, 203.
Hauser, Mark W., 117.
Hawkins, John Palmer, 204.
Hayes, Tanya M., 573.
Haynes, Jason, 937.
Hecht, Ana Carolina, 309.
Hecht, Susanna B., 778.
Héctor, J.G.F., 216.
Heidbrink, Lauren, 1576.
Heller, Carlos, 1384.
Hellwig, Timothy, 1255.
Helmke, Christophe, 106–107, 110, 484.
Henrique, Karen Paiva, 779.
Henríquez Ruiz, Cristián, 422.
Hepp, Guy David, 59.
Her cup for sweet cacao: food in ancient Maya society, 11.
Heredia, Luis Fernando, 592.
Heredia, Mariana, 1101.
Herlihy, Peter H., 474, 534.
Hermes, Bernard, 107.
Hernández, Anabel, 1484.
Hernández, Maricarmen, 1683.
Hernández Aracena, Javier, 717.
Hernández Bonilla, Sindy, 1566.
Hernández Cabrera, Porfirio Miguel, 1485.
Hernández Campos, Carlos, 1545.
Hernández Cordero, Adrián, 388.
Hernández Favale, Jorge, 441.
Hernández López, Mario Humberto, 1297.
Hernández Oliva, Carlos, 133.
Hernández Ramos, Ricardo Alejandro, 832.
Hernández Reyes, Carlos, 60.
Hernández Rodríguez, Rogelio, 822.
Hernandez Sandoval, Betzy E., 483.
Hernández-Stefanoni, José Luis, 495.
Hernández Urías, Mariana, 1511.
Hernández Veleros, Zeus Salvador, 1413.
Herrera, Cristóbal, 697.
Herrera, Gioconda, 1000.
Herrera, José, 558.
Herrera Abad, Luis, 1707.
Herrera León, Fabián, 1170.
Herrera Tapia, Francisco, 419.
Hesketh, Chris, 1305.
Hevia de la Jara, Felipe, 194.
Heyman, Josiah, 1577.
Hidalgo, F. Daniel, 1250.
High, Casey, 287.
Hilburn, Andrew M., 534.
Hilsenrad Grünpeter, Marcelo, 1067.
Hinds, Kristina, 1194.
Hinojosa, Magda, 1074.
Hinostroza Rivera, Dino, 1708.
Hirsch, Silvia María, 316, 330.
Hirtzel, Vincent, 317.
Historia ambiental comparada de ciudades mexicanas, 535.
História ambiental e história indígena no Semiárido brasileiro, 255.
História ambiental e migrações: diálogos, 780.
Historia necesaria del Banco Central de la República Argentina: entre la búsqueda de la estabilidad y la promoción del desarrollo, 1395.
Historical archaeologies of the Caribbean: contextualizing sites through colonialism, capitalism, and globalism, 125.
Hodara B., Joseph, 1312.
Hoffmann, Bert, 982, 1621.
Hofman, Corinne Lisette, 121, 135.
Hofmann, Susanne, 385, 1438.
Hogares y familias transnacionales: un encuentro desde la perspectiva humana, 1486.
Hoggarth, Julie A., 101, 482.
Höhl, Johanna, 700.
Holguín, Carmen Jimena, 1673.
Holland, Bradley E., 1264.
Holzinger, Katharina, 828.
Hölzl, Corinna, 637.
Holzner, Claudio A., 1253.
Hoogland, Menno L.P., 135.
Hooper, Paul L., 315.
Hopkins, Nicholas A., 205.
Hora, Roy, 1392.
Horbath Corredor, Jorge Enrique, 1439.

Horn, Philipp, 318.
Horn, Sally P., 487.
Horta Cruz, Juan, 823.
Horton, John, 782.
Hosannah, Luciana Dornelles, 781.
Hosein, Gabrielle, 1630.
Hosein, Roger, 946.
Hostetler-Díaz, Jean, 969.
Houle, Christian, 1265.
Houston, Stephen D., 1.
Hualde Alfaro, Alfredo, 1487.
Huatulco: espacio y tiempo, 536.
Huerta, Benjamín, 504.
Huerta González, Arturo, 1306.
Huertas, Daniel M., 1421.
Hughes, David McDermott, 973.
Humacata, Luis, 638–639.
Hummel, Calla, 1422.
Humphreys Bebbington, Denise, 470.
Huneeus, Carlos, 1079.
Hunter, R. Alexander, 166.
Hunter, Wendy, 1105, 1136.
Hurst, Heather, 50.
Hurtado, Adriana, 1237.
Hutson, Scott, 105.
Ibañez Martín, María, 1388.
Ibarra, Macarena, 427, 701.
Ibarra Chávez, Héctor Angel, 1578.
ICAR (institute), 419.
Íconos: Revista de Ciencias Sociales, 386.
Identidad y postnacionalismo en la cultura cubana, 1622.
Iglesias, Fernando A., 1091.
Iglesias Martínez, Juan, 1684.
Imilan, Walter, 702.
Impactos de la homologación del IVA en zonas fronterizas: análisis desde la plataforma informática OCEF, 1307.
INAPI Sinaloa, 1503.
Inclán, María, 824.
Inclán Oseguera, Silvia, 817.
Inclusión social en Bolivia: avances y desafíos, 2006–2014: política pública, estructura económica y tierra, 1739.
Indígenas e indios en el Caribe: presencia, legado y estudio, 126.
Indígenas en las ciudades de las Américas: condiciones de vida, procesos de discriminación e identificación y lucha por la ciudadanía étnica, 1439.
Indigenous struggles for autonomy: the Caribbean coast of Nicaragua, 206.
Innovation and inclusion in Latin America: strategies to avoid the middle-income trap, 1266.
Inoa, Orlando, 1623.
La inolvidable edad: jóvenes en la Costa Rica del siglo XX, 1579.
Inomata, Takeshi, 61, 91.
Institute for Defence Studies and Analyses, 1182.
Instituto Centroamericano de Estudios Fiscales, 1337.
Instituto Colombiano de Antropología e Historia, 158, 1647.
Instituto Colombiano de Desarrollo Rural, 1647.
Instituto de Altos Estudios Nacionales (Ecuador), 1241.
Instituto de Estudios en Salud, Sexualidad y Desarrollo Humano, 1731.
Instituto de Estudos de Política Econômica, Casa das Garças, 1419.
Instituto de Investigaciones Dr. José María Luis Mora, 526.
Instituto Latinoamericano de Investigaciones Sociales, 1689.
Instituto Nacional de Antropología e Historia (Mexico), 3, 23, 53, 100.
Instituto Nacional de Medicina Legal y Ciencias Forenses (Colombia). Regional Noroccidente, 1662.
Instituto Nacional de Migración (Dominican Republic). Departamento de Investigación y Estudios Migratorios, 1638.
Instituto Nacional de Tecnología Agropecuaria (Argentina), 358.
Instituto Nacional Electoral (Mexico), 802.
Instituto Tecnológico de Estudios Superiores de Occidente (Guadalajara, Mexico), 371.
Integração regional na América Latina: o papel do estado nas políticas públicas para o desenvolvimento, os direitos humanos e sociais e uma estratégia Sul-Sul, 1145.
Integración y desintegración del espacio económico mexicano: mercado interno y abastecimiento de las carnes desde la colonia al siglo XX, 1308.
Integración y paradiplomacia transfronteriza: experiencias comparadas del Río Bravo hasta la Patagonia, 1146.
Integridad electoral: México en perspectiva global, 825.
Inter-American Commission on Human Rights, 904, 913.
Inter-American Development Bank, 1251.

Inter-American Institute of Agricultural Sciences, 359.
Interculturalidad, arte y saberes tradicionales, 207.
International Conference on Hydrometeorological Risks and Climate Change (ICHRCC), 2nd, Cholula de Rivadabia, Mexico, 2015, 387.
International Crisis Group, 898.
International Development Research Centre (Canada), 194.
International Monetary Fund, 1345.
International volunteer tourism: critical reflections on good works in Central America, 475.
International Work Group for Indigenous Affairs, 583.
Interpretación del patrimonio cultural: pasos hacia una divulgación significativa en México, 12.
Interregional interaction in ancient Mesoamerica, 13.
Inuca Lechón, José Benjamín, 353.
La invariable crisis, 1624.
La invención de la memoria: fotografía y arqueología en México, 62.
Investigaciones arqueológicas en Nariño (Colombia), 158.
Irizarry Mora, Edwin, 1339.
Irusta, Silvina, 1737.
Irwin, Daniel, 483.
Islas Domínguez, Alicia, 38.
Ismael Simental, María Emilia, 388.
Itzcovitz, Victoria, 1093.
Iucci, María Emilia, 144.
Izcara Palacios, Simón Pedro, 1580.
Jabin, David, 319.
Jackson, Jean Elizabeth, 275.
Jackson, Sarah E., 63, 109.
Jaeggi, Adrian V., 315.
Jain, Meha, 480.
James C., Johannie, 443.
Jaramillo Nieves, Lorna Gisela, 451.
Jarquín Calderón, Edmundo, 918.
Jarquín Ortega, María Teresa, 208.
Jennings, Justin, 162.
Jepson, Wendy, 797.
Jiménez, Javier Donoso, 1488.
Jiménez Abollado, Francisco, 33.
Jiménez Badillo, Diego, 3.
Jiménez Frei, Cheryl, 640.
Jiménez Izarraraz, María Antonieta, 12, 21.
Jiménez López, José Concepción, 29.
Jiménez Marce, Rogelio, 551.
Jiménez Martín, Carolina, 1661.
Jiménez Martínez, Nancy Merary, 521.
Jiménez-Sánchez, Fernando, 897.
Jirón Martínez, Paola, 418.
Jobbová, Eva, 110, 484.
Johannessen, Peter G., 1121.
Johanson, Erik N., 487.
Johnson, Adrienne, 574.
Johnson, Erlend M., 95, 111.
Jokisch, Brad D., 249.
Jornadas de Acumulación y Dominación en la Argentina: Debates sobre el Modo de Acumulación en la Posconvertibilidad, 5th, Quilmes, Argentina, 2016, 1398.
Jornadas Puebla: Ciudad, Capital y Cultura, 3rd, San Andrés Cholula, Mexico, 2016, 388.
Joseph, Tonny, 434.
Journal of Latin American Geography, 389.
Joyce, Arthur A., 26.
Juániz Maya, José Ramón, 878.
Juárez Elías, Erick, 892.
Juárez Ramírez, Clara, 194.
Juchari eratsikua, Cherán keri: retrospectiva histórica, territorio e identidad étnica, 209.
Justo, Liborio, 1068.
Juventud y espacios de participación en Chile y América Latina, 1069.
Juventudes indígenas: estudos interdisciplinares, saberes interculturais: conexões entre Brasil e México, 256.
Kadiwel, Idjahure, 257, 266, 270.
Kahn, Jeffrey S., 1625.
Kalakonas, Petros, 503.
Kalisch, Hannes, 329.
Kamenov, George D., 91.
Kan, Julián, 1210.
Kaplan, Hillard, 315.
Kaplan, Jonathan H., 64.
Kappers, Michiel, 123.
Keller, Héctor, 320.
Kellner, Corina M., 24.
Kelly, John H., 534.
Kelly, Mary K., 111.
Kennett, Douglas J., 65.
Keyser, Ulrike, 209.
Kidd, Stephen, 321.
Kidder, Barry, 105.
Kim, Sun, 765.
Kimball, Natalie L., 1740.

Kingstone, Peter R., 1114, 1267.
Kivland, Chelsey L., 1626.
Kjerfve, Björn, 476.
Klašnja, Marko, 1122.
Klaufus, Christien, 1685.
Knaf, Alice C.S., 121.
Knight, Christopher A.C.J., 471.
Knight, Vernon J., 127.
Knowlton, Timothy, 112.
Knudson, Kelly J., 77.
Koechlin, José, 1670.
Kohut, Lauren E., 590.
Kolinjivad, Vijay, 578.
Komadina, George, 1056.
Koppel, Martín, 1201.
Korpisaari, Antti, 138.
Kosiba, Steve, 166.
Kosoy, Nicolas, 578.
Koszkuł, Wiesław, 106–107.
Kotschack, Linda, 634.
Kouba, Karel, 909.
Kovacevich, Brigitte, 66.
Kraftl, Peter, 782.
Kras, Helen, 1110.
Krenak, Ailton, 257.
Krigbaum, John, 91.
Kröger, Markus, 390, 749.
Kubota, Yuichi, 893.
Kuemmerle, Tobias, 660.
Kulfas, Matías, 1401.
Kulstad González, Pauline, 128.
Kumar, Sanjeev, 508.
Kurjenoja, Anne Kristiina, 388.
Kury, Lorelai Brilhante, 263.
Kustov, Alexander, 1123.
Kuzdas, Christopher, 496.
Lacarrieu, Mónica B., 367.
Ladrón de Guevara, Sara, 4.
Ladronis, Julieta, 472.
Laffoon, Jason E., 135.
Lagrou, Els, 258.
Laguardia Martínez, Jacqueline, 1188.
Laguarta Ramírez, José A., 967.
Lakhani, Nina, 905.
Lalo, Eduardo, 968.
Lamas, Marta, 1489.
Lambe, Jennifer L., 979.
Lamina Luguana, Alexandra Magaly, 416.
Lanari, María Rosa, 358.
Landa, Carlos, 641.
Landscapes of inequity: environmental justice in the Andes-Amazon region, 391.
Lane, Chad S., 487.

Lange, Charlotte, 374.
Lange, Victoria, 642.
Langer, Karen, 671.
Lanzelotti, Sonia L., 609.
Lanzilotta, Bibiana, 744–745.
Lara Martínez, Carlos Benjamín, 1581.
Lara Pinto, Gloria, 203.
Larco Chacón, Carolina, 1687.
Larios Deniz, Jonás, 1490.
Larratt-Smith, Charles, 990.
Lascurain, Maite, 524.
Laserna, Roberto, 1736.
Latin America in times of global environmental change, 392.
Latin American Migration Project, 1646.
Latin American Perspectives, 393, 969.
Latorre Restrepo, Sergio, 987.
Latorre Tomás, Sara, 1686.
LaVanchy, G. Thomas, 411.
Layton, Matthew L., 1124.
Le Clerq Ortega, Juan Antonio, 1466.
Leal Buitrago, Francisco, 991.
Leaño Espejo, Jimmy, 1732.
Leavy, Pia, 322.
Lecaros, Véronique, 1709.
Lechón Gómez, Domingo Manuel, 1515.
Leco Tomás, Casimiro, 209, 1171.
Lederman, Daniel, 1184.
Lee, Thomas A., 49.
Lee Alardín, Gabriela, 528.
Lee-DiStefano, Debbie, 1433.
Legatzke, Hannah L., 501.
Leguizamón, Amalia, 643.
Leighton, Mary, 151.
Leiva, Favio, 1696.
Lema, Carolina, 644.
Lemus, Leslie, 1570.
Lemus Jiménez, Alicia, 209.
Lenguas minorizadas: documentación, revitalización y políticas lingüísticas, 210.
Lentino, Miguel, 116.
León Cortés, Jorge Leonel, 1172.
León-Escribano Schlotter, Carmen Rosa de, 1603.
León-Sicard, Tomás Enrique, 562.
Lerma Gómez, María del Carmen, 67.
Lessing, Benjamin, 1125.
Lesure, Richard G., 78.
Letelier Eltit, Matías, 1232.
Levine, Marc N., 68.
Levita, Gabriel, 1092.
Levoyer, Saudia, 1011.
Lewis, Patsy, 452, 929.

Ley, Sandra, 826, 843.
Leyva Muñoz, Olivia, 1517.
Leyva Remón, Arisbel, 1351.
Lezama, José Luis, 521.
Li, Yan, 1331.
Liang, Fuyuan, 482.
Libertun, Nora, 394.
Lichtenstein, Gabriela, 617.
Lieske, Rosemary, 14.
Ligi, Gianluca, 303.
Lima, Maria Regina Soares de, 1207.
Lima, Nísia Trindade, 263.
Limaye, Ashutosh S., 483.
Lind, Michael, 69.
Lineamientos estratégicos y agenda de políticas públicas para la región metropolitana cruceña, 593.
Lira, Elizabeth, 1377.
Lizano-Araya, Melvin, 488.
Lizano-Rodríguez, Omar Gerardo, 488.
Lizarazo, Tania, 1654.
Llach, Lucas, 1391.
Llopis Hernández, José Octavio, 1570.
Lloréns, Hilda, 453, 1615, 1627.
Loeza Reyes, Laura, 1466.
La lógica neoliberal y su impacto en el estado mexicano: un enfoque multidisciplinario, 1309.
Lohse, Jon C., 26.
Lois, Carla, 395.
Looper, Matthew George, 15.
Lopes, Alberto Pereira, 783.
López, Alejandro Martín, 323.
Lopez, Felix, 1133.
López, Mario, 703.
López, Octavio Tixtha, 1491.
López, Pabel, 345, 370.
López Bárcenas, Francisco, 537.
López Caballero, Paula, 183.
López Castaño, Carlos Eduardo, 337.
López Castellanos, Nayar, 847, 1593.
López Castro, Gustavo, 1502.
López Contreras, Guillermo, 1170.
López Díaz, Martha Alicia, 114.
López-Dietz, Sandra, 699.
López Estrada, Silvia, 820.
López Guerrero, Jahel, 1504.
López Hernández, Haydeé, 16.
López Luján, Leonardo, 70.
López Montero, María Elena, 1174.
López Nájera, Verónica Renata, 1440.
López Nava, Karla Joana, 521.
López Ortega, Antonio, 1671.
López Pardo, Gustavo, 538.
López Ricoy, Eugenia, 194.
López Salazar, Roberto Oswaldo, 1555.
López Sánchez, Oliva, 1495.
López Segrera, Francisco, 976.
López-Torrijos, Ricardo, 88.
López-Vázquez, Carlos, 604.
Lora, Quisqueya, 949.
Lorda, María Amalia, 647.
Lorenzo, Cristian, 392.
Loreto López, Rosalva, 535.
Loritz, Erika, 211.
Loughlin, Michael L., 25.
Loughmiller-Cardinal, Jennifer A., 7, 71.
Louis, Jean Guy-Marie, 1195.
Lovato, Roberto, 1582.
Love, Michael W., 2, 72.
Love, Thomas F., 1710.
Lovell, W. George, 477.
Lowe, Kelsey M., 123.
Lowrey, Kathleen Bolling, 324.
Loyola Díaz, Rafael, 1316.
Loza Otero, Nicolás, 825.
Lucatello, Simone, 526, 1166.
Lucero, Gustavo, 143.
Lucio, Carlos, 525.
Lugares de memória: ditadura militar e resistências no Estado do Rio de Janeiro, 784.
Lukas, Michael, 688, 704.
Luna, Juan Pablo, 1061.
Luna Alfaro, Ángel Christian, 1492.
Luna Osorio, Luis, 1239.
Luna Tavera, Francisco, 212.
Lunde Seefeldt, Jennapher, 705.
Luzar, Jeffrey B., 276.
Lyall, Victoria I., 18.
Lyko Marczak, Halina, 1240.
Maawad, David, 89.
Maca Urbano, Deidi, 1657–1658.
Macchi, Leandro, 660.
Macedo, Alexandre Cordeiro, 1428.
Maceira, Nestor, 610.
Machuca, Luciano, 361.
Maciel, David, 1493.
Macusaya, Carlos, 1042.
Madrazo Lajous, Alejandro, 844.
Madrigal Sánchez, Víctor, 1711.
Maffini, Manuel Alfredo, 645.
Magaloni, Beatriz, 827–828, 1126.
Magliocca, Nicholas R., 480–481.
Maglione, Dora Silvia, 608.
Mahabir, Joy, 1628.

Maillet, Antoine, 1059.
Maisterrena, Javier, 177.
Makaran, Gaya, 345.
Malamud, Carlos, 953.
Malan, Pedro S., 1419.
Malas notas: voces e ideas del Club Político Argentino, 1093.
Maldonado, Carlos Eduardo, 337.
Maldonado, Gabriela Inés, 645.
Maldonado, Valentín, 45.
Maldonado Hernández, Gerardo, 956.
Maldonado LaFontaine, Mariecel, 441.
Maldonado Tomás, Rocío Elizabeth, 1570.
Malone, Mary Fran T., 912.
Mamani Ramírez, Pablo, 1043.
Manak, Leah, 505.
Mangonnet, Jorge, 1268.
Manjarrez Rosas, Josefina, 1587.
Manrique, Irma, 1318.
Mansilla, Pablo, 418.
Manson, Robert H., 530.
Mantilla Valbuena, Silvia, 443.
Manuschevich, Daniela, 706.
Manzanilla, Linda, 37, 1467.
Manzi, Maya, 372, 785.
Mao, Xianglin, 977.
Mapping South-South connections: Australia and Latin America, 396.
La maquinaria agrícola argentina: desafíos de la producción nacional en el nuevo desarrollismo, 1396.
Marandola Junior, Eduardo, 790.
Marchi Moyano, Bianca de, 1745.
Marconi Ojeda, Reynaldo, 1739.
Marcus, Alan P., 786.
Mardones Peñaloza, Marcelo Mauricio, 362.
Margalho, Maurício, 1423.
Marins, Mani Tebet A. de, 1424.
Markert, Kel N., 483.
Maroto Arce, Steven, 377.
Marques, Eduardo, 759.
Marques, Luiz C., 397.
Martí i Puig, Salvador, 914.
Martín, Eloísa, 1142.
Martinet, Gilles, 605.
Martínez, Christopher, 1070.
Martínez, Edin, 1583.
Martínez, Emilio, 1712.
Martínez, Gustavo A., 145.
Martínez, Polioptro, 387, 523.
Martínez Delgado, Gerardo, 539.
Martínez Espinoza, Manuel Ignacio, 398.
Martínez Flores, Verónica, 1494.

Martínez García, Claudia Cristina, 552.
Martínez González, Gloria, 1330.
Martínez i Coma, Ferran, 825.
Martínez Meléndez, Ángel, 1310.
Martínez Osorio, Margarita, 986.
Martínez-Reyes, Alberto, 872.
Martínez Ruiz, Rosaura, 1511.
Martínez Sánchez, Gloriana, 853.
Martínez Valdés, Valentina, 524.
Martins, Carlos Eduardo, 1269.
Martins, Luis Carlos dos Passos, 1425.
Martins, Sckarleth, 259.
Martner, Gonzalo, 1379.
Martos López, Luis Alberto, 213.
Martz de la Vega, Hans, 79.
Marulanda, José J., 1147.
Marvel, Lucilla Fuller, 441.
Más allá de las fronteras: integración, vecindad y gobernanza: Colombia, Ecuador, Perú, 1209.
Masculinidades, familias y comunidades afectivas, 1495.
Masek, Vaclav, 895.
Masferrer K., Elio, 829.
Massidda, Adriana Laura, 373.
Massol Deyá, Arturo A., 454.
Mata Zenteno, Ximena, 809.
Matanock, Aila M., 827.
Mateos Inchauspe, Macarena, 646.
Mathewson, Kent, 380.
Matsumoto, Yuichi, 167.
Matta, Raúl, 369.
Mattei, Lauro, 1418.
Mattiace, Shannan L., 806, 826.
Mattos, César Costa Alves de, 1428.
Matus Acuña, Alejandra, 1380.
Maurial, Álvaro, 1713.
Maya, Mario Alejandro, 647.
Maya kingship: rupture and transformation from Classic to Postclassic times, 17.
Mayer Center Symposium, *17th, Denver Art Museum, 2017*, 18.
Mayka, Lindsay, 992, 1127.
Maza, Francisca de la, 348.
Maza García de Alba, Rocío, 73.
Mazzanti, Diana L., 145.
McCall, Michael K., 420.
McClung de Tapia, Emily, 96.
McCool, Weston C., 168.
McCordic, Cameron, 455.
McCullich, Cindy, 525.
McField, Melanie, 476.
McIntyre, Alister, 938.

McIntyre, Meredith A., 938.
McKay, Ben M., 357.
McKenzie, Gabrielle, 939.
McNeil, Cameron L., 76.
McPherson, Alan L., 1230.
McSweeney, Kendra, 249, 469, 478, 480–481, 505.
Medel, Rodrigo, 1080.
Medina, Arely, 1496.
Medina Garzón, Camilo Andrés, 1270.
Medina Martínez, Fuensanta, 830.
Medina Miranda, Héctor M., 214.
Medina-Mora, María Elena, 1467.
Medina Sánchez, Fabián, 915.
Medios públicos: políticas, actores, estrategias, 1094.
Medrano de Luna, Gabriel, 207.
Medwinter, Sancha Doxilly, 940.
Megaminería en América Latina: estados, empresas transnacionales y conflictos socioambientales, 399.
Mejia, Daniel, 984.
Mejía-Guinand, Luis Bernardo, 993.
Mejía Navarrete, Julio Víctor, 1441.
Mejía Sanabria, Carlos Alberto, 1657–1658.
Meléndez, Carlos, 1071.
Melgar Tísoc, Emiliano Ricardo, 37, 74.
Mellon, Jonathan, 1132.
Melo, Vanessa, 1126.
Melosi, Martin V., 405.
Memoria y resistencia en Xoxocotla, 215.
Memorias del presente: ensayos sobre juventud, violencia y el horizonte democrático, 1713.
Méndez de Hoyos, Irma, 825.
Mendieta Ocampo, Jorge Alirio, 564.
Mendizabal, Tomás, 511.
Mendoza, Liz, 1056.
Mendoza, Marcos, 648.
Mendoza García, Leticia, 1497.
Menéndez, Mariana, 1547.
Menéndez González, Irene, 1271.
Meneses Herrera, Luis, 1044.
Menjívar, Cecilia, 1597.
Meraz Ruiz, Lino, 1311.
Mercadal, Silvina, 1094.
Mercado, Alejandro, 1290.
Mercado Ibarra, Santa Magdalena, 180.
Merchán, Yelitza Osorio, 400.
Mereles, Fátima, 734.
Mérida Martínez, Israel, 1045–1046.
Meridians: Feminism, Race, Transnationalism, 941.

Merk, Stephan, 54.
Mesa-Lago, Carmelo, 1356–1358.
Metamorfoses florestais: culturas, ecologias e as transformações históricas da Mata Atlântica, 787.
Métodos cuantitativos en geografía humana, 649.
México, Mexico (state). Secretaría de Educación, 23.
México: represión, resistencia y rebeldía: L@s zapatistas, el Congreso Nacional Indígena, las madres y padres de Ayotzinapa, l@s normalistas, l@s jornaler@as, l@s maestr@s disidentes, las luchas por la autonomía y el territorio, otros movimientos sociales y la necesidad de una filosofía de la revolución, 216.
México y la Sociedad de Naciones: una antología documental, 1170.
México y Uruguay ante la Gran Recesión, 1413.
Mexico's human rights crisis, 1498.
Meyer, Lorenzo, 1173.
Meza Peñaloza, Abigail, 19.
Meza Torres, Andrea, 1540.
Meza Velarde, Alejandra, 1321.
Mezzadra, Sandro, 1435.
Mezzenzana, Francesca, 288.
Michelet, Dominique, 40.
Micheli T., Jordy, 1301.
Michelotti, Fernando, 795.
Migración de tránsito por la ruta del Pacífico mexicano: caso Sinaloa: analizando al fenómeno y sus actores, 217.
La migración intrarregional en América Latina: sociedad, legislación y desafíos en un mundo complejo, 401.
Migración miradas y reflexiones desde la universidad, 1499.
Migración: nuevos actores, procesos y retos, 1500.
Migración, remesas y actividad económica en las relaciones bilaterales México-Estados Unidos, 1171.
Migraciones y movilidades en el centro de México, 1501.
Migrants, refugees, and asylum seekers in Latin America, 402.
Miguel, Vinicius Valentin Raduan, 271.
Miguel S. Wionczek y el Prointergemex: travesías en el petróleo mexicano, 1312.
Miklos, Tomás, 540.
Milani, Carlos R.S., 1207.

Milei, Javier Gerardo, 1397.
Millán, René, 1453.
Millán Valenzuela, Henio, 1313.
Miller, Errol, 959.
Miller, Jacob C., 707.
Miller, Michael K., 1265.
Mimica, Nicolás, 1072.
Miranda, Bruno, 406.
La misión de la máquina: técnica, extractivismo y conversión en las tierras bajas sudamericanas, 325.
Mita Machaca, Julio Cesar, 1741.
Moctezuma Longoria, Miguel, 1486.
Moctezuma Pérez, Sergio, 419, 548–549.
Modelos económicos de las regiones de México, 1314.
Modeste, Denneth M., 1196.
Modificaciones cefálicas culturales en Mesoamérica: una perspectiva continental, 20.
El modo de acumulación en la Argentina contemporánea, 1398.
Mohammadi, Elham, 455–456.
Mojica Madrigal, Óscar Ariel, 1502.
Molenaar, Fransje, 1584.
Molina, Fernando, 1742.
Molina Camacho, Francisco, 708.
Molina Jiménez, Iván, 1579.
Molina O., Raúl, 710.
Mollett, Sharlene, 403, 512.
Mombello, Laura, 650.
Mommer, Bernard, 1368–1369.
Moncayo Moncayo, Patricio, 1012.
Mondragón González, Araceli, 541.
Monje, Daniela, 1094.
Monje Penha, Felix Eney, 563.
Monreal Ávila, Ricardo, 831.
Monsalve, Mauricio, 697.
Montanari, Emanuel Guillermo, 641.
Montani, Rodrigo, 326.
Montás, Juan Temístocles, 1341.
Monte, Antonio, 916.
Montenegro, Germán, 1218.
Montero, Sergio, 1276.
Monterrosa Desruelles, Hervé Victor, 74.
Monterroso Salvatierra, Neptalí, 410.
Montes, Nahuel, 651.
Montes de Oca Barrera, Laura Beatriz, 1315.
Montes de Oca Hernández, Acela, 419.
Montes Galbán, Eloy José, 616, 652–654.
Montgomery, Shane M., 101.
Monti, Alejandra I., 655.
Montobbio, Manuel, 894.

Montoute, Annita, 934.
Montoya, Ainhoa, 498, 873.
Montoya, Francisco, 753.
Montoya Gómez, Brígida, 1662.
Montoya Rodríguez, Paola, 377.
Montoya Ruiz, Sandra, 1235.
Montoya Zavala, Erika, 1503.
Monzón Flores, Martha, 218.
Mora, Marie T., 1342.
Mora Cortés, Luis Fernando Ricardo, 552.
Mora Cortés, María Teresa del Carmen, 552.
Mora-García, Claudio A., 1585.
Mora Mora, José U., 1139.
Moraes, Flávia D., 457.
Morais, Fernando, 1197.
Moral Pajares, Encarnación, 517.
Morales, Fabiola, 1743.
Morales, Helda, 502.
Morales Álvarez, Manuel, 1047.
Morales-Arilla, Jose, 1023.
Morales Franco, Fabiola, 1743.
Morales Gamarra, Ricardo, 173.
Morales Olmos, Virginia, 1416.
Morales Quiroga, Mauricio, 1075.
Morales Raya, Eva, 735.
Morales-Salinas, Luis, 689.
Morán Alvarez, Julio César, 192.
Morando, Agustina, 327.
Moratto Vásquez, Nadia Semenova, 1649.
Mordecki, Gabriela, 1413.
Morea, Juan Pablo, 656.
Moreano, Melissa, 386, 570, 576.
Morell-Hart, Shanti, 75–76.
Moreno Hernández, Hugo César, 1586.
Moreno Jiménez, Antonio, 613, 694.
Moreno León, Carlos Enrique, 994.
Moreno Mora, Rodrigo, 691.
Moreno Ortiz, Evelyn, 441.
Moreno Pineda, Edgar Adrián, 210.
Moreno Rodríguez, Laura Beatriz, 1169.
Moreno Rubio, Sergio, 1661.
Morera Beita, Carlos, 381.
Moretto, Samira Peruchi, 780.
Morgenfeld, Leandro Ariel, 1223.
Moris, Roberto, 697.
Morrell, Patricia Alejandra, 646.
Morton, Douglas C., 792.
Morton, Shawn, 28.
Mosinger, Eric S., 917.
Mota, Dalva, 761.
Mote, Thomas L., 457.
Motta, Angélica, 1714.
Moulton, Holly, 581.

Mouyiannou, Amaryllis, 503.
Moya, Cristóbal, 1063.
Muehe, Dieter, 788.
Muench, Rebekke E., 483.
Mujeres bolivianas: desde el Parlamento hasta la Asamblea Legislativa Plurinacional, 1744–1745.
Mujeres en la policía: miradas feministas sobre su experiencia y su entorno laboral, 1504.
Mujeres, migración centroamericana y violencia: un diagnóstico para el caso de Puebla, 1587.
Mujeres y participación política: proceso electoral 2015–2016 de Aguascalientes, 832.
Mujica Barrera, Elías, 173.
Müller, Ingrid, 316.
Mulrennan, Monica E., 695.
O mundo indígena na América Latina: olhares e perspectivas, 250.
Muniz, Antônio Walber Matias, 1145.
Muñiz Zúñiga, Viviana, 978.
Munizaga, Juan, 719.
Munoz, Ercio, 458.
Muñoz Martínez, Aurora del Socorro, 219.
Muñoz Mata, Laura, 1162.
Muñoz-Nájar Rojas, Teresina, 1715.
Muñoz-Portillo, Juan, 857, 906.
Muñoz S., Camila, 154.
Muñoz Sánchez, Hernando, 1655.
Muñoz Velasco, Luis Alfredo, 1656.
Muriente Pérez, Julio A., 971.
Murillo, Diana, 576.
Murillo, María Victoria, 1268.
Murillo Garnica, Jacqueline, 1629.
Murtinho, Felipe, 573.
Museo del Templo Mayor (Mexico), 74.
Museo Nacional de Antropología (Mexico), 48, 100.
Musto, Ryan A., 1148.
Mustoni, Nora, 671.
La nación petrolera: Venezuela, 1914–2014, 1370.
Nacionalismo, globalización y participación social: re-visiones sobre el manejo del patrimonio cultural en México, 21.
NACLA Report on the Americas, 970.
Nadarajah, Yaso, 449.
Nägele, Kathrin, 129.
Nahón, Cecilia, 1223.
Nahuelhual, Laura, 610.

Name, Leonardo, 737.
Napoletano, Brian, 420.
Natanson, José, 1095.
Nates Cruz, Beatriz, 564.
National Endowment for the Humanities, 1613.
Native peoples, politics, and society in contemporary Paraguay: multidisciplinary perspectives, 328.
Navarrete, Jorge Eduardo, 1287.
Navarrete-Hernández, Pablo, 709.
Navarrete Linares, Federico, 229.
Navarrete Yáñez, Bernardo, 1075.
Navarro Arredondo, Alejandro, 361.
Navarro Chávez, José César Lenin, 1171.
Navarro-Pérez, José Javier, 872.
Navarro Smith, Alejandra, 80.
Navia, Patricio, 858, 895, 1072, 1381.
Nazareno, Marcelo, 1098.
Negociación de paz, escenarios para el desarrollo y la integración fronteriza Ecuador-Colombia, 1241.
Negotiating gender, policy and politics in the Caribbean: feminist strategies, masculinist resistance and transformational possibilities, 1630.
Negotiating space in Latin America, 404.
Nehe, Börries, 1746.
Neira Orjuela, Fernando, 1442.
Nelson, Stephen C., 1282.
Nelson-Nuñez, Jami, 389, 411.
Nengvaanemquescama Nempayvaam Enlhet, 329.
Nerome, Mariela, 669.
Netflix (firm), 1113.
Netzahualcoyotzi, Raúl, 1298.
Neumann, Pamela J., 1588.
New political culture in the Caribbean, 942.
New World cities: challenges of urbanization and globalization in the Americas, 405.
Nicaragua, el cambio azul y blanco: dejando atrás el régimen de Ortega, 918.
A Nicaraguan exceptionalism?: debating the legacy of the Sandinista revolution, 919.
Nicolau, Jairo Marconi, 1128.
Nicoletti, María Andrea, 1213.
Niedzwiecki, Sara, 1129.
Nielsen, Erik A., 480–481, 505.
Niesenbaum, Richard A., 489.
Night and darkness in ancient Mesoamerica, 22.

Niñez detenida, los derechos de los niños, niñas y adolescentes migrantes en la frontera México-Guatemala: diagnóstico y propuesta para pasar del control migratorio a la protección integral de la niñez, 1505.
Niño, César Augusto, 1149.
Niño Martínez, José Javier, 1645.
Niveles de vida en un país en ciernes: dimensiones de la desigualdad en la Argentina en el largo plazo, 1700–1900, 1399.
El no al ALCA diez años después: la Cumbre de Mar del Plata y la integración latinoamericana reciente, 1210.
Nobbs-Thiessen, Ben, 736.
Nociones sobre seguridad y paz en las relaciones internacionales contemporáneas, 1149.
Nodari, Eunice Sueli, 780.
Noguera Santaella, José, 1371.
Non-humans in Amerindian South America: ethnographies of Indigenous cosmologies, rituals and songs, 251.
Nondédéo, Philippe, 17.
Norman, Susan Virginia, 995.
Norte-sur: diálogos de frontera, 1172.
Nosotros que nos quisimos tanto: rupturas y continuidades en la relación con los sindicatos en las administraciones kirchneristas, 1096.
Nostti, Raúl Bringas, 1506.
Notaro, Jorge, 1414.
Novaes, Lucas M., 1130.
Novellino, Paula Silvana, 148.
Novelo, Victoria, 196.
Novkovic, Sonja, 1349.
Novotny, Anna C., 77.
Nueva Historia Económica de la Argentina: temas, problemas, autores; el último medio siglo: ensayos de historiografía económica desde 1810 a 2016, 1400.
Nuevo mapa de actores en Bolivia: crisis, polarización e incertidumbre (2019–2020), 1048.
Nuevo modelo energético y cambio climático en México, 1316.
Núñez, Andrés G., 710.
Núñez, Lautaro, 155.
Núñez, Paula Gabriela, 644, 1214.
Núñez Castellano, Rogelio, 953.
Núñez González, Leonardo, 809.
Núñez Tapia, Francisco Alberto, 362.
Nurse Allende, Lester, 1613.

Nygren, Anja, 368, 390.
Oakley, R. Elliott, 277.
Observatorio Político Nacional (Santa Cruz de la Sierra, Bolivia), 1051.
Ocampo, Emilio, 1100.
Ocasio, Rafael, 1631.
Ochoa Ávila, Eneida, 180.
Ochoa Nájera, José Daniel, 220.
Ochoa Rivera, Teresa, 221.
Octubre y el derecho a la resistencia: revuelta popular y neoliberalismo autoritario en Ecuador, 1013.
Oddone, Nahuel, 1146.
Offen, Karl H., 479.
Ojeda, Alex, 1055.
Ojeda Dávila, Lorena, 222.
O'Keefe, Thomas Andrew, 1150.
Okoshi Harada, Tsubasa, 17.
Oliva Medina, Mario, 1169.
Oliva Quiñones, Aurora Lucía, 236.
Olivares Dysli, Luis Benjamín, 1231.
Olivares L., Alejandro, 1070.
Olivas Hernández, Olga Lidia, 223.
Oliveira, Ana Luíza Matos de, 1420.
Oliveira, Assis da Costa, 256.
Oliveira, Edivania Granja da Silva, 255.
Oliveira, Gustavo de L.T., 789.
Oliveira, Lívia de, 790.
Oliveira Filho, Luiz Chrysostomo de, 1419.
Olivera, Julio H.G., 1406.
Oliveros, Virginia, 954, 1272.
Olmeda, Juan C., 812.
Olmedo Vera, Bertina, 46.
Olvera Muñoz, Omar Alejandro, 1507.
O'Meally, Rosalie, 938.
O'Neill, Kevin L., 1574.
Onofre Rodríguez, Dora Julia, 1508.
Ontaneda, Constanza, 289.
Opas, Minna, 252.
Opillard, Florian, 605.
Ordaz, Mario, 504.
Ordenar el territorio: un desafío para Mendoza, 657.
Ordóñez, Angélica, 351.
Ordoñez, María, 658.
Orellana Peña, Jorge Humberto, 1589.
Organization of American States (OAS), 904, 913.
Organized violence: capitalist warfare in Latin America, 1273.
Los orígenes latinoamericanos de Podemos, 1151.
Orihuela, José Carlos, 1274.

Oropeza García, Arturo, 1152.
Orrantia, Daniela, 1014.
Orrego Echeverría, Israel Arturo, 338.
Ortega, Daniel, 910.
Ortega, José Emilio, 1205.
Ortega Canto, Judith, 187.
Ortega González, Jorge Manuel, 190.
Ortiz, Agustin, 43.
Ortiz, Pablo, 662.
Ortiz Ceballos, Ponciano, 25.
Ortiz Flores, Enrique, 1583.
Ortiz Ocaña, Alexander, 1443.
Ortiz Sandoval, Luis Alberto, 740.
Ortiz-T., Pablo, 290.
Ortiz Véliz, Jorge, 691.
Osorio, Hloreley, 920.
Osorio, Rodrigo, 1381.
Osorio-Caballero, María Isabel, 1139.
Ospina Peralta, Pablo, 1015.
Ossa, Luisa Marcela, 1433.
Osses, Pablo Eugenio, 711.
Ostapkowicz, Joanna, 130.
Otero, Álvaro, 753.
Ötker, Inci, 1345.
Oulhaj, Leïla, 1471.
Out of the shadow: revisiting the revolution from post-peace Guatemala, 896.
Pachano, Simón, 1677.
Pacheco, Pablo, 761.
Pacheco-Pailahua, Stefanie, 699.
Pachón Buitrago, Mónica, 996.
Padilla, Suyapa, 1591.
Padilla Delgado, Héctor Antonio, 1298.
Padilla Gutiérrez, Eliseo Francisco, 48.
Padrón Innamorato, Mauricio, 1501.
Páez, Katherine, 716.
Painting the skin: pigments on bodies and codices in pre-Columbian Mesoamerica, 113.
Paisajes laborales postfordistas en el sur occidente colombiano, 1657–1658.
Paisajes multiversos: reflexiones en torno a la construcción del espacio social, 541.
Las palabras que en mí dormían: discursos indígenas de Bolivia, Ecuador, Chile y México, 224.
Palacios, Hugo, 1509.
Palacios-Valladares, Indira, 1073.
Palet, Andrea, 1378.
Paley, Dawn, 1273.
Palma, Romina M., 300.
Palma Campos, Claudia, 1590.
Palma Leotta, María, 658.
Palma Solís, Marco A., 187.
Palmas Castrejón, Yanelli Daniela, 421.
Palmer-Rubin, Brian, 1275.
Palomino, Bertha, 538.
Paltán López, Homero, 351.
Pansters, Wil G., 1527.
Pantin, Shane J., 1637.
Pantoja Díaz, Luis, 105.
Pardelli, Giuliana, 1123.
Pardo Fernández, Rodrigo, 1499.
Pardo Montaño, Ana Melisa, 1510.
Paré, Luisa, 530.
Paredes, Beatriz, 250.
Paredes Gudiño, Blanca Luz Mireya, 21.
Paredes-Umaña, Federico, 64.
Pareja Cucalón, Francisco, 1156.
Parga Figueroa, Orlando, 971.
Parodi, Camila, 1004.
Parpart, Jane L., 1630.
Parra Ávila, Juan, 1548.
Parra Molina, José Antonio, 842.
Parrish, Elizabeth, 459.
Parthenay, Kevin, 1138.
Participación política indígena en México: experiencias de gestión comunitaria, participación institucional y consulta previa, 833.
Participación, políticas públicas y territorio: aportes para la construcción de una perspectiva integral, 1097.
Los partidos de izquierda ante la cuestión indígena, 1920–1977, 1049.
Pasaron cosas: política y políticas públicas en el gobierno de Cambiemos, 1098.
Paso de la Amada: an early Mesoamerican ceremonial center, 78.
Pastore, Affonso Celso, 1419.
Pastrana Buelvas, Eduardo, 1154, 1233.
Patiño-Gómez, Carlos, 387.
Patiño Gómez, Zaida Liz, 559.
Un patrimonio universal: las pirámides de México: cosmovisión, cultura y ciencia, 23.
Patrucco Núñez-Carvalho, Sandro, 584.
Patterson, Orlando, 1632.
Patterson, Percival James, 1343.
Paulsen Bilbao, Abraham, 712.
Paulsen Espinoza, Alex, 713.
Pavão, Nara, 1131.
Pavlic, Rodolfo, 1080.
Paz Arauco, Verónica, 1739.
Paz en el territorio: diálogo intercultural y justicia social, 1659.

Paz Frayre, Miguel Ángel, 225.
Paz Reverol, Carmen Laura, 278.
Pearson, Zoe, 481.
Peate, Ailsa, 374.
Pedone, Claudia, 406.
Pedraza Álvarez, Laura Nayeli, 1481.
Pedrini, Giovanni, 303.
Pedrozo Conedo, Zaira Esther, 1443.
Peixoto, Tiago, 1132.
Pelfini, Alejandro, 1212.
Peluso, Daniela, 291.
Peña, Carlos, 1373.
Peña Farias, Ángela I., 1633.
Peñaloza, Fernanda, 396.
El pensamiento político de los movimientos sociales, 1687.
Pensando Bolivia desde México: estado, movimientos, territorios y representaciones, 1746.
Pensar Ayotzinapa, 1511.
Pensar la economía argentina: por una macroeconomía compatible con el desarrollo, 1401.
Pensar Palestina desde el Sur Global, 1153.
Peralta, Sebastián, 340.
Peralta Beltrán, José Orlando, 1050.
Peralta de Legarreta, Alberto, 226.
Peraza Noriega, Brianda Elena, 217.
Perdomo Gamboa, Óscar, 1660.
Pereira, Anthony W., 1418.
Pereira, Carlos, 1133.
Pereira, Edwina E., 964.
Pereira, Grégory, 48, 100.
Pereira, Luiz Carlos Bresser, 1426.
Pereira, Ritaumaria, 795.
Pereira, Sonia Maria Couto, 260.
Pereira, Wagner Pinheiro, 250.
Pereira Júnior, Davi, 416.
Pereira M., Rodney, 1739.
Perelló, Lucas, 858, 895.
Peresini, Natalí del Valle, 631.
Perevochtchikova, María, 521.
Pérez, Gilberto, 98.
Pérez, Kelita, 169.
Pérez, Laura, 316.
Pérez, Louis A., 1359.
Pérez Brito, Antonio Emmanuel, 1302.
Pérez-Bustos, Tania, 1650.
Pérez Caldentey, Esteban, 1283.
Pérez-Campos, Xyoli, 504.
Pérez Centeno, Marcelo Javier, 358.
Pérez de Heredia, Eduardo, 42.
Pérez-Escamilla, Rafael, 508.

Pérez Leiva, Pablo, 686.
Pérez-Lizasuain, César, 1634.
Pérez Morales, Faustino, 807.
Pérez Mutul, José, 187.
Pérez Negrete, Miguel, 79.
Pérez Pineda, Jorge A., 1317.
Pérez-Ramírez, Carlos Alberto, 542.
Pérez Rodríguez, Verónica, 24.
Pérez Sáinz, Juan Pablo, 1601.
Pérez Sánchez, José Manuel, 548.
Périplos: Revista de Pesquisa sobre Migrações, 406.
Perlès, Catherine, 155.
Perló Cohen, Manuel, 527, 817.
Pernudi Chavarría, Vilma, 227.
Perreira, Krista Marlyn, 1597.
Perspectiva Geográfica, 407.
Perú: crónicas y perfiles, 1716.
Peru. Ministerio del Ambiente, 584.
Petersen, German, 834.
Petersen Farah, Carlos, 371.
Petrocelli, Santiago Pablo, 669–670.
Peuramaki-Brown, Meaghan, 28.
Pezoa, Mario, 693.
Picardo Joao, Óscar, 1591.
Picciani, Ana Laura, 659.
Picco Plencovich, Pablo, 1212.
Pick, James B., 459.
Pieces of eight: more archaeology of piracy, 131.
Piedras Feria, Ernesto, 1335.
Pienknagura, Samuel, 1184.
Pignataro, Adrián, 859.
Pilar Trujillo, María del, 1237.
Pinassi, Andrés, 341.
Pineau, Virginia Giselle, 641.
Pineda Camacho, Roberto, 279.
Pineda Duque, Javier Armando, 983.
Pineda Gómez, José Alfredo, 219.
Pinheiro, Lidriana, 788.
Pinkus Rendón, Manuel Jesús, 545.
Pinto, Juan Pablo, 1688.
Pinto Santa Cruz, Aníbal, 1382.
Piquer-Rodríguez, María, 660.
Piraux, Marc, 761.
Pires do Rio, Gisela Aquino, 737.
Piscopo, Jennifer M., 1074.
Pittman, Jeremy, 455.
Piva, Adrián, 1398.
Piwowar, Katarzyna, 175.
Planeación, gobernanza y sustentabilidad: retos y desafíos desde el enfoque territorial, 542.

Plascencia López, Ismael, 1325.
Plata Vázquez, José Luis, 177.
Pleasant, Traben, 513.
Pleyers, Geoffrey, 1444.
Plotinsky, Daniel, 1402.
PNUD Chile, 1378.
Pobreza y vulnerabilidad: debates y estudios contemporáneos en México, 1512.
Poder(es) en contexto: lecturas teológicas, socioculturales y de género en torno al poder, 1717.
Poder(es) en movimiento(s): procesos y dinámicas (re)constituyentes en Colombia durante el siglo XXI, 1661.
Pohl, John M.D., 30.
La política energética y petrolera vista desde *Foro internacional*, 1173.
La política exterior de México: entre la responsabilidad global y el interés nacional, 1174.
Política migratoria y derechos de los migrantes en México, 1513.
Política subnacional en Chile: instituciones, partidos, elecciones, 1075.
Política y elecciones en México: nuevas historias regionales, 1980–2015, 835.
Políticas de juventudes y participación política: perspectivas, agendas y ámbitos de militancia, 1099.
Políticas proactivas en lo fiscal y financiero: México y América Latina, 1318.
Políticas públicas en Paraguay: avances y desafíos 1989–2020, 1411.
Políticas y estrategias de resistencia, 1514.
Polo Amashta, Giselle Paola, 1648.
Ponce, María Gabriela, 1032.
Ponce de León, Ricardo Higelín, 24.
Ponce Ortiz, Esteban, 1682.
Ponstingel, Daria, 473.
Ponstingel, John, 481.
Pontificia Universidad Católica de Valparaíso. Programa de Magister en Relaciones Internacionales, 1227.
Pontificia Universidad Javeriana. Instituto de Estudios Interculturales, 1647.
Pontón C., Daniel, 1241.
Ponzi, Brenda Sofía, 661.
Pool, Christopher A., 25.
Pope, Cynthia, 379, 485.
Populações litorâneas e ribeirinhas na América Latina: estudos interdisciplinares, 408.
El populismo en la Argentina y en el mundo, 1100.
Porcayo Michelini, Antonio, 80.
Porter, Jennifer, 490.
Portillo, Ana, 738.
Portillo-Quintero, Carlos, 495.
Porto-Gonçalves, Carlos Walter, 370.
Portugal Loayza, Jimena, 152.
Posas, Mario, 1592.
Postero, Nancy Grey, 310.
Pou, Sonia Alexandra, 662.
Power, Timothy Joseph, 1114.
Powis, Terry G., 93.
Pozo Serrano, Francisco José del, 1648.
Praça, Sérgio, 1133.
Prácticas comunicativas y prefiguraciones políticas en tiempos inciertos, 1515.
Prada-Trigo, José, 575.
Prado Ramírez, Rogelio, 519.
Prado Salmón, Fernando, 593–594.
Prado Zanini, Isabella, 593.
Prates, Luciano, 141.
Praxis en América Latina (organization), 216.
Preceramic Mesoamerica, 26.
Price, Jessica J., 836.
Price, Richard, 1635.
Price, Sally, 1635.
Price, T. Douglas, 81.
Priego Brito, Erik Manuel, 1316.
Prieto, Alfredo, 975.
Prieto Corredor, Germán Camilo, 1211.
Prieto Sánchez, Roberto, 1718.
Procesos migratorios en la Centroamérica del siglo XXI, 1593.
Prouse, Carolyn, 791.
Provencio Durazo, Enrique, 1287.
La proyección de China en América Latina y el Caribe, 1154.
Pueblos indígenas y estado en México: la disputa por la justicia y los derechos, 228.
Puello-Socarrás, José Francisco, 1661.
Puente Aguilar, Sergio, 521.
Puente Martínez, Khemvirg, 837.
Los puentes y las puertas: las fronteras de la política argentina a través de sus elites, 1101.
Puga, Ismael, 1063.
Pugh, Jeffrey D., 1016.
Pugh, Timothy W., 47, 82.
Pugliese, Melanie, 76.
Pulgar Pinaud, Claudio, 605.

¿Qué hacemos con la(s) masculinidad(es)?: reflexiones antipatriarcales para pasar del privilegio al cuidado, 1689.
¡Que hermosa es tu voz!: relatos de los Enlhet sobre la historia de su pueblo, 329.
Querejazu Lewis, Roy, 153.
Quesada-Román, Adolfo, 491, 494.
Quick, Joe, 351.
Quiñones Calderón, Antonio, 971.
Quintal López, Rocío, 1516.
Quintana Jara, Yonatan, 698.
Quintero Novoa, Raúl Teobaldo de Jesús, 1524.
Quiroga, Aníbal Alejandro, 622.
Quiroga, Diego, 351.
Quirós, Julieta, 663.
Quiroz, Enriqueta, 1308.
Quiroz Londoño, Orlando Mauricio, 664.
Racismo y desigualdad: una visión multidisciplinar, 1517.
Radical cartographies: participatory map-making from Latin America, 409.
Radiografía de la violencia regional: indicadores de diversos tópicos de violencia en el departamento de Antioquia, 1662.
Ragazzini, Irene, 211.
Rahier, Jean Muteba, 1690–1691.
Rahman, Eric, 874.
Railsback, Loren Bruce, 482.
Rainer, Gerhard, 665.
Rajão, Raoni, 778.
Ramakrishnan, Uma, 1345.
Ramassote, Rodrigo Martins, 189.
Ramírez, Erna, 329.
Ramírez, Martín, 378.
Ramírez, Sócrates, 1026.
Ramírez Bautista, Bernardino, 1719.
Ramírez Cañedo, Elier, 1198.
Ramírez Frías, Clemente Hugo, 1636.
Ramírez Gallegos, René, 1017.
Ramírez Gröbli, María del Pilar, 1663.
Ramírez Hernández, Marcos, 210.
Ramírez Hernández, Roberto, 1319.
Ramírez López, Dulce Karol, 1518.
Ramírez Pascualli, Carlos A., 706.
Ramos, Ventura, 1554.
Ramos Bonilla, Andrea, 586.
Ramos de Castro, Edna Maria, 795.
Ramos García, José María, 1146.
Ramos Viera, Aida, 534.
Rampazo, Adriana Vinholi, 770.
Rangel, Lucia Helena, 256.
Rangel Cáceres, Antonio, 1672.
Rao, Anirudh, 503.
Raponi, Livia, 267.
Rapoport, Mario, 1403.
Rappoport, Luis, 1093.
Rausch, Gisela Ariana, 666–667.
Rausch, Lisa L., 792.
Raventós Vorst, Ciska, 860, 1336.
Raymond, Christopher D., 838.
Raynal, José A., 387.
Raynal-Gutiérrez, María E., 387.
Rearte, Astrid, 641.
Rebollar, Maria Dolores Campos, 253.
Recalde, Eulalia Flor, 1009.
Recalde, Marina Yesica, 1388.
La reciente crisis financiera y el debate sobre migración y desarrollo: propuestas para América Latina y México, 1320.
Recientes investigaciones sobre sitios con quilcas o arte rupestre en el Perú, 170.
Reconfiguraciones socioterritoriales: entre el despojo capitalista y las resistencias comunitarias, 1321.
Red Internacional de Procesos Participativos, Género y Desarrollo Territorial, 419.
Red Temática: "Tecnologías Digitales para la Difusión del Patrimonio Cultural", 3.
Redes Arawa: ensaios de etnologia do Médio Purus, 261.
Reed, David M., 22.
Reflexiones interdisciplinarias sobre la ciudadanía de género: mujeres en la Ciudad de México, 1519.
Regional discourses on society and history: shaping the Caribbean, 1637.
Regiones periféricas, gobernanza frágil: desarrollo económico local desde América Latina, 1276.
Regnier, Amanda, 68.
Reifschneider, Meredith, 132.
Reimagining the Gran Chaco: identities, politics, and the environment in South America, 330.
Rein, Raanan, 402.
Reinoso, Diego, 800.
Reinoso Niche, Jorgelina, 244.
Las relaciones entre Sudamérica y Asia-Pacífico en un mundo incierto: los casos de Argentina, Chile y Brasil, 1212.
Religiones, 229.
Religiosidades transplantadas: recomposiciones religiosas en nuevos escenarios transnacionales, 1520.
Rennó, Lúcio R., 1124.

Renta básica universal: más libertad, más igualdad, más empleo, más bienestar: una propuesta para Guatemala (2019–2030), 1337.
Repensando el turismo sustentable, 410.
Resende, André Lara, 1427.
Reséndiz Rivera, Nelly Erandy, 1594.
La restauración ecológica productiva: el camino para recuperar el patrimonio biocultural de los pueblos mesoamericanos, 543.
Los retos del desarrollo local en el ámbito rural, 544.
Retos demográficos en Colombia y Cuba, 460.
Retos, oportunidades y fracasos del ecoturismo: Reserva de la Biosfera Ría Celestún, México, 545.
A revolução do antitruste no Brasil: a era dos cartéis, 1428.
The revolution from within: Cuba, 1959–1980, 979.
Reyes, Raimy, 1638.
Reyes Albarracín, Fredy Leonardo, 273.
Reyes Hernández, Humberto, 381.
Reyes Montes, Laura, 548.
Reyes Morales, Rafael G., 1521.
Reyes Pérez, Óscar, 381.
Reygadas Langarica, Yununen, 500.
Rezagos de la economía de Jalisco en la apertura económica (1980–2015), 1322.
Rezende, Vinícius de, 1429.
Ribeiro, Ana Freitas, 765.
Ribeiro, Karina Braga, 765.
Ribeiro Hoffmann, Andrea, 1199.
Rice, Mark, 587.
Rice, Prudence M., 83.
Richard, Analiese, 1466.
Richard, Matthew A., 775.
Richard, Nicolas, 325.
Richmond, Matthew Aaron, 793.
Rico-Rodríguez, Tyanif, 420.
Riggio, Milla Cozart, 1639.
Rinaldi, Arturo, 714.
Rinke, Stefan H., 402.
Riofrancos, Thea N., 1018, 1258.
Riojas López, Carlos, 1322.
Ríos, Diego Martín, 667.
Ríos, Mariana, 755.
Rios, Viridiana, 1264.
Riquelme Brevis, Hernán, 715.
Riquelme Brevis, Matías, 715.
Riris, Philip, 171.

Riva Palacio Guerrero, Felipe, 1288.
Rivas Otero, José Manuel, 1151.
Rivas Sada, Eva Luisa, 529.
Rivera Andía, Juan Javier, 251.
Rivera Cusicanqui, Silvia, 1747.
Rivera García, Óscar Bernardo, 1522.
Rivera Heredia, María Elena, 1499.
Rivera Sosa, Andrea, 481.
Rivera Vélez, Fredy, 1019.
Rivero, Ariel, 340.
Roa Martínez, María Gertrudis, 1646.
Robayo Lemarie, Anibal, 1240.
Robertini, Camillo, 1404.
Robertson, Raymond, 1184.
Robins, Nicholas A., 391.
Robinson, Eugenia J., 61.
Robledo Silvestre, Carolina, 1523.
Robles, Gustavo, 827.
Robles Robles, María del Rosario Fátima, 1323.
Rocca Torres, Luis, 1720–1721.
Rocha, Heder Leandro, 668.
Rocha, José Luis, 921, 1595.
Rodas Ziadé, Fadia Paola, 1692.
Rodgers, David, 248.
Rodríguez, Bernardo, 98.
Rodríguez, Carlos Armando, 159.
Rodríguez, Cecilia Graciela, 907.
Rodríguez, Havidán, 1342.
Rodríguez, Indhira Libertad, 1025.
Rodríguez, Jorge, 716.
Rodríguez, José Luis, 980.
Rodríguez, Mariana, 492, 870, 881.
Rodríguez, Tomás, 672.
Rodríguez Arechavaleta, Carlos Manuel, 981.
Rodríguez Cancel, Jaime L., 1200.
Rodríguez Elizondo, José, 1076, 1232.
Rodríguez Franco, Diana, 565.
Rodríguez Galván, María Guadalupe, 358.
Rodríguez Garavito, César A., 565.
Rodríguez García, Huascar, 1049.
Rodríguez Gutiérrez, José Guadalupe, 1486.
Rodríguez Hernández, Leyde E., 1155.
Rodríguez Hernández, Rogelio, 1524.
Rodríguez Herrejón, Guillermo Fernando, 362.
Rodríguez López, Mercedes, 1664.
Rodríguez-Luna, Ernesto, 524.
Rodríguez Miranda, Adrián, 751.
Rodríguez Mota, Francisco Manuel, 84.
Rodríguez-Mourelo, Belén, 1622.

Rodríguez Muñoz, Gregoria, 421.
Rodríguez Ortiz, Lauriano Eliseo, 1309.
Rodríguez Pastor, Humberto, 1722.
Rodríguez-Ramírez, Rony, 920.
Rodríguez Ramos, Alexis, 1624.
Rodríguez-Rivera, Luis E., 461.
Rodríguez Sánchez Lara, Gerardo, 839.
Rodríguez-Silva, Ileana M., 462.
Rodríguez Sumano, Abelardo, 840, 1175.
Rodríguez Vargas, Rafael A., 463.
Rofman, Adriana, 1097.
Rogan, John, 865.
Rogers, Alexander K., 85.
Rogers, Melissa Ziegler, 863.
Rojas, Mara Leticia, 1388.
Rojas Casimiro, Mauricio, 1077.
Rojas Hernández, Jorge, 393.
Rojas Herrera, Inés, 535.
Rojo Mendoza, Félix, 717.
Rojo Negrete, Iskra A., 521.
Rolande, Josinelma Ferreira, 262.
Román, Carolina, 1415.
Román, Madeline, 1617.
Román Alarcón, Rigoberto Arturo, 546.
Román Jáquez, Juana Gabriela, 552.
Román R., Raúl, 443.
Román Reyes, Rosa Patricia, 1501.
Romanelli, Asunción, 664.
Romano, Sarah T., 411.
Romero, Nadia, 576.
Romero, Ramón, 1554.
Romero, Vidal, 827.
Romero Aravena, Hugo, 422.
Romero Luna, Monzerrat, 235.
Romero Robles, David Daniel, 230.
Romero-Toledo, Hugo, 718.
Romero Vadillo, Jorge Javier, 844.
Romero-Vargas, Marilyn, 493.
Romeu Aldaya, Vivian, 1723.
Rommen, Timothy, 944.
Romo Viramontes, Raúl, 1501.
Rondon: inventários do Brasil, 1900–1930, 263.
Roniger, Luis, 606–607, 1277, 1445.
Ronzón Hernández, Zoraida, 1501.
Roriz, João, 758.
Ros, Jaime, 1292.
Rosa, Herman, 470.
Rosa Gutiérrez, Yuri Leopoldo de la, 86.
Rosales, Antulio, 1364, 1372.
Rosas Salas, Sergio Francisco, 551.
Rosendo Chávez, Alejandro, 419.
Rosenswig, Robert M., 27, 87–88.
Rosique Cañas, José Antonio, 547.
Rossi, Alejandro M., 1096.
Rossi, Franco, 1.
Rossi, Pedro Linhares, 1420.
Rosso, Beatriz, 701.
Rosso, Cintia N., 331.
Rosso, Lucila, 1210.
Los "rostros invisibles" de la desigualdad social: un estudio sobre arte, política, educación y consumo cultural en América Latina: los casos de Lima y la Ciudad de México, 1723.
Rougier, Eric, 1430.
Rougier, Marcelo, 1395.
Roura Álvarez, Lisette, 133.
Rousseau, Isabelle, 1173.
Rovira Kaltwasser, Cristóbal, 1071.
Rozario, Tannuja D., 940.
Ruales, Gabriela, 576.
Rubial García, Antonio, 229.
Rubinzal, Diego, 1384.
Rubio Correa, Jorge Félix, 1244.
Rubio González, Ricardo, 712.
Rueda, Miguel R., 1278.
Ruhl, J. Mark, 922.
Ruiz, Irma, 332.
Ruiz, Nelson A., 1278.
Ruiz, Vannia, 719.
Ruiz Euler, Alexander, 828.
Ruiz Peyré, Fernando, 624.
Ruiz Ponce, Heriberto, 231.
Ruiz-Rodríguez, Leticia M., 956.
Ruiz Romero, Gabriel, 1645.
Rumbo al auto del futuro: innovación, sistemas de calidad y trabajo en la industria automotriz de México, 1324.
Lo rural en redefinición: aproximaciones y estrategias desde la geografía, 412.
Rurange Espinoza, Jacqueline de, 687.
Russo Garrido, Anahi, 1525.
Ruvalcaba Mercado, Jesús, 195.
Ryburn, Megan, 720.
Sá, Magali Romero, 263.
Sá Carvalho, Carolina, 292.
Saavedra, Valentina, 721.
Saborit, Antonio, 62, 89.
Sacher, William, 399.
Sachs, Jeffrey D., 1033.
Saelzer Canouet, Gerardo, 722.
Sagot, Montserrat, 1436.
Sain, Marcelo Fabián, 1102, 1218.
Sajuria, Javier, 1071.
Salas Acarapi, Juan Carlos, 1739.

Salas Alfaro, Renato, 1461, 1526.
Salas Maturana, Alejandro, 401.
Salazar, Lucy C., 164.
Salazar Burrows, Alejandro, 719.
Salazar Cachi, Ladislao, 1735.
Salazar Chávez, Víctor E., 6.
Salazar de la Torre, Cecilia, 1746.
Salazar Lohman, Huáscar, 1038.
Salcedo Ávila, Gustavo Enrique, 1246.
Salega, María Soledad, 148.
Salgado Espinoza, Raúl, 1242.
Salgado-Gálvez, Mario A., 504.
Salgado López, Héctor, 159.
Salgado Peñaherrera, Germánico, 1156.
Salim Grau, Jacqueline, 629.
Salinas, Cecilia, 333.
Salisbury, David S., 589.
Samaniego Mesías, Augusto, 1078.
Sámano Rentería, Miguel Ángel, 232.
Samaroo, Brinsley, 464, 947.
Samet, Robert, 1031.
San Martín, José, 1725.
Sanabria-Coto, Iván J., 494.
Sánchez, Francisco, 1677.
Sánchez, Gabriel, 1226.
Sánchez, Jhon Antón, 1691.
Sánchez, Martha Judith, 414.
Sánchez Aguilar, Aníbal, 1724.
Sánchez Albarrán, Armando, 1514.
Sánchez Almanza, Adolfo, 520.
Sánchez-Azofeifa, Gerardo-Arturo, 495.
Sánchez González, Mónica Elivier, 1586.
Sánchez Gutiérrez, Gabriela, 1187.
Sánchez Nava, Pedro Francisco, 23.
Sánchez Osorio, Ever, 519, 1447.
Sánchez Peña, Landy, 521.
Sánchez Reséndiz, Victor Hugo, 215.
Sánchez Soria, David, 662.
Sánchez Suárez, Aurelio, 243.
Sánchez Vázquez, Sergio, 92.
Sandi Bernal, Ruben, 595.
Sandoval, Iván, 690, 723.
Sandoval Díaz, José, 683.
Sandoval Godoy, Sergio A., 1324.
Sandoval Hormazabal, Marfilda, 685.
Sandoval Palacios, Juan Manuel, 1298.
Sanguinetty, Jorge A., 1360.
La Santa Muerte in Mexico: history, devotion, & society, 1527.
Santamaría, Gema, 1528.
Santana Juárez, Marcela Virginia, 649.
Sant'Anna, Sérgio Luiz Pinheiro, 1145.
Santasilia, Catharina E., 77.
Santelices Spikin, Andrea, 393.
Santi Huaranca, Inés Fanny, 1730.
Santiago, Mario Alberto, 1331.
Santiago, Ruth, 1615.
Santilli, Daniel, 1399.
Santos, Boaventura de Sousa, 1004, 1444.
Santos, Carlos Alberto Batista, 255.
Santos, Gilton Mendes dos, 261.
Santos, Jader de Oliveira, 797.
Santos, María Josefa, 1290.
Santos, Miguel Angel, 1023.
Santos, Saúl de los, 1325.
Santos Alvite, Eduardo, 1156.
Sanz-Levia, Laura, 897.
Sarachu, Gerardo, 756.
Saraiva, Luiz Alex Silva, 770.
Saraví, Gonzalo Andrés, 1512.
Sardo, Daniel Enrique, 371.
Sarkar, Avijit, 459.
Sarmiento Barletti, Juan Pablo, 293–294.
Sauls, Laura Aileen, 470–471, 501.
Savenije, Wim, 867.
Saving Guatemala's fight against crime and impunity, 898.
Saviola, Donatella, 130.
Scarato, Luciane, 372.
Scardino, Marisa, 669–670.
Scarpa, Gustavo F., 331.
Scartascini, Carlos G., 1251.
Scartascini, Federico Luis, 146.
Schabasser, Christoph, 179.
Schackt, Jon, 280.
Schelly, Ian, 792.
Schenoni, Luis L., 1279.
Schlink Ruiz, Carlos, 593.
Schmalz, Stefan, 378.
Schneider, Cathy Lisa, 1457.
Schneider, Cecilia, 1088.
Schoneveld, George, 761.
Schorr, Martín, 1409.
Schrank, Andrew, 955.
Schroedl, Gerald F., 125.
Schulting, Rick, 130.
Schulz, Carsten-Andreas, 1157.
Schumann Gálvez, Otto, 233.
Schurster, Karl, 1029.
Schuster, Christian, 954, 1272.
Schweitzer, Mariana, 669–670.
Schweitzer, Pablo, 669.
Scullin, Dianne, 172.
Sedevich, Ana, 671.
Seecharan, Ranita, 946.
Seedhouse, Lexy, 294.

Seeking conflict in Mesoamerica: operational, cognitive, and experiential approaches, 28.
Seemann, Jörn, 413, 602.
Seemann, Miriam, 556.
Segura, María Soledad, 1098.
Seguridad humana y violencia crónica en México: nuevas lecturas y propuestas desde abajo, 1528.
Seguridad y construcción de ciudadanía: perspectivas locales, discusiones globales, 841.
Selección de los Archivos Económicos de la Secretaría de Hacienda y Crédito Público, Biblioteca Miguel Lerdo de Tejada, 1326.
Selección de *Realidad y Perspectivas*, 1232.
Selfa, Theresa, 598.
Sells, Cameron J., 1134.
Sember, Florencia, 1395.
Seminario Institucional La Crisis, el Poder y los Movimientos Sociales, 1529.
Seminario Internacional, "Zonas Vitivinícolas, Trabajadores Inmigrantes y Transformaciones Sociales," *Mexico City, 2015*, 414.
Sempio Durán, Camilo, 235.
Senkman, Leonardo, 607, 1277, 1445.
Sentido y tendencias de la transformación en México, 842.
Seoane, Javier, 1373.
Sequera, Jorge, 672.
Serbin, Andrés, 1154.
Serna Pérez, María Guadalupe, 1530.
Serra, Macià, 914.
Serra Yoldi, Inmaculada, 414.
Serrano, Mariana, 741.
Serrano, Sandra, 1513.
Serrano-Barquín, Carolina, 190.
Serrano Barquín, Héctor, 190.
Serrano Barquín, Rocío del Carmen, 421.
Serrano Sánchez, Carlos, 20.
Sesnie, Steven E., 480–481, 505.
Sexton, Renard, 1280.
Sexualidades andinas: otras formas posibles del sexo y el erotismo, 1725.
Seymour, Lynne, 457.
Shapiro, Jacob, 1256.
Sharpe, Ashley E., 50, 90–91.
Shearn, Isaac, 134.
Sheinin, David, 402.
Sheller, Mimi, 465.
Shepard, Glenn, 247.
Siavelis, Peter M., 1074.
Sierra Camacho, María Teresa, 228.
Signorelli, Gisela, 361.
Sili, Marcelo, 679, 739.
Silva, Bernardino Coelho da, 1431.
Silva, Edson, 255.
Silva, Joseli Maria, 428.
Silva, Ricardo Barbosa da, 794.
Silva, Vitor, 503.
Silva Rivera, Evodia, 524.
Silva Santisteban, Rocío, 415.
Silveira, Claudinei Taborda da, 754.
Silveira, Manuela, 567, 576.
Silveira, Ricardo Pinheiro, 754.
Silvius, Kirsten M., 276.
Simmons, Cynthia S., 795.
Simonassi, Silvia, 1446.
Simonsen, Aká, 449.
Simposio de Arqueología del Estado de Hidalgo, 2nd, *Pachuca, Mexico, 2011*, 92.
Simposio Internacional El hombre temprano en América, 7th, *Museo Nacional de Antropología, México, 2014*, 29.
Simposio "Políticas de Juventud y Participación Política en la Argentina Reciente: Perspectivas, Problemáticas y Ámbitos de Militancia," *Buenos Aires, 2017*, 1099.
Singer, André, 1135.
Singh, Shri K., 504.
Singh, Simron Jit, 455–456.
El sistema fronterizo global en América Latina: un estado del arte, 1158.
El sistema político de Chile, 1079.
Sistemas, agrícolas tradicionales: biodiversidad y cultura, 548.
El sitio Chenque I, un cementerio prehispánico en la Pampa occidental: estilo de vida e interacciones culturales de cazadores-recolectores del Cono Sur americano, 147.
Sjoberg, Fredrik M., 1132.
Skaggs, Sheldon, 93.
Skarbun, Fabiana, 673.
Skoggard, Ian, 321.
Skowronek, Russell K., 131.
Slack, Jeremy, 1577.
Sletto, Bjørn, 409, 416.
Smart, Sebastián, 1377.
Smith, Derek A., 534.
Smith, Faith, 943.
Smith, Kimbra, 1693.
Smith, Vaughn, 495.
Smorkaloff, Pamela María, 975.
Soares, Paulo Valladares, 782.

Soboroff, Jacob, 1531.
Sobrino, Jaime, 521.
Sociedad Argentina de Análisis Político, 1099.
Sociedad Geográfica de Lima, 586.
Sociedad Minera Cerro Verde, 161.
Sociedad Puertorriqueña de Planificación, 441.
Sociología y género: estudios en torno a performances, violencias y temporalidades, 1532.
Soifer, Hillel David, 1666.
Solano, Angélica, 993.
Solano Ramírez, Mario Antonio, 875.
Solares, Mateo Rodrigo, 1731.
Solís Avendaño, Manuel Antonio, 861.
Solís Ciriaco, Reyna Beatríz, 74, 94.
Solís Cruz, Jesús, 848.
Solíz T., María Fernanda, 376.
Soltmann, Claudio, 308.
Somma, Nicolas, 1080.
Sonora: la sierra, el desierto y la costa en el contexto de los guajiríos, 549.
Sonora: problemas de ayer y hoy, desafíos y soluciones, 1327.
Sorcery in Mesoamerica, 30.
Soria, Nélida, 734.
Soria Galvarro Sánchez de Lozada, Harry, 1733.
Sosa, Alberto J., 1215.
Sosa, Arturo, 1369.
Sosa Hernández, Guadalupe Georgina, 1533.
Sosa Núñez, Gustavo, 526.
Sosnowski, Saúl, 607, 1277, 1445.
Sotelo, Laura, 106.
Sotelo, Nélida, 739.
Soto Barrientos, Francisco, 1081.
Soto Caro, Marcela, 722.
Soto Coloballes, Natalia Verónica, 521.
Soto Víquez, Carlos, 364.
Sounds of vacation: political economies of Caribbean tourism, 944.
Southeastern Mesoamerica: Indigenous interaction, resilience, and change, 95.
Souto, Cintia P., 674.
Soutullo, Alvaro, 755.
Souverein, Jan, 1048.
Souza, Catiúscia Custódio de, 264.
Souza, Vanderlei Sebastião de, 265.
Spada, Paolo, 1115.
Spalding, Ana K., 513–514.
Spalding, Rose J., 876.
Spence-Morrow, Giles, 162.
Spiritto, Fernando, 1027.
Šprajc, Ivan, 31.
Sprenkels, Ralph, 877.
Srinivasan, Krishna, 1345.
Staab, Silke, 1082.
Stahlschmidt, Mareike Cordula, 96.
Stallings, Barbara, 1266.
Stamm, Caroline, 688.
Stanford, Catherine M., 923.
Stanish, Charles, 169.
Stark, Barbara L., 97.
State and nation making in Latin America and Spain: the rise and fall of the developmental state, 1281.
Staudt, Kathleen A., 1328.
Steele, Abbey, 1256.
Steenge, Albert E., 964.
Steinberg, David A., 1282.
Steinberg, Philip, 466.
Stella, Alessandro, 234.
Stemp, James, 56.
Stensrud, Astrid B., 588.
Sticotti, Nicolás, 1004.
Stocker, Karen, 1596.
Stocks, Gabriela, 496.
Stockwell, Diane, 821.
Stoll, David, 1598.
Stone, Livia K., 1534.
Stoner, Wesley D., 97.
Straka, Tomás, 1370.
Strassburg, Bernardo, 792.
Stresser-Péan, Claude, 100.
Stresser-Péan, Guy, 100.
Stuhldreher, Amalia Margarita, 1416.
Sturtevant, Chuck, 334.
Su, Ping, 449.
Suárez, Ginés, 509.
Suárez, Hugo José, 596, 1748.
Suárez Diez, Lourdes, 114.
Suárez Salazar, Luis, 1350.
Sugiyama, Natasha Borges, 1136–1137.
Sugiyama, Nawa, 98.
Surasky, Javier, 1207.
Suremain, Charles-Edouard de, 369.
Susani, Bruno, 1405.
Sutton, Constance R., 932.
Sutton, David Evan, 932.
Svampa, Maristella, 417.
Svejnar, Jan, 1357.
Świerk, Kacper, 295.
Sznajder, Mario, 607, 1277, 1445.
Sztulwark, Diego, 1104.
Szulc, Andrea P., 322.

Tacher Contreras, Daniel, 1535.
Tadey, Mariana, 674.
Talledos Sánchez, Edgar, 536.
Taller Binacional Argentino-Chileno "Araucanía-Norpatagonia: Cultura y Espacio," *3rd, Pucón, Chile, 2013*, 1213.
Taller Binacional Argentino-Chileno "Araucanía-Norpatagonia: Cultura y Espacio," *4th, San Carlos de Bariloche, Argentina, 2015*, 1214.
Taller Nacional de Bioarqueología y Paleopatología, *4th, Córdoba, Argentina, 2018*, 148.
Tamez Valedez, Blanca Mirthala, 1536.
Tamisari, Franca, 303.
Tanaka, Martín, 1697.
Tantaleán, Henry, 169.
Tapia, Luis, 1038.
Tapia, Mike, 1537.
Tapia Barría, Verónica, 724.
Tapia Landeros, Alberto, 80.
Tapiero, Eddie, 1179.
Tappan, Taylor A., 474.
Taveira, Germán, 750.
Taylor, Lucy, 675.
Taylor, Matthew MacLeod, 1432.
Technology and tradition in Mesoamerica after the Spanish invasion: archaeological perspectives, 32.
Teelucksingh, Jerome, 1637.
Teixeira-de-Mello, Franco, 755.
Téllez Contreras, León Felipe, 1538.
Tellman, Beth, 473, 480–481, 500, 505.
Tena, Olivia, 1504.
Teoría y política económica: ensayos en honor al profesor Dr. Julio H.G. Olivera, 1406.
Termes, Laura, 123.
Términos clave para los estudios de movilidad en América Latina, 418.
Territorialidades, migración y política pública en el contexto rural latinoamericano, 419.
Territorialising space in Latin America: processes and perceptions, 420.
Tetreault, Darcy Victor, 525.
Thaler, Gregory M., 796.
Thame, Maziki, 960.
Thattai, Deeptha, 476.
Theodossopoulos, Dimitrios, 511.
Thomas, Deborah A., 932.
Thomas, Evert, 562.
Thomas, Gwynn, 1074.
Thomas, Marc Anthony, 961.
Thompson, Canute S., 1343.
Thongs, Gabrielle, 448.
Thornton, Erin Kennedy, 99.
Tiesler, Vera, 20, 81.
Tigani, Eugenio Pablo, 1407.
Time and space: Latin American regional development in historical perspective, 1417.
Tinat, Karine, 1532.
Ting, Carmen, 107.
Tirado, Daniel A., 1417.
Tirado Villegas, Gloria, 1539.
Titiunik, Rocío, 1122.
Tobasura Acuña, Isaías, 564.
¿Todo cambia?: reflexiones sobre el "proceso de cambio" en Bolivia, 1748.
Tognolli, Claudio Julio, 1431.
Tokatlian, Juan Gabriel, 1218.
Tola, Florencia C., 335.
Tomaselli, Alexandra, 349.
Tomaz, Paula, 797.
Tominaga, Yasutaka, 1159.
Toni, Fabiano, 796.
Toral, Guillermo, 1250.
Torcal, Mariano, 956.
Toro, Fernando, 709.
Torre, André, 688.
Torre, Renée de la, 1483, 1520.
Torrelli, Milton, 756.
Torres, Fabiola, 98.
Torres, Fernanda Valeria, 636.
Torres, Gerver, 1024.
Torres, Jorge Alberto, 658.
Torres, Nataly, 572, 576.
Torres, Rodrigo A., 1069.
Torres Bonilla, Daniel, 441.
Torres Curiel, Yesenia, 1143.
Torres Falcón, Marta, 1571.
Torres Guevara, Juan, 584.
Torres-Obregón, Reyna, 1508.
Torres Parra, Camilo Alberto, 1652.
Torres Pérez, Francisco, 414.
Torres Pérez, Ricardo, 1361.
Torres Rodríguez, Alfonso, 92.
Torres Rodríguez, Alicia, 517.
Touchton, Michael, 1137.
Tourism resilience and recovery for global sustainability and development: navigating COVID-19 and the future, 945.
Toussaint Ribot, Mónica, 1180.
Toxqui Furlong, Mayra Gabriela, 551.

Trabajadores y sindicatos en Latinoamérica: conceptos, problemas y escalas de análisis, 1446.
Trabajo colectivo en el siglo XXI: formas y contextos entre grupos étnicos de Oaxaca, 235.
Trabichet, Florencia Cecilia, 676.
Trade and development issues in CARICOM: key considerations for navigating development, 946.
Trak, Juan Manuel, 1032.
Transfiguraciones de danzas tradicionales: ensayos y entrevistas, 236.
Transiciones territoriales, ciudad y campo: reflexiones teóricas sobre el espacio contemporáneo, 550.
Traslaviña, Abel, 590.
35 años de democracia: resultados y tendencias: ensayo, 1051.
Trejo, Guillermo, 826, 843.
Trejos Rosero, Luis Fernando, 987, 1209, 1234.
Treminio, Ilka, 859.
Triadan, Daniela, 91.
Tribunal Internacional para la Aplicación de la Justicia Restaurativa en El Salvador, 878.
Trienekens, Jacques, 752.
Trigo, María de los Angeles, 1344.
Trujillo Montalvo, Patricio, 296.
Tschakert, Petra, 779.
¡Tú, migrante!: la construcción de las representaciones de la migración en el contexto de América del Norte y Centroamérica, 1540.
Tuaza Castro, Luis Alberto, 1694.
Tukano, Álvaro, 266.
Tula y su jurisdicción: arqueología e historia, 33.
Tumas, Natalia, 662.
Turismo y género: una mirada desde Iberoamérica, 421.
Turits, Richard Lee, 1191.
Turning tides: Caribbean intersections in the Americas and beyond, 1639.
Tushingham, Shannon, 105.
Tutino, John, 405.
Tykot, Robert H., 81, 93.
Tzul Tzul, Gladys, 237, 899.
Ubieta Gómez, Enrique, 1201.
Uc, Pablo, 848, 1052.
Uceda, Santiago Castillo, 173.
Ugalde, Luis Carlos, 809.
Ugalde, María Fernanda, 140.
Ugalde, Vicente, 521.
Ugarteche, Oscar, 1329.
Ugolini, Agustina, 1103.
Ulibarri, Eduardo, 1181.
Ulloa, Félix, 879.
Ulloa Hung, Jorge, 126.
Ulmer, Gordon, 297.
Umaña Reyes, Lorena Margarita, 1519, 1541.
Undocumented and unaccompanied: children of migration in the European Union and the United States, 1597.
UNESCO Chair on Hydrometeorological Risks, 387, 523.
A única vida possível: itinerários de Ermanno Stradelli na Amazônia, 267.
Unidas tejemos la vida: testimonios de mujeres indígenas y afromexicanas radicadas en Acapulco, 238.
Uniremington (university), 1662.
Universidad Andina Simón Bolívar. Sede Ecuador, 1009.
Universidad Andina Simón Bolívar. Sede Ecuador. Cátedra de Estudios Afro-Andinos, 1680.
Universidad Autónoma de Chiapas. Instituto de Estudios Indígenas, 358.
Universidad Autónoma de Coahuila. Escuela de Ciencias Sociales, 552.
Universidad Autónoma de Yucatán, 20, 187.
Universidad Autónoma del Estado de Hidalgo. Área Académica de Economía, 1413.
Universidad Autónoma del Estado de México. Centro de Investigación en Ciencias Sociales y Humanidades, 419.
Universidad Autónoma del Estado de México. Facultad de Planeación Urbana y Regional, 542.
Universidad Autónoma Metropolitana. Unidad Azcapotzalco. División de Ciencias Sociales y Humanidades, 1571.
Universidad Autónoma Metropolitana. Unidad Xochimilco. División de Ciencias Sociales y Humanidades, 547.
Universidad Católica Andrés Bello. Centro de Estudios Políticos, 1032.
Universidad Católica Andrés Bello. Centro de Estudios Políticos y de Gobierno, 1026.
Universidad Católica Andrés Bello. Instituto de Investigaciones Económicas y Sociales, 1669.

Universidad Católica de Chile. Instituto de Estudios Urbanos, 427.
Universidad Católica Nuestra Señora de la Asunción. Centro de Estudios Antropológicos, 320.
Universidad de Buenos Aires. Grupo de Estudios de Políticas y Juventudes, 1099.
Universidad de Chile, 427.
Universidad de Ciencias y Artes del Estado de Chiapas. Centro de Estudios Superiores de México y Centroamérica, 1456.
Universidad de Ciencias y Artes del Estado de Chiapas. Observatorio de las Democracias: Sur de México y Centroamérica, 848.
Universidad de Guadalajara. Centro de Estudios Estratégicos para el Desarrollo, 845.
Universidad de Guadalajara. Departamento de Estudios Regionales-INESER, 1322.
Universidad de las Américas Puebla, 387–388.
Universidad de los Andes (Bogotá). Centro Interdisciplinario de Estudios sobre Desarrollo, 1276.
Universidad de los Andes (Bogotá). Maestría en Estudios Interdisciplinarios sobre Desarrollo, 983.
Universidad de Santo Tomás (Bogotá). Facultad de Gobierno y Relaciones Internacionales, 1149.
Universidad del Este, 1200.
Universidad del Norte (Barranquilla, Colombia), 1648.
Universidad del Norte (Barranquilla, Colombia). Departamento de Ciencia Política y Relaciones Internacionales, 1234.
Universidad del Valle, 1646, 1657–1658.
Universidad Mayor de San Andrés. Instituto de Investigaciones Antropológicas y Arqueológicas, 1732.
Universidad Mayor de San Andrés. Post Grado en Ciencias del Desarrollo, 1746.
Universidad Michoacana. Centro Nicolaita de Estudios Migratorios, 1499.
Universidad Nacional Autónoma de México, 20.
Universidad Nacional Autónoma de México. Centro de Investigaciones sobre América Latina y el Caribe, 1594.
Universidad Nacional Autónoma de México. Dirección General de Asuntos del Personal Académico, 1593.
Universidad Nacional Autónoma de México. Facultad de Contaduría y Administración, 1297.
Universidad Nacional Autónoma de México. Instituto de Investigaciones Sociales, 817, 1453, 1529.
Universidad Nacional Autónoma de México. Programa de Posgrado en Estudios Latinoamericanos, 1746.
Universidad Nacional Autónoma de México. Programa Universitario de Estudios del Desarrollo, 1287.
Universidad Nacional Autónoma de México. Seminario Permanente Cultura y Representaciones Sociales, 1542.
Universidad Nacional de Quilmes. Centro de Investigaciones sobre Economía y Sociedad en la Argentina Contemporánea, 1398.
Universidad Nacional de Quilmes. Programa de Investigación: Acumulación, dominación y luchas de clases en la Argentina contemporánea, 1989–2011, 1398.
Universidad Nacional de Rosario. Grupo de Estudio sobre Juventudes y Políticas de Juventud, 1099.
Universidad Rafael Landívar. Instituto de Investigación y Proyección sobre Dinámicas Globales y Territoriales, 1566.
Universidad Santo Tomás (Bogotá). Grupo de Investigación Comunicación, Paz-Conflicto, 273.
Universidad Torcuato di Tella, 1099.
University of Puerto Rico (Río Piedras Campus). Facultad de Estudios Generales, 1613.
University of Puerto Rico (Río Piedras Campus). Instituto de Investigación Violencia y Complejidad, 1617.
Unleashing growth and strengthening resilience in the Caribbean, 1345.
Unruh, Ernesto, 329.
Urban climates in Latin America, 422.
Urban Latin America: inequalities and neoliberal reforms, 423.
Urdinez, Francisco, 1254.
Uribe Castro, Hernando, 1673.
Urioste Fernández de Córdova, Miguel, 1749.
Urquijo Torres, Pedro Sergio, 382, 424.
Urquizo Valdeiglesias, Luis, 1726.
Urrutia Reveco, Santiago, 725.
Urteaga, Maritza, 256.
Urtubia Odekerken, Ximena, 1083.

Usos e historias del agua en México: riego, ciudad y legislación, 551.
Uvas, tierra y memoria: Coahuila: raíz de la vitivinicultura en América, 552.
Vaccotti, Luciana, 677.
Valadez, Raúl, 98.
Valcárcel Rojas, Roberto, 126, 135.
Valdano, Silvia G., 137.
Valdez Carrasco, Bettina, 1727.
Valdéz Rodas, Julio Alejandro, 1598–1599.
Valdivia, Gabriela, 602.
Vale Nieves, Otomie, 1619.
Valencia García, Guadalupe, 1746.
Valencia Londoño, Paula Andrea, 1645.
Valencia Rivera, Rogelio, 115.
Valentín Maldonado, Norma, 70.
Valenzuela, Andrea, 703.
Valenzuela, Arturo, 1084.
Valenzuela, Cristina, 678.
Valenzuela Aguilera, Alfonso, 841.
Valenzuela Marroquín, Manuel Luis, 1728.
Valle Álvarez, Luis, 161.
Valle Baeza, Alejandro, 1330.
Valle-Castillo, Julio, 1560.
Valle Fonrouge, Marcelo F., 1160.
Valle González, Carlos Del, 441.
Vallejo, Ivette, 1695.
Vallejo, Sebastián, 1020.
Valtierra García, Magdalena, 238.
Valverde Bravo, Carlos, 1053.
Valverde Díaz de León, Francisco, 553.
Van Damme, Patrick, 562.
Van den Berk, Jorrit, 849.
Van Der Hoek, Yntze, 577.
Vanzolini, Marina, 268.
Varela, Héctor H., 137.
Varela Huerta, Amarela, 1435.
Vargas, Constanza, 711.
Vargas, Juan F., 1256.
Vargas Arenas, Iraida, 1025.
Vargas Morúa, Elizarda, 1600.
Vargas Sarmiento, Patricia, 566.
Vasconcellos, Eduardo Alcântara de, 425.
Vásquez, Alexis, 704.
Vásquez, Eduardo, 746.
Vasquez, Jessica M., 1543.
Vazquez, Alberto, 679.
Vázquez, Georgiane Garabely Heil, 428.
Vázquez, Guillermo Javier, 1098.
Vázquez, Martin, 156.
Vázquez, Raquel, 216.
Vázquez Carmona, Homero, 1511.
Vázquez de Agredos Pascual, M. Luisa, 113.
Vázquez Dzul, Gabriel, 239.
Vázquez Zárate, Sergio R., 89.
Vecchio, Carlos, 1674.
Vega, Rosalynn A., 1544.
Vega López, Eduardo, 1292.
Vega Tapia, Héctor, 1383.
Vegliò, Simone, 426.
Vela-Almeida, Diana, 578.
Velasco, Marcela, 997.
Velasco Alarcón, C. Melissa, 589.
Velasco Jaramillo, Marcela, 281.
Velasco Orozco, Juan Jesús, 549.
Velasco Ortiz, M. Laura, 1545.
Velasco Santos, Paola, 554.
Velásquez, Teresa A., 354.
Velásquez Atehortúa, Juan Fernando, 1665.
Velásquez C., Carolina, 443.
Velásquez Luna, Gabriella, 50.
Velásquez Pérez, Luis Guillermo, 850.
Velázquez Castro, Adrián, 45.
Velázquez Galindo, Yuribia, 240.
Velázquez García, Mario Alberto, 1546.
Velázquez Gatica, Belén, 1474.
Velázquez Orihuela, Daniel, 1413.
Veloso, André, 798.
Veltmeyer, Henry, 1349.
Venezuela: la caída sin fin ¿hasta cuándo?: Encuesta Nacional de Condiciones de Vida 2016, 1675.
Venezuela y su tradición rentista: visiones, enfoques y evidencias, 1373.
Venter, Marcie L., 4.
Vepretskii, Sergei, 41.
Vera, Paula, 680.
Vera, Ricardo Alberto, 1307.
Vera, Sofia, 985.
Verbitsky, Horacio, 1104.
Vereda, Marisol, 620.
Vergara, Karla, 586.
Vergara Tenorio, María del Carmen, 543.
Vernengo, Matias, 1283.
Verwiebe, Roland, 637.
Vial, Camilo, 1075.
Viales Hurtado, Ronny José, 862.
Viana, Cecilia, 796.
Viaña Uzieda, Jorge, 1054.
Victorino Ramírez, Nicolás A., 1237.
La vida en el centro: feminismo, reproducción y tramas comunitarias, 1547.
Vidal Alejandro, Pavel, 1362.
Vidas sitiadas: jóvenes, exclusión laboral y violencia urbana en Centroamérica, 1601.
Videla, Gabriela, 215.

Vidoni, Flavio, 1408.
Vieira, Ima, 761.
El viejo y el nuevo poder económico en la Argentina: del siglo XIX a nuestros días, 1409.
Vieyra, Antonio, 382.
Vigil, José Ignacio, 1396.
Vila Benites, Gisselle, 356.
Vilaça, Aparecida M.N., 269.
Vilanova, Mateus Ricardo Nogueira, 782.
Vilar, José Rafael, 339.
Vilches, Patricia, 404.
Vilches Hinojosa, Miguel, 814.
Villagra Carron, Rodrigo, 312, 321.
Villalobos A., Víctor M., 359.
Villalobos Cavazos, Oswaldo, 555.
Villariny Marrero, Mari A., 441.
Villavicencio, Daniel, 1325.
Villegas, María Cecilia, 1729.
Villegas Chádez, Rubén, 1351.
Villegas Mariscal, Leobardo, 241.
La violencia contra las mujeres en las empresas: nuevas visiones de jóvenes valores, 1730.
Violencia y crisis social en el último rincón de la frontera: Piedras Negras y Acuña, 1548.
Las violencias: en busca de la política pública detrás de la guerra contra las drogas, 844.
Visconti, Giancarlo, 1085.
Vísperas del urbanismo en Latinoamérica, 1870–1930: imaginarios, pioneros y disciplinas, 427.
Vista Hermosa: nobles, artesanos y mercaderes en los confines del mundo huasteco: estudio arqueológico de un sitio Posclásico Tardío del municipio de Nuevo Morelos, Tamaulipas, México, 100.
Vivencias de mulheres no tempo e espaço da pandemia de COVID-19: perspectivas transnacionais, 428.
Vizcarra Bordi, Ivonne, 242.
Voeks, Robert A., 429.
Voices of Latin America: social movements and the new activism, 430.
Volante, José N., 660.
Volcanes, cenizas y ocupaciones antiguas en perspectiva geoarqueológica en América Latina, 140.
Volteando la tortilla: género y maíz en la alimentación actual de México, 242.
vom Hau, Matthias, 1666.

von Rueden, Chris, 315.
Voorhies, Barbara, 65.
El votante dominicano: ciudadanos y elecciones en la República Dominicana, 956.
Vrana, Heather A., 896.
Vranckx, An, 562.
Vukovic, Sinîsa, 874.
The W. Arthur Lewis reader, 1346.
Wade, Christine J., 924.
Walden, John P., 101.
Walker, Catherine, 782.
Walker, Kendra L., 515.
Walker, Robert, 795.
Walker, Thomas W., 924.
Wallace, Wendell C., 935.
Waller, Lloyd G., 945.
Wallerstein, Immanuel Maurice, 804.
Wallman, Diane E., 117, 136.
Walsh, Catherine, 1680.
Walsh, Sarah, 396.
Walsh-Dilley, Marygold, 389.
Walters, Shinique, 962.
Wampler, Brian, 1137.
Warnecke-Berger, Hannes, 851.
Warner, Benjamin P., 389, 496.
Washington, John, 1484.
Washington Office on Latin America, 885, 891.
Wasserstrom, Robert, 298.
Wassink, Joshua T., 1304.
Waters, Mary-Alice, 1201.
Watkins, Case, 799.
Watson, Hilbourne A., 963.
Waylen, Georgina, 1082.
Waylen, Michael, 795.
Webster, David L., 102.
Weisbrot, Mark, 1033.
Wellhausen, Rachel L., 1280.
Welp, Yanina, 1081.
Werner, Marion, 1347.
Wernke, Steven A., 590.
Weston, Darlene A., 135.
Weston, Gavin Michael, 900.
White, Nigel D., 1202.
Whitehead, Laurence, 982.
Why Latin American nations fail: development strategies in the twenty-first century, 1283.
Wiedenhoeft, Alex C., 130.
Wilhelmy von Wolff, Manfred, 1227.
Wilkinson, Darryl, 174.
Willebald, Henry, 1413, 1415, 1417.
Willers, Susanne, 1571.

Williams, Eric Eustace, 947.
Williams, Ernest H., 467.
Williams, Julie, 351.
Wills Otero, Laura, 991.
Wilson, Japhy, 579.
WinklerPrins, Antoinette M.G.A., 380.
Winocur, Diego, 143.
Winters, Zachary S., 468.
Wionczek, Miguel S., 1312.
Wise, Carol, 1284.
Woitowicz, Karina Janz, 428.
Wojcik, Dariusz, 766.
Wolff, Hendrik, 573.
Woloszyn, Janusz Z., 175.
Wong, María Belén, 1240.
Wood, Andrew Grant, 363.
Woodfill, Brent, 103.
World Bank Group, 1184.
Worrell, Rodney, 948.
Wrathall, David J., 473, 480–481, 500.
Wright, Claire, 833.
Wright, Glenn D., 886.
Wu Brading, Celia, 1245.
Xa' anil naj: la gran casa de los mayas, 243.
Xiap Riscajché, Rosa Liberta, 1602.
Xu, Yanran, 1161.
Xunfo Deni—Santa Rosa: trance enteogénico y ritualidad otomí, 244.
¿Y ahora que?: México ante el 2018, 845.
Yánez, Ivonne, 570.
Yang, Jianmin, 977.
Yashar, Deborah J., 1285.
Yawanawá, Biraci, 270.
Yepez Alvarez, Willy, 162.
Yin-Hang To, Emma Miriam, 1374.
Yllescas Illescas, Jorge Adrián, 1549.
Yohe, Robert M., 85.
Young, Harold A., 852.
Young, Jason, 591.
Zack, Guido, 1401.
Zalaquett Rock, Francisca A., 104.
Zaldúa, Natalia, 755.
Zambrana, Rocío, 972.
Zambrano Solarte, Hugo Ibsen, 563.
Zamora, Edgar, 1236.
Zamora Carmona, Gabriela, 1550.
Zamora Sáenz, Itzkuauhtli, 527.
Zangrando, Francisco, 156.
Zapata, María Cecilia, 622.
Zapata Macías, Helena, 832.
Zara, Cristana, 782.
Zaragocin, Sofía, 386, 431–432.
Zaragoza Martínez, María de Lourdes, 358.
Zárate, Alfonso, 846.
Zárate Botía, Carlos Gilberto, 1237.
Zarza Delgado, Martha Patricia, 190.
Zavattiero Tornatore, Georgina, 740.
Zeballos Videla, Mabel Luz, 757.
Zechmeister, Elizabeth J., 870, 881, 911.
Zegada, María Teresa, 1055–1056.
Zendejas Romero, Sergio, 1551.
Zepeda, Beatriz, 1158, 1603.
Zícari, Julián, 1410.
Ziccardi, Alicia, 384.
Zilio, Leandro, 149.
Zimmermann, Mario, 105.
Zizumbo Villarreal, Lilia, 410.
Zomo newen: relatos de vida de mujeres mapuche en su lucha por los derechos indígenas, 350.
Zottele Allende, Aníbal, 1331.
Żrałka, Jaroslaw, 106–107.
Zucco, Cesar, 1286.
Zuin, Aparecida Luzia Alzira, 271.
Zúñiga, Claudia, 723.
Zúñiga Arellano, Belem, 70.
Zunino Singh, Dhan, 418.
Zurita, Alfonso, 1750.
Zusman, Perla, 433.
Zygadło, Gabriela W., 82.

www.ingramcontent.com/pod-product-compliance
Lightning Source LLC
Chambersburg PA
CBHW030821210225
22220CB00001B/1